OFFICIAL ORGAN OF THE RADIATION RESEARCH SOCIETY

RADIATION RESEARCH

MANAGING EDITOR: TITUS C. EVANS

Volume 10, 1959

Academic Press, New York and London

CONTENTS OF VOLUME 10

NUMBER 1, JANUARY 1959

M. A. SICARD AND DREW SCHWARZ. The Effect of High Doses of Radiation on Seedling Growth 1
PAUL N. GOODWIN. Calorimetric Measurements on a Cesium-137 Teletherapy Unit 6
C. C. MOH AND R. B. WITHROW. Nonionizing Radiant Energy as an Agent in Altering the Incidence of X-Ray-Induced Chromatid Aberration. II. Reversal of the Far-Red Potentiating Effect in *Vicia* by Red Radiant Energy 13
V. P. BOND AND O. D. EASTERDAY. Effects of Heavy Particle Irradiation on Acute Mortality and Survival Time in the Mouse 20
ARMON F. YANDERS. The Effect of Dose Rate on Genetic Damage from Fast Electrons in *Drosophila* Sperm 30
M. L. WOLFROM, W. W. BINKLEY, L. J. MCCABE, T. M. SHEN HAN AND A. M. MICHELAKIS. The Effect of Ionizing Radiations on Carbohydrates 37
K. A. MADSEN, D. K. SALUNKHE AND M. SIMON. Certain Morphological and Biochemical Changes in Gamma-Irradiated Carrots (*Daucus carota* L.) and Potatoes (*Solanum tuberosum* L.) 48
JOHN E. PARKINSON. The Effect of Internal Emitters on Red Cell Survival in Beagle Dogs 63
KENNETH L. JACKSON AND CECIL ENTENMAN. The Role of Bile Secretion in the Gastrointestinal Radiation Syndrome 67
JOHN S. KREBS, RALPH W. BRAUER, AND HARVEY KALBACH. The Estimation of the Nonrecuperable Injury Caused by Ionizing Radiation 80

NUMBER 2, FEBRUARY 1959

LEROY AUGENSTINE. Indirect Inactivation of Macromolecules in Solution by Ionizing Radiation. A Method of Analysis 89
WILLIAM S. WILCOX. The Gamma Radiolysis of Butyl Bromides 112
MICHAEL P. DACQUISTO. Acquired Radioresistance. A Review of the Literature and Report of a Confirmatory Experiment 118
BETSY J. STOVER, D. R. ATHERTON, AND N. KELLER. Metabolism of Pu^{239} in Adult Beagle Dogs 130
W. A. RAMBACH, J. A. D. COOPER, H. L. ALT, H. H. VOGEL, JR., J. W. CLARK, AND D. L. JORDAN. The Effect of Single and Multiple Doses of Co^{60}

Gamma-Radiation and Fission Neutron Radiation on the Incorporation of Fe^{59} into the Rat Erythropoietic System 148
ALBERT A. BARBER AND KARL M. WILBUR. The Effect of X-Irradiation on the Antioxidant Activity of Mammalian Tissues 167
J. F. SPALDING, V. G. STRANG, AND J. A. SAYEG. Relative Biological Effect of Fission Neutrons with the Broad Bean Root (*Vicia faba*) as a Test System 176
JOHN B. STORER. Rate of Recovery from Radiation Damage and its Possible Relationship to Life Shortening in Mice 180
SUPPLEMENT
J. H. MARSHALL, V. K. WHITE, AND J. COHEN. Microscopic Metabolism of Calcium in Bone. I. Three-Dimensional Deposition of Ca^{45} in Canine Osteons 197
J. H. MARSHALL, R. E. ROWLAND, AND J. JOWSEY. Microscopic Metabolism of Calcium in Bone. II. Quantitative Autoradiography 213
R. E. ROWLAND, J. JOWSEY, AND J. H. MARSHALL. Microscopic Metabolism of Calcium in Bone. III. Microradiographic Measurements of Mineral Density 234
J. H. MARSHALL, J. JOWSEY, AND R. E. ROWLAND. Microscopic Metabolism of Calcium in Bone. IV. Ca^{45} Deposition and Growth Rate in Canine Osteons 243
J. H. MARSHALL, R. E. ROWLAND, AND J. JOWSEY. Microscopic Metabolism of Calcium in Bone. V. The Paradox of Diffuse Activity and Long-Term Exchange 258
Announcements 271

NUMBER 3, MARCH 1959

WARREN M. GARRISON, HERMAN R. HAYMOND, WINIFRED BENNETT AND SIBYL COLE. Radiation-Induced Oxidation of Aqueous Acetic Acid-Oxygen Solutions 273
M. M. ELKIND AND HARRIET SUTTON. The Relationship between Division and X-ray Sensitivity, Ultraviolet Sensitivity, and Photoreactivation in Yeast 283
M. M. ELKIND AND HARRIET SUTTON. Sites of Action of Lethal Irradiation: Overlap in Sites for X-Ray, Ultraviolet, Photoreactivation, and Ultraviolet Protection and Reactivation in Dividing Yeast Cells 296
D. METCALF. Long-Term Effects of Whole-body Irradiation on Lymphocyte Homeostasis in the Mouse 313
R. E. ROWLAND, J. H. MARSHALL, AND J. JOWSEY. Radium in Human Bone: The Microradiographic Appearance 323
DOUGLAS E. SMITH. Protection of the Irradiated Ground Squirrel by Cysteine 335
O. VOS, F. WENSINCK, AND D. W. VAN BEKKUM. Lesions of the Tongue in Irradiated Mice 339
RAYMOND G. MURRAY. The Effects of Single and Divided Doses of X-Radiation on Bone Marrow of Partially Shielded Rats 347

Charles A. Leone, Anne Rimkus Hartnett, Robert Crist, and Carolee McBeth. Paper Electrophoretic Analyses of Sera from Irradiated Rhesus Monkeys 357
Carl Woese. Radiation Destruction of the Plaque-Forming Ability of Spores of Lysogenic *Bacillus megaterium* 370
Sidney P. Kent. Further Observations on the Effect of X-Irradiation on the Glycogen Content and Histology of the Rabbit Retina 380

Number 4, April 1959

W. F. Baldwin and T. N. Salthouse. Latent Radiation Damage and Synchronous Cell Division in the Epidermis of an Insect. I. Nonreversible Effects Leading to Local Radiation Burns 387
W. F. Baldwin and T. N. Salthouse. Latent Radiation Damage and Synchronous Cell Division in the Epidermis of an Insect. II. Reversible Effects in Burn Repair 397
Howard E. Noyes. A Chronic Irradiation Source for Small Animals 400
Henry Quastler and Marion Zucker. The Hierarchy of Modes of Radiation Death in Specifically Protected Mice 402
Clyde M. Williams and George M. Krise. The Effect of Pitressin on Postirradiation Polydipsia and Polyuria in the Rat 410
W. K. Sinclair, S. E. Gunter, and A. Cole. The Relative Biological Effectiveness of 200-Kvp X-Rays, Cobalt-60 Gamma-Rays, and 22-Mevp X-Rays, Determined from the Dose-Survival Curve of *Saccharomyces cerevisiae* 418
Ann C. Birge and Joseph A. Sayeg. The Effects of Accelerated Carbon Nuclei and Other Radiations on the Survival of Haploid Yeast. I. Dosimetry of the Cyclotron Beams 433
Joseph A. Sayeg, Ann C. Birge, Carl A. Beam, and Cornelius A. Tobias. The Effects of Accelerated Carbon Nuclei and Other Radiations on the Survival of Haploid Yeast. II. Biological Experiments 449
Oddvar F. Nygaard and Richard L. Potter. Effect of X-Radiation on DNA Metabolism in Various Tissues of the Rat. I. Incorporation of C^{14}-Thymidine into DNA during the First 24 Hours Postirradiation 462
F. Hutchinson and D. A. Ross. Some Kinetics of the Indirect Effect of Ionizing Radiation on Aqueous Solutions 477
R. F. Kimball, Nenita Gaither, and Stella M. Wilson. Reduction of Mutation by Postirradiation Treatment after Ultraviolet and Various Kinds of Ionizing Radiations 490

Number 5, May 1959

Gisuke Meshitsuka and Milton Burton. Hydrogen Iodide Production in Radiolysis of Organic Liquids Containing Dissolved Iodine: Cyclohexane, *n*-Hexane, Benzene 499

Donald R. Anderson and Betty J. Joseph. Radiation Effects on Aqueous Solutions of *S*-(2-Aminoethyl) thiuronium Salts 507
L. I. Grossweiner and W. A. Mulac. Primary Processes in the Flash Photolysis of Ovalbumin and Constituents 515
Harald H. Rossi. Specification of Radiation Quality 522
W. Rosenzweig and H. H. Rossi. Determination of the Quality of the Absorbed Dose Delivered by Monoenergetic Neutrons 532
E. R. Gordon, E. Gassner, S. Okada, and L. H. Hempelmann. Deoxyribonuclease II Activity in Lymphoid Tissues of Rats 545
M. J. Berger and L. V. Spencer. Some Radiological Applications of Gamma-Ray Transport Theory 552
Edwin I. Goldenthal, M. V. Nadkarni, and Paul K. Smith. A Study of Comparative Protection against Lethality of Triethylenemelamine, Nitrogen Mustard, and X-Irradiation in Mice 571
Edward W. Daniels and Howard H. Vogel, Jr. Effects of Nonirradiated Protoplasm on Recovery of Amoebae Exposed to Supralethal Doses of Fission Neutrons 584
A. Szutka, J. F. Hazel, and Wallace M. McNabb. Synthesis of Porphine-like Substances Induced by Gamma-Irradiation 597

Number 6, June 1959

Robert Livingston. Samuel Colville Lind: The First Eighty Years 605
Leon M. Dorfman. The Radiation Chemistry of Gases: Introduction to the Symposium 607
D. P. Stevenson. On the Average Energies of Molecular Ions 610
John L. Magee and Koichi Funabashi. The Clustering of Ions in Irradiated Gases 622
Aron Kuppermann and Milton Burton. Decomposition of *n*-Butane in an Electric Discharge 636
A. Russell Jones. Radiation-Induced Reactions in the N_2–O_2–H_2O System 655
R. F. Pottie, R. Barker, and W. H. Hamill. Ion-Molecule Reactions of Methyl and Ethyl Iodides 664
O. A. Schaeffer and S. O. Thompson. The Exchange of Hydrogen and Deuterium in the Presence of Electrons and Ultraviolet Radiation 671
Leon M. Dorfman and A. C. Wahl. The Radiation Chemistry of Acetylene. I. Rare Gas Sensitization. II. Wall Effect in Benzene Formation 680
F. W. Lampe. The Direct Radiolysis and the Radiation-Sensitized Hydrogenation of Ethylene 691
Author Index 703
Subject Index 705

RADIATION RESEARCH 10, 1–5 (1959)

The Effect of High Doses of Radiation on Seedling Growth

M. A. SICARD[1] AND DREW SCHWARTZ

Biology Division, Oak Ridge National Laboratory,[2] Oak Ridge, Tennessee

INTRODUCTION

In experiments involving irradiation of dry maize seeds, Schwartz (*1*) has described a reversal in the seedling height-dose curve at very high doses of ionizing radiation. At doses above 125,000 r of γ-rays, there is a positive correlation between seedling height and dose. A plateau is reached at about 400,000 r. The reversal has been explained (*2*) as the result of interaction between chromosome damage and mitotic inhibition. Extensive chromosome breakage in dividing cells will result in a high degree of lethality of daughter cells because of aneuploidy. At the very high doses there is an increase in chromosome breakage; however, the inhibition of mitosis serves to prevent aneuploidy and hence lethality. The reversal phenomenon has since been confirmed by Moutschen *et al.* (*3*) with the barley coleoptile. This paper deals with a further investigation of the growth response of seedlings to ionizing radiation.

Comparison of Coleoptile and Leaf Growth

Dormant wheat seeds with a moisture content of about 11% were exposed to γ-radiation from a Co^{60} source similar to that described by Ghormley and Hochanadel (*4*) with doses ranging to a maximum of 380,000 r. The intensity was 1150 r/min. Fifty seeds were treated at each dose. After treatment, the seeds were planted in sand in the greenhouse. Fifteen days after planting, the seedlings were harvested and the height of the coleoptile and of the first leaf of each plant was measured. At this time the coleoptile and first leaf had attained their maximum growth. These measurements are plotted against dose in Fig. 1.

The first leaf of wheat responded to radiation in a manner similar to that described for corn. Growth decreases with increasing doses up to 110,000 r; beyond this dose the relation is reversed and growth increases. The coleoptile does not show this reversal, although the plateau in the curve between 50,000 and 150,000 r may be indicative of a slight effect.

[1] On Fulbright Fellowship.

[2] Operated by Union Carbide Corporation for the U. S. Atomic Energy Commission.

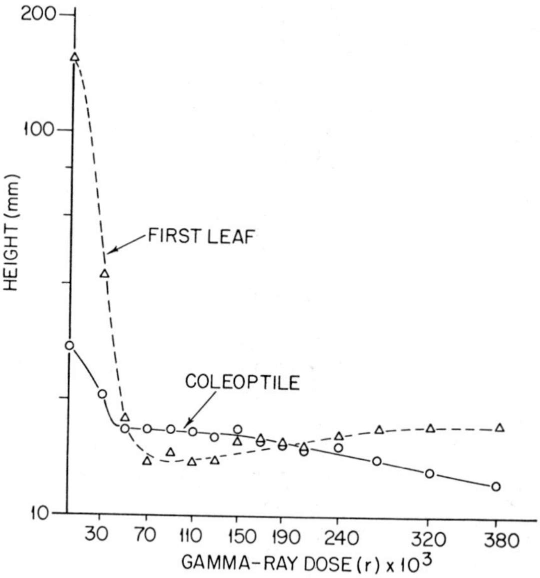

FIG. 1. Seedling height-dose curve for wheat.

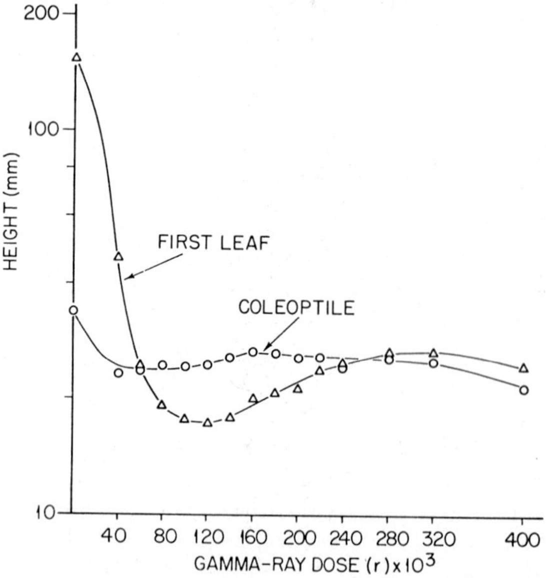

FIG. 2. Seedling height-dose curve for barley.

The comparison of the coleoptile and leaf dose curves of wheat is interpreted as a confirmation of the explanation advanced above. There is a large difference in the frequency of mitoses in these two tissues. The involvement of mitotic inhibition to explain the reversal phenomenon would predict that the reversal would be much less striking in the coleoptile, where there are fewer cell divisions.

The appearance of the seedlings at the low, intermediate, and high dose ranges is of interest. At the low and high dose ranges, the first leaf of each seedling grows out beyond the coleoptile, but in the intermediate dose range the leaf is short and does not protrude.

Similar results have been obtained with Himalaya barley except that here there may be a slight reversal with the coleoptile (Fig. 2), as was previously reported by Moutschen (*3*). The difference in the dose curves of the wheat and barley coleoptiles can be correlated with the mitotic rate in the two tissues. Twenty-four hours after germination in unirradiated material, when the number of mitoses is at a maximum, an average of 224 cells in metaphase were counted in the wheat coleoptile as compared to 2700 such cells in the barley coleoptile.

Storage Effect

Moutschen reported that storage of the seeds after irradiation caused a diminution of the reversal phenomenon in the barley coleoptile; the reversal was completely

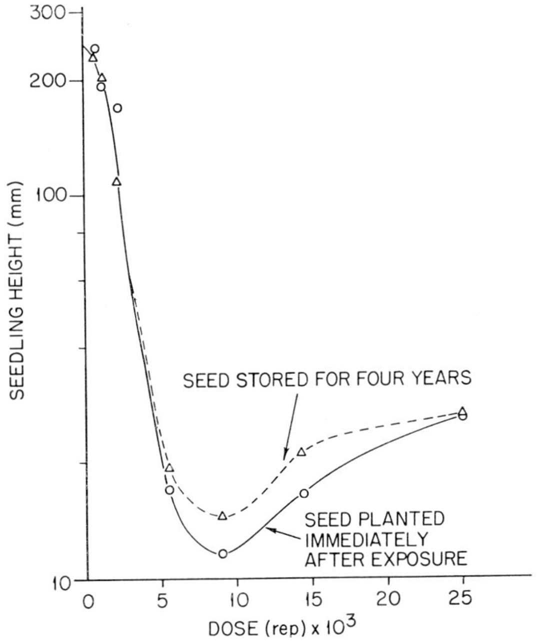

FIG. 3. Effect of long-term seed storage on the reversal phenomenon in maize.

eliminated after 20 days of storage. This was confirmed in our laboratory only under certain conditions, namely, when the barley was grown under strong light. However, the reversal in the coleoptile was unaffected by storage when the seedlings were grown in darkness. Furthermore, storage up to 21 days caused no change in the shape of the leaf growth-dose curve for barley, wheat, or corn even when grown under strong light. The reason for the storage effect on the barley coleoptile grown in light is not known.

The effect of long-term storage was also investigated. Samples of maize seed that had been exposed to radiation from a nuclear detonation in 1953 were planted in 1957 after storage for more than 4 years. The seeds had been kept in the laboratory at room temperature. Seedling height at the various doses was measured 10 days after planting, and the dose curve obtained was compared to the original curve plotted for the same samples of seed planted 4 years earlier, before storage (Fig. 3). It is evident from these curves that the reversal phenomenon in maize persists even after a long-term storage of the irradiated seed. The dip in the dose curve for the stored seeds is less pronounced, but this could reflect a difference in culture conditions at the time of planting.

Influence of Water Content

Ehrenberg and Nybom (*5*) and Caldecott (*6*) reported an inverse relation between radiation sensitivity and water content of seeds below 15%. They used relatively low doses, the highest being 35,000 r of X-rays.

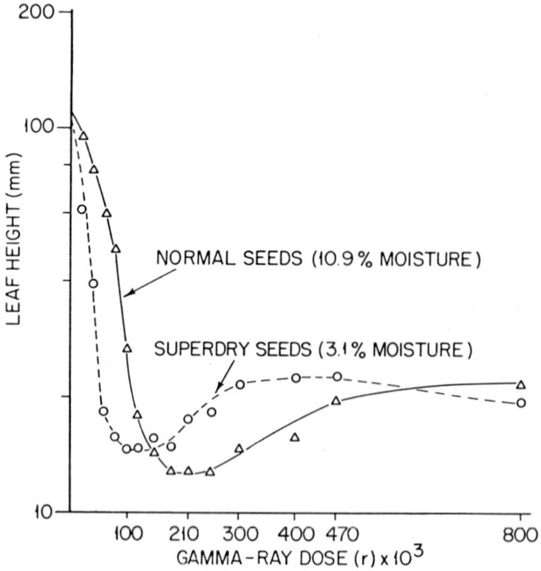

FIG. 4. Effect of moisture content of barley seeds at time of irradiation. The height of the first leaf is plotted against dose. Seeds planted immediately after irradiation.

This work has been repeated and substantiated in our laboratory with doses ranging up to 800,000 r of γ-rays. Himalaya barley seeds with moisture contents of 3.1% (superdry) and 10.9% (air-dry) were irradiated and planted in sand in the greenhouse. Seedling heights were measured after 14 days, and the results are plotted in Fig. 4. The reversal phenomenon at high doses necessitates a comparison of the whole dose curve rather than just seedling height at any one dose to determine the comparative radiosensitivity of seeds with high and low moisture contents. For example, at 100,000 and 800,000 r, the air-dry seeds show more growth than the superdry ones, but at 300,000 r this condition is reversed and the seedlings from the superdry seeds are taller. When the dose curve as a whole is considered, it is clear that there has been a shift to greater sensitivity in the seeds with the 3.1% moisture content in that the reversal in the curve occurs at a lower dose. The dose reduction factor is approximately 2. If plotted with this conversion factor, the curves are almost superimposable. These results point to an equivalence in the effect of moisture content on the radiosensitivity of all the factors governing seedling growth.

SUMMARY

Further studies on the phenomenon of reversal in the seedling height-dose curve are reported. A comparison of the coleoptile and leaf growth in barley and wheat lends support to the postulate that the reversal is caused by an interaction of chromosome damage and mitotic inhibition. In corn, the phenomenon persisted even after a postirradiation storage of the seeds for more than 4 years. The dose at which the reversal occurs was shown to be dependent on the moisture content of the seed at the time of irradiation. With superdry seeds, which show increased radiosensitivity as compared to air-dry seeds, the reversal occurs at a lower dose.
RECEIVED: April 18, 1958

REFERENCES

1. D. SCHWARTZ, An interesting phenomenon associated with irradiation of dry maize seeds. *Science* **119**, 45–46 (1954).
2. D. SCHWARTZ, and C. E. BAY, Further studies on the reversal in seedling height dose curve at very high levels of ionizing radiation. *Am. Naturalist* **90**, 323–327 (1956).
3. J. MOUTSCHEN, Z. M. BACQ, and A. HERVE, Action du rayonnement X sur la croissance de la plantule d'orge. *Experientia* **12**, 314–315 (1956).
4. J. A. GHORMLEY, and C. J. HOCHANADEL, A cobalt gamma-ray source used for studies in radiation chemistry. *Rev. Sci. Instr.* **22**, 473–475 (1951).
5. L. EHRENBERG, and N. NYBOM, Ion density and biological effectiveness of radiations. *Acta Agr. Scand.* **4**, 396–418 (1954).
6. R. S. CALDECOTT, Inverse relationship between the water content of seeds and their sensitivity to X rays. *Science* **120**, 809–810 (1954).

RADIATION RESEARCH 10, 6–12 (1959)

Calorimetric Measurements on a Cesium-137 Teletherapy Unit

PAUL N. GOODWIN[1]

Physics Department, Institute of Cancer Research, Royal Cancer Hospital, London, England

INTRODUCTION

The conventional means of measuring the intensity of a beam of X- or γ-radiation has long been the measurement of the ionization produced in air, as required when the roentgen is the unit of dose. But with the introduction, and recommended use, of the rad as the fundamental unit of absorbed dose, the direct measurement of energy absorption by calorimetric methods has become of great interest. Among the first such measurements were those of Laughlin and his co-workers (*1*), who have used calorimeters on a 22-Mev betatron, a 400-kev generator, and a Co^{60} unit. More recently, calorimetric measurements have been made at 0.5 and 1 Mev by Dolphin and Innes (*2*), at 1.4 Mev by McElhinney *et al.* (*3*), and at 22 Mev and with Co^{60} by Johns and his co-workers (*4*, *5*). Calorimetric measurements determine the intensity of an X- or γ-ray beam directly in ergs per square centimeter per second; and, together with suitable ionization measurements, yield the ergs per square centimeter per roentgen, and thus relate rads to roentgens at a particular quantum energy. This factor, the quantity of radiation per roentgen, was calculated over a wide range of energies by Mayneord (*6*). Its rapid variation with photon energy makes it essential to have measurements made at a number of different photon energies.

This report describes calorimetric measurements made on a 1400-curie Cs^{137} teletherapy unit installed at the Downs branch of the Royal Marsden Hospital. Cs^{137} offers certain advantages over X-ray units for calorimetric measurements, such as constant output and a monochromatic primary beam (662 kev), but also some disadvantages, such as the low output (about 14 r/min) at the minimum source-absorber distance (50 cm) and large penumbra due to the large source diameter (2.7 cm).

DESCRIPTION OF CALORIMETER

The construction of the calorimeter is shown in Fig. 1. The absorber was a lead cylinder 10.2 cm in diameter and 5.7 cm thick with an embedded spiral heating

[1] U. S. Public Health Service Research Fellow of the National Cancer Institute.

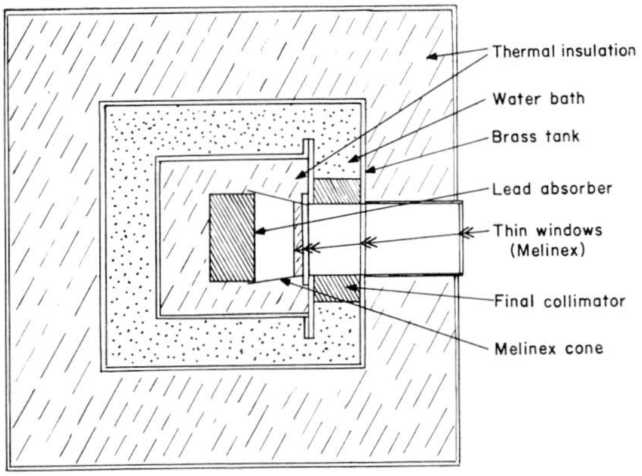

FIG. 1. The layout of the calorimeter.

coil of enameled Eureka wire. The temperature-detecting element was a thermistor (Stantel type KB) embedded in the rear surface of the absorber, and covered over with Wood's metal. The lead cylinder was suspended by nylon threads inside a brass tank and surrounded by insulation, except on the front face, where a thin plastic cone allowed entry of the beam. The insulation was Santocell made by Monsanto Chemical Co. The observed thermal conductivity of this arrangement averaged about 4×10^{-3} cal/sec/deg, which was as low as that observed with the best readily obtainable vacuum; and the use of insulation offered practical advantages over the evacuation of the brass tank. The brass tank was immersed in a tank of water, but, since it was necessary that the water temperature vary by less than 10^{-3} °C per minute, no attempt was made to control it thermostatically. The water tank was, however, surrounded with 10 cm of Santocell, and the room kept at a fairly constant temperature. Under normal conditions this arrangement resulted in the temperature drift of the water being less than 5×10^{-4} °C per minute, as measured with a type F thermistor immersed in the water. The tunnel through which the beam entered contained a number of thin windows of aluminized Melinex film, having a total thickness of about 10 mg/cm^2. To further reduce heat loss through the tunnel, a 1-cm layer of Santocell was sandwiched between two films as shown in Fig. 1. The absorption coefficient of Santocell for Cs γ-rays was measured, and the absorption in this layer calculated to be 0.7%.

The electrical connections to the calorimeter are shown in Fig. 2. The thermistor and heater coil leads were No. 36 enameled copper wire, fed through plastic sleeving to the cable connection which was embedded in the outer insulating jacket. The resistance of the heater coil was measured on a Kelvin double bridge constructed from 0.1% grade elements; the current through the coil was measured by a milliameter calibrated by the National Physical Laboratory to ± 0.1%.

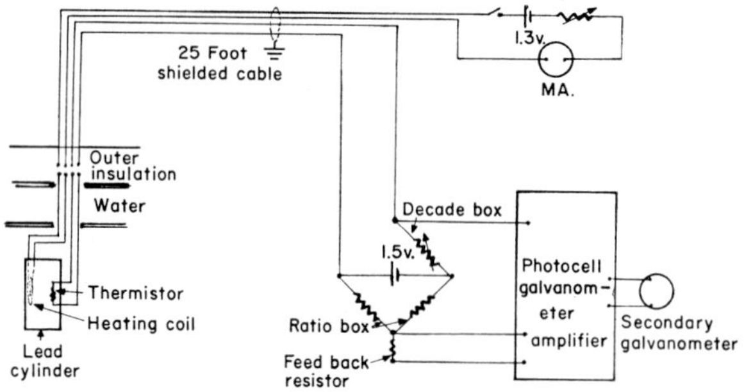

FIG. 2. Schematic diagram showing electrical connections.

The thermistor, which had a resistance of about 2600 ohms at 20° C and a resistance change of about 110 ohms per degree centigrade, was connected in one arm of a Wheatstone bridge. The variable arm was a six-decade box, 0.1% grade, with steps of 0.01 ohm; the fixed resistances were a 0.1% grade ratio box. The bridge unbalance was detected by a galvanometer amplifier of the twin photocell type, based on a circuit described by Brinton and O'Konski (7). The secondary detector was a multirange spotlight galvanometer. The over-all sensitivity of the system was limited only by zero drift in the amplifier, and under normal conditions temperature changes of 10^{-5} °C could be readily detected.

CALORIMETER DATA

In making temperature measurements, the bridge was kept balanced, and the amplifier and secondary galvanometer used as a null detector, so as to avoid the question of linearity of response. Since each 0.01-ohm change in the balancing resistance produced a wide sweep of the secondary galvanometer, the time of zero deflection corresponding to each step was noted and plotted against the balancing resistance. Figure 3 shows a typical plot obtained when the calorimeter was alternately irradiated with the Cs^{137} beam or the embedded coil. The two times were the same, and the heater current was such that the two energy inputs were approximately equal.

The beam energy may then be obtained from the following considerations:

1. The thermistor resistance varies exponentially with temperature, but over the temperature change involved here ($<3 \times 10^{-3}$ °C) the variation in linearity is less than 0.01%. Thus the same equations apply to both resistance and temperature differences.

2. From Newton's cooling law, the temperature drift of the absorber when not being heated (regions A, C, and E of Fig. 3) may be written: $dT/dt_A = K(T - T_0)$, where K is the cooling constant and T_0 is the ambient temperature. Since, during the time involved here, the temperature change is very small compared to $T - T_0$,

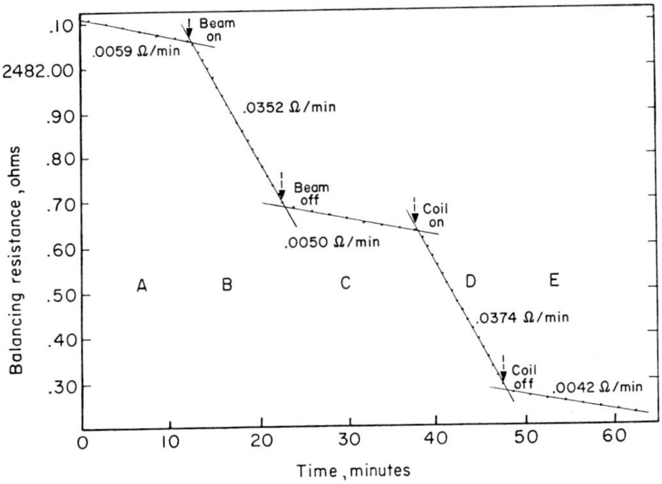

FIG. 3. Typical plot of the resistance changes during an experimental run. The letters *A* to *E* denote the regions referred to in the text.

T is a linear function of time; T_0 need not be a constant, but may be assumed also to change linearly with time. Thermistor measurements of the water-tank temperature verify this relationship.

3. In regions *B* and *D* there is a constant rate of energy input. If it is assumed that all the absorbed energy is eventually degraded to heat, then the temperature rise (with no heat loss) will be proportional to the energy input.

From 1, 2, and 3, it is clear that the net rate of resistance change due to irradiation by the beam may be written

$$\left(\frac{dR}{dt}\right)_{\text{beam}} = \frac{dR}{dt_B} - \frac{1}{2}\left(\frac{dR}{dt_A} + \frac{dR}{dt_C}\right) \tag{1}$$

where the subscripts refer to regions in Fig. 3.

Similarly, the resistance change due to coil heating may be written

$$\left(\frac{dR}{dt}\right)_{\text{coil}} = \frac{dR}{dt_D} - \frac{1}{2}\left(\frac{dR}{dt_C} + \frac{dR}{dt_E}\right) \tag{2}$$

Then for the ratio of equations 1 and 2

$$\frac{(dR/dt)_{\text{beam}}}{(dR/dt)_{\text{coil}}} = \frac{(dT/dt)_{\text{beam}}}{(dT/dt)_{\text{coil}}} = \frac{(dE/dt)_{\text{beam}}}{(dE/dt)_{\text{coil}}}$$

Thus it is merely necessary to measure the slopes of the plotted curves (Fig. 3) and from them to determine the ratio of the net slopes, as given by equations 1 and 2, and also to determine the rate of energy input in the coil, which is found by measuring the current flowing through the known coil resistance; the result is the energy absorbed from the beam directly in ergs per minute. With this analysis, it is not necessary to know the cooling constant, K, the equilibrium temperature, T_0, the exact irradiation time, or even the calorimeter sensitivity, dR/dE. Measurements of these constants have been made but generally yield slightly varying results, owing to changes in temperature differences, previous temperatures, and other variables. Use of the above approach eliminates all these uncertainties.

Certain corrections must be applied to the calorimeter data:

1. Transmission through the lead absorber, using the measured attenuation coefficient, was calculated at 0.1%.

2. Backscatter from the face of the absorber was taken as 0.1% in agreement with calculations by Hayward and Hubbel (*8*) on 1-Mev photons and measurements by Laughlin *et al.* (*1*) on 400-kv X-rays, both of whom found about 0.1% backscatter at these energies.

3. Window absorption, mainly in the insulation, was calculated at 0.7%.

4. Energy loss due to sidescatter within the absorber was calculated to be approximately 0.1%. Thus the calorimetric readings must be increased by a total of 1.0% to correct for the above losses.

BEAM AREA

The determination of the effective area of the Cs^{137} beam proved to be the most critical measurement in the whole experiment, since an error of 1 ml in the measurement of the effective diameter would result in a final error of 2.5%. Measurements of the beam area were made with Ilford Process film placed in paper envelopes with a 1/16-inch sheet of Perspex placed directly in front of the film. The Perspex prevented scattered electrons from unduly blackening the film just outside the beam edge; it also ensured electronic equilibrium at the position corresponding to the front face of the absorber.

It was first established that there was a linear relation between exposure and film density; a series of films exposed for varying times to the Cs^{137} beam showed a strictly linear exposure-density relation from background up to a density of about 2.0. The lead absorber and the back and sides of the brass tank were removed, and films were placed in a position corresponding to the front face of the absorber. A large number of films were thus exposed, and each scanned with a densitometer. Readings were taken every millimeter in both the horizontal and vertical directions and plotted on millimeter graph paper. The maximum net intensity, as determined from the average value across the central 2 cm of the plot, was divided into the net area under the plotted curve as read with a planimeter; this quotient was then taken as the effective diameter of the beam. This method thus took into account any nonuniform intensity across the beam, and also any radiation scattered outside the geometrical edge of the beam but still absorbed by the lead absorber, although such scattered radiation amounted to less than 2% of the total beam intensity. The effective beam diameters determined in this manner were 8.02 ± 0.07 cm at a 50-cm source-absorbed distance and 7.88 ± 0.02 cm at a 55-cm distance.

IONIZATION MEASUREMENTS

In order to measure the conversion factor, ergs per square centimeter per roentgen, it was desired to obtain an accurate measurement of the ionization produced by the beam as it was actually used for the calorimetric measurements. The calorimeter was constructed in such a way that the sides and back of the brass tank could be removed, leaving the final collimator and front of the tank in place. The thimble chamber of a Baldwin-Farmer substandard dosimeter was then placed inside the Perspex tank, in a position corresponding to the front of the lead absorber. The Baldwin-Farmer thimble chamber had an active length of 2 cm, and inside diameter of 4 mm, and a wall thickness of 0.7 mm; a 2-mm Perspex buildup cap was added to ensure electronic equilibrium. The dosimeter was then calibrated on the Cs^{137} unit by J. C. Jones and T. C. Sinclair of this department, who used a carbon chamber to obtain an absolute measurement of the ionization produced by the beam. Their results showed that the readings on the Baldwin-Farmer should be multiplied by 1.04 to give the correct reading for the Cs^{137} γ-ray beam (HVL = 11 mm Cu). This correction is in good agreement with the results of a calibration performed on the same chamber by the National Physical Laboratory, which yielded a correction factor of 1.05 for a 2 Mev X-ray beam with a HVL of 12.5 mm Cu.

RESULTS

All the measurements mentioned above were made at two different source-absorber distances, with slightly different field sizes. The final results at the different distances differed by less than 1%. The energy in the beam at 50 cm was found to be $4.36 \pm 0.05 \times 10^4$ ergs/cm²/min as determined from runs made during August, 1957. The statistical fluctuations and systematic errors involved in this measurement are: 0.9% in the area of beam; 0.5% in the radiation and heater curves; 0.2% in the heater coil resistance; 0.2% in the heater coil current.

The uncertainties involved in the ionization measurement are 0.3% variations in readings and 1.0% calibration of ionization chamber.

Combining the energy absorption measurements at the different distances with the corresponding ionization measurements gives the value for the conversion factor for 662 Kev of 2959 ± 44 ergs/cm²/r. This factor can be calculated by the method outlined by Mayneord (*6*). Since at this energy only the Compton effect is significant, this calculation reduces to the formula

$$F = \frac{W\ (\text{ev/ion pair}) \times 1.59\ (\text{ergs/ev})}{4.8 \times 10^{-10}\ (\text{esu/ion pair}) \times \rho_{\text{air}} \times \mu_a\ (\text{cm}^2/\text{gm})}$$

when μ_a is the "true" absorption coefficient in air.

The value of the theoretical conversion factor thus depends on one's choice of

W. A review by Bay (*9*) of recent measurements of W gives an average value of 33.6; this would give a calculated value of 2928 ergs/cm²/r.

This calculation assumes a monochromatic 662-kev γ-ray beam: it is probable that the beam contains a small amount of X- and γ-rays of lower energy due to bremsstrahlung from the cesium β-rays, and scattering within the source. Absorption measurements and theoretical considerations, however, show that low-energy radiations contribute less than 1% of the energy of the beam, and thus their effect here can be neglected.

If the experimentally measured conversion factor and the calculated "true" absorption coefficient are put into the above formula, a value for W is obtained. This was found to be

$$W = 33.9 \pm 0.5 \text{ ev/ion pair}$$

SUMMARY

The power in the γ-ray beam from a Cs^{137} teletherapy unit has been measured with a calorimeter. Comparison with ionization measurements gives a conversion factor of 2959 ± 44 ergs/cm²/r, and combining this result with the calculated absorption coefficient gives a value for W of 33.9 ± 0.5 ev/ion pair.

ACKNOWLEDGMENTS

The author wishes to thank Professor W. V. Mayneord for his advice and encouragement throughout this project, and the workshop staff for their help in building the apparatus.

RECEIVED: February 17, 1958

REFERENCES

1. J. S. LAUGHLIN, J. W. BEATTIE, W. J. HENDERSON, and R. A. HARVEY, Calorimetric evaluation of the roentgen for 400 Kv and 22.5 Mev roentgen rays. *Am. J. Roentgenol. Radium Therapy Nuclear Med.* **70,** 294 (1953).

2. G. W. DOLPHIN and G. S. INNES, A calorimetric method used in the dosimetry of X-ray beams from a 1 Mev generator. *Phys. Med. Biol.* **1,** 161–174 (1956).

3. J. MCELHINNEY, B. ZENDLE, and S. R. DOMEN, Calorimetric determination of the power in a 1400-kv X-ray beam. *Radiation Research* **6,** 40–54 (1957).

4. J. P. BERNIER, L. D. SKARSGARD, D. V. CORMACK, and H. E. JOHNS, A calorimetric determination of the energy required to produce an ion pair in air for cobalt-60 gamma-rays. *Radiation Research* **5,** 613–633 (1957).

5. L. D. SKARSGARD, J. P. BERNIER, D. V. CORMACK, and H. E. JOHNS, Calorimetric determination of the ratio of energy absorption to ionization for 22-Mev X-rays. *Radiation Research* **7,** 217–228 (1957).

6. W. V. MAYNEORD, Some application of nuclear physics to medicine. *Brit. J. Radiol.* Suppl. 2, pp. 133–136 (1950).

7. R. K. BRINTON and C. T. O'KONSKI, A phototube measuring circuit for thermopiles. *Rev. Sci. Instr.* **24,** 1102–1104 (1953).

8. E. HAYWARD and J. HUBBEL, The albedo of various materials for 1-Mev photons. *Phys. Rev.* **93,** 955 (1954).

9. Z. BAY, W. B. MANN, H. H. SELIGER, and H. O. WYKOFF, Absolute measurement of W for sulfur-35 beta-rays. *Radiation Research* **7,** 567 (1957).

RADIATION RESEARCH 10, 13–19 (1959)

Nonionizing Radiant Energy as an Agent in Altering the Incidence of X-Ray-Induced Chromatid Aberrations

II. Reversal of the Far-Red Potentiating Effect in *Vicia* by Red Radiant Energy[1]

C. C. MOH[2] AND R. B. WITHROW

Smithsonian Institution, Washington, D. C.

INTRODUCTION

In a previous report (*1*) evidence was presented that radiant energy from about 710 to 820 mμ can increase the frequency of chromatid aberrations induced by X-rays in *Tradescantia* and *Vicia*, whereas infrared beyond about 820 mμ is relatively ineffective. These findings indicated that the potentiating effect of nonionizing radiation is due to far-red energy rather than infrared in the vicinity of 1000 mμ, as concluded by previous workers (*2, 3*). We presented a kinetical hypothesis based on the assumption that red energy of wavelengths shorter than about 700 mμ is capable of reversing the far-red potentiation. This is analogous to the reversible photosystems found in a great variety of higher plants. In seed germination (*4*), flowering, and seedling development (*5*), the red induces certain growth reactions that can be inhibited by the far-red. The present report shows evidence of a similar photoreversible system at the nuclear level.

MATERIALS AND METHODS

Plant Material

The root tips of broad bean (*Vicia faba*) were used for all experiments. A sample of roots grown from each newly purchased batch of seed was examined cytologically for significant spontaneous chromosomal breakage. In some batches, the spontaneous chromosomal breakage rate was as much as 10% or more, and these were discarded. Seed used in the present experiments were purchased from Sutton and Sons

[1] This study was supported by the U. S. Atomic Energy Commission under Contract AT-(30-1)-1661 and is published with the approval of the Secretary of the Smithsonian Institution.

[2] Present address: Inter-American Institute of Agricultural Sciences, Turrialba, Costa Rica.

Ltd., Reading, England. The method of culture of the bean roots has been described in detail previously (*1*). Seven-day-old, dark-grown seedlings with primary roots 6 to 9 cm long were selected for the irradiations.

Filter Systems

Most of the filters were prepared from organic dye solutions because such solutions have a sharper cutoff than gelatin or glass and can be kept cooled more readily. The compositions of filter systems for four wavebands and the approximate irradiances obtained are given in Table I. The relative spectral energy distributions of the radiant flux transmitted by the filter systems are presented in Fig. 1.

Filter A transmitted wavelengths from 715 to 940 mμ, involving most of the far-red and a relatively small proportion of near infrared. Since it has been shown previously that the potentiating effect was most effectively induced by the far-red from about 710 to 820 mμ and that wavelengths longer than about 820 mμ were ineffective, we have designated filter A as a far-red filter throughout this paper as a matter of convenience. Filter B transmitted a waveband from 670 to 940 mμ, passing most of the far-red and a small proportion of the red. Filter C was similar to B but transmitted a greater bandwidth of red radiant energy. Filter D passed wavelengths from 620 to 700 mμ which will be referred to as red, in contrast with the term far-red. The glass filter cell and cooling system were the same as previously described (*1*). The radiation source was a 500- or 1000-watt GE projection lamp, and the intensity was

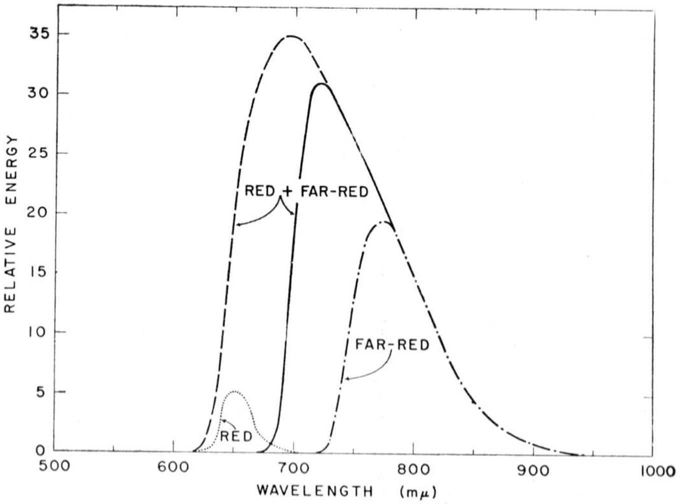

FIG. 1. Relative spectral energy distribution of the flux transmitted by the four filter systems.

TABLE I
COMPOSITION OF FILTER SYSTEMS

Waveband ($m\mu$)	*Primary filter*	*Secondary filter*	*Irradiance* ($\mu w/cm^2$)
A. Far-red 715–940	Ferrous ammonium sulfate, 100 gm/l, in 2% H_2SO_4; path length, 5 cm	DuPont acid green No. 1854 new, 0.32 gm/l, and Pontamine fast red 8BL, 0.4 gm/l; path length, 5 cm	3000
B. Far-red and Red 670–940	Ferrous ammonium sulfate, 100 gm/l, in 2% H_2SO_4; path length, 5 cm	Pontacyl green BL extra conc., 200% 0.06 gm/l, and Pontamine fast red 8BL, 0.14 gm/l; path length, 5 cm	6000
C. Far-red and Red 620–940	Ferrous ammonium sulfate, 100 gm/l, in 2% H_2SO_4; path length, 5 cm	Orange G, 0.4 gm/l, and Pontamine fast red, 0.8 gm/l; path length, 5 cm	8500
D. Red 620–700	$CuSO_4 \cdot 5H_2O$, 10 gm/l in 0.5% H_2SO_4; path length, 10 cm	Corning Glass No. 2403	300

regulated by a variable transformer. A glass condensing lens produced an intense and relatively parallel beam.

Irradiation Method

The primary roots to be irradiated were matched in length and size and divided into two or three groups, depending on the experiment. They were arranged for irradiation in a linear pattern in a 1-cm rectangular glass water cell. Four experimental series were conducted to investigate the influence of red and/or far-red radiant energy on the induction of X-ray-induced chromatid aberrations. The sequence of application of various types of radiant energy to the roots is shown in Table II. In the experimental series I*a* and I*b*, the red was applied as a 3-hour treatment immediately after a 3-hour far-red exposure. In series II and III, the red and far-red were applied simultaneously by extending the transmission band of the filter to shorter wavelengths. In series II, the level of red to far-red energy was relatively low, as determined by the position of the short wavelength limit at 670 mμ. In III, the filter transmitted to 620 mμ and included a greater proportion of the red, without appreciably altering the amount of far-red energy. In series IV, only red energy was used as a pretreatment.

After the visible irradiation treatment, the roots were simultaneously irradiated with X-rays. All roots received 120 r except those of series I*b*, which were given 100

r. A group of roots subjected to X-rays alone was used as a control; it was necessary to have a control group for each experimental series, since the response of chromatid aberrations to X-radiation fluctuated somewhat from experiment to experiment. The X-ray machine was a therapy type and was operated at 120 kvp and 10 ma, with a 1-mm aluminum filter. The dosage rate was approximately 50 r/min, as measured with a Victoreen roentgen meter. A constant temperature of 17° C was maintained for all phases of the various treatments.

Cytological Technique

Twenty-four hours after X-irradiation, the root tips were excised, pretreated with chilled saturated aqueous *p*-dichlorobenzene for an hour, and fixed in Carnoy's fluid. The slides were prepared by the aceto-orcein smear technique, one root tip per slide. The chromatid aberrations were observed at metaphase, and no more than

TABLE II

EFFECT OF PRETREATMENT WITH RED (620–680 Mμ) AND/OR FAR-RED (715–940 Mμ) RADIANT ENERGY ON THE FREQUENCY OF CHROMATID ABERRATIONS INDUCED BY X-RAYS IN *Vicia* ROOT TIPS

Experimental series	*Irradiation sequence*[a]			*Number of cells observed*	*Aberrations per cell*					
					Chromatid breaks		*Isochromatid breaks*		*Chromatid exchanges*	
	3 hr	*3 hr*	*2–2.5 min*		*Number*	*Increase (%)*	*Number*	*Increase (%)*	*Number*	*Increase (%)*
I*a*	D	D	X 120 r	444	0.53 ± 0.04	—	0.63 ± 0.04	—	0.20 ± 0.02	—
	FR	D	X 120 r	446	0.72 ± 0.04	+36	0.61 ± 0.04	−3	0.27 ± 0.02	+35
	FR	R	X 120 r	433	0.49 ± 0.03	−7	0.57 ± 0.04	−9	0.21 ± 0.02	+5
I*b*	D	D	X 100 r	490	0.24 ± 0.02	—	0.28 ± 0.02	—	0.12 ± 0.01	—
	FR	D	X 100 r	476	0.34 ± 0.03	+42	0.40 ± 0.03	+43	0.19 ± 0.02	+59
	FR	R	X 100 r	500	0.24 ± 0.02	—	0.30 ± 0.02	+7	0.11 ± 0.01	−8
II	—	D	X 120 r	304	0.47 ± 0.04	—	0.62 ± 0.04	—	0.18 ± 0.02	—
	—	R, FR	X 120 r	271	0.58 ± 0.05	+23	0.70 ± 0.05	+13	0.25 ± 0.03	+39
III	—	D	X 120 r	450	0.51 ± 0.03	—	0.60 ± 0.04	—	0.19 ± 0.02	—
	—	R, FR	X 120 r	450	0.51 ± 0.03	0	0.63 ± 0.04	+5	0.20 ± 0.02	+5
IV	—	D	X 120 r	650	0.60 ± 0.03	—	0.74 ± 0.03	—	0.18 ± 0.02	—
	—	R	X 120 r	625	0.53 ± 0.03	−12	0.68 ± 0.03	−8	0.20 ± 0.02	+11

[a]D: Dark period.
FR: Far-red, 715–940 mμ, 3000 μw/cm².
R: Red, 620–680 mμ, 300 μw/cm².
R, FR: 670–940 mμ, 6000 μw/cm² in series II; 620–940 mμ, 8000 μw/cm² in series III.
X: X-irradiation.

50 metaphases were scored from each slide. The standard errors were calculated according to the Poisson distribution.

RESULTS

The results of cytological observations of all experimental series are summarized in Table II. As shown in the experimental series I*a* and I*b*, a 3-hour far-red pretreatment increased the frequency of chromatid breaks and exchanges about 40% (average of two experiments), as compared with the control, which was subjected to X-ray treatment alone. The differences are statistically significant at the 5% level. The frequency of isochromatid aberration showed a rather erratic response to the far-red treatment and, in most series, no statistical significance was found. Because of this inconsistent response, only the frequency of chromatid breaks and exchanges were used for comparison.

When the red energy was given immediately after the far-red treatment, no significant increase in either type of chromatid aberration was observed, indicating that the red can completely nullify or reverse the far-red potentiating effect on X-ray-induced chromatid breakage.

In series II, the red and far-red were applied simultaneously. The proportion of red to far-red energy was relatively low, and this low level of red energy did not reduce the far-red effect to a significant degree. When the proportion of red energy was increased as in series III, however, the far-red effect was almost completely nullified.

The red in the range of 620 to 680 mμ did not significantly alter chromosomal aberrations when used alone with X-rays, as shown in series IV of Table II. This region of the red appears to be effective only in nullifying the effects of a far-red exposure.

DISCUSSION

The preceding experiments verify that far-red radiant energy is capable of increasing the frequency of chromatid breaks and exchanges in *Vicia* root tips. When red energy is applied, either simultaneously or immediately after the far-red treatment, far-red potentiation cannot be observed. From these results, we conclude that the red is capable of nullifying or reversing the ability of the far-red to potentiate the X-ray effect on chromatid aberrations.

The results of this study might explain the observation of previous workers in regard to the absence of any effect with direct unfiltered sunlight. Swanson *et al.* (*6*) first noted that the number of X-ray-induced chromatid aberrations in *Tradescantia* inflorescences from plants grown in a heavily shaded greenhouse were similar to those in inflorescences from an open field exposed to the intense radiation of a summer sun. One would have expected some difference, since the plants grown in open-field conditions received much more far-red energy. This anomalous phenomenon led us to speculate that a red, far-red reversible system might be involved (*1*).

Although Swanson and Yost (*7*) found that a high temperature shock (48° C for 30 seconds) applied to the inflorescences after the irradiation could completely remove the potentiation, there was no evidence that such temperatures were involved in the field experiments. The present results make it possible to interpret the similarity of X-ray effects in the two conditions as resulting from a blocking of far-red potentiation by simultaneous exposure to red energy.

It has been noted that the red versus far-red system has been found in many plant morphological and physiological expressions. In all the reported cases, the red induces the reaction and the far-red reverses it. In the potentiation of chromosomal aberrations, the active region of induction is in the far-red and the reversal is in the red. The total incident energy required to counteract plant photomorphogenic induction has been studied by a few workers. It has been shown by Klein *et al.* (*8*) that a relatively small amount of far-red can counteract a relatively large dose of red. The present study shows that in the red, far-red effect on the nuclear system complete reversal may be obtained with red energy equivalent to only 10% of the far-red.

The energy level of far-red required for an induction of potentiating effect on chromosome breakage, however, is extremely high. Yost (*9*) used an irradiance of 56,000 $\mu w/cm^2$ for an irradiation period of 3 hours in order to obtain a significant potentiating effect on *Tradescantia* microspore chromosomes. In general, a detectable response requires an order of 10,000 times as much as the more sensitive photomorphogenic systems. It is possible that this extremely high energy requirement is due to a very small amount of photosensitive pigment and the low quantum-capturing capabilities of the system.

Lea (*10*) has shown that exchanges between chromosome breaks in *Tradescantia* microspores are limited to breaks which, at the moment of their production, are separated by distances up to about 1 micron. Such breaks remain capable of exchange for only a few minutes, and then the majority restitute. Observations of Wolff and Luippold (*11*) indicate that in *Vicia* the repair of radiation-induced chromosome breaks is dependent on oxidative phosphorylation, especially that part mediated by cytochrome oxidase. They concluded that oxidative metabolism with its concurrent formation of ATP is necessary for rejoining.

Gordon and Surrey have recently carried this one step further. They have reported (*12*) that a high rate of phosphate esterification takes place when isolated rat mitochondria are incubated with succinate as a substrate and ADP as an acceptor, with a constant rate for about 30 minutes. The rate then decays exponentially in the dark. The decay constant is increased by 1.6 if far-red radiant energy (722 to 727 mμ) is given and decreased by 0.29 with red (648 to 652 mμ), both at about 18 $ergs/mm^2/sec$. The inhibition of the mitochondrial activity by the far-red is repeatedly reversible by the red given in alternating sequence.

These observations strongly imply that the far-red does not directly increase chromosomal aberrations but rather reduces the level of oxidative phosphorylation and thereby reduces the rate of chromosomal repair of aberrations induced by the X-irradiation. It is possible that an exposure to red radiant energy, simultaneous with or subsequent to the far-red, prevents the reduced availability of high-energy phosphate and thereby permits normal restitution to take place.

SUMMARY

Far-red radiant energy given in a waveband from 715 to 940 mμ, with an irradiance of 3000 μw/cm^2, was capable of inducing a potentiating effect on chromatid aberrations in *Vicia* root tips induced by 100 to 120 r of X-rays. When red energy from 620 to 680 mμ, at an irradiance of 300 μw/cm^2, was applied for 3 hours either simultaneously with or immediately after the far-red treatment, no increase in frequency was obtained. These results indicate that the red is capable of nullifying or reversing the far-red potentiating effect. Apparently, the red, far-red reversible system, which has been demonstrated in a wide variety of systems in higher plants, also occurs at the nuclear level.

RECEIVED: March 18, 1958

REFERENCES

1. R. B. WITHROW and C. C. MOH, Nonionizing radiant energy as an agent in altering the incidence of X-ray-induced chromatid aberrations. I. Effects of far-red and infrared radiant energy on *Tradescantia* and *Vicia*. *Radiation Research* **6,** 491–500 (1957).
2. BERWIN P. KAUFMANN, ALEXANDER HOLLAENDER, and HELEN GAY, Modification of the frequency of chromosomal rearrangements induced by X-rays in *Drosophila*. I. Use of near infrared radiation. *Genetics* **31,** 349–367 (1946).
3. C. P. SWANSON and ALEXANDER HOLLAENDER, The frequency of X-ray-induced chromatid breaks in *Tradescantia* as modified by near infrared radiation. *Proc. Natl. Acad. Sci. U. S.* **32,** 295–302 (1946).
4. E. H. TOOLE, V. K. TOOLE, H. A. BORTHWICK, and S. B. HENDRICKS, Photocontrol of *Lepidium* seed germination. *Plant Physiol.* **30,** 15–21 (1955).
5. W. H. KLEIN, R. B. WITHROW, and V. B. ELSTAD, Response of the hypocotyl hook of bean seedlings to radiant energy and other factors. *Plant Physiol.* **31,** 289–294 (1956).
6. C. P. SWANSON, CLAUD S. RUPERT, and HENRY T. YOST, JR., Infrared absorption and temperature studies on the buds and chromosomes of *Tradescantia paludosa*. *Am. J. Botany* **40,** 557–565 (1953).
7. C. P. SWANSON and HENRY T. YOST, JR., The induction of activated, stable states in the chromosomes of *Tradescantia* by infra-red and X-rays. *Proc. Natl. Acad. Sci. U. S.* **37,** 796–802 (1951).
8. W. H. KLEIN, R. B. WITHROW, A. P. WITHROW, and V. ELSTAD, Time course of far-red inactivation of photomorphogenesis. *Science* **125,** 1146–1147 (1957).
9. HENRY T. YOST, JR., The effect of intensity of infrared on X-ray induced chromosome aberrations in *Tradescantia*. *Genetics* **37,** 457–468 (1952).
10. D. E. LEA, The induction of chromosome structural changes by radiation; detailed quantitative interpretation. *Brit. J. Radiol. Suppl.* **1,** 85–93 (1947).
11. SHELDON WOLFF and HENRY E. LUIPPOLD, Metabolism and chromosome-break rejoining. *Science* **122,** 231–232 (1955).
12. SOLON A. GORDON and KENNETH SURREY, A biological basis for the far-red potentiation of X-ray induced chromosomal breaks. (Abstract, 94) *Proc. Intern. Congr. Radiation Research* **9,** 121 (1958).

RADIATION RESEARCH 10, 20–29 (1959)

Effects of Heavy Particle Irradiation on Acute Mortality and Survival Time in the Mouse[1]

V. P. BOND AND O. D. EASTERDAY

Medical Department, Brookhaven National Laboratory, Upton, New York

INTRODUCTION

Acute total-body irradiation of the mouse with heavy particles can be accomplished by thermal neutron exposure of animals injected previously with isotopes such as B^{10} or Li^6 that have a high capture cross section for thermal neutrons. The short-range heavy recoil particles liberated instantaneously in the resulting nuclear reaction irradiate the tissues with a distribution of dose determined by the distribution of the capture element in the tissues. With B^{10}, a 1.473-Mev α-particle and a 0.841-Mev recoil Li^7 particle are liberated in the process (*1*). A 0.479-Mev γ-ray is liberated in 94.1% of the disintegrations. In the Li^6 capture process, a 2.051-Mev α-particle and a 2.748-Mev tritium particle (no γ-particle) are liberated (*2*).

In a previous communication (*3*), the procedure for such irradiation was presented in detail, and the effects of heavy particles from boron capture as determined from the spleen-thymus weight loss end points in mice were described. In the present paper, the effects of B^{10} and Li^6 capture radiations on acute mortality and survival time in the mouse are presented. This material has been presented in part previously (*4*).

METHODS

Mice were irradiated in the medical facility of the Brookhaven Research reactor (*3, 5*). The thermal neutron flux, determined at each exposure with gold foil monitors, was approximately 1.35×10^9 n/cm²-sec at the surface of the mouse. The γ-particle contamination at this flux was approximately 220 r/hr from the intrinsic reactor radiation, 30 r/hr from hydrogen capture in the Lucite exposure apparatus, and 50 r/hr from inter-mouse hydrogen capture in tissue (*3*). All exposures in which B^{10} or Li^6 were used were 30 minutes or less in duration.

For comparison, mice were exposed in a cobalt-60 γ-irradiator maintained in the Brookhaven Medical Department. The exposure dose rate in tissue was approxi-

[1] This research was supported by the U. S. Atomic Energy Commission.

mately 8 r/min with the exposure apparatus and animals in place (approximately 2% higher than the exposure dose-free in air). Exposure dose rates were measured with a Victoreen chamber calibrated for cobalt-60 γ-radiation by the National Bureau of Standards. Exposure dose rates in tissue were converted to rads by the factor of 0.96 (*6*).

Female CF1 mice, obtained from Carworth Farms, were used in these studies. The animals were 3 to 4 weeks old when received and 10 to 12 weeks old when used for mortality studies. Mice were exposed at the reactor, 10 at one time, in thin Lusteroid centrifuge cones; 30 per group were exposed in a plastic box in the cobalt-60 γ-irradiator. Exposure groups were of essentially equal weight distribution; control groups were subjected to procedures identical to those used for exposure groups, with the exception of actual irradiations. The numbers per group are presented below under results. Mortality observations were made twice daily for 28 days after exposure.

Boron was administered intravenously as B^{10}-enriched borax 5 minutes prior to neutron exposure. Approximately 96% of the boron was B^{10}. A dose of 25 μg/gm of tissue was administered in a volume of 0.01 ml/gm. Lithium was given intravenously in the form of enriched Li^6Cl (96% of Li was Li^6). The dose of Li^6 was 33.3 μg/gm in a volume of 0.01 mg/gm. Studies previously reported indicated acceptably uniform distribution of borax throughout the tissues (*3*), and the concentrations in the marrow and gut were essentially identical. Distribution studies

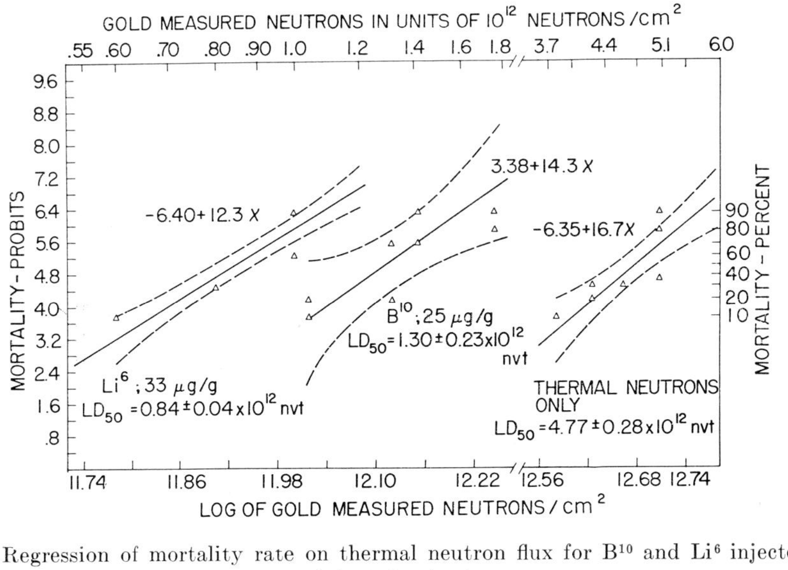

FIG. 1. Regression of mortality rate on thermal neutron flux for B^{10} and Li^6 injected and uninjected animals.

were not done with LiCl. Previous studies (*3*) indicated that the combination of injected B^{10} and Co^{60} γ-irradiation did not enhance the γ-radiation effect.

RESULTS

The mortality results are tabulated in Tables I and II. The data were analyzed by the probit transformation technique and the maximum likelihood solution (*7*, *8*). The calculations were performed by the Computer Center of this laboratory on a Remington Rand Model 409-2R punch card electronic computer. The regression of mortality rate on exposure dose for the several radiations employed are shown in Fig. 1. The LD_{50} values obtained are as follows: cobalt-60 γ-radiation, 789 $\pm$ 31 rads; thermal neutrons only, $4.77 \pm 0.14 \times 10^{12}$ n/cm^2; B^{10} plus thermal neutrons, $1.30 \pm 0.11 \times 10^{12}$ n/cm^2; Li^6 plus thermal neutrons, $0.84 \pm 0.04 \times 10^{12}$ n/cm^2. No mortality occurred in control animals injected with the B^{10} or Li^6 compounds.

It is apparent that the presence of the capture elements in the tissue markedly increased the mortality rate in mice exposed to thermal neutron irradiation. The slopes of the regression lines are not significantly different among the several radiations employed.

TABLE I

MORTALITY RATE IN MICE EXPOSED TO THERMAL NEUTRONS AND γ-RADIATIONS

Co^{60} γ-rays				*Thermal neutrons*			
Dose (rads)	*Dead/total*	*Mortality (%)*	*MST*[a]	*Neutron dose*[b]	*Dead/total*	*Mortality (%)*	*MST*[a]
630	1/25	4.0	15.0	3.82	0/10	0	12.3
					1/10	10	
675	1/24	4.2	14.0		2/10	20	
720	2/25	8.0	15.0	4.21	2/10	20	8.5
					3/10	30	
765	13/25	52.0	13.2		3/10	30	
					0/10	0	
810	14/25	56.0	15.4				
				4.60	1/10	10	8.5
					3/10	30	
				5.10	9/10	90	8.8
					4/10	40	
					8/10	80	
				5.46	9/10	90	10.4
					6/10	60	
					9/10	90	
				5.92	10/10	100	5.3
					10/10	100	
					10/10	100	

[a] Mean survival time of decedents in days. Groups at equal dose levels of thermal neutrons were combined.

[b] Total thermal neutrons, units of 10^{12}/cm^2.

TABLE II

MORTALITY RATE IN MICE EXPOSED TO HEAVY PARTICLE RADIATION

B^{10} borax + thermal neutrons (25 μg B^{10}/gm)				Li^6Cl + thermal neutrons (33.3 μg Li^6/gm)			
Neutron dose[a]	*Dead/total*	*Mortality* (%)	*MST*[b]	*Neutron dose*[a]	*Dead/total*	*Mortality* (%)	*MST*[b]
1.04	2/10	20	8.7	0.60	1/10	10	4.3
	1/10	0			1/10	10	
	1/10	10			1/10	10	
1.32	7/10	70	4.3	0.80	3/10	30	9.0[c]
	2/10	20			3/10	30	
	7/10	70			3/10	30	
	0/10	0			2/10	20	
1.42	10/10	100	4.7	1.00	9/10	90	5.1
	9/10	90			9/10	90	
	7/10	70			9/10	90	
1.59	10/10	100	4.5	1.20	10/10	100	3.2
	10/10	100			10/10	100	
					10/10	100	
					10/10	100	
1.76	10/10	100	4.1	1.39	10/10	100	3.3
	10/10	100			10/10	100	
	9/10	90			10/10	100	
	8/10	80			10/10	100	
2.13	10/10	100	3.2	1.52	10/10	100	3.2
	10/10	100			10/10	100	
	10/10	100			10/10	100	
	10/10	100					
	10/10	100					
	10/10	100					
2.37	10/10	100	3.0	1.85	10/10	100	3.2
	10/10	100			10/10	100	
	10/10	100			10/10	100	

[a] Total thermal neutrons, units of $10^{12}/cm^2$.
[b] Mean survival time of decedents in days. Groups at equal dose levels were combined.
[c] Mean value influenced markedly by 2 mice dying on the twenty-sixth day.

Dosage calculation. The apparent relative biological effectiveness (RBE) of the recoil heavy particle radiations can be estimated from the calculated dose to the tissues delivered by the heavy particles. The rem dose rates due to recoil particles alone can be determined by subtracting the rem dose rate resulting from the thermal neutron and associated radiations alone from the total rem dose rate observed. The effects of thermal neutrons and γ-radiations on mortality rate on the mouse have been found to be additive (*9*). The method of calculation has been presented in detail (*3*). It is convenient to use the LD_{50} values in the calculations, equal to 789 rads or rem of the standard cobalt-60 γ-radiation, and thus equal to 789 rem of the other radiations employed.

For boron, the rem dose rate from the recoil particles was 442 rem per 10^{12} nvt (nvt indicates total neutrons per square centimeter). The rad dose rate, based on the mean tissue concentration of 25 μg of B^{10} per gram, the capture cross section of 4010 barns, and a value of 2.34 Mev for the total energy liberated by the two recoil particles (*3*), is 223 rads per 10^{12} nvt. The RBE for this particle radiation is accordingly 442/223, or 2.0. If the energy of the α-ray only (1.473 Mev) is used in the rad calculation, the RBE becomes 3.2.

For lithium, the rem dose rate for the particles liberated from Li^6 is 774 rem per 10^{12} nvt. The calculated rad dose rate (*3*), based on the mean tissue Li^6 dose of 33.3 μg/gm, the cross section of 950 barns, and the total energy liberated by both the recoil α- and tritium particles (4.80 Mev), is 241 rads per 10^{12} nvt. The RBE is thus 774/241 = 3.2.

The survival time of mice irradiated with heavy particles was different from those observed with either thermal neutron only or γ-irradiation. From Table I it can

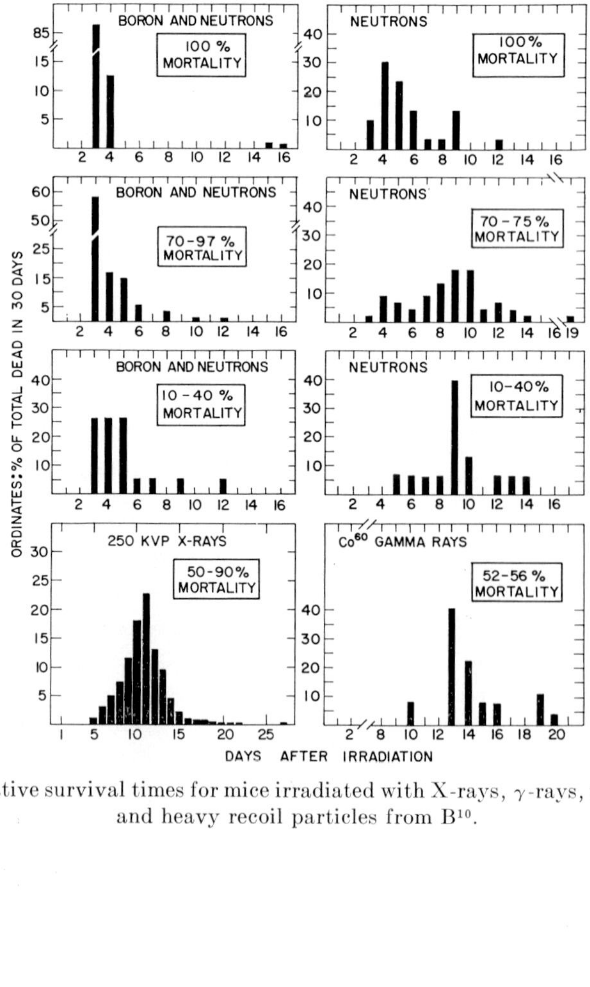

FIG. 2. Comparative survival times for mice irradiated with X-rays, γ-rays, thermal neutrons, and heavy recoil particles from B^{10}.

be seen that with cobalt-60 γ-irradiation all mean survival times are of the order of 13 to 15 days. From these data and from the published literature it is clear that throughout the 30-day lethal range (LD_1 to LD_{99}) the survival time for X- or γ-irradiated mice is approximately 10 to 15 days. With thermal neutrons (Table I), the mean survival time in the lethal range is shorter, approximately 8 to 10 days, as has been noted previously for thermal (*1*) and fast neutron (*10*) irradiation. The shortened survival time is considerably more marked with heavy particle irradiation (Table II) and is of the order of 4 to 5 days throughout the 30-day lethality range.

The differences in survival times are shown more clearly in Fig. 2 in which the daily deaths are compared for several types of radiations. It is seen that for comparable 30-day mortality levels, as one goes from X- or γ-, to thermal neutron, to boron plus thermal neutron irradiation, more animals die in the early period (3 to 5 days), leaving fewer to die in the later period (8 to 15 days). This results, of course, in a lower mean survival time.

In order to determine if the degree of biological effect varies appreciably from that anticipated with differing boron doses, additional LD_{50} values were determined on mice given 25, 40, 80, and 120 mg of B^{10} as borax per kilogram and then irradiated with thermal neutrons. The rem dose rates per nvt from the boron capture reaction alone were calculated by subtracting out the rem dose due to the thermal neutron beam alone (*1*). The increasing B^{10} doses, in the ratios of 1:1.6:3.2:4.8, resulted in increasing rem per nvt dose rates from the B^{10} alone, in the ratios of 1:1.5:4.1:6.3. The apparent relative increase in effect with increasing B^{10} dosage is not significant statistically.

DISCUSSION

The intravenous injection of B^{10} or Li^6 compounds prior to thermal neutron irradiation markedly increases the biological effect of the neutrons. The dose of B^{10} used in this study, 25 μg of B^{10} as borax per gram, was well below toxic levels for this compound. The borax dose, and thus approximately the effect of B^{10} neutron capture, could be raised by a factor of approximately 8 (LD_1 for B^{10} as borax in the female CF1 mouse is approximately 195 $\pm$ 19 μg of B^{10} per gram). With Li^6 as LiCl, however, the maximum effect possible was more nearly attained. (The LD_1 for Li as LiCl in the female CF1 mouse is 29 $\pm$ 9 μg of Li per gram, approximately the dose used in these studies.) These experimental results indicate that, because of the greater toxicity of lithium compared to boron compounds, boron may be the element of choice in considering neutron capture therapy. The toxicity factor largely offsets other theoretical advantages of lithium compounds (*11*).

The RBE of 2.0 for the recoil particles in this study is in good agreement with the value of 1.7 obtained previously, based on the degree of spleen and thymus weight loss in the mouse as the criterion of effect (*3*). It differs, however, from the

RBE of 1.3 obtained by another group (*12*) for acute mortality in the mouse; however, the LD_{50} for the standard Co^{60} γ-radiation differs in the two studies, as do the details of the method of calculation of dose from the $B^{10}(n, \alpha)Li^7$ reaction. The RBE values are not in agreement with the value of 3.2 obtained in the present study for the recoil α- and tritium particles from Li^6 neutron capture. (In unreported studies, a value of 2.8 was obtained for Li^6 neutron capture particles with spleen-thymus weight loss as the biological end point.) Possible explanations for the difference are offered in the following discussion.

The absolute values for the RBE figures obtained depend on the parameters used in the calculations, for which different values can be assumed. The relative values, however, should be valid unless drug concentrations grossly different from the average administered are present. The results thus probably indicate a real difference in the degree of effects of the particles from the two reactions. If the difference reflects a true difference in RBE, it would indicate that the boron recoil particles, with a higher mean linear energy transfer (LET) value, have the lower RBE. There is evidence from studies with microorganisms that the RBE may pass through a maximum and decrease with particles of very high LET (*13*). An alternative explanation lies in considering which particles should be used in the dose calculation. If, in the calculation of rads from the B^{10} capture reaction, only the energy of the recoil α-particle is used (with the recoil Li^7 particles neglected), the RBE becomes 3.2, in close agreement with the value of 3.2 obtained for both of the recoil particles from Li^6 capture. This could be taken to indicate that the recoil Li^7 nucleus from B^{10} capture does not contribute appreciably to the biological effect because, with its short range of 3 microns, it cannot penetrate sufficiently far in cells. The ranges in soft tissue of the other particles involved are: α from B^{10}, 1.473 Mev, 8 microns; α from Li^6, 2.051 Mev, 10 microns; tritium from Li^6, 2.748 Mev, 65 microns. Some support for this interpretation is found in the unpublished work of the present authors, in which neutron irradiation after intravenous injection of uranyl nitrate, $U^{235}O_2(NO_3)_2 \cdot 6H_2O$, failed to produce an appreciable effect of the recoil fission products on testis weight loss in the mouse. The β-particles from tritium injected as $H_2{}^3O$ are known to have an apparent RBE of 1.3 to 1.5 for acute effects on the mouse (*14*), even though the mean range of the β-particles in soft tissue is only about 4 microns (*15*). It should be pointed out, however, that the $H_2{}^3O$ quickly distributes as body water and appears intracellularly where the short-range β-particles would be expected to be effective. It appears that, where particles with ranges short as compared to the cell diameter are considered, the usual concept of "dose" or total energy absorbed per gram of tissue may be too gross for prediction of biological effect. The biological effects depend on the precise microscopic distribution of the chemical administered, which in turn determines the exact location of the deposited radiation energy and its accessibility to vulnerable intracellular structure.

The shortening of survival time after total-body heavy particle irradiation is more pronounced than that after thermal neutron (*16*) or fast neutron (*10*) irradiation. That the phenomenon was seen in B^{10}- and Li^{6}-treated animals would argue against postulated explanations for the shortened survival time with neutron irradiation—that it may result from decreased energy absorption from neutrons in the relative hydrogen, from poor bone (*10*), or from a high boron content of the gut or its contents. The early deaths are associated with gut damage, the latter with bone marrow damage (*17*). The most likely explanation at present is a marked sensitivity of the mouse intestine to changes in LET.

As pointed out above, in the mouse the phenomenon of shortened survival time increases in degree with different radiations in the following order: γ-rays, thermal neutrons, fast neutrons, heavy particles from neutron capture. Although the LET's of the heavy particles are different, the contribution from γ-radiation generated in tissue changes also (*18*). This undoubtedly contributes to the degree of the phenomenon seen in the mouse exposed to different radiations and probably accounts for the absence of the phenomenon in large animals exposed to fast neutrons in which the degree of contribution from γ-radiation is quite appreciable (*18*). The phenomenon is seen minimally or not at all in rats (M. N. Swift and V. P. Bond, unpublished data) and not at all in dogs (*19*).

In the present experiments, although some mice died on the sixth or seventh day, no evidence of a distinct mode of death characterized by this survival time was seen (*20*). This is in keeping with the results of the very large series of mice exposed to γ-radiation (*21*), in which two modes, a 4- to 5-day and a 10- to 12-day death, were seen. As seen clearly for X-rays in Fig. 2, the deaths group around a mean with a distribution over several days. Thus the 6- and 7-day deaths may well be the trailing portion of the 3- and 4-day death distribution, or the earlier part of the later death distribution. The time of death bears on the RBE value (*10*). The γ-ray dose to kill mice in 3 to 5 days is considerably higher than that needed to kill in 30 days. From reference *10*, the 5-day LD_{50} is higher than the 30-day LD_{50} by a factor of 1.6. If the 5-day LD_{50} values for the different radiations are compared as representing more comparable end points than do the 30-day LD_{50} values, the calculated RBE values are raised by a factor of approximately 1.6.

SUMMARY

The 28-day mortality rate was determined for female CF1 mice given B^{10}-enriched borax or Li^{6}-enriched LiCl intravenously and exposed 5 minutes later to graded doses of total-body thermal neutron radiation. The LD_{50} values were as follows: 25 μg of B^{10} per gram, $1.30 \pm 0.11 \times 10^{12}$ n/cm^2; 33.3 μg of Li^{6} per gram, $0.84 \pm 0.04 \times 10^{12}$ n/cm^2; thermal neutrons alone, $4.77 \pm 0.14 \times 10^{12}$ n/cm; and cobalt-60 γ-radiation, 789 ± 30 r. The RBE for the heavy particles (α and Li^{7}) from B^{10} neutron capture was calculated to be 2.0; a value of 3.2 was obtained for the particles (α and tritium) from Li^6 neutron capture. The tendency to 3- and 4-day deaths was found to be much more pronounced in animals exposed to heavy particle irradiation as compared to those exposed to X-ray, γ-, fast neutron, or thermal neutron irradiation.

ACKNOWLEDGMENTS

The authors are indebted for the advice and assistance of Drs. J. S. Robertson and E. E. Stickley, and for the excellent technical assistance of J. S. Gilmartin, C. A. Meyer, and M. N. Canner.

RECEIVED: March 13, 1958

REFERENCES

1. J. RHODES, W. FRANZEN, and W. E. STEPHENS, Ionization measurement of $B^{10}(n, \alpha)Li^7$. *Phys. Rev.* **87,** 141–145 (1952).
2. V. FACCHINI, E. GATTI, and E. GERMAGNOLI, The $Li^6(n, \alpha)H^3$ reaction spectrum. *Phys. Rev.* **81,** 475–476 (1951).
3. V. P. BOND, O. D. EASTERDAY, E. E. STICKLEY, and J. S. ROBERTSON, The relative biological effectiveness of thermal neutrons and of the heavy particles from the $B^{10}(n, \alpha)Li^7$ reaction for acute effects in the mouse. *Radiology* **67,** 650–664 (1956).
4. V. P. BOND and O. D. EASTERDAY, The effect of heavy particles from the $B^{10}(n, \alpha)Li^7$ reaction on acute mortality in the mouse. *Federation Proc.* **15,** 21 (1956).
5. L. E. FARR, J. S. ROBERTSON, and E. E. STICKLEY, Physics and physiology of neutron capture therapy. *Proc. Natl. Acad. Sci. U. S.* **40,** 1087–1093 (1954).
6. Report of the International Commission on Radiological Units and Measurements (ICRU), 1956. *Nat. Bur. Standards Handbook* **62** (available from the Government Printing Office, Washington, D. C.).
7. C. I. BLISS, *The Statistics of Bioassay,* Academic Press, New York, 1952.
8. D. J. FINNEY, *Probit Analysis,* Cambridge University Press, Cambridge, 1952.
9. J. B. STORER and J. E. FURCHNER, Studies on the mechanism of action of thermal neutrons in producing biological effects. II. Comparative effectiveness in producing intestinal damage, lethality and marrow damage in rats. U. S. Atomic Energy Commission Document LA-1848 (1954).
10. R. E. CARTER, V. P. BOND, and P. N. SEYMOUR, The relative biological effectiveness of fast neutrons in mice. *Radiation Research* **4,** 413–423 (1956).
11. A. J. LUESSENHOP, W. H. SWEET, and J. ROBINSON, Possible use of the neutron capturing isotope lithium-6 in the radiation therapy of brain tumors. *Am. J. Roentgenol. Radium Therapy Nuclear Med.* **76,** 376–392 (1956).
12. J. B. STORER, P. S. HARRIS, J. E. FURCHNER, and W. H. LANGHAM, The relative biological effectiveness of various ionizing radiations in mammalian systems. *Radiation Research* **6,** 188–288 (1957).
13. J. A. SAYEG, The effect of highly ionizing radiations on cell survival. U. S. Atomic Energy Commission Document UCRL-2293 (April, 1954).
14. F. C. V. WORMAN, The relative biological effectiveness of tritium beta rays in producing splenic and thymic weight loss in mice. U. S. Atomic Energy Commission Document LA-1641 (1954).
15. J. S. ROBERTSON and W. L. HUGHES, Theoretic considerations of the radiation dose from discrete tritium sources. *Radiology* **68,** 100–105 (1957).

16. J. T. Brennan, P. S. Harris, R. E. Carter, and W. H. Langham, The biological effectiveness of thermal neutrons in mice. Parts I and II. *Nucleonics* **12,** 48–56 (February, 1954); *ibid.* **12,** 31–35 (April, 1954).

17. V. P. Bond, M. S. Silverman, and E. P. Cronkite, Pathogenesis and pathology of post-irradiation infection. *Radiation Research* **1,** 389–400 (1954).

18. W. S. Snyder and J. Neufeld, Calculated depth-dose curves in tissue for broad beams of fast neutrons. *Brit. J. Radiol.* **28,** 342–350 (1955).

19. V. P. Bond, R. E. Carter, J. S. Robertson, P. H. Seymour, and H. H. Hechter, The effects of fast neutron irradiation in dogs. *Radiation Research* **4,** 139–153 (1956).

20. M. K. Austin, M. Miller, and H. Quastler, Five- to eight-day radiation death in mice. *Radiation Research* **5,** 303–307 (1956).

21. E. P. Cronkite, V. P. Bond, W. H. Chapman, and R. H. Lee, The relative biological effectiveness of atomic bomb gamma radiation. Naval Medical Research Institute Report NM-006-012.04.86 (1955). Condensed report in *Science* **122,** 148–50 (1955).

RADIATION RESEARCH 10, 30–36 (1959)

The Effect of Dose Rate on Genetic Damage from Fast Electrons in *Drosophila* Sperm[1]

ARMON F. YANDERS

U. S. Naval Radiological Defense Laboratory, San Francisco, California

INTRODUCTION

An assumption implicit in many studies involving the genetic effects of radiation in *Drosophila* is that the rate at which a dose of ionizing radiation is administered to spermatozoa is not effective in quantitatively influencing the effect produced (*1*). This hypothesis seemingly rests on a firm experimental foundation, since dose rates ranging from about 20,000,000 r/min (*2*) to 0.001 r/min (*3*) have been reported, and in neither case are the results significantly different from those obtained with the more usual rate of 100 r/min, although these extremes represent a 2×10^{10} range of dose rates. The hypothesis has been challenged, however, by two recent studies employing rapid dose rates. Haas *et al.* (*4*), measuring the production of translocations in *D. virilis* sperm, found the amount of induced effect to be nearly one-fifth greater when the dose was administered at 1800 r/min, rather than 100 r/min. Clark (*5*), using similar dose rates (2000 r/min versus 100 r/min) and measuring the induction of sex-linked recessive lethal mutations, found the effect to be nearly one-third greater at the faster rate.

This paper presents the results of a study in which *Drosophila* sperm were irradiated with fast electrons at several widely different dose rates. No significant differences due to dose rate can be found in the amount of effect produced, although the highest rates used were markedly higher than those employed in the two studies in which an effect was demonstrated.

MATERIALS AND METHODS

The effectiveness of the radiation was measured by two types of genetic damage: sex-linked recessive lethals, and dominant Minute characters. The first group, exhibiting a linear increase with dose over the ranges commonly employed, is a reflection of several kinds of genetic changes, from point mutations to gross chro-

[1] The opinions or assertions contained herein are those of the writer and are not to be construed as official or reflecting the views of the Navy Department or the Naval Establishment at large.

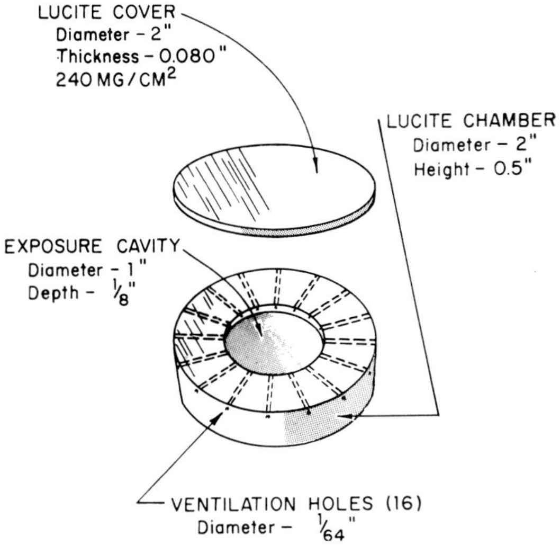

FIG. 1. Lucite exposure chamber used in fast electron studies with *Drosophila*.

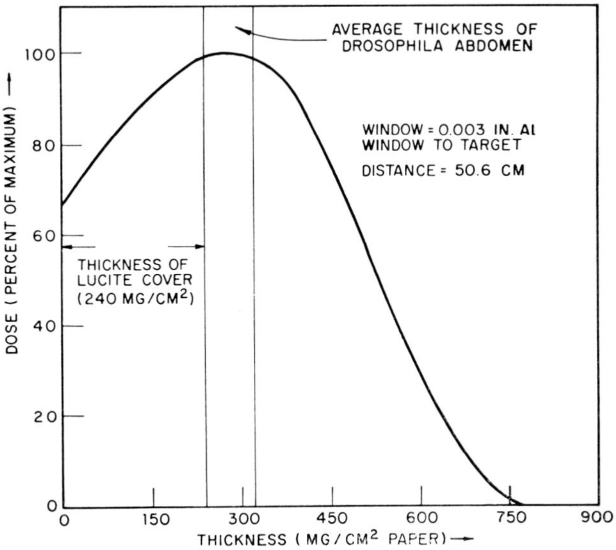

FIG. 2. Van de Graaff electron depth-dose curve for 1.6-Mev electron energy.

mosomal aberrations (*6*). The second group, also exhibiting a linear response with dose, is presumably the result of small deletions (*7*) and has been used to estimate genetic damage (*8*).

Fast electrons from a 2.0-Mev Van de Graaff accelerator were chosen as the radiation to be employed, since extremely high dose rates are obtainable with this machine. It was originally planned to use a total dose of 4000 rads, but midway in the study it was found that the dosimeter correction factor was nearly 20% too high. The revised figure gives an estimate of total dose of 3200 rads, which is a constant figure for the entire series of exposures, since the geometry remained the same over all. The voltage of the beam and the distance at which irradiation took place were constant; the rate of dose was varied only by changing the beam current. The dose rates ranged between 210 rads/min, a rather customary rate in work with *Drosophila*, and 6400 rads/min, a rate higher than that used by either Haas *et al.* (*4*) or Clark (*5*), although not so high as that used by Lüning *et al.* (*2*) with a special type of X-ray equipment capable of giving 1000 r in 50 μsec.

Male *Drosophila melanogaster* (Oregon-R strain) were irradiated with 1.6-Mev electrons in specially fabricated Lucite chambers (shown in Fig. 1). These chambers will accommodate as many as 100 males without crowding. The covering plate of each exposure chamber was machined to the thickness necessary to produce maximum dosage to the fly (for 1.6 Mev, a thickness of 0.080 inch, equivalent to 240 mg/cm^2). The maximum dose is about 1.6 times the dose to the surface of the Lucite chamber. It results from the electron scatter and the production of secondary electrons within the material. Figure 2 illustrates the experimental depth-dose curve obtained for a broad beam of 1.6-Mev electrons. It can be seen that the flies received uniform dosage, within about 1%, throughout their abdominal volume. The dose of 3200 rads was administered in time intervals of 30, 60, 135, 304, 683, or 900 seconds.

Immediately after irradiation, each treated group was anesthetized and divided into halves, one of which was placed with Muller-5 females for determination of the incidence of sex-linked recessive lethals, and the other with Oregon-R females for the determination of occurrence of Minute offspring. The parents were permitted to remain together for 48 hours (sperm batch I); the males were then transferred to new females for a second period of mating of 48 hours (sperm batch II). In one replication, the number of sex-linked recessive lethal tests was increased by a third 48-hour period of mating. These results (610 chromosomes tested) are included with sperm batch II.

After removal of the irradiated males, the Muller-5 females were placed in large culture vials and permitted to lay eggs; they were transferred en masse at 24-hour intervals to give four subcultures. The F_1 females to be tested for sex-linked recessive lethals were products of these mass cultures. On emergence, they were placed in mating vials with an excess of Muller-5 males, either sibs or stock, and permitted to mate for several days to increase the probability of successful insemination. After this period, single females were placed in individual small vials with one or two males. The resulting F_2 cultures were scored as lethal only if no normal males, and at least seven Muller-5 males, emerged. In doubtful cases, F_2 females were retested.

In testing for Minutes, each Oregon-R female was placed in a separate small culture vial after mass matings with irradiated males. The progeny were scored on emergence. Flies having only Minute bristles were scored as "total." Those with three or more Minute bristles, but not "total," were scored as "partial."

Quantitative estimates of Minute production can be meaningful only if great care is taken to recover each F_1 fly. Not only do Minute individuals develop more slowly than do wild-type flies, but they often are so weak as to live but a short time after emergence. To ensure complete recovery, at every collection in each of these experiments the surface of the food and the sides of each vial were inspected, and any flies remaining stuck were removed and examined. Since the characteristic Minute bristles can be identified even after the death of the flies, those recovered in this way are included in the results. As an additional precaution, the culture vials for each group were retained for several days after the last successful collection and reinspected carefully for late emergers before discarding.

Groups of controls were handled in the manner outlined above, with the exception of the irradiation.

RESULTS

Sex-linked recessive lethals. No effect of dose rate on genetic damage is found in the results of the tests for sex-linked recessive lethals. The data are given in Table I; each value represents the total of two to five replications. The differences in lethal frequency between exposures are not statistically significant; the summed data are homogeneous ($P = 0.67$), and, although the mean percentage of lethals induced (8.38%) is lower than would be predicted by X-ray data [an expected 9.4%, based on the estimate of 2.9% per 1000 r, as given by Herskowitz (*6*)], it is not seriously different.

Data from the subcultures exhibit only random variability, but a detectable difference ($P < 0.01$) is present between the ratios of lethals recovered in sperm

TABLE I

PRODUCTION OF SEX-LINKED RECESSIVE LETHALS IN MATURE *Drosophila* SPERM BY 3200 RADS OF 1.6-MEV ELECTRONS GIVEN AT VARIOUS DOSE RATES

Time of irradiation (sec)	*Number of chromosomes tested*	*Lethal chromosomes*	*Per cent lethal*
30	2143	182	8.49
60	887	76	8.57
135	1113	102	9.16
304	1014	81	7.99
683	1324	105	7.93
900	2250	186	8.27
Total	8731	732	8.38
Control	1423	2	0.14

TABLE II

COMPARISON OF INDUCED EFFECTS CONSIDERED BY SPERM BATCHES (See text)

Effect	Sperm batch I N	Sperm batch I Total	Sperm batch I %	Sperm batch II N	Sperm batch II Total	Sperm batch II %	P value (I vs. II)
Sex-linked lethals	355	3,792	9.36	377	4,939	7.63	0.01[a]
Dominant Minutes	151	16,955	0.89	182	24,744	0.74	0.08[b]

[a] Difference highly significant.
[b] Difference not significant.

TABLE III

PRODUCTION OF DOMINANT MINUTE CHARACTERS IN MATURE *Drosophila* SPERM BY 3200 RADS OF 1.6-MEV ELECTRONS GIVEN AT VARIOUS DOSE RATES

Time of irradiation (sec)	Number of flies observed	Number of Minutes observed P[a]	T[b]	P + T	% P + T
30	9,957	14	72	86	0.864
60	4,038	7	18	25	0.619
135	5,246	7	31	38	0.724
304	4,647	13	46	59	1.269
683	5,431	9	25	34	0.626
900	12,380	16	75	91	0.735
Total..........	41,699	66	267	333	0.799
Control........	5,429	1	1	2	0.037

[a] "Partials": 3 or more bristles Minute.
[b] "Totals": all bristles Minute.

batches I and II (see Table II). This represents the differential sensitivity at the time of irradiation of sperm of different ages, as has been shown previously for sex-linked recessive lethals (*9*).

Dominant Minutes. No effect of dose rate on Minute production can be detected. The recovery of Minutes after irradiation at the various exposure times is given in Table III. Each value in the table represents the total of two to five replications. These data, although heterogeneous enough to be significantly different (P = 0.05), exhibit no clear-cut trend and certainly no evidence that fast dose rates are more effective than slow. It is of interest to note that the high value for the irradiation time of 304 seconds (1.27%) contributes most of the variability in the test for significance. When the other values are tested, excluding this high value, no difference is detectable. Why this value should be so discrepant is not known.

The apparently higher value for recovery of Minutes in sperm batch I, compared to sperm batch II (see Table II), is not great enough to be significant in these results ($P = 0.08$).

DISCUSSION

The data collected during this study indicate that the rate at which a dose of fast electrons is given to mature spermatozoa of *Drosophila* does not influence the amount of genetic damage produced. It is difficult to reconcile these results with studies in which a rate effect is demonstrated, but two possibilities, not necessarily mutually exclusive, can be suggested.

First, since the irradiation employed in the present study was fast electrons rather than X-rays, it might be contended that this constitutes a difference. Why the two types of radiation should differ can be only speculative. In the production of genetic damage, fast-electron radiation should not be qualitatively different from X-radiation on purely theoretical grounds, since X-rays, after all, produce their effect by ionization due to recoil electrons. There is a great difference, however, in the linear energy transfer (LET) between the average electron from 250-kvp X-rays and 1.6-Mev electrons, the former having an LET about ten times as great as the latter. This difference in LET might be responsible for the existence of a rate effect with X-rays and not with electrons.

On the other hand, there may be an optimum rate of dose at which the greatest amount of damage is produced. If this is true, rates substantially higher or lower than the optimum would not exhibit pronounced differences in effectiveness. This can neither be confirmed nor denied on the basis of the present study, but the fact that no difference is found in dominant lethal production between irradiation times of 50 μsec and 15 minutes (*3*) could be interpreted in this light. Haas *et al.* (*4*) and Clark (*5*) may have been using the critical rate at which an effect can be demonstrated. The fractionation data of Clark are especially suggestive from this point of view, as he found that the production of hyperploid males at his fastest rate (2000 r given in 1 minute, no fractionation) and his slowest rate (2000 r, fractionated over a 90-minute period) was not significantly different; a detectable difference is exhibited only by intermediate time intervals of fractionation.

SUMMARY

Mature sperm of male *Drosophila melanogaster* were exposed to 3200 rads of fast (1.6-Mev) electrons from a Van de Graaff accelerator, given at rates ranging from 210 rads/min to 6400 rads/min. The amount of genetic damage was assessed by measurements of the frequency of induction of sex-linked recessive lethal mutations and dominant Minute effects.

No significant differences attributable to radiation dose rate were found between treated groups. The dose-rate effects reported by other authors using X-rays are not found with fast electrons. Possible reasons for the disagreement are discussed.

ACKNOWLEDGMENTS

I am grateful to Messrs. Bruce W. Shumway and Frank G. Watson for their interested cooperation with the irradiation and dosimetry, and to Mr. H. H. Hechter for discussions concerning the experimental design and statistical treatment.

RECEIVED: April 11, 1958

REFERENCES

1. H. J. MULLER, The manner of production of mutations by radiation. In *Radiation Biology* (A. Hollaender, ed.), Vol. 1, Chapter 8, McGraw-Hill Book Company, New York, 1954.
2. K. G. LÜNING, B. LINDELL, and R. FALK, The effect of high and low roentgen intensity on dominant lethals in *Drosophila melanogaster*. *Acta Radiol.* **43,** 89–92 (1955).
3. D. E. UPHOFF and C. STERN, The genetic effects of low intensity irradiation. *Science* **109,** 609–610 (1949).
4. F. L. HAAS, E. DUDGEON, F. E. CLAYTON, and W. S. STONE, Measurement and control of some direct and indirect effects of X-radiation. *Genetics* **39,** 453–471 (1954).
5. A. M. CLARK, Genetic effects of X-rays in relation to dose-rate in *Drosophila*. *Nature* **177,** 787 (1956).
6. I. H. HERSKOWITZ, The genetic basis of X-ray induced recessive lethal mutations. *Genetics* **36,** 356–363 (1951).
7. H. B. GLASS, Dosage curves for sex-linked lethals and dominant Minutes in *Drosophila melanogaster* females. *Genetics* **37,** 584–585 (1952).
8. G. H. MICKEY and A. F. YANDERS, The production of dcminant Minutes in *Drosophila* sperm irradiated with X rays, gamma rays, and fast neutrons. *Records Genet. Soc. Amer.* **23,** 56 (1954).
9. A. F. YANDERS, An influence of aging mature sperm upon X-ray induction of sex-linked recessive lethals. *Records Genet. Soc. Amer.* **25,** 667 (1956).

RADIATION RESEARCH **10**, 37–47 (1959)

The Effect of Ionizing Radiations on Carbohydrates[1]

M. L. WOLFROM, W. W. BINKLEY, L. J. McCABE, T. M. SHEN HAN, AND A. M. MICHELAKIS

Department of Chemistry, The Ohio State University, Columbus, Ohio

INTRODUCTION

Although the literature on the effects of ionizing radiations on carbohydrates and related substances is increasing rapidly, most of the reported work is concerned with changes in physical properties, with little emphasis placed on product isolation and characterization. For this reason and in recognition of the current interest in the effect of ionizing radiation on carbon compounds as well as in the potential utility of these radiations for the sterilization of foods, deinfestation of grains and cereals, and increasing the shelf-life of foods and medicinals, a program was initiated in this laboratory concerned with the effects of ionizing radiations on carbohydrates. Included in this study are the detection and determination of physical, chemical, and organoleptic changes, and the isolation and characterization of irradiation products.

RESULTS

Irradiation sources. The high-speed electrons (cathode rays) utilized in these experiments were supplied by a 1-Mev resonant transformer in conjunction with a permanently evacuated cathode-ray tube (*1*). This source was located at the General Electric Company, Milwaukee, Wisconsin. A 2000-curie Co^{60} source located at the Battelle Memorial Institute, Columbus, Ohio, provided the γ-rays. All samples exposed to γ-rays were irradiated at the rate of 400,000 rep/hr.

Cathode-ray irradiation of selected carbohydrates as crystalline solids. Two-gram samples of D-glucitol (sorbitol), methyl α-D-glucopyranoside, methyl β-D-glucopyranoside, maltose, cellobiose, α-D-glucose monohydrate, β-D-fructose, sucrose, and amylopectin (waxy maize starch) were weighed into plastic boxes (polystyrene,

[1] This paper represents research undertaken in cooperation with the Quartermaster Institute for the Armed Forces QM Research and Engineering Command, U. S. Army, under Contracts DA44-109-qm-1772 and DA-19-QM-515 with The Ohio State University Research Foundation (Projects 597 and 661), and has been assigned No. 839 in the series of papers approved for publication. The views or conclusions contained in this report are those of the authors. They are not to be construed as necessarily reflecting the view or indorsement of the Department of Defense. Preliminary communication: *Abstracts Papers Am. Chem. Soc.* **130,** 16A (1956).

rectangular, 1.9 × 4.8 × 4.8 cm, supplied by Cargille, 117 Liberty Street, New York, New York) and shipped to the cathode-ray source where they were irradiated with high-energy electrons at a dose of 13 Mrep at the rate of 6.5 Mrep/min. The materials were irradiated in air in open containers, which were closed and sealed immediately after the irradiation treatment. The time lapse between completion of irradiation and arrival at this laboratory was 2 to 3 days for this and subsequent series. The irradiated powders had changed color. Irradiated sucrose was pink, and the other irradiated carbohydrate powders varied in color from cream to yellow to tan. All the irradiated samples fluoresced when exposed to an ultraviolet lamp.

A number of samples of α-D-glucose monohydrate and β-D-fructose (as crystalline powders) were exposed to cathode-ray irradiation in varying doses. The reducing values (Somogyi method, *2*) of both monosaccharides decreased with irradiation. Unirradiated α-D-glucose monohydrate reduced 7.42 ml of 0.005 N Cu^{++} solution; α-D-glucose monohydrate (50 Mrep), 6.68 ml; unirradiated D-fructose, 7.49 ml; and D-fructose (50 Mrep), 6.06 ml. These sugars decreased in sweetness as the irradiation dose increased.

Two-gram samples of powdered sucrose were irradiated in air in open plastic boxes. The boxes and their containers were precooled for 30 minutes at about 5° C just prior to irradiation under cooling in an ice-water bath. The irradiated samples were dried under reduced pressure over Drierite (anhydrous calcium sulfate, as soluble anhydrite, a product of the W. A. Hammond Drierite Co., Xenia, Ohio) for several days. The rate and extent of reduction of Benedict reagent increased to a maximum at 26 Mrep and then decreased at 39 Mrep.

A descending paper chromatogram of the irradiated sucrose samples was prepared according to the method of Partridge (*3*, *4*). The chromatogram was developed for 16 hours with 1-butanol:ethanol:water (40:11:19, volume ratio). The developed chromatogram was air-dried and sprayed with aniline-phthalate indicator (1.66 gm of phthalic acid and 0.93 gm of aniline in 100 ml of 1-butanol saturated with water) and then placed in a moist oven at 110° C for 5 minutes (*5*). In all the irradiated samples, spots with the same mobilities as sucrose, glucose, and fructose were observed. The spot corresponding to fructose was visible only under ultraviolet light.

Irradiation of D-glucitol (sorbitol) and D-mannitol in frozen aqueous solutions. Fifty per cent aqueous solutions of D-glucitol (sorbitol) and D-mannitol were exposed to cathode-ray irradiation in doses ranging from 50 to 200 Mrep at the rate of 10 Mrep/min. The samples were cooled in an ethanol–solid carbon dioxide bath during irradiation. The irradiated products were yellow sirups. All the irradiated samples gave positive tests with Benedict and Molisch reagents. On arrival at this laboratory the irradiated samples were stored at −20° C.

Most of the unchanged D-glucitol was removed from the sample which had been exposed to 150 Mrep of cathode-ray irradiation by crystallization from absolute ethanol. A descending paper chromatogram was prepared from the mother liquor and developed according to the method described above for sucrose. The chromatogram so obtained was dried in air and developed further with this same developer for an additional 16 hours. The chromatogram was sprayed with aniline phthalate reagent (*5*). Spots with the same mobilities as glucose, gulose, arabinose, and xylose were observed; comparative known substances were run simultaneously. Two other chromatograms were developed for 16 hours with 1-butanol:acetic acid: water (4:1:5, volume ratio) (*6*) and allowed to stand overnight to remove the volatile acetic acid. One chromatogram was sprayed with *p*-anisidine hydrochloride reagent (*7*). The other was sprayed with sodium metaperiodate, potassium permanganate, and benzidine according to the method of Wolfrom and Miller (*8*). No gluconic or glucuronic acids were detected; the method detected known samples of these substances.

The sample of 50% aqueous D-mannitol which had been exposed to 150 Mrep of cathode-ray irradiation was concentrated to a sirup. A large portion of the unaltered D-mannitol was removed by crystallization from ethanol. The mother liquor was subjected to descending paper chromatography in the same manner as described above for the irradiated D-glucitol. Spots were detected with the same mobilities as mannose, arabinose, and mannuronic acid.

A sample of D-mannitol, as a 2.0 M aqueous solution, was sealed in a tinned can of 20-ounce capacity and exposed to γ-radiation from a Co^{60} source at the temperature ($\sim$25° C) of the "swimming pool" unit. The can was coated on the inside with lacquer. The sample received a dose of 4 Mrep delivered at the rate of 400,000 rep/hr. The irradiated sample gave positive tests with Benedict and Molisch reagents. After concentration of the irradiated sample to a sirup, the bulk of the unchanged D-mannitol was removed by crystallization from ethanol. Two paper chromatograms were prepared from the residual alcoholic solution as described above for irradiated D-glucitol, and the chromatograms were developed with 1-butanol:acetic acid:water. Spots corresponding to mannose and arabinose were observed. No mannonic or mannuronic acids were detected.

The mother liquor used for the above-described chromatography was concentrated to dryness under vacuum. The solid residue obtained gave a positive Benedict test. This solid residue was acetylated with 14 ml of pyridine (dried over barium oxide) and 9 ml of acetic anhydride at 0° C. After 24 hours the solution was poured into a mixture of ice and water. The gummy precipitate obtained was filtered, washed with water, and allowed to crystallize from ethanol. The product was recrystallized from hot ethanol; melting point 124° to 125° C undepressed on admixture with authentic D-mannitol hexaacetate, $[\alpha]_D^{25}$ +25° (c 4, $CHCl_3$). The filtrate, after removal of the D-mannitol hexaacetate, was neutralized with aqueous sodium bicarbonate solution and then extracted with chloroform. The pyridine was removed from the chloroform extract by the addition of a few drops of saturated cadmium chloride solution. The solid residue obtained on solvent removal, dissolved in a small amount of benzene, was added to the top of a 3.2 × 22-cm column of a mixture of "Silene EF" (synthetic hydrated calcium acid silicate, a product of the Columbia Chemical Division, Pittsburgh Plate Glass Co., Barberton, Ohio) and Celite (Celite 545, a siliceous filter aid, manufactured by the Johns-Manville Co., New York, New York) (5:1 by weight). The chromatogram was developed with 350 ml of benzene:ethanol (500:1 by volume). The extruded column was streaked with a freshly prepared solution of 1% potassium permanganate in 2.5 *N* sodium hydroxide. One distinct zone was observed. This zone was eluted with acetone, and the eluate was concentrated to a sirup which crystallized on the addition of ethanol. This material was recrystallized from ethanol; melting point 117° to 118° C undepressed on admixture with authentic β-D-mannopyranose pentaacetate, $[\alpha]_D^{25}$ −25° (*c* 3.2, $CHCl_3$). No other crystalline products were isolated.

Irradiation of maltose and cellobiose in aqueous solution at 0°. A number of samples of aqueous maltose (50%) and aqueous cellobiose (50%) were placed in open aluminum dishes (9.9 cm in diameter) and exposed to cathode-ray irradiation in doses ranging from 50 to 400 Mrep at the rate of 5 Mrep/min. During irradiation the samples were cooled in an ice-water bath. The sugar-water mixtures were prepared just prior to irradiation. The irradiated samples were lyophilized and stored in an evacuated desiccator over Drierite. Two per cent aqueous solutions were prepared from the lyophilized irradiated samples and were chromatographed on paper in a descending manner according to the method described above for irradiated sucrose. The air-dried chromatogram was sprayed according to the method of Wolfrom and Miller (*8*). Unirradiated maltose and cellobiose gave single spots, indicating chromatographic purity. All the irradiated maltose samples gave two spots, one of which in all cases corresponded to glucose. No spot other than that corresponding to the unirradiated disaccharide was detected in the irradiated cellobiose samples.

Five samples of 20% aqueous maltose (in open aluminum containers) were exposed to cathode-ray irradiation in doses ranging from 20 to 100 Mrep at the rate of 10 Mrep/min. On arrival at this laboratory the irradiated samples were lyophilized and placed over Drierite under reduced pressure. Descending paper chromatography indicated the formation of glucose in the irradiated products. The intensity of the spots corresponding to glucose increased with increasing irradiation dosage. The reducing sugar values of the irradiated products were determined by the method of Somogyi (*2*). The apparent per cent maltose hydrolyzed was calculated on the basis that glucose was the only reducing substance formed; 1 mg of glucose reduced 7.5 ml of 0.005 *N* Cu^{++}. The results are shown in Fig. 1.

Irradiation of raffinose with gamma-rays. Two per cent aqueous solutions of raffinose in tinned cans (lacquered inside) of 20-ounce capacity were exposed to γ-rays from a Co^{60} source in doses ranging from 2.5 to 10.0 Mrep at the rate of 400,000 rep/hr. The irradiation temperature was approximately 24° C. The ir-

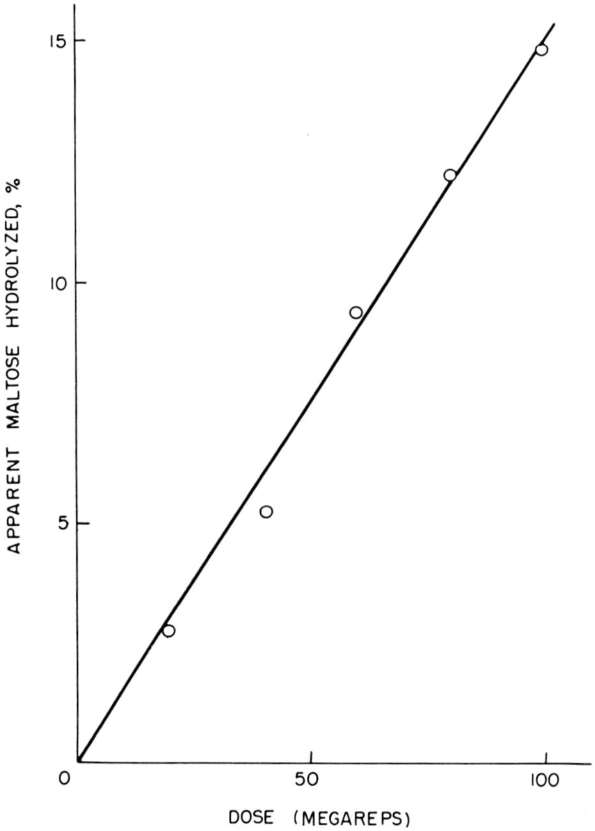

FIG. 1. Irradiation of 20% aqueous solutions of maltose at 0° C with cathode rays at the rate of 5 Mrep/min. Reducing values by method of Somogyi (*2*).

radiated samples were lyophilized and placed in an evacuated desiccator over Drierite.

Two per cent aqueous solutions were prepared from the lyophilized irradiated product and chromatographed on paper as described above for irradiated sucrose. In all the irradiated samples, spots were observed corresponding to raffinose, melibiose, sucrose, galactose, fructose, and glucose. The intensity of the spot coinciding with raffinose decreased with increasing irradiation dosage. The solutions prepared for the chromatography of irradiated aqueous raffinose were subsequently used for paper ionophoresis investigation (*9*). The ionophoretogram was run for 1.5 hour, and indication was effected with aniline-phthalic acid reagent (*5*). Spots corresponding to raffinose, melibiose, sucrose, galactose, glucose, and fructose were observed. The intensity of the raffinose spot decreased with increasing irradiation dosage. The reducing sugar values of the irradiated products, as determined by the Somogyi method (*2*), increased in a nonlinear fashion and were: at 2.5 Mrep, 0.64 ml of 0.005 *N* Cu^{++} reduced per milligram of sample; at 5.0 Mrep, 1.36 ml; at 7.5 Mrep, 1.76 ml; and at 10.0 Mrep, 2.08 ml.

DISCUSSION

A number of samples of carbohydrate crystalline solids were exposed to cathode-ray irradiation. The appearance of the irradiated samples was altered in color. It is interesting to note that all the irradiated samples fluoresced. The change in color along with the observed fluorescence indicates excitation of the molecule with the possible formation of stable free radicals.

D-Glucose, and to a lesser extent D-fructose, are among the sugar end products in the depolymerization of carbohydrates in foods. These sugars (as solids) were exposed to varying doses of cathode radiation. In both cases a decrease in reducing sugar value with irradiation was observed. D-Fructose was destroyed to a greater extent than D-glucose under the same irradiation conditions.

Sucrose is one of the most important constituents of foodstuffs. If ionizing radiations are to be used for sterilizing foods, then the effects of these radiations on sucrose will be of prime importance. Early workers reported that X-rays color crystalline sucrose to reddish brown (*10*). In the present work it was noted that sucrose turned pink on exposure to ionizing radiation. The inversion of aqueous solutions of sucrose was also observed (*10*). Other workers reported that when a dilute aqueous solution of sucrose with added lead nitrate was exposed to X-rays some inversion occurred (*11*). When no lead nitrate was present the amount of inversion was minimal. The authors believed that the increase in inversion with added lead nitrate was due to a resulting lowering of pH. In the present work, sucrose, as a powder, was irradiated with cathode rays in doses of 13, 26, and 39 Mrep. The sample exposed to 26 Mrep possessed the largest amount of reducing groups. At 39 Mrep it appears that irradiation destroyed some of the carbonyl compounds initially formed in the product. Further indication that sucrose was hydrolyzed by the action of ionizing radiations was obtained by paper chromatography. Glucose and fructose were detected in the irradiation product. The chromatographic work suggested that the fructose formed in the hydrolysis of sucrose was altered by the irradiation process. It is possible, though not probable, that the hydrolyses observed were due to acid catalysis by organic acids which may have been produced in the irradiation process. If so, the irradiation still remains as the primary cause. A more detailed investigation of the irradiation of sucrose will be presented in a later communication.

In 1954 Phillips (*12*) reported the production of mannose when D-mannitol was irradiated with cathode rays. After prolonged irradiation, mannuronic acid was reported. No experimental details were given in support of these observations.

In the present work the action of ionizing radiations on selected alditols was investigated initially by studying the effects of cathode rays on 50% aqueous solutions of D-glucitol (sorbitol) and D-mannitol. All the irradiated samples gave positive tests with Benedict and Molisch reagents. Descending paper chromatography of irradiated aqueous D-glucitol indicated the presence of D-glucitol, glucose, gulose, arabinose, and xylose in the irradiation product; although not established, the gulose and xylose should be of the L-series. No sugar acids were detected. Chromatography of irradiated aqueous D-mannitol indicated the presence of D-mannitol, mannose, arabinose, and mannuronic acid in the irradiation product. In order to obtain sufficient material for isolative purposes, a 2.0 *M* aqueous solution of D-mannitol was prepared and exposed to γ-rays at a dose of 4 Mrep. Paper chromatography indicated that mannose and arabinose were formed. The presence of D-mannose in the irradiation product was demonstrated by the isolation and characterization of a crystalline derivative, β-D-mannopyranose pentaacetate.

These results are tentative, inasmuch as not all the products have been isolated and characterized on a crystalline basis; nevertheless an interpretation can be made through known reactions in the carbohydrate field. It has been established that primary alcohols are oxidized to aldehydes by Fenton's reagent (ferrous ions and hydrogen peroxide). D-Mannose was synthesized from D-mannitol in 40% yield by this method *(13)*. Haber and Weiss *(14)* have suggested that hydroxyl radicals are formed by the action of hydrogen peroxide on ferrous salts.

$$Fe^{++} + H_2O_2 \rightarrow Fe^{+++} + \cdot OH + OH^-$$

In the Fenton reaction, the aldehyde could be produced by radical-induced oxidation of the alcohol. The oxidation of aqueous hexitols to aldohexoses could follow a similar path. It has been postulated that OH radicals are formed when water is exposed to ionizing radiation *(15–17)*. The production of the hexoses (II and III) from D-glucitol (I) could result from a secondary reaction involving attack of hydroxyl radicals on either end of the D-glucitol (sorbitol) molecule (I). Dehydrogenation of the primary alcohol group at one end will yield the glucose, and dehydrogenation at the other end will give rise to gulose. The formation of glucose and gulose, without hydroxyl radical attack, by direct radiation alone, is not excluded. Similarly, arabinose (IV) and xylose (V) could result from the attack of hydroxyl radicals on glucose and gulose, yielding intermediate osones, which, on decarbonylation would give the aldopentoses. (Osones have been produced by the action of Fenton's reagent on the hexoses; *18, 19*). An alternate path for the formation of the aldopentoses would be the oxidation of the formed hexose to the hexonic acid, followed by the oxidation of the secondary alcohol group at carbon 2 with subsequent decarboxylation to yield the aldopentose. As yet, no acids have been detected in the irradiation products of D-glucitol. Radical induced oxidation of D-mannitol (VI) produces only one hexose, since oxidation of either primary hydroxyl group would give D-mannose (VII). The characterization of D-mannose was probably made easier, since it was the only hexose produced in the irradiation of D-mannitol. As expected, if the radiation process proceeds through the same path as the Fenton reaction, the only pentose detected in the irradiation of D-mannitol (VI) was D-arabinose (IV). It was also observed that mannuronic acid was formed in the irradiation of aqueous D-mannitol with a high dose of cathode rays at ethanol–solid carbon dioxide temperature. This indicates selective oxidation which is dependent on radiation dosage and irradiation temperature and is in agreement with the work reported by Phillips (*12*).

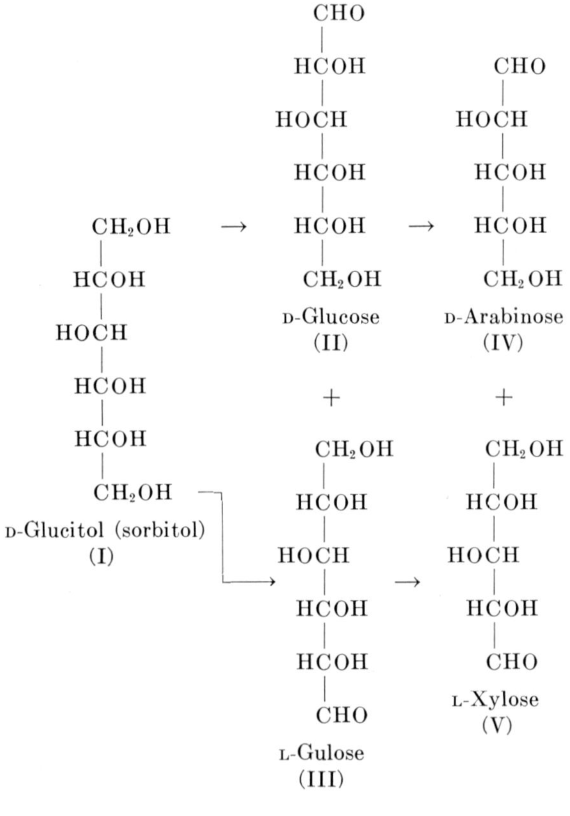

Maltose and cellobiose, as 50% aqueous solutions, were irradiated with cathode rays of varying dosages. This study was conducted to determine the relative ease of hydrolysis of the α-D and β-D glycosidic linkages in these disaccharides. The results suggest that the α-D linkage is the more labile and is in accord with the relative hydrolysis of these disaccharides by acids. The exact path of the hydrolysis of these disaccharides in the irradiation process is not known.

A number of samples of 20% aqueous maltose were irradiated with cathode rays in doses ranging from 20 to 100 Mrep. The apparent per cent hydrolysis of the dried, lyophilized, irradiated samples was determined (Fig. 1) and was found to increase with increasing irradiation dosage in a linear fashion, probably owing to the fact that only one bond was being hydrolyzed.

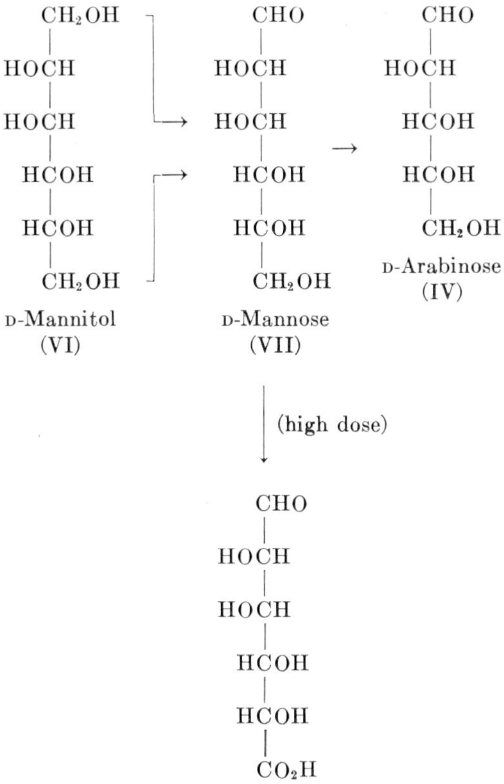

D-Mannitol (VI)

D-Mannose (VII)

D-Arabinose (IV)

D-Mannuronic acid (VIII)

The trisaccharide raffinose in 2% aqueous solution was exposed to γ-rays in doses ranging from 2.5 to 10 Mrep. Descending paper chromatography and ionophoresis indicated that raffinose was hydrolyzed. Khenokh (*20*) reported only two spots (corresponding to sucrose and fructose) on chromatography of the product of γ-irradiated dilute aqueous solutions of raffinose. The chromatographic work in the present investigation suggested also that the extent of hydrolysis increased with increasing irradiation, and this was substantiated by copper reduction methods. The relation between dosage and reduction was nonlinear, since two different bonds were being hydrolyzed.

SUMMARY

Selected carbohydrates underwent color and organoleptic changes on irradiation in the solid state. On irradiation in aqueous solution, a selective oxidation of the terminal primary hydroxyl groups of D-glucitol (sorbitol) and D-mannitol occurred, with the formation of glucose and gulose from the former and of D-mannose (isolated as β-D-mannopyranose pentaacetate) from the latter. Arabinose and xylose (from D-glucitol) and arabinose alone (from D-mannitol) were also formed, and at high doses D-mannitol yielded mannuronic acid. These changes were established by paper chromatographic methods. D-Glucose and D-fructose (especially) undergo radiation damage in aqueous solution. Irradiation of the disaccharides sucrose, maltose, and cellobiose, and the trisaccharide raffinose, demonstrated that the glycosidic bond is especially sensitive to the action of ionizing radiations and that the order of hydrolysis is qualitatively that found with acid hydrolysis. Hydrolysis of the disaccharides and trisaccharides increased with increasing irradiation dosage.

ACKNOWLEDGMENT

Acknowledgment is made of the counsel of Dr. Don S. Miyada in portions of this work.

RECEIVED: April 29, 1958

REFERENCES

1. J. A. KNOWLTON, G. R. MAHN, and J. W. RANFTL, The resonant transformer: a source of high-energy electrons. *Nucleonics* **11**, No. 11, 64–66 (1953).
2. M. SOMOGYI, A new reagent for the determination of sugars. *J. Biol. Chem.* **160**, 61–68 (1945).
3. S. M. PARTRIDGE, Application of the paper partition chromatogram to the qualitative analysis of reducing sugars. *Nature* **158**, 270–271 (1946).
4. S. M. PARTRIDGE and R. G. WESTALL, Filter paper partition chromatography of sugars. *Biochem. J.* **42**, 238–248 (1948).
5. S. M. PARTRIDGE, Aniline hydrogen phthalate as a spraying reagent for chromatography of sugars. *Nature* **164**, 443 (1949).
6. J. G. BUCHANAN, C. A. DEKKER, and A. G. LONG, The detection of glycosides and non-reducing carbohydrate derivatives in paper partition chromatography. *J. Chem. Soc.* **1950**, 3162–3167.
7. L. HOUGH, J. K. N. JONES, and W. H. WADMAN, Improved methods for the separation and detection of the sugars and their methylated derivatives. *J. Chem. Soc.* **1950**, 1702–1706.
8. M. L. WOLFROM and J. B. MILLER, Detection of carbohydrates on paper chromatograms. *Anal. Chem.* **28**, 1037 (1956).
9. A. B. FOSTER, A simplified apparatus for filter paper ionophoresis. *Chem. & Ind. (London)* **1952**, 1050–1051.
10. M. C. REINHARD and K. L. TUCKER, The effects of X-radiation on crystalline and dissolved sucrose. *Radiology* **12**, 151–153 (1929).
11. G. L. CLARK and L. W. RICKETT, Some experiments on the chemical effects of X-rays and energy relations involved. *J. Am. Chem. Soc.* **52**, 465–479 (1930).
12. G. O. PHILLIPS, Action of ionizing radiations on aqueous solutions of carbohydrates. *Nature* **173**, 1044–1045 (1954).

13. H. J. H. Fenton and H. Jackson, The oxidation of polyhydric alcohols in presence of iron. *J. Chem. Soc.* **75,** 1–11 (1899).

14. F. Haber and W. Weiss, The catalytic decomposition of hydrogen peroxide by iron salts. *Proc. Roy. Soc.* **147A,** 332–351 (1934).

15. A. O. Allen, The yields of free H and OH in the irradiation of water. *Radiation Research* **1,** 85–96 (1954).

16. E. J. Hart, Molecular product and free radical yields of ionizing radiations in aqueous solutions. *Radiation Research* **1,** 53–61 (1954).

17. H. A. Dewhurst, A. H. Samuel, and J. L. Magee, A theoretical survey of the radiation chemistry of water and aqueous solutions. *Radiation Research* **1,** 62–84 (1954).

18. R. S. Morrell and J. M. Crafts, Action of hydrogen peroxide on carbohydrates in the presence of ferrous salts. *J. Chem. Soc.* **75,** 786–792 (1899).

19. S. Bayne and J. W. Fewster, The osones. *Advances in Carbohydrate Chem.* **11,** 44–96 (1956).

20. M. A. Khenokh, Action of gamma radiation of Co-60 on carbohydrates. *Doklady Akad. Nauk S. S. S. R.* **104,** 746–749 (1955).

RADIATION RESEARCH 10, 48–62 (1959)

Certain Morphological and Biochemical Changes in Gamma-Irradiated Carrots (*Daucus carota L.*) and Potatoes (*Solanum tuberosum L.*)[1, 2]

K. A. MADSEN,[3] D. K. SALUNKHE, AND M. SIMON

Department of Horticulture, Utah State University, Logan, Utah, and Quartermaster Food and Container Institute for the Armed Forces, Chicago, Illinois

INTRODUCTION

Through the ages, people have been confronted with the problem of storing food after the harvest season for consumption during the winter months. They have preserved food by dehydration, canning, and by cold storage. People usually prefer fresh vegetables if available, however. Carrots and potatoes can be stored fresh, but they start sprouting and shriveling unless the temperature and humidity are carefully controlled. Every year many tons of these vegetables become unfit for human consumption as a result of sprouting and breakdown in storage.

Some chemicals have been used with various degrees of success in preventing sprouting of certain vegetables. The chemicals were applied as a preharvest foliar spray or directly on the tubers or on the roots.

In 1954, a law was passed by the U. S. Congress authorizing the release of small amounts of radioactive materials to study the peaceful uses of atomic energy. Through this program, the investigations presented in this paper were conducted. They were mainly to show the effects of the dose and the rate of γ-radiation on sprout inhibition, chemical, histological, and organoleptic (taste) quality changes in carrots and potatoes when stored at different temperatures. In addition, studies

[1] This paper is based on a dissertation submitted (by K. A. Madsen) to the Faculty of Graduate School of Utah State University in candidacy for the Degree of Master of Science (1958). Contribution No. 63(a) from Utah State Agricultural Experiment Station, Logan, Utah.

[2] This paper reports research undertaken in cooperation with the Quartermaster Food and Container Institute for the Armed Forces and has been assigned No. 818 in the series of papers approved for publication. The views or conclusions contained in this paper are those of the authors. They are not to be construed as necessarily reflecting the views or endorsement of the Department of Defense.

[3] Present address: Fulbright Research Fellow (1958–59), The Institute of Horticultural Plant Breeding, Wageningen, Netherlands.

were conducted to combine the thermal and the radiation treatments with the assumption that the "threshold" radiation dose may be lowered. The application of the work presented herein constitutes a new approach to the problems of vegetable preservation (*1*). The success of this new field will depend on improved methods and techniques of handling the material, and on the economics of the γ-ray source.

METHODS AND MATERIALS

Gamma-Radiation Technique

Carrots and potatoes were irradiated at the Material Testing Reactor Station near Arco, Idaho. The source of γ-rays was active, spent fuel (U^{235}) rods, 3 $\times$ 26 inches. These rods were placed around an aluminum tube at the bottom of a canal filled with 18 feet of water. The rate of radiation was arranged by placing the fuel rods at varying distances from the aluminum tube. The rate of radiation was determined by dosimeter measurements, and from this the time required for the particular dose was calculated. Two No. 10 cans containing either carrots or potatoes were placed one on top of the other in a wire cage with a lead weight attached to the cage. The cans in this wire cage were lowered inside the aluminum tube to the level of the fuel rod and irradiated for half the calculated time required for the dose. The cans were then raised to the surface, and the top can placed at the bottom. The cans were re-arranged, because the fuel rods do not emit rays at the same rate along their length. By changing the cans in this manner, both of them received the same amount of radiation. Subsequently, the cans were again lowered down into the tube for the last half of the dose. The cans were transported at 40° F before and after the radiation process.

The following five experiments were arranged to study the sprout inhibition, physiochemical changes, and quality of γ-irradiated carrots (variety—Long Imperator) and potatoes (variety—Russet Burbank).

Experiment 1: Effect of radiation dose on sprout inhibition and taste quality of carrots. The carrots were irradiated with doses of 0, 9.3, 18.6, 37.2, 65.1, and 93.0 krad at 93.0 krad/hr at 78° F. Subsequent to irradiation, the total weight of the carrots in each can was recorded. Half of the nonirradiated cans of carrots and half of the irradiated carrots at each dose were stored in rooms at 50° F and 70° F for sprouting studies. The cans containing the carrots were covered with moist burlap sacks to maintain higher moisture in the air around the carrots, in an attempt to decrease the moisture loss from the carrots. The length of the carrot sprouts was measured at 2-week intervals for those stored at 70° F and at 4-week intervals for those stored at 50° F. The experiment was terminated after 4 weeks for the carrots stored at 70° F and after 12 weeks for the carrots stored at 50° F. The sprouts were removed from the carrots which were stored at 50° F at the end of the experiment. The carrots and sprouts were weighed separately to determine weight losses. Carrots stored at 50° F for 3 months were evaluated for taste quality (*2*).

Experiment 2: Effect of radiation dose and radiation rate on sprout inhibition and taste quality of carrots. Carrots for this experiment were irradiated with doses of 0, 27.9, 37.2, 46.5, 55.8, and 65.1 krad at 9.3, 53.0, and 99.5 krad/hr at 78° F. Subsequent to radiation, the carrots were individually weighed and marked for identification. The carrots were packed in a sand-sawdust mixture with the tops of the carrots just above the surface of the packing. The packing was kept moist during the experiment. Half of the nonirradiated carrots and half of the irradiated carrots were stored in rooms at 50° F and 70° F for sprouting studies.

The measurement and the weight of sprouts and roots of the carrots from the respective storage rooms were recorded as explained under experiment 1. Taste tests were conducted before and after the storage.

Experiment 3: Effect of radiation dose and preirradiation thermal treatments on sprout inhibition and taste quality of carrots. Carrots for this experiment were sealed in perforated cans and then divided into the following three categories.

Category 1: The cans containing carrots were stored at 40° F before and after irradiation.

Category 2: The cans containing carrots were removed from storage at 40° F and placed in water at 80° F for 15 minutes prior to radiation. The water was allowed to enter the cans through the perforations and then drained off before they were placed in the chamber for irradiation.

Category 3: The cans containing carrots were treated as described for category 2 with the water at 120° F.

The carrots were irradiated with doses of 0, 2.3, 4.7, 9.3, 18.6, and 37.2 krad at 287.4 krad/hr at 78° F. Prior to radiation and subsequent to storage at 50° F for 4 months, the experiment was conducted as discussed under experiments 1 and 2.

Experiment 4: Effect of radiation dose on sprout inhibition and physical changes in potatoes. The cans of potatoes were irradiated with doses of 0, 4.7, 9.3, and 13.9 krad at 93.0 krad/hr at 78° F. The potatoes were placed in storage at 50° F for 9 months. The sprouting of the potatoes was noted during this time.

At the end of the experiment, three potatoes from the 0-, 4.7-, and 9.3-krad lots were used for shear-press determinations (*3*). From each potato, a 60-gm sample was removed and sheared. The maximum pressure (pounds) required to shear each sample was recorded.

Experiment 5: Effect of radiation dose on physical, chemical, and histological changes in potatoes. Cans containing potatoes were irradiated with doses of 0, 0.9, 1.9, 3.7, 7.4, 9.3, 18.6, and 37.2 Mrad at 0.93 Mrad/hr at 78° F.

On return to the Horticultural Laboratories of Utah State University, the cans were opened. The color and physical appearance of the potatoes were noted. Representative samples were taken from the potatoes to prepared slurries with 95%

ethanol in a Waring blendor for the following chemical analyses: total solids, total starch, amylose, alcohol-insoluble solids, reducing sugars, and pH.

Histological Effects. Microscopic studies were conducted according to the method of Salunkhe and Pollard (*4*). Sprouting, physical, chemical, and organoleptic determinations were analyzed for statistical significance (*5*).

RESULTS

Experiment 1: Effect of radiation dose on sprout inhibition and taste quality of carrots. During the second week of postirradiation storage, an unidentified black mold appeared on some of the carrots in the 70° F room. The carrots in both the 50° F and 70° F rooms were therefore packed in the cans with moist sand. The surface of the sand was just below the growing point of the carrots and was kept moist by sprinkling with water during the remaining storage period. A weak solution of mercuric chloride was sprinkled on the mold that developed later on some carrots in the 70° F room.

It is evident from Table I that carrots irradiated to 37.2 krad and higher did not sprout when stored at 70° F. There was a sharp decrease in the amount of sprouting of the carrots receiving 9.3 krad and a significant drop at 18.6 krad but no significant difference in sprout inhibition above 18.6 krad. Some of the carrots stored at 70° F started to rot after 6 weeks' storage and had to be discarded.

The carrots stored at 50° F did not sprout as fast as those stored at 70° F, nor did

TABLE I

EFFECT OF RADIATION DOSE ON THE LENGTH OF SPROUTS, WEIGHT OF SPROUTS, AND WEIGHT LOSS OF CARROTS STORED AT 70°F AND 50°F SUBSEQUENT TO IRRADIATION

Dose (Krad)	Stored at 70° F			Stored at 50° F				
	Average length of sprouts (inches)			Average length of spouts (inches)			Weight of sprouts (%)	Weight loss of carrots (%)[a]
	2 weeks	4 weeks	6 ueeks	1 month	2 months	3 months		
0	0.7	3.1	4.8	0.7	5.3	9.2	16.4	9.2
9.3	0.3	1.1	2.0	0.2	0.7	1.7	2.0	0.0
18.6	0.1	0.2	0.3	0.1	0.2	0.2	0.1	0.0
37.2	0.0	0.0	0.0	0.0	0.1	0.1	0.0	0.0
65.1	0.0	0.0	[b]	0.0	0.1	0.1	0.0	0.0
93.0	0.0	0.0	[b]	0.0	0.0	0.0	0.0	0.0

Standard error of difference for doses	0.4
Standard error of difference for time intervals	0.3
Standard error of difference for weight of sprouts	0.4
Standard error of difference for weight loss of carrots	1.4

[a] Per cent of original carrot weight.

[b] Rotten.

any rotting occur at the low temperature during the 3-month storage period. There was a significant increase in sprout inhibition from the control to the 9.3-krad group but not from the carrots irradiated to 18.6 krad and the higher doses (Fig. 1). Only the nonirradiated and the carrots receiving a dose of 9.3 krad showed significant growth during the 1-month intervals after irradiation between sprout growth measurements.

The weight of the carrot sprouts decreased in the same manner as the length of the sprouts. The nonirradiated carrots lost 9.2% of their original weight during the 3-month storage, but the irradiated carrots did not lose any weight.

When the carrots were evaluated for quality changes, after 3 months' storage, there was a slight increase in acceptability of irradiated carrots over the nonirradiated carrots.

The reason for sprout inhibition by radiation has not been definitely established, but some explanations have been suggested by various workers. A breakdown in the process of auxin synthesis rather than the auxin has been postulated as the result of work which shows that 10 r of X-radiation was found to inhibit the activity of the enzymes converting tryptophan to auxin (*6*). Brownell *et al.* (*7*) found varying results in determining the effect of γ-radiation on plant growth regulators in potatoes. In addition to the degradiation of the plant growth regulators, it seems that the disintegration of the cells and/or inhibition of cell division in the apical meristems may have occurred during the process of radiation.

FIG. 1. Effect of radiation dose on the sprout inhibition of carrots stored for 12 weeks at 50° F. Left to right—nonirradiated, 9.3, 18.6, and 37.2 krad.

TABLE II

EFFECT OF RADIATION RATE AND RADIATION DOSE ON THE SPROUT LENGTH AND WEIGHT LOSS OF CARROTS STORED AT 50°F AND 70°F SUBSEQUENT TO IRRADIATION

Rate (krad)	*Dose (krad)*	*Average length of sprouts (inches)*			*Weight loss (%)*[a]
		1 month	*2 months*	*3 months*	
0	0 (70° F)[b]	2.7	c	c	c
0	0 (50° F)	1.0	4.0	8.2	16.8
9.3	27.9	0.0	0.1	0.1	11.5
	37.2	0.0	0.1	0.1	3.2
	46.5	0.0	0.1	0.1	7.7
	55.8	0.0	0.1	0.1	2.3
	65.1	0.1	0.1	0.1	2.3
				Mean	*5.4*
53.0	27.9	0.0	0.0	0.1	12.1
	37.2	0.0	0.1	0.1	9.7
	46.5	0.0	0.0	0.0	12.5
	55.8	0.0	0.0	0.0	5.3
	65.1	0.0	0.0	0.1	7.7
				Mean	*9.4*
99.5	27.9	0.0	0.0	0.0	7.8
	37.2	0.0	0.1	0.1	6.0
	46.5	0.0	0.1	0.1	10.1
	55.8	0.0	0.1	0.1	13.5
	65.1	0.0	0.1	0.1	10.5
				Mean	*9.6*
Dose means	0				16.8
	27.9				10.4
	37.2				6.3
	46.5				10.1
	55.8				7.0
	65.1				6.8
Standard error of difference for rate means					2.3
Standard error of difference for dose means					3.0

[a] Per cent of original carrot weight.

[b] At 1 month, the complete sprout inhibition of the irradiated carrots (27.9, 37.2, 46.5, 55.8, and 65.1 krad at the rate of 9.3, 53.0, and 99.5 krad/hr) when stored at 70° F was observed.

[c] Rotten.

Doses higher than 18.6 krad did not result in additional decreases in carrot sprout inhibition that were significant. The dose required for complete sprout inhibition under the conditions of this experiment was higher than that found by Mikaelsen *et al.* (*8*).

Experiment 2: Effect of radiation dose and radiation rate on sprout inhibition and taste quality of carrots. The nonirradiated carrots stored at 70° F sprouted and continued to grow, but none of the irradiated samples sprouted more than ⅛ inch; these sprouts turned black and did not grow farther. The carrots started to rot after 6 weeks and were discarded from the experiment.

The carrots stored at 50° F were kept for 3 months. During this time, 95% of the nonirradiated carrots sprouted and continued to grow. Thirty-five per cent of the irradiated carrots sprouted, and only 4% had sprouts longer than ¼ inch. The sprouting was not extensive enough to show difference between the rates of radiation used. The carrots sprouted about the same length at all five dose levels. The data in Table II indicate that the nonirradiated carrots lost a higher per cent of their original weight than the irradiated carrots. The carrots irradiated at 9.3 krad/hr did not lose as much weight as the carrots irradiated at the higher rates of 53.0 and 99.5 krad/hr.

In the carrots evaluated by taste test prior to storage, there was an increase in the acceptability as the rate of radiation increased, but subsequent to storage there was a decrease in the acceptance as the rate of radiation increased. As the dose of radiation increased, there was a slight decrease in flavor acceptance of the carrots tested before storage but no trend after the storage. The sprouts did not grow enough at the doses studied to provide information as to the effect of rates of radiation on sprout growth.

Experiment 3: Effect of radiation dose and preirradiation thermal treatments on sprout inhibition and taste quality of carrots. The carrots were given a preradiation mild thermal treatment with the idea of reducing the radiation dose required to inhibit sprouting, but the results did not support this idea.

According to data presented in Table III, it is apparent that the growth of the carrot sprouts increased as the temperature of the treatment increased, with a significant increase of sprouting from the 40° F to the 80° F treatments; however, no significant difference was noted from the 80° F to the 120° F treatments.

Carrots irradiated to 2.3, 4.7, and 9.3 krad and the nonirradiated carrots showed significant sprout growth during the 1-month intervals, but the carrots given higher doses did not.

As the dose of radiation increased, there was a decrease in the carrot sprouting, although there was not a significant decrease of sprouting when doses of over 18.6 krad were used. The sprouts on the carrots in this experiment were longer than in the first experiment; this may be because these carrots were cut above the apical meristem region so that there were only a few sprouts from each carrot. The preradiation thermal treatments resulted in an increase of carrot sprouting as the treatments increased in temperature (Fig. 2). This may be due to the degradation of antiauxin, rather than auxins by hot-water treatments. Previous work (*6*) also indicates that heat treatments would suppress the auxin-producing system. This

TABLE III

EFFECT OF PRERADIATION THERMAL TREATMENT AND RADIATION DOSE ON THE SPROUT INHIBITION, WEIGHT LOSS, AND WEIGHT OF CARROT SPROUTS STORED AT 50° F AFTER IRRADIATION

Temperature (°F)	*Dose (krad)*	*Average length of sprouts (inches)*				*After 4 months at 50° F*	
		1 month	*2 months*	*3 months*	*4 months*	*Weight loss of carrots (%)*[a]	*Weight of carrot sprouts (%)*[a]
40	0	2.9	13.2	15.7	20.4	17.0	11.3
	2.3	2.4	10.4	12.1	16.7	23.1	9.2
	4.7	1.7	4.5	5.5	6.6	29.9	4.6
	9.3	1.6	2.4	2.2	1.7	25.8	0.3
	18.6	0.5	1.2	1.3	1.1	12.2	0.1
	37.2	0.2	0.6	0.7	0.6	19.8	0.1
	Mean	*1.5*	*5.4*	*6.3*	*7.8*	*21.3*	*4.3*
80	0	4.3	12.8	15.4	20.1	20.5	11.6
	2.3	3.3	10.4	12.5	17.6	26.9	10.6
	4.7	3.6	10.2	12.9	17.1	26.3	10.3
	9.3	1.5	3.8	4.5	6.1	24.9	3.2
	18.6	1.0	1.7	1.7	1.3	15.4	0.3
	37.2	0.7	1.6	1.6	1.3	21.4	0.1
	Mean	*2.4*	*6.8*	*8.1*	*10.6*	*22.6*	*6.0*
120	0	5.2	15.9	18.5	22.9	21.7	13.9
	2.3	4.5	10.7	13.7	14.8	33.1	8.9
	4.7	3.2	10.0	12.5	16.5	23.0	10.5
	9.3	2.1	4.7	6.2	8.9	27.7	5.4
	18.6	1.4	2.8	3.0	3.8	18.9	2.5
	27.2	0.4	1.3	1.3	1.0	23.0	0.1
	Mean	*2.8*	*7.5*	*9.2*	*11.3*	*24.6*	*6.9*
Dose means	0	4.1	13.6	16.6	21.1	19.7	12.2
	2.3	3.4	10.5	12.7	16.4	27.7	9.6
	4.7	2.8	8.2	10.3	13.4	26.5	8.5
	9.3	1.7	3.6	4.3	5.6	26.2	3.0
	18.6	0.9	1.9	2.0	2.0	15.5	1.0
	37.2	0.4	1.2	1.2	1.0	21.4	0.1
Standard error of difference for temperature means 1.3						2.2	0.3
Standard error of difference for dose means 1.9						3.1	1.2
Standard error of difference for time intervals 0.6							

[a] Per cent of original carrot weight.

FIG. 2. Effect of preradiation thermal treatments and dose of radiation on the sprout inhibition of carrots radiated to 4.7 krad and stored at 50° F for 4 months. Left to right—40° F, 80° F, and 120° F.

would result in a decrease in sprouting rather than an increase, as the data in this experiment indicate. The weight loss of the carrots increased as the preradiation thermal treatment increased (Table III). There was a higher weight loss of the irradiated carrots at the lower doses. The weight of the carrot sprouts changed in the same manner as the length of the carrots with respect to dose and preradiation thermal treatments.

The carrots given preradiation thermal treatments were tested organoleptically before storage and no significant difference was found between the treatments. After 4 months' storage, the 120° F treatment was not rated as high as the 40° F or the 80° F treatment. There was some difference between the flavor scores of carrots receiving different doses of radiation but no trends before or after storage.

The data in this experiment are in general agreement with the experiment on the dose required for effective sprout inhibition.

Experiment 4: Effect of radiation dose on sprout inhibition and physical changes in potatoes. Potatoes were irradiated to 0, 4.7, 9.3, and 13.9 krad at 93.0 krad/hr at 78° F before storage at 50° F.

The nonirradiated potatoes sprouted profusely, whereas potatoes irradiated to 4.7 krad had shorter sprouts. Potatoes receiving 9.3 krad had a few sprouts ⅛ inch long, but these did not develop. The dose required for the sprout inhibition for carrots was 18.6 krad, whereas for potatoes it was 9.3 krad. Hence the sprout re-

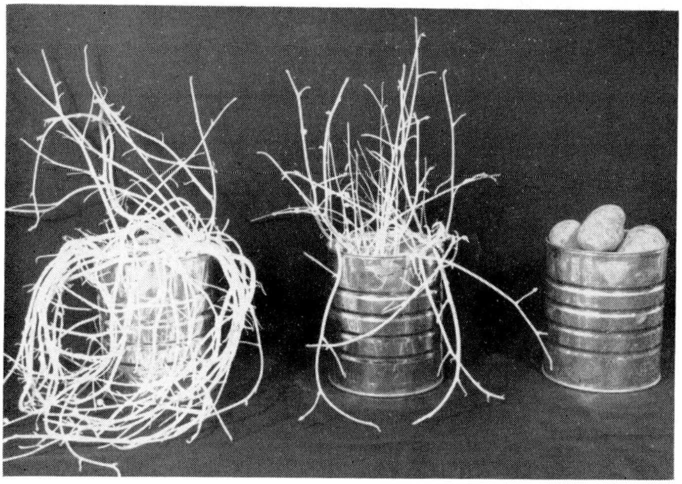

FIG. 3. Effect of radiation dose on the sprout inhibition of potatoes stored for 5 months at 50° F. Left to right—nonirradiated, 4.7, and 9.3 krad.

tardation dose depends on the type of plant.[4] Small secondary tubers were formed on the vines of the nonirradiated potatoes and the potatoes irradiated to 4.7 krad (Fig. 3).

In this experiment, the dose required to inhibit potato sprouting completely is in agreement with that determined by other workers (*9–15*).

The shear-press values (Table IV) indicate that the nonirradiated potatoes that sprouted profusely were tough, as would be expected. The potatoes that received a dose of 9.3 krad were still firm and turgid, thereby requiring less pressure to shear.

Experiment 5: Effect of radiation dose on physical, chemical, and histological changes in potatoes. Potatoes were irradiated at 78° F to 0, 0.93, 1.86, 3.72, 7.44, 9.30, 18.60, and 37.20 Mrad at the rate of 0.93 Mrad/hr.

The potatoes became progressively softer and darker as the dose of radiation increased, and the potatoes irradiated to 3.72 Mrad were rather mushy. The physical appearance of the dehydrated (158° F) potato slurry, made with 95% ethanol, changed as the dose of radiation increased. From the nonirradiated to the potatoes irradiated to 3.72 Mrad the dehydrated potato slurry at the bottom of an aluminum pan appeared as one light-colored chip; at 7.44 and 9.30 Mrad the chip was broken and darker in color; and at 18.60 and 37.20 Mrad the dehydrated slurry was dark and adhered to the drying pan. This pigment development may be attributed to the condensation of soluble nitrogenous and sugar fractions or probably the carameliza-

[4] Preliminary unpublished data on sprout inhibition of beets, onions, parsnips, and turnips by γ-radiation by K. A. Madsen and D. K. Salunkhe, Department of Horticulture, Utah State University, Logan, Utah, 1957.

TABLE IV

EFFECT OF RADIATION DOSE ON SHEAR-PRESS VALUES OF POTATO TUBERS STORED AT 50° F FOR 9 MONTHS AFTER IRRADIATION

Dose (krad)	*Pressure (lb)*			*Means*
	Sample I	*Sample II*	*Sample III*	
0	1240	1210	830	1093
4.7	990	920	1100	1003
9.3	890	810	870	857
Standard error of difference for dose means				118

TABLE V

EFFECT OF RADIATION DOSE ON CERTAIN CHEMICAL CHANGES IN POTATO TUBERS

Dose (Mrad)	*Total solids (%)*	*Starch (%)*	*Amylose (%)*	*Alcohol-insoluble solids (%)*	*Reducing sugars (%)*	*pH*	*Total acidity*
0	21.55	14.34	5.28	19.26	1.39	6.52	0.36
0.93	20.33	13.41	5.09	18.29	1.15	6.25	0.48
1.86	22.79	16.39	5.65	21.01	1.34	6.17	0.45
3.72	22.33	15.51	5.12	20.24	1.57	6.10	0.46
7.44	22.66	16.03	4.38	20.61	1.29	6.05	0.46
9.30	21.59	15.24	3.99	19.27	1.41	5.94	0.50
18.60	25.70	19.12	3.46	23.08	1.24	5.67	0.55
37.20	24.83	17.70	1.74	21.52	1.17	5.45	0.67
Standard error of difference	0.60	0.76	0.34	0.71	0.14	0.05	0.03

tion sugars; or perhaps it is the catalytic effect of certain components on the process of condensation or caramelization or on both at high doses of radiation (over 7.44 Mrad).

The chemical analyses of the irradiated potato slurries indicated that the total solids, alcohol-insoluble solids, total starch, and total acidity increased and the pH and amylose decreased as the dose of radiation advanced, but the content of reducing sugars did not change appreciably (Table V). The potatoes were not tested for specific gravity before being selected for radiation; therefore it was not known if the starch content or total dry matter was identical in all the potatoes used. In this experiment, the potatoes irradiated at high doses had more starch than in the nonirradiated. The content of reducing sugars did not change significantly, which is in disagreement with Roberts (*16*), Salunkhe (*17*), Salunkhe and Moser (*18*), and Schwimmer *et al.* (*19*), who found a decrease in starch or inulin and an increase in sugars as the dose of radiation advanced. The possible explanations for these con-

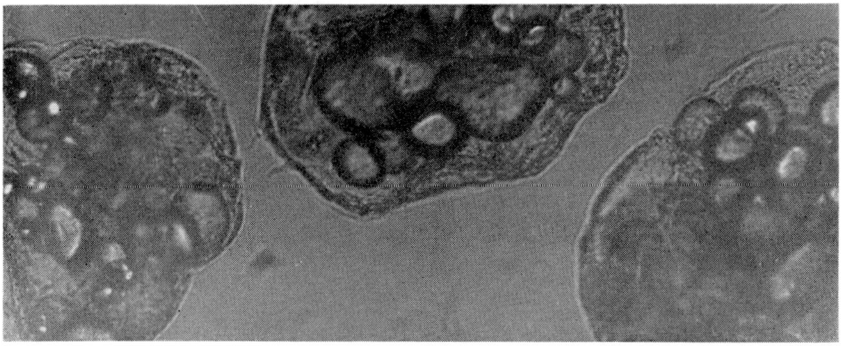

FIG. 4. Separation of cells of irradiated (over 3.72 Mrad) tubers of potatoes.

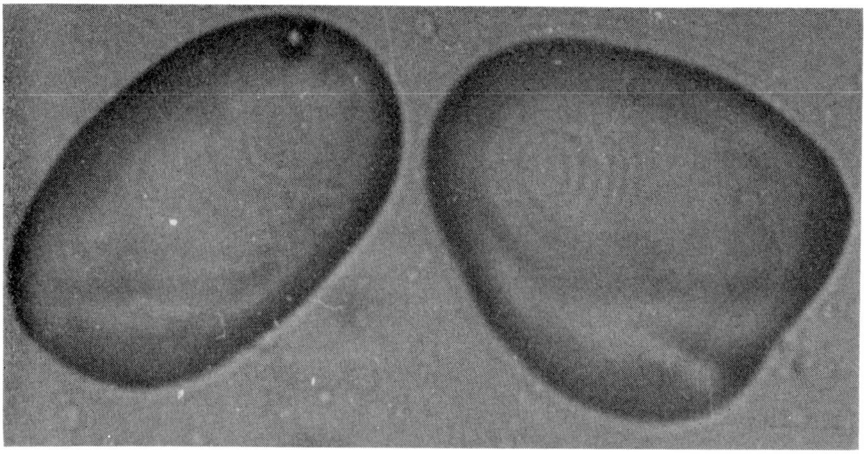

FIG. 5. Starch grains of nonirradiated tubers of potatoes (note lamellae intact).

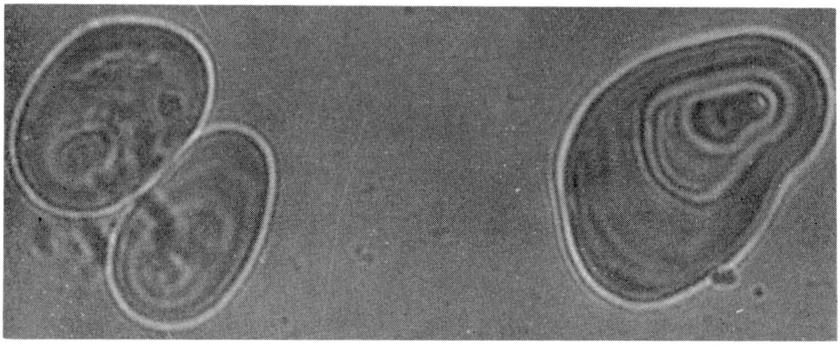

FIG. 6. Starch grains of irradiated (7.44-Mrad) tubers of potatoes (note loose lamellae and distortions on the surface of the starch grains).

tradictory results may be the heterogenity of the chemical makeup of the potato samples studied and/or the high doses of radiation dehydrated the potato tubers.

As the dose of radiation increased over 3.72 Mrad, the cells of the potato tubers were separating from each other (Fig. 4), which may be the result of the degradation of the components of middle lamellae, mainly calcium pectate. This concurs with the findings of Salunkhe (*17*). Radiation perhaps made the cell walls rather rubbery, thereby preventing the cell walls from breaking easily and liberating the starch grains. The starch grains of nonirradiated potato tubers had intact lamellae (Fig. 5), but the lamellae of the starch grains of potato tubers irradiated to 7.44 Mrad were loose and starting to separate (Fig. 6). These results in general follow the pattern of observations of Roberts (*16*). In addition, the progressive distortion on the surface of starch grains occurred as the dose of radiation advanced over 7.44 Mrad.

SUMMARY

Experiments were conducted to study the effects of γ-radiation (dose and rate) and preradiation thermal treatments on morphological, chemical, histological, and taste quality changes in carrots and potatoes. The results and observations are summarized below.

Morphological Changes

In general, the radiation doses of 9.3 krad for potatoes (variety—Russet Burbank) and 18.6 krad for carrots (variety—Long Imperator) for practical purposes inhibited the sprouting.

There was no significant difference in the effect of radiation rate on carrot sprouting at the doses studied. The length and weight of the carrot sprouts increased as the preradiation thermal treatment increased from 40° F to 80° F to 120° F.

Chemical Changes

In general, the chemical analysis of the irradiated potatoes indicated that the total solids, alcohol-insoluble solids, total starch, and total acidity increased, the pH values and amylose content decreased as the dose of radiation increased, and the amount of reducing sugars remained fairly constant.

Histological Changes

The cells of potato tubers, when irradiated to over 3.72 Mrad, were separating from each other. The starch grains of irradiated potatoes (7.44 Mrad) had loose lamellae separating from each other and also had ramifications on the surface of the starch grains.

Taste Quality Changes

In general, the dose and the rate of radiation and preradiation thermal treatments did not result in the significant changes in carrots tested for taste quality immediately after radiation, but the quality of the irradiated carrots (18.6 krad) stored at 50° F for 3 to 4 months had significantly better flavor than the unirradiated profusely sprouted carrots.

ACKNOWLEDGMENTS

The authors wish to thank Dr. W. S. Boyle for his assistance in taking the photomicrographs; Dr. E. B. Wilcox for her assistance in the preparation for organoleptic appraisal studies; and Mr. D. L. Hunke and his staff at the Material Testing Reactor Station, Phillips Petroleum Co., Idaho Falls, Idaho, for their assistance and co-operation in making the necessary arrangements for γ-radiation. The senior author also expresses deep gratitude to the Quartermaster Food and Container Institute for the Armed Forces, Chicago, for financial support during this study.

RECEIVED: May 12, 1958

REFERENCES

1. D. K. SALUNKHE, L. H. POLLARD, R. K. GERBER, E. B. WILCOX, and M. SIMON, Effects of different environments prior to, during, and subsequent to gamma-radiation on the quality, shelf-life, and physio-chemical changes in certain fruit and vegetable products. *Food Technology 12*, No. 4, 44 (1958).
2. D. R. PERYAM and F. J. PILGRAM, Hedonic scale method of measuring food preference. *Food Technol.* **11,** 9–14 (1957).
3. A. KRAMER, G. J. BURKHARDT, and H. P. ROGERS, The shear-press; a device for measuring food quality. *Canner* **112,** No. 5, 34–36 (1951).
4. D. K. SALUNKHE and L. H. POLLARD, Microscopic observations of starch grains in relation to maturity of potatoes. *Proc. Am. Soc. Hort. Sci.* **64,** 331–334 (1954).
5. B. OSTLE, *Statistics in Research*, The Iowa State College Press, Ames, Iowa, 1956.
6. S. A. GORDON, Physiology of hormone action. In *Growth and Differentiation in Plants* (W. E. Loomis, ed.), pp. 265–266, The Iowa State College Press, Ames, Iowa, 1953.
7. L. E. BROWNELL, C. H. BURNS, F. G. GUSTAFSON, W. J. HOOKER, D. ISLEIB, J. V. NEHEMIAS, R. A. MARTENS, A. PENDILL, and F. HEILIGMAN, Gamma ray sprout inhibition of potatoes. *Quartermaster Food and Container Inst. Final Rept.* (1957).
8. K. MIKAELSEN, H. BRENNA, and L. ROER, Effects of gamma-rays on sprouting and growth during storage in carrots and potatoes. *Proc. Intern. Conf. Peaceful Uses Atomic Energy, Geneva, 1955* **12,** 208–210 (1956).
9. F. HEILIGMAN, Effects of ionizing radiation on white potatoes. *Am. Potato J.* **34,** No. 6, 153–157 (1957).
10. K. MIKAELSEN and L. ROER, Improved storage ability of potatoes exposed to gamma radiation. *Acta Agr. Scand.* **6,** 124–154 (1956).
11. S. PEDERSEN, The effect of ionizing radiations on sprout prevention and chemical composition of potatoes. *Food Technol.* **10,** 532–536 (1956).
12. R. L. SAWYER and S. L. DALLYN, The effect of gamma radiation on storage life of potatoes. *Am. Potato J.* **32,** 141–143 (1955).
13. W. C. SPARKS, The effect of gamma-rays from fission product wastes on the storage and anatomy of potato tubers. *Am. Soc. Hort. Sci.* (Abstracts 54th annual meeting) (1957).
14. A. H. SPARROW and E. CHRISTENSEN, Effects of X-ray, neutron, and chronic gamma irradiation on growth and yield of potatoes. *Am. J. Botany* **37,** 667 (1950).
15. A. H. SPARROW and E. CHRISTENSEN, Improved storage quality of potato tubers after exposure to Co^{60} gammas. *Nucleonics* **12,** No. 8, 16–17 (1954).

16. E. A. Roberts, *The Microstructure of Starch Grains*. Spaulding-Moss Company, Boston, Massachusetts, 1956.

17. D. K. Salunkhe, Histological and histo-chemical changes in gamma-irradiated lima beans, *Phaseolus lunatus*. *Nature* **179,** 585–586 (1957).

18. D. K. Salunkhe and F. Y. Moser, Cheaper fructose on way? *Food Eng*. **30,** No. 5, 110 (1958).

19. S. Schwimmer, H. K. Burr, W. O. Harrington, and W. J. Weston, Gamma irradiation of potatoes: Effects on sugar content, chip color, germination, greening and susceptibility to mold. *Am. Potato J*. **34,** 31–41 (1957).

RADIATION RESEARCH **10**, 63–66 (1959)

The Effect of Internal Emitters on Red Cell Survival in Beagle Dogs[1]

JOHN E. PARKINSON

Radiobiology Laboratory, Department of Anatomy, University of Utah

INTRODUCTION

Plutonium, radium, radiothorium, and mesothorium deposited internally have produced anemias in beagle dogs. This has been reported in semi-annual and annual progress reports of this laboratory since March, 1953. The pattern produced by plutonium and radium for the first year of exposure has been summarized (*1*). An associated hemolytic component has been observed in the anemia of chronic bone-marrow failure from other causes (*2*). The Cr^{51}-tagged red-cell survival method was employed to evaluate a possible hemolytic factor in the anemia of chronic internal irradiation. The acute anemia from external X-ray is mostly the result of capillary leakage of red cells (*3–5*), but evidence of intravascular red-cell damage has also been demonstrated (*6*). In dogs studied here an anemia is produced by potent α-, β-, and γ-emitters which deliver continuous radiation at close proximity to the bone marrow. The potent ionizing properties of α-irradiation delivered at a cellular level probably represent the chief mode of biologic damage of these isotopes.

METHODS

The 25 control and 37 isotope-injected animals are a part of a colony of about 350 beagle dogs. They are housed in modern kennels and are under the care of a full-time veterinarian and kennel personnel. Adult dogs were injected intravenously with graded doses of isotopes. Animals at different dose levels and times of exposure were examined. Isotope burdens on a retained basis were as follows: for mesothorium and radiothorium, 0.27, 0.81, and 2.5 $\mu c/kg$; for radium and plutonium, 0.81 and 2.5 $\mu c/kg$. Lower dose levels were not studied, since these dogs had not yet developed anemias. Anemia occurred at 1 to 6 months postinjection, with recoveries and relapses at later times. Grouping of animals with regard to parameters of dosage, isotope, and exposure time was not done because the dogs

[1] This research was supported by the Division of Biology and Medicine, U. S. Atomic Energy Commission.

were injected in serial groups leaving, at a given time, only one dog at a given dosage and exposure. Red-cell survivals were done 1 to 34 months postinjection.

Red-cell survival was determined by a modification of a previously described method (*7*). About 50 ml of blood was collected in a plastic Fenwall bag containing 10 ml of ACD solution and 20 to 25 μc (5 to 10 μg of Cr^{51} per milliliter of red blood cells) Rachromate.[2] After 45 minutes the Cr^{51} uptake was stopped with 50 mg of sodium ascorbate. The total counts injected were determined by obtaining an aliquot sample for counting and by weighing the bag before and after transfusion (specific gravity of blood was determined with solutions of graded copper sulfate concentrations) (*8*). At 1 hour postinjection a sample was obtained to be used as a 100% value for Cr^{51} survival and to serve as the dilution sample for red-cell volume. Hematocrits were determined in Wintrobe tubes without correction for trapped plasma. The samples were counted in sealed glass vials in a shielded well-type scintillation counter with pulse height analyzer (992,950 counts/min/μc Cr^{51} with background of 200 to 210 counts/min), and the counts were expressed per milliliter of packed red cells. Blood was placed in weighed vials, centrifuged, and the plasma withdrawn into weighed vials so that the counts from the packed red cells could be corrected for the small amount of remaining plasma.

Apparent 50% red-cell Cr^{51} survivals were read from semilogarithmic plots of the data, represented as per cent of the original 1-hour sample. Five to eight points at 7- to 10-day intervals determined a best-fit line. Samples were counted with the appropriate 1-hour sample standard to correct for Cr^{51} decay.

RESULTS

Red-cell Cr^{51} uptake ranged from 72 to 91%. Red-cell volume in 25 controls ranged from 35.4 to 69.9 ml/kg (average = 42.7 ml/kg). Isotope-injected animals with red-cell volumes below 35.4 ml/kg were considered anemic (range = 22.7 to 35.2 ml/kg; average = 28.7 ml/kg.)

Figure 1 shows the frequency distribution of 50% red-cell survivals ($T_{1/2}$) for 25 controls (average = 24 days) and 37 isotope-injected dogs. In general the $T_{1/2}$ for isotope-injected animals followed the same distribution as controls, though there were more anemic dogs at the low range of normal. There was no evidence in these animals of hemorrhagic tendency or external blood loss. Except for those dogs noted in Fig. 1, hematocrits remained stable over the period of study.

Five per cent ($T_{1/20}$) survivals, beyond which counting errors became too large, were followed in 9 control dogs (range = 89 to 105 days) and in the isotope-injected dog with the shortest $T_{1/2}$ ($T_{1/20}$ = 82 days).

Two normal control littermates were run simultaneously. The combined data were fit to a formula of postulated red-cell destruction by least-squares fit employing Taylor's expansion. The formula, $Y = Ae^{-ct}(1 - Bt)$, has been used to

[2] Abbott Laboratories.

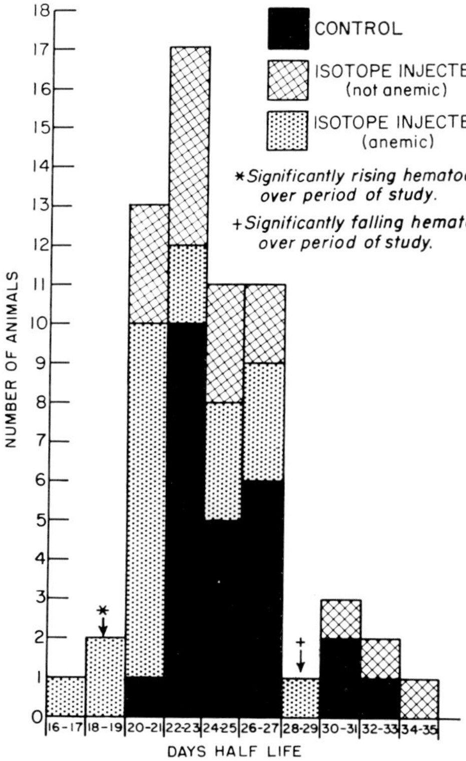

FIG. 1. Distribution of Cr^{51} red-cell survivals measured as apparent half-life ($T_{1/2}$) in beagle dogs.

characterize the Cr^{51} curve of red-cell survival (*9*). Accordingly Y is the number of cells surviving on a given day T, A is the number of cells on day 0, c is a constant of random loss, and B is the reciprocal of the life span. A detailed discussion with references concerning the steps in derivation has been published (*9*). Survival was followed for 91 days, determining 30 points on the graph. The calculated life span was 158 days with a variance of errors for the fit of $0.143\% \pm 0.98$.

SUMMARY

The time for reduction in survival of red cells to 50% of normal beagle dogs in this study (20 to 32 days) compares closely with that of normal mongrel dogs (21 to 30 days) (*10*). There was no definite hemolytic component as indicated by Cr^{51}-labeled red-cell studies in the anemia secondary to internal irradiation in beagle dogs. Slight damage to red cells is suggested, however, by the fact that survivals for many of the anemic irradiated dogs fell into the low normal range.

Evidence for red-cell damage with shortening of the Cr^{51} red-cell survival time has been found in dogs subjected to external X-ray (*6*). Two control dogs with pooled data appeared to fit a formula of postulated red-cell destruction.

ACKNOWLEDGMENTS

The author wishes to express appreciation to Dr. J. H. Dougherty, Dr. T. F. Dougherty, and Dr. B. J. Stover for advice and assistance; to Dr. M. A. Van Dilla for advice on counting techniques; to Kathryn Seymour, Warren Fisher, and David Atherton for technical assistance; and to John Fedako for help with statistical analysis.

RECEIVED: March 31, 1958

REFERENCES

1. J. H. DOUGHERTY, J. Z. BOWERS, R. C. BAY, and P. KEYANONDA. Comparison of hematologic effects of internally deposited radium and plutonium in dogs. *Radiology* **65**, 253–259 (1955).

2. V. LOEB, JR., C. V. MOORE, and R. DUBACH, The physiologic evaluation and management of chronic bone marrow failure. *Am. J. Med.* **15**, 499–517 (1953).

3. J. B. KAHN, JR., and J. FURTH, The pathogenesis of post irradiation anemia. *Blood* **7**, 404–416 (1952).

4. M. H. ROSS, J. FURTH, and R. R. BIGELOW, Changes in cellular composition of the lymph caused by ionizing radiations. *Blood* **7**, 417–428 (1952).

5. L. F. LAMERTON and C. F. BAXTER, An experimental study of radiation-induced anaemia with reference to shielding procedures and platelet changes. *Brit. J. Radiol.* **28**, 87–94 (1955).

6. F. STOHLMAN, JR., G. BRECHER, M. SCHNEIDERMAN, and E. P. CRONKITE, The hemolytic effect of ionizing radiations and its relationship to the hemorrhagic phase of radiation injury. *Blood* **12**, 1061–1085 (1957).

7. R. C. READ, Studies of red-cell volume and turnover using radiochromium. Description of a new "closed" method of red-cell-volume measurement. *New Engl. J. Med.* **250**, 1021–1027 (1954).

8. R. A. PHILLIPS, D. D. VAN SLYKE, P. B. HAMILTON, V. P. DOLE, K. EMERSON, JR., and R. M. ARCHIBALD, Measurement of specific gravities of whole blood and plasma by standard copper sulfate solutions. *J. Biol. Chem.* **183**, 305–330 (1950).

9. G. S. EADIE and I. W. BROWN, JR., The potential life span and ultimate survival of fresh red blood cells in normal healthy recipients as studied by simultaneous Cr^{51} tagging and differential hemolysis. *J. Clin. Invest.* **34**, 629–636 (1955).

10. F. STOHLMAN, JR., and M. SCHNEIDERMAN, Application of the Cr^{51} technique to the study of experimental hemolysis in the dog. *J. Lab. Clin. Med.* **47**, 72–82 (1956).

RADIATION RESEARCH 10, 67–79 (1959)

The Role of Bile Secretion in the Gastrointestinal Radiation Syndrome[1]

KENNETH L. JACKSON AND CECIL ENTENMAN

Biochemistry Branch, U. S. Naval Radiological Defense Laboratory, San Francisco, California

INTRODUCTION

The existence of a distinct radiation syndrome in mammals associated with exposure of the intestine is well established (*1*, *2*). That loss of fluid and electrolyte is an important aspect of the syndrome has been shown by recent studies in this laboratory indicating that whole-body X-irradiation of the fasted rat with 1500 r leads to severe diarrhea which commences on the third postirradiation day, followed by death during the fourth day. During the postirradiation period excessive loss of body sodium occurs, principally by way of the gastrointestinal tract, and the magnitude of the loss of this electrolyte is sufficient to account for the death of the animal (*3*). Successful treatment of the syndrome in dogs has been carried out by Conard *et al.* (*4*) by means of therapy with blood plasma, polyelectrolyte solution, concentrates of white blood cells and platelets, antibiotics, vitamins, and protein hydrolyzate.

The mechanism of excessive sodium loss after high doses of X-radiation is poorly understood. It seems reasonable to assume, however, that alteration in enteric absorption is involved, since after irradiation there is decreased absorption of sugars (*5*), sodium (*6*), water (*6*), and acute damage to the mucosa is apparent (*7*). Goodner *et al.* (*6*) interpret the results of their study on rats to indicate net leakage of sodium from blood to lumen of the gut after irradiation.

If a considerable reduction in the ability of the intestine to absorb sodium occurs after irradiation, then sodium entering the gastrointestinal tract in bile may be an important route for the loss of body sodium. Bile flow in the normal rat (as measured in bile fistula rats) is considerable, amounting to 5 ml per 100 gm of body weight per day (*8*). The concentration of sodium in bile is about 0.15 meq/ml (*9*, *10*) and, consequently, amounts to a daily influx to the gastrointestinal tract of approxi-

[1] This work was supported, in part, by funds provided by the Bureau of Medicine and Surgery, U. S. Navy Department, and the Federal Civil Defense Administration. The opinions or assertions contained herein are the private ones of the authors and are not to be construed as official or as reflecting the views of the Navy Department.

mately 15% of the rat's total body sodium. The present investigation is, therefore, concerned with the role played by bile secretion in the "gastrointestinal radiation syndrome." This has been approached by a study of bile secretion of electrolyte and the effect of bile duct ligation on survival time and electrolyte excretion in the 1500-r X-irradiated rat.

METHODS

Adult female Sprague-Dawley rats, 2½ to 3 months old, were used. In each experiment rats of the same age and approximately the same body weight were used. The animals were maintained on a diet of Purina laboratory chow. Food was given ad libitum during the experimental period unless otherwise indicated. Tap water was given ad libitum except during periods of fasting, in which case the animals were given distilled water.

The rats received a whole-body X-ray dose of 1500 r delivered from a Westinghouse therapy unit at 250 kvp and at a dose rate of 27 to 28 r/min (in air). Other irradiation factors were: target-to-midline distance, 40 inches; 15 ma; 0.5 mm Cu, 1 mm Al filter. During irradiation the rats were held in sector-shaped acetate plastic containers which were rotated under the beam. All rats in each experiment were irradiated simultaneously.

After irradiation the rats were caged in groups of 3 to 5 per cage except when excreta were being collected, in which case the animals were housed individually in metabolism cages. Urine and feces were collected together in beakers placed under the metabolism cages. At the end of each collection period the cages were scraped and rinsed with distilled water, the washings being combined with the collected excreta. In one experiment the gastrointestinal tract was removed and the contents of the stomach, small intestine, cecum, and large intestine were rinsed out with 0.25 *M* sucrose solution. Excreta samples and gastrointestinal tract content samples were diluted with water and homogenized until a fine suspension was obtained; after standing for several days, the supernatants were decanted and used for sodium and potassium analyses.

Bile was collected from bile fistula rats by the technique of Friedman *et al.* (*8*) which allows the rat freedom of movement with the exception that one hind foot is secured to the bottom of the cage. Bile duct cannulation was performed under ether anesthesia immediately before the collection period. The animals were then transferred to metabolism cages allowing simultaneous collection of bile and excreta. The delivery end of the cannula was placed at the same level as that of the rat. During bile collection the sham-operated controls were also secured to the bottom of the cage. Sodium and potassium analyses of bile, excreta, and gastrointestinal samples were performed with the Baird Associates flame photometer.

Bile duct ligation was performed under ether anesthesia with a single ligature of silk placed about 5 mm distal to the point where the hepatic ducts join to become

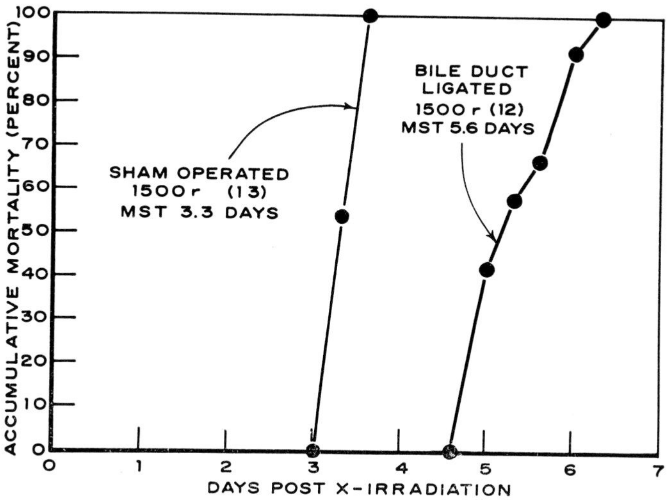

FIG. 1. Alteration in survival time by means of bile duct ligation performed immediately before X-irradiation. The number in parentheses indicates the number of animals used, and MST denotes mean survival time. The body-weight range of the rats used was 175 to 233 gm before irradiation.

the bile duct. In each experiment the control animals were subjected to sham operations, the sham operations being alternated with the operations of the experimental group.

Survival times were calculated as described below. Irradiation was performed between 8 and 10 o'clock in the morning. The animals were inspected each day after irradiation at 8:00 A.M., 4:00 P.M., and 10:00 P.M., and animals found dead at these times were recorded as surviving up to these times. Thus, survival times are reported to the following fractions of a day: 0.0, 0.3, and 0.6.

RESULTS

Survival Time

The effect of bile duct ligation performed immediately before irradiation is shown in Fig. 1. The data are combined from two separate experiments, since the results were essentially the same. It may be seen that bile duct ligation caused a significant increase in survival time. Mean survival time was increased from 3.3 days to 5.6 days. Since it has previously been found that the amount of sodium lost by the irradiated rat is sufficient to account for death (*3*), a possible interpretation of the effect of bile duct ligation on survival time is that elimination of bile secretion into the intestine has reduced sodium loss via the gastrointestinal tract.

If the results of the above experiment are to be explained on the basis postulated, bile duct ligation after irradiation but before the onset of excessive sodium loss

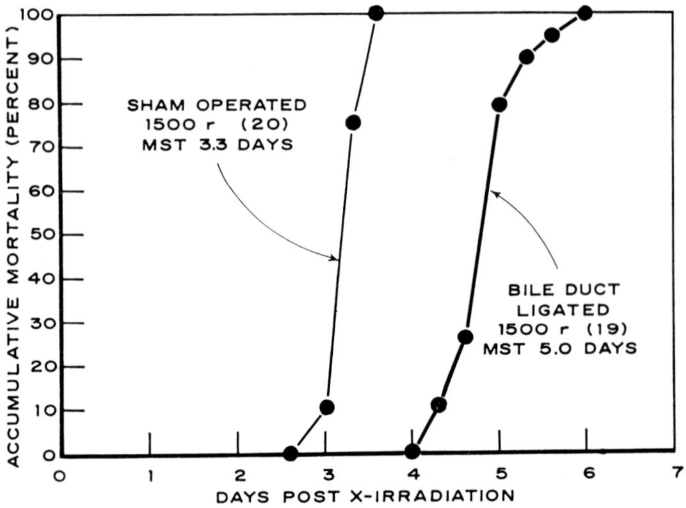

FIG. 2. Alteration in survival time by means of bile duct ligation performed 1 day after the time of X-irradiation. The number in parentheses indicates the number of animals used, and MST denotes mean survival time. The body-weight range of the rats used was 185 to 228 gm before irradiation.

should also be effective.[2] The effect of bile duct ligation 1 day after irradiation is shown in Fig. 2. The data are combined from two separate experiments. Mean survival time was increased from 3.3 days to 5.0 days, indicating that bile duct ligation after irradiation is almost as effective as when performed before irradiation.

Electrolyte Excretion

In order to make a quantitative evaluation of the effect of bile duct ligation on loss of electrolyte after irradiation, sodium and potassium excretions from 1500-r X-irradiated bile-duct-ligated rats were measured. In this experiment the rats were fed ad libitum up to the time of bile duct ligation but were fasted subsequent to this time. Bile duct ligation was performed 1 day after irradiation. Urine and feces were collected together daily from the time of bile duct ligation until the death of the animal. The effects observed on survival time are shown in Fig. 3. Alteration in mean survival time was somewhat less than in previous experiments, being increased from 3.3 days to 4.6 days. This may have been due to the increased handling of the rats necessitated by daily excreta collections and to fasting for part of the postirradiation period. The latter effect is shown in Fig. 4 for rats fasted for 24 hours prior to and for the period after irradiation. It may be seen that increase in survival time by means of bile duct ligation was less effective in the fasted-

[2] Excessive sodium loss commences on the third day post 1500 r of X-irradiation (*3*).

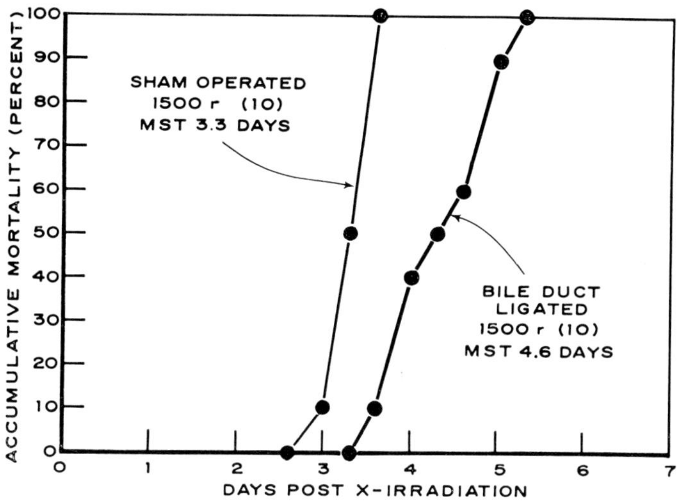

FIG. 3. Survival time of bile-duct-ligated rats used for the measurement of sodium and potassium excretions after irradiation (Figs. 5 and 6). Bile duct ligation was performed 1 day after irradiation. The number in parentheses indicates the number of animals used, and MST denotes mean survival time. The body-weight range of the rats used was 192 to 227 gm before irradiation.

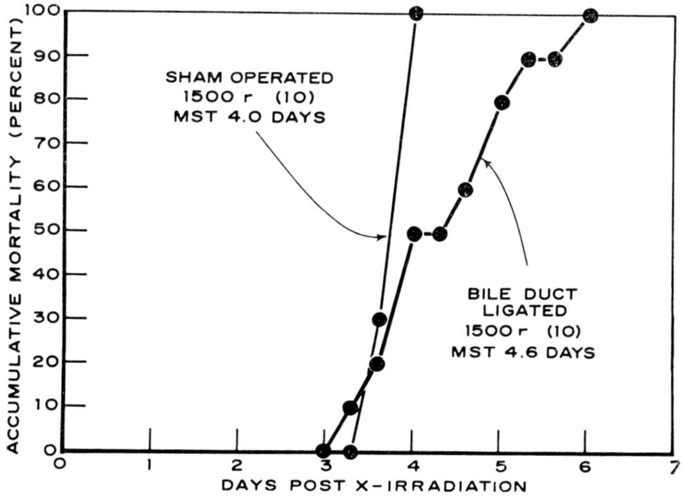

FIG. 4. Alteration in survival time of fasted rats by means of bile duct ligation performed immediately before X-irradiation. The rats were fasted for 24 hours prior to and for the period after irradiation. The number in parentheses indicates the number of rats used, and MST denotes mean survival time. The body-weight range of the rats used was 202 to 219 gm before fasting.

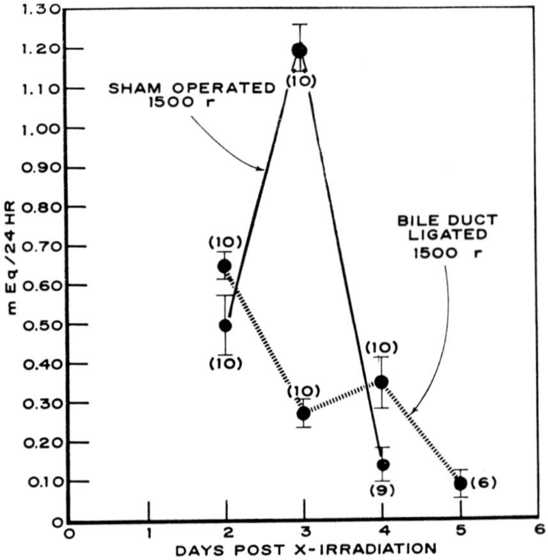

FIG. 5. The effect of bile duct ligation on sodium excretion by the rat after 1500 r of X-irradiation. The rats used in this experiment are the same as those indicated in Fig. 3. The rats were fasted during the excreta collection period which was initiated 1 day after irradiation. The number in parentheses indicates the number of rats from which the mean daily sodium excretion was derived. Bars indicate the standard errors of the means.

irradiated rat as compared to previous data obtained with the fed-irradiated rat (Fig. 1). Nevertheless, there was a significant difference in survival time due to bile duct ligation in the experiment in which excreta were collected, thereby allowing a comparison to be made between increase in survival time and possible alteration in electrolyte excretion.

Excretions of sodium and potassium are shown in Figs. 5 and 6. It may be seen (Fig. 5) that bile duct ligation effectively reduced the excessive loss of sodium normally seen on the third day postirradiation. Sodium excretion was changed from 1.20 meq to 0.27 meq, a reduction in sodium loss of 78%. Although only combined urine and fecal sodium was measured, it is assumed that the effect of bile duct ligation on reduced sodium excretion was primarily an effect on loss of sodium via the intestinal tract, since previous study has shown that sodium loss at this time is principally by way of the intestinal tract (*3*).

Sodium excretion was correlated with severity of diarrhea as observed qualitatively by the character of the stools on the bottom of the metabolism cage. Severe diarrhea was present on day 3 in all the animals of the sham-operated group, whereas diarrhea had commenced in only 3 out of the 10 animals of the bile-duct-ligated group at this time. On the fourth day, however, diarrhea was evident in the

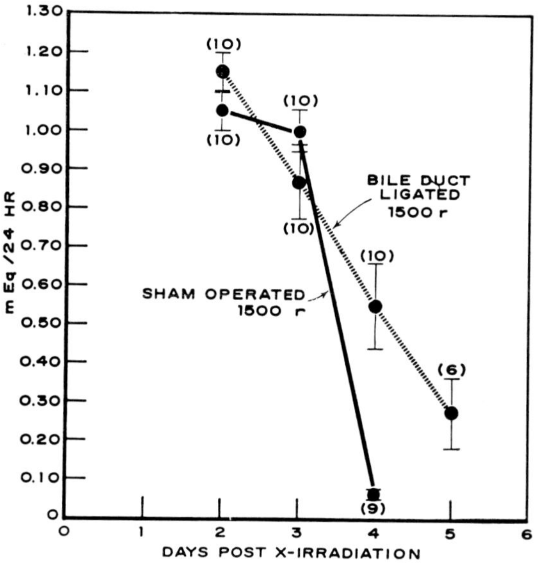

FIG. 6. The effect of bile duct ligation on potassium excretion by the rat after 1500 r of X-irradiation. The rats used in this experiment are the same as those indicated in Figs. 3 and 5. The number in parentheses indicates the number of rats from which the mean daily potassium excretion was derived. Bars indicate the standard errors of the means.

remainder of the bile-duct-ligated rats. The fact that sodium excretion was slightly lower in the sham-operated group as compared to the duct-ligated group on day 4 is probably because a large percentage of the rats of this group died before the end of the collection period and hence did not complete the fourth-day collection period.

The effect of bile duct ligation on potassium excretion by the irradiated rat should, by theory, be different from that of sodium excretion. Excess potassium excretion after irradiation occurs mainly by way of the urine (*3*) and hence should not be greatly affected by bile duct ligation. The experimental results indicate this to be correct (Fig. 6). Potassium excretion in the bile-duct-ligated rats was not significantly different from that of the sham-operated rats on the second and third days. The lower potassium excretion by the sham-operated group on day 4 may be explained on the same basis as that given previously for sodium excretion on day 4.

It should be pointed out that up to the beginning of the second day postirradiation both groups of rats were treated in an identical manner. Thus, by comparing the difference in the amount of sodium or potassium excreted from day 2 until death, one can calculate the difference in total-body excretory loss of sodium or potassium as a result of bile duct ligation. The total excretory loss of potassium from day 2 until death by the sham-operated group was 2.11 ± 0.08 (standard error) meq, and by the bile-duct-ligated group 2.73 ± 0.25 meq. One may conclude, therefore, that the bile-duct-ligated group, which had a greater survival time, excreted, on the average, a slightly greater amount of body potassium. Sodium excretion, on the other hand, exhibited a reversal of this finding. Mean sodium excretion during the same period was 1.83 ± 0.12 meq in the sham-operated group and 1.32 ± 0.09 meq in the bile-duct-ligated group. Thus, although the bile-duct-ligated rats lived longer, they had excreted less of their body sodium at the time of death than had the sham-operated group.

Sodium in the Gastrointestinal Tract Contents

An experiment was performed in order to rule out the possibility that reduction in sodium excretion after bile duct ligation of irradiated rats is due to a pooling of sodium within the gastrointestinal tract. Such a possibility might arise as follows: An irradiation-induced net leakage of sodium across the intestinal wall could occur, but the subsequent elimination of this sodium by the fecal route is impaired by bile duct ligation. If this were the case, the amount of sodium found in the gastrointestinal tract of the bile-duct-ligated irradiated rat would be greater than that found in the sham-operated irradiated rat. Consequently, the luminal sodium content of the gastrointestinal tracts of bile-duct-ligated and sham-operated rats was measured after 1500 r of X-irradiation. Bile duct ligation was performed 1 day after irradiation, and the rats were fasted subsequent to the time of ligation. Three days after X-irradiation the stomach, small intestine, cecum, and large intestine were removed and the amount of sodium in the contents of each structure was measured. The results are presented in Table I. The mean sodium content of

TABLE I

SODIUM IN THE GASTROINTESTINAL TRACT CONTENTS 3 DAYS AFTER 1500 R OF X-IRRADIATION

Treatment[a]	*Number of rats*[b]	*Luminal sodium content (meq)*[c]				
		Stomach	*Small intestine*	*Cecum*	*Large intestine*	*Total*
Bile-duct-ligated (1500 r)	8	0.414 ± 0.034	0.253[d] ± 0.021	0.256 ± 0.063	0.063 ± 0.018	0.985[d] ± 0.057
Sham-operated (1500 r)	8	0.475 ± 0.027	0.466 ± 0.070	0.372 ± 0.087	0.089 ± 0.016	1.40 ± 0.06

[a] The rats were fasted subsequent to time of bile duct ligation which was performed 1 day after X-irradiation.

[b] The body-weight range of the rats was 199 to 226 gm before irradiation.

[c] The mean value is followed by the standard error of the mean.

[d] The difference between means of bile-duct-ligated and sham-operated groups is greater than twice the sum of the standard errors.

each structure in the bile-duct-ligated group was lower than in the corresponding structure of the sham-operated group. This difference was significant only in the small intestine. The total amount of sodium in the contents of the whole gastrointestinal tract at the end of the third postirradiation day was significantly lower in the bile-duct-ligated group as compared to the sham-operated group, however. This indicates that reduced third-day sodium excretion, brought about by bile duct ligation, cannot be the result of pooling of sodium within the gastrointestinal tract. In fact, a decreased fecal excretion of sodium combined with a decreased amount of sodium in the gastrointestinal contents indicates that the net rate of sodium movement into the intestine of the irradiated rat is reduced by bile duct ligation.

Bile Secretion of Electrolyte

Volume of bile and amount of electrolyte secreted by the irradiated rat were also studied in order to determine whether enough sodium is secreted in the bile to account for the reduction in sodium excretion brought about by bile duct ligation.

A 24-hour collection of bile from rats with biliary fistulae was initiated at the beginning of the third day post 1500 r of X-irradiation. Fasting was started 1 day after irradiation, thus duplicating the fasting sequence of the two previous experiments. The results are given in Table II. Some of the rats in both the fistula and control groups died before the end of the third postirradiation day, which was probably due to the rather severe treatment used to obtain bile samples. Some conclusions can be formulated, however. Bile flow on the third day after 1500 r of X-irradiation was not different from normal. The mean bile flow on the third post-

TABLE II

EXCRETION AND BILE SECRETION OF SODIUM AND POTASSIUM ON THE THIRD DAY POST X-IRRADIATION

Treatment[a]	*Number of rats*[b]	*Number of rats dead during collection period*	*Volume of bile (ml/day)*[c]	*Sodium (meq/day)*[c]			*Potassium (meq/day)*[c]		
				Bile	*Excreta*	*Total*	*Bile*	*Excreta*	*Total*
Bile fistula (1500 r)	9	6	9.8 ± 0.5	1.53 ± 0.08	0.06 ± 0.01	1.59 ± 0.09	0.058 ± 0.004	0.409 ± 0.033	0.467 ± 0.032
Sham-operated (1500 r)	8	3	—	—	0.832 ± 0.163	0.832 ± 0.163	—	0.830 ± 0.079	0.830 ± 0.079

[a] The rats were fasted subsequent to the first day post 1500 r of X-irradiation. Bile was collected only during the third postirradiation day.

[b] The body-weight range of the rats used was 200 to 225 gm before irradiation.

[c] The mean value is followed by the standard error of the mean.

TABLE III

BILE SECRETION RATE IN VARIOUS SPECIES[a]

Species[b]	*Cubic centimeters of bile per kilogram body weight per 24 hours*	*Concentration of gall bladder bile relative to hepatic bile*[c]	*Estimated time period to secrete 20% body sodium in bile (days)*[d]
Mouse	34.9	4–5	1.9
Rat	47.1	—	1.4
Guinea pig	228.0	1–2	0.29
Rabbit	118.6	5	0.57
Cat	14.0	5–10	4.8
Dog	12.0	5–10	5.6
Sheep	12.1	0	5.5
Pig	25.2	0	2.7
Man	16.0	5–10	4.2

[a] Values for bile secretion rate and concentrating ability of the gall bladder are taken from data of Schmidt and Ivy (*11*).

[b] The rat is the only animal of the species listed that lacks a gall bladder.

[c] The concentration of gall bladder bile relative to hepatic bile is based on the pigment concentration ratios.

[d] Estimate is based on hepatic bile flow rate given in the table and sodium in hepatic bile at a concentration of 0.15 meq/ml (*9, 10*). Total body sodium is estimated to be 50 meq/kg of body weight.

irradiation day, calculated on the basis of body weight, was 46 ml per 24 hours per kilogram, which is close to the value measured for the normal rat (Table III).[3] The mean concentration of sodium in the bile was likewise normal, being 156 meq/l (*9, 10*).

The amount of potassium secreted in the bile was small compared to the total excretory loss of potassium. This is consistent with the effect of bile duct ligation on potassium loss by the irradiated rat (Fig. 6), which shows that bile duct ligation does not appreciably affect potassium excretion.

The amount of sodium secreted in bile, on the other hand, was relatively large, being 1.53 ± 0.08 meq. This amount is greater than either the magnitude of reduction of sodium loss brought about by bile duct ligation (0.93 meq, Fig. 5) or the total excretory loss of sodium (1.20 meq, Fig. 5) on the third postirradiation day. In the fistula rats (Table II) the amount of sodium appearing in the excreta was extremely small. This correlates with the incidence of diarrhea. None of the irradiated fistula rats exhibited diarrhea, whereas all the control irradiated rats had diarrhea.

DISCUSSION

From the data presented it is clear that ligation of the bile duct increases the mean survival time of the 1500-r X-irradiated rat as much as 70%. This effect

[3] The value was calculated on the basis of all rats studied. The average value calculated for the 3 rats which survived the 24-hour collection period was 47 ml per 24 hours per kilogram.

of bile duct ligation is correlated with a decrease in the rate of loss of body sodium and postponement of the onset of diarrhea. Mean sodium excretion on the third postirradiation day was reduced by 0.93 meq because of bile duct ligation (Fig. 5). A further reduction in loss of body sodium due to bile duct ligation is indicated by the reduced sodium content of the gastrointestinal tract at the end of the third postirradiation day. The mean magnitude of this reduction was 0.41 meq (Table I). Since sodium excretion on the *second day* after the time of X-irradiation does not differ significantly between irradiated and nonirradiated rats (*3*) or between irradiated sham-operated and irradiated bile-duct-ligated rats, it is assumed that the difference in sodium content of the gastrointestinal tracts of bile-duct-ligated rats and sham-operated rats, observed at the end of the third day, takes place, primarily, *during* the third postirradiation day. On the basis of this reasoning, it is estimated that the total reduction in body sodium loss on the third postirradiation day, due to bile duct ligation, is the reduced sodium excretion, 0.93 meq, plus the reduced sodium content of the gastrointestinal tract at the end of the third day, 0.41 meq, which equals 1.34 meq. Since the amount of sodium secreted in bile during this period by the irradiated rat was 1.53 meq, it is apparent that prevention of bile sodium from reaching the intestinal tract could account for the magnitude of the reduction of sodium loss after bile duct ligation.

In view of these and previous findings (*3*), a preliminary characterization of the mechanism of "gastrointestinal radiation death" in the rat can be made. It seems justifiable to conclude that an important factor in the mechanism of death is the excessive loss of fluid and sodium by way of the gastrointestinal tract. This is based on the fact that the amount of sodium lost by fasted-irradiated rats is sufficient to cause death (*3*) and that, when sodium excretion is reduced by bile duct ligation, survival time is increased. The immediate problem of interest is, therefore, the mechanism involved in excessive sodium loss. As pointed out previously, there is evidence that enteric absorption is altered after irradiation (*5, 6*). A question is raised, however, as to what extent net leakage of sodium occurs directly across the mucosal barrier into the lumen of the gastrointestinal tract. The results obtained in the present study indicate that this represents a minor contribution during the early period of extensive fluid and electrolyte loss. This is evidenced by the fact that prevention of bile from reaching the gastrointestinal tract in the irradiated rat reduced the third-day sodium excretion by 78% and that when bile was collected from fistula rats irradiated with 1500 r the amount of sodium excreted by way of the gastrointestinal tract was exceedingly small.

On the basis of the above considerations and the evidence that the amount of sodium secreted in bile is sufficient to account for the magnitude of the loss in body sodium on the third day, induced by bile duct ligation, it is concluded that the principal route for the third-day sodium loss is via the bile. This conclusion implies that the major route for irradiation-induced body sodium loss, up to the time of death, is via the bile because the major portion of the irradiation-induced loss of sodium, from the time of irradiation until the time of death, takes place by way of the fecal route on the third postirradiation day (*3*). Because diarrhea eventually developed in irradiated rats subjected to bile duct ligation, however, leakage of fluid and electrolyte directly across the intestinal mucosa may become an important route for sodium loss when some treatment is initiated that causes a prolongation of survival time.

Finally, it is of interest to consider the possible relationship of bile secretion to the gastrointestinal radiation syndrome of other species, especially in view of the fact that the rat's extrahepatic biliary system differs from that of most other mammals in that the rat does not possess a gall bladder. Values for bile flow rates and gall bladder concentrating ability in various species, shown in Table III, are taken from the data of Schmidt and Ivy (*11*). The values for bile flow refer to hepatic bile flow and hence do not indicate the volume of bile entering the intestine which may be lower than indicated because of the gall bladder's ability to absorb sodium and water (*9*). Nonetheless, an estimate of the upper limit for daily input of sodium into the gastrointestinal tract can be made. For purposes of comparing various species, the time necessary for the animal to secrete 20% of his body sodium in bile has been calculated. Loss of this amount of body sodium would lead to serious consequences (*12*). By inspection of the data in Table III it may be seen there is considerable variation in the bile volume output in various species. The upper limit for the amount of bile sodium entering the intestine in most of the larger species (cat, dog, sheep, and man) is small compared to that of the rat, indicating that loss of body sodium due to defective intestinal absorption of bile sodium would be a relatively slow process. On the other hand, the small laboratory animals have relatively high rates of bile secretion, and loss of bile sodium may play an important role in the gastrointestinal radiation syndrome, as has been shown to be the case with the rat. It is of interest in this respect that preliminary studies have shown that bile duct ligation also increases the survival time of the hamster (gall bladder present) after irradiation (Taketa and Swift, personal communication). Consequently it may prove valuable to consider the magnitudes of bile secretion when evaluating differences in the response of various species to gastrointestinal radiation injury.

SUMMARY

The role of bile secretion in the gastrointestinal radiation syndrome of the 1500-r X-irradiated rat was studied. Ligation of the bile duct increased the survival time of irradiated rats and reduced the excretory loss of sodium. When changes in the sodium content of the gastrointestinal tract were taken into consideration, the estimated body sodium loss was almost as great as the measured sodium secreted in bile by irradiated rats during the same period.

It is concluded that after X-irradiation of the rat with 1500 r: (1) the loss of body sodium due to net leakage of this electrolyte directly across the intestinal wall is of minor importance; (2) the major portion of the body sodium loss is the result of an inadequate absorption of bile sodium, which is secreted into the intestine at a normal rate; and (3) the loss of sodium via the bile is an important factor in the cause of death.

ACKNOWLEDGMENTS

The authors wish to express their appreciation for technical assistance rendered by G. E. Caldwell, HM2; R. L. Rhodes, HM2; and C. H. Sanders, HM3.

Received: May 19, 1958

REFERENCES

1. E. P. Cronkite and G. Brecher, Effects of whole-body irradiation. *Ann. Rev. Med.* **3,** 193–214 (1952).
2. H. Quastler, The nature of intestinal radiation death. *Radiation Research* **4,** 303–320 (1956).
3. K. L. Jackson, C. Entenman, and R. L. Rhodes, Electrolyte excretion in the rat following severe intestinal damage by X-irradiation. *Radiation Research* **8,** 361–373 (1958).
4. R. A. Conard, E. P. Cronkite, G. Brecher, and C. P. A. Strome, Experimental therapy of the gastrointestinal syndrome produced by lethal doses of ionizing radiation. *J. Appl. Physiol.* **9,** 227–233 (1956).
5. W. T. Moss, The effect of irradiating the exteriorized small bowel on sugar absorption. *Am. J. Roentgenol. Radium Therapy Nuclear Med.* **78,** 850–854 (1957).
6. C. J. Goodner, T. E. Moore, J. Z. Bowers, and W. D. Armstrong, Effects of acute whole-body X-irradiation on the absorption and distribution of Na^{22} and H^3OH from the gastrointestinal tract of the fasted rat. *Am. J. Physiol.* **183,** 475–484 (1955).
7. G. Brecher, E. P., Cronkite, R. A. Conard, and W. W. Smith, Gastric lesions in experimental animals following single exposures to ionizing radiation. *Am. J. Pathol.* **34,** 105–119 (1958).
8. M. Friedman, S. O. Byers, and F. Michaelis, Observations concerning production and excretion of cholesterol in mammals. II. Excretion of bile in the rat. *Am. J. Physiol.* **162,** 575–578 (1950).
9. J. P. Peters, *Body Water*, Charles C Thomas Co., Springfield, Illinois, 1935.
10. H. Sobotka, *Physiological Chemistry of the Bile*, Williams & Wilkins Co., Baltimore, Maryland, 1937.
11. C. R. Schmidt and A. C. Ivy, The general function of the gall bladder. Do species lacking a gall bladder possess its functional equivalent? The bile and pigment output of various species of animals. *J. Cellular Comp. Physiol.* **10,** 365–383 (1937).
12. G. Nichols and N. Nichols, Changes in tissue composition during acute sodium depletion. *Am. J. Physiol.* **186,** 383–392 (1956).

RADIATION RESEARCH 10, 80–88 (1959)

The Estimation of the Nonrecuperable Injury Caused by Ionizing Radiation

JOHN S. KREBS, RALPH W. BRAUER, AND HARVEY KALBACH

Biological and Medical Sciences Division, U. S. Naval Radiological Defense Laboratory, San Francisco, California

INTRODUCTION

Evidence has been accumulating in the recent literature to show that exposure of animals to doses of ionizing radiation which fail to cause acute death results in a variety of late pathological lesions leading in most cases to reduced life expectancy in the animals (*1*). Although it must be supposed that exposure to radiation results in a latent injury from which the animals do not recover, the presence of the injury is usually masked by an extended period of apparent normalcy prior to the development of the late lesions and foreshortened survival. In a previous communication (*2*) the authors pointed out a method which could be used to unmask this injury. If the word "injury" is allowed to take on the somewhat restricted meaning of "susceptibility to acute death," then the amount of such injury in an animal caused by a sublethal dose of ionizing radiation can be measured at any time after exposure to the radiation in terms of the amount of additional radiation necessary to cause acute death. This technique has been used in several investigations of the kinetics of recovery of animals from acute radiation injury (*3–10*).

In the application of the technique to the present study, the animals were irradiated in a fractionated-dose scheme so that a large dose could be given to animals without significant loss of animals by acute death, and a sufficient time after completion of the irradiation was allowed before testing for injury, so that the injury would have decreased to a level where further recovery was not demonstrable. Under such conditions the injury found represents nonrecuperable injury caused by ionizing radiation.

METHODS

All animals used in these studies were C3H female mice.[1] The irradiation to establish nonrecuperable injury, called the conditioning irradiation, was begun when the animals were 9 ± 1 weeks old.

[1] Obtained from the Cancer Research and Genetics Department of the University of California.

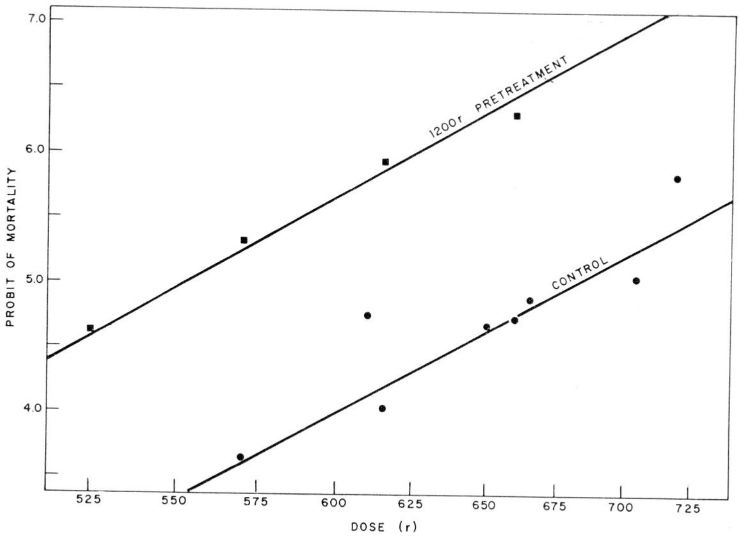

FIG. 1. Dose-mortality plot for pool of all control animals and pool of all animals receiving 1200 r of conditioning radiation.

Mice were irradiated in Lucite boxes measuring 6 × 9 × 16 cm, in groups of 3 or 4 mice per box. The radiation source was a 250-kvp X-ray machine, HVL 2.7 mm Cu, delivering between 12 and 15 r/min at a mean target-skin distance of 115 cm.

The conditioning irradiation was performed in two or more doses of 300 r each, separately by intervals of 3 weeks. After completion of the course of conditioning exposures, the mice were held to 4 to 20 weeks and were then tested for injury by exposure to additional radiation to determine the dose-response curve. The amounts of conditioning radiation and times allowed for recovery are shown in Table I, the numbers of animals used in each test are shown in Table II, and the nature of the test performed is illustrated in Fig. 1.

During the recovery period between the time of completion of the conditioning irradiation and the time of administration of the test radiation none of the mice receiving 900 r or less died, about 3% of those receiving 1200 r died, 7% of those receiving 1500 r died, and 40 to 50% of those receiving 1800 r died. The animals receiving 1800 r were discarded from the experiment, and the administration of the 1800-r conditioning dose was discontinued.

To test the response of conditioned animals, four separate groups were exposed a single time to one of a graded series of dose levels which were increased in steps of 45 r. The irradiation was done by placing all the mice to be tested under the X-ray, giving the minimum dose, removing the first group of animals, and continuing the irradiation in steps of 45 r, with removal of a group of animals after each step, until all the animals had been irradiated. Control mice, which had not received conditioning radiation, were given the test radiation along with each group of mice that had previously received conditioning radiation.

The LD_{50} for X-rays was determined by calculating the regression of the probit of 30-day mortality on the logarithm of the dose and obtaining the estimated log dose for a probit of 5.0, according to standard methods of treatment (*11*). In the final compilation of data the results from two studies with conditioning doses of 1200 r were rejected because the observed mortalities were greater than 50% for all doses tested. The data from these studies were combined with other data from similarly treated groups to obtain a pooled estimate of LD_{50}.

RESULTS

Nonrecuperable Injury in Relation to Dose of Conditioning Radiation

The basic data on nonrecuperable injury are shown in Table I. The columns of the table list, in order, the amount of conditioning radiation, the time allowed for recovery, the LD_{50} for X-ray of animals receiving the conditioning dose, and the LD_{50} for X-ray of control animals not previously irradiated. It can be seen that in all cases the mice that had received the conditioning radiation had LD_{50} values for X-ray significantly lower than those of mice not previously irradiated. The amount by which the LD_{50} is lowered, column 5 of Table I, is the amount of unrecovered injury resulting from the conditioning irradiation.

In Fig. 2 the amount of unrecovered injury, column 5 of Table I, is plotted against amount of conditioning radiation given to the animals. It can be seen that, to a

TABLE I

EFFECT OF CONDITIONING IRRADIATION IN DISPLACING THE DOSE-RESPONSE CURVE OF MICE TO X-IRRADIATION

Conditioning dose (r)	*Time for recovery (weeks)*	*LD_{50} (r)*	*Control LD_{50} (r)*	*Difference*
600	10	668.2 ± 17.9	706.6 ± 16.2	38.4 ± 24.2
600	10	641.0 ± 14.1	708.1 ± 15.2	67.1 ± 20.8
900	4	568.7 ± 17.4	650.3 ± 13.4	81.6 ± 22.0
900	8	592.8 ± 14.8	650.3 ± 13.4	57.5 ± 20.0
1200	5	608.9 ± 10.4	706.6 ± 16.2	97.7 ± 19.3
1200	10	Not measurable		
1200	20	595.5 ± 11.5	687.0 ± 18.7	91.5 ± 22.0
1500	10	552.0 ± 25.4	696.8 ± 18.7	144.8 ± 31.6
Combined 900	—	573.6 ± 11.4	679.9 ± 6.9	106.3 ± 13.3
Combined 1200	—	552.5 ± 6.2	679.9 ± 6.9	127.4 ± 9.3

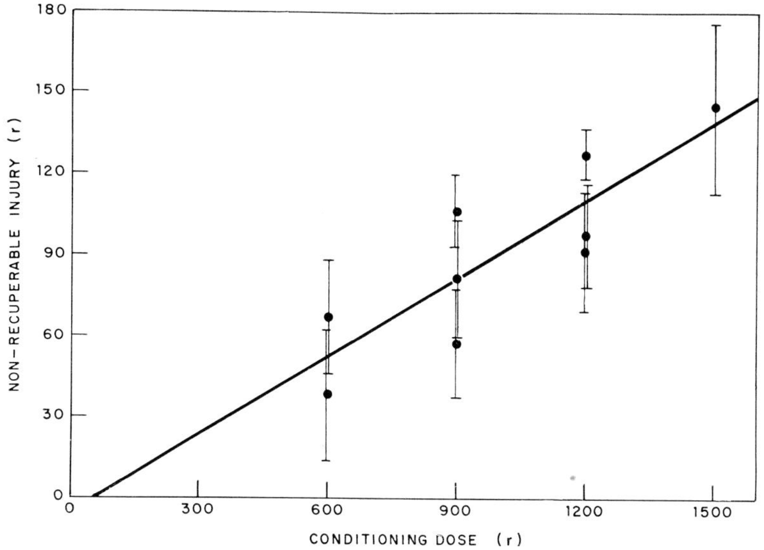

FIG. 2. Nonrecuperable injury in relation to dose of conditioning radiation given.

fair approximation, the amount of injury is linearly related to the amount of conditioning radiation. The regression equation for the data of Fig. 2 is

$$Y = 90.26 + 0.0958(X - 1000)$$

where Y is the amount of injury and X is the conditioning dose.

Effect of Prior Conditioning Irradiation on the Characteristics of Acute Death after the Test Radiation

The mean value of the slopes of the dose-response curves for the acute death after the test radiation was 16.47 ± 4.90 for the mice that had received conditioning radiation and 15.84 ± 2.64 for the control mice, which had not previously been irradiated. The difference in mean values is probably not significant.

The time distribution of death of the mice is shown in Table II. It can be seen that for the death occurring during the first 30 days after the test radiation the mean time of death is essentially the same in both the control and the conditioning-irradiated animals. During the period from 31 to 90 days after the test radiation the proportion of conditioning-irradiated mice that died was significantly greater than that of control mice.

Survival of Mice under Repeated Weekly Irradiation

In a separate experiment small groups of mice were exposed to doses of X-ray repeated at intervals of 1 week until all the animals were dead. The data for this

TABLE II

TIME DISTRIBUTION OF DEATH OF MICE IRRADIATED IN THE MIDLETHAL RANGE

onditioning dose (r) and Crecovery time, (weeks)	Number of animals	Number dead, 1–30 days	Mean time of death, 1–30 days	Number dead, 31–60 days	Number dead, 61–90 days
Control	50	32	12.6 ± 3.1	1	0
900 (4)	71	45	16.4 ± 3.6	9	4
900 (8)	64	38	13.2 ± 3.9	3	5
Control	95	24	17.6 ± 5.6	3	2
600 (10)	91	28	16.9 ± 5.6	3	4
1200 (5)	68	29	13.0 ± 4.4	20	1
Control	71	24	17.7 ± 5.4	8	6
1200 (20)	59	27	15.9 ± 5.7	7	4

TABLE III

SURVIVAL OF MICE TO IRRADIATION REPEATED AT WEEKLY INTERVALS

Dose rate (r/week)	Observed mean lethal dose (r)	Maximum lethal dose (r)	Calculated mean lethal dose (r)
200	2100 ± 97	2200	3200
150	2250 ± 129	2400	4100
100	2660 ± 430	3100	5000
50	1860 ± 301	2250	5900

study are shown in Table III. The lethal dose for each mouse was calculated as the total dose accumulated up to 24 hours prior to death; the mean lethal dose for a group of mice was calculated in the usual fashion; and the standard error was estimated from the range of lethal doses. The calculated mean lethal dose is the value obtained by assuming that the injury caused by each dose consists of 10% nonrecoverable injury and 90% recoverable injury, that the recoverable injury disappears from the animal with a half-life of 7 days, and that the mean lethal dose for periodic irradiation is the dose at which the accumulated total of injury in the animal, recoverable and nonrecoverable, equals the acute single dose LD_{50}. It can be seen that at all dose rates studied the observed lethal doses are significantly lower than calculated values.

DISCUSSION

It appears from the above data that, when mice are given a sublethal course of X-ray treatment and allowed to recover, then at a time when the effect of the irradiation should have vanished completely there is present in the animals an injury resulting from the X-ray treatment which manifests itself as a reduction in the ability of the irradiated animals to sustain further X-ray injury. The amount by which the tolerance of the animals to X-ray is reduced is called the nonrecuperable radiation injury.

From Fig. 2 it can be seen that the amount of nonrecuperable injury is linearly proportional to the amount of conditioning radiation given to the animals. From the regression equation estimated from the data it can be formally calculated that the nonrecuperable injury has a threshold at 58 r of conditioning radiation and thereafter rises at a rate of 9.58% of the conditioning dose. It is probable that this value of threshold is not significantly different from the origin of the plot and that there may be no threshold at all.

The central problem in connection with the injury measured in the foregoing experiments is whether or not the injury is truly nonrecuperable. In planning the experiments the authors used the studies of Patterson *et al.* (*4*) on the kinetics of recovery of mice from a nonlethal dose of radiation as the basis for setting the times after completion of the conditioning radiation when the injury would be tested. According to Patterson *et al.* the injury from the radiation, measured in the same way as the experiments currently being reported, decreases as an exponential function of time after the conditioning dose, with a half-life of approximately 7 days. If we assume that the half-life is correct and that the exponential recovery process applies to the conditioning radiation sequence used in the current experiments, it can be calculated that the amounts of injury remaining in a mouse at various times after completion of a 900-r or 1200-r course of conditioning radiation would be as follows: 4 weeks, 20 r; 5 weeks, 10 r; 8 weeks, 1 r; 20 weeks, 0 r. In Table I it can be seen that the injury from the 900-r conditioning dose was tested at 4 and 8 weeks after completion of the conditioning radiation, and that from the 1200-r dose at 5 and 20 weeks after conditioning treatment. The experimental results and calculations may be summarized thus:

900-r conditioning dose:	
Injury remaining at 4 weeks	81.6 r
Injury remaining at 8 weeks	57.5 r
Recovery, 4–8 weeks	24.1 r
Calculated recovery, 4–8 weeks	19 r
1200-r conditioning dose	
Injury remaining at 5 weeks	97.7 r
Injury remaining at 20 weeks	91.5 r
Recovery, 5–20 weeks	6.2 r
Calculated recovery, 5–20 weeks	10 r

It should be noted that the amount of recovery from either conditioning dose is over 90% at the time of the first test, but that the amount of injury still present is significantly greater than would be predicted from exponential recovery. The amount of recovery observed in the period after the first test is of the order of magnitude expected from the continued exponential recovery of a portion of the injury.

The observations of Patterson *et al.*, were repeated in an extensive study by Kohn and Kallman (*6*). The latter authors confirmed the exponential nature of the recovery and obtained half-time recovery values of 1.6 to 2.8 days, depending on the strain of mouse used. The differences between their values and those of Patterson are ascribed to differences in the age of the animals at the time of first irradiation. On this basis the animals used in the current experiments are more nearly comparable to those of Patterson than those of Kohn, and the calculations above appear to be justified. If values of half-recovery time reported by Kohn were used, then the amount of injury that should be present at 4 to 5 weeks after completion of the conditioning radiation would be zero, and the significance of the amount found would be heightened. In passing, it should be noted that the exponential recovery process for radiation does not have unrestricted applicability. As indicated by the data of Table III, the exponential recovery process must break down at some point when radiation is repeated regularly. Observations similar to those of Table III have been reported by Patterson *et al.* (*4*) and by Mole (*10*).

Granted that there is nonrecuperable injury, there is a major hazard in underestimating its value. Accordingly, in the plot of nonrecuperable injury versus dose in Fig. 2, the values of nonrecuperable injury are assigned equal weight, irrespective of the time after conditioning dose at which the measurement is made. In view of the large standard errors associated with each value of nonrecuperable injury, the procedure is not unreasonable.

Another aspect of the nature of the nonrecuperable injury is the problem of whether or not the conditioning radiation alters the nature or manner of death in the animals after the test irradiation is given. From Table II is can be seen that the mean time of death during the first 30 days after the test radiation is not different for control and conditioning-irradiated animals, suggesting that the basic course of illness leading to acute death is the same for both groups. The fact that the slope of the dose-response curve is not changed by the conditioning radiation indicates that the conditioning does not change the distribution of radiation sensitivity in the population but rather shifts the sensitivity of the population as a whole to lower levels. The incidence of a higher death rate among the 30-day survivors of the test radiation in the conditioning-irradiated animals, as opposed to the control animals, suggests that the conditioning irradiation has effects in addition to the change in radiation sensitivity, possibly related to survival potential of the animals. In view of the known effect of irradiation in reducing life expectancy in animals, the result in the above case is not unreasonable.

In view of the high post-30-day mortality among the conditioning-irradiated animals, the possibility was considered that the period of observation of mortality for inclusion in the computation of the dose-response curves might be extended to—say—60 days after the test radiation. Such a procedure has been suggested previously (*9*). But the choice of time is necessarily arbitrary, unless one wishes to wait until all the animals are dead, and the choice of 30 days is based on the experience that most of the acute mortality occurring after lethal radiation is usually between the twelfth and twentieth days. Further deaths occur, to be sure, but the incidence tends to be sporadic and subject to influence from random causes not readily controlled by the investigator.

The investigation of nonrecuperable radiation injury was originally suggested by the studies of Blair (*12*) which predicted the existence of nonrecuperable injury on the basis of the observed survival of animals under chronic irradiation. The present investigation seems to support Blair's prediction, in that sublethal irradiation results in a nonrecuperable injury proportional to dose. The results presented in Table III, however, indicate that the available information on nonrecuperable injury and rates of decrease of recoverable injury in the animal is not sufficient to account for the survival of animals subjected to regularly repeated radiation. In all cases the calculated value for mean lethal dose is greater than the mean lethal dose actually observed, and the discrepancy becomes larger as the dose rate is decreased. A number of factors might be cited to account for the discrepancy, of which potentially the most fruitful is the study by Mole (*10*) indicating that exposure to radiation decreases the rate of recovery of mice when exposed to additional radiation.

The authors of the present communication have found evidence of nonrecoverable injury in every experiment in which the measurement was made. The failure of others to find evidence of nonrecoverable injury (*4*, *6*) cannot be readily explained but perhaps results from the fact that in the latter cases the conditioning doses given to the animals were small, less than half of the smallest dose used in the present study. Under such conditions the amount of residual injury would be sufficiently small so that it would be difficult to detect.

SUMMARY

Exposure of mice to a nonlethal course of X-ray treatment results in a reduction in tolerance of mice to further X-ray treatment. The reduction in tolerance to X-ray, measured as a lowering of the LD_{50}, is linearly proportional to dose to which the animals were previously exposed and thus can serve as a measure of permanent injury induced by the X-ray. The evidence does not indicate that the exposure to X-ray changes either the mechanism of acute death from X-ray or the distribution of sensitivity to X-ray. The injury found does not account for the observed mortality of animals from chronically imposed radiation.

RECEIVED: May 5, 1958

REFERENCES

1. J. FURTH, A. C. UPTON, K. W. CHRISTENBERRY, W. H. BENEDICT, and J. MOSHMAN, Some late effects in mice of ionizing radiation from an experimental nuclear detonation. *Radiology* **63**, 562–570 (1954).
2. R. W. BRAUER, J. S. KREBS, and R. L. PESSOTTI, The "non-recuperable" fraction of X-ray irradiation injury as the basis for an experimental approach to the problem of delayed effects of ionizing radiation. *In Progress in Radiobiology*, pp. 396–400, Oliver & Boyd, London, 1954.
3. C. W. HAGEN and E. L. SIMMONS, Effects of total body X-irradiation on rats. Part I. Lethal action of single, paired, and periodic doses. University of Chicago Metallurgical Laboratory Report CH-3815 (1947); U. S. Atomic Energy Commission Document MDDC-1210 (1947).
4. E. PATTERSON, C. W. GILBERT, and J. MATTHEWS, Time intensity factors and whole body irradiation. *Brit. J. Radiol.* **25**, 427–433 (1952).
5. H. I. KOHN and R. F. KALLMAN, Acute X-ray studies with the hamster. The LD_{50}, death rate, and recovery rate. *Radiation Research* **6**, 137–147 (1957).
6. H. I. KOHN and R. F. KALLMAN, The influence of strain on acute X-ray lethality in the mouse. II. Recovery rate studies. *Radiation Research* **6**, 329–338 (1957).
7. H. I. KOHN and R. F. KALLMAN, Acute lethality studies with the rat: The LD_{50}, death rate, and recovery rate. *Radiation Research* **7**, 85–97 (1957).
8. A. L. CARSTEN and T. R. NOONAN, Determination of the recovery from lethal effects of lower body irradiation in rats. (Abstract) *Radiation Research* **5**, 472–473 (1956).
9. R. H. MOLE, Quantitative observations on recovery from whole body irradiation in mice. I. Recovery after single large doses of radiation. *Brit. J. Radiol.* **29**, 563–569 (1956).
10. R. H. MOLE, Quantitative observations on recovery from whole body irradiation in mice. II. Recovery during and after daily irradiation. *Brit J. Radiol.* **30**, 40–46 (1957).
11. D. J. FINNEY, *Probit Analysis*, Cambridge University Press, London, 1947.
12. H. A. BLAIR, A formulation of the injury, life span, dose relations for ionizing radiations. I. Application to the mouse. University of Rochester Atomic Energy Project Report UR-206 (1952).

RADIATION RESEARCH **10**, 89–111 (1959)

Indirect Inactivation of Macromolecules in Solution by Ionizing Radiation

A Method of Analysis[1]

LEROY AUGENSTINE

Biology Department, Brookhaven National Laboratory Upton, New York

INTRODUCTION

The early work of Fricke's group (*1–3*) demonstrated that the effects of radiation on aqueous solutions of inorganic and simple organic compounds are mediated by "activated water" (*4*). Reactions between the elements of "activated water"—identified subsequently as radicals—and compounds in solution have been defined as *indirect effects* of the radiation. In contrast, primary interactions between radiation and compounds are defined as *direct effects* of radiation. Dale (*5*) first showed that very dilute solutions of pure enzyme could be inactivated by doses of the order of 10^4 instead of the 10^6 r or greater necessary for direct inactivation of impure solutions (*6, 7*) or dry (*8*) preparations. Barron (*9*) later found that the sensitivity of molecules to indirect inactivation depended markedly on their surface composition. For instance, sulfhydryl enzymes in solution were inactivated by doses as low as 10^2 r, with the largest fraction of the damage apparently being the oxidation of free —SH groups necessary for activity. At least two different types of indirect inactivation, one immediate and one delayed, have been observed in enzymes (*10–11*), hemoglobin (*12*) and DNA (*13*). McDonald's work with trypsin (*11*) and that of Bachofer and Pottinger (*14*) with bacteriophage T1 showed that inactivation yield (i.e., units of solute inactivated per unit of radiation) is greatly affected by hydrogen and other ions. Although constant yields have been observed for some solutes over a considerable concentration range (*1–3, 15*), the inactivation yield of macromolecules usually decreases if their initial solute concentration is decreased (*5, 9, 15–19*).

In the first section of this paper a theoretical method will be developed for characterizing indirect inactivation due to radiation-produced radicals. Next, data will

[1] Portions of this manuscript were presented before the Radiation Research Society, Rochester, New York, May 13–15, 1957. Research carried out at Brookhaven National Laboratory under the auspices of the U. S. Atomic Energy Commission.

be presented which appear to demonstrate satisfactorily the validity of that method of analysis. In the third section, earlier data for proteins will be reanalyzed. The occurrence—under certain conditions—of yields larger than those expected from a single species of radicals will be taken in Section IV as evidence that either more than one species of radical can inactivate a particular solute or else two modes of inactivation can occur in solution.

I. THEORY

The model on which the present method of analysis is based can be defined by three propositions:

1. Radiation produces activated solvent molecules, including ions as well as the oxidizing and reducing radicals to be dealt with here.
2. Inactivation,[2] if it occurs at all, is the result of a single collision with a radiation-produced radical (this excludes those situations where multiple collisions either with additional radicals or other solute molecules play a major role).
3. Inactivation is produced solely by collisions with radicals (the theory applies only where direct inactivation is negligible).

It is important to recognize that, although the present development will be restricted to radicals produced by radiation, it has a much larger realm of validity. The equations to be derived are applicable to any system in which the reaction mechanism is consistent with the basic propositions—independent of whether the activated molecules are radicals produced by radiation or not.

Glossary of Terms

N_i—the number of solute molecules of kind i in unit volume.
X_j—the number of radicals of kind j in unit volume.
z_{ij}—the probability that any given collision involves a specific one of the jth radicals and a specific molecule of solute i.
R_{ij}—the probability that a collision between an ith solute molecule and a jth radical will destroy the *radical*.
S_{ij}—the probability that a collision which results in radical elimination will cause inactivation of the *solute* molecule.
n—the number of solutes reactive to the jth type of radical.
Y_{1j}—the number of solute 1 molecules inactivated per jth radical produced, the "yield."
m—the slope of the straight line obtained by plotting the reciprocal of the yield against the reciprocal of solute concentration.

The probability that any collision is between an i molecule and a j radical is

[2] In this paper the term inactivation includes any solute changes which fall into the particular category being measured experimentally.

$z_{ij}N_iX_j$. Thus, the fraction of jth radicals destroyed by collisions with solute 1 molecules

$$\frac{z_{1j}\, N_1\, X_j\, R_{1j}}{\sum_{i=1}^{n} z_{ij}\, N_i\, X_j\, R_{ij}} = \frac{z_{1j}\, N_1\, R_{1j}}{\sum_{i=1}^{n} z_{ij}\, N_i\, R_{ij}}$$

does not depend on X_j and is independent of the frequency and total number of collisions. (Later $z_{ij}R_{ij}N_i$ will be referred to as the reactive capacity of solute i toward j radicals.) If dX_j radicals are produced by an increment of dose, dD,

$$\frac{z_{1j}\, N_1\, R_{1j}}{\sum_{i=1}^{n} z_{ij}\, N_i\, R_{ij}}\, dXj$$

is the number of those radicals destroyed by collisions with solute 1 molecules. Multiplying by S_{1j} gives the number of solute 1 molecules inactivated by the dXj radicals:

$$-dN_1 = \frac{z_{1j}\, N_1\, R_{1j}\, S_{1j}}{z_{1j}N_1R_{1j} + \sum_{i=2}^{n} z_{ij}N_iR_{ij}}\, dXj \qquad (1)$$

The n terms in the denominator include the reactive capacity toward radicals of the jth kind of added solutes including solute 1, impurities, and potentially *other* radicals formed by the radiation (however, the many observations of independence of inactivation and dosage rates indicate that the latter factor is normally insignificant). Henceforth the reactive capacity of those components in the solvent other than *added* solutes will be designated by $z_{cj}R_{cj}N_c$ and referred to as the "solvent capability."

The factors of interest in equation 1 are R_{1j}, S_{1j}, and $z_{ij}R_{ij}$: they are respective *measures* of the reactive capacity of the macromolecular surface for jth radicals; the proportion of molecular surface both reactive to jth radicals and also necessary for function; and the relative reactive capacity or "protective effect" of solute i. Various authors (*5*, *15*, *20–22*) have formulated relations similar to equation 1, and Lea has summarized methods for determining these factors. The methods are based on a number of assumptions of which the most important is that the reactive capacity of the solvent components is much less than that of added solutes and can be neglected (i.e., there is a region in which $z_1R_1N_1 \gg z_cR_cN_c$, so that yield is independent of solute concentration). The assumptions can often be satisfied if the solute concentration is large enough (for instance, see Table 4, p. 101, in reference (*16*). However, in systems where it is advantageous to work with very dilute solutions (*15*)—e.g., those containing two or more macromolecular solutes—it is often impossible or undesirable to meet the above conditions even if the solvent and reagents are carefully purified. The revised treatment of the data presented below provides a means of obtaining the desired information with less restrictive assumptions.

Equation 1 can be inverted, factored, and written as

$$\frac{1}{Y_{1j}} = \frac{1}{S_{1j}} + \left[\frac{\sum_{i=2}^{n} z_{ij} R_{ij} N_i}{z_{1j} R_{1j} S_{1j}}\right] \frac{1}{N_1} \tag{2}$$

where $-dN_1/dX_j$ is designated the yield Y_{1j}. Thus, if the reciprocal, $1/Y_{1j}$, of the yield is plotted against the reciprocal, $1/N_1$, of the solute concentration, a straight line should result, whose intercept is $1/S_{1j}$ and whose slope is the quantity in parentheses. This not only provides a measure of S_{1j}—which in this case is the *yield* at *infinite concentration*—irrespective of Lea's assumptions, but also permits relative determinations of both $z_{cj}R_{cj}N_c$ and the R_{ij} of a protective solute without finding the exact N_i which reduces the yield 50% (*20*).

Using the methods of least squares to "fit" the straight line predicted above gives two experimental quantities—the intercept, $1/S_{1j}$, and the slope, m—and measures of the reliability of both. For the case of a single added solute the slope is

$$m^c = \frac{\sum_{i=2}^{n} z_{ij} R_{ij} N_i}{z_{1j} R_{1j} S_{1j}} = \frac{z_{cj} R_{cj} N_c}{z_{1j} R_{1j} S_{1j}^c} \tag{3a}$$

Or a very useful alternative parameter can be calculated from the slope and intercept: if N_1^d denotes the concentration of solute 1 for which the value of the reciprocal of the yield would be twice the intercept, then

$$z_{1j} R_{1j} N_1^d = \sum_{i=2}^{n} z_{ij} R_{ij} N_i = z_{cj} R_{cj} N_c = z_{1j} R_{1j} N_1^c \tag{3b}$$

where the c superscripts are used to indicate that only a single solute is present and N_1^c is the concentration of solute 1 which has a reactive capacity equivalent to $z_{cj}R_{cj}N_c$. If Lea's previous assumptions were to be fulfilled, the slope would be zero. It is important that the solvent capability be determined for *each* experimental situation, because it depends on many factors. One of these is the radiation quality—both the spatial distribution and the ratios of the various species of radicals are thereby affected; e.g., the more densely ionizing the radiation, the more likely is radical recombination. However, impurities in the solute sample will be added proportionally with the amount of solute. Therefore, they will change the intercept rather than the slope.

Once m^c and S_{1j}^c—or equivalently N_1^c—have been found for a given experimental situation, the determination of m^p and S_{1j}^p—or N_1^d—on the addition of a second "protector" solute allows an evaluation of R_{1j} in terms of the R_{2j} of the protector by either

$$R_{1j} = \left(\frac{z_{2j}}{z_{1j}}\right)\left(\frac{N_2}{m^p S_{1j}^p - m^c S_{1j}^c}\right) R_{2j} \tag{4a}$$

$$R_{1j} = \left(\frac{z_{2j}}{z_{1j}}\right)\left(\frac{N_2}{N_1^d - N_1^c}\right) R_{2j} \tag{4b}$$

The absolute values of the z's would be affected by any environmental factors which would affect the velocity or direction of migration of individual molecules (whether on a micro or macro scale) (*23*). However, since only the ratio (z_{2j}/z_{1j}) is required, the z values given by Lea (p. 53 of reference *20*) are probably adequate. An ideal "protective standard" would be one in which the effects of oxidation and reduction could be distinguished, since it seems feasible that proteins can be inactivated by both.

It is necessary to designate both the slope and intercept with c and p superscripts because the separation of the S and R parameters permits a distinction between two types of "protector" effects—one of which affects the slope and the other the intercept. In the first effect, designated "competitive protection" (because it is analogous to the "competitive inhibition" of antimetabolites), the protector molecules compete with solute 1 molecules for the radicals: this causes an increased slope but leaves the intercept unchanged. In the second, designated "reactive protection," the protector molecules react with solute 1 molecules so as to alter the critical surface site or else make it unavailable to inactivating radicals (*9*): this will increase the intercept (i.e., decrease S_{1j}). When an enzyme is irradiated at the proper pH in the presence of its substrate, the substrate may provide both types of protection. The critical enzyme site is expected to be unavailable to radical inactivation for the duration of each enzyme-substrate complex, so that the "reactive protection" would produce a reduction in the measure of S_{ej} (i.e., $S_{ej}^p - S_{ej}^c$) proportional to the fraction of the time the enzyme is effectively complexed with a protector molecule. In addition, some substrates will scavenge radicals, thus providing "competitive protection" and, accordingly, increase the slope (i.e., $m^p - m^c$).

For relation 2, the basic equation of this method, to be applicable, the following conditions must be satisfied in addition to the three propositions given initially: (1)The sum of the reactive *capacities* of *all* solutes must remain constant during an experiment; and (2) the solute inactivation must not be reversible.

This method is not the first to employ reciprocal functions or plots: Dale *et al.* (*21*) utilized similar plots to "fit" the parameters they used to describe protein inactivation; and, the use of Lineweaver-Burke (*24*) plots for determining the rate constants of enzyme-controlled reactions is valuable in studies of competitive inhibition. However, in the present development reaction probabilities are associated with the slope and intercept. Thus not only is a predictable behavior (linear) established for the data, but separate estimates of the S and R parameters can be made, and all measures of the pertinent parameters are obtained from linear regression lines rather than point estimates, so that a measure of the variance of each of the parameters is provided.

It is to be emphasized that this method, like previous ones (*15*, *20*) provides estimates of R_{ij} in *relative units* of a *standard* R_{sj}. Thus, these estimates, as well as those of solvent capability, N_1^c, and protective effects depend only on *relative* dosage measures. However, values of S_{1j}, require a correct conversion of *absolute* dosage measurements into numbers of radicals, dX_j, and are correspondingly biased. In many cases it may be possible to measure dX_j using chemical dosimeters so that potentially S_{1j} can also be determined in relative units of a standard S_{sj}.

In the results presented in this paper no attempts have been made experimentally to identify the radical(s) responsible for inactivation, so that $1/Y_1$, the reciprocal of the yield due to *all* radicals, has been plotted instead of $1/Y_{1j}$ (and correspondingly the j terminology has been dropped on all other parameters). However, either inactivation by one type of radical must predominate or else two or more types of radicals contribute proportionally to the total inactivation, since all the plots (except Fig. 5*C*) have a linear portion (see Table II). Further, all values of Y are in units of ionic yield; i.e., the number of ion pairs produced per unit of radiation (see next section) has been used for the value of dX. Comparable units—such as *G*—could have been used, since they differ only by a multiplicative factor. The possibility of using other more exact estimates of dX_j (*25*) must await the determination of the species of inactivating radicals.

II. TESTING THE THEORY

Materials and Methods

Water. Three sources of water were used: (A) "normal" distilled water obtained from a commercial Aetna tin-lined still and run through about 150 feet of aluminum pipe to a chrome-plated spigot; (B) type A water triple-distilled in a Barnstead three-stage still; and (C) type A water redistilled from an alkaline $KMnO_4$ solution (*16*) in an all-Pyrex glass apparatus. Both type B and C water were stored in an all-Pyrex system with a soda-lime-activated charcoal air trap. In a given experiment all solutions were prepared with water from the same source.

Stock solutions. Methylene blue (MB)—1-liter portions of 10^{-4} *M* were prepared from USP crystals (obtained from either Coleman and Bell Co. or National Aniline Division) and stored in a Pyrex volumetric flask which had been surface-treated with a silicone (Desicote).

Trypsin—500 mg of twice-recrystallized, salt-free crystals (Worthington Biochemical Co.) were sprinkled on the surface of 10^{-4} *M* H_3PO_4 in a Desicoted Pyrex container. Agitation was avoided, and the solution was kept in a refrigerator for at least 12 hours, after which the volume was made up to 1 liter. Portions of this solution (10 and 25 ml) were frozen in polyethylene vials[3] and stored at $-7°C$ until needed.

Acetyltrypsin—500 mg of salt-free crystals prepared by lyophilization (Worthington) were dissolved in 1 liter of H_2O in a Desicoted Pyrex flask, and portions were frozen as above.

Samples to be irradiated were prepared by dilution of the stock solutions with appropriate buffer solutions.

Irradiation technique. Radiation was from a G.E. Maxitron operated at 250 kvp and 30 ma with either 0.25 mm Al or 10 mm Bakelite filtration. Either filter absorbed the "white tail" of the X-ray emission sufficiently so that resulting plots of log dosage versus depth of absorbing solution were linear. Precautions were taken so that dosages within a given solution varied less than 15%: (1) solutions and containers were surrounded by Lucite, paraffin, or water to provide as continuous a scattering medium as possible; (2) irradiating distances were kept as large as feasible. Dosage rates in roentgens were determined with either a Fricke dosimeter (*26*) (comparable as to container, solution depth, etc., with the samples being irradiated) or a calibrated 250-*r* Victoreen nylon thimble, which was semisurrounded with a Lucite block so as to simulate the scattering conditions at the surface of a liquid. In general, dosage estimates obtained with the Fricke dosimeter were lower than comparable ones from the Victoreen method. Since solution depths of 1 to 4 cm and widths of 2 to 15 cm were used, all Victoreen determinations included measurements of the effect of irradiating distance, depth of solution, and radial distance from the axis of the principle beam. These factors were inserted into an integral equation to estimate the average dose (in roentgens) in solution. By using the conversion factor (*20*)—1 r corresponds to 1.76×10^{12} ion pairs/cc/r—the reciprocal of the yield, $1/Y$ (in ion pairs per molecule), is

$$\frac{1}{Y_1} = \frac{2.92}{y_1} \qquad (5)$$

where y_1 is the micromoles of solute inactivated by 1000 r.

Most irradiations were made in either a 5-cm-diameter cup cast from Kel-F (a polymer of trifluorochloroethylene made by M. W. Kellogg Co.), in polystyrene vials 2.5 cm in diameter and 5.5 cm long, or in 2×15-cm glass tubes. Crude tests showed these containers to be less subject to contamination and/or aging effects than those of Lucite or polyethylene (see Table I).[4]

The MB solutions contained 2.6 to 12.0 μM MB; 0, 1, or 2 μM/l of either trypsin

[3] McDonald "questions the advisability of using polyethylene vials even for storage in the frozen state, because of the possibility of inadvertant contamination" (personal communication).

[4] Glass was slightly less desirable than Kel-F or polystyrene, since it "browned" with use. This could be counteracted by heating the tubes at 45°C overnight.

or acetyltrypsin (assuming molecular weights of 20,000) as protector solutes; buffer; and those gases adsorbed from the atmosphere. Irradiations were carried out at room temperature (21° to 25°C). Dose rates of 200 to 3000 r/min were investigated. Optical densities, measured at 6300 A with either a Bausch and Lomb "spectronic 20" or a Beckman model DU spectrophotometer, decreased essentially linearly with dose (for dosages producing 25% or less inactivation). Multiplication of the slope of the optical density *vs* dose regression line by the extinction coefficient (obtained from a plot of optical density of unirradiated samples versus MB concentration) converts optical density units per 1000 r to micromoles per 1000 r (see equation 5).

In trypsin inactivation studies, 1-ml aliquots of trypsin in 0.004 M NaH_2PO_4 buffer were irradiated in polystyrene vials at 0°C at a dose rate of 255 r/min (Fricke dosimeter). The solutions were 1 to 5 μM in trypsin and contained 0, 2, or 4 μMs/l of MB as a protector solute. The proteolytic activity of the trypsin was assayed within 3 hours after irradiation by the hemoglobin digestion method of Anson (*27*). When log fraction activity remaining after a dose D was plotted against dose, a straight line with negative slope was obtained. This indicated that inactivation could be described by

$$-\frac{dN_1}{dD} = \frac{N_1}{D_{37}} \tag{6}$$

where D_{37} is the dose necessary to reduce activity to $1/e$ its initial value. Thus, equation 5 can be revised to

$$\frac{1}{Y_{tr}} = \frac{2.92D_{37}\text{ (in } r)}{10^3 N_{tr}\text{ (in } \mu M)} \tag{7}$$

Results

Methylene blue alone. The data in Fig. 1 are consistent with equation 2, which is the basis of the method. These results indicate that a reproducibility of about ±5% between daily runs can be achieved by the techniques described here; further, any large deviations from the fitted curves usually represent decreased yields, probably caused by random contamination. The solvent capability in Fig. 1 is equivalent to the reactive capacity of 1.8 μM of MB. Preliminary determinations, with only limited accuracy, of the effect caused by the types of water, buffer, and container on the solvent capability and variance of the data are summarized in Table I. Numerous features are readily apparent from these order-of-magnitude measurements. First either type B or type C but not type A water is suitable; second, N_{mb}^c is very large in polyethylene containers; third, S_{mb} and N_{mb}^c depend on the anions present; and S_{mb} depends on the type of container. This latter is possibly indicative of differences between actual and calculated dosages. Different amounts of scatter originating in the container walls (*26*) as well as the surrounding scattering material could cause such differences (Kel-F and Lucite containers were surrounded by

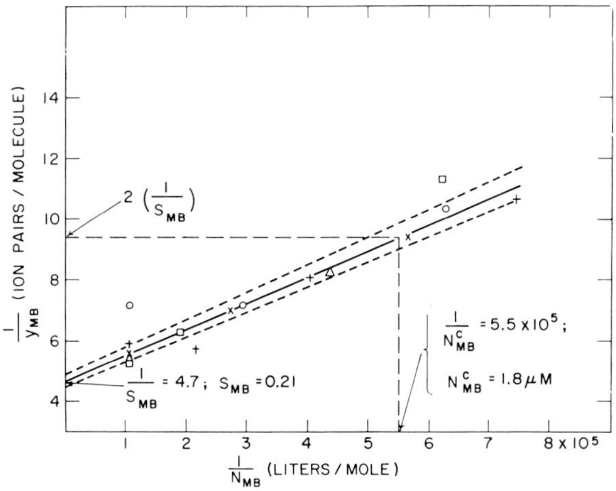

FIG. 1. Relation between the reciprocal of inactivation yield ($1/Y_{mb}$) and the reciprocal of the concentration ($1/N_{mb}$) (see equation 2) for methylene blue solutions. Experimental factors: 0.02 *M* Na_2HPO_4, 10-mm Bakelite filter, 2000-r maximum dose, 3000-r/min dose rate, Kel-F container surrounded by 1-inch Lucite scattering block, 5-mm solution depth, type C water. Like symbols indicate measurements made on the same day. Other nomenclature is explained in text.

Lucite, glass by water or paraffin, polyethylene by paraffin, and polystyrene by Lucite on the sides and brass on the bottom). The rate of inactivation did not vary significantly over the fifteenfold dosage range. This indicates that the loss of inactivating radicals by recombination with other types of radicals is insignificant compared to those destroyed by contaminants.

Effect of pH and anions. The data in Table I as well as experiments now in progress indicate that both S_{mb} and R_{mb} vary with pH and the anionic complement of the solution. Other workers (*28*) have reported G values (molecules inactivated per 100 ev absorbed) of 0.33 for methylene blue irradiated in the presence of air at neutral pH. Our values at pH 4 to 5 are two to three times as large (multiplying the S_{mb} values by 3 converts from molecules per ion pair to molecules per 100 ev). However, further discussion of these MB effects will be deferred until the experiments now in progress are completed. Data for trypsin (*16*) also showing anion effects have been reanalyzed and plotted in Fig. 5*A*. Intuitively such changes are not unexpected in molecules as complex as proteins, since the ratio between reactive sites and those reactive sites critical for activity may well vary with pH.

Methylene blue with other solutes. The data in Fig. 2 can be used to illustrate the determination of R_1 in units of a standard solute and also the "protective coefficient," z_2R_2, of an added solute. The values of $z_{at}R_{at}$ (acetyltrypsin) for the experiment shown in Fig. 2 have the most variability of four such determinations: the

TABLE I

EFFECT OF TYPE OF CONTAINER, BUFFER, AND TYPE OF WATER ON THE APPROXIMATE STANDARD DEVIATIONS, σ, OF DAILY DETERMINATIONS OF N_{mb} AND S_{mb} OF METHYLENE BLUE (COLEMAN AND BELL CO.) SOLUTIONS

(Dosage measurements were made either with a method utilizing a Victoreen thimble, V, or with a Fricke dosimeter, F.)

Type of container	Type of water	Dosage method	Buffer	Number of experiments	N^c_{mb} (μM)	S_{mb} (molecules per ion pair)	σ (%)
Kel-F	A	V	0.001 M Na_2HPO_4–NaCl	1	⩾7	0.21	10–15
Kel-F	B	V	Na_2HPO_4–NaCl	3	1.7–5	0.21	5–10
Kel-F	C	V	Na_2HPO_4–NaCl	6	1.2–2.1	0.21	5
Lucite	B	V	Na_2HPO_4–NaCl	2	2–5	0.23	10
Glass	C	V	Na_2HPO_4–NaCl	2	1–3	0.27	5–10
Glass	B	V–F	Na_2HPO_4 NaCl	3	2–5	0.26–0.32	5–10
Polyethylene	C	V	Na_2HPO_4–NaCl	2	7	0.22	10
Polystyrene	B	F	0.001 M Na_2HPO_4	1	2.2	0.28	5
Polystyrene	B	F	0.002 M Na_2HPO_4	3	2.5	0.32	5
Polystyrene	B	F	0.002 M NaH_2PO_4	2	0.9	0.20	5–7
Polystyrene	B	F	0.002 M NaCl	1	0.7	0.24	5

mean and standard deviation of the eight values was $z_{at}R_{at} = (4.2 \pm 0.8)\ z_{mb}R_{mb}$. The value of $z_{tr}R_{tr}$ in Fig. 2 is typical of four such determinations in which it was found that $z_{tr}R_{tr} = (5.8 \pm 0.2)\ z_{mb}R_{mb}$. In terms of R_{mb}, R_{tr} is calculated by

$$R_{tr} = \left(\frac{z_{mb}}{z_{tr}}\right)\left(\frac{N^d_{mb} - N^c_{mb}}{N_{tr}}\right)R_{mb} = \left(\frac{4.5}{4.0}\right)\left(\frac{7.7 - 1.7}{1.0}\right)R_{mb} = 0.65R_{mb} \qquad \text{(4b)}$$

(if the molecular weight of trypsin is 20,000, 20 mg/l is 1 μM/l; taking values from p. 53 of Lea (*20*) gives z_{mb} [M.W. of 374] $= 4.5 \times 10^{11}$ and z_{tr} [M.W. of 20,000] $= 4.0 \times 10^{12}$ collisions/sec/gm M.W.). Thus, in pH 7.4 Na_2HPO_4–NaCl buffer the number of radicals which can inactivate MB and which are destroyed by a given number of collisions with trypsin molecules is only 0.65 times as great as those destroyed by the same number of collisions between radicals and methylene blue molecules.

The acetyltrypsin data emphasize two points. First, when working with the very dilute solutions necessary in this method care must be taken to avoid any danger of chance contamination if reasonable reproducibility is to be obtained; second, acetylation changes the reactive capacity of the trypsin surface toward activated radicals by about 25%. Although the source of the large variability in the determinations of

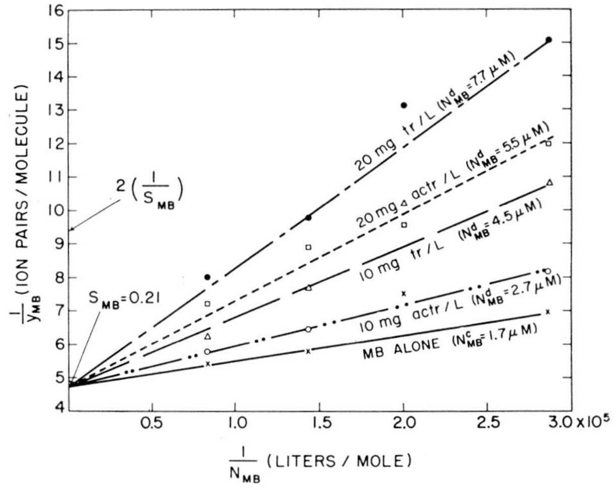

FIG. 2. Simultaneous determination of the protective effects of trypsin and acetyltrypsin for methylene blue. Experimental factors: 0.001 *M* Na_2HPO_4-NaCl, 0.25 mm Al filter, 6700-r maximum dose, 1830-r/min dose rate, Kel-F container with 1-inch Lucite scattering block, 15-mm solution depth, type B water.

$z_{at}R_{at}$ is not known, the fluctuations appear to be random rather than a function of N_{at}. Dale *et. al.* (*15, 29*) also reported essentially constant protective values, Q, for the range of protector concentrations employed in the present study (10 to 40 μg/ml, which is 0.5 to 2 μ*M*) in contrast to the decreases in Q they found at higher concentrations. Alexander *et al.* (*30*) also reported protection coefficients which were concentration-dependent. The results in Fig. 2 demonstrate how such discrepancies can arise when a 50% reduction in the inactivation of a *single* concentration of standard solute is used as the criterion of protection. There 10 mg/l of trypsin would reduce the yield in a 1.1 μ*M* MB solution by 50%, whereas 20 mg/l would halve the yield in a 4.3 μ*M* solution, i.e., about 100% difference in the measured protective power on doubling of the protector concentration.

Trypsin. The line of least slope in Fig. 3 is typical for trypsin irradiated alone—with respect both to the values obtained and to the variance of the data. The values of S_{tr} obtained in this experiment and three others varied between 0.11 and 0.13: the solvent capability, N^c_{tr} (in this case 0.1 μ*M*), was normally less than the reactive capacity of 1.0 μ*M* trypsin. The decreased yields (i.e., increases in slope) in Fig. 3 were obtained when the Coleman and Bell Co. sample of methylene blue was used as a "protector solute." Similar results were obtained with the National Aniline samples of MB. The increase in slope without a change in intercept on the addition of MB indicates that it provides "competitive" but not "reactive" protection for trypsin (see Theory section).

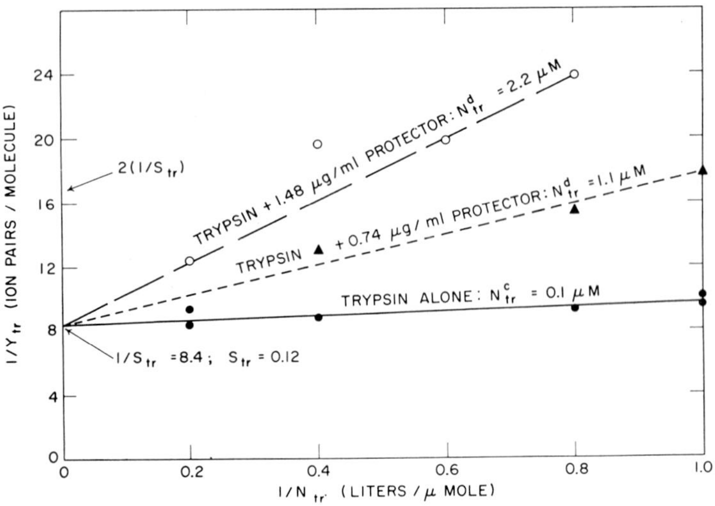

FIG. 3. The relation between the reciprocal ($1/Y_{tr}$) of the irradiation yield and the reciprocal of the concentration ($1/N_{tr}$) for trypsin in solution alone as well as in the presence of a protector solute. See text for experimental conditions.

Substituting into equation 4 the average values of $(N_1{}^d - N^c)$ and N_2 from Fig. 3 along with the values of z_{tr} and z_{mb} cited earlier gives

$$R_{tr} = \left(\frac{4.5}{40}\right)\left(\frac{2\ \mu M}{1.05\ \mu M}\right) R_{mb} = 0.21 R_{mb} \tag{4b}$$

It is possible that the difference in the values of 0.65 and 0.21 obtained for R_{tr}/R_{mb} are not entirely due to the different pH's at which they were measured. The first was obtained when trypsin "protected" MB. Therefore, it represents an average of $\sum_j R_{tr,j}$ for *those* jth radicals which *can inactivate MB*. The 0.21 was obtained when MB "protected" trypsin. Therefore, it represents a similar average but for *those* jth radicals which *can inactivate trypsin*. The two values will be the same only when the two solutes are inactivated by exactly the same species of radicals.

In another paper (*31*) the product $R_{tr}S_{tr} = (0.21)\ (0.12)$ has been used to estimate that 2.5% of the trypsin surface is critical for activity and can react with radiation-produced radicals. There it was assumed that: (1) there is a one-to-one correspondence between reaction probability (in units of molecules per ion pair) and molecular surface area and (2) R_{mb} is unity. If trypsin is a spherical molecule of molecular weight of 20,000 and density of 1.35, 2.5% of its surface area would be occupied by about two amino acids. With different experimental conditions estimates as large as eight amino acids have been obtained.

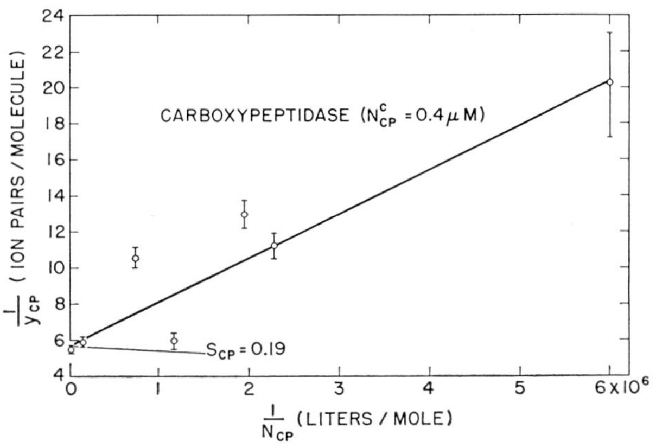

FIG. 4A

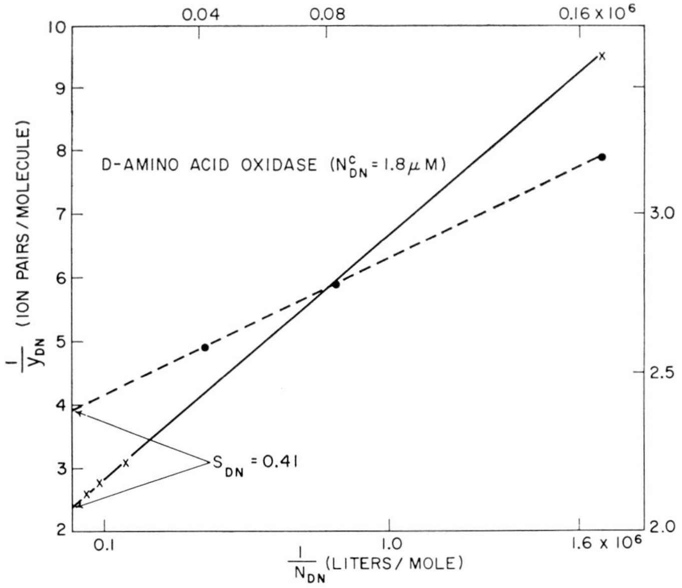

FIG. 4B

FIG. 4. The relation between $1/Y$ and $1/N$ for four enzymes. The data have all been recalculated from the original references. Experimental factors and the calculated parameters are listed in Table II. In the plots for D-amino acid oxidase and deoxyribonuclease the data are plotted on two different scales to utilize properly the wide range of concentrations tested; the scales on the left and bottom apply to the X's connected by the solid lines, and the scales on the right and top to the ●'s connected by the dashed lines.

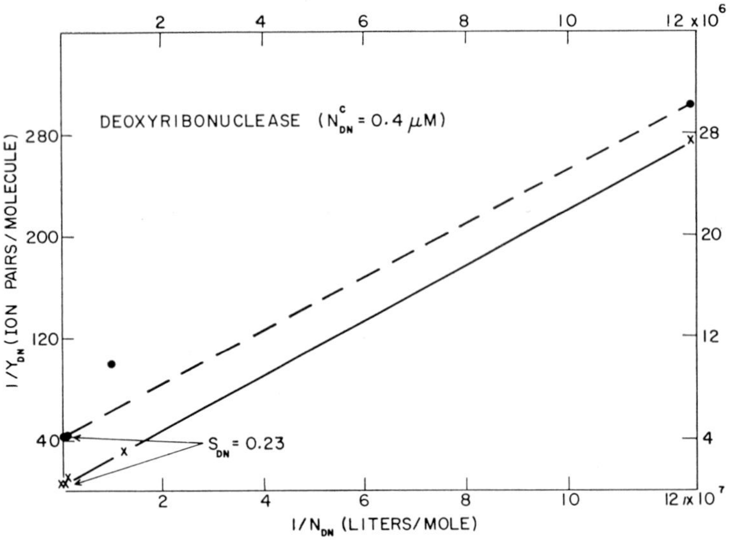

FIG. 4C

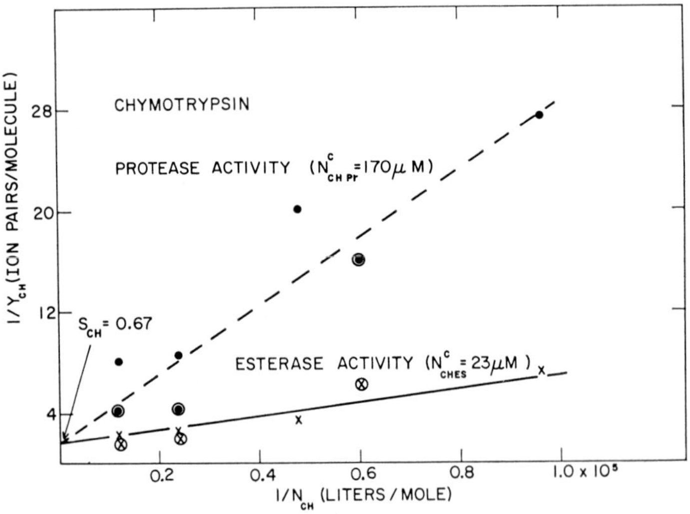

FIG. 4D

III. APPLICATION TO ENZYME DATA

In addition to the trypsin data just discussed, results of previous enzyme irradiation studies (*5*, *9*, *16*, *17*, *32*, *33*) have been reanalyzed according to the present method and are plotted in Figs. 4 and 5. Numerous others were not amenable to

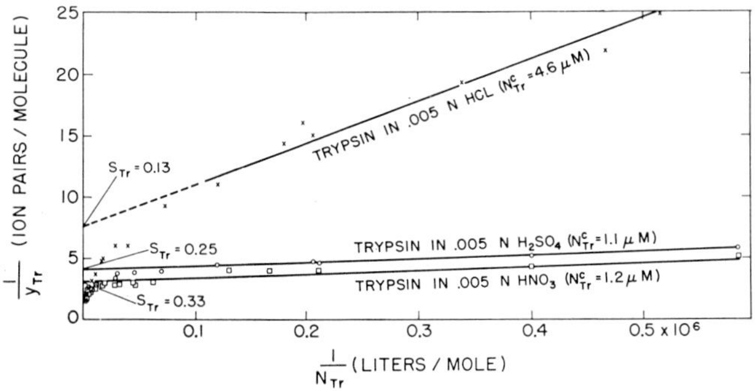

FIG. 5A

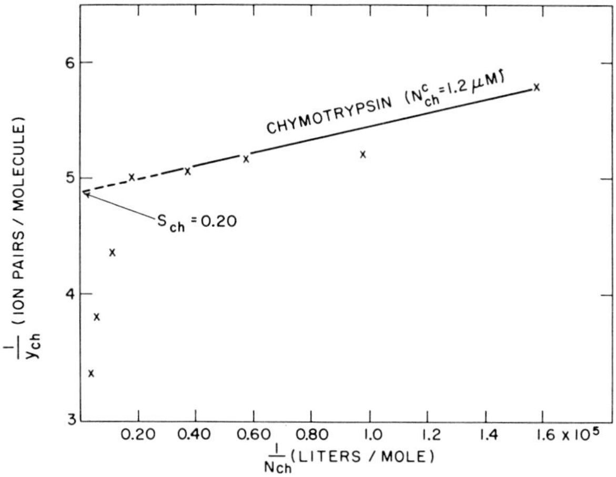

FIG. 5B

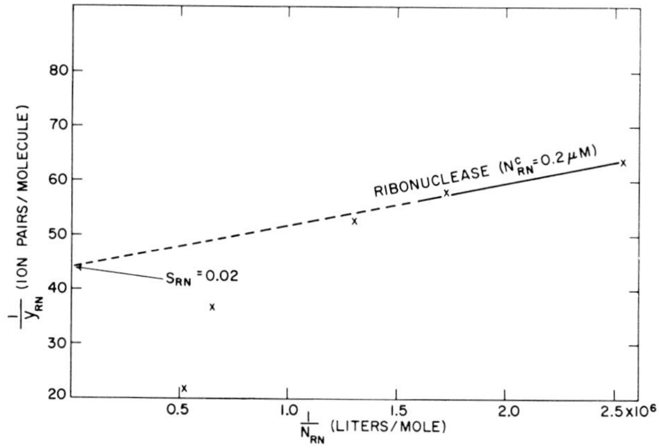

FIG. 5C

FIG. 5. The relation between $1/Y$ and $1/N$ for three enzymes. These data, recalculated from the original references, satisfy equation 2 only at the lower concentrations. See Table II for references, experimental factors, and calculated parameters.

TABLE II

SUMMARY OF ENZYME IRRADIATION DATA PRESENTED IN FIGS. 3 TO 5

Enzyme	*Figure*	*Reference*	*pH*	*Assumed Molecular weight*	S_e *(molecules per ion pair)*	N_e^c (μM)	*Concentration range consistent with equation 2* (μM)
Trypsin	3		4.6	20,000	0.12	<1.0	1–5
Trypsin:							
Cl^-	5*A*	*16*	2.4	20,000	0.13	4.6	2–14
$SO_4^=$	5*A*	*16*	2.4	20,000	0.25	1.1	1.6–20
NO_3^-	5*A*	*16*	2.4	20,000	0.33	1.2	1.6–50
Chymotrypsin:							
Protease	5*B*	*17*	3.1	21,500	0.20	1.2	6–50
Protease	4*D*	*33*	Unbuffered	24,500	0.67	170	10–80
Esterase	4*D*	*33*	Unbuffered	24,500	0.67	33	10–80
Carboxypeptidase	4*A*	*5*	8.5–10	35,000	0.19	0.4	0.2–10
D-amino acid oxidase	4*B*	*5*	8.3	70,000	0.41	1.8	0.6–25
Deoxyribonuclease	4*C*	*32*	Unbuffered (5.6–6)	63,000	0.23	0.4	0.008–80
Ribonuclease	5*C*	*9*	9.1	13,000	0.02	0.2	(<6?)

such treatment, even though the yield was determined as a function of concentration, because either very large increments in concentration were investigated (*18*, *34*, *35*), or the accuracy of the data was too low (*34*) or else the concentrations used were too great (*20*). Actually the first two objections apply in limited degree to some of the data shown, and the last applies to data for the deamination of amino acids (*15*, *36*).

Obvious features of the data are: (1) each plot—with the exception of Fig. 5*C*—has at least a sevenfold range of concentration in which equation 1 is valid (i.e., a linear relation occurs) (see Table II), and (2) when irradiation was carried out at a pH quite different from the isoelectric point the yields at higher concentration became increasingly larger than predicted by an extrapolation of the linear portion to those concentrations. This latter deviation will be treated in the next section in much greater detail. The maximum concentration consistent with equation 1 ranged from 0.008 to 100 μM for those enzymes represented. Thus, studies which employ only one large solute concentration may provide poor determinations of the parameters of indirect inactivation if the concentration used is larger than the range consistent with equation 1; this is in spite of the fact that a large concentration should minimize the effects of contaminants (see a discussion of Lea's assumptions in the Theory section). Although the maximum concentration for which equation 1 is valid varies among the proteins treated, the expected linear relation invariably extends to the lowest concentration tested (usually corresponding to the limits of precision of the assay method) and likely extends to infinite dilution.

The effect of different anions on both the intercept and slope of the reciprocal plots for trypsin is well illustrated in the plot of Fig. 5*A*. Nitrate and sulfate ions differ very little in their influence on the inactivation parameters; on the other hand S_{tr} is lower and N^c_{tr} higher in the presence of chloride[5] than with NO_3^- or SO_4^{--}. Apparently the Cl^- effect also depends on the cations present, ionic concentration and pH (*16*). Since yields were not determined as a function of concentration in the additional data of McDonald (*16*) and that of Bachofer and Pottinger (*14*), it is difficult to determine if the other pH and ionic effects they report are the result of changes in the intercept or both.

Aronson *et al.* (*33*) have speculated that chymotrypsin probably contains only one localized area of activity but that its protease and esterase activities require different charge configurations. They suggest that different inactivation sensitivities are observed for those activities because the two charge configurations cover different surface areas. The "visual fit" we have imposed on their data (Fig. 4*D*) suggests that the surface areas may be the same but that the two activities are destroyed by different kinds of radicals. However, their data are only moderately consistent with the present theoretical expectations (and similarly with their fitted curves). Thus, experiments to select between these possibilities are planned for the near future.

IV. EVIDENCE FOR TWO MODES OF PROTEIN INACTIVATION

In accord with the discussion in the Theory section, Hutchinson (personal communication) has suggested that the data in Fig. 5 may indicate that inactivation was produced by more than one kind of radical. The data in Fig. 5*A* and 5*B* are consistent with such an explanation; however, the author believes that the interpretation presented below is a more likely alternative on the basis of available data. A main argument against inactivation by two types of radicals is that that explanation leads to apparently unrealistic values for the inactivation parameters. "Fitted values" of S_1 (molecules per 32.5 ev) and N_1^c(μM/l) in the "low" and "high" concentrations are listed below:

	Trypsin in HNO_3	*Trypsin in* H_2SO_4	*Trypsin in* HCl	*Chymotrypsin*	*RNase*
S (low)	0.22	0.22	0.23	0.19	?
S (high)	0.28	0.63	2.1	0.22	Undoubtedly negative
N^c (low)	0.32	.28	2.1	0.84	—
N^c (high)	32	170	250	350	—

Of note are the order-of-magnitude differences between the "high" and "low" values. However, in favor of this proposal is the constancy of S (low) for trypsin.

[5] McDonald (*16*) claims that the differences noted between sulfuric and hydrochloric acid were not due to impurities which could be removed by redistillation; rather she suggests that chloride ions compete more effectively for radicals.

This suggests the possibility of two kinds of radicals—one independent of and one markedly dependent on anion composition.

Other possible mechanisms to account for the deviations observed at "high" concentrations have been discussed. For instance, Dale (*15*) in attempting to account for similar deviations in the yields of X-ray deamination of amino acids suggested that at very high solute concentrations energy may be handed from one molecule to the other in the form of energy of excitation, or that protector molecules, including previously inactivated ones, may be capable of further reaction with the active solute molecules, thus increasing the yield above that for simple indirect inactivation. Another possibility considered both by Dale and by McDonald (*16*) is that direct inactivation produces the increased yield. However, McDonald rejected this potential explanation by pointing out that, if one assumes a direct-action yield for the dissolved state of the solute *equal* to that in its dry state, the contribution of direct inactivation to the reaction yield for solutions of trypsin up to 1% (the highest concentration she investigated) would be negligible.

The possibility that the yield for direct action in solution and the dry state *are* different (F. Krenz, personal communication to W. Dale; see pp. 269 and 280 of reference *15*) is considered in the following discussion. The total or observed yields, Y_t, in Fig. 5 were assumed to consist of two components—one due to indirect inactivation, Y_{in}, and the other due to direct inactivation, Y_d. The extent of Y_d is thus obtained by subtracting Y_{in} (obtained from the extrapolated linear plots) from the observed yields, Y_t. Since a given incremental dosage, dD, should produce direct inactivation of a given fraction of the molecules present according to the differential relation 6, a plot of Y_d versus enzyme concentration, N, should be linear. Figure 6 contains such plots for trypsin, chymotrypsin, and ribonuclease. The results for ribonuclease are inconclusive; however, the concentration range of the data is small. The results for the other two enzymes suggest strongly that such a relation does exist between Y_d and N. Such agreement implies that equation 1 should be revised to

$$-dN_1 = N_1 \left[\sum_j \frac{k_{1j} R_{1j} S_{1j} dX_j}{\sum_i k_{ij} R_{ij} N_i} + \frac{dD}{D_{37}} \right] \tag{9}$$

The striking feature in the plots of figs. 6*A* and 6*B* is that target volumes calculated[6] from the fitted straight lines are 200 times (trypsin) and 45 times (chymo-

[6] The slopes of the fitted straight lines provide an estimate of dN/N for a dose $dD = 10^3$ r. so that the $1/e$ dose, D_{37}, can be calculated by relation 6. The values of D_{37} *in water* are 2.6×10^5 r for trypsin and 1.1×10^6 r for chymotrypsin. These compare with expected D_{37} doses in the *dry state* of about 5×10^7 r calculated by Lea's "method of associated volumes" (see Fig. 9, p. 90, reference 20). If these results are taken to be exact, then the target volume of chymotrypsin *in water* is about 45 times that in the *dry state*, and for trypsin the ratio is about 200:1; or, translated into the diameters of spherical targets, the ratios *in water*:*dry state* are about 3.5:1 for chymotrypsin and 6:1 for trypsin.

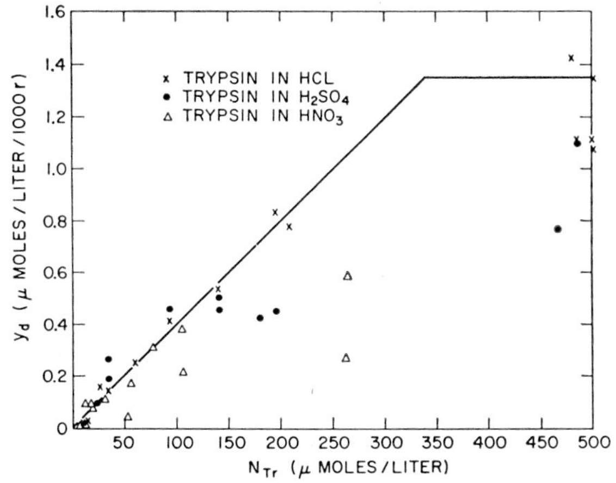

FIG. 6A

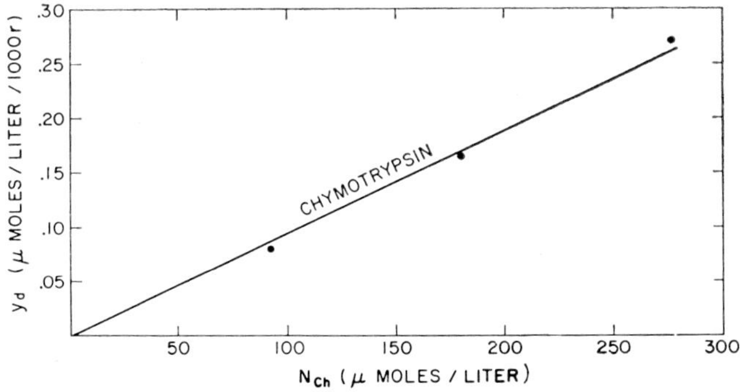

FIG. 6B

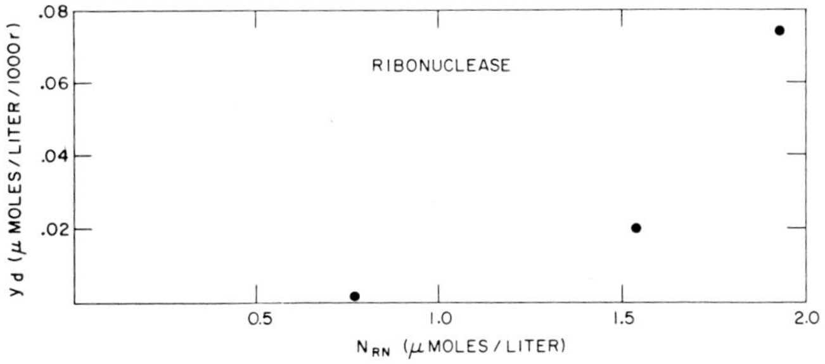

FIG. 6C

FIG. 6. Plots of the difference (Y_d) between the observed (Y_t) and predicted (Y_{in}—due to radical inactivation) yields versus enzyme concentration (N) for those enzymes represented in Fig. 5. See text for a discussion of the significance of these plots.

trypsin) those anticipated for the two enzymes in the dry state. That this represents a corresponding increase in protein volume seems remote; rather, the author wishes to treat the possibility that under the experimental conditions employed the volume within which the production of an ion pair causes inactivation is 45 or 200 times as large as the actual molecular volume. It is not intended to specify the nature of the process by which the production of an ion within this target volume leads to inactivation—perhaps a negative ion formed within this region has a very high probability of migrating to the protein as the result of electrostatic attraction between the ion and the relatively highly charged colloidal particle (these irradiations were carried out at fairly acid pH's). Or possibly the ion does not migrate per se; but, rather the energy associated with the ion is transmitted in some fashion such as the polarization mechanism recently suggested by Platzman and Franck (*37*). Thus, whether the target volume corresponds to an ordered region in the solvent similar to some of the recent suggestions of Szent-Györgyi (*38*), Frey-Wyssling (*39*), and Buswell and Rodebush (*40*) or merely to the distance over which the colloidal charge of the protein (*41*) exerts an effective force on migrating ions is unknown. Mechanisms to account for the migration of an effect due to primary ionizations have also been discussed by Alexander (*42*).

Although mechanisms other than a direct effect could also be consistent with first-order kinetics, as depicted by equation 6, nevertheless at least three observations tend to support the tentative model of an ionic effect occurring within an enlarged volume surrounding the molecule: (1) Although the over-all yield for trypsin depends strongly on the anion composition of the solvent (fig. 5*A*), the values of Y_d are essentially independent of this factor, as would be expected for a direct type of inactivation (fig. 6*A*). (2) The target volume for such a process should depend on the net charge on the protein molecule—McDonald (*16*, *17*) has reported that there is a 200% and a 100% difference in reaction yield (i.e., Y_t) between the minimum and the optimum pH for trypsin and chymotrypsin, respectively. (3) The value of Y_d should increase linearly with enzyme concentration until the target volumes associated with the individual molecules begin to overlap—for this and larger concentrations Y_d should assume the value expected for the yield in the dry state. These expectations are shown for monomeric trypsin by the two-component solid line in fig. 6*A*. This implies that proteins behave as ion traps or sinks; otherwise, Y_d would increase even after overlapping of the target volumes.

Considering the stated accuracy of the data, the agreement seems adequate to warrant careful consideration of this model and further experimentation. If the model is found to be correct, then it would seem preferable to refer to direct effects which occur in the dry state as a special or limiting case (i.e., where no water is present) of indirect effects which occur in solution, where the indirect effects can be produced either by freely diffusing *radicals* or by *ions* produced in a target volume surrounding charged solute molecules.

SUMMARY

The theoretical developments presented in this paper provide an improved method of treating indirect inactivation. Features of the method are: (1) the probabilities associated with radical destruction and solute inactivation can be measured separately; (2) a predictable behavior is established for the data; (3) the reliability of each of the parameters can be determined; (4) the "solvent capability" (which includes radical recombinants as well as impurities) can be readily measured and corrected for; (5) the determination of "protection coefficients" is simplified; and (6) two types of protection can be distinguished. Methylene blue and trypsin have been used as solutes to demonstrate applications of the revised method.

The theory and results not only established an improved method of treating indirect inactivation but provide a criterion for discriminating between indirect and other types of inactivation. The criteria provide a means of differentiating mechanisms by which radiation interacts with biological material and of showing how these mechanisms and their associated probabilities are affected by pH and the ionic complement of the solvent. Reanalysis of previously published protein data showed that the linear relation predicted by this method is applicable at the lowest protein concentrations. At high concentrations the yield may—depending on experimental conditions—become larger than expected for indirect inactivation by one kind of radical alone. Such deviations were taken as evidence that either more than one species of radical was producing inactivation or that more likely there was an effect arising from the production of ions in a target volume larger than the protein molecule.

ACKNOWLEDGMENTS

The author takes pleasure in thanking Drs. H. Quastler, L. Nims, A. Allen, and R. Klein for their criticisms of style and content and in particular for their suggestions concerning the applicability of this method.

RECEIVED: April 3, 1958

REFERENCES

1. H. FRICKE and S. MORSE, The action of X-rays on $FeSO_4$ solutions. *Phil. Mag.* **7**, 129–141 (1929).
2. H. FRICKE and E. HART, The oxidation of ferrous, ferrocyanide, arsenite, and selenite ions by the irradiation of their aqueous solutions with x-rays. *J. Chem. Phys.* **3**, 60–61, 596 (1935).
3. H. FRICKE, E. HART, and H. SMITH, Chemical reactions of organic compounds with X-ray-activated water. *J. Chem. Phys.* **6**, 229–240 (1938).
4. O. RISSE, Einige Bemerkungen zum Mechanismus chemischer Röntgenreaktionen in wässrigen Lösungen. *Strahlentherapie* **34**, 578–581 (1929).
5. W. DALE, The effect of X-rays on enzymes. *Biochem. J.* **34**, 1367–1373 (1940); The effect of X-rays on the conjugated protein D-amino-acid oxidase. *ibid.* **36**, 80–85 (1942).
6. R. HAVARD, The action of X-rays upon the lactate, glucose, citrate and succinate dehydrogenases. *Brit. J. Radiol.* **8**, 787–792 (1935).

7. C. SCOTT, "Some quantitative aspects of the biological action of X- and rays." *Med. Research Council (Brit.) Spec. Rept. Ser.*, **No. 223** (1937).
8. E. POLLARD, Primary ionization as a test of molecular organization. *Advances in Biol. Med. Phys.* **3,** 153–190 (1953).
9. E. S. G. BARRON, S. DICKMAN, J. MUNTZ, and T. SINGER, Studies on the mechanism of action of ionizing radiations. I and II. *J. Gen. Physiol.* **32,** 537–552, 595–605 (1949).
10. R. ANDERSON, A delayed effect of X-rays on pepsin. *Biol. Bull.* **92,** 189 (1947); A delayed effect of X-rays on pepsin. *Brit. J. Radiol.* **27,** 56–61 (1954).
11. M. MCDONALD, The effects of X-radiation on dilute solutions of crystalline trypsin: Continued inactivation after termination of irradiation. *Brit. J. Radiol.* **27,** 62–63 (1954).
12. H. FRICKE AND B. PETERSEN, "Action of roentgen rays in solutions of oxyhemoglobin in water." *Am. J. Roentgenol. Radium Therapy* **17,** 611–620 (1927).
13. B. TAYLOR, J. GREENSTEIN and A. HOLLAENDER, Effects of X-radiation on thymus nucleic acid. *Science* **105,** 263–264 (1947).
14. C. BACHOFER and M. POTTINGER, The role of high ionic concentrations in protection against X-irradiation. *J. Gen. Physiol.* **37,** 663–675 (1954).
15. W. DALE, Basic radiation biochemistry. In *Radiation Biology* (A. Hollaender, ed.), Vol. I, Part 1, pp. 255–282, McGraw-Hill Book Company, New York, 1954.
16. M. MCDONALD, The inactivation of dilute solutions of crystalline trypsin by X-radiation. I and II. *J. Gen. Physiol.* **38,** 93–103, 581–598 (1955).
17. C. MOORE and M. MCDONALD, The inactivation of dilute solutions of crystalline chymotrypsin by X-radiation. *Radiation Research* **3,** 38–44 (1955).
18. A. TYTELL and H. KERSTEN, Effects of soft X-rays on urease and catalase. *Proc. Soc. Exptl. Biol. Med.* **48,** 521–525 (1941).
19. W. BELLAMY and E. LAWTON, Problems in using high-voltage electrons for sterilization. *Nucleonics* **12,** 54–57 (April, 1954).
20. D. LEA, *Actions of Radiations on Living Cells*, The Macmillan Company, New York, 1947.
21. W. DALE, L. GRAY, and W. MEREDITH, The inactivation of carboxypeptidase by X- and α-radiation. *Phil. Trans. Roy. Soc.* **A242,** 33–62 (1949).
22. J. WEISS, Radiochemistry of aqueous solutions. *Nature* **153,** 748–750 (1944).
23. F. HUTCHINSON, The distance that a radical formed by ionizing radiation can diffuse in a yeast cell. *Radiation Research* **7,** 473–483 (1957).
24. H. LINEWEAVER and D. BURK, The determination of enzyme dissociation constants. *J. Am. Chem. Soc.* **56,** 658–666 (1934).
25. A. ALLEN, The yields of free H and OH in the irradiation of water. *Radiation Research* **1,** 85–96 (1954).
26. J. WEISS, A. ALLEN, and H. SCHWARTZ, Use of the Fricke ferrous sulfate dosimeter for gamma-ray doses in the range 4 to 40 kr. *Proc. Intern. Conf. Peaceful Uses Atomic Energy, Geneva, 1955* **14,** 179–181 (1956).
27. M. ANSON, The estimation of pepsin, trypsin, papain and cathepsin with hemoglobin. *J. Gen. Physiol.* **22,** 79–89 (1938).
28. M. DAY and G. STEIN, The action of ionizing radiations on aqueous solutions of methylene blue. *Radiation Research* **6,** 666–679 (1957).
29. W. DALE, J. DAVIES, and W. Meredith, Further observations on the protection effect in radiation chemistry. *Brit. J. Cancer* **3,** 31–41 (1949).
30. P. ALEXANDER, Z. BACQ, S. COUSENS, M. FOX, A. HERVE, and J. LAZAR, Mode of action of some substances which protest against the lethal effects of X-rays. *Radiation Research* **2,** 392–415 (1955).

31. L. AUGENSTINE, A method for the estimation of the surface area occupied by active enzyme sites. *Proc. 1st Natl. Biophys. Conf., 1958* in press.
32. S. OKADA, Inactivation of deoxyribonuclease by X-rays. *Arch. Biochem. Biophys.* **67,** 102–112 (1957).
33. D. ARONSON, L. MEE, and C. SMITH, Comparison of the inactivation of the esterase and protease activities of α-chymotrypsin solution with X-rays. In *Progress in Radiobiology* (J. Mitchell, B. Holmes, and C. Smith, eds.), pp. 61–69, Oliver & Boyd, Edinburgh, 1955.
34. W. FRIEDEWALD and R. ANDERSON, Influence of extraneous protein and virus concentration on the inactivation the rabbit papilloma virus by X-rays. *J. Exptl. Med.* **74,** 463–487 (1941).
35. D. LEA, K. SMITH, B. HOLMES, and R. MARKHAM, Direct and indirect actions of radiation on viruses and enzymes. *Parasitology* **36,** 110–118 (1944).
36. W. DALE, J. DAVIES, and C. GILBERT, The kinetics and specificities of deamination of nitrogenous compounds by X-radiation. *Biochem. J.* **45,** 93–99 (1949).
37. R. PLATZMAN and J. FRANCK, A physical mechanism for the inactivation of proteins by ionizing radiation. In *Information Theory in Biology* (H. Yockey, ed.), pp. 262–275 Pergamon Press, London, 1957.
38. A. SZENT-GYÖRGYI, Bioenergetics. *Science* **124,** 873–875 (1956).
39. A. FREY-WYSSLING, *Submicroscopic Morphology of Protoplasm*, 2nd English ed., Chapter 1. Elsevier Publishing Co., New York, 1953.
40. A. BUSWELL and W. RODEBUSH, Water. *Sci. Amer.* **194,** 76–92 (April, 1956).
41. A. ALEXANDER and P. JOHNSON, *Colloid Science*, Vols. I and II. Oxford University Press, London, 1949.
42. P. ALEXANDER, Effect of oxygen on inactivation of trypsin by the direct action of electrons and alpha-particles. *Radiation Research* **6,** 653–660 (1957).

RADIATION RESEARCH 10, 112–117 (1959)

The Gamma Radiolysis of Butyl Bromides

WILLIAM S. WILCOX

Southern Research Institute, Birmingham, Alabama

INTRODUCTION

The four isomeric butyl bromides constitute a series of compounds in which some effects of structure on the course of radiation-induced reactions can be observed. A study of the electron bombardment of liquid butanes (*1*) showed the formation of a rather large number of products in more or less comparable yields, as well as numerous minor products. Such a result would be expected, since it has been found (*2*, *3*) that the initial splitting of saturated hydrocarbons occurs at relatively random points in the carbon skeleton. The radiation-induced decomposition of the butyl bromides follows a simpler course, because the predominant primary effect of the radiation apparently is to break the carbon-bromine bond. There is effectively a single major reaction for each isomer, accompanied by a number of minor side reactions.

EXPERIMENTAL METHODS

Liquid samples of 1 to 2 ml were sealed in Pyrex vials and subjected to the γ-radiation from a water-shielded Co^{60} source of about 750 curies. The temperature was approximately 25°C. The dose rate, determined by ferrous sulfate dosimetry, was 3.2×10^5 r/hr.

Both commerical reagent-grade (Eastman White Label) compounds and specially purified compounds were irradiated. Each of the four commerical compounds contained a total of approximately 1% of impurities detectable by gas chromatography. Of those impurities that could reasonably be expected, saturated and unsaturated hydrocarbons, alcohols, and bromides lighter or heavier than the monobromobutanes were detectable by the gas chromatographic method used. The limit of detectability was about 0.05%. Neither HBr nor free bromine would pass through the column. Bromine was undetectable by chemical analysis, the sensitivity being estimated at about 0.01%. Titration showed traces of acid, possibly HBr, less than 0.01% in each case. It was estimated that unsaturated compounds, if any were present, totaled less than 0.1%, inasmuch as infrared spectra showed no detectable absorption characteristic of ethylenic compounds. Most of the observed impurities were appreciably more volatile than the butyl bromides.

Traces of a less volatile impurity were found in some instances. Definite identification of the impurities was not attempted.

A sample of *n*-butyl bromide was purified by fractional distillation in a dry nitrogen atmosphere. The material used boiled within about 0.2°C and contained no individual impurity in concentration great enough to be detected by the gas chromatographic analysis. Less exhaustively purified samples of the other bromides were prepared by taking the center fraction from a simple distillation under vacuum.

Samples for irradiation were prepared in three ways: (1) sealed under air, (2) degassed by freezing and pumping and sealed under vacuum, and (3) deaerated by prolonged sweeping with dry nitrogen and sealed under nitrogen. Since most of the impurities in the commercial compounds were more volatile than the butyl bromides, the last-named procedure tended to give a sample somewhat purer than the starting material. The radiation yields reported are for samples sealed under nitrogen.

Analyses were made by gas chromatography on a Burrell Kromo-Tog, Model I-1. The absorbent was dinonylphthalate on acid-washed C-22 firebrick, and the sweep gas was helium. Chromatograms were prepared at 120°C, except for *tert*-butyl bromide, which had to be run at 70°C because of significant thermal decomposition at higher temperatures.

Identification of the major volatile products was confirmed by recording infrared spectra of relatively large samples separated on the chromatographic column.

The amount of noncondensable gas formed, assumed to be hydrogen, was roughly estimated from the extent of pressure buildup in the sealed vials.

The acid formed, assumed to be HBr, was determined by titration. Sodium hydroxide in isopropyl alcohol was used to titrate the irradiated tertiary butyl bromide to avoid hydrolysis.

RESULTS

Table I gives the calculated yields of identified products, expressed as number of molecules formed per 100 ev of energy absorbed. Some uncertainty is introduced into the yield determinations by the chance that some loss of volatile products may occur in transferring samples to the gas chromatograph and by the limitations on determining the amount of products by measuring areas on the chromatograph charts. The yields for which numerical values are given, except for the dibromobutanes, are probably accurate within 10 to 20%. Dibromobutane yields are subject to more uncertainty, perhaps twice as much, because of greater difficulty encountered in making quantitative determinations of these compounds. In making the calculations, it was assumed that the bromides absorbed more energy than the aqueous dosimeter in proportion to their greater electron density. The electron density in the bromides is about 1.1 times as great as in water. Yields for the major volatile products and for the isomerization of isobutyl bromide were computed for samples receiving doses of 1.9×10^{21} ev/gm. The yields of dibromobutanes were

TABLE I

APPROXIMATE RADIATION YIELDS OF PRODUCTS IDENTIFIED IN IRRADIATED BUTYL BROMIDES

Product	*G-value of product from indicated isomer*			
	Normal	*Secondary*	*Iso-*	*Tertiary*
Hydrogen[a]	Very small	Very small	Appreciable	Appreciable
Methane[b, c]	Very small	Very small	Very small	Very small
n-Butane[c, d]	3.4	6.2	0[e]	0
Isobutylene[c, d]	0	0	6.2	9.0
n-butyl bromide[d]	—	0.9	0	0
sec-butyl bromide[d]	0.2	—	0	0
isobutyl bromide[d]	0	0	—	1.8[h]
tert-Butyl bromide[c, d]	0	0	4.5	—
1,2-dibromo-2-methylpropane[d]	0	0	2.0	3.0
1,2-dibromobutane[d]	1.0	0.7	0	0
2,3-dibromobutane[d]	~0.2[f]	1.5	0	0
HBr[g]	<0.2	<0.2	<0.2	<0.2

[a] The noncondensable gas formed is assumed to be hydrogen.

[b] Methane was not determined quantitatively, but more was produced from the branched compounds than from the straight-chain compounds.

[c] Identified by infrared spectra.

[d] Identified by chromatographic retention time.

[e] Throughout the table a "zero" yield means that the product was undetectable by the analytical method used. In most cases it may be considered that G is certainly <0.1.

[f] This product had virtually the same retention time as 2,3-dibromobutane. Its presence seems difficult to explain, however, especially since little isomerization of *n*- to *sec*-butyl bromide was detectable. The amount of it collected was insufficient for spectroscopic study.

[g] The acid formed is assumed to be HBr.

[h] The identification of this product is not conclusive.

determined in samples irradiated to 3.0×10^{21} ev/gm. Some samples were given doses of 9.5×10^{21} ev/gm, and for them the yields in isomerization of normal, secondary, and tertiary butyl bromides were estimated. These samples showed minor amounts of five to ten products, mostly more volatile than the parent compounds, that were not identified conclusively.

All results in the table are for samples sealed under nitrogen. The air- or vacuum-sealed samples apparently gave the same set of products, and the yields seemed to be at least of comparable orders of magnitude. Only a few air-saturated samples of each compound were run, however; no conclusions have been drawn about quantitative effects that oxygen may have on the yields, especially in the initial stages of the irradiation.

Yields for the reagent-grade commercial compounds and for the more highly

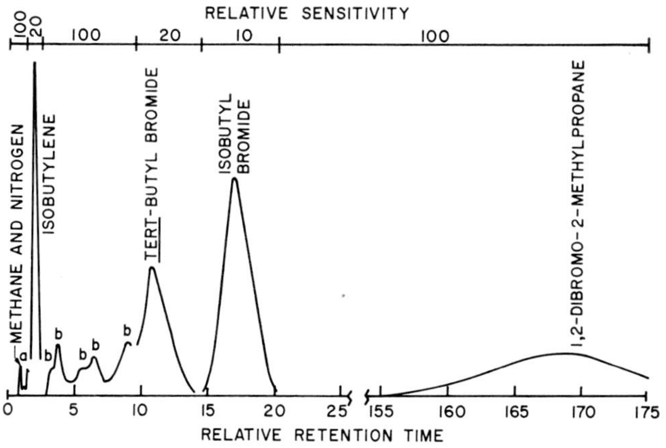

FIG. 1. Gas chromatogram of isobutyl bromide irradiated to a dose of 9.5×10^{21} ev/gm. (*a*) The minor peaks in this region are probably C_2 and C_3 hydrocarbons. (*b*) Products of thermal decomposition of *tert*-butyl bromide. There may also be minor radiation products in this region.

purified samples differed by less than the estimated experimental error. The impurities may have more significant effects during the initial stages of the radiation-induced reactions than on the ultimate results for samples given these comparatively high doses.

The chromatogram for irradiated isobutyl bromide is shown in Fig. 1. It illustrates most of the phenomena encountered: the formation of one predominant hydrocarbon product, the isomerization reaction, the formation of a dibromobutane, and the thermal instability of *tert*-butyl bromide.

Several products that might reasonably be expected were present in very minute amounts or not at all: free bromine, methyl bromide and other lower bromides, and various hydrocarbons such as octanes.

DISCUSSION

Two features stand out on inspecting the products of irradiation: (1) The two straight-chain compounds react similarly. The two branched compounds react much like each other, but they differ from the straight-chain compounds. (2) Isobutyl bromide undergoes more extensive isomerization than the other compounds.

Normal butane and isobutylene are by far the predominant volatile products, except for the *tert*-butyl bromide formed in about the same yield by the isomerization of the isobutyl compound. Very little of the bromine corresponding to the hydrocarbons formed can be accounted for amoung the volatile products. A considerable part of it is found in various dibromobutanes, at least one of which has been identified among the products of each isomer. All the dibromo compounds definitely identified were vicinal dibromides with the second bromine on a carbon atom adjacent to the one bonded to the bromine of the original compound. One and in some cases two other products of low volatility were observed in appreciable amounts; they could possibly be dibromobutanes of different configurations. The yields of these compounds were smaller than those of the identified dibromobutanes, however.

The radiolysis of organic compounds is known to involve highly complex processes. Nevertheless, the fact that very small numbers of products predominate in yield over all others in the irradiation of butyl bromides makes it seem reasonable to assume that there are a few reactions that predominate even though there may be many others occurring.

The observed small number of products and the nature of the products found seem most readily explained if it is assumed that the effect of the radiation is almost always to rupture the carbon-bromine bond. This idea is in agreement with earlier work on halogenated hydrocarbons (*2*, *4*, *5*), and it means that a mechanism must exist for transferring energy from other parts of the irradiated molecule to the carbon-bromine bond.

The isomerization of isobutyl bromide into the tertiary compound is probably related to the known relative stability of the tertiary butyl free radical.

The difference, in regard to the formation of unsaturated hydrocarbons, between the straight-chain and branched compounds was quite clear-cut and reproducible under the conditions of these experiments, but the reason for the difference is not apparent from the structure of the starting materials.

SUMMARY

The γ-ray-induced decomposition of the four isomeric butyl bromides has been studied. Normal butane is the major product from the two straight-chain compounds, and isobutylene from the two branched-chain isomers. A considerable portion of the bromine corresponding to the production of these hydrocarbons has been found to occur, under the conditions of the experiments, as various dibromobutanes. Isobutyl bromide isomerizes extensively into the tertiary bromide. Some implications of the experimental findings have been discussed.

ACKNOWLEDGMENTS

The author is indebted to C. E. Flanagan for the irradiations, and to B. B. Baker, W. C. Coburn, E. B. Dismukes, and Mrs. Ruby H. James for the analytical work.

RECEIVED: April 7, 1958

REFERENCES

1. V. J. KEENAN, R. M. LINCOLN, R. L. ROGERS, and H. BURWASSER, Irradiation of petroleum hydrocarbons. I. Electron bombardment of liquid butanes. *J. Am. Chem. Soc.* **79**, 5125–5128 (1957).

2. L. H. Gevantman and R. R. Williams, Detection and identification of free radicals in the radiolysis of alkanes and alkyl iodides. *J. Phys. Chem.* **56,** 569–574 (1952).
3. R. R. Williams and W. H. Hamill, Identification of free radicals by radio-halogens in the radiolysis of hydrocarbons. *J. Am. Chem. Soc.* **72,** 1857–1858 (1950).
4. E. Collinson and A. J. Swallow, The radiation chemistry of organic substances. *Chem. Revs.* **56,** 471–568 (1956).
5. R. H. Schuler and R. C. Petry, Decomposition of the liquid alkyl iodides by 120-kvp X-radiation. *J. Am. Chem. Soc.* **78,** 3954–3958 (1956).

RADIATION RESEARCH 10, 118–129 (1959)

Acquired Radioresistance

A Review of the Literature and Report of a Confirmatory Experiment

MICHAEL P. DACQUISTO, Major, MC

Radiobiology Section, Department of Nuclear Medicine, Walter Reed Army Institute of Research, Walter Reed Army Medical Center, Washington, D. C.

INTRODUCTION

Acquired resistance to X-radiation is not an uncommon event in clinical medicine. Certain malignancies respond to small doses of X-radiation originally but in time become "radioresistant." Still others fail to respond at all, suggesting an inherent resistance. Although such factors as tumor size or duration of the disease are possible explanations (*1*, *2*), the actual cause of the resistance is unknown.

A thorough but not exhaustive review of the available literature reveals a number of experiments that seem to indicate that animals can be made radioresistant by prior exposure to small doses of X-radiation. Bloom (*3*) gave mice 60 r of whole-body X-radiation (WBR) daily for 16 days and then an additional 200 r WBR either 1 day or 7 days after completion of the 16-day course. The latter animals showed evidence of many more mitoses in the crypt epithelium of the duodenum and no increase in the amount of cellular debris, as contrasted to controls which received 200 r WBR only. Overcompensation in mitoses as a response to small doses of X-radiation in several types of mouse tissue has been noted (*4*). Pape (*5–7*) in several reports in 1950 and 1951 stated that small doses of X-radiation (from 1 to 20 r), locally to the spleen led to definite cellular changes and to enhanced resistance of the animal to whole-body X-radiation delivered later. He ascribed this protective effect to "cellular resistance" and proliferation of the reticuloendothelial system as a result of the small local exposure.

In 1947 Raper (*8*) reported that prior nonlethal doses of whole-body β-radiation increased significantly the LD_{50} in 45 days, from 4700 rep in control mice to a maximum of 8400 rep occurring from 28 to 56 days after the "conditioning dose" of 3000 rep. He offered no explanation for this finding.

Betz (*9*) gave three groups of mice (40 in a group) 500 r WBR and at 7, 10, and 15 days thereafter subjected one of the groups to an additional 700 r WBR. Controls that received 700 r WBR alone had 100% mortality by the tenth day.

The 30-day survival figures (starting with the day 700 r was given) for the three experimental groups are not reported, but enhanced survival for the first 20 days as contrasted to the controls is apparent even in the abbreviated results given. The author proposed Selye's adaptation theory as the mechanism of this protection. Bacq and Alexander *(10)* report the following, based on a later paper by Betz: "In 57 mice, 500 r produces a mortality of 10 to 15 percent; if 700 r (a 100% fatal dose) is given 7, 10, 15 or 33 days after the 500r dose, the survivals recorded are 20, 26, 36 and 0 percent respectively, that is to say, the radioresistance is greatest about the fifteenth day, and disappears completely by the thirty-third day." Unfortunately, the 10 to 15% mortality from the "conditioning dose" itself might be interpreted as natural selection of the more resistant animals. If this is true there can be no valid comparison with a control group not so selected.

Cronkite *et al.* *(11)* used a "conditioning dose" of 144 r WBR weekly for a total of three doses. Thirty days after the last exposure of 144 r, 703 r was given to 100 mice as well as to 100 controls. (There was no mortality in a third group that received only the "conditioning dose.") Control mice showed a 41% mortality in 28 days, in contrast to a 26% mortality for the experimental group. The authors noted that this result was significant at the 0.02 to 0.05 level and concluded that "no adequate explanation for this phenomenon of increased tolerance to X-ray radiation is available at the present time." A recent attempt to duplicate Cronkite's results failed to wait 30 days after the "conditioning dose" but gave 703 r 7 days after the third dose of 144 r with no difference in survival *(12)*. This does not invalidate Cronkite's report but shows simply that a 7-day interval is too short to allow for expression of radioresistance.

Using a somewhat similar scheme of repeated small doses of X-radiation—in this case 417 r WBR over a 1-month period to mice followed by 800 r in one exposure (which in controls causes 100% mortality in an average of 99 hours, range 68 to 138 hours)—Bonet-Maury and Patti found a 213-hour survival in such treated animals *(13)*. A 45% mortality from the "conditioning dose" creates the same doubt of, perhaps, selection of more resistant animals and invalidates comparison with control values. In a personal communication (1957) Bonet-Maury described a later experiment in which 415 r was given over a period of 55 days in multiple small doses (17 to 72 r). Sixteen days after completion of this "conditioning dose" 800 r was delivered. The average survival time was 212 hours, compared to 100 hours for controls. There was no mortality associated with the conditioning dose.

Further evidence to support the concept of the development of tolerance to lethal WBR by prior small doses of WBR can also be inferred from several reports dealing with the problem of recovery from WBR in experimental animals. Paterson *et al.* *(14)* gave mice one-half their known $LD_{50(30)}$ and at intervals of time thereafter gave an additional increment of WBR to establish a new LD_{50}. After a 20-day interval mice given 260 r required an additional 546 r to cause an LD_{50}. This not only shows complete recovery from the original 260 r but also contains a faint suggestion of resistance. The same type of experiment performed on rhesus monkeys (*15*) showed that, 20 days after a dose of 260 r WBR, 623 r was necessary to effect an LD_{50}, in contrast to 570 for controls. The authors state, "The animals apparently tolerated at the second irradiation a larger dose than the LD_{50} for a single exposure. Recovery from the initial 260 r was, therefore, complete, as far as survival of the animal was concerned. Since, however, the standard deviation is rather large it would not be justifiable to say a heightened resistance has been achieved." One can reasonably say, however, that heightened resistance is suggested. Several additional reports also allude to radioresistance (*16–20*) and offer theories which will be discussed later.

In spite of the number of reports quoted that seem either to confirm or to suggest the concept of acquired radioresistance in experimental animals (mainly mice), this method of investigation of the acute radiation syndrome as yet lacks precise time-dose clarification. If acquired radioresistance is indeed possible, it offers a new avenue of approach to explore the inherent defense mechanisms initiated by the insult of X-radiation. With this in mind an experiment is reported which attempts to delineate some time and exposure relationships in the development of radioresistance by prior exposure to nonlethal X-radiation.

PROCEDURE

Experiment 1

For this experiment 320 young adult female white Swiss mice, Walter Reed strain, were used. The animals were divided into three groups of 100 mice, and the remaining 20 mice served as controls throughout the duration of the procedure. One group of 100 mice received 50 r WBR 10 days prior to the larger exposure to WBR; the second group received 50 r WBR 17 days before; the third group received no prior X-radiation.

To determine the $LD_{50(30)}$ each group of 100 mice was subdivided into five smaller groups of 20 each and exposed to 350 r, 460 r, 600 r, 770 r, and 1000 r, respectively. The experiment was timed so that the lethal X-radiation was delivered all on the same day, approximately 5 weeks after the mice were obtained, at an average age of 14 weeks. This uniform age was selected to be well beyond the point where age is reported to influence X-ray mortality (*21*). The average weight at this time was 32.0 gm.

The mice were exposed to X-ray in groups of 30, and all three groups were represented equally in each exposure. The exposure was uneventful except that with 1000 r there were 5 deaths "under the beam"—1 control, 3 who had received 50 r 10 days prior, and 1 who had received 50 r 17 days prior. These deaths were excluded from the groups; consequently, these three groups were considered to have been originally 19, 17, and 19 respectively, whereas all others were 20.

After the exposure the mice were returned to their original cages and observed once daily for the next 30 days to determine survival. All surviving animals were weighed once daily over the same period. Water and standard laboratory animal food was available ad lib. Cages were changed and cleaned when necessary.

Throughout the experiment animal selection was always random. To avoid the reported "cage effect" (*22*) each batch of 20 mice was housed in four cages, 5 to a cage. Each cage of 10 animals, therefore, contained equal numbers of two different groups, identified by ear clipping and/or picric acid staining. All animals were handled identically with blank X-ray exposures when indicated.

A 250-kv 30-ma Maxitron unit was used for all X-radiation. The TSD was 70 cm, and the rate was relatively constant at 30 r/min as measured in air in the approximate midposition of the animal. Inherent filtration was 3.2 mm Be, and added filtration 1.0 mm Al and 1.0 mm Cu. All mice were exposed in a round cylinder, 11 inches in diameter, 1¼ inches in depth, with plywood bottom and sides and a perforated plastic top.

Experiment 2

The experiment just described was repeated in every detail, with the same number of mice, of the same age, weight, etc. For this study, however, all animals were sacrificed 72 hours after their lethal exposure. The spleen was removed and weighed promptly; the thymus was preserved in 10% buffered formalin, and 24 hours later the adherent fat was removed and the thymus weighed. Each value listed is the average of 20 weights.

In addition 60 mice were exposed to 50 r WBR, and at 3, 10, 17, and 24 days thereafter a group of 15 was sacrificed for spleen and thymus weights. A similar group of controls was studied in the same manner at each point. Each value given is the average of 15 weights for that group.

The X-radiation factors were as described before; that is, all X-radiation was at 250 kv, 30 ma, with a TSD of 70 cm, and a rate of about 30 r/min. Analysis of the spleen and thymus was limited to gross organ weight alone; no histology was attempted.

RESULTS

Experiment 1

Preliminary experiments confirmed the fact 50 r WBR would cause no 30-day mortality in these mice. Previously quoted reports (*9, 10, 14, 15, 19*) as well as unpublished data (Dacquisto) suggested that the most fruitful area for investigation was from about the tenth to the twentieth day after the small X-radiation dose. For this reason the tenth and seventeenth days were selected.

The improved 30-day survival of the animals who received 50 r WBR 17 days prior to lethal X-radiation is evident at every exposure except for 1000 r (Fig. 1).

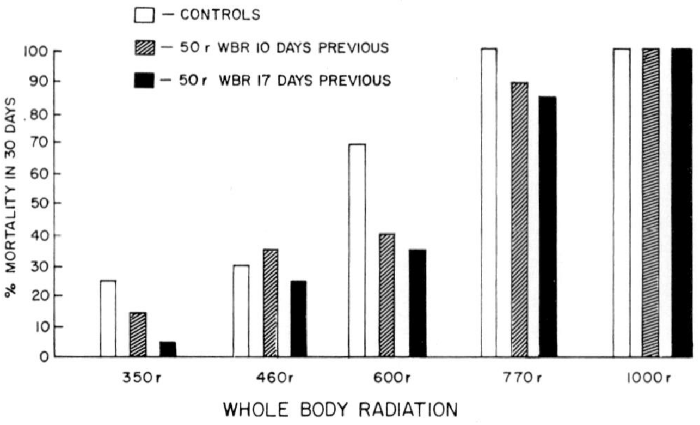

FIG. 1. Graph showing 30-day mortality versus dose in female mice. Enhanced 30-day survival for the treated groups is evident at every exposure except at 1000 r. With a few exceptions each group consisted of 20 mice originally.

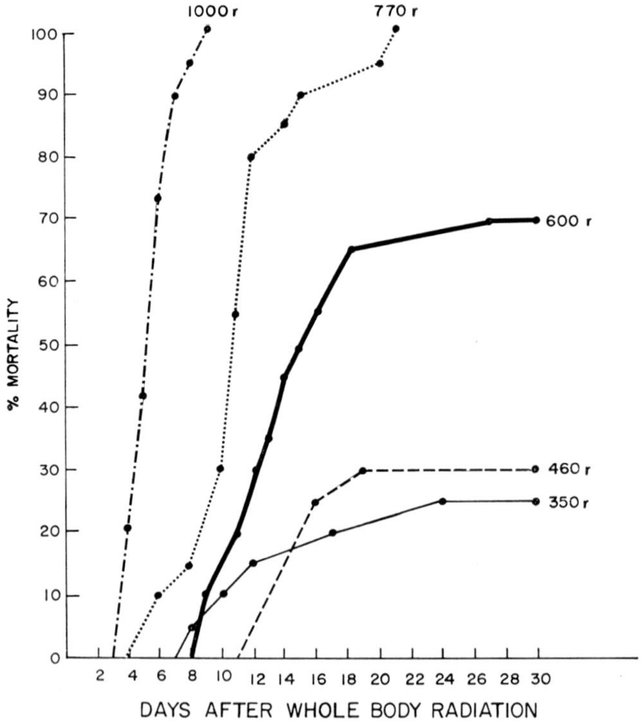

FIG. 2. Cumulative 30-day mortality for control mice at exposures and times shown. This graph should be compared with Figs. 3 and 4.

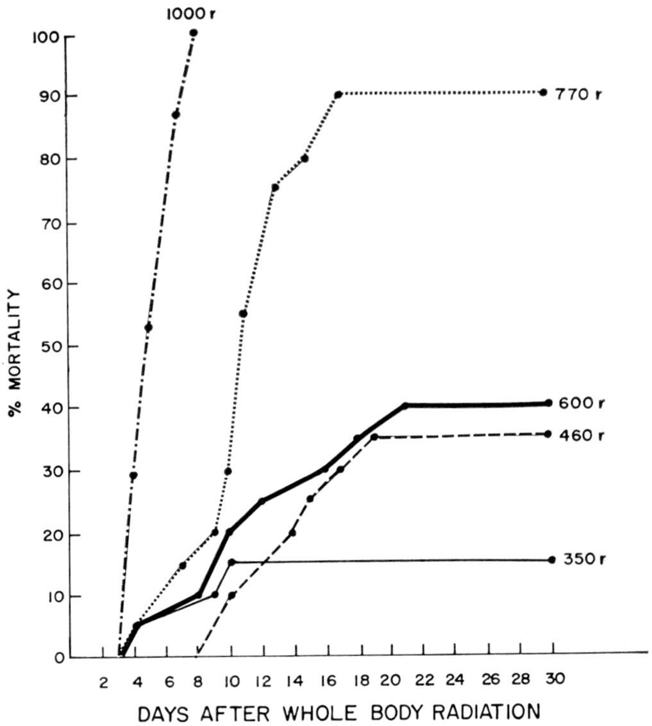

FIG. 3. Cumulative 30-day mortality in female mice conditioned by 50 r WBR 10 days prior to varying doses of radiation. Comparison of the cumulative mortality shown here with Fig. 2 shows the same pattern of mortality in relation to time but at a decreased rate. This is more apparent at the lower exposures.

The results show that tolerance is overwhelmed at this level of exposure. This indicates that there is no resistance to the gastrointestinal syndrome. A 10-day interval also allows for some development of tolerance, but it would appear that an additional week is necessary for its more prominent manifestation, although there is no statistically significant difference in the survival figures at either time.

Study of the 30-day cumulative mortality figures gives no clue as to what time period of the acute radiation syndrome is most affected (Figs. 2, 3, and 4). The median survival time is essentially the same for both the experimental and the control animals. This implies that the beneficial effects of the small exposure are manifested throughout the 30-day period equally. The $LD_{50(30)}$ for each group was obtained by probit analysis with the least-squares regression construction of the best-fitting line. Table I shows these values, their confidence limits, and their statistical significance. These data are considered to be firm evidence favoring the development of radioresistance within the time and dose schedules employed, although the protection obtained is not dramatic.

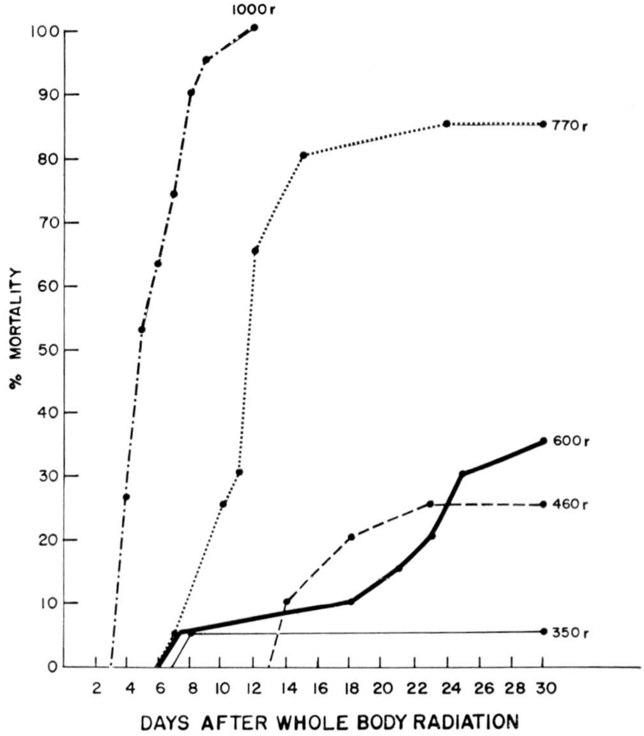

FIG. 4. Cumulative 30-day mortality in female mice conditioned by 50 r WBR 17 days prior to varying doses of radiation. In contrast to the results for control animals, the lowered mortality is quite obvious here. There is no clear-cut change in the cumulative mortality patterns, however.

TABLE I

THE $LD_{50(30)}$ FOR ADULT FEMALE WHITE MICE (WALTER REED STRAIN)

Interval between first and second dose	*Number of mice/ Number of batches*	$LD_{50(30)}$	*S.E.*	*95% Confidence limits*
None (controls)	99/5	487 r	25.7	487 ± 50 r
10 days	97/5	560 r	31.0	560 ± 60 r[a]
17 days	99/5	617 r	32.0	617 ± 63 r[b]

[a] Significant at the 90% (*t*-test) compared to control value.

[b] Significant at the 98% level (*t*-test) compared to control value.

TABLE II

SPLEEN AND THYMUS WEIGHT LOSS IN FEMALE MICE AFTER VARIOUS EXPOSURES TO WHOLE-BODY X-RADIATION

(Each value listed is the mean of 20 weights, 72 hours X-radiation exposure as indicated.)

Exposure (r)	*Spleen*			*Thymus*		
	Control	*50 r 10 days prior*	*50 r 17 days prior*	*Control*	*50 r 10 days prior*	*50 r 17 days prior*
350	86	72	86	19	26	21
460	72	67	66	11	22	21
600	69	64	54	19	22	35
770	77	79	52	9	8	6
1000	53	54	53	6	6	7
0	309			86		

Daily body weight of the survivors revealed no difference among the three groups. The magnitude of weight loss was proportional to the dose delivered in all instances. The small control group, 20 mice, had no mortality during the experiment and showed a slow weight gain over the 30-day period from 30.5 to 33.0 gm.

At 150 days postradiation the experiment was terminated owing to animal space limitations. During this 120-day period additional deaths occurred in all groups but at a rate no greater than in mice of similar age who had received no X-radiation. The enhanced early survival, therefore, persisted throughout the whole period of observation.

Experiment 2

In Table II are listed the average spleen and thymus weights for mice who had received 50 r WBR followed by lethal exposures at later dates, as well as controls. The spleen exhibits the expected loss in weight, which is dose-dependent. There is no evidence here that 50 r WBR either 10 days or 17 days before made any difference in the 72-hour postexposure weight.

Thymus weights are also noninformative and show only a dose dependency without regard to previous nonlethal X-radiation. Conversely, in neither the spleen nor thymus data is there evidence of any cumulative effect of the 50 r WBR with the later lethal exposure.

The results of 50 r alone on these same two parameters is interesting. There is no evidence of hypertrophy of either the spleen or the thymus for 24 days after such a low exposure (see Fig. 5). If anything, spleen weight may be slightly less in the ten- to twenty-day period, and the thymus weight seems normal. The rate of recovery and growth of the spleen subjected to 50 r WBR may be increased in the first 10 days after X-radiation, however.

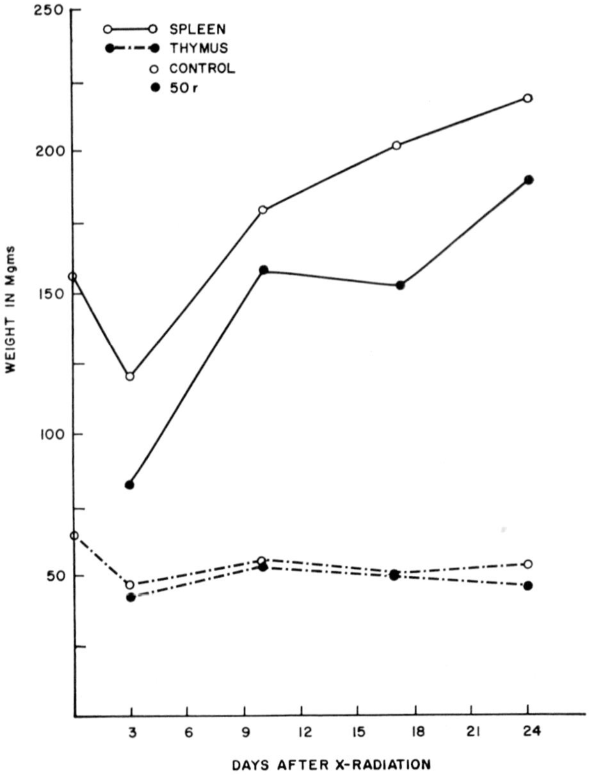

FIG. 5. There is no evidence of splenic or thymic hypertrophy for 24 days after a single 50-r exposure. The rate of recovery and growth of the spleen may be increased in the first 10 days after exposure.

DISCUSSION

Speculation as to the mechanism of action of small exposures to X-radiation in inducing tolerance to lethal X-radiation delivered later raises some interesting points, although no convincing explanation is at hand. Temporary stimulation of hematopoiesis may be a possible explanation. The results of experiment 2, however, do not confirm the presence of hypertrophy during the period when radioresistance is present. During the third postexposure week splenic hypertrophy has been reported, but the dose of X-radiation required was much greater than 50 r (*23–25*). This might explain the positive results obtained by Betz (*9*, *10*), Cronkite *et al.* (*11*), Paterson *et al.* (*14*, *15*), and others, as in these experiments the first X-radiation dose was in the range known to cause splenic hypertrophy, and the increased resistance was found during this period only. This cannot explain the positive results reported in this paper, however, for, as can be seen in Table II, 72 hours after a lethal exposure all spleen and thymus weights were essentially the same. Under such circumstances the enhanced survival provoked by prior X-radiation should be sought elsewhere.

Mole (*17*) makes this statement: "If death after single large doses of radiation is due to cellular depletion of the bone marrow, it might be expected that the dose needed to kill would be increased by a preliminary sub-lethal dose of radiation for the bone marrow is normally partly fatty and would be expected to become more fully hematopoietic during recovery. A larger proportion of the marrow cells would then need killing before the surviving number of cells fell below the critical number required to ensure survival of the whole animal. The mouse would not be a satisfactory animal in which to demonstrate such an effect since so little of its marrow is normally fatty, and in fact mice show only a small increase in radioresistance." Bone marrow study was not done in these experiments, as it was felt that thymus and spleen weight analyses would yield equally good evidence concerning X-radiation recovery and hematopoiesis, respectively. This may not be true. Certainly other species should be studied, for to date only the mouse has been investigated extensively, with brief remarks available on the monkey (*15*) and the rat (*19*).

Sacher (*16*) reports that he has evidence showing "an as yet unexplained action of small repeated dosages which leads to a decreased mortality from infectious disease. We have confirmed the existence of this effect and have it under further study at present." In 1942 Warren and Dunlap (*26*) stated that small doses of X-radiation, 25 to 200 r, had a favorable effect on some infectious processes in animals and man. The two latter reports again point to hematopoietic stimulation as the responsible mechanism.

Because of the time interval involved for the manifestation of tolerance, 2 to 3 weeks, one should consider the possibility of some kind of temporary protection against toxic products, a reaction akin to an antigen-antibody immune response without implying elaboration of a specific, classical antibody with its long-lasting effect. Further investigation of this hypothesis requires only a belief that toxic products are an important factor in the acute radiation syndrome, and, although this does not appear to be the predominant opinion, ample reports favoring this theory are available (*17*, *27–34*).

Another possible mechanism postulates that the conditioning dose given leads to a natural selection of the more radioresistant animals (*13*; Bonet-Maury, personal communication). When there is no mortality from the conditioning dose, however, this becomes a most improbable explanation. In addition, if the reason for the enhanced survival is indeed selection of the radioresistant animals, this should be a lifelong characteristic; but experimental evidence refutes this (*10*; Dacquisto, unpublished data). Natural selection as an explanation therefore seems unlikely.

CONCLUSIONS

1. The ability of experimental animals (mice) to develop significant radioresistance by prior exposure to small doses of X-radiation seems to be well established.

2. An experiment is reported which shows that for control adult female white Swiss mice, Walter Reed strain, the $LD_{50(30)}$ is 487 $\pm$ 25.7 r. If they are given 50 r WBR 10 days prior, it increases to 560 r $\pm$ 31.0 r; and if the interval is 17 days, it is 617 r $\pm$ 32.0 r.

3. In this experiment radioresistance was manifest at both 10 and 17 days after the small exposure.

4. Analysis of spleen and thymus weights under the conditions of these experiments gave no clue to the mechanism of the acquired radioresistance.

5. Alternate hypotheses have been suggested, but the phenomenon remains unexplained.

ACKNOWLEDGMENTS

Willie Smith of the National Institutes of Health and Lt. Cols. J. B. Hartgering and J. T. Brennan of the Walter Reed Army Institute of Research gave helpful advice to the author; Lt. E. Blackburn, R. Failer, and R. Zaveson were of valuable technical assistance. The illustrations were prepared by the Medical Audio-Visual Dept., Walter Reed Army Institute of Research.

RECEIVED: February 13, 1958

REFERENCES

1. C. C. STURGIS, Treatment and prognosis in leukemia and allied disorders. *Postgrad. Med.* **9,** 375–382 (1951).
2. C. M. NICE, Relation of tumor size to radioresistance. *Radiology* **68,** 555–557 (1957).
3. M. A. BLOOM, Acquired radioresistance of the crypt epithelium of the duodenum. *Radiology* **55,** 104–115 (1950).
4. N. P. KNOWLTON, JR., and L. H. HEMPELMANN, The effect of X-rays on the mitotic activity of the adrenal gland, jejunum, lymph node and epidermis of the mouse. *J. Cellular Comp. Physiol.* **33,** 73–92 (1949).
5. R. PAPE, Histological findings after very small doses of irradiation. *6th Intern. Congr. Radiol., London* 162–163 (1950).
6. R. PAPE and N. JELLINKE, Important variations in the organic findings after total and local radiation and the particular effects of small scale dosages. The spleen as a test for various radiation effects. *Radiol. Austriaca* **3,** 43–62 (1950).
7. R. PAPE, New observations and experimental findings on the effect of very small roentgen doses. *Radiol. Austriaca* **4,** 35–51 (1951).
8. J. R. RAPER, Effects of total surface beta irradiation. *Radiology* **49,** 314–324 (1947).
9. H. BETZ, The importance of the resistance phase of the organism at the time of application of a lethal dose of X-radiation. *Compt. rend. soc. biol.* **144,** 1439–1442 (1950).
10. Z. M. BACQ and P. ALEXANDER, *Fundamentals of Radiobiology*, p. 271, Academic Press, New York, 1955.
11. E. P. CRONKITE, C. R. SIPE, D. C. ELTZHOLTZ, W. H. CHAPMAN, and F. W. CHAMBERS, JR., Increased tolerance of mice to lethal X-radiation as a result of previous sub-lethal exposures. *Proc. Soc. Exptl. Biol. Med.* **73,** 184–186 (1950).

12. A. T. Krebs and J. B. Storer, Adaptation to ionizing radiation. Army Medical Research Laboratory Report 175, Fort Knox, Kentucky (Feb. 2, 1955).
13. P. Bonet-Maury and F. Patti, Protection of mice after whole-body X-irradiation. *Brit. J. Radiol.* **313,** 72–76 (1954).
14. E. Paterson, C. W. Gilbert, and J. Matthews, Time intensity factors and whole body irradiation. *Brit. J. Radiol.* **25,** 427–433 (1952).
15. E. Paterson, C. W. Gilbert, and M. V. Haigh, Effects of paired doses of whole body irradiation in the Rhesus monkey. *Brit. J. Radiol.* **29,** 218–226 (1956).
16. G. A. Sacher, On the statistical nature of mortality, with especial reference to chronic radiation mortality. *Radiology* **67,** 250–257 (1956).
17. R. H. Mole, Quantitative observations on recovery from whole body irradiation in mice. I. Recovery after single large doses of radiation. *Brit. J. Radiol.* **29,** 563–569 (1956).
18. R. M. Mole, Quantitative observations on recovery from whole body irradiation in mice. II. Recovery during and after daily irradiation. *Brit. J. Radiol.* **30,** 40–46 (1957).
19. H. I. Kohn and R. F. Kallman, Acute lethality studies with the rat: The LD_{50}, death rate, and recovery rate. *Radiation Research* **7,** 85–97 (1957).
20. R. Rugh and J. Wolff, Fetal conditioning against X-irradiation lethality. *Radiation Research* **7,** 462–463 (1957).
21. H. L. Abrams, Influence of age, body weight and sex on susceptibility of mice to lethal effects of X-radiation. *Proc. Soc. Exptl. Biol. Med.* **76,** 729-732 (1951).
22. A. Raventos, A factor influencing the significance of radiation mortality experiments. *Brit. J. Radiol.* **28,** 410–414 (1955).
23. W. W. Smith, W. Anderson, Jr., and G. Ashwell, Spleen adenosine triphosphate activity in irradiated mice treated with spleen homogenate. *Am. J. Physiol.* **178,** 471–473 (1954).
24. W. W. Smith, I. M. Alderman, and H. J. Ruth, Functional studies of the hyperplastic spleen of mice recovering from radiation damage. *Am. J. Physiol.* **182,** 403–406 (1955).
25. A. N. Stroud, Recovery and regeneration of spleens after single and divided doses of X-irradiation. Argonne National Laboratory Report ANL-5378, pp. 95–99 (1955).
26. S. Warren and C. E. Dunlap, Effects of radiation on normal tissues. III. Effects of radiation on the blood and the hemopoietic tissues, including the spleen, thymus and lymph nodes. *A.M.A. Arch. Pathol.* **34,** 562–608 (1942).
27. A. Edelmann, New evidence for a toxic substance elaborated after radiation. *Federation Proc.* **14,** 42 (1955).
28. R. A. Conard, Some effects of ionizing radiation on the physiology of the gastrointestinal tract: A review. *Radiation Research* **5,** 167–188 (1956).
29. M. Berenbom, Nucleic acid changes in rat spleen after localized X-irradiation. *Radiation Research* **5,** 650–656 (1956).
30. J. W. Osborne, Prevention of intestinal radiation death by removal of the irradiated intestine. *Radiation Research* **4,** 541–546 (1956).
31. W. M. Court Brown and R. F. Mahler, The X-ray dose-body size relationship in radiation sickness. *Science* **118,** 271–272 (1953).
32. W. M. Court Brown and R. F. Mahler, Some clinical and biochemical observations following a single therapeutic dose of X-rays. *Proc. Roy. Soc. Med.* **46,** 245–250 (1953).
33. W. M. Court Brown and R. F. Mahler, Integral dose, body size and the site of irradiation as factors determining the severity of radiation sickness. *J. Fac. Radiol.* **5,** 200–209 (1955).
34. M. N. Swift, S. T. Kaketa, and V. P. Bond, Regionally fractionated X-irradiation equivalent in dose to total-body exposure. *Radiation Research* **1,** 241–252 (1954).

RADIATION RESEARCH **10**, 130–147 (1959)

Metabolism of Pu^{239} in Adult Beagle Dogs[1]

BETSY J. STOVER, D. R. ATHERTON, AND N. KELLER
Radiobiology Laboratory, University of Utah, Salt Lake City, Utah

INTRODUCTION

The currently accepted maximum permissible level for Pu^{239} in man (*1*) is derived from the relative effectiveness of Pu^{239} and Ra^{226} in rodents and the effect of Ra^{226} in man. Because of the great dissimilarities in both the skeleton and life span of man and rodent, there is a great need for a comparison of the chronic effects of Pu^{239} and Ra^{226} in a larger, longer-lived animal. Young adult beagle dogs are being used for these studies.

A comparison of the toxicities of Ra^{226} and Pu^{239} on an absorbed-dose basis requires detailed knowledge of their metabolism as a function of time. The metabolism of Ra^{226} and its daughter Rn^{222} have been reported previously (*2*, *3*). Ra^{226} in human subjects is the basis of the dose-level scheme (*2*) for both the radium and plutonium studies in beagles. Since that value, 0.1 μc of "retained" Ra^{226} per 70 kg, contains a safety factor of 10, our lowest dose level is

$$(10 \times 0.1\ \mu c\ \text{"retained"})/70\ \text{kg} = 0.0143\ \mu c/\text{kg}$$

To allow for the fact that the maximum permissible level of radium in man is defined as a retained amount, our actual injected doses of plutonium were based on an assumed average plutonium retention of 90 %. The spread in dose levels is such that the highest is about 150 times the lowest. The injected doses appear in Table I. The dogs were injected in groups of six, one at each dose level[2] plus one control. Twelve such groups (six male and six female) were injected during a period of 3.5 years.

METHODS

Injection solutions. Each dog is given a single intravenous injection of tetravalent plutonium in a citric acid–sodium citrate buffer, 0.08 *M* in total citrate and pH = 3.5. Since PuIV disproportionates, radiation-induced decomposition occurs, and molds grow in these solutions, fresh solutions are prepared for each injection group

[1] This work was done under Atomic Energy Commission Contract AT(11-1)-119.

[2] Except the 1.7-level dogs, which were injected later.

so that all groups receive chemically similar material. The amount of Pu^{239} required for a group of dogs and the corresponding injection standards is about a milligram, which makes it possible to use a precipitation method to prepare solutions of monomeric PuIV suitable for intravenous injection.

All operations (except for final dilutions) are performed in a Berkeley-style glove box. An appropriate amount of the stock solution is transferred to a 15-ml centrifuge cone by means of micropipets. To reduce the plutonium (*4*), SO_2 is introduced through a fine glass capillary, immersed so that a stream of small bubbles rises through the solution. The capillary bubbler is connected to a glass trap inside the box, and the trap to the SO_2 tank outside the box. When the solution is saturated, the bubbler is rinsed, then removed. After about 15 minutes, the solution, which is now the bright blue characteristic of PuIII (*5*), is cooled to 0° C by immersing the tube in an ice-water bath. A dark-colored hydroxide is precipitated by adding 5 *N* NaOH dropwise while stirring to dissipate the heat. The tube is centrifuged, completeness of precipitation is checked, and, after the supernatant is aspirated, the precipitate is washed with distilled water. The hydroxide, still in the 0° C bath, is dissolved in 0.2 ml of concentrated HNO_3. In this step, PuIII is oxidized to PuIV, the PuIV forms a strong complex with the nitrate ions (*6*), and the resulting solution is a brilliant green. The complexing of PuIV by nitrate inhibits further oxidation.

The PuIV solution and measured amounts of 0.08 *M* citric acid rinses are transferred to a 30-ml serum bottle. Then appropriate amounts of 0.08 *M* citric acid and 0.08 *M* sodium citrate are added to give a pH of 3.5 and a PuIV concentration such that the injection of the dog receiving the highest dose level requires about 10 ml. Injection solutions for the other dose levels are prepared by successive dilution with the citric acid-sodium citrate buffer, so that all injection volumes are about 10 ml. Aliquots of several of the injection solutions were dialyzed, and, as anticipated from other work (*7*), essentially all the plutonium was diffusible. Nojax[3] cellulose casing was used, and the injection solutions were dialyzed against some of the same citrate buffer solutions that had been used in their preparation.

An injection standard is obtained for each dog by delivering an equal dose to a volumetric flask with the syringe subsequently used to inject the dog. The standards are diluted with 0.1 *N* HNO_3, and aliquots are pipetted onto stainless steel disks for α-particle activity measurements. The total volumes and aliquots are chosen so that the count rates measured are of the same order of magnitude for all dose levels. The α-particle activity measurements are made with a conventional 2π proportional counter,[4] which is standardized with a U_3O_8 standard provided by the U. S. National Bureau of Standards. No correction is made for backscattering of the α-particles, since the effect is negligible compared to other uncertainties in

[3] The Visking Corporation, Chicago, Illinois.

[4] Nuclear Measurements Co., Model PC-1.

TABLE I

Pu Excretion by Dose Level

Dose level	*Injected dose* ($\mu c/kg$)	*Cumulative excretion, 0–22 days* (%)	*Retention at 22 days* (%)	*Cumulative excretion, 22 days to 4 years* (%)	*Retention at 4 years* (%)
All		12.1	87.9	16.4	71.5
5	2.78	10.8	89.2	14.3	74.9
4	0.900	10.6	89.4	16.9	72.5
3	0.300	13.4	86.6	16.4	70.2
2	0.0955	13.3	86.7	16.5	70.2
1.7	0.0477	—	—	—	—
1	0.0159	14.2	85.8	—	—

the experiment. The average actual injected doses are within a few per cent of the desired injected doses of Table I (*8*, *9*).

Blood studies. Blood samples are collected with heparin as an anticoagulant and centrifuged without delay. Plasma samples collected soon after injection are pipetted directly onto stainless steel disks 1 inch in diameter. The maximum amount which can be handled in this manner is 0.25 ml. To measure these plasma volumes, we use micropipets which are calibrated "to contain" and which must be rinsed with a fluid that will not coagulate the plasma protein. Distilled water proved satisfactory. After thorough drying at room temperature (faster drying causes clumping and humping), the disks can be flamed with negligible sample loss from flaking.

Later plasma samples are wet-ashed with nitric acid, and the plutonium is concentrated by the standard double coprecipitation method (*10*). First the plutonium is carried with bismuth phosphate, then with lanthanum fluoride. The LaF_3 is dissolved by adding 1 to 3 drops of concentrated nitric acid and an equal amount of saturated boric acid, and the solution is transferred to a stainless steel disk. Alpha particles are detected as described above. Mass absorption curves have been determined to correct the observed sample count rates when necessary.

In the dialysis studies, serum is used. Tubes of Nojax cellulose casing, each containing 1 ml of serum of known plutonium concentration, are suspended in 25 ml of the solutions, which are analyzed for plutonium at various times. To minimize the growth of bacteria and molds, the dialyses are done at 2° C.

Excreta, soft tissues, and bones. For the excretion studies, the dogs are housed in stainless steel metabolism cages constructed so that the urine drains through Tygon tubing into polyethylene bottles and the feces are deposited on perforated plates, which serve as the floors. Since the dogs usually defecate soon after being fed, the feces can be collected shortly thereafter, resulting in a good separation of urine and feces. To make the collections as quantitative as possible, the cages are rinsed daily with 10^{-3} N HNO_3, and the rinsings are added to the day's urine samples. When the excretion rate is changing rapidly, daily measurements are made; for the long-term points 96-hour samples are analyzed.

The urine samples and soft tissues are wet-ashed with nitric acid; the fecal samples and bones are incinerated in a muffle furnace, then digested with nitric acid. Aliquots of ashed samples are pipetted onto weighed stainless steel disks 1 inch in diameter, dried, flamed, cooled, and weighed. When the amount of plutonium becomes too low for the direct method, the double coprecipitation method described above is employed.

RESULTS

Concentration of plutonium in plasma. The concentration of Pu^{239} in plasma has been measured from 1 minute to 4.5 years after injection, and the data appear in Figs. 1 and 2. Except for the 4.5-year point, each is the average of samples from two or more dogs, and, nearly all samples are from dogs of the two highest dose levels. The plasma concentration at 1 minute after injection is 0.193% dose per gram of plasma, the average injection weight of these dogs is 9.0 kg, and the average plasma volume is 49.3 ml/kg (*11*). Thus, about $0.193 \times 49.3 \times 9.0 = 85\%$ of the injected dose is circulating at 1 minute. Between 1 minute and 10 hours, the concentration drops only by a factor of about 2. From then until 3 weeks after injection, the decrease is by a factor of 250. Then the decrease in concentration becomes slower, and at 4 years the value is still one-fourth that at 3 weeks.

The first attempts at mathematical description consisted in fitting sums of exponentials to the plasma concentration data. The resulting equations, in addition to being cumbersome, did not give as satisfactory a description as desired, and this approach was abandoned. A log-log plot suggested division of the data into three

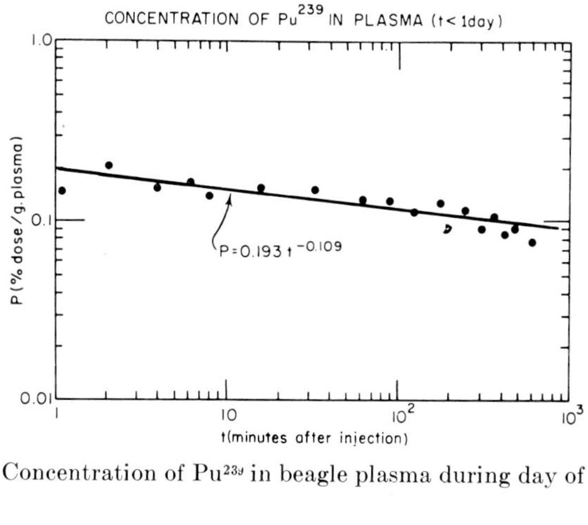

FIG. 1. Concentration of Pu^{239} in beagle plasma during day of injection

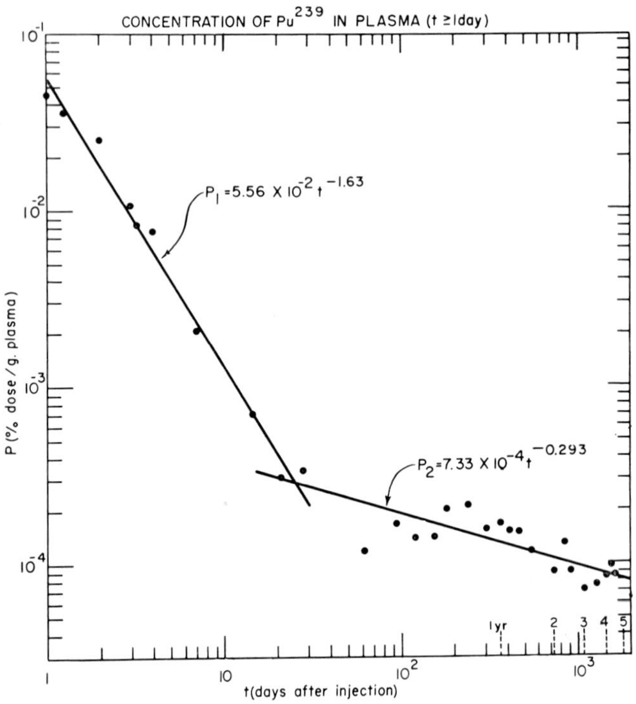

FIG. 2. Concentration of Pu^{239} in plasma from 1 day through 4 years after injection.

time periods and fitting a power function to each period (see Figs. 1 and 2). The day of the injection was chosen as the first period for the plasma data, and the calculated equation[5] is

$$P = 0.193t^{-0.109} \quad (1)$$

where P is per cent dose per gram of plasma, and t is minutes. The second arbitrary time period chosen is 1 through 22 days after injection; the third is 22 days through 4 years. With t now expressed in days, the calculated equations for these two periods are

$$P_1 = 5.56 \times 10^{-2}\, t^{-1.63} \qquad (1 \leq t \leq 22 \text{ days}) \quad (2)$$

$$P_2 = 7.33 \times 10^{-4}\, t^{-0.293} \qquad (t \geq 22 \text{ days}) \quad (3)$$

Dialysis studies. The results of our dialysis experiments are in agreement with the previously reported binding of plutonium by the blood proteins (*12*). When

[5] This equation was calculated by minimizing Σr_i^2, where $r_i = \log P_i - \log a + b \log t_i$. Succeeding equations were obtained similarly.

the sera were dialyzed against 0.31 *M* NaCl, pH = 7, for as long as 5 days, no significant amount of plutonium was found in the outside solution. Similar results were obtained with 0.16 *M* sodium carbonate, 0.16 *M* sodium oxalate, 0.16 *M* sodium acetate, and 0.08 *M* glycine solutions (all solutions adjusted to pH = 7.2 to 7.5). In contrast, when 0.16 *M* sodium citrate, pH = 7.5, was used, more than 90% of the plutonium was dialyzable, appearing in the outside solution with a half-period of about 9 hours. This finding shows that the plutonium citrate complex is stronger than the plutonium protein complex (or complexes). With a citric acid–sodium citrate buffer of pH = 3.5, no plutonium appeared in the outside solution. This may be explained by the fact that Cit^{3-} forms a stronger plutonium complex than does H_2Cit^-; however, the fact that the isoelectric points of the blood proteins lie between 3.5 and 7.0 also must be remembered. Dialyses against 0.31 *M* NaCl, pH = 2, resulted in variable but significant amounts of plutonium in the outside solutions. Perhaps hydrogen ion displaces plutonium from its protein complex.

Excretion studies. The excretion of plutonium has been measured continuously through the first 22 days after injection. Nineteen dogs, representing all dose levels,[2] excreted an average of 12.1% of the injected dose during this interval. Continuous measurements were made on fewer dogs through 36 days. For later measurements, dogs were returned to the metabolism cages for 4-day collection periods. Twelve dogs, representing the top four dose levels equally, were measured at 6-month intervals from 6 months through 4 years after injection.

The daily total excretion, X, and the daily urinary excretion, U, are plotted in Fig. 3. Both sets of data have been divided into two time groups corresponding to the second and third periods chosen for the plasma concentration data. For the first 22 days after injection, the calculated equations for daily total and urinary excretion are, respectively,

$$X_1 = 6.98t^{-1.59} \qquad (t \leq 22 \text{ days}) \tag{4}$$

$$U_1 = 1.44t^{-1.52} \tag{5}$$

where X_1 and U_1 are expressed in per cent dose per day, and t is in days. For the second period from 22 days through 4 years, the corresponding equations, with the same units, are

$$X_2 = 0.223t^{-0.485} \qquad (t \geq 22 \text{ days}) \tag{6}$$

$$U_2 = 0.0605t^{-0.409} \tag{7}$$

As illustrated in Fig. 4, the relative amounts excreted in the urine and feces vary during the first 20 to 30 days, then remain approximately constant through 4 years. For the 22-day continuous study, the cumulative fecal excretion is 2.14 times the cumulative urinary excretion. The average value of the individual daily fecal to urinary excretion ratios, $\overline{F/U}$, is 3.9; the average value of the ratio of average daily

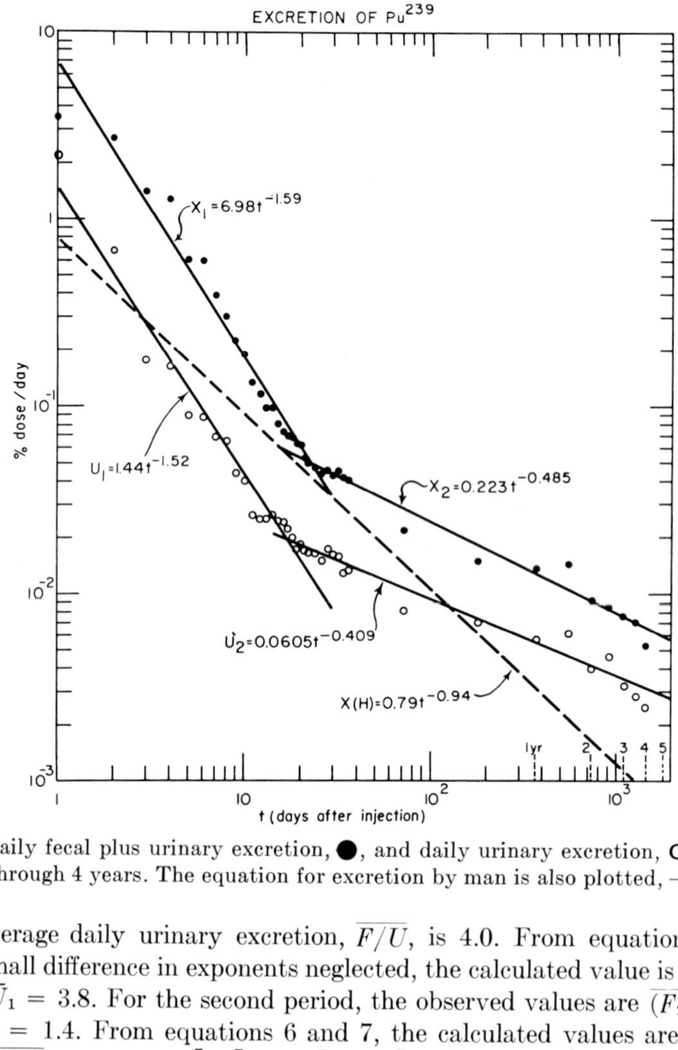

FIG. 3. Daily fecal plus urinary excretion, ●, and daily urinary excretion, O, of Pu^{239} by the beagle through 4 years. The equation for excretion by man is also plotted, — — — .

fecal to average daily urinary excretion, $\overline{F/U}$, is 4.0. From equations 4 and 5, with the small difference in exponents neglected, the calculated value is $(\bar{X}_1 - \bar{U}_1)/\bar{U}_1 = \bar{F}_1/\bar{U}_1 = 3.8$. For the second period, the observed values are $\overline{(F_2/U_2)} = 1.6$ and $\bar{F}_2/\bar{U}_2 = 1.4$. From equations 6 and 7, the calculated values are $\overline{(F_2/U_2)} = \overline{(X_2 - U_2)/U_2} = 1.2$ and $\bar{F}_2/\bar{U}_2 = (\bar{X}_2 - \bar{U}_2)/\bar{U}_2 = 1.4$.

The renal clearance of plutonium can be calculated from equations 2 and 5 and from equations 3 and 7. For 1 to 22 days, $\overline{(U/P)}_1 = 33$ gm of plasma per day, and for 22 days to 4 years, $\overline{(U/P)}_2 = 40$ gm of plasma per day, in good agreement with the early value. Since the total plasma volume is 440 ml, it follows that the kidneys clear only 7.5 to 9% of the plasma of plutonium in the course of a day.

Of the nineteen dogs in the continuous 22-day excretion study, eleven were males

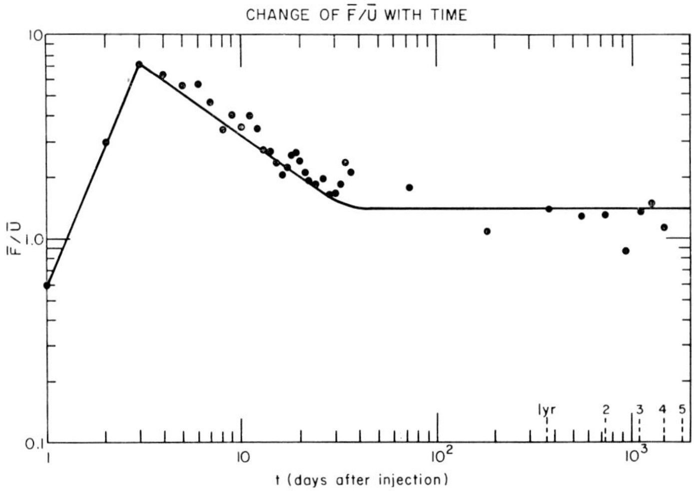

FIG. 4. The change with time of the ratio of average daily fecal excretion, $\bar{F}$, to average daily urinary excretion, $\bar{U}$.

and eight females. No correlation between sex and plutonium excretion was observed. Fourteen were 1.2 to 1.6 years old at injection; the others ranged from 2.2 to 4.3 years. No correlation between age and excretion was observed.

The excretion data of both time periods have been examined carefully for dose-level effect, and none has been found. All dose levels[2] are represented in the 22-day continuous period, and the total amounts excreted by each dose level are compared in Table I. Dose levels 2 through 5 were studied in the second period. The data were separated according to dose level, and a power function was calculated for each dose level. From these four equations, the cumulative excretion was calculated for the period 22 days through 4 years. From equation 6, the same calculation was made for all dose levels. The results appear in Table I.

Plutonium in liver, spleen, and kidney. Although the major part of the plutonium deposits in the skeleton, a significant amount is found in the soft tissues, especially in the liver. A number of dogs from two experimental categories have been autopsied, and the amount of plutonium in the liver, spleen, and kidneys determined. The first category consists of 5-level dogs which were injected for special studies and sacrificed at times ranging from 1 day to 2.5 years after injection. The second one consists of dogs that have succumbed from the effects of plutonium and includes dogs of dose levels 3, 4, and 5.

The results for all three tissues show a slight decrease with time, incomplete deposition at 1 day, and considerable scatter. The total plutonium in the liver is

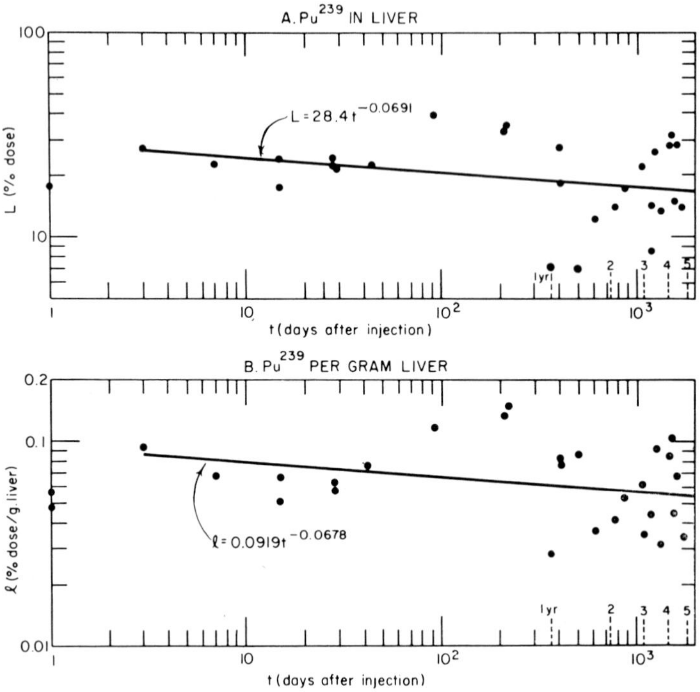

FIG. 5. *A*, total amount of Pu^{239} in the beagle liver. *B*, concentration of Pu^{239} in the liver.

plotted in Fig. 5*A*, and the concentration appears in Fig. 5*B*. Most of the liver values fall between 15 and 30% of the injected dose, and there is perhaps less scatter in the concentration points. Equations to describe the decrease in both amount and concentration are

$$L = 28.4t^{-0.0691} \tag{8}$$

$$l = 0.0919t^{-0.0678} \tag{8a}$$

where L is per cent dose per liver, l is per cent dose per gram, and t is in days. The amount in the spleen is small and variable and decreases with time, as shown in Fig. 6*A*. The equation for S (per cent dose per spleen) is

$$S = 0.391t^{-0.119} \tag{9}$$

The amount in the kidneys is also small but decreases a little more rapidly than in the liver and spleen. The data appear in Fig. 6*B*, and the equation for K (per cent dose per two kidneys) is

$$K = 0.476t^{-0.167} \tag{10}$$

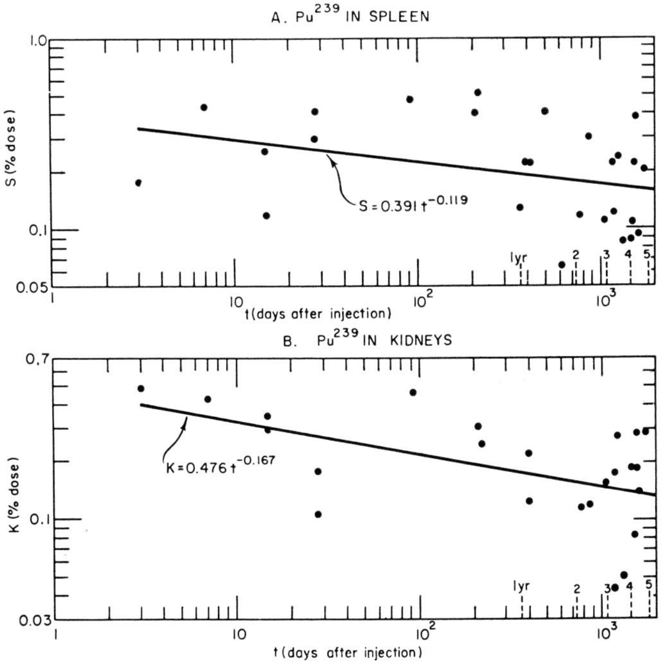

FIG. 6. *A*, amount of Pu^{239} in the spleen. *B*, amount of Pu^{239} in two kidneys.

The kidney concentration is about ten times the plasma concentration and thus cannot be accounted for merely by the amount of blood in the kidneys. (The 1-day values were not used in calculating equations 8, 8a, 9, and 10.)

Plutonium in the skeleton. One humerus and the third lumbar vertebra from a number of dogs have been analyzed for plutonium. The results in Fig. 7*A* and 7*B* show considerably less scatter than those for the soft tissues. The amount in the humerus is constant, whereas that in the third lumbar decreases with time. For H (per cent dose per humerus) and V (per cent dose per third lumbar vertebra), with the 1-day values excluded, we calculate

$$H = 2.08\ (\pm 0.49) \tag{11}$$

$$V = 1.12t^{-0.104} \tag{12}$$

In addition, the entire skeletons of four dogs were analyzed. The skeletons of two dogs sacrificed at 29 and 44 days were divided into five samples for measurement, and these skeletons contained 62 and 66% of the injected dose, respectively. Each bone of the other two skeletons was measured separately (increasing the error in the total). At 365 days, 53% was found in the skeleton, and at 610 days,

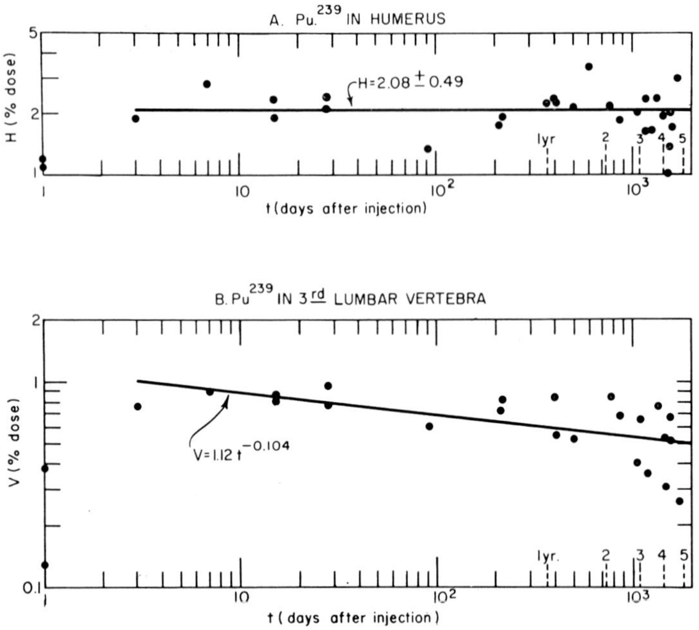

FIG. 7. *A*, amount of Pu^{239} in one humerus. *B*, amount of Pu^{239} in the third lumbar vertebra.

the observed value was 55%. These results are consistent with a decrease with time as shown below.

Calculated retention. From the results of the excretion studies we can calculate plutonium retention as a function of time. Since we are mainly concerned with fairly long times after injection, we shall use the average cumulative excretion for the first 22 days and X_2 (equation 6). The retention, R, at $t \geq 22$ days, is

$$R(t) = 100 - 12.1 - \int_{22}^{t} X_2 \, dt = 90.0 - 0.434t^{0.515} \tag{13}$$

where R is per cent injected dose and t is days after injection. From Table I we see that $R(22) = 87.9\%$ and $R(1461) = 71.5\%$, or that 16.4% has been excreted between 22 days and 4 years. Is this consistent with the results from our measurements of bones and soft tissues?

The two dogs sacrificed at 29 and 44 days averaged 64% in skeleton, 22% in the liver (in good agreement with equation 8), and 2 to 3% in blood, pelt, and other soft tissues to give a total of 88 to 89%, which is in excellent agreement with $R(22)$. At 22 days $L = 23\%$, and at 4 years $L = 17\%$ and $R = 71.5\%$, from equations 8 and 13, respectively. Since the blood, pelt, and other soft tissues at 4 years contain less than 1%, there must be $71 - 17 = 54\%$ in the skeleton. Thus, of the 16% excreted between 22 days and 4 years, 6% comes from the liver and about 10% from the skeleton. These values apply to our composite "average" dog, and, of course, there will be individual variation. Our measurements of the humerus showed no decrease with time, however. On the basis of the above discussion, the anticipated decrease is by a factor of 54/64. Accordingly, if $H(22) = 2.08\%$, we expect that $H(1461) = (54/64) \times 2.15 = 1.76\%$, a decrease of only 0.3%, which is less than one standard deviation of our average value for H (equation 11). Thus, we cannot determine the decrease in skeletal plutonium by measuring a sample which represents only 3% of the total, for the dog-to-dog variation masks the slight change with time. The fact that we do seem to notice a decrease in V suggests a nonuniform skeletal decrease. Since we know the total retention and the soft tissue amounts, we can determine the amount in bone by difference. This has been done, and the results can be approximated by the following equation for B, the per cent of injected dose in bone at t days after injection:

$$B = 72t^{-0.040} \tag{14}$$

DISCUSSION

Blood, tissue, and excretion measurements. The agreement between excretion measurements and tissue measurements has been demonstrated above in the calculation of retention. Also, the dogs with lower than average amounts in the skeletal samples had higher tissue values, and vice versa. The general aspects of plutonium metabolism, such as high retention and principal deposition in skeleton and liver, are in agreement with many prior studies (*13*) and will not be discussed further.

The slow removal of plutonium from the blood during the first day undoubtedly results from the protein binding of the plutonium. The success of citrate in competing with the blood proteins was anticipated from *in vivo* studies (*13*) in which citrate increased early plutonium excretion.

In view of the changing fecal-to-urinary excretion ratio (Fig. 4) during the early time period, it is at first surprising that the power functions for P_1, X_1, and U_1 (equations 2, 4, and 5) have very similar exponents. A careful inspection of the data shows, however, that the variable early F/U ratio results mainly from the inherent lag in fecal excretion which is accentuated by the very rapid decrease in early excretion rate. No elaborate mechanism is needed to explain the data, although an initial biliary excretion of a small amount of plutonium may well be a factor.

The agreement among the exponents of P_2, X_2, and U_2 (equations 3, 6, and 7) is quite good, especially since they are slowly changing functions and the amounts of plutonium measured were very small. The value for the renal clearance of plutonium, 33 to 40 gm of plasma per day, is very low. The corresponding value observed for radium (*2*) is 1690 gm of plasma per day!

Comparison with other dog studies. Early in the history of plutonium, Painter *et al.* (*14*) studied the metabolism and toxicity of plutonium in mongrel adult dogs. Their dose levels were 1.7 to 17 times as high as our highest; the plutonium was given in the hexavalent form in citrate solution (but no description of the preparation is given); and intravenous and intramuscular administration were compared. The results of the plasma and excretion studies made on the mongrels given plutonium intravenously are amazingly similar to those obtained with our beagles. The plasma concentration decreased slowly during the first 10 hours, then fell according to a power function with the exponent 1.55 as compared with 1.63 of equation 2. Also, the urinary excretion decreased according to $0.817t^{-1.53}$. Between 2 and 20 days, individual renal clearance values for the mongrels ranged from 12 to 48 gm of plasma per day, and the average retention at 15 days was 85.7%. Most of their dogs died early, so comparisons during the second time period are limited. There are sufficient excretion data, however, for two of the mongrels to show the same change of slope (in a log-log plot) which led us to treat our data in two time periods.

Comparison with rats and man. The metabolism of plutonium in rats has been studied extensively. The most significant difference between the metabolism in the rat and the dog is in the liver deposition. The initial deposition in the rat liver is about the same as that of the dog, but it decreases much more rapidly (*15, 16*). Studies at this laboratory in which rats were injected with material similar to that given the beagles showed a maximum liver deposition of 33% occurring by the fourth day, which subsequently decreased according to $t^{-0.75}$.

The metabolism of plutonium has also been studied in man (*17, 18*). These individuals received tetravalent plutonium in 0.014 *M* citrate buffer, pH = 5.5, by intravenous injection. The excretion rate was measured through 5 years after injection, and the data were described by a single power function:

$$X(\mathrm{H}) = 0.79t^{-0.94} \tag{15}$$

The human excretion rate is compared with that of the beagles in Fig. 3 and is seen to be less throughout the 5-year period. Langham's (*17*) calculated retention for human beings is 96.7% at 22 days after injection and 90.7% at 4 years, as compared with 87.9% and 71.5% for beagles at the same times. Some tissue measurements were also made by Langham and co-workers. From these data they estimated that 65.7% of the injected dose deposited in the skeleton, 23.1% in liver, 0.4% in spleen, and 0.4% in kidneys. This distribution is remarkably similar to what we have measured in the beagles. In addition, the liver deposition was like that of the beagles in that it persisted over long periods of time (in contrast with the observations on rats).

Calculation of radiation dose. This exhaustive study of the metabolism of plutonium in adult beagle dogs was made primarily to enable us to calculate radiation dose to the various tissues. Pu^{239} decays by α-particle emission to U^{235} with a half-period of 24,300 years, and hence decay is negligible in the periods with which we are concerned. The half-period of U^{235} is so long that we may consider U^{235} a stable isotope. The decay energy of Pu^{239} is 5.24 Mev per disintegration; hence the energy per day from 1 μc of Pu^{239} is

$$5.24 \frac{\text{Mev}}{\text{dis}} \times \frac{3.7 \times 10^4 \times 60 \times 60 \times 24 \text{ dis}}{1 \mu c \text{ Pu}^{239}} \frac{}{\text{day}} \times \frac{1.60 \times 10^{-6} \text{ erg}}{\text{Mev}} \quad (16)$$

$$= (2.68 \times 10^4 \text{ ergs/day})/\mu c \text{ Pu}^{239}$$

First, let us consider the soft tissues. Radioautographic studies show that the plutonium deposits both in the reticuloendothelial system and in the parenchymal cells of the liver (W. S. S. Jee, private communication). Let us assume that the distribution is uniform and calculate the dose rate to the liver, dD_L/dt, which is just the product of the plutonium concentration in the liver (equation 8a) and the rate of energy release by the plutonium. If A is the injected dose in microcuries,

$$\begin{aligned} dD_L/dt &= (9.2 \times 10^{-4}\, t^{-0.068}\, A \times 2.68 \times 10^{-4} \text{ ergs/gm})/\text{day} \quad (17) \\ &= (0.25t^{-0.068}\, A) \text{ rads/day} \end{aligned}$$

since 1 rad = 100 ergs/gm tissue. The cumulative dose to the liver at any time, t, is

$$D_L = \int_1^t (0.25t^{-0.068}A) + D_L^1 = 0.26(t^{0.93} - 1)A + D_L^1 \quad (18)$$

where $D^1{}_L$ is the dose for the first day. For times of interest in a chronic study, i.e., $t \geq 100$ days, $(t^{0.93} - 1) \simeq t^{0.93}$, and $D^1{}_L$ can be neglected to give

$$D_L \simeq 0.26t^{0.93}\, A \text{ rads} \quad (18a)$$

If uniform distribution in the kidneys is assumed, similar calculations can be made from equation 10, and the average weight of two kidneys equals 55.6 gm. The dose rate to the kidneys is

$$dD_K/dt = (0.023t^{-0.17}A) \text{ rads/day} \quad (19)$$

and the cumulative dose at time t is

$$D_K = \int_1^t (0.023t^{-0.17}A)\, dt + D_K^1 \simeq 0.028t^{0.83}A \text{ rads} \quad (20)$$

There is about a fourfold variation in the weights of spleens, since the dog spleen is to a certain extent an elastic container for blood. For this reason, even an average dose calculation may not have much significance and will not be made.

Since the major long-term effects of plutonium are skeletal ones, the calculation of skeletal dose is of considerable importance. The average weight of the beagles at injection was 9.0 kg, which gives a skeleton weight of 900 gm, since our dogs are about 10% skeleton (B. J. Stover, D. R. Atherton, and W. Stevens, unpublished data). The lack of uniformity of plutonium deposition in the skeleton is well known, and the assumption of uniform distribution leads to poor estimates of localized radiation dose but does permit the calculation of average dose. The average dose rate to the skeleton of a dog injected with A μc's is, from equations 14 and 16,

$$dD_B/dt = (0.21t^{-0.04} A) \text{ rads/day} \quad (21)$$

The cumulative skeletal dose at t days is

$$D_B = \int_1^t (0.21t^{-0.04} A)\, dt + D_B^1 \simeq 0.22t^{0.96} A \text{ rads} \quad (22)$$

Comparison with Ra^{226}. When radium is administered to an adult dog in a single intravenous injection, the skeletal distribution is also far from uniform. Since radium is chemically and hence metabolically similar to calcium, in contrast with plutonium which has no metabolic analog and which is insoluble at physiological pH's, the microscopic distribution of radium in the skeleton is quite different from that of plutonium.[6] Another important difference is that the amount of radium in the soft tissues is negligible and essentially all the radiation dose is delivered to the skeleton. The cumulative skeletal dose at t days for an adult beagle dog (*2*),[7] injected with A μc of Ra^{226} is

$$D_B(Ra^{226}) \simeq 0.48t^{0.80} A \text{ rads} \quad (23)$$

In Fig. 8, the average cumulative dose to bone, liver, and kidneys per microcurie of Pu^{239} injected and the average cumulative dose to bone per microcurie of Ra^{226} injected are compared. Uniform distribution and a 900-gm skeleton are assumed. The doses to the liver and to bone of plutonium dogs are essentially the same, yet skeletal damage predominates. This finding indicates that the assumption of uniform distribution is more valid for liver than for bone,[8] which is in agreement with radioautographic findings (*19*; W. S. S. Jee, private communication).

Let us now neglect the soft tissues completely and make a preliminary qualified comparison of the skeletal damage occurring in dogs injected with plutonium and radium. In general, we are seeing a greater variation in skeletal pathology in plutonium dogs than in radium dogs. This observation correlates with the greater individual variation in plutonium metabolism. A less generalized comparison must be

[6] Space does not permit reviewing the extensive literature on the different modes of plutonium and alkaline earth deposition in the skeleton. For an early report, see Hamilton (*19*).

[7] The calculation in reference (*2*) assumes 1000 gm of skeleton, and equation 23 assumes 900 gm.

[8] Another point of view is, of course, that the skeleton is more "radiosensitive" than is the liver.

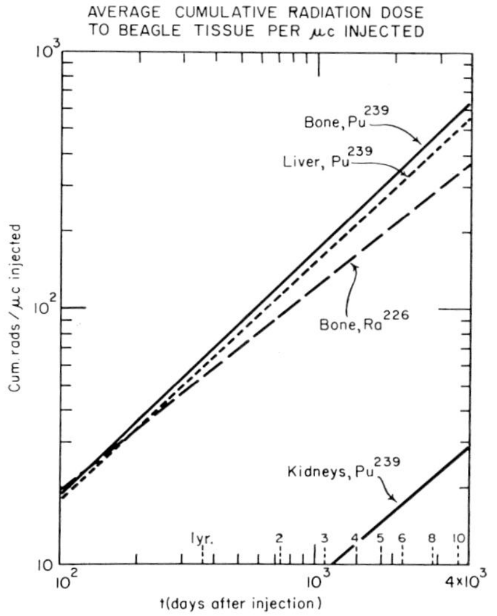

FIG. 8. The average cumulative radiation dose to bone, liver, and kidneys after the intravenous injection of 1 μc of Pu^{239} into a 9-kg adult beagle dog, and the average cumulative dose to beagle bone after the injection of 1 μc of Ra^{226}.

carefully qualified, since the majority of these dogs are still living and different lengths of time have elapsed since they were injected. Bone tumors have developed in plutonium dogs with average skeletal doses of 500 to 7400 rads,[9] and in radium dogs over the range 5600 to 15,000 rads. The minima differ by a factor of 10, and the maxima by a factor of 2. Frequent careful radiological examinations of the dogs are made to detect the earliest changes in bone architecture. The earliest minimal changes are seen in the jaw (*20*) at average doses of about 140 rads for plutonium and about 290 for radium, a difference of about a factor of 2. Thus, a preliminary comparison of skeletal damage on the basis of amount of energy dissipated in bone shows that plutonium is roughly twice as damaging as radium.

SUMMARY

1. The metabolism of plutonium in young adult beagle dogs has been studied over a period of 4 years after a single intravenous injection of PuIV in citrate buffer of pH 3.5.

2. Three time periods were arbitrarily chosen to facilitate treatment of the plasma concentration and excretion rate data. For times greater than 3 weeks after injection, the per cent retention calculated from excretion measurement is

$$R = 90.0 - 0.434t^{0.515} \qquad (t \text{ in days})$$

[9] Time of death was used in these calculations since the difference between latent period and survival is small.

The major part of the plutonium deposits in the skeleton and the liver, and the results of tissue measurements agree well with the retention calculated from excretion.

3. No effect of dose level, age at injection, or sex could be demonstrated in the excretion studies. Comparison of our results with those of some early studies in which mongrel dogs were given much larger doses showed remarkable similarities.

4. Plutonium metabolism in the dog is more like that in man than in rat. The liver deposition persists for long times in man and dog, but not in the rat. The retention in man is a little higher than in beagles, but the distributions are quite similar.

5. The average dose rates and average cumulative doses to the skeleton and to the liver of our beagles are about equal (when calculated on the basis of uniform distribution). Skeletal damage greatly predominates, however.

6. A limited preliminary comparison of skeletal effects of Pu^{239} and Ra^{226} on the basis of the amount of energy dissipated in bone shows that plutonium is more toxic.

ACKNOWLEDGMENTS

Since this work was done over a period of years, it is difficult to give individual recognition to all who have participated. We especially wish to acknowledge the assistance of K. C. Humpheries, Mrs. D. S. Buster, G. D. Westenskow, C. E. Rehfeld, and R. C. Bay. In addition, we wish to mention that many other members of the Radiobiology Laboratory, both past and present, have contributed to these studies.

RECEIVED: March 5, 1958

REFERENCES

1. Chalk River, Canada, Conference of September 29–30, 1949, reported in *Natl. Bur. Standards (U. S.) Handbook* **52,** 14 (1953).
2. M. A. VAN DILLA, B. J. STOVER, R. L. FLOYD, D. R. ATHERTON, and D. H. TAYSUM, Radium (Ra^{226}) and radon (Em^{222}) metabolism in dogs. *Radiation Research* **8,** 417–437 (1958).
3. C. W. MAYS, M. A. VAN DILLA, R. L. FLOYD, and J. S. ARNOLD, Radon retention in radium-injected beagles. *Radiation Research,* **8,** 480–489 (1958).
4. J. C. HINDMAN, K. A. KRAUS, J. J. HOWLAND, JR., and B. B. CUNNINGHAM, in *The Transuranium Elements* (G. T. Seaborg, J. J. Katz, and W. M. Manning, eds.), pp. 121–132, McGraw-Hill Book Company, New York, 1949.
5. R. E. CONNICK, W. H. MCVEY, and G. E. SHELINE, *The Transuranium Elements* (G. T. Seaborg, J. J. Katz, and W. M. Manning, eds.), pp. 175–179, McGraw-Hill Book Company, New York, 1949.
6. K. A. KRAUS, in *The Transuranium Elements* (G. T. Seaborg, J. J. Katz, and W. M. Manning, eds.), pp. 264–267, McGraw-Hill Book Company, New York, 1949; J. C. HINDMAN, pp. 388–404 *ibid.*
7. J. SCHUBERT and D. REVINSON, Studies on PuIV solutions in the presence and absence of citric acid. U. S. Atomic Energy Commission Report CH-3578 (1946).*

* Available at USAEC depository libraries.

8. B. J. Stover, D. R. Atherton, and N. Keller, University of Utah Radiobiology Laboratory Progress Report, pp. 13–15 (September 30, 1956).
9. B. J. Stover and D. R. Atherton, University of Utah Radiobiology Laboratory Progress Report AECU-3522, pp. 135–143 (March 31, 1957).
10. J. Schubert, L. S. Meyers, Jr., and J. A. Jackson, The analytical procedures of the bioassay group at the Argonne National Laboratory. Argonne National Laboratory Report ANL-4509 (1951).*
11. J. H. Dougherty and K. Seymour, University of Utah Radiobiology Laboratory Progress Report AECU-3522, pp. 69–70 (March 31, 1957).
12. J. A. Muntz and E. S. G. Barron, Combination of plutonium with plasma proteins. U. S. Atomic Energy Commission Report CH-3757 (1947).*
13. J. Katz, Plutonium metabolism. A literature review. U. S. Atomic Energy Commission Report HW-21868 (1951).*
14. E. Painter, E. Russell, C. L. Prosser, M. N. Swift, W. Kisieleski, and G. Sacher, Clinical physiology of dogs injected with plutonium. U. S. Atomic Energy Commission Report AEDC-2042 (June, 1946).*
15. J. Carritt, R. Fryxell, J. Kleinschmidt, R. Kleinschmidt, W. Langham, A. San Pietro, R. Schaffer, and B. Schnap, The distribution and excretion of plutonium administered intravenously to the rat. *J. Biol. Chem.* **171,** 273 (1947).
16. D. R. Atherton, R. G. Horne, W. Stevens, and B. J. Stover, University of Utah Radiobiology Laboratory Progress Report, pp. 45–47 (September 30, 1956).
17. W. H. Langham, Determination of internally deposited radioactive isotopes from excretion analyses, *Am. Ind. Hyg. Assoc. Quart.* **17,** 305–318 (1956).
18. W. H. Langham, S. H. Bassett, P. S. Harris, and R. E. Carter, Distribution and excretion of plutonium administered intravenously to man, Los Alamos Scientific Laboratory Report LA-1151 (1950).
19. J. G. Hamilton, The metabolic properties of the fission products and actinide elements. *Revs. Mod. Phys.* **20,** 718–728 (1948).
20. W. R. Christensen, C. E. Rehfeld, G. N. Taylor, and W. Fisher, University of Utah Radiobiology Laboratory Progress Report AECU-3522, pp. 23–27 (March 31, 1957).

RADIATION RESEARCH **10**, 148–166 (1959)

The Effect of Single and Multiple Doses of Co^{60} Gamma-Radiation and Fission Neutron Radiation on the Incorporation of Fe^{59} into the Rat Erythropoietic System[1]

W. A. RAMBACH, J. A. D. COOPER, H. L. ALT, H. H. VOGEL, JR., J. W. CLARK,[2] AND D. L. JORDAN

Departments of Medicine and Biochemistry, Northwestern University Medical School, Chicago, Illinois, and Division of Biological and Medical Research, Argonne National Laboratory, Lemont, Illinois

INTRODUCTION

The detrimental effect of acutely delivered ionizing radiation on the erythropoietic system of man and animals has been well established by numerous histopathological investigations and extensively reviewed (*1–7*). Quantitative studies (*8–12*) of the effect of acute ionizing radiation on the erythropoietic system, utilizing Fe^{59}, have been shown to reflect radiation-induced functional changes. The present work has been concerned with a study of the effect of both single and multiple doses of Co^{60} γ-rays and fission neutrons on the distribution of Fe^{59} in rat plasma, bone marrow, red blood cells, liver, and spleen. From the data we have derived a comparison of the relative biological effectiveness of acute γ-radiation and neutron radiation, and, in conjunction with morphologic studies, have evaluated the functional capacity of the rat erythropoietic system.

MATERIALS AND METHODS

Animals and Radiation Exposure

Female albino rats of the Sprague-Dawley strain, with an average weight of 190 gm, were used in this study. On receipt from commercial sources, the animals were isolated for a 2-week period and then were selected at random for control or experimental use. One hundred and ninety animals, equally divided between experi-

[1] This work was supported in part by Contract AF 18(600)-1265 with the School of Aviation Medicine, USAF, and in part was performed under the auspices of the U. S. Atomic Energy Commission.

[2] Present address: Department of Radiology, Presbyterian-St. Luke's Hospital, Chicago, Illinois.

mental and control, were utilized for the acute radiation experiments, and 142 similarly divided were studied in the chronic phase.

The rats were exposed either to fission neutrons or to Co^{60} γ-rays in the γ-neutron radiation chamber (*13*) at the CP-5 research reactor of the Argonne National Laboratory.

In the acute radiation experiments groups of animals were exposed to ten dosages of 38 to 549 rads of γ-radiation and nine dosages of 40 to 283 rads of fission neutron radiation. In the chronic radiation experiments groups of animals were exposed once per week at weekly intervals as follows: γ-radiation: 16 rads × 5, 16 rads × 10, 32 rads × 5, 32 rads × 10, and 150 rads × 5; neutron radiation: 27 rads × 5, 27 rads × 10, and 81 rads × 5.

The animals were contained in a circular Lucite cage consisting of ten radially arranged compartments. Of the ten compartments, nine held one animal each and the tenth was occupied by a Victoreen dosimeter (Fig. 1). The radial arrangement permitted simultaneous isodose exposure. For all exposures the sensitive volume of the Victoreen chamber was held in the same standard position, approximating the mid-body region of the animals. The circular cage was contained within an aluminum cage holder and rotated by an electric motor one revolution per minute through the radiation field. Temperature-controlled room air (24°C) was fed by a blower system to the radiation chamber and to a control chamber, containing 9 animals and a dosimeter.

In order to ensure comparable radiation dosimetry, 9 animals were exposed simultaneously; however, at times fewer animals (never less than 4) were studied subsequently.

Radiation Dosimetry

Gamma-radiation. Gamma-radiation was obtained from eighteen sources of Co^{60} located in a radiation chamber as previously described (*13*). The sources were used at their closest proximity to the animal position. This produced a dose rate of 17 rads/min. At the conclusion of the experiments the dose rate had decayed to approximately 14 rads/min.

The γ-radiation dose was measured by a 25-r Victoreen chamber with a 4-mm plastic cap. The instrument had been previously calibrated for Co^{60} γ-radiation by the National Bureau of Standards.

Neutron radiation. Neutrons were obtained from the CP-5 reactor, operating at 1000 kw during the majority of the experiments, by the method of Zirkle (*14*), in which the thermal column of a reactor is used in conjunction with a plate of uranium to convert slow neutrons to fission neutrons. In the present work the uranium converter plate was inserted in the thermal column approximately 4 feet from the animal exposure position, and the fission neutrons were appropriately filtered to reduce contamination from either pile and fission γ-rays or thermal neutrons (*13*).

Fig. 1. Radiation exposure cage and holder.

A ¼-inch boral attenuator (Fig. 2) for thermal neutrons (*15*) was inserted between the CP-5 reactor and the uranium converter plate in order to control the flux of thermal neutrons reaching the converter and thus, indirectly, the flux of fission neutrons reaching the animals. Constructed as a variable-position shutter, the boral attenuator permitted the flux of fission neutrons to be altered for different experiments even though the power level of the reactor was kept constant.

The spectrum of fast neutrons used in these experiments was essentially the fission spectrum (*16*) modified by transmission through either 3 inches of lithium fluoride or ¼-inch boral and 4 inches of bismuth. This spectrum (for neutrons of 0.5 Mev and above) is illustrated in Fig. 3.[3] It is seen that the relative neutron flux

[3] The spectrum determination was accomplished by G. Kohler, E. Tochilin, and B. W. Shumway of the United States Naval Radiological Defense Laboratory. Ilford, type C-2, 200-micron nuclear track plates were exposed to the neutron field within the biological facility. After development by standard procedures (*17*), the lengths of proton tracks in the emulsion were measured according to a method for using the track plate as both radiator and detector (*18*). The number of neutrons in four overlapping energy regions was determined to obtain accurate estimates of flux in regions of low neutron population. The results were adjusted to bring overlapping flux values into agreement so that a smooth curve could be drawn.

Fig. 2. Boral filter plate used at CP-5 to alter flux of thermal neutrons reaching uranium converter plate.

density reaches its maximum value at about 0.5 Mev and falls to 10% of this peak value at 2.0 Mev. Beyond 3.0 Mev the slope of the curve is similar to that obtained by Watt for thermal fission neutrons from U^{235} (*16*).

The neutron radiation dose was measured by a 25-r Victoreen chamber (25 II) calibrated against a tissue-equivalent ionization chamber of the Failla-Rossi type.[4]

[4] This calibration was obtained with the aid of H. H. Rossi of the Radiological Research Laboratory, Columbia University. A conversion factor of 2.6 was used at CP-5 to convert readings on a Victoreen 25-r chamber to total rads. Corroboration of this calibration was obtained through (1) the use of chemical dosimeters supplied and evaluated by Lt. Sanford C. Sigoloff of the Radiobiological Laboratory of the University of Texas and the United States Air Force, Austin, Texas; (2) the use of film detectors, gold foils, and sulfur disks supplied and evaluated

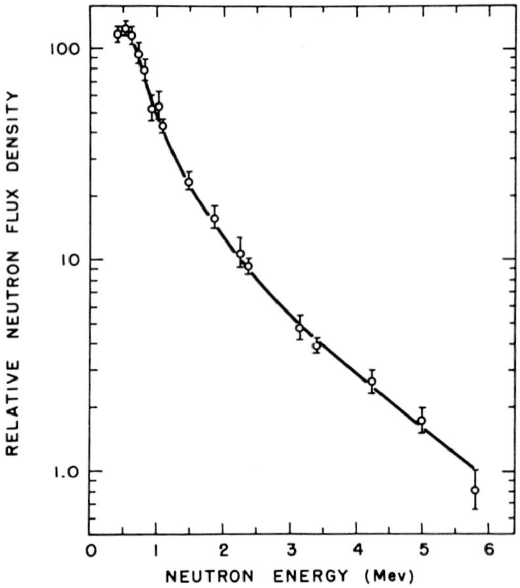

FIG. 3. Neutron fission spectrum within the biological facility at the Argonne CP-5 reactor.

The Victoreen readings were corrected for temperature, barometric pressure, and a chamber factor relating the instrument to a "standard" 25-r Victoreen chamber. The neutron doses are total doses containing 10 to 15% γ-ray contamination.[4] All radiation doses are reported and discussed in terms of the international radiation unit, the rad (that quantity of ionizing radiation which will deposit 100 ergs of energy per gram of tissue).[5] The intensity of the fission neutrons was 3 to 4 rads/min.

---

by E. Tochilin and collaborators of the U. S. Naval Radiological Defense Laboratory; and (3) the use of Hurst-type, small proportional counters (*19*) under the direction of J. A. Auxier and E. B. Wagner of the Oak Ridge National Laboratory. The dosimetry supplied by these groups was also used to ascertain the percentage of γ-ray contamination of the neutron flux. An additional check of the neutron dosimetry has been obtained from two boron trifluoride counters, surrounded by a cadmium shield and paraffin moderator, and installed in the shielding above the radiation chamber.

[5] For a conversion factor from roentgens to rads for Co^{60} X-ray we have used a figure of 0.97, calculated by John S. Laughlin, Division of Biophysics, Memorial Center for Cancer and Allied Diseases, New York. This absorbed dose was calculated for Co^{60} γ-rays using a "whole mouse" of the following chemical composition: O, 69.8%; H, 9.8%; C, 13.9%; N, 4.4%; Ca, 0.75%; P, 1.3%; K, 0.3%; S, 0.2%.

A conversion factor of 2.58 to 2.62 was used to convert readings on Victoreen r-chamber to total rads of neutrons.

Biological Measurements

Studies of Fe^{59} utilization in the normal rat (*10, 20*) show that the bone marrow achieves a maximum label in 6 hours. This 6-hour uptake is maximally depressed when measured 24 hours after X-irradiation (*10*; Rambach, Cooper, and Alt, unpublished observations). Accordingly, in the present acute radiation experiments, Fe^{59} was injected 24 hours after irradiation, and its 6-hour incorporation into bone marrow, red blood cells, liver, spleen and plasma was then studied. In the chronic radiation experiments the 6-hour uptake was determined 10 to 11 days after the last irradiation in order to obviate the acute effect of the last radiation dose. Control animals for both acute and chronic experiments were similarly studied.

The rats were given an intracardiac injection of approximately 0.5 μc of Fe^{59} as ferrous citrate contained in 0.5 ml of solution with a pH of 6.0. Six hours later the animals were sacrificed by aortic exsanguination under ether anesthesia. The blood of all groups was collected in disodium ethylenediaminetetraacetic acid (Na_2EDTA), and microhematocrits were obtained. One milliliter of well-mixed whole blood was set aside in a plastic test tube for later determination of activity. The remainder of the whole blood was centrifuged, and 2.0-ml aliquots of plasma were removed and saved in plastic tubes for counting. The femora were removed and stripped of surrounding tissue. The spleen and liver were removed and weighed. Subsequently, the aliquots of whole blood, the plasma aliquots, the femora, the whole spleen, and a weighed portion of liver were counted by standard scintillation techniques. The activity per unit of plasma was subtracted from the activity per unit of whole blood to obtain red cell activity. From the hematocrit and an average blood volume of 5.18 ml per 100 gm of body weight (obtained from Fe^{59} blood volume studies on 15 animals of the same strain and age range as the experimental animals), the per cent injected dose of Fe^{59} appearing in the total red cell mass was calculated. The per cent Fe^{59} appearing in the total bone marrow was calculated on the assumption that the femoral marrow represented 16% of the total marrow mass, as demonstrated by Baxter *et al.* (*10*) and corroborated in this laboratory by Fe^{59} labeling and counting of all the skeletal components. (Counts contributed by the iron content of bone and by the labeled circulating cells in the marrow have been shown in this laboratory to contribute a negligible proportion of the total count.) Fe^{59} uptake by liver and spleen were calculated for the total organ.

Peripheral blood studies including hemoglobin, hematocrit, red cell count, white cell count, reticulocyte count, platelet count, and differential white cell count were done on the animals exposed to repeated doses of radiation. Hemoglobin was measured by the oxyhemoglobin photoelectric method; hematocrits were determined by the microhematocrit procedure; reticulocytes were enumerated by the wet cresyl blue method; differential counts were done on Wright-stained films; and the platelet, white, and red cell counts were determined by the usual standard laboratory procedures.

TABLE I

EFFECT OF ACUTE γ-RADIATION ON Fe^{59} DISTRIBUTION[a]

Radiation dose (rads)	*Number of animals*	*6-Hour Fe^{59} uptake (% injected dose)*				
		Bone marrow	*RBC*	*Plasma*	*Liver*	*Spleen*
38	5	19.63 ±2.43	3.31 ±1.26	5.05 ±0.70	14.68 ±1.06	0.71 ±0.19
Control (no radiation)	5	23.04 ±1.44	7.78 ±1.12	3.04 ±1.24	12.34 ±1.17	1.98 ±0.57
49	4	16.55 ±4.26	4.28 ±0.84	6.37 ±1.99	17.31 ±2.71	0.52 ±0.08
Control	5	21.46 ±2.81	5.92 ±2.76	4.28 ±2.30	14.93 ±2.71	1.01 ±0.42
69	5	14.19 ±5.41	1.37 ±0.77	6.09 ±1.48	12.88 ±4.34	0.54 ±0.19
Control	5	17.28 ±5.82	4.45 ±1.91	3.72 ±1.13	10.91 ±4.99	1.24 ±1.18
92	5	13.40 ±1.51	2.20 ±1.17	7.40 ±1.65	21.82 ±3.56	0.58 ±0.09
Control	5	21.61 ±3.02	5.91 ±1.23	5.37 ±3.03	15.03 ±2.35	1.53 ±0.45
91	4	11.74 ±2.73	2.13 ±2.93	10.22 ±3.99	17.05 ±6.89	0.54 ±0.10
Control	5	22.90 ±4.91	5.14 ±2.46	5.03 ±4.45	10.89 ±1.94	1.55 ±1.28
140	5	6.54 ±2.12	0.63 ±0.60	11.90 ±1.18	20.34 ±4.41	0.36 ±0.08
Control	4	21.00 ±2.78	5.10 ±1.59	4.04 ±0.75	13.56 ±1.99	1.18 ±0.49
143	5	6.75 ±1.16	0.06 ±0.13	14.10 ±1.06	20.22 ±2.23	0.50 ±0.05
Control	4	22.72 ±2.80	3.96 ±0.20	3.84 ±2.15	12.88 ±7.00	1.11 ±0.18
315	5	5.17 ±0.41	0.34 ±0.34	11.38 ±0.73	48.51 ±3.97	0.90 ±0.87
Control	5	14.27 ±1.52	2.41 ±0.78	6.22 ±0.83	48.76 ±3.03	1.84 ±0.87
334	5	4.44 ±0.33	0.05 ±1.12	15.51 ±0.50	23.46 ±1.06	0.34 ±0.08
Control	5	20.99 ±1.86	4.20 ±1.17	5.40 ±1.67	13.55 ±2.59	1.11 ±0.19
549	5	3.69 ±0.48	0.37 ±0.51	21.76 ±2.94	22.72 ±3.66	0.43 ±0.59
Control	5	16.93 ±5.57	3.54 ±1.59	10.21 ±2.42	16.54 ±3.00	0.80 ±0.41

[a] Underlined values are statistically significant at the 0.95 level or better.

TABLE II

EFFECT OF ACUTE NEUTRON RADIATION ON FE^{59} DISTRIBUTION[a]

Radiation dose (rads)	*Number of animals*	*6-Hour Fe^{59} uptake (% injected dose)*				
		Bone marrow	*RBC*	*Plasma*	*Liver*	*Spleen*
40	4	16.44	2.16	11.74	17.96	0.87
		±5.30	±1.78	±3.45	±2.36	±0.36
Control	5	19.36	6.23	7.39	15.58	2.57
		±5.73	±3.93	±3.01	±4.05	±1.66
41	4	21.99	2.91	4.64	17.49	0.90
		±1.71	±1.32	±0.80	±1.98	±0.40
Control	4	24.27	8.03	3.88	11.09	2.05
		±4.66	±1.54	±3.03	±0.44	±2.22
56	5	16.08	1.67	5.33	21.10	0.64
		±2.61	±0.79	±1.14	±3.48	±0.24
Control	5	20.66	6.13	2.91	14.44	2.84
		±2.36	±1.59	±1.78	±1.26	±1.32
66	5	13.11	1.32	8.36	19.60	0.56
		±1.94	±0.99	±1.15	±0.74	±0.12
Control	5	19.29	3.69	5.52	13.76	1.13
		±3.73	±1.20	±1.16	±1.59	±0.41
66	5	10.81	0.14	15.67	17.83	0.50
		±2.06	±0.40	±3.21	±3.89	±0.12
Control	4	24.72	4.76	4.82	11.19	1.32
		±3.25	±0.86	±1.07	±2.42	±0.28
86	5	10.69	0.54	8.74	20.40	0.57
		±3.36	±0.26	±1.87	±4.62	±0.16
Control	4	23.30	7.62	1.72	10.37	2.61
		±3.02	±1.58	±0.78	±2.12	±0.79
115	5	5.78	0.00	14.33	21.06	0.37
		±1.04	±0.00	±2.75	±2.82	±0.04
Control	4	20.34	2.60	7.68	14.24	0.67
		±2.00	±0.81	±2.27	±1.55	±0.10
162	4	7.22	0.16	17.67	23.94	0.42
		±1.18	±0.28	±4.26	±1.75	±0.06
Control	5	21.26	5.52	6.12	13.08	1.16
		±3.94	±2.07	±2.60	±3.73	±0.63
283	5	5.46	0.20	9.04	53.00	0.82
		±0.43	±0.19	±1.84	±3.31	±0.12
Control	5	14.89	2.73	4.96	46.20	1.55
		±1.13	±1.47	±0.51	±2.16	±0.44

[a] Underlined values are statistically significant at the 0.95 level or better.

RESULTS

The effects of acute γ-radiation and neutron radiation on the 6-hour Fe^{59} distribution are presented in Tables I and II. As the radiation dose is increased, the percentage of Fe^{59} appearing in the marrow declines, the red-cell label decreases, and the plasma level of Fe^{59} increases. In the irradiated animals the level of Fe^{59} in the spleen is consistently lower than control values, and the amount of labeled iron appearing in the liver is always greater than that seen in the controls.

A combined plot of the bone-marrow data for neutron- and γ-irradiated animals is presented in Figs. 4 and 5. It appears that there is little difference between the effects exerted by equal doses of the two types of radiation and that doses greater than approximately 150 rads produce little additional depression of bone-marrow uptake.

The effects of chronic radiation on 6-hour Fe^{59} distribution and on peripheral blood morphology 10 to 11 days after radiation are presented in Tables III through

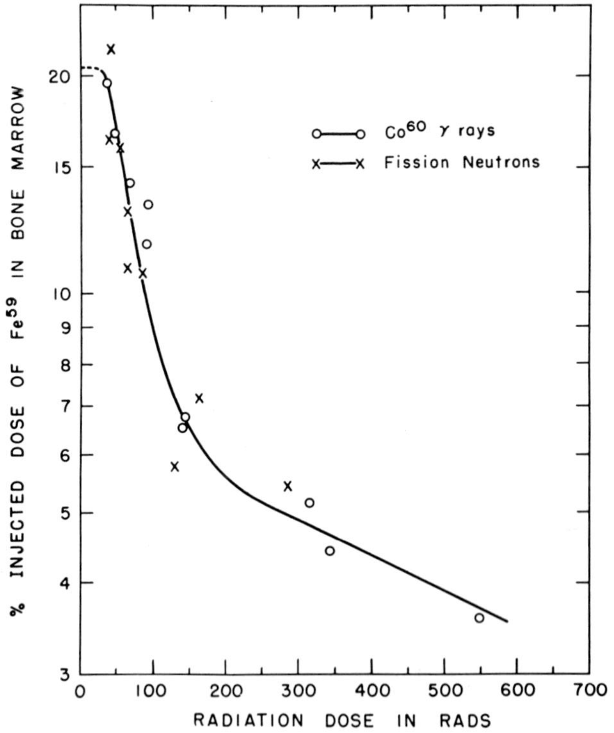

FIG. 4. Semilogarithmic plot of Fe^{59} incorporation into bone marrow as a function of Co^{60} γ-radiation and fission neutron radiation. (The absolute value at zero dose is the average of all controls.)

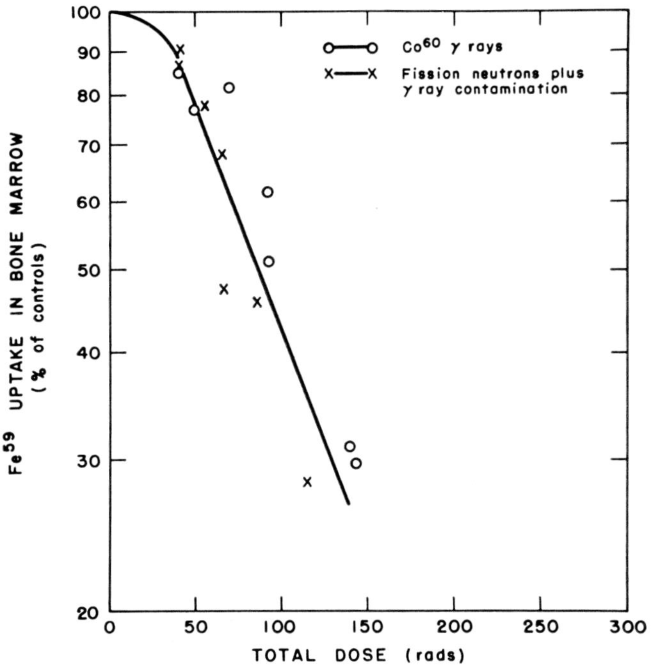

FIG. 5. Semilogarithmic plot of total dose and Fe^{59} uptake by rat bone marrow, calculated as per cent of controls for each irradiation.

V. Except for the higher Fe^{59} incorporation in the spleens of those animals exposed either to five doses of 150 rads of γ-rays or to 81 rads of neutrons, there is no statistically significant difference between the Fe^{59} distribution of any of the irradiated groups and their respective controls. Morphologically, however, certain changes are apparent. Significant depression of the hematocrit is observed in the highest dose groups both in the γ-ray and in the neutron series, and this is accompanied by an elevation in the reticulocyte count. There is no significant difference between the control and irradiated animals in terms of red-cell count, hemoglobin, or platelet count, with two unexplained exceptions noted in the 32 rads $\times$ 5 group (Table IV). The total white-blood-cell count is lower, with statistical significance, in the 16 rads $\times$ 10, 150 rads $\times$ 5, 27 rads $\times$ 5, and 81 rads $\times$ 5 groups, and there is a consistent trend to lower values in all irradiated animals. Statistically significant depressions of lymphocyte levels are noted in the 16 rads $\times$ 10, 32 rads $\times$ 5, 150 rads $\times$ 5, 27 rads $\times$ 5, and 81 rads $\times$ 5 groups.

Abnormally elevated Fe^{59} values for the liver, decreases for marrow and red cells, and a trend toward higher plasma levels are to be noted in control and experimental animals in the 283-rad and 315-rad acute neutron and γ-ray groups, and in the

TABLE III

EFFECT OF CHRONIC RADIATION ON Fe^{59} DISTRIBUTION[a]

Radiation dose per week (rads)	*Group*	*Number of animals*	*6-Hour Fe^{59} uptake (% injected dose)*				
			Bone marrow	*RBC*	*Plasma*	*Liver*	*Spleen*
			Gamma-irradiation				
16	5 week	8	23.38 ±2.70	5.01 ±1.48	5.80 ±2.48	13.77 ±2.78	1.70 ±0.41
Control	5 week	8	21.82 ±2.58	4.70 ±1.72	5.85 ±0.98	13.15 ±2.14	1.66 ±0.73
16	10 week	9	27.33 ±3.94	12.15 ±2.25	2.81 ±1.13	9.27 ±1.54	3.50 ±0.74
Control	10 week	5	27.71 ±4.09	9.45 ±2.47	4.74 ±3.90	9.56 ±1.19	3.64 ±1.40
32	5 week	9	28.94 ±3.82	7.90 ±4.28	4.46 ±1.59	12.93 ±1.52	2.27 ±1.46
Control	5 week	8	29.78 ±4.91	6.46 ±2.89	3.83 ±1.76	10.55 ±2.87	2.51 ±1.05
32	10 week	8	19.09 ±6.78	2.83 ±1.57	8.90 ±2.26	9.19 ±3.18	1.19 ±0.57
Control	10 week	9	24.57 ±6.17	4.65 ±2.55	7.68 ±2.66	9.77 ±4.04	1.41 ±0.64
150	5 week	9	11.11 ±2.47	3.30 ±1.65	5.75 ±0.84	39.65 ±8.69	$\underline{2.06 \pm 0.53}$
Control	5 week	8	12.94 ±2.07	2.16 ±0.61	6.32 ±1.14	41.22 ±7.05	1.38 ±0.21
			Neutron-irradiation				
27	5 week	9	26.74 ±3.73	10.24 ±3.62	4.39 ±1.06	$\underline{14.50 \pm 1.69}$	3.33 ±1.05
Control	5 week	9	27.21 ±3.52	8.09 ±2.55	3.96 ±2.30	11.91 ±2.29	2.78 ±1.16
27	10 week	9	24.41 ±2.39	3.67 ±1.46	6.22 ±1.29	13.95 ±1.31	0.89 ±0.33
Control	10 week	5	23.42 ±3.14	4.02 ±1.08	8.05 ±0.92	13.85 ±2.04	0.78 ±0.13
81	5 week	8	11.70 ±1.46	$\underline{6.16 \pm 2.07}$	6.08 ±0.99	38.53 ±3.43	$\underline{3.08 \pm 0.58}$
Control	5 week	8	12.02 ±1.16	1.16 ±0.64	6.58 ±0.77	39.68 ±2.70	1.37 ±0.33

[a] Underlined values are significant at the 0.95 level or better.

TABLE IV

EFFECT OF CHRONIC RADIATION ON PERIPHERAL BLOOD MORPHOLOGY[a]

Radiation dose per week (rads)	*Group*	*Number of animals*	*RBC (× 10⁶)*	*Hematocrit (%)*	*Hemoglobin (gm.)*	*WBC*	*Platelet (× 10³)*	*Reticulocyte (%)*
				Gamma-irradiation				
16	5 week	9	8.62 ±0.33	46.2 ±1.7	13.08 ±0.64	13,561 ±3,089	562 ±147	2.4 ±0.28
Control	5 week	9	8.61 ±0.68	45.4 ±1.8	13.24 ±0.73	16,372 ±4,135	427 ±124	2.3 ±0.27
16	10 week	9	8.35 ±0.84	42.4 ±1.7	15.00 ±0.66	13,017 ±2,506	584 ±109	2.5 ±0.48
Control	10 week	7	8.67 ±0.61	45.4 ±2.3	14.64 ±0.85	19,043 ±4,254	648 ±71	2.6 ±0.49
32	5 week	9	8.07 ±1.01	42.5 ±4.3	13.86 ±0.67	14,000 ±4,816	538 ±104	2.8 ±0.54
Control	5 week	9	8.38 ±0.71	45.2 ±3.0	14.51 ±0.40	17,183 ±3,898	362 ±226	2.9 ±0.58
32	10 week	9	8.37 ±0.36	46.9 ±2.2	14.20 ±0.79	11,106 ±4,049	660 ±53	2.2 ±0.34
Control	10 week	9	8.57 ±0.48	47.7 ±1.7	14.20 ±0.63	13,350 ±3,911	681 ±119	1.9 ±0.44
150	5 week	9	7.43 ±0.99	44.4 ±2.6	14.01 ±0.58	4,856 ±1,372	512 ±49	4.2 ±1.5
Control	5 week	9	8.44 ±0.99	48.3 ±2.5	16.11 ±1.23	13,228 ±3,930	564 ±63	2.1 ±0.91
				Neutron-irradiation				
27	5 week	9	7.83 ±0.72	45.7 ±2.5	13.30 ±0.65	10,322 ±4,242	577 ±146	2.0 ±0.41
Control	5 week	9	8.10 ±0.48	46.3 ±3.5	13.77 ±0.50	19,333 ±3,301	499 ±110	3.1 ±1.20
27	10 week	8	7.96 ±1.01	45.3 ±2.3	14.51 ±0.93	15,788 ±4,393	633 ±118	
Control	10 week	6	8.57 ±0.63	46.7 ±1.6	14.90 ±0.72	21,167 ±6,964	802 ±215	
81	5 week	9	6.48 ±0.73	37.9 ±2.1	12.94 ±0.91	1,811 ±511	445 ±58	3.5 ±1.69
Control	5 week	9	8.62 ±1.15	45.3 ±2.3	14.56 ±0.66	17,300 ±3,495	445 ±105	2.4 ±0.72

[a] Underlined values are significant at the 0.95 level or better.

TABLE V

EFFECT OF CHRONIC RADIATION ON THE DIFFERENTIAL CELL COUNTS[a]

Radiation dose per week (rads)	Group	Number of animals	Neutrophils: Segmented (%)	Neutrophils: Bands (%)	Eosinophils (%)	Basophils (%)	Lymphocytes (%)	Monocytes (%)
Gamma-irradiation								
16	5 week	9	14.22 ±7.20	0.11 ±0.33	0.78 ±0.44	0.00 ±0.00	84.67 ±6.86	0.22 ±0.44
Control	5 week	9	12.10 ±6.45	0.44 ±0.73	0.78 ±1.17	0.11 ±0.33	85.67 ±7.11	0.89 ±1.17
16	10 week	9	20.22 ±2.82	1.11 ±0.93	1.67 ±1.41	0.11 ±0.33	77.11 ±3.89	0.89 ±1.17
Control	10 week	7	11.86 ±3.89	0.43 ±0.53	1.71 ±1.60	0.29 ±0.49	85.29 ±3.95	0.43 ±0.79
32	5 week	9	20.56 ±6.14	0.44 ±0.53	1.33 ±0.87	0.11 ±0.33	77.33 ±9.28	0.22 ±0.41
Control	5 week	9	10.33 ±3.83	0.78 ±1.09	1.44 ±2.13	0.11 ±0.33	87.00 ±5.36	0.33 ±0.71
32	10 week	9	18.11 ±6.02	1.33 ±2.24	1.22 ±0.97	0.00 ±0.00	77.67 ±7.53	0.00 ±0.00
Control	10 week	9	17.44 ±7.11	1.11 ±1.27	1.44 ±1.13	0.00 ±0.00	79.78 ±9.35	0.22 ±0.44
150	5 week	9	23.10 ±5.28	0.00 ±0.00	1.60 ±1.67	0.40 ±0.88	74.90 ±7.34	0.00 ±0.00
Control	5 week	8	14.90 ±1.61	0.10 ±0.34	0.40 ±0.77	0.00 ±0.00	83.50 ±5.74	0.30 ±0.71
Neutron-irradiation								
27	5 week	9	21.67 ±5.92	0.67 ±0.50	0.89 ±1.45	0.11 ±0.33	76.00 ±7.04	0.11 ±0.33
Control	5 week	9	14.33 ±5.29	0.78 ±0.67	2.78 ±1.85	0.11 ±0.33	81.44 ±4.95	0.11 ±0.33
27	10 week	8	26.38 ±9.13	0.00 ±0.00	0.75 ±0.96	0.20 ±0.54	72.25 ±9.24	0.13 ±0.35
Control	10 week	6	19.00 ±8.65	0.00 ±0.00	0.50 ±0.84	0.00 ±0.00	79.50 ±9.14	1.00 ±1.10
81	5 week	9	27.70 ±7.69	0.00 ±0.00	0.40 ±0.88	0.10 ±0.34	70.20 ±1.11	0.20 0.67
Control	5 week	9	10.10 ±4.73	0.00 ±0.00	0.70 ±0.11	0.00 ±0.00	88.90 ±6.05	0.30 ±0.71

[a] Underlined values are significant at the 0.95 level or better.

chronic 150-rad γ-ray and 81-rad neutron groups. These animals were injected with Fe^{59} from a vial repeatedly used over a period of several months, with a lapse in time between their injection and the last previous use of the isotope. It is probable that entry of air into the vial resulted in oxidation of the iron to the ferric state. Iron in the ferric form is bound in part not only to β-globulin (which constitutes the major binding of the ferrous form) but also appreciably to albumin, with the result that some 95% of the iron is protein-bound. It is thus considered likely that these changes in binding resulted in a decreased availability of transferrin iron for direct erythropoietic utilization, and, therefore, increases in iron entering the liver stores.

DISCUSSION

Our previously reported studies on Fe^{59} distribution in the normal rat after the intracardiac injection of the isotope are in substantial agreement with those of Baxter *et al.* (*10*). After the injection of Fe^{59}, maximum levels are reached in the bone marrow in 6 to 8 hours, and this is followed by a linear decline to 48 hours when the slope sharply flattens and becomes asymptotic through 168 hours. The appearance of Fe^{59} in the circulating red cells after 6 hours follows a rising curve complementary to a declining concentration in marrow. (The labeling of the red cells during the first 6 hours is largely due to the uptake of radioiron by circulating reticulocytes.) Radioactivity of the spleen, reflecting the active erythropoietic role of the rat spleen, follows a curve similar to that of the bone marrow, but at a reduced level of uptake. Liver stores of iron are maximally labeled in 24 to 48 hours. The rapid flow of radioiron to the major sources of utilization is reflected in the plasma clearance which is essentially complete in 6 hours.

Acute Radiation

Hennessy and Huff (*8*) have demonstrated a depression of erythropoiesis in the rat after X-irradiation with as little as 5 r, when the Fe^{59} was injected 24 hours after irradiation and determinations made on a daily basis thereafter. When rats were injected 48 hours after irradiation and the uptake in cells measured 24 hours after injection, Belcher *et al.* (*9*) found that a minimum observable response was obtained with 30 r. In the present acute experiments, changes in 6-hour uptake, 24 hours after irradiation, do not achieve consistent statistical validity until approximately 60 to 70 rads of radiation has been delivered. These data suggest, however, that functional change may begin to be observed with doses of 40 rads.

Exposure of the erythropoietic tissue to ionizing radiation is reflected in an initial change in iron incorporation in the bone marrow and spleen. The Fe^{59} levels in marrow and spleen decline, and there follows a decrease in the appearance of the label in the peripheral red cell. Two possible mechanisms may account for these changes: a decrease in the mitotic activity of developing red cells, resulting in a reduction of erythropoietic population and a consequent decreased demand for iron in hemoglobin synthesis, or a direct suppression of the formation of hemoglobin. From many previous studies (*10*, *11*, *21–23*) it is probable that the mitotic inhibition and destruction of erythropoietic tissue in the bone marrow accounts in large measure for the decreased Fe^{59} label in the peripheral cells.

The decreased uptake of Fe^{59} by bone marrow is reflected in the delay in plasma clearance of the isotope and the appearance of a higher level in the liver. These findings are in agreement with the results of Chanutin and Ludewig (*24*, *25*), who found elevated levels of nonradioactive serum and liver iron in rats after whole-body X-irradiation. It is probable that the increased Fe^{59} content of the liver is due to a simple shunt of iron, no longer in demand for erythropoiesis, to storage. It is possible, however, that radiation may evoke a mechanism by which iron is preferentially directed to the liver.

As the radiation is increased, its effect on erythropoiesis becomes more profound as revealed by the declining curve of Fe^{59} level in the bone marrow (Figs. 4 and 5). Radiation doses greater than 150 rads produce little further effect. If the radioiron measure accurately reflects erythropoiesis, we may state that in the rat a dose of 150 rads is sufficient to cause a cessation of mitosis in the erythrocytic series. The 4 to 6% Fe^{59} incorporation seen in doses above 100 rads may be accounted for by iron uptake for hemoglobin synthesis in surviving late red-cell elements, plus the extremely small amounts representing marrow hemosiderin or ferritin and the iron content of bone.

In keeping with the primary effect of radiation on marrow, the secondary manifestations of radiation damage, i.e., the amount of Fe^{59} appearing in the plasma, red cells, and liver, are further changed by increased radiation in a direction and magnitude in general accord with the increased suppression of erythropoiesis.

The bone-marrow curve of Fig. 4 is probably a two-component curve, with the steep slope related to inhibition of mitosis and cell destruction, and the shallow slope related to the residual Fe^{59} as described above. A statistical regression analysis of the neutron data and γ-ray data for both slopes, with subsequent t-testing, revealed no significant difference between the γ-ray and neutron effects as represented in the individual slopes. Accordingly, the results of the present study indicate an approximate relative biologic effect (RBE) of 1.0, fission neutron to Co^{60} γ-ray, when the biologic endpoint is suppression of erythropoiesis as measured by Fe^{59} incorporation into the bone marrow of the rat. Utilizing depression of Fe^{59} uptake by the red cells of the rat as the biologic test system, Furchner (*12*) found an RBE of 1.14 when thermal column neutrons were compared with 250-kvp X-rays, and an RBE of 0.6 when the 4.0-Mev radiation of the thermal column was similarly compared.

Chronic Radiation

The lack of impairment of erythropoietic function in the chronic experiments, in all dose regimes, as measured by Fe^{59} distribution 10 to 11 days after the last radiation exposure, is outstanding. There is apparently complete functional recovery even from the larger doses which when administered acutely are capable of severe suppression of erythropoiesis and which in total exceed any respective neutron or γ-ray dose used in the acute experiments.

The normal values for Fe^{59} distribution 10 to 11 days after irradiation are compatible with the recent Fe^{59} data of Hennessy and O'Kunewick (*26*). These authors submitted rats to 100 r of X-radiation and made daily measurements of the 24-hour Fe^{59} in the peripheral red cells for 33 days after irradiation. They demonstrated elevated values of Fe^{59} red-cell label on postirradiation days 4 through 8, with normal values after that period. These results indirectly revealed an acute compensatory rise above normal in marrow activity. As the authors point out, this is not unexpected, since such an increase is necessary to maintain the subsequent normal peripheral blood values which would otherwise drop as a result of the initial radiation-induced mitotic arrest in the marrow. In accordance, in the present work one would expect erythropoietic activity to recover fully within a period of 7 days. The exact time of recovery is probably a dose-dependent phenomenon; the smaller the acute dose, the shorter is the recovery period. With a higher dose of X-radiation, 400 r, Baxter *et al.* (*10*), using the 24-hour red-cell uptake technique, showed that 15 days was required for a return of normal erythropoietic function. From this it may be surmised that doses of radiation below 100 rads would be attended by correspondingly shorter periods of recovery.

Despite the great functional reserve of the erythropoietic system, if repeated radiation doses are sufficiently large, the bone marrow is unable to compensate completely for the loss of red-cell elements engendered by central mitotic suppression and destruction, and anemia ensues. In those animals exposed to 150 rads of γ-radiation or 81 rads of neutron radiation per week, statistically significant decreases in the hematocrits are noted. Although there is no apparent statistical relevance to the change in red count or hemoglobin at this time, a decrease is suggested and mean corpuscular volume determinations indicate a possible macrocytosis. A macrocytic anemia has been noted in human beings chronically exposed to radiation (*27*) and has also been commented on in irradiated rats by Baum *et al.* (*28*) and Stearner *et al.* (*29*).

Except in the high-dose γ-ray and neutron groups no severe alteration is noted in the total leukocyte counts of the chronically irradiated animals. In the rats irradiated with 150 rads $\times$ 5 and 81 rads $\times$ 5, a marked supression of the white count is seen. Whether this represents the total effect of the last given dose or is indicative of a cumulative effect cannot be ascertained from the present data. Comparison of our results, however, with the changes observed by Baum *et al.* (*28*) in a serial study of rat white-cell counts after doses of X-irradiation comparable to those used in the present study suggests that it is reasonable to assume some additive effect.

Changes in the absolute values of the differential counts agree with the well-known sensitivity of the lymphocytic series. In the 16 rads × 5 γ-ray group no change is noted in the absolute numbers of lymphocytes or neutrophils, and it is assumed that, if the unit dose is capable of effecting a change, complete recovery ensues during the interval between irradiations. Since the 16 rads × 10 γ-ray group reveals significant changes in absolute differential values, however, it is possible that there is some cumulative radiation effect not observable during the first 5 weeks of exposure. The fact that the decrease in absolute numbers of lymphocytes may be made apparent at the end of 5 weeks by giving the total dose of 16 rads × 10 in 5 weeks (32 rads × 5 group) lends support to the assumption of cumulative effect. Elevation of the absolute values for neutrophils in the 16 rads × 10, 32 rads × 5, and 27 rads × 5 groups suggests myelopoietic recovery. The highest doses of chronic radiation cause further suppression of the absolute values for neutrophils. We are unable to account for the lack of effect on the differential count observed in the 32 rads × 10 γ-ray and 27 rads × 10 neutron exposure groups.

It is apparent from these studies that repeated exposure to doses of neutron or γ-radiation below 32 rads produces little or no immediate irreparable damage to the hematopoietic system. Higher doses of repetitive exposure, 81 rads and 150 rads, are, however, capable of producing change from which recovery is obviously slower. It is possible that some residual effect of radiation, at present not measurable, may be present which in future time will reveal itself in hematopoietic aberration.

SUMMARY

Rats have been exposed to single and multiple doses of Co^{60} γ-radiation and fission neutron radiation, and a subsequent study has been made of the distribution of Fe^{59} within the erythropoietic system.

Irradiation causes a decreased incorporation of radioiron into bone marrow and spleen, with a consequent decrease in the level of Fe^{59} in the peripheral red cells and an increase in the levels in plasma and liver iron. The mechanism of this redistribution has been discussed.

From the data on acute exposure, with the incorporation of Fe^{59} into bone marrow as a biologic endpoint, an approximate RBE of 1.0, fission neutron to Co^{60} γ-ray, has been derived.

An analysis of the acute and chronic exposure data has revealed the great propensity for recovery of the erythrocytic system.

RECEIVED: April 2, 1958

REFERENCES

1. W. BLOOM, *Histopathology of Irradiation from External and Internal Sources*, McGraw-Hill Book Company, New York, 1948.
2. L. H. HEMPELMANN, H. LISCO, and J. G. HOFFMAN, The acute radiation syndrome. A study of nine cases and a review of the problem. *Ann. Internal Med.* **36**, 279 (1952).

3. W. BLOOM and M. BLOOM, The radiosensitivity of erythroblasts. *J. Lab. Clin. Med.* **32,** 654 (1947).
4. C. E. DUNLAP, Effect of radiation on the blood and the hemopoietic tissues, including spleen, thymus and lymph nodes. *A.M.A. Arch. Pathol.* **34,** 562 (1942).
5. L. O. JACOBSON, E. K. MARKS, and E. LORENZ, The hematological effects of ionizing radiations. *Radiology* **52,** 371 (1949).
6. E. P. CRONKITE and G. BRECHER, Effects of whole body irradiation. *Ann. Rev. Med.* **3,** 193 (1952).
7. J. S. LAWRENCE, A. H. DOWDY, and W. VALENTINE, Effects of radiation on hemopoiesis. *Radiology* **51,** 400 (1948).
8. T. G. HENNESSY and R. L. HUFF, Depression of tracer iron uptake curve in rat erythrocytes following total body X-irradiation. *Proc. Soc. Exptl. Biol. Med.* **73,** 436 (1950).
9. E. H. BELCHER, I. G. F. GILBERT, and L. F. LAMERTON, Experimental studies with radioactive iron. *Brit. J. Radiol.* **27,** 387 (1954).
10. C. F. BAXTER, E. H. BELCHER, E. B. HARRISS, and L. F. LAMERTON. Anemia and erythropoiesis in the irradiated rat: An experimental study with particular reference to techniques involving radioactive iron. *Brit. J. Haematol.* **1,** 86 (1955).
11. L. G. LAJTHA and H. D. SUIT, Uptake of radioactive iron (Fe^{59}) by nucleated red cells *in vitro*. *Brit. J. Haematol.* **1,** 55 (1955).
12. J. B. STORER, P. S. HARRIS, J. E. FURCHNER, and W. H. LANGHAM, The relative biological effectiveness of various ionizing radiations in mammalian systems. *Radiation Research* **6,** 188 (1957).
13. H. H. VOGEL, JR., R. A. BLOMGREN, and N. J. G. BOHLIN. Gamma-neutron radiation chamber for radiobiological studies. *Nucleonics* **11,** 28 (March, 1953).
14. R. E. ZIRKLE, J. R. RAPER, E. F. RILEY, JR., and G. E. STAPLETON, Additivity of fast neutrons and gamma rays in their acute lethal action on mice. U. S. Atomic Energy Commission Report AECD-2328 (1945).
15. H. H. VOGEL, JR., J. W. CLARK, and D. L. JORDAN, Modification of the gamma-neutron radiation chamber for use at the Argonne research reactor. Quarterly Report of Biological and Medical Research Division, Argonne National Laboratory, Report ANL-5288, p. 35 (1954).
16. B. E. WATT, Energy spectrum of neutrons from thermal fission of U^{235}. *Phys. Rev.* **87,** 1037 (1952).
17. J. ALLRED and A. ARMSTRONG, Laboratory handbook of nuclear microscopy. Los Alamos Scientific Laboratory Report LA-1510 (1953).
18. L. ROSEN, Nuclear emulsion techniques for the measurement of neutron energy spectra. *Nucleonics* **11,** 32 (July, 1953).
19. G. S. HURST, An absolute tissue dosimeter for fast neutrons. *Brit. J. Radiol.* **27,** 353 (1954).
20. W. A. RAMBACH, J. A. D. COOPER, and H. L. ALT, The uptake of radioiron in the bone marrow as a measure of erythropoiesis. *Proc. Central Soc. Clin. Research* **28,** 62 (1955).
21. K. SALOMON, K. I. ALTMAN, G. W. CASARETT, and T. R. NOONAN, Effect of X-ray radiation and of starvation on hemoglobin synthesis in the rat. *Federation Proc.* **8,** 247 (1949).
22. J. E. RICHMOND, K. I. ALTMAN, and K. SALOMON, The effect of X-radiation on the biosynthesis of hemoglobin. *J. Biol. Chem.* **190,** 817 (1951).
23. W. A. RAMBACH, H. L. ALT, and J. A. D. COOPER, Protective effect of hypoxia against irradiation injury of the rat bone marrow and spleen. *Proc. Soc. Exptl. Biol. Med.* **86,** 159 (1954).
24. A. CHANUTIN and S. LUDEWIG, Effect of whole body X-irradiation on serum iron concentration of rats. *Am. J. Physiol.* **166,** 380 (1951).
25. S. LUDEWIG and A. CHANUTIN, Effect of whole body X-irradiation on the storage of iron in liver, spleen and kidney of rats. *Am. J. Physiol.* **166,** 384 (1951).

26. T. G. Hennessy and J. P. O'Kunewick, Radioiron study of erythropoiesis after X-irradiation. University of California at Los Angeles Report UCLA-383 (1956).
27. M. M. Wintrobe, *Clinical Hematology*. Lea and Febiger, Philadelphia, 1956.
28. S. J. Baum, D. J. Kimeldorf, and E. M. Jacobsen, Effect of repetitive exposures to gamma rays on the hematopoietic system of the rat. *Blood* **10,** 926 (1955).
29. S. P. Stearner, E. L. Simmons, and L. O. Jacobson, The effects of total body radiation on the peripheral blood and blood forming tissues of the rat. Argonne National Laboratory Report ANL-4001 (MDDC-1319) (1947).

RADIATION RESEARCH **10**, 167–175 (1959)

The Effect of X-Irradiation on the Antioxidant Activity of Mammalian Tissues[1]

ALBERT A. BARBER[2] AND KARL M. WILBUR

Department of Zoology, Duke University, Durham, North Carolina

INTRODUCTION

Two lines of investigation have indicated that oxidation reactions are of significance during the initial phases of radiation damage. The first concerns radical production in aqueous media exposed to ionizing radiation, and the second is the study of chemical protection both *in vitro* and *in vivo*. Various biological compounds are oxidized by the action of radicals produced by radiation (*1*). The radiochemical yield of these oxidations is increased by the presence of heavy metals and oxygen, indicating that metal-catalyzed oxidations may be important in radiation effects. The possible mechanisms of oxidation of biological compounds exposed to ionizing radiation have been discussed by Barron (*1*). The studies on chemical protection have indicated that one of the mechanisms might involve the inhibition of the oxidation reactions due to free radical activity (*2*). In fact, many of the protective agents such as reducing agents and chelating agents do have antioxidant properties. Chelating agents would be effective against metal-catalyzed oxidations such as the Fenton reaction (*1*) and lipid peroxide formation (*3*).

Lipid peroxides have been demonstrated in certain animal tissues after X-irradiation (*4–6*), whereas they are not normally found in these tissues (*7*). These substances are toxic when fed to mice (*8*). Among their *in vitro* effects are: inhibition of respiration and glycolysis in ascites tumor metabolism (*9*), inhibition of certain oxidative enzymes in rat liver mitochondria (*10*), decrease in viscosity of deoxyribonucleoprotein (*11*), inhibition of cell division (*12*), and inhibition of the activity of the Rous sarcoma virus (*13*).

The absence of lipid peroxides in normal animal tissues suggests that some antioxidant mechanism prevents their formation. The antioxidant activity of a number of mammalian tissues has been investigated in the present study. One of

[1] Aided by a grant from the U. S. Atomic Energy Commission.

[2] Present address: Department of Zoology, University of California, Los Angeles 24, California.

the explanations for the formation of lipid peroxides in irradiated tissues is the destruction of the normal antioxidant activity by radiation. To determine whether this is the case, the antioxidant activity of tissues from normal and irradiated animals was compared.

MATERIALS AND METHODS

Tissue preparation. Male Sprague-Dawley rats of 175 to 200 gm, male strain A mice, and male New Zealand rabbits of 1.4 to 1.8 kg were used. Rats were killed by cervical dislocation followed by decapitation, and the tissues were quickly placed in containers at 0°C and weighed. Intestinal mucosa was collected by scraping the duodenum with a microscope slide. Blood from the ear vein of rabbits and ascitic fluid from mice were collected directly into cold buffered medium. Bone marrow was aspirated from the long bones of the hind limbs of rabbits. Homogenization of tissues was carried out in cold buffer with a Teflon-glass homogenizer. All tissues including blood and ascitic fluid were brought to volume in buffered medium prepared by combining 100 ml of 0.154 *M* NaCl, 4.0 ml of 0.154 *M* KCl, and 12 ml of 0.10 *M* Na–K phosphate buffer at pH 7.0. Homogenates were centrifuged at 1000 $\times g$ for 5 minutes. The supernatants or, in some cases, the original homogenates were immediately assayed for antioxidant activity by one of the three test systems described below. The protein content of supernatants was determined by the Folin-Ciocalteu reagent with bovine serum albumen as the reference standard (*14*).

Test systems. Three test systems were used to investigate the antioxidant activity of tissues: peroxide formation in incubated rat liver homogenates; peroxide formation in methyl linolenate emulsions; and melanin formation in incubated solutions of dihydroxyphenylalanine (DOPA).

In the rat liver homogenate test system the antioxidant activity was determined by measuring the inhibition of peroxide formation resulting from the addition of tissue supernatants. Rat livers were homogenized in cold salt–buffer and diluted 1:15 (w/v). Three milliliters of this homogenate was incubated with 1.0 ml of tissue supernatant for 90 minutes at 36°C with shaking. Peroxide formation was then determined by the thiobarbituric acid (TBA) test (see below).

The methyl linolenate emulsion, a highly purified peroxide-forming system, was utilized to test the antioxidant and catalytic activities of normal and irradiated mucosa. One-tenth milliliter of the ester was emulsified in 50 ml of salt–buffer, pH 7.0, in a Waring blendor. Mucosal supernatants were added to 0.5 ml of this emulsion in a final volume of 4.0 ml, and the mixtures were incubated at 36°C for 2 hours. Peroxide formation was then determined by the TBA test.

The DOPA-melanin test system was used to measure the antioxidant activity of normal and irradiated mucosa on a test system other than a lipid peroxide-forming system. The antioxidant activity was expressed as per cent inhibition of melanin formation after 15 hours of incubation at 36°C. The test system was similar to that described by Hirsch (*15*) except that Tween 80 was used for the suspension of melanin. Supernatants were added to 4.5 mg of DOPA in a final volume of 7.0 ml.

Thiobarbituric acid (TBA) test. The extent of lipid peroxide formation in the liver homogenate and methyl linolenate test systems was measured by the TBA test (*16*). The contents of the incubating vessels were transferred to test tubes containing 1 ml of 30% trichloroacetic acid (TCA). Two milliliters of 0.75% TBA was then added. The tubes were placed in a boiling water bath for 15 minutes and then cooled. One milliliter of 70% TCA was added to the tubes containing the liver homogenate test system, whereas 1 ml of chloroform was added to those containing the methyl linolenate. The tubes were then centrifuged, and the optical density of the chromogen was read spectrophotometrically at 525 mμ.

X-Irradiation. Animals were irradiated in perforated wooden boxes with a Picker industrial X-ray unit operated at 250 kv and 15 ma. Intrinsic filtration HVL 0.26 mm Cu equivalent; added filtration 3 mm Al and 0.25 mm Cu. Target distance, 78 cm; rate, 40 r/min; total dose, 800 r.

RESULTS

Antioxidant Activity of Normal Tissues

The antioxidant activity of mammalian tissues was found in the supernatant fraction except in the rabbit bone marrow and rat testis where 20 to 40% of the total activity remained in the pellet. Rabbit plasma and bone marrow, rat intestinal mucosa, and mouse ascitic fluid formed no peroxides when incubated aerobically and exhibited strong antioxidant activity. Comparisons of antioxidant activity were based on the protein content of tissue supernatants. Figure 1 shows the antioxidant activity of plasma and supernatants of bone marrow. The protein content required for 50% inhibition was 1.7 mg/ml for plasma and 3.3 mg/ml for marrow. Curves of antioxidant activity for intestinal mucosa (Fig. 2) and ascitic fluid (not shown) were intermediate between those of plasma and marrow, and the protein contents for 50% inhibition were 2.0 mg/ml for the mucosa and 2.2 mg/ml for the ascitic fluid.

Rat testis, spleen, brain, and liver, in contrast to the tissues mentioned above, formed peroxides on incubation. The testis formed the least and was the only peroxide-forming tissue which had significant antioxidant activity. A relatively high protein content of 9.6 mg/ml was required for 50% inhibition. The spleen was slightly inhibitory, and in eight experiments with protein concentrations of 12.5 to 15.4 mg/ml the inhibition was only 22% and showed great variability.

Lipid peroxide formation in liver homogenates was catalyzed by low concentrations of iron and ascorbic acid (Table I). Iron and ascorbic acid catalysis of oxidation has also been reported for pure unsaturated lipids (*17*). Citrate and chelating agents, such as EDTA, were inhibitory (Table I), indicating that traces of iron may be responsible for lipid peroxide formation in incubating tissues.

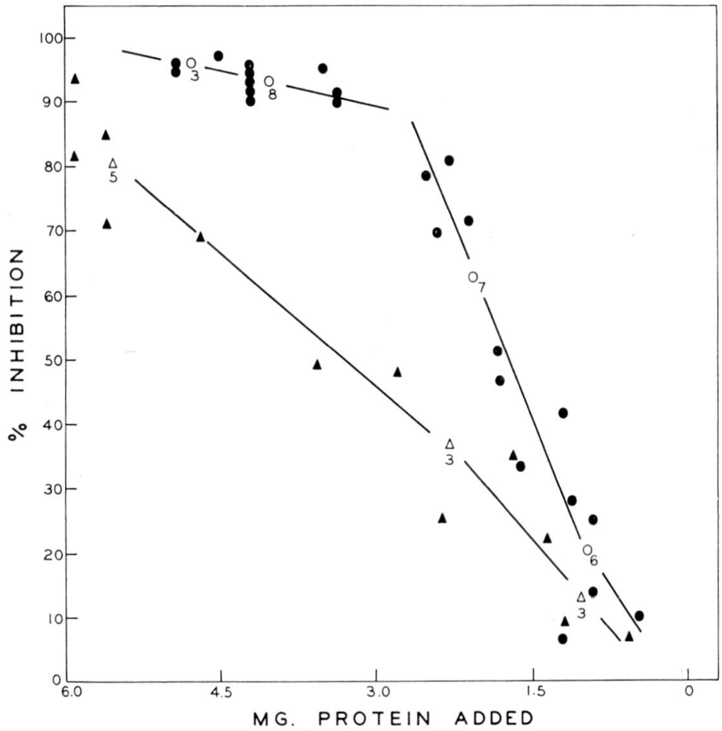

FIG. 1. Inhibition of peroxide formation by rabbit plasma and bone marrow supernatants: ● represents plasma; ○ represents averages of plasma values within the designated 1.5-mg increments; ▲ represents bone-marrow supernatants; △ represents averages of bone-marrow values within the designated 1.5-mg increments.

X-Irradiation Effects

Liver homogenate test system. The antioxidant activity of the rat intestinal mucosa was destroyed by 800 r of whole-body X-irradiation, whereas the activity of blood, bone marrow, ascitic fluid, testis, and spleen was unchanged. In the mucosa the antioxidant activity was decreased 24 hours after irradiation, and by 48 hours many of the samples catalyzed peroxide formation (Fig. 3). Mucosa taken 72 hours or later after irradiation was always catalytic. The protein content per unit wet weight of mucosa dropped to a minimum after 48 hours and then increased to a value somewhat below normal by 96 hours (Fig. 3). The antioxidant activity, however, did not show recovery during this period. Mucosa taken from rats 96 hours postirradiation contained lipid peroxides when analyzed immediately after removal from the animal, whereas peroxides were never found in the mucosa from unirradiated animals. A decreased food intake by the irradiated animal was not responsible

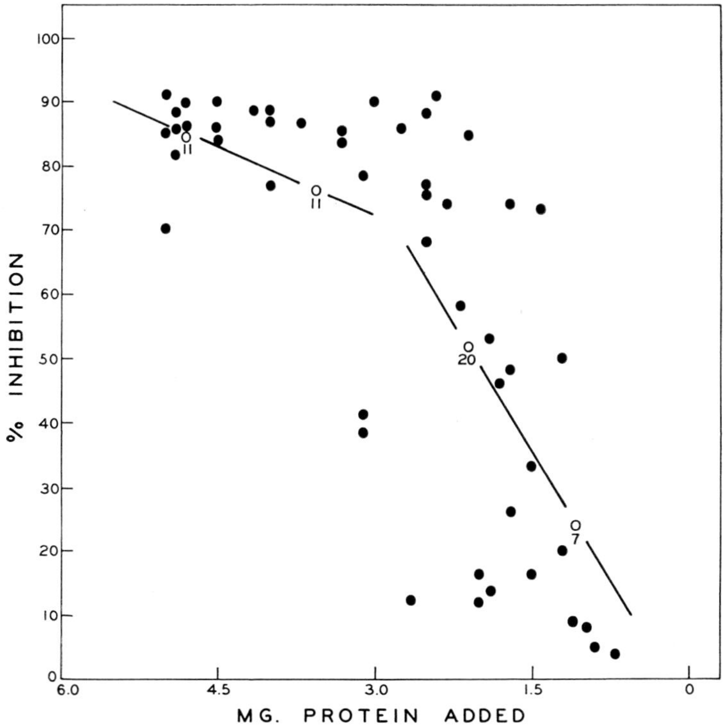

FIG. 2. Inhibition of peroxide formation by rat intestinal mucosa supernatants: ● represents experimental values; ○ represents the averages of values within the designated 1.5-mg increments.

TABLE I

EFFECT OF VARIOUS COMPOUNDS ON PEROXIDE FORMATION IN LIVER HOMOGENATES

(Liver homogenate test system used as described under Methods. The compounds were added in 1 ml of buffer. Peroxides were determined after 90 minutes of incubation at 36° C.)

Compound	*Concentration (M)*	*Inhibition (%)*	*Catalysis (%)*
$FeCl_3$	5.0×10^{-4}		215
$FeCl_3$	5.0×10^{-5}		17
Ascorbic acid	2.5×10^{-3}	87	
Ascorbic acid	2.5×10^{-4}	13	
Ascorbic acid	1.2×10^{-4}		42
EDTA	2.5×10^{-5}	95	
EDTA	2.5×10^{-6}	12	
Citrate	2.5×10^{-3}	79	

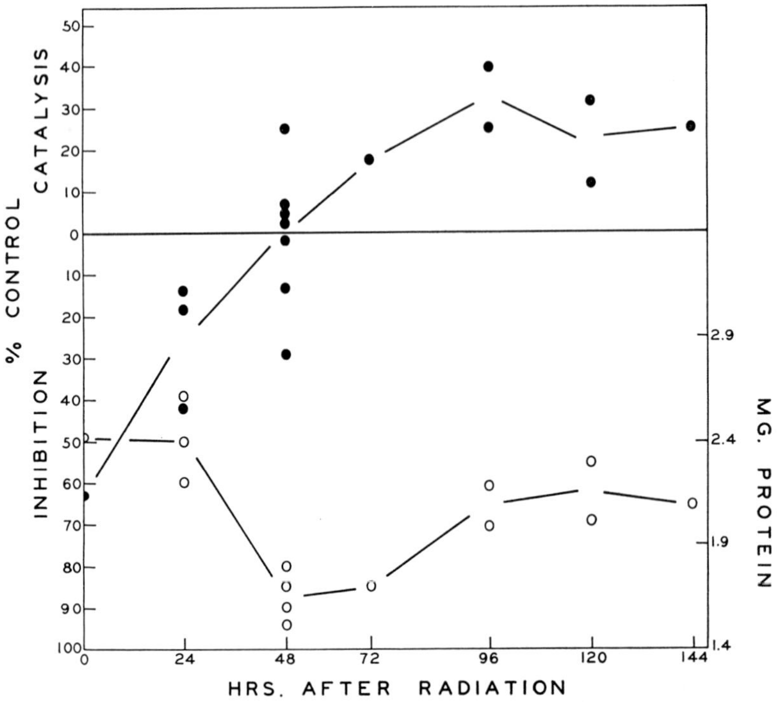

FIG. 3. Effect of whole-body X-irradiation on the antioxidant activity of rat intestinal mucosa supernatants: Rats received 800 r and were sacrificed at 24-hour intervals for 6 days; ● represents antioxidant activity; ○ represents protein concentration per milliliter of mucosa supernatant prepared from 1:30 homogenates.

for the changes, since the mucosa of rats starved for 72 hours had normal antioxidant activity.

DOPA–melanin and methyl linolenate test systems. The loss of antioxidant activity in the mucosa after irradiation could be explained either by a destruction of antioxidant or by an increase in catalyst for peroxide formation. An attempt was made to resolve this problem by using the DOPA-melanin and the methyl linolenate test systems.

Melanin formation was inhibited by normal intestinal mucosa (Table II). Mucosa from irradiated animals inhibited to a lesser extent than the unirradiated preparations. None of the preparations was catalytic.

Peroxide formation in methyl linolenate emulsions was catalyzed by mucosa from rats irradiated 72 and 96 hours previously (Table III). The mucosa from unirradiated controls was slightly inhibitory.

TABLE II

EFFECT OF WHOLE-BODY X-IRRADIATION ON THE INHIBITION OF MELANIN FORMATION BY RAT INTESTINAL MUCOSA

(Irradiated animals received 800 r of X-rays. Melanin formation was determined after 15 hours of incubation at 36°C. All mucosa supernatants were tested at dilutions containing 2 mg of protein.)

Inhibition of melanin formation (%)		
Control	*72 hours postirradiation*	*96 hours postirradiation*
61	40	—
61	11	—
55	—	23
55	—	31

TABLE III

EFFECT OF WHOLE-BODY X-IRRADIATION ON THE ACTIVITY OF RAT INTESTINAL MUCOSA ON THE OXIDATION OF METHYL LINOLENATE EMULSIONS

(Lipid peroxides were determined after 2 hours of incubation at 36°C. Numerical values indicate the optical density of the TBA reaction. Mucosal preparations containing 1 mg of protein were added to the emulsions. The values are averages of two cases. Irradiated animals received 800 r of X-rays.)

Peroxide formation			
No tissue	*Control*	*72 hours postirradiation*	*96 hours postirradiation*
0.100	0.060	0.315	0.560

DISCUSSION

Mammalian tissues may be divided into two groups with respect to their capacity to form lipid peroxides on aerobic incubation. One group, including liver, brain, kidney, and spleen, forms peroxides; the other, including intestinal mucosa, blood, and bone marrow, does not. The difference appears to be in the antioxidant activity. The peroxide-forming group has little or no antioxidant activity. By breaking the cell structure some substances, possibly iron, may be released resulting in the catalysis of peroxide formation. Addition of citrate and EDTA, a chelating agent, inhibits peroxide formation of homogenates, presumably by removing the catalyst.

In intestinal mucosa, blood, and bone marrow, antioxidants, which may be naturally occurring chelating agents, are present. They can be demonstrated by the inhibition of lipid peroxide formation resulting from the addition of extracts of bone marrow and mucosa to liver homogenates. This antioxidant activity could explain the lack of peroxide formation in aerobically incubated homogenates of bone marrow and mucosa.

The capacity of a tissue to form lipid peroxides would be expected to be enhanced when the ratio of catalyst to antioxidant is increased either by an increase in catalyst or a decrease in antioxidant. Addition of the catalyst $FeCl_3$ to tissue homogenates brought about this result (unpublished experiments of A. Ottolenghi). After irradiation the ratio in the mucosa shifted toward increased catalytic activity, as shown by the catalysis of peroxide formation brought about by the addition of irradiated mucosa to the liver homogenate and to the methyl linolenate test systems. Whether this increased catalytic activity is accompanied by a concomitant decrease in antioxidant is unknown. The antioxidant activity when tested on the DOPA reaction was decreased after irradiation, however. This decrease may or may not be due to increased catalyst.

The tissues which showed the greatest antioxidant activity are known to have a relatively high mitotic rate. A similar relationship is indicated in regenerating rat liver in which peroxide formation is diminished during periods of high mitotic activity (*18*). These findings may be of significance in view of the inhibition of cell division by lipid peroxide (*12*).

A decrease in antioxidant activity after irradiation could lead to the formation of peroxides, and these peroxides may contribute to the radiation damage. The effectiveness of EDTA as a protective agent against whole-body irradiation (*2*) may have some basis in its chelation of a catalyst released by the irradiation, although Alexander *et al.* (*2*) do not favor this explanation.

SUMMARY

Tissue antioxidant activity was measured by the capacity of tissue supernatants to inhibit peroxide formation when added to rat liver homogenate. Blood, ascitic fluid, intestinal mucosa, and bone marrow had the highest antioxidant activity. Testis and spleen had less, and liver and brain had none. Peroxide formation in this test system was inhibited by citrate and EDTA. $FeCl_3$ and low concentrations of ascorbic acid were catalytic.

Whole-body irradiation destroyed the antioxidant activity of the mucosa but had no effect on that of other tissues. The mucosa from irradiated animals catalyzed peroxide formation in incubated methyl linolenate emulsions as well as in the liver homogenate. When tested by the inhibition of melanin formation, the antioxidant activity of irradiated mucosa was somewhat less than that of the unirradiated controls, but it never catalyzed this reaction.

RECEIVED: April 25, 1958

REFERENCES

1. E. S. G. BARRON, The effect of ionizing radiations on systems of biological importance. *Ann. N. Y. Acad. Sci.* **59**, 574–593 (1955).

2. P. Alexander, Z. M. Bacq, S. F. Cousens, M. Fox, A. Herve, and J. Lazar, Mode of action of some substances which protect against lethal effects of X-rays. *Radiation Research* **2,** 392–415 (1955).
3. A. A. Barber and A. Ottolenghi, Effect of ethylenediaminetetraacetate on lipid peroxide formation and succinoxidase inactivation by ultraviolet light. *Proc. Soc. Exptl. Biol. Med.* **96,** 471–473 (1957).
4. F. Bernheim, A. Ottolenghi, and K. M. Wilbur, Studies on bone marrow lipid in normal and irradiated rabbits. *Radiation Research* **4,** 132–138 (1956).
5. P. Dubouloz and J. Dumas, Sur le métabolisme des peroxydes lipidiques. IV. Presence de peroxydes lipidiques dans le peau au cours des processus "inflammatoires." *Bull. soc. chim. biol.* **36,** 983–991 (1954).
6. V. J. Horgan and J. St. L. Philpot, The nature of the peroxide-like substances formed in mice by X-rays. In *Radiobiology Symposium* (Z. Bacq and P. Alexander, eds.), pp. 26–29, Academic Press, New York, 1955.
7. P. Dubouloz, J. Fondarai, and J. P. Pracchia, Sur le métabolisme des peroxydes lipidiques. III. Méchanisme de la destruction des peroxydes lipidiques par les tissus animaux. *Bull. soc. chim. biol.* **36,** 893–900 (1954).
8. T. Kaneda and S. Ishii, Nutritive value or toxicity of highly unsaturated fatty acids. 1. *J. Biochem.* **41,** 327–335 (1954).
9. C. W. Shuster, Effects of oxidized fatty acids on ascites tumor metabolism. *Proc. Soc. Exptl. Biol. Med.* **90,** 423–426 (1955).
10. A. Ottolenghi, F. Bernheim, and K. M. Wilbur, The inhibition of certain mitochondrial enzymes by fatty acids oxidized by ultraviolet light or ascorbic acid. *Arch. Biochem. Biophys.* **56,** 157–164 (1955).
11. W. D. Fisher and K. M. Wilbur, Depolymerization of desoxyribonucleic acid preparations by oxidized methyl linolenate. *J. Elisha Mitchell Soc.* **70,** 124–125 (1954).
12. K. M. Wilbur, N. Wolfson, C. B. Kenaston, A. Ottolenghi, M. E. Gaulden, and F. Bernheim, Inhibition of cell division by ultraviolet irradiated unsaturated fatty acids. *Exptl. Cell Research* **13,** 503–509 (1957).
13. J. B. Maloney, Inhibition of Rous sarcoma virus activity by oxidized tumor lipids. *J. Natl. Cancer Inst.* **18,** 515–527 (1957).
14. O. H. Lowry, N. J. Rosebrough, A. L. Farr, and R. J. Randall, Protein measurement with the Folin phenol reagent. *J. Biol. Chem.* **193,** 265–275 (1951).
15. H. M. Hirsch, Tissue autoxidation inhibitors. 1. The inhibition of DOPA autoxidation by extracts from normal and neoplastic tissues. *Cancer Research* **15,** 249–255 (1955).
16. F. Bernheim, K. M. Wilbur, and D. B. Fitzgerald, Studies on a new metabolite and its oxidation in the presence of ascorbic acid. *J. Gen. Physiol.* **31,** 195–201 (1947).
17. K. A. C. Elliott and B. Libet, Oxidation of phospholipid catalyzed by iron compounds with ascorbic acid. *J. Biol. Chem.* **152,** 617–626 (1944).
18. N. Wolfson, K. M. Wilbur, and F. Bernheim, Lipid peroxide formation in regenerating rat liver. *Exptl. Cell Research* **10,** 556–558 (1956).

RADIATION RESEARCH **10**, 176–179 (1959)

Relative Biological Effect of Fission Neutrons with the Broad Bean Root (*Vicia faba*) as a Test System[1]

J. F. SPALDING, V. G. STRANG, AND J. A. SAYEG

Los Alamos Scientific Laboratory, University of California, Los Alamos, New Mexico

INTRODUCTION

This study is one of a series of experiments designed to determine the relative effect of a number of types of radiation using the broad bean root as a biological test system. In earlier investigations (*1–4*) the relative biological effectiveness (RBE) of β-particles, α-particles, and 14-Mev neutrons was reported. The present study was designed to obtain the RBE for degraded fission neutrons with an average energy of 1.4 Mev.

METHODS AND MATERIAL

Sutton's Long Pod Broad Beans (*Vicia faba*) were germinated and cultured in the same manner as described in an earlier paper (*1*). When the roots were 5 to 8 cm in length, they were exposed to ionizing radiation. Cobalt-60 γ-rays were used as a base-line radiation, and the Godiva II, an untamped U^{235} critical assembly, was used as a source of fission neutrons. Daily root growth was measured from 2 days prior to exposure to 9 days after exposure. The LD_{50} was determined for each type of radiation, with cessation of root growth for 4 consecutive days as the criterion for death.

A 106-curie Co^{60} source was used for cobalt γ-ray exposure. Source-to-specimen distance was 57.2 cm, and the dose rate was 7.0 rads/min. Gamma dose measurements were made with a Victoreen (Model 621) 100-r high-energy-range chamber. Victoreen readings were corrected for temperature and barometric pressure and converted to a water dose in rads by the conversion factor 1 r = 0.975 rad (*5*). The bean roots exposed to γ-rays were exposed at room temperature (22° to 24°C) in tap water with an initial aeration of approximately 4.63 cc of oxygen per liter of water (normal oxygen content of tap water at the temperature and barometric

[1] This work was performed under the auspices of the U. S. Atomic Energy Commission.

TABLE I
RELATIVE EFFECTIVENESS OF FISSION NEUTRONS IN THE PRODUCTION OF DEATH OF THE BROAD BEAN ROOT

	Co⁶⁰ γ-rays[a]			*Fission neutrons ($\overline{E}$ = 1.4 Mev)*[a]		
	Number of beans	*Dose (rads)*	*Number killed (%)*	*Number of beans*	*Dose (rads)*	*Number killed (%)*
	20	275	30	24	28	25
	20	324	45	23	39	35
	19	381	58	24	59	58
	20	447	70	21	83	88
	20	525	85	22	127	95
	20	Control	0	24	190	100
LD_{50}		345.6 ± 21.4			46.4 ± 3.8	
RBE				7.4 ± 0.8		

[a] Dose rates for both neutron and γ-ray exposures were in the same range (approximately 7 rads/min).

pressure of this laboratory).[2] The roots were arranged on the arc of a circle (57.2-cm radius) with the Co^{60} at the center. Five doses (275 to 525 rads) with 20 beans per dose were used (Table I).

Neutrons from the Godiva II critical assembly were degraded fission neutrons with an average energy of 1.4 Mev. Dose measurements were made with the Hurst proportional counter (*6*), condenser-type beryllium-shelled tissue-equivalent and graphite–CO_2 ionization chambers (*7*), and threshold detectors of Pu^{239}, Np^{237}, U^{238}, and S^{32}. The neutron dose measurements obtained by the above methods agreed to within 10%. The total γ-ray dose during exposure was approximately 15% of the neutron dose. The effect of the total γ-ray dose delivered during the neutron exposures, however, was considered to be negligible and was ignored in the dose calculations. The bean roots were arranged on the arc of a circle (1-meter radius) around the critical assembly and situated in tap water in the same manner as described for Co^{60} γ-ray exposures. Six doses (28 to 190 rads) with 24 beans per dose group were used (Table I).

RESULTS AND DISCUSSION

The lethality data for Co^{60} γ-rays and fission neutrons are summarized in Table I. Probit analysis of the Co^{60} lethality data showed the LD_{50} dose for γ-rays to be

[2] Bean roots were not aerated during exposure to ionizing radiations because in preliminary studies reported earlier (*1*) it was observed that within the limits of these RBE studies the oxygen effect was not significant, and it was not practical to aerate radon or tritium solutions, so it was felt that the γ-ray base-line exposures should also be made in tap water.

345.6 ± 21.4 rads. The expression

$$Y = -8.50 + 5.32X$$

in which Y is the probit of per cent mortality and X is the log of the radiation dose, best represents the Co^{60} data.

A probit of the lethality data for fission neutrons showed the LD_{50} to be 46.4 ± 3.8 rads, and the data were best represented by the expression

$$Y = -1.41 + 3.85X$$

where Y is the probit of per cent mortality and X is the log of neutron dose.

The RBE for fission neutrons was 7.4 ± 0.8 when the γ-ray LD_{50} dose was used as a base line. The RBE value for 2.5- to 2.8-Mev neutrons reported by Gray and Read (*8*) was 8.7 ± 1.6. The LD_{50} value for fission neutrons (46.4 ± 3.8 rads) was considerably lower than that of 75 ± 16 energy units reported by Gray (*8*) for neutrons in the energy range of 2.5 to 2.8 Mev.

The results of this and earlier studies (*1–4*) indicate a maximum in the RBE curve as a function of LET with the bean root as a test system. This maximum appears to occur with ionizing radiations having LET values between 50 and 100 kev/μ.

SUMMARY

Lethality of the broad bean root was used as a test system to obtain the RBE for fission neutrons. The LD_{50} dose for fission neutrons was 46.4 ± 3.8 rads; comparison to the γ-ray LD_{50} of 345.6 ± 21.4 rads gave an RBE of 7.4 ± 0.8.

ACKNOWLEDGMENTS

We wish to acknowledge the cooperation of O. S. Johnson for providing the γ-ray exposures and dosimetry for this study, and the technical assistance of S. B. Hawkins.

RECEIVED: May 26, 1958

REFERENCES

1. J. F. SPALDING, W. H. LANGHAM, and E. C. ANDERSON, The relative biological effectiveness of tritium β-radiation with the broad bean root (*Vicia faba*) as a test system. *Radiation Research* **4**, 221–227 (1956).

2. J. F. SPALDING, E. C. ANDERSON, and W. LANGHAM, The relative biological effectiveness of X-rays and β-rays with the broad bean root (*Vicia faba*) as a test system. *Radiation Research* **3**, 348–349 (1955).

3. J. F. SPALDING, W. H. LANGHAM, and E. C. ANDERSON, Relative biological effectiveness of alpha-radiation with the broad bean root (*Vicia faba*) as a test system. *Radiation Research* **8**, 322–328 (1958).

4. J. F. SPALDING, S. B. HAWKINS, and J. A. SAYEG, Relative biological effect of 14-Mev neutrons with the broad bean root (*Vicia faba*) as a test system. *Radiation Research* in press.

5. L. H. GRAY, Conversion from the roentgen to the rad. *Brit. J. Radiol.* **29**, 355 (1956).
6. G. S. HURST, An absolute tissue dosimeter for fast neutrons. *Brit. J. Radiol.* **27**, 353–357 (1954).
7. J. A. SAYEG, J. H. LARKINS, and P. S. HARRIS, Experimental determination of fast and thermal neutron tissue dose. Los Alamos Scientific Laboratory Report LA-2174 (1958).
8. L. H. GRAY and J. READ, The effect of ionizing radiations on the broad bean root. Part III. The lethal action of neutron radiation. *Brit. J. Radiol.* **15**, 72–76 (1942).

RADIATION RESEARCH 10, 180–196 (1959)

Rate of Recovery from Radiation Damage and Its Possible Relationship to Life Shortening in Mice[1]

JOHN B. STORER[2]

Los Alamos Scientific Laboratory, University of California, Los Alamos, New Mexico

INTRODUCTION

The recovery rate of animals exposed to sublethal doses of radiation and subsequently challenged by a second dose of radiation has been studied in detail by a number of authors (*1–10*). In these studies, which utilize lethality as the biological end point, it has generally been found that in mice and rats recovery can be described as a simple exponential function. When the recovery rate so determined has been utilized to predict median lethal doses for fractionated exposures extending over several days, however, the observed LD_{50} has generally been lower than that predicted on the assumption of a constant recovery rate. This finding has led to the suggestion that repeated exposures cause a progressive decline in recovery rate (*1*, *4*, *5*), but an analysis of the rate of decline has not as yet been performed.

Blair (*11–13*), utilizing the concept of a constant repair rate for reparable radiation damage and the premise that a portion of the damage does not repair, has advanced an interesting hypothesis that attempts to relate the acute LD_{50} to mean survival time (life shortening) at very long times after radiation exposures.

Since there are now a number of published reports on the survival times of mice exposed to a great variety of daily doses of radiation, it was considered worth while to re-examine these data and to calculate mean recovery rate constants for animals exposed to different numbers of daily radiation doses. If a systematic variation in recovery rate with number of fractions could be demonstrated, it was then planned to modify certain aspects of Blair's hypothesis accordingly and to apply the modified hypothesis to certain cases of experimentally produced life shortening from radiation. These calculations and modifications of the Blair hypothesis are the subject of the present report.

[1] Work done under the auspices of the U. S. Atomic Energy Commission.

[2] Present address: Roscoe B. Jackson Memorial Laboratory, Bar Harbor, Maine.

ASSUMPTIONS

The rationale for determining recovery rates from split-dose or daily-dose lethality data, the limitations and reservations that must be attached to these rates, and the assumptions involved in their derivation have been discussed adequately by other authors (*1–10*). The assumptions used in the present study may be briefly stated as follows:

1. Radiation damage is linearly proportional to dose.
2. Recovery from radiation damage which contributes to death within 30 days after exposure may be described as a simple exponential function. This assumption for mice appears to be supported adequately by the many split-dose studies in which it has been possible to determine the extent of recovery at frequent intervals after a single sublethal dose (see Table I).
3. In the case of daily exposures to equal-sized doses, the recovery process remains a simple exponential although the recovery rate for each successive dose does not necessarily remain constant. It is assumed, however, that the mean rate of recovery for successive doses can be calculated from:

$$D_e = D_d \frac{1 - e^{-\beta(n-1)}}{1 - e^{-\beta}}$$

where D_e = "effective" dose in roentgens. In the case in which the equation is solved for β, D_e is set equal to the single dose $LD_{50(30)}$.
D_d = daily dose in roentgens.
β = mean fractional recovery per day or mean recovery rate.
n = number of daily doses which are effective in producing 50% lethality. In the case of radiation to death, it is assumed that radiation during the last 10 days of life is "wasted".[3] Therefore, n is taken as the mean or median survival time minus 10 days. In the following calculations it was necessary to use median survival time and mean survival time interchangeably because of the methods used by various authors in reporting data. In view of other errors involved, it was considered that this usage introduced negligible additional errors.

The equation shown above is that derived by Mole (*14*) and by Davidson (*15*) for a similar treatment of data.

[3] Mice given a single, lethal dose of X-rays typically die 8 to 14 days after the exposure. If additional radiation is given during the latent period between the time of accumulation of a lethal level of damage and actual death this additional radiation presumably does not affect the lethal outcome or the time of death. In this sense the additional radiation is "wasted." For purposes of computing the number of doses required to produce 50% deaths it was decided arbitrarily to assume that radiation exposures during the last 10 days of life were "wasted."

4. Fifty per cent of the mice will die when the accumulated damage (measured in "effective roentgens" as described by Hagen and Simmons (*1*) reaches a level equal to the single dose $LD_{50(30)}$.

5. The $LD_{50(30)}$ is constant over about 80% of the life span of mice. It is known that very young (*16–18*) and very old (*19*) mice show an increased sensitivity to radiation. The data examined, however, were obtained in mice over the age range in which the LD_{50} changes very little with age (*18–20*).

6. There is no irreparable component of injury which is measurable by the split-dose technique. Although there can be no doubt that radiation exposure permanently injures an animal, there is no unequivocal evidence for mice that this injury takes the form of an increased sensitivity to a second single radiation exposure. Rather, as will be discussed later, it appears that the permanent damage consists of a decrement in the recovery rate.

MEAN RECOVERY RATE AS A FUNCTION OF THE NUMBER OF DAILY DOSES OF X- OR GAMMA RAYS

Table I summarizes the results of a number of studies on the rate of recovery of mice exposed to an initial sublethal dose of X-rays and later challenged with a second dose. It can be seen that the recovery half-times varied markedly and that this variation appeared to be due more to differences in strains of mice than to

TABLE I

RECOVERY RATES AND HALF-TIMES FOR MICE EXPOSED TO PAIRED X-RADIATION DOSES

Strain of mice[a]	*Initial dose (r)*	*Recovery half-time (days)*	*Recovery rate* (β)[b]	*Reference*
A/He	350	1.6	0.43	Kohn and Kallman (*9*)
Balb/C	350	2.8	0.25	Kohn and Kallman (*9*)
C3H	350	2.0	0.35	Kohn and Kallman (*9*)
C57BL	350	1.8	0.39	Kohn and Kallman (*9*)
CAF_1	350	2.1	0.33	Kohn and Kallman (*9*)
RF (female)	½LD_{50}	3.4	0.20	Melville *et al.* (*10*)
RF (male)	½LD_{50}	2.4	0.29	Melville *et al.* (*10*)
A manch	260	7.4	0.09	Paterson *et al.* (*4*)
CBA (female)	400	3.0	0.23	Mole (*6*)
CBA (male)	600	8.7	0.08	Mole (*6*)
CF-1	400	3.6	0.19	Storer and Sanders, unpublished data, 1956)

[a] Unless specified, data for males and females were pooled.

[b] A simple exponential equation of the type $D_t = D_0e^{-\beta t}$ gave an adequate fit to the data from all authors if (in cases where it applied) the results for very early times (t = 24 hours or less) were ignored. In this equation β represents the fractional amount of damage repairing per day.

TABLE II

RECOVERY RATES FOR MICE IRRADIATED DAILY TO DEATH WITH X- OR GAMMA RAYS

Strain of mice	*Type of radiation*	*Daily dose (r)*	*Mean or median survival (days)*	*Number of effective doses (n)*[a]	*Mean recovery rate (β)*	*Reference*
CF-1	X-rays	104	16.6	7	0.12	Sacher (*21*)
ABC	X-rays	88	20.6	11	0.16	Sacher (*21*)
CF-1	γ-rays	140	22	12	0.17	Thomson *et al.* (*5*)
CF-1	X-rays	68	24	14	0.12	Sacher (*21*)
C3H	X-rays	57	28	18	0.10	Henshaw (*22*)
ABC	X-rays	67	30	20	0.13	Sacher (*21*)
CF-1	γ-rays	115	37	27	0.16	Thomson *et al.* (*5*)
ABC	X-rays	42	37	27	0.08	Sacher (*21*)
CF-1	X-rays	53	37	27	0.10	Sacher (*21*)
ABC	X-rays	50	39	29	0.10	Sacher (*21*)
C3H	X-rays	43	49	39	0.09	Henshaw (*22*)
CF-1	γ-rays	90	52	42	0.12	Thomson *et al.* (*5*)
CF-1	X-rays	33	63	53	0.07	Sacher (*21*)
C3H	X-rays	29	77	67	0.06	Henshaw (*22*)
ABC	X-rays	33	79	69	0.07	Sacher (*21*)
C3H	X-rays	18	134	124	0.036	Henshaw (*22*)
C3H	X-rays	14	169	159	0.028	Henshaw (*22*)
C3H	X-rays	11	193	183	0.021	Henshaw (*22*)
ABC	X-rays	16.5	213	203	0.030	Sacher (*21*)
Swiss and CF-1	X-rays	7.9	263	253	0.012	Evans (*23*)
C3H	X-rays	7.1	265	255	0.014	Henshaw (*22*)
C3H	X-rays	3.6	279	269	0.006	Henshaw (*22*)
CF-1	γ-rays	7.4	336	326	0.008	Henshaw *et al.* (*24*)
LAF_1	γ-rays	8.8	488	478	0.014	Lorenz (*25*)
LAF_1	γ-rays	4.4	591	581	0.007	Lorenz (*25*)
LAF_1	γ-rays	2.2	630	620	0.003	Lorenz (*25*)
LAF_1	γ-rays	1.1	684	674	0.0017	Lorenz (*25*)

[a] See text.

differences in the size of the initial dose. Intuitively, one would expect the size of the initial dose to influence the rate of repair. On the basis of available information, however, it does not appear possible to correlate dose size and repair half-time.

Table II summarizes the calculated mean recovery rates for mice exposed to repeated doses of radiation to death. Some of the investigators cited exposed their animals for 5 or 6 days a week rather than daily. In those cases, the total weekly doses were spread over 7 days for convenience in computation. In a few cases, no $LD_{50(30)}$ values were reported, and it was necessary to estimate this value from the data of other authors using the same strain of mice and type of radiation. Inspection of this table indicates that, in general, the calculated mean repair rate declined as the number of daily exposures increased. There are other factors besides the total

TABLE III

RECOVERY RATES FOR MICE X-IRRADIATED DAILY FOR LIMITED PERIODS OF TIME (NO WASTED RADIATION)

Strain of mice	*Daily dose (r)*	*Number of doses (n)*	*Mean recovery rate (β)*	*Reference*
C57BL	a	2	0.23	Kaplan and Brown (*3*)
C57BL	a	4	0.25	Kaplan and Brown (*3*)
A manch	a	5	0.08	Paterson *et al.* (*4*)
CF-1	a	5	0.18	Storer and Sanders (unpublished data, 1956)
CBA	143	7[b]	0.12	Mole (*14*)
C57BL	a	8	0.18	Kaplan and Brown (*3*)
A manch	a	10	0.11	Paterson *et al.* (*4*)
CBA	71	18[b]	0.11	Mole (*14*)
A manch	a	21	0.08	Paterson *et al.* (*4*)
CBA	36	49[b]	0.045	Mole (*14*)
CBA	18	203[b]	0.025	Mole (*14*)

[a] Graded daily doses were given to a number of groups and the LD_{50} for each regimen was calculated. The value for β is based on the LD_{50} values.

[b] Constant daily doses were given to the entire subsample of mice, but radiation was discontinued at various times for various groups in the subsample. The value for n is an estimate of the number of doses for an LD_{50}.

number of exposures that probably contribute to this decline. Increasing age and the size of the daily dose are, in all likelihood, involved in this progressive decrease. Existing data are inadequate to assess the contribution of these factors, however, and for the present the decline will be considered as a function of the number of exposures.

The data in Table II are based on experiments in which the mice were irradiated to death, and, although 10 days was subtracted from the mean or median survival time to obtain the number of doses effective in producing this survival time, there is no absolute assurance that this procedure corrected adequately for "wasted" radiation. A few experiments have been performed in which mice were irradiated daily for a predetermined number of days and the LD_{50} computed for animals dying within 30 to 60 days after the end of exposure. In those cases in which radiation was delivered for only 5 days a week the reported dose levels and numbers of doses delivered were adjusted to the levels that would have given comparable total doses had they been delivered daily. The mean repair rates for this type of experiment are shown in Table III.

When the values for the mean repair rates shown in Tables I, II, and III were plotted as a function of $(n - 1)$ number of doses, it appeared that a simple exponential function would adequately describe the relationship. Such a plot is shown

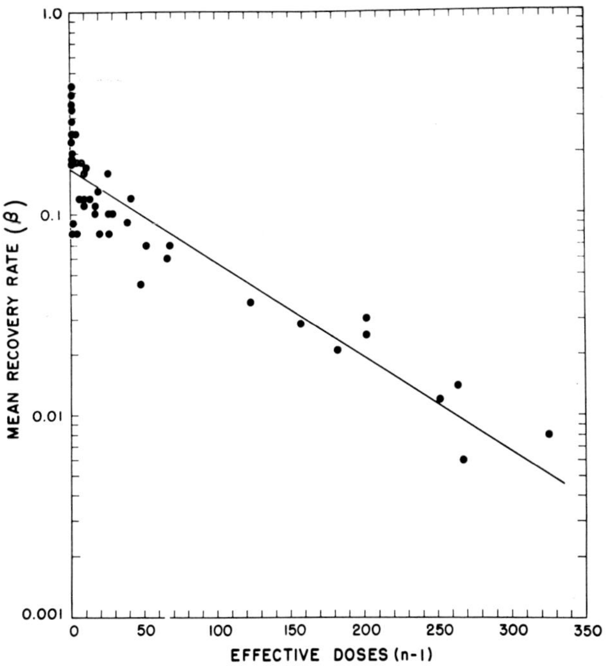

FIG. 1. Mean recovery rate as a function of $(n - 1)$ effective daily doses of X- or γ-rays.

in Fig. 1. The rationale for using $(n - 1)$, rather than n, on the abscissa was as follows. It was assumed that, as soon as the nth dose was accumulated, then the lethal level for 50% of the animals had been reached and repair of this nth dose did not affect the lethal outcome. Therefore, the mean rate of repair of $(n - 1)$ doses was the value of principal interest because this repair constant determined whether the nth dose would be fatal. A regression line relating the mean repair rate to $(n - 1)$ number of doses was calculated on the assumption that the relationship was exponential. The equation for the line was

$$\text{Mean repair rate, } \beta = 0.166e^{-0.0106(n-1)}$$

It is interesting to note that this equation appeared to hold even for high values of $(n - 1)$, where radiation had been continued for many days, and there was no reason to believe that death of the animals was due to acute causes as is the case with the single dose $LD_{50(30)}$. This fact is noteworthy because in the calculation of mean repair rates it was assumed that when the "residual effective roentgens" or unrepaired damage measured in roentgens reached the level of the acute LD_{50} half the animals would die regardless of the cause of death. The apparently smooth fit to the data suggests that either the animals dying at the long time intervals at relatively low daily doses were in reality dying from acute radiation effects or that death from other causes ensued when the effective damage reached the lethal level measured by LD_{50} studies. If this latter explanation is correct, then it is apparent that there is a relationship between acute radiation sensitivity and shortened life span.

The equation derived for mean recovery rates as a function of $(n - 1)$ doses represents a composite of a number of mouse populations sampled. Because it is based on mean or median survival times, it is, of course, possible to synthesize curves showing mean accumulated dose as a function of dose rate, per cent shortening of life span as a function of daily dose, etc. The form of such curves would necessarily be similar to those observed experimentally. Data from experiments designed to measure mean survival times at very low dose rates (sufficiently low that the total dose delivered over the life span did not equal the acute LD_{50}) were not included, however, and it was of interest to see whether the equation would hold down to these very low rates. In order to calculate survival times at these low dose rates, it was necessary to postulate that at some time in the life span of the mice the acute LD_{50} declines from the level observed in young adults. Existing evidence suggests that the $LD_{50(30)}$ remains reasonable constant throughout most of the adult life of mice (*18–20*) and decreases rapidly in old age (*19*). This finding conflicts with Blair's postulated progressive decrease with age (*11–13*). We have, therefore, set up a hypothetical population of mice with the following characteristics:

1. Mean recovery rate is given by

$$\beta = 0.166e^{-0.0106(n-1)}$$

for the daily exposure situation.

2. Radiation is begun at 3 months of age. The control mice have a mean after-expectation of life of 500 days.

3. The acute LD_{50} is 500 r of X-rays for the first 400 days, then declines linearly to 0 r at 500 days.

The mean accumulated dose at death was calculated for this hypothetical population using various daily doses ranging from 0.5 to 90 r/day. The basic equation used in the calculation was

$$LD_{50} = D_d \frac{1 - e^{-\beta n}}{1 - e^{-\beta}}$$

The approach was to select various values for n (which equals mean survival time minus 10 days), calculate the appropriate value for β for each value of n, calculate the appropriate LD_{50} from assumption 3 above, and solve for D_d (the daily dose required for 50% deaths in $n + 10$ days). The mean accumulated dose was calculated from $D_d \times (n + 10)$. The results of these calculations are shown in Fig. 2. The general shape of this curve is the same as that reported by other authors who

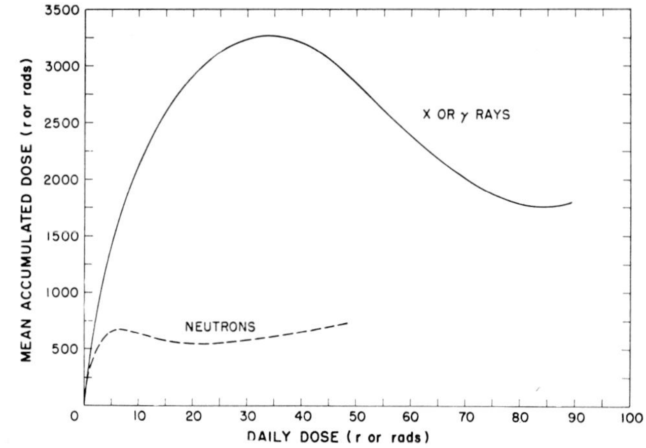

FIG. 2. Calculated values for mean accumulated dose at death as a function of daily dose of X-rays or fast neutrons.

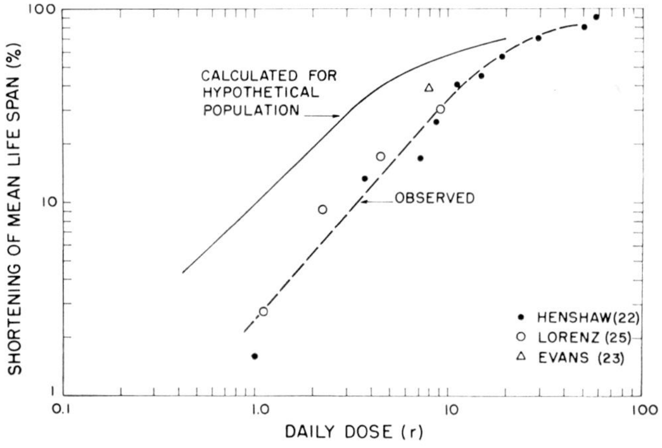

FIG. 3. Per cent shortening of mean life span as a function of daily dose.

have plotted the same variables (*1*, *21*, *26*). It should be noted that the decrease in mean accumulated dose at the very low daily dose rates described a smooth curve all the way to the zero intercept, suggesting that the model chosen was reasonable.

To determine whether life shortening predicted for the hypothetical population by this method of calculation was in general agreement with observed values for very low to reasonably high dose rates, the per cent shortening of mean survival was plotted as a function of daily dose. The theoretically derived line is shown in Fig. 3, along with a plot of some values from the literature. It can be seen that the general form of the relationship was similar for the theoretical and the observed values. A similar theoretical form was obtained by Brues and Sacher (*26*) using a different analytical approach.

APPLICATION TO THE PROBLEM OF INCREASED SENSITIVITY TO SINGLE LARGE DOSES AFTER VARIABLE SCHEDULES OF SMALL CONDITIONING DOSES

If the equation derived for decrement in mean repair rate as a function of the number of radiation exposures applies to the general case rather than only to the specific case of radiation to death, then it should be possible to predict the sensitivity of mice to large single doses of radiation at various times after the delivery of repeated small doses. The most complete experimental study utilizing this type of design appears to be that reported by Mole (*14*). He exposed CBA mice daily to doses of 10, 25, or 50 r, 5 days a week, for various lengths of time. At intervals of 0 to 18 days after the last daily dose, he determined the LD_{50} for each group.

From another portion of his study, it was possible to calculate the decrease in mean recovery rate as a function of the number of doses delivered for the strain of mice under investigation. The equation obtained was

$$\beta = 0.125e^{-0.0089(n-1)}$$

where these symbols have the same meaning as described previously. From this equation it was possible to calculate the mean repair rate for each regimen of daily treatment employed. (For simplicity of computation, it was assumed that slightly smaller doses were given 7 days a week to the same total dose over the same elapsed time as was actually employed.) Then, from the equation

$$D_e = D_d \frac{1 - e^{-\beta n}}{1 - e^{-\beta}}$$

the "effective" dose (D_e) remaining at the end of the treatment period was calculated. When there was a delay between the end of treatment and the delivery of the single doses for LD_{50} determination, the "effective" dose remaining at the time of delivery of the large single doses was obtained from

$$D_t = D_e(e^{-\beta t})$$

where D_t = "effective" dose present at time of delivery of the large single doses.
D_e = "effective" dose present at termination of the repeated conditioning doses.
β = mean recovery rate.
t = time in days between the end of the conditioning doses and delivery of the large single doses.

The $LD_{50(30)}$ for each of these experimental groups was estimated from:

$$LD_{50} \text{ of untreated controls} - D_t = LD_{50} \text{ for experimental group}$$

TABLE IV

PREDICTION OF $LD_{50\,(30)}$ FOR MOLE'S (*14*) EXPERIMENTAL DESIGN

Daily dose (r) (5 days a week)	*Total dose*	*Time from end of daily exposure to delivery of LD_{50} dose*	*Observed LD_{50} (r)*	*Predicted LD_{50} (r)*	*Per cent difference*
50	250	0	541 ± 13	550	+1.7
	500	0	467 ± 34	492	+5.4
	500	5	600 ± 18	617	+2.8
	500	11	695 ± 7	741	+6.6
	750	0	373 ± 19	426	+14.2
	1000	0	239 ± 27	394	+64.9
25	250	0	671 ± 13	630	−6.1
	500	0	622 ± 13	628	+1.0
	500	5	718 ± 13	702	−2.2
	1000	0	574 ± 22	577	+0.5
	1000	5	656 ± 21	655	−0.2
	1000	18	701 ± 77	759	+8.3
	1500	0	593 ± 8	526	−11.3
	1500	5	660 ± 19	607	−8.0
	1500	18	687 ± 11	725	+5.5
10	200	0	769 ± 36	693	−9.9
	500	0	762 ± 12	714	−6.3
	500	11	807 ± 37	771	−4.5
Controls	—		750 ± ?	—	
	—		768 ± 6	—	
	—		815 ± 8	—	

The results of these calculations are shown in Table IV. It can be seen from this table that our predicted values agreed within ±10% of the observed LD_{50} values with only three exceptions. There does not appear to be any systematic overestimation or underestimation of the LD_{50}, the two types of errors appearing with about equal frequency.

The good agreement between predicted and observed LD_{50} values suggests that the equations utilized may apply equally well to radiation to death and to increased susceptibility to acute death.

APPLICATION TO CONTINUOUS NEUTRON EXPOSURE EXPERIMENTS

It has been shown that the lethal effects of neutron exposures are relatively rate-independent over a fairly large range of exposure rates in contrast to the marked rate dependence observed for X- or γ-rays (*27,28*). It also appears that the biological effectiveness of neutrons relative to X- or γ-rays is increased in experiments in which small daily doses of each are given to shorten the mean survival time (*23, 29, 30*). These findings have led Blair (*12, 13*) to postulate that densely ionizing radiations produce a greater fraction of irreparable damage than do X- or γ-rays. His hypothesis also

TABLE V

RECOVERY RATES FOR MICE EXPOSED TO NEUTRONS

Strain of mice	*Daily dose*	*Number of effective doses (n)*	*Mean recovery rate (β)*	*Reference*
RF	a	2	0.12	Melville *et al.* (*10*)
CF-1	11 n[b]	12	0.07	Henshaw *et al.* (*24*)
CF-1	3.7 n	63	0.04	Henshaw *et al.* (*24*)
Swiss and CF-1	1 n	176	0.011	Evans (*23*)
CF-1	0.9 n	193	0.009	Henshaw *et al.* (*24*)

[a] Recovery rate determined by the split-dose technique.

[b] One n of neutrons is that amount of radiation that produces the same reading in a Victoreen ionization chamber as 1 r of X-rays.

holds that this irreparable damage (which may amount to as much as 80% of the total damage from α-particles) is manifest as a permanently increased sensitivity to acute radiation damage (a permanently lowered LD_{50}). Bond *et al.* (*31*) were unable to detect this postulated lowered LD_{50} in mice exposed to the densely ionizing particles from the $B^{10}(n, \alpha)Li^7$ reaction. Storer and Saunders (unpublished data, 1956) were similarly unable to detect an increased sensitivity of mice to X-rays 125 days after neutron exposures of as much as 420 rads. For these reasons, it was of interest to determine whether effects on the mean repair rate for continuously or repeatedly exposed mice would explain the relative rate independence of neutron effects and the increased relative potency at small daily dose rates.

The assumptions and methods of calculation of mean recovery rates were covered earlier. There were relatively few data available for analysis, but Table V summarizes the results obtained. It can be seen from this table that the recovery constants for neutrons were, in general, considerably lower than those calculated for equal numbers of exposures to X- or γ-rays. A plot of the mean recovery rate constants as a function of $(n - 1)$ number of effective doses again suggested a simple exponential relationship. Since the slope constant did not differ significantly from that obtained for X- and γ-rays, this constant was adjusted to coincide with the one previously obtained. The adjusted regression equation for mean recovery rate as a function of number of doses was

$$\beta = 0.082e^{-0.0106(n-1)}$$

This regression line is shown in Fig. 4.

In order to use this equation to synthesize a curve showing the relationship between daily dose and mean accumulated dose, a hypothetical population of mice with the following characteristics was used:

1. Mean recovery rate is given by

$$\beta = 0.082e^{-0.0106(n-1)}$$

2. Irradiation is begun at 3 months of age. The control mice have a mean after-expectation of life of 500 days.

3. The acute LD_{50} is 200 rads for the first 400 days and declines linearly to zero at 500 days.

The calculated mean accumulated dose as a function of daily dose is plotted in Fig. 2. It can be seen from this plot that neutrons show far less rate dependence for the production of lethal effects than do X-rays. A plot of per cent life shortening against daily dose (Fig. 5) indicates that the form of the relationship is the same as that for X-rays, but the slope of the line is different. Because of this difference in slope and the marked difference between the radiations with respect to rate de-

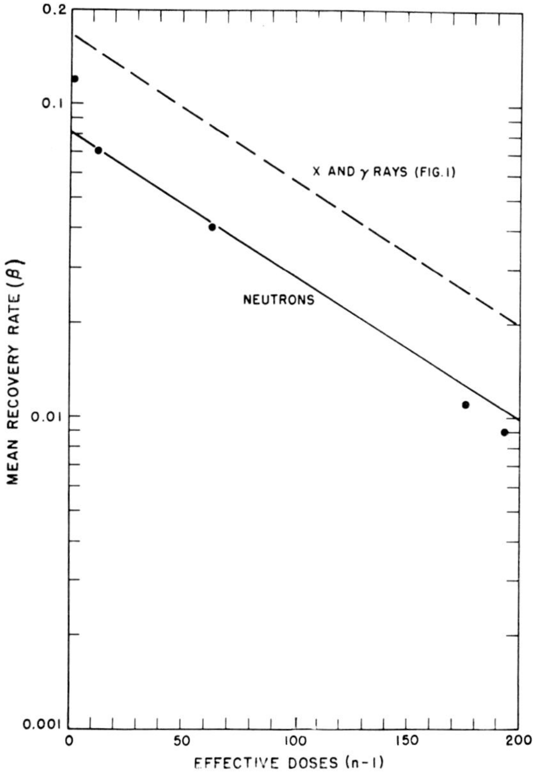

FIG. 4. Mean recovery rate as a function of $(n - 1)$ effective daily doses of fast neutrons.

pendence for effect, it follows that the relative effectiveness of the neutrons will vary with daily dose rate. Table VI summarizes the daily dose required for death at various time intervals for X-ray and neutron exposures to our hypothetical population of mice. If we assume that 1 r of X-rays is roughly equivalent to 1 rad, then the relative effectiveness or relative potency of the radiations for various dosage schedules can be calculated. With the assumptions used as to the single dose LD_{50}, the relative potency of neutrons for a single exposure is 2.5. As the number of daily doses to 50% death is increased, the relative potency values rise rapidly to a maxi-

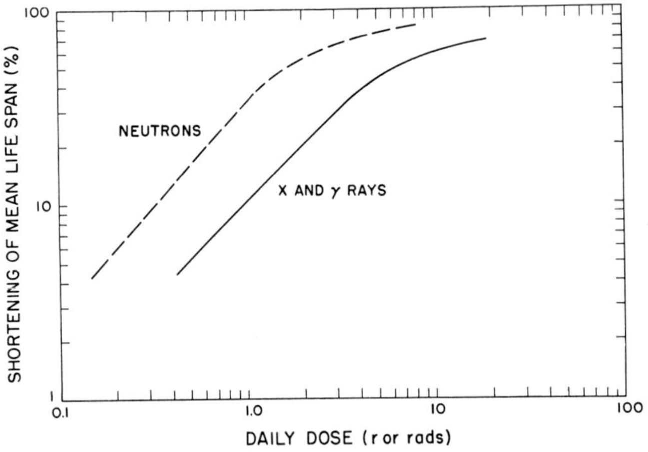

FIG. 5. Per cent shortening of mean life span as a function of daily dose of X-rays and fast neutrons.

TABLE VI

VARIATION IN RELATIVE EFFECTIVENESS OF NEUTRONS WITH SIZE OF DAILY DOSE

Mean survival time (days)	*Daily dose of X-rays (r)*	*Daily dose of neutrons (rads)*	*Relative effectiveness*
—	500[a]	200[a]	2.5
25	75	22	3.4
50	60	12	5.0
100	33	6.8	4.9
150	19	4.1	4.6
200	11	2.5	4.4
250	6.8	1.7	4.0
300	4.3	1.2	3.6
350	2.9	0.84	3.5
400	2.1	0.66	3.2
450	0.93	0.32	2.9
475	0.49	0.17	2.9

[a] Single dose LD_{50}.

mum of 5 and then gradually decline as radiation is protracted over very long times, but these values never reach the single-dose value. The model suggests, therefore, that fractionated neutron exposures may result in relative potency values at least twice as high as those obtained for single exposures. This consequence of the hypothesis is in general agreement with experimental results (*23*, *29*, *30*).

APPLICATION TO LIFE SHORTENING FROM SINGLE OR LIMITED FRACTIONAL EXPOSURES

The equations derived above appear to relate, empirically at least, the acute LD_{50} to the life shortening produced by daily exposure to death. At present, the hypothesis cannot be applied to life shortening from a single dose. A hypothesis which might relate the concepts presented here to the single-dose life-shortening phenomenon is as follows. Assume that with increasing age in normal animals there is a progressive loss of ability to repair both radiation damage and damage that normally accumulates in the course of everyday living. This assumption holds that the recovery process is identical for the two types of damage, although the types of damage may not necessarily be identical. Assume further that a single exposure causes a permanent decrease in the repair function and that aging continues to contribute to the progressive decrease. Then, if death occurs in the animals at the point at which the recovery rate is too slow to keep up with the rate at which damage from any cause is spontaneously accumulating, the recovery rate as determined by paired-dose experiments may be related to life shortening for single doses. There are not enough data available at present to evaluate this hypothesis. Two corollaries to it are easily amenable to testing, however, and some information relating to these corollaries is at hand. The first corollary holds that a single radiation exposure causes a permanent decrement in the recovery rate. Sacher (*32*) has found that, if he exposes mice to a single sublethal dose and challenges these mice at a much later time with a large single dose, they do not show an increased sensitivity to the second dose. If, however, the second exposure consists of daily irradiation to death, the animals die at lower mean accumulated doses than do controls having no previous exposure. This finding of no increased sensitivity to a second single dose is in agreement with the assumptions used in the present report, which hold that damage repairs exponentially to levels not detectable by a second single exposure and that, once a lethal level of damage is accumulated, the animal will die regardless of the rate of repair between the time of the accumulation of this lethal level and actual death. The finding of increased sensitivity to repeated daily doses supports the concept of a permanent slowing of the recovery rate as a result of a single radiation exposure.

The second corollary holds that the extent of the permanent decrease in recovery rate would necessarily be proportional to dose. This corollary to the hypothesis has not as yet been studied in sufficient detail to warrant acceptance or rejection. It appears from the literature that strain differences in recovery rates are so great that a comparison of the effect of dose size from one set of experiments to another in which different strains are used is not justified. The technique of radiation to death as employed by Sacher appears very promising for evaluation of the effect of the size of the initial dose.

GENERAL COMMENTS

In the present analysis of the effect of repeated exposures on the mean recovery rate, the decline in mean rate was related to the number of exposures without regard to the size of the exposure. Intuitively, it seems likely that the size of the daily dose as well as increasing age must contribute to the general decrement in repair. Since it was not possible to evaluate separately the contribution of each factor, the relationship was established arbitrarily as a function of the number of doses. It should be pointed out that Mole (*14*) has offered an alternative explanation of the low repair rate for a large number of small doses. He has suggested that each small dose simply does not produce enough damage to stimulate maximum repair and, as a result, the mean recovery rate for multiple small doses is lower than for a small number of large doses. Fortunately, these alternative hypotheses can be tested experimentally.

Finally, the concept of no residual injury detectable by the split-dose technique should not be interpreted as meaning that there is no permanent damage from radiation exposure. Rather, the suggestion is made that the permanent damage is manifest as an irreversible decrease in the rate at which subsequent damage can be repaired and a hypothesis has been advanced which attempts to relate this effect to a decreased life span.

SUMMARY

It was shown that the mean rate at which mice recover from the radiation damage contributing to acute death can be related empirically to the number of daily radiation doses delivered. Neutron-induced damage recovers more slowly at all time intervals than does X- or γ-radiation damage. By using the empirically derived relationships and certain assumptions about the change in LD_{50} with age, it was possible to predict the general form of the relation between daily dose and shortening of life span. The application of the equations to the problem of increased sensitivity to further exposure after various regimens of small daily doses was discussed. A further consequence of the hypothesis was shown to be that the relative lethal effectiveness of neutrons will vary with the size of the daily exposure. A hypothesis relating recovery rate to life shortening in general was advanced.

RECEIVED: June 2, 1958

REFERENCES

1. C. W. HAGEN, JR., and E. L. SIMMONS, Effects of total-body X irradiation on rats. Lethal action of single, paired, and periodic doses. University of Chicago Metallurgical Laboratory Report CH-3815 (1947).

2. F. W. FURTH, M. P. COULTER, and J. W. HOWLAND, Effect of a second large dose of X radiation on dogs surviving one dose of X radiation. University of Rochester Report UR-152, pp. 47–53 (1951).
3. H. S. KAPLAN and M. B. BROWN, Mortality of mice after total body irradiation as influenced by alterations in total dose, fractionation, and periodicity of treatment. *J. Natl. Cancer Inst.* **12,** 765–775 (1952).
4. E. PATERSON, C. W. GILBERT, and J. MATTHEWS, Time intensity factors and whole body irradiation. *Brit. J. Radiol.* **25,** 427–433 (1952).
5. J. F. THOMSON, W. W. TOURTELLOTTE, M. S. CARTTAR, R. S. COX, JR., and J. E. WILSON, Studies on effects of continuous exposure of animals to cobalt 60 plane sources. *Am. J. Roentgenol. Radium Therapy Nuclear Med.* **69,** 830–838 (1953).
6. R. H. MOLE, Quantitative observations on recovery from whole body irradiation in mice. I. Recovery after single large doses of radiation. *Brit. J. Radiol.* **29,** 563–569 (1956).
7. A. L. CARSTEN and T. R. NOONAN, Determination of the recovery from lethal effects of lower body irradiation in rats. University of Rochester Report UR-455 (1956).
8. H. I. KOHN and R. F. KALLMAN, The influence of strain on acute X-ray lethality in the mouse. II. Recovery rate studies. *Radiation Research* **6,** 329–338 (1957).
9. H. I. KOHN and R. F. KALLMAN, Acute lethality studies with the rat: The LD_{50}, death rate, and recovery rate. *Radiation Research* **7,** 85–97 (1957).
10. G. S. MELVILLE, JR., F. P. CONTE, M. SLATER, and A. C. UPTON, Acute lethality of mice as influenced by the periodicity of paired exposures to fast neutrons or X rays. *Brit. J. Radiol.* **30,** 196–199 (1957).
11. H. A. BLAIR, A formulation of the injury, life span, dose relations for ionizing radiations. I. Application to the mouse. University of Rochester Report UR-206 (1952).
12. H. A. BLAIR, A formulation of the injury, life span, dose relations for ionizing radiations. II. Application to the guinea pig, rat and dog. University of Rochester Report UR-207 (1952).
13. H. A. BLAIR, A formulation of the relation between radiation dose and shortening of life span. *Proc. Intern. Conf. Peaceful Uses Atomic Energy, Geneva, 1955* **11,** 118–120 (1956).
14. R. H. MOLE, Quantitative observations on recovery from whole body irradiation in mice. II. Recovery during and after daily irradiation. *Brit. J. Radiol.* **30,** 40–46 (1957).
15. H. O. DAVIDSON, *Biological Effects of Whole-Body Gamma Radiation on Human Beings*, p. 74, The Johns Hopkins Press, Baltimore, 1957.
16. H. QUASTLER, Studies on roentgen death in mice. II. Body weight and sensitivity. *Am. J. Roentgenol. Radium Therapy* **54,** 457–461 (1945).
17. H. L. ABRAMS, Influence of age, body weight, and sex on susceptibility of mice to the lethal effects of X radiation. *Proc. Soc. Exptl. Biol. Med.* **76,** 729–732 (1951).
18. H. I. KOHN and R. F. KALLMAN, Age, growth, and the LD_{50} of X rays. *Science* **124,** 1078 (1956).
19. G. A. SACHER, Dependence of acute radiosensitivity on age in the adult female mouse. *Science* **125,** 1039–1040 (1957).
20. R. E. ZIRKLE, E. ANDERSON, E. F. RILEY, and H. J. CURTIS, The effect of age on the radiosensitivity of mice. Manhattan Project Report MDDC-418 (1946).
21. G. A. SACHER, The survival of mice under duration-of-life exposure to X rays at various dose rates. University of Chicago Metallurgical Laboratory Report CH-3900 (1946).
22. P. S. HENSHAW, Experimental roentgen injury. IV. Effects of repeated small doses of X rays on blood picture, tissue morphology, and life span in mice. *J. Natl. Cancer Inst.* **4,** 513–522 (1944).
23. T. C. EVANS, Effects of small daily doses of neutrons on mice. *Radiology* **50,** 811–833 (1948).

24. P. S. Henshaw, R. S. Snider, E. F. Riley, G. E. Stapleton, and R. E. Zirkle, Comparative late effects of periodic doses of fission neutrons and of gamma rays. Manhattan Project Report MonH-115 (1946).
25. E. Lorenz, Some biologic effects of long-continued irradiation. *Am. J. Roentgenol. Radium Therapy* **63,** 176–185 (1950).
26. A. M. Brues and G. A. Sacher, Analysis of mammalian radiation injury and lethality. In *Symposium on Radiobiology* (J. J. Nickson, ed.), Chapter 23, John Wiley & Sons, New York, 1952.
27. L. H. Gray, Comparative studies of the biological effects of X rays, neutrons and other ionizing radiations. *Brit. Med. Bull.* **4,** 11–18 (1946).
28. J. W. Clark, D. L. Jordan, and H. H. Vogel, Jr., Biological effects of fast neutrons and gamma rays. *Proc. Intern. Conf. Peaceful Uses Atomic Energy, Geneva, 1955* **11,** 110–114 (1956).
29. P. S. Henshaw, E. F. Riley, and G. E. Stapleton, The biologic effects of pile radiations. *Radiology* **49,** 349–360 (1947).
30. T. C. Evans, The influence of quantity and quality of radiation on the biologic effect. In *Symposium on Radiobiology* (J. J. Nickson, ed.), Chapter 20, John Wiley & Sons, New York, 1952.
31. V. P. Bond, E. P. Cronkite, and O. D. Easterday, Degree to which recovery from acute alpha-irradiation is possible. *Radiation Research* **7,** 304 (1957).
32. G. A. Sacher, A new procedure for the investigation of X ray injury and recovery, and some preliminary results. Argonne National Laboratory Report ANL-4163, pp. 83–85 (1948).

RADIATION RESEARCH 10, 197–212 (1959)

Microscopic Metabolism of Calcium in Bone

I. Three-Dimensional Deposition of Ca^{45} in Canine Osteons[1]

J. H. MARSHALL,[2] V. K. WHITE,[3] AND J. COHEN[4]

INTRODUCTION

Recent concern about the long-term effects of radioactivity deposited in the skeleton has emphasized the need for quantitative knowledge of fundamental processes in bone on a microscopic scale. It is well known that the deposition and retention of radioactive elements in bone is nonuniform. Some of the radioactivity concentrates in discrete histological structures and then is subject to widely varying but quantitatively unknown rates of turnover. We should like to know more about these radioactive concentrations, or "hotspots." How intense are they? Where do they occur in bone? How long do they last? Can hotspots migrate from one location to another? What fraction of bone do hotspots occupy? How much of the total skeletal activity is *not* represented by hotspots? And, finally, how do differences in age, species, and timing of radioactive intake affect the distribution of radioactivity in bone?

The development of two quantitative microscopic techniques has made it possible to approach the answer to some of these questions. Quantitative autoradiography and quantitative X-ray microradiography, together with kinetic analysis of the specific activity of the blood after a single injection of Ca^{45}, can yield the rates of accretion and exchange of calcium in volumes of bone of the order of 10^{-6} cm^3. An investigation of calcium metabolism on this microscopic scale is valuable for three reasons. First, the measurements can be focused on volumes of bone so small that one can investigate the histological elements of bone structure which in different proportions are common to all bone. Thus we may hope to obtain data which describe bone in general rather than bone limited to particular parts of particular animals. Second, the results may begin to bridge the experimental gap between *in vivo* measurements of calcium metabolism in the body as a whole and *in vitro* measurements of the physical chemistry of bone mineral. Third, the chemical

[1] Work performed under the auspices of the U. S. Atomic Energy Commission.

[2] Radiological Physics Division, Argonne National Laboratory, Lemont, Illinois; formerly at Radioactivity Center, Massachusetts Institute of Technology, Cambridge, Massachusetts.

[3] Radioactivity Center, Massachusetts Institute of Technology, Cambridge, Massachusetts.

[4] Children's Medical Center, Boston, Massachusetts.

similarity of calcium to the other alkaline earth metals makes it probable that the results will elucidate the behavior of radium and strontium in bone.

This investigation began during a Ca^{45} tracer study of bone grafts in dogs (*1*). There it was found that the autoradiographic darkening over large areas of callus in dogs given a single injection of Ca^{45} could be quantitatively related to the average specific activity of the blood during callus calcification. This indicated that callus Ca^{45} represented primarily accretion and yielded approximately the timing of callus calcification. Measurements were also made of the darkening produced by osteon hotspots, by diffuse activity, and by periosteal activity, and we wondered whether these values could similarly be related to blood-specific activities and the timing of calcification. If so, we might be able not only to measure rates of growth but also to relate them directly to radiation dose under different conditions of radioactive injection.

These normal components of Ca^{45} uptake turned out to be more difficult than callus to analyze for two reasons. First, the Ca^{45} uptake does not necessarily correspond simply to accretion, particularly in the diffuse component (*2*). This complication has been elucidated by combining autoradiography with quantitative microradiography and blood curve analysis. Second, osteon and periosteal deposits of Ca^{45} after single injections are nonuniform and confined to regions of bone with at least one dimension much smaller than β-particle range. It is therefore practically impossible to relate autoradiographic darkening directly to specific activity or calcification rate. One must first know something about the size or three-dimensional continuity of such a deposit before attempting autoradiographic quantification.

Therefore, the purpose of the present paper is to present a three-dimensional study of the deposition of Ca^{45} in osteon hotspots. Particular emphasis has been placed on their longitudinal continuity, their length, and their relationship with the structure of the osteon network in bone. In subsequent papers we shall describe the autoradiographic technique suggested by these results, the microradiographic technique, and quantitative results concerning hotspots, diffuse, and periosteal activity.

The three-dimensional pattern of deposition of Ca^{45} in the osteons of canine cortical bone to be discussed below has been investigated by two techniques: serial facing (*3*) and serial sectioning. The description and results will be given separately for the two techniques, since they were in fact applied at different laboratories and to different animals. All results reported here were obtained by qualitative observation of hotspot intensities; quantitative densitometry will be described in the later papers. From reported quantitative work (*1*), however, it can be estimated that the hotspots discussed here have net linear autoradiographic darkening values between three and thirty times the net darkening of the diffuse component. The minimum detectable hotspot darkening is, by the present qualitative technique, roughly twice the net diffuse darkening.

SERIAL FACING

Method

A middle-aged mongrel dog (C119) weighing 8 kg was injected intravenously with Ca^{45} (0.06 mc/kg) and sacrificed 14 days after injection. Both femurs were dehydrated in alcohol and embedded in Bioplastic. Six cross-section blocks 1 mm thick were taken, four from the middle of the right femur shaft (CF 35, 36, 37, 38), one from the middle of the left femur shaft (CF 79), and one from the distal end of the left femur shaft (CF 97). These undecalcified cross-section blocks were faced repeatedly on a lathe (*3*), the cutting tool removing 50 μ of the bone surface between faces and advancing toward the distal end of each block. Each face was autoradiographed on an Eastman No Screen autoradiographic plate, which required an exposure of 20 hours. A typical autoradiogram is shown in Fig. 1. The autoradiograms and the bone blocks, which were mounted on slides, were held during exposure in a right-angled jig identical to the slide holder on the microscope, so that alternate examination of the plate and the bone gave an unambiguous identification of the hotspots with their corresponding osteons. A few (5 to 15) of the more intense hotspots on the initial autoradiogram from each block were chosen to be followed. Then at each bone face photomicrographs centered on each of the chosen hotspots were taken of the bone surface.

The 50-μ interval between successive faces was chosen to yield a maximum of information about the continuity of the Ca^{45} deposition in the osteons. The range of the Ca^{45} β-particle in bone is such that the half-value thickness for absorption is about 30 μ. Thus, intervals of less than 50 μ, though feasible, would have resulted in a useless overlap of autoradiographic information, and intervals larger than 50 μ might have allowed us to miss significant variations in the deposition. The initial thickness of each block was limited to about 1 mm to permit photography with transmitted light.

Comparison of Ca^{45} Deposition with Osteon Anatomy

The autoradiograms and photomicrographs from the left femur shaft were compared in detail in an effort to reveal any correlation between the ending of a hotspot and the characteristics or vascular connections of the corresponding osteon. This comparison is illustrated by Figs. 2 to 5. The number of hotspots chosen at the start of facing was 33. Of these 33 hotspots, 21 were observed to end, and 12 persisted through all facings.

The results may be classified as follows:

1. Hotspot disappearance as an osteon with a large canal is followed into a region of resorption. (The temporal sequence of events must be just the opposite, since a resorption cavity is the first step in the formation of an osteon.) The central spot in Fig. 2 is an example of this class, of which there were four instances.

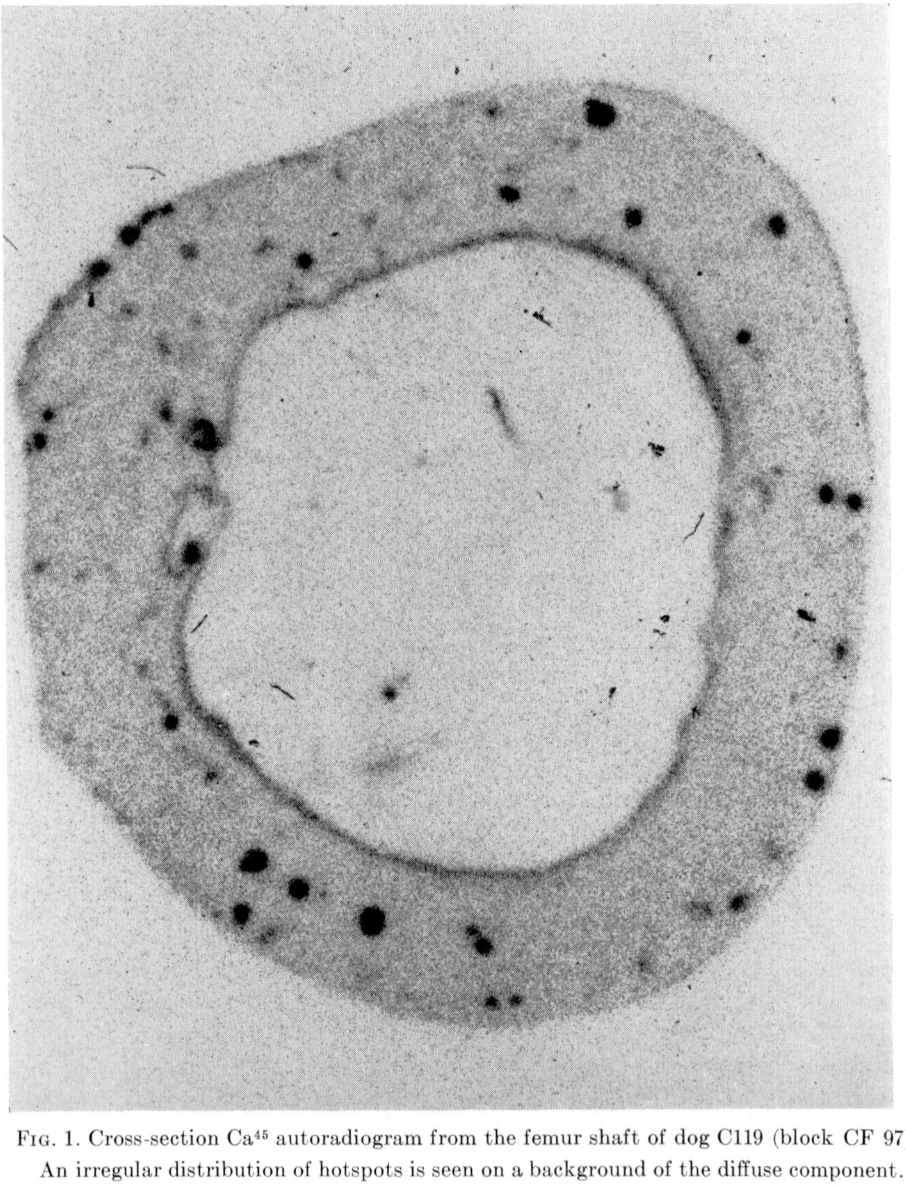

FIG. 1. Cross-section Ca^{45} autoradiogram from the femur shaft of dog C119 (block CF 97). An irregular distribution of hotspots is seen on a background of the diffuse component.

2. Hotspot disappearance as the diameter of the osteon's canal decreases to the common minimum diameter (about 20 μ); no evidence of branches. Two instances.

3. Hotspot disappearance coincident with the blind ending of the osteon itself. Six instances, of which Fig. 3 is typical. Although they were not apparent on the

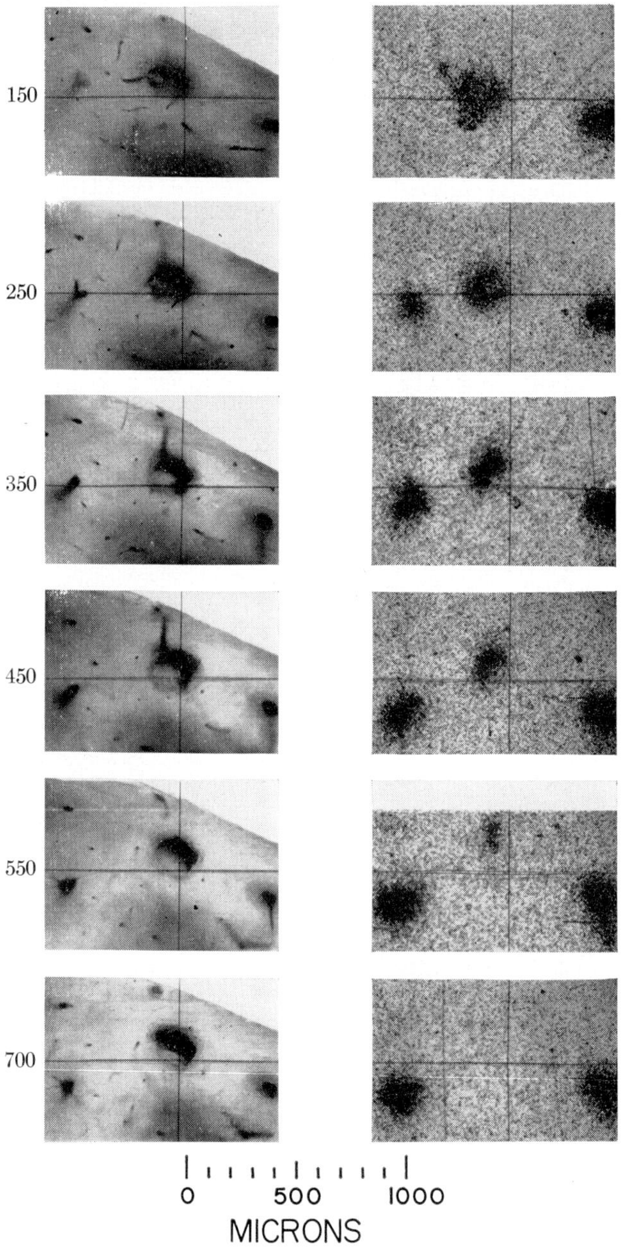

FIG. 2. Serial photomicrographs and corresponding autoradiograms of individual osteon hotspots in the femur midshaft of dog C119. Numbers at the left refer to the depth of the bone face in microns.

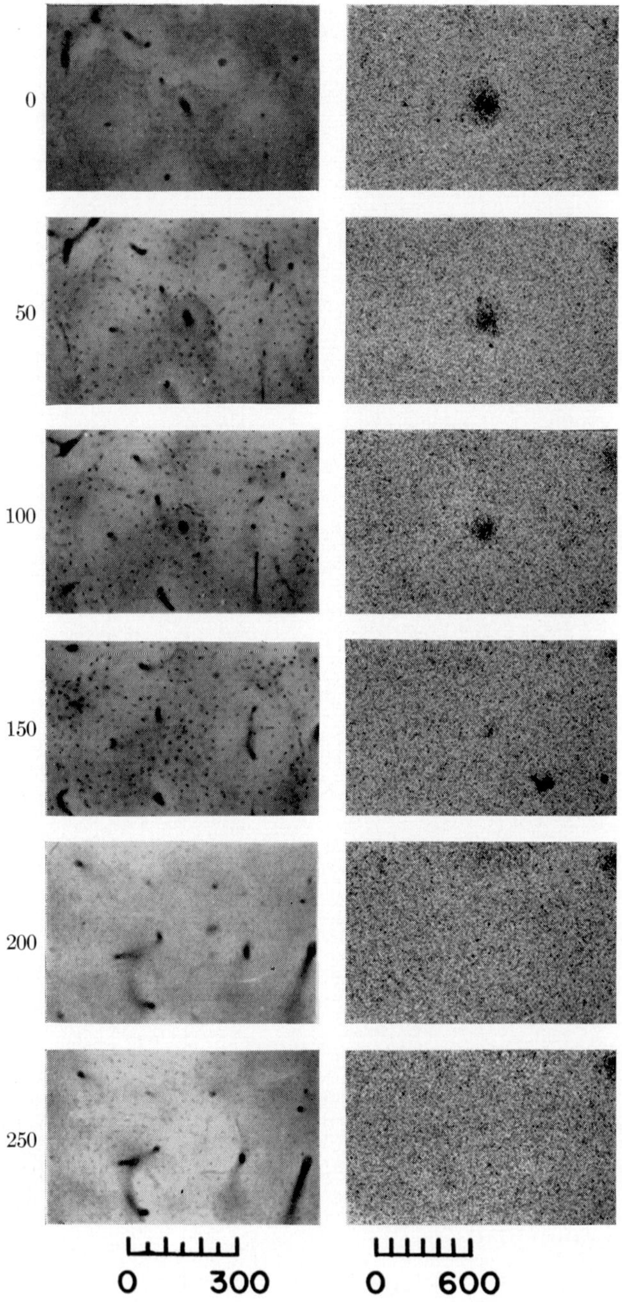

FIG. 3. Same as Fig. 2. Blindly ending osteon and hotspot. Note that the autoradiogram scale is reduced to include more than one spot for reference.

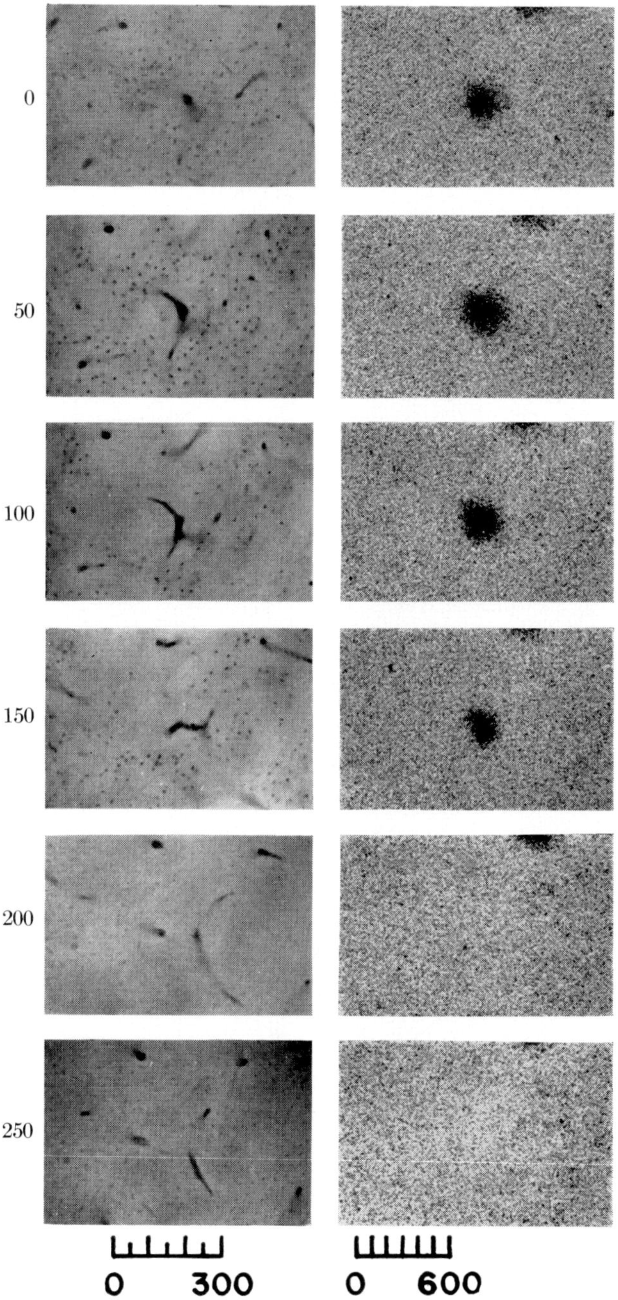

FIG. 4. Same as Fig. 2. Disappearance of hotspot at branching of osteon.

photomicrographs, the central canals of some of these osteons may have continued beyond the lamellae of the osteons. Anatomical demonstration has also indicated, however, that some blindly ending systems (*4*) may show active deposition of bone.

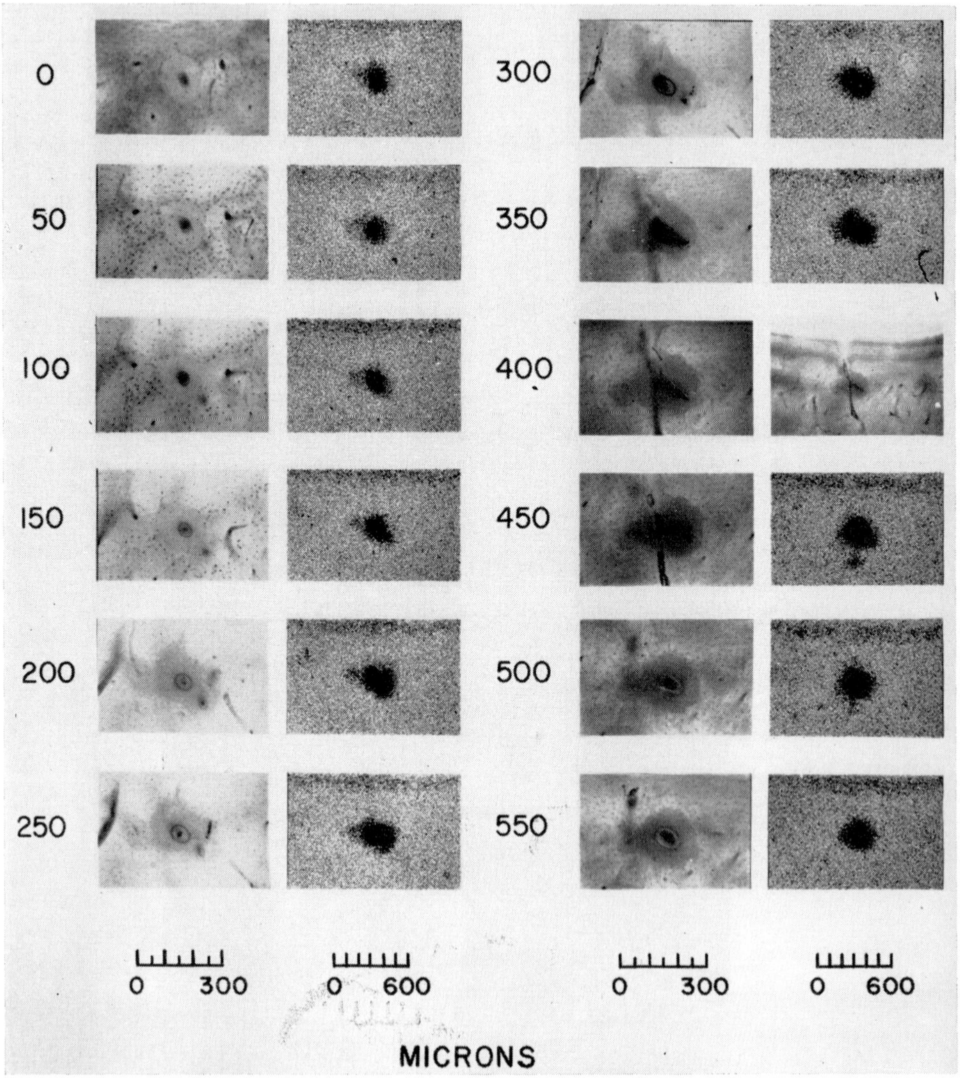

FIG. 5. Same as Fig. 2. Persistence of hotspot despite nonradioactive branching canal at 400 to 450. Photomicrograph substitutes for missing autoradiogram at 400. Note correlation between canal diameter and hotspot darkening area in 0 to 250. This correlation will be analyzed quantitatively in paper IV of this series.

4. Hotspot disappearance coincident with branching of the osteon's canal or junction with other canals. There were nine instances of this class, in two of which the joining canal itself was radioactive and in seven of which the joining canal(s) contained no detectable Ca^{45} in excess of the diffuse component. Figure 4 shows an example of hotspot disappearance coincident with a branching point in which the branches are not detectably radioactive.

5. Hotspot persistence through all sections examined, despite branching canals which are radioactive. In Fig. 2, the spot on the right illustrates this. Two instances.

6. Hotspot persistence through all sections examined, despite branching canals which are not radioactive. Three instances, one of which is shown in Fig. 5.

7. Hotspot persistence through all sections examined without branching canals. Seven instances.

The Length of a Hotrod

The above results of serial facing suggest that "hotrod" might be better than "hotspot" as a three-dimensional description of the Ca^{45} deposition in osteons. A cross-section autoradiogram through a three-dimensional "hotrod" would then record a two-dimensional "hotspot."

From the observed number of hotspots which disappear in a given depth of bone we can calculate approximately the average length of a hotrod. Let us assume

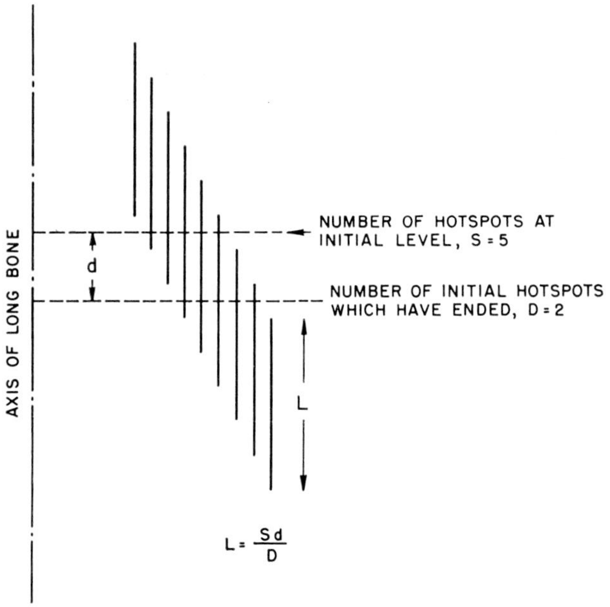

FIG. 6. Derivation of hotrod length, L, from the observed disappearance of hotspots in serial facing, with all hotrods assumed to be the same length.

for the moment that every hotrod is the same length, and that their distribution is random along the length of the bone; this situation is schematically represented in Fig. 6. If the number of hotspots present in the starting cross sections is S, and the number of hotspots which have disappeared within a distance d below the given section is D, then the hotrod length is $L = Sd/D$. From this relation, the data in Table I give $L = 1.3 \pm 0.3$ mm. The χ^2 test for these data gives $P = 0.2$, so the deviations in the data in Table I may be considered random. No correction has been made for β-particle range because the half-value thickness for Ca^{45} is only about 0.03 mm. This hotrod length, L, was derived with the over-simplified assumption that all hotrods were the same length. If we take a distribution of lengths like that in Fig. 9, however, and perform the same analysis indicated by Fig. 6, the value for the average hotrod length is only 20 to 30% larger than that derived above.

The fact that the average osteon hotrod was found to be over a millimeter in length suggested that for tracing hotrods it was not necessary to use serial autoradiogram intervals as small as 50 μ. By using a small segment of a cross section, it was found to be possible to section undecalcified bone at 300-μ intervals and to obtain autoradiograms at 150-μ intervals. This serial sectioning technique, de-

TABLE I

Calculation of Average Hotrod Length from Serial Facing

Block number	*Initial number of hotspots, S*	*Observed endings, D*	*Depth faced, d*	*Sd*	*Expected endings,* $\frac{Sd}{L}$	χ^2, $\frac{(Sd/L - D)^2}{Sd/L}$
CF 35	7	0	450 μ	3,150 μ	2.4	2.4
CF 36	5	3	450	2,250	1.7	1.0
CF 37	7	2	450	3,150	2.4	0.1
CF 38	14	4	450	6,300	4.8	0.1
CF 79	14	10	550	7,700	5.8	3.0
CF 97	15	6	700	10,500	7.9	0.5
		$\sum D = 25$		$\sum Sd = 33{,}050\ \mu$		$\chi^2 = 7.1$

If all hotrods are assumed to be the same length:

$$L \cong \frac{\sum Sd}{\sum D} = \frac{33{,}050\ \mu}{25} = 1320\ \mu$$

or

$$L = 1.3 \pm 0.3 \text{ mm}$$

The total number of observed events is $\sum D = 25$, so the standard error is 20%, or 0.3 mm. Probability that repetition of the observations would show greater statistical deviations than $\chi^2 = 7.1$ is $P = 0.2$, so the given data are self-consistent. Assuming a reasonable distribution of hotrod lengths raises L 20 to 30%.

scribed below, made it possible to follow hotrods much further than 1 mm, the limitation imposed by the need for light transmission through the bone block in the serial facing technique. For convenience, the serial sectioning technique was applied to a young animal in the midst of rapid osteon formation so that many hotspots could be found in a small segment of bone.

SERIAL SECTIONING

Method

A young adult mongrel dog (C120) weighing 9.8 kg was injected intravenously with Ca^{45} (0.04 mc/kg) and sacrificed 12 hours after injection. This short time interval should not affect the present results, since here we are concerned only with the pattern of deposition and not absolute hotspot intensities. A cross-section block about 1 cm long was taken from the midshaft of the right humerus, dehydrated in alcohol, and embedded in Bioplastic. This undecalcified block was cut longitudinally into quadrants, so that subsequent sectioning could be performed with a small circular saw. One quadrant was sectioned twenty-six times at 300-μ intervals with a circular saw 150 μ (0.006 inch) thick and 1¾ inches in diameter.

Autoradiograms were then made at 150-μ intervals by sandwiching each of the 150-μ-thick bone sections between autoradiographic plates. When the plates were analyzed under the microscope, every other plate was turned upside down so that the hotspots on adjacent plates could be superimposed. Since the majority of hotspots changed very little from plate to plate, it was simple to maintain the identity of each hotrod on the successive plates. The analysis of the plates was greatly facilitated by projecting each plate at a magnification of 20× on the ground glass of an Eastman Contour projector. The position of each hotspot was traced in black pencil, and its relative intensity was recorded in a color code directly on the ground glass. When the next plate was projected and superimposed on the tracing, the modification in the tracing necessary to make it correspond to the new plate could be made.

Osteon Hotrods in Three Dimensions

The hotspots in 52 serial autoradiograms were analyzed by choosing section 24 as the master section, of which Fig. 7 is the autoradiogram. Every prominent hotspot (52 in all) which appeared in the master section was followed either until it disappeared or for 23 sections proximal and 28 sections distal to this master section, a total distance of 7.65 mm.

Figure 8 shows the results of this three-dimensional mapping. Hotrods which interconnect are placed side by side in order to simplify the map. The width of the hotrods is drawn to the same scale as their length. Each hotrod is drawn vertically in a single column even though individual osteon hotrods may not run perfectly parallel to the axis of the bone. No attempt was made to distinguish between

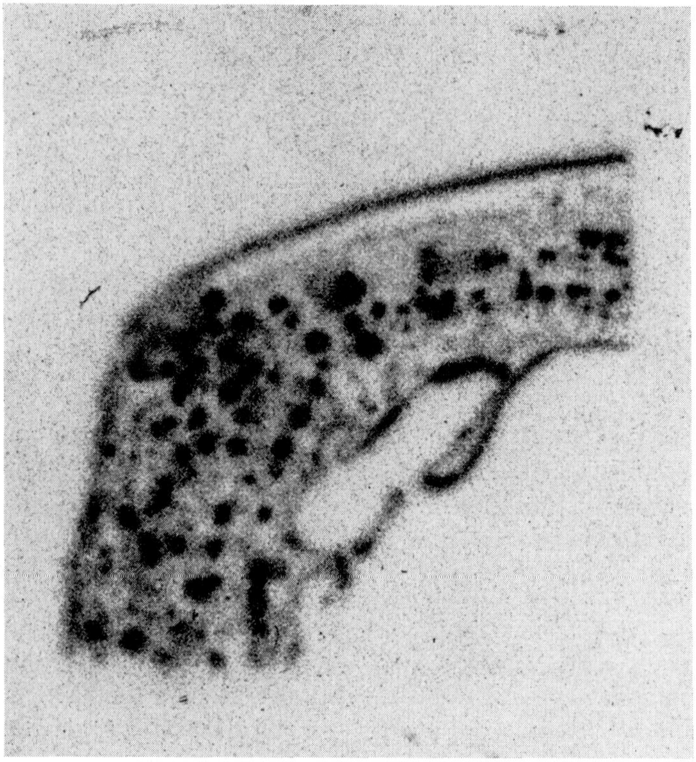

FIG. 7. Cross-section Ca^{45} autoradiogram of the humeral midshaft of dog C120. This is the number 24 in a series of 52 autoradiograms from which Fig. 8 was constructed.

hotspots that appeared on the autoradiograms merely as spots and those that were large enough and well enough resolved to appear as crescents or rings. The widths of the activity distributions shown in Fig. 8 were obtained by subtracting 100 μ from the average width of the hotspot as measured on the autoradiogram, a procedure which compensates approximately for the effect of resolution; no hotspot smaller than 100 μ in diameter (full width at half maximum) was observed. In Fig. 8, the most intense Ca^{45} darkening is represented by black, with lesser darkening values in gray, and those barely detectable in white. (See end of Introduction for quantitative estimates.) Points along a hotrod at which active branches occurred but which were not followed are indicated by bulges.

Distribution of Hotrod Lengths

The distribution of the lengths of hotrods appearing in Fig. 8 is given in Fig. 9. The length of every hotrod which appeared in the master section was measured from the first point of detectable activity above the master section to the last

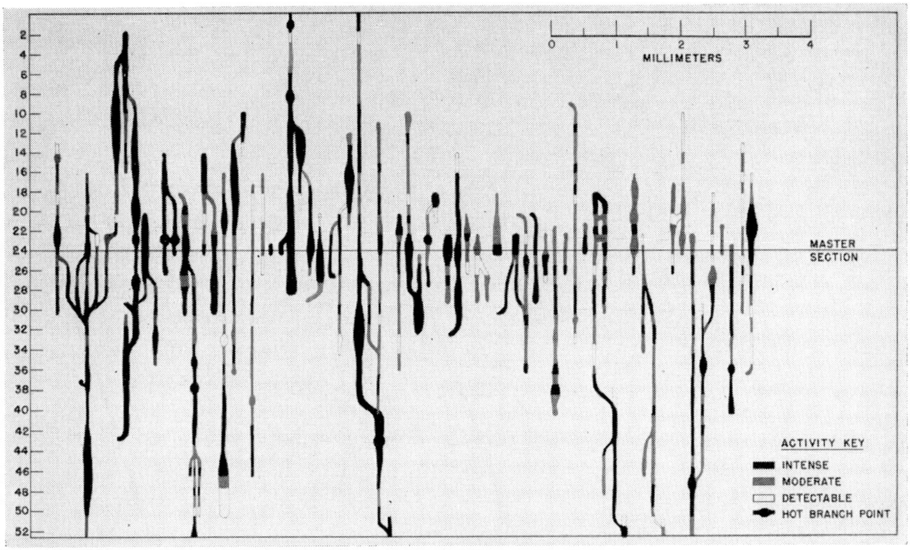

FIG. 8. Three-dimensional extension of 52 of the more intense hotrods intersecting Fig. 7. The ordinates refer to serial autoradiogram number. Approximate hotrod widths were obtained by subtracting 0.1 mm from observed hotspot widths. A millimeter scale for both ordinate and abscissa is shown at upper right. Convenience in graphing determined placement of hotrods on the abscissa. Minimum detectable activity refers to autoradiographic darkening about twice, and maximum intense to about thirty times the diffuse darkening. Intensity alternation of a hotrod at successive levels indicates classification uncertainty rather than true alternation.

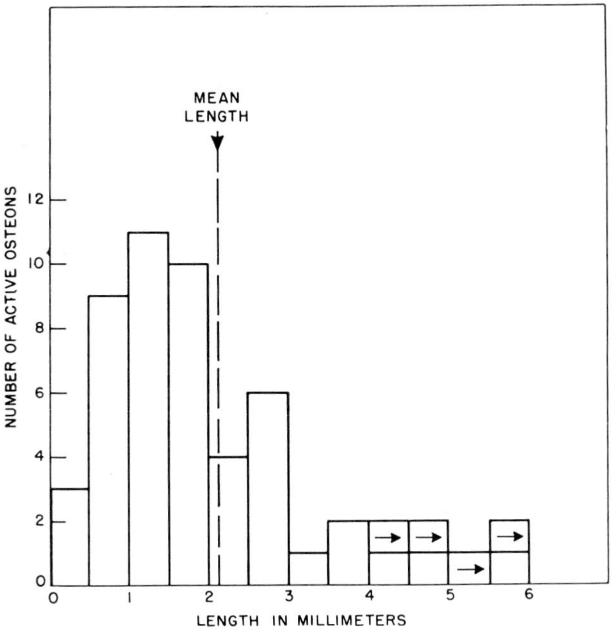

FIG. 9. Distribution of hotrod lengths measured from Fig. 8. Measurements were restricted to hotrods present in section 24, radioactive lateral branches (connections between vertical columns) being neglected. Arrows indicate hotrods extending beyond observed sections and hence represent partial lengths.

detectable activity below the master section. In those cases in which one of the hotrods of the master section connected laterally with another hotrod not present in the master section, the length includes only the original hotrod and does not extend beyond the branch point. Only 4 of the 52 hotrods present in the master section continued beyond the limits of the segment analyzed. These systems are recorded in Fig. 9 (at the partial lengths measured) with arrows pointing to the right. The mean length of the hotrods in Fig. 9 is thus somewhat over 2.1 mm.

DISCUSSION

It is well known that hotspots in cortical bone are related to secondary haversian systems or osteons (*2*, *5*, *6*). This is also shown clearly in Figs. 2 through 5. Three stages are known to occur in the formation of an osteon. First, by the process of resorption an approximately cylindrical cavity 100 to 150 μ in diameter[5] is dug within previously existing bone. Second, new bone is laid down in layers around the walls of this cavity until the remaining canal has a diameter of about 20 μ.[5] Third, the mineral density of the new bone increases very slowly to that of the surrounding bone (*7*). The seven classes into which the data concerning comparison of Ca^{45} deposition with osteon anatomy have been divided above can be qualitatively linked to this process of osteon formation. In class 1 the appearance of Ca^{45} activity in the osteon evidently corresponds to the beginning of the second or apposition stage of osteon formation. The fact that a resorption cavity becomes a filling osteon as one moves along the canal suggests that the region of new calcification also advances along the resorption cavity as time goes on. Class 2 probably represents the cessation of the formation of new bone within an osteon after the diameter of the osteon's canal has decreased to its final value. (The rate of increase in mineral density during the third stage of osteon formation is slow so that the Ca^{45} deposited by this process is probably part of the diffuse component which forms the autoradiographic background for the observed hotspots.) Class 3 is probably associated with the tunneling and formation of an osteon in a volume of bone which did not previously contain a blood vessel. Despite the existence of class 3, most of the hotrods are associated with canals which extend for indefinite distances beyond both longitudinal limits of the hotrod.

Classes 4, 5, 6, and 7 have a bearing on whatever local mechanism determines the location and length of resorption cavities; since a resorption cavity must precede the formation of a hotrod, it is reasonable to assume that the longitudinal limits of the cavity determine the longitudinal limits of the subsequent hotrod (with the exception of class 1, which represents a hotrod which has not yet expanded into all the available cavity). Thus the many examples of class 4 suggest that most resorption cavities begin or terminate at vascular branches. Class 7 might also support this view. The finding of classes 5 and 6, however, prevent us from coming

[5] These figures apply to osteons in dog. Those for man are twice as large.

to any general conclusion about the location of resorption cavity limits because there seems to be no consistent correlation between the beginning and ends of hotrods and the locations of branch canals.

Now let us consider the measured average length of hotrods. The value derived from serial facing compares favorably with the value of about 2 mm derived by serial sectioning. This agreement is remarkable, considering the differences between the animals. The former value was measured for a middle-aged dog in which the rate of bone replacement by resorption and osteon formation was so slow that a cross section through the shaft of a long bone contained only 10 to 20 hotspots. In contrast, the latter measurement was obtained from a young, adult dog in a burst of new osteon formation which was revealed by the presence of several hundred hotspots in a corresponding long-bone shaft cross section.

The observed distribution and average length of canine hotrods corresponds well to the lengths of resorption cavities (or haversian spaces) which have recently been determined in dog by histological examination of serial sections of unlabeled bone (*4*). For comparison, Hoecker and Roofe (*5*) reported cylinders of activity essentially uniform for distances of at least 2 mm in osteon deposits of radium in human bone.

A glance at Fig. 8 will indicate that somewhat arbitrary criteria are required for defining the total length of a hotrod when there are many hotspots per unit area. Thus of greater significance than the total length is the fact (Fig. 8) that the most intense, large-diameter regions of canine hotrods are the order of a millimeter in length. A relation between this millimeter length and the rates of calcium supply and deposition in osteons will be discussed in paper IV of this series.

For development of an applicable quantitative autoradiographic technique, it is significant that most osteon deposits of Ca^{45} have considerable longitudinal extent. From Fig. 8, it appears it should not be difficult to find many osteon hotrods in 100-μ-thick cross sections of bone which have activity distributions practically invariant with depth through the section. An autoradiographic technique based on such depth invariance will be developed in the following paper.

SUMMARY

1. From data obtained from two adult dogs, one young, the other middle-aged, regions of Ca^{45} uptake in canine osteons were found to have a wide distribution of lengths parallel to the axis of a long bone which averaged about 2 mm. This distribution and average length correspond well to the lengths of canine resorption cavities found histologically. The most active regions of Ca^{45} uptake had lengths of the order of a millimeter.

2. No consistent correlation was found between the locations of vascular connections to osteons and the limits of the regions of Ca^{45} deposition.

3. The deposits of Ca^{45} in osteons can be explained qualitatively in terms of the

formation of new bone in locations governed primarily by the locations of previous resorption tunneling.

4. It should be possible to find many osteons in dog in which the distribution of Ca^{45} is approximately invariant in the longitudinal direction within distances of the order of 10^{-2} cm.

ACKNOWLEDGMENTS

We should like to thank R. D. Evans and J. B. Bulkley of the Massachusetts Institute of Technology, F. C. McLean of the University of Chicago, and J. E. Rose, L. D. Marinelli, R. E. Rowland, and J. Jowsey of the Argonne National Laboratory for their support and interest in this work.

RECEIVED: March 4, 1958

REFERENCES

1. J. COHEN, C. J. MALETSKOS, J. H. MARSHALL, and J. B. WILLIAMS, Radioactive calcium tracer studies in bone grafts. *J. Bone and Joint Surg.* **39A**, 561–577 (1957).
2. J. S. ARNOLD, W. S. S. JEE, and K. JOHNSON, Observations and quantitative radioautographic studies of calcium^{45} deposited in vivo in forming haversian systems and old bone of rabbit. *Am. J. Anat.* **99**, 291–313 (1956).
3. J. H. MARSHALL, V. K. WHITE, and J. COHEN, Autoradiography of serial cross-sections of undecalcified bone. *Intern. J. Appl. Radiation and Isotopes* **1**, 191 (1956).
4. J. COHEN and W. H. HARRIS, Three dimensional anatomy of haversian systems. *J. Bone and Joint Surg.* **40A**, 419–434 (1958).
5. F. E. HOECKER and P. G. ROOFE, Studies of radium in human bone. *Radiology* **56**, 89–98 (1951).
6. J. VINCENT, Recherches sur la Constitution de l'Os Adulte. Dissertation under P. LaCroix, Université Catholique de Louvain, Belgium (1955).
7. R. AMPRINO, Rapporti fra processi di ricostruzione e distribusione dei minerali nelle ossa. *Z. Zellforsch. u. mikroskop. Anat.* **37**, 144–183 (1952).

RADIATION RESEARCH **10**, 213–233 (1959)

Microscopic Metabolism of Calcium in Bone[1]
II. Quantitative Autoradiography

J. H. MARSHALL, R. E. ROWLAND, AND J. JOWSEY
Radiological Physics Division, Argonne National Laboratory, Lemont, Illinois

INTRODUCTION

Autoradiographic investigation of the metabolism of calcium in bone on a microscopic scale (*1*) required a technique capable of measuring the amount of Ca^{45} in an individual osteon or in a segment of periosteal surface. Some of the linear dimensions of these regions are comparable to the range of the Ca^{45} β-particle and contain nonuniform distributions of activity. Hence, none of the simplifying assumptions applicable either to sources of known size or to macroscopically homogeneous volumes of activity could be used with impunity. Similar difficulties have been met in the past by quantitative autoradiographic techniques (*2*) of greater or lesser complexity, according to the nature of the problem involved. Thus, β-particle autoradiograms were grain-counted by Nadler *et al.* (*3*) in their investigation of the relative radioiodine concentrations in thyroid follicles of different size. An absolute method for quantifying β-particle autoradiography has been described by Odeblad (*4*), who used a microphotometer to measure the blackening of autoradiographic plates. Odeblad calibrated his film with a β-ray source in air and then calculated the effects of the β-particle absorption, scattering, and distribution from the actual tissue sample. Dudley and Dobyns (*5*) have described the use of a thick plaster-of-Paris radiator in the quantitative determination of radiation dosages from Ca^{45} in bone. The present paper analyzes the radiator calibration technique of Dudley and Dobyns and extends it to densitometric measurements of the activities of β-emitters in both uniform and nonuniform microscopic distributions in cortical bone.[2]

The essence of the present method is a reduction of the general three-dimensional problem of autoradiography to two dimensions. This reduction can be made for those distributions of β-particle activity which extend unchanged for a short

[1] Work performed under the auspices of the U. S. Atomic Energy Commission.

[2] A somewhat similar method has been reported which, however, depends for its derivation on the assumption of a uniform source distribution and exponential absorption (*6*).

distance in at least one direction. In what follows, this distance within which the activity distribution must be invariant will be assumed to be equal to or greater than β-particle range. In Section VI, however, we show that the same analysis may be applied when one-dimensional invariance exists only within the thickness of a section which may be as little as 5% of the β-particle range. If an autoradiographic plate is exposed at right angles to this direction of invariance, quantitative analysis is greatly simplified, because the activity distribution can be analyzed in terms of line sources rather than point sources. Thus the dimension perpendicular to the emulsion is eliminated from the analysis and with it the necessity of calculating the effects of absorption, scattering, emulsion thickness, emulsion backing, and source-emulsion interspace. Absolute activity values even for certain nonuniform sources can be obtained directly from densitometer measurements calibrated with a thick uniform radiator. Though the requirement of depth invariance of the source limits the general application of this method, the simplicity and flexibility which result from the natural symmetry of a line source at right angles to the plane of an autoradiogram should make the method useful for many autoradiographic problems.

II. DERIVATION OF s, THE ACTIVITY PER GRAM OF A UNIFORM, EXTENDED SOURCE OF BETA-PARTICLES

The absolute calibration of the present method depends on the comparison of the exposure produced by a thick uniform source in bone with that produced by a plaster-of-Paris radiator of known activity per gram. In order to elucidate the effect of density (grams per cubic centimeter) on this comparison, let us assume that we have two materials with identical atomic compositions and equal, uniform specific activities, s (millicuries per gram). Let one have a uniform density ρ, and

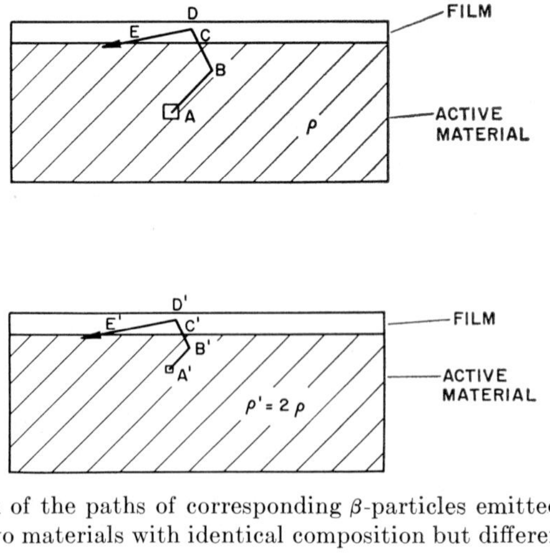

FIG. 1. Comparison of the paths of corresponding β-particles emitted from corresponding volume elements of two materials with identical composition but different densities.

the other a uniform density $\rho' = 2\rho$. As discussed by Failla (7), the pattern of β-particle paths in the first material is the same as that in the second material except for a change in linear scale of a factor of 2. This "expansion" principle follows from the fact that the absorption and scattering processes for β-particles are atomic in nature, so that the requirement of "identical atomic composition" ensures identical angular distributions in scattering and ensures path lengths inversely proportional to ρ.

Consider the path of a typical β-particle when these two materials are placed in contact with an autoradiographic film (Fig. 1). In the material of density ρ, the β-particle is emitted from a volume element at A, scatters at B, traverses the emulsion at C, backscatters in the glass plate above the emulsion at D, and traverses the emulsion again at E. For the material with density $\rho' = 2\rho$, the angles of scattering for the corresponding particle will be unchanged and the path segments within the material will be half as long: $(A'B') = \frac{1}{2}(AB)$, $(B'C') = \frac{1}{2}(BC)$. Similar relations will hold for every pair of corresponding particle paths in the two materials. Therefore the distribution of particles (angles and energies) incident on the emulsion for the first time, as at point C, is identical for corresponding volume elements in the two materials. A volume element of the first material has eight times the volume and four times the mass of a corresponding element of the second material. Since the specific activities are equal, the number of particles emitted from the corresponding volume elements to equal areas of emulsion is the same in the two cases (a linear scale change of 2 means a factor of 4 in area).

When we trace the path of a particle through the emulsion or backing, the expansion principle clearly no longer applies: the path lengths $C'D'$ and $D'E'$ certainly do not vary inversely with the density of the source material but remain equal to CD and DE, respectively. Therefore the distributions of exposed grains produced by β-particles originating in corresponding volume elements of the two materials will not be related simply by a change in linear scale. The *total number* of grains exposed, however, by a given distribution of initially incident particles will be a fixed property of the autoradiographic plate, and hence the total number of exposed grains will be the same in each case.

The particle flux incident on the film is the sum of the fluxes from every volume element within β-particle range of the emulsion, each of which is proportional to the specific activity of the source material. Therefore the resultant film darkening for an extended, uniform source depends directly on its specific activity and is independent of its density.

Now what is the effect of the atomic composition of the absorber? To a first approximation, the flux of β-particles transmitted by a material depends only on its superficial density (grams per square centimeter), so that the darkening effect of a uniform source may be expected to be roughly independent of the atomic composition of the source material. As shown above, however, the comparison of a source

TABLE I

APPROXIMATE COMPOSITION OF DRY FAT-FREE BONE

Component	*Element*	*Z*	*Weight*	*Z × Weight*
$Ca_{10}(PO_4)_6\ (OH)_2$, 65% by weight	Ca	20	26%	5.2
	P	15	12%	1.8
	O	8	27%	2.2
	H	1	0.1%	0.0
Organic and other C, H, O, Na, etc., 35% by weight		7.5	35%	2.6
			Average Z =	11.8
HARDENED PLASTER OF PARIS (GYPSUM)				
$CaSO_4 \cdot 2H_2O$	Ca	20	23%	4.6
	S	16	19%	3.0
	O	8	56%	4.5
	H	1	2%	0.0
			Average Z =	12.1

with a radiator will give an accurate result only if the probabilities of electron energy loss and scattering per atom are approximately the same.

Let us compare the atomic compositions of bone and plaster of Paris, taking the weight of dry, fat-free bone to be 65% hydroxyapatite and the remaining 35% to be organic matrix and other inorganic materials (Table I). A plaster-of-Paris radiator with $\bar{Z} = 12.1$ is seen to have an atomic composition closely equivalent to that of bone, $\bar{Z} = 11.8$. The composition of bone is not constant, however, the relative weight of mineral and organic matrix varying during the process of calcification. If the above figures are taken to represent full mineralization, then at 75% mineralization the average atomic number of bone becomes about 10.7.

What order of magnitude of error is introduced in the present analysis by an increase in $\bar{Z}$ from 10.7 to 12.1? We note that the effect of backscattering from a thick source mount increases the counting rate about 2% in a 2π counter for the above change in Z (*8*). The energy loss per unit path length for electrons of 70 kev (approximately the average energy of Ca^{45}) decreases about 2% for the same increase in Z (*9*). From wide-angle ionization chamber measurements of the absorption of β-particles in different elements (*10*) one may estimate that the apparent absorption coefficient (square centimeters per gram) for plaster of Paris may exceed that for bone by 2 to 5%, depending on whether the bone is 100% or 75% mineralized, respectively: Therefore, the differences between the atomic compositions of bone and plaster of Paris may be expected to introduce an error of not more than a few per cent into our analysis for Ca^{45} activity.

Film darkening[3] due to a uniformly distributed, thick β-particle source may therefore be written

$$D = ksF \tag{1}$$

where D = darkening corrected for nonlinearity and for film background.
s = specific activity of the source (mc/gm).
F = exposure time (corrected for radioactive decay, if necessary) (days).
k = calibration factor (darkening gm/mc-day).

From the argument above, the value of k for autoradiograms made with the same film, the same β-emitter, and the same exposure and development procedure will hold for both bone and a plaster-of-Paris radiator, or

$$\boxed{s = \frac{D}{kF}} \tag{2}$$

and

$$\boxed{k = \frac{D^*}{s^*F^*}} \tag{3}$$

where the starred quantities refer to radiator exposures and the unstarred quantities to bone. Expression 3 provides the desired relation between the specific activity of a uniform source in bone and the known specific activity of the radiator in terms of corrected densitometer readings.

For most films, darkening is approximately proportional to exposure over at least part of the range; a calibration curve can thus easily be constructed from measurements of various exposure times or specific activities which allows one to correct a densitometer reading for exact linearity with exposure.

III. DERIVATION OF THE ACTIVITY PER UNIT LENGTH OF A LINE SOURCE

Consider a long thin filament of β-activity embedded in a material of density ρ and exposed end-on, at right angles to an autoradiographic plate (Fig. 2). We shall call such a distribution of activity a line source, ascribing to it negligible thickness, a length greater than the β-particle range, and a uniform activity per unit length, h.

The developed plate will show a "hotspot," the darkening of which can be measured in the plane of the film as a function of radial distance from the peak.

Let H be the peak darkening value for the line source, and let the function $u(r)$

[3] We define darkening as $D = \log_{10} I_0/I$, where I_0 and I are the incident and transmitted light intensities, respectively. "Darkening" is used in place of photographic "density" to avoid confusion with mass density (grams per cubic centimeter).

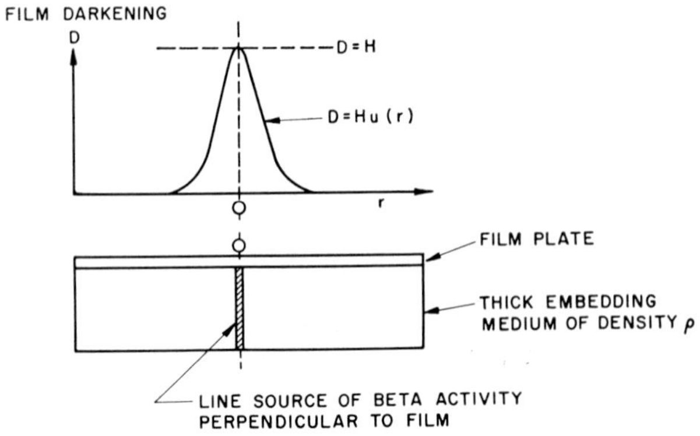

FIG. 2. Diagram of a line source of β-activity perpendicular to an autoradiographic film together with the profile of film darkening it would produce.

describe the decrease in darkening as the radial distance from the peak position increases:

$$D = Hu(r) \tag{4}$$

where $u(0) = 1$.
$u(\infty) = 0$.

Now what is the relation between peak darkening, H, and activity per unit length, h? Since all densitometer readings are corrected for linearity with exposure, the value of H for any line source in a given medium must be directly proportional to the exposure time, F, and to the activity per unit length, h. Let us try the expression

$$H = \frac{qhF}{\rho} \tag{5}$$

where H = peak darkening over line source.
h = activity per unit length (mc/cm).
ρ = gm/cm^3 of embedding material.
F = exposure time (days).
q = unknown factor to be determined.

We make no assumptions here as to the nature of q or its dependence on the density or atomic number of the embedding material.

The relation between the unknown factor, q, for a line source and the uniform source calibration factor, k, which was derived in Section II, can be found by mathematically constructing a uniform source out of an assembly of line sources, holding constant the density and atomic composition of the embedding material (see Fig. 3). Consider the effect on the darkening at a point P of many line sources, each with the same activity per unit length, h, evenly spaced at right angles to the

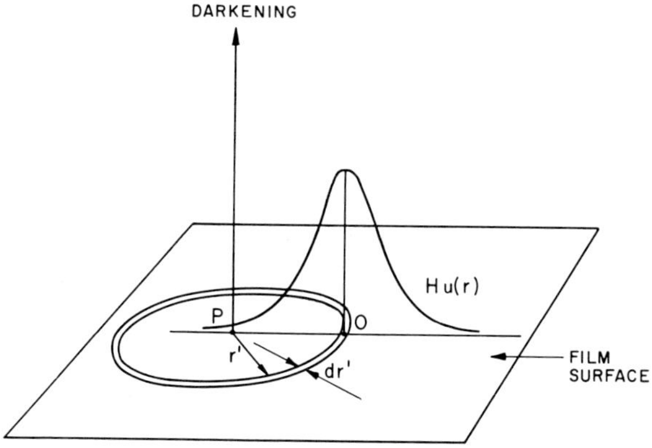

FIG. 3. Construction for generating a uniform source from an assembly of line sources.

film surface. Each line at a distance r' from point P will contribute a darkening of $Hu(r')$. If there are n line sources per unit area of film surface, the increment in the darkening at point P due to those lines between r' and $r' + dr'$ from P will be

$$dD = nHu(r')2\pi r'\, dr' \tag{6}$$

Substitute for H the relation in equation 5 above, and

$$dD = \frac{qF}{\rho} nhu(r')2\pi r'\, dr' \tag{7}$$

Now let the number of line sources per unit area, n, approach infinity and h approach zero in such a way that the product nh remains constant. The assembly of line sources will then become effectively a uniformly distributed source with specific activity $s = nh/\rho$. If we substitute s for nh/ρ in equation 7 and integrate over the whole surface around P, we obtain

$$D = qFs \int_0^\infty 2\pi r' u(r')\, dr' \tag{8}$$

The only variable within the integral is r', the radial distance from point P. Now if we substitute r for r' we obtain an integral with exactly the same value as that in equation 8:

$$D = qFs \int_0^\infty 2\pi r u(r)\, dr \tag{9}$$

but now the integral refers to a single line source with the profile function $u(r)$.

Comparing expressions 9 and 2, both of which apply to uniform sources, we see that

$$q = k/A \qquad \text{where} \qquad A = \int_0^\infty 2\pi r u(r)\, dr \tag{10}$$

Substituting equation 10 into equation 5, we obtain the desired expression for the activity per unit length of a line source embedded in material of density ρ:

$$h = \frac{H\rho}{kF} \int_0^\infty 2\pi r u(r)\, dr \tag{11}$$

Notice that the integral A is a measure of the area of the hotspot as seen on the film. If the hotspot were a perfectly resolved disk of radius b, $u(r) = 1$ for $r < b$, and $u(r) = 0$ for $r > b$, then the area A would be simply πb^2. The actual A is a weighted average of area elements, the weighting factor being the function $u(r)$, namely, the profile of a hotspot due to a line source.

From the discussion of Section II, it is apparent that the shape of a line source profile, $u(r)$, depends not only on the density of the embedding medium but also on the emulsion thickness and backing and on the source-to-emulsion interspace.

In the above derivation, D must be linear with β-particle exposure. This requirement does not restrict the general nature of the derivation, however, for as long as film darkening is a single-valued, increasing function of exposure it is possible to associate a linear D value with each exposure. In other words, for D to be linear we need only assume that the actual film darkening is additive.

Note that the construction of a uniform source from an assembly of line sources automatically takes into account the effects of angular distribution and energy spectrum of the β-particles on the darkening of the film. A line source is the simplest element of a uniform source in contact with a plane film, so it must produce the same distribution of particle paths through the emulsion.

IV. ACTIVITY PER UNIT LENGTH OF ARBITRARY DISTRIBUTIONS GENERATED FROM LINE SOURCES

Expression 11 can be generalized to apply to any distribution of activity which can be generated by line sources, that is, to any distribution which is invariant in the direction perpendicular to the film for a distance comparable to the β-particle range. Rewriting expression 11 so that H appears inside the integral, we have

$$h = \frac{\rho}{kF} \int_0^\infty H u(r) 2\pi r\, dr \tag{12}$$

Rewriting equation 12 in rectangular coordinates, the activity per unit length for a line source becomes

$$h = \frac{\rho}{kF} \int \int D(x, y)\, dx\, dy \tag{13}$$

where $D(x, y)$ = the two-dimensional darkening distribution for a line source, identical with $Hu(r)$. The integration is over the whole film surface for which $D(x, y) > 0$, just as before.

Consider a large assembly of line sources as in Section III, but this time as their number approaches infinity let the product of their activity and concentration vary with position on the film, dropping to zero eventually in each direction. The continuous darkening distribution thus generated will be the sum of the distributions due to each line source taken separately:

$$D(x, y) = D_1(x, y) + D_2(x, y) + \cdots$$

and the activity per unit length of the entire distribution will be the sum of the individual h values.

Therefore the activity per unit length of a two-dimensionally arbitrary distribution of activity is formally similar to expression 13:

$$\boxed{h = \frac{\rho}{kF} \iint D\,(x, y)\,dx\,dy} \tag{14}$$

where now h = total activity per unit length in the entire distribution; and $D(x, y)$ = any darkening distribution which is bounded by zero values in the xy plane and which is produced by a distribution of activity invariant with z. If the darkening is not required to fall to zero, the integral will not converge. In other words, the darkening distribution must be resolvable from neighboring distributions and from the edges of the film or embedding material.

Expression 14 can be evaluated by adding a series of densitometer readings spread over the distribution (as shown in Fig. 4):

$$h \cong \frac{\rho(\Delta x)(\Delta y)}{kF} \sum D_{ij} \tag{15}$$

where h = activity per unit length (mc/cm).
ρ = density of material (gm/cm^3).
k = calibration factor from radiator (expression 3).
F = exposure time corrected for decay (days).
Δx = horizontal spacing on the film between successive densitometer readings (cm).
Δy = vertical spacing of readings (cm).
D_{ij} = typical densitometer reading corrected for linearity and background.

The sum is over all D_{ij} values not zero.

Note particularly that the area $(\Delta x)(\Delta y)$ that enters expression 15 is *not* the densitometer aperture. The only requirement on the aperture size or shape is that it be small enough so that there is no large change of darkening within the aperture

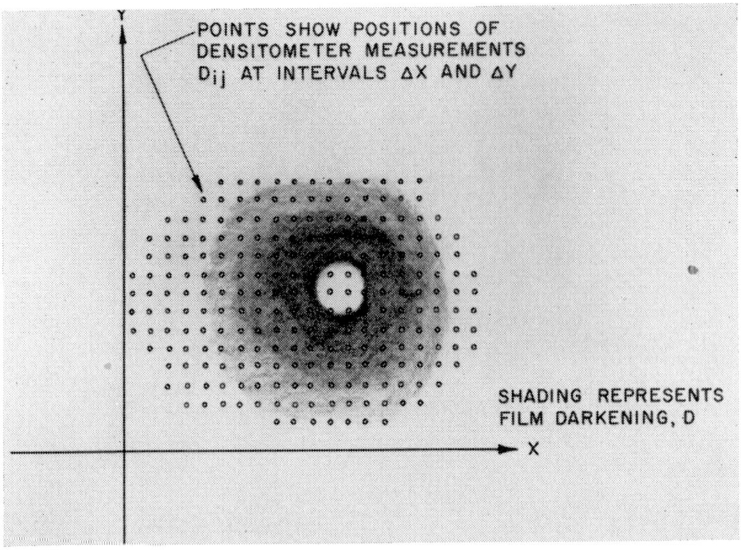

FIG. 4. Autoradiographic analysis for activity distributions that vary with x and y but are invariant in the z direction (perpendicular to the film) within β-particle range or within a given section.

(see Appendix A). The same requirement must be made on Δx and Δy to ensure an accurate integration.

Expression 15 has been evaluated by using a microscope-densitometer combination with micrometer indicators on the microscope stage and apertures of 10 to 30 μ in diameter. Once a number of typical distributions have been measured as in Fig. 4, values of the summation can be plotted as a function of two or three more quickly measurable parameters such as peak darkening and major and minor half-widths. Expression 15 has been used for the analysis of Ca^{45} in osteons or haversian systems whose radial distributions of activity are not uniform enough or large enough in extent to be treated as uniform sources by expression 2.

V. ACTIVITY PER UNIT AREA OF SURFACES

The activity per unit area of a surface can be derived directly from expression 14. Let the active surface be perpendicular to the film (Fig. 5). Take rectangular axes x and y in the plane of the film, and let the yz plane be parallel to the active surface. Then we can measure the total activity per unit area in all yz planes of a distribution of activity which is arbitrary in the x direction but remains constant in the y and z directions for a distance comparable to the β-particle range.

Since by our choice of axes we have made the $D(x, y)$ values for such distributions independent of y, we may replace $D(x, y)$ in expression 14 by $D(x)$. Setting dy equal

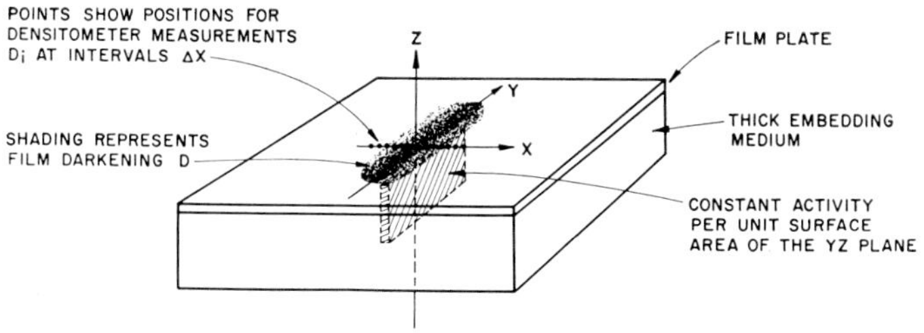

FIG. 5. Autoradiographic analysis for activity distributions that vary with x but are invariant in the y and z directions within β-particle range or within a given section.

to unit length and dividing through by it, we obtain the total activity per unit area for the distribution:

$$L = \frac{\rho}{kF} \int D(x)\ dx \tag{16}$$

This is evaluated by adding a single row of densitometer readings (Fig. 5):

$$L \cong \frac{\rho \Delta x}{kF} \sum D_i \tag{17}$$

where L = activity per unit area (mc/cm^2) in all yz planes of the activity distribution.
Δx = spacing between successive densitometer readings (cm).
ρ = density of material (gm/cm^3).
D_i = typical densitometer reading corrected for linearity and background.
k = calibration factor from radiator (expression 3).
F = exposure time corrected for decay (days).

Expression 17 is being used to obtain the total Ca^{45} activity per unit area deposited on or near a growing bone surface after a single injection of the isotope.

VI. EXTENSION OF METHOD TO SOURCES THAT ARE NOT THICK COMPARED TO BETA-PARTICLE RANGE AND TO SOURCES COVERED BY ABSORBERS

Expressions 2, 14, and 16 may now be extended to sources that are not thick compared to the β-particle range. Note that the thickness of the source did not enter specifically into any of the geometrical derivations. If the medium in which the source is embedded extends uniformly in all directions for distances greater than β-particle range, the radioactive source itself may be made thinner than β-particle range without modifying anything in the previous derivations except the calibration factor, k. In other words, provided we knew the film darkening which would be produced by a uniform radiator that was *not* thick compared to the β-

particle range, then we could derive results for uniform or nonuniform, depth-invariant β-particle sources of equivalent thickness.

In order to find the calibration factor, k, as a function of radiator thickness, it is not necessary to construct many different radiators; an absorption curve, measured with autoradiographic plates, aluminum absorbers, and a thick plaster-of-Paris radiator, yields the same information. This may be demonstrated by comparing the film darkening produced by a thick uniform radiator of density ρ in contact with an autoradiographic plate with that produced by the same radiator separated from the same plate by an absorber with the same density and atomic composition as the radiator. This comparison is illustrated by the upper and middle diagrams in Fig. 6. By the same arguments that we employed for Fig. 1, it can be seen that the darkening produced in the film by the infinitely thick radiator indicated by II (upper diagram) will be the same as the darkening produced by the infinitely thick radiator indicated by II′ (middle diagram). Then the difference between the darkening of the upper film and that of the middle film must be produced by the less-than-thick active material indicated by I. Therefore, if only layer I were active and layer II were replaced by an absorber of the same density and atomic composition, then the darkening produced on the film by the less-than-thick radiator, I, would be identical to the difference in the darkening produced by

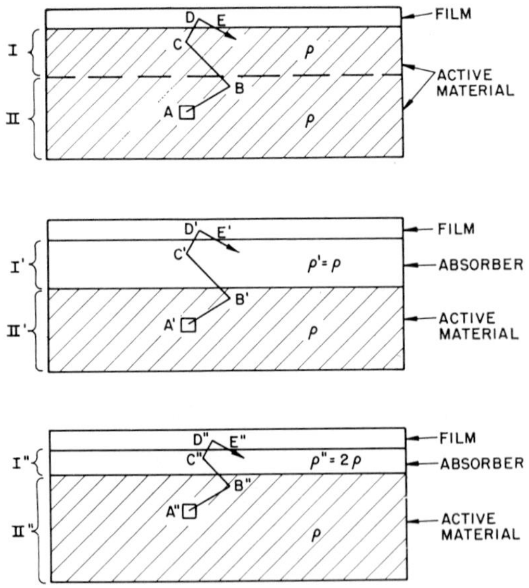

FIG. 6. Demonstration of the use of an absorber with a thick radiator to obtain the calibration factor for a less-than-thick source. The different media are assumed to have identical atomic composition. Sectors II, II′, and II″ are assumed to be thick to β-particles, and sectors I, I′, and I″ are not thick.

a thick radiator with and without the absorber of equivalent thickness, I′. Thus, a thick radiator, together with an absorption curve, may be used to calibrate less-than-thick bone sources.

Now consider the effect of using an absorber of the same atomic composition but of different density, ρ''. The situation in which $\rho'' = 2\rho$ is shown in the lower diagram of Fig. 6. Since the angles of scattering are independent of the density and depend merely on the atomic composition of the medium, the only difference between the middle and lower diagrams in Fig. 6 is that the segments of β-particle paths in the absorber are inversely proportional to the density of the absorber. As before, the total flux, the angular distribution, and the energy distribution of the β-particles incident on the film are all independent of the density of the absorber provided that its mass per unit area is held constant. Therefore, in measuring an absorption curve with the thick radiator we need absorbers with the same atomic composition but not necessarily the same density as that of the radiator or of bone. As indicated in Section II, this requirement as to the atomic composition is not restrictive, since small differences in atomic composition would produce errors of at most a few per cent. We may therefore use aluminum for the absorbing material, since its atomic number is close to the average atomic number of bone.

Let us measure the darkening produced by our thick plaster-of-Paris radiator as a function of the mass per unit area, m, of aluminum absorber inserted between radiator and autoradiographic plate. These darkening values, corrected for background and linearity, and referred to the same time of exposure, constitute the absorption curve, $a(m)$, applicable to our particular experimental conditions. If we normalize these values so that the darkening with zero absorber is unity, then

$$\boxed{k_m = k\,[1 - a(m)]} \qquad (18)$$

where k = calibration factor for infinitely thick source (expression 3).
k_m = calibration factor for source with mass per unit area m.
$a(m)$ = absorption curve factor for absorber with mass per unit area m: $a(0) = 1$; $a(\infty) = 0$.

We may further extend the method to a thick source covered by an aluminum absorber, using the same absorption curve measured above:

$$\boxed{k_n = ka(n)} \qquad (19)$$

where k_n = calibration factor for thick source covered by absorber with mass per unit area n.
$a(n)$ = absorption curve factor for mass per unit area n.

If an absorber is to be used with a less-than-thick source, expressions 18 and 19 cannot be used independently, since, in general, a β-particle absorption curve is not strictly exponential. It follows directly from the above analysis, however, that

$$\boxed{k_{mn} = k\,[a(n) - a(m+n)]} \qquad (20)$$

where k_{mn} = calibration factor for source with mass per unit area m covered by an absorber with mass per unit area n.

$a(m + n)$ = absorption curve factor for absorber with mass per unit area $m + n$.

For the accurate evaluation of a less-than-thick source by this subtraction technique, one should back the source with a material of approximately the same atomic composition as bone in order to provide the infinitely thick embedding medium assumed in the derivation.

It should be noted that reducing source thickness or adding an absorber not only reduces film darkening values but also changes the darkening distributions for nonuniform sources. It is the power of the present method that such changes in resolution do not affect the derivation of the relations 14 and 16 for nonuniform, depth-invariant sources.

The experimental error in evaluating expression 18 or 20 becomes large for small values of m. For Ca^{45} with maximum range 58 mg/cm^2, $a \cong 0.5$ for an absorber thickness of 6 mg/cm^2. We may conclude that it becomes increasingly difficult to apply this method of calibration with accuracy when the source thickness is less than 5 to 10% of β-particle range. It is not applicable to very thin sources. This simple method of calibration is independent of β-emitter, however, and makes expressions 2, 14, and 16 applicable to a wide range of intermediate source thicknesses with practically the same experimental accuracy as for thick sources. Expression 20 has been used to apply the present method of analysis to double tracer autoradiograms of bone sections containing both Sr^{90}–Y^{90} and Ca^{45}.

SUMMARY

A quantitative autoradiographic technique has been developed for evaluating the β-particle activity in radioactive sources in which the distribution of activity is invariant in at least one dimension for a distance of more than 5 to 10% of the maximum particle range. The method is applicable to any β-emitter or mixture of β-emitters and to any autoradiographic film because it depends on symmetry arguments rather than on calculation of β-particle absorption and scattering.

The radioactive material is assumed to be embedded in a medium of uniform density and composition. This source-containing medium is sectioned so that a direction of invariance in the source distribution is perpendicular to the autoradiographic emulsion. The exposed emulsion is densitometered through a small aperture in order to obtain either film darkening or the surface or line integral of film darkening. The densitometer is calibrated by exposing the same type of autoradiographic emulsion to a thick, uniform radiator of approximately the same atomic composition but not necessarily the same density as the embedding medium, the radiator containing a known activity per gram of the desired β-particle activity. This calibration may be used directly for thick sources; for thin sources of thickness greater than about 5% of β-particle range or for sources covered by absorbers, the same calibration may be used together with a correction factor derived from an autoradiographic absorption curve.

In practice, the required invariance of the activity distribution with depth below the emulsion may be partially verified by comparing two autoradiograms exposed over and under the source-containing medium; invariance of the activity distribution itself is inferred from the similarity of the two exposure patterns and from the invariance with depth of the structure which contains the activity.

For measurements of Ca^{45} or Sr^{90} in bone, the technique yields the specific activity of the diffuse component, the activity per unit area of growing surfaces such as the periosteum, or the activity per unit length of osteons.

The accuracy of this technique for evaluating the activity of a small nonuniform source depends inversely on β-particle range and *inversely* on the autoradiographic resolution. The relation between accuracy, range, and resolution has been estimated by calculating line source dose distributions in an infinite homogeneous medium (Appendix B).

ACKNOWLEDGMENTS

The authors wish to thank J. E. Rose and L. D. Marinelli for their generous support and encouragement in this work.

APPENDIX A—APERTURE ERROR

For evaluating expression 14 or 16, a small densitometer aperture must be used because each reading should correspond to the average film darkening within the aperture. When there is a large change in darkening within the aperture, a detector depending on light transmission will not record an average darkening value. The magnitude of this aperture error can be determined from the definition of darkening, D:

$$D = \log_{10} \frac{I_0}{I} \tag{21}$$

where I_0 and I are the incident and transmitted light intensities, respectively. Let us assume that we have a square aperture focused on a linear gradient of film darkening. Let the true average darkening within the aperture be $\bar{D}$, and let the darkening at one side of the aperture be $\bar{D} + V\bar{D}$, and at the other side $\bar{D} - V\bar{D}$. The average intensity of transmitted light will depend not only on $\bar{D}$ but also on the fractional change in darkening, V, between the center and edge of the aperture.

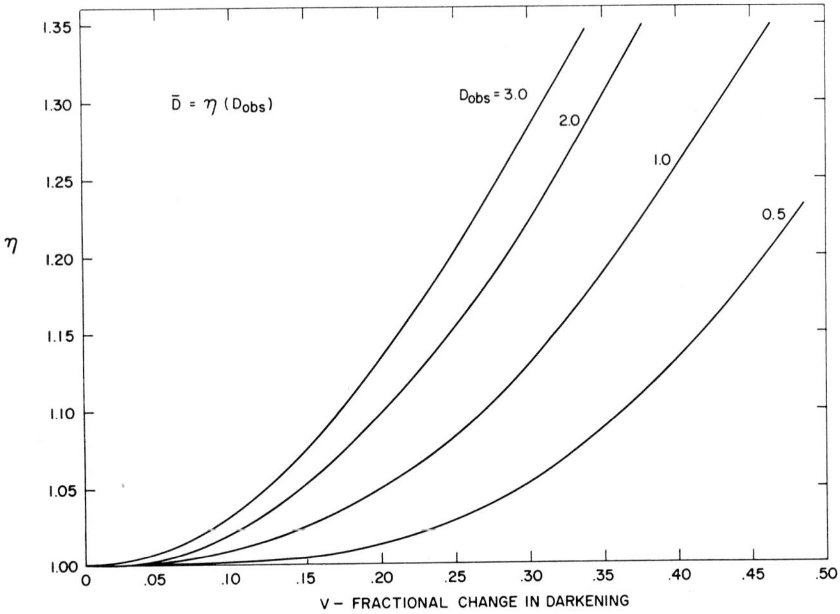

FIG. 7. The ratio, η, of the true average film darkening, $\bar{D}$, to the value D_{obs} measured with a densitometer aperture within which darkening changes linearly from a fraction V above to a fraction V below $\bar{D}$.

Numerical calculation using expression 21 shows that the desired darkening value, $\bar{D}$, will be higher than the value indicated by the densitometer, D_{obs}, by a factor η:

$$\bar{D} = \eta(D_{obs}) \tag{22}$$

In Fig. 7, values of η are plotted as a function of V for different values of D_{obs}. For example, when there is a darkening gradient from 20% above to 20% below the true average darkening within the aperture, the densitometer reading will be 5 to 10% low. For Ca^{45} hotspots with the present technique, the aperture error in individual densitometer readings may be made less than this only by using an aperture $\leqq 30\ \mu$ in diameter. In practice one must collimate both the photomultiplier and the incident light in order to reduce scattering and achieve an effectively small aperture. The incident light can be collimated by placing an aperture below the microscope substage condenser and by focusing this aperture in the plane of the film.

APPENDIX B—ESTIMATION OF EXPERIMENTAL ERROR IN EVALUATING THE SURFACE INTEGRAL OF DARKENING

Evaluation of the surface integral of darkening (expression 14) requires that densitometer measurements be made over the whole area in which darkening is significantly above background. For small sources and high-energy β-particles considerable error may be made due to the difficulty of measuring darkening values close to background over a large area. Therefore it is useful to know approximately the theoretical shape of the darkening distribution for a line source so that we may estimate the area over which densitometer readings must be made in order to include all significant contributions to a given surface integral. It would be extremely difficult to make such a calculation exactly applicable to given experimental conditions. Instead, we have calculated the dosage distribution produced by a line source in an infinite homogeneous medium. Since darkening (corrected for linearity with exposure) is approximately proportional to dose (*11*), this calculated line source dose profile gives a valuable indication as to the approximate distribution of line source darkening.

From the point source dose function developed by Loevinger (*12*) with parameter $c = 2$, the dosage distribution in a plane at right angles to a semi-infinite line source was calculated by numerical integration. The dimensionless unit of length used in this calculation is based on the apparent absorption coefficient, ν, for which Loevinger gives values as a function of maximum β-particle range, R_{max}. The

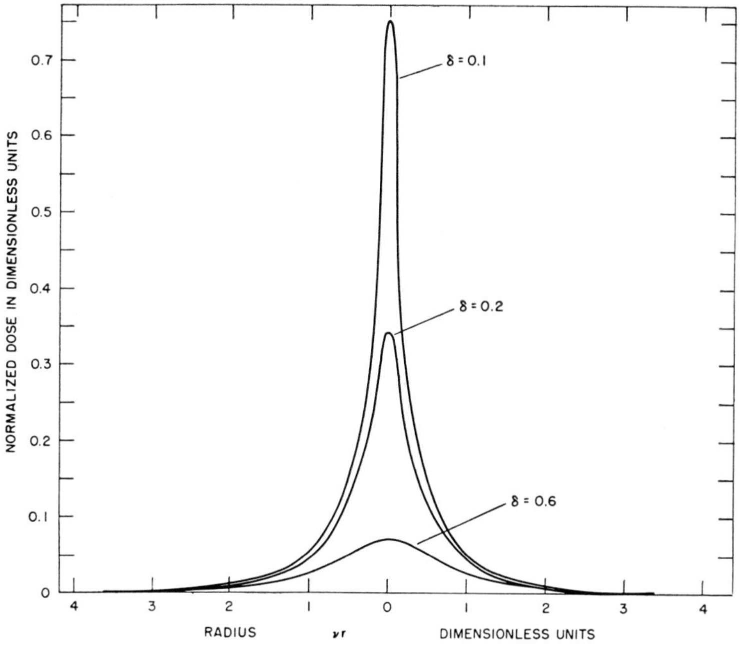

FIG. 8. The dose distribution in a homogeneous medium in a plane at right angles to and at a distance δ from the end of a semi-infinite line source of β-particle activity. (See diagram in Fig. 9.) The dimensionless unit of length corresponds approximately to $0.12\ R_{max}$ (maximum β-particle range). Dose values are normalized so that the surface integral of dose for $\delta = 0$ is unity.

product νR_{max} for soft tissue is very nearly constant, being 9.5 for S^{35} and falling to 6.8 for Y^{90}. The dose at the point at which the line source touches the plane becomes infinite. A line source profile such as that in Fig. 2, however, does not go infinite at $r = 0$ because the detector was specified to be an actual emulsion with a finite section-to-emulsion interspace. Line source calculations (*13*) have demonstrated this interspace effect for thin sources. In order to approximate actual resolution losses in the present line source dose calculation, dosage distributions were calculated for planes separated by absorbers of different thickness, δ, from the end of the embedded line source (see diagram in Fig. 9). In Fig. 8, calculated line source dose profiles are given for three values of δ in the same dimensionless units as the radius. Thus Fig. 8 shows the dosage distribution over a semi-infinite line source covered by different thicknesses of absorber of the same composition and density as the embedding medium. Figure 8 has been normalized so that the total surface integral of dose for $\delta = 0$ is unity.

In Fig. 9, the fraction γ, that lies within radius r, of the total surface integral of dose for each line source profile is shown for the different values of δ. Note that the profile for $\delta = 0$, which goes infinite at $r = 0$, still has a finite surface integral. Figure 9 provides an estimate of the radius over which densitometer measurements

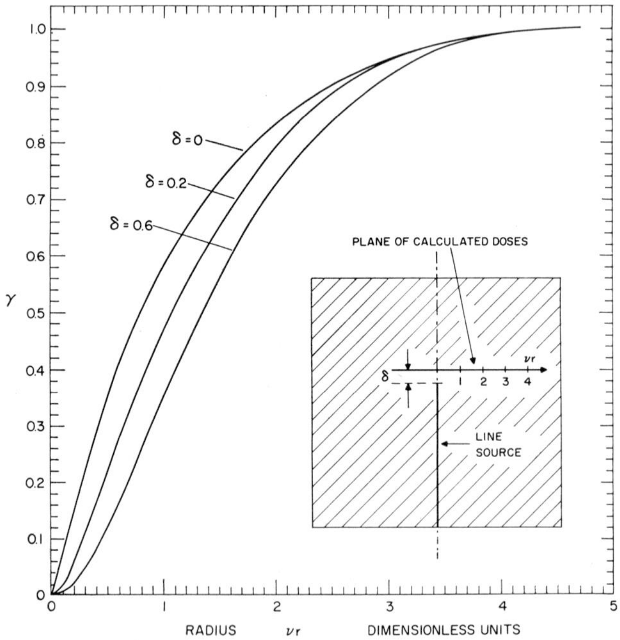

FIG. 9. The fraction γ, that lies within radius r, of the total surface integral of dose for a line source. The total surface integral of dose for *each* value of δ is here unity (unlike Fig. 8). Note that the surface integral of dose for $\delta = 0$ remains finite although the dose at $r = 0$ is infinite.

should be made in order to include a fraction, γ, of all the darkening contributions to the total activity per unit length of a line source.

For Ca^{45}, $\nu = 154\ cm^2/gm$; in bone with density $\rho = 2\ gm/cm^3$, unit length for Ca^{45} ($\nu r = 1$) is about 32 μ. The Loevinger function does not fit Sr^{90}-Y^{90} exactly, but for our purposes we may take $\nu = 6.2\ cm^2/gm$ (the value for Y^{90}) and parameter $c = 2$ to include the effect of the Sr^{90} spectrum. Then with density $\rho = 2\ gm/cm^3$, unit length for Sr^{90}-Y^{90} is about 810 μ. Hotspot darkening profiles measured for Ca^{45} deposits which approximate line sources in bone show a full width at half-maximum darkening, λ, of about 100 μ. Hotspot profiles for Sr^{90}-Y^{90} in bone, however, show a full width at half-maximum darkening as small as $\lambda = 200\ \mu$, only twice that for Ca^{45} despite the fact that the range of Sr^{90}-Y^{90} β-particles is twenty times as great. This apparent discrepancy may be understood by referring to Fig. 8.

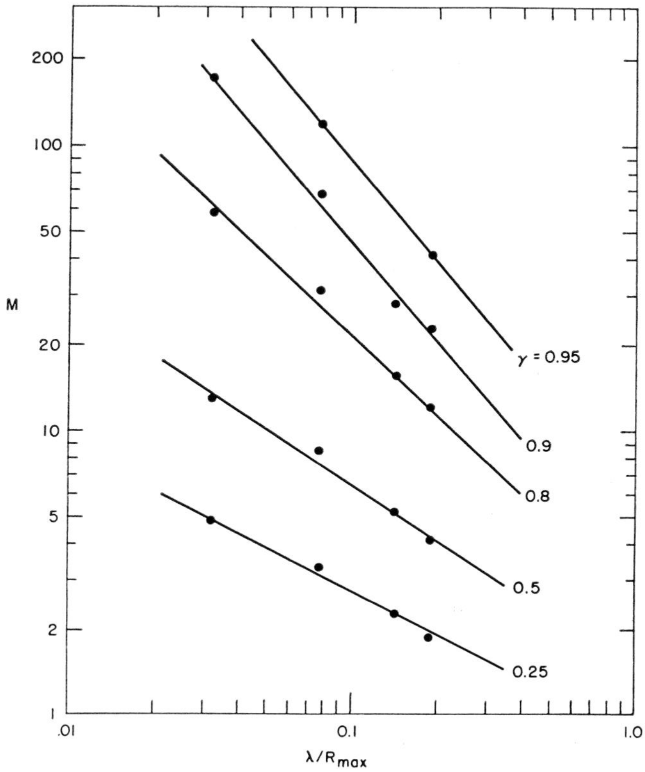

FIG. 10. Estimate of the experimental difficulty, M, of measuring a fraction, γ, of the total surface integral of darkening (expression 14) as a function of autoradiographic resolution and β-particle range. Figure 10 combines the calculations of Figs. 8 and 9. M is the ratio of the maximum to the minimum net darkening included within the integral; λ is the full width at half-maximum darkening of the actual darkening distribution; and R_{max} is maximum β-particle range.

If we approximate the resolution losses of our autoradiographic technique for Ca^{45} by an absorber thickness $\delta = 0.6$, the calculated profile for Ca^{45} and $\rho = 2$ gm/cm^3 has the observed width $\lambda = 100\ \mu$; the absorber thickness corresponding to $\delta = 0.6$ is 20 μ. If the same absorber thickness is taken to represent the resolution losses for Sr^{90}-Y^{90}, the corresponding value of δ is 0.03. Thus the resolution of our thick-source autoradiographic plate technique is much better for Sr^{90}-Y^{90} than it is for Ca^{45} when expressed in units relative to β-particle range. In Fig. 8 the full width at half maximum for each profile is a smaller fraction of β-particle range for smaller values of δ. Therefore, for longer range β-emitters it becomes more difficult to evaluate the total surface integral of darkening for small sources because densitometer readings $D(r)$ at νr values of 1 and 2 become very small compared to the peak densitometer reading D_{max} at $r = 0$ (Fig. 8), but the contribution of these readings to the integral is still significant (Fig. 9).

The relation between β-particle range, resolution, and difficulty in evaluating the surface integral of darkening is summarized by combining the information of Figs. 8 and 9 in Fig. 10. The abscissa is the full width at half maximum, λ, of the calculated line source dose profiles divided by the maximum β-particle range R_{max}. An average value of $\nu R_{max} = 8.5$ has been used for all β-emitters as sufficiently accurate for our purpose. The ordinate M is the ratio of the peak dose D_{max} to the dose $D(r)$ at the radius r within which there lies a fraction, γ, of the total surface integral of dose for a given dose profile. For example, if densitometer measurements were made across a single darkening distribution in order to evaluate expression 14, and if D values from D_{max} to one-tenth D_{max} were included, then $M = 10$. If the darkening distribution were due to a Ca^{45} line source and showed $\lambda/R_{max} = 0.4$, then $\gamma = 0.9$ which would indicate that roughly 90% of the total surface integral of darkening had been evaluated. For a Sr^{90}-Y^{90} line source with $\lambda/R_{max} = 0.04$ and the same ratio of included densitometer readings, $M = 10$, $\gamma = 0.4$, so that only 40% of the total integral would be obtained.

These calculations should be used only as estimates for autoradiographic measurements because they were derived for dose in an infinite homogeneous medium, not for darkening of an autoradiographic plate exposed to bone. Figure 10, however, indicates an experimental limit to the accuracy of the present quantitative autoradiographic method. The calculations apply to a line source, so that for actual depth-invariant sources of finite width the value of γ from Fig. 10 should underestimate the accuracy of measurements.

RECEIVED March 4, 1958

REFERENCES

1. J. H. MARSHALL, V. K. WHITE, and J. COHEN, Microscopic metabolism of calcium in bone. I. Three-dimensional deposition of Ca^{45} in canine osteons. *Radiation Research* **10**, 197–212 (1959).
2. W. P. NORRIS and L. A. WOODRUFF, Fundamentals of radioautography. *Ann. Rev. Nuclear Sci.* **5**, 297 (1955).

3. J. J. NADLER, C. P. LEBLOND, and R. BOGOROCH, The rate of iodine metabolism by the thyroid follicle as a function of its size. *Endocrinology* **54,** 154 (1954).
4. E. ODEBLAD, Matrix theory of quantitative apposition autoradiography. *Acta Radiol.* **45,** 323 (1956).
5. R. A. DUDLEY and B. M. DOBYNS, The use of autoradiographs in the quantitative determination of radiation dosages from Ca^{45} in bone. *Science* **109,** 327 (1949).
6. F. J. DOMINGUES, A. SARKO, and R. R. BALDWIN, A simplified method for quantitation of autoradiography. *Intern. J. Appl. Radiation and Isotopes* **1,** 94 (1956).
7. G. FAILLA, The distribution of energy imparted to a homogeneous medium nonuniformly irradiated. *Radiation Research* **5,** 205 (1956).
8. E. P. STEINBERG, Interpretation of counting data. Argonne National Laboratory Report ANL-5622, p. 26 (1956).
9. A. T. NELMS, Energy loss and range of electrons and positrons. *Natl. Bur. Standards (U. S.) Circ.* **No. 577** (1956)
10. J. A. CROWTHER, *Phil. Mag.* **12,** 379 (1906); or E. RUTHERFORD, *Radioactive Substances and Their Radiations*, p. 26, Cambridge, 1913.
11. R. A. DUDLEY, Photographic detection and dosimetry of beta rays. *Nucleonics* **12,** no. 5, 24 (1954).
12. R. LOEVINGER, The point source function. In *Radiation Dosimetry* (G. J. HINE and G. L. BROWNELL, eds.), pp. 709–715, Academic Press, New York, 1956.
13. I. DONIACH and S. R. PELC, Autoradiograph technique. *Brit. J. Radiol.* **23,** 184 (1950).

RADIATION RESEARCH **10**, 234–242 (1959)

Microscopic Metabolism of Calcium in Bone
III. Microradiographic Measurements of Mineral Density[1]

R. E. ROWLAND, J. JOWSEY, AND J. H. MARSHALL

Radiological Physics Division, Argonne National Laboratory, Lemont, Illinois

INTRODUCTION

The density of bone mineral in microscopic volumes of bone containing no cavities larger than canalicules can be measured by quantitative microradiography. The technique employed and the results of some measurements of the microscopic calcium density of compact bone from man, dog, and a few other species are described.

THEORY

Microradiography can be made quantitative (1) by exposing an aluminum step wedge and a bone section to the same beam of X-rays; (2) by determining from the resulting microradiograph the thickness of aluminum which produces the same absorption of the X-rays as a given region of the bone section; and (3) by measuring the thickness of the given region of the bone section.

For the microradiograph it is convenient to employ a rather wide band of X-rays rather than the monochromatic source employed by Engstrom (*1*); the analysis of the results, however, is essentially the same if the band of X-rays is chosen so that the mass absorption coefficients of the materials in question are in a constant ratio to each other throughout its width. Calcium, phosphorus, and the step wedge material, aluminum, satisfy this criterion for the X-rays produced by a tungsten target tube operated at 10 kv and filtered by at least 1 mm of beryllium.

Figure 1 shows these mass absorption coefficients (*2*) and indicates the band of X-rays which are produced by the tube and passed by the filter. This distribution has been calculated by means of the expression given by Kramer as described by Lindell (*3*) and has been checked experimentally by measuring the photon distribution with a proportional counter and a single-channel pulse height analyzer. We find that over this energy band

$$\begin{aligned} \mu_{\mathrm{Ca}} &= 3.29 \cdot \mu_{\mathrm{Al}} \\ \mu_{\mathrm{P}} &= 1.47 \cdot \mu_{\mathrm{Al}} \end{aligned} \tag{1}$$

[1] Work performed under the auspices of the U. S. Atomic Energy Commission.

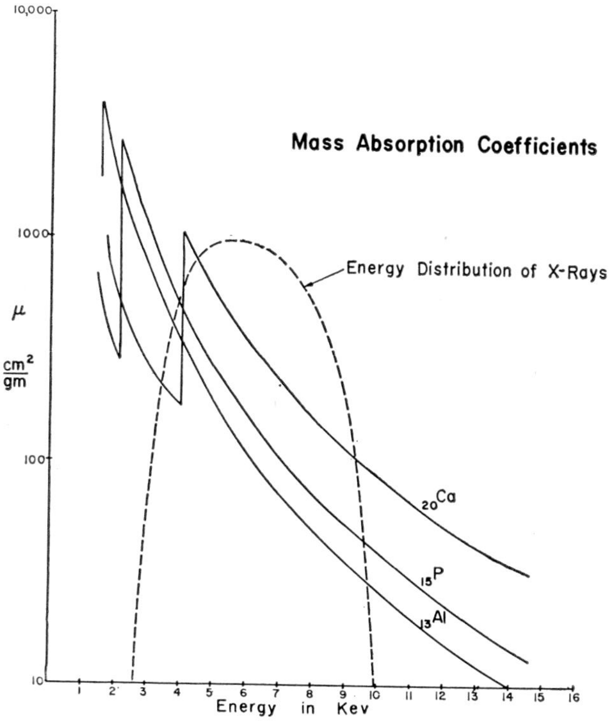

FIG. 1. A semilog plot of the mass absorption coefficients (μ) for aluminum, phosphorus, and calcium as a function of energy. Superimposed is the energy distribution of the photons emitted from the X-ray tube operated at 10 kv, with a total filtration of 1 mm of beryllium. (The characteristic X-rays from the tungsten anode, at 8.4 kev, have been ignored.)

where μ is the mass absorption coefficient of the element denoted by the subscript, in units of square centimeters per gram.

The absorption of X-rays is given by

$$I = I_0 e^{-\mu \rho d} \tag{2}$$

where I_0 = the original intensity of the beam, a measure of the number of X-rays.
I = the intensity after passing through a thickness, d, of a material.
μ = the mass absorption coefficient of the material (cm²/gm).
ρ = the density of the material (gm/cm³).
d = the thickness of the material (cm).

The mass absorption coefficient, μ, is a function of X-ray energy, so the equation as written above is energy-dependent.

The absorption of X-rays by a thin bone section is given by

$$I = I_0 e^{-(\mu \rho d)_{\mathrm{Ca}} - (\mu \rho d)_{\mathrm{P}}} \tag{3}$$

Here we have neglected the X-ray absorption due to O, H, and the trace elements present in bone because they account for less than 1% of the total absorption.

From the step wedge of aluminum which was radiographed simultaneously with the bone section we can determine the thickness of aluminum which produced the same absorption of the X-rays as any given area of the section. For this thickness we write

$$I = I_0 e^{-(\mu\rho d)_{\mathrm{Al}}} \quad (4)$$

Then, since I/I_0 has the same value in equations 3 and 4, we have

$$[\mu\rho d]_{\mathrm{Al}} = [\mu\rho d]_{\mathrm{Ca}} + [\mu\rho d]_{\mathrm{P}} \quad (5)$$

Substituting the values of μ from equation 1, we have

$$[\rho d]_{\mathrm{Al}} = 3.29\ [\rho d]_{\mathrm{Ca}} + 1.47\ [\rho d]_{\mathrm{P}} \quad (6)$$

Here we have eliminated the energy dependence and find that the numerical value of the left-hand side of this equation is a measurable quantity. If we assume that all the calcium present in the bone is in the form of hydroxyapatite

$$Ca_{10}(PO_4)_6 \cdot (OH)_2$$

then

$$[\rho d]_{\mathrm{Ca}} = 2.15\ [\rho d]_{\mathrm{P}} \quad (7)$$

From equation 6, by substitution,

$$[\rho d]_{\mathrm{Ca}} = 0.252\ [\rho d]_{\mathrm{Al}} \quad (8)$$

Hence, we have shown that a microradiograph of a thin bone section and suitable aluminum step wedge can be employed to obtain the mass per unit area of calcium in a given area of the bone section. The densitometer with which the photographic darkening is measured has an aperture 10 μ in diameter. Since the sections analyzed are normally 50 μ thick, the volume analyzed is a cylinder containing 4×10^{-9} cm^3.

The second required measurement, the thickness, enables us to transform the mass determination into density, the mass per unit volume. In practice the thickness of the bone section must be obtained at each spot to be analyzed, because the section cannot be assumed to be free from fluctuations in thickness. The ideal instrument should measure the average thickness of the section over the same area as covered by the densitometer beam. Our instrument approaches these requirements in that it measures the maximum thickness of a spot 40 μ in diameter instead of the average over 10 μ. It works as follows: On the substage condenser of a Leitz Ortholux microscope is mounted a metal cone. The end of this cone is ground flat and smooth, as seen through a 22× Ultropak objective (surface illumination). The diameter of this circular flat end is 40 μ. Employing the vernier of the microscope, we can reproducibly locate the position of proper focus of this surface within ± 1 μ.

To measure the thickness of any given region of a bone section, the section is mounted horizontally over the cone, and the cone raised until it touches and lifts the bone. When the flat end of the cone touches the bone section, it can be readily seen through the section; thus the section can be moved to place any desired region directly over the cone. The objective lens is focused on the top surface of the bone; then the section is removed, and the objective moved down to focus on the top of the cone. The difference in the two vernier readings gives the thickness of the desired region of the bone section.

Most of the absorption of X-rays with energies between 4 and 10 kev by bone mineral is due to calcium, with absorption by phosphorus being secondary in importance; and the contributions due to the components of lower atomic number may be neglected. We have assumed in the calculations of the calcium density that the atomic ratio of Ca/P in bone was 10/6. A change in this ratio from 10/6 to 9/6 will change the results by only 2%. On the basis of a 10/6 ratio the measured calcium density has been also expressed as the mineral density of hydroxyapatite in the results which follow.

Although there exists no doubt as to the ability of the microradiographic technique to measure relative differences in the degree of calcification, there might be question of the absolute values determined by the technique described above. To verify these results, a section previously analyzed in this fashion was microradiographed with the fluorescent radiation produced by titanium, 4.51 kev. A 2-mm-square piece of titanium was placed in the direct beam of the X-ray tube, and the characteristic X-rays produced at 90° to the direct beam employed to make the X-ray image. The spectrum produced was analyzed with a proportional counter and pulse height analyzer; with 20 kv applied to the X-ray tube, 88% of the X-rays produced were found to be due to Kα emission of titanium. The resulting microradiograph was quite satisfactory but required an exposure of 275 hours on Kodak Spectroscopic plate, Type 548-0. This is to be compared to the direct-beam exposure, on a plate approximately half as fast (649-0), of 10 minutes with 10 kv applied to the tube. The results obtained by monochromatic analysis differed by less than 2% from the direct-beam analysis, a difference well within the limits of error of these measurements.

RESULTS

The measured values of calcium density, expressed in terms of grams of calcium per cubic centimeter and in grams of hydroxyapatite per cubic centimeter, found in bone sections from man, dog, and several other species, are listed in Tables I, II, and III, respectively. These measurements are the lowest mineral density observed, usually in newly formed secondary haversian bone, and the highest density, either a remnant of an old system between secondary haversian systems or primary bone. The values obtained are in accord with the relative density measurements reported by Amprino (*4*) in that newly formed mineral contains 70 to 75% of the mineral content of the most highly calcified bone in a given bone section.

Human Bones

The densities found in the cortical cross sections of the femurs of individuals of ages 7, 29, 31, and 76 years are tabulated in Table I. Also included are the corresponding densities found in the clavicles. These thus represent values from bones both of which contain secondary haversian systems but which differ in size and shape.

Dog Bones

In Table II are tabulated the values obtained from sections of the femurs of five dogs, of ages 6 weeks to 5 years. The values from two dogs burdened with Sr^{90} for 10 years have also been included; these were 11 and 12 years old.

TABLE I

OBSERVED VALUES OF MINERAL DENSITY IN HUMAN BONES

	Femur				Clavicle			
	Low density		High density		Low density		High density	
Age	*gm Ca/cm³*	*gm HA[a] /cm³*	*gm Ca/cm³*	*gm HA /cm³*	*gm Ca/cm³*	*gm HA /cm³*	*gm Ca/cm³*	*gm HA /cm³*
7 yr	0.360	0.90	0.516	1.29	0.360	0.90	0.484	1.21
29 yr	0.480	1.20	0.576	1.44				
31 yr	0.444	1.11	0.560	1.40	0.412	1.03	0.524	1.31
76 yr	0.392	0.98	0.512	1.28	0.448	1.12	0.548	1.37

[a] gm HA/cm³ = grams of hydroxyapatite per cubic centimeter.

TABLE II

OBSERVED VALUES OF MINERAL DENSITY IN THE FEMUR OF DOGS OF VARIOUS AGES

	Low density		High density	
Age	*gm Ca/cm³*	*gm HA/cm³*	*gm Ca/cm³*	*gm HA/cm³*
6 wk	0.468	1.17	0.536	1.34
6 wk	0.456	1.14	0.612	1.53
9 mo.	0.408	1.02	0.492	1.23
1–2 yr	0.440	1.10	0.609	1.52
5¼ yr	0.482	1.23	0.612	1.53
11 yr	0.512	1.28	0.616	1.54
12 yr	0.500	1.25	0.612	1.53

[a] gm HA/cm³ = grams of hydroxyapatite per cubic centimeter.

TABLE III

OBSERVED VALUES OF MINERAL DENSITY IN VARIOUS ANIMALS

Animal	Low density		High Density		Number of sections
	gm Ca/cm³	gm HA/cm³	gm Ca/cm³	gm HA/cm³	
Man	0.360–0.480	0.90–1.20	0.484–0.576	1.21–1.44	22
Cow	0.444	1.11	0.600	1.50	2
Dog	0.408–0.512	1.02–1.28	0.492–0.616	1.23–1.54	28
Mouse	0.472–0.500	1.18–1.25	0.544–0.556	1.36–1.39	2
Rabbit	0.556	1.39	0.612	1.53	2
Rat	0.56–0.569	1.40–1.42	0.676–0.680	1.69–1.70	2

[a] gm HA/cm³ = grams of hydroxyapatite per cubic centimeter.

Bones from Other Animals

In Table III are tabulated values obtained from the bone sections of single animals of several other species. Of the animals examined, the bone from the rat had the highest microscopic density.

DISCUSSION

The density of hydroxyapatite, $Ca_{10}(PO_4)_6 \cdot (OH)_2$, is 3.15 gm/cm^3, if calculated from the weight of a unit cell and the volume it occupies. The unit cell dimensions, obtained from Carlstrom (*5*), are: *a*-axis, 9.42 A; *c*-axis, 6.88 A. The largest value of mineral density found, that of 1.70 gm/cm^3 in the rat, requires that 54% of the analyzed volume be occupied by mineral, whereas the highest value in man, 1.44 gm/cm^3, implies that 46% of the volume is occupied. If both of these values represent the maximum possible levels of calcification, and at maximum calcification the water content of bone is at an absolute minimum, then the organic fraction of bone is less in rat bone than in human bone.

The density of microscopic volumes of bone has been measured by Davies and Engstrom (*6*), who employed both microradiography and interference microscopy to measure both the organic and inorganic components of bone. Unfortunately, their results are not directly comparable to ours, because they reported and employed an effective thickness, namely, the actual thickness reduced by the fraction of the volume occupied by immersion medium. Wallgren and Holmstrand (*7*) have described a system of quantitative microradiography for bone which they state can detect mass differences as small as ±1.66%, but they have not reported any measured values.

Holmstrand (*8*) has reported microscopic density measurements of the intermediary callus for autogenous and homogenous cortical transplants in rabbit bone in terms of the linear absorption coefficient, μ (cm^{-1}). If we convert his values to calcium densities, on the basis of an atomic Ca/P ratio of 10/6, his maximum density is 0.640 gm Ca per cubic centimeter, and the lowest value is 0.462 gm Ca. These values, employed to show the increase in density of the callus with time, have a greater spread than the values we found in two sections of rabbit bone.

Macroscopic densities of canine bone have been described in considerable detail by Robinson and Elliott (*9*), who carefully describe the frame of reference for their work. Considering that the volume analyzed in our work is a factor of 10^8 smaller than that analyzed by Robinson, the agreement between his values of ash volume, 49 to 51% of 1 cm^3 of dry bone, and our values of mineral volume, 32 to 53% of a volume 4×10^{-9} cm^3, is remarkable. His values are an average over a volume of 1 cm^3, whereas ours represent the extremes that exist in various structural units of bone.

It should also be noted that Robinson calls attention to the fact that his ratio of ash weight to dry bone weight for dogs is higher than the values Vogt and Tonsager (*10*) report for human subjects and states that this might be a species difference, the osteoid in dogs being able to hold more mineral crystals per unit volume than human bone when fully calcified. Our results verify his tentative conclusion.

Figures 2 and 3 were made to illustrate our findings that the absolute quantity of calcium per unit volume of bone is species-dependent. Newly formed mineral,

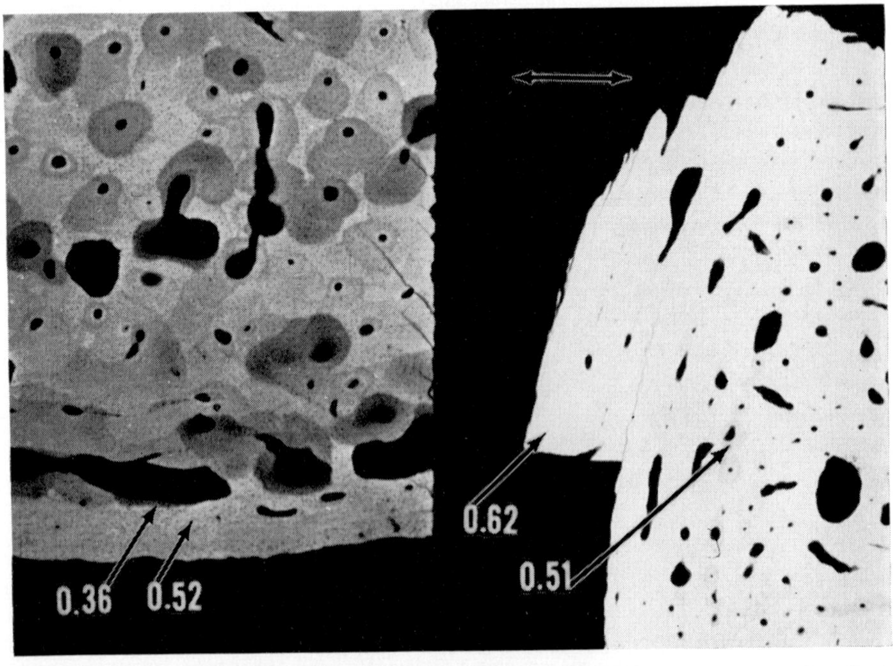

FIG. 2. A microradiograph of two fragments of bone. On the left, a femur section from a 7-year-old human being is 45.4 μ thick at the points analyzed; the 11-year-old dog femur is 44.9 μ thick at the indicated points. The scale arrow is 0.5 mm long; the units of density are grams Ca per cubic centimeter.

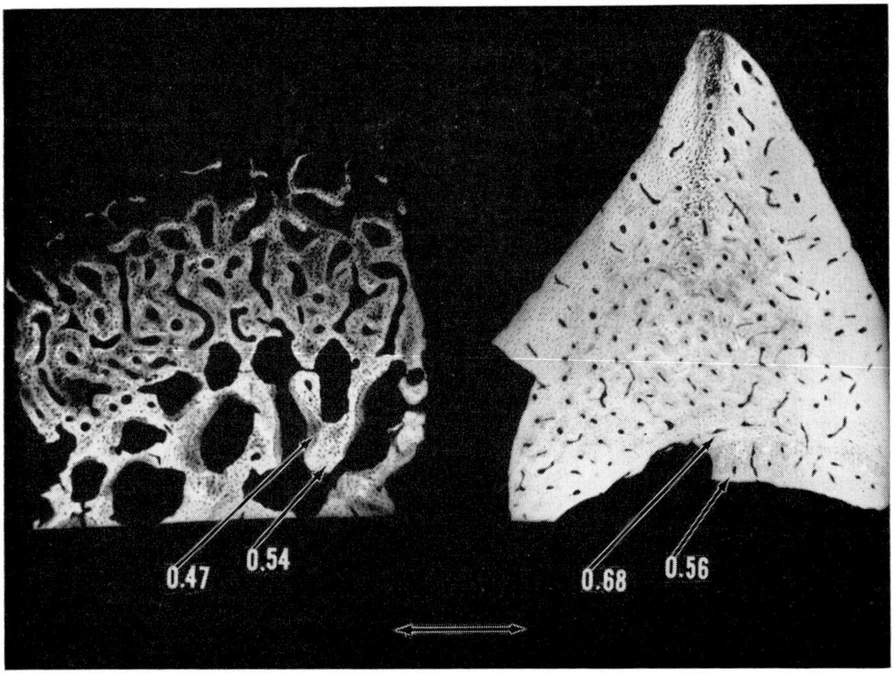

FIG. 3. A microradiograph of two fragments of bone. On the left, the bone from the 6-week-old puppy is 67 μ thick at the points analyzed; the rat bone on the right is 64 μ thick at the indicated points. The scale arrow is 0.5 mm long; the units of density are grams of Ca per cubic centimeter.

such as is laid down appositionally in secondary haversian systems, is formed at different densities in the different species. Likewise, the ultimate level of calcium density, such as found in old haversian systems, or in nonhaversian bone, is different in the different species. Figure 2 is a microradiograph of two femur fragments, one from a human being, 7 years old, the other from an 11-year-old dog. Both were equally thick (within 1%), so that a proper X-ray exposure for the human bone resulted in a very underexposed radiograph of the more dense dog bone. Figure 3, in addition, shows the contrast in macroscopic density to be expected between the bone from a 6-week-old dog and a mature rat.

Such differences in the initial and final levels of calcium density might be expected to produce differences in the uptake of alkaline earths by appositional growth processes and differences in time constants and rates for exchange processes.

CONCLUSION

The range of microscopic calcium densities observed in man and in dog does not change with the age of the individual. The ranges, however, are not the same in the two species. New bone mineral in the dog is formed at higher density than similar mineral in man, and highly mineralized bone in the dog is more dense than the most dense bone in man. Thus species differences in calcium metabolism of bone do exist and should not be overlooked in the intercomparison of the uptake and retention of the alkaline earths in mammalian skeletons.

ACKNOWLEDGMENT

These studies were carried out at the suggestion of L. D. Marinelli, to whom we are also indebted for many helpful suggestions and advice.

RECEIVED March 4, 1958

REFERENCES

1. A. ENGSTROM, Quantitative micro- and histochemical elementary analysis by Roentgen absorption spectrography. *Acta Radiol. Suppl.* **63** (1946).
2. A. H. COMPTON and S. K. ALLISON, *X-Ray in Theory and Experiment*, D. Van Nostrand Co., New York, 1943.
3. B. LINDELL, Frequency or wavelength in Roentgen energy diagrams. *Acta Radiol.* **37,** 28–32 (1952).
4. R. AMPRINO, Relationship between the processes of reconstruction and distribution of minerals in bone. 1. Investigations conducted with the method of study of absorption of Roentgen rays. *Z. Zellforsch. u. mikroskop. Anat.* **37,** 144–183 (1952).
5. D. CARLSTROM, X-Ray crystallographic studies on apatites and calcified structures. *Acta Radiol. Suppl.* **121** (1955).
6. H. G. DAVIES and A. ENGSTROM, Interferometric and X-ray absorption studies of bone tissue. *Exptl. Cell Research* **7,** 243–255 (1954).
7. G. WALLGREN and K. HOLMSTRAND, Technical considerations on quantitative microradiography on bone. *Exptl. Cell Research* **12,** 188–191 (1956).
8. K. HOLMSTRAND, Biophysical investigations of bone transplants and bone implants. *Acta Orthopaed. Scand. Suppl.* **No. 26** (1957).
9. R. A. ROBINSON and S. R. ELLIOTT, The water content of bone. *J. Bone and Joint Surg.* **39A,** 167–188 (1957).
10. J. H. VOGT and A. TONSAGER, Investigations on bone chemistry of man. II. Phosphatase, calcium, phosphorus, and nitrogen in the substantia spongiosa, cristae ilei. *Acta Med. Scand.* **135,** 231–244 (1949).

RADIATION RESEARCH 10, 243–257 (1959)

Microscopic Metabolism of Calcium in Bone

IV. Ca^{45} Deposition and Growth Rate in Canine Osteons[1]

J. H. MARSHALL, J. JOWSEY, AND R. E. ROWLAND

Radiological Physics Division, Argonne National Laboratory, Lemont, Illinois

I. INTRODUCTION

When calciumlike radioactive nuclides are injected into the blood stream, they are deposited in high concentrations in some of the osteons in cortical bone. These concentrations of activity are interesting both because they may be a factor in the long-term radiation damage produced by Sr^{90} or Ra^{226} in bone and because, at least for Ca^{45}, they reflect the dynamics of calcium metabolism between the blood and individual osteons in living bone. A three-dimensional autoradiographic study of Ca^{45} in osteons has been reported (*1*).

If Ca^{45} is present in the blood, it will be taken up by an osteon during appositional growth and during secondary mineralization along with stable calcium and be built into bone mineral. In addition to this accretion of calcium, an exchange of Ca^{45} for already-deposited Ca^{40} may be expected to occur. Such exchange has been demonstrated *in vitro* by Neuman (*2*), Amprino (*3*), and others, and has been invoked as the process of P^{32} deposition in living osteons (*4*). On the other hand, Arnold *et al.* (*5*) have attributed the Ca^{45} concentrations in growing osteons of rabbits to accretion of calcium.

It is our purpose to present autoradiographic measurements of the total Ca^{45} content of individual osteons in dogs after a single injection and to compare them with the Ca^{45} uptake expected from accretion of calcium during appositional growth. An expression for the appositional growth rate of an average osteon is derived which is consistent with the observed Ca^{45} content of forming osteons as well as with direct measurements of osteon growth.

II. METHOD

Three adult mongrel dogs were given single low-level[2] intravenous injections of Ca^{45} (0.05 mc/kg body weight) at pH 4 to 5 and specific activity >1000 mc/gm$_{Ca}$.

[1] Work performed under the auspices of the U. S. Atomic Energy Commission.

[2] This level of injected activity should have no significant effect on the observed growth processes. The average skeletal dose was about 1 rad/day; some hotspots delivered 5 to 10 rads/day.

TABLE I
EXPERIMENTAL ANIMALS

Dog	Time between Ca^{45} injection and sacrifice, T_s	Age	Region from which data in Fig. 3 were taken: Approximate number of forming osteons per cm^2 with $b > 40\ \mu$	Region from which data in Fig. 3 were taken: Bone location
C119	2 weeks	Adult	10	Femur midshaft
		(4 ± 2 years)	20	Femur end of shaft
C120	12 hours	1 year	300	Humerus midshaft
C122	12 hours	6 years	10	Femur midshaft

Two were sacrificed 12 hours after injection, and the other was sacrificed 2 weeks after injection, as shown in Table I. The diaphyses of long bones from each dog were dehydrated in alcohol and ether and embedded in Bioplastic. Cross sections were cut to a thickness of 125 μ, a distance short compared to the length of most Ca^{45} deposits in osteons (*1*) but comparable to Ca^{45} β-particle range so that the β-particle emission from a section was over 95% that of a thick source. Each cross section was sandwiched between two No Screen Autoradiographic plates. A typical autoradiogram is shown in Fig. 1.

Selection of Ca^{45} Deposits in Osteons for Longitudinal Invariance

In order to relate the observed quantities of Ca^{45} to the properties of osteons, it is necessary to eliminate the complexity introduced by the interconnecting osteon network. This has been done by using cross sections of long bones so that most osteons are perpendicular to the film and by choosing Ca^{45} deposits which are relatively invariant with depth in the given section. The two autoradiograms from each cross section were compared by projecting them alternately on a ground-glass screen at a magnification of 30 to 100 and by tracing the spots of Ca^{45} darkening. Spots which were not practically identical on the two autoradiograms were eliminated from further analysis. Microradiographs of each bone section, taken with X-rays from a tube operating at 12 kv, were similarly projected and compared with the autoradiograms. Two different microradiographic exposures were used: one to reveal the small differences in high calcium density between osteons and primary bone, and another, shorter exposure to reveal differences in low calcium density so as to distinguish between osteon canals which were oblique and those which continued perpendicularly through a section. By this comparison of two autoradiograms and two microradiographs, Ca^{45} deposits were selected which ran perpendicular to, and continued through, a section without noticeable variation either in the Ca^{45} activity distribution or in the structure of the corresponding osteon. This selection eliminated from further analysis about half the Ca^{45} hotspots from an average autoradiogram, as was to be expected from the three-dimensional pattern of Ca^{45} deposits (*1*). The present analysis does not include osteons with arrested

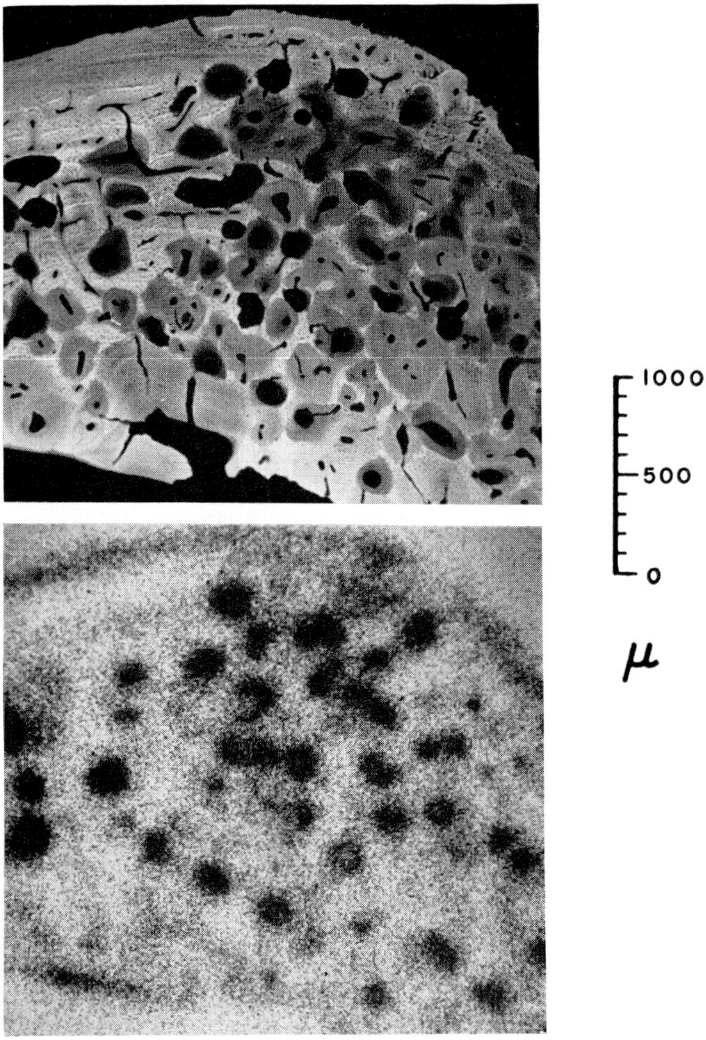

FIG. 1. Ca^{45} autoradiogram and corresponding long-exposure microradiograph from the midshaft of the humerus of dog C120. The autoradiogram is at the bottom.

growth—that is, low-density osteons with canals larger than 20-μ diameter but negligible Ca^{45} uptake—though several were observed. The activity per unit length and the canal diameter of each of the selected active osteons were measured as follows.

Activity per unit length, h. The total activity per unit length of a Ca^{45} deposit was determined from the surface integral of the film darkening which it produced. Measurements from each of the pair of autoradiograms were averaged.

Provided that (1) the distribution of Ca^{45} activity in the deposit is invariant with depth in the (thick) bone section, and (2) the osteon's canal is filled with an embedding medium of the same density, and approximately the same atomic composition as the surrounding bone, it follows (*6*) that

$$h = \frac{\rho}{kF} \iint D \, dx \, dy \qquad (1)$$

where h = activity per unit length (μc/cm) of Ca^{45} deposit in bone.
ρ = density of bone and embedding material seen by β-particles (gm/cm^3).
F = exposure time for bone (days), corrected for decay if necessary.
k = calibration factor for film derived from exposure to thick uniform radiator (darkening gm/μc-day).
D = film darkening, a function of position, corrected for linearity and film background.

The first of the above provisions, depth invariance, was satisfied by the selection of data. The second provision, homogeneity of the source, was not exactly satisfied. The bone of a young or forming osteon is generally surrounded by bone of about 30% higher density, whereas the Bioplastic embedding medium within its canal had a density about 30% lower than that of the newly formed bone. In osteons with large-diameter canals, for which the inhomogeneity is greatest, the two errors work in opposite directions. That Bioplastic actually filled canal spaces was checked under an incident illumination microscope. Thus by ignoring inhomogeneity and using the density of newly formed bone for ρ in equation 1, we should not introduce an uncertainty in h greater than 30%. The value $\rho = 2$ gm/cm^3 has been used in equation 1 but cancels out in the results given by expression 4 or 7.

The measured activity per unit length for an osteon corresponds to the total Ca^{45} activity in the osteon whether that activity is associated with the newly forming lamellae around the canal or with a diffuse uptake in the recently formed bone between canal and cement line. All measurements of h are normalized to an injected Ca^{45} activity of 0.1 mc/kg body weight.

Canal diameter, b. The diameter of the canal in each osteon was measured from the longer exposure microradiograph and corresponds to the inner diameter of the calcified region or, more exactly, to the sharply defined perimeter at which calcium density changes from zero to approximately 70% that of primary bone. For canals not approximately circular, the average of the maximum and minimum diameter was used. No osteons were included whose maximum diameter exceeded their minimum diameter by a factor of 2 or more.

Blood specific activity, B. Previously reported measurements (*7*) of blood specific

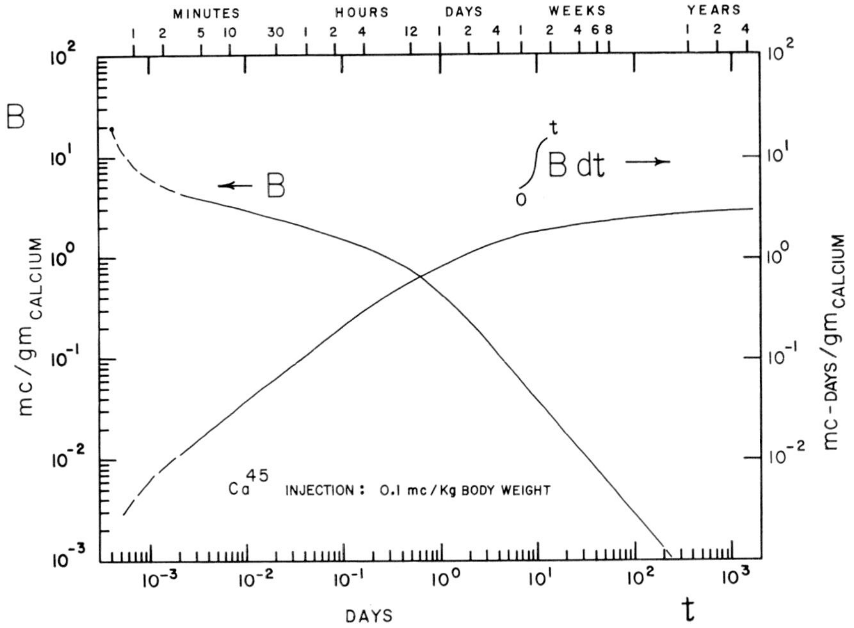

FIG. 2. Blood specific activity, B, in mc/gm$_{Ca}$, as a function of time, t, after a single injection of Ca^{45} taken from data for five adult dogs used in reference 7. The initial point on the B curve is the total injected activity divided by the calcium content of the blood plotted at about one circulation time (8). The time integral of B from injection to time t is given in mc-days/gm$_{Ca}$. Only 5% of the value of the integral at 12 hours is contributed by the first 10 minutes after injection.

activity, B (mc$_{Ca^{45}}$/gm$_{Ca}$), as a function of time, t, for five Ca^{45}-injected adult dogs are shown in Fig. 2. Measured values extend from 10 minutes to 100 days and are normalized to an injection of 0.1 mc/kg body weight. The integral increases a factor of 3 between 12 hours and 2 weeks. Since the integral is not strongly dependent on the values of blood specific activity at an hour or less, a time delay before interstitial fluid reaches equilibrium with the blood (probably of the order of 15 minutes) can be neglected.

The three dogs used here were also injected by J. Cohen with Ca^{45} standardized in the MIT 4π counter, but blood samples were not taken. Individual variation from the data of Fig. 2, however, is expected to be less than a factor of 2.

III. RESULTS

Experimental

The measured activity per unit length versus canal diameter for the selected osteons in the three dogs is plotted in Fig. 3. The relative numbers of points do not

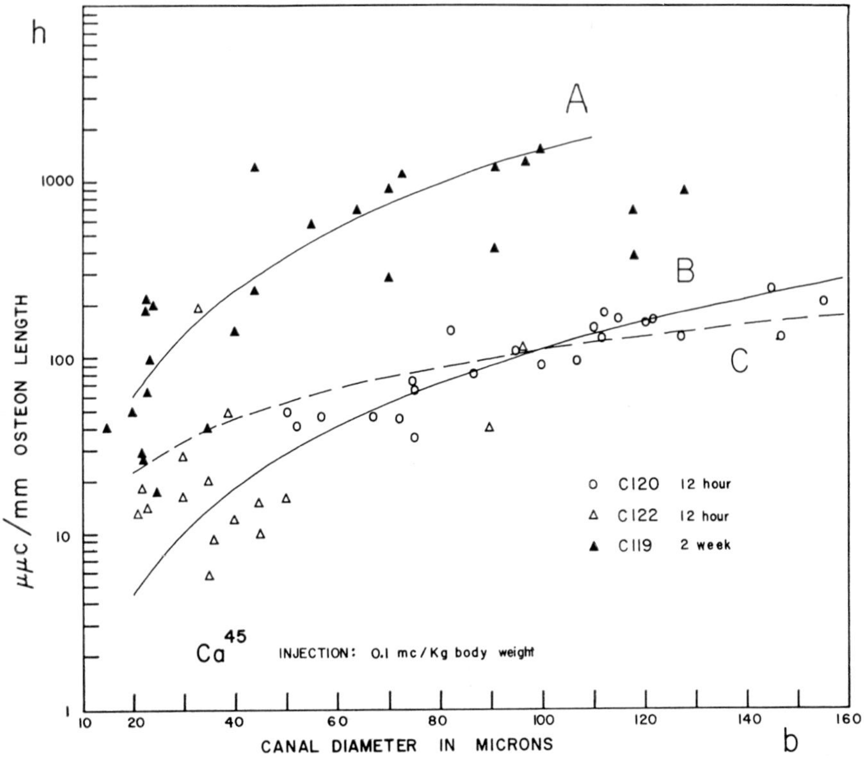

FIG. 3. The total Ca^{45} activity per unit length, h, in $\mu\mu c$/mm, in individual osteons of dogs listed in Table I plotted against the diameter of the osteon canal, b, in microns, both h and b being measured either 12 hours or 2 weeks after injection. The values have been normalized to a Ca^{45} injection of 0.1 mc/kg body weight. Curve A is given by expression 7 with $T_s = 2$ weeks, $\beta = 0.04$ day^{-1}; and curve B by $T_s = 12$ hours, $\beta = 0.024$ day^{-1}. Curve A does not extend to the largest values of b because for $T_s = 2$ weeks these values represent osteons which started forming during the 2-week interval after injection and which therefore should contain less than the activity given by expression 7.

indicate a frequency distribution because many sections were examined to find the larger values of canal diameter. The points for the two dogs sacrificed at 12 hours fall considerably lower than the points for the 2-week dog, and separate curves have been fitted to the data as described below. A displacement of the two sets of points may be expected for two reasons: the uptake of Ca^{45} in osteons in 2 weeks may be greater than in 12 hours; and the canal diameter of a forming osteon would decrease more owing to osteon growth in the 2-week interval than in the 12-hour interval after injection. There may also be a displacement due to differences in the actual blood curves or in the animals used.

Theoretical

Let us calculate the Ca^{45} deposition expected in osteons for given rates of appositional growth and then compare the calculated values with the data. Let us assume that (1) the specific activity (Ca^{45}/Ca) seen by an osteon is equal to the specific activity of the blood measured in the large veins, and that (2) the Ca^{45} activity observed in osteons at 12 hours and 2 weeks has been deposited by accretion of calcium (and does not represent exchange of Ca^{45} for Ca^{40}). Under these two assumptions, which we shall discuss in view of the results, we can calculate the rate of calcium accretion per unit length in an osteon from the observed Ca^{45} activity per unit length and blood specific activity measurements. The activity per unit length, h, is given by

$$h = \int_0^{T_s} gB \; dt \qquad (2)$$

where h = total activity ($\mu c/cm$) in osteon.
g = accretion rate per unit length of osteon (gm_{Ca}/cm day).
B = blood specific activity ($\mu c/gm_{Ca}$).
T_s = interval between injection and sacrifice (days).

We can describe a forming osteon as a cylindrical shell with a fixed outer diameter and with an inner diameter, b, which decreases with time, owing to appositional growth of new bone. The rate of calcium deposition, g, resulting from a given rate, db/dt, of decrease of canal diameter is

$$g = -\frac{\pi \rho c}{2}\left(b\,\frac{db}{dt}\right) \qquad (3)$$

where b = inner (canal) diameter (cm).
ρ = density of newly formed bone (gm_{bone}/cm^3).
c = calcium content of newly formed bone (gm_{Ca}/gm_{bone}).[3]

There will also be some accretion associated with the slow increase of ρc with time, but, to a good approximation, we can neglect this secondary mineralization in comparison with appositional growth and use a constant value of ρc. Because we desire the total accretion per unit length in an osteon, we may take a value of ρc that is representative of the osteon mineral as a whole and thereby avoid the difficult task of describing the rapid variation of mineral density near the growing surface.

Combining expressions 2 and 3 we can calculate the total Ca^{45} activity per unit length that would be deposited in an osteon of given canal diameter by a rate of appositional growth db/dt:

$$h = -\frac{\pi \rho c}{2}\int_0^{T_s} b\left(\frac{db}{dt}\right) B \; dt \qquad (4)$$

[3] The value $c = 0.25$ gm_{Ca}/gm_{bone} has been used throughout this paper.

For short intervals between injection and sacrifice in which b and db/dt may be considered constant, expression 4 yields rates of appositional growth db/dt from measurements of h and b. For $T_s = 12$ hours in Fig. 3, any point on curve C (dashed) corresponds to a value of h and b such that $db/dt = -2.4\ \mu$/day. Therefore the assumption of constant canal diameter, b, and db/dt for $T_s = 12$ hours in expression 4 is self-consistent because the canal diameter decrease during 12 hours at the rate of 2.4 μ/day is negligible. For an interval as long as 2 weeks between injection and sacrifice, however, the decrease in canal diameter for an individual osteon will no longer be negligible and we must take into account changing values of the accretion rate, g, within the integral (expression 2).

The simplest assumption for the variation of g with time would be that the osteon canal diameter have a constant rate of decrease, db/dt, in which case an average of the 12-hour data would indicate that a 120-μ-diameter osteon takes 6 weeks to fill in to a final canal diameter of 20 μ. The data are better fitted, however, when we take into account the fact that an osteon fills in more rapidly at first than it does when nearing completion (unpublished results of J. Jowsey and also reference *9*). Let us represent a decreasing rate of linear growth by an exponential:

$$b = b_o e^{-\beta t} \tag{5}$$

$$db/dt = -\beta b \tag{6}$$

where b is the canal diameter as a function of time after the beginning of appositional growth, and β is the fractional decrease in canal diameter per unit time. The constant b_o is the outer or cement line diameter of the osteon. The time required for a forming osteon to reduce its canal diameter to half any given diameter is thus $0.693/\beta$, which we shall refer to as the half-diameter time. This somewhat arbitrary description of the average forming osteon in dog provides a reasonably good fit to the data. Of course when the final diameter of about 20 μ is reached, expressions 5 and 6 can no longer be applied.

Inserting expressions 5 and 6 into expression 4 gives an expression in which activity per unit length is proportional to the square of the canal diameter at any time after injection:

$$h = b_s^2 \left[\left(\frac{\pi \rho c}{2} \right) \beta e^{2\beta T_s} \int_0^{T_s} e^{-2\beta t} \ B \ dt \right] \tag{7}$$

where b_s is the canal diameter observed at the time of sacrifice, and other symbols are as defined above.

Expression 7 yields the solid curves through the data in Fig. 3, the C119 data giving $\beta = 0.04$ day^{-1}, and the C120 and C122 data giving $\beta = 0.024$ day^{-1}. The difference between these values is probably not significant considering the possible errors of the measurements, and we therefore report the average value below.

Summary of Results

Under our assumptions that the observed Ca^{45} was deposited by accretion at the specific activity of the blood, at either 12 hours or 2 weeks after injection, the data may be described by an osteon apposition rate given by expression 6 with $\beta = 0.03 \pm 0.01 \text{ day}^{-1}$. This is equivalent to a rate of formation of an average osteon such that its canal diameter decreases to half its value every 3 ± 1 weeks. At this rate, an average osteon with an outer diameter of 120 μ would have almost completed appositional growth by reaching a canal diameter of 30 μ in 6 ± 2 weeks.

IV. DISCUSSION

Comparison of 12-Hour and 2-Week Data

Although intercomparison between animals is here subject to an error of perhaps a factor of 2, the similarity of the values of β derived from the 12-hour and 2-week data suggests that forming osteons contain no large amount of Ca^{45} in an exchangeable fraction of bone salt in equilibrium with the blood at 12 hours or more after injection. The presence of such short-term exchangeable activity[4] would make the 12-hour value of β larger than the 2-week value because during this period blood specific activity falls by a factor of 25 to 30. Such a comparison by itself is not sufficient, however, to prove that the observed Ca^{45} activity is associated primarily with accretion. Although the possible influence of resorption is eliminated by the nature of the data (on the microradiographs resorption cavities are easily recognizable and did not encroach on any of the selected osteons), we have not yet eliminated the possibility of nonequilibrium or long-term exchange[4] which might arise from such processes as recrystallization or intracrystalline diffusion in bone existing at the time of injection (*2*).

Comparison of Results with Direct Observations of Osteon Growth—Conclusions

How does the canal half-diameter time of 3 weeks which we have derived compare with direct observations of osteon growth? High-resolution osteon-labeling studies by Jee and Arnold (*9*) in young rabbits indicated that of the osteons which were just beginning formation at the time of Ca^{45} administration, 20 to 30% were completed in 21 days though they did not show the distribution of growth rates. Vincent (*10*), using high-resolution S^{35} labeling, concluded that an osteon in adult dog takes about 6 weeks to complete appositional growth. (Vincent finds secondary mineralization still not complete in 18 weeks.) Thus the rate of appositional growth which we have derived from the total Ca^{45} activity in an osteon after a single injection agrees at least within a factor of 2 with the rate of growth observed directly by the use of high-resolution labels. Therefore we may conclude that our basic assumptions are essentially correct and that (1) the intense deposits of Ca^{45} which we have

[4] Definitions of these terms appear in the appendix to paper V of this series.

observed in osteons are due primarily to accretion of calcium in appositional growth, and (2) the specific activity (Ca^{45}/Ca) of new bone being deposited in an osteon is practically the same as that in the blood as measured in the large veins.

Strictly speaking, these two conclusions are not independent: If the specific activity of the blood in a bone capillary were significantly lower than that measured in the large veins, then the observed Ca^{45} uptake in an osteon might indicate a correspondingly larger gross rate of calcium uptake than that due to accretion alone. Several of the following calculations, however, give us confidence that both conclusions are essentially correct.

The present data should not be taken as evidence that all Ca^{45} hotspots in osteons are produced by appositional growth. The nature of the Ca^{45} uptake in osteons of small canal diameter cannot be determined by our present technique: part of the uptake may be accretion due to almost-completed appositional growth, part accretion due to secondary mineralization, and part long-term exchange. These different possible mechanisms of Ca^{45} uptake in osteons of small canal diameter may be partially differentiated by high-resolution autoradiography in that a relatively uniform deposition throughout an osteon after a single Ca^{45} injection cannot possibly have been produced by appositional growth. Such uniform distributions of activity after a single injection have occasionally been observed (unpublished observations of J. Jowsey and reference *4*) and may contain activity several times in excess of the diffuse component. From Fig. 3, however, it appears that the total Ca^{45} uptake at small canal diameters due to all processes is about an order of magnitude less than that at large canal diameters. We have shown that this large-diameter uptake of Ca^{45} *in vivo* is comparable to that which would be produced by purely appositional growth. Therefore, although some hotspots may be produced by other processes, we have shown that the more intense depositions *in vivo* are produced by appositional growth.

Observations of occasional arrested growth in an osteon—that is, the failure of an osteon with a large-diameter canal to deposit a radioactive tracer in appositional growth—have been interpreted as evidence that the normal process of calcium deposition in a forming osteon may be intermittent. We have found, however, that the Ca^{45} uptake by a forming osteon does not exceed that which would be required for the completion of appositional growth in about 6 weeks at a continuous rate. Of course intermittent calcium deposition with a period of a few hours or less might produce the observed rate as an average value, but given a resolving time of perhaps half a day our result indicates that calcium deposition in most osteons is continuous.

V. CALCULATIONS BASED ON THE GROWTH RATE OF AN OSTEON

Distributions of Forming Osteons and Ca^{45} Deposits

If in a large group of osteons the number which have just started to form per day has remained constant for 2 months or more, we would expect to find forming osteons with all possible values of canal diameter, b. Since according to expression 5 an individual osteon spends more time at small diameters than at large, small-diameter osteons should predominate, the number of canal diameters per unit diameter being inversely proportional to diameter. The distribution of activities per unit length, h, after a single injection would also be hyperbolic, the number of osteons with activity between h and $h + dh$ being inversely proportional to h. Observed distributions of b or h in C119 and C122 agree with this hyperbolic shape fairly well. C120, however, shows a peaked distribution of both b and h, probably because a burst of new osteon formation in this 1-year-old dog had recently occurred so that equilibrium did not exist.

The bell-shaped maximum darkening distribution for osteon hotspots in rabbits reported by Arnold (*5*) may thus be partly the result of a nonequilibrium population of osteons. A maximum darkening distribution is not strictly comparable to an activity per unit length distribution, however, because the former depends on a single measurement of darkening whereas the latter depends on the surface integral of the darkening in a distribution whose shape depends on canal diameter.

Time for Formation of a Resorption Cavity

The number of resorption cavities in an average cross section from the femur of C119 was smaller than the number of forming osteons by a factor of 2 to 3; assuming an equilibrium between resorption and osteon replacement in this animal, we estimate that the formation of a resorption cavity at a given site takes roughly 3 weeks.

Total Accretion Rate Due to Osteon Formation

A rate of accretion and bone turnover can be related to the number of forming osteons observed in bone. If the average cross section contains ten hotspots per square centimeter corresponding to forming osteons with canal diameters larger than 40 μ at the time of injection, then it follows from expression 5 that the accretion rate in the bone sample due to osteon formation is about 0.004% per day. Accretion rate is here calculated as grams of bone per day per gram of bone for $b_o = 120\ \mu$ and $\beta = 0.03\ \text{day}^{-1}$, and it includes secondary mineralization as well as apposition, if we assume equilibrium numbers of osteons at each stage of formation. The number of forming osteons per unit area is difficult to predict for individual animals because it depends strongly on their metabolic state (see Table I). This very low value of 0.004% per day derived for the femur midshaft of C119 or C122 is probably typical of normal adult dogs, however. The corresponding mean time of bone turnover by resorption and osteon formation is thus about 70 years. The osteon accretion rate in C120 with thirty times as many hotspots per square centimeter is about 0.12% per day, and the mean turnover time by osteon formation is about 2.3 years. If the mean time of bone turnover by resorption and new osteon formation is as slow in adult human subjects as it is in the older adult dogs, it is difficult to explain the elimination of radium from human subjects in terms of this process, though it is then easy to understand the persistence of hotspots for many decades. In the next paper of this series, the possibility of a long-term loss of calcium-like radioactivity from mature bone without discrete resorption will be discussed.

Calculation of Calcium Supply to an Individual Osteon

The calcium accretion rate of an individual osteon which we have derived may be compared to the quantity of calcium supplied to it by its capillary. The rate of blood flow in a capillary of 8-μ diameter in dog has been calculated[5] to be very roughly 0.7 mm/sec (*8*), and if we take a normal calcium concentration of 55 μg of Ca per milliliter of blood, then the calcium which flows by a particular point in an osteon is about 0.16 μg of Ca per day. Using expression 5 with $\beta = 0.03$ day^{-1}, we find that the calcium accretion rate per unit length in an osteon with a canal diameter of 100 μ is about 0.2 μg of Ca per millimeter day. The length of canine osteon over which the most rapid calcification occurs at any given time is of the order of a millimeter (*1*), so that the rate of calcium deposition is of the same order of magnitude as the rate of calcium supply. This suggests that the length of an osteon over which rapid calcification can occur may be limited to the order of a millimeter by a limitation in the calcium deliverable by a capillary, and that a rapidly forming osteon probably retains a large fraction of the calcium flowing by it. This limitation in the calcium supplied by a single capillary may also explain the failure of a forming osteon to achieve full mineralization as rapidly as periosteally-formed bone.

Specific Activity of the Blood in a Capillary within Bone

The slope of the curve of specific activity of the blood in the large veins versus time (Fig. 2) provides an estimate of the average arterio-venous difference in blood specific activity within bone at any time after injection. If we take 5 % of the cardiac output as the fraction of blood which flows through bone and (to be on the safe side) assume that calcium leaves the blood only within bone, then the average specific activity drop within bone during one circulation time ($\sim$30 seconds, reference *8*) would become less than a few per cent at times an hour or more after injection; at times less than an hour specific activity differences have a negligible effect on the integral of specific activity 12 hours or more after injection (Fig. 2). Thus the specific activity in an average bone capillary at any time of importance to our measurements is practically the same as that in the large veins.

We now wish to estimate what local variations from this average capillary specific activity might be produced by resorption and osteon formation. The fall in blood

[5] The diameter of the capillaries found in haversian canals is roughly 8 μ. The flow calculation was not made specifically for bone, however, and must be used only for order of magnitude calculations; in particular, the flow calculation assumes a capillary length of 1 mm which is too short for cortical bone capillaries.

calcium concentration in a capillary passing a growing osteon which may be inferred from the calculation of the previous section would not reduce the specific activity (Ca^{45}/Ca) in the capillary because both Ca^{45} and Ca would be removed. The comparable rate of release of calcium from a resorbing cavity would reduce the downstream specific activity, however. If the number of resorbing cavities per unit volume were large, and if the resorption process immediately releases calcium to the ionic form (not known), then the release by resorption of relatively inactive calcium to capillaries might reduce the Ca^{45} uptake by downstream osteons. Cohen and Harris (*12*) have found that longitudinal capillaries in cortical bone of dogs spiral slowly from endosteum to periosteum over a distance of about a centimeter. The thickness of the cortex in a long bone of a dog is usually a couple of millimeters. Thus, although we do not know the pattern or direction of blood flow in the capillaries, it is reasonable to assume that the average capillary path from artery to vein in cortical bone is more than a couple of millimeters but not much more than a centimeter. In an animal such as C120, which was in a burst of osteon formation, a cross section shows that about one out of every ten capillaries was in a rapidly growing osteon. If we take the length of rapid growth to be 1 mm (reference *1*) and the capillary blood path between artery and vein to be 1 cm, then an average blood pass through cortical bone will encounter one region of active osteon growth, and one out of two or three passes will encounter a resorbing cavity. The chance of a resorbing cavity lying upstream from a rapidly forming osteon will thus be about one out of five. Therefore in C120 there may be some reductions of capillary specific activity below that of the large vessels due to dilution from resorbing cavities. Thus in C120 we may underestimate the rate of calcium uptake in the average osteon by ~ 20 %, but such an effect would be negligible in C119 or C122 which showed less than one capillary in a hundred to be in a rapidly-growing osteon.

Hotspot Migration

This same type of calculation may be applied to the hypothesis of hotspot migration (*13*) in which it is postulated than an intense radium deposit may have moved from a previous location in bone to its present position without appreciable dilution with inactive mineral. In the light of the above calculation we would conclude that migration of calciumlike radioactivity by resorption and redeposition in a single capillary pass through bone is conceivable but improbable, especially in adult animals. Once the resorbed activity reached the general circulation it would be diluted rapidly in the whole blood volume and be redeposited all over the skeleton only at the existing specific activity of the blood as a whole.

SUMMARY

The Ca^{45} content of individual osteons in three dogs given single intravenous injections has been measured autoradiographically and correlated with osteon canal diameter measured from microradiographs. An osteon was found to contain up to 10^{-6} of the injected activity, its total activity per unit length being approximately proportional to the square of its canal diameter at the time of injection. The activities observed at 12 hours or 2 weeks after injection divided by the corresponding time integral of the blood specific activity yield an accretion rate for calcium at each canal diameter such that the half-diameter time for the canal of an average forming osteon in a rather wide distribution is 3 ± 1 weeks, which is consistent with direct observations of osteon growth. It is concluded that the intense concentrations of *in vivo*-deposited Ca^{45} which we have observed in canine osteons 12 hours or more after injection are due to accretion of calcium in appositional growth at approximately the specific activity measured in the large veins. The nature of the Ca^{45} uptake in osteons which have completed or arrested appositional growth before injection cannot be inferred from the present data, but such uptake is here of an order of magnitude less than that due to appositional growth. Comparison of calculated blood flow with observed osteon growth rate indicates that an osteon in the early stages of appositional growth accretes a large fraction of the calcium reaching it by its capillary. The total rates of accretion and resorption due to osteon formation, the shapes of osteon hotspot distributions, the specific activity in a capillary, and hotspot migration are discussed.

ACKNOWLEDGMENTS

We wish to thank R. D. Evans and the staff of the Radioactivity Center of the Massachusetts Institute of Technology, J. Cohen of Children's Hospital, Boston, F. C. McLean of the University of Chicago, and J. E. Rose and L. D. Marinelli of the Radiological Physics Division of Argonne National Laboratory for valuable support and assistance.

RECEIVED: March 4, 1958

REFERENCES

1. J. H. MARSHALL, V. K. WHITE, and J. COHEN, Microscopic metabolism of calcium in bone. I. Three-dimensional deposition of Ca^{45} in canine osteons. *Radiation Research* **10,** 197–212 (1959).
2. W. F. NEUMAN and M. W. NEUMAN, *The Chemical Dynamics of Bone Mineral,* University of Chicago Press, Chicago, 1958.
3. R. AMPRINO, Rapporti fra processi di ricostruzione e distribuzione dei minerali nelle ossa. *Z. Zellforsch. u. mikroskop. Anat.* **37,** 144–183, 240–273 (1952).
4. B. ENGFELDT, A. ENGSTROM, and R. ZETTERSTROM, Renewal of phosphate in bone minerals. II. Radioautographic studies of the renewal of phosphate in different structures of bone. *Biochim. et Biophys. Acta* **8,** 375–380 (1952).
5. J. S. ARNOLD, W. S. S. JEE, and K. JOHNSON, Observations and quantitative radioautographic studies of Ca^{45} deposited *in Vivo* in forming haversian systems and old bone of rabbit. *Am. J. Anat.* **99,** 291–314 (1956).
6. J. H. MARSHALL, R. E. ROWLAND, and J. JOWSEY, Microscopic metabolism of calcium in bone. II. Quantitative autoradiography. *Radiation Research* **10,** 213–233 (1959).
7. J. COHEN, C. J. MALETSKOS, J. H. MARSHALL, and J. B. WILLIAMS, Radioactive calcium tracer studies in bone grafts. *J. Bone and Joint Surg.* **39A,** 561–577 (1957).

8. H. D. GREEN, The circulatory system: Physical principles. In *Medical Physics* (O. Glasser, ed.), Vol. II, p. 231, Year Book Publishers, Chicago, 1950.

9. W. S. S. JEE and J. S. ARNOLD, Rate of individual haversian system formation. *Anat. Record* **118,** 315 (1954).

10. J. VINCENT, Recherches sur la Constitution de L'Os Adulte. Dissertation under P. La-Croix, Université Catholique de Louvain, Belgium, p. 52 (1955).

12. J. COHEN and W. H. HARRIS, The three dimensional anatomy of haversian systems. *J. Bone and Joint Surg.* **40A,** 419–434 (1958).

13. J. C. AUB, R. D. EVANS, L. H. HEMPELMANN, and H. S. MARTLAND, The late effects of internally-deposited radioactive materials in man. *Medicine* **31,** 221–329 (1952) (see pages 324–327).

RADIATION RESEARCH **10**, 258–270 (1959)

Microscopic Metabolism of Calcium in Bone

V. The Paradox of Diffuse Activity and Long-Term Exchange[1]

J. H. MARSHALL, R. E. ROWLAND, AND J. JOWSEY

Radiological Physics Division, Argonne National Laboratory, Lemont, Illinois

INTRODUCTION

When Ca^{45} is taken up by bone, activity deposits not only in regions of appositional growth but also in bone already existing at the time of injection. This Ca^{45} deposition in pre-existing bone, which we shall refer to as *diffuse* activity, produces a relatively uniform low level of darkening in an autoradiogram. The mechanism of this diffuse uptake of Ca^{45} is not clear. If it represents exchange of Ca^{45} atoms from the blood with Ca^{40} atoms in bone mineral, why does the Ca^{45} activity remain in bone long after the specific activity of the blood has dropped to a negligible level? If, as some suggest, this diffuse Ca^{45} deposition is irreversible, then why is there not a large increase with time in the calcium density of the bone? This paradoxical situation has been discussed in terms of recrystallization (*1*), but most of the pertinent experiments (*2*) have been performed *in vitro* under conditions which may differ from those in living bone. There have been many excellent experiments *in vivo* which support the findings *in vitro*, but it has been difficult completely to avoid ambiguity in the results, because accretion followed by resorption of Ca^{45} activity is macroscopically indistinguishable from exchange, and because at least part of the diffuse uptake of Ca^{45} in existing bone may be associated with secondary mineralization. (Definitions of these terms as used in this paper are given in the Appendix.)

The purpose of the present investigation is to measure autoradiographically the magnitude of the diffuse component of Ca^{45} uptake in cortical canine bone, to relate this uptake to the specific activity of the blood after a single Ca^{45} injection in order to derive the local rate of calcium uptake, and to obtain microradiographic measurements of the microscopic calcium density in the same region of bone as a function of time. Thus, we have studied the phenomenon of Ca^{45} uptake by pre-existing bone *in vivo*, independently of the effects of appositional growth and resorption in neighboring regions of bone or elsewhere in the skeleton, and with discrimination

[1] Work performed under the auspices of the U. S. Atomic Energy Commission.

between the irreversible Ca^{45} uptake due to secondary mineralization and an apparently irreversible Ca^{45} uptake due to long-term exchange.[2]

METHOD

Adult mongrel dogs were given single low-level (0.02 to 0.2 mc/kg body weight) intravenous injections of Ca^{45} chloride at pH 4 to 5 and specific activity >1000 mc/gm_{Ca}. Blood specific activity measurements ($mc_{Ca^{45}}/gm_{Ca}$) were made on 5 of the animals (*3*), and a Ca^{45} blood curve and its integral derived (*4*). Long bones were scraped clean, dehydrated in alcohol and ether, and embedded in Bioplastic. Cross sections 150 μ or more in thickness were cut through the shaft with a circular saw, smoothed on ground glass, and autoradiographed on Eastman No Screen Autoradiographic plates. Control sections of bone containing no activity produced no exposure. The diffuse darkening was found to be proportional to exposure time and to injected activity per unit body weight. The specific activity of the diffuse component was derived from densitometer measurements of film darkening calibrated with thick plaster-of-Paris radiators containing known Ca^{45} activities per gram (*5*). The calcium content of highly mineralized dehydrated cortical bone was taken to be 0.25 gm_{Ca}/gm_{bone}. All specific activity values have been normalized to an injected activity of 0.1 mc/kg body weight.

Microradiographs were made of bone sections 100 μ in thickness with continuous X-rays from a 12-kv tube filtered above the calcium absorption edge by 1 mm of beryllium. The superficial calcium density (gm_{Ca}/cm^2) was determined by comparison with an aluminum step wedge, and section thickness at the point of interest was measured by the substage probe method using incident illumination (*6*).

Microscopic Scale of Measurement

The microscopic measurements of diffuse specific activity reported here refer to specific activity as observed on an autoradiogram by a microscope densitometer with an aperture of 30 μ. The half-thickness for absorption of Ca^{45} β-particles is also about 30 μ, so structures smaller than this are not resolved by the present technique. In regions of cortical bone containing no secondary haversian systems or resorption cavities, the Ca^{45} diffuse activity appears to be uniform (with the exception of the rare avascular regions mentioned below), but this observation, of course, implies nothing about uniformity of specific activity on the crystallite level (tens or hundreds of angstroms).

The microscopic measurements of calcium density refer to the grams of calcium per cubic centimeter as observed on a microradiograph through a 10-μ aperture. The volumes measured are thus $10 \times 10 \times 100$ microns and appear uniform in density because they contain no cavities larger than canalicules, which are not resolved on the microradiographs. The present measurements of calcium density

[2] See terminology in Appendix.

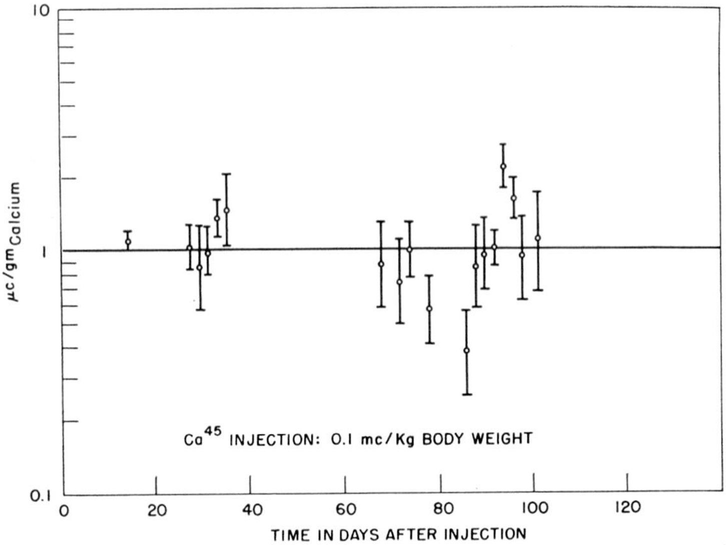

FIG. 1. Diffuse specific activity ($\mu c\ Ca^{45}/gm_{Ca}$) in the femoral or tibial shafts of six adult mongrel dogs sacrificed at different times after a single Ca^{45} injection (*3*). Values have been normalized to an injected activity of 0.1 mc/kg body weight and plotted as a function of time after injection. Dog ages were unknown, but epiphyseal and periosteal growth were complete.

are thus not directly comparable to those measured for bone on the cubic centimeter level. They of course measure only the net effect of any changes in the number, volume, or density of individual crystallites on the angstrom level.

RESULTS

Magnitude of Ca^{45} Diffuse Activity as a Function of Time

Autoradiographic measurements of the specific activity of the diffuse component in the shafts of the long bones of 6 dogs are plotted in Fig. 1 as a function of time after Ca^{45} injection. The dogs were adult mongrels of unknown age which were used in a previous experiment (*3*). The estimated standard error of each measurement is indicated by the error bar. Different low-level injections were used, the plotted values being normalized to an injected activity of 0.1 mc/kg body weight. The average value of about 1 $\mu c/gm_{Ca}$ corresponds to about one-half the average specific activity of the skeleton. The values of diffuse specific activity remain constant within a factor of 2 from 2 weeks to 3 months after injection. During this period the blood specific activity falls by a factor of 10, and the integral of the blood curve rises by a factor of only 1.3 (*4*). Within the error of our measurements, therefore, practically all the Ca^{45} diffuse activity at 2 weeks or longer after injection follows the integral of the blood specific activity rather than the blood specific activity itself. Therefore the activity observed indicates a substantially one-way flow of Ca^{45} from blood to bone.

Rate of Calcium Uptake Indicated by Ca^{45} Diffuse Activity

Since Ca^{45} is retained in the diffuse component at least over the period indicated above, Ca^{40} must similarly be retained. Certainly the skeleton does not distinguish between these isotopes. Therefore, we can calculate the rate of uptake of calcium in bone which gives rise to the diffuse component, knowing that in times of the order of a month after this calcium is deposited it is not returned to the blood. Let us define this rate of calcium uptake as a calcium *augmentation* rate, since if unopposed by a corresponding rate of loss it would increase the calcium density of a microscopic region of existing bone.

[It is shown below that, curiously enough, there is no corresponding increase in calcium density in the areas of periosteal bone studied, so that the augmentation in these regions is not the net uptake of calcium but is opposed by a comparable rate of *diminution*. These two new words are useful because they represent observable quantities which pertain to phenomena the molecular description of which is not yet clear (variously referred to as recrystallization, intracrystalline diffusion, irreversible exchange, etc.). The rate of increase of microscopic calcium density in secondary mineralization is thus the augmentation rate minus whatever rate of diminution may exist at a particular location.]

Under the assumption that the diffuse activity is deposited at the specific activity of the blood, the increment to the Ca^{45} diffuse activity in a microscopic region of bone per gram of calcium per unit time is

$$da = fB\,dt \tag{1}$$

where f = augmentation rate (gm_{Ca}/gm_{Ca} day).
B = blood specific activity ($\mu c/gm_{Ca}$).
da = diffuse specific activity increment ($\mu c/gm_{Ca}$).
dt = time increment (days).

Since comparable results are obtained for adult dogs of different age, the augmentation rate, f, may be assumed to remain constant at least for times of the order of a month, and expression 1 may be integrated and solved for f:

$$f = \frac{a}{\int_0^{T_s} B\,dt} \tag{2}$$

where a = diffuse specific activity at time T_s ($\mu c/gm_{Ca}$).
T_s = time of sacrifice or sampling (days).
Time zero refers to time of injection.

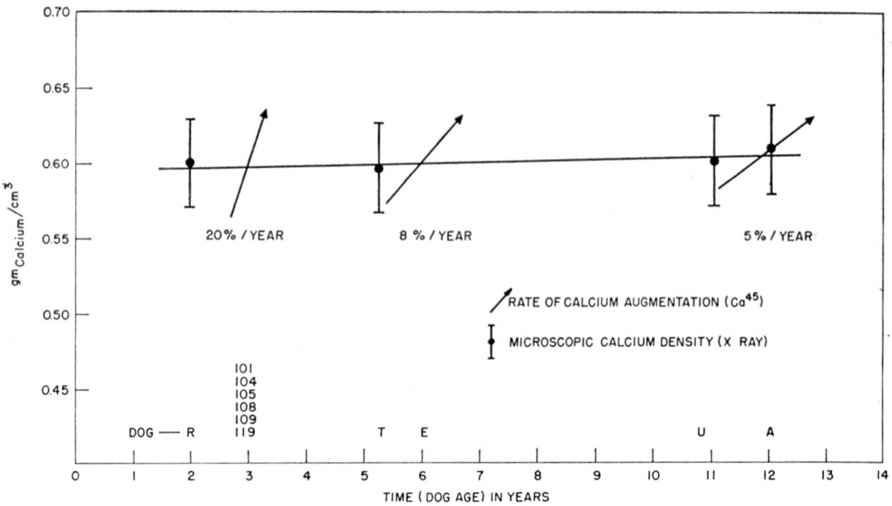

FIG. 2. Microscopic calcium density of periosteal bone containing no secondary haversian systems plotted as a function of age in 4 dogs, in the oldest of which the augmentation rate in the same region of bone has also been measured. Points show standard error bars of 5%. The slope of the plotted arrows indicates values of augmentation rate derived from the diffuse Ca^{45} activity in corresponding regions of bone. The arrow plotted at 3 years refers to the average augmentation rate for all the dogs of Fig. 1. Since calcium density does not detectably increase with time, the augmentation must be primarily long term exchange.

The augmentation rate corresponding to the diffuse specific activity of 1 $\mu c/gm_{Ca}$ observed at long periods after injection is then $f = 0.05\%$ per day, or approximately 20% per year. This rate which describes the data for the adult mongrels of unknown age (Fig. 1) has been plotted as a sloping arrow in Fig. 2 at an age of 3 years.

A diffuse activity at $T_s = 12$ hours in a 1-year-old dog (C120) has been found as high as 1.5 $\mu c/gm_{Ca}$, in spite of the fact that the integral of B is then only one-third of its value at 2 weeks. The diffuse component therefore probably contains a short-term exchangeable fraction (*7*), which probably explains the rapid initial uptake reported (*1*). Such a short-term exchangeable fraction, which has reached equilibrium with the blood with respect to labeled atoms, would contain negligible Ca^{45} at more than a week after injection.

Histological Location of Diffuse Activity; Use of Periosteal Bone of Known Age

The values of diffuse activity used above were obtained by scanning and averaging values from autoradiograms. Some of the values were measured over secondary haversian bone, some over millimeter-wide regions of periosteal bone containing no secondary haversian systems and no resorption cavities. A systematic study of diffuse uptake as a function of location and mineral density has not yet been made.

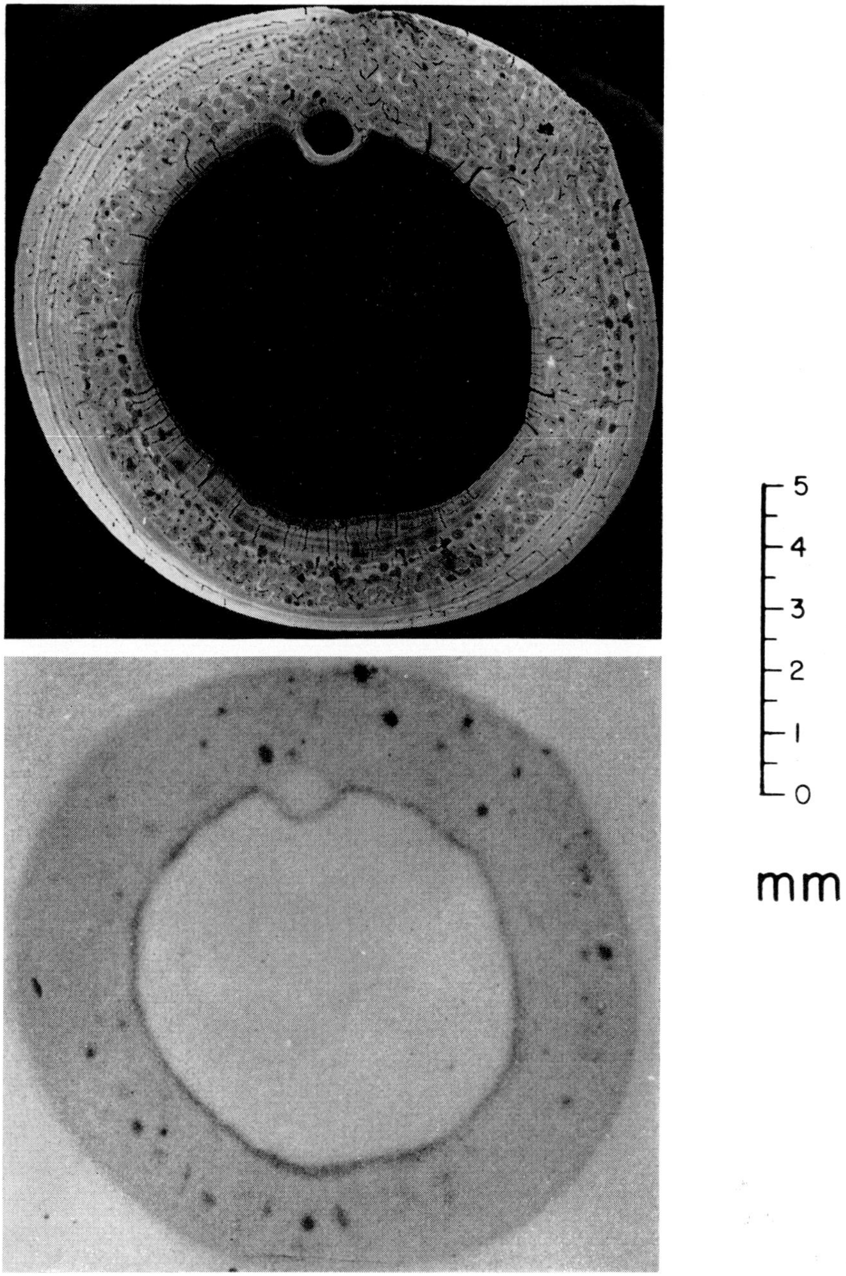

FIG. 3. Autoradiogram and microradiograph of a cross section through the femoral midshaft of an adult dog (119 or C119). Note the uniformity of the diffuse component whether or not the underlying bone has been replaced by secondary haversian systems. The large cavity in the cortex is the nutrient canal close to its junction with the marrow cavity.

The diffuse activity in adult dogs with few forming osteons is remarkably uniform, however, whether the measurements are made for periosteal bone or secondary haversian bone (Fig. 3). In areas filled with many comparatively young but completed osteons with mineral densities 80 to 90% that of highly mineralized periosteal bone, the diffuse specific activity is perhaps 50% higher than that in the periosteal bone. Occasionally a small region of nonhaversian bone has been found which deposits less than one-fifth the usual diffuse activity of 1 $\mu c/gm_{Ca}$. These regions of low diffuse uptake have a somewhat *lower* mineral density than ordinary periosteal bone, so that an inverse correlation between mineral density and diffuse uptake does not always hold. These regions of low diffuse uptake are believed to be rare but require investigation. A few recently formed osteons of low mineral density may possibly take up considerably more than the average diffuse activity. This point also remains to be investigated.

In spite of these known variations in diffuse activity, a value of augmentation rate of 10 to 20% per year may be taken as typical of periosteal bone containing no secondary haversian systems in an adult dog a few years of age. This bone, in contrast to secondary haversian bone, may confidently be assigned an age and hence will be taken as the experimental material for the remainder of this paper.

Microscopic Calcium Density of Periosteal Bone as a Function of Dog Age

Measurements of the microscopic calcium density (gm_{Ca}/cm^3) of periosteal bone by quantitative microradiography in corresponding regions of femur midshaft are shown in Fig. 2 for dogs which were 2, 5, 11, and 12 years of age. Within the 5% standard error of the measurements, there is no detectable increase in the microscopic calcium density with time.

The Diffuse Paradox

There is thus a curious paradox. A microscopic volume of bone that contains no osteons and no resorption cavities is observed to be receiving and retaining calcium atoms with no corresponding increase in the total number of calcium atoms it contains. We conclude that there is a corresponding loss of calcium atoms from the same microscopic volume so that the total number of calcium atoms, the microscopic calcium density, does not change. But since the same number of calcium atoms are leaving as are arriving, the augmentation rate measured for periosteal bone does not represent accretion. Instead, the measured augmentation rate must be the blood-to-bone transfer rate of two-way exchange between blood and bone. But then why, over a period of weeks or months, has there been no loss of Ca^{45} atoms along with the calcium atoms transferring from bone to blood? Is there some gross error in our measurements or assumptions?

Re-examination of Assumptions

The three most crucial assumptions we have made are the following:

Assumption 1. The diffuse Ca^{45} activity is deposited at the measured specific activity of the blood. From our previous work (*3, 4*) this seems a good assumption. But suppose that the extracellular fluid did not reach equilibrium with blood specific activity for a long period, so that the specific activity seen by bone crystallites was less than we have assumed. In that case the time integral of B in expression 2 would be less than we have calculated, so that the value of f would be greater and the paradox aggravated, not resolved.

Assumption 2. The augmentation rate, f, does not vary significantly over long periods of time. Most of the measured values of diffuse activity come from mongrels of unknown age. One 6-year-old dog showed a diffuse uptake even at 12 hours, which was less than half the others (E or C122). If f were decreasing sharply, the diffuse retention of Ca^{45} might be more easily explained. We might then postulate that a comparatively rapid exchange had been occurring during the time the blood was active but that the rate of exchange was decreasing sharply so that the Ca^{45} was trapped.

Assumption 3. The periosteal bone we have measured was laid down in the first year or two of life and is not recently deposited bone. If the observed diffuse uptake corresponded to comparatively young bone, we might postulate that the Ca^{45} activity represented accretion due to secondary mineralization and that the microradiographic measurements referred only to older bone which had reached maximum mineralization.

The second and third of these assumptions were submitted to test by the following experiment.

Eleven-Year Double-Tracer Experiment

A 12-year-old mongrel dog (QA122 or A) which had been injected with Sr^{90} late in 1945 in connection with a toxicity experiment (*8*) was injected with Ca^{45} in 1957; blood specific activity measurements (Ca^{45}/Ca) were made, and the animal was sacrificed 11 days after Ca^{45} injection. Cross sections through the midshaft of the femur were autoradiographed on No-Screen plates, both with and without 4-mil aluminum filters, so that the Sr^{90} diffuse component and the Ca^{45} diffuse component could be measured separately.

[In December, 1945, the dog was a young adult weighing 10.7 kg; it was injected with 0.30 mc of Sr^{89} per kilogram, together with roughly 15 to 30 μc of Sr^{90} per kilogram as an impurity. The Sr^{89} (half-life 54 days) has long since decayed, leaving only the Sr^{90}-Y^{90}. In November, 1955, the Sr^{90} burden was 5.4 μc as determined by bremsstrahlung counting. The dog was failing rapidly, owing to the long-term effects of his radioactive burden.]

In regions of periosteal bone over a millimeter wide which contained no secondary haversian systems and therefore no regions of growth more recent than the original periosteal apposition, both Sr^{90} diffuse activity and Ca^{45} diffuse activity were found. The Ca^{45} diffuse activity in this old dog averaged 0.7 $\mu c/gm_{Ca}$ (with the usual normalization to 0.1 mc/kg body weight injected), a value comparable to the Ca^{45} uptake in all the younger animals. The Ca^{45} blood specific activity fell more slowly after injection than our standard Ca^{45} blood curve (*4*), so that the corresponding calcium augmentation rate was 0.015% per day or 5% per year, only a little lower than the augmentation rate for the younger dogs. The measured microscopic calcium density in the same region of bone is plotted in Fig. 2 at 12 years of age together with an arrow indicating the rate of augmentation measured at age 12 with Ca^{45}. Thus assumption 2 is substantially correct in that there is not a large decrease of augmentation rate with age. The precise age dependence of f requires further study.

The presence of uniform Sr^{90} diffuse activity throughout this same region of bone indicates that periosteal growth was complete at the time of Sr^{90} injection. If periosteal growth of even 1 μ/day had been proceeding in this region in December, 1945, the Sr^{90} ring of darkening would be detectable above the Sr^{90} diffuse component, and the bone outside such a ring would contain negligible Sr^{90}. Assumption 3 is therefore verified for measurements on this animal.

CONCLUSIONS

Diminution and Long-Term Exchange

Since our measurements and assumptions appear to be substantially correct, how can we resolve the paradox? We have focused our attention on a microscopic volume of bone containing neither osteons nor resorption cavities, and we have waited 11 or more days after Ca^{45} injection before making activity measurements. Therefore the complications of appositional growth, resorption, and short-term exchange have been eliminated. By tagging every millionth calcium atom in the blood, we have counted the calcium atoms going into this microscopic volume of bone, but by shooting X-rays through it we find that the total number of calcium atoms it contains has not been increasing. We must therefore conclude that calcium atoms are leaving this microscopic volume of bone at a rate comparable to the measured augmentation rate. Since these departing atoms are different from the arriving atoms—Ca^{45} atoms are not among them—it is convenient to define another term: the *diminution rate* or rate of loss of calcium from our microscopic volume. Then our result may be stated: highly mineralized periosteal canine bone has been observed to be undergoing simultaneous augmentation and diminution of calcium at a rate the order of 10% per year (0.1 gm_{Ca}/gm_{Ca} year). This is an enormous rate of calcium turnover to be found in what has hitherto been considered unavailable bone mineral. It has been generally believed that only recently-formed osteons provide bone mineral available for exchange with body fluids. It now appears that augmentation-diminution in highly mineralized bone probably accounts for a larger rate of calcium turnover in adult cortical bone in dogs than accretion, resorption, or exchange associated with osteons (*4*). The importance of this diffuse component of skeletal metabolism has also been pointed out by Arnold (*1*) and by Tomlin (*9*). If the rate of 10% per year were extrapolated to the whole skeleton, the total rates of augmentation and diminution would be of the same order of magnitude as the total adult accretion rate for dog or man and would turn over an amount of calcium equal to that in the blood every day (taking blood calcium content to be 1/3000 that of the skeleton); however, such an extrapolation in detail is not justified by the data available at this time.

Balanced rates of augmentation and diminution represent an exchange of calcium atoms: there are equal and opposite rates of transfer of calcium atoms between blood and bone occurring at the same microscopic location. But this exchange cannot have reached equilibrium with respect to Ca^{45} atoms, even over the 3 months of our experiments, because the diminution rate is not yet labeled (within the accuracy of our present measurements). Thus, although the equal and opposite rate of transfer of calcium atoms is large, the time necessary to reach equilibrium with respect to Ca^{45} atoms must be longer than the period of our measurements. We are therefore dealing with what may be called *long-term exchange*. We conclude that, if the augmentation rate is maintained, then a loss of Ca^{45} activity due to continuous calcium diminution should become significant if we wait long enough.

There are several molecular mechanisms which might be responsible for long-term exchange: recrystallization in its original sense of continual dissolution and redeposition of submicroscopic crystallites (*2*); deposition and long-delayed thermal re-emission of calcium atoms in the first calcium layer of a crystallite coupled perhaps with diffusion of calcium within the crystallite's lattice structure (*2*); or some barrier to calcium atoms between extracellular fluid and crystallite that has a low probability of penetration per unit time. The long-term time dependence of elimination of calciumlike radioactivity by diminution would depend not only on the diminution rate as here defined but also on the molecular mechanism responsible. Is all the mineral in a single microscopic volume of bone involved directly in the long-term exchange, or is a several-step process involved such as diffusion into crystallite interiors? Whether or not one would expect the effect of diminution on hotspots to be quantitatively the same as its effect on diffuse activity would likewise depend on the molecular mechanism and cannot be predicted from the present data.

Our results are comparable to those of Tomlin (*9*), though the interpretations differ to some extent. Tomlin maintains the specific activity of the blood of young rats at a constant level for many weeks by including Ca^{45} in their food and measures autoradiographically the diffuse component of Ca^{45} uptake. He derives a rate of "interstitial calcium uptake" of about 1% of the total cortical bone calcium per week. According to our terminology, Tomlin has measured a calcium augmentation rate of 1 % per week for cortical bone of young rats, whereas we have found values of 0.1 to 0.4 % per week for cortical bone of adult dogs. Tomlin observes that the (short-term) exchangeable fraction was <0.2 % of cortical bone calcium; we have not yet made comparable measurements. Since the augmentation rate measured by Tomlin is comparable to the rate of increase of the percentage content of calcium in the long bones of similar rats, Tomlin concludes (in our terminology) that the diminution rate is zero and that all the observed Ca^{45} uptake represents secondary mineralization. No microradiographic measurements were made, however, and from our present results we would suspect that at least a significant part of the calcium augmentation in young rats is balanced by diminution and thus partly represents long-term exchange. Tomlin did not detect a loss of Ca^{45} by diminution over a 70-day interval after a 2-week Ca^{45} dietary period, but if half of the observed augmentation were balanced by diminution and if all cortical calcium were directly involved in the long-term exchange, the Ca^{45} loss would be only about 5 % and still undetectable.

In view of the magnitude and persistence in the older dogs of the augmentation (and diminution) rate here measured, a loss of Ca^{45} by diminution from the diffuse component in periosteal canine bone should be just detectable over a period of a year.

SUMMARY

By quantitative autoradiography and quantitative microradiography the *in vivo* diffuse uptake of Ca^{45} in highly mineralized canine bone many years old has been measured and identified primarily with long-term exchange of calcium. By long-term exchange we mean an equal rate of transfer of calcium atoms in opposite directions between blood and bone in which the mean residence time of an individual calcium atom in bone is long, here of the order of a month or longer. In microscopic regions of canine cortical bone with a calcium density of 0.60 ± 0.03 gm_{Ca}/cm^3, the rate of transfer of calcium atoms between blood and bone in this exchange is 0.05 to 0.20 gm_{Ca} per year per gram of calcium in bone. This rate of calcium transfer represents a significant fraction of the total calcium turnover in the skeleton of an adult dog and may play an important part in the calcium regulation of the blood. The possible implications for the distribution of long-term radiation dose to the skeleton due to internally deposited Sr^{90} or Ra^{226} are being examined. The observed rate of calcium transfer suggests that loss of Ca^{45} activity from highly mineralized canine bone by a process other than resorption should be just detectable over a period of a year.

APPENDIX

The following terminology is used in this paper; for clarity, specific reference is made to calcium though, of course, the terms need not be so restricted. We have attempted to use familiar terms in their accepted sense.

Microscopic volume. A cube of the order of 10 μ on a side which may or may not be occupied by bone mineral but in which no resorption is taking place. (This arbitrary definition is used to simplify the following definitions.)

Exchange. Any process involving equal and opposite rates of transfer of calcium atoms to and from a single microscopic volume.

Time constant of an exchange process. The number of calcium atoms available for this exchange in a single microscopic volume divided by the rate of transfer of calcium atoms (number per unit time); approximately equal to the time necessary for labeled calcium atoms to reach equilibrium, that is, for equal and opposite rates of transfer of labeled calcium atoms to be established.

Short-term exchange. Any exchange processes with time constants much less than a week.* Labeled calcium atoms will be in equilibrium in most tracer experiments.

Long-term exchange. Any exchange processes with time constants much greater than a week.* Labeled calcium atoms will not be in equilibrium in most tracer experiments.

Accretion. Any process involving the net transfer of calcium atoms to a single microscopic volume.

Apposition. The process of accretion involving the formation of new bone and resulting in an increase in mineral *volume* as observed microscopically.

Secondary mineralization. The process of accretion in existing bone mineral by which the mineral *density* is increased as observed microscopically.

Resorption. The process by which bone is eroded resulting in a decrease in mineral *volume* as observed microscopically.

Augmentation. A gross uptake in a microscopic volume of existing bone mineral of calcium atoms which remain much longer than a week.*

Diminution. A gross loss from a microscopic volume of bone mineral of calcium atoms which have resided there much longer than a week.*

In terms of these definitions, the following quantitative relations may be expressed either for small volumes of bone or for a whole bone or skeleton:

Accretion = Apposition + secondary mineralization
Secondary mineralization = Augmentation − diminution
Accretion − resorption = Net increase of mineral

In terms of our definitions above, the quantity A measured and defined mathematically by Bauer *et al.* (*7*) is:

* The time dependence of the concepts indicated by an asterisk is obvious. If the times of observation are specifically referred to, however these concepts are valuable for analyzing data short of a more complex analog computer analysis. The value of such a separation of time constants rests on the apparent absence of important exchange processes with time constants of the order of magnitude of a week.

$$A = \text{Apposition rate} + \text{Augmentation rate}$$

or

$$A = \text{Accretion rate} + \text{Diminution rate}$$

and the exchangeable fraction, E, refers to short-term exchange.

Evaluation of the diminution rate for the skeleton as a whole may be a difficult task but will probably not affect the utility of the quantities A and E as presently derived from activity measurements (*7*).

ACKNOWLEDGMENTS

We are much indebted to M. P. Finkel of Argonne National Laboratory, to J. Cohen of Children's Hospital, Boston, and to C. J. Maletskos, V. K. White, and M. J. Helmick of the Radioactivity Center at the Massachusetts Institute of Technology for material assistance in this work. We wish also to thank J. E. Rose and L. D. Marinelli, Radiological Physics Division of Argonne National Laboratory, and F. C. McLean, University of Chicago, for valuable support and encouragement.

RECEIVED: March 4, 1958

REFERENCES

1. J. S. Arnold, W. S. S. Jee, and K. Johnson, Observations and quantitative radioautographic studies of Ca^{45} deposited *in vivo* in forming haversian systems and old bone of rabbit. *Am. J. Anat.* **99**, 291–313 (1956).

2. W. F. Neuman and M. W. Neuman, *The Chemical Dynamics of Bone Mineral*, University of Chicago Press, Chicago, 1958.

3. J. Cohen, C. J. Maletskos, J. H. Marshall, and J. B. Williams, Radioactive calcium tracer studies in bone grafts. *J. Bone and Joint Surg.* **39A**, 561–577 (1957).

4. J. H. Marshall, J. Jowsey, and R. E. Rowland, Microscopic metabolism of calcium in bone. IV. Ca^{45} deposition and growth rate in canine osteons. *Radiation Research* in press.

5. J. H. Marshall, R. E. Rowland, and J. Jowsey, Microscopic metabolism of calcium in bone. II. Quantitative autoradiography. *Radiation Research* **10**, 213–233 (1959).

6. R. E. Rowland, J. Jowsey, and J. H. Marshall, Microscopic metabolism of calcium in bone. III. Microradiographic measurements of mineral density. *Radiation Research* **10**, 234–242 (1959).

7. G. C. H. Bauer, A. Carlsson, and B. Lindquist, Evaluation of accretion, resorption, and exchange reactions in the skeleton. *Kgl. Fysiograf. Sällskap. Lund Förh.* **25**, No. 1 (1955).

8. M. P. Finkel, R. J. Flynn, J. W. Clark, G. Scribner, J. Lestina, H. Lisco, A. M. Brues, Toxicity of radiostrontium in carnivores: current status of the long term cat and dog experiment, Quarterly Report of Biological and Medical Research Division, Argonne National Laboratory Report ANL-5696, p. 18 (March, 1957).

9. D. H. Tomlin, K. M. Henry, and S. K. Kon, Autoradiographic study of growth and calcium metabolism in the long bones of the rat. *Brit. J. Nutrition* **7**, 235–252 (1953); Interstitial metabolism of calcium in the bones and teeth of rats. *ibid.* **9**, 144–156 (1955).

RADIATION RESEARCH **10**, 273–282 (1959)

Radiation-Induced Oxidation of Aqueous Acetic Acid-Oxygen Solutions[1]

WARREN M. GARRISON, HERMAN R. HAYMOND[2], WINIFRED BENNETT, AND SIBYL COLE

Crocker Laboratory, University of California Radiation Laboratory, Berkeley, California

INTRODUCTION

In the radiolysis of oxygen-free acetic acid solutions, the primary radicals, H and OH, are removed via the steps

$$H + CH_3COOH \rightarrow H_2 + CH_2COOH \tag{1}$$

$$OH + CH_3COOH \rightarrow H_2O + CH_2COOH \tag{2}$$

and the resultant organic intermediate, CH_2COOH, is removed in turn by the combination reaction

$$2CH_2COOH \rightarrow COOH(CH_2)_2COOH \tag{3}$$

to yield succinic acid as the principal organic product (*1*).

If dissolved oxygen is present, the competing processes

$$H + O_2 \rightarrow HO_2 \tag{4}$$

$$CH_2COOH + O_2 \rightarrow O_2CH_2COOH \tag{5}$$

lead to a suppression of the succinic acid production and a concomitant oxidation of the acetic acid molecule. Products of this oxidation include glyoxylic, glycolic, and oxalic acids, formaldehyde, and carbon dioxide. The present paper reports (1) experimental evidence for the formation of these products, (2) product yield measurements for several different conditions of irradiation, and (3) a consideration of the intermediate processes ensuant to steps 4 and 5 above.

[1] This work was performed under the auspices of the U. S. Atomic Energy Commission.

[2] Present address: Department of Radiology, University of Southern California, Los Angeles.

EXPERIMENTAL PROCEDURE

Irradiation

Studies were made with γ-rays from Co^{60} and with helium ion, proton, and neutrons beams from the Crocker Laboratory 60-inch cyclotron.

A 2000-curie cobalt source was used for the γ-irradiations. Solutions (3 ml) were exposed under oxygen (5 ml) at 1 atmosphere in sealed Pyrex tubes. Contents were shaken at intervals to prevent depletion of oxygen in the solution during exposure. The irradiation dose rate was $\sim 7.8 \times 10^{18}$ ev/ml-min.

The all-glass cells used in the helium ion and proton irradiations were of the tubular, aerated type previously described (*2*). Target solutions (10 ml) were aerated continuously with oxygen during exposure. Product yields obtained at beam intensities of 0.01 μa and below were essentially independent of the gas flow rate at values above 30 to 40 ml/min. Details of the target assembly, beam monitoring circuits, and dosimetry methods have been given (*1*, *2*). Energy of the helium ions and protons incident on the cell window were 40 Mev and 10 Mev, respectively. Corrections for energy loss were calculated from range-energy data (*3*).

Neutrons were produced by bombardment of beryllium with 24-Mev deuterons. Solutions (10 ml) were exposed under oxygen (10 ml) at 1 atmosphere in Pyrex tubes mounted uniformly in a motor-driven reel situated a standard distance from the source. Experimental techniques including methods used in establishing the dosimetry have been reported elsewhere (*4*, *5*).

Materials

Water from a Barnstead still was redistilled in Pyrex first from alkaline permanganate and then from dilute phosphoric or sulfuric acid. Baker and Adamson reagent-grade glacial acetic acid was redistilled twice. The middle fraction (~30%) was retained each time. The C^{14}-labeled acetic acid was purified chromatographically on a silicic acid column (see below).

Analysis

The analytical scheme of the present study is very similar to that developed as part of our work on the synthesis of higher molecular weight products in the radiolysis of aqueous solutions of formic acid (*6*). The present discussion will emphasize those modifications found to be necessary in adapting the methods to the acetic acid–oxygen system. Other experimental details may be found in the earlier paper.

1. *Organic acids.* Acid products were determined by methods of partition chromatography adapted from the work of Marvel and Rands (*7*) and Bulen *et al.* (*8*). Water absorbed on silicic acid acts as the immobile phase. Chloroform containing increasing amounts of butyl alcohol is used as the developing liquid.

In the preliminary studies, 10-ml volumes of oxygen-aerated 0.25 *M* acetic acid containing 100 to 200 μc of $CH_3C^{14}OOH$ (or $C^{14}H_3COOH$) were irradiated with

40-Mev helium ions at a beam intensity of 0.01 μa. The solutions were distilled to dryness *in vacuo* at room temperature to remove acetic acid. The nonvolatile fraction was chromatographed using the standard survey method of Bulen *et al.* (*8*). Solvents in sequence were 5, 15, 20, 25, 35, and 50% (v/v) *n*-butyl alcohol in chloroform saturated with 0.5 *N* sulfuric acid. Appropriate aliquots of each 10-ml fraction of the effluent were neutralized with a few drops of 0.01 *N* sodium hydroxide, evaporated to dryness, and assayed for C^{14} activity. The specific activity of the target solution was set so that any acid produced in significant yield would give a product peak with a total C^{14} activity of several hundred counts per second and an associated titer of less than 0.1 ml of 0.01 *N* sodium hydroxide. Two major activity peaks were observed at radiation doses as low as 1×10^{18} ev/ml.

The position of peak I indicated that the C^{14} activity of this fraction could be associated with succinic acid and/or glyoxylic acid. These acids are eluted very close together in the standard survey method. Usually separation of such pairs can be accomplished by changing the elution procedure. No adequate separation of succinic and glyoxylic acids could be accomplished, however, although numerous control runs were made under various column conditions. The composition of peak I was established as follows. A sample of the C^{14} activity plus added succinic acid and glyoxylic acid in milligram amounts was treated with 2,4-dinitrophenylhydrazine-hydrochloric acid solution (*9*) to form the glyoxylic acid hydrazone derivative. The solution was evaporated to dryness *in vacuo*, and the residue was chromatographed with 25% *n*-butyl alcohol in chloroform. The glyoxylic acid hydrazone and excess reagent were recovered in the "break-through" volume. The succinic acid was eluted on further addition of developing liquid and showed only back-ground activity. All the C^{14} activity of peak I was subsequently found to be retained by the glyoxylic acid hydrazone derivative after it had been separated and purified chromatographically on filter paper with a butanol-ammonia solvent system (*6*).

Peak II from its position on the elution curve was suspected of being oxalic acid acid and/or glycolic acid. Samples of the C^{14} activity plus added authentic acids in milligram amounts were chromatographed with 25% *n*-butyl alcohol in chloroform saturated with 0.50 *N* sulfuric acid. This procedure effects a satisfactory separation of the oxalic and glycolic acids (also glyoxylic acid). The activity of peak II was found to be divided into two fractions which showed exact correspondence with the titers of the added oxalic and glycolic acids. Typical co-chromatographs for this particular separation are published in reference *6*.

In determining quantitative yield data, known amounts of oxalic, glycolic, and glyoxylic acids were added to the target solution immediately after irradiation, recovered as a nonvolatile fraction (not necessarily quantitatively), and chromatographed as described in the preceding paragraph. Each of the three separated acid peaks was then rechromatographed individually and assayed for specific activity. Corrections for self-absorption were obtained experimentally for the actual counting geometry employed.

2. *Carbonyl products.* Carbonyl products were identified as the 2,4-dinitrophenylhydrazone derivatives. Since these can be readily detected in amounts as low as 10^{-7} mole, preliminary studies were made on target solutions that did not contain $C^{14}H_3COOH$. Aliquots of the irradiated solutions were treated with platinum black to remove hydrogen peroxide and were then added to 2,4-dinitrophenylhydrazine-hydrochloric acid solution. Hydrazones and excess reagent were extracted with chloroform and separated chromatographically on filter paper by use of the solvent systems: (1) butanol saturated with 3% aqueous ammonia, (2) heptane (pract) saturated with methanol. The first method separates the carbonyl acid hydrazones; the second develops the "nonacid" hydrazones, i.e., those of formaldehyde, acetaldehyde, etc. (*6*). Only glyoxylic acid and formaldehyde derivatives were observed.

In the quantitative studies, known amounts of formaldehyde carrier were added to irradiated solutions containing $C^{14}H_3COOH$ and precipitated as the 2,4-dinitrophenylhydrazone derivative. This was washed several times with dilute base and chromatographed by method 2. The appropriate area of the filter paper chromatogram was then extracted with methanol and assayed for C^{14} activity and for total hydrazone (*6*).

3. *Carbon dioxide.* Yield data for carbon dioxide were obtained only for the case of helium ion irradiation. Target cells containing C^{14}-labeled acetic acid were aerated with oxygen containing 1% carbon dioxide. The effluent gas was scrubbed with a dilute solution of sodium hydroxide. Flow was continued several minutes after irradiation to ensure complete recovery of the $C^{14}O_2$. Carbonate in the sodium hydroxide trap was quantitatively recovered as barium carbonate and assayed for C^{14} activity (thick sample geometry).

4. *Peroxides.* Hydrogen peroxide was routinely determined by titration with ceric sulfate in the cold (*10*). A series of control runs with simulated target solutions showed that the organic products of acetic acid oxidation do not interfere. Organic hydroperoxides were also measured (*10, 11*).

RESULTS AND DISCUSSION

Table I gives the 100-ev yields, or G values, for the formation of organic products in oxygen-saturated 0.25 M acetic acid solution by irradiation with helium ions, protons, neutrons, and γ-rays for approximately the same total dose (electron volts per milliliter). All the acid products appear in appreciable yield at concentrations which are lower than that of the parent solute by a factor of about 10^{-4}. This observation would suggest that the glycolic, glyoxylic, and oxalic acids, for example, are not formed in sequence through a series of consecutive oxidation steps. Support for this conclusion is to be found in the data of Table II, which shows that the measured G values for the acid products are essentially independent of radiation dosage over a fairly wide range. Note also that the carbon dioxide yield data

TABLE I

PRODUCT YIELDS IN THE RADIOLYSIS OF OXYGEN-SATURATED 0.25 *M* ACETIC ACID SOLUTIONS BY VARIOUS TYPES OF RADIATION

Radiation	100-ev yield, G[a]			
	Helium ions[b] *(40 Mev)*	*Protons (10 Mev)*	*Neutrons*[c] *(10 Mev)*	*Gamma-rays*[d] *(Co^{60})*
Dose (ev/ml)[e]	4.31×10^{19}	1.50×10^{19}	1.29×10^{19}	1.80×10^{19}
Hydrogen peroxide	1.82	2.58	2.82	—
Glyoxylic acid	0.54	1.10	0.75	1.35
Glycolic acid	0.10	0.39	0.65	0.45
Oxalic acid	0.13	0.22	0.10	0.28
Formaldehyde	0.10	0.20	0.10	—

[a] Data are average values based on the results of at least two runs for each condition. Duplicate runs were reproducible to within 10%.

[b] Although the results reported for the helium ion irradiations were obtained at a somewhat higher dose, the data given represent initial *G* values (see Table II) and may be compared directly with the other data shown.

[c] The neutron spectrum had a population maximum at about 10 Mev. Dose was based on measurements made with the formic acid dosimeter. Assumptions involved in the use of this system for evaluating dose to dilute aqueous solutions is described in references *4* and *5*.

[d] Based on $G(Fe^{+3}) = 15.6$ for the Fricke dosimeter (*23*).

[e] Calculated in each case as total dose/total volume of irradiated solution.

TABLE II

EFFECT OF DOSE ON PRODUCT YIELDS IN THE RADIOLYSIS OF OXYGEN-SATURATED 0.25 *M* ACETIC ACID SOLUTIONS BY 40-MEV HELIUM IONS

Dose (ev/ml)	100-ev yield, G		
	4.31×10^{19}	1.29×10^{20}	4.31×10^{20}
Glyoxylic acid	0.54	0.60	0.35
Glycolic acid	0.10	0.11	0.11
Oxalic acid	0.13	0.12	0.19
Formaldehyde	0.10	—	—
Carbon dioxide			
$CH_3C^{14}OOH$	0.07	0.15	0.20
$C^{14}H_3COOH$	0.006	0.009	0.03

obtained with $C^{14}H_3COOH$ are consistently lower than those obtained with $CH_3C^{14}OOH$. The inference is that carbon dioxide is produced preferentially by some intermediate decarboxylation process, not through oxidation of oxalic acid. We also found that irradiation of solutions of unlabeled acetic acid (0.25 *M*) containing added $C^{14}H_2OHCOOH$ (10^{-3} *M*) gave *G* values for glyoxylic acid which were less than 0.001. The irradiation conditions were identical with those of column 1, Table II. The foregoing observations lead to the conclusion that the radiation-induced oxidation of acetic acid occurs primarily through parallel reactions initiated by the formation of the common precursor O_2CH_2COOH via reaction 5 above.

In considering possible reaction paths involving O_2CH_2COOH radicals, we note first that processes which lead to chain reactions, e.g.,

$$O_2CH_2COOH \rightarrow CHOCOOH + OH \quad (6)$$

$$O_2CH_2COOH + CH_3COOH \rightarrow HO_2CH_2COOH + CH_2COOH \quad (7)$$

probably do not contribute appreciably to the yields of observed products. Reactions 6 and 7 in conjunction with reactions 2 and 5, respectively, each initiate a chain reaction. There is, however, no evidence from the present work that more than one acetic acid molecule is removed per OH radical initially formed in the primary radiation-induced reaction.

The reaction

$$HO_2 + O_2CH_2COOH \rightarrow HO_2CH_2COOH + O_2 \quad (8)$$

may also be ruled out, since specific tests for organic hydroperoxides give an upper limit for G(ROOH) of $\sim$0.3 under the conditions of the present study. This result is in agreement with the work of Weiss and co-workers (*11*), who have detected organic hydroperoxides as major products in several irradiated aquo-organic systems but only at the higher pH values under which conditions $HO_2(O_2^-)$ is a more effective reducing agent. At the pH of 0.25 M acetic acid we may assume that HO_2 is preferentially removed by the well-established disproportionation reaction

$$2HO_2 \rightarrow H_2O_2 + O_2 \quad (9)$$

We come, therefore, to the conclusion that formation of organic products in the radiolysis of oxygen-saturated acetic acid solution occurs primarily through interactions of O_2CH_2COOH radicals. The problem of elucidating the various reactions of peroxy radicals in the present study would appear to be closely related to the classical problem of formulating the mechanism of chain termination in hydrocarbon oxidation as denoted by the general reaction $2RO_2 \rightarrow$ products. In attempting to formulate the possible interactions of O_2CH_2COOH we shall consider first those processes which are indicated on the basis of the more qualitative evidence and then will attempt to ascribe relative importance in terms of the quantitative results obtained under the several experimental conditions studied.

The simplest mechanism for the formation of the aldehyde functions, glyoxylic acid, and formaldehyde is given by the sequence

$$2O_2CH_2COOH \rightarrow O_2 + 2OCH_2COOH \quad (10)$$

$$O_2 + OCH_2COOH \rightarrow CHOCOOH + HO_2 \quad (11)$$

$$\rightarrow CH_2O + CO_2 + HO_2 \quad (11a)$$

Reaction of type 10 has been considered by Vaughan and co-workers to be of importance as a chain-ending process in the low-temperature oxidation of hydrocarbons (*12*). More recently, Jolley employed the equivalent of reactions 10, 11, and 11a in interpreting studies of the photochemically induced oxidation of diethylketone (*13*).

The removal of O_2CH_2COOH may also be written as a type of disproportionation reaction to give glyoxylic and glycolic acids directly, i.e.,

$$2O_2CH_2COOH \rightarrow O_2 + CHOCOOH + CH_2OHCOOH \quad (10a)$$

Evidence for reaction of type 10a has been given by Russell (*14*).

The presence of oxalic acid as an initial product is somewhat more difficult to account for. Bach (*15*) observed a rather similar phenomenon in radiolysis studies of liquid hydrocarbon systems containing dissolved oxygen. It was found that organic acids (in addition to carbonyls and organic peroxides) are produced initially as a linear function of radiation dosage. The author interprets the formation of the carboxyl function in terms of the early studies of Rieche and Meister (*16*), who showed that organic free radicals of the type $RCHO_2$ undergo isomerization according to $RCHO_2 \rightarrow RCOOH$. The formation of oxalic acid as an initial product in the present work could be interpreted on the assumption that a small fraction of the O_2CH_2COOH radicals undergo hydrogen abstraction:

$$2O_2CH_2COOH \rightarrow O_2CHCOOH + HO_2CH_2COOH \quad (10b)$$

followed by isomerization:

$$O_2CHCOOH \rightarrow (COOH)_2 \quad (12)$$

The correspondingly small amount of organic hydroperoxide formed in step 10b would be below the experimentally observed upper limit for hydroperoxide production, i.e., $G(ROOH) \leq 0.3$.

Disregarding for the moment the question of absolute product yields, it is seen that the helium ion, proton, and γ-ray data (Table I) are generally consistent with a mechanism in which reaction 10 represents the principal path for removal of O_2CH_2COOH. The lower yields of oxalic and glycolic acids are interpreted simply by ascribing proportionately lower rates to the parallel steps 10a and 10b. Note, however, that the results obtained with neutrons show glyoxylic and glycolic acids to be formed in almost equivalent amounts for this particular irradiation condition. Obviously, the latter result is not consistent with the idea that the yields of oxalic, glyoxylic, and glycolic acids are wholly determined by the relative rates of parallel paths 10, 10a, and 10b. This apparent anomaly is resolved, however, if we include in the reaction scheme the recognized hydrolytic process

$$H_2O + O_2CH_2COOH \rightarrow CH_2OHCOOH + HO_2 \quad (13)$$

Reaction of type 13 has been proposed by Sworski (*17*) and by Phung and Burton (*18*) as a mechanism for the formation of phenol in the radiolysis of aqueous benzene-oxygen solutions. We postulate that the relatively higher yield of glycolic acid from neutron irradiation in the present study may be attributed to an effect of dose rate on the relative rates of reactions 10, 10a, and 10b as compared to 13. The former, being of second order in O_2CH_2COOH, would, of course, be favored over the pseudo first-order reaction 13 at the higher dose rates. In the helium ion and proton irradiations the dose rate was $\sim 5 \times 10^{18}$ ev/ml-min; in the γ-ray irradiations about 7.8×10^{18} ev/ml-min. The corresponding value in the neutron runs was $\sim 1 \times 10^{17}$ ev/ml-min.

The absolute yields of observed final products can be related only approximately to the primary radical and molecular product yields for water decomposition. The notation of Dewhurst and Burton is used here to represent the initial chemical reaction (*19*):

$$H_2O \rightsquigarrow H, OH, H_2, H_2O_2$$

The 100-ev yields of initial products are denoted $G_w(H)$, $G_w(OH)$, $G_w(H_2)$, and $G_w(H_2O_2)$. Hart has shown that the aqueous formic acid–oxygen dosimeter provides a convenient chemical system for the determination of these values because of the relative simplicity of the radiation-induced oxidation mechanism (*20*). Data are available for Co^{60} γ-rays (*20*) and for the 10-Mev proton beam used in the present study (*5*); the following primary yield values may be taken: (1) γ-rays: $G_w(H) \simeq G_w(OH) \simeq 3.0$, $G_w(H_2) \simeq G_w(H_2O_2) \simeq 0.4$; (2) 10-Mev protons: $G_w(H) \simeq G_w(OH) \simeq 2.4$, $G_w(H_2) \simeq G_w(H_2O_2) \simeq 0.6$. It is noted that these values provide only a first approximation in the present system, since the specific yields of H, OH, H_2, and H_2O_2 are somewhat dependent on the nature and concentration of the solute (*21*).

Now the scheme proposed for the radiation-induced oxidation of acetic acid predicts that the sum $G(CHOCOOH) + G(CH_2OHCOOH) + 2G(COOH)_2 + G(CH_2O)$ should approximate $G_w(OH)$. It is readily apparent from inspection of the data obtained in 0.25 *M* acetic acid (Table I) that *G* for total organic product as defined above is considerably less than $G_w(OH)$ for both the γ-ray and proton irradiations as measured in the formic acid–oxygen system. This discrepancy could be a reflection of the uncertainties referred to regarding the assumed $G_w(OH)$ values. The possibility that not all OH radicals available in the bulk of the solution are removed by reaction with acetic acid in 0.25 *M* solutions is considered unlikely in view of the fact that $G(H_2O_2)$ was found to decrease but a few per cent when the acetic acid concentration was decreased by a factor of 5. On the other hand, it is quite possible that we have not identified all organic products formed in the radiation-induced oxidation of the acetic acid molecule. An interesting possibility which we are now investigating is that dialkyl peroxide derivatives are produced via reaction of type $2RO_2 \rightarrow ROOR + O_2$. This reaction has frequently been cited as a path for removal of RO_2 radicals in hydrocarbon oxidation (*22*). Dialkyl peroxides are relatively inert and are not detected by methods employed in the determination of the hydroperoxides, ROOH.

SUMMARY

Radiation-induced oxidation of acetic acid in oxygenated aqueous solution yields glycolic, glyoxylic, and oxalic acids, formaldehyde, and carbon dioxide. Formation of these products apparently occurs through parallel processes initiated by formation of a common precursor, viz., the peroxy radicals, O_2CH_2COOH. There is no evidence for a chain reaction. Possible reaction paths for removal of O_2CH_2COOH are treated. The experimental results are shown to be consistent with the concept that the removal steps involve $2RO_2 \rightarrow$ products, $RO_2 + H_2O \rightarrow$ products. A detailed mechanism is presented.

ACKNOWLEDGMENTS

The authors wish to thank Mr. William B. Jones and the staff of the Crocker Laboratory 60-inch cyclotron for their assistance in certain of the irradiation procedures. The cobalt source was made available through the courtesy of the bio-organic chemistry group of the University of California Radiation Laboratory. We are also indebted to Mr. Joseph Ward for certain of the radioactivity measurements.

RECEIVED: August 4, 1958

REFERENCES

1. W. M. GARRISON, W. BENNETT, S. COLE, H. R. HAYMOND, and B. M. WEEKS, Indirect and direct action of heavy-particle radiation on acetic acid in aqueous solution. *J. Am. Chem. Soc.* **77,** 2720–2727 (1955).

2. W. M. GARRISON, H. R. HAYMOND, and B. M. WEEKS, Some effects of heavy-particle irradiation of aqueous acetic acid. *Radiation Research* **1,** 97–108 (1954).

3. W. A. ARON, B. G. HOFFMAN, and F. C. WILLIAMS, Range-energy curves. U. S. Atomic Energy Commission Report AECU-663 (May, 1951).

4. M. E. JAYKO and W. M. GARRISON, Formation of >C=O bonds in the radiation-induced oxidation of protein in aqueous systems. *Nature* **181,** 413–414 (1958).

5. W. M. GARRISON, B. M. WEEKS, J. O. WARD, and W. BENNETT, Water decomposition yields in the radiolysis of aqueous formic acid-oxygen solutions by cyclotron-produced radiations. *J. Chem. Phys.* **27,** 1214–1215 (1957).

6. W. M. GARRISON, W. BENNETT, and S. COLE, Synthesis of higher molecular weight products in the radiolysis of aqueous solutions of formic acid. *Radiation Research.* **9,** 647 (1958).

7. C. S. MARVEL and R. D. RANDS, JR., Separation of organic acids. *J. Am. Chem. Soc.* **72,** 2642–2646 (1950).

8. W. A. BULEN, J. E. VARNER, and R. C. BURRELL, Separation of organic acids from plant tissues. *Anal. Chem.* **24,** 187–190 (1952).

9. H. A. IDDLES and C. E. JACKSON, Determination of carbonyl compounds by means of 2,4-dinitrophenylhydrazine. *Ind. Eng. Chem. Anal. Ed.* **6,** 454–456 (1934).

10. F. P. GREENSPAN and D. G. MACKELLAR, Analysis of aliphatic per acids. *Anal. Chem.* **20,** 1061–1063 (1948).

11. G. R. A. JOHNSON and J. WEISS, The formation of methyl hydroperoxide from methane

irradiated by X-rays in aqueous solution in the presence of dissolved oxygen. *Chem. & Ind. (London)* **1955,** 358–359.
12. J. G. Raley, L. M. Porter, F. F. Rust, and W. E. Vaughan, The oxidation of free methyl radicals. *J. Am. Chem. Soc.* **73,** 15–17 (1951).
13. J. E. Jolley, The photoöxidation of diethyl ketone. *J. Am. Chem. Soc.* **79,** 1537–1542 (1957).
14. G. A. Russell, Mechanism of the termination step in autoöxidation reactions. *Chem. & Ind. (London)* **1956,** 1483.
15. N. A. Bach, Radiolytic oxidation of organic compounds. *Proc. Intern. Conf. Peaceful Uses Atomic Energy, Geneva, 1955* **7,** 538–542 (1956).
16. A. Rieche and R. Meister, Alkyl peroxides. VIII. Ethylidene peroxide. *Ber.* **64B,** 2335–40 (1931).
17. T. J. Sworski, Some effects of cobalt gamma radiation on aqueous benzene solutions. *Radiation Research* **1,** 231 (1954).
18. P. V. Phung and M. Burton, Radiolysis of aqueous solutions of hydrocarbons, benzene, benzene-d_6, cyclohexane. *Radiation Research* **7,** 199–216 (1957).
19. H. A. Dewhurst and M. Burton, Radiolysis of aqueous solutions of hydrazine. *J. Am. Chem. Soc.* **77,** 5781–5785 (1955).
20. E. J. Hart, Gamma-ray induced oxidation of aqueous formic acid-oxygen solutions. Effect of oxygen and formic acid concentration. *J. Am. Chem. Soc.* **76,** 4312–4315 (1954).
21. C. J. Hochanadel and S. C. Lind, Radiation chemistry. *Ann. Rev. Phys. Chem.* **7,** 83–106 (1956).
22. *Fifth Symposium (International) on Combustion*, Reinhold Publishing Corp. New York, 1955.
23. C. J. Hochanadel and J. A. Ghormley, Calorimetric calibration of gamma-ray actinometers. *J. Chem. Phys.* **21,** 880–885 (1953).

RADIATION RESEARCH **10**, 283–295 (1959)

The Relationship between Division and X-ray Sensitivity, Ultraviolet Sensitivity, and Photoreactivation in Yeast

M. M. ELKIND AND HARRIET SUTTON

Radiation Branch, National Cancer Institute, National Institutes of Health, Public Health Service, Department of Health, Education, and Welfare, Bethesda, Maryland

INTRODUCTION

The use of various irradiations in additivity or coupling experiments affords a means of identifying those types of sensitive sites which are common to two or more types of radiation. For instance, using additivity experiments in the case of interdivisional haploid and diploid yeast cells, Uretz (*1*) concluded that the same sites are involved to a large extent in both ultraviolet (UV) and X-ray inactivation. A similar conclusion was reached by Blum *et al.* (*2*) in connection with the production of cleavage delay in sea urchin eggs.

When coupling experiments with UV (e.g., 254-mμ Hg line) include a study of the decoupling effects of photoreactivation, it is also possible to gain some knowledge of the UV-absorbing chromophore and hence the chemical nature of the sites sensitive to the other irradiations which couple with UV. This follows from anology with the appreciable number of instances, referred to by Brandt and Giese (*3*), in which it has been found that UV effects which can be photoreactivated have nucleic acid action spectra.

When yeast cells are harvested from log phase growth (*4*) or from nutrient agar surfaces after incubation for a day or two (*5*), an appreciable fraction of the population consists of budding cells. Beam and coauthors (*5*) showed, particularly for haploid cells, that this moiety was considerably less sensitive to X-rays than interdivisional cells, and subsequently Elkind and Beam (*4*) showed that this situation also obtained in the case of α-particles, suggesting, therefore, that dividing cells are appreciably less sensitive to ionizing radiations in general. In contrast to the preceding observations, published yeast survival curves for UV exposure have not indicated a moiety of lesser UV sensitivity (*6–10*), even though the conditions of growth could have been expected to have yielded an appreciable fraction of budding cells. Since UV-sensitive sites have been shown to be closely associated with nucleic acid chromophores in a number of instances, and since Uretz (*1*) presented evidence of coupling between UV and X-ray sites in *interdivisional* cells, the apparent homogeneous nature of UV survival curves suggests either that the lethal sites in interdivisional cells are nongenic or, at least, that UV and X-ray sites in dividing cells do not overlap. This follows from the reasonable requirement that, if X-ray and UV lethality sites are common to any appreciable extent, then both survival curves should display the presence of a dividing cell moiety having reduced sensitivity.

In addition to the apparent uniform sensitivity of dividing and non-dividing yeast cells to UV, the degree of radioresistance (e.g., resistance to X-rays) of dividing cells is also anomalous. Beam and associates (*5*) also showed that the radioresistant "tail" on the haploid yeast survival curve could not be explained by a simple duplication of the interdivisional X-ray site structure attendant with mitosis. This means either that the X-ray sites in dividing cells are unrelated to those in interdivisional cells or that the latter are transformed during division in at least an operational sense.

Thus the question arises, what is the nature of the lethal sites in dividing yeast cells? Preparatory to the examination of this question through the use of additivity experiments, it was recognized that it would first be necessary to answer definitively the question of whether or not dividing yeast cells are less sensitive to UV than are interdivisional cells. That a lesser UV-sensitive moiety had not been previously reported suggested that the relative difference involved might appear to be small. Nevertheless, the point of significance in these connections is whether or not dividing cells are less sensitive at all. The purpose of this report is to present evidence which proves that budding cells are less sensitive to UV than are nonbudding cells. In a subsequent paper (*11*), data will be presented which implicates chromosomal deoxyribonucleic acid as the site(s) of lethal action of UV and X-rays in dividing yeast cells.

MATERIALS, APPARATUS, AND METHODS

Cell lines. Two haploid and one diploid *Saccharomyces cerevisiae* strains, all genetically related, were used in this work. The lines have been designated SC-7, SC-7 (ρ), and SC-6. The SC-7-strain[1] was isolated from SC-6, and both are respiring strains; their lineage has been described by Zirkle and Tobias (*12*). Strain SC-7(ρ) is a respiration-deficient subline presumably derived from SC-7 at some time during the past decade. Recent work has shown that log phase SC-7 and SC-7(ρ) can be lethally affected by small doses of visible radiation administered after specific, though not uncommon, storage conditions. The detailed nature of this visible light sensitivity has been reported for SC-7(ρ) (*13, 14*). Strain SC-6 and its haploid derivatives have been used in a number of radiobiological studies, many of which are referred to in reference *13*. Of the two haploid lines, it is known with certainty only that SC-7(ρ) was the subline used in reference *4* of this paper.

[1] Obtained from H. E. Kubitschek via R. K. Mortimer.

X-ray exposure. A 150-kvp Westinghouse power supply converted to 75-kvp full-wave rectification was used to power a Machlett OEG-60 X-ray tube (exit window 1 mm beryllium) at 55 kvp and 25 ma. No additional filtration was used; the half-value layer of the beam was 2.3 mils of aluminum. The absorbed dose rate (*15*) was 30.2 krad/min; details of the dose measurement are given in reference *4*. For studies of this type, a very high dose rate is essential. The longest exposures used with the equipment described were less than 7 minutes. Equipment of higher voltage would have required exposures ten to thirty times as long, exposures which are comparable to the times for significant cellular events.

Because of the weak penetrating ability of the X-ray beam, in all cases cells were exposed while resting on solid agar (at room temperature) and after the suspending buffer had been absorbed (2 to 3 minutes after spreading). For survival curves, the agar contained growth media in 9-cm petri plates which were placed in a 30°C incubator after exposure. For additivity or coupling experiments requiring pre-X-ray exposure, 1 to 2 $\times$ 10^6 cells were deposited on an agar planchard (2 cm in diameter) which enabled the cells to be resuspended after exposure.

Ultraviolet. The UV source consisted of three tubular 8-watt General Electric germicidal lamps, type G8T5. The lamps were parallel, 2 inches apart, and the plane of their center lines was 24 inches from the irradiated samples. The UV flux emitted by these low-pressure Hg lamps, primarily the 254-mμ line, was measured with a General Electric detector consisting of a cadmium cathode phototube and an electrometer circuit. The wavelength response of this phototube lies between 200 and 300 mμ and peaks at close to 254 mμ. As measured with this meter, the UV intensity varied from 22.1 to 20.5 ergs/sq mm-sec during the course of the work, owing to tube aging. For some survival curves, cells were exposed on solid growth media (as described for X-ray exposure) with the petri plates rotated about their perpendicular center line at 24 rpm. For coupling experiments and in some instances for survival curves, cells were suspended in buffer and exposed in 10-ml aliquots contained in a Pyrex cup (inverted, truncated cone: 4.8-cm upper diameter, 3.3-cm lower diameter, 2.9 cm high). On the survival curves to be discussed, the labels "agar" or "buffer" refer to exposure on agar or in buffer, respectively. For the same survival of budding cells, the UV exposure required in buffer was 1.5 times that required on agar. The cups rotated around their center lines at 50 rpm while the center lines of the cups rotated around a circle of radius 3.5 cm at 24 rpm. Mixing of the suspensions was further ensured by four dimples blown into the bottom of each cup. Cell densities exposed in buffer were about 10^6 per milliliter. As measured in a 1-cm cuvette with a Beckman DU spectrometer, at the highest cell concentrations used the transmission was not less than 87% at 254 mμ, with no indication of specific absorption from 220 to 400 mμ. Precautions were taken to avoid incidental photoreaction and/or photolethality.

Visible-light source. The setup used for photoreactivation was essentially that shown in Fig. 1 of reference *13* with the exceptions that a 500-watt projector was used and the cell suspension temperature was controlled by pumping 30°C water through the Pyrex water jacket surrounding the Pyrex suspension container. About 10 ml of suspension mixed by an air stream could be photoreactivated at one time with maximum reactivation exposures up to 2 hours being used, depending on the UV dose. The projector contained a heat-absorbing filter; the remaining integral intensity measured with a thermopile was 118 mw/cm^2.

Experimental procedure. For most of the experiments to be discussed, the cells were grown at 30°C overnight on YED agar (½% Difco yeast extract, 1% dextrose, 2% Difco bacto-agar) from stocks stored at 4°C on YED agar. Suspensions of the latter cells had X-ray-resistant moieties of about 10%. In some experiments, cells harvested from overnight YED plates were used to inoculate liquid YED of the same composition (no agar), and in a few instances cells were grown on potato dextrose (PD) agar. After suitable periods of growth in log phase, the former cells produced X-ray-resistant moieties of about 30% (*4*).

After growth, cells were harvested in chilled 0.05 *M* KH_2PO_4 (which was the standard buffer used in this work) and washed at least two times by centrifugation in 250-ml bottles at 0°C. Microscopically no clumps were observed. Subsequently all suspensions were maintained at about 2°C in shielded tubes. In some pre-UV coupling experiments the suspensions were concentrated by centrifugation at 0°C after exposure. Cell survival was taken as the ability of a single or a budding cell to grow on YED agar (autoclaved for 45 minutes at 18 psi) into a visible colony after at least 5 days in a 30°C incubator.

Respiration-deficient colonies were scored by the tetrazolium overlay technique (2,3,5-triphenyltetrazolium chloride, TTC) of Ogur *et al.* (*16*). In essence, this simple technique consists in scoring those colonies that still appear white about 3 hours after overlay as respiration-deficient (*aer*), and scoring those that appear red as having normal respiration (*AER*). Sectored colonies and mixed colonies (base white, apex of papilla red), which usually constituted less than 15% of the total deficient population, were also easily scored.

Most of the data to be discussed are in the form of survival curves, and in each case the standard error in survival is indicated unless smaller than the plotted point.

EXPERIMENTAL RESULTS

Survival curves. Figure 1 shows four sets of UV and X-ray survival curves for the cell lines used in this work. The curves in Fig. 1*C* were obtained with cells grown from a respiration-deficient colony which appeared spontaneously on an SC-7 control plate. Several other *aer* isolates gave similar results, and of course similar results were obtained many times for the other cell lines. In each case, it can be seen that the X-ray tail (X-ray-resistant portion of the curve) extrapolates to about the same survival at zero dose as does what is tentatively identified as the UV tail. For hap-

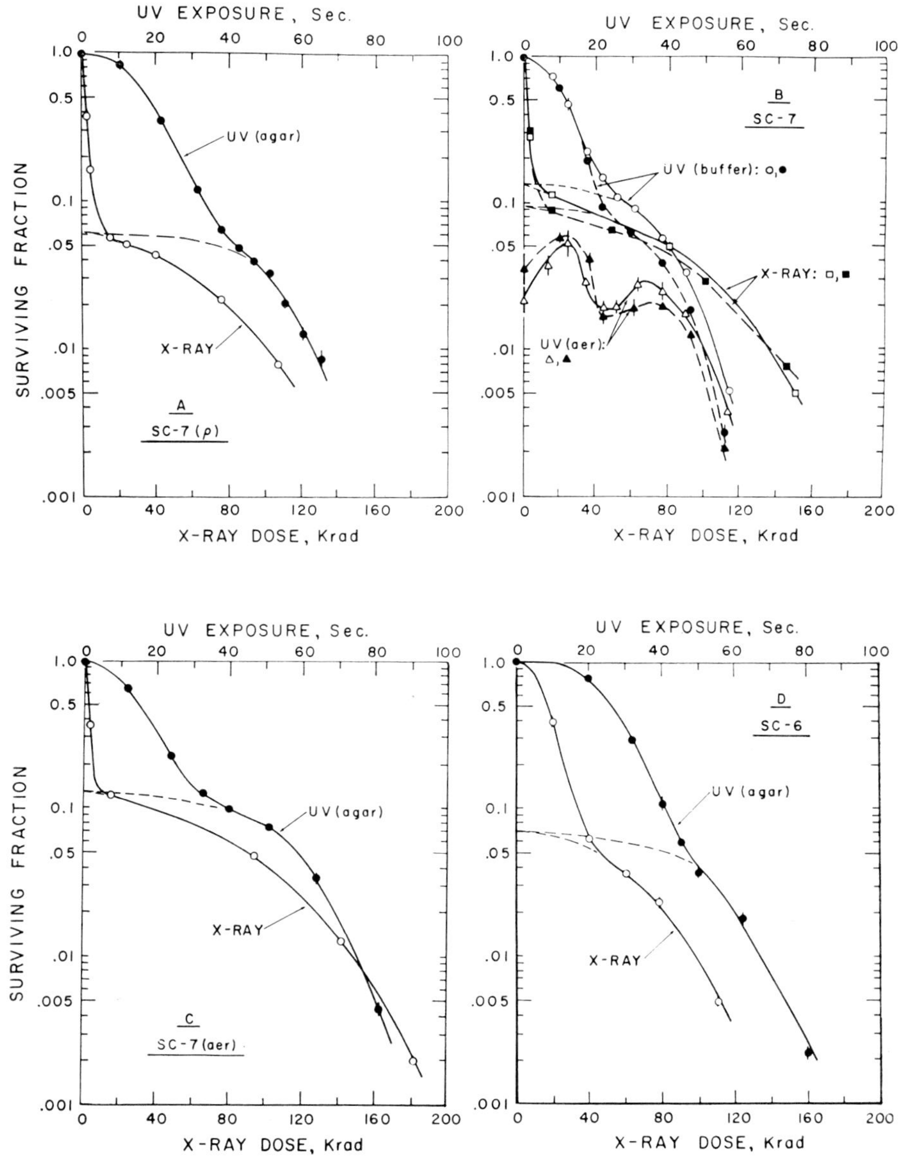

FIG. 1. Ultraviolet and X-ray survival curves for yeast cells showing the presence of a moiety less sensitive to UV as well as to X-rays. *A*, respiration-deficient haploid strain SC-7 (ρ). *B*, respiration-sufficient haploid strain SC-7 (UV production of respiration-deficient survivors, *aer*, also shown for two different batches of cells). *C*, respiration-deficient, spontaneously occurring mutant of SC-7. *D*, respiration-sufficient diploid strain SC-6.

loid cells, the zero dose level can be identified with ease because the survival curve consists of a rapidly decreasing exponential added to a slowly decreasing multihit curve (*4*). However, just as the zero dose level of the X-ray tail for the diploid line, determined by extrapolation, is less certain than it is for the haploid lines, so also are the zero dose levels determined from the UV tails less certain for the haploid lines and even less certain still for the diploid line. In both the latter instances, the survival curves are sums of at least two multihit curves each. For similar reasons, the inflection point on the UV curve for the diploid line is less pronounced than those for the haploid lines. In general consistency with the UV survival curves determined by Uretz for *interdivisional* cells only (*1*), the initial portions of the UV survival curves in Fig. 1, tentatively attributed to interdivisional cells, show that the interdivisional cells of the diploid stock are less sensitive than similar cells from the haploid stocks.

Figure 1*B* also shows the *aer* survivors of UV irradiation of SC-7 for two different batches of cells. That *aer* mutants are copiously produced with UV was shown by Raut (*9*), who also concluded that the vast majority (more than 95%) of *aer* survivors were cytoplasmic mutants. The *aer* production curves strongly suggest, however, that the *aer* cells are being produced from two different moieties of the initial, essentially homogeneous *AER* population. The second rise in the *aer* curve correlates well with the UV-resistant portion of the total survival curve. This is further evidence to support differential UV effects in yeast populations containing budding and nonbudding cells.

The results in Fig. 1 suggest, therefore, that populations of yeast cells generally contain a UV-resistant moiety identified by an inflection point in the UV survival curve, and that this moiety corresponds to the X-ray-resistant moiety which has been shown to be due to cells which are in the early phase(s) of divisions (*5*).

Existence of the UV tail. Proof of the existence of a UV tail and its correlation with the level of the X-ray tail is shown in Fig. 2. In the coupling or additivity experiments shown, labels such as UV(0.39 ± 0.01)–X mean that the unirradiated population was given a single UV dose which reduced the survival to 0.39 ± 0.01 and that this pre-UV exposure was followed by a graded series of X-ray exposures.

Figure 2*A* shows the initial portion of the X-ray and UV survival curves as well as three UV–X coupling curves. For the coupling experiments, the control survival was that resulting from the pre-UV exposure. Now if the UV survival curves do not have tails representing cells of both decreased UV as well as decreased X-ray sensitivity, then small pre-UV doses would not affect the level of the tail observed with subsequent X-ray exposure. That is, if the UV survival curves do not have inflection points and therefore represent a homogeneous population as far as UV sensitivity is concerned, then the survivors of a pre-UV dose should have the same percentage of budding cells as the original population. Figure 2*A* shows that this is not the case, but rather that the level of the X-ray tail is raised progressively as the pre-UV

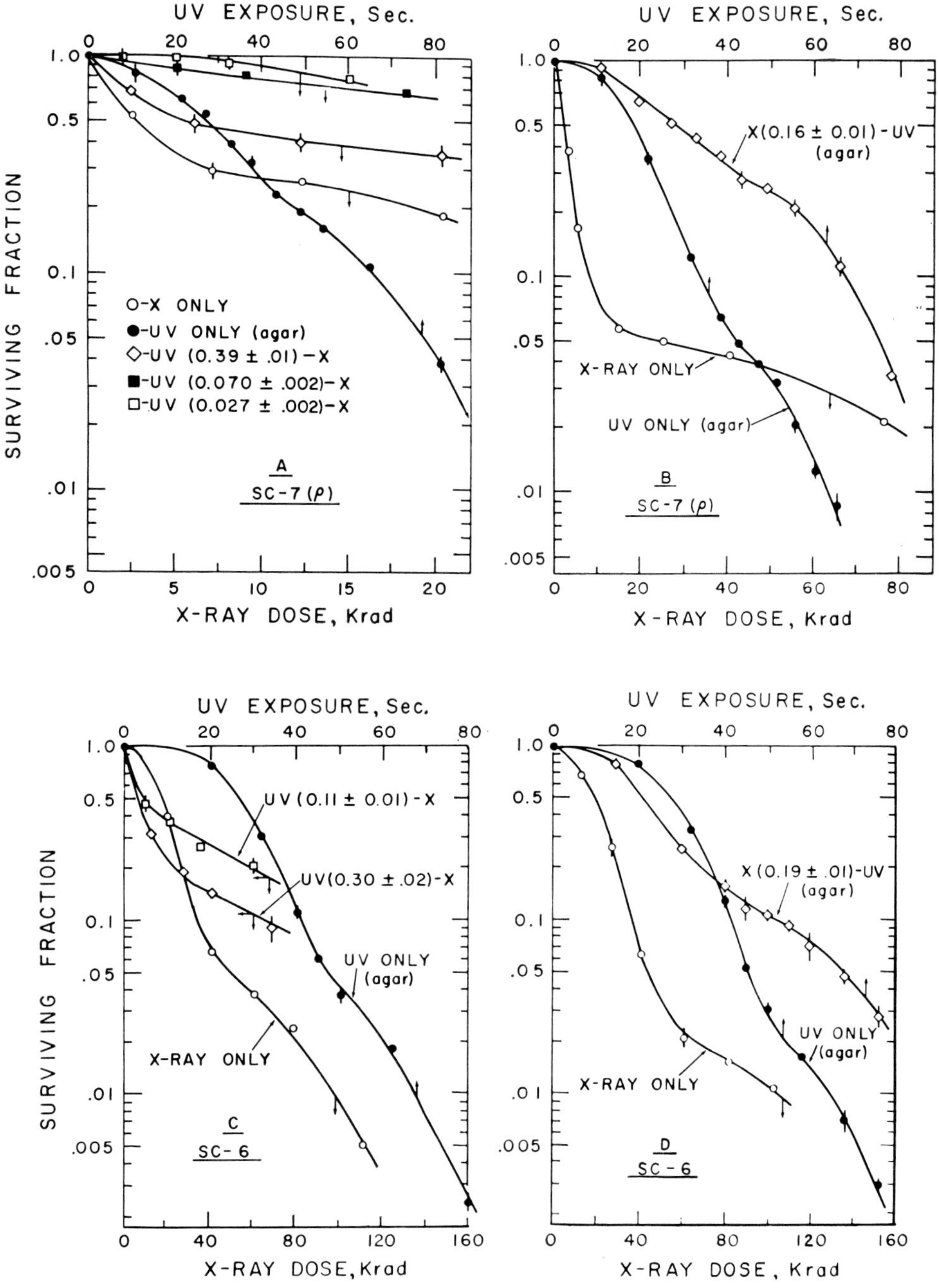

FIG. 2. X-Ray and ultraviolet additivity experiments which show that dividing yeast cells are less sensitive to UV than are interdivisional cells. *A*, UV–X-ray coupling experiments for SC-7(ρ). *B*, X-ray–UV coupling experiments for SC-7(ρ). *C*, UV–X-ray coupling experiments for SC-6. *D*, X-ray–UV coupling experiments for SC-6.

dose is increased. Alternatively, if budding cells are less sensitive to UV, as they are to X-rays, then the results shown in Fig. 2*A* would follow both qualitatively and quantitatively.

To illustrate this, consider the first coupling curve plotted in Fig. 1*A*. The level of the tail (i.e., the fraction of budding cells) is 0.29 from the "X-ray only" survival curve. With this fact and from the "UV only" survival curve, the 0.39 surviving fraction of the pre-UV exposure contains about 56% dividing cells determined from an extrapolation of the UV tail to the ordinate 0.29. The tail on the UV(0.39 $\pm$ 0.01)–X survival curve extrapolates to about 56%, as it should if the moiety which is less UV-sensitive corresponds to the moiety which is less X-ray-sensitive. The other two coupling curves in Fig. 1*A* consist essentially of an X-ray tail only, as they should because of the higher pre-UV exposures used. Additional quantitative checks of the relative shifts in the X-ray tail level can be seen in Figs. 6, 7, and 8 of reference *11*, although in the latter instances the UV–X curves are plotted starting from the fraction which survive the pre-UV dose.

The results in Fig. 2*B* show the reverse experiments on another batch of SC-7(ρ). Here, a pre-X-ray exposure to 0.16 $\pm$ 0.01 survival followed by graded UV exposures show an inflection and bump in the curve which extrapolates back to about 0.30 survival. If the unirradiated population was homogeneous and consisted only of interdivisional cells, then the X–UV survival curve superimposes over the initial UV survival curve, as Uretz has shown (*1*).

Figures 2*C* and *D* show the corresponding results for diploid cells with good quantitative checks of the assumption that dividing cells are less UV-sensitive. In passing, it is noted that the initial portions of the coupling curves in Fig. 2*C* and D show evidence of overlap in UV and X-ray sites for *interdivisional* cells, as previously reported (*1*).

Photoreactivation. As shown by Novick and Szilard for *E. coli* (*17*), and by Warshaw for yeast (*18*), the UV survival curve is related to the photoreactivation survival curve by a constant dose-reduction factor. In the case of yeast, homogeneous populations consisting of interdivisional cells only (*18*) can be obtained from PD agar surfaces after incubation for a number of days (e.g., 7 days in reference *1*); such populations do not display a radioresistant tail. If a mixed population of yeast cells is photoreactivated, the lesser UV sensitivity of dividing cells should affect photoreactivation, providing that the sites of photoreactivation are closely associated with those of UV lethality. The results of an examination of this point will be given for the diploid line SC-6.

Figure 3 shows a set of curves for a population of SC-6 consisting of interdivisional cells only. As previously shown (*1*) and as also verified in this work for the haploid line SC-7(ρ), after a 1-week incubation on PD agar the UV and X-ray survival curves have no inflection points and reflect a homogeneous population. The plots of surviving fraction versus photoreactivation time, t, can be analyzed by

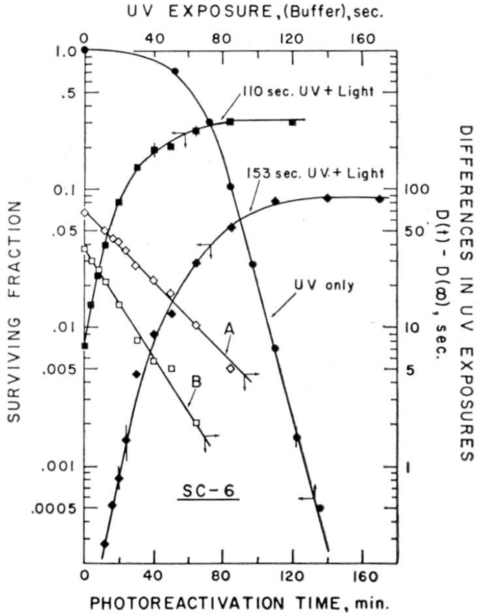

FIG. 3. Photoreactivation and UV dose reactivation plots for interdivisional diploid cells, SC-6. Curve *A* refers to the "153 sec. UV + light" curve. Curve *B* refers to the "110 sec. UV + light" curve.

plotting the UV dose reduction, $D(t) - D(\infty)$, as a function of t (*17*). Here $D(t)$ is the UV dose taken from the UV survival curve (dark) corresponding to the survival resulting from a visible-light exposure, t, and $D(\infty)$ is the UV dose corresponding to maximum photoreactivation, $t = \infty$. Curves *A* and *B* are semilog plots of this type obtained from the survival versus photoreactivation time plots shown, indicating that dose reactivation is exponential for a population of interdivisional cells only.

Figure 4 shows a similar set of curves for a population consisting of about 10% budding cells. In contrast to the previous case, the dose reactivation curve appears to be the sum of two exponentials with the break in the curve at $D(t) - D(\infty) =$ 16 seconds. Since $D(\infty) = 54$ seconds in this case, $D(t) = 70$ seconds. This agrees well with the location of the inflection point in the UV survival curve (dark).

Hence, it is seen that a mixed population of yeast cells photoreactivates as though it consisted of two moieties, and that these appear to be the interdivisional and dividing cell fractions. In addition, it is worth noting that in reference *11* curve *e* in Fig. 1*C* and curves *d* in Figs. 1*A* and 2*A* show that dividing cells are photoreactivated first, and therefore from our Fig. 4 it can be seen that the rate of photoreactivation is considerably greater for dividing cells than it is for interdivisional cells.

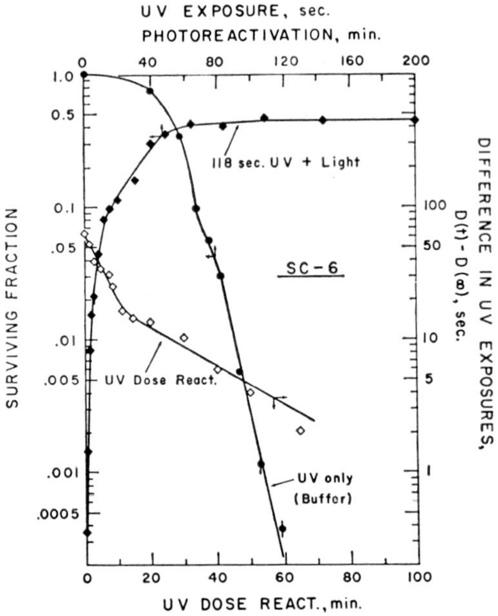

FIG. 4. Photoreactivation and UV dose reactivation of a population of diploid cells, SC-6, containing about 10% dividing cells.

Site replication for division. One possible explanation of the lesser sensitivity of dividing cells to UV is that in such cells there are two sets of sites identical to those in interdivisional cells which must be independently inactivated to suppress visible colony formation. This mode of inactivation is in distinction to the recessive-dominant hit theory model of Zirkle and Tobias (*12*), which requires the inactivation of allelic sets in polyploid cells. In connection with the X-ray response of dividing cells, Beam and coauthors (*5*) were able to rule out simple multiplicity (increase in hitness number only) by just comparing the multihit curves generated from the exponential survival of the nonbudding cells with the X-ray tail. The situation for UV is by no means as clear cut, and in the Appendix a "two-hitness" theorem is derived which proves that duplication alone of the UV sites present in interdivisional cells cannot account for the inflection points in the UV survival curves. In reference *11* it is shown further that the lesser UV sensitivity of dividing cells represents an intrinsic change in sensitivity and is not due to a kind of artifact like a larger amount of nucleic acid in dividing cells.

SUMMARY AND CONCLUSIONS

Evidence has been presented which shows that a mixed population of yeast contains a moiety which is of lesser UV sensitivity, and that this moiety is the dividing cell fraction of the population. It also shows that the existence of a UV-resistant fraction is independent of the ploidy, respiration competence, and sensitivity to other types of irradiation such as the visible-light sensitivity of the haploid lines.

Although the apparent lesser UV sensitivity of dividing cells appears to be small relative to that of interdivisional cells, the existence of this difference alone makes it plausible that UV lethal sites overlap X-ray lethal sites in dividing cells. This, in turn, makes it likely that the overlap in interdivisional cells (*1*) involves the same type(s) of sites (molecular and/or anatomical) as those involved in dividing cells. That neither the lesser UV nor X-ray sensitivity can be explained on the basis of a simple duplication of the respective site structures present in interdivisional cells represents another consistency in the over-all picture. No detailed insight into the relationship between the site structures in interdivisional as compared to dividing cells is afforded by these results, however.

It should be noted that the existence of the UV tail may be an important factor to consider in connection with effects other than lethality. The saddle-shaped curve for production of respiration-deficient (*aer*) mutants, as shown in Fig. 1*B*, is one illustration of results which might otherwise have appeared to be quite unrelated to the UV survival curve. The apparent correlation between the second rise in the production of *aer* mutants and the inflection in the UV survival curve is probably not fortuitous and probably reflects changes in or duplication of cytoplasmic constituents which occur during division. The attribution of the differential production of *aer* mutants to the duplication and division of nuclear material requires that cytoplasmic mutants result from specific absorption by deoxyribonucleic acid, since Raut and Simpson (*10*) have shown that the action spectrum for *aer* production is very similar to the absorption spectrum of nucleic acid.

In a subsequent paper (*11*), the evidence presented here is extended to show that in dividing yeast cells there is considerable overlap among the sites of UV and X-ray lethality and that these sites are probably located in the chromosomes.

APPENDIX

The question is raised in the text: Can the inflection points in the UV survival curves of haploid and diploid cells be due to the presence in dividing cells of two identical sets of interdivision cell sites, each set of which must be inactivated independently?

Let f represent the survival function of interdivisional cells; $f = f(D)$, where D is the UV dose. It has been shown (*1, 18*) and confirmed in this study that for

$$0 < f \leqslant 1 \tag{1}$$

$$f^2 \frac{\partial^2(\ln f)}{\partial D^2} = f \frac{\partial^2 f}{\partial D^2} - \left(\frac{\partial f}{\partial D}\right)^2 \leqslant 0 \tag{2}$$

which also requires that

$$\frac{\partial(\ln f)}{\partial D} \leqslant 0 \tag{3}$$

These equations state that the semilog plot of the interdivisional cell survival curve starts from 1.0, has no inflection point, and has a negative slope. For cells grown under the proper conditions (i.e., potato-dextrose agar for 7 or more days), this has been found to be true down to survivals of 10^{-5}. The question is, can any mixture of f and its two-hitness counterpart have at least one inflection point? That is, if c_1 and c_2 are positive constants, and $c_1 + c_2 = 1$, can

$$\frac{\partial^2(\ln F)}{\partial D^2} > 0 \tag{4}$$

where

$$F = c_1 f + c_2[1 - (1 - f)^2] \tag{5}$$

Since $F^2 > 0$, this requires that at least for some range of values of F

$$F \frac{\partial^2 F}{\partial D^2} - \left(\frac{\partial F}{\partial D}\right)^2 > 0 \tag{6}$$

which from equation 5 can be expressed in the form

$$\frac{A}{B}\left(f \frac{\partial^2 f}{\partial D^2}\right) - \left(\frac{\partial f}{\partial D}\right)^2 > 0 \tag{7}$$

In equation 7, A and B are positive and contain the mixing coefficients c_1 and c_2 as well as f.

From equation 2 it is seen that for equation 7 to be satisfied it is at least necessary that $A/B > 1$ or $A - B > 0$. The latter expression, however, is

$$- c_2(c_1 + 2c_2)f \leqslant 0 \tag{8}$$

and hence equation 4 cannot be true. This result applies for f exponential as well as sigmoid. For hitness mixtures of one and moieties greater than two, f must be known in order to verify equation 4. For f exponential, it can be shown that higher multiplicities will not mix without an inflection point.

RECEIVED: May 26, 1958.

REFERENCES

1. R. B. URETZ, Additivity of X-rays and ultraviolet light in the inactivation of haploid and diploid yeast. *Radiation Research* **2**, 240–252 (1955).
2. H. F. BLUM, J. C. ROBINSON, and G. M. LOOS, The loci of action of ultraviolet and X-irradiation and of photorecovery in the egg and sperm of the sea urchin *Arbacia punctulata*. *J. Gen. Physiol.* **35**, 323–342 (1951).

3. C. L. Brandt and A. C. Giese, Photoreversal of nuclear and cytoplasmic effects of short ultraviolet radiation on *Paramecium caudatum*. *J. Gen. Physiol.* **39,** 735–751 (1956).
4. M. M. Elkind and C. A. Beam, Variation of the biological effectiveness of X-rays and α-particles on haploid *Saccharomyces cerevisiae*. *Radiation Research* **3,** 88–104 (1955).
5. C. A. Beam, R. K. Mortimer, R. G. Wolfe, and C. A. Tobias, The relation of radioresistance to budding in *Saccharomyces cerevisiae*. *Arch. Biochem. Biophys.* **49,** 110–122 (1954).
6. A. Sarachek, Ultraviolet inactivation of *Saccharomyces* during the budding cycle. *Exptl. Cell Research* **6,** 45–55 (1954).
7. A. Sarachek and W. H. Lucke, Induction of resistance to X-ray inactivation in *Saccharomyces* by pre-exposure to 2537Å ultraviolet radiation. *Experientia,* **9,** 1–5 (1953).
8. A. Sarachek, A comparative study of the retardation of budding and cellular inactivation by ultraviolet radiation in a polyploid *Saccharomyces* with special reference to photoreactivation. *Cytologia* **19,** 77–85 (1954).
9. C. Raut, Heritable non-genic changes induced in yeast by ultraviolet light. *J. Cellular Comp. Physiol.* **44,** 463–475 (1954).
10. C. Raut and W. L. Simpson, The effect of X-rays and of ultraviolet light of different wavelengths on the production of cytochrome-deficient yeasts. *Arch. Biochem. Biophys.* **57,** 218–228 (1955).
11. M. M. Elkind and H. Sutton, Sites of action of lethal irradiation: Overlap in sites for X-ray, ultraviolet, photoreactivation, and ultraviolet protection and reactivation in dividing yeast cells. *Radiation Research* **10,** 296–312 (1959).
12. R. E. Zirkle and C. A. Tobias, Effects of ploidy and linear energy transfer on radiobiological survival curves. *Arch. Biochem. Biophys.* **47,** 282–306 (1953).
13. M. M. Elkind and H. Sutton, Lethal effect of visible light on a mutant strain of haploid yeast. I. General dependencies. *Arch. Biochem. Biophys.* **72,** 84–95 (1957).
14. M. M. Elkind and H. Sutton, Lethal effect of visible light on a mutant strain of haploid yeast. II. Absorption and action spectra. *Arch. Biochem. Biophys.* **72,** 96–111 (1957).
15. Report of the International Commission on Radiological Units and Measurements (ICRU). *Natl. Bur. Standards (U. S.) Handbook* No. **62,** 16 (April 10, 1957).
16. M. Ogur, R. St. John, and S. Nagae, Tetrazolium overlay technique for population studies of respiration deficiency in yeast. *Science* **125,** 928–929 (1957).
17. A. Novick and L. Szilard, Experiments on light-reactivation of ultraviolet inactivated bacteria. *Proc. Natl. Acad. Sci. U. S.* **35,** 591–600 (1949).
18. S. D. Warshaw, Effect of ploidy in photoreactivation. *Proc. Soc. Exptl. Biol. Med.* **79,** 268–271 (1952).

RADIATION RESEARCH 10, 296–312 (1959)

Sites of Action of Lethal Irradiation: Overlap in Sites for X-Ray, Ultraviolet, Photoreactivation, and Ultraviolet Protection and Reactivation in Dividing Yeast Cells

M. M. ELKIND AND HARRIET SUTTON

Radiation Branch, National Cancer Institute, National Institutes of Health, Public Health Service, Department of Health, Education, and Welfare, Bethesda, Maryland

INTRODUCTION

The questions of where and what, on a cellular level, are the sites of action of lethal irradiation are principal ones in radiobiology. Although much evidence exists which implicates the nucleus as the anatomical domain of the sites of many irradiation effects (*1*), at least for ultraviolet (UV) irradiation it has been suggested that effects can be nuclear and specific for nucleic acid (or nucleoprotein) but in part nongenic (*2*, *3*); specific for nucleic acid but nonnuclear (*4*, *5*); and nonnuclear as well as nonspecific for nucleic acid (*6*). In *E. coli*, Kelner has shown (*7*) that UV stops deoxyribonucleic acid (DNA) synthesis whereas ribonucleic acid (RNA) synthesis proceeds at a rate paralleling that of residual cell growth.

Although the preceding observations imply that the sites for UV effects can be nuclear and/or cytoplasmic, specific for nucleic acid (or nucleoprotein) as well as not, for some effects it has been shown that the sites for UV and X-ray damage are the same. Blum *et al.* (*8*) have shown that cleavage delay in sea urchin eggs can be produced by both UV and X-rays and that in both instances it is necessary that a nucleus (whole egg, nucleated half, or sperm) be irradiated. Using additivity experiments, Uretz (*9*) concluded that in interdivisional haploid and diploid yeast cells the same sites are involved to a large extent in both UV and X-ray inactivation. In view of the evidence, at least from Mortimer and coauthors' single-cell crossing experiments with *interdivisional* yeast cells (*10–12*), that X-ray lethality in yeast is probably nuclear and related to ploidy, it would appear that sites of UV lethality are also located in the nucleus.

As concerns yeast, however, there are some anomalies in this picture. The results of UV irradiation of uninucleate and multinucleate *Neurospora conidia*, interpreted by Norman with considerable interval consistency as indicating nuclear sites of action (*2*, *3*), show that the survival curve of the haploid nucleus is exponential. Giles (*13*) has shown that the X-ray survival curve of uninucleate conidia is multihit, and recently Gafford (*14*) has attributed the multihit shape to the combined effects of exponential nuclear lethality and multihit cytoplasmic lethality. The UV survival curve of *interdivisional* haploid yeast cells (*9*, *15*) is multihit, although, as is well known, the X-ray survival curve of interdivisional cells is exponential.

Raut and Simpson (*5*) reported that the UV production of "petits" (respiration-deficient cytoplasmic mutants) as well as lethality in a haploid yeast strain are closely correlated and have action spectra similar to the absorption spectrum of nucleic acid. This suggested that UV sites of petit production and lethality are closely associated and cytoplasmic.

Lastly, although it is well known that dividing yeast cells (cells in division when irradiated) are much more resistant to X-rays than are interdivisional cells (*16–18*), a corresponding change in the UV response of budding cells had not been reported (*4*, *5*, *19–21*). This absence of a UV-insensitive moiety had been a key point against the view that UV and X-ray lethal effects have many sites in common. In our preceding paper (*22*), we have shown that dividing cells are indeed less sensitive to UV than are nondividing cells, although the relative difference in sensitivity is small. Although the existence of a UV-resistant moiety (or tail on the UV survival curve) is not by itself a sufficient condition to prove the existence of overlap, it would appear to be a necessary condition for almost any reasonable model of the organization of sites and their inactivation.

In the work to be described, the existence of overlap in the sites of action of X-rays, UV, and photoreaction in dividing cells is examined in detail. This point is critical for a coherent interpretation of site overlap experiments with yeast as well as for consistency of the results with the latter and other biological material. In addition, the uniqueness of the response of dividing yeast cells to ionizing radiation (*16–18*) lends considerable interest to investigations which examine the latter response in relation to other radiations.

MATERIALS, APPARATUS, AND METHODS

A characterization of the cell lines used in this work is given in Table I. These lines are genetically related and have been used in a number of other radiobiological studies, including those described in reference *22*. Of the two haploid lines, it is known with certainty only that SC-7(ρ), a visible-light-sensitive strain, was the subline used in reference *17*. Additional details with regard to the materials, apparatus, and methods used in this work are given in reference *22*.

Most of the data to be discussed are in the form of survival curves, and in each case the standard error in survival is indicated unless smaller than the plotted point.

TABLE I
YEAST CELL LINES USED

Designation	*Ploidy*	*Respiration*	*Visible light sensitivity*
SC-7[a]	1	+	+
SC-7(ρ)	1	−	+
SC-6	2	+	−

[a] Obtained from H. E. Kubitschek via R. K. Mortimer.

EXPERIMENTAL RESULTS

X-ray and UV lethality sites. In our preceding paper (*22*), it was shown that dividing yeast cells are less sensitive to UV as well as to X-rays and that these lesser sensitivities cannot be attributed to a simple duplication of the site structures present in interdivision cells. Four general possibilities relating to the question of possible overlap in these sites will now be considered. One (I), there is no overlap; the decreased UV sensitivity of dividing cells is a reflection, for instance, of a larger amount of nucleic acid in dividing cells which absorbs the 254-mμ line specifically but nonactively. The first possibility is, therefore, that dividing cells have the same UV sites as interdivisional cells and no others. Two (II), there are at least two independent sets of UV sites, one of which governs the survival of the cell and another which can potentiate or mitigate the lethal effects of X-rays without appreciably affecting cell survival. Three (III), there is complete overlap of UV and X-ray lethality sites, although the detailed manner (accumulation of hits, etc.) in which these sites are inactivated may or may not be the same. And four (IV), there is partial overlap with or without the detailed manner of inactivation being the same. A series of additivity experiments will now be described which bear on these possibilities.

In fig. *1A*, curves *b* and *c* show the coupling effect of two different pre-UV doses. In the coupling or additivity experiments shown in this figure, as well as those to follow, labels such as UV(0.107 ± 0.004)–X mean that the unirradiated population was given a single pre-UV dose which, in this case, reduced survival to 0.11 and that this exposure was followed by a graded series of X-ray exposures. For curve *b*, the UV dose was large enough to inactivate essentially all the interdivisional cells without appreciably affecting the viability of the budding cells. For curve *c*, the UV dose was large enough to inactivate the interdivisional as well as 90% of the budding cells. Curve *b* has essentially the same shape as the X-ray tail (curve *a*), but curve *c*, plotted from the zero-dose extrapolation of *a*, shows a considerable increase in the X-ray sensitivity of the cells which survived the pre-UV exposure. Similar results are shown in Fig. *2A*, curves *a*, *b*, and *c*, for diploid cells, and Fig. *1B* shows that a spontaneous, respiration-deficient mutant of SC-7 responds similarly.

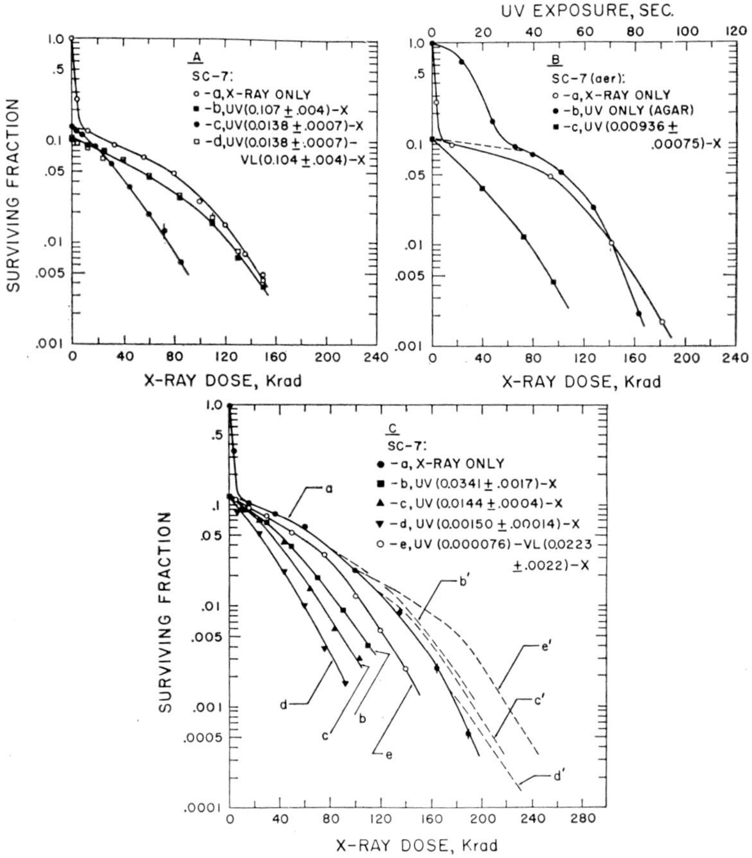

FIG. 1. The effect of UV and of UV plus photoreactivation (VL) pre-exposures on the X-ray sensitivity of dividing yeast cells. (See text for explanation of legends.) *A*, SC-7. *B*, respiration-deficient, spontaneously occurring mutant of SC-7. *C*, the effect of increasing UV exposures and photoreactivation on the X-ray sensitivity of dividing cells for SC-7.

If dividing cells are less sensitive to UV for artifactual reasons (possibility I), then survivors of pre-UV doses large enough to inactivate all the interdivisional cells plus an appreciable fraction of dividing cells should have an UV-X survival curve similar in shape to the "X-ray only" survival curve of dividing cells. The increase in X-ray sensitivity of the dividing haploid and diploid pre-UV survivors rules out possibility I. That pre-UV doses which do not appreciably affect the viability of the budding cells (curves *b*, Figs. 1*A* and 2*A*) also do not appreciably affect the shape of the X-ray tail, whereas large pre-UV doses affect both, makes possibility II quite unlikely. (Curves *d* in Figs. 1*A* and 2*A* further support this conclusion and will be discussed in the next section.)

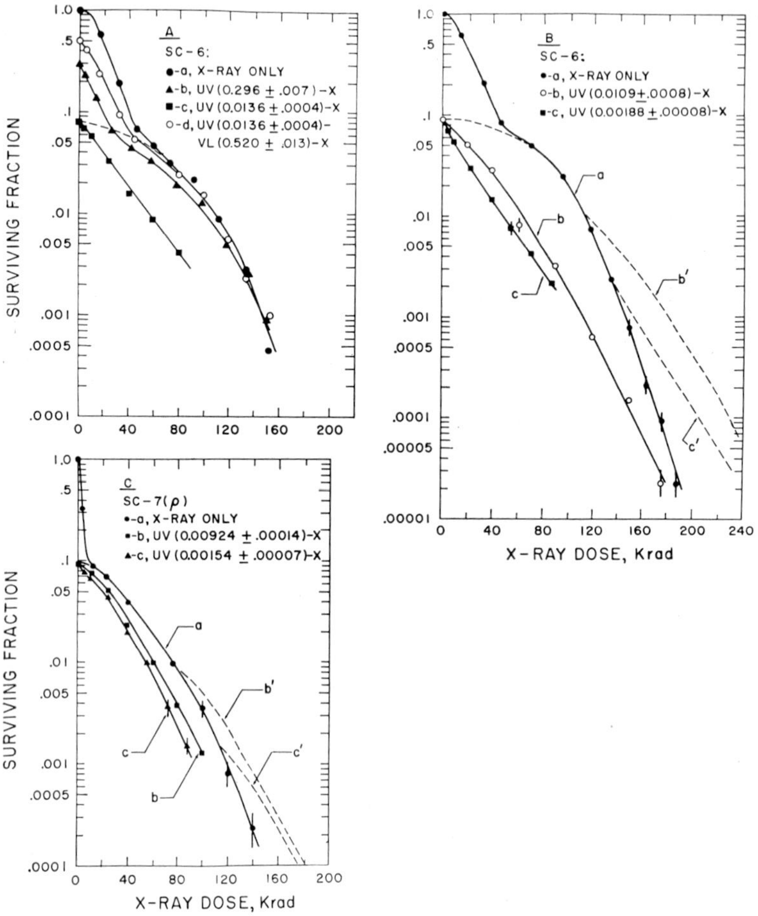

FIG. 2. The effect of UV and of UV plus photoreactivation (VL) pre-exposures on the X-ray sensitivity of dividing yeast cells. (See text for explanation of legends.) *A* and *B*, SC-6. *C*, SC-7(ρ).

In Figs. 1*C*, 2*B*, and 2*C*, the results of a series of UV–X experiments in each case are compared with the X-ray tails (curves *a*). The curves denoted by primes are plotted starting from the X-ray tails at the surviving fraction resulting from the pre-UV exposure. In each instance, the survivors of pre-UV were increasingly more sensitive to X-rays as the pre-UV exposure was increased. At a given surviving fraction, the coupling appears to be largest for SC-7, and least for SC-7(ρ). It is also seen that the primed curves do not superimpose on the X-ray tails, and in each case they lie above the "X-ray only" curves.

These results show that, although all three cell lines display evidences of overlap, the degree and/or nature of the overlap is different in each case. Since the primed curves do not superimpose on the X-ray control curves, it is also clear that the detailed manner in which UV inactivates cells is not the same as for X-rays in all respects. That the primed curves all lie above the X-ray tails may indicate that not all the X-ray sites are overlapped by UV sites. Another possibility is that there are some UV lethality sites in addition to those which couple with the X-ray tail sites. If this were true, it would be expected that a UV-X survival curve might overlap the X-ray tail starting from a survival larger than that resulting from the pre-UV exposure. For the primed curves of SC-7 and SC-7(ρ) this may be the case, although the SC-6 curves would still lie above the X-ray tail. In either event, possibility IV appears more likely than III.

Figure 3 shows a series of X–UV coupling experiments for the haploid line SC-7. As would be expected from the results shown in Fig. 2*A*, curve *c* of Fig. 3 shows that a pre-X-ray exposure which is not large enough to affect appreciably the survival of dividing cells also does not affect the shape of the UV tail. (Indeed, curve *c* can be taken to represent the UV survival curve of dividing cells only.) When the exposure is increased so that only 18 % of the dividing cells survive the pre-X-ray dose, then the resulting UV sensitivity is markedly increased (curve *d*). Although it is clear that curve *d′* does not overlap the UV tail, the roughly parallel shapes of curves

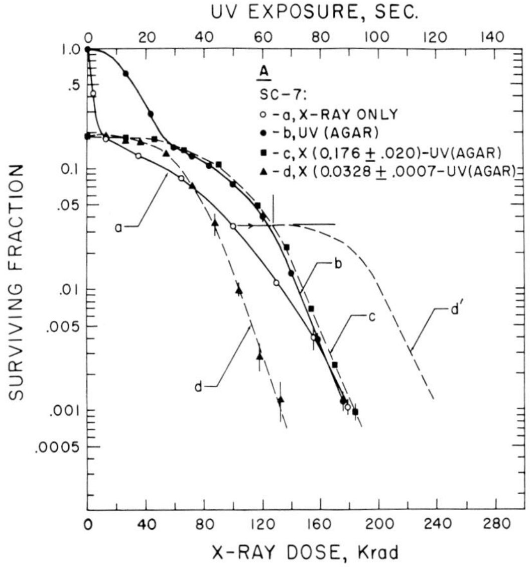

FIG. 3. The effect of X-ray pre-exposures on the ultraviolet sensitivity of dividing haploid cells, SC-7. (See text for explanation of the legends.)

b and *d* suggest that pre-X-rays reduce the number of "viable" targets per site without appreciably altering the number of sites. A similar result was obtained by Uretz for interdivisional diploid cells (*9*).

Photoreactivation. Returning to curves *d* in Figs. 1*A* and 2*A*, the effect of photoreactivation on UV–X coupling will now be discussed. In the labels of each of these curves, VL stands for visible light (photoreactivation). Curves *d* in each case were obtained by maximally photoreactivating a subaliquot of the cell suspensions which gave curves *c*, and then performing an X-ray experiment with the reactivated population (i.e., UV–VL–X). The resulting survival curves have shapes which are very similar to the tails of the X-ray control experiments, curves *a*. This shows that sites of photoreactivation overlap UV and X-ray sites, in at least an operational sense, which were shown to overlap each other, and further supports the inapplicability of possibility II as previously discussed. In the photoreactivation experiment shown in Fig. 1*C*, curve *e*, the pre-UV dose reduced the survival to to 7.6×10^{-5}, and the subsequent photoreactivating exposure increased the survival to 2.2×10^{-2}. This latter survival is larger than those corresponding to curves *c* and *d* after pre-UV, 1.4×10^{-2} and 1.5×10^{-3}, respectively, but smaller than that for curve *b*, 3.4×10^{-2}. Still curve *e* lies above curves *b*, *c*, and *d*, and *e* is closer in shape to the X-ray tail than the others. If there are UV lethality sites in addition to those which overlap X-ray lethality sites, this result suggests that the former can be reactivated to a lesser extent than the latter. If the UV–X-ray site overlap structure is more closely described by complete UV overlap but fewer UV sites than there are X-ray sites, then these results could mean that UV–X-ray coupling is reversed more effectively by visible light than is UV lethality.

Concerning the UV dose-reactivation curves discussed in reference *22* (Figs. 3 and 4), all the photoreactivation experiments just described indicate that the budding cell moiety of the UV-inactivated cells are photoreactivated first. Curve *e* of Fig. 1*C* shows that the reactivated population displays an X-ray survival curve more distinctly similar in shape to the X-ray tail than to the exponential, initial portion of the "X-ray only" survival curve. These cells were maximally photoreactivated to a survival of 0.022, which is well below the fraction of dividing cells in the unirradiated population, 0.12. Curve *d* of Fig. 1*A* is a case where maximal photoreactivation returned the surviving fraction to the same fraction, 0.11, as that corresponding to dividing cells in the unirradiated population. Here too, the UV–VL–X survival curve is very similar to that of the tail of the "X-ray only" curve. And curve *d* of Fig. 2*A* shows a case where maximal photoreactivation restored viability to some interdivisional as well as dividing cells with the presence of both moieties being apparent in the shape of the survival curve. Hence it is clear that, when UV-inactivated cells include cells in division, the latter are photoreactivated first. Consistent with this conclusion, Fig. 4 of reference *22* shows that the rate of photoreactivation is considerably greater for dividing cells than it is for interdivisional cells.

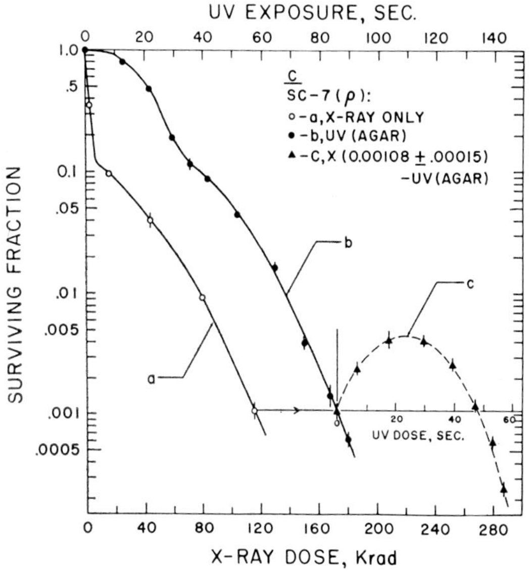

FIG. 4. The effect of X-ray pre-exposure on the ultraviolet sensitivity of dividing haploid cells, SC-7(ρ). (See text for explanation of the legends.) Note that the initial UV exposures, curve *c*, reactivate X-ray-inactivated cells.

Mitigating action of UV on X-ray lethality. To extend the X–UV coupling experiments to SC-7(ρ) and SC-6, experiments similar in every detail to those shown in Fig. 3 for SC-7 were performed. The results of these experiments, Figs. 4 and 5, show that before post-UV produces inactivation it first reactivates a fraction of the X-ray–inactivated cells. That this unexpected result was due to UV only was determined by: (1) the observation that plated cells exposed to the UV lamps with the plate covers on displayed neither reactivation nor additional inactivation; and (2) in the case of SC-7(ρ) (cells harvested from an overnight YED agar surface), a pre–X-ray exposure to a survival of 8×10^{-4} followed by exposure to visible light for 1 hour at 30°C in the photoreactivation apparatus described (*22*) did not alter the surviving fraction.

From Fig. 5, it is seen that the amount of reactivation appears to increase with increasing pre-X-ray exposure, and, as was the case with SC-7, the final shapes of the X–UV curves appear to parallel the UV tail. [Other experiments with SC-7(ρ) in which the pre-X-ray dose was smaller than that in Fig. 4 more clearly illustrated this point for SC-7(ρ).] If these latter X–UV curves were considered to be sigmoid starting from survivals somewhat larger than their maxima, the relative positions of these curves would be similar to those for SC-7. Evidence lending support to such a comparison will be presented in connection with SC-7(ρ), since it was found that these cells displayed the most UV reactivation of X-ray lethality and were there-

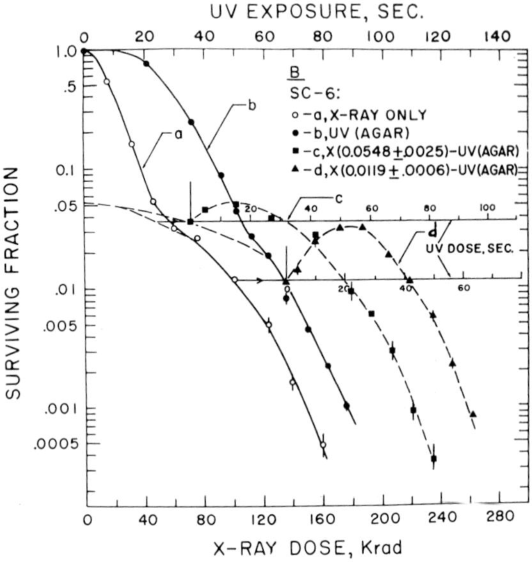

FIG. 5. The effect of X-ray pre-exposures on the ultraviolet sensitivity of dividing diploid cells, SC-6. (See text for explanation of the legends.) Note that the amount of UV reactivation depends on the pre-X-ray dose.

fore studied in detail. Although the results in Fig. 3 do not show any UV reactivation, other experiments suggested that the response of SC-7 differed only in degree (20 % post-UV reactivation at a pre-X-ray survival of 1.4×10^{-3}).

In Fig. 6, the mitigating action of pre- and post-UV exposure are compared. Curves *a* and *b* are the X-ray and UV survival curves, respectively. Curve *c* is an X-UV coupling experiment showing a maximum reactivation of a factor of 3. Curves *d* and *e* were obtained by first giving unirradiated suspensions small UV exposures (in buffer) and then performing X-ray survival experiments with the survivors. That the pre-UV doses were small can be seen from the zero X-ray dose survivals, 0.87 and 0.35, respectively. Plotted with the unirradiated titer as controls, *d* and *e* show that the portions of the survival curve corresponding to non-budding and budding cells lie, respectively, below and above the "X-ray only" survival curve. This shows that only the dividing cells were protected. Further, it can be seen from the zero X-ray dose points of *d* and *e* and the curves *b* and *c* that there is the same amount of protection if the UV is given before as there is reactivation if the UV dose is given after the X-ray exposure. Curve *e* in Fig. 7 is an X–UV–X coupling experiment showing that the UV dose can also be given during the X-ray sequence of exposures and still produce essentially the same degree of protection.

In Fig. 7, curve *b* resulted from a pre-UV exposure chosen to yield about maximum

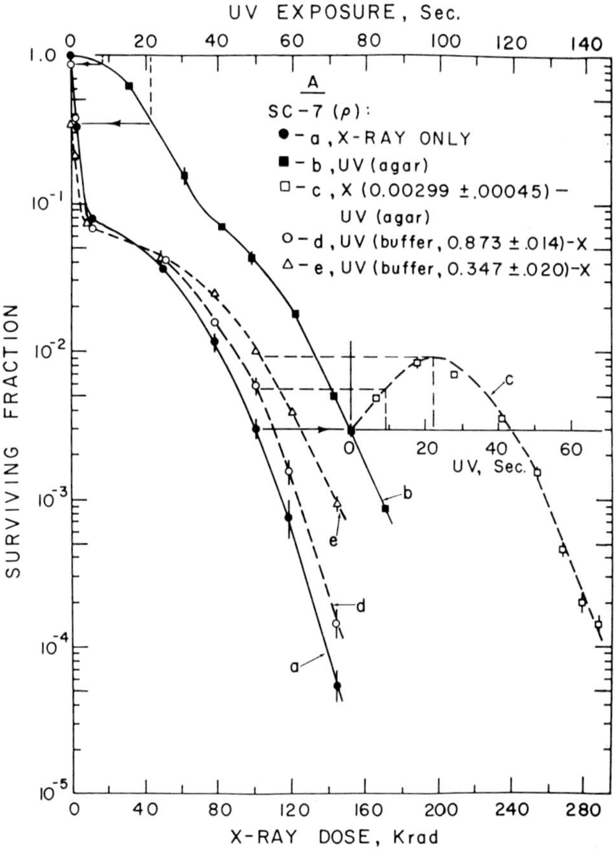

FIG. 6. The reactivation and protection effects of ultraviolet on the X-ray survival of dividing haploid cells, SC-7(ρ). (See text for an explanation of the legends.) Note the equivalent mitigating effects of pre-UV, curves *d* and *e*, and post-UV, curve *c*, exposure.

protection. Curve *b* appears functionally similar to curve *a* (X-ray only), the dose-reduction factor being 0.77. In the case of photoreactivation of yeast, dose-reduction factors of 0.4 to 0.5 (*15*), and 0.63 (*21*) have been reported. In view of the generally injurious nature of UV irradiation, a dose-reduction factor of even 0.8 is significant.

For curves *c* and *d* in Fig. 7, two subaliquots of the pre-UV-exposed suspension used for *b* were placed at 30°C. One subaliquot, curve *c*, was exposed to photoreactivating light for a maximum increase in survival, 30 minutes, and the second was shielded from the light for the same period of time, curve *d*. Curve *d* compared to *b* shows that, whatever may be the detailed nature of the protective effect produced by a small pre-UV dose, it is fairly temperature-stable. The small increase

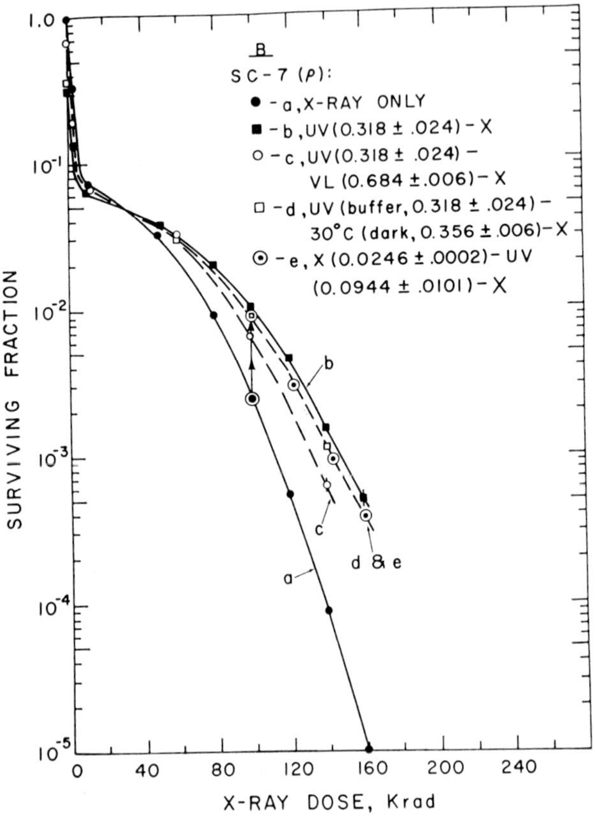

FIG. 7. Portection effect of ultraviolet on the X-ray survival of dividing haploid cells, SC-7(ρ). (See text for an explanation of the legends.) This figure shows that photoreactivation increases survival and decreases the protection effect, curve *c* compared to curve *b*.

in the zero X-ray dose survival (from 0.32 to 0.36) is accompanied by a small decrease in survival of dividing cells (curve *d* compared to *b*). Comparing curves *b* and *c*, it is seen that photoreactivation increased the zero X-ray dose titer from 0.32 to 0.68 with a corresponding larger decrease in the survival of dividing cells to subsequent X-ray exposure. This shows that photoreactivation reverses the UV effect on viability (primarily interdivisional cells) as well as the UV protection effect against X-ray inactivation. That this effect was due to visible light only is clear, since curve *d* shows the effect of the elevated temperature alone.

Figure 8 shows that UV reactivation can be increased as well as decreased by visible light. In this case, the pre-UV dose was large enough to show some amount of increased X-ray sensitivity in dividing cells (curve *b* lies below *a*). The specific

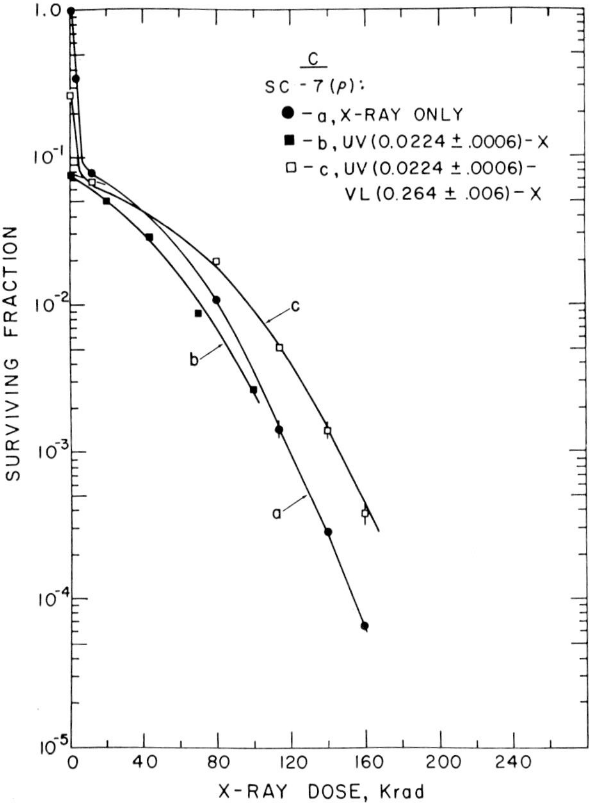

FIG. 8. Protection effect of ultraviolet on the X-ray survival of dividing haploid cells, SC-7(ρ). (See text for an explanation of the legends.) This figure shows that photoreactivation can increase survival as well as the protection effect if the pre-UV dose is in the right range.

pre-UV dose chosen was such that subsequent maximal photoreactivation could be expected to increase the surviving fraction to a level corresponding to that produced by a protective pre-UV dose alone. Curve *c* was obtained after photoreactivation of a subaliquot of the suspension used for curve *b*. The somewhat smaller degree of protection compared to curve *b* in Fig. 7 is consistent with the zero X-ray dose survival in *c* of Fig. 8, being only 0.26 as opposed to 0.32 in *B* of Fig. 7.

These results show, therefore, that photoreactivation and UV protection or reactivation of X-ray lethality in dividing cells are closely linked. Further, in a functional sense at least, sites for both of the latter effects must also overlap sites for the production of UV and X-ray lethality.

In view of the results shown in Figs. 6, 7, and 8, the effect of pre-X-rays on the

UV tail (Figs. 4 and 5) can now be more reasonably described. The post-UV survival curve appears to be a composite of an ascending reactivation curve and a descending inactivation curve. The ascending portion, in effect, reduces the amount of the pre-X-ray dose. The descending portion could be reasonably expected to start out with zero slope from a survival slightly larger than the maxima in the X–UV curves. Such curves would be similar in shape to that of curve *d*, Fig. 3, and their positions relative to the UV tail would also be similar to that shown in Fig. 3 for SC-7. Hence, it seems reasonable that all three cell lines involve similar X–UV coupling for large UV doses (as far as the lethal effects of these irradiations are concerned) and that this coupling, in terms of hit theory, is suggestive of a decrease in the number of viable targets per site without affecting the number of sites. The suggested composite nature of the X–UV curves does not alter the conclusions concerning overlap, since the sites for UV reactivation and inactivation could be the same or separate (molecularly and anatomically) and still overlap X-ray sites.

Visible-light lethality versus X-ray and UV lethality. From the results presented thus far plus those presented in reference *22*, it might reasonably be expected that all types of lethal irradiation are coupled and display differential effects on the dividing and nondividing moieties of a yeast population. That this is not generally true is shown in Fig. 9 in connection with the visible-light-sensitive strain SC-7(ρ), whose visible-light response has been previously described (*23*, *24*).

First, in order to obtain cells capable of developing light sensitivity, the cells were harvested from log phase growth in liquid YED (*23*). After washing, they were incubated at 30°C in $M/20$ neutral potassium phosphate buffer with aeration for 2½ hours. This storage period is required in order for the cells to synthesize the hemoprotein-like material which is responsible for the light sensitivity of the cells (*24*). The suspension was then transferred to about 2°C, and aliquots were removed for X-ray and UV experiments. Curves *a* and *b* are the results of these experiments and show, particularly in connection with the X-ray curve, that the population consisted of 30% dividing cells. Another aliquot of the stored suspension was used for a visible-light experiment in the manner described in reference *23* except that a 500-watt projector (*22*) was employed. During visible-light exposure, the temperature of the cell suspension was 1½°C.

The inset in Fig. 9 is the visible-light survival curve. Survivors of the last light exposure, 8.3% of the original population, were used for a second set of X-ray and UV experiments, curves *d* and *e*, respectively. Now if the population possessed a differential sensitivity to light related to the states of division of the cells, then, particularly in the case of curve *d*, the inflection point would have been shifted. Indeed, a situation comparable to that shown in Fig. 2*A* of reference *22* for UV–X coupling experiments might have been expected if dividing cells were less sensitive to light than are nondividing cells. The superimposition of curves *a* and *d* is consistent with the absence of an inflection point in curve *c* and requires the conclusions that the

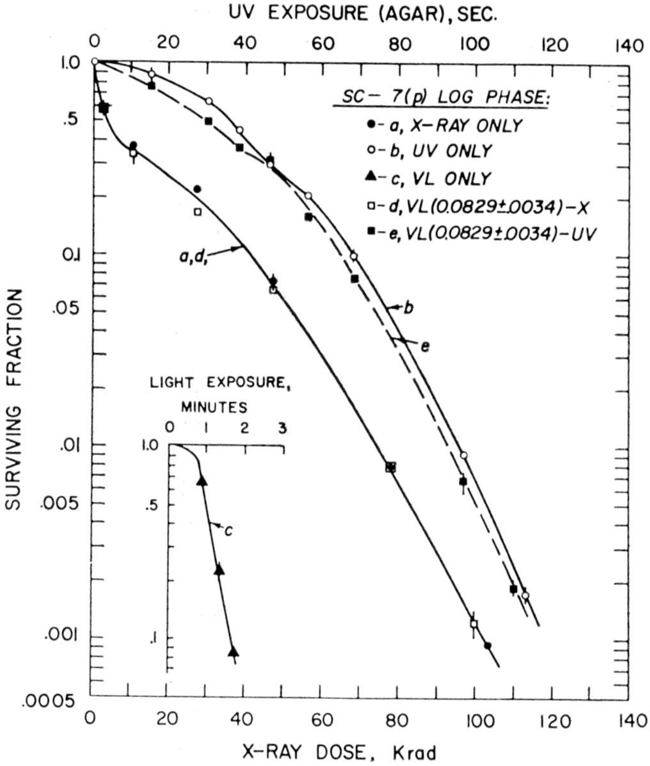

FIG. 9. Evidence for the lack of both visible-light coupling with X-ray and ultraviolet lethality as well as the absence of differential visible-light effects in a log phase population of haploid cells, SC-7(ρ). (See text for an explanation of the legends.)

state of division is unrelated to light sensitivity and that visible light does not couple with X-rays. A comparison of curves *b* and *e* show, however, that visible light couples to a small extent with UV lethality.

SUMMARY AND CONCLUSIONS

From the data presented, the general conclusion can be stated that in dividing yeast cells, irrespective of their ploidy, the competence of their respiratory systems, and their sensitivity to visible light, there is considerable overlap in sites sensitive to X-rays, ultraviolet (UV), photoreactivation (visible-light reversal of UV lethality), and the new effect, UV reactivation of or protection against X-ray lethality. Proof that the effects of these different irradiations are coupled was predicted on the lesser sensitivity to UV of dividing cells relative to interdivisional cells. This was shown to be true in reference *22*, and that the relative difference was small, which is probably the reason why this fact had not been noted earlier. Nevertheless, the existence of the difference is the significant point, and, as shown in the Appendix of reference *22*, this difference cannot be due to a simple duplication of the UV-sensitive site structure present in interdivisional cells.

Although the UV–X-ray coupling experiments described yielded indirect evidence for considerable overlap in these sites, the X-ray–UV experiments gave direct evidence of a strong interaction. Ultraviolet reactivation of X-ray lethality was shown to occur only in dividing cells, the resulting survival curve being suggestive of the composite effect of two separate processes. The initial reactivation is obviously coupled to X-ray lethality (and UV lethality through photoreactivation); the subsequent inactivation was also shown to be coupled, at least in the case of SC-7 which displayed essentially no UV reactivation. It is possible, therefore, that there are at least two types of UV sites both of which overlap X-ray sites. That the survival curves resulting from coupling experiments did not superimpose on their respective "X-ray only" or "UV only" survival curves indicates a lack of detailed and/or complete overlap of all sites. In addition, the evidence presented does not permit a choice to be made between there being fewer UV sites than X-ray sites and/or there being some UV sites in addition to those which overlap X-ray sites.

The striking correlation between the marked reduction in radiosensitivity and the incidence of budding, which is characteristic of yeast, has been taken as an indication of the effect of mitosis on the inherent radiosensitivity of genic material. This evidence is presumptive, since at the time of division cytoplasmic structures may also be undergoing changes which could be reflected in the over-all radiosensitivity of the cell. From the evidence presented here alone, no clear choice between the cytoplasm and the nucleus can be made.

There are, however, a number of experiments with which these results are consistent and which favor the nucleus. Kelner has shown in *E. coli* (*7*) that the UV inhibition of DNA synthesis could be effectively reversed by visible light but the effect of UV and visible light on RNA synthesis was minor. Brandt and Giese (*6*) and von Borstel and Wolff (*25*) have shown that the particular nuclear effects of UV that they had observed could be photoreversed, whereas the cytoplasmic effects could not be. On the basis of their own as well as a number of other observations to which they refer, Brandt and Giese postulated that photoreversible UV effects are due to nucleic acid (or nucleoprotein) as the absorbing chromophore and that in general nuclear effects would be photo-reversible but cytoplasmic effects would not be. An exception, in part, to this view may be the production of respiration-deficient cytoplasmic mutants in yeast which Raut and Simpson (*5*) showed had a nucleic acid action spectrum and which in this work (data not presented) was found to be photoreversible.

Raut and Simpson reported further that the action spectrum for lethality (visible colony suppression) also implicated nucleic acid. This they found to be true for the evaluation of the wavelength dependence at survival levels from 37 to 0.1%. Since their yeast populations consisted of about 5% budding cells, as evidenced by the level of the tail of the X-ray survival curve they published (*5*), in view of the data presented here, this also means that nucleic acid is the absorbing chromophore in dividing cells. All this is consistent with the view that the nucleus is the location of the coupled effects described in this study, and that the sites of action consist of or are closely associated with genic material.

There is additional evidence, complementing the preceding, which is concerned with the protective and reactive effect of UV on X-ray lethality. In cytogenetic studies, Swanson (*26*) found that pre- or post-UV treatment of X-irradiated *Tradescantia* pollen tubes significantly reduced the number of chromosome breaks. Also, Kaufmann and Hollaender (*27*) found that post-UV treatment of X-irradiated *Drosophila* sperm produced a similar effect. In both instances, the mitigating effect of UV was thought to be due to an increase in the probability of chromosome restitution resulting from UV exposure. The similarity of these observations with the UV protection and reactivation described here is additional evidence favoring the chromosomes as the cellular components containing the sites of action of the effects described and nucleic acid as the primary absorbing molecule.

Lastly, it should be pointed out that not all lethal irradiations couple or display differential lethality capabilities related to the state of division of the cell. This was shown to be true particularly for the case of the visible-light sensitivity of the haploid line SC-7(ρ). Since UV and X-ray lethality sites are probably nuclear, visible-light-sensitive sites are probably cytoplasmic, as one might expect from the correlation observed between the development of light sensitivity and the synthesis of an hemoprotein-like material which is probably the absorbing chromophore (*24*).

RECEIVED: May 26, 1958

REFERENCES

1. A. HOLLAENDER, *Radiation Biology*, Vols. I and II, McGraw-Hill Book Company, New York, 1954 and 1955.

2. A. NORMAN, Inactivation of *Neurospora* conidia by ultraviolet radiation. *Exptl. Cell Research* **2,** 454–473 (1951).

3. A. NORMAN, The nuclear role in the ultraviolet inactivation of *Neurospora* conidia. *J. Cellular Comp. Physiol.* **44,** 1–10 (1954).

4. C. RAUT, Heritable non-genic changes induced in yeast by ultraviolet light. *J. Cellular Comp. Physiol.* **44,** 463–475 (1954).

5. C. RAUT and W. L. SIMPSON, The effect of X-rays and of ultraviolet light of different wavelengths on the production of cytochrome-deficient yeasts. *Arch. Biochem. Biophys.* **57,** 218–228 (1955).

6. C. L. BRANDT and A. C. GIESE, Photoreversal of nuclear and cytoplasmic effects of short ultraviolet radiation on *Paramecium caudatum*. *J. Gen. Physiol.* **39,** 735–751 (1956).

7. A. KELNER, Growth, respiration, and nucleic acid synthesis in ultraviolet-irradiated and photoreactivated *Escherichia coli*. *J. Bacteriol.* **65,** 252–262 (1953).

8. H. F. BLUM, J. C. ROBINSON, and G. M. LOOS, The loci of action of ultraviolet and X-irradiation and of photorecovery in the egg and sperm of the sea urchin *Arbacia punctulata*. *J. Gen. Physiol.* **35,** 323-342 (1951).

9. R. B. Uretz, Additivity of X-rays and ultraviolet light in the inactivation of haploid and diploid yeast. *Radiation Research* **2,** 240–252 (1955).
10. R. K. Mortimer and C. A. Tobias, Evidence for X-ray induced recessive lethal mutations in yeast. *Science* **118,** 517–518 (1953).
11. R. K. Mortimer, Evidence for two types of X-ray-induced lethal damage in *Saccharomyces cerevisiae*. *Radiation Research* **2,** 361–368 (1955).
12. M. E. Owen and R. K. Mortimer, Dominant lethality induced by X-rays in haploid and diploid *Saccharomyces cerevisiae*. *Nature* **177,** 625–626 (1956).
13. N. H. Giles, Jr., Studies on the mechanism of reversion in biochemical mutants of *Neurospora crassa*. *Cold Spring Harbor Symposia Quant. Biol.* **16,** 283–313 (1951).
14. R. D. Gafford, The observation of two-process survival curves in gamma-irradiated *Neurospora* conidia. *Radiation Research* **9,** 248–259 (1958).
15. S. D. Warshaw, Effect of ploidy in photoreactivation. *Proc. Soc. Exptl. Biol. Med.* **79,** 268–271 (1952).
16. C. A. Beam, R. K. Mortimer, R. G. Wolfe, and C. A. Tobias, The relation of radioresistance to budding in *Saccharomyces cerevisiae*. *Arch. Biochem. Biophys.* **49,** 110–122 (1954).
17. M. M. Elkind and C. A. Beam, Variation of the biological effectiveness of X-rays and α-particles on haploid *Saccharomyces cerevisiae*. *Radiation Research* **3,** 88–104 (1955).
18. C. A. Beam, The influence of ploidy and division stage on the anoxic protection of *Saccharomyces cerevisiae* against X-ray inactivation. *Proc. Natl. Acad. Sci. U. S.* **41,** 857–861 (1955).
19. A. Sarachek, Ultraviolet inactivation of *Saccharomyces* during the budding cycle. *Exptl. Cell Research* **6,** 45–55 (1954).
20. A. Sarachek and W. H. Lucke, Introduction of resistance to X-ray inactivation in *Saccharomyces* by pre-exposure to 2537 Å ultraviolet radiation. *Experientia* **9,** 1–5 (1953).
21. A. Sarachek, A comparative study of the retardation of budding and cellular inactivation by ultraviolet radiation in a polyploid *Saccharomyces* with special reference to photoreactivation. *Cytologia* **19,** 77–85 (1954).
22. M. M. Elkind and H. Sutton, The relationship between division and X-ray sensitivity, ultraviolet sensitivity, and photoreactivation in yeast. *Radiation Research,* **10,** 283–295 (1959).
23. M. M. Elkind and H. Sutton, Lethal effect of visible light on a mutant strain of haploid yeast. I. General dependencies. *Arch. Biochem. Biophys.* **72,** 84–95 (1957).
24. M. M. Elkind and H. Sutton, Lethal effect of visible light on a mutant strain of haploid yeast. II. Absorption and action spectra. *Arch. Biochem. Biophys.* **72,** 96–111 (1957).
25. R. C. von Borstel and S. Wolff, Photoreactivation experiments on the nucleus and cytoplasm of the *Habrobracon* egg. *Proc. Natl. Acad. Sci. U. S.* **41,** 1004–1009 (1955).
26. C. P. Swanson, X-ray and ultraviolet studies on pollen tube chromosomes. I. The effect of ultraviolet on X-ray-induced chromosomal aberrations. *Genetics* **29,** 61–68 (1944).
27. B. P. Kaufmann and A. Hollaender, Modification of the frequency of chromosomal rearrangements induced by X-rays in *Drosophila*. II. Use of ultraviolet radiation. *Genetics* **31,** 368–376 (1946).

RADIATION RESEARCH 10, 313–322 (1959)

Long-Term Effects of Whole-body Irradiation on Lymphocyte Homeostasis in the Mouse[1]

D. METCALF[2]

The Children's Cancer Research Foundation, The Children's Medical Center, Boston, Massachusetts

INTRODUCTION

The occurrence of leukemia in man after exposure to ionizing irradiation was first documented by Aubertin (*1*). Subsequently, Krebs *et al.* (*2*) and Furth and Furth (*3*) described the induction of leukemia in mice by whole-body irradiation. These observations have been amply confirmed.

The importance of the thymus in the pathogenesis of spontaneous lymphoid leukemia was first shown by Furth (*4*). Later, it was shown by Kaplan (*5*) that thymectomy also prevented the occurrence of radiation-induced lymphoid leukemia. The exact role of the thymus in leukemogenesis is not certain. It has been shown (*6, 7*) that the thymic lymphoid tissue is a major site of leukemic transformation; hence part of the effect of thymectomy is attributable to removal of potentially neoplastic cells. On the other hand, Law (*8, 9*) has produced evidence indicating that the thymus exerts a noncellular leukemogenic influence on the remaining lymphoid tissues of the irradiated animal.

The thymus has been shown to produce a lymphocytosis-stimulating factor (LSF) (*10*). This factor is present in excessive amounts in mice with spontaneous lymphatic leukemia.

This paper describes the long-term effects of whole-body irradiation in mice on lymphocyte and LSF levels and the responsiveness of the tissues of irradiated mice to stimulation by LSF.

It has been found that, after initial depression of lymphoid tissues, irradiated mice showed persistently elevated lymphocyte and circulating LSF levels. The mice also developed an apparent unresponsiveness to LSF which was shown to be secondary to the elevated circulating levels of LSF.

[1] This investigation was supported by the National Institutes of Health (Grant C-2547), the U. S. Atomic Energy Commission, and the Anti-Cancer Council of Victoria.

[2] Present address: Walter and Eliza Hall Institute; Royal Melbourne Hospital, Parkville, Victoria, Australia.

MATERIALS AND METHODS

Mice

Male mice of the $C_{57}Bl$ strain, 4 to 6 weeks old, were obtained from the Jackson Memorial Laboratory, Bar Harbor, Maine. In two experiments, male Rf and LAF_1 mice of the same origin were used.

All mice were housed in pans in groups of 4 and given water and Purina chow ad libitum. The temperature of the animal room was kept constant at 75° to 80° F.

Irradiation

Mice received whole-body irradiation from a 250-kv X-ray source with a half-value layer of 0.5 mm Cu. The target distance was 100 cm, and the air dosage rate was 36 r/min. No additional filter was used.[3]

After irradiation, the mice were placed on oral terramycin (100 mg/l) throughout the experiments to minimize the risk of bacterial infection.

Lymphocyte Levels

White cell counts were performed on tail blood with standard human diluting pipets and counting chambers. Blood was obtained from the tail veins by pricking with a sharp scalpel, and care was taken to ensure uniformity of blood flow. All counts were performed between 10 A.M. and 12 noon to minimize any diurnal variation.

Assay for LSF

Serum from irradiated mice was assayed in 1-day-old mice of strains Rf or $C_{57}Bl$. Blood was collected aseptically from the axillary artery, allowed to clot, and the serum collected after centrifugation at $3000 \times g$ for 15 minutes. The technique for assay was as previously described (*10*).

LSF Preparations

LSF extracts were prepared by removing thymuses aseptically from young adult $C_{57}Bl$ mice. These were homogenized in penicillin/saline (1000 U/ml) with a pestle and mortar. Cellular debris was removed by centrifugation at $3000 \times g$ for 15 minutes. Four milliliters of supernatant contained material extracted from one thymus.

The LSF extract was injected into adult experimental recipient mice subcutaneously under the skin folds of the neck in such a manner that the injected material lay ventral to the injection site. One milliliter of extract was injected into each recipient mouse. Thus, each mouse received LSF extracted from one-quarter of an adult mouse thymus.

[3] For the dosimetry and irradiations we are grateful to Mr. Russell Cowing and Dr. Shields Warren, of the Cancer Research Institute, New England Deaconess Hospital, Boston.

RESULTS

Lymphocyte Levels in Irradiated Mice

In Fig. 1 are shown the lymphocyte levels found in C_{57}Bl mice receiving 250 r whole-body irradiation as compared to unirradiated controls. These figures are the mean values from three experiments using 8 mice per group.

It may be seen that in the initial phase a sharp lymphopenia occurred. Lymphocyte levels rose progressively after the first 2 weeks, reaching the levels of unirradiated mice between the third and fourth week. By the third month, lymphocyte levels had risen to about 30 to 60% above those of the nonirradiated mice. This relative lymphocytosis persisted in the irradiated mice for the remainder of the 15-months observation period, despite a gradual rise, with age, in the lymphocyte levels of nonirradiated mice. Although there was considerable individual variation in lymphocyte levels within each group, the levels of the two groups were significantly different ($P < 0.01$) at all points after the third month.

Serum LSF Levels in Irradiated Mice

A survey was made of LSF levels in irradiated and nonirradiated mice. Because of the labor involved in assaying the thymic LSF content in such mice, estimations were confined to serum LSF. Theoretically, this information is more meaningful, since serum LSF represents the circulating LSF stimulation reaching the lymphopoietic cells throughout the body.

Observations were made on mice 11 to 13 months after 350 r whole-body irradiation. No nonirradiated mice of the same age of either strain C_{57}Bl or Rf showed detectable serum LSF (Table I). On the contrary, sera of all but one of the irradiated mice produced a lymphocytosis in the test mice. Thus, it may be concluded that elevated quantities of LSF were present in the sera of these mice.

All these mice were examined postmortem. Macroscopically, no difference was

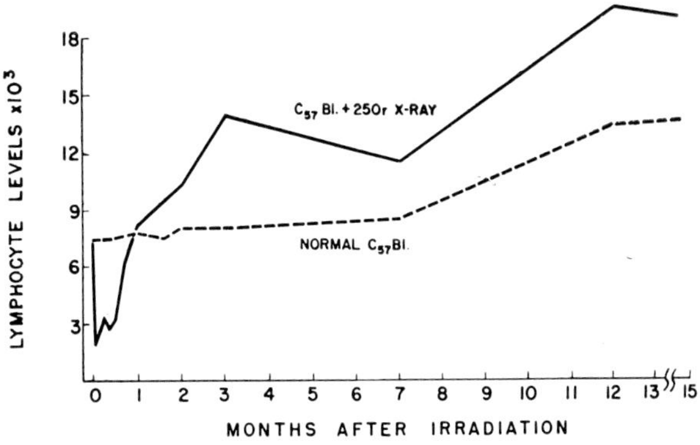

FIG. 1. Lymphocyte levels in C_{57}Bl mice receiving 250 r whole-body irradiation. Each point represents mean value of 24 mice.

TABLE I
ASSAY FOR DETECTABLE SERUM LSF IN IRRADIATED AND CONTROL MICE
(X-ray dose, 350 r)

Strain	*Number of mice tested*	*Average time after irradiation (months)*	*Average age at testing (months)*	*Lymphocyte: polymorph ratios of injected assay mice (Mean ± S.E.)*	*Number of sera with detectable LSF*
C_{57}Bl	9	11.7	12.7	4.0 ± 0.23	8/9
	10	—	13.1	2.7 ± 0.05	0/10
Rf	4	13	14	3.7 ±.0.19	4/4
	4	—	14	2.2 ± 0.08	0/4

observable between the thymuses of the two groups. They were of normal size or slightly atrophic. No gross signs of leukemia were observable in any of the mice. Microscopically, no evidence of early thymic or generalized lymphoid leukemia was found in any of the mice.

Effect of Whole-Body Irradiaton on Responsiveness to LSF

When daily white cell counts are performed on normal C_{57}Bl mice, they develop a persistent lymphocytosis in response to the trauma involved. This lymphocytosis has been shown to be mediated through thymic LSF (*11*). Groups of irradiated and nonirradiated control C_{57}Bl mice were tested at various periods after irradiation for their ability to show a lymphocytosis response.

Figure 2 shows the results obtained from six groups of C_{57}Bl mice, 2 months after a single dose of 250 r. It will be noted that, although the control mice developed a

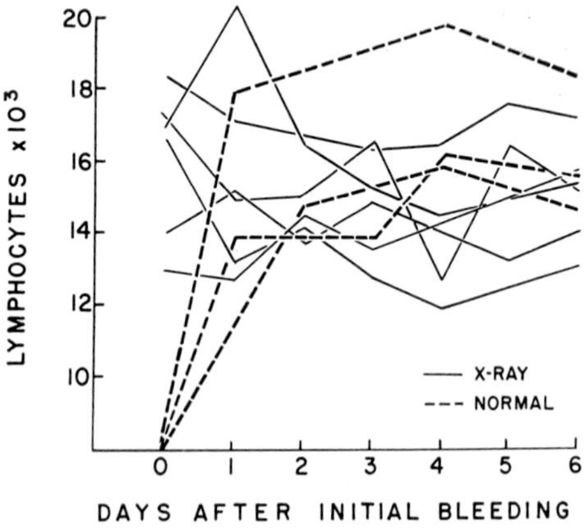

FIG. 2. Effect of 250 r whole-body irradiation in C_{57}Bl mice on ability to develop lymphocytosis response. Mice tested 2 months after irradiation. Each point represents mean value of 4 mice.

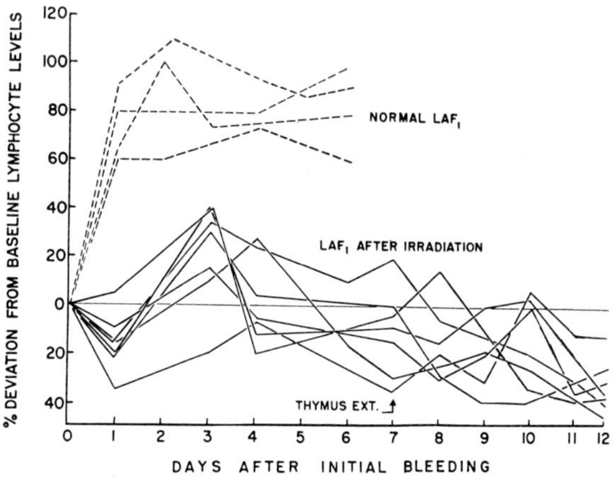

FIG. 3. Effect of 350 r whole-body irradiation in LAF_1 mice on ability to develop lymphocytosis response. Mice tested 14 months after irradiation. Each point represents a single mouse.

prompt lymphocytosis, the irradiated mice did not. It will also be noted that the initial lymphocyte levels were higher in the irradiated mice and that the lymphocytosis response in the control mice elevated their lymphocyte levels to approximately those of the irradiated groups. Similar results were obtained with mice tested 6 months after 250 r whole-body irradiation.

Figure 3 shows the results obtained from a group of LAF_1 mice irradiated with 350 r, 14 months before testing. Here the lymphocyte levels are plotted for individual mice, and subsequent changes are recorded as percentage deviations from the values on the first day. Again, no lymphocytosis occurred in the irradiated mice. On the seventh day of testing, these mice were injected with an active preparation of isologous thymic LSF. None of the mice developed a lymphocytosis in response to the LSF preparation. One month after this test, the sera from all 7 of these irradiated mice were individually assayed for LSF content, and all were found to contain elevated amounts of LSF. It should be noted in this experiment that the irradiated mice behaved as a homogeneous population.

Effect of Thymectomy on Responsiveness of Irradiated Mice to LSF

In analyzing the failure of irradiated mice to develop a lymphocytosis response to trauma, the possibility of a nonfunctional thymus was felt to be excluded. Extracts from thymuses of such mice were tested in baby mice and were found to produce a lymphocytosis. Indeed, assay of the sera from irradiated mice, as described above, showed elevated LSF levels, indicating that the thymuses in these animals were probably hyperfunctional. Further, the injection of active LSF into irradiated mice, although circumventing a possibly nonfunctional thymus, still did not result in a lymphocytosis.

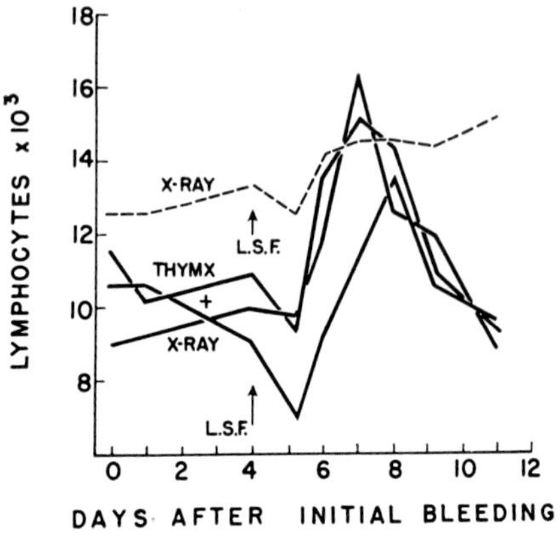

FIG. 4. Effect of preirradiation thymectomy on responsiveness of irradiated C_{57}Bl mice to stimulation by LSF. X-Ray dose 450 r. Each point represents mean value of 4 mice.

Because of these findings, the possibility was investigated that irradiated mice were already responding maximally to the elevated endogenous levels of LSF and hence were unable to develop a lymphocytosis in response to either trauma or the injection of additional LSF.

The effect of thymectomy on the responsiveness of the lymphoid tissues to LSF was therefore investigated. Groups of C_{57}Bl mice were thymectomized, others sham-thymectomized. Two weeks after operation, all groups were given 450 r whole-body irradiation in three doses of 150 r at 4-day intervals. Two months later, these mice were tested for their ability to develop a lymphocytosis response to trauma. Neither group developed a lymphocytosis. It was also noted that the thymectomized irradiated mice showed lymphocyte levels about 30% lower than the sham-operated irradiated animals. When injections of C_{57}Bl thymus extract were made, the sham-operated irradiated mice again failed to develop a lymphocytosis (Fig. 4). The thymectomized irradiated mice, however, responded with a lymphocytosis of a degree and duration similar to that previously described in thymectomized nonirradiated mice (*11*). It was also noted that the levels reached in the stimulated thymectomized irradiated mice approximated those of the sham-operated irradiated mice. This experiment was repeated with 250 r single-dose irradiation, and, as seen in Fig. 5, similar results were obtained. Thus, irradiation of thymectomized animals did not appear to affect the responsiveness of the lymphoid tissues to LSF.

It was possible that, after irradiation, the thymus might induce some change in the responsiveness of the lymphoid tissues to LSF. This was investigated by studying the effect of thymectomy performed subsequent to irradiation. Groups of C_{57}Bl mice were given 250 r whole-body irradiation. Six months later these mice

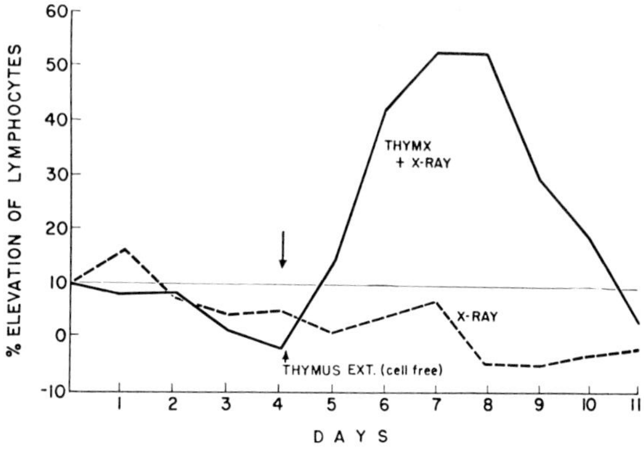

FIG. 5. Effect of preirradiation thymectomy on responsiveness of irradiated C_{57}Bl mice to stimulation by LSF. X-Ray dose 250 r. Each point represents mean value of 20 mice.

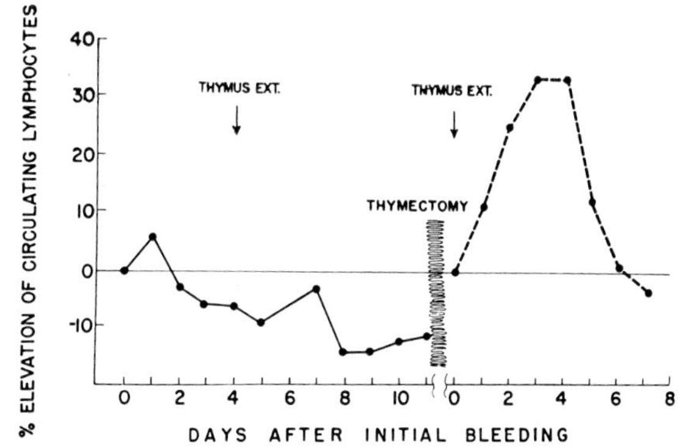

FIG. 6. Effect of postirradiation thymectomy in restoring responsiveness of irradiated C_{57}Bl mice to stimulation by LSF. X-Ray dose 250 r. Each point represents mean value of 16 mice.

were tested and found to be unable to develop a lymphocytosis in response either to trauma or to injected LSF (Fig. 6). These mice were then thymectomized. Four weeks later they were injected with C_{57}Bl thymus extract. This time a lymphocytosis did develop as in the mice thymectomized before irradiation. Thus the irradiated thymus does not appear to induce changes in the responsiveness of the lymphoid tissues to stimulation by LSF.

DISCUSSION

In the present investigation, consistently elevated lymphocyte levels were found in whole-body-irradiated mice during the period 3 to 15 months after exposure. The initial lymphopenia was exactly as described by other workers.

It is possible that considerable variation exists between species in long-term effects of irradiation on lymphocyte levels, since similar investigations in man and various animals have not shown lymphocytosis as a late effect of whole-body irradiation (*12*). It is also likely that strain differences in the response to irradiation may occur within species which might prevent the recognition of any consistent pattern in members of an irradiated non-inbred species.

The underlying mechanism of this lymphocytosis has not been fully elucidated. The present work has indicated that excess levels of LSF circulate in irradiated mice after the first few months. That this excess LSF is, in part, responsible for the lymphocytosis is suggested by the finding that thymectomized mice, after irradiation, show lymphocyte levels similar to those of nonirradiated mice. Injection of LSF into thymectomized irradiated mice elevates the lymphocyte levels in these mice to those of irradiated sham-operated mice.

The evidence, from serum assays of LSF, that thymic LSF production is excessive in irradiated mice was supported by the finding that such mice were unable to develop a lymphocytosis in response to trauma or to injection of LSF. Mice have been shown to exhibit a plateau type of response to increasing amounts of LSF (*13*). This suggested that irradiated mice might already be responding maximally to LSF and hence would be unable to respond to further increases in LSF.

Thymectomy, possibly by removing the intrinsic source of such excess LSF, enabled irradiated mice to respond normally to injected LSF. The effect of thymectomy was the same whether it was performed before or 6 months after irradiation. No evidence was obtained that irradiation had altered the responsiveness of the lymphoid cells to the stimulation of injected LSF.

It has previously been observed (*14*) that normal mice of the high-leukemia strains AkR and C_{58} show elevated lymphocyte and LSF levels as compared to low-leukemia strain mice. In addition, an apparently primary unresponsiveness to LSF is also present in strains AkR and C_{58}.

Thus, whole-body irradiation appears to convert the low-leukemia type of lymphocyte and LSF levels to the high-leukemia type. In the case of irradiated mice, however, the observed unresponsiveness to LSF was found to be secondary to elevated circulating LSF levels in these animals. It is tempting to speculate that the observed changes in thymic function and lymphocyte homeostasis reported here represent an intrinsic part of the leukemogenic process after irradiation. If this is true, then two features of these changes should be commented on. First, the changes were observed in virtually all irradiated mice. This is in contradistinction to the leukemogenic effect where only 70 to 80% of mice of strain C_{57}Bl develop leukemia, even after optimal doses of irradiation. This situation in no way differs, however, from that found in the high-leukemia strains where, although every mouse shows abnormal lymphocyte homeostasis (*14*) and all carry the genes potentiating leukemia development (*15*), only 80 to 90% of the mice develop leukemia. Second, the dose of irradiation used in some of these experiments was a low-leukemogenic one. Despite this, such irradiated mice showed the same changes as did mice receiving higher doses of irradiation. Thus, if the changes in lymphocyte homeostasis reported here are related to the pathogenesis of lymphoid leukemia, then either quantitative factors are important or other cofactors are required for the subsequent development of leukemia.

SUMMARY

1. After whole-body irradiation with 250 or 350 r, a persistent lymphocytosis develops in C_{57}Bl mice, subsequent to the initial lymphopenia.
2. Serum assays of irradiated mice showing this lymphocytosis reveal elevated levels of the thymic lymphocytosis stimulating factor (LSF).
3. Irradiated mice do not develop a lymphocytosis in response to either trauma or the injection of LSF.
4. Thymectomy, either before or after irradiation, allows normal responsiveness of irradiated mice to LSF.

ACKNOWLEDGMENT

I wish to thank Mrs. Sah Cook Cho for her technical assistance throughout this work.

RECEIVED: June 4, 1958

REFERENCES

1. C. AUBERTIN, Leucemie myéloide chez les radiologists. *Bull. soc. franç. électrothér. et radiol.* **40,** 218–226 (1931).
2. C. KREBS, A. WAGNER, and H. C. RASK-NIELSEN, The origin of lymphosarcomatosis and its relation to other forms of leucosis in white mice. *Acta Radiol. Suppl.* **10,** 1–53 (1930).
3. J. FURTH and O. B. FURTH, Neoplastic diseases produced in mice by general irradiation with X-rays. I. Incidence and types of neoplasms. *Am. J. Cancer* **28,** 54–65 (1936).
4. D. P. MCENDY, M. C. BOON, and J. FURTH, On the role of the thymus, spleen and gonads in the development of leukemia in a high leukemia stock of mice. *Cancer Research* **4,** 377–383 (1944).
5. H. S. KAPLAN, Influence of thymectomy, splenectomy and gonadectomy on incidence of radiation induced lymphoid tumors in strain C_{57}Bl mice. *J. Natl. Cancer Inst.* **11,** 83–90 (1950).
6. J. FURTH, Prolongation of life with prevention of leukemia by thymectomy in mice. *J. Gerontol.* **1,** 46–52 (1946).
7. H. S. KAPLAN, Comparative susceptibility of the lymphoid tissues of strain C_{57}Bl mice to the induction of lymphoid tumors by irradiation. *J. Natl. Cancer Inst.* **8,** 191–197 (1948).
8. L. W. LAW, Increase in incidence of leukemia in hybrid mice bearing thymic transplants from a high leukemic strain. *J. Natl. Cancer Inst.* **12,** 789–796 (1951).
9. L. W. LAW and M. POTTER, The behaviour in transplant of lymphocytic neoplasms arising from parental thymic grafts in irradiated thymectomized hybrid mice. *Proc. Natl. Acad. Sci. U. S.* **42,** 160–167 (1956).
10. D. METCALF, The thymic origin of the plasma lymphocytosis stimulating factor. *Brit. J. Cancer* **10,** 442–457 (1956).

11. D. METCALF and R. F. BUFFETT, Lymphocytosis response in mice and its relation to thymus and adrenal. *Proc. Soc. Exptl. Biol. Med.* **95,** 576–579 (1957).
12. W. BLOOM and L. O. JACOBSON, Some hematologic effects of irradiation. *Blood* **3,** 586–592 (1948).
13. D. METCALF, The thymic lymphocytosis stimulating factor. *Ann. N. Y. Acad. Sci.* (Conference on Hodgkin's Disease, November, 1957) **73,** 113–119 (1958).
14. D. METCALF and R. F. BUFFETT, Abnormal lymphocyte homeostasis in high leukemia strain mice. *Proc. Am. Assoc. Cancer Research* **2,** 326–327 (1958).
15. R. K. COLE and J. FURTH, Experimental studies on the genetics of spontaneous leukemia in mice. *Cancer Research* **1,** 957–965 (1941).

RADIATION RESEARCH **10**, 323–334 (1959)

Radium in Human Bone: The Microradiographic Appearance[1]

R. E. ROWLAND, J. H. MARSHALL, AND J. JOWSEY

Radiological Physics Division, Argonne National Laboratory, Lemont, Illinois

INTRODUCTION

Radium-burdened human beings who have carried their radioactivity for periods of 20 to 40 years provide a unique source of information on the effects of uninterrupted irradiation of bone for long periods of time. The large number of patients potentially available (*1*) suggests the possibility of studying many details of radium poisoning on a statistical basis. Such studies may reveal factors that influence the biological effects under these conditions of irradiation.

Several excellent reports have described the gross changes appearing in bones of individuals burdened with radium (*1–4*). In this report we describe lesions in bone as revealed by microradiographic analysis of thin bone sections and make a first attempt at correlation between these phenomena and the local concentrations of radium.

MATERIAL

Samples of cortical bone from the tibia and/or femur from 15 individuals with terminal Ra^{226} burdens of 0.8 to 10.5 μc have been examined. Twelve of these cases who have carried a radium burden for more than 20 years are listed in Table I, with their terminal burden, the route of acquisition of their radium, and the age at which it was acquired.

Skeletal samples have also been examined from 17 human beings, most of whom were from 50 to 80 years old and had no history of radium exposure. These control bones were for the most part from normal individuals, a few of whom had senile osteoporosis, but none of whom had any history of bone cancer.

QUANTITATIVE MICRORADIOGRAPHY

In microradiographs of thin sections of undecalcified bone the pattern of mineral densities that exist in various structures, such as the haversian systems, are revealed by regions of various opacities, whereas the blood-carrying haversian canals, the

[1] Work performed under the auspices of the U. S. Atomic Energy Comission.

TABLE I

Radium Patients

Patient	*Terminal radium burden (μc)*	*Sex*	*Age when acquired*	*Method of acquisition*	*Age at death*	*Years radium carried*	*Comments*
118	10.5	F	48	Medically: Ra water?	84	36	Low Ca diet at time of Ra acquisition
103	6.8	F	36	Medically: I.V.?	64	28	Fibrosarcoma
302	3.8	F	15	Dial painter for 2 months	47	32	Osteogenic sarcoma
R	3.6	F	32	Medically: I.V. 41 weekly injections	56	24	10 μc Ra^{226} per injection, osteogenic sarcoma
RB	2.7	F	20	Dial painter for 1 year	53	33	Carcinoma of right mastoid
313	1.3	F	18–47	Dial painter for 28 years	48	30	Tipped brush with lips for first 2 years, fibrosarcoma
IJ	1.2	F	18–21	Dial painter for 3½ years		31	Sample obtained age 49; resection of upper third of femur, sarcoma
Q	1.2	M	33	Medically: I.V. 45 weekly injections	59	26	10 μc Ra^{226} per injection
BM	1.2	M	21–23	Medically: I.V. injections	51	28–30	Osteogenic sarcoma
112	1.2	F	25	Medically: oral	48	23	Fibrosarcoma
ML	~1	F	16–17	Dial painter for 18 months		39	Amputation, age 55, osteogenic sarcoma
I	0.8	F	28	Medically: I.V. 18 weekly injections	53	26	10 μc Ra^{226} per injection

lacunae of the osteocytes, and the resorption tunnels appear as dark regions in which no material is present. The differences between normal and radium-bearing bone that can be shown by the microradiographic technique are therefore changes in the inorganic content of these structures.

The most characteristic change appearing in bones burdened with radium is the plugging of the haversian canal with mineral of a density higher than that of normal bone (Fig. 1). These plugged canals have been found in 14 of our 15 cases, and their widespread occurrence in cortical bone can be seen by reference to Table II, where the percentage of haversian systems[2] seen to have plugs is tabulated. These percentages were obtained from counts over at least 1000 different haversian systems from each individual and, whenever possible, from sections cut from different bones. Often these plugged systems occur in groups, as shown in Fig. 2, and in such cases the fraction of the systems plugged was obtained by counting the plugs in a com-

[2] In this paper we use the term "haversian system" to refer to a 100-μ-long segment of an osteon.

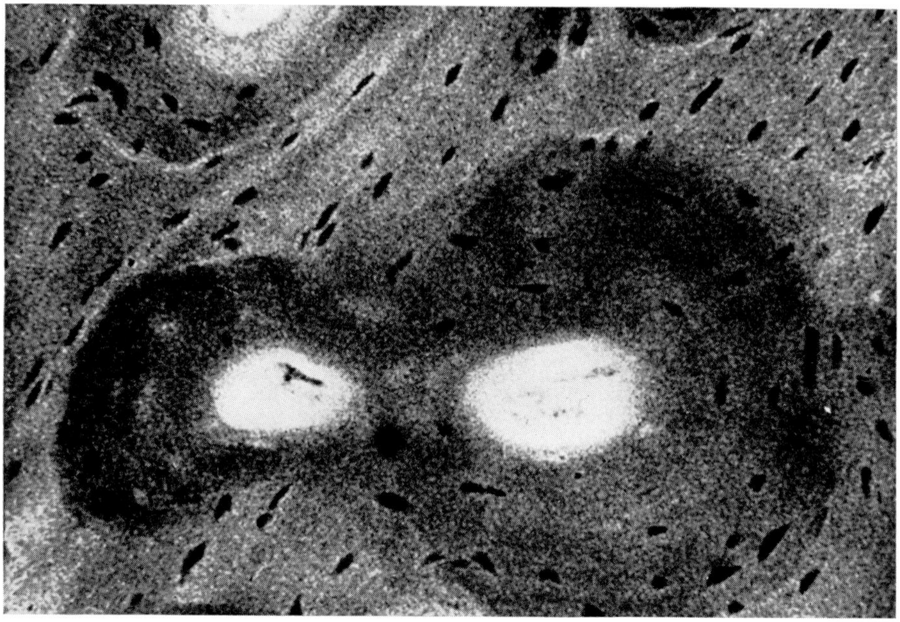

FIG. 1. A microradiograph of two merging haversian systems with plugged canals. Case R. (376 ×)

TABLE II

OCCURRENCE OF THE MICRORADIOGRAPHIC CHANGES

Patient	*Terminal radium burden* (μc)	*Initial activity ratio:* Ra^{228}/Ra^{226}	*Percentage of haversian canals plugged*	*Abnormally dense haversian systems*[a]	*Filled lacunae*[a]	*Bizarre resorption*[a]	*Enlarged lacunae*[a]
118	10.5	0.0003	25%	+	+	+	0
103	6.8	0.0004	22%	+	+	+	+
302	3.8	—	29%	+	0	0	0
R	3.6	0.0002	10%	+	0	0	0
RB	2.7	—	29%	+	+	+	+
313	1.3	0.0013	22%	+	0	0	0
IJ	1.2	0.02	9.5%	+	+	+	+
Q	1.2	0.0002[b]	8%	+	0	0	+
BM	1.2	—	5.5%	0	+	+	0
112	1.2	0.012	2%	+	0	0	0
ML	~1	—	9%	+	+	+	0
I	0.8	0.0002[b]	<0.01%	0	0	0	0

[a] Symbol + = microradiographic change was observed; symbol 0 = change was not observed.

[b] Not measured, but assumed to be identical to case R, for these patients acquired their radium at the same time and from the same source (5).

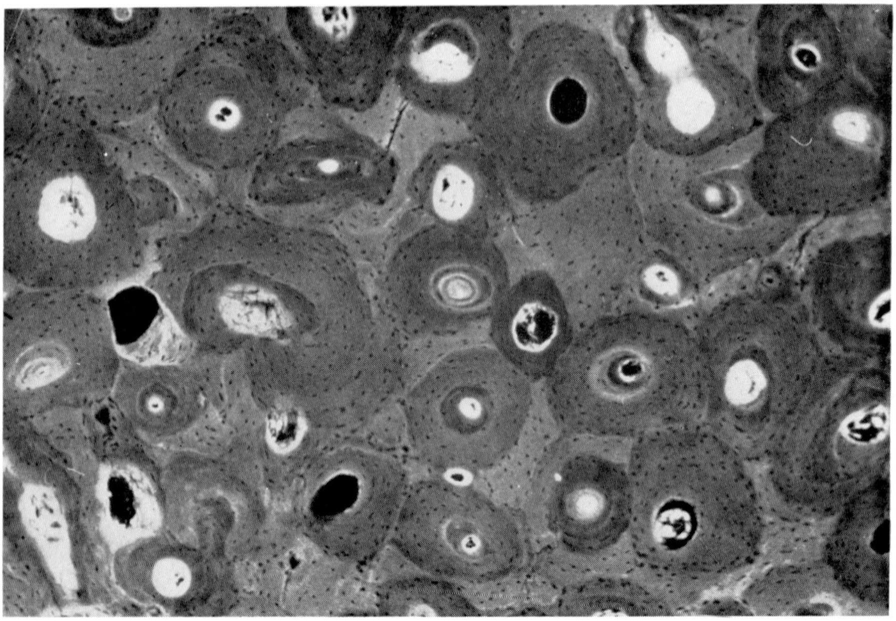

FIG. 2. A microradiograph of a region in the cortex of the tibia in which a large number of haversian systems are plugged. Case 118. (73 ×)

plete cross section of the femur or tibia. Plugged canals are rarely found in normal bone; three plugs were found in one control, none in all the sections examined from the other 16 controls.

These plugs have been traced through centimeter lengths of cortical bone to determine their length. Microradiographs were made of 30 sections, each 100 μ thick, and separated by 150 μ, the thickness of the saw employed to cut the sections. Osteons in which the central canal was plugged could easily be traced from one section to the next with these microradiographs. This three-dimensional analysis indicated that, although some canals were plugged for as much as 3 mm or more, most of them were plugged for only about 0.5 mm, a distance short compared with the length of the osteon. This observation implies that the fraction of osteons which contained a plug somewhere along their length was quite large, larger than the percentage of haversian systems showing plugs, as tabulated in Table II.

To determine whether or not any correlation exists between these plugged canals and the local high concentrations of radium, a careful comparison between stripping film autoradiographs and the corresponding microradiographs has been made. This comparison showed no correlation between plugged canals and hotspots.[3] The frac-

[3] The term "hot spot" refers to a region of high concentration of radium, often found in haversian systems and in subperiosteal or endeosteal bands of bone.

tion of hotspots containing plugged canals is virtually the same as the fraction of all haversian systems which contain plugs, implying a random distribution of the plugged canals with respect to concentration of radium. The fact that there are several times as many plugged canals as hotspots per bone section is also an indication that the occurrence of plugs is not directly related to the concentrations of activity left 20 years or more after the initial radium deposition. As for the relationship between plugged canals and initial concentrations of activity, not much can be said until the long-term behavior of the latter, both as to number and to specific activity, is known in sufficient detail.

The mineral composition of the plugs has been studied by quantitative microradiographic techniques. The maximum density of normal human bone is 0.58 gm of Ca per cubic centimeter (*6*), whereas these plugs contain 0.65 gm of Ca per cubic centimeter. Expressed in terms of hydroxyapatite, these values are 1.44 gm and 1.62 gm of hydroxyapatite per cubic centimeter, respectively. The density of solid hydroxyapatite is 3.15 gm/cm^3, so these plugs are far from being solid mineral. The Ca/P ratio in the plug was measured by microradiographing bone sections with monoenergetic X-rays of energy just greater than the K-absorption edge of calcium, 4.04 kev, and then making a second radiograph with X-rays of energy less than this edge. Quantitative analysis of these two plates showed the same Ca/P ratio in the plugs as in the adjacent osteons.

A second abnormality noted in the microradiographs is shown in Fig. 3. A major fraction of, or even an entire, haversian system will appear at a mineral density as high as that found in the plugged canals. These systems contain apparently normal lacunae and an unplugged central canal, and they usually extend about 1 mm in length. Often they appear to end in a resorption cavity. Such systems have not been found to be hotspots; we cannot tell whether they contain less activity than the surrounding mineral, for the statistical accuracy of α-track counting over such a small area is very poor. The cases in which these abnormally dense haversian systems have been observed are indicated in Table II, as is also the occurrence of the other abnormalities discussed below. Only one such hypercalcified system has been found in the control sections.

A third type of increased mineralization is shown in Fig. 4. Here the lacunae, which normally contain osteocytes, are filled with mineral and appear more dense than the surrounding bone. If the mineral in these cavities 10 to 12 μ deep is hydroxyapatite, a density of about 3 gm/cm^3 is required to produce the observed appearance, implying that the cavities contain almost solid hydroxyapatite. Monoenergetic X-ray analysis of these regions indicates that they contain both calcium and phosphorus, although they are too small in area to permit quantitative analysis. Since hydroxyapatite is one of the most dense minerals containing both of these elements, it appears reasonable to assume this composition for the mineral in the cavities.

Such filled lacunae are often seen in microradiographs of bone sections from hu-

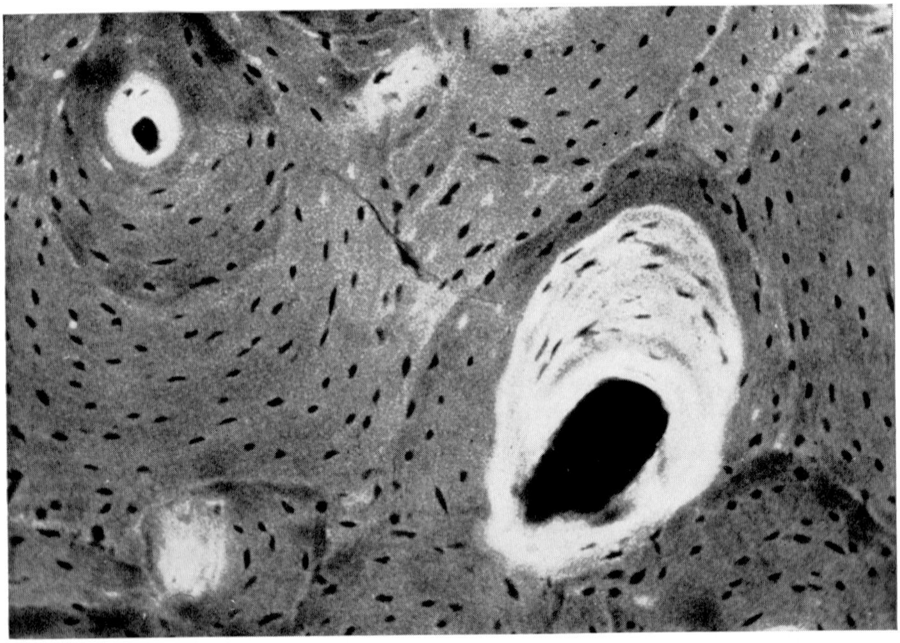

FIG. 3. A microradiograph showing haversian systems of abnormally high density. Case 103. (189 ×)

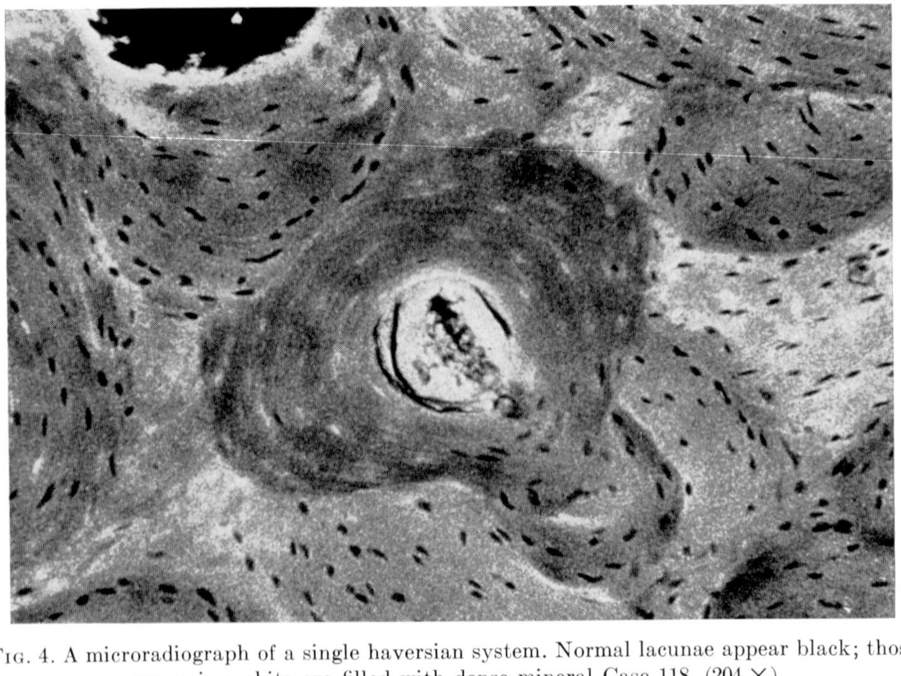

FIG. 4. A microradiograph of a single haversian system. Normal lacunae appear black; those appearing white are filled with dense mineral Case 118. (204 ×)

man subjects over 50 years old. Those seen in the control samples, however, always have had apparently normal lacunae intermixed with them, whereas in these radium cases often all the lacunae in a region are filled. The filled regions may be followed from section to section, although no quantitative measure of the length of such regions has been attempted. The regions containing filled lacunae are not radium hotspots.

Two unusual types of mineral resorption are found in the microradiographs of radium-bearing bone. The first of these, illustrated in Fig. 5, we have called enlarged lacunae. These lacunae have poorly defined edges and give the impression that the mineral is dissolving around them. The lacunae have usually been found in haversian systems of low mineral density; three or four adjacent osteons will show these peculiar lacunae, but the change seems to be confined to the osteon, for lacunae in adjacent bone are not affected. The osteons containing these characteristic lacunae have been traced by serial sectioning and found to contain such lacunae for about 1 mm of their length. These systems never have been found to contain high concentrations of radium.

The second type of resorption, illustrated in Fig. 6, is characterized by smooth-walled alcoves which define the edges of a resorption cavity. Often a line of spherical cavities, 20 to 30 μ in diameter, will extend out from the area of resorption into the

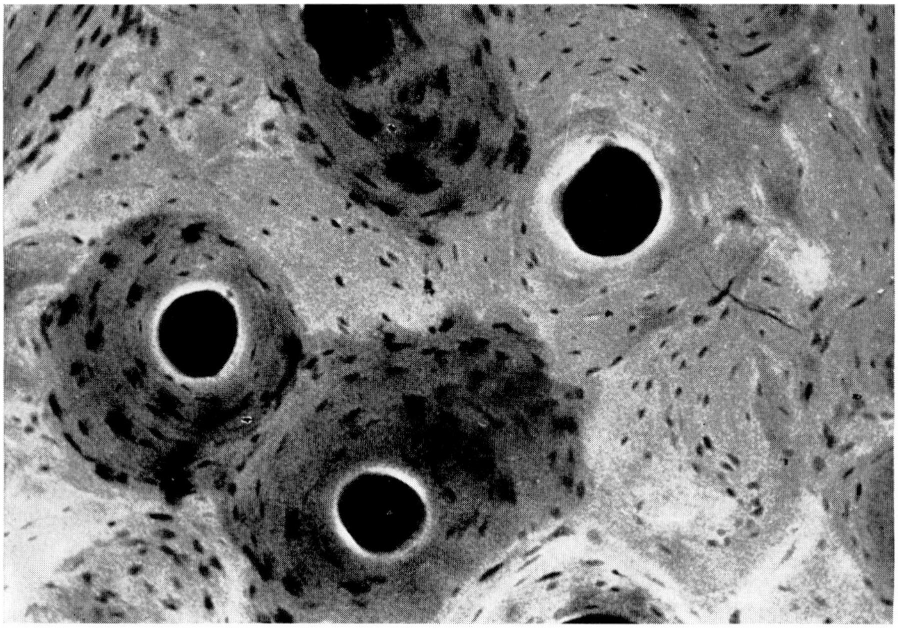

FIG. 5. A microradiograph of an area of bone showing enlarged lacunae. Case 103. (194 ×)

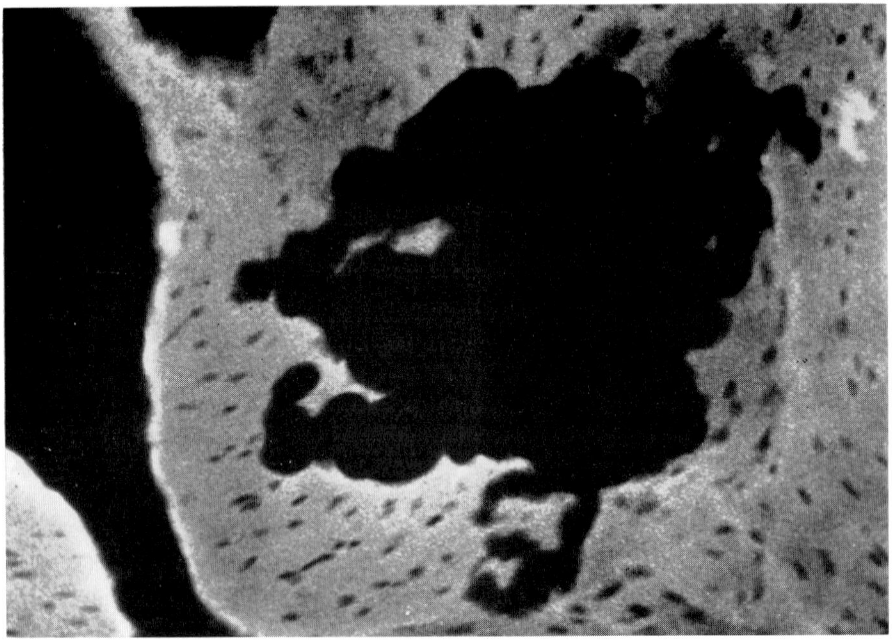

FIG. 6. A microradiograph of a small region of bizarre resorption. Note the unusual tunnels and the scalloped edges. Case RB. (237 ×)

compact bone, looking very much like a tunnel formed by a chain of hollow beads. Often these cells of resorption extend only a part of the way through a bone section, as in the extension from the central cavity at the bottom of Fig. 6. These cavities do not appear to coincide in position with the lacunae. This bizarre resorption has been found to occur to a much smaller extent in control bone sections where rapid resorption is known to be taking place.

Gross X-rays of the long bones of human beings burdened with radium show regions of reduced density in the cortex. When such regions are examined by the microradiographic technique they are often found to be made up of many large cavities in the cortical bone, rather than one large hole (Fig. 7). Sometimes, however, the resorption seems to start at the periosteal or endosteal surface and erode a single large hole into the cortical bone (Fig. 8). In agreement with what has been pointed out previously (7), we find that these regions never contain large concentrations of radium. Although it is obvious from the microradiograph that such a region should not be expected to show a radium concentration, for there is no mineral left within the region to retain it, it is unlikely that the resorption in this rather vast region took place in exactly the same areas where radium deposition was high. To form a hotspot, bone remodeling must be taking place during the period when

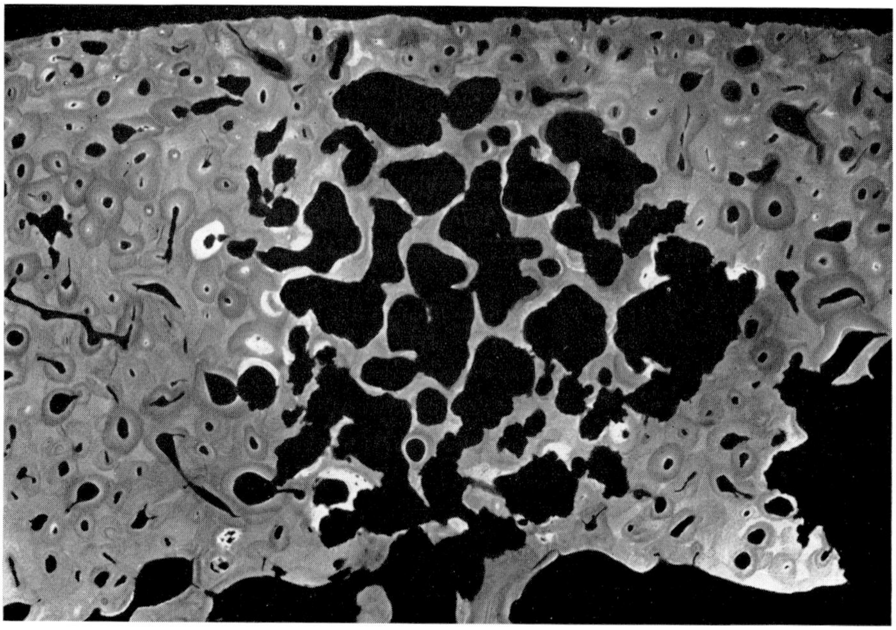

FIG. 7. A microradiograph of a gross region of destruction in the cortex of the femur. Case 103. (16 ×)

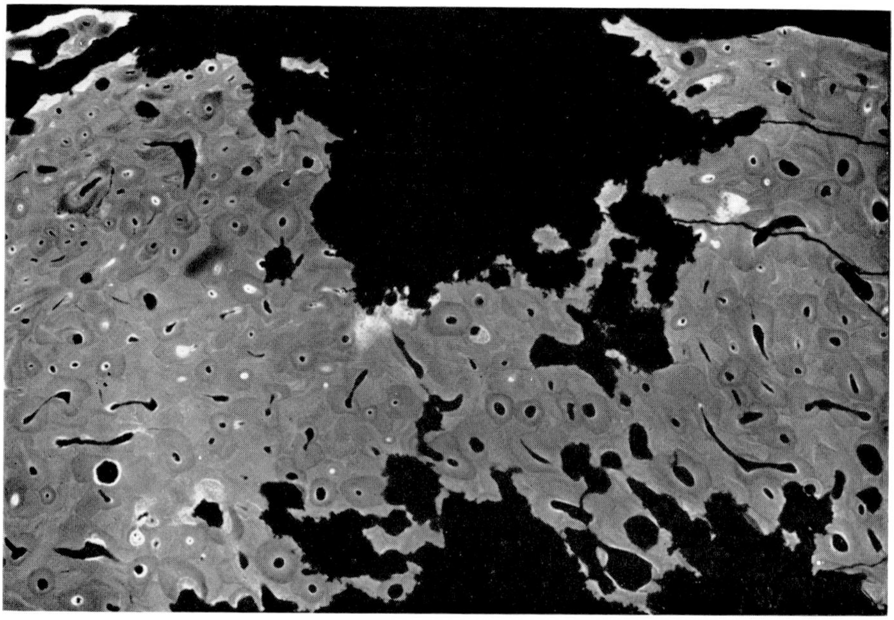

FIG. 8. A microradiograph of a gross region of destruction in the cortex of the femur. Case RB. (16 ×)

radium was in the blood or must have taken place immediately before or after the radium was acquired. This process does not label all the osteons in a given region of bone in an adult but rather produces a spotty distribution of labelled systems throughout the bone. Hence, we are inclined to believe that these gross regions of resorption do not remove exclusively volumes of radiation-damaged bone but are rather an indication of increased resorption followed by failure of the rebuilding processes.

DISCUSSION

These particular microradiographic changes have been reported here not in the sense that they may be specific to radiation-damaged bone but rather because their frequency and widespread occurrence in radium-bearing bone may give an indication of the abnormal metabolic processes occurring under the influence of continued irradiation. The plugged canals, for example, indicate disruption of the blood flow; the many regions which exist similar to that illustrated in Fig. 2 imply the existence of widespread circulatory damage throughout the cortical bone.

Some of these changes have been observed in isotope-burdened dogs; hypercalcified plugs and abnormally dense haversian systems have been reported in dogs burdened with radium and in those burdened with radiothorium (*8*). In two Sr^{90}-burdened dogs we have found plugged canals, but none of the other changes described above. One dog, to which 2 mc was administered, had carried the burden for 3 years; the other had retained 10 μc of Sr^{90} at the end of $10\frac{1}{2}$ years after administration of mixed Sr^{89} and Sr^{90}. It would be of interest to determine which, if any, of these changes could be produced by X- or γ-irradiation of bone, and the dose required.

None of the lesions which we have described appears to be located in a region of high radium concentrations. Radium, however, is also distributed uniformly throughout the mineral of bone as well as in the hotspots. Thus all volumes of bone receive a radiation dose from this diffuse distribution of radium. The possibility still exists, then, that the diffuse dose may cause these changes. In the hotspots the dose might be high enough to kill all the cells, whereas in the remaining bone the dose may be sufficient only to injure them, and hence produce abnormalities. This argument fails, however, when we examine in detail the dose distributions; in high-level patients the dose due to the diffuse radium deposits approaches in magnitude the dose due to hotspots in the patients with the lowest burdens. Hence, there should be a higher incidence of bone changes in hotspots in low-level patients if a comparable dose produced by the diffuse radium distribution was responsible for the randomly distributed changes in the high-level patients. This is not observed.

There is always doubt, when attempting to correlate damage with the radium body burden, as to whether the acquired burden was pure Ra^{226} or a mixture of Ra^{228} and Ra^{226}. In the latter case, since Ra^{228} has a 6.7-year half-life, most of it would have decayed by the time the *in vivo* measurements were made. We are fortunate in that bone samples from six of these cases have been analyzed by Wallace and Stehney (*9*) for Ra^{228}. The Ra^{228} content has been expressed in Table II as the ratio of Ra^{228} activity to Ra^{226} activity that existed at the time the radium was acquired. It is apparent that the dose from Ra^{228} was not appreciable in any of these measured cases.

The increase in number of plugged canals with terminal body burden suggests that the two are related. There are a few cases, such as 302, RB, 313, and ML, that appear to have an abnormally high fraction of plugs for their body burden. For three of these cases—302, RB, and ML—Ra^{228} measurements have not yet been made, so these high values might be the result of a higher dose than the Ra^{226} body burden indicates. On the other hand, these particular cases acquired their radium when they were less than 20 years old, so that the changes we see today may well have been the result of the initial high uptake in younger bone.

Hindmarsh and Vaughan (*10*) state that in the microradiographs made from a case in which the terminal burden was 0.48 μc no gross morphological differences from the controls were apparent. In our case with the lowest terminal burden (I at 0.8 μc) none of the microradiographic abnormalities present at the higher levels were found. Before any conclusions can be safely drawn, however, regarding the frequency of occurrence of mineral changes at low body burdens, many more low-level cases will have to be examined. Moreover, since after two decades less than 1% of the original radium administered remains in the bones, and since one-half of the total dose delivered to the bones over this period occurred in the first 3 years (*11*), it is apparent that a study of cause and effect must take into account an accurate description of radiation dose *in situ* at much earlier times.

CONCLUSIONS

Changes occur in the mineral components of human bone when it contains Ra^{226}. These changes are not necessarily found in the regions of high concentration of radioactivity. The uniformity with which these microradiographic abnormalities are seen throughout cortical bone suggests that these lesions are probably only symptomatic of the primary radiation damage.

ACKNOWLEDGMENTS

This study would not have been possible without the continued support of Dr. R. J. Hasterlik, of the Argonne Cancer Hospital, and Dr. A. J. Finkel, of the Argonne National Laboratory. It has been undertaken at the suggestion of L. D. Marinelli, to whom we are also indebted for continued advice and criticism. Some of the human bone samples were provided by Dr. R. D. Evans, of the Massachusetts Institute of Technology, Dr. F. E. Hoecker, of the University of Kansas, Dr. W. P. Norris, of the Argonne National Laboratory, and Dr. H. Q. Woodard, of the Sloan-Kettering Institute, New York. Dr. M. Finkel kindly supplied the samples from the Sr^{90} dogs.

RECEIVED: June 17, 1958

REFERENCES

1. W. B. LOONEY, R. J. HASTERLIK, A. M. BRUES, and E. SKIRMONT, A clinical investigation of the chronic effects of radium salts administered therapeutically (1915–1931). *Am. J. Roentgenol. Radium Therapy Nuclear Med.* **73,** 1006–1037 (1955).
2. H. S. MARTLAND, Occupational poisoning in the manufacture of luminous watch dials. *J. Am. Med. Assoc.* **92,** 466–552 (1929).
3. J. C. AUB, R. D. EVANS, L. H. HEMPELMANN, and H. S. MARTLAND, The late effects of internally-deposited radioactive materials in man. *Medicine* **31,** 221–329 (1952).
4. R. J. HASTERLIK, The delayed toxicity of radium deposited in the skeleton of human beings. *Proc. Intern. Conf. Peaceful Uses Atomic Energy, Geneva, 1955* **11,** 149–155 (1955).
5. H. SCHLUNDT, J. T. NERANCY, and J. P. MORRIS, The detection and estimation of radium in living persons. IV. The retention of soluble radium salts administered intravenously. *Am. J. Roentgenol.* **30,** 515–22 (1933).
6. R. E. ROWLAND, J. JOWSEY, and J. H. MARSHALL, Microscopic metabolism of calcium in bone. III. Microradiographic measurements of mineral density. *Radiation Research* **10,** 234–242 (1959).
7. W. B. LOONEY and L. A. WOODRUFF, Investigation of radium depositions in human skeleton by gross and detailed autoradiography. *A. M. A. Arch. Pathol.* **56,** 1–12 (1953).
8. W. S. S. JEE and J. S. ARNOLD, Microradiographic studies of cortical bone of chronic toxicity dogs. Semi-annual Progress Report, pp. 56–57, Radiobiological Laboratory, College of Medicine, University Utah (September 30, 1957).
9. D. E. WALLACE and A. F. STEHNEY, Th^{228}, Ra^{228} and Ra^{226} in normal bone and in bone specimens from radium patients. Radiological Physics Division Semiannual Report, Argonne National Laboratory Report ANL-5829, pp. 115–120 (January, 1958).
10. M. HINDMARSH and J. VAUGHAN, The distribution of radium in certain bones from a man exposed to radium for thirty-four years. *Brit. J. Radiol. Suppl.* **7,** 71–80 (1957).
11. M. A. VAN DILLA, B. J. STOVER, R. L. FLOYD, D. R. ATHERTON, and D. H. TAYSUM, Radium (Ra^{226}) and radon (Em^{222}) metabolism in dogs. *Radiation Research* **8,** 417–437 (1958).

RADIATION RESEARCH **10**, 335–338 (1959)

Protection of the Irradiated Ground Squirrel by Cysteine[1]

DOUGLAS E. SMITH

Division of Biological and Medical Research, Argonne National Laboratory, Lemont, Illinois

INTRODUCTION

Marked protection against the lethal effects of ionizing radiations is obtained in mammals when sulfhydryl compounds are administered before irradiation but not when such treatment is given after irradiation (*1*). It is of great interest, therefore, that significant protection by cysteine has been reported (*2*) in the dormouse (*Glis glis*) irradiated while hibernating at 4°C but not treated with the sulfhydryl compound until 3 weeks after irradiation when the animals were removed to a warm (20°C) room. In these experiments (*2*) no irradiated animals died during the 3-week period in the cold. During the ensuing 30 days in the warm environment, however, 67% of non-cysteine-treated, irradiated dormice died; none of the animals injected with cysteine died during this time. The present paper is concerned with the question of whether similar protection can be obtained in the hibernating ground squirrel. It is important that the findings in the dormouse be confirmed and extended. In all previous animal experiments, sulfhydryl compounds were protective only when they were administered prior to irradiation (*1*). It has been postulated (*1*) that they exert their protective effect during irradiation by reacting with the decomposition products of irradiated water, by causing tissue anoxia, or by forming complexes with important constituents of tissue. It should be anticipated that the mechanism of action of sulfhydryl compounds would be entirely different in the case of protection from their administration after irradiation.

EXPERIMENTAL PROCEDURE

Ground squirrels (*Citellus tridecemlineatus*) were collected in the autumn in Northern Illinois and kept in the laboratory in an air-conditioned room at 23°C. The animals had free access to Rockland guinea pig diet and were given supplements of raw carrots twice weekly. Hibernation was induced by transferring the animals to a cold (5°C) room where they were deprived of food and water.

The possibility of cysteine protection in the ground squirrel was tested in animals kept in the 23°C environment. A group of 10 animals under ether anesthesia was

[1] This work was performed under the auspices of the U. S. Atomic Energy Commission.

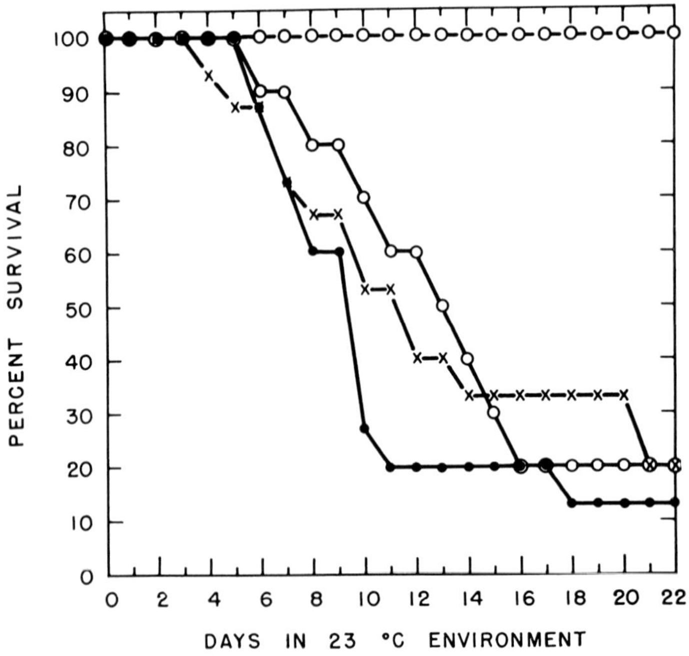

FIG. 1. Survival of X-irradiated (1000 r) ground squirrels under different environmental conditions. ○—○, 10 animals kept always in 23°C room; ○- ○-, 10 animals kept always in 23°C room and injected with cysteine prior to irradiation; ●—●, 15 animals irradiated (at 5°C) while hibernating, kept 22 days in 5°C room after irradiation, and then removed to 23°C environment; X—X, 15 animals irradiated (at 5°C) while hibernating, kept 22 days in 5°C room after irradiation, then removed to 23°C environment and injected with cysteine.

injected intravenously (femoral vein) with cysteine hydrochloride (950 mg/kg body weight, neutralized) about 10 minutes prior to a single, total-body exposure to 1000 r of X-rays (250 kv, 15 ma, 0.5 mm Cu and 3.0 mm Bakelite filters, 35 cm target distance, 1.5 mm Cu half-value layer, and 135 r/min). A control group of 10 squirrels was anesthetized, sham-operated, and irradiated, but not treated with cysteine. At 30 days after exposure all the cysteine-treated and 2 of the control animals were alive. The survival curves of these experiments are found in Fig. 1. In a similar experiment it was found that cysteine injected intraperitoneally was without such a protective effect.

To test the possibility of protection by cysteine given after irradiation, 30 ground squirrels that had been in hibernation for 1 week were given single, total-body exposures of 1000 r in chambers maintained at 5°C. After 22 additional days at 5°C (during which no animals died), the squirrels were removed to a room at 23°C. Immediately before they awoke from hibernation, 15 of the animals were injected intravenously with cysteine-HCl (950 mg/kg body weight). The remaining animals were sham-operated but not injected. The survival curves of this experiment are found in Fig. 1 and show no evidence of a significant protective action by cysteine. In a similar experiment, cysteine injected intraperitoneally was also without protective effect.

An incidental finding was noted. Within 30 to 60 minutes after irradiation at 5°C, half of the 30 hibernating ground squirrels kept at 5°C became fully awake and active. By the end of the next 36 hours these animals were in deep hibernation once again. During the ensuing 20 days in the cold all but 3 of the 30 animals awoke from hibernation two to four times. These periods of wakefulness lasted no longer than 24 hours and occurred apparently at random throughout the period in the cold. In a simultaneously observed group of 12 nonirradiated, hibernating ground squirrels there were no spontaneous awakenings.

DISCUSSION

The present data clearly show that cysteine when injected intravenously prior to irradiation protects the nonhibernating ground squirrel against the lethal effects of X-radiation. We have no explanation of the failure of intraperitoneally administered cysteine to afford similar protection.

The absence of deaths during the 22-day period in the 5°C room after irradiation of hibernating ground squirrels indicates that radiation damage contributing to mortality develops slowly in the dormant animal. This finding confirms previous reports on the hibernating ground squirrel (*3*), the marmot (*4*), and the dormouse (*2*). The differences in time to 50% mortality (Fig. 1) and in average survival time (11.6 days for the group exposed to 1000 r and always kept at 23°C, 9.3 days for the group exposed to 1000 r while hibernating, and 8.9 days for the group exposed to 1000 r while hibernating and subsequently injected with cysteine) between the animals always in the 23°C room and those irradiated while hibernating indicate, however, that radiation damage contributing to lethality does develop during the period at 5°C.

The present data do not afford an explanation of the discrepancy between the hibernating dormouse (*2*) and the hibernating ground squirrel with respect to protection afforded by cysteine. We suggest, however, that the failure to find protection by cysteine in the ground squirrel may be related to the periods of wakefulness observed after irradiation. The heightened metabolism accompanying these periods could allow the development of the radiation damage which contributed to lethality and which was unaffected by cysteine. (We plan to test this explanation in future experiments in which cysteine is injected within 30 minutes after the irradiation of the hibernating ground squirrel.) It is also possible that species differences exist with respect to protection afforded by cysteine given after irradiation of the hibernating animal.

It has been reported previously that ground squirrels which were exposed to 800 r of X-rays during hibernation and which awoke spontaneously could not re-enter hibernation (*3*). We have no sure explanation of the discrepancy between these observations and those of the present experiments where re-entrance into hibernation always followed spontaneous awakening from hibernation. It is possible that differences in the nutritional status of the animal in the two sets of experiments might account for the differences in result. It may be of interest to note that the same workers (*3*) have reported that homeothermic ground squirrels exposed to 800 r did not enter hibernation when subsequently exposed to 5°C. In another study we have found that nonhibernating ground squirrels given a single, total-body exposure to 800 to 1200 r enter hibernation within 48 hours of exposure to 5°C.

The present observations indicate that irradiation interferes with the ability of the ground squirrel to stay in hibernation continuously. This may be taken as a further indication that radiation-induced changes occur in this hibernating animal.

SUMMARY

Intravenous injection of cysteine prior to irradiation significantly protects the nonhibernating ground squirrel from the lethal effects of X-rays. Such protection was not demonstrated when cysteine was administered to the hibernating ground squirrel after irradiation. Some ground squirrels irradiated while hibernating spontaneously awake from hibernation for short periods of time. The significance of these findings and their relation to previous work are discussed.

RECEIVED: June 24, 1958

REFERENCES

1. V. P. BOND and E. P. CRONKITE, Effects of radiation on mammals. *Ann. Rev. Physiol.* **19,** 299–328 (1957).

2. H. A. KÜNKEL, G. HÖHNE, and H. MAAS, Der Einfluss von Cystein und Winterschlaf auf die Überlebensrate röntgenbestrahlter Siebenschläfer (*Glis glis*). *Z. Naturforsch.* **12,** 144–147 (1957).

3. J. DOULL and K. P. DUBOIS, Influence of hibernation on survival time and weight loss of X-irradiated ground squirrels. *Proc. Soc. Exptl. Biol. Med.* **84,** 367–370 (1953).

4. F. SMITH and M. M. GRENAN, Effect of hibernation upon survival time following whole-body irradiation in the marmot (*Marmota monax*). *Science* **113,** 686–688 (1951).

RADIATION RESEARCH 10, 339–346 (1959)

Lesions of the Tongue in Irradiated Mice

O. VOS, F. WENSINCK, AND D. W. VAN BEKKUM

Medical Biological Laboratory of the National Defence Research Council TNO, Rijswijk (Z.H.), The Netherlands

INTRODUCTION

The majority of bacteremias in CBA mice irradiated with 675 r has been found to be caused by group G streptococci. In normal and irradiated mice this organism is a common inhabitant of the upper respiratory tract (*1*, *2*). Since group G streptococci were not found in the lymph nodes during the period immediately preceding the onset of bacteremia, a direct invasion of the blood stream seems likely. Consequently, a search was made for epithelial lesions which might be the portal of entry in these cases of bacteremia. In a number of irradiated mice lesions of the tongue resembling an ulcer or an abscess were found. So far, we have not been able to find a description of a similar lesion in mice. In this paper data are presented on the occurrence of the lesion in irradiated mice. The macroscopic and microscopic appearance is described. The significance of the lesion with regard to the development of bacteremia has been evaluated by studying the tongue flora of normal and irradiated mice.

MATERIALS AND METHODS

Animals

Inbred CBA male and female as well as C57BL male mice were used. Details of the care of the mice before and after the irradiation have been given previously (*3*). Most of the animals had been subjected to pre- or postirradiation treatment with chemical substances or hematopoietic tissue preparations, which were in these cases ineffective with regard to the prevention of death. These and the control animals injected with distilled water were autopsied within 18 hours after death. Eighty-nine untreated mice were killed in the terminal stage of the acute radiation syndrome. These mice were autopsied immediately afterward.

Irradiation

The method of irradiation with 200-kv X-rays and the dose-mortality response of both mouse strains have been described elsewhere (*4*). The mean survival time of the mice used in the present study was slightly longer than reported before, probably as a result of the administration of prophylactic and therapeutic agents. The X-ray dose varied between 675 and 1200 r.

Histological Methods

The tongue with the tongue base and the adhering epiglottis was dissected out and fixed in Bouin's fluid. In other cases the larynx, pharynx, and part of the tongue base were dissected out and fixed. Serial paraffin sections of 7-μ thickness were stained with hematoxylin and eosin or with a trichrome stain according to Mallory-Petersen.

Bacteriological Methods

Methods of culture and identification of organisms have been described in a previous paper (*1*).

RESULTS

The Occurrence of Tongue Lesions after Irradiation

The occurrence of lesions in mice dying after total-body irradiation is shown in Table I. It may be seen that the frequency of the lesion varies considerably in

TABLE I

INCIDENCE OF LESIONS OF THE TONGUE IN IRRADIATED MICE

Group	*Strain*	*Sex*	*Treatment*[a]	*X-ray dose (r)*	*Number of mice*	
					With lesions	*Total*
A	CBA	♂	c.p.	675	46	175
	CBA	♂	b.m.	675	23	79
	CBA	♂	c.p.	950	2	10
	CBA	♂	c.p.	1200	16	37
	CBA	♀	c.p.	675	17	116
	C57BL	♂	b.m.	700	14	156
B	CBA	♂	d.w.	675	3	17
	CBA	♂	d.w.	800	2	9
	CBA	♂	d.w.	950	0	8
	CBA	♂	d.w.	1200	0	10
	CBA	♀	d.w.	675	8	25
	CBA	♀	d.w.	800	0	9
	CBA	♀	d.w.	900	10	10
	C57BL	♂	d.w.	700	1	20
C	CBA	♀	No	675	4	27
	CBA	♀	No	750	22	53
	CBA	♂	No	750	4	9

[a] The animals of group A had been treated with chemical protectors (c.p.) or with bone marrow (b.m.). Group B had been injected with distilled water (d.w.). The mice of group A and B died spontaneously; animals of group C were killed when moribund.

different groups of mice. A greater incidence has been found in CBA male mice as compared with C57BL males. In the groups of CBA mice (271 animals, 675 r) 27% showed lesions; in the C57BL mice (176 animals, 700 r) the incidence was 9%. The data in Table I, group A, suggest that the lesion occurs less frequently in CBA females than in CBA males. When all the CBA females and males of the groups A and B are compared, however, the incidence is nearly the same—22% in 160 females and 27% in 345 males.

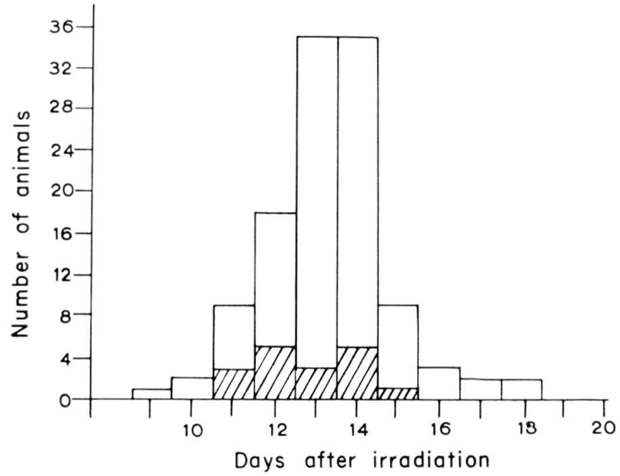

FIG. 1. The incidence of lesions of the tongue in CBA females: 116 mice were irradiated with 675 r and treated with chemical protectors. □ Deaths; ▨ animals with tongue lesion.

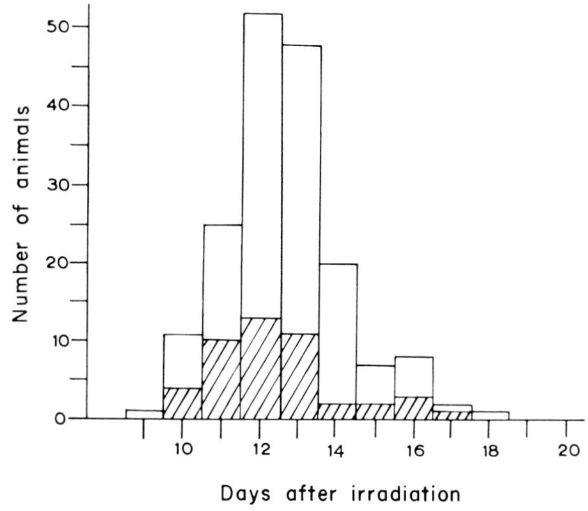

FIG. 2. The incidence of lesions of the tongue in CBA males: 175 mice were irradiated with 675 r and treated with chemical protectors. □ Deaths; ▨ animals with tongue lesion.

Within the dose range of X-rays employed there was no clear relation between the dose and the frequency of the lesion. Some mice in group A (Table I), although dying, may have received some protection, which resulted in less radiation damage and a longer survival time. Therefore the incidence found in the 1200-r group (Table I, group A) cannot be considered as typical for this radiation dose. The data presented in Figs. 1 and 2 suggest that the proportion of mice with tongue lesions does not vary with the survival time. The results obtained with mice that were killed in the final stage of the radiation sickness (Table I, group C) were similar to those reported for the animals that died spontaneously.

Description of the Lesion

In most cases the lesion was located on the dorsal surface of the tongue in the region of the papilla circumvallata (Fig. 3). Exceptionally two separate ulcers were found (Fig. 4). In a few cases an ulcer was located at the lateral surface of the tongue or in the upper part of the larynx.

The size of the lesion varied between pinpoint and a few millimeters. Usually the lesion revealed itself as a slight, grayish yellow elevation; occasionally it resembled an ulcer. A large number of mice showed either a demarcated edema or a discolored

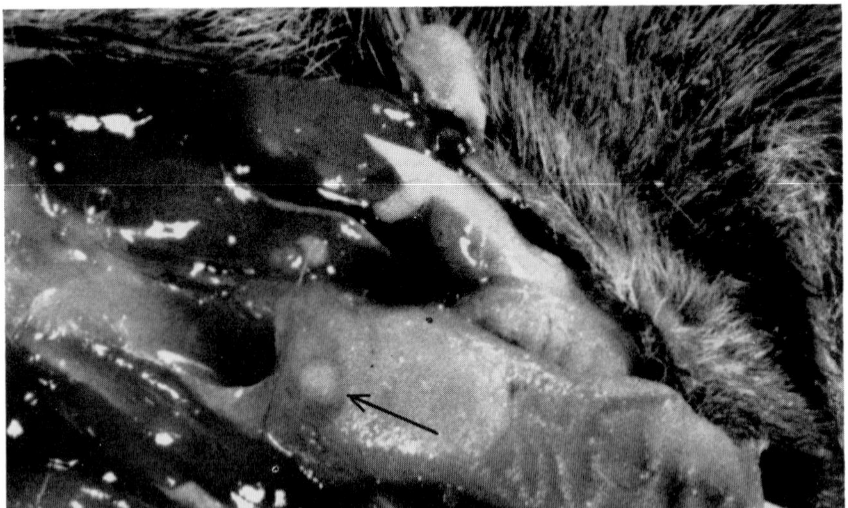

FIG. 3. Tongue showing the typical lesion.

patch at the place where typical tongue lesions were found in other animals. In the preceding section these changes were not classified with the lesions. Microscopic lesions were found, however, in 7 out of 8 tongues showing edema or discoloration. Furthermore the histological investigation revealed small foci of degeneration in 3 out of 7 tongues that were essentially normal on macroscopic inspection (Table II).

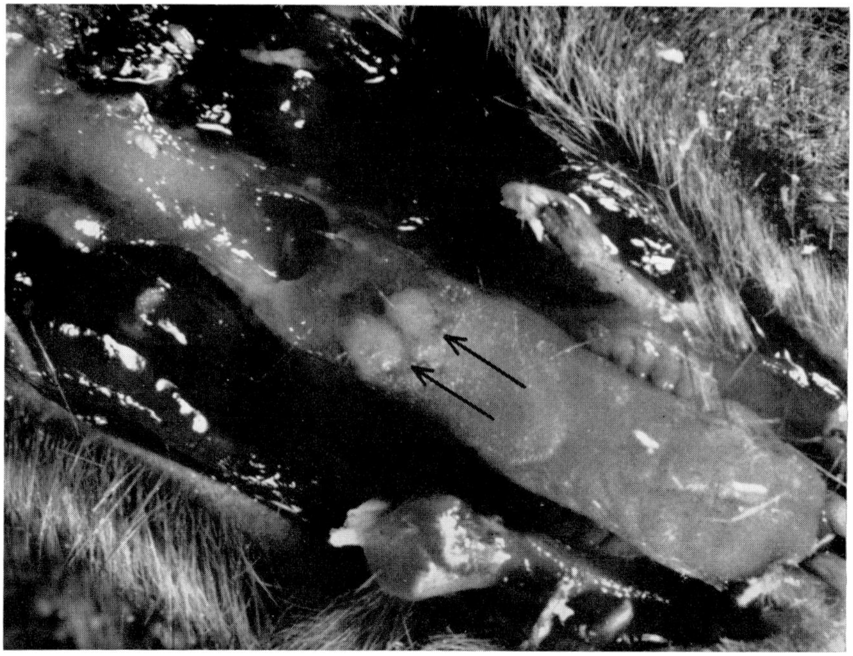

FIG. 4. Tongue showing the typical lesion.

TABLE II

INCIDENCE OF MICROSCOPIC LESIONS OF THE TONGUE IN MICE IRRADIATED WITH 675 TO 750 R

Strain	*Number of tongues examined*	*Number of tongues showing lesions*	
		Macroscopic	*Microscopic*
C57BL	4	0	2
CBA	3	1 (edema)	1
		2 (abscess)	2
CBA	11	1 (edema)	1
		1 (abscess)	1
		3 (negative)	1
		6 (dubious[a])	5

[a] Tongues showing discolored patches.

This finding suggests that the lesion is much more frequent than appears from autopsy. Microscopically the lesions were found to consist of a necrotic center in which no definite tissue structure could be observed (Fig. 5). Instead granular masses were observed, which apparently consisted mostly of densely packed bacteria. In the peripheral parts of the lesion bacteria could easily be recognized. In some preparations bacteria had infiltrated into the surrounding tissue. Characteristically, cellular reaction was never observed. Interstitial edema was often present, and small hemorrhages were found in the immediate vicinity of the necrotic area. In some cases the lesion extended to the surface; in others it was separated from the oral cavity by normal tissue. In a number of tongues more than one microscopic lesion was found. There was no obvious connection with the ducts of the intralingual salivary glands which end near the papilla circumvallata. Only in a few cases necrotic foci were observed in the larynx.

Bacteriological Observations

Cultures from tongues of normal CBA mice were markedly uniform. On blood-agar comparable numbers of colonies of *Streptococcus equinus* and a gram-negative rod, probably a *Haemophilus* species, were found. Endo-agar and salt-agar were

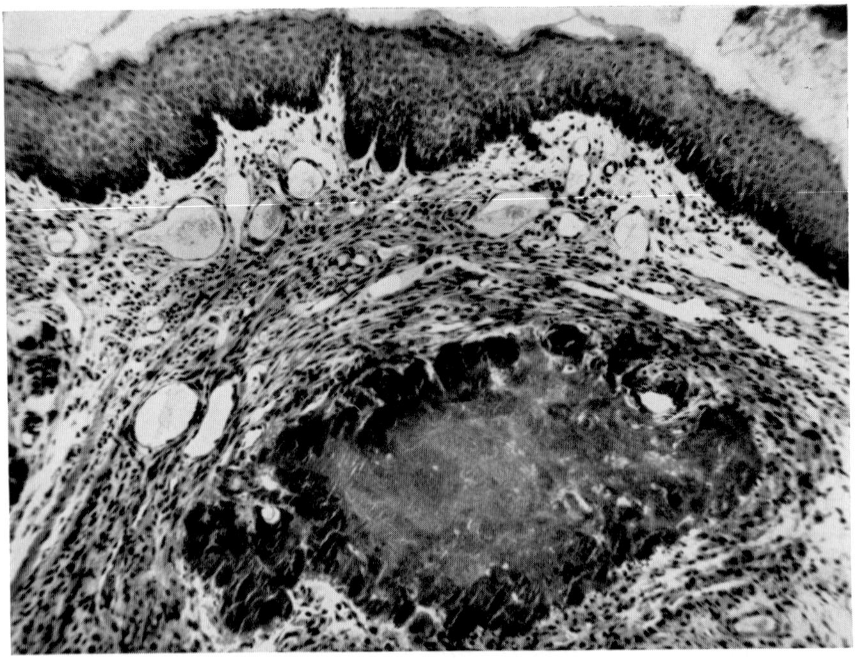

FIG. 5. Section of the tongue showing the necrotic area. Fixation Bouin, hematoxylin and eosin-stained. (110 ×)

TABLE III

BACTERIAL FLORA OF THE TONGUE OF MICE IRRADIATED WITH 675 TO 750 R AND SHOWING GROUP G STREPTOCOCCUS BACTEREMIA

Flora of the tongue	*Number of cultures*
Normal[a]	2
Group G streptococcus	16
Group G streptococcus + enteric organisms[b]	21
Enteric organisms[b]	12

[a] *Str. equinus* and *Haemophilus* species.
[b] *E. coli* and *Str. faecalis*.

always negative, indicating the absence of the characteristic enteric organisms. Apparently there is a rapid elimination of these organisms which are introduced into the oral cavity by coprophagy.

The tongues of irradiated CBA mice were examined 3 to 8 days after irradiation with 675 and 750 r. The heart's blood was cultured also. The findings in cultures from the tongue were arranged in a prebacteremic and a bacteremic group. In mice showing no bacteremia a normal tongue flora was found in 18 out of 24 cases. Varying numbers of *Str. faecalis* were found in 6 specimens. Group G streptococci were not found in any culture during the prebacteremic period. The data concerning tongue cultures from bacteremic mice are presented in Table III. In 70% of these cases, group G streptococci were found in the tongue cultures, which frequently contained enteric organisms as well. About 20% of the cultures were overgrown with *E. coli* or *Str. faecalis*. This rather high incidence of intestinal bacteria in cultures of the tongue indicates that the clearing mechanism of the oral cavity may be deficient in irradiated animals.

DISCUSSION

The results of a microscopic study of tongues from irradiated mice indicate that necrotic lesions are much more frequent than appears from macroscopic inspection. The data presented indicate that the incidence amounts to 90% of the tongues. The lesion may be compared with the ulceration of the oral cavity observed after irradiation in dogs (*5*), pigs (*6*), mules (*7*), and monkeys (*8*, *9*). These ulcers contained numerous microorganisms and showed very little inflammatory reaction, similar to the lesions described in this paper. Ulcerative tonsillitis was frequently found in the Japanese atomic bomb victims; in some of these cases ulcers of the tongue developed (*10*).

The significance of the necrotic lesions of the tongue and larynx with regard to the developing bacteremias in our mice is not completely understood. In this laboratory the majority of bacteremias associated with the bone marrow syndrome in CBA mice has found to be caused by group G streptococci. These organisms have been found to be normal inhabitants of the respiratory tract in this mouse strain, which suggests the above lesions to be involved as portal of entry. Group G streptococci were never found, however, in tongue cultures from irradiated mice before the onset of bacteremia.

Whatever the precise mechanism of invasion be, the data contained in this paper suggest a role of the lesions of the oropharyngeal region in the development of bacteremia after total-body irradiation.

SUMMARY

Postmortem examination of nearly 700 CBA and C57BL mice that died after total-body exposure to 675 and 750 r revealed macroscopic lesions of the tongue in 23% of the cases. Microscopic lesions were found to be much more frequent. The lesions resemble an abscess or an ulcer and consist of a heavily infected necrotic mass. Cellular reaction is absent. The possibility that the lesions are the portal of entry for microorganisms in the development of the bacteremia associated with the bone marrow syndrome is discussed.

RECEIVED: June 24, 1958

REFERENCES

1. F. WENSINCK and H. RENAUD, Bacteremia in irradiated mice. *Brit. J. Exptl. Pathol.* **38**, 483–488 (1957).
2. F. WENSINCK and H. RENAUD, Murine group G streptococci. *Brit. J. Exptl. Pathol.* **38**, 489–492 (1957).
3. F. WENSINCK, D. W. VAN BEKKUM, and H. RENAUD, The prevention of *Pseudomonas aeruginosa* infections in irradiated mice and rats. *Radiation Research* **7**, 491–499 (1957).
4. D. W. VAN BEKKUM, The protective action of dithiocarbamates against the lethal effects of X-irradiation in mice. *Acta Physiol. et Pharmacol. Neerl.* **4**, 508–523 (1956).
5. G. BRECHER and E. P. CRONKITE, Lesions of the alimentary tract of dogs exposed to whole body X-radiation of 300–3,000 R. *Am. J. Pathol.* **27**, 676–677 (1951).
6. J. L. TULLIS, B. G. LAMSON, and S. C. MADDEN, Pathology of swine exposed to total body gamma radiation from an atomic bomb source. *Am. J. Pathol.* **31**, 41–71 (1955).
7. B. F. TRUM, Whole body irradiation of large animals. *Military Surgeon* **112**, 333–341 (1953).
8. H. G. SCHLUMBERGER and J. J. VAZQUEZ, Pathology of total body irradiation in the monkey. *Am. J. Pathol.* **30**, 1013–1047 (1954).
9. M. V. HAIGH and E. PATERSON, Effects of a single session of whole body irradiation in the rhesus monkey. *Brit. J. Radiol.* **29**, 148–157 (1956).
10. A. W. OUGHTERSON and S. WARREN, *Medical Effects of the Atomic Bomb in Japan*, McGraw-Hill Book Company, New York, 1956.

RADIATION RESEARCH **10**, 347–356 (1959)

The Effects of Single and Divided Doses of X-Radiation on Bone Marrow of Partially Shielded Rats

RAYMOND G. MURRAY

Department of Anatomy, Indiana University School of Medicine, Bloomington, Indiana

INTRODUCTION

To test the degree of radioresistance developed in bone marrow by previous exposure to X-radiation, rats were given 180 r/day for 5 days to the right lower quadrant only and "tested" with a single whole-body dose of 525 r. It was found, however, that as long as 12 days after the preliminary irradiation the exposed marrows were still so poorly recovered that acquired resistance, if any, could not be measured. The recovery was less than that seen in marrows of rats 10 days after 525 r of single whole-body irradiation. This result is surprising in view of the high degree of protection which either partial shielding (*1*) or divided dose (*2, 3*) acting independently can produce. It was possible, however, to demonstrate slight resistance to 525 r at 3 and 10 days in the marrows from the shielded portions of these rats.

MATERIALS AND METHODS

A total of 48 female Sprague-Dawley rats, 3½ months of age, ranging in weight from 185 to 220 gm, were used. They were maintained on a diet of rat pellets and water ad libitum supplemented with cabbage or lettuce.

For the divided doses 4 rats were tied (on their backs) to a board, and each was covered by a lead shield, 3⁄32 inch thick, shaped to protect all but the lower right quadrant. For total-body irradiation, the rats were confined in a special ventilated plastic box holding 6 rats at a time in separate compartments and exposed to a current of air during irradiation. Rotation of the rats twice during the treatment increased the uniformity of the dose.

The radiation was delivered by a 200-kvp machine at 15 ma, through 0.5 mm copper and 1 mm of aluminum at a distance of 70 cm. The delivery rate as measured in air with a Victoreen chamber was approximately 10 r/min on the board, 8.5 r/min in the box, and 0.7 r/min under the shield in the position of the protected femur.

The rats were killed by a blow on the head. Marrow pencils, removed from the femurs by carefully chipping away the bone with forceps, were fixed in Zenker-formol, embedded and sectioned in celloidin, and stained with hematoxylin-eosin-Azure II.

The rats were separated into five groups for treatment (see Table I). Rats of groups A and B received five daily "pretreatments" of 180 r to the right lower quadrant. After a "rest" of 3 days (group B) or 10 days (group A) a "test dose" of 525 r was administered to the whole body. Group C rats were tied down for periods comparable to that required for the pretreatment and after a 2-day rest were given the same test dose, 525 r. The $LD_{50(30)}$ for these rats was about 600 r. Pairs of rats were sacrificed at 4 hours, 2 days, 5 days, and 10 days after the midpoint of the test dose. Group D consisted of 6 rats given the same pretreatment as in groups A and B and sacrificed in pairs, at 2, 5, and 12 days after the midpoint of the pretreatment, without receiving the test dose. Fourteen untreated rats (group U) were sacrificed in pairs at various times throughout the experimental period. From these groups of rats, seven experimental series of marrows were examined and compared, as indicated in Table II, which also compares the per cent of recovery, or degree of return to normal, in each series.

The degree of damage or recovery was roughly judged by estimating in the sections the area occupied by developing cells, exclusive of fat, vessels, extravasated blood, or edema fluid, with some weight given to the quality of recovery. It was felt that other methods, particularly those involving smear and touch preparations (*4–8*) for which quantitative validity has been claimed, do not substantially eliminate the sources of error in the estimations. By relying on detailed examination of well-prepared sections the qualitative impressions become more reliable.

TABLE I

Schedule of Treatments and Autopsies

Group	*Pretreatment*	*Exposed area*	*Rest*	*Second exposure or test dose*	*Autopsy intervals from midpoint of dose (Number of rats in parenthesis)*
A	180 r/day for 5 days	Lower right quadrant	10 days	525 r, total body	4 hours (2), 2 days (2), 5 days (2), 10 days (3)
B	180 r/day for 5 days	Lower right quadrant	3 days	525 r, total body	4 hours (2), 2 days (2), 5 days (2), 10 days (3)
C	Sham Rx, for 5 days	—	2 days	525 r, total body	4 hours (2), 2 days (2), 5 days (3), 10 days (2)
D	180 r/day for 5 days	Lower right quadrant	None	None	2 days (2), 5 days (2), 12 days (2)
U	None	None	None	None	Throughout the experiment (14).

TABLE II

RECOVERY OF HEMATOPOIESIS IN THE BONE MARROW

Series	*Group*	*Treatment*	*Percent return to normal*
AR	A, right femur	5 × 180 r—other ¾ of rat shielded—10-day rest—525 r, total body.	15–20
AL	A, left femur	5 × 13 r—opposite quadrant had 5 × 180 r—10-day rest—525 r, total body.	65–100
BR	B, right femur	5 × 180 r—other ¾ of rat shielded—3-day rest—525 r, total body.	15–20
BL	B, left femur	5 × 13 r—opposite quadrant had 5 × 180 r—3-day rest—525 r, total body.	65–100
C	C, both femurs	Sham 5 × 180 r—2-day rest—525 r, total body.	40–65
DR	D, right femur	5 × 180 r—other ¾ of rat shielded—no further treatment	20–35
DL	D, left femur	5 × 13 r—opposite quadrant had 5 × 180 r—no further treatment	100

OBSERVATIONS

The effects of 525 r (group C) of total-body irradiation were used as a reference "base line." The type of destruction, its distribution among the several cell lines, and the sequence of events in this series closely paralleled those described by Bloom (*9*). Here, as in the previous work, the sensitivity of erythroblasts was striking, megakaryocytes were subtly but gradually lost, waves of regeneration and regression were suggested, regeneration was primarily focal in type, and giant forms of granulocytic cells were found. One feature not emphasized in the previous report was the consistent finding of increased numbers of plasma cells. These seemed to represent abortive erythroblast production, or in some cases even suggested transformations or early myelocytes to plasma cells. Also, no evidence of gelatinous marrow, as reported by Bloom (*9*), was noted in this series.

In quantitative terms, the degree of destruction was only moderately less and the rate of recovery slightly greater than Bloom (*9*) reported for 600 r, which is consistent with the measured dose of 525 r for this series. It was estimated from the total number of hematopoietic cells and the quality of the cells (i.e., young normal cells, mitotic activity) that recovery at 10 days represented return toward normal of about 40 to 65% (see Table II).

Series DR marrows received 5 × 180 r while most of the rat was shielded and were examined at 2, 5, and 12 days after the midpoint of the third dose, or 4 hours, 3 days, and 10 days after the middle of the last dose. At the early interval in both rats the depletion of cells resembled that at 2 days after 525 r (group C). The cells present were relatively mature, and proliferative activity was low. Plasma cells were more numerous than normal, though perhaps not so prominent as at 5 days after 525 r. At 5 days both specimens were more severely depleted than at 2 days, and the predominance of late forms continued. Myelocytes were relatively more severely depressed than erythroblasts, in contrast to any stage after 525 r. Mitoses were rare, and there were many plasma cells among the groups of late erythroblasts.

At 12 days, cellularity was in the range of one-third or less of normal, an amount not significantly increased over the value at 3 days. This represents, on the whole, less general recovery than at the comparable period after 525 r. Moreover, the preponderance of erythrocytic precursors, noted at 5 days, was even more striking at 12 days here. Myelocytes were quite few and scattered irregularly rather than developing in organized groups. Erythropoiesis was active but less so than at the comparable interval after 525 r. Megakaryocytes were very few, probably relatively more depressed than the general cellularity. Mitotic activity was probably within the normal range. Plasma cells were distinctly more numerous than at the comparable interval in series C. These appearances taken together seemed to indicate both qualitative and quantitative recovery distinctly below that at the 10-day interval after the single unshielded dose of 525 r.

In the marrows of series DL, which received the very mild pretreatment (i.e., 5 × 13 r plus irradiation of the opposite quadrant), the appearance prior to the test dose (see Table II) was indistinguishable from that of untreated rats. Marrows similarly "pretreated" which subsequently received the test dose (series AL and BL) showed a pattern of destruction, depletion, and recovery through the 5-day specimens similar to that seen in series C (525 r, no pretreatment). It is probable that there was less destruction of cells at the 4-hour interval than in series C, but within the limits of variation in this material the degree of loss of hematopoiesis at 2 and 5 days was the same as in group C, and there was no difference between series AL (10-day rest) and series BL (3-day rest) marrows. A comparison of the 10-day intervals, however, indicated a significantly greater recovery of cellularity and return to normal distributional pattern in the marrows in both AL and BL than after 525 r alone, without pretreatment. Of the six marrows examined, five were well above the 10-day series C marrows in cellularity, and the sixth was about equal to the least populated of the series C marrows. Several of these marrows were difficult to distinguish from normal, which was not true of any of the series C specimens.

After a combination of 5 × 180 r and 525 r (series AR and BR) the marrow was depleted to levels never reached in the other series and at 10 days showed extremely variable recovery which in all but one rat was below that in any other series. This was equally true whether the rest interval was 3 days or 10 days. A large part of the marrow was completely lacking in hematopoiesis, but a few sharply circumscribed areas were intensely proliferative. This was a striking exaggeration of the general tendency in marrows of all series for recovery to be focal rather than diffuse. The marrows of these two series differed from series C also in that almost no debris was noticeable at the earliest interval, and the occurrence of plasma cells at all intervals after the earliest was in amounts greater than in the other series. Their occurrence in fairly large groups, frequent association with a few erythroblasts, and occasional transitional forms between erythroblast and plasma cell very strongly indicated that erythroblasts were being formed only to transform into plasma cells rather than continue to differentiate further into erythrocytes.

DISCUSSION

In previous work (*3*) the author studied the effects of repeated daily doses of 80 r to the thymus of mice. Specimens examined at intervals after one, two, and up to twenty doses indicated that, after an initial period of destruction and moderate depletion of free cells, there was some recovery in general cellularity and continued high activity of lymphopoiesis. This suggested that some degree of resistance to the radiation might have developed in this organ. The present experiment was originally designed (1) to see whether bone marrow acted similarly to thymus and (2) to determine more precisely the extent and time relations of the effect. Femoral bone marrow was chosen because of the opportunity of comparing on opposite sides of the same animal the effects of a test dose on a previously treated organ as opposed to an untreated, or much more mildly treated, one.

The choice of pretreatment dose and the time interval between pretreatment and test dose worked out in such a way that there was so much residual damage from the pretreatment that the effects of the test dose on the two sides could not reasonably be compared, as was originally intended. It might at first seem reasonable that a marrow which had received 900 r would be poorly recovered by 12 days, but two factors should operate to reduce the damage. As Jacobson (*1*) and others have shown, shielding of part of the rat or mouse, particularly the spleen (which is included in the shielded area in the rats used here), can increase the $LD_{50(30)}$ by a factor of $2X$, and the marrow of rats with the spleen so shielded shows comparable protection. One would expect, then, less damage from 900 r partially shielded than from 525 r to the whole body.

At the same time, fractionation of the dose greatly reduces the effectiveness of the radiation. Since the size of the dose fractions may be an important factor in the degree of protection offered by this mechanism, and in order to have information from more nearly comparable material, a few additional rats were given 5×180 r of total-body irradiation. Recovery over a 10-day period was as great as or greater than that after the single 525-r dose.

It would appear that two factors acting together produced a protective effect less than each of these factors was capable of producing independently. How can we explain the apparent discrepancy between these results and previous work?

De Bruyn and Tornova-Svehlik (*10*) have emphasized the fact that, after severe irradiation, recovery in the rabbit appendix is extremely variable at the late intervals after treatment. Since there are very few samples in the groups of this series, individual variation may account for the discrepancy. Pairs of rats at each interval were consistent in their qualitative recovery, however, and reasonably so in quantitative evaluation so far as this could be measured. Not only did the two marrows at 12 days after 5 × 180 r show less recovery than marrows 10 days after 525 r, but the pairs at 5 days showed the same difference in approximately the same degree, particularly with regard to the granulocytic series.

It is possible that the mechanism in shielded areas which affords protection is so sensitive that a low dose of radiation would destroy it. Measurements in air with a Victoreen chamber indicated about 0.7 r/min beneath the shield, which would mean that the protected part received five doses of 13 r. This figure included a high proportion of soft radiation from scatter, so the depth dose was probably lower than this. Since examination of the shielded marrow from these animals after five treatments revealed no evidence of damage, it does not seem likely that this very limited irradiation could destroy the protective mechanism.

The two protective factors in question might not be additive if they operated through stimulation of the same mechanism. Jacobson (*1*) discusses possible mechanisms in the protective effect of partial shielding and concludes that a humoral rather than a cellular mechanism is probably most important in recovery. Let us assume that, on the other hand, protection in partial shielding depends on the saving from destruction of a reserve of cells which can be distributed to damaged areas and furnish centers for regrowth. Dividing the dose into moderate-sized fractions, each of which would normally leave a large percentage of "intact" cells, might provide the same protection. But since a reserve of cells is already available from the shielded parts, the additional undamaged cells from dividing the dose might have little or no additional recuperative value.

Another possible explanation of the discrepancy is that the damaged marrow of series DR represented such a small part of the total hemopoietic tissue that the stimulus to regenerate was not very great. This would be particularly true if a large reserve of mature cells were available from the protected areas. The number of circulating granulocytes in the rat is less than that of erythrocytes by a factor of about 2000. The erythrocyte survives about 45 to 50 days in the rat circulatory system (*11*, *12*), whereas the estimates of survival time for heterophil leukocytes vary from a few days to a few weeks (*13–15*). Therefore the ratio of the life span of heterophil and erythrocyte in the blood is certainly no more than $1/100$ and probably much less. From these values it would appear that 20 erythrocytes must be replaced by the marrow production for each heterophil that needs replacement. One would expect many more erythrocytic than granulocytic precursors in the marrow. There are, on the other hand, usually more granulocytic cells, which suggests, in agreement with Bloom and Bloom (*16*), that the marrow stores large numbers of mature granulocytic cells. The release of these cells from the unirradiated portions of the marrow might temporarily supply the needs of the organism for this cell type. If the erythrocyte supply is more directly dependent on continued rate of production than is the supply of granulocytes, erythropoietic activity might be favored over granulopoiesis.

The distinctly focal nature of regenerative activity, with at times as many as 50 or 100 cells in virtually the same stage of development grouped together, suggests one or very few common ancestors at that location for the entire group. If this be so, such appearances do not support the conception of repopulation in the marrow being affected in any large part by extensive influx of stem cells from other parts of the body (*17*, *18*). Since most of the hemopoietic tissue of the body was not irradiated, large numbers of cells would be available, if this mechanism were operative, and presumably would spread more evenly throughout the damaged marrow. This interpretation would tend to favor Jacobson's (*1*) conclusion that the protection offered by partial shielding is by a humoral mechanism. Apparently undamaged reticular cells, however, capable of transforming into blood cells, were present throughout the marrow without undergoing these transformations, a fact which does not support the humoral concept.

It is widely held (*19*) that plasma cells may be derived from lymphocytes. There are numerous reports of plasma cells being increased in number in hemopoietic tissue after irradiation (*20–24*). Presumably the lymphocytes are the source of the new plasma cells, but in the bone marrow other possibilities have been considered. The frequent transformation of reticular cells into plasma cells is reported in the marrow of persons exposed to the radiation of the Hiroshima and Nagasaki atomic explosions (*21*). In the present work, plasma cells in large numbers were present in regenerating marrows, frequently associated with sharply demarcated foci of developing cells, usually erythroblasts. The changes from hemocytoblast (or lymphocyte) to plasma cell involve increasing basophilia of the cytoplasm and concentration of the chromatin into a few coarse granules, mostly along the nuclear membrane in the classic case. The typical plasma cell has, moreover, a relatively small, round, eccentrically placed nucleus. But the ratio of cytoplasmic to nuclear areas, and nuclear size and position in developing plasma cells, may vary widely with the size of the precursor cell (reticular cell, large, medium, or small hemocytoblast). Also the nucleus of developing erythroblasts passes through stages identical with certain stages in the developing plasma cell, while the deep basophilia of the early erythroblast may still be present in the cytoplasm. Thus the distinction between developing plasma cell and developing erythrocyte is not clear, and it is not certain whether hemocytoblasts were differentiating toward erythroblasts first and then further into plasma cells, or directly into plasma cells. There was, however, a definite increase in the number of plasma cells present, and primarily in the foci of erythrocyte production.

There were occasional instances of young plasma cells with nuclear pattern resembling early myelocytes, and with a slight pink color in the area of the attraction sphere, as well as many otherwise typical plasma cells with a pink color in the attraction sphere. In the myelocyte series, the pink color always preceded the appearance of the first specific granules. These appearances suggest transformation to plasma cells from cells in the very early stage of myelocyte development.

There was no positive instance of transformation of reticular cell to plasma cell. Since the changes from reticular cell to either hemocytoblast or plasma cell will at first be the same, it may be that in the atomic casualties cited above an intermediate hemocytoblast stage was present in the plasma cell transformations. Whether the plasma cells are developing from lymphocytes in the conventionally accepted manner or from a variety of other cells, the net result in the hemopoietic tissue after irradiation appears to be an effort to produce blood cells, which results in an abnormally high production of plasma cells. Several authors (*25*, *26*) have suggested that plasma cells are responsible for the production of antibody, and their hypothesis has been supported by Coons (*27*) by demonstration of antibody in these cells. Another possible relation of the plasma cell to antibody formation is suggested by Fitch *et al.* (*28*) in a study which showed that plasma cells increase in number only after the height of antibody production has been passed. It is known that antibody is reduced in acute radiation damage (*29*), and the present work confirms earlier observations (*22*) that plasma cells are not damaged at the $LD_{50(30)}$ dose level. Possibly the antibody-producing potential of the undamaged lymphocytes is expressed under the stimulus of radiation damage to the rest of the body, much as a lymphoid cell in inflammation differentiates to a phagocytic cell. When the stimulus is past, the lymphocyte is no longer capable of returning to the highly undifferentiated state but rather further differentiates into an antibody-storing cell which might be the typical plasma cell. The stimulus to produce antibodies may be so strong in the animals of the present series that cells partially differentiated toward erythroblast or myelocyte may be diverted and eventually form antibody-storing plasma cells.

The greater percentage of recovery in series AL and BL compared to series C suggests that treatment with mild irradiation conferred some degree of resistance to severe irradiation on these marrows which was still active 10 days after the pretreatment. Although this confirms the findings of Bloom (*30*) and others that irradiation results in acquired radioresistance, the present results differ in two respects. Bloom found resistance to moderate doses (200 r) but not to large doses (600 r and 1200 r) after pretreatment, and noted that evidence of resistance was lacking if more than a week elapsed between pretreatment and test dose. It is possible that the resistance acquired by the rat marrows from the mild direct radiation in series AL and BL was enhanced by indirect effects from the heavily irradiated opposite quadrant. This possibility of indirectly acquired radioresistance should be investigated further.

SUMMARY

A total of 48 rats were exposed in a variety of ways to 200-kvp X-rays with the following results:

1. Bone marrow in an exposed lower quadrant which received 900 r in five daily fractions of 180 r while the remaining three-fourths of the rat was shielded showed less recovery at 10 to 12 days than marrow which received 525 r of total-body irradiation in a single dose. The fact that partial shielding and dividing the dose did not give more protection suggests that these two protective mechanisms are not additive.

2. Mild irradiation (5 × 13 r) appeared to produce slight but measurable resistance to a heavy (525-r) dose of X-ray at 3 days or 10 days after the mild treatment.

3. Plasma cells were undamaged by 525 r or 5 × 180 r and increased significantly in the marrow 5 and 10 days after irradiation by transformations from hemocytoblasts, and possibly from early erythroblasts and myelocytes.

RECEIVED: June 24, 1958

REFERENCES

1. L. O. JACOBSON, The hematologic effects of ionizing radiation. In *Radiation Biology* (A. Hollaender, ed.), Vol. 1, Part 2, pp. 1029–1090, McGraw-Hill Book Company, New York, 1954.

2. C. W. HAGEN and E. L. SIMMONS, Effects of total body X-irradiation on rats. I. Lethal action of single, paired and periodic doses. U. S. Atomic Energy Commission Report CH-3815 (1947).

3. R. G. MURRAY, Thymus. *Natl. Nuclear Energy Ser. Div. IV*, **22-II,** 446-501 (1948).

4. G. BRECKER, K. M. ENDICOTT, H. GRUMP, and N. P. BROWNEN, Effects of X-ray on lymphoid and hematopoietic tissue of albino mice. *Blood* **3,** 1259–1274 (1943).

5. K. M. ENDICOTT and N. OTT, The normal myelogram in albino rats. *Anat. Record* **92,** 61–69 (1945).

6. A. S. WEISBERGER and R. HEINLE, Study of fixed tissue sections of sternal bone marrow obtained by needle aspirations. I. Method and morphology in various conditions. *Am. J. Med. Sci.* **215,** 170–176 (1948).

7. R. L. ROSENTHAL, B. I. PICKERING, and N. GOLDSCHMIDT, A semiquantitative study of bone marrow in rats following total body X-irradiation. *Blood* **6,** 600–613 (1951).

8. J. STASNEY and G. M. HIGGINS, A quantitative cytologic study of the bone marrow of the adult albino rat. *Anat. Record* **63,** 77–99 (1935).

9. M. BLOOM, The bone marrow. *Natl. Nuclear Energy Ser. Div. IV*, **22-II,** 162–242 (1948).

10. P. P. H. DE BRUYN and M. M. TORNOVA-SVEHLIK, Quantitative aspects of the effects of X-rays on lymphatic tissue. *Radiation Research* **6,** 573–584 (1957).

11. E. L. BURWELL, B. A. BRICKLEY, and C. A. FINCH, Erythrocyte life span in small animals. *Am. J. Physiol.* **172,** 718–725 (1953).

12. W. M. DAVIS, E. L. ALPEN, and A. K. DAVIS, Studies of radioiron utilization and erythrocyte life span in rats following thermal injury. *J. Clin. Invest.* **34,** 67–74 (1955).

13. H. G. WEISKOTTON, The normal life span of the neutrophile leukocyte. *Am. J. Pathol.* **6,** 183–190 (1930).

14. D. L. KLINE and E. E. CLIFTON, Life span of leukocytes in man. *J. Appl. Physiol.* **5,** 79–84 (1952).

15. J. OTTESEN, On the age of human white cells in peripheral blood. *Acta Physiol. Scand.* **32,** 75–93 (1954).

16. W. BLOOM and M. A. BLOOM, Histological changes after irradiation. In *Radiation Biology* (A. Hollaender, ed.), Vol. 1, Part 2, pp. 1097–1143, McGraw-Hill Book Company, New York, 1954.

17. R. S. FARR, Experiments on the fate of the lymphocyte. *Anat. Record* **109,** 515–533 (1951).

18. H. E. JORDAN and C. C. SPEIDEL, The fate of the mammalian lymphocyte. *Anat. Record* **26,** 223–234 (1923).

19. A. A. MAXIMOW, Lymphocytes and plasma cells. In *Special Cytology* (E. V. Cowdry, ed.), Vol. 2, pp. 603–650, Paul B. Hoeber, New York, 1932.

20. P. P. H. DE BRUYN, Lymph node and intestinal lymphatic tissue. *Natl. Nuclear Energy Ser. Div. IV* **22-II,** 348–445 (1948).

21. A. A. LIEBOW, SHIELDS WARREN, and E. DECOURSEY, Pathology of atomic bomb casualties. *Am. J. Pathol.* **25,** 853–1027 (1949).

22. R. G. MURRAY, The spleen. *Natl. Nuclear Energy Ser. Div. IV* **22-II,** 243–347 (1948).

23. J. M. ROSS, A case illustrating the prolonged action of radiation. *J. Pathol. Bacteriol.* **35,** 899–912 (1932).

24. H. F. THOMAS and F. H. BRUNER, Chronic radium poisoning in rats. *Am. J. Roentgenol.* **29,** 641–662 (1933).

25. A. FAGRAEUS, The plasma cellular reaction and its relation to the formation of antibodies *in vitro*. *J. Immunol.* **58,** 1–13 (1948).

26. T. MAKINODAN, R. F. RUTH, and H. R. WOLF, Precipitin production in chickens. XI. Site of antibody production. *J. Immunol.* **72,** 45–51 (1953).

27. A. H. COONS, E. L. LEDUC, and J. M. CONNOLLY, Leukocytes involved in antibody production. *Ann. N. Y. Acad. Sci.* **59,** 951–955 (1955).

28. F. W. FITCH, R. W. WISSLER, M. LAVIA, and P. BARKER, The timing of antigen injections relative to whole body X-irradiation and the development of circulating antibody and the splenic histologic reaction in the rat. *J. Immunol.* **76,** 151–160 (1956).

29. H. M. PATT and A. BRUES, The pathological physiology of radiation injury in the mammal. II. Specific aspects of the physiology of radiation injury. In *Radiation Biology* (A. Hollaender, ed.), Vol. 1, Part 2, pp. 959–1028, McGraw-Hill Book Company, New York, 1954.

30. M. A. BLOOM, Acquired radioresistance of the crypt epithelium of the duodenum. *Radiology* **55,** 104–115 (1950).

RADIATION RESEARCH 10, 357–369 (1959)

Paper Electrophoretic Analyses of Sera from Irradiated Rhesus Monkeys[1]

CHARLES A. LEONE,[2] ANNE RIMKUS HARTNETT,[3]
ROBERT CRIST, AND CAROLEE McBETH

Argonne National Laboratory, Lemont, Illinois, and University of Kansas, Lawrence, Kansas

INTRODUCTION

Most studies that present comparative electrophoretic data on plasmas or sera of animals have one or two "normal" or "control" samples and one or at most four or five "experimental" samples. Long series of samples from control and experimental animals, or long series of normal and experimental samples from one animal, are generally not available. Largely responsible for the absence of comparative information on electrophoresis has been the difficulty of working with the standard, moving boundary method. Paper-strip electrophoresis has greatly simplified this kind of comparative analysis of protein systems.

As part of some experiments designed to follow histological and hematological changes in irradiated monkeys, it was possible to obtain extensive series of samples of sera. This study presents and describes the changes that were found in samples of sera taken periodically from *Rhesus* monkeys before and after irradiations, as revealed by paper-strip electrophoresis.

MATERIALS AND METHODS

Monkeys. Twenty-three irradiated monkeys (Table I) and one unirradiated monkey were used in these experiments. The monkeys were maintained individually in cages in an air-conditioned kennel, fed a standard ration and left unhandled except when they were being irradiated or bled. Eight of the irradiated monkeys were initially free of tuberculosis but subsequently developed positive clinical symptoms for the disease. Fifteen of the irradiated monkeys and the one non-irradiated monkey were TB-positive throughout the entire course of experimentation.

[1] This work was performed in part under the auspices of the U. S. Atomic Energy Commission and AEC contract AT(11-1)-83, Project No. 4.

[2] Resident Research Associate, Argonne National Laboratory, from University of Kansas.

[3] Student Assistant (Summer), Argonne National Laboratory. Present address: University of Ottawa.

Irradiations. Whole-body exposures were employed in all irradiations. During exposures the monkeys were held in a harness that covered their legs and body and permitted their arms to be strapped to the outside. If the animals were suspended in a hammock-type of position during an exposure, they remained relatively quiet.

Seven monkeys were given 600 r of X-irradiation in a single bilateral exposure at a rate of 5 r/min. Irradiation conditions were: 250 kv, 15 ma, 1 mm Cu and 3 mm Bakelite filters, half-value layer 2.3 mm Cu. The monkeys were placed in an exposure field whose maximum variation was 5%. Two other groups (11 monkeys and 5 monkeys) were given repeated doses of Co^{60} γ-rays, 60 r every 2 weeks, or 100 r every week, respectively, at 5 r/min, until they died (Table I).

Serum samples. The samples of serum were derived from slightly heparinized plasmas by freezing the latter at −20°C. Fibrin clots inevitably formed when the plasmas were thawed. Each sample of plasma was frozen within 48 hours after collection and was kept in this condition until all samples from a given monkey had been collected.

Protein determinations. A standard curve was plotted from color reactions obtained with Biuret reagent and human serum the protein content of which was determined from micro-Kjeldahl analyses of both total and nonprotein nitrogen. The values for protein nitrogen were converted to protein on the assumption that the nitrogen was 16% of the total weight of the protein. Dittebrandt's (*1*) modification of the Biuret reagent was employed throughout. Tubes containing the protein and the reagent were incubated at 37°C for 30 minutes and then were read in a Coleman junior spectrophotometer set at 555 mμ. The reagent-protein mixtures produced color reactions that were stable for 2 hours after incubation.

Electrophoresis. The sera were analyzed by means of the Spinco Model R paper electrophoresis apparatus and the Spinco Analytrol scanner. Standardized procedures were employed (*2*); runs were made with Spinco barbituate buffer B-2 at pH 8.5 for 18 hours at 5 ma. Two Model R cells were used in each run; this permitted, for a majority of the monkeys, the simultaneous handling of all samples of serum obtained from a single animal. When more samples were obtained than could be handled by the two cells—that is, 16 strips—preirradiation samples of sera from these monkeys were included in the second run with the postirradiation samples so that comparative controls were obtained. All strips were placed in a still-air drying oven at 120°C for 30 minutes, after which they were stained for 6 hours in Spinco Dye B-1, rinsed twice in baths of 5% acetic acid, carefully dried between clean blotters, and returned to the drying oven for 15 minutes. Fresh stain, rinse, and fixing solutions were used to process the strips from each monkey. One hour before the strips were scanned in the Analytrol instrument they were placed for 1 minute in an atmosphere saturated with vapor from concentrated ammonium hydroxide (28 to 30% NH_3) to further develop color.

The Analytrol scanner traced a curve that indicated the relative concentration of the individual serum proteins as these were stained and fixed along the electrophoretic paper strip. The curves were automatically integrated by the scanner which, simultaneously with the tracing, recorded "counts" that were proportional to the area under each portion of the curve. Each tracing of serum was divided into four components representing the albumins and the α-, β-, and γ-globulins. No attempt was made to divide the α- and β-globulins into their subcomponents. In any sample that exhibited hemolysis the tracing representing the hemoglobin (Hb) was deducted from all calculations derived from the curve.

TABLE I

SURVIVAL OF MONKEYS EXPOSED TO X- AND GAMMA RADIATION

Exposure	*Monkey Number*	*TB*	*Sex*	*Number of doses*	*Total dose (r)*	*Survival (days)*[a]
X-rays, 600-r single dose	MC4	−	M	1	600	3
	19	−	M	1	600	16
	20	−	M	1	600	39
	21	−	M	1	600	32
	24	−	M	1	600	210
	27	−	M	1	600	60
	30	−	M	1	600	25
Average				1	600	55
γ-rays, 60 r/2 weeks	1	+	M	12	720	161
	7	+	F	14	840	182
	8	+	F	2	120	21
	9	+	F	3	180	35
	10	+	F	3	180	28
	11	+	F	11	660	147
	12	+	F	7	420	84
	13	−	Preg. F	11	660	140
	16	+	F	7	420	91
	23	+	?	2	120	14
	31	+	?	2	120	14
Average				7	404	83
γ-rays, 100 r/ week	14	+	F	9	900	56
	18	+	M	9	900	56
	22	+	M	5	500	28
	29	+	M	7	700	42
	32	+	M	11	1100	70
Average				8	820	50

[a] Days after the first exposure to irradiation. MC4 was a cynomologous monkey, *Macaca irus;* all other animals were rhesus monkeys, *Macaca mulatta.*

The per cent of each component in a sample of serum was calculated from (1) the counts of the total protein minus Hb and (2) the counts for the proteins of each type. The amount of protein represented by the tracing was calculated as follows:

$$\left(\frac{\text{Individual protein count}}{\text{Total count minus Hb count}}\right)(\text{Total protein in gm/100 ml}) = \text{Individual protein in gm/100 ml}$$

EXPERIMENTAL DATA

Table I shows the general plan of the experiment and gives the relation between radiation dosage and survival. Monkeys receiving 60 r per 2 weeks on the average were exposed seven times, accumulated a dose of 404 r, and survived 83 days. Monkeys receiving 100 r/week on the average were exposed eight times, accumulated a dose of 820 r, and survived 50 days. Monkeys that received a single dose of 600 r survived an average of 55 days.

Plots were made of the amounts of the various component proteins found in each sample of serum from every monkey. Representative data, illustrating the responses of monkeys to the irradiations, are presented in Figs. 1 to 4.

Examination of all the data for the groups receiving 60 r per 2 weeks and 100 r/week suggested that the postirradiation data could, in most cases, be divided into two phases; the end of the first phase was estimated to occur at 90 days in the former group and at 25 days in the latter. The total protein curves in Figs. 2 and 3 are illustrative. When no change in response was obvious, the postirradiation data were not divided into two phases.

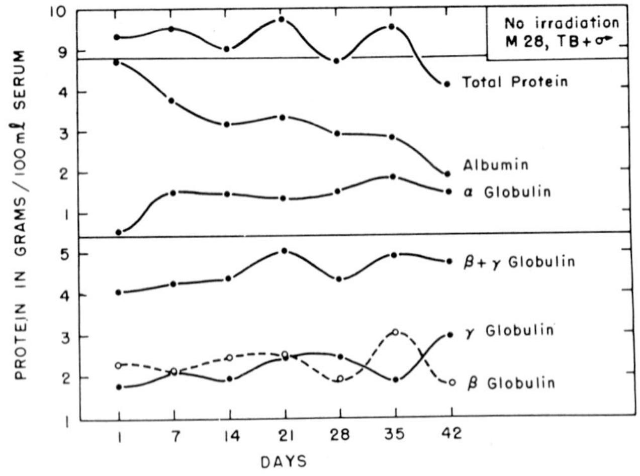

FIG. 1. Variations in the levels of the proteins in the serum of an unirradiated TB+ monkey (M28).

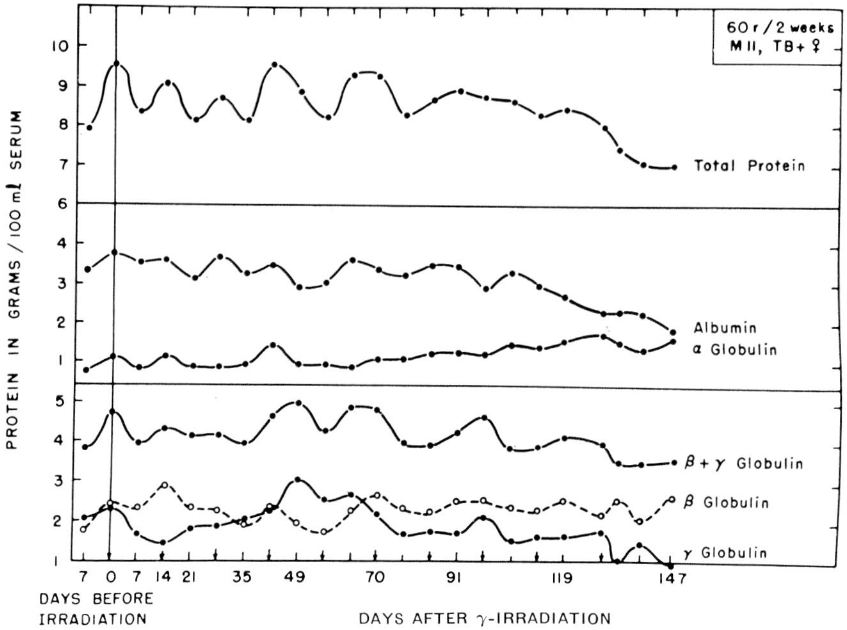

FIG. 2. Variations in the levels of the proteins in the serum of a monkey (M11) that received 60 r of γ-rays every 2 weeks. Two samples were obtained prior to irradiation. Blood taken on any day of irradiation, indicated on the abscissa (↓), was obtained prior to exposure.

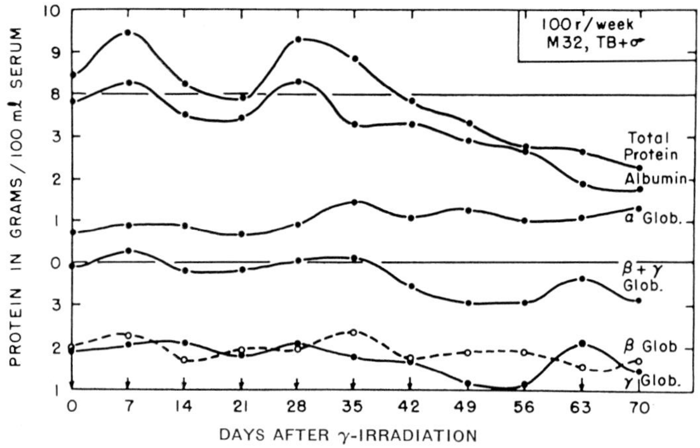

FIG. 3. Variations in the levels of the proteins in the serum of a monkey (M32) that received 100 r of γ-rays every week. Blood taken on any day of irradiation, indicated on the abscissa (↓), was obtained prior to exposure.

In general only two or three preirradiation samples were obtained from the monkeys that received 60 r per 2 weeks and 100 r/week, and hence there were insufficient numbers of normal samples to provide adequate data for comparison with the postirradiation samples. From the monkeys that received 600 r in a single exposure, eight to ten samples of blood at 4- to 5-day intervals were obtained prior to irradiation, and adequate comparisons of preirradiation and postirradiation data were possible. The responses of the monkeys in the 600-r group were generally acute, and the two phases were not observable in the postirradiation data.

An attempt was made to characterize, for each monkey, the responses to irradiation, as indicated by the changes in amount (grams per 100 ml) of total protein, albumin, and globulin of the serum and with respect to time in days. The data for the first phase and the second phase (where both were evident in the postirradiation response of a monkey), the entire postirradiation response (when it could not be conveniently divided), as well as the preirradiation data for the 600-r group were separately fitted to the equation for a straight line by the method of "least squares" (*3*).

Each group of data was placed on an x-y coordinate system. The intersect of the axes was adjusted so that all values for x and y would be positive. The data were then employed in the equation for a 3 × 3 determinant as follows:

$$\begin{vmatrix} x & y & 1 \\ \sum_{i=1}^{n} xi & \sum_{i=1}^{n} yi & \sum_{i=1}^{n} 1 \\ \sum_{i=1}^{n} x^2i & \sum_{i=1}^{n} xiyi & \sum_{i=1}^{n} xi \end{vmatrix} = 0$$

The equation was solved for all values of x and y to give for each group of data the generalized equation for a straight line:

$$Ax + By + C = 0$$

The slopes of the resultant lines are equal to the expression A/B.

The values for the slopes of the lines are given in Tables II and III for 13 of the 24 monkeys that were studied. These monkeys were selected for analyses because the data on them were the most extensive. Positive values for slopes indicate a general increase in amounts of protein, negative values a general decrease in the amounts of protein.

Among the monkeys that received 60 r every 2 weeks and 100 r every week (Table II), the second phase of the postirradiation response showed a decrease in the amount of total protein and albumin and an increase in the amount of α-globulin. Similarly, among monkeys in these exposure groups for which the postirradiation phase was not divided, the total protein and albumin decreased and the α-globu-

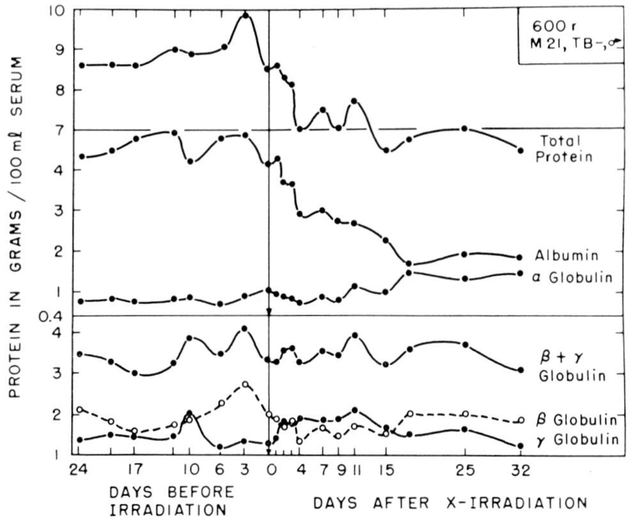

FIG. 4. Variations in the levels of the proteins in the serum of a monkey (M21) that received 600 r of X-rays in a single exposure. Blood taken on the day of irradiation, day zero on the abscissa, was obtained prior to exposure.

TABLE II

SLOPES OF CURVES DETERMINED FROM THE FIRST- AND SECOND-PHASE POSTIRRADIATION VALUES OF AMOUNTS OF PROTEIN IN THE SERA OF MONKEYS SUBJECTED TO REPEATED EXPOSURES TO GAMMA RAYS

Exposure group	*Monkey number*	*Total protein*		*Albumin*		*α-Globulin*	
		1st	*2nd*	*1st*	*2nd*	*1st*	*2nd*
60 r/2 weeks	7	0.767	−2.851	0.380	−3.137	−0.107	0.794
	11	0.344	−3.598	−0.177	−2.661	0.226	0.615
	13	0.263	−1.665	0.368	−2.690	0.092	0.252
	Average	0.458	−2.705	0.190	−2.829	0.071	0.554
100 r/week	14	4.400	−7.686	0.614	−6.342	−0.371	1.300
	32	0.229	−7.336	0.243	−5.587	0.343	0.168
	Average	2.314	−7.611	0.429	−5.965	−0.142	0.734
No irradiation	28	−1.847		−5.434		1.857	
60 r/2 weeks	12	−0.900		−2.464		0.849	
100 r/week	18	−5.391		−3.779		0.014	
	29	−5.192		−4.641		1.763	
	Average	−5.291		−4.210		0.888	

lins increased. The rate of decrease was greater in the monkeys that received 100 r/week.

Among the monkeys that received 600 r (Table III) the preirradiation phase showed a general decrease in total protein and albumin, and the postirradiation

TABLE III

SLOPES OF CURVES DETERMINED FROM THE PREIRRADIATION AND POSTIRRADIATION VALUES OF AMOUNTS OF PROTEIN IN THE SERA OF MONKEYS EXPOSED TO 600 R OF X-IRRADIATION

Monkey number	*Total protein*		*Albumin*		*α-Globulin*	
	Before irradiation	*After irradiation*	*Before irradiation*	*After irradiation*	*Before irradiation*	*After irradiation*
20	−1.533	−2.995	−3.016	−4.836	1.611	1.723
21	2.491	−5.479	0.170	−7.354	0.607	2.234
27	−0.401	−0.445	−0.297	−1.102	0.310	0.397
30	−1.367	−7.128	−2.360	−6.007	1.078	1.161
Average	−0.203	−3.790	−1.376	−4.825	0.901	1.379

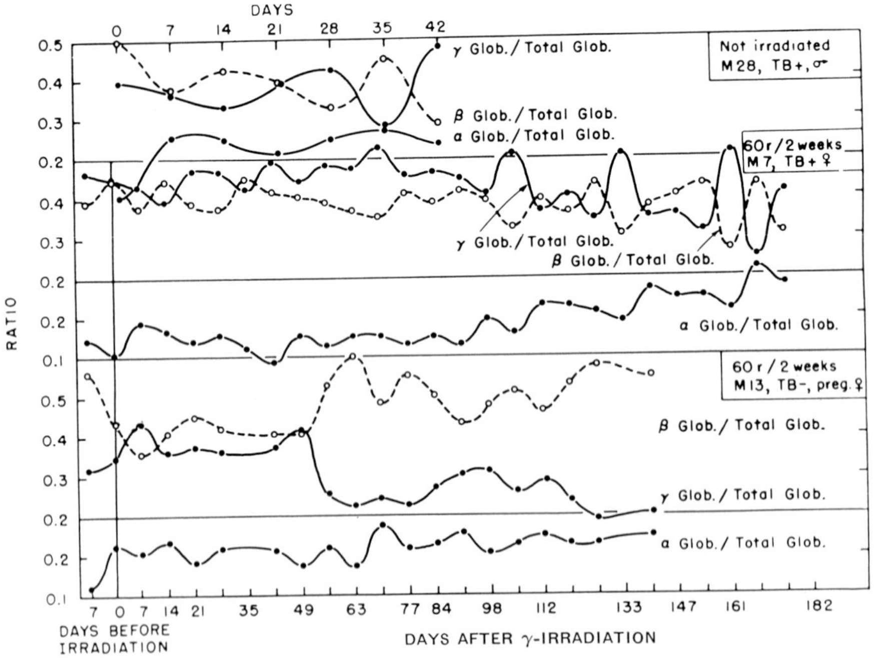

FIG. 5. Ratios of each kind of globulin to the total globulins in the serum of a monkey (M28) that was not irradiated and in the sera of two monkeys (M7 and M13) that received 60 r of γ-rays every 2 weeks.

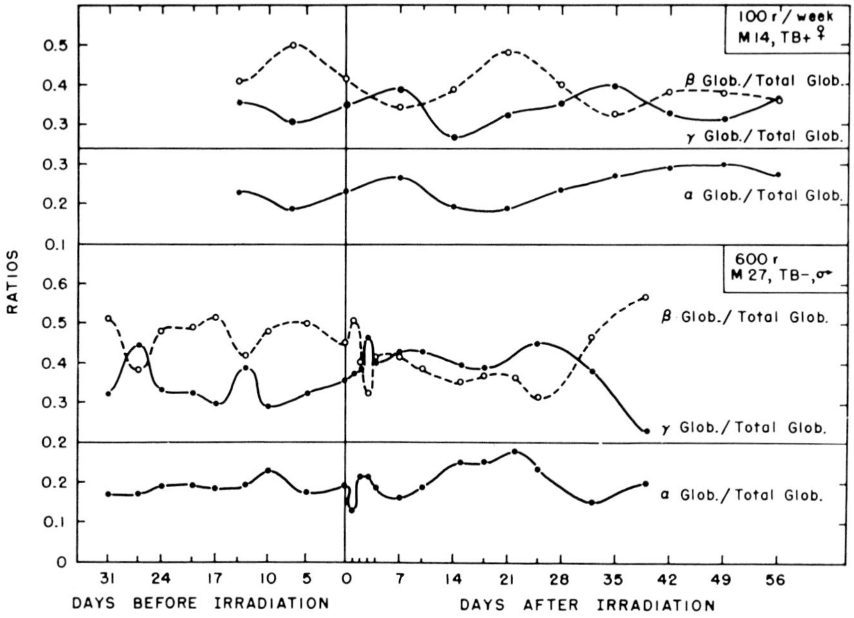

FIG. 6. Ratios of each kind of globulin to the total globulins in the serum of a monkey (M14) that received 100 r of γ-rays each week and a monkey (M27) that received 600 r of X-rays in a single exposure.

phase showed a greater decrease. The α-globulins increased during both preirradiation and postirradiation phases.

Regardless of the exposure groups, 20 of the 23 irradiated monkeys exhibited a decrease in total proteins of the sera after irradiation. In 22 monkeys the albumins of the sera likewise decreased. In all 23 animals, the α-globulins of the sera increased after irradiation.

From data such as those presented in Figs. 1 to 4, it appeared that the β- and γ-globulins might be interdependent and complementary. In order to reveal any such relationship, values for the ratio of single globulin to total globulin were determined for each sample. These ratios, when plotted, had the effect of smoothing out the globulin curves and made more apparent the relationship of each kind of globulin to the others. Illustrative curves obtained with values for the globulin ratios are presented in Figs. 5 and 6. It is clear that the β- and γ-globulins are complementary to each other, since the curves for these globulins, in every monkey, are nearly mirror images. The curves for the α-globulins, on the other hand, indicate that these proteins are not metabolically interrelated to the other globulins.

Figures 7 to 9 are plots of the albumin-to-globulin (A/G) ratios for the sera from monkeys of each of the irradiation exposure groups. Superimposed on the cyclic

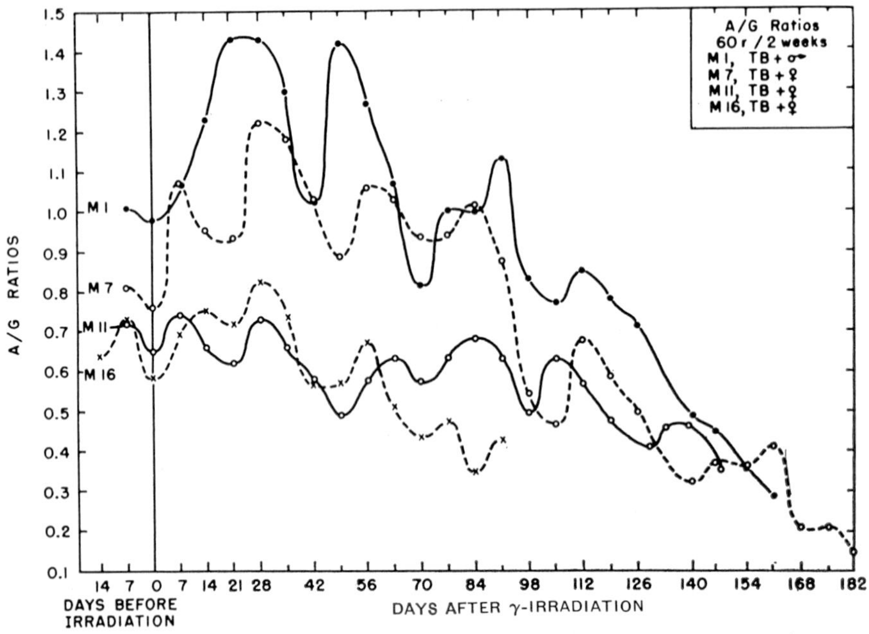

FIG. 7. The albumin-to-globulin (A/G) ratios of 4 monkeys (M1, M7, M11, M16) that received 60 r of γ-rays every 2 weeks until death.

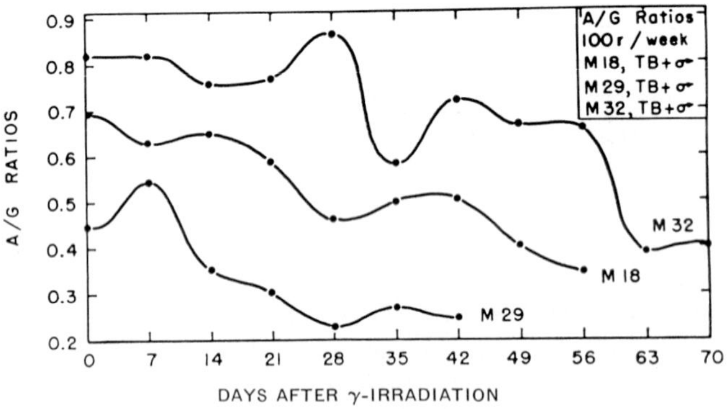

FIG. 8. The albumin-to-globulin (A/G) ratios of 3 monkeys (M18, M29, M32) that received 100 r of γ-rays every 2 weeks until death.

variation of the ratios is a steady decline in the values after irradiation. The concordance of the cycles among the monkeys from each exposure group implies an innate rhythmic metabolic interrelationship between the albumins and the globulins of the sera.

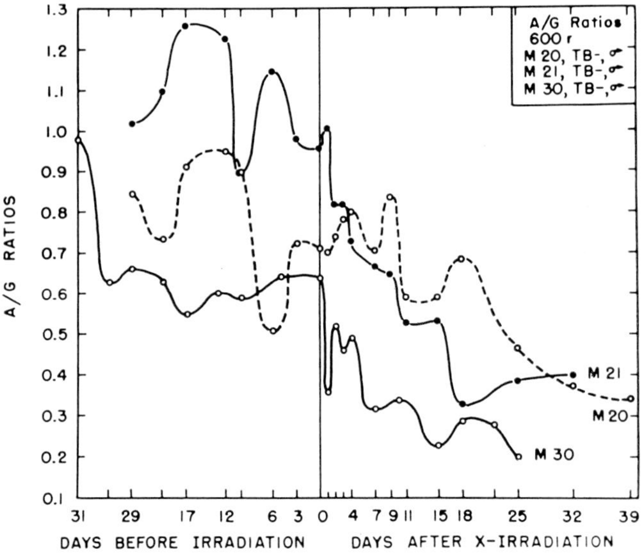

FIG. 9. The albumin-to-globulin (A/G) ratios of 3 monkeys (M20, M21, M30) that received 600 r of X-rays in a single exposure.

DISCUSSION

The mortality data in Table I for the monkeys that received 600 r of X-irradiation agree with those of Henschke (*4*), who estimates the 30-day LD_{50} for monkeys to be 530 ± 21 r.

For the monkeys that received 60 r of γ-rays every 2 weeks, the range of survival values was greater than expected. All monkeys in this group were tuberculin-positive, and, despite the administration of antibiotics, this undoubtedly shortened their survival time; it is unlikely that 120 r in two exposures of 60 r or 180 r in three such exposures would have resulted in the death of 5 of 11 monkeys. Those monkeys that survived between 84 and 182 days probably represent the more normal response to repeated irradiations at the rate of 60 r every 2 weeks. If only these latter monkeys are considered, the average survival time is 134 days.

Similarly, the tuberculin-positive condition of the 5 monkeys that received 100 r of γ-rays every week (Table I) probably had an adverse influence on their survival, but the observed average of 50 days and 8 exposures would probably be reasonable even for healthy monkeys.

Tuberculosis in humans has been reported by several workers to cause a decrease in serum albumins and an increase in α-globulins (*5–8*). Observations of these workers on the β- and γ-globulins were at variance; increases, decreases, and no changes were observed. From an inspection of Figs. 1 to 6 one can understand how observations by separate workers on the behavior of the β- and γ-globulins could be contradictory and yet true, depending on the moment the sample of blood was taken. Monkey 28, the only unirradiated animal in our experiments, was tuberculin-positive and showed, in agreement with the above workers, a decrease in total protein and albumin and an increase in α-globulin (Fig. 1).

The loss of serum albumin and the increase of α-globulin observed as responses to ionizing radiations in our experiments with monkeys have been reported for other laboratory animals: dogs (*9*), rabbits and guinea pigs (*10*), rabbits (*11*), and rats (*12–14*). These two responses are not peculiar to tuberculosis and irradiation and have been reported in the literature as the regular consequence of a wide variety of infectious and systemic diseases and for physiological stresses such as aging, pregnancy, burns, and extremes of environmental temperatures.

The complementary behavior of the β- and γ-globulins of the serum implies a physiological interrelationship. Tentatively, it is suggested that the site of formation for these two classes of proteins is the same. The stimuli and regulatory mechanisms that cause the suppression of the synthesis of one globulin in favor of the other is unknown to us.

The α-globulins seem to be independent of the β- and γ-globulins and more intimately related to the serum albumins. As the albumins begin their general decline after irradiation, the α-globulins begin to increase in amount; however, the rise in the amount of α-globulin does not quantitatively compensate for the loss of albumin.

It is obvious from a study of the data for serum changes in any one monkey that there is considerable fluctuation in the total amount of protein in the serum, even in normal animals. The component proteins do not rise and fall proportionately with each change in total protein. The complementary responses of the β- and γ-globulins coupled with the independent changes of the α-globulins and the albumins establish a picture of continuously altering proportionalities among the components.

SUMMARY

Periodic preirradiation and postirradiation samples of sera from 23 monkeys were studied by means of paper-strip electrophoresis. The changes in concentration of the total proteins, the albumins, the α-globulins, the β-globulins, and the γ-globulins were followed. Eleven TB+ animals received 60 r of Co^{60} γ-rays every 2 weeks until they died; 5 TB+ animals received 100 r of γ-rays every week until they died; 7 TB− animals received 600 r of X-rays in a single exposure; 1 TB+ animal was not irradiated. In 20 of the 23 irradiated monkeys there was a decrease in serum albumin. In all irradiated monkeys there was an increase in α-globulin. All proteins of the sera fluctuated considerably in their absolute concentration. The β- and γ-globulins appear to be complementary with respect to one another.

RECEIVED: June 3, 1958

REFERENCES

1. M. DITTEBRANDT, Application of the Wechselbaum biuret reagent to the determination of spinal fluid protein. *Am. J. Clin. Pathol.* **18,** 439–441 (1948).
2. Operating Instructions, Spinco Model R Paper Electrophoresis Apparatus. Special Instruments Corporation, Belmont, California.
3. D. V. WIDDER, *Advanced Calculus*, p. 108, Prentice-Hall, New York, 1947.
4. U. K. HENSCHKE and J. L. MORTON, Mortality of rhesus monkeys after single total-body irradiation. *Am. J. Roentgenol. Radium Therapy Nuclear Med.* **77,** 899–909 (1957).
5. E. H. KOLN, The electrophoretic diagram in infantile tb. *Monatsschr. Kinderheilk.* **98**(4), 150–151 (1950).
6. H. BRODHAGE, Serum observations in tuberculosis with the hemagglutination reaction and electrophoresis. *Beitr. Klin. Tuberk.* **107,** 494–511 (1952).
7. R. W. BALDWIN and C. N. ILAND, Electrophoretic studies of serum proteins in tuberculosis. *Am. Rev. Tuberc.* **68,** 372–381 (1953).
8. H. KANAGAMI, On the electrophoretic analysis of serum protein of pulmonary tuberculosis. Part II. The relation between the qualitative classification of pulmonary tuberculosis and serum protein components. *Repts. Research Inst. Tuberc. Leprosy* **5**(4), 415–423 (1954).
9. W. H. GOLDWATER and C. ENTENMAN, Nature of serum protein changes in the X-irradiated dog. *Am. J. Physiol.* **188,** 409–414 (1957).
10. G. MEYNIEL and S. DEMENDE, Electrophoretic study of serum proteins of irradiated animals. *Bull. soc. chim. biol.* **37,** 127–131 (1955).
11. O. ANDREONI, M. DOMPE, and A. M. RUSSO, Proteins and lipoproteins of the serum in rabbits subjected to total-body irradiation. *Ricerca sci.* **25,** 1393–1399 (1955).
12. M. A. FISCHER, M. Z. MAGEE, and E. P. COULTER, Studies on the serum proteins of the X-irradiated rat. *Arch. Biochem. Biophys.* **56,** 66–74 (1955).
13. G. HOHNE, R. JASTER, and H. A. KUNKEL, Electrophoretic measurements on the serum of roentgen-irradiated rats. *Klin. Wochschr.* **30,** 952 (1952).
14. G. HOHNE, H. A. KUNKEL, and R. ANGER, Serum proteins of the rat after whole-body irradiation with 3000 r. *Klin. Wochschr.* **33,** 284 (1955).

RADIATION RESEARCH 10, 370–379 (1959)

Radiation Destruction of the Plaque-Forming Ability of Spores of Lysogenic *Bacillus megaterium*

CARL WOESE

Biophysics Department, Yale University, New Haven, Connecticut

INTRODUCTION

It has been shown (*1*) that spores of lysogenic *B. megaterium* lose very little of their ability to produce virus (on germination) when given doses of ionizing radiation which destroy 99% of their colony-forming ability. This applies to spores of inducible strains of *B. megaterium* (inducible in the sense that ultraviolet and H_2O_2 cause lysis of a turbid growing culture and virus production) as well as to spores of non-inducible lysogenic *B. megaterium*. The kinetics of inactivation of the plaque-forming ability of lysogenic vegetative cells is, in general, a multiple-target curve whose multiplicity correlates, at least roughly, with the number of nuclear bodies (*2*). It appears, therefore, that, as long as at least one prophage (or one nuclear body) remains unhit by radiation, the cell may function to produce virus. The present paper deals with the kinetics of the radiation inactivation of virus production by spores of lysogenic *B. megaterium*.

MATERIALS AND METHODS

The strains of *B. megaterium* used in these experiments were as follows:

S —a nonspore-forming strain sensitive to all phages used in this experiment. This strain has a very low rate of lysogenization by the phages used.

D(1) —the classical inducible lysogenic strain of *B. megaterium* (known more commonly as *B. megaterium* 899) lysogenic for phage M1 (*3*).

D —a variant of D(1), producing no detectable phage and sensitive to all phages used in this experiment.

D(5) —D strain lysogenic for phage M5 (*3*); vegetative cells of this strain are noninducible.

D(25)—D strain lysogenic for phage M25 (*3*); vegetative cells of this strain are noninducible,

C —a strain of *B. megaterium* which produces no phage detectable on strain S or any other available indicator strain.

C(1) —C strain lysogenic for phage M1; this strain is inducible.

C(1L)—C strain lysogenic for phage M1L, a clear plaque mutant of phage M1; this strain is inducible.

C(5) —C strain lysogenic for phage M5; vegetative cells of this strain are noninducible.

All these bacterial strains and phages were a gift of Dr. Philip Cowles of the Yale University School of Medicine, Department of Microbiology.

Phage stocks were prepared by infecting a log phase culture of S grown in yeast extract broth with the appropriate phage strain and storing the resulting lysate in a refrigerator until use. Lysogenization was accomplished by adding phage to a broth suspension of spores of the strain to be lysogenized. After one day of incubation of the mixture at room temperature, single-colony isolates were made and tested for phage-producing ability; stable lysogenic systems were then sporulated.

Plaque-count assays for phage or lysogenic spores were done by an agar layer technique on yeast extract agar plates with *B. megaterium* S as the indicator strain; this procedure has been described fully previously (*1*).

Irradiation procedures were as follows:

a. For spores—spores to be X-irradiated were taken from a potato agar slant and suspended in 2 ml of ice-cold yeast extract broth (*4*), heated rapidly to a temperature of 72°C for 10 minutes (which destroys all free phage and nonspore forms of bacteria), and rapidly cooled again to ice temperatures. The sample was then X-irradiated and periodically sampled (*4*), being kept at ice temperatures throughout to prevent germination of the spores.

b. For phage—all phage irradiations were carried out with the phage either dried onto glass cover slips from a broth suspension, or in yeast extract broth under the conditions described above for spores.

RESULTS

Figure 1 shows the survival of plaque-forming ability of D(1), D(5), and D(25) spores as a function of X-ray dose, given in the figure as minutes of irradiation at 4700 r/min. The colony-survival curve has a much steeper slope and different shape. It is discussed in ref. *4*. The solid curves for destruction of plaque-forming ability shown on the graph are theoretical two-target curves of the form (*5*)

$$N/N_0 = e^{-V_r I}(2 - e^{-V_r I}) \qquad (1)$$

where N/N_0 is the fractional survival, I is the dose of radiation in arbitrary units, and V_r is a parameter measuring the "target volume" for the specific inactivation process in appropriate units.

It should be noticed that the fraction of plaques rises as a function of dose for strain D(25) before it falls. For spores of this strain, then, there is an induction component in addition to an inactivation component to the plaque-survival curve (*2*). All the strains used except D(25) have a control plaque count equal to the

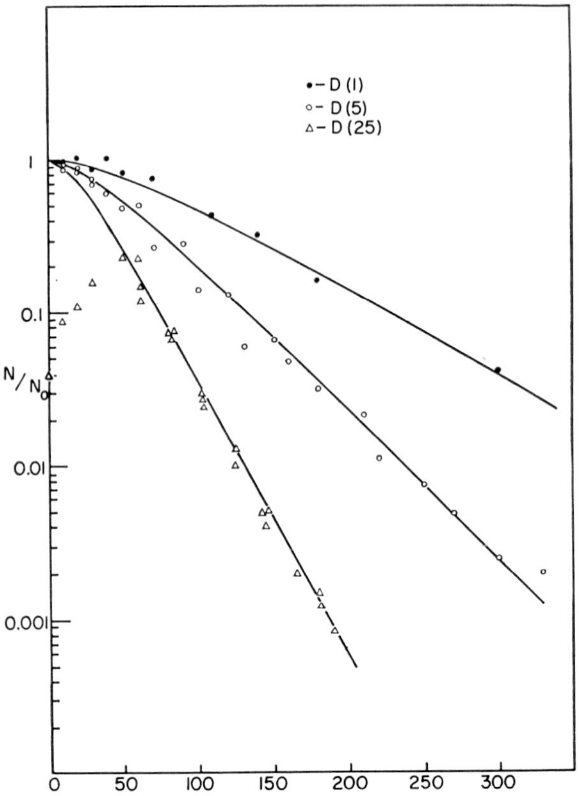

FIG. 1. Survival of the plaque-forming ability of lysogenic *B. megaterium* D spores as a function of X-ray exposure (given as minutes of irradiation at 4700 r/min).

control colony count within a few per cent (1), so that there can be no rise in plaque count with radiation dose. In the case of strain D(25) the control colony count is used to determine the fractional survival of plaques (i.e., N_0 equals the control colony count, as the plaque count can never reach 100% of the control colony count, owing to the fact that the dose range which gives appreciable inactivation overlaps that which gives induction).

Figure 2 shows the results of X-irradiating spores of C(1), C(1L), and C(5). In Fig. 3 the results of irradiating the viruses M1, M5, and M25 are plotted; dose is given in minutes of irradiation at 3800 r/min. The viruses were irradiated in cold broth, as were the spores. It is probable that there is little or no indirect effect of the radiation under these conditions, owing to the protective effect of the yeast extract broth (*6*). Phage M1L shows an inactivation curve identical to that of phage M1 (this result is not presented in Fig. 3).

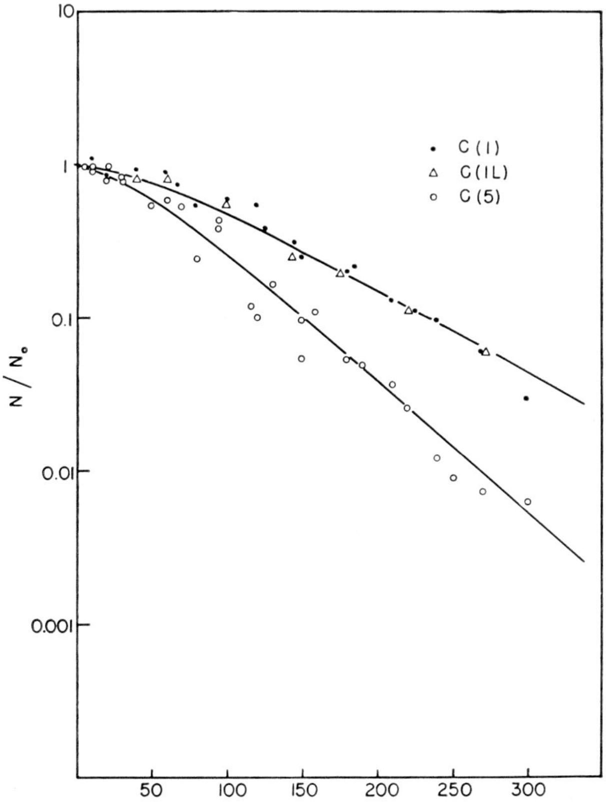

FIG. 2. Survival of the plaque-forming ability of lysogenic *B. megaterium* C spores as a function of X-ray exposure (given as minutes of irradiation at 4700 r/min).

The data presented in the figures are summarized and compared in Table I. Also included in the table are the relative target-volume parameters for irradiation of the free viruses in the dry state. The comparison reveals several interesting points. First, the destruction of plaque-forming ability of a spore carrying a given prophage is independent of the bacterial strain carrying the prophage, as the results are essentially the same whether the C or D strain is used. Second, the radiation-sensitive volumes, V_r, for destruction of plaque-forming ability of spores carrying different prophages vary as the V_r's of the corresponding free phages. Third, the V_r for destruction of plaque-forming ability by a given type of lysogenic spore is one-third of the radiation-sensitive volume of the corresponding free phage irradiated in yeast extract broth. Another point of comparison is that, whereas the free virus is inactivated in a single-target fashion (i.e., straight line on a semilog plot), the spore inactivations are two-target.

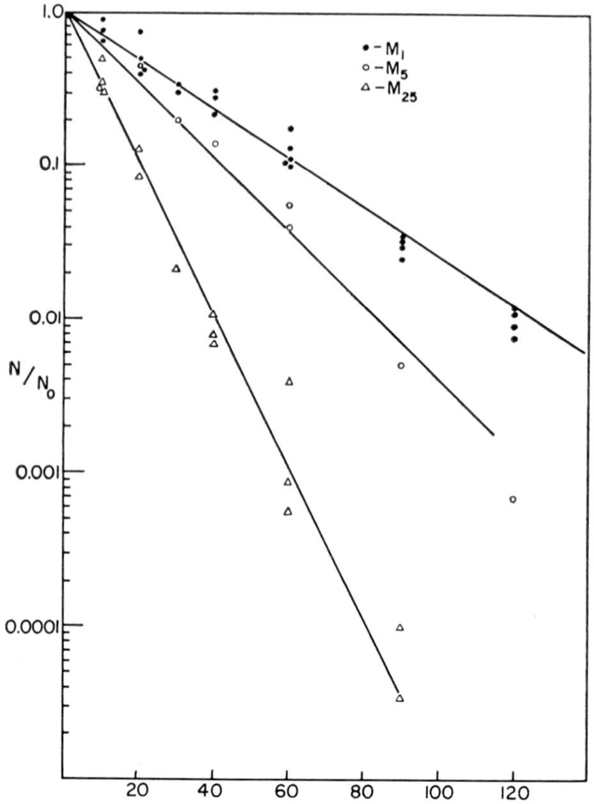

FIG. 3. Survival of the plaque-forming ability of free phages as a function of X-ray exposure (given as minutes of irradiation at 3800 r/min).

It is clear from the results presented in ref. *1* that colony-forming ability of a spore can be destroyed by radiation without destroying the plaque-forming ability. There remains the question as to whether the reverse of this can occur; i.e., can the plaque-forming ability of a spore be destroyed without destroying the colony-forming ability? The following experiment shows that this is not the case. When lysogenic spores are given a dose of X-radiation sufficient to reduce the fraction of colony formers to 10^{-4} to 10^{-5}, the corresponding plaque survivals range from 0.8 to 0.02 (depending on the strain used, etc.). In other words, if the colony-forming ability and the plaque-forming ability of the spore were destroyed independently of each other, at the very least 20% of the colony survivors at 10^{-4} to 10^{-5} survival would not produce virus. Direct tests on colony survivors can check this possibility, but one must avoid possible reinfection of sensitive cells by free virus.

Cowles (personal communication) has shown that citrate ion prevents infection of

TABLE I

COMPARISON OF THE RELATIVE X-RAY SENSITIVITY PARAMETERS FOR FREE PHAGES AND SPORES OF BACTERIAL STRAINS LYSOGENIC FOR THESE STRAINS

Phage Mx	*Target volume free phage broth irradiated*[a]	*Target volume, free phage dry irradiated*[a]	*Dry target volume: broth target volume ratio*	*Target volume, plaque formation by spore $D(x)$*[a]	$C(x)/D(x)$	$D(x)/Mx$ *virus irradiated*	
						In broth	*Dry*
M1	1.0	0.40	2.5	0.33	1.05	0.33	0.82
M5	1.5	0.76	2.0	0.53	1.08	0.35	0.69
M25	2.9	3.0	1.0	1.0	—	0.34	0.33

[a] Relative to target volume of M1 irradiated in broth.

cells by the viruses used in this study but does not prevent the production and release of these viruses from cells lysogenic for them. We have repeated this observation and find that without citrate addition roughly 50% of nonlysogenic cells produce lysogenic colonies when plated in the presence of virus under the experimental conditions we use. With the addition of citrate to the assay medium, however, we have never observed the lysogenization of nonlysogenic cells.

The actual experiment in question is to irradiate spores until their colony survival is 10^{-4} to 10^{-5} of controls, plate on minimal citrate medium (*1*), and test the resulting colonies for their ability to produce virus. For bacterial strains lysogenic for phages M1L, M5, and M25, we have never observed a nonlysogenic (nonphage-producing) colony resulting from irradiation. For strains carrying phage M1 the situation is complicated by the fact that about 3% of such spores prove to be nonlysogenic on germination when unirradiated. There is, however, no increase or decrease in the percentage of nonlysogenic colonies in the heavily irradiated C(1) and D(1) spores. The number of colonies of each lysogenic strain tested ranges from 100 to 300. Speaking in terms of probabilities, the above negative result means that the probability of destroying the virus-producing ability of the spore *without* destroying the colony-forming ability is less than one-tenth the probability of destroying the plaque-forming ability of the spore.

DISCUSSION

The striking feature of the above data is that there is a constant ratio between V_r of the free virus irradiated in broth and V_r of the unit(s) responsible for the plaque-forming ability of the spore (on germination), even though the V_r's themselves vary over a factor of 3. This suggests that when radiation destroys the plaque-forming ability of the spore it acts mainly on the prophage itself, and perhaps the prophage is about one-third the size of the radiosensitive portion of the free virus. Another explanation of the data, however, is that not the prophage but the "capacity" of the cell to produce virus is being destroyed in the case of the spore irradiations, and that the V_r for capacity is directly proportional to free-virus sensitive volume. A third possibility is that radiation is destroying the ability of the spore to germinate to the point where it can support virus growth; this is a nonspecific effect. It is extremely unlikely, however, that this last-mentioned effect would correlate with free-virus radiation-sensitive volume.

It is difficult to determine what portion of the V_r involved in plaque-forming ability of the lysogenic spore is due to prophage and what portion is due to capacity. Partly this is a function of defining capacity for a lysogenic system. We shall consider prophage as any genetic material of the lysogenic cell identical with that of the virus (assuming that it takes identical genetic material to produce identical genetic material), and capacity to be any other bacterial components necessary to production of virus from prophage. There is no a priori reason to assume that capacity for a superinfecting phage is the same as that for phage production from a prophage. It is likely that the latter capacity is equal to or smaller than the former capacity, as most of the steps in phage production from prophage are the same as those for phage production from external phage infection (*7*). There are probably not so many steps involved in the prophage case, however, as the prophage does not have the problem of entering the bacterium. A comparison of the capacities for external infection by the phages used in this study can give strong suggestions as to the role capacity plays in the data reported above, though the comparison may not decide the matter unequivocally.

A study of capacity by irradiating spores has an additional complicating factor over the same study on vegetative cells, namely, radiation may affect the ability of the spore to germinate to the point where it develops the requisite capacity (this includes phage receptors, etc.). We have attempted to measure "spore capacity" of strain D for external infection by phages M1 and M5. The technique is to irradiate strain D spores, germinate them for about 2½ hours (which allows maximum development of irradiated spores), then adsorb phage (about 1 phage per 100 cells) to the germinated cells, centrifuge off unadsorbed phage, and finally plate for plaque count. The data show that the capacities for infection by phages M1 and M5 have essentially the same V_r, which is *larger* than the V_r for destruction of plaque-forming ability in strain D(1), but about the same size as the V_r for destruction of plaque-forming ability in strain D(5). The V_r for M25 capacity is smaller than that for M5 and M1 capacity. Such data do not give an unambiguous answer to the question.

Capacity studies on vegetative cells are more informative, however. For phage M11 (*3*) the result is clear-cut; the capacity for external phage infection is far more radiation-resistant than is the plaque-forming ability of the vegetative cells of the same strain lysogenic for phage M11 (which sensitive volume is about the same size as that for the same strain lysogenic for phage M1). The same is true for phage M25; the V_r for lysogenic phage production (in the vegetative cell) is over ten times the V_r for capacity for external phage infection. In the case of M5 and M1, however, the V_r's for lysogenic phage production are only two to four times the V_r's for capacity for external infection.

It is clear that the V_r for capacity for external phage infection bears no direct correlation with free-phage V_r, and that in two cases at least the capacity for external phage infection has a negligible V_r compared to that for phage production by corresponding lysogenic strains. In view of this, though it is not definitely proved, it seems likely that the prophage itself is the major radiosensitive target involved in the destruction of the plaque-forming ability of spores of lysogenic bacilli. The question could possibly be resolved completely by irradiating spores of doubly lysogenic strains carrying two closely related prophages, for in this case capacity would be the same for both prophages; such a strain would presumably produce mixed plaques if unirradiated, and the radiation kinetics for production of plaques containing only one type of phage could unequivocally decide the point in question. We have been unable to isolate and/or sporulate such strains to date.

If we consider the radiosensitive target in the spores to be prophage, several further conclusions can be arrived at. First, there are two prophages, as shown by the fact that the survival curve is a two-target curve, and it is necessary to destroy both of them in order to destroy the plaque-forming ability of the spore. This is in keeping with the multiple-target curves for destruction of plaque-forming ability observed in other lysogenic systems (*2, 8*). The radiation inactivation of the colony-forming ability of *B. megaterium* spores can be analyzed in terms of a model which postulates the radiosensitive targets of the spore to consist of n pairs of targets, survival being possible so long as at least one member of each pair is intact (*4*). This implies that the genetic material of the spore is duplicated. That there are two prophages agrees with a model postulating duplication of targets.

Under conditions that eliminate the contribution of indirect effects, radiation has been shown to be a reasonably accurate measure of molecular weights (*9*). We have shown previously that there is no indirect effect involved in the irradiation of spores, as the spore contains little or no unbound water (*10*) and the results of irradiation are the same whether the spores are irradiated dry *in vacuo* or in cold yeast extract broth (*4*). Further, there should be no indirect effects involved in the irradiation of free phage in yeast extract broth, as Latarjet (*6*) has shown protection of phages against indirect effects when irradiated under these conditions. In the case of M1 and M5, however, there is a difference between a particular phage irradiated in yeast extract broth and that phage irradiated dry. The exact correlation between free-phage sensitive volume and prophage sensitive volume exists only for the case where the free phage is irradiated in yeast extract broth. It is possible that the state of the virus radiosensitive material approximates more closely that of the spore radiosensitive material when the virus is in the "wet" state.

Comparing the V_r's for free phage irradiated in broth to those for prophage (Table I) we see that the latter is 33% of the former. Levinthal (*11*) has found that in phage infection 40% of the virus DNA is passed on intact to the progeny phage; it is tempting to equate this intact fraction to prophage in the case of lysogenic infections. Caution must be used in interpreting radiation target sizes for spores, however, as the response of spores to radiations of varying ion density is very atypical (*4*).

Prophage is considered to be intimately associated with the bacterial genetic material (*12*), but there is no evidence which unequivocally shows whether or not prophage is an *addition* to already existing bacterial genetic material, or in some manner a piece of bacterial genetic material of equivalent size is replaced by (or becomes transformed into) virus genetic material in forming a prophage. The following argument bears on th s question if three assumptions are made: first, that prophage is the entity being measured in these studies (which seems reasonable for at least one if not all the cases); second, that destruction of the colony-forming ability of spores is due to genetic damage, as the data suggest (*13*); and third, that a prophage hit by radiation has about the same probability (within a factor of 2) of undergoing a radiation recovery process, whether the spore itself can or cannot form a colony. If the presence of prophage does produce *additional* genetic material in the spore, then the radiosensitive volume for the spore colony-forming ability will be increased by this amount, provided that the additional material is also essential to spore colony-forming ability. If the additional material is not essential to spore colony-forming ability, however, it can be destroyed without affecting colony-forming ability, and the radiosensitive volume for colony formation will not be increased by its presence; but such destruction should destroy the virus-producing ability of the surviving cell. On the other hand, if the presence of prophage does not produce additional genetic material in the spore, one would expect that the radiosensitive volume for the spore colony-forming ability will not change, and that there could be no destruction of prophage without destroying colony-forming ability also.

The data (presented above, and in ref. *1*) show that in the case of spores of noninducible lysogenic strains there is no increase in radio-sensitive volume of the colony-forming ability over that of nonlysogenic strains, and that there is no destruction of plaque-forming ability which does not result in loss of colony-forming ability (i.e., all colony survivors are lysogenic). Therefore, for noninducible strains the prophage is not an addition to the existing bacterial genetic material but is the result of replacement (or transformation) of existing bacterial genetic material by (into) virus genetic material. For the case of spores of inducible lysogenic strains, there is also no destruction of plaque-forming ability without destruction of colony-forming ability, but there is an increase in the radiosensitive volume of the colony-forming ability over that of the nonlysogenic spores. This fact is not open to a single interpretation, though one possibility is that, in the case of inducible lysogenic strains only, there is extra genetic material in which ionizations or excitations induce phage synthesis.

SUMMARY

The destruction by X-rays of the plaque-forming ability of three phages and spores of *Bacillus megaterium* strains lysogenic for these phages is studied. It is found that the phages inactivate in a "single-target" fashion, whereas the spores inactivate in a "two-target" fashion as a function of X-ray dose. There is in every case a constant ratio between radiation size of the free phage and radiation size of the corresponding plaque-forming ability of the lysogenic spore.

These results are interpreted to mean (1) that the plaque-forming ability of the spore is destroyed by destroying the prophage, (2) that there are two prophages per spore, and (3) that for noninducible lysogenic strains the prophage is not an *addition* to already existing bacterial genetic material, but results from the replacement of existing bacterial genetic by (or its transformation into) phage genetic material.

RECEIVED: July 7, 1958

REFERENCES

1. C. WOESE, Induction of spores of lysogenic *Bacillus megaterium* by X-rays. *Arch. Biochem. Biophys.* **79,** 55–66 (1959).
2. F. JACOB and E. L. WOLLMAN, Induction of phage development in lysogenic bacteria. *Cold Spring Harbor Symposia Quant. Biol.* **18,** 101–121 (1953).
3. M. FRIEDMAN and P. B. COWLES, The bacteriophages of *Bacillus megaterium.* I. Serological, physical, and biological properties. *J. Bacteriol.* **66,** 379–385 (1953).
4. C. WOESE, Interpretation of inactivation kinetics of spores of *Bacillus megaterium. Arch. Biochem. Biophys.* **74,** 28–45 (1958).
5. K. C. ATWOOD and A. NORMAN, On the interpretation of multi-hit survival curves. *Proc. Natl. Acad. Sci. U. S.* **35,** 696–709 (1949).
6. H. EPHRUSSI-TAYLOR and R. LATERJET, Inactivation, par les rayons x, d'un facteur tranformant du pneumocoque. *Biochim. et Biophys. Acta* **16,** 183–197 (1955).
7. G. BERTANI, Lysogenic versus lytic cycle of phage multiplication. *Cold Spring Harbor Symposia Quant. Biol.* **18,** 65–73 (1955).
8. H. RAPPAPORT, Induction of a lysogenic *Escherichia coli* with alpha and deuteron particles. *Arch. Biochem. Biophys.* **76,** 1–14 (1958).
9. E. C. POLLARD, W. R. GUILD, F. HUTCHINSON, and R. B. SETLOW, The direct action of ionizing radiation on enzymes and antigens. *Progress in Biophys.* **5,** 72–108 (1955).
10. J. F. POWELL and R. E. STRANGE, Biochemical changes occurring during the germination of bacterial spores. *Biochem. J.* **54,** 205–209 (1953).
11. C. LEVINTHAL, The mechanism of DNA replication and genetic recombination in phage. *Proc. Natl. Acad. Sci. U. S.* **42,** 394–404 (1956).
12. F. JACOB, Transduction of lysogeny in *Escherichia coli. Virology* **1,** 207–220 (1955).
13. C. WOESE, Comparison of the X-ray sensitivity of bacterial spores. *J. Bacteriol.* **75,** 5–8 (1958).

RADIATION RESEARCH 10, 380–385 (1959)

Further Observations on the Effect of X-Irradiation on the Glycogen Content and Histology of the Rabbit Retina[1]

SIDNEY P. KENT

Department of Pathology, University of Alabama Medical Center, Birmingham, Alabama

INTRODUCTION

Morphological changes indicative of cell injury have been reported in the outer nuclear layer of the retina of rabbits receiving high doses of X-irradiation (*1*, *2*). More recently the glycogen content of the outer nuclear layer of the retina has been shown to increase within 4 hours after the administration of approximately 6000 r to the whole head (*3*). The glycogen content of the rat liver has been reported to increase after as little as 300 r of whole-body X-irradiation (*4*). Further, the liver glycogen increase even when the liver was shielded during the course of whole-body irradiation. This suggests that the effect of X-irradiation on liver glycogen is indirect. The purpose of this study was to determine, first, the effect of varying doses of X-irradiation on the histology and glycogen content of the retina and, second, whether these effects are indirect.

MATERIAL AND METHODS

Fifty New Zealand white male rabbits weighing from 2.2 to 3.2 kg were used in this study. The animals were maintained for at least 1 week on Purina chow ad libitum before use. As the irradiated animals refused food, the controls were starved for the same length of time. They were divided into nine groups: Eight groups contained 5 animals, and one group 10 animals. The latter was a nonirradiated control group. Six groups received whole-head irradiation to the following dose levels: 3000 r, 4000 r, 5000 r, 6000 r, 7000 r, and 10,000 r. One eye of each animal (the right eye of 5 and the left eye of 5) in the last two groups was shielded with 3 mm of lead while the rest of the head received 6000 r.

Animals to be irradiated were bound to a Y-shaped board with the head immobilized at a 45° angle with the board (*3*). A Picker deep-therapy X-ray unit was the

[1] This work was performed at the Radiobiology Laboratory of the University of Texas and the U.S.A.F., Austin, Texas. Presented at the annual meeting of the Society for Experimental Pathology, April, 1958.

source. With a Victoreen chamber dosimeter the dose rate was measured at a point in air corresponding to the center of the rabbit eye when in place for irradiation. Irradiation factors were: 260 kv. 18 ma; source-target distance 26 cm; dose rate in air 413 r/min. The inherent filtration of the X-ray tube was equivalent to 0.25 mm Cu; 1 mm Al and 0.25 mm Cu were added.

All animals were sacrificed 48 hours postirradiation with intravenous Nembutal. Both eyes were removed immediately and cut parallel to the longitudinal axis into strips 4 to 5 ml wide. Strips from each eye were fixed in 95% alcohol, Rossman's fluid, and Gendre's fluid at 0°C for 24 hours. The tissue was embedded in paraffin, and sections were cut at 6μ. Alternate sections were stained by the hematoxylin and eosin, the periodic acid–Schiff (PAS), and the diastase-periodic acid–Schiff methods (*5*, *6*).

RESULTS

The morphological changes in the retina of the irradiated animals consisted of pyknosis and edema in the outer nuclear layer and fragmentation in the bacillary

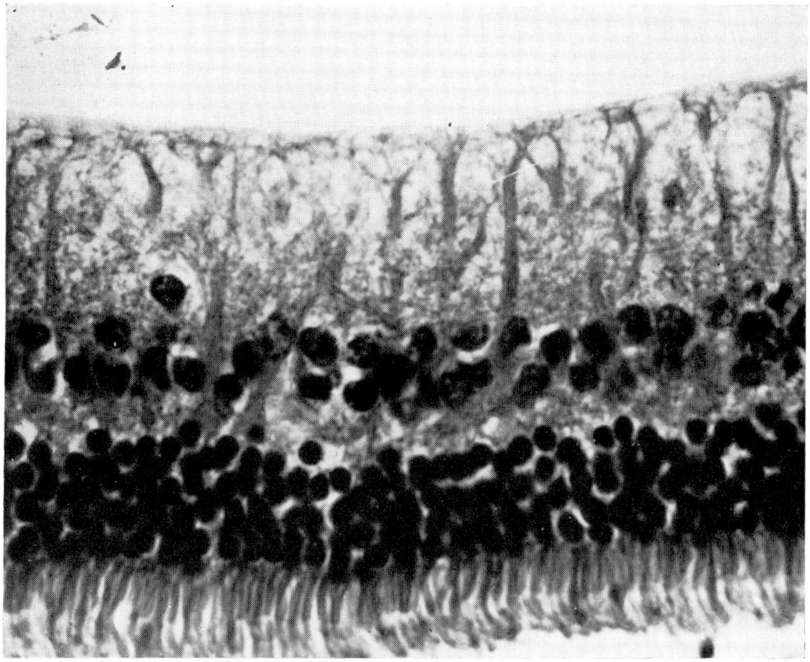

FIG. 1. Retina from nonirradiated control. Note the straight and regular arrangement of the rods (bottom layer), and the homogenous appearance of the outer nuclear layer immediately above for comparison to Fig. 2. Hematoxylin and eosin. (658 ×)

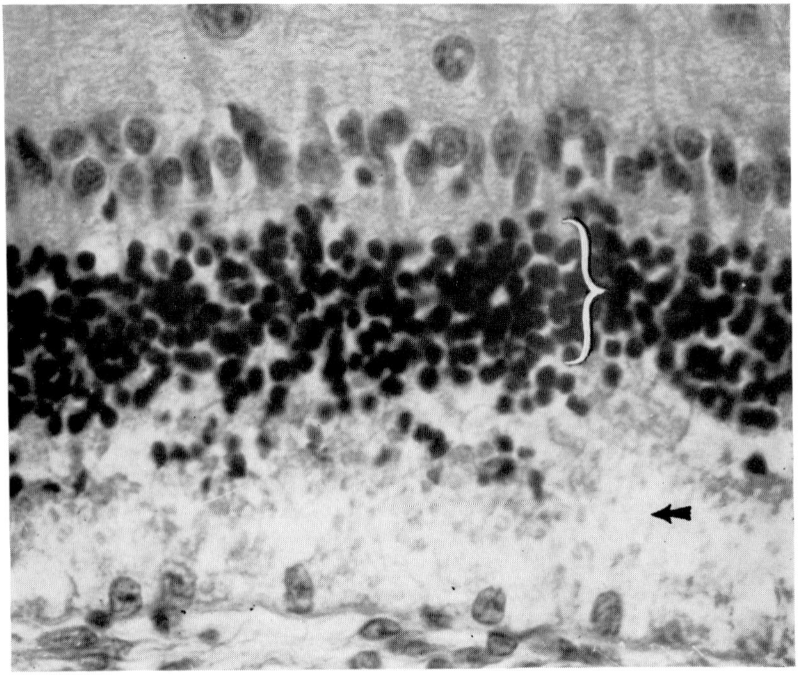

FIG. 2. Retina. Animal received 7000 r 48 hours before death. Note the fragmentation of the rods (arrow), the pyknosis of the nuclei, and the disruption of the outer nuclear layer (bracket). Hematoxylin and eosin. (658 ×)

layer (Figs. 1 and 2). Only 2 of the animals in the 3000-r group had morphological changes. Those consisted of fragmentation of the bacillary layer. There was little change noted in the outer nuclear layer. All animals receiving 4000 r or more showed severe morphological changes. In the lower dose groups, these changes tended to be focal. Some areas showed definite damage, whereas others looked normal. The distribution of the lesions appeared to be random with the exception of the ora serrata; it was less often involved. This sparing of some areas in the retina was also found in the 5000-r, 6000-r, and to some extent the 7000-r group; however, all areas examined in the 10,000-r group showed severe morphological change, including fragmentation of the nuclei in the outer nuclear layer.

The retina of the control animals contained a considerable amount of glycogen, most of which was in the inner layers of the retina (Fig. 3). Ordinarily only a few granules of glycogen were found in the outer nuclear layer. The amount of glycogen in the outer nuclear layer was graded from 0 to 4+: 4+ = maximum amount seen in any animal, and 3+, 2+, and 1+ = 75%, 50%, and 25% of the maximum. The values for the control animals varied from 0 to 1+. The animals receiving 3000 r

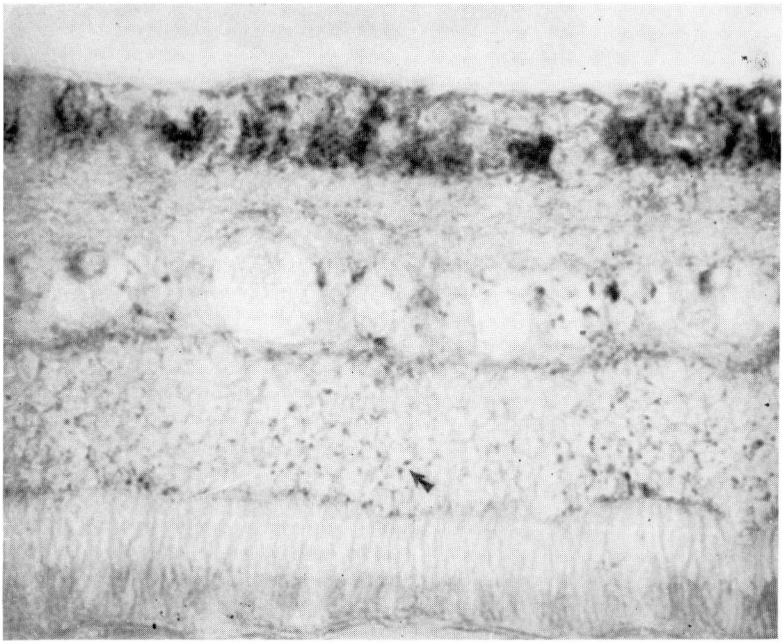

FIG. 3. Retina from nonirradiated control. Note the dark granules of glycogen in the inner layer of the retina and occasionally in the outer nuclear layer (arrow). These granules were removed by diastase digestion. Periodic acid–Schiff. (658 ×)

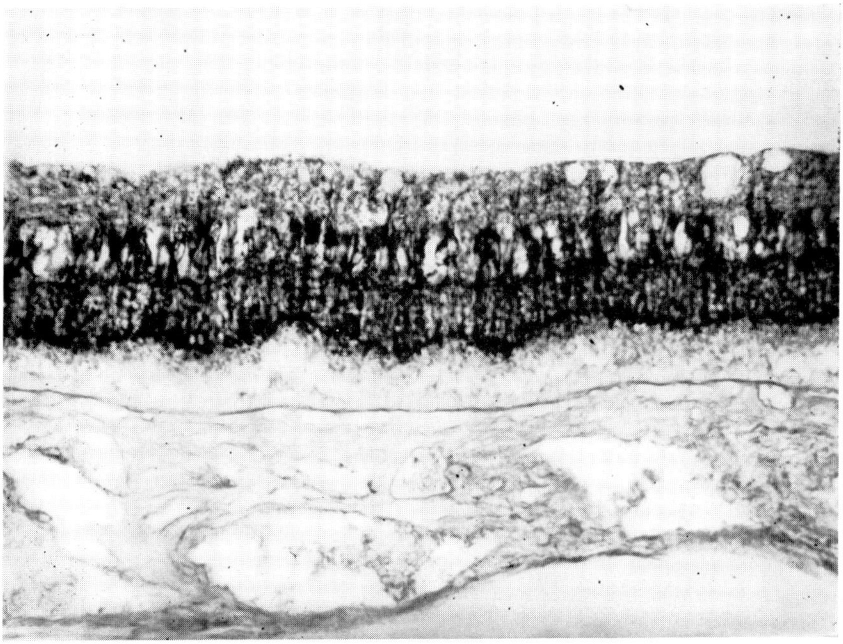

FIG. 4. Retina. Animal received 7000 r 48 hours before death. Note the abundance of glycogen (dark granules) in the outer nuclear layer. These granules were removed by diastase digestion. Periodic acid–Schiff. (280 ×)

did not show any increase in glycogen over the control group. All animals in the 4000-r to 10,000-r categories showed increase in glycogen in the outer nuclear layer (Fig. 4). In the lower dose groups of 4000 r to 6000 r some areas showed this change more than others; the areas showing morphological damage were the ones in which the increase in glycogen was most striking. The distribution of glycogen in the 7000-r and 10,000-r groups was more homogeneous.

The animals with one eye covered by lead during the whole-head irradiation did not show morphological evidence of cell damage or alteration of glycogen content in the shielded eye. The unshielded eye always showed morphological evidence of damage and an increase in glycogen similar to that found in the other irradiated animals.

DISCUSSION

In a previous study where groups of rabbits received approximately 6000 r or whole-head X-irradiation and were sacrificed at intervals after irradiation (½, 1, 2, 4, 6, 12, 24, 48, and 72 hours), glycogen was shown to accumulate in the outer nuclear layer of the retina within 4 hours after irradiation (*3*). As the time after irradiation increased, the amount of glycogen tended to increase. In the present study, where the time of sacrifice, 48 hours postirradiation was constant and the dose of irradiation varied, the threshold for glycogen accumulation in the outer nuclear layer of the retina under the conditions of the experiment appears to be between 3000 r and 4000 r. Further, in both experiments the increase in glycogen occurred only when there was definite evidence of cell damage in the outer nuclear layer. This accumulation of glycogen in cells that show evidence of cell injury is of particular interest, as other causes of cell death, such as in the ischemic myocardium, result in a decrease in the glycogen content rather than an increase (*7*). This suggests that irradiation injury to these cells does not impair the ability of the cells to produce glycogen but does in some way result in a decrease in catabolism of glycogen. One wonders whether this accompaniment of cell death is peculiar to irradiation injury.

Ross and Ely, and others, have reported an increase in liver glycogen after as little as 300 r of whole-body X-irradiation, which is not sufficient to ensure the death of liver cells (*4, 8*). Further the accumulation occurred even if the liver was shielded during the whole-body irradiation. Therefore, the accumulation of glycogen in the eye is probably by a mechanism different from that found in the liver.

SUMMARY

The heads of groups of New Zealand white male rabbits were exposed to 3000 r, 4000 r, 5000 r, 6000 r, 7000 r, and 10,000 r of X-irradiation. Another group of rabbits received 6000 r of head irradiation with one eye shielded by lead. The morphological changes and glycogen content were studied. Glycogen accumulated in the outer nuclear layer of the retina in all irradiated groups except the 3000-r group. This accumulaton was associated with morphological changes suggestive of cell death. Shielding one eye with lead completely protected that eye from these changes.

The relation of this glycogen accumulation to the accumulation of liver glycogen after whole-body irradiation was discussed.

RECEIVED: July 13, 1958

REFERENCES

1. P. A. CIBIS, W. K. NOELL, and B. EICHEL, Ocular effects produced by high intensity X-radiation. *A.M.A. Arch. Ophthalmol.* **53,** 651–663 (1955).
2. D. V. L. BROWN, P. A. CIBIS, and J. E. PICKERING, Radiation studies on the monkey eye. *A.M.A. Arch. Ophthalmol.* **54,** 249–256 (1955).
3. S. P. KENT and A. A. SWANSON, Effects of high-intensity X-irradiation on the retina; a histological, histochemical and chemical study in the rabbit. *Radiation Research* **6,** 111–120 (1957).
4. M. H. ROSS and J. O. ELY, Radiation effects on liver glycogen in the rat. *J. Cellular Comp. Physiol.* **37,** 163 (1951).
5. J. F. A. MCMANUS, Histological and histochemical uses of periodic acid. *Stain Technol.* **22,** 67 (1948).
6. R. D. LILLIE and J. GRECO, Malt diastase and Ptyalin in place of saliva in identification of glycogen. *Stain Technol.* **22,** 67 (1947).
7. S. P. KENT and M. DISEKER, Early myocardial ischemia; study of histochemical changes in dogs. *Lab. Invest.* **4,** 398–405 (1955).
8. N. NORTH and L. A. NIMS, Time-dose study of biochemical responses of rats to X-radiation. *Federation Proc.* **8,** 119 (1949).

RADIATION RESEARCH 10, 387–396 (1959)

Latent Radiation Damage and Synchronous Cell Division in the Epidermis of an Insect

I. Nonreversible Effects Leading to Local Radiation Burns

W. F. BALDWIN AND T. N. SALTHOUSE

Biology Branch, Atomic Energy of Canada Limited, Chalk River, Ontario.

INTRODUCTION

With very few exceptions, cells and tissues are highly resistant to destruction by radiation if they do not undergo subsequent cell division. This is generally true, for example, of the central nervous system in mammals, and also of most tissues in whole adult insects. Usually, the first functions to be destroyed by radiation are those affecting the capacity for successful cell division. Further, the appearance of radiation burns in mammals is delayed until some time after the exposure. It may be that the expression of latent damage in the case of burns occurs only when the irradiated cells attempt to divide. In most animal tissues, cells may be at any stage of division during irradiation, making it impossible to correlate precisely the expressed damage with the stage of cell development at the time of exposure. Cell destruction at the next postirradiation division has been proved only in a few instances such as in pollen grains (*1*) and in the eye and brain of frog tadpoles (*2*).

Ideally, one would like to test this common interpretation both of the radioresistance of nondividing cells and of the observed delayed appearance of radiation lesions using some tissue in which the divisions take place simultaneously. For this purpose, an experimental animal was sought which could be irradiated while all the cells were in a "resting" phase, but in which cell divisions could be induced experimentally at a selected period after irradiation. Insects were chosen because they are highly resistant to radiation destruction in any stage lacking cell divisions. It was predicted on the above hypothesis that the damage would become apparent if cell division were induced subsequent to irradiation.

In the bloodsucking bug *Rhodnius prolixus* Stål., cell division preparatory to molting takes place in the nymphal epidermis only during a fixed period after a meal of blood (*3*); thus, feeding will determine the time of mitosis in the epidermis, which can be irradiated at suitably chosen doses and observed as a discrete tissue. The present report deals with the conversion of latent radiation damage in the epidermal layer into visible burns in *Rhodnius*, after a blood meal.

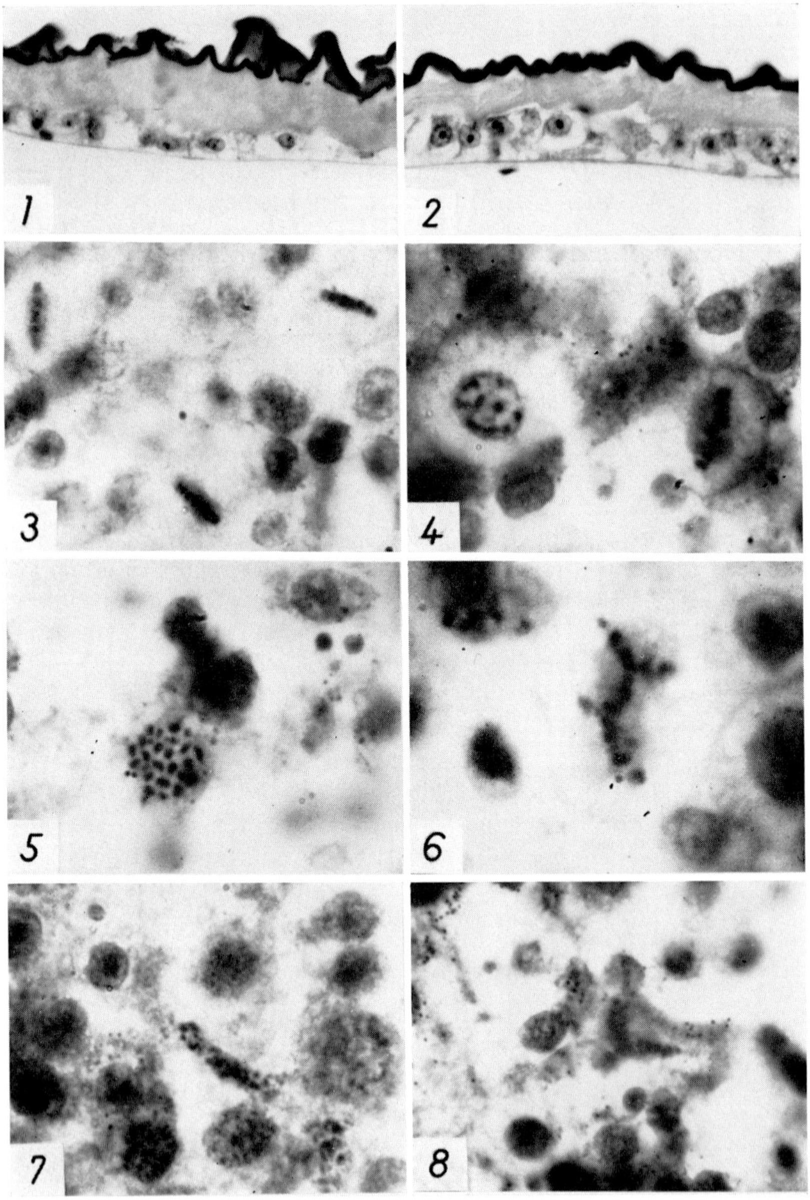

PLATE I

FIG. 1. Section from irradiated area, 1 day after exposure. From below, basement membrane underlying dormant epidermal layer; above lies endocuticle with folded epicuticle (stellate folds) as dark layer on surface. Regaud's iron hematoxylin. (225 ×)

METHODS

Rhodnius has been reared in our laboratory by methods given by Buxton (*4*). The insects are fed simply by inverting their gauze-covered jars on a rabbit's ear; the bugs promptly engorge with blood. The insects have been reared, and held during experiments, in incubators at 25°C and a relative humidity of 75%.

Irradiations were confined to a small area on the abdomen (1.6-mm diameter) as shown in Fig. 17. The insects, fourth-stage *Rhodnius* nymphs, were strapped over a 1.6-mm hole in a 5-cm-thick lead shield, the hole being centered along the main beam of a 2-Mev X-ray machine at 16 cm from the target (dose rate, 6000 r/min without the collimator). Test insects were given a meal of rabbit blood immediately after irradiation, in all except one of the experiments; irradiated controls were not fed.

For histological studies we used both paraffin-embedded material and whole abdominal tergites (the body wall from the dorsal side of the abdomen). Paraffin-embedded insects were previously fixed in Eltringham's fixative, and the sections were stained with Regaud's iron hematoxylin and Giemsa's stain. For whole mounts, the abdominal tergites were dissected from the abdomen, and all organs such as tracheae and fat body were removed under a binocular dissecting microscope, leaving the basement membrane and epidermal layer intact (*3*). The tergites were fixed in Carnoy's and stained with Lillie's hemalum.

RADIATION BURNS

Cell division in the normal epidermis occurs in the period 5 to 9 days after feeding in fourth-stage *Rhodnius* nymphs, and the first appearance of new cuticle coincides with the cessation of mitosis on the ninth day (*3*). In the experimental insects irradiated at 50,000 r, the epidermal cells follow their normal development until approximately 5 days after feeding, when they begin to alter in appearance, and cytological evidence of cell destruction during mitosis can be found in "burned" areas. After 14 or 15 days, the developing radiation burns could be seen in the new cuticle through the unshed, old body wall. On molting to a fifth stage at about 22 to 25 days after feeding, each of the burns appeared as an unpigmented area (Fig.

FIG. 2. Same as above, at 5 days after exposure. Epidermal cell layer much thicker, nuclei increased in volume. Regaud's iron hematoxylin. (225 ×)

FIG. 3. Whole tergite mount at seventh day. Several mitotic figures (metaphase) shown in area of future radiation burn. Lillie's hemalum. (500 ×)

FIG. 4. Whole tergite mount at eighth day, showing destruction of cells during mitosis with cloud of cytoplasmic material between mitotic figures. Hemalum. (600 ×)

FIG. 5. Whole tergite mount at eighth day, showing disruption of cell in prophase and nuclear debris from disintegration of cells. Hemalum. (750 ×)

FIG. 6. Whole tergite mount at eighth day; abnormal metaphase figure. Hemalum. (750 ×)

FIGS. 7 and 8. Whole tergite mounts at ninth day; typical fields in irradiated area. Hemalum. (750 ×)

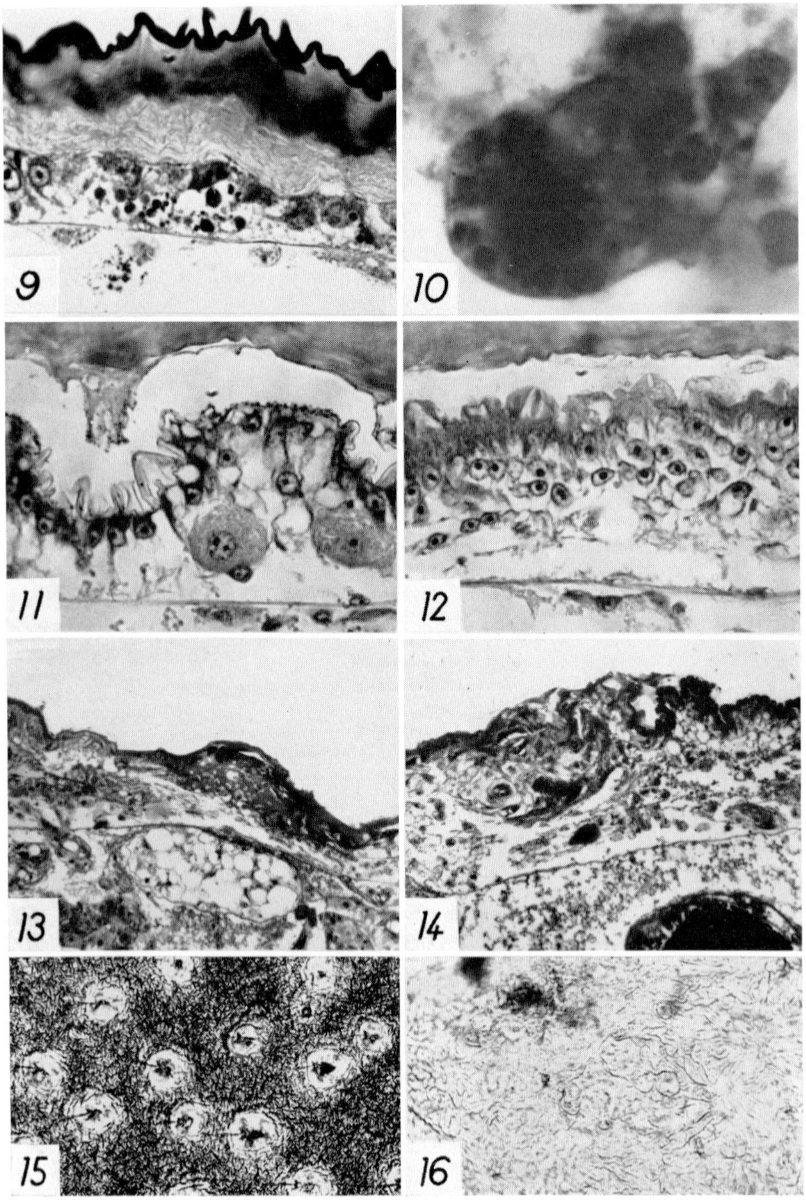

PLATE II

FIG. 9. Section from irradiated area on tenth day. Nuclear pyknosis evident in epidermal layer, with spherical globules of chromatin. Two normal cells can be seen on the far left. Regaud's iron hematoxylin. (300 ×)

17) lacking the spine-bearing plaques and stellate folds found in normal cuticle. A number of irradiated controls have been held without food for as long as 2 months after exposure; the damage persists in a latent state, however, and burns have still appeared after feeding and subsequent molting.

HISTOLOGY

The normal development of the epidermal layer after feeding and prior to molting in *Rhodnius* has been recorded at some length by Wigglesworth (*3*, *5*, *6*). In unfed fourth-instar nymphs, the single layer of epidermis contains comparatively small cells. The cells start to enlarge within a day or two after feeding (Fig. 1); about the fifth day they separate from the old cuticle, and mitosis begins. Numerous mitotic figures can be found over the whole tergite by the sixth and seventh days. Division is completed by the ninth day, when the epidermal layer has begun to form the thin epicuticle of the new body wall; by the tenth day this epicuticle forms conspicuous "stellate" folds (Figs. 11 and 15). The formation of the endocuticle (which lies under the epicuticle) begins as soon as the epicuticle is formed; by the thirteenth day, when the endocuticle is about one-third its final thickness, the epicuticle and bristles are becoming slightly colored. Molting takes place about the fifteenth day. The new cuticle is fully developed about 4 days after molting.

In experimental insects irradiated with 50,000 r, the cells of the epidermal layer in the burned area develop quite normally during the first 4 or 5 days after feeding (Fig. 2). During the next few days an excess of cells in prophase and metaphase appear in the irradiated area, apparently the result of mitosis proceeding to a developmental block at prophase or metaphase (Fig. 3). On the seventh day after feeding it has been possible to find as many as seven metaphase figures in a single field (i.e., at magnifications of 675×) in the burn; in normal unirradiated tergites, on the other hand, we have never found more than one metaphase in five fields, except in areas along the intersegmental membranes, where divisions are numerous owing to crowding of the cells. Evidence of cell destruction appears on the ninth and tenth days, with abnormal aggregations of chromatin material gathering within

FIG. 10. Whole tergite mount on tenth day. Phagocyte containing nuclear chromatin debris from destroyed cells. Hemalum. (750 ×)

FIG. 11. Section from unirradiated area away from burn at fifteenth day. Normal epicuticle forming under old cuticle. Two large oenocytes at base of epidermal layer. This latter type of cell does not appear in irradiated areas. Giemsa's stain. (250 ×)

FIG. 12. Section from periphery of irradiated area on fifteenth day. Massing of epidermal cells resulting from proliferation around burn. Giemsa's stain. (250 ×)

FIGS. 13 and 14. Typical sections in irradiated area after molting. Thick irregular chitin-protein deposit forming burn. Absence of epicuticle. Hematoxylin-eosin. (75 ×)

FIG. 15. Whole tergite mount of unirradiated area after molt. Plaques bearing setae surrounded by stellate folds of epicuticle. Unstained mount. (40 ×)

FIG. 16. Surface of burn from same tergite as above, showing absence of stellate folds, plaques, and pigment. Unstained. (40 ×)

and outside the cell walls, sometimes in the form of perfectly spherical globules (Fig. 9). Abnormal metaphase figures can be found throughout the burn (Figs. 4–8). Occasional normal nuclei occur in the burned area rather too early to be attributable to cell migration, suggesting that a small number of cells can remain normal in appearance after an exposure to 50,000 r. Cytoplasmic contents freed by the disintegration of cell walls appear as a cloud of pink-staining material (Fig. 4) when counterstained with eosin. A few large phagocytic cells, filled with chromatin material, can be found in the area (Fig. 10). About the sixteenth day, a great many normal cells appear, cells which apparently spread inward from the periphery of the irradiated area. The migration and spreading of epidermal cells has been described by Wigglesworth (*6*) in studies on the healing of thermal burns. He concludes that the substances responsible for migration are protein degradation

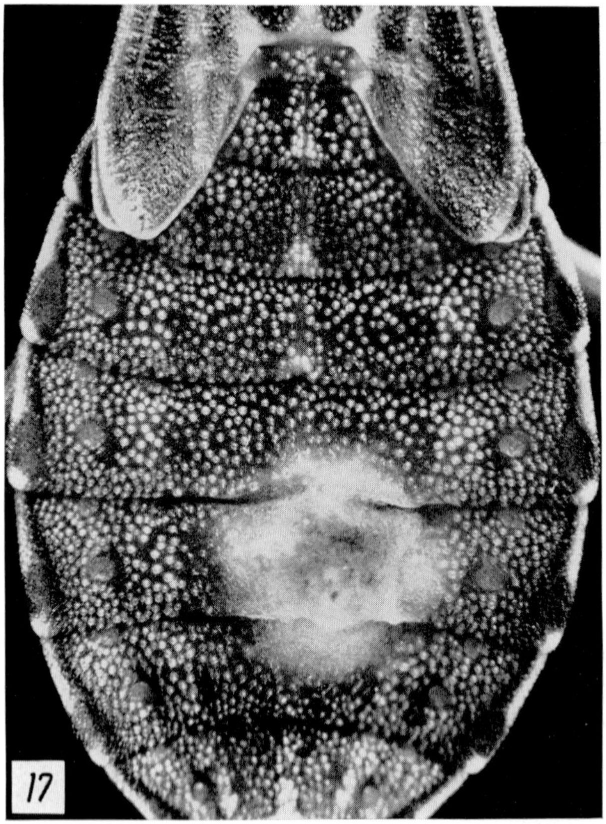

PLATE III

FIG. 17. Photograph of abdominal tergite of *Rhodnius* with burn showing after molting to fifth-instar nymph. (15 ×)

products. The migratory cells form a thickened, irregular epidermis, sometimes three or four cell layers in thickness (Figs. 13 and 14). By the seventeenth day, the deposition of a thin surface layer can be noticed between the epidermal layer and the old cuticle in irradiated areas, a layer which increases in thickness until molt. In the unirradiated tergite of the same insect, an abundant supply of oenocytes, which normally form the epicuticle (*5*), can be found between the epidermis and the basement membrane (Fig. 11). Here, a normal epicuticle develops; in the irradiated areas, where oenocytes are not found, there is no evidence of epicuticle formation.

Around the periphery of the burn a great abundance of mitotic figures suddenly appears on the eleventh or twelfth day; by the fifteenth day large numbers of cells are present at the periphery (Fig. 12). According to Wigglesworth (*5*), cellular proliferation in thermal burns is stimulated either by an absence of cells or by toxic materials in injured areas. It would appear that a similar mechanism initiates proliferation with radiation burns. The multiplication of cells in this band of epidermal tissue is undoubtedly the source of the migratory cells mentioned above.

The first appearance of new epicuticle occurs on the tenth day in the body wall of normal nymphs. In irradiated insects, epicuticle formation in areas outside the burn is delayed for 1 or 2 days and appears first in areas furthest away from the center of the developing burn; the epicuticle gradually develops inward toward the burn periphery, forming the normal stellate folds and bristle plaques (Figs. 11 and 15). Over the burn the undifferentiated surface layer appears, lacking the plaques, setae, and pore canals of normal areas (Fig. 16). Chemical tests and staining reactions have shown that this layer has a chitin-protein composition similar to that of the endocuticle of normal body wall. The chitin layer is formed wholly or largely by the migrating epidermal cells. It is significant that the burned areas were devoid of specialized cells such as oenocytes, dermal gland cells, trichogen, and tormogen cells.

A further proof that the cells are active and functional during the first few days after irradiation and feeding was found in tests for oxidase enzymes on whole tergites (using the G. Nadi reaction as recommended by Pearse, *7*). The tests showed that this enzyme increases to a maximum in unirradiated epidermal layer until the ninth day. The irradiated area, however, showed a diminution in activity after the seventh day, until only a very slight reaction occurred on the tenth day; as a result the site of the future burn was outlined in great contrast from the seventh day onward. Subsequent to the fourteenth day the amount of oxidase began to increase again in the irradiated area, apparently as a result of cell migration, until by molting time oxidase activity was only slightly less than in surrounding normal areas. Thus, as far as production of oxidase is concerned, the cells in the area were functional during a latent period of 7 days, and cell damage commenced at this time, being followed by migration to replace the damaged cells.

The sequence of events during the whole period from feed to molt in irradiated

TABLE I

TIMETABLE OF EVENTS DURING DEVELOPMENT OF LATENT RADIATION DAMAGE IN THE EPIDERMIS OF *Rhodnius* (IRRADIATED AT 50,000 R), COMPARED WITH A NORMAL CONTROL

Day	*Cells in prophage*		*Cells in metaphase*		*G. Nadi reaction*		*Presence of normal cells*	
	Normal	*Irradiated*	*Normal*	*Irradiated*	*Normal*	*Irradiated*	*Normal*	*Irradiated*
1	−	−	−	−	Trace	Trace	+++	+++
2	−	−	−	−	+	+	+++	+++
3	−	−	−	−	++	++	+++	+++
4	−	−	−	−	++	++	+++	+++
5	+	+	−	−	++	++	+++	+++
6	+	++	+	++	++	++	+++	+++
7	+	+	+	++++	++	+	+++	++
8	−	+	+	++	+++	+	+++	+
9	−	+	−	++	+++	±	+++	+
10	−	±	−	+	+++	−	+++	+
11	−	−	−	+	+++	−	+++	+
12	−	−		−	+++	−	+++	+
13	−	−	−	−	+++	−	+++	++
14	−	−	−	−	+++	+	+++	+++
15[a]	−	−	−	−	+++	+	+++	+++

[a] Normal controls molted at 15 days after feeding, irradiated insects molted at 22 to 25 days

and nonirradiated insects has been summarized for greater clarity in Table I. The developmental block at prophase and metaphase, and the absence of oxidase enzyme and normal cells following the appearance of these stages, illustrate that the effects of radiation did not become apparent until the cells attempted to divide, and that development was normal during a period leading to the appearance of mitotic prophases at about the fifth day. Cell damage begins to show after about the seventh day. In irradiated insects, about 22 to 25 days was required for molting; in contrast, unirradiated control insects required only 15 days.

SUMMARY AND DISCUSSION

In *Rhodnius*, latent damage from exposure of the epidermis to X-irradiation, during a resting phase, does not become evident until the time of cell division. The cellular destruction is expressed after division as a burn in the new cuticle of the insect, clearly visible after molting. The occurrence of damage after X-irradiation and at cell division in other animals regardless of the time of division has been reported by Spear and Glucksmann (*2*), and Lasnitzki (*8*). Other workers (*9*) have shown that cell degradation can take place during prophase and metaphase, a phenomenon which is even more clearly illustrated in *Rhodnius*, where it is possible to irradiate epidermal cells during a resting stage, and in which a wave of mitoses can be induced at will, at any time after the exposure.

The repair of the irradiated area is similar to the healing process in thermal burns and is accomplished by the deposition of a chitin-protein layer by migratory epidermal cells which have moved in from the periphery of the burn. The absence of epicuticle and other cuticular structures in irradiated areas indicates that migratory cells do not assume specialized functions. In experiments not reported in this paper, in which nymphs went through a further molt, the burn reappeared, showing that cells with these specialized functions could not be replaced.

Molting time was found in these studies to be lengthened in the irradiated insects. The delay can be attributed to two factors: firstly, the developmental "block" in cell division lasting 2 or 3 days during prophase and metaphase and leading to cell destruction; secondly, the additional longer period required for healing processes to be completed in the irradiated area. The sequence of events in the burn is as follows:

1. Destruction of cells in prophase or metaphase.
2. Assimilation and removal of cellular debris by phagocytic cells.
3. Migration of epidermal cells into the injured area.
4. Deposition by these cells of the chitin-protein layer.

While these events are taking place, normal cuticle formation has been proceeding inward toward the periphery of the burn from unirradiated areas; molting does not take place until the covering over the burn has been secreted.

Thus, under the experimental conditions of this study, it has been shown in work with the epidermis of *Rhodnius*, in which cells develop concurrently and come to division simultaneusly, that destruction occurs at mitosis. The abruptness of the appearance of cell destruction is due entirely to the essentially synchronous division of all epidermal cells. This is in direct contrast to the more gradual appearance of radiation damage in other animals.

ACKNOWLEDGMENTS

We wish to express our appreciation to Dr. V. B. Wigglesworth for the original stock of *Rhodnius* used in this study, to Dr. H. B. Newcombe for advice and editorial comments, and to Messrs. P. Knight and C. M. Gravelle for their technical assistance.

RECEIVED: March 18, 1958

REFERENCES

1. H. B. NEWCOMBE, The action of X-rays on the cell. The chromosome variable. *J. Genet.* **43,** 145–171 (1942).

2. F. G. SPEAR AND A. GLUCKSMANN, The effect of gamma radiation on cells *in vivo*. Part III. Spaced radiation. *Brit. J. Radiol.* **14,** 65–76 (1941).

3. V. B. WIGGLESWORTH, The physiology of the cuticle and of ecdysis in *Rhodnius prolixus* (Triatomidae, Hemiptera); with special reference to the function of the oenocytes and of the dermal glands. *Quart. J. Microscop. Sci.* **76,** 269–317 (1933).

4. P. A. BUXTON, The biology of a blood-sucking bug, *Rhodnius prolixus*. *Trans. Entomol. Soc. London* **78,** 227–236 (1930).

5. V. B. Wigglesworth, The epicuticle in an insect. *Proc. Roy. Soc.* **B134,** 163–181 (1946).
6. V. B. Wigglesworth, Wound healing in an insect (*Rhodnius prolixus* Hemiptera). *J. Exptl. Biol.* **14,** 364–381 (1937).
7. A. G. E. Pearse, *Histochemistry,* J. and A. Churchill, London, 1953.
8. I. Lasnitzki, The effect of X-rays on cells cultivated *in vitro*. Part II. Recovery factor. *Brit. J. Radiol.* **16,** 61–67 (1943).
9. H. M. Patt, Protective mechanisms in ionizing radiation injury. *Physiol. Revs.* **33,** 35–76 (1953).

RADIATION RESEARCH 10, 397–399 (1959)

Latent Radiation Damage and Synchronous Cell Division in the Epidermis of an Insect

II. Reversible Effects in Burn Repair

W. F. BALDWIN AND T. N. SALTHOUSE

Biology Branch, Atomic Energy of Canada Limited, Chalk River, Ontario.

Work with the bloodsucking bug *Rhodnius prolixus* has shown that latent damage to resting cells of the epidermis by exposure to a small beam of X-radiation prior to feeding does not become evident until cell division (*1*). Cell division in the epidermal layer occurs at 5 to 9 days after feeding (*2*). Cellular destruction in the epidermal cells of fourth-instar nymphs at division is expressed later as a burn in the cuticle of newly molted fifth-instar insects. Further, the healing of the wound and subsequent molting of insects which have received 25,000 to 50,000 r in a localized (1.6-mm diameter) area is prolonged if they are fed immediately after the irradiation. In fact, owing to division delay and healing processes (*1*), the normal period of 13 or 14 days from feeding to molting is sometimes extended to as much as 30 days at the higher doses. As reported here, however, the time required for healing and molting in irradiated nymphs can be reduced almost to normal if they are given a period in which to recover from some of the effects of irradiation before being fed.

Groups of unfed fourth-instar *Rhodnius* were irradiated through the abdomen with a 1.6-mm beam of X-rays (see Baldwin and Salthouse, *1*). The insects were given a meal of rabbit blood at 2, 3, and 4 weeks after irradiation (dose 40,000 r at 6000 r/min). Molting times and the sizes of burns are recorded below. The insects were kept at a constant temperature (26°C) and a constant humidity (75% relative humidity) throughout the experiment.

Number of days between irradiation and feeding	*Number of insects*	*Time to molt (days)*	*Diameter of burns (mm)*
0	10	25.5 ± 2.7	1.48 ± 0.62
14	10	21.1 ± 2.2	1.63 ± 0.63
21	10	18.3 ± 3.1	1.22 ± 0.74
28	8	15.5 ± 2.6	1.78 ± 0.51
Controls (no irradiation)	10	13.7 ± 1.2	—

When the insects were fed immediately after irradiation, molting was delayed for about 12 days (25 days from the time of feeding); however, if feeding was delayed for several weeks, molting times returned nearly to the normal period of 13 days. The sizes of the burns (which are dose-dependent) did not differ significantly with similar delays. The latter result was not unexpected, however, since it had been shown previously (*1*) that latent damage would produce a burn after cell division, even if feeding was delayed for as long a period as 3 months. The absence of any reduction in the sizes of the burns shows that all cells irradiated in the main beam of X-rays are eventually destroyed, making it impossible for recovery to take place in the central burn area. Replacement cells from the periphery of the burn, produced by proliferation of epidermal cells under the stimulation of cell degradation products (*3*), form the typical burn covering. It is probable that molting time recovery has its origin in this region, where the dose of radiation was less than in the main beam, and where many cell divisions take place. With a lapse of 4 weeks between irradiation and feeding it appears that the "delaying" effect of the radiation has almost disappeared and that the marginal cells can reproduce at a high rate. The production and movement of the replacement cells in insects which molt within the normal period after irradiation must be prompt, since molting cannot take place until the wound covering is complete and the new epicuticle has been formed in unirradiated areas (*1*).

The return of molting times to near normal after irradiation is a concrete example of a reversible radiation phenomenon. In the period between irradiation and feeding, the epidermal cells around the periphery are in a resting phase, and the recovery reported here is occurring during the resting period. It is obvious that a reversible radiation effect has been produced from which spontaneous recovery occurs with the passage of time, a recovery which will allow healing and subsequent molting to proceed more rapidly.

Preliminary cytological studies with insects whose whole bodies have been irradiated, at doses which will not produce burns and which will permit molting, have supported these conclusions. The delay in molting is the result of a delay in the completion of mitosis which starts at the normal time but proceeds more slowly. If an extended latent period is interposed between exposure and feeding, mitotic division and the whole molting cycle proceed at a rate comparable to that in unirradiated insects. Thus it can be inferred, in the case of the spot irradiations, that recovery in the cells around the periphery of burns must lead to a reduction in molting time through a more rapid division of replacement cells.

It may be that partial recovery could take place in all cells if a prolonged resting period occurred after irradiation. As an experimental material, *Rhodnius* epidermal cells may be exceptional in the ease with which the cell divisions can be delayed at will and the extent to which the onset of division is synchronous. These characteristics have permitted a clearer distinction between the reversible and the irreversible components of radiation injury than has been possible with vertebrate animals.

RECEIVED: July 1, 1958

REFERENCES

1. W. F. BALDWIN and T. N. SALTHOUSE, Latent radiation damage and synchronous cell division in the epidermis of an insect. I. Nonreversible effects leading to local radiation burns. *Radiation Research* **10,** 387–396 (1959).
2. V. B. WIGGLESWORTH, The physiology of the cuticle and of ecdysis in *Rhodnius prolixus* (Triatomidae, Hemiptera); with special reference to the function of the oenocytes and of the dermal glands. *Quart. J. Microscop. Sci.* **76,** 269–317 (1933).
3. V. B. WIGGLESWORTH, Wound healing in an insect (*Rhodnius prolixus* Hemiptera). *J. Exptl. Biol.* **14,** 364–381 (1937).

RADIATION RESEARCH 10, 400–401 (1959)

A Chronic Irradiation Source for Small Animals

HOWARD E. NOYES

Department of Experimental Surgery, Walter Reed Army Institute of Research, Walter Reed Army Medical Center, Washington, D. C.

Most studies on the effects of chronic irradiation have been carried out by subjecting laboratory animals to daily doses of total-body X-irradiation. This method is often cumbersome and may or may not approximate the effects resulting from the use of a chronic irradiation source. A simple chamber used for chronic irradiation of small animals has been designed and used in this laboratory (Fig. 1).

Briefly, the chamber consists of two pieces of double-thickness glass embedded in 7.0 mm of lead with an air space of 2 mm between them. The two pieces of glass are sealed in position with hypoxy[1] resin. A cover of 7.0 mm of lead (supported by aluminum to provide rigidity) is used to reduce irradiation when the chamber is not in use.

The chamber is filled as follows: Dilute the isotope to the volume needed to fill the chamber. Then, using polyethylene tubing, let the radioactive solution siphon between the sheets of glass through a small hole in the corner of the top sheet. No air bubbles will be trapped if the chamber is tilted during the time of filling. The hole in the corner of the glass is later closed by sealing a rubber stopper into it with the hypoxy resin mentioned above.

A wooden frame supports a stainless steel pan containing the experimental animals. The pan used in this laboratory is 22 inches square and 8 inches deep. Food and water are provided to last one week, so the investigator needs to go into the irradiation area one time a week to remove the pan to another room where cleaning, feeding, etc., are done. Exposure to irradiation under these conditions need not exceed 10 to 20 seconds per week.

The pan described above will house 60 mice or 15 to 20 rats or guinea pigs. The isotope in use is cesium-134 with a half-life of 2.3 years. The radiation dose can be varied by inserting sheets of lead between the glass and the pan or by raising the pan. When a dose of 100 mc is placed in the chamber and a sheet of lead 7.0 mm thick is placed between the chamber and the pan, the mice at the bottom of the

[1] Epon Adhesive VI, using Curing Agent A, Shell Chemical Corporation, New York, New York.

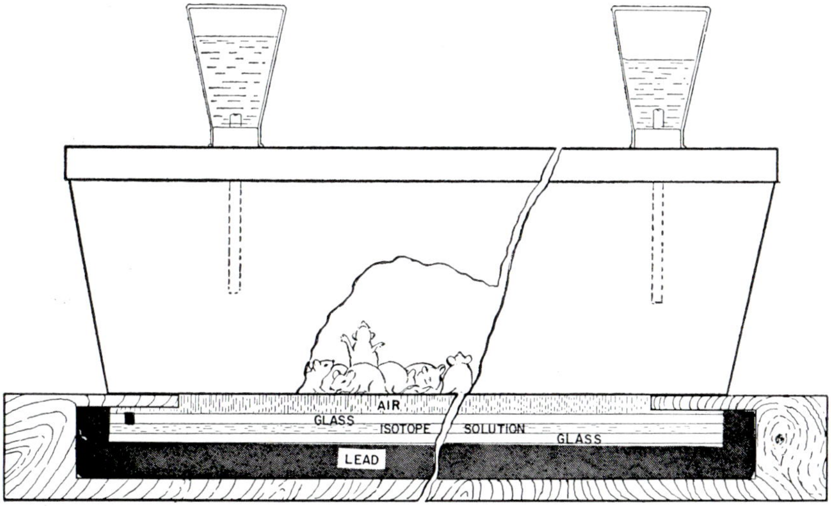

FIG. 1. Chronic irradiation source with animals in place.

pan receive 25 roentgen equivalents per day. The cost of this chamber including the isotope was $200.

This chamber could be modified by evenly saturating an absorbent material such as filter paper with isotope solution and then sealing it between two pieces of glass or laminating it with plastic, which would preclude any danger of leakage. This modification has not been tried but would seem to be desirable from the standpoint of safety.

RECEIVED: October 27, 1958

RADIATION RESEARCH 10, 402–409 (1959)

The Hierarchy of Modes of Radiation Death in Specifically Protected Mice[1]

HENRY QUASTLER AND MARION ZUCKER[2]

Biology Department, Brookhaven National Laboratory, Upton, New York

INTRODUCTION

There are several modes of acute radiation death. Which of them occurs in a particular instance depends on the quantity and quality of the radiation used, the species of animal, the parts which were irradiated or shielded, concomitant treatments, and a number of other factors which are not controllable or, at least, not controlled (*1–3*). In mice and rats, the mode of death which is the earliest to occur after the smallest lethal dose (about 600 rads applied to the whole body) is called "marrow death"; it is associated with aplasia of the hemopoietic tissues and can be prevented by providing some normal hemopoietic tissue, either by partial shielding or by transplantation (*4*). Animals so protected tolerate doses up to about 1200 rads; after doses above this, animals die from intestinal damage. Death occurs before hemopoietic recovery can begin. In order to study hemopoietic recovery in heavily irradiated animals, one has to protect them from lethal intestinal damage.

Intestinal death is due to a radiation response of the small bowel (*5*) and can be prevented by shielding most of the small bowel or by parenteral administration of fluids and electrolytes (*6*). Mice specifically protected against both marrow and intestinal death will survive still higher doses until another system is so severely impaired that the animal succumbs. It seems, thus, that successive elimination of modes of radiation death by specific protection is an interesting approach to the modal analysis of radiation death. It might reveal new syndromes which are ordinarily masked and furnish new information on known syndromes. Specific protection (such as that afforded by spleen shielding) must be distinguished from the more diffuse protection afforded by certain drugs such as cysteine which act; their use in modal analysis is limited by the fact that the differences in the degree to which they affect the various syndromes are comparatively small.

[1] Work carried out at Brookhaven National Laboratory under the auspices of the U. S. Atomic Energy Commission.

[2] Present address: Medical School, Albert Einstein College, New York.

MATERIAL AND METHODS

Animals

We used a total of 409 young adult mice of both sexes and three strains: RF1, CF1, and C57 Brown. The animals were kept in an air-conditioned room, up to 10 to a cage, supplied with Purina dog chow and water ad libitum, and pretreated with terramycin which was added to the water for one week. The amount of time spent with each animal made it necessary to perform the whole investigation in a sequence of many small experiments.

Irradiation Procedures

Bone marrow protection was provided by shielding the exteriorized spleen or both hind legs with lead; intestinal protection, by shielding as much of the intestine as could be exteriorized (which means all but the duodenum, a small part of the proximal jejunum, and the distal colon); oral protection, by wrapping a thin lead foil around the lower jaw. As specific controls, animals were used in which gut (and sometimes spleen) was exteriorized but not shielded, animals in which the exteriorized intestine was irradiated with the rest of the body shielded, and animals in which the duodenum alone was surgically exposed and irradiated with the remainder of the body shielded as far as possible.

Preceding partial irradiations, animals were anesthesized (Nembutal, 0.11 mg/gm intraperitoneally), and laparotomy was performed by transverse incision of skin and sagittal incision of muscle or fascia and peritoneum. For the irradiation, animals were arranged, singly, in the device shown in Fig. 1.

Radiation factors used were: G.E. Maximar, operated at 200 or 240 kv and 30 ma, filter 1 mm Al (HVL 0.5 mm Cu), target distance 27 cm, dosage rates around 2000 rads/min. Doses were measured in roentgens inside a plastic phantom of appropriate size and shape and converted into rads, assuming 1 r = 0.93 rad.

Histology

Animals were sacrificed by perfusion with Bouin's fluid or neutral formalin. Paraffin was used as embedding medium, and hematoxylin-eosin as stain.

RESULTS AND DISCUSSION

Marrow Syndrome

The median lethal dose for marrow death, $LD_{50(marrow)}$, is about 600 rads in C57 Brown and about 550 rads in the two other strains. (As it is well known that LD_{50}'s fluctuate not inconsiderably under standard laboratory conditions, no attempt was made to obtain precise estimates of these and other LD_{50}'s.) With good technique, the LD_{50} in animals with surgically exteriorized but not shielded gut and spleen is about the same as with whole-body irradiation without surgery.[3]

[3] In some of our earlier experiments, high LD_{50}'s (about 900 rads) were found in animals in which spleen and intestines were exteriorized but not shielded. It was suspected that this was

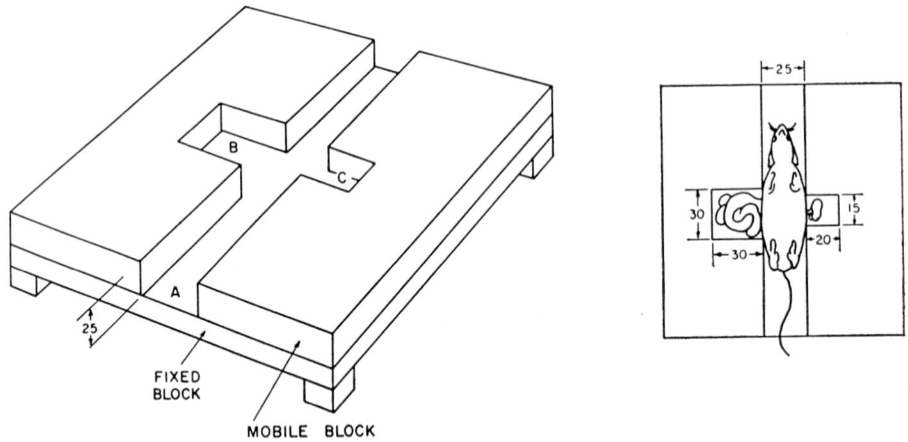

Fig. 1. Device for partial irradiation. The device is made of Lucite, covered with a lead foil to reduce backscatter, and varnished. A single animal is laid into groove *A*. The exteriorized intestine is placed upon platform *B*, between layers of cotton soaked in warm saline. The exteriorized spleen is placed on the smaller platform, *C*. Lower jaw and hind legs are protected, if desired, by wrapping with lead foil ($\frac{1}{32}$-inch). After the animal is in position, a thin ($\frac{1}{16}$-inch) sheet of Lucite is laid on top; additional protection, when needed, is provided by lead sheets ($\frac{3}{16}$-inch) placed on the Lucite sheet. The whole assembly can be secured with C-clamps or by surrounding lead blocks.

Hemopoietic recovery after irradiation with 3000 rads was studied histologically in animals in which both hind legs, the lower jaw, and as much of the intestine as could be exteriorized had been shielded. Animals so treated die in about 8 days (see Table III). Our studies are based on animals sacrificed on schedule or when about to die. In all specimens, hemopoiesis in the *protected femur* was active, and so was lymphopoiesis in the Peyer's plaques of the shielded intestine. *Spleens* were examined in 2 animals sacrificed 4 days after irradiation: one was depleted, the other showed some activity. Of 2 animals sacrificed 7 days after irradiation, one spleen appeared normal, one still showed evidence of previous destruction. In all 7 animals sacrificed while dying 8 to 11 days after irradiation, the spleens appeared normal. Marrow in the *sternum* showed a somewhat slower recovery: depletion at 4 days, still low cellularity at 7 days, but normal appearance from 9 days on. The *white counts* of these animals are given in Table I; it is seen that the depression has virtually disappeared. These studies in animals protected against lethal intestinal damage show that hemopoietic recovery can proceed normally even in animals which were heavily irradiated and are fatally damaged. It seems that the specific protection afforded by some normal bone marrow is not limited to moderate doses.

due to accidental interference with arterial circulation, with resulting protection by anemic hypoxia; this was corroborated by the histological finding of strong hemopoietic activity in spleens examined 9 days after administration of 650 rads.

TABLE I
WHITE BLOOD COUNTS
(Single counts, white blood corpuscles per cubic millimeter)

Protection	*Dose (rads)*	*Day after irradiation*	*Counts*
None	650	5	210, 320, 350
None	650	9	200, 740, 800
Spleen and gut	1200	5	180, 270, 300
	1200	9	4600, 5650, 5700
	2800	5	Very low (2 cases)
	2800	8	400
Both hind legs, gut, and lower jaw	3000	4	1040, 3070
	3000	7	1250, 5500
	3000	9	6020
	3000	11	2575, 3800

Note: Spleen shielding was done in 1956, hind leg shielding in 1957; we are not certain whether there is a real difference in effectiveness as indicated by the tabulated counts.

Intestinal Syndrome

The $LD_{50(\text{intestinal})}$ for acute intestinal death (in 3½ to 4½ days) is about 1200 rads. Death in the intestinal mode does not occur, as a rule, with doses up to 6000 rads (possibly more) if the exteriorized intestine is shielded during irradiation (see Table III). The procedure we use leaves the duodenum unprotected. It is remarkable that a sizable and notoriously radiosensitive portion of the small bowel can be treated with high doses without causing death. To analyze this situation further we irradiated the duodenal region after laparotomy, with the mobile parts of the bowels pushed aside; the field includes parts of kidneys, stomach, pancreas, a portion of the spine, and the dorsal abdominal wall. This treatment was given with doses up to 6000 rads; 5 out of 10 animals so treated survived the acute phase. We utilized this situation to obtain histological preparations of heavily irradiated duodena from animals sacrificed at various times and compare them with duodena from animals totally irradiated with smaller doses.

The pathological findings are summarized in Table II and illustrated in Fig. 2. The degenerative process follows the well-established pattern: production of new cells in the crypts is stopped, the crypts are emptied by cell death and cell maturation (*7*), the population of cells covering the villi is reduced to a thin sheet; continued DNA synthesis without division results in presumably hyperploid, large, misshapen cells (*8*) (Fig. 2*A*). Somewhat later, these cells fall off, and the lumen is completely denuded (Fig. 2*B*). Regeneration in these heavily irradiated intestines proceeds in similar fashion as found after much smaller doses (*9–12*). It seems to start from a few centers which become very hyperplastic; these crypts do not always connect with the surface, and some become cystic. The surface cells produced are

TABLE II

HISTOLOGICAL FINDINGS AFTER HIGH DOSES OF X-IRRADIATION TO ONLY THE DUODENUM

Strain	*Dose (krad)*	*Days irradiated to sacrifice*	*Crypts*[a]	*Villi*
C57	3	3	Empty except for occasional nests of Paneth cells	Barely covered by few large, misshapen cells
CF1	3	3½	Empty	Denuded and collapsed
C57	3	4	Normal	Normal? (questionable villar changes)
C57	3	4	*a*—Normal *b*—Empty	*a*—Normal *b*—Few large misshapen cells
CF1	3	4	*a*—Normal or slightly hyperactive *b*—Empty	*a*-Normal *b*—Denuded
C1	3	4	Normal	Normal
CF1	3	5	Normal	Normal
CF1	3	5	Empty	Denuded
C57	2	6	Normal	Normal
C57	3	6	Empty except for Paneth cell nests	Denuded
C57	3	7	Normal	Normal
C57	3	7	Most crypts empty, but hyperplasia in several spots	Cover partly regenerated, with many abnormal cells
CF1	6	8	*a*—Normal *b*—Empty in one spot	*a*—Normal *b*—Denuded
C57	3	8	Normal	Normal
CF1	3	8	*a*—Empty (on top of damaged Brunner glands) *b*—Hyperplastic to normal	*a*—Denuded *b*—Normal and abnormal patches
C57	3	9	Normal	Normal
CF1	6	29	Empty	Denuded

[a] Two descriptions (*a* and *b*) for one animal refer to patches of radically different appearance.

sometimes definitely abnormal (Fig. 2*C*). Once the process gets going, however, a mucosa of fairly normal appearance is reconstructed quickly. We find denuded places alternating with fairly normal-looking ones (Fig. 2*D*), as well as a wide variety of findings in animals treated the same way (see Table II); we are reasonably certain that these differences are not due to accidental shielding. In some cases, the only evidence of regeneration after serious derangement is the finding of depolarized nuclei in the distal portion of the villi (where the older cells are), while the nuclei in the cells covering the proximal portion are normally polarized. The depolarization of cells in the villus epithelium has been observed by Sternberg (*13*) in rats treated with radiomimetic drugs and occurs equally after X-irradiation. But the

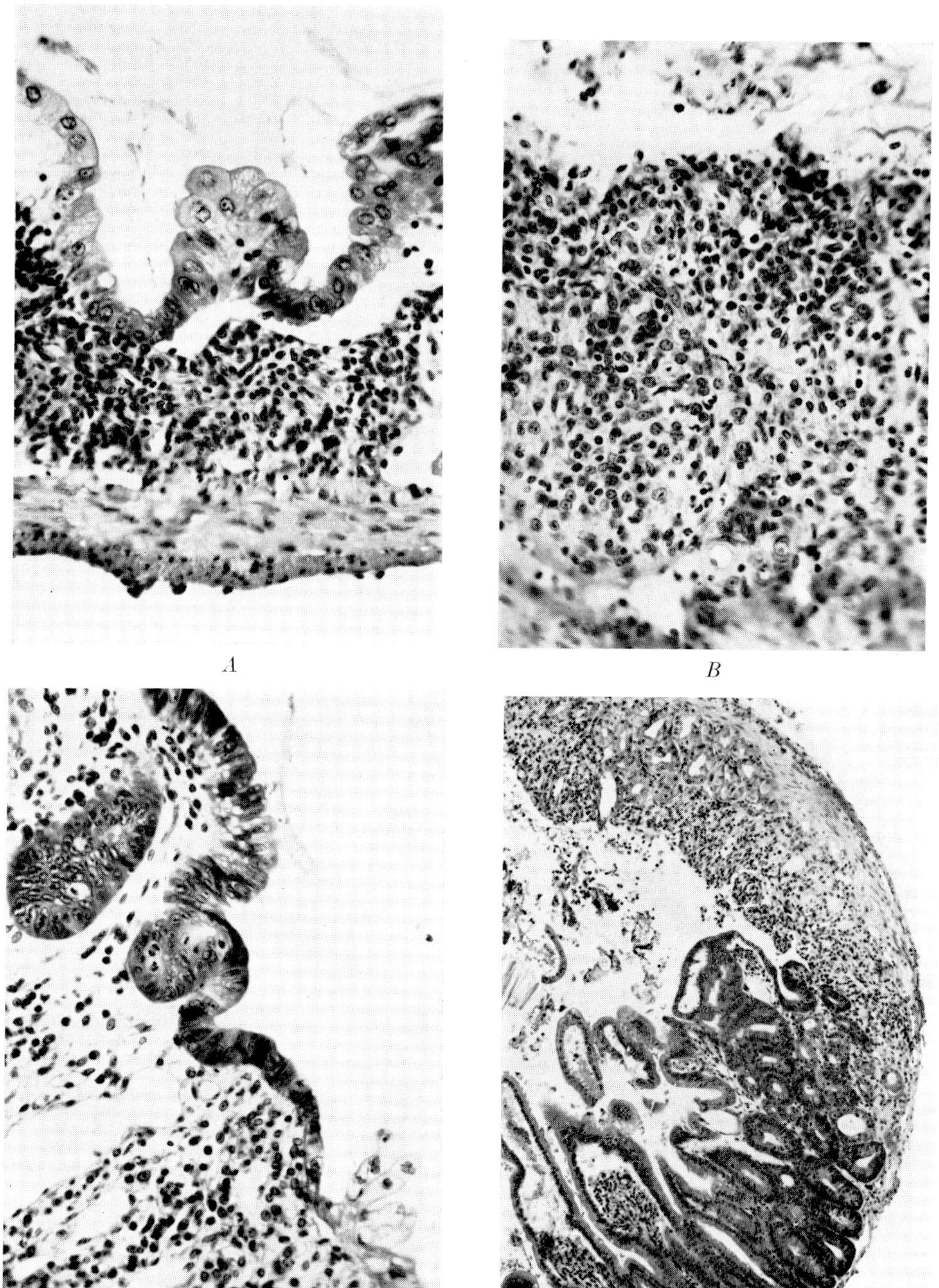

FIG. 2. Duodena after localized irradiation with 3 kilorads. Bouin, hematoxylin-eosin. *A*, crypts empty, villi covered with few abnormal (hyperploid ?) cells, 3 days after irradiation. (140 ×). *B*, complete denudation of intestinal wall, 4 days after irradiation. (140 ×). *C*, a center of regeneration, 6 days after irradiation. (140 ×). *D*, denudation and regenerated cover in close proximity, 3 days after irradiation (30 ×).

TABLE III

Mortality in Mice Irradiated with Shielded Hind Legs, Gut, and Lower Jaw

Dose (krad)	Mice		Killing time (days)		
	treated	% died	Min.	Max.	Mean
1–2	46	17%	3.5	17.0	7.8
3	19	100%	4.0	10.5	8.5
5	10	100%	2.5	8.5	5.3

duodenum may also remain denuded for a long time without the animal's dying (see last entry in Table II); the denudation presumably occurred within 4 days after irradiation.

Five- to Eight-Day Death

There are at least two modes of death which are associated with survival times between 5 and 8 days: one we call "intestinal syndrome II," which differs from the earlier described syndrome (*1, 5*) in that the cell cover over the villi is never entirely lost but becomes an inadequate barrier against massive bacterial invasion (*9–12*; and another, of unknown nature, which occurs with dose around 800 rads (*14*).

In this series of experiments we have observed death in 5 to 8 days quite commonly after doses between the $LD_{50(marrow)}$ and the $LD_{50(intestinal)}$, including one experiment in which the gut was shielded. We found only infrequent instances of death at that time in mice in which the spleen was shielded. No histological studies were made in these animals.

Oral Death

The $LD_{50(oral)}$ was about 1700 rads. We found no oral death in mice in which the lower jaw had been shielded by wrapping in lead foil.

Death in Mice Protected against Marrow, Intestinal, and Oral Syndrome

The LD_{50} for this kind of treatment is between 2 and 3 krad; for time of death, see Table III. This mode of death was not analyzed beyond ascertaining that neither marrow aplasia nor intestinal denudation was involved.

SUMMARY

1. Specific protection prevents one particular mode of radiation death without strongly affecting other syndromes; in the case of marrow, intestinal, and oral death, this can be accomplished by partial shielding. This method allows the study of situations which cannot be realized with total-body irradiation with or without unspecific protection.

2. Marrow syndrome: the protective effect of partial shielding is not affected by doses up to several kilorads; this can be seen if intestinal death is prevented.

3. Intestinal syndrome: denudation of the duodenum is compatible with survival; regeneration occurs even after doses of several kilorads.

4. Mice irradiated with several kilorads, even though protected against marrow, intestinal, and oral death, succumb to an unidentified disturbance.

RECEIVED: June 5, 1958.

REFERENCES

1. H. QUASTLER, Modes of acute radiation death. *Proc. 1st Conf. Peaceful Uses Atomic Energy, Geneva, 1955* **11,** 121–124 (1956).
2. L. T. STEADMAN, The immediate causes of early death in lethally X-irradiated rabbits. (Abstract) *Radiation* **7,** 453 (1957).
3. S. P. STEARNER and S. A. TYLER, Indicators of injury in the chick and chick embryo. (Abstract) *Radiation Research* **7,** 453–454 (1957).
4. C. C. CONGDON, Bone marrow transplantation in animals exposed to whole-body irradiation. *J. Cellular Comp. Physiol* **50,** *Suppl.* **1,** 103–108 (1957).
5. H. QUASTLER, E. F. LANZL, M. E. KELLER, and J. W. OSBORNE, Acute intestinal radiation death. *Am. J. Physiol.* **164,** 546–556 (1951).
6. R. A. CONARD, E. P. CRONKITE, G. BRECHER, and C. P. A. STROME, Experimental therapy of the gastro-intestinal syndrome produced by lethal doses of ionizing radiations. *J. Appl. Physiol.* **9,** 227–233 (1956).
7. W. L. HUGHES, V. P. BOND, G. BRECHER, E. P. CRONKITE, R. B. PAINTER, H. QUASTLER, and F. G. SHERMAN, Studies with tritiated thymidine on cell renewal in mice. *Proc. Natl. Acad. Sci. (U. S.)* in press.
8. H. QUASTLER, F. G. SHERMAN, G. BRECHER, and E. P. CRONKITE, Cell renewal, maturation and decay in the gastro-intestinal epithelia of normal and irradiated animals. *Proc. 2nd Intern. Conf. Peaceful Uses Atomic Energy, Geneva, 1958* in press.
9. G. BRECHER, E. P. CRONKITE, R. A. CONARD, and W. W. SMITH, Gastric lesions in experimental animals following single exposures to ionizing radiations. *Am. J. Pathol.* **34,** 105–119 (1958).
10. W. W. SMITH, R. Q. MARSTON, L. GONSHERY, I. M. ALDERMAN, and H. J. RUSH, X-irradiation in hamsters and effects of streptomycin and marrow-spleen homogenate treatment. *Am. J. Physiol.* **183,** 98–110 (1955).
11. M. F. SULLIVAN, S. MARKS, P. L. HACKETT and R. C. THOMPSON, X-irradiation of the exteriorized or *in situ* intestine of the rat. To be published.
12. S. LESHER and H. H. VOGEL, JR., A comparative histological study of duodenal damage produced by fission neutrons and Co^{60} gamma-rays, Radiation Research **9,** 560–571 (1958).
13. S. S. STERNBERG and F. S. PHILIPS, Azaserine: pathological and pharmacological studies. *Cancer* **10,** 889–901 (1957).
14. M. K. AUSTIN, M. MILLER, and H. QUASTLER, Five-to-eight day radiation death in mice. *Radiation Research* **5,** 303–307 (1956).

RADIATION RESEARCH **10**, 410–417 (1959)

The Effect of Pitressin on Postirradiation Polydipsia and Polyuria in the Rat[1]

CLYDE M. WILLIAMS[2] AND GEORGE M. KRISE[3]

The Radiobiological Laboratory of the University of Texas and the United States Air Force, Balcones Research Center, Austin, Texas

INTRODUCTION

Postirradiation polydipsia and polyuria have been studied in the rat by Edelmann (*1*), Edelmann and Eversole (*2*), Smith and Tyree (*3*), Pentz and Hasterlik (*4*) and Pentz (*5*). Although all these authors have suggested the possible role of hormonal imbalance in this phenomenon, no one to our knowledge has measured the effect of the antidiuretic hormone on postirradiation thirst and diuresis. Recent experiments in this laboratory have shown that postirradiation polydipsia and polyuria may be reduced to normal levels by the injection of the antidiuretic hormone vasopressin (Pitressin). A preliminary report has been published (*6*).

MATERIALS AND METHODS

One hundred and sixty young (75 days old) female and 24 young male Holtzman rats each weighing 150 to 200 gm were used. Pitressin tannate in peanut oil or aqueous Pitressin (Parke, Davis and Co.) was used in all experiments. When control injections or dilutions were necessary, commercial peanut oil (Sargent Co.) was used. All injections were made into the thigh muscles with tuberculin syringes using 22- or 23-gauge needles. Prior to testing, all animals were allowed free access to Lab-blox pellets and water. After irradiation and/or injection, each animal was placed in an individual metabolism cage (Acme Sheet Metal Co., Chicago, Illinois) and allowed free access to water from feeder bottles having a capacity of at least 100 ml. All animals were deprived of food during the course of the experiment. Water intakes and urine outputs were measured at 24 and 48 hours. Irradiations were carried out in a 1240-curie Co^{60} source designed by Auxier (*7*). Dosimetry

[1] This work was supported with funds provided under Contract AF 41(657)-149 and the School of Aviation Medicine, USAF.

[2] Present address: Radioisotope Unit, Veterans Administration Hospital, University Drive, Pittsburgh 40, Pennsylvania.

[3] Present address: Department of Biology, Agricultural and Mechanical College of Texas, College Station, Texas.

TABLE I

AVERAGE WATER INTAKE AND URINE OUTPUT PER ANIMAL FOR 48 HOURS AFTER 1500 R OF Co^{60} GAMMA-IRRADIATION

Time (hours)	*No irradiation; no injection (15 animals)*		*1500 r irradiation; no injection (15 animals)*		*1500 r irradiation; injected with 0.1 ml of peanut oil immediately after irradiation (15 animals)*		*1500 r irradiation; injected with 500 mU of Pitressin tannate in 0.1 ml of peanut oil immediately after irradiation (15 animals)*	
	Intake ml	*Output ml*	*Intake ml*	*Output ml*	*Intake ml*	*Output ml*	*Intake ml*	*Output ml*
0–24	15 (±8)	10 (±3)	58 (±21)	52 (±18)	52 (±21)	44 (±17)	16 (±5)	6 (±3)
24–48	5 (±3)	6 (±3)	21 (±7)	19 (±6)	19 (±16)	16 (±8)	5 (±4)	6 (±3)

was accomplished with two-phase water-equivalent trichloroethylene chemical dosimeters (*8*).

RESULTS

Effect of Pitressin Tannate in Peanut Oil on Postirradiation Polydipsia and Polyuria Evoked by 1500 R of Whole-Body Co^{60} Gamma-Irradiation

An experiment using female rats was designed with 5 animals in each of four groups. This experiment was repeated three times, and the data were treated together (Table I). All animals irradiated received a dose of 1500 r at the rate of 1500 r/min, and injections of Pitressin tannate in peanut oil were made within 1 minute after irradiation. For each group the water intakes did not differ significantly from the urine outputs during any period examined, with one exception. That exception was the group irradiated with 1500 r and then injected with 500 milliunits (mU) of Pitressin tannate in peanut oil. In this group the intakes were significantly greater ($P < 0.001$) than the outputs during the first 24 hours after irradiation. The intakes of the nonirradiated, noninjected controls were not significantly different from the intakes of the irradiated Pitressin-injected animals. The outputs of the nonirradiated, noninjected controls were significantly greater ($P < 0.001$) than those of the irradiated Pitressin-injected animals. It was concluded that the injection of 500 mU of Pitressin reduced postirradiation thirst to normal levels and postirradiation diuresis to levels significantly below normal. Water intakes and urine outputs of the irradiated, nontreated and of the irradiated peanut-oil-injected animals were significantly greater ($P < 0.001$) by a factor of 4 to 5 than the intakes and outputs of the untreated controls or the Pitressin-injected animals. The injection of peanut oil did not significantly affect the degree of antidiuresis.

The Effect of Pitressin Tannate in Peanut Oil Injected Prior to 1500 R of Co^{60} Gamma-Irradiation

In order to test the effect of the antidiuretic hormone injected prior to irradiation, 10 female rats were selected at random from a holding colony. Five animals served

TABLE II

AVERAGE WATER INTAKE AND URINE OUTPUT PER ANIMAL FOR 48 HOURS AFTER INJECTION OF PITRESSIN PRIOR TO 1500 R OF Co^{60} GAMMA-IRRADIATION

Time (hours)	*No irradiation; no injection (5 animals)*		*Injected with 500 mU of Pitressin tannate in 0.1 ml of peanut oil immediately before 1500 r irradiation (5 animals)*	
	Intake ml	*Output ml*	*Intake ml*	*Output ml*
0–24	3 (±2)	5 (±2)	13 (±3)	7 (±1)
24–48	5 (±3)	4 (±2)	4 (±2)	5 (±1)

TABLE III

AVERAGE WATER INTAKE AND URINE OUTPUT PER ANIMAL FOR 48 HOURS AFTER INJECTION OF AQUEOUS PITRESSIN PRIOR TO AND AFTER 1500 R OF Co^{60} GAMMA-IRRADIATION

Time (hours)	*No irradiation; no injection (5 animals)*		*Injected with 0.025 ml of water immediately before 1500 r irradiation (5 animals)*		*Injected with 500 mU of Pitressin in 0.025 ml of water immediately before 1500 r irradiation (5 animals)*		*1500 r irradiation injected with 500 mU of Pitressin in 0.025 ml of water immediately after irradiation (5 animals)*	
	Intake (ml)	*Output (ml)*	*Intake (ml)*	*Output (ml)*	*Intake (ml)*	*Output (ml)*	*Intake (ml)*	*Output (ml)*
0–24	5 (±3)	7 (±4)	40 (±16)	34 (±12)	52 (±14)	47 (±12)	48 (±11)	42 (±9)
24–48	12 (±7)	12 (±5)	18 (±10)	17 (±7)	20 (±5)	21 (±7)	15 (±7)	15 (±5)

as controls, and 5 animals were injected with 500 mU of Pitressin tannate in peanut oil immediately prior to irradiation. A dose of 1500 r was delivered at the rate of 1500 r/min. The injection of Pitressin prevented diuresis to a degree significantly different from that in the controls, but the intakes of the Pitressin-injected animals were significantly higher than the intakes of the controls during the first 24-hour period, as shown in Table II. By comparing the results with those in Table I, it was concluded that Pitressin tannate in peanut oil reduces postirradiation thirst and inhibits postirradiation diuresis when administered immediately prior to irradiation.

Effect of Aqueous Solutions of Pitressin on the Polydipsia and Polyuria evoked by 1500 R of Co^{60} Gamma-Irradiation

In order to test the effect of aqueous solutions of Pitressin on postirradiation polydipsia and polyuria, 20 female rats were treated as described in Table III. It is obvious from this table that aqueous Pitressin is ineffective in suppressing postirradiation polydipsia and polyuria, when administered either just prior to irradiation or just after. In no case was the intake of a group significantly different from the output during the 0- to 24-hour period or the 24- to 48-hour period. The average water intakes and urine outputs of the three irradiated groups were not significantly different from each other during the first 24 hours postirradiation.

Effect of Water Deprivation after 500 R of Co^{60} Gamma-Irradiation

Fifteen female rats were treated as shown in Table IV. The dose of 500 r was delivered at the rate of 200 r/min. One group of 5 animals was deprived of water for the first 24 hours after irradiation. As can be seen in Table IV, 500 r evoked a pronounced polydipsia and polyuria during the first 24 hours. Animals deprived of water for this same period did not exhibit a 24-hour urine excretion significantly different from that of the nonirradiated controls. With the return of water to their cages, however, the deprived animals exhibited a polydipsia and polyuria of the same magnitude as those of the nondeprived animals and greater than those of the controls during the subsequent 24- to 48-hour period.

Threshold Dose of Pitressin for Inhibition of Polydipsia and Polyuria Evoked by 1500 R of Co^{60} Gamma-Irradiation

In order to establish the minimum dose required to inhibit the effect, 55 females were selected at random from the holding colony and treated as described in Table V. During the first 24-hour period after irradiation, the average water intakes and urine outputs fell linearly with increasing dose of injected Pitressin. Figure 1 shows the mean values for each group of animals plotted against the dose of Pitressin injected. The lines for the irradiated animals were calculated by the method of least squares. Because of the large standard deviations of the mean values, it is impossible to be precise about the exact value of the threshold dose. The water intakes and urine outputs of the group injected with 100 mU of Pitressin were significantly higher ($P < 0.001$) than the corresponding values for the control group during the 0- to 24-hour period. The water intakes and urine outputs of the group injected with 150 mU were not significantly different, however, from the corresponding values for the control group during this time. During the 24- to 48-hour period, there was a rise in the urine output of the animals injected with 150 mU of Pitressin, but it was not significantly different from the control values for the same period.

TABLE IV

AVERAGE WATER INTAKE AND URINE OUTPUT PER ANIMAL FOR 48 HOURS AFTER 500 R OF Co^{60} GAMMA-IRRADIATION

Time (hours)	*No irradiation; no injection (5 animals)*		*500 r irradiation; injected with 0.1 ml of peanut oil immediately after irradiation; free access to water from 0 to 48 hours. (5 animals)*		*500 r irradiation; injected with 0.1 ml of peanut oil immediately after irradiation; no access to water for first 24 hours; free access to water from 24 to 48 hours (5 animals)*	
	Intake (ml)	*Output (ml)*	*Intake (ml)*	*Output (ml)*	*Intake (ml)*	*Output (ml)*
0–24	7 (±3)	8 (±3)	71 (±15)	50 (±14)	—	4 (±1)
24–48	8 (±7)	7 (±3)	21 (±10)	15 (±8)	25 (±17)	24 (±17)

TABLE V

THE EFFECT OF THRESHOLD AND SUBTHRESHOLD DOSES OF PITRESSIN ON THE AVERAGE WATER INTAKE AND URINE OUTPUT PER ANIMAL AFTER 1500 R OF Co^{60} GAMMA-IRRADIATION

Time (hours)	*No irradiation; no injection (10 animals)*		*1500 r irradiation injected with 0.1 ml peanut oil immediately after irradiation (10 animals)*		*1500 r irradiation injected with 50 mU of Pitressin in 0.1 ml peanut oil immediately after irradiation (15 animals)*		*1500 r irradiation injected with 100 mU of Pitressin in 0.1 ml peanut oil immediately after irradiation (10 animals)*		*1500 r irradiation injected with 150 mU Pitressin in 0.1 ml peanut oil immediately after irradiation (10 animals)*	
	Intake (ml)	*Output (ml)*	*Intake (ml)*	*Output (ml)*	*Intake (ml)*	*Output (ml)*	*Intake (ml)*	*Output (ml)*	*Intake (ml)*	*Output (ml)*
0–24	13 (±10)	11 (±8)	71 (±24)	55 (±20)	59 (±19)	45 (±28)	41 (±17)	25 (±13)	18 (±13)	7 (±4)
24–48	15 (±8)	9 (±5)	32 (±10)	25 (±8)	30 (±16)	28 (±11)	31 (±8)	33 (±9)	18 (±7)	19 (±9)
48–72	12 (±4)	7 (±3)	20 (±11)	16 (±15)	17 (±15)	16 (±14)	18 (±22)	20 (±20)	4 (±4)	8 (±3)

TABLE VI

THE EFFECT OF IRRADIATION OF PITRESSIN TANNATE IN PEANUT OIL ON ITS ABILITY TO INHIBIT POSTIRRADIATION POLYDIPSIA AND POLYURIA

Time (hours)	*No irradiation no injection (5 animals)*		*1500 r irradiation; injected with 0.1 ml peanut oil immediately after irradiation (4 animals)*		*1500 r irradiation; injected with 150 mU of Pitressin in 0.1 ml of peanut oil; Pitressin irradiated with 1500 r Co^{60} γ-rays immediately before injection (5 animals)*		*1500 r irradiation; injected with 150 mU of Pitressin in 0.1 ml of peanut oil; Pitressin irradiated with 5000 r Co^{60} γ-rays immediately before injection (5 animals)*		*1500 r irradiation; injected with 150 mU of Pitressin in 0.1 ml peanut oil Pitressin irradiated with 20,000 or CO^{60} γ-rays immediately before injection (5 animals)*	
	Intake (ml)	*Output (ml)*	*Intake (ml)*	*Output (ml)*	*Intake (ml)*	*Output (ml)*	*Intake (ml)*	*Output (ml)*	*Intake (ml)*	*Output (ml)*
0–24	8 (±7)	8 (±6)	64 (±23)	51 (±20)	19 (±3)	10 (±2)	15 (±4)	7 (±2)	8 (±5)	10 (±5)
24–48	11 (±7)	8 (±3)	31 (±14)	22 (±11)	19 (±5)	19 (±6)	6 (±5)	11 (±8)	6 (±5)	11 (±4)

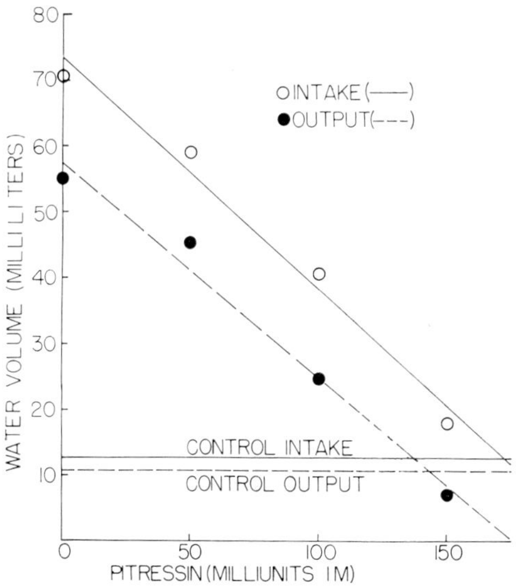

FIG. 1. The effect of injected Pitressin tannate in peanut oil on water intake and urine output during the first 24 hours after 1500 r of whole-body irradiation.

Effect of Irradiated Pitressin Tannate in Peanut Oil on Postirradiation Polydipsia and Polyuria

Pitressin tannate in peanut oil in a concentration of 1500 mU/ml was irradiated for total doses of 1500, 5000, and 20,000 r. The mixture was rotated during irradiation to ensure uniform suspension of the hormone. Immediately after this, 19 male rats were irradiated with 1500 r at the rate of 1500 r/min and then injected with either 0.1 ml of peanut oil or 150 mU of the irradiated hormone (Table VI). The intakes and outputs of the animals irradiated with 1500 r and then injected with peanut oil were significantly elevated ($0.01 < P < 0.001$) during the first 24 hours postirradiation. The outputs of the three groups of animals injected with irradiated Pitressin were significantly different from the outputs of the noninjected, nonirradiated controls during the first 24 hours postirradiation. The intakes of the three groups of irradiated animals injected with irradiated Pitressin were not significantly different from those of the nonirradiated, noninjected controls. It was concluded that irradiation in doses up to 20,000 r of Pitressin in peanut oil in the concentration examined, 1500 mU/ml, did not interfere with the ability of the hormone to suppress postirradiation polydipsia and polyuria.

DISCUSSION

Aqueous Pitressin (100 mU per 100 gm) injected into the venous circulation of anesthetized rats is cleared from the blood (or inactivated) within about 5 minutes;

the removal is accomplished in part by the kidney and the splanchnic vascular bed (*9*). The observation that aqueous solutions of Pitressin do not inhibit postirradiation thirst and diuresis is most easily explained by supposing that irradiation does not affect the mechanisms which inactivate (or clear) the hormone. The fact that irradiation of Pitressin tannate in peanut oil (1500 mU/ml) by doses up to 20,000 r does not affect the ability of the hormone to suppress postirradiation polydipsia and polyuria is consistent with the observation that the antidiuretic factor is as effective when injected before irradiation as when injected immediately after irradiation.

These results show that postirradiation thirst and diuresis are not an obligatory renal tubular water loss. This conclusion is also a consequence of the observation that no diuresis occurs when irradiated animals are denied access to water (*5*). That the antidiuretic hormone of the posterior pituitary is implicated in the phenomenon seems a reasonable conclusion, but none of our observations necessarily support any of the proposed hypotheses concerning the mechanisms of postirradiation polydipsia and polyuria. It has been repeatedly suggested (*2–4*) that postirradiation polydipsia and polyuria result from a hormonal imbalance between adrenal cortical diuretic and posterior pituitary antidiuretic factors. The main evidence in favor of this hypothesis is the fact that the phenomenon does not occur in animals previously subjected to anterior hypophysectomy or adrenalectomy, but is not obliterated when the animal has been subjected to posterior hypophysectomy (*4*). This apparently straightforward interpretation has been complicated, however, by the observations of Pentz, who has shown that the diuretic response to irradiation is not abolished for at least 12 days after adrenalectomy (*5*). Moreover, as Gaunt has pointed out, it is impossible to speak simply of corticoid-vasopressin antagonism: "The effects of vasopressin may be either antagonized, enhanced or unaltered by a corticoid depending on the steroid used, its dose or the variable measured" (*10*).

SUMMARY

1. The intramuscular injection of 500 mU of Pitressin tannate in peanut oil, either immediately before or immediately after whole-body irradiation by 1500 r of Co^{60} γ-rays, was found to inhibit polydipsia and polyuria in the adult rat.

2. Aqueous solutions of Pitressin, when injected intramuscularly either before or after irradiation, did not inhibit the postirradiation polydipsia and polyuria evoked by 1500 r of whole-body irradiation.

3. Rats deprived of water for the first 24 hours after 500 r of whole-body irradiation did not excrete urine in amounts significantly greater than were excreted by nonirradiated controls.

4. Water intakes and urine outputs during the first 24 hours after 1500 r of whole-body irradiation decreased linearly with increasing dose of injected Pitressin tannate

in peanut oil; 150 mU was found to be the minimum dose of Pitressin which produced a water intake and urine output not significantly different from those of the nonirradiated controls during the first 24 hours postirradiation.

5. The irradiation of Pitressin tannate in peanut oil (in a concentration of 1500 mU/ml) by doses up to 20,000 r did not alter the ability of Pitressin to inhibit the polydipsia and polyuria evoked by 1500 r of whole-body irradiation.

RECEIVED: June 24, 1958

REFERENCES

1. A. EDELMANN, Effects of X-radiation on water and electrolyte metabolism in the rat. *Federation Proc.* **8,** 39 (1949).
2. A. EDELMANN and W. J. EVERSOLE, Changes in antidiuretic activity of rat serum after X-irradiation. *Am. J. Physiol.* **163,** 709 (1950).
3. D. E. SMITH and E. B. TYREE, Influence of X-irradiation upon water consumption by the rat. *Am. J. Physiol.* **184,** 127–133 (1956).
4. E. I. PENTZ and R. J. HASTERLIK, Factors influencing diuresis in rats following total-body X-irradiation. *Am. J. Physiol.* **189,** 11–14 (1957).
5. E. I. PENTZ, Further studies on diuresis in normal and adrenalectomized rats following total-body X-irradiation. *Proc. Soc. Exptl. Biol. Med.* **96,** 829–833 (1957).
6. C. M. WILLIAMS and G. M. KRISE, Inhibition of postirradiation diuresis by Pitressin in rats. *Science* **128,** 475–476 (1958).
7. J. A. AUXIER, A high level Co^{60} irradiation facility. School of Aviation Medicine Report No. 55-40 (1955).[4]
8. S. C. SIGOLOFF, Fast neutron insensitive chemical gamma-ray dosimeters. *Nucleonics* **14,** (10), 54–56 (1956).
9. M. GINSBURG and H. HELLER, The clearance of injected vasopressin from the circulation and its fate in the body. *J. Endocrinol.* **9,** 283–291 (1953).
10. R. GAUNT, C. W. LLOYD, and J. J. CHART, The adrenal-neurohypophysial interrelationship. In *The Neurohypophysis* (H. Heller, ed.), pp. 233–251, Academic Press, New York, 1957.

[4] Copies available at Air University, School of Aviation Medicine, USAF, Randolph AFB, Texas.

RADIATION RESEARCH **10**, 418–432 (1959)

The Relative Biological Effectiveness of 200-Kvp X-Rays, Cobalt-60 Gamma-Rays, and 22-Mevp X-Rays, Determined from the Dose-Survival Curve of *Saccharomyces cerevisiae*[1]

W. K. SINCLAIR,[2] S. E. GUNTER,[3] AND A. COLE[2]

INTRODUCTION

During the past four years a series of RBE determinations for high-energy X-rays has been carried out using the dose-survival curve (LD_{50}) of a haploid strain of the yeast *Saccharomyces cerevisiae*, determined by macrocolony counts, as the biological endpoint. The studies were planned to establish the reproducibility of the biological test in interlaboratory comparisons as well as to provide information concerning the relative effectiveness of radiation in the supervoltage range. The RBE of 1-Mevp and 250-kvp X-rays was found to be 0.86 ± 0.02 by Kohn and Gunter (*1*) (work carried out in San Francisco, 1955). Previously, however, an RBE of 1.06 ± 0.04 for 22.5-Mevp X-rays and 180-kvp X-rays was found by Gunter *et al.* (*2*) (work done in New York, 1954). Considering the relation of RBE with LET, these results would require the effectiveness to decrease and then increase again as the mean value of LET decreased from 2.5 kev/μ. It was of interest, therefore, to check the results in a third laboratory (M. D. Anderson Hospital), where sources of 200-kvp X-rays, 1.25-Mev γ-rays, and 22-Mevp X-rays were available, and determinations with these radiations could be carried out simultaneously. The results of these experiments are reported below.

MATERIALS AND METHODS

Biological Procedure

The haploid strain 93.1C(α) of *Saccharomyces cerevisiae* was grown and plated on yeast-dextrose agar with incubation at about 30°C. A suspension of washed cells in

[1] This work was carried out under a project sponsored by the U. S. Atomic Energy Commission, Grant AT-(40-1)-2028.

[2] Physics Department, The University of Texas M. D. Anderson Hospital and Tumor Institute, Houston, Texas.

[3] Radiological Laboratory, University of California Medical Center, San Francisco, California.

potassium phosphate buffer adjusted to 2×10^4 cells/ml was irradiated in Teflon cups. The irradiations were carried out simultaneously with the three machines. After irradiation the samples were diluted and plated, and macrocolony counts were made after 2 days of incubation.

The method outlined above is the standard procedure described in detail by Gunter and Kohn (*3*) and has been used in all RBE determinations of this series. A diagram and description of the Teflon cups used as containers for the yeast suspension have been presented (*1*).

This procedure, referred to as method 1 (Kohn and Gunter, 1), gives a resting cell suspension containing 4 to 8% radioresistant cells, the presence of which results in a modified exponential survival curve for the total population. By correcting for the resistant fraction, the exponential survival curves for the sensitive population were obtained. The slopes of the latter were determined and used in the calculation of the RBE.

Radiological Procedure

Exposure method and dose distribution. The physical procedures were planned to deliver a uniform dose to replicate samples under reproducible conditions and to permit an accurate measurement of the absorbed dose in rads at the location of the samples. To accomplish this, the samples were irradiated at the center of a mass of unit density under conditions of full scatter and electron equilibrium. The central core containing the samples was rotated and/or inverted halfway through each exposure in such a way as to give a final dose distribution uniform to within $\pm 2\%$. The exposure dose rate in roentgens, or the relative ionization in the case of the betatron, was determined with a 250-r Victoreen thimble chamber inserted into the mass at the location of the samples. The readings have been converted to absorbed dose in rads by use of the appropriate factors.

The sample holders used for the irradiations with 200-kvp X-rays and 1.25-Mev γ-rays were blocks of Mix D wax (tissue-equivalent wax) $15 \times 15 \times 22$ cm. In the case of the 200-kvp machine the block was surrounded by 5 cm of Masonite on all sides except that toward the beam. The block was attached directly to the 200-kvp machine, or mounted against the nose of the teletherapy unit in the case of cobalt-60. Each block contained a removable central core into which were inserted six Teflon cups. The sample holder used with the betatron was a Lucite block $9 \times 9 \times 11$ cm which filled the collimating space and was pushed into a stop against the front of the collimator. The center of the block contained a removable section of tissue-equivalent wax consisting of four right circular cylinders with each of the two central members holding three Teflon cups. The exposure arrangement, the design of each sample holder, and the method of moving the central core to give a uniform dose to all cups is shown in parts *A* and *B* of Figs. 1–3.

The standard beam was obtained from a constant-potential machine operated at 200 kvp and 8.5 ma. The filtration consisted of 0.5 mm Cu + 1 mm Al, providing

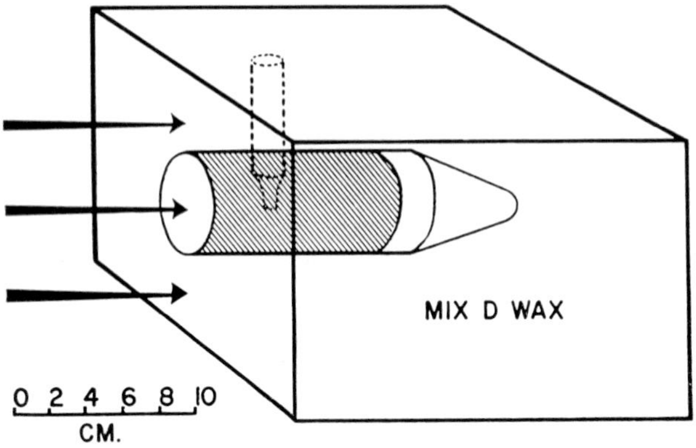

FIG. 1*A*. Exposure arrangement, 200 kvp. The central core (shaded) is interchangeable. One plug is used for calibration purposes, and the other for exposure of the yeast suspension. This block of Mix D wax is further surrounded on all sides with 5 cm of masonite.

FIG. 1*B*. Exposure arrangement, 200 kvp. Six Teflon cups are mounted in the Mix D wax core, the position of which is reversed halfway through the exposure.

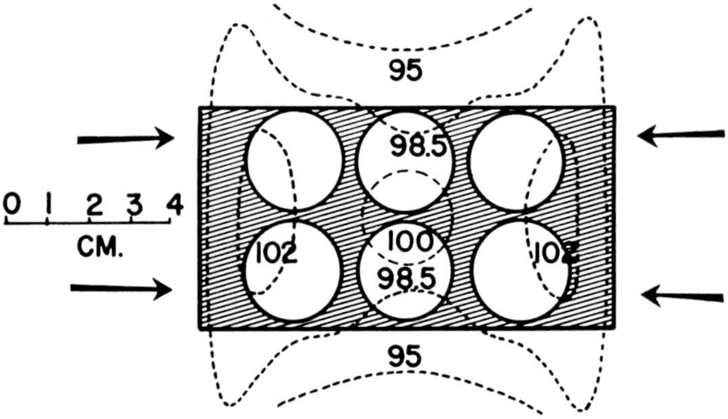

FIG. 1*C*. Isodose curves for yeast exposure, 200 kvp. Section of exposure core for six Teflon cups, each containing 2 ml of yeast suspension. Two parallel opposing fields are obtained by reversing the position of the core (along the long axis) after each half exposure. This produces the isodose curves shown, expressed as percentages of the measured exposure dose at the center.

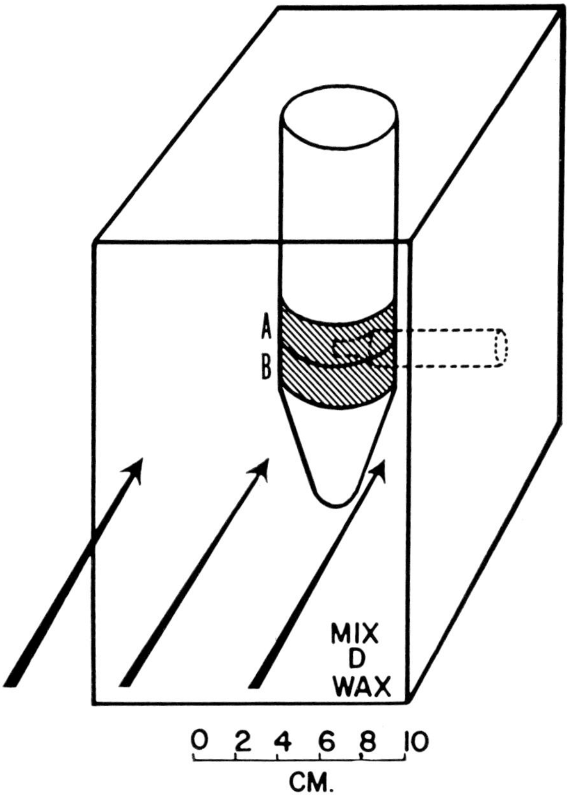

FIG. 2*A*. Exposure arrangement, cobalt-60. The shaded area shows the uniformly irradiated volume. The core is interchangeable, one plug for calibration and one to carry cylinders A and B, each holding three Teflon cups containing yeast suspension.

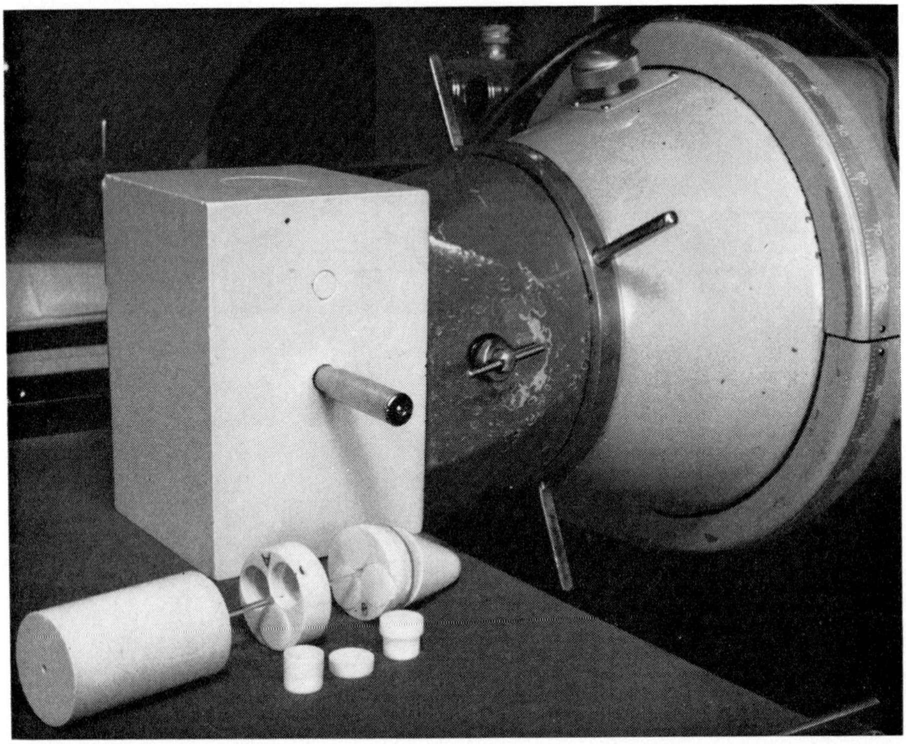

FIG. 2*B*. Exposure arrangement, cobalt-60 The six Teflon cups are mounted in two Mix D wax cylinders forming the central core, the position of which is reversed relative to the beam halfway through the exposure.

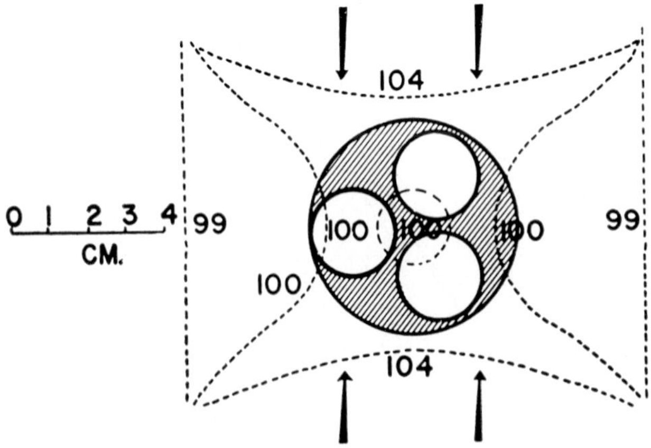

FIG. 2*C*. Isodose curves for yeast exposure, cobalt-60. One of the cylinders A and B is shown in section. Two parallel opposing fields are obtained by rotating through 180° after each half exposure. This produces the isodose curves shown, expressed as percentages of the measured exposure dose at the center.

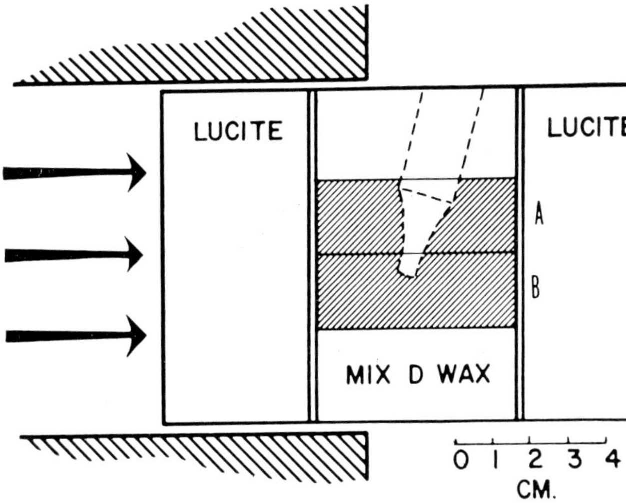

FIG. 3*A*. Exposure arrangement, betatron. Central core has interchangeable plugs of Mix D wax, one for calibration and one containing two cylinders, each with three Teflon cups of yeast suspension.

FIG. 3*B*. Exposure arrangement, betatron. The six Teflon cups are mounted in two Mix D wax cylinders forming the central core, the position of which is reversed and interchanged halfway through the exposure.

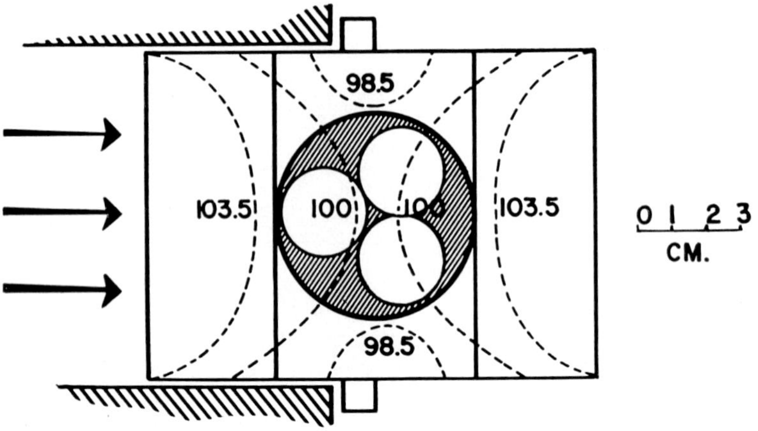

FIG. 3*C*. Isodose curves for yeast exposure, betatron. One of the cylinders is shown in section. Two parallel opposing fields are obtained by rotating through 180° after each half exposure. This produces the isodose curves shown, expressed as percentages of the measured exposure dose at the center.

an HVL of 1.4 mm Cu. With a target-to-surface distance of 25 cm, the absorbed dose rate was 135 to 140 rads/min at the exposure depth.

The source of the 1.25-Mev γ-radiation was a cobalt-60 teletherapy unit containing approximately 2000 curies of cobalt-60. The distance from the source to the surface of the sample holder was 36 cm, and the absorbed dose rate at the location of the samples was 135 to 140 rads/min. The exposures were controlled both by timer and independent clock, as with all other machines.

The third radiation was from an Allis-Chalmers betatron operating at 22 million volts with a compensating aluminum filter. A dose rate of 120 to 150 rads/min was provided at a target-to-sample distance of 60 cm. This distance is at the end of the standard collimating arrangement and is about the shortest distance possible if the calibration is to be made with a Victoreen chamber at the center of the sample arrangement.

To determine the dose distribution throughout the region occupied by the samples, measurements of the 200-kvp and 22-Mevp X-rays were made in a water phantom simulating the exposure geometry with a small ionization chamber as detector and the automatic iso-signal plotter designed by Cole (*4*). Similar measurements of the γ-radiation were carried out with an anthracene crystal and photomultiplier assembly with the automatic recording device, and confirmed by film exposures in the actual exposure setup. The isodose curves obtained by the irradiation procedure described above are shown in part *C* of Figs. 1–3.

Calibration procedure. The exposure-dose rate (200-kvp X-rays and 1.25-Mev γ-rays) or the relative ionization in air (22-Mevp X-rays) was determined at the beginning and end of each experiment (more frequently in the case of the betatron) by exposing a 250-r Victoreen thimble chamber at the center of the volume usually occupied by the cups. The Victoreen chamber was inserted into a special calibration core identical in composition to the sample core and interchangeable with it.

A single 250-r chamber and the same electrometer were used throughout these measurements. The chamber was calibrated directly at the National Bureau of Standards (NBS) for radiation with an HVL of 1.2 mm Cu. For cobalt-60 radiation only 25-r chambers are calibrated at NBS, and it was necessary to compare the 250-r chamber against the 25-r chamber under conditions (half stem irradiated) which differed from the NBS calibration (whole stem). Consequently, a greater error is possible in the cobalt-60 calibration than in the 200-kvp X-ray calibration. In the case of 22-Mevp X-rays no NBS calibration is available. Measurements made by Laughlin of the ionization at a depth in polystyrene have been used instead to provide a direct conversion of ionization measurements into rads (*5*).

Corrections and estimation of absorbed dose. Some corrections to the reading on the chamber are necessary in order to estimate the exposure dose correctly at the sample depth. These include a correction for the difference between the calibration conditions and the exposure conditions in the phantom—occasioned, for example, by material displaced by the chamber in order to make the calibration measurement, for which a negative correction of 1.75% for 200 kvp, 0.96% for cobalt-60, and 0.61% for 22 Mevp was estimated to be necessary.

In the eventual estimation of the absorbed dose to the yeast suspension, both the medium and the radiation quality at the exposure depth must be taken into account. The medium consists in part of Mix D wax, Teflon cups, and the yeast cell suspension (and Lucite in the betatron case), and its composition may affect both the measurement of exposure dose and the absorbed dose estimation. The yeast cell suspension has substantially the same composition as water, but its surrounding materials differ slightly. This problem was considered for each of the three radiations and the pertinent exposure circumstances. With 200-kvp X-radiation the range of the secondary electrons produced is so short that only those from the Teflon cup need be considered. In the case of cobalt-60 radiation, electrons from the Mix D wax will affect both the measurement and the absorbed dose very slightly. In the case of the betatron, electrons from the Mix D wax affect the measurement and those from the Lucite affect the estimate of absorbed dose to the suspension. Based on electron range data from NBS Circular 577 (*6*) and absorption coefficient data from NBS Handbook 62 (*7*), calculations for each situation showed that in no case did the error amount to as much as 1%. Since these corrections are complex and of limited accuracy, no correction was made in any of the three cases.

The quality of the radiation must also be considered in cases where the samples are placed at a depth in a scattering medium. In the case of 200-kvp X-rays this is important because the relation between exposure dose and absorbed dose varies

TABLE I

Estimation of Absorbed Dose

Radiation	*Equivalent energy at exposure depth*	*Conversion factor (rads/r)*	*Error in absorbed dose estimate*
200-kvp X-ray, HVL 1.4 mm Cu	75.2 kev	0.933	±2.5%
Cobalt-60 γ-ray	1.25 Mev	0.979	±3.1%
22-Mevp X-ray (betatron)	10 Mev	[a]	±3.3%

[a] Converted directly; see text and reference *5*.

quite rapidly with quality. Primary radiation of HVL of 1.4 mm Cu can be shown (*8*) to be softened from an initial equivalent energy of 96.5 kev to 75.2 kev with an effective HVL of about 0.78 mm Cu at a depth of 5 cm in water (the average depth of the samples. For this softened beam, data from NBS Handbook 62 (*7*) indicate that the conversion factor for water from exposure dose to absorbed dose is 0.933 rad/r.[4]

No correction for beam softening has been considered necessary in the case of the cobalt-60 and betatron beams. Average beam quality and conversion factor from exposure dose to absorbed dose are summarized in Table I. It may be noted that in the case of the betatron no measurement of the exposure dose has been made. The Victoreen chamber was compared against similar chambers of Dr. J. S. Laughlin at the center of a Lucite calibration block (11.5-cm cube). These chambers in turn were calibrated by Laughlin against measurements with an extrapolation chamber of polystyrene, yielding the true ionization per cubic centimeter at a given point in a polystyrene medium. With polarization taken into account, the absorbed dose in polystyrene can be estimated for that point (the peak of the buildup curve). The absorbed dose in water can then be estimated by the ratio of the respective absorption coefficients in water and polystyrene, weighting appropriately for the betatron spectrum. The procedure is outlined in a previous communication (*5*). The number of steps involved is considerable, and consequently there is a possibility of small additive errors accumulating. The final factor, however, converts the reading on the chamber directly to the absorbed dose in a water-like medium such as yeast.

Chemical measurement. If the G value (number of molecules oxidized per 100 ev) for a system such as ferrous sulfate were sufficiently well known, it would be possible to replace the yeast suspension by dosimeter fluid and measure the absorbed dose

[4] In the experiments of Kohn and Gunter (*1*) yeast irradiations were carried out with two beams, one of 0.6 mm Cu HVL and the other of 1.6 mm Cu HVL, and the RBE between these beams was found to be unity (exposure dose estimate). It may be noted that, had the absorbed dose been estimated, the factor would have been 0.926 for 0.6 mm Cu HVL and 0.959 for 1.6 mm Cu HVL (*7*, *9*), but the difference of about 3% may not have been detectable.

directly. The only correction required would be for the elementary composition of the dosimeter solution which differs sufficiently from water to cause errors of a few per cent for 200-kvp X-rays. The G value for ferrous sulfate for cobalt-60 γ-radiation appears to be well established (15.6 molecules per 100 ev), but it is less certain for 22-Mevp X-radiation and 200-kvp X-radiation. Measurements of this G value for these three radiations (*10*) yield values of 14.6 ± 0.4 for 200-kvp X-rays, 15.8 ± 0.5 for cobalt-60 γ-radiation, and 15.5 ± 0.5 for 22-Mevp X-radiation. These values were obtained from exactly the same exposure arrangements as in the yeast experiments. In fact, the three series of exposures for the chemical determinations were made on the same days as three of the yeast experiments. Consequently, if these G values are correct (and in the reference quoted the good agreement between these values and others outside the range is pointed out), the estimate of the absorbed dose based on these chemical measurements is in exact agreement with the ionization estimate of absorbed dose.

It is interesting to consider the error to which the ionization estimate of the absorbed dose may be liable in each instance. The various sources of error have been discussed in connection with the G value determinations for the ferrous sulfate dosimeter (*10*) and, since the exposure conditions were identical, apply here. The analysis of errors indicates uncertainties in the estimate of absorbed dose of ±2.5% for 200-kvp X-rays, ±3.1% for cobalt-60 γ-rays, and ±3.3% for betatron 22-Mevp X-rays (Table I).

RESULTS

Five experiments[5] were carried out during a period of four months, and the results for individual determinations are shown in Table II. In each case the slope of the regression line was calculated by conventional methods (*11*) from the macrocolony counts which had been corrected for the resistant population. The data for one experiment are presented graphically in Fig. 4. Although the data may not exhibit a strictly normal distribution, as assumed in the calculations, it was found previously (*1*) that this method gave practically the same values as a more complicated one which assumed a Poisson distribution of the plate counts. The lack of consistency in the slopes determined through this series was disappointing, particularly as the last two determinations yielded slopes for 200-kvp X-rays which were rather high in comparison with those found in the earlier experiments. The RBE was obtained from the slopes, and the standard deviation of the RBE was calculated from the formula for the standard deviation of a quotient, $q = u/v$:

$$\sigma_q^2 = (\sigma_u^2 + q^2\sigma_v^2)/v^2$$

[5] It may be noted that two initial preliminary experiments were conducted but have not been included because they were technically unsatisfactory. The inclusion of the results of either one or both of these experiments would not affect the final results by more than 2 to 4%, however.

TABLE II
SUMMARY OF YEAST EXPERIMENTS

Experiment	Slope			RBE		
	200 kvp	*Cobalt-60*	*22 Mevp*	*Cobalt-60 versus 200 kvp*	*22 Mevp versus 200 kvp*	*22 Mevp versus cobalt-60*
I	0.3892	0.3484	0.3478	0.8952	0.8936	0.9983
(4/20/57)	±0.0077	±0.0142	±0.0182	±0.0404	±0.0499	±0.0661
II	0.3933	0.3511	0.3506	0.8927	0.8914	0.9986
(4/22/57)	±0.0052	±0.0163	±0.0070	±0.0435	±0.0216	±0.0509
III	0.3909	0.3360	0.3276	0.8596	0.8381	0.9750
(6/29/57)	±0.0088	±0.0115	±0.0128	±0.0351	±0.0375	±0.0514
IV	0.4229	0.3561	0.3395	0.8420	0.8028	0.9534
(7/13/57)	±0.0155	±0.0235	±0.0145	±0.0634	±0.0451	±0.0784
V	0.4387	0.3391	0.3752	0.7730	0.8553	1.1065
(8/17/57)	±0.0147	±0.0159	±0.0121	±0.0445	±0.0401	±0.0568

To determine if the differences between the slopes of the survival curves obtained with the various radiations were significant, the *t*-test was employed. The difference between the slopes for a given pair of radiations was determined for each experiment. The mean and standard deviation of the series of differences were then calculated and used to obtain *t*. The values of *t* found for three pairs of radiations (cobalt-60 and 200-kvp X-rays, betatron and 200-kvp X-rays, betatron X-rays and cobalt-60 γ-rays) were 5.645, 7.562, and 0.243, respectively.[6]

The hypothesis tested was that the true difference between the slopes of the survival curves was zero; i.e., the two radiations were equally effective. It can be seen by reference to tables of *t* values that with cobalt-60 γ-rays versus 200-kvp X-rays and for betatron 22-Mevp X-rays and 200-kvp X-rays the probability of finding by chance alone values of *t* as large or larger than the calculated value is less than 1% if the slopes for the two radiations are really the same. Thus it is evident that both the cobalt-60 beam and betatron beam differ significantly from the 200-kvp beam in their effectiveness. There is a very reasonable probability, however, that the cobalt-60 and betatron beams are equally effective.

Both the average slopes for each machine and the RBE values have been calculated in two ways: first, by simple averaging of the results from the individual experiments and, second, by pooling the counts for each dose level in all five experiments and calculating the slopes (Table III) and subsequently the RBE's from the pooled data. The results are shown in Table IV.

The combined slopes (from the pooled data) are within a fraction of 1% of the average slope in each case. The RBE values obtained from the combined slopes are again in good agreement with those representing simple averages for the five experi-

[6] The first two correspond to a significance level of less than 1%, and the last one corresponds to a level of greater than 50%.

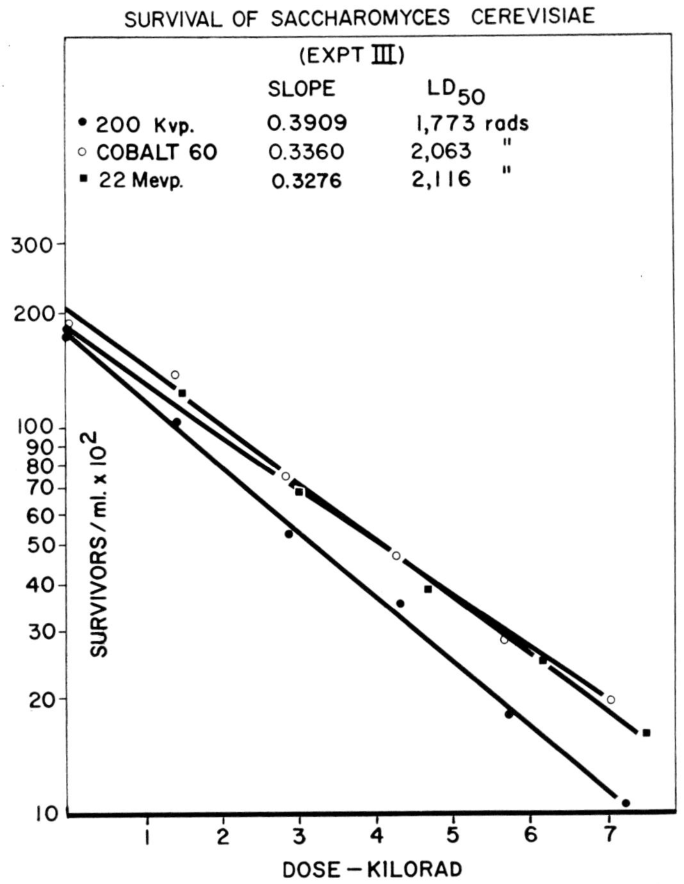

FIG. 4. Survival of *Saccharomyces cerevisiae* after irradiation from 200-kvp X-rays, cobalt-60 γ-rays, and 22-Mevp X-rays after correction for budding radioresistant cells.

TABLE III

POOLED DATA OF FIVE EXPERIMENTS

($\log S = \log S_0 - \beta D$)

Radiation	*Slope β*	*Variance of β (σ_β)*	*LD_{50} (rads)*	*σLD_{50} (rads)*
200-kvp X-ray	0.4065	0.0042	1705	18
Cobalt-60 γ-ray	0.3445	0.0069	2012	40
22-Mevp X-ray	0.3465	0.0057	2000	33

TABLE IV

SUMMARY OF RELATIVE BIOLOGICAL EFFECTIVENESS DETERMINED BY FIVE EXPERIMENTS

Value	Cobalt-60 versus 200 kvp	22 Mevp versus 200 kvp	22 Mevp versus cobalt-60
Average RBE from pooled data	0.848	0.852	1.006
	±0.019	±0.017	±0.026
Simple average RBE of five experiments (standard deviation)	0.853	0.856	1.006
	±0.045	±0.034	±0.053
t (for 4 degrees of freedom)	5.645[a]	7.562[a]	0.243[b]

[a] Less than 1%.
[b] Greater than 50%.

TABLE V

INTERLABORATORY COMPARISON OF LD_{50} OF YEAST

Test beam		Reference beam			RBE	Year	Laboratory location
Source	LD_{50} (rads)	Kvp	HVL (mm Cu)	LD_{50}			
1-Mevp Maxitron	2018	250	0.6	1739	0.86	1955	San Francisco
1.25-Mev cobalt-60	2012	200	0.8	1705	0.85	1957	Houston
22-Mevp betatron	2000	200	0.8	1705	0.85	1957	Houston
22.5-Mevp betatron	1914	180	0.75	2036	1.06	1954	New York

ments, although in the latter case the standard deviations from the mean are larger than those estimated from the variances of the combined slopes. It is clear, however, that both the cobalt-60 and the betatron differ significantly from unity as represented by the 200-kvp X-rays and do not differ significantly from one another.

DISCUSSION

Although the spread of results in this series of experiments is greater than one would desire in a set of presumably identical determinations, the final results appear valid. The values of the RBE determined from these experiments are believed to be 0.85 for cobalt-60 γ-rays and 0.85 for 22-Mevp X-rays from the betatron, with 200-kvp X-rays as the standard of comparison. It is believed that these results are reliable to about ± 0.05. No significant difference between betatron 22-Mevp X-rays and cobalt-60 γ-rays has been demonstrated.

The reason for the discrepancy between the value for 22-Mevp X-rays of 0.85 obtained in this work and that of 1.06 obtained at Memorial Hospital (New York) is not known. The same basic absolute determinations made by Dr. Laughlin, with the betatron, were used in calculations of the dose in both cases. Although the estimate of dose requires derivation through a number of pathways, each giving rise to small errors in both instances, the difference is greater than one would expect, even with due allowance for possible cumulative errors. The independent confirmation supplied by the agreement with expected values of G for ferrous sulfate, determined under the experimental conditions employed in this series, leaves little room for a substantial margin of error in the dosimetry. It may be pointed out, for example, that, if all three radiations had the same G value (15.6), as is sometimes assumed, the two supervoltage radiations would be even more different from 200-kvp X-rays than these results indicate.

It was of interest, therefore, to compare the LD_{50} values obtained in the three series of RBE determinations in which the same culture and procedure were employed. They are summarized in Table V. The LD_{50} for 200-kvp X-rays determined in Houston (1957) differed from that for 250-kvp X-rays determined in San Francisco (1955) by only 34 rads, or less than 2%, whereas the LD_{50} for 180-kvp X-rays (New York) differed by 17.1%. The LD_{50} for 22-Mevp X-rays obtained in Houston differed from that obtained in New York by only 4.5%, however. The difference in the LD_{50} of 1.25-Mev cobalt-60 γ-rays (Houston) and 1-Mevp X-rays (San Francisco) was 0.3%. The very good agreement among the results obtained with three groups of comparable radiations in three different laboratories, with the exception of the LD_{50} for 180-kvp X-rays (New York), suggests that this may be a source of the discrepancy between the RBE values obtained for 22-Mevp X-rays in Houston and in New York. Plans for the investigation of this possibility are being made (J. S. Laughlin, personal communication).

SUMMARY

The relative biological effectiveness of cobalt-60 γ-rays (1.17, 1.33 Mev) and 22-Mevp X-rays from a betatron with reference to 200-kvp X-rays (primary HVL 1.4 mm Cu) has been determined by using the slope of the survival curve of the yeast *Saccharomyces cerevisiae* (based on macrocolony counts) as the biological end point. The average RBE of five experiments was found to be 0.85 for cobalt-60 γ-radiation and 0.85 for 22-Mevp X-radiation, with uncertainties of the order of ± 0.05 in each case. No significant difference between cobalt-60 γ-radiation and 22-Mevp X-radiation was demonstrated.

ACKNOWLEDGMENT

The authors wish to acknowledge the important contributions of Dr. H. I. Kohn, Radiological Laboratory, University of California Medical Center, who suggested the undertaking and offered much helpful criticism and advice at important stages in the experiment.

RECEIVED: July 31, 1958

REFERENCES

1. H. I. KOHN and S. E. GUNTER, Relative biological efficiency of 1000-kvp and 250-kvcp X-rays. I. General introduction. Determinations based on the dose-survival curves of *Saccharomyces cerevisiae*, haploid and diploid. *Radiation Research* **5**, 674–687 (1956).

2. S. E. GUNTER, H. I. KOHN, E. B. TYREE, J. S. LAUGHLIN, JACQUES OVADIA, G. SHAPIRO, and PAT THOMPSON, The relative biological effectiveness of 180-kevp and 22.5-Mevp X-rays determined from the dose-survival curve of *Saccharomyces cerevisiae*. *Radiation Research* **4,** 326–338 (1956).
3. S. E. GUNTER and H. I. KOHN, The effect of X-rays on the survival of bacteria and yeast. I. A comparative study of the dose-survival curves of *Azotobacter agile*, *Escherichia coli*, *Pseudomonas fluorescens*, *Rhodopseudomonas spheroides*, and *Saccharomyces cerevisiae* irradiated in the resting state. *J. Bacteriol.* **71,** 571–581 (1956).
4. A. COLE, An automatic iso-signal plotter. To be published.
5. W. K. SINCLAIR, J. S. LAUGHLIN, H. H. ROSSI, M. TERPOGOSSIAN, and W. S. MOOS, Intercomparison of X-ray exposure dose using Victoreen dose meters at various energies, particularly 22 Mevp. *Radiology* **70,** 736–743 (1958).
6. A. T. NELMS, Energy loss and range of electrons and positrons. *Natl. Bur. Standards (U. S.) Circ.* **577** (July 26, 1956).
7. Report of the International Commission on Radiological Units and Measurements, ICRU, 1956. *Natl. Bur. Standards (U. S.) Handbook* **No. 62** (1957)
8. J. R. GREENING and C. W. WILSON, The wavelength of the X radiation at a depth in water irradiated by beams of X rays. *Brit. J. Radiol.* **24,** 605–612 (1951).
9. G. W. GRODSTEIN, X-ray attenuation coefficients from 10 kev to 100 Mev. *Natl. Bur. Standards (U. S.)* **583,** (April 30, 1957).
10. R. J. SHALEK and W. K. SINCLAIR, The use of the ferrous sulfate dosimeter for X- and γ-ray beams, *Radiation Biology and Cancer*, Symposium at M. D. Anderson Hospital and Tumor Institute, University of Texas Press, 1958.
11. G. W. SNEDECOR, *Statistical Methods Applied to Experiments in Agriculture and Biology*, The Collegiate Press, Ames, Iowa, 1946.

RADIATION RESEARCH 10, 433–448 (1959)

The Effects of Accelerated Carbon Nuclei and Other Radiations on the Survival of Haploid Yeast

I. Dosimetry of the Cyclotron Beams[1]

ANN C. BIRGE AND JOSEPH A. SAYEG[2]

Donner Laboratory of Biophysics and Medical Physics, University of California, Berkeley, California

INTRODUCTION

It is well known that the effects of ionizing radiation on a biological system are dependent not only on the energy delivered to the system, i.e., the total dose, but also on the spatial distribution of that energy. There have been many studies of relative biological effectiveness (RBE) between radiations of different rates of energy loss or linear energy transfer (LET) (*1*, *2*), but there are only a few instances in which the same biological system has been studied systematically with a wide range of radiations. In the investigation reported here, cell survival of the haploid yeast, *Saccharomyces cerevisiae*, was studied for LET values ranging between 2 and 500 kev/μ. It is not possible to obtain such high and uniform values of LET with conventional radiations such as polonium α-particles. Furthermore, the dose is uncertain near the Bragg ionization peak, where the LET varies rapidly with absorber thickness. Hence for this study we used the beams available at the Berkeley 60-inch cyclotron: 20-Mev deuterons, 40-Mev α-particles, and 120-Mev carbon nuclei with mass 12 and charge 6 (*3*), in addition to X-rays and polonium α-particles.

For any study of relative biological effectiveness it is essential to have accurate dose measurements for all the radiations used. The successful measurement of dose from a cyclotron beam depends on a series of physical measurements to determine the beam characteristics. For this purpose equipment was designed to measure Bragg ionization curves and particle ranges as a function of absorber thickness, and a special ionization chamber was built to measure the dose to biological samples.

[1] This work was supported by the U. S. Atomic Energy Commission and the Cancer Fund of the State of California. A preliminary report of part of this work is contained in J. A. Sayeg, "The effect of highly ionizing radiations on cell survival," Thesis, University of California Radiation Laboratory Report UCRL-2293 (1954).

[2] Present address: Los Alamos Scientific Laboratory, Los Alamos, New Mexico.

Special emphasis was placed on the work with the carbon particles because of their uniqueness and the difficulties inherent in their use. The first paper of this pair deals with the physical problem of determining the linear energy transfer and the doses delivered by the various cyclotron beams. The second paper describes the biological experiments and their results, including additional data obtained with 50-kv and 220-kv X-rays, as well as Po^{210} α-particles.

Because the frequency of the 60-inch cyclotron is fixed, the resonance conditions for accelerating particles of slightly different charge-to-mass ratio are satisfied by adjusting the magnetic field. For ions that originate with their full charge at the ion source—e.g., deuterons and α-particles—the resonance peak is sharp and the machine can be adjusted to give a known beam with only a small spread in energy. For carbon ions, however, the voltages in the ion source are not sufficient to strip off all the electrons. Since the cyclotron resonance conditions are met by carbon ions with a charge of 2 as well as by those with a charge of 6, it is believed that the ions to be accelerated leave the ion source with a charge of 2 and are converted to a charge of 6 after gaining some energy (*4*). As a consequence, the magnetic-field resonance for carbon ions is not a sharp peak in the position expected from calculations of the charge-to-mass ratio, but is a very broad maximum that overlaps the sharp resonance peak of the α-particles. Hence the mean energy and energy spread of carbon particles in the external beam are determined by the position and width of slits in the external equipment, which in our experiments was located in the fringing magnetic field of the cyclotron. During each run measurements were made to determine the beam energy and hence the LET, and to be sure that the number of α-particles mixed with the carbon ions was negligible. Measurements were also made to determine the intensity distribution of the beams to ensure adequate uniformity over the area of the biological samples. Various other checks were made to provide accurate dose measurements for each run.

EXPERIMENTAL ARRANGEMENT

Figure 1 shows a schematic plan view of the cyclotron with our equipment for using the external beams. The ions originally formed at the ion source, I_s, are accelerated by the oscillating electric field between the dees and are held in spiral trajectories by the magnetic field of the cyclotron. Those particles which come down the deflector channel with suitable energy pass through the series of adjustable slits, S_1, S_2, and S_3, which are needed to exclude particles of unsuitable energy or charge-to-mass ratio. The beam passes out of the vacuum system through the thin Dural window, W, into the monitor ionization chamber, I_1, thence through the aluminum absorbers controlled remotely in the pair of selector wheels, and finally through the analyzer ionization chamber, I_2. The sample to be irradiated is placed behind the second ionization chamber. The position of the evacuated snout and the attached ionization chambers can be adjusted remotely in a horizontal

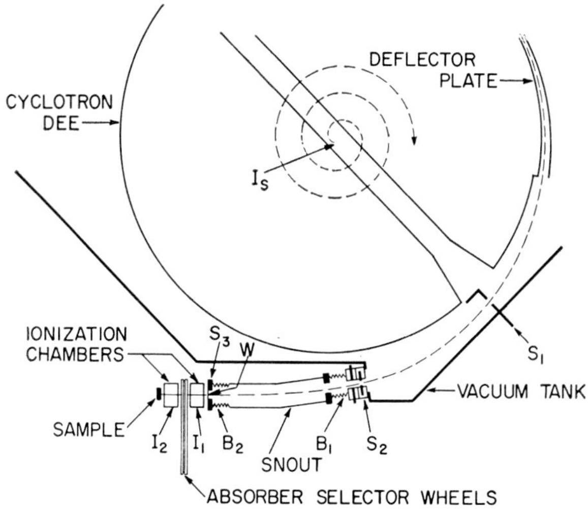

FIG. 1. Schematic plan view of the cyclotron and the equipment used for biological experiments.

plane by bending the two Sylphon bellows, B_1 and B_2, and in a vertical plane by raising or lowering the supporting ¼-inch Dural plate with adjustment screws. Thus the equipment can be moved to center the beam in the ionization chambers. In Fig. 2 is shown a photograph of this equipment in place between the magnet coils of the cyclotron.

For measuring the range and specific ionization of the carbon particles, ionization chambers were constructed in which individual particle pulses could be counted. The beam passed through the ionization chambers in a direction parallel to the collection of charge, so that a uniform pulse height was produced by particles passing through different parts of the chamber. The monitor ionization chamber, I_1, consisted of two 0.00025-inch-thick aluminum foils, spaced $^{29}/_{32}$ inch apart, with an effective area 1¼ inches in diameter. Teflon insulation and a grounded guard ring between the high-voltage foil and collector foil minimized leakage currents. The chamber was housed in a brass cylinder which also supported the coaxial connectors to the high-voltage supply and to the electronic equipment.

For much of the work the analyzer ionization chamber was identical to the monitor chamber. The best results were obtained, however, with a pair of analyzer chambers. The first analyzer chamber, only ⅛ inch thick, was used for integrating the total charge produced. Such a thin chamber gives good resolution for measuring the average specific ionization produced by the particles. An adjacent thick chamber with 0.82-inch spacing was used for counting individual particle pulses. The large collection space was necessary in order that an individual particle would produce

FIG. 2. Photograph showing the irradiation equipment connected to the exit port of the cyclotron.

enough ions to be counted as a pulse above the noise level of the electronic equipment. The two chambers were separated by a thin aluminum foil, weighing 1.6 mg/cm^2. In these chambers the collector foil was placed between a pair of high-voltage foils and was constructed of aluminum leaf, 0.12 mg/cm^2 in thickness. The voltage on the foils was adjusted so that the electric field was the same in all parts of the chambers.

The charge collected in each ionization chamber was determined by measuring the voltage produced across a known capacitance or resistance with an integrating electrometer. Since the electrometer held the collector plate effectively at ground potential, a constant voltage was supplied to the ionization chamber. At the same time the total charge or ionization current was being measured, the individual pulses were fed through a low-capacity cable and blocking condenser to a preamplifier located just outside the magnetic field of the cyclotron, and into a linear amplifier and scaler. A Tektronix oscilloscope was used to monitor the output pulses visually.

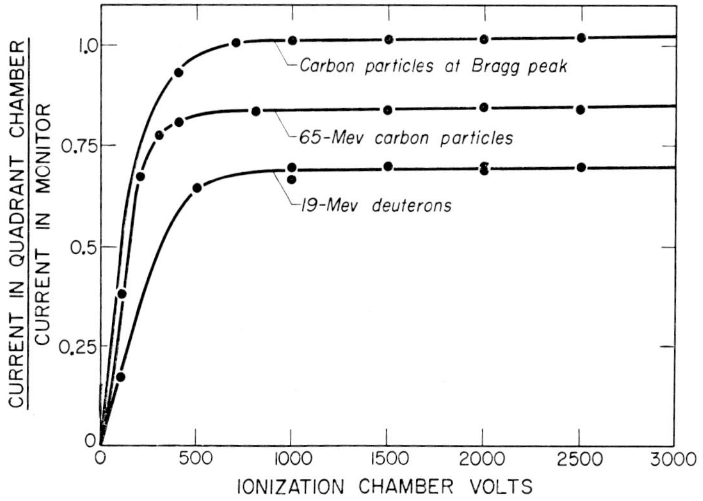

FIG. 3. Typical voltage saturation curves for the dose-measuring quadrant ionization chamber.

To minimize problems of ion recombination and assure fast electron collection, the formation of negative ions was prevented by flowing dry nitrogen gas through the ionization chambers at a slow rate. Curves of ionization current as a function of collection voltage showed that with a voltage gradient of 1000 volts/cm the chambers were being operated in the region of saturation, where a negligible number of ions was being lost by recombination. Typical voltage saturation curves are shown in Fig. 3. Observation of the heights and shapes of individual particle pulses as functions of collection voltage showed that the charge was collected in a time shorter than the amplifier rise time and supported the conclusion that fast electron collection was maintained at the voltages used.

The counting rate for a given amplifier gain is a function of the discriminator-bias setting on the scaler. For both ionization chambers a curve of counting rate as a function of bias setting showed a broad plateau, approximately 20 volts wide, where amplifier noise pulses were excluded but carbon-particle pulses were counted. Although special precautions were taken to minimize amplifier noise, calculations showed that a particle had to loose nearly 1 Mev in the ionization-chamber gas in order to produce a pulse barely visible at the lower end of the plateau curve. The final bias settings used were far enough up on the plateau so that a small shift in bias voltage would produce a negligible change in counting rate; the settings for different runs corresponded to energy losses between 1.5 and 2.5 Mev.

Because of the fringing magnetic field of the cyclotron, the various beams were confined to a vertical dimension between ⅛ and ¼ inch but extended horizontally across the full ¾ inch allowed by the defining aperture S_3 in Fig. 1. Since it is

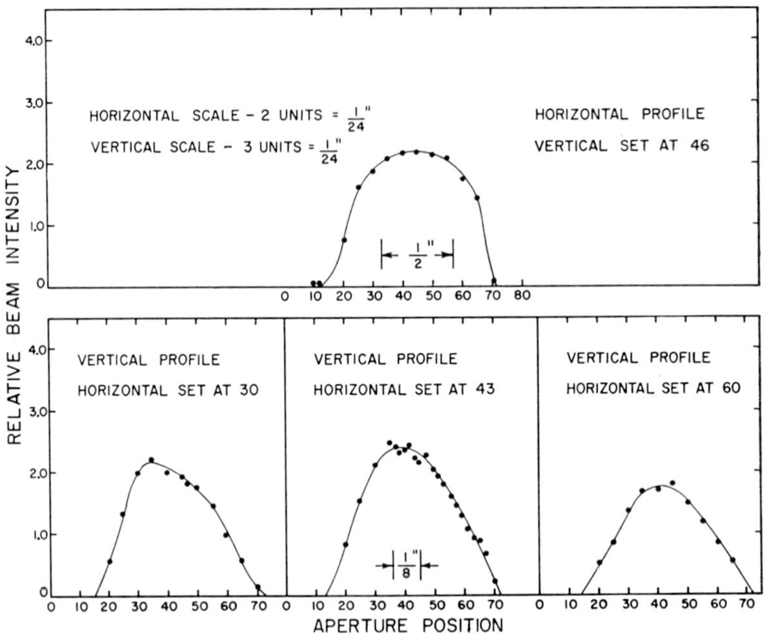

FIG. 4. Profiles of the carbon-particle beam used in experiment 2.

important to have the radiation as nearly as possible uniform in intensity over the biological sample, a profile-scanning apparatus was used to measure the intensity distribution of the cyclotron beams. This apparatus consisted of a movable aluminum flag, $\frac{1}{16}$ inch thick, with a $\frac{1}{32}$-inch circular aperture at the center, and was inserted between the absorber wheels and the second ionization chamber. The flag could be moved by remote control from outside the cyclotron target area. For each experiment a series of beam profiles was taken, each consisting of a plot of relative beam intensity as the scanning aperture was moved horizontally or vertically across the radiation field. Figures 4 and 5 show profiles of the carbon and α-particle beams obtained in this manner. The peculiar pattern shown in Fig. 5 was apparently related to the operating conditions of the cyclotron and was most persistent for the α-particles. For carbon particles, which exhibited a very broad cyclotron resonance, such a nonuniform pattern was avoided by adjustment of the position of the external equipment.

Because of the peculiar distribution of the beam, its alignment with respect to the biological samples was critical; therefore a special quadrant ionization chamber was constructed for measuring the dose and indicating the beam alignment during the actual biological irradiations. The design of this plane parallel chamber, $\frac{17}{32}$ inch deep, was basically similar to the monitor ionization chamber, except that the

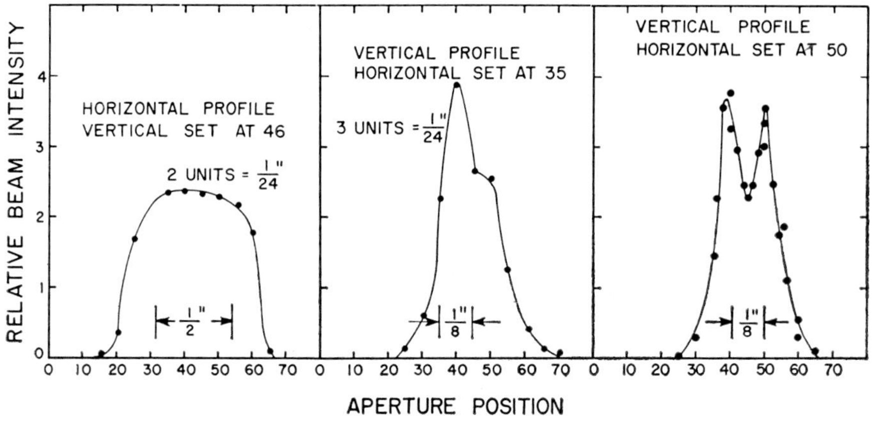

FIG. 5. Profiles of the α-particle beam used in experiment 1.

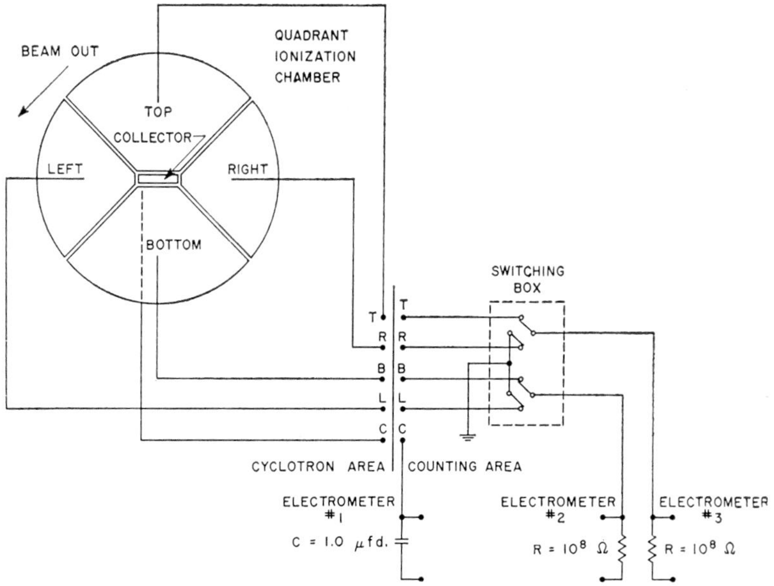

FIG. 6. A schematic diagram of the quadrant ionization chamber plates connected to the electrometers.

collector foil was divided into a central region—smaller than the dimensions of the beam—and four surrounding quadrant plates, shown schematically in Fig. 6. The area of the central 0.0005-inch aluminum collector foil, very nearly a rectangle 13.4 mm wide by 3.8 mm high, was measured accurately with a traveling micro-

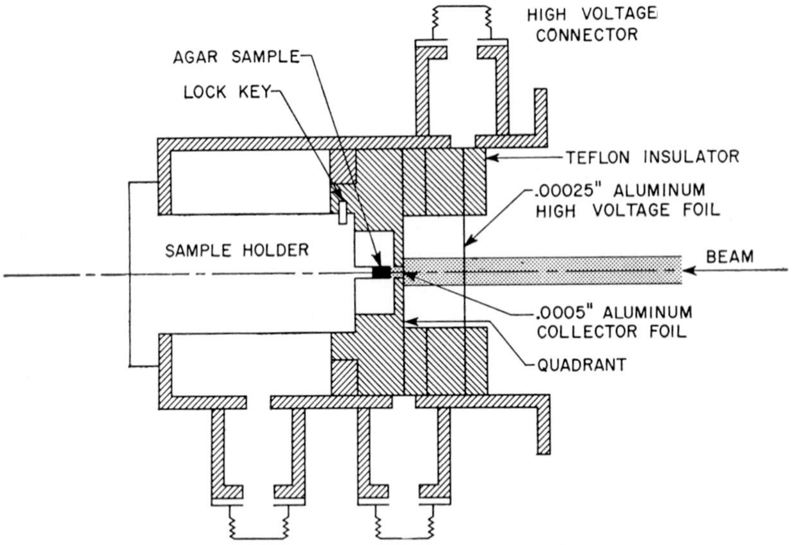

FIG. 7. Schematic diagram of the dose-measuring quadrant ionization chamber showing the position of the biological sample relative to the cyclotron beam.

scope and served to define the collection volume used in the dose calculation. The biological sample consisted of cells plated on the surface of an agar block 9.9 mm by 2.6 mm, and smaller in area than the collector foil. The sample was accurately positioned just behind the foil (see Fig. 7). The four quadrant electrodes were made of a conducting layer of silver paint on Teflon backing. When the ionization current collected from the top quadrant equaled that from the bottom, and the current from the left equaled that from the right, the beam was assumed to be centered over the collector and hence over the biological sample. Since the beam had to be turned off while the samples were changed, it was important to check the beam alignment during each bombardment. As with the other chambers, a continuous flow of dry nitrogen gas was maintained. For each experiment a curve of ion current as a function of collection voltage (Fig. 3) showed that the chamber was being operated in the region of saturation for the collection voltage of 2000 volts.

PHYSICAL MEASUREMENTS

In order to do practical biological experiments with the external beam of carbon particles, it was necessary to use the maximum beam obtainable, which gave dose rates around 1000 rads/min. To obtain the maximum beam, and because of variations in cyclotron operating conditions between different runs, many measurements and adjustments had to be made during each run before the beams could be used for irradiation of biological materials.

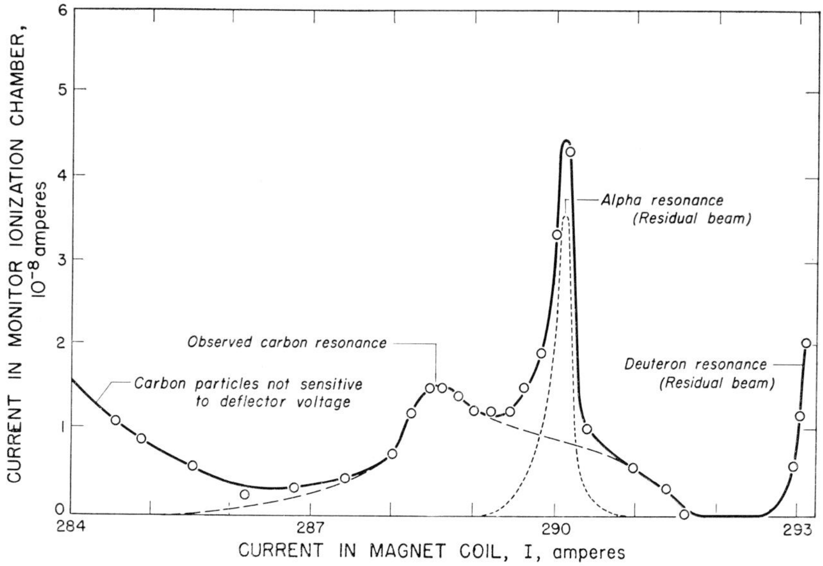

FIG. 8. A graph of the ionization-chamber current as a function of the current in the cyclotron magnet coils.

At the beginning of each cyclotron run, the equipment was set up in the position used in the preceding run, and the beam intensity was measured as a function of cyclotron magnetic field (Fig. 8). The carbon particles, identified by observation of their pulse heights and ranges, were found to lie in a broad resonance. Toward higher magnetic fields they overlapped the sharp resonance of α-particles accelerated from residual helium gas in the cyclotron tank, and toward lower magnetic fields they disappeared into a group of carbon particles of unknown trajectory that were not sensitive to the voltage on the cyclotron deflector. For bombardments with carbon ions the magnetic field was adjusted to give the maximum deflected beam of carbon particles with a minimum of α-particles. The ionization produced by the spurious α-particles was measured by inserting sufficient absorber to stop all carbon particles. During bombardments frequent checks were made; the ionization due to α-particles was kept to a maximum of 1% of the total and was usually considerably lower.

After the cyclotron magnetic field was adjusted properly, a radioautograph of the beam was obtained to show what adjustments should be made in the position of the snout and ionization chambers in order to center the equipment on the beam and to give a visual estimate of the intensity distribution. Small X-ray films, wrapped in 0.0005-inch aluminum foil, were exposed to the beam by placing them in the blank position of the absorber wheel behind the first ionization chamber.

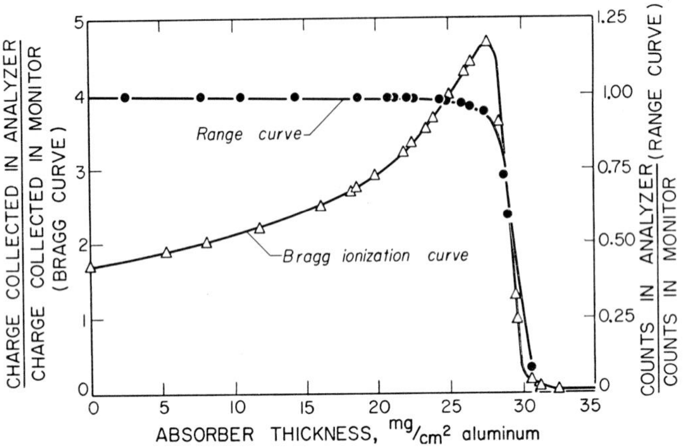

FIG. 9. A Bragg ionization curve and range curve for carbon particles.

When the beam alignment was satisfactory, a Bragg ionization curve was obtained by plotting the ratio of charge collected in the analyzer ionization chamber to that collected in the monitor chamber as a function of the absorber thickness between the two ionization chambers. Simultaneously, individual particle pulses were counted in the two chambers, and a range curve was obtained by plotting the fraction of particles penetrating the absorber as a function of its thickness. Range and Bragg curves obtained in this manner are shown in Fig. 9. As explained above, the particles were actually counted in a thick chamber separated by a thin aluminum foil (1.6 mg/cm^2) from the chamber used in obtaining the ionization curve. Furthermore, with the discriminator settings used for these data, a minimum energy loss of 2.0 Mev was required in the second ionization chamber in order for a particle to be counted. It is estimated that this corresponds to a residual range for carbon particles of 0.6 ± 0.2 mg/cm^2 of aluminum. The collector foils of aluminum leaf and the gas of the ionization chambers accounted for an additional 0.4 mg/cm^2 between the two analyzer ionization chambers. Hence in the range curve of Fig. 9 an additional absorber thickness of 2.6 mg/cm^2 has been added to each measured value in order to make the range curve correspond to the Bragg curve.

From the simultaneous collection of charge and the counting of particles in the ionization chambers it was possible to compute the average charge produced per particle. When this value was compared with that calculated for a carbon ion in nitrogen, the discrepancy of 2% was well within the expected uncertainty of $\pm 6\%$.

Because of the finite resolving time of the electronic equipment, for counting individual particle pulses it was necessary to limit the beam intensity to approximately $1/500$ of that used in the biological experiments. Various attempts were made to lower the beam intensity by changing cyclotron operating conditions, with the hope that a low-intensity beam could be obtained with the same slit widths as the maximum-intensity beam used in the biological experiments. A comparison of the Bragg ionization curves showed that this was not possible, however, and the best physical data were obtained during runs in which biological irradiations were not attempted. For the data in Fig. 9 a ⅛-inch-diameter aperture was inserted in front of the first ionization chamber, and the first two slits were narrowed until a reasonable counting rate was observed. By comparing the range and Bragg curves measured simultaneously under different cyclotron running conditions and at different slit widths, the mean range of the carbon particles was found to correspond to a point on the Bragg curve of 0.45 ± 0.30 times the maximum ionization. For the high-intensity beams used in the biological irradiations, for which individual particles could not be counted, this ordinate on the Bragg curve was used to determine the mean range and hence the energy and LET of the carbon particles.

While data for the range and Bragg curves were being obtained, particle pulses were also observed on the oscilloscope. The uniformity of pulse height for small absorber thickness showed that the particles had a uniform average LET. As a result of range straggling, however, pulses of all heights were produced near the peak of the Bragg curve and beyond. Care was taken that the cell bombardments were made in the region of homogeneous LET.

After the measurement of range and Bragg curves was completed, the profile-scanning apparatus was inserted in front of the second ionization chamber, and the intensity distribution of the beam was obtained with the wide slits to be used for the cell bombardments. On the basis of these data further adjustments were made in the alignment of the apparatus. When the beam characteristics were considered satisfactory, the second analyzer ionization chamber was replaced by the dose-measuring quadrant chamber described above, and a fine adjustment was made in position in order to balance the ionization currents collected in the quadrants. Subsequent checks of beam centering were made frequently throughout the experiment. At this point the voltage saturation curve was checked, and a Bragg ionization curve was obtained with the dose-measuring chamber in its final geometry. For bombardment the biological samples, each consisting of a monolayer of cells plated on a block of agar, were placed in turn on a special receptacle just behind the ionization chamber. After the samples were irradiated, the Bragg-curve measurement was repeated and the temperature was determined.

CALCULATION OF DOSE AND LET WITH ESTIMATED UNCERTAINTIES

For determination of the dose delivered to the cells, the quantity actually measured was the voltage produced on a condenser by the charge collected from an ionization chamber. For each volt measured on the integrating electrometer, a dose D (in rads) was delivered to the cells, where D was calculated by the equation

$$D = \frac{CWS_mKP\ 10^5}{V\rho} \text{ rads/volt}$$

TABLE I

DOSE CALCULATION FACTORS FOR THE CYCLOTRON BEAMS

(1) Experiment number	(2) Bombarding particle	(3) Absorber thickness (mg/cm² Al)	(4) Integrating capacitance, C (10^{-6} farad)	(5) Density of N_2 gas (mg/cm³)	(6) Profile correction factor, P	(7) Beam uniformity over sample	(8) Bragg correction factor, K	(9) Particle energy at cell (Mev)	(10) Energy per nucleon (Mev)	(11) Relative mass stopping power, S_m tissue to N_2	(12) Average LET in cells (Mev cm²/gm)	(13) Dose, D (rads/volt)	(14) Error in dose (%)
1a	Alpha	56.3	1.095	1.138	1.00 ± 0.05	±22%	1.022 ± 0.011	26.8 ± 0.7	6.7 ± 0.2	1.153 ± 0.036	258 ± 6	5850	6.7
1b	Alpha	130.3	1.095	1.138	1.00 ± 0.05	±22%	1.340 ± 0.050	5.9 ± 0.8	1.5 ± 0.2	1.210 ± 0.067	850 ± 100	8130	8.8
1c	Deuteron	Zero	1.095	1.138	1.020 ± 0.015	±14%	1.00 ± 0.00	19.1 ± 0.5	9.6 ± 0.2	1.144 ± 0.033	48 ± 2	5790	4.5
2a	Carbon	Zero	1.095	1.127	1.024 ± 0.005	±4%	1.099 ± 0.008	65 ± 5	5.4 ± 0.4	1.161 ± 0.039	2680 ± 300	6550	4.6
2b	Carbon	13.4	1.095	1.127	1.024 ± 0.005	±4%	1.298 ± 0.033	30 ± 10	2.5 ± 0.8	1.186 ± 0.051	4450 ± 540	7900	5.9
3a	Carbon	Zero	1.057	1.150	1.027 ± 0.010	±6%	1.067 ± 0.016	67 ± 5	5.6 ± 0.4	1.159 ± 0.038	2600 ± 200	5990	4.8
3b	Carbon	16.1	1.057	1.150	1.027 ± 0.010	±6%	1.353 ± 0.027	24 ± 9	2.0 ± 0.7	1.194 ± 0.056	5080 ± 460	7840	6.1

In this expression C is the capacitance of the integrating condenser in farads, W is the energy in electron volts per ion pair for the formation of ions in dry nitrogen, S_m is the relative mass stopping power for the cell composition relative to that of nitrogen, K is the Bragg correction due to the stopping material located between the dose-measuring chamber and the irradiated cells, P is the correction for the nonuniformity of the beam, V is the volume of the ionization chamber in cubic centimeters, and ρ is the density of the ionization-chamber gas in grams per cubic centimeter. The factor 10^5 comes from the conversion of units into rads, since 1 joule per gram is 10^5 rads. The quantities for each experiment with estimated standard deviations are given in Table I; their values are discussed below.

The most certain quantities in the dose measurement are the values C of the integrating capacitances (which were calibrated with an error of $\pm 0.5\%$), the sensitive volume, V, of the ionization chamber (0.677 ± 0.010) and the density, ρ, of the gas (for which a temperature variation of $\pm 1°C$ was assumed). Together these uncertainties contribute less than 2% to the resultant standard error.

The correction factor, P, takes account of the nonuniform intensity distribution of the beam and the fact that the sample area is smaller than the area over which the dose is measured. The value of P was found by integrating the beam intensity graphically from profiles such as those in Figs. 4 and 5. The estimated uncertainty in P allows for variations in the position of the sample relative to the observed profile and for uncertainties in the dimensions of the sample. In addition, in column 7 of Table I we have given the maximum variation in beam intensity over the sample. This figure was obtained by taking the high and low points of the beam profiles relative to their average. Even for the large variation observed with α-particles, this nonuniformity has small effect on an exponential survival curve for survival levels above 5%.

The Bragg correction factor, K, is the ratio of ionization produced in nitrogen in the position occupied by the cells to that measured in the chamber. For each experiment it was determined graphically from a Bragg curve (similar to that in Fig. 9), measured with the quadrant ionization chamber just before or after the cell irradiation. The uncertainty in K was estimated from the consistency among different Bragg curves obtained during the same experiment, as well as the uncertainty in the thickness of absorber between the center of the ionization chamber and the center of the cells. The material between these two positions consisted of half of the gas of the ionization chamber (0.79 mg/cm² N_2), the collector foil (3.56 ± 0.04 mg/cm² Al), the air between the collector foil and the cells (0.48 ± 0.10 mg/cm² air), and half the cell diameter (0.25 ± 0.12 mg/cm² tissue). The total is equivalent to 5.44 ± 0.33 mg/cm² of Al.

In order to convert the ionization produced in a gas to cellular dose it is necessary to multiply by the energy per ion pair, W, and the relative mass stopping power, S_m. These quantities, as well as the linear energy transfer (LET), are functions of particle velocity. Hence it is necessary to determine the energy of the particles used in each experiment.

In the case of deuterons and α-particles, for which individual particles could not be counted, the particle ranges were obtained from the measured Bragg curves. For the particular beams used here, we do not know what point on the Bragg curve corresponds to the mean range of the particles; hence the limits of error in the measured range were set by the peak of the Bragg curve on one hand and the extrapolated ionization range on the other. Then the particle energies and the values of LET were obtained by using the range-energy curves of Aron *et al.* (*5*). The large uncertainty allowed in the range measurement produces small errors in S_m and LET, since both quantities are slowly varying functions of particle energy.

In the case of carbon particles, the physical measurements in the previous section indicated that the mean range corresponded to a point on the Bragg curve of 0.45 $\pm$ 0.30 times the maximum ionization. Since there are no published range-energy curves for carbon particles in aluminum, a semiempirical curve was constructed from the calculations by Smith for protons (*6*). The range extension due to charge pickup was estimated as 7.5 $\pm$ 2.5 mg/cm^2 from the data of Miller (*7*) and Barkas (*8*) for nuclear emulsion. The uncertainty in our range measurement was considerably larger than the error in the range-energy relation. For carbon particles, the uncertainty in the range measurement introduces a substantial error in the linear energy transfer. Fortunately the LET does not appear in the dose calculation; the corresponding error in S_m is less than 1% and is small compared with errors from other sources. The curves calculated by Snyder and Neufeld (*9*) were used to give the LET values in Table I for high-energy carbon ions. For these energies, where the stripped nuclear charge of 6 may be assumed (*10*), the values are in good agreement with those obtained from the semiempirical curves for protons (*5, 11, 12*).

For both α-particles and carbon ions, the LET for each high absorber point was obtained from the low absorber value by taking the observed ratio of ionization for the two absorbers, with suitable corrections between tissue and nitrogen. The particle energies were then obtained from the energy-loss curves (*5, 9*) and were found to lie within the values obtained from the range estimates.

For each particle energy, column 10 in Table I gives the energy per nucleon, i.e., the energy of a proton traveling with the same velocity. For each proton energy, the value of the relative mass stopping power, S_m, was obtained from semiempirical curves (*5, 12*) as explained in Birge *et al.* (*11*), but modified to fit the experimental data for the stopping power of water and nitrogen at low energies (*13–15*). The errors assigned to S_m in Table I allow for the rather large discrepancy between the calculated and experimental values of the stopping power of nitrogen for protons below 1 Mev, in addition to the estimated uncertaintites of $\pm$2% each in the calculated values for water and nitrogen. The elemental composition used for yeast cells was 9.9% hydrogen, 11.5% carbon, 4.7% nitrogen, 72.3% oxygen, 0.03%

sodium, 0.06% magnesium, 0.02% silicon, 0.6% phosphorus, 0.06% sulfur, 0.8% potassium, and 0.04% calcium (*16–18*). For the calculation of the energy loss of fast particles there is a negligible difference between this composition and that given by Lea for soft tissue (*19*). Both yeast and soft tissue have the same effective excitation potential as water, but they have 1% fewer electrons per gram. Hence the stopping power for these compositions is 1% less than that of water for particles of all energies (*11*).

For all particle energies above 2 Mev per nucleon the value of W for dry nitrogen was taken as 34.8 ± 0.9 ev per ion pair (*11, 20–23*). For the slow α-particles (experiment 1b) the value $W = 35.1$ was used (*11*).

For each experiment the last two columns in Table I give the calculated dose in rads per volt and the estimated per cent standard deviation. The resultant error was obtained by summing the squares of the fractional errors for all the factors in the calculation (*24*). The resultant errors range from 4.5 to 8.8%. It should be noted that, since the same experimental arrangement was used for all the cyclotron irradiations, some of the errors would be expected to cancel out in the calculations of relative biological effectiveness. Of course this does not apply to comparisons with other radiations.

SUMMARY

The experimental apparatus used for the irradiation of yeast cells with cyclotron beams of 20-Mev deuterons, 40-Mev α-particles, and 120-Mev carbon nuclei is described. The physical measurements necessary for an accurate determination of dose and average LET are also described. The dose calculation from ionization-chamber measurements is given, along with the estimated uncertainties that produce an over-all error ranging between 5 and 10%.

ACKNOWLEDGMENTS

The authors wish to express their sincere appreciation to Professor Cornelius A. Tobias, whose continued direction and support made this work possible. We should also like to express indebtedness to the late Professor Joseph G. Hamilton and Mr. G. Bernard Rossi for their encouragement and extended efforts in providing the carbon beam. In addition we thank Mr. W. Barclay Jones and members of the cyclotron crew, the various electronics groups, and members of the biophysics group, whose help throughout the work was invaluable.

RECEIVED: August 4, 1958

REFERENCES

1. R. E. ZIRKLE, The radiobiological importance of linear energy transfer. In *Radiation Biology* (A. Hollaender, ed.), Vol. I, pp. 315–350, McGraw-Hill Book Company, New York, 1954.

2. J. W. BOAG, The relative biological efficiency of different ionizing radiations. *Natl. Bur. Standards (U. S.) Rept.* **2946** (1953).

3. J. F. MILLER, J. G. HAMILTON, T. M. PUTNAM, H. R. HAYMOND, and G. B. ROSSI, Acceleration of stripped C^{12} and C^{13} nuclei in the cyclotron. *Phys. Rev.* **80,** 486(L) (1950).

4. D. WALKER and J. H. FREMLIN, Acceleration of heavy ions to high energies. *Nature* **171,** 189–191 (1953).
5. W. A. ARON, B. G. HOFFMAN, and F. C. WILLIAMS, Range-energy curves. U. S. Atomic Energy Commission Document AECU-663, Technical Information Service, Oak Ridge, Tennessee, 1951.
6. J. H. SMITH, Theoretical range-energy values for protons in air and aluminum. *Phys. Rev.* **71,** 32–33, (1947).
7. J. F. MILLER, Reactions of fast carbon nuclei in photographic emulsions. Thesis, University of California Radiation Laboratory Report UCRL-1902 (1952).
8. W. H. Barkas, The range correction for electron pick-up. *Phys. Rev.* **89,** 1019–1022 (1953).
9. W. S, SNYDER AND J. NEUFELD, On the passage of heavy particles through tissue. *Radiation Research* **6,** 67–78 (1957).
10. J. KNIPP and E. TELLER, On the energy loss of heavy ions. *Phys. Rev.* **59,** 659–669 (1941).
11. A. C. BIRGE, H. O. ANGER, and C. A. TOBIAS, Heavy charged-particle beams. In *Radiation Dosimetry* (G. J. Hine and G. L. Brownell, eds.), pp. 623–665, Academic Press, New York, 1956.
12. M. RICH and R. MADEY, Range-energy tables. University of California Radiation Laboratory Report UCRL-2301 (1954).
13. H. K. REYNOLDS, D. N. F. DUNBAR, W. A. WENZEL, and W. WHALING, The stopping cross section of gases for protons, 30–600 kev. *Phys. Rev.* **92,** 742–748 (1953).
14. A. B. CHILTON, J. N. COOPER, and J. C. HARRIS, The stopping powers of various elements for protons of energies from 400 to 1050 kev. *Phys. Rev.* **93,** 413–418 (1954).
15. J. E. BROLLEY, JR., and F. L. RIBE, Energy loss by 8.86-Mev deuterons and 4.43-Mev protons. *Phys. Rev.* **98,** 1112–1117 (1955).
16. C. N. FREY, History and development of the modern yeast industry. *Ind. Eng. Chem.* **22,** 1154–1162 (1930).
17. G. SYKES (ed.), Constituents of bacterial culture media. *Soc. of Gen. Microbiol., Spec. Rept.* Cambridge (1956).
18. S. SPIEGELMAN, H. O. HALVORSON, and R. BEN-ISHAI, Free amino acids and the enzyme-forming mechanism. In *A Symposium on Amino Acid Metabolism* (W. D. McElroy and H. B. Glass, eds.), pp. 124–170, Johns Hopkins Press, Baltimore, Maryland, 1955.
19. D. E. LEA, *Actions of Radiations on Living Cells*, The Macmillan Co., New York, 1947.
20. W. P. JESSE and J. SADAUSKIS, Ionization in pure gases and the average energy to make an ion pair for alpha and beta particles. *Phys. Rev.* **97,** 1668–1670 (1955).
21. W. P. JESSE and J. SADAUSKIS, Absolute energy to produce an ion pair by beta particles from S^{35}. *Phys. Rev.* **107,** 766–771 (1957).
22. W. C. BARBER, Specific ionization by high-energy electrons. *Phys. Rev.* **97,** 1071–1077 (1955).
23. J. WEISS and W. BERNSTEIN, The current status of *W*, the energy to produce one ion pair in a gas. *Radiation Research* **6,** 603–610 (1957).
24. R. T. BIRGE, The propagation of errors. *Am. J. Phys.* **7,** 351–357 (1939).

RADIATION RESEARCH 10, 449–461 (1959)

The Effects of Accelerated Carbon Nuclei and Other Radiations on the Survival of Haploid Yeast

II. Biological Experiments[1]

JOSEPH A. SAYEG,[2] ANN C. BIRGE, CARL A. BEAM,[3] AND CORNELIUS A. TOBIAS

Donner Laboratory of Biophysics and Medical Physics, University of California, Berkeley, California

INTRODUCTION

During the past several decades experiments have indicated that radiation-induced damage in biological systems varies not only with the administered radiation dose but also with the linear energy transfer (LET) of the radiation employed. The difference in biological effect has been described in terms of relative biological effectiveness (RBE). The RBE is defined as the ratio of the dose of a standard radiation, frequently 220-kv X-rays, to the dose of the radiation being studied, in order for both to produce an equal biological effect (*2*). The reviews presented by Zirkle (*3*) and Boag (*4*) illustrate that the RBE varies with LET in different ways, depending on the biological effect studied, the environment, and the physiological state of the system.

The maximum LET values previously available for RBE studies (excluding those involving fission fragments, which have presented many difficulties) were obtained with α-particles from natural radioactive sources (e.g., Po^{210}). In the investigation reported here, the LET was extended to higher values by using the beam of carbon nuclei with a charge of 6 accelerated by the Berkeley 60-inch cyclotron. Furthermore, the use of several different cyclotron beams, as well as of polonium α-particles and X-rays, made possible a systematic study of the response of the same biological system to radiations varying in LET between 20 and 5000 Mev cm^2/gm.[4] The physical properties and dosimetry of the cyclotron beams have

[1] This work was supported by the U. S. Atomic Energy Commission and the Cancer Fund of the State of California. Part of this work has previously been reported by Sayeg (*1*).

[2] Present address: Los Alamos Scientific Laboratory, Los Alamos, New Mexico.

[3] Present address: Department of Biophysics, Yale University, New Haven, Connecticut.

[4] When expressed in units of Mev cm^2/gm, the LET is independent of the density of the material irradiated. For material of unit density, 10 Mev cm^2/gm is 1 kev/μ.

been described in the preceding paper (*5*). In this paper we describe the biological experiments and their results. In addition, the dosimetry for the Po^{210} α-particles and both 50-kv and 220-kv X-rays is included in this part.

The biological effect studied in this investigation was the inhibition of colony formation in the haploid yeast, *Saccharomyces cerevisiae*. This test system was chosen for the following reasons:

1. The total range of 120-Mev carbon particles is less than 0.6 mm in tissue. Therefore, studies with this beam are limited to thin layers of material.
2. Since the yeast cell is only about 5 μ in diameter, the mean LET of the radiations studied does not vary appreciably throughout the target material (*3*).
3. Large numbers of yeast cells can be handled with ease. This is an advantage in obtaining statistically significant results.
4. The RBE for haploid *Saccharomyces cerevisiae* is not a function of dose, because the survival curves for all radiations are exponential under suitable conditions.
5. The earlier results obtained by Zirkle and Tobias with *Saccharomyces cerevisiae* (*6*) indicated a very rapid rise in the RBE with increasing LET in the low-energy α-particle region. On the other hand, one would expect that the RBE for any system must decrease with LET at sufficiently high values. Hence it appeared particularly significant to determine whether or not the RBE for this system would show a decrease in the region of LET made available with carbon particles.

BIOLOGICAL PROCEDURES

The strain of yeast used, designated SC-7 by Zirkle and Tobias (*6*), has been used in many studies in this laboratory and others (*7–10*). The preparation of the yeast culture was essentially that used by Beam *et al.* (*7*), employing cells treated in dextrose and phosphate buffer. This method was followed in order to obtain survival curves that were exponential down to a low level of survival (0.2%). A summary of the technique is as follows: A 48-hour yeast culture, grown on yeast extract–dextrose–agar (YED),[5] was harvested from a Petri dish and suspended in sterile 0.05 *M* KH_2PO_4 buffer solution. The concentration of cells was approximately 10^8 cells/ml. To reduce clumping the cells were shaken for ½ hour. One milliliter of a sterile 33 wt % dextrose solution was added to 20 ml of the phosphate buffer cell suspension. This suspension was aerated and incubated in a water bath at 30°C for 48 hours. After incubation 0.003-ml aliquots of the treated cells were pipetted onto the surfaces of $\frac{3}{8} \times \frac{3}{32} \times \frac{1}{8}$-inch nonnutrient 4% agar blocks. Each block was allowed to dry for approximately ½ hour at room temperature, so that a monolayer of cells was left on its surface. The blocks were then refrigerated until time for bombardment.

For the cyclotron irradiations each sample block was mounted on a Lucite holder

[5] This medium contained 20 gm of agar, 10 gm of dextrose, and 5 gm of yeast extract per liter of H_2O.

and placed directly behind the collector foil of the dose-measuring ionization chamber (Fig. 7 of Part I). The sample holder was held in a fixed position by a lock and key. The determination of the dose delivered to the cells has already been described in Part I. The bombardment time for each sample block was between 2 and 45 minutes, depending on the dose delivered and the stability of the cyclotron beam.

After bombardment the samples were removed from the chamber and the cells resuspended in 0.05 *M* KH_2PO_4 buffer. The cells were then refrigerated until time for plating. At this time the suspensions were diluted so that a 0.1-ml aliquot contained 100 to 400 viable cells. Each 0.1-ml aliquot was pipetted onto a layer of YED agar contained in a Petri dish. The irradiated cells were then spread over the nutrient medium with a glass rod. The Petri dishes were incubated at 30°C for a sufficient time (about 48 hours) for surviving cells to develop into visible colonies, which were then counted. At least three samples were taken for each dose point, and three to five Petri plates were prepared from each sample block. The percentage survival was computed by comparison with unirradiated controls treated in the same manner as the irradiated samples.

IRRADIATIONS WITH POLONIUM-210 ALPHA-PARTICLES

Figure 1 shows a schematic diagram of the arrangement used for the Po^{210} α-particle irradiations. The source, $\frac{3}{16}$ inch in diameter, was electroplated and centered on the surface of a $\frac{3}{8}$-inch nickel disk. The nickel disk in turn was mounted on the

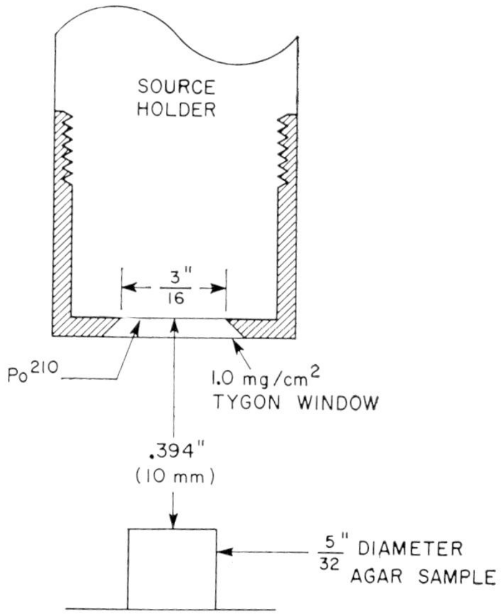

FIG. 1. A schematic diagram showing the geometry used in the Po^{210} α-particle irradiations.

lower end of a micrometer screw assembly which was housed in a Lucite chamber. The micrometer assembly made possible an accurate adjustment of the distance between the source and the yeast cells, an important quantity in the dose determination. The sample, prepared by allowing a 0.003-ml aliquot of the treated cell suspension to dry on the surface of a nonnutrient agar block, 5⁄32 inch in diameter, was accurately centered in a drawer near the bottom of the housing of the α-particle source. The source was covered by a 0.00025-inch Tygon film to prevent radioactive contamination of the samples and surroundings. The duration of exposure was timed with a stopwatch, starting at the instant when the closing of the drawer put the sample directly beneath the source.

Two different sources, varying in strength by a factor of 10, were used. Their activities were determined by means of a calibrated "low-geometry" scintillation counter with an accuracy of $\pm 2\%$ and were corrected for subsequent decay of the radioactive material. The dose rate, D', at any point on the sample can be calculated by the expression (*1*, *6*, *9*)

$$D' = k\frac{n}{4}\sigma_m G \tag{1}$$

where G is a geometry factor given by

$$G = \ln \frac{\sqrt{(a^2 + b^2)^2 + 2(a^2 - b^2)r^2 + r^4} + r^2 + a^2 - b^2}{2a^2} \tag{2}$$

In equations 1 and 2, n is the activity per unit area of the source (disintegrations/cm² sec), a is the distance between sample and source (cm), r is the radius of the source (cm), and b is the distance of any given point on the sample from the point directly below the center of the source. The quantity σ_m is the mass stopping power or total average LET (Mev cm²/gm) for the α-particles in cellular material and is assumed to be the same for all the α-particle trajectories. The constant k relates different units of dosage and is 1.602×10^{-8} rad gm/Mev.

The derivation of equations 1 and 2 is given by Sayeg (*1*). In essence the dose is obtained by calculating the flux density of α-particles through the sample at any point and then multiplying by the LET or energy loss of the particles in traversing a thin layer of cellular material (see references in Part I). In calculating the LET it is necessary to know the amount of material traversed and hence the energy lost by the α-particles between the source and the centers of the cells, a quantity that varies for different particle trajectories. For the geometry used in this experiment (Fig. 1), the maximum path length is 9.1% longer than the minimum path length. The corresponding increase in LET, however, is only 4.2%. There is a larger proportion of particles with an increased path length at the edges of the sample than at the center. The geometry factor, G, on the other hand, shows that the particle flux density is 3.5% less at the edges of the sample than at the center. Hence these two variations tend to cancel each other, and the dose rate is nearly uniform over the area of the sample.

TABLE I

DOSIMETRY FOR Po^{210} ALPHA-PARTICLE IRRADIATIONS

(1) Experiment number	(2) Equivalent air path between source and centers of cells (cm)	(3) Particle energy at centers of cells (Mev)	(4) Average total LET in cellular material (Mev. cm²/gm)	(5) Dose Rate (rads/min)
4a	1.91 ± 0.11	3.34 ± 0.14	1250 ± 50	$4.18 \pm 0.21 \times 10^4$
5	1.82 ± 0.10	3.45 ± 0.13	1230 ± 50	$5.17 \pm 0.26 \times 10^3$

The values used in the dose calculations are given in Table I. The total amount of material traversed by an α-particle traveling at right angles to the source and the sample was found by summing the equivalent dry-air paths of Tygon (a polyvinyl choride with relative mass stopping power of 0.903) (*11*), room air, and the yeast-cell radius (*5*), with estimates for the uncertainties in each quantity. The total equivalent dry-air path at 15°C and 760 mm Hg for each experiment is given in column 2 of Table I. The resultant energy for α-particles with an initial energy of 5.30 Mev was found from range-energy curves in air (*12*) and is given in column 3 of Table I. The corresponding values of average total LET in cellular material were obtained from the semi-empirical energy-loss curves for water (*5, 13*), extended to low energy by experimental data for protons (*14*) (column 4, Table I). For both experiments the uncertainty in LET is ±4%, compounded from the uncertainty in α-particle energy and ±3% assumed for the error in the energy-loss curves. The dose rate for both experiments is given in column 5 of Table I. The over-all error in both cases is ±5%. For a cell thickness of 5 μ the LET and dose rate are decreased by 2.9% and increased by 4.5%, respectively, at the top and bottom surfaces of the cell. In the cyclotron experiments the corresponding change was only ±2% in the worst case, that of low-energy carbon particles.

X-IRRADIATIONS

A control experiment with 50-kv X-rays was carried out with each cyclotron and α-particle experiment. A Picker X-ray machine containing a Machlett OEG-60 beryllium window tube was used. The only filter was that inherent in the tube and air path. The operating conditions were: voltage 50 kv, current 25 ma, and target-to-sample distance 15.4 cm. The exposure-dose rate for these conditions was measured by Mortimer (*8*) and was 250 r/sec with an estimated error of ±2.5%. Agar sample blocks identical to those used in the cyclotron experiments were placed in a dish within a radius of 2 cm from the axis of the X-ray tube. Irradiation was briefly interrupted for removal of the samples so that a series of graded doses was delivered. In each X-ray experiment three small agar samples were irradiated for each dose point, and three Petri plates were prepared from each sample.

A 220-kv G.E. Maximar machine was also used in order to obtain survival curves with a radiation comparable to that used in other RBE studies. The samples were placed in a specially designed Lucite holder which had inserted in the center a Victoreen integron chamber used for the dose measurement. The integron chamber was calibrated against several portable Victoreen ionization chambers, and the error in the dose measurement was estimated to be ±4.5%. The radiation conditions were: voltage 220 kv, current 15 ma, target-to-sample distance 28 cm, and dose rate approximately 800 r/min. There was no external filter other than the Lucite cover of the irradiation chamber. The same irradiation technique was employed as with the 50-kv experiments.

The conversion factor, f, between exposure dose in roentgens and absorbed dose in rads was calculated for the yeast composition given in the first paper of this pair (*5*) by using the mass energy-absorption coefficients of G. R. White (*2*). The value of $W = 34 \pm 1$ ev per ion pair in air was assumed. For X-ray energies between 15 and 40 kv, f was 1.01 rads/r. In this energy region, however, the conversion factor is very sensitive to the elemental composition of the material irradiated. For example, at 20 kv the 0.8% potassium present in yeast accounts for 15% of the energy absorbed. Hence for the 50-kv X-rays an error in the absorbed dose of ±7% was estimated to arise from the uncertainties in the composition of yeast. An additional error of ±5% was estimated in the calculated absorption coefficients. When the square root is taken of the sum of the fractional errors squared for all factors, the resultant standard error in absorbed dose for the 50-kv irradiations is ±10%.

For X-ray energies between 80 and 200 kv, the conversion factor, f, calculated for yeast is 0.97 rad/r, with an estimated error of ±3% in the calculated absorption coefficients. For these X-ray energies the uncertainty in composition introduces a negligible error. The resultant over-all error in absorbed dose for the 220-kv irradiations is ±6%. The mean LET for X-rays does not change very much for tube voltages between 40 and 200 kv (*15*). The value of 20 ± 5 Mev cm^2/gm has been used in plotting the results for both sets of X-ray data (*16*).

EXPERIMENTAL RESULTS

In preliminary experiments with 50-kv X-rays, the survival curve for cells treated by the method described above was a single exponential for doses up to 25,000 rads, or a survival level of 0.2% (*1*), where the radioresistant population associated with budding cells appeared (*7*). No correction was made in the initial slopes of the survival curves, since the resistant population represents a negligible error at this low survival level. During the final series of experiments the survival curves were taken down to levels varying between 1% and 10%. All the curves were of the form $N = N_0 e^{-\alpha D}$, where N is the number of cells surviving at the dose D, and N_0 is the number at zero dose. For each curve, a weighted least-squares calculation was made of the logarithmic slope, α, which is a direct measure of the

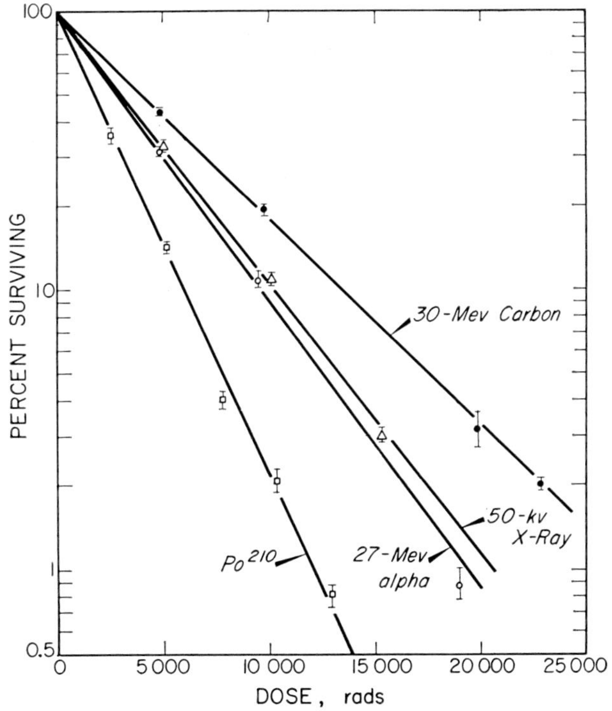

FIG. 2. The per cent survival of haploid *Saccharomyces cerevisiae* as a function of absorbed dose for four different radiations: ● 30-Mev carbon particles (experiment 2b); ○ 27-Mev α-particles (experiment 1a); △ 50-kv X-rays (control experiment 3); □ Po^{210} α-particles (experiment 5). The errors shown are standard deviations of the mean values.

radiosensitivity of the cells. Several of the observed survival curves are shown in Fig. 2.

The results obtained during five different experiments are summarized in Table II. For each radiation described in column 2 the total average LET in cellular material is given in column 3, and the logarithmic slope of the survival curve is given in column 4. The quoted error in column 4 results from the statistical error in the calculated slope of each survival curve, and the estimated error in each dose measurement (cf. above and Part I). In all cases except experiment 1b, the error in the dose measurement is several times the statistical error in the calculated slope of the survival curve. Column 5 of Table II gives the dose in rads for 50% survival, and column 6 gives the slope of the 50-kv X-ray control curve for each run.

For the three cyclotron runs, the slope of the 50-kv X-ray curve remained constant within ±2% and was in agreement with the value obtained in the preliminary

TABLE II

EXPERIMENTAL RESULTS ON HAPLOID *Saccharomyces Cerevisiae*

(1) Experiment number	(2) Radiation	(3) Total average LET (Mev cm²/gm)	(4) Slope of survival curve (10^{-4} rad^{-1})	(5) Dose for 50% survival (rads)	(6) Slope of 50-kv X-ray survival curve (10^{-4} rad^{-1})	(7) Cross section for inactivation (10^{-8} cm² /particle)	(8) Approximate dose rate (rads/min)
1a	Alpha (27 Mev)	258 ± 6	2.40 ± 0.18	2890	2.24 ± 0.22	0.0991 ± 0.0076	1100–2300
1b	Alpha (6 Mev)	850 ± 100	3.05 ± 0.41	2270	2.24 ± 0.22	0.416 ± 0.074	3300–10,000
1c	Deuteron (19 Mev)	48 ± 2	1.96 ± 0.11	3550	2.24 ± 0.22	0.0150 ± 0.0010	1100–2100
2a	Carbon (65 Mev)	2680 ± 300	2.57 ± 0.12	2700	2.24 ± 0.22	1.10 ± 0.13	900–1800
2b	Carbon (30 Mev)	4450 ± 540	1.72 ± 0.10	4030	2.24 ± 0.22	1.23 ± 0.17	1200–3000
3a	Carbon (67 Mev)	2600 ± 200	2.51 ± 0.12	2760	2.29 ± 0.22	1.04 ± 0.09	400–750
3b	Carbon (24 Mev)	5080 ± 460	1.29 ± 0.08	5370	2.29 ± 0.22	1.05 ± 0.12	1000–1500
4a	Alpha (Po^{210})	1250 ± 50	4.30 ± 0.23	1610	1.95 ± 0.20	0.862 ± 0.035	42,000
4b	X-ray (220 kv)	20 ± 5	2.16 ± 0.14	3200	1.95 ± 0.20	— —	800
5	Alpha (Po^{210})	1230 ± 50	3.86 ± 0.23	1800	2.12 ± 0.20	0.761 ± 0.037	5000

X-ray experiments. Although every attempt was made to perform the last two series of experiments involving polonium α-particles with the same techniques as the cyclotron experiments, the slope of the 50-kv survival curve is shifted by 7% in these runs. We believe that this shift is related to the known variation of the radiosensitivity of haploid yeast to X-rays with the treatment time in dextrose-buffer medium, and it does not affect the results obtained with α-particles (*9*). Unfortunately the only experiment performed with 220-kv X-rays shows the same shift in sensitivity, but the uncertainty in dose measurement for this point is as large as the change in sensitivity.

In Fig. 3 the radiosensitivity for each radiation is plotted as a function of the total average LET in cellular material. Here the radiosensitivity is defined as the logarithmic slope, α, of the survival curve; it is the reciprocal of the absorbed dose in rads for 37% survival.

For an exponential dose-effect relationship, the RBE is the ratio of logarithmic slopes between the curve for the radiation under consideration and that of a standard radiation such as 220-kv X-rays. Hence the sensitivity plotted in Fig. 3 is directly

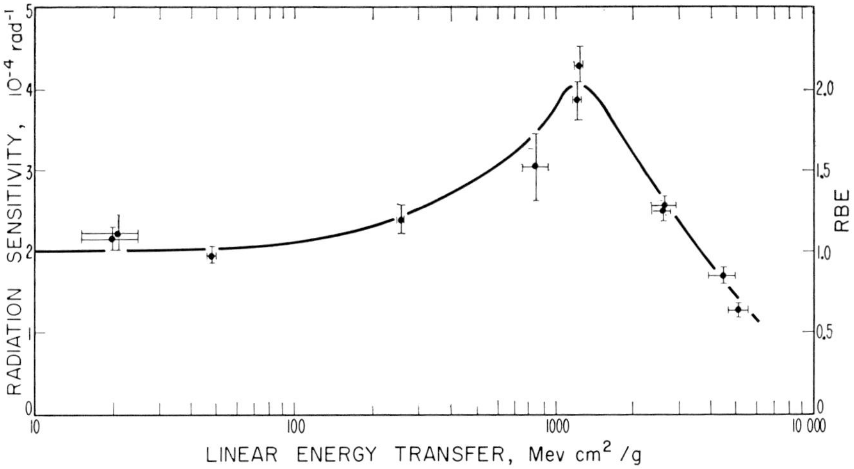

FIG. 3. The radiosensitivity and RBE for the inhibition of colony formation in haploid *Saccharomyces cerevisiae* as functions of the total average LET in cellular material. The errors shown are standard deviations.

proportional to the RBE, but it does not involve a comparison with any preferred radiation. For convenience, units of RBE are included on the right-hand side of Fig. 3, where a standard sensitivity of 2.0×10^{-4} per rad has been assumed for an RBE of unity. From Fig. 3 it is seen that at low LET the radiosensitivity is approximately constant; it shows a region of increasing sensitivity with increasing LET for deuterons and α-particles; and finally at high LET values it shows a region of decreasing sensitivity. The maximum observed RBE of approximately 2.0 was obtained with 3.4-Mev α-particles from Po^{210}. The carbon particles, on the other hand, exhibit about the same effectiveness as 220-kv X-rays.

The RBE compares the effectiveness of two radiations in terms of the energy absorbed to produce the same biological effect. Another useful measure of biological effectiveness is provided when the dose is expressed as f, the number of particles per square centimeter bombarding the biological sample. Then the survival curve takes the form $N = N_0 e^{-\sigma f}$, where the logarithmic slope, σ, has the units of square centimeters per particle and is sometimes called the cross section for inactivation (*17*). It is easily shown that σ in square centimeters per particle is related to α in rads^{-1} by the equation

$$\sigma = 1.602 \times 10^{-8} \text{ (LET) } \alpha$$

where the LET in cellular material is expressed in units of Mev cm^2/gm.

For each experiment the value of σ is given in column 7 of Table II and is shown graphically in Fig. 4. For comparison the line of constant RBE is also shown in the log-log plot of Fig. 4. Here it is apparent that, after a region of increasing cross

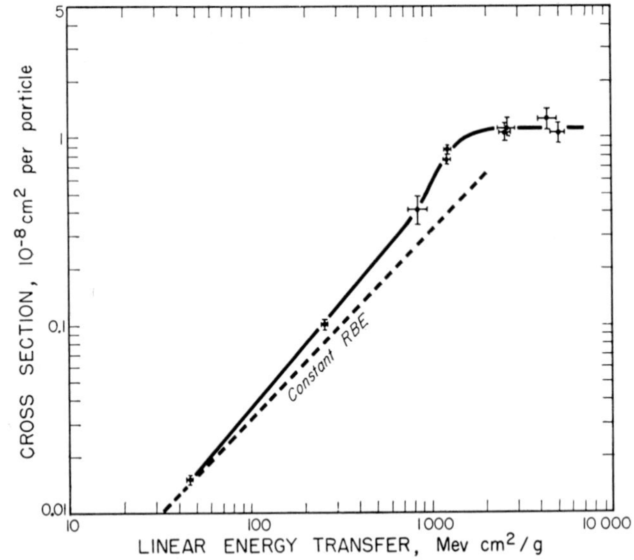

FIG. 4. The measured cross section in square centimeters per particle for the inhibition of colony formation in haploid *Saccharomyces cerevisiae* as a function of the total average LET of the incident radiation. The errors shown are standard deviations.

section with increasing LET, σ for haploid yeast approaches a constant value of approximately 1.1 μ^2 at very high LET values.

DISCUSSION

The data presented here are in qualitative agreement with the earlier results of Zirkle and Tobias in the region of low and intermediate LET (*6*). This study shows that for the survival of haploid *Saccharomyces cerevisiae* the sensitivity to radiation is maximum at the LET of polonium α-particles and that the sensitivity falls progressively as the LET is increased above this value, a region of LET which had not previously been studied. Employing a technique different from ours, Kohn and Gunter obtained RBE data on yeast at very low LET by using high-energy X-rays (*18*).

The exponential nature of the yeast survival curves supports the conclusion that a single ionizing particle is responsible for the inhibition of colony formation; it permits the description of radiosensitivity in terms of the apparent cross section per particle for inactivation (*17*). The observations at high LET values are consistent with an approximately constant cross section (Fig. 4), as predicted by classical target theory. The constant cross section and decreasing RBE at high LET are explained in terms of a saturation mechanism whereby more energy is transferred by the ionizing particle than is required to produce the observed biological effect.

A comparison of the observed value of the cross section at high LET with the estimated area of a single cell shows that only one particle out of approximately 20 that traverse the cell is effective in the lethal action. Exact knowledge of the nature and size of the yeast cell nucleus is not available, but electron-microscope (*19*) and Feulgen staining studies (*20*) lead to estimates of the nuclear area approximating the value of 1 μ^2 and agree with the maximum inactivation cross section observed in this experiment. This observation supports the view that a single particle track of high LET has a high efficiency for producing lethal damage when it passes through nuclear material but is ineffective when passing through the cytoplasm (cf. the review by Gray, *21*). A similar result has been demonstrated directly in the work of Zirkle and Bloom, in which a microbeam of protons was ineffective in producing aberrations in mitotic cells of newt heart unless the radiation was directed at chromosome material (*22*). The extensive literature in this field has been reviewed by Zirkle (*23*). Since the maximum cross section now observed for yeast is only one-twentieth of the cellular area, it will be interesting in the future to extend the observations to even higher LET values to determine whether or not a further increase in inactivation cross section is possible.

Although the target theory correctly predicts the constant cross section observed at high LET, we now know that such a theory masks a complicated sequence of events in the production of radiation damage. Furthermore, if the target theory is restricted to biological effects produced by a single ionization or a single primary energy transfer, it does not explain the rise in RBE with increasing LET observed for intermediate values of LET. For this reason Zirkle and Tobias postulated a migration model, in which chemical intermediates operate between the energy transfer and the final biological effect (*6*). According to this model, the increase of RBE as a function of LET observed for yeast is explained by assuming that one type of intermediate predominates in causing damage at low LET, and another longer-lived species predominates at high LET. The rise in RBE is then explained in terms of the increased ionic yield at high LET for the production of the second type of intermediate. Adjustment of the values of the ionic yields and diffusion lengths for the two chemical species makes it possible to fit the migration model to the type of curve observed for haploid yeast.

The target theory also predicts a curve of the general shape observed in this experiment on yeast, if it is assumed that the radiation effect is caused by the cooperative action of a group of n or more ion pairs produced simultaneously within the sensitive region of the cell (*4*, *24*). Howard-Flanders has developed this theory in detail and has given a track-segment method for calculating the variation of radiation sensitivity with LET (*25*). According to this formulation the particle track is considered in terms of the number of ion pairs produced in the distance t. The distance t is characteristic of the biological material irradiated but is not necessarily the thickness of a biological target. In order to explain the influence of oxygen on sensitivity to different radiations, two types of radiation damage are postulated, the first requiring several ions (but less than n ions) in the presence of oxygen, and the other requiring at least n ions with or without oxygen present. When the two types of damage are summed and the value obtained for each LET is compared with the experimental results for the track core alone, with the effects of δ-rays subtracted, good agreement is obtained with the haploid yeast data of this experiment when n equals 8 ions and t is 4×10^{-7} gm/cm^2 (40 A in material of unit density).

The main significance of the experiment reported here is that it extends radiobiological measurements to LET values beyond those that can be obtained with α-particles and that it demonstrates for one unicellular organism that the radiation sensitivity decreases with increasing LET after passing through a maximum. It is hoped that further studies of this kind on different biological systems under various environmental conditions may eventually lead to a unified theory of the action of ionizing radiations.

SUMMARY

The radiation sensitivity for the inhibition of colony formation in the haploid yeast, *Saccharomyces cerevisiae*, has been measured with a series of radiations that cover a range in LET from 20 to 5000 Mev cm^2/gm. In addition to X-rays and Po^{210} α-particles, the radiations employed include cyclotron deuterons, α-particles, and carbon nuclei with a charge of 6. The radiation sensitivity increases with increasing LET until it reaches a maximum corresponding to an RBE of 2 for 3.4-Mev α-particles. At still higher LET values, the radiosensitivity decreases progressively and corresponds to an approximately constant inactivation cross section of 1 μ^2. Implications of the experimental results are considered in terms of target theory, the migration model, and the track-segment calculation.

ACKNOWLEDGMENTS

The authors wish to express their appreciation to Albert Salo, Herman P. Robinson, and Elinor G. Potter of the Chemistry Division of the University of California Radiation Laboratory for the preparation and calibration of the Po^{210} α-particle sources, and to the members of the Biophysics Group of Donner Laboratory for help in carrying out the experiments. We are also indebted to Dr. Robert A. Wijsman and Dr. Paul Howard-Flanders for many helpful discussions.

RECEIVED: August 4, 1958

REFERENCES

1. J. A. SAYEG, The effect of highly ionizing radiations on cell survival: Thesis, University of California Radiation Laboratory Report UCRL-2293 (1954).
2. Report of the International Commission on Radiological Units and Measurements (ICRU) 1956. *Natl. Bur. Standards (U. S.) Handbook* **No. 62** (1957).
3. R. E. ZIRKLE, The radiobiological importance of linear energy transfer. In *Radiation Biology* (A. Hollaender, ed.), Vol. I, pp. 315–350. McGraw-Hill Book Company, New York, 1954.

4. J. W. Boag, The relative biological efficiency of different ionizing radiations. *Natl. Bur. Standards (U. S.) Rept.* **2946** (1953).
5. A. C. Birge and J. A. Sayeg, The effects of accelerated carbon nuclei and other radiations on the survival of haploid yeast. I. Dosimetry of the cyclotron beams. *Radiation Research* in press.
6. R. E. Zirkle and C. A. Tobias, Effects of ploidy and linear energy transfer on radiobiological survival curves. *Arch. Biochem. Biophys.* **47,** 282–306 (1953).
7. C. A. Beam, R. K. Mortimer, R. G. Wolfe, and C. A. Tobias, The relation of radioresistance to budding in *Saccharomyces cerevisiae*. *Arch. Biochem. Biophys.* **49,** 110–122 (1954).
8. R. K. Mortimer, Cytological and environmental factors related to the effects of radiation on yeast cells. Thesis, University of California, 1953 (unpublished).
9. M. M. Elkind and C. A. Beam, Variation of the biological effectiveness of X-rays and α-particles on haploid *Saccharomyces cerevisiae*. *Radiation Research* **3,** 88–104 (1955).
10. A. C. Birge and C. A. Tobias, Radiation sensitivity of yeast cells grown in aerobic and anaerobic environments. *Arch. Biochem. Biophys.* **52,** 388–393 (1954).
11. W. A. Aron, B. G. Hoffman, and F. C. Williams, Range-energy curves. U. S. Atomic Energy Commission Report AECU-663, Technical Information Service, Oak Ridge, Tennessee, 1951.
12. H. A. Bethe, The range-energy relation for slow alpha-particles and protons in air. *Revs. Mod. Phys.* **22,** 213–219 (1950).
13. A. C. Birge, H. O. Anger, and C. A. Tobias, Heavy charged-particle beams. In *Radiation Dosimetry* (G. J. Hine and G. L. Brownell, eds.), pp. 623–665. Academic Press, New York, 1956.
14. H. K. Reynolds, D. N. F. Dunbar, W. A. Wenzel, and W. Whaling, The stopping cross section of gases for protons, 30–600 kev. *Phys. Rev.* **92,** 742–748 (1953).
15. L. H. Gray, The distribution of the ions resulting from the irradiation of living cells. *Brit. J. Radiol. Suppl.* **1,** pp. 7–15 (1947).
16. D. V. Cormack and H. E. Johns, Electron energies and ion densities in water irradiated with 200 kev, 1 Mev and 25 Mev radiation. *Brit. J. Radiol.* **25,** 369–381 (1952).
17. E. Pollard, Primary ionization as a test of molecular organization. *Advances in Biol. and Med. Phys.* **3,** 153–189 (1953).
18. H. I. Kohn and S. E. Gunter, Relative biological efficiency of 1000-Kvp and 250-Kvcp X-rays. *Radiation Research* **5,** 674–687 (1956).
19. H. D. Agar and H. C. Douglas, Studies on the cytological structure of yeast: electron microscopy of thin sections. *J. Bacteriol.* **73,** 365–375 (1957).
20. E. D. DeLamater, The nuclear cytology of the vegetative diplophase of *Saccharomyces cerevisiae*. *J. Bacteriol.* **60,** 321–332 (1950).
21. L. H. Gray, Primary sites of energy deposition associated with radiobiological lesions. *Ciba Foundation Symposium, Ionizing Radiations and Cell Metabolism* 255–270 (1956).
22. R. E. Zirkle and W. Bloom, Irradiation of parts of individual cells. *Science* **117,** 487–493 (1953).
23. R. E. Zirkle, Partial-cell irradiation. *Advances Biol. and Med. Phys.* **5,** 103–146 (1957).
24. D. E. Lea, *Actions of Radiations on Living Cells*, Cambridge University Press, Cambridge, 1946.
25. P. Howard-Flanders, Physical and chemical mechanisms in the injury of cells by ionizing radiations. *Advances in Biol. and Med. Phys.* **6,** 553–603 (1959).

RADIATION RESEARCH 10, 462–476 (1959)

Effect of X-Radiation on DNA Metabolism in Various Tissues of the Rat[1]

I. Incorporation of C^{14}-Thymidine into DNA during the First 24 Hours Postirradiation

ODDVAR F. NYGAARD AND RICHARD L. POTTER

Atomic Energy Commission, Biological Effects of Irradiation Laboratory, and the Department of Biological Chemistry, Medical School, University of Michigan, Ann Arbor, Michigan

INTRODUCTION

More than fifteen years ago von Euler and Hevesy (*1*) reported that X-radiation inhibited the incorporation of radioactive phosphate into deoxyribonucleic acid (DNA) of Jensen sarcoma, a finding which was interpreted as inhibition of DNA synthesis in this material. It has since been established that this initial observation represents a universal effect of ionizing radiations on living cells.

Unfortunately, the many contributions to this field contain data obtained under such a variety of experimental conditions that integrating the available data into an over-all picture is exceedingly difficult. In the present investigation and in subsequent work we shall attempt to study extensively the effect of radiation on DNA metabolism under standardized experimental conditions.

The work reported here concerns the early effect of total-body X-irradiation on the incorporation of thymidine-2-C^{14} into DNA of the thymus, spleen, the small intestine of the rat. The labeling of DNA was measured over 1-hour periods throughout the first 24 hours after doses of 50 to 800 r.

It has been demonstrated (*2*, *3*) that thymidine is a specific precursor of DNA and that it is rapidly and efficiently incorporated into most tissues. This makes thymidine the precursor of choice for studying transitory changes in the synthesis of DNA.

[1] This work was performed under U. S. Atomic Energy Commission contract AT (11-1)-75. A preliminary report was presented at the annual meeting of the Federation of American Societies for Experimental Biology, 1958.

EXPERIMENTAL PROCEDURE

Preparation of radioactive thymidine. Thymidine-2-C^{14} was prepared by an exchange reaction between thymine-2-C^{14} and nonlabeled thymidine in the presence of a nucleoside phosphorylase, essentially as described by Reichard (*4*). The enzyme was prepared from lyophilized *Escherichia coli* B which had been grown on a synthetic medium (*5*). The dried material was suspended in 10 volumes of ice-cold 0.1 *M* sodium bicarbonate and shaken with glass beads in a Nossal bacterial disintegrator (*6*) for a total of 60 seconds, with chilling after each 15 seconds. The suspension was centrifuged at high speed, and nucleic acids were removed by precipitation with manganous chloride. The resulting extract was used without dialysis.

In a typical preparation, the extract from 0.5 gm of lyophilized bacteria was incubated for 2 hours at 38°C with 200 μM of thymine-2-C^{14} and 300 μM of unlabeled thymidine in 20 ml of 0.1 *M* phosphate buffer at pH 7.0. The mixture also contained sodium fluoride at a final concentration of 0.7 *M*. The reaction was stopped by chilling and adding 1 ml of 12 *N* perchloric acid. The precipitated proteins were centrifuged down; the supernatant liquid was neutralized with potassium hydroxide, and potassium perchlorate was removed in the cold. The thymine–thymidine mixture was resolved on a 2 × 30-cm column of Dowex 2-X8 in acetate form (*7*). The mixture was added at pH 9.5, and the column was eluted with a system consisting of a constant-volume mixer containing 400 ml of 0.1 *M* ammonium acetate at pH 8.9 and a reservoir containing 0.1 *M* ammonium acetate at pH 9.3. The use of an increasing pH gradient gave a better resolution of the two compounds than did elution at a constant pH, and the system described was found satisfactory for the separation of at least 2 to 3 mM of the compounds. Thymidine was eluted with approximately 13 resin-bed-volumes of eluent (about 1200 ml) as compared with 17.5 resin-bed-volumes for thymine.

From a comparison of the specific activities of the added thymine and the recovered thymidine it was calculated that the isotope exchange was at least 96% complete. The chemical recovery of thymidine was 70 to 75%, giving an over-all recovery of radioactivity as thymidine-2-C^{14} of 40 to 45%.

Animals. Male rats, of the Sprague-Dawley strain, were received 1 week prior to their use and were kept in individual cages in an air-conditioned room. The animals were maintained on Rockland rat diet supplemented with green lettuce and had free access to water. Food was removed at 7 A.M. on the day of the experiment. Unless otherwise stated, all animals weighed 180 ± 10 gm and were usually 45 days old at the beginning of an experiment.

Irradiation. An X-ray machine was operated at 245 kv with added filtration of ½ mm copper and 1 mm aluminum. During the irradiation period the animals were kept in a sectioned Plexiglas cage on a slowly rotating turntable underneath the X-ray machine. The irradiation was always carried out between 9 and 10 A.M.

The exposure time was kept constant at 27 ± 2 minutes for all doses by varying the tube current and the distance from the target, the shortest distance employed being 75 cm. For the 50-r dose the irradiation was delivered intermittently, with 3-minute "on" and 2-minute "off" periods, to obtain the desired total time for the delivery of the dose. The dose rates in air were determined with a Victoreen r-meter, placed in the rotating rat cage during the test exposures.

Administration of precursor. The rats were given the radioactive thymidine by intraperitoneal injection. The standard injection dose was 10 μM of thymidine-2-C^{14}, with specific activity of 0.3 μc/μM, dissolved in 1.0 ml of physiological saline, adjusted to pH 7.4 with 0.05 *M* phosphate buffer.

It was found that the efficiency of incorporation of radioactivity into DNA of spleen and intestine depended on the number of micromoles of thymidine injected into the animals. Although maximum efficiency was obtained for doses of 1 μM or less, the specific activity of the radioactive thymidine proved to be a limiting factor; hence the 10-μM precursor level was used. In thymus the efficiency of incorporation was not affected by the size of the dose up to 50 μM of thymidine per injection.

Preparation of samples. The rats were killed by decapitation; spleen and thymus were quickly excised, trimmed, and weighed. The major part of the small intestine, from 1 inch below the stomach to within 1 inch of the large intestine, was excised, pancreas tissue removed, and the lumen flushed with ice-cold physiological saline buffered with 0.02 *M* phosphate at pH 7.4. The tissues were immediately frozen in liquid nitrogen and stored at −20° C.

Isolation of mixed nucleic acids. Spleen and thymus were homogenized individually for 30 seconds in a glass Potter-Elvehjem homogenizer with 10 volumes of ice-cold water. An aliquot was removed for analysis of total content of nucleic acids according to Schneider (*8*), and the remainder was homogenized for another 10 to 20 seconds after the addition of ¼ volume of 2.5 *N* perchloric acid. The intestine was homogenized in a semimicro Waring blendor. As it proved extremely difficult to obtain representative aliquots of the homogenized intestine, total nucleic acids were determined from the isolated nucleates.

The acid homogenates were centrifuged in the cold, and the precipitates washed twice with cold 0.3 *N* perchloric acid. The excess perchloric acid was neutralized with sodium hydroxide. The insoluble material was extracted for 30 minutes at 100° C with 10% sodium chloride buffered at pH 7 with 0.1 *M* phosphate, and the residue re-extracted for 15 minutes under the same conditions. Sodium nucleates were precipitated from the combined extracts by the addition of 2 to 2.5 volumes of ethanol. For further purification, the nucleates were dissolved in water and an excess of hydrochloric acid was added in the cold. The precipitated nucleic acids were washed with 65% ethanol and finally dissolved in water by addition of small amounts of sodium hydroxide.

Determination of radioactivity. Since it is known that thymidine is incorporated into DNA only, and not into RNA (*2, 3*), the specific activity of the DNA was obtained by determining the radioactivity and DNA content on aliquots of the solutions of mixed nucleates. The radioactivity was measured with a thin-window flow counter (Nuclear Chicago, Model D-47) with an estimated over-all efficiency of 42% for C^{14}. The DNA content was determined with the diphenylamine reaction (*9*).

To prove the validity of this procedure, radioactive DNA was isolated from several samples of mixed nucleates from the small intestine of animals injected with radioactive thymidine by using a modification of the Schmidt-Thannhauser procedure (*10*). The isolated DNA contained all the radioactivity in the original sample. By degrading the DNA with 7.5 *N* perchloric acid (*11*) and isolating the liberated purine and pyrimidine bases by chromatography, it was shown that thymine was the only radioactive component.[2]

The specific activity data have been normalized by conversion to "biological concentration coefficients" (*13*), defined as follows:[3]

$$\text{BCC} = \frac{\text{cpm/mM DNA thymine}}{\text{cpm injected/body weight}} \times 100$$

As an expression of total activity, the specific activity has been multiplied by the total amount of DNA thymine found in the organ.

RESULTS

Time course for the incorporation of thymidine into DNA. Thirty rats were injected with radioactive thymidine and killed 15, 30, 60, 120, or 240 minutes later. The specific activity of the DNA was determined as described. The data are recorded in Fig. 1. The curve for liver is included for comparison. It will be noticed that, for spleen and thymus, maximum incorporation is reached 1 hour after the injection. In the small intestine the radioactivity of the DNA continues to increase for another hour, but at a much reduced rate. The rapid attainment of maximum incorporation agrees well with our finding (unpublished observations) that the amounts of radioactive thymidine in the blood and in the acid-soluble fractions of the various organs fall off very rapidly. Thus the radioactivity found at 2 hours after the injection is less than 3% of the radioactivity at 15 minutes.

In the case of irradiated animals we have found that only the maximum levels, but not the shapes of the incorporation curves, are altered. We therefore feel that

[2] From the specific activities of the DNA and of the isolated thymine, it was calculated that the molar ratio of thymine to total nitrogen bases in DNA from rat intestine is 0.272, in fair agreement with the value of 0.284 reported for rat bone marrow DNA (*12*).

[3] For 3 μc of C^{14} injected into a 180-gm rat, BCC is approximately equal to (cpm/μM) $\times$ 6.5, with our counting equipment.

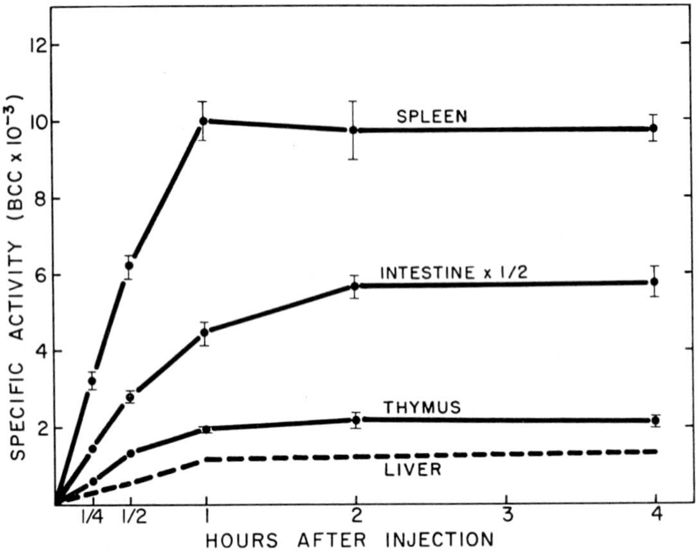

FIG. 1. Specific activity of DNA from spleen, intestine, thymus, and liver of control rats, after single injections of thymidine-2-C^{14} (3 μc in 10 μM). The vertical bars indicate the standard errors for the points on the graph. The values for intestine have been multiplied by ½.

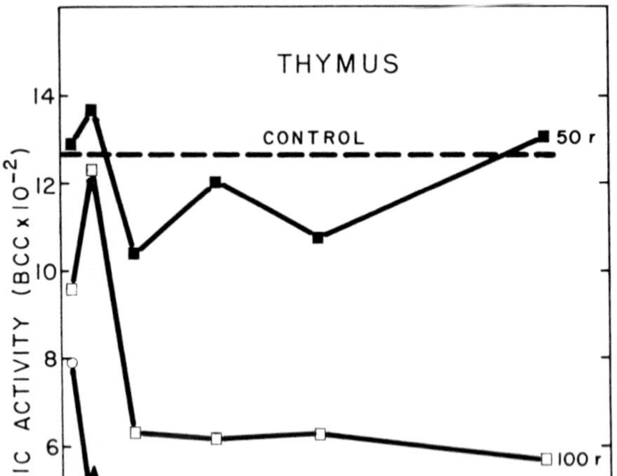

FIG. 2A

FIG. 2. Variations in specific activity of DNA from thymus, spleen, and small intestine, after different doses of total-body X-irradiation. The values are plotted at the mid-points of the 1-hour periods for incorporation of thymidine-2-C^{14}.

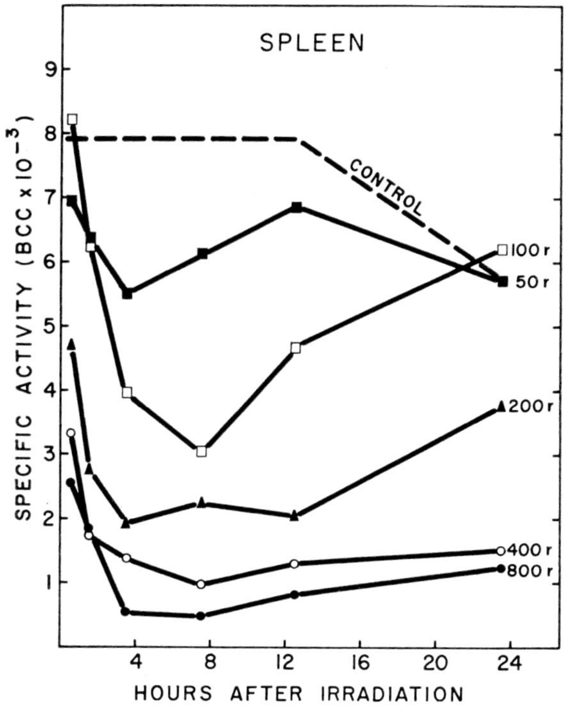
SPLEEN
SPECIFIC ACTIVITY (BCC x 10⁻³)
CONTROL
100 r
50 r
200 r
400 r
800 r
HOURS AFTER IRRADIATION

FIG. 2B

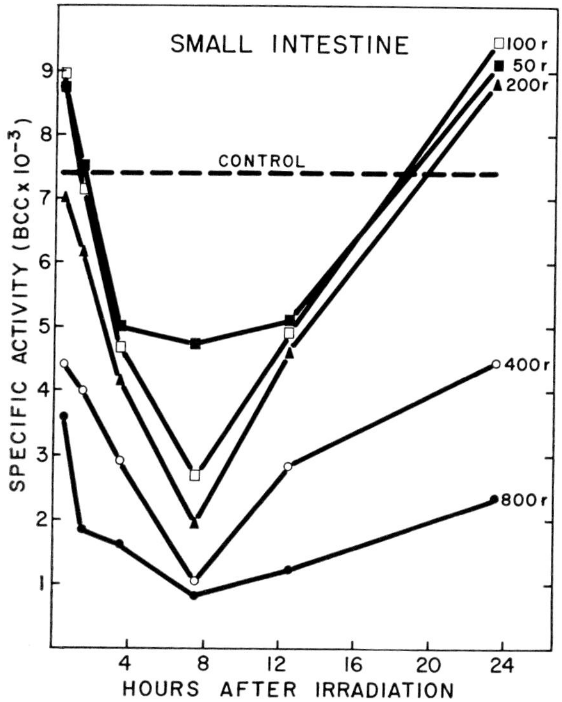
SMALL INTESTINE
SPECIFIC ACTIVITY (BCC x 10⁻³)
CONTROL
100 r
50 r
200 r
400 r
800 r
HOURS AFTER IRRADIATION

FIG. 2C

the use of 1-hour incorporation periods, which we have employed in the following, will yield data reflecting the ability of a tissue to incorporate thymidine into DNA.

Effect of X-radiation on the incorporation of thymidine into DNA. In this series of experiments the rats were given single injections of radioactive thymidine at 0, 1, 3, 7, 12, or 23 hours after the end of the irradiation period and were killed 60 minutes later. Normally two rats were used for each time point. The levels of radiation were 50, 100, 200, 400, and 800 r. Figure 2 shows the data obtained for the different organs in terms of specific activity of the isolated DNA. The control values indicated were obtained in sham-irradiated animals in late fall, after the completion of the irradiation series, which were run from the higher to the lower dose levels. It was noticed that data on control animals obtained during the summer showed approximately 50% greater incorporation in the case of thymus. For spleen the discrepancy was less than 10%, and for intestine no significant difference was noted. In contrast

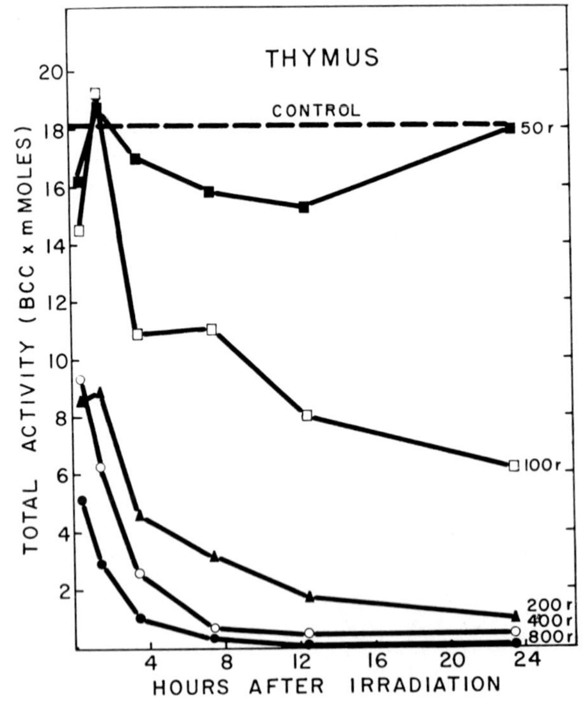

FIG. 3A

FIG. 3. Variations in total activity of DNA in thymus, spleen, and small intestine, after different doses of total-body X-irradiation. The values are plotted at the mid-points of the 1-hour periods for incorporation of thymidine-2-C^{14}.

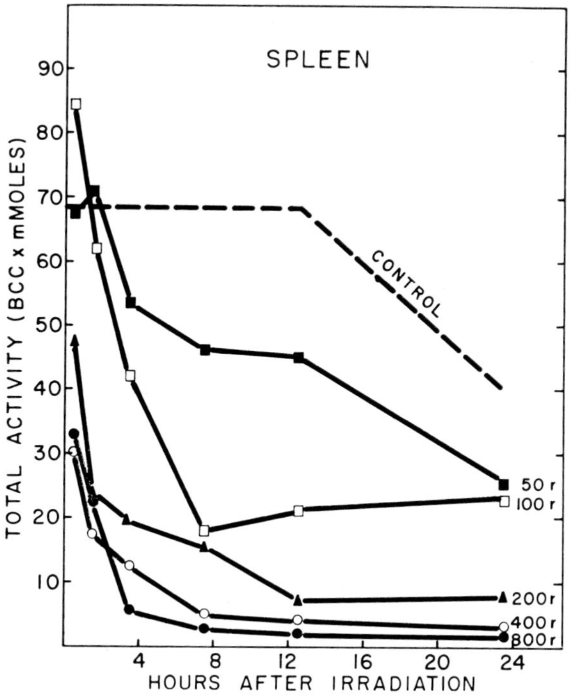
SPLEEN
CONTROL
TOTAL ACTIVITY (BCC x mMOLES)
90
80
70
60
50
40
30
20
10
50 r
100 r
200 r
400 r
800 r
4
8
12
16
20
24
HOURS AFTER IRRADIATION
FIG. 3B

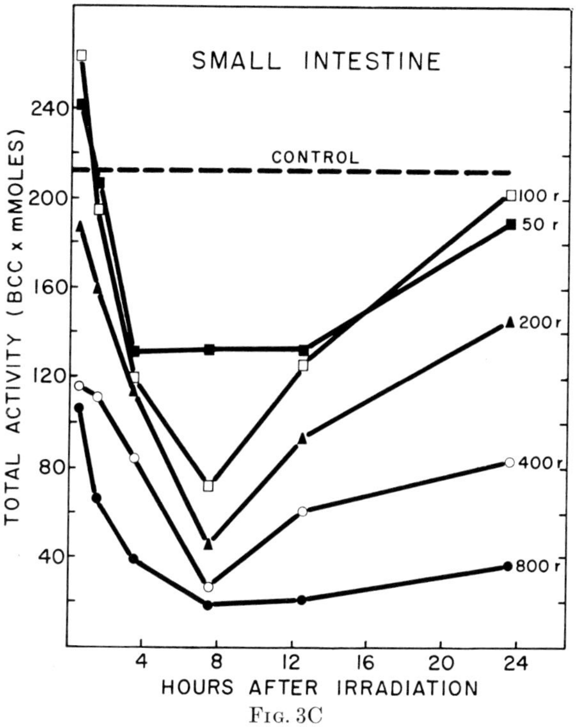
SMALL INTESTINE
CONTROL
TOTAL ACTIVITY (BCC x mMOLES)
240
200
160
120
80
40
100 r
50 r
200 r
400 r
800 r
4
8
12
16
20
24
HOURS AFTER IRRADIATION
FIG. 3C

to this seasonal variation there was no indication of diurnal variation in the control groups, except for the drop in spleen activity after 24 hours of fasting.[4]

It will be observed that in all three tissues there is a rapid and extensive inhibition of the incorporation of thymidine into DNA with the higher doses of radiation. In the case of the intestine, and to a lesser degree the spleen, the specific activity increases after 8 hours postirradiation. With the lower doses the depression is less in all tissues, as would be expected. Note that thymus, which shows the greatest depression after the highest doses, shows little effect after 50 r. The incorporation maximum which occurs during the second hour after irradiation with the lowest doses is another interesting feature of the data for thymus.

In Fig. 3 the data are expressed as total radioactivity per organ. The extensive loss of DNA which is known to accompany the involution of thymus and spleen after irradiation (14–16) was also observed in our animals. It will be seen that there is no increase in total labeling of the spleen after 8 hours. This suggests that the increase in specific activity (Fig. 2B) after this time is due to the progressive loss of dead cells with concomitant loss of metabolically inactive DNA from this organ. Thus, in both spleen and thymus there is no recovery of the capacity of the total organs to incorporate thymidine into DNA during the first 24 hours postirradiation. As for the small intestine, the data suggest that the recovery in this tissue is real.

The drop in the control value for spleen activity between 13 and 24 hours is a result of the fasting of the animals in these experiments. This factor also seems to have affected the 50- and 100-r curves for spleen. In other experiments we have found that results at 24 hours for fasted and fed animals were not significantly different with doses greater than 100 r.

The data reported here are essentially in agreement with previous studies on the effect of X-radiation on incorporation of different precursors into DNA of thymus (*14*, *17*, *18*), spleen (*18–20*), and intestine (*19–22*). In all cases a decrease was observed at an early time after the irradiation, with the exception of a single report on the incorporation of adenine into thymus DNA after a dose of 100 r (*17*). The majority of these studies involved observations at a single or a few, widely separated times after the exposures, and only in the work by Kelly and co-workers (*19*, *20*) have the time and dose response been investigated. Although they give fewer observations in the period we have studied, their data for mice and ours for rats show similar features.

DISCUSSION

Incorporation of thymidine as a measure of DNA synthesis. Up to this point we have considered the effect of X-radiation on the incorporation of thymidine into

[4] The variation in the values obtained within each control group was greater than the difference between duplicate animals in the irradiated groups, but, expressed as per cent of the means, the "mean deviations" were quite similar in all experiments. For thymus, spleen, and small intestine the over-all averages for the "mean deviations" were 11, 10, and 6%, respectively.

DNA. Whether the observed changes in incorporation can be interpreted as evidence for similar changes in DNA synthesis will now be discussed.

From our data on control animals it appears that the incorporation of thymidine into DNA is not a measure of the absolute rate of DNA synthesis. This becomes evident when we compare our values for incorporation into the various tissues with results obtained with other precursors. In particular, it has been found that thymus, in rats as well as in rabbits, is one of the most active organs with respect to incorporation of radioactive phosphate (*18*, *23*, *24*), whereas our data (Fig. 1) show that thymus incorporates thymidine relatively poorly in comparison to spleen and small intestine. Since all three tissues are known to have high rates of cell division, and hence a high rate of DNA synthesis, it is surprising to find that incorporation of radioactive thymidine in the thymus is only slightly greater than in the liver, which has a relatively low mitotic activity.

There are several possible reasons for this apparent lack of proportionality between incorporation of thymidine and DNA synthesis. Differences in permeability to thymidine might be a factor. Preliminary studies (unpublished observations) indicate, however, that the magnitude of such differences is too small to account for the present observations. A more likely explanation, we feel, is that the discrepancy among the various tissues is due mainly to differences in pool size for one or more of the intermediates between the injected precursor and DNA. This hypothesis is supported by the difference in response of the three tissues to changes in the "carrier level" or the size of the precursor dose in terms of micromoles of thymidine. Thus, varying the "carrier level" from 1 to 50 μM had little or no effect on the efficiency of the incorporation of thymidine into DNA of thymus. This is to be expected if there is a great dilution of precursor, or a large intermediate "pool," at some point in the reaction chain. Spleen and intestine, on the other hand, exhibited great dependence on the "carrier level," with a three- to sixfold increase in efficiency of incorporation when the dose was reduced from 50 to 1 μM of thymidine. This indicates the presence of a smaller "pool" and hence a lesser dilution of the precursor.

Further support for our conclusions on the relative "pool" sizes has been provided by Rotherham and Schneider (*25*), who reported that, in the rat, the concentration of acid-soluble deoxynucleoside derivatives is far greater in the thymus than in any other tissue analyzed, including the spleen.

Inhibition of incorporation by X-radiation has been observed with all precursors of DNA so far tested. In one instance the simultaneous inhibition of the incorporation of orotic acid and of the net synthesis of DNA has been recorded (*26*). This supports the view that in the irradiated animals we are dealing with a general inhibition of DNA synthesis, rather than with a specific inhibition of the metabolism of thymidine. Although the incorporation of thymidine into DNA was not found to provide a valid basis for comparing the rates of DNA synthesis among different tissues, we feel justified in assuming that the variations in incorporation are at least a semiquantitative measure of the variations in DNA synthesis, so long as we restrict the comparison to data obtained for a single tissue.

Evaluation of results. The interpretation of data on the labeling of DNA is complicated by the fact that few tissues consist of a single population of cells. When an organ contains cell populations of different mitotic activities, the specific activity of the isolated DNA will depend on the relative abundance of the different cell types and on their mitotic activities. In measuring the effect of irradiation on the organ we obtain the summation value for the effect on the various cell types. Also, after irradiation we are often dealing with a changing cell population, owing to the loss of cells from the radiosensitive tissues, as has been emphasized by Kelly *et al.* (*19*). This loss of cells might affect the relative abundance of the various cell types as well as the total number of cells in the tissues.

The situation is somewhat simplified where one of the relatively abundant types of cell exhibits a greater rate of reproduction than the others, in which case the observed changes in incorporation will essentially reflect the changes in these normally more active cells. In the intestine, cells of the crypts of Lieberkühn show by far the greatest mitotic activity. For this reason our observations on the small intestine may likely reflect the effect of radiation on the DNA synthesis in the crypt cells. Since the results for thymus and spleen seem more difficult to interpret, the remainder of the discussion will mainly concern the intestine, although some of the conclusions may have general validity.

If one compares in Fig. 2 (small intestine) the time curves for the different doses at their minima, one observes a graded response to the increase in radiation dose. If, on the other hand, one were to compare the values for the 23- to 24-hour period, without the knowledge of the other points on the curve, one might erroneously conclude that doses up to 200 r have no effect on the synthesis of DNA in the small intestine. This points out a potential pitfall in evaluating the radiosensitivity of a tissue from observations at a single time after irradiation, in the absence of an extensive knowledge of the time course for the particular response studied.

It is perhaps significant that the minimum activity in intestine is reached at the same time postirradiation for all dose levels tested. From their studies on the effect of X-rays on various mouse tissues, Knowlton and co-workers (*27*, *28*) have concluded that the time from the irradiation to the minimum for the mitotic index is a measure of the duration of mitosis. In analogy to this, the time from irradiation to the minimum for the incorporation of thymidine into DNA might indicate the duration of the DNA synthesis in the individual cells. For this discussion we shall assume that, after moderate doses of X-rays, cells which are already synthesizing DNA will carry the process to completion (*29–33*). The initial decrease in labeling can then be explained as a reduction in the number of cells entering the period of DNA synthesis. In part this might be due to a delay in the initiation of synthesis (*29*, *30*, *33*), and in part it might be due to irreversible inhibition and general cell death. It is to be expected that cell death will become more prominent at the higher dose levels, which might explain the less regular shapes of the curves for 400 and 800 r.

The minimum at 8 hours would mean that the duration of DNA synthesis in the more active cells of the small intestine is somewhat longer than 8 hours, and that the sensitive period, prior to synthesis, is somewhat shorter than 8 hours. The resumption of DNA synthesis is likely caused by cells that were not inhibited and would normally have entered DNA synthesis at this time, and by the recovery of cells that were originally delayed by the irradiation. The summation of synthesis in these two groups of cells would explain the "overshoot" in specific activity seen at 24 hours (Fig. 2).

In analogy to the above, the DNA synthesis in spleen and thymus cells might last approximately 8 and 4 hours, respectively. In these organs, cell death is much more pronounced. The sensitive period of the block must also be longer, since there is no evidence of recovery within the 24-hour period studied.

Although the work of Knowlton *et al.*, referred to earlier, was carried out with mice, a comparison of some of their data with ours may be justified, since the intermitotic times of cells in the intestinal epithelium of mice and rats have been found to be similar (*28*, *34*). According to Knowlton and Hempelmann (*27*), a dose of 325 r of total-body irradiation caused an immediate fall of the mitotic counts in the crypts of Lieberkühn of the jejunum. The number of mitoses reached a minimum in less than 2 hours, returned to an approximately normal value at 6 hours, and showed a second minimum at 20 to 24 hours. The initial drop in mitotic activity has also been recorded for rat intestine (*34*). Since DNA synthesis and mitosis do not occur simultaneously in any one cell, the immediate fall in both mitotic activity and DNA synthesis in various tissues suggests that the two processes are inhibited independently. This does not preclude that the inhibition in both cases may be due to a common block in the metabolism of the cell. The temporary return to normal of the mitotic activity (*27*) would further indicate such independence. The second minimum in mitotic activity may, however, be a result of the failure of DNA synthesis, since the replication of DNA is a necessary prerequisite for mitotic division. The data so far available from mammalian cells indicate that DNA synthesis takes place during the later part of interphase (*31*, *35*). We would therefore expect that the failure in DNA synthesis would affect the mitotic index at an earlier time than inhibition of mitosis would affect DNA synthesis.

The independent inhibition of mitosis and DNA synthesis was first observed by Howard and Pelc in irradiated bean root meristems (*29*). Later data by Cater *et al.* (*31*) and by Kelly *et al.* (*32*) on regenerating rat livers, as well as by Kelly and co-workers on ascites tumor cells (*36*), are in support of this concept. The data referred to also suggest that the relative sensitivities of these two processes may vary with the material employed. It would seem, therefore, that studies on the effect of ionizing radiation on DNA synthesis and on mitosis would yield more information if carried out simultaneously in the same material.

SUMMARY

The effect of total-body X-irradiation on the DNA synthesis in thymus, spleen, and small intestine of the rat has been studied throughout the first 24 hours after exposure to doses ranging from 50 r to 800 r. The amounts of radioactivity, from thymidine-2-C^{14}, incorporated into DNA over 1-hour periods were used as a relative measure of synthesis.

A rapid and extensive decrease in the incorporation of radioactivity was observed in all three tissues after the highest doses, with a gradually decreasing effect with lowering of the dose. In thymus and spleen there was no indication of recovery within the 24-hour period, whereas in the intestine there was an increase in labeling after 8 hours at all dose levels.

The data obtained for the small intestine are compatible with the assumption that the decreased incorporation is, in part, caused by a delayed onset of DNA synthesis in some of the cells. This delay, at least at the earliest times after irradiation, is not the result of inhibition of mitosis.

ACKNOWLEDGMENTS

The assistance of Mrs. Jeanette McLaughlin and Mrs. Vina Buettner-Janusch in this work is gratefully acknowledged.

We are indebted to Dr. P. Gerhardt of the Department of Bacteriology for the lyophilized *Escherichia coli* B used in the preparation of the nucleoside phosphorylase.

RECEIVED: August 19, 1958

REFERENCES

1. H. VON EULER and G. HEVESY, Wirkung der Röntgenstrahlen auf den Umsatz der Nukleinsäure im Jensen-Sarkom. *Kgl. Danske Videnskab. Selskab. Biol. Medd.* **17,** No. 8, 3–38 (1942).
2. P. REICHARD and B. ESTBORN, Utilization of desoxyribosides in the synthesis of polynucleotides. *J. Biol. Chem.* **188,** 839–846 (1951).
3. M. FRIEDKIN, D. TILSON, and D. ROBERTS, *In vitro* studies of desoxyribonucleic acid synthesis with C^{14}-thymidine. *Federation Proc.* **13,** 214 (1954).
4. P. REICHARD, Utilization of deoxyuridine and 5-methyluridine for the biosynthesis of thymine by the rat. *Acta Chem. Scand.* **9,** 1275–1285 (1955).
5. E. H. ANDERSON, Growth requirements of virus-resistant mutants of *Escherichia coli* Strain B. *Proc. Natl. Acad. Sci. U. S.* **32,** 120–128 (1946).
6. P. M. NOSSAL, A mechanical cell disintegrator. *Australian J. Exptl. Biol.* **31,** 583–590 (1953).
7. M. FRIEDKIN and D. ROBERTS, The enzymatic synthesis of nucleosides. II. Thymidine and related pyrimidine nucleosides. *J. Biol. Chem.* **207,** 257–266 (1954).
8. W. C. SCHNEIDER, Phosphorus compounds in animal tissues. I. Extraction and estimation of desoxypentose nucleic acid and of pentose nucleic acid. *J. Biol. Chem.* **161,** 293–303 (1945).

9. Z. Dische, Some new color reactions of the thymonucleic acids and their application to their determination. *Microchemie* **8,** 4–20 (1930).

10. O. Nygaard and H. P. Rusch, Incorporation of radioactive phosphate into nucleic acids of regenerating rat liver. *Cancer Research* **15,** 240–245 (1955).

11. A. Marshak and H. J. Vogel, Microdetermination of purines and pyrimidines in biological material. *J. Biol. Chem.* **189,** 597–605 (1951).

12. G. R. Wyatt, The purine and pyrimidine composition of deoxypentose nucleic acids. *Biochem. J.* **48,** 584–590 (1951).

13. J. Schulman and M. Falkenheim, Review of conventions in radiotracer studies. *Nucleonics* **3,** No. 10, 13–23 (1948).

14. J. F. Thomson, W. W. Tourtelotte, and M. S. Carttar, Some observations on effect of gamma radiation on the biochemistry of the rat thymus. *Proc. Soc. Exptl. Biol. Med.* **80,** 268–272 (1952).

15. H. Harrington and P. S. Lavik, A study of the phosphorus composition and P^{32} incorporation in irradiated lymphatic tissue. *J. Cellular Comp. Physiol.* **46,** 503–515 (1955).

16. L. J. Cole and M. Ellis, Spleen desoxyribonucleic acid content as an index of recovery in X-radiated mice treated with spleen homogenate. *Cancer Research* **14,** 738–744 (1954).

17. H. Harrington and P. S. Lavik, The differential effect of X-irradiation on the incorporation of various precursors into rat thymus deoxyribonucleic acid. *Arch. Biochem. Biophys.* **54,** 6–14 (1955).

18. M. G. Ord and L. A. Stocken, The effects of X- and γ-radiation on nucleic acid metabolism in the rat *in vivo* and *in vitro*. *Biochem. J.* **63,** 3–8 (1956).

19. L. S. Kelly, J. D. Hirsch, G. Beach, and A. H. Payne, Post-irradiation time and dose-response studies on the incorporation of P^{32} into DNA of mouse tissues. *Radiation Research* **2,** 490–501 (1955).

20. E. L. Bennet, L. S. Kelly, and B. Kreuckel, Effect of X-irradiation upon the incorporation of adenine-4,6-C^{14} in mice. *Federation Proc.* **13,** 181 (1954).

21. G. Hevesy, Effect of X-rays on the incorporation of carbon-14 into desoxyribonucleic acid. *Nature* **163,** 869–870 (1949).

22. R. Abrams, Effect of X-rays on nucleic acid and protein synthesis. *Arch. Biochem.* **30,** 90–99 (1951).

23. E. Andreasen and J. Ottesen, Significance of the various lymphoid organs to the lymphocyte production in the albino rat. *Acta Pathol. Microbiol. Scand., Suppl.* **54,** 25–32 (1944).

24. R. M. S. Smellie, G. F. Humphrey, E. R. M. Kay, and J. N. Davidson, The incorporation of radioactive phosphorus into the nucleic acids of different rabbit tissues. *Biochem. J.* **60,** 177–185 (1955).

25. J. Rotherham and W. C. Schneider, Deoxyribosyl compounds in animal tissues. *J. Biol. Chem.* **232,** 853–858 (1958).

26. R. E. Beltz, J. van Lancker, and V. R. Potter, Nucleic acid metabolism in regenerating liver. IV. The effect of X-radiation of the whole body on nucleic acid synthesis *in vivo*. *Cancer Research* **17,** 688–697 (1957).

27. N. P. Knowlton and L. H. Hempelmann, The effect of X-rays on the mitotic activity of the adrenal gland, jejunum, lymph node and epidermis of the mouse. *J. Cellular Comp. Physiol.* **33,** 73–91 (1949).

28. N. P. Knowlton and W. R. Widner, The use of X-rays to determine the mitotic and intermitotic time of various mouse tissues. *Cancer Research* **10,** 59–63 (1950).

29. A. Howard and S. R. Pelc, Synthesis of desoxyribonucleic acid in normal and irradiated cells and its relation to chromosome breakage. *Heredity (Suppl.)* **6,** 261–273 (1953).

30. S. R. Pelc and A. Howard, Effect of various doses of X-rays on the number of cells synthesizing deoxyribonucleic acid. *Radiation Research* **3,** 135–142 (1955).
31. D. B. Cater, B. E. Holmes, and L. K. Mee, Cell division and nucleic acid synthesis in the regenerating liver of the rat. *Acta Radiol.* **46,** 655–667 (1956).
32. L. S. Kelly, J. D. Hirsch, G. Beach, and W. Palmer, The time function of P^{32} incorporation into DNA of regenerating liver; the effect of irradiation. *Cancer Research* **17,** 117–121 (1957).
33. L. G. Lajtha, R. Oliver, T. Kumatori, and F. Ellis, On the mechanism of radiation effect on DNA synthesis. *Radiation Research* **8,** 1–16 (1958).
34. W. R. Widner, J. B. Storer, and C. C. Lushbaugh, The use of X-ray and nitrogen mustard to determine the mitotic and intermitotic times in normal and malignant rat tissues. *Cancer Research* **11,** 877–884 (1951).
35. L. G. Lajtha, R. Oliver, and F. Ellis, Incorporation of P^{32} and adenine C^{14} into DNA by human bone marrow cells *in vitro*. *Brit. J. Cancer* **8,** 367–379 (1954).
36. L. S. Kelly, J. D. Hirsch, G. Beach, and N. L. Petrakis, DNA synthesis and incorporation of P^{32} in irradiated Ehrlich ascites cells. *Proc. Soc. Exptl. Biol. Med.* **94,** 83–86 (1957).

RADIATION RESEARCH **10**, 477–489 (1959)

Some Kinetics of the Indirect Effect of Ionizing Radiation on Aqueous Solutions[1]

F. HUTCHINSON AND D. A. ROSS[2, 3]

Biophysics Department, Gibbs Research Laboratories, Yale University, New Haven, Connecticut

INTRODUCTION

The inactivation with ionizing radiation of many dilute solutions appears to obey first-order kinetics, indicating that the products of a reaction between a radical and a solute molecule have essentially the same affinity for radicals as the original molecule. Some simple relations between experimental observables will be derived for such systems, using the concepts of ordinary chemical kinetics, and experimental evidence will be presented to confirm the theory.

THEORY

The following symbols will be used in discussing the action of ionizing radiation in dilute aqueous systems:

N_s = concentration of the *s*th type of solute.
X_j = concentration of the *j*th type of radiation-produced radical.
D = dose delivered in units of 100 ev per unit volume.
$G(j)$ = yield of the *j*th radical species per unit dose.
$G_j(s)$ = number of solute molecules per unit volume of type *s* inactivated per unit dose by radicals of type *j* under conditions where all the *j* radicals react with the solute *s*, i.e., the yield due to *j*-type radicals when N_s is large.
k_{js} = rate at which molecules of type *s* react with radicals of type *j* at unit concentration of each.

[1] This study was supported by funds provided under contract AF 41(657)-124 with the School of Aviation Medicine, USAF, Randolph Air Force Base, Texas.

[2] This work is part of a dissertation presented by D. A. Ross for the degree of Doctor of Philosophy in Yale University, 1957.

[3] Present address: David Sarnoff Research Center, R.C.A., Princeton, New Jersey.

If $(N_s)_a$ is the concentration of molecules of type s which are still active, i.e., have not lost some assayable property,

$$-\frac{d(N_s)_a}{dt} = \sum_j k_{sj}\,(N_s)_a\,X_j\,\frac{G_j(s)}{G(j)} \tag{1}$$

where the ratio $G_j(s)/G(j)$ represents the fraction of radicals reacting with molecules s which inactivates them.

In the steady state the rate of production of radicals equals the rate at which they are removed by all solutes:

$$G(j)\,\frac{dD}{dt} = \sum_s k_{sj}\,N_s\,X_j$$

or (2)

$$X_j = \frac{G(j)}{\sum_s k_{sj}\,N_s}\,\frac{dD}{dt}$$

Substituting for X_j in equation 1 gives

$$-\frac{d(N_s)_a}{dt} = (N_s)_a\,\frac{dD}{dt}\sum_j\frac{k_{sj}\,G_j(s)}{\sum_s k_{sj}\,N_s} \tag{3}$$

which can be rewritten as

$$-\frac{d(N_s)_a}{dD} = (N_s)_a\sum_j\frac{k_{sj}\,G_j(s)}{\sum_s k_{sj}\,N_s} \tag{4}$$

From the definition of the 37% dose, D_{37},

$$(N_s)_a = N_s\,e^{-D/D_{37}}$$

or (5)

$$-\left.\frac{d(N_s)_a}{dD}\right|_{D=0} = \frac{N_s}{D_{37}}$$

Comparing equations 4 and 5 gives

$$\frac{1}{D_{37}(s)} = \sum_j\frac{k_{sj}\,G_j(s)}{\sum_s k_{sj}\,N_s} \tag{6}$$

where $D_{37}(s)$ represents the dose needed to inactivate s to 37%.

Because of the double summation in equation 6 it is difficult to arrange it in a form in which the parameters can be readily obtained from experimental data. If one of the radicals predominates, or if the several radicals can be replaced by an "average," the summation over j can be omitted. By inverting,

$$D_{37}(t) = \frac{N_t}{G(t)} + \frac{1}{G(t)} \sum_{s \neq t} \frac{k_s}{k_t} N_s \qquad (7)$$

Thus equation 7 predicts that a plot of the 37% dose versus solute concentration is a straight line with a positive intercept. This intercept is a measure of the scavenging effect of other materials in the solution on the radicals, and the slope of the line is the reciprocal of the yield, $G(s)$, for the inactivation of solute N_s.

L. Augenstine (private communication) has devised a similar treatment, in which equation 7 is divided by N_t, and D_{37}/N_t is plotted as a function of $1/N_t$. In this plot, the intercept measures the maximum yield, and the slope measures the radical scavengers present in the solution.

It should be noted that it is possible to include the scavenging effect of the radical-radical reactions in this equation by suitable definition of the solutes N_s. The absence, however, of a dose rate effect at rates as high as 10^6 r/sec (*1*) indicates that radical-radical reactions are not important at ordinary dose rates.

Equation 7 implicitly assumes that, once a radical has reacted with one of the solutes, no further reaction of the organic radicals thus formed will alter the activity of the solute N_s whose activity is assayed. Such interactions have been shown with other systems (*2*).

The second term on the right-hand side of equation 7 indicates that the addition of a second solute, N_2, will displace the curve of $D_{37}(t)$ versus N_t by a constant amount equal to $k_2N_2/k_tG_j(t)$. There is thus an experimental method available to measure the relative rate constants, k_s/k_2, for the radical which predominates in the inactivation of s. The significance of this ratio can be better comprehended if the rate constant k_{sj} is first evaluated in terms of more easily visualized parameters.

Wisjman (*3*) has shown that the probability, P, of a radical, j, reacting with a solute molecule, s, when they are initially separated by a distance r_1 in a medium which absorbs radicals at a rate $a_j = \sum_t k_{jt}N_t$ per unit volume per unit time is given by

$$P = q_{js} \frac{r_{js}}{r_1} \exp - \left(\frac{r_1 - r_{js}}{\rho_j} \right) \qquad (8)$$

where $r_{js} = r_j + r_s =$ collision radius of the radical j and molecule s.

$$\rho_j = \sqrt{\frac{d_{js}}{a_j}}.$$

$d_{js} = d_j + d_s =$ sum of the diffusion coefficients of the radical j and molecule s, respectively.

Physically ρ_j is the distance at which the probability of reaction of a radical with solute s has been decreased by absorption by the medium of the radicals to 37% of what the rate would be in the absence of absorption. The subscript j indicates that ρ_j depends almost entirely on the radical diffusion coefficient, which is usually much greater than that of the solute molecules.

The factor q_{js} has been evaluated (*3–5*) and may be written in the alternative forms:

$$q_{js} = \frac{1}{1 + k_d/k_c} = \frac{1}{1 + \epsilon \dfrac{l_j}{r_{js}} \dfrac{(1 + r_{js}/\rho_j)}{p_{js}}} \tag{9}$$

where k_d = the rate constant for encounters between molecule and radical, the diffusion-limited rate constant.

k_c = the rate constant for chemical reactions between the radicals at the surface of the molecule and the molecule.

l_j = the mean "jump" distance of the radical in diffusion through the liquid.

p_{js} = the probability of reaction between j and s on an encounter.

ϵ = a number of order of magnitude unity whose exact value depends on the detailed model of the liquid.

If k_c (or p_{js}) is large, q_{js} approaches unity. When k_c (or p_{js}) is small, q_{js} also becomes small.

The rate at which j and s react is then

$$N_s G(s) \frac{dD}{dt} \int_{r_{js}}^{\infty} q_{js} 4\pi r_1^2 dr_1 \frac{r_{js}}{r_1} \exp - \left(\frac{r_1 - r_{js}}{\rho_j}\right)$$
$$= N_s G(s) \frac{dD}{dt} q_{js} 4\pi r_{js} \rho_j^2 (1 + r_{js}/\rho_j) = k_{sj} N_s X_j \tag{10}$$

Substituting the value of X_j from equation 2 and ρ_j from equation 8 gives

$$k_{sj} = 4\pi r_{js} d_{js} q_{js} (1 + r_{js}/\rho_j) \tag{11}$$

Equation 11 is valid only in dilute solutions, since in the integration of equation 10 it is assumed that the presence of solute molecules does not interfere with the generation of free radicals from the solvent. For this case $\rho_j \gg r_{js}$, and

$$k_{sj} = 4\pi j_{js} d_{js} q_{js} \tag{11a}$$

By applying equation 11a to equation 7 it can be seen that, if an increase in dose, $\Delta D_{37}(s)$, is caused by the addition of an additive, N_2,

$$\Delta D_{37}(s) = \frac{k_2}{k_s} \frac{N_2}{G(s)} = \frac{r_{j2}}{r_{js}} \frac{N_2}{G(s)} \frac{q_z}{q_s} \tag{12}$$

TABLE I

G VALUES FOR THE INACTIVATION OF ORGANIC MOLECULES IN DILUTE AQUEOUS SOLUTION

Solute	*Molecular weight*	r_{js} (*A*)	*G* (*molecules/100 ev*)
Methylene blue	374	6.2	0.9
Thiourea	76	4.2	—
Sulfanilamide	172	5.15	1.9
Coenzyme A	767	7.6	2.8
Ribonuclease	13,000		0.48

This assumes that the molecular diffusion coefficients, d_s, are so much smaller than the radical diffusion coefficients that they can be ignored, eliminating the diffusion term. Thus from experimental data it is possible to calculate relative values of q.

EXPERIMENTAL DATA

To verify the linearity of the N_s versus D_{37} curves of equation 7, a number of organic and biological materials were irradiated in dilute solutions. An 1100-curie cobalt-60 source was used for the radiation source. Dose calibration was carried out with ferrous sulfate solutions as described by Weiss *et al.* (*6*).

All solutions were made up with triply distilled water except where noted. Ordinary distilled water was passed through a de-ionizer and then distilled from acid and basic permanganate solutions in a quartz still and stored in Vycor containers until ready for use. The sample solutions were irradiated in 1-ml glass-stoppered volumetric flasks which were thoroughly soaked and rinsed before being filled with the sample solution. Multiple runs were made with each solution, and the assay method was carefully calibrated prior to use.

For purposes of calculation the solute molecule was assumed to have a density of 1.3 and to have a spherical shape. The radius, r_{js}, was determined by using this density and the molecular weight and assuming that the radical radius was 1.5 A. The values of r_{js} are given in Table I.

Methylene Blue

Methylene blue was used as a solute because it has been studied extensively and is easy to assay. It is probably affected only by the OH radical in aerated solutions (*2*, *7*), and its chemical structure is well known. Radiation causes a color change which was measured at 630 mμ on a Beckman Model DU spectrophotometer.

To ensure that first-order kinetics could be used, survival curves were taken at a number of different concentrations. In all cases these were exponential, indicating that the reaction was monomolecular. Figure 1 shows several such curves for aerated solutions.

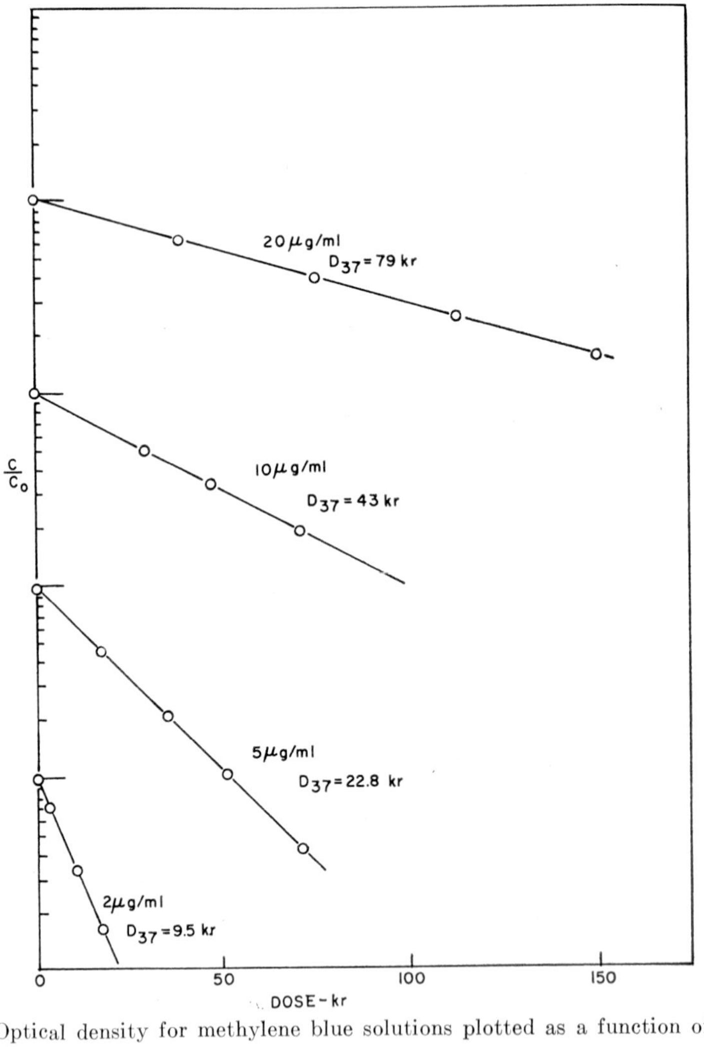

FIG. 1. Optical density for methylene blue solutions plotted as a function of dose from cobalt-60 γ-rays.

The bottom curve in Fig. 2 shows the straight line which results when the measured D_{37} dose is plotted against dye concentration. The small intercept on the dose axis indicates that the impurities in the water have been reduced to a very low level. By extrapolating the line to negative concentration values, it can be determined that in radical-trapping ability the impurities are equivalent to about 1 μg/ml of dye. The ionic yield is given by the slope of the line, or $G = 0.9$ molecule inactivated per 100 ev absorbed.

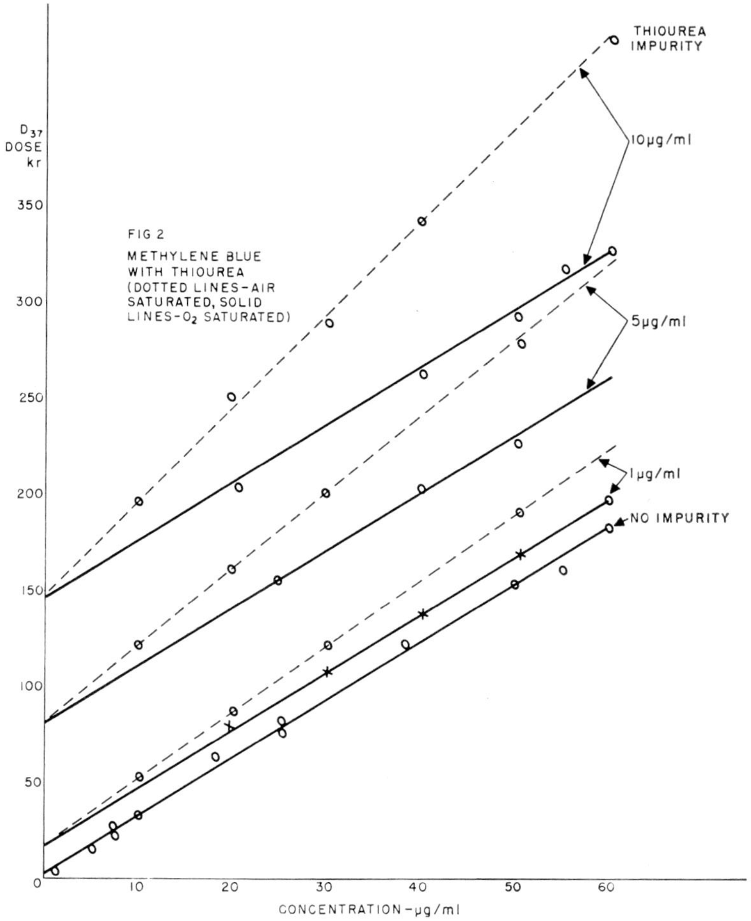

FIG. 2. The D_{37} dose for methylene blue plotted as a function of concentration, with different amounts of thiourea added.

To investigate the effect of additives as described in equations 7 and 12, measured amounts of thiourea were added to the methylene blue solution prior to irradiation. Tests were run to look for interaction between the thiourea and the dye, and all were negative. The results are shown in Fig. 2. It should be noted that the slopes changed for the higher concentrations of thiourea when the solutions were air-saturated, as shown by the dotted curves. When oxygen was bubbled through the solutions prior to irradiation, however, the slopes of the curves became the same, indicating that on the average the same number of radicals are still needed to inactivate.

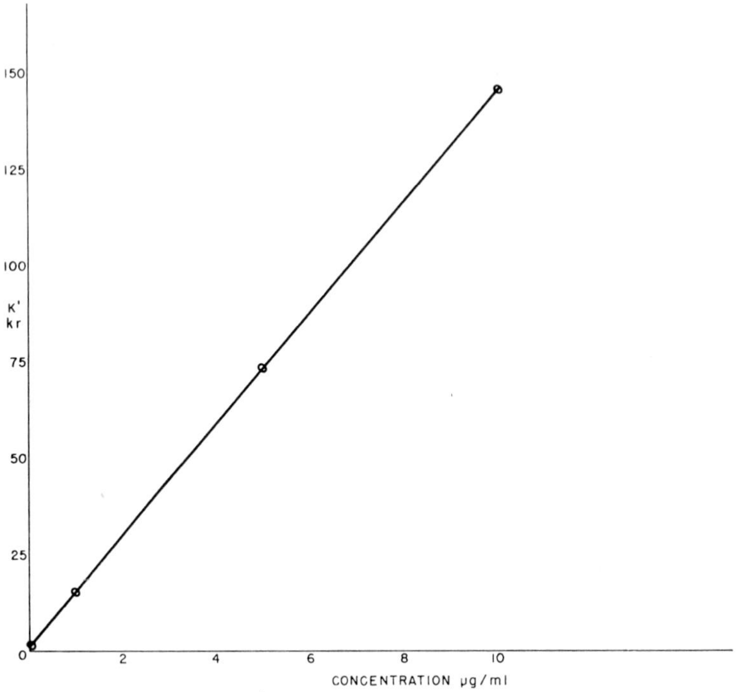

FIG. 3. The intercept on the dose axis, K', of the curves of D_{37} versus methylene blue concentration, plotted against concentration of added thiourea.

The effect of the additive was linear with added weight and independent of solute concentration. This is shown in Fig. 3, which is a plot of the intercept at zero solute concentration. Within experimental error this is a straight line whose slope indicates that the energy absorbed per thiourea molecule was 107 ev.

The possibility of the radiation-produced molecular products H_2 and H_2O_2 becoming radical-trapping centers was considered. Saturating solutions of methylene blue with hydrogen gas did not change results. Solutions were made up with hydrogen peroxide concentrations to 10^{-3} M. On standing, no effect was noticed over periods many times as long as that required to carry out an irradiation experiment. When the dye was irradiated in the hydrogen peroxide solution, the results were as shown by the dotted curve in Fig. 4. Possibly the hydrogen peroxide is dissociated by the radiation to form a high concentration of OH radicals, increasing the yield initially as indicated by the lower slope at low concentrations. The significant point is the relatively small change introduced by the relatively large increase in peroxide concentration.

A further experiment using coenzyme A as an impurity gave similar curves to Fig. 4, with CoA absorbing 130 ev per molecule.

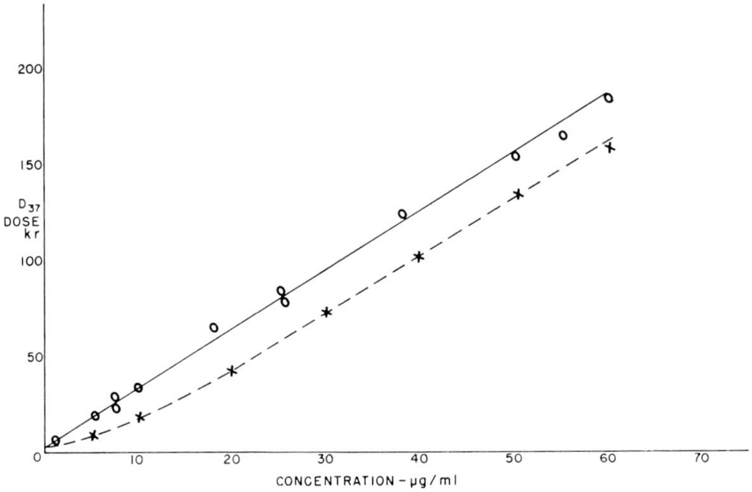

FIG. 4. Plot of D_{37} dose versus methylene blue concentration in water (solid curve) and in 10^{-3} M hydrogen peroxide (dashed curve).

Sulfanilamide

Sulfanilamide was used as a solute because of its sensitivity to radiation and its use in part of the assay for coenzyme A, which was selected as a biological solute. It has a molecular weight of 172 and is easily assayed by adding sodium nitrite and ammonium sulfamate to the solution and developing with a 1% solution of NED (1-naphthylethylene dihydrochloride). The purple color produced is read at 545 mμ in a Coleman spectrophotometer (*8*). Calibration runs were made to ensure that the solution obeyed Beer's law and that the radiation reaction was first-order.

Figure 5 shows the results for aerated solutions at a number of concentrations. The slope of the curves give the yield as 1.9 molecules per 100 ev. Thiourea was added after making sure it did not interact with the solute. The energy absorbed by the thiourea was obtained by measuring the distance between the parallel curves. It is 62 ev per molecule.

A run was also made with coenzyme A as an added impurity. The assay was not affected by the presence of the impurity and gave an energy absorption of 71 ev per molecule of coenzyme A.

Coenzyme A

Co-enzyme A was used as a biological solute. Its chemical formula is completely known, and it has a molecular weight of 767 (*9*). Radiation studies were carried

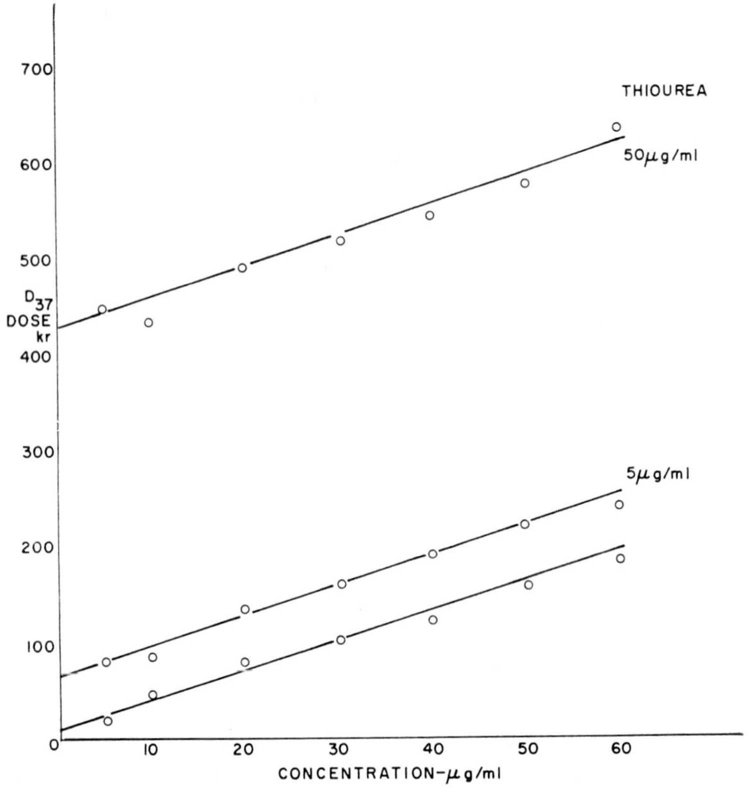

FIG. 5. The D_{37} dose for sulfanilamide plotted as a function of concentration, with different amounts of thiourea added. The bottom curve is with no added thiourea.

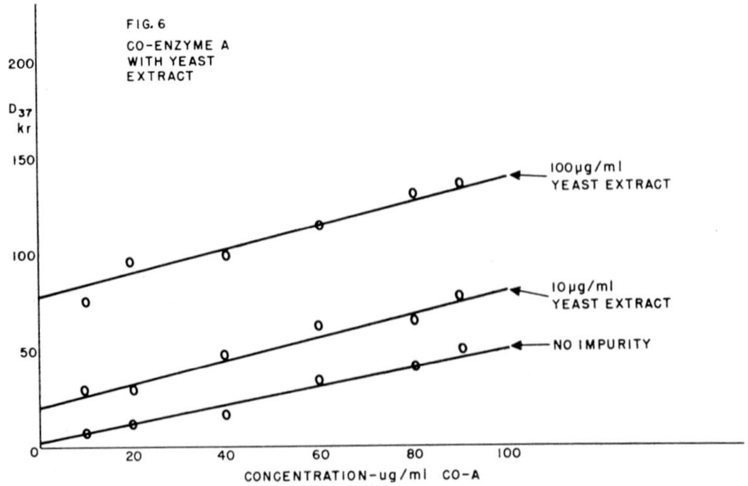

FIG. 6. The D_{37} dose for coenzyme A plotted against concentration with varying amounts of yeast extract (Difco) added.

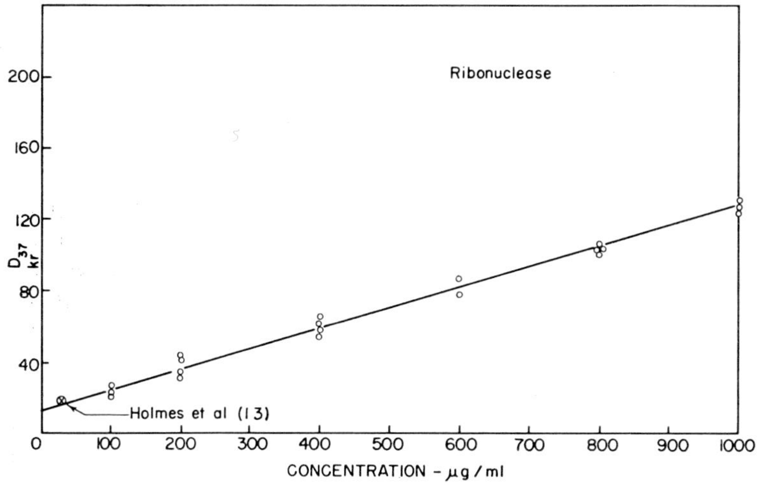

FIG. 7. The D_{37} dose for ribonuclease plotted as a function of concentration.

out in aerated aqueous solutions made up with triply distilled water. The active enzyme concentration was determined by measuring the free sulfanilamide not acetylated by an enzyme system from pigeon liver operating with CoA, as described by Kaplan and Lipmann (*10*). Calibration curves were determined and checks made to ensure that the solute obeyed first-order kinetics.

Runs were made in the pure state and with yeast extract as an additive. The results are shown in Fig. 6. From the slope of the curve without impurity the yield is 2.8 molecules per 100 ev. The interpretation of the data obtained with the yeast extract is not simple, but it shows that the D_{37} dose is a linear function of solute concentration in the presence of a complex substance of biological origin. It can be noted that the increase in dose is not linear with increased additive.

Ribonuclease

Ribonuclease is an enzyme with a molecular weight of 13,000; it is stable in aqueous solutions for long periods of time. Irradiation was carried out at concentrations from 100 to 1000 μg/ml at room temperature. The method of assay was that described by Kunitz (*11*). It measures by optical absorption at 260 mμ the depolymerized ribonucleic acid which cannot be precipitated by trichloroacetic acid after the nucleic acid has been treated by the enzyme. The yield obtained from the slope of the D_{37} versus N curve shown in Fig. 7 was 0.48 molecule per 100 ev. This is much higher than that reported by Holmes *et al.* (*12*). This is believed to be due to the impurities in their solutions, the effects of which were eliminated in these experiments by the method of analysis.

DISCUSSION

From the material presented it is clear that the experimental data confirm the predicted linear relationship between solute concentration and 37% dose. This being so, using the slope of the line to determine ionic yields is an efficient way to extract the most information about the ionic yield from all the data available. The yield data in this paper is summarized in Table I.

It might be asked whether the existence of such a linear relationship is evidence that only one radical is effective. To answer this it is necessary to go back to equation 6. Unfortunately, no good method of handling this rather awkward equation, with its double summations, has been found. By a rather complicated study of this equation for various assumed values of the parameters, however, it has been found that with two or three radicals there are wide ranges of G values and relative rate constants for which the deviations of a N_s–D_{37} plot from linearity will be surprizingly difficult to recognize. Therefore, we must conclude that, although a visible break in such a curve is clear evidence of more than one radical, the existence of a linear relation, even over a wide range of concentration, is not necessarily evidence for only one effective radical.

From the change in D_{37} doses with the concentration of additives, the relative q's of the additive and of the substance assayed may be calculated by use of equation 12. In Table II are summarized the increase in D_{37} caused by adding another substance, the ratio expressed in electron volts per molecule, and the ratio of the q values calculated from these data. It should be noticed that these values are consistent within themselves—that is, from the first three sets of data,

$$\frac{q_{\text{CoA}}}{q_{\text{sulfa}}} = \frac{q_{\text{CoA}}}{q_{MB}} \times \frac{q_{\text{MB}}}{q_{\text{thio}}} \times \frac{q_{\text{thio}}}{q_{\text{sulfa}}}$$

$$= 0.91 \times \frac{1}{1.41} \times 1.44 = 0.92$$

which happens to be exactly the measured value, although the accuracy of the individual numbers would be consistent with agreement to within 20%.

The most striking point is the nearness of these ratios to unity. In ordinary chemical reactions the ratios of these numbers are given by a term $e^{-\Delta E/kT}$, where

TABLE II

RELATIVE REACTIVITIES OF SEVERAL ORGANIC MOLECULES FOR WATER RADICALS

Solute assayed	*Additive*	D/N_2 (*ev/molecule*)	$\frac{q_{additive}}{q_{solute}}$
Methylene blue	Thiourea	107	1.41
	CoA	129	0.91
Sulfanilamide	Thiourea	62	1.44
	CoA	71	0.92

ΔE is the difference of the activation energies. The ratios can thus range over many orders of magnitude. The present ratios cannot be said to be different from unity, both because of experimental errors and because of various uncertainties in the calculations, a major one being the assumed values of the collision radii, r_{js}. The nearness to unity is somewhat indicative of a reaction's taking place on every encounter between a radical and a molecule, but it is by no means a proof of this.

SUMMARY

The relationship between solute concentration and the dose to inactivate to 37% of the solute activity in dilute aqueous solutions is shown experimentally to be a straight line for four organic solutes. The linear relationship is confirmed by an analysis, and the slope is shown to be the reciprocal of the ionic yield of the solute. From experiments in which solutes are irradiated with various additives present in solution, the ratio of the reactivity for radicals of the additive to that of the solute can be determined. These ratios are shown in four cases to be unity within experimental error.

ACKNOWLEDGMENTS

The authors wish to thank Miss Jane Rusk for her invaluable technical assistance in carrying out the experiments reported in this paper. They also wish to thank various members of the Biophysics Department for help and discussion.

RECEIVED: September 15, 1958

REFERENCES

1. D. A. ROSS and F. HUTCHINSON, Lower limit to the rate with which OH radicals react with methylene blue. *J. Chem. Phys.* **28,** 745 (1958).
2. M. J. DAY and G. STEIN, Action of ionizing radiation on aqueous solutions of methylene blue. *Radiation Research* **6,** 666–679 (1957).
3. R. A. WISJMAN, Probability that two diffusing molecules will collide. *Bull. Math. Biophys.* **14,** 327–383 (1955).
4. F. HUTCHINSON, The distance that a radical formed by ionizing radiation can diffuse in a yeast cell. *Radiation Research* **7,** 473–483 (1957).
5. F. C. COLLINS and G. E. KIMBALL, Diffusion controlled reaction rates. *J. Colloid Sci.* **4,** 425–437 (1949).
6. J. WEISS, A. O. ALLEN, and H. A. SCHWARZ, Use of the Fricke ferrous sulfate dosimeter for gamma ray doses in the range 4 to 40 kr. *Proc. 1st Intern. Conf. Peaceful Uses Atomic Energy, Geneva, 1955* **14,** 179–181 (1956).
7. E. HAYON, G. SCHOLES, and J. WEISS, Chemical action of ionizing radiation in solution: Part XIX. Some aspects of the reduction of methylene blue by X-rays in aqueous solutions. *J. Chem. Soc.* **1957,** 301–311.
8. A. C. BRATTON and E. K. MARSHALL, A new coupling component for sulfanilamide determination. *J. Biol. Chem.* **128,** 537–550 (1939).
9. J. BADDILEY, The structure of coenzyme A. *Advances in Enzymol.* **16,** 1–21 (1955).
10. N. O. KAPLAN and F. LIPMANN, The assay and distribution of coenzyme A. *J. Biol. Chem.* **174,** 37–44 (1948).
11. M. KUNITZ, A spectrophotometric method for the measurement of ribonuclease activity *J. Biol. Chem.* **164,** 563–568 (1946).
12. B. HOLMES, E. COLLINSON, and F. DAINTON, Inactivation of ribonuclease in dilute aqueous solutions. *Nature* **165,** 266–269 (1950).

RADIATION RESEARCH **10**, 490–497 (1959)

Reduction of Mutation by Postirradiation Treatment after Ultraviolet and Various Kinds of Ionizing Radiations

R. F. KIMBALL, NENITA GAITHER, AND STELLA M. WILSON

Biology Division, Oak Ridge National Laboratory[1], Oak Ridge, Tennessee

INTRODUCTION

It is now well established that mutational processes can be modified by treatment after the irradiation that initiated them. A review of this problem has been given by Hollaender and Kimball (*1*). Other references and more recent investigations are found in papers by Kimball *et al.* (*2*), Witkin (*3*), and Ehrenberg and Lundquist (*4*). The results are not yet ready for organization into a comprehensive and orderly picture, but the indications are that all three main processes in radiation damage to chromosomes—breakage, reunion, and gene mutation—can be modified by one or another postirradiation treatment.

In the specific case of *Paramecium aurelia*, Kimball *et al.* (*2*) have shown that posttreatment with streptomycin decreases the frequency of X-ray-induced lethal and deleterious mutations. The effect is on the mutational process itself and is not an artifact of an effect of the treatment on selection or detection of mutations. The hypothesis was advanced (*2, 5*) that streptomycin and similar agents act by slowing growth and division to allow more time for spontaneous recovery from the initial radiation damage before the mutations are irrevocably established. The work of Doudney and Haas (*6*) and Witkin (*3*) suggests a similar time limit for the mutational process, though some other features of their hypotheses are different.

Most posttreatments have been used with only one kind of radiation or have been of very different effectiveness after different kinds of radiation. We were therefore somewhat surprised to find that the number of lethal and deleterious mutations in *Paramecium aurelia* was decreased by posttreatment with streptomycin not only after X-irradiation, as previously reported by Kimball and associates (*2, 5*), but also after exposure to ultraviolet light and α-particles. Thus it would seem that this particular posttreatment acts on some process that is common to the mutational pathway initiated by any mutagenic radiation.

[1] Operated by Union Carbide Corporation for the U. S. Atomic Energy Commission.

MATERIALS AND METHODS

As in previous work, individuals of *Paramecium aurelia*, variety 4, stock 51, were irradiated at about 1½ hours after division and either exposed immediately after irradiation to culture medium with streptomycin sulfate (Lilly) equivalent to 3 mg/ml of streptomycin base for 4 hours or kept in culture medium without the antibiotic. X-Irradiation was carried out as previously except that, in experiments involving gases, the paramecia were in small hanging drops over a Lucite chamber filled with either nitrogen (Linde, 99%) or a 20% oxygen–80% helium mixture.

The α-particle exposures were as follows. The source was a Pu^{239} disk, 1.12 cm in diameter, with a total emission of about 3×10^5 α-particles per second. It was mounted in a metal holder that could be positioned accurately in an exposure rack with the beam directed vertically downward. About 15 paramecia were placed in a small drop on a sheet of Mylar 0.79 mg cm^{-2} previously sealed with Vaseline over a 0.5-cm-diameter hole in a thicker piece of Mylar for mechanical support. Fluid was withdrawn from the drop with a capillary pipet until the paramecia were compressed as much as possible without injury by the surface film. The preparation was then sealed with Vaseline over a depression slide containing a small amount of water to reduce evaporation from the drop. The depression slide was pushed into a slot in the exposure rack so that the hanging drop was centered about 0.15 cm below the source. The animals were exposed for 10 minutes, and immediately after each exposure half of them were put into culture medium and the rest into streptomycin. Several exposures were made on different days to obtain adequate numbers.

A rough estimate of the dose was made as follows. The compressed animals probably ranged in thickness from 20 to 30 μ. The plutonium α-particles, having an energy of 5.15 Mev, penetrated about 25 μ into the animals after passing through 0.15 cm of air and the Mylar film. The α-particle flux reaching the animals was estimated to be 1.1×10^5 α-particles sec^{-1} cm^{-2} when the geometry of the arrangement was taken into account. The average dose rate was then estimated to be 2.8 rad sec^{-1} in 25-μ-thick animals when allowance was made for energy lost in air and Mylar. A more accurate estimate of the dose did not seem warranted, since knowledge of the precise dose is not necessary for the experiment.

Ultraviolet irradiations were made with a 15-watt G. E. germicidal lamp. The animals were exposed in small drops in uncovered depression slides 39 cm from the lamp. Immediately after each exposure, half the animals were put into streptomycin and half into culture medium. All manipulations after irradiation were carried out in a darkened room with a low-intensity yellow light; the animals were kept in the dark until the next day. The dose rate was about 40 ergs mm^{-2} sec^{-1}, as measured with a photocell meter (7).

As in previous work, the irradiated paramecia were isolated and kept as daily isolation lines for several days. Autogamy was then induced, 25 autogamous animals

TABLE I

INFLUENCE OF STREPTOMYCIN POSTTREATMENT ON MUTATION BY X-RAYS AND ALPHA-PARTICLES

Radiation	*Gas*	*Posttreatment*	*Number of treated paramecia*	*Percentage frequency of exautogamous clones with good growth*
X-rays (4.5 kr)	20% O_2 and 80% He	None	60	21
		Streptomycin	60	32
	N_2	None	60	50
		Streptomycin	60	63
Alpha-particles	Air	None	120	51
		Streptomycin	120	63

were isolated from the descendants of each treated animal, and the percentage frequency of exautogamous clones with good growth was determined for each group of 25. This frequency is inversely related to the number of recessive lethal and deleterious mutations. For tests of significance, the percentage frequencies were transformed to a variable having nearly the same variance over most of the dose range. This transformation is given by the formula

$$y = \sin^{-1}\left(\frac{n-1}{n+3}\right) + \sin^{-1}\left[\frac{2p^{1/2}(n+1) - (n-1)}{n+3}\right] \qquad (1)$$

where p is the proportion of exautogamous clones with good growth and n is the number of exautogamous clones per treated animal, in this case 25.

RESULTS

The results of the α-particle experiments and of X-irradiation in nitrogen are summarized in Table I. There is no doubt that streptomycin is at least as effective after α-particle irradiation and after X-irradiation in nitrogen as it is after X-irradiation in air. The difference between the posttreated groups and those not posttreated is significant at the 1% level for α-particles and for X-rays in nitrogen, and at the 5% level for X-rays in 20% oxygen.

In preliminary experiments, a streptomycin effect was found with a low dose of ultraviolet but not with a high one. For comparison, we obtained dose curves for ultraviolet (Fig. 1) and for X-rays (Fig. 2). The means of the transformed data were plotted because standard errors were more readily available for the data in this form. Direct transformation of these means to percentage frequencies by the equation gives values that depart considerably from the arithmetic means of the original frequencies. The latter means are therefore given alongside the points to facilitate comparison with data in Table I and in earlier publications.

Figure 1 demonstrates beyond question that streptomycin decreases mutation

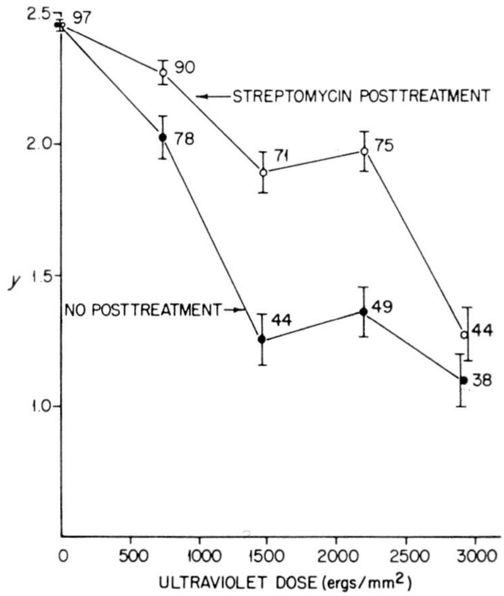

FIG. 1. The relation of dose of ultraviolet to a transformation (equation 1) of the frequency of normal exautogamous clones. Mean percentage frequencies are given alongside the points. Each point is a mean for 80 irradiated paramecia with 25 autogamous animals from each.

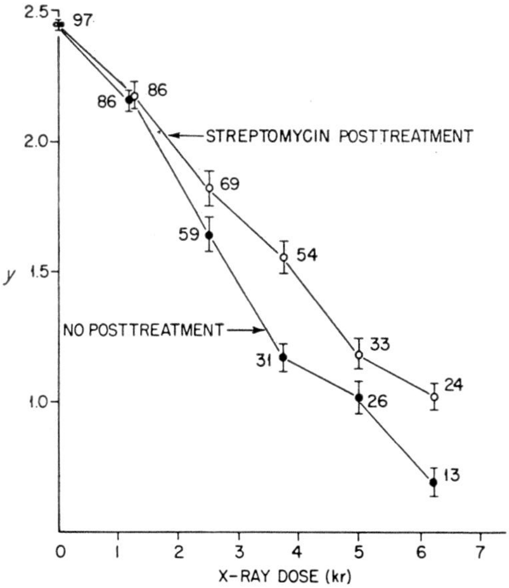

FIG. 2. Same as Fig. 1, except that X-rays were used instead of ultraviolet. Each point is a mean for 60 irradiated paramecia with 25 autogamous animals from each.

induced by ultraviolet, but the relation between dose and effect varies with radiation dose. The X-ray curves in Fig. 2 are obviously different. In the first place, the ultraviolet curves (Fig. 1) show a marked plateau at doses producing only a moderate amount of mutation; but the curves in Fig. 2 show little, if any, evidence of a plateau, though one may occur at still higher doses (*8*). In the second place, streptomycin is not equally effective at all doses of ultraviolet; but with X-rays it seems to act as a simple dose-reducing agent.

DISCUSSION

The differences between X-rays and ultraviolet in dose curves and in response to streptomycin require discussion. Kimball and co-workers (*2*, *5*) have proposed that streptomycin and similar agents decrease mutation by slowing growth and division, thereby allowing more time for spontaneous recovery from the lesions produced by radiation before mutations are irrevocably established. Ultraviolet has marked effects on growth and division in the dose range used, but X-rays do not. Ultraviolet may therefore act not only as a mutagen but, like streptomycin, to favor recovery, whereas X-rays may act more nearly as a simple mutagen. This interpretation is strongly supported by the observation that X-rays followed by ultraviolet resulted in somewhat less mutation than X-rays alone and considerably less than would have been expected from the addition of the mutations produced by the two radiations. The percentage frequencies of normal exautogamous clones were, for ultraviolet, 57 %; for X-rays, 18 %; and for the combined radiations, 28 %. With such a situation, the increased effect on growth at higher doses of ultraviolet might balance or even reverse the increased mutagenic effect. At still higher doses mutation might increase again if, for some reason, further effects on growth proved ineffective in decreasing mutation.

The possibility that some part of the postautogamous lethality after ultraviolet is the result of inherited cytoplasmic or macronuclear effects of undefined nature has been raised by Mitchison (*9*) and may complicate the situation, especially at higher doses. His data are, however, too limited to be at all conclusive; and a careful genetic analysis on a more extensive material, with various complicating factors taken into account, is still lacking. As a working hypothesis, the micronuclear mutation hypothesis still seems to us much the best, and we are further encouraged in this view by the basic similarity between our results with posttreatments and those with known mutations in bacteria (*3*, *6*). There seems little doubt that the postautogamous lethality after X-rays is indeed caused by micronuclear mutation (*10*), and this is substantiated by unpublished data which demonstrate that the streptomycin-sensitive portion of the X-ray effect is inherited in crosses in the way expected for micronuclear mutations.

There are several other indications that radiations, especially ultraviolet, have double or multiple actions on the mutational process. Thus it has been known for some time (*11*) that the dose curve for ultraviolet-induced mutation often reaches a maximum, and decreases again. A number of possible explanations have been suggested for this phenomenon. Muller (*12*) discusses the idea, among others, that ultraviolet can both produce and prevent mutation. Evidence that an ultraviolet pre- or posttreatment can decrease the frequncy of chromosome aberrations has been given by Swanson (*13*) and by Kaufmann and Hollaender (*14*), but Swanson (*15*) finds that ultraviolet plus X-rays gives more mutations than expected from their individual effects. A somewhat different concept of a double action of radiation has been suggested by Wolff and Luippold (*16*) for X-ray-induced chromosome aberrations. Now that it is becoming increasingly evident that the amount of mutation and chromosome aberration can be influenced by the physiological state of the cell after irradiation, it is obvious that the mutagenic effects of radiation cannot be considered apart from the physiological effects. The detectable mutation may usually result from opposing mutagenic and recovery actions of the radiation, with the relative importance of these two roles varying considerably with the kind of radiation and the type of cell.

The nearly identical effect of streptomycin after a variety of radiations, with the exceptions just noted, suggests that the reversible step in the mutational process demonstrated by this agent is not one of the initial events in the absorption of energy, such as the production of diffusible mutagens or of activated states in the molecules. Such events would be expected to be of very different relative importance with the different kinds of radiation. On the other hand, the number of kinds of relatively stable chemical changes that can be produced in the chromosomes is probably quite limited. Eventually, these chemical events must be responsible for the chromosome aberrations and gene mutations that are detected, but meanwhile the damage they represent is reparable.

This repair may be the relatively well-known process of restitutional reunion of broken chromosomes, but there are some grounds for skepticism about this being the repair process that is shown by our data. We (*2*) have given reasons for thinking that the mutations detected in *Paramecium* are primarily small changes, such as gene mutations or perhaps small deletions. Thus it is not impossible that we are investigating, primarily, gene mutations. Moreover, the *Paramecium* results have their closest parallels in studies on reversional mutations in bacteria (*3, 17*). This similarity is given added support by the finding of the streptomycin effect after ultraviolet, since Witkin's work was with this radiation. Finally, breakage and reunion phenomena are usually reported to be quite different for different radiations (*12, 18*). None of these considerations excludes the possibility that the phenomenon we are investigating in *Paramecium* is breakage followed by recovery through restitutional reunion. But they do make it necessary to consider seriously the possibility that gene mutation induced by any radiation involves a reversible step of appreciable duration.

SUMMARY

Postirradiation exposure to streptomycin reduces the amount of recessive lethal and deleterious mutation produced in *Paramecium aurelia* by X-rays in the absence of oxygen as well as in its presence, by α-particles, and by ultraviolet light. Thus the reversible step that is influenced by the posttreatment is common to the mutational processes initiated by all these radiations, making it probable that this step is more closely related to the structure and activities of the chromosomes than to the nature of the initial physical events in them. Certain pecularities of the ultraviolet dose curves lead to the suggestion that this radiation acts not only as a mutagen but also as a recovery agent through its effects on growth and division.

ACKNOWLEDGMENTS

We are indebted to Dr. J. S. Kirby-Smith for putting the α-particle source and exposure rack at our disposal, to Dr. M. L. Randolph for estimating the dose rate, and to both Dr. Kirby-Smith and Dr. Randolph for valuable discussions and advice. We are also indebted to Dr. A. W. Kimball of the Mathematics Panel of this Laboratory for developing the transformation for our data.

RECEIVED: May 22, 1958

REFERENCES

1. A. HOLLAENDER and R. F. KIMBALL, Modification of radiation-induced genetic damage. *Nature* **177,** 726–730 (1956).
2. R. F. KIMBALL, NENITA GAITHER, and STELLA M. WILSON, Postirradiation modification of mutagenesis in *Paramecium* by streptomycin. *Genetics* **42,** 661–669 (1957).
3. E. M. WITKIN, Time, temperature, and protein synthesis: A study of ultraviolet-induced mutation in bacteria. *Cold Spring Harbor Symposia Quant. Biol.* **21,** 123–140 (1956).
4. L. EHRENBERG and U. LUNDQUIST, Post-irradiation effects on X-ray-induced mutation in barley seeds. *Hereditas* **43,** 390–402 (1957).
5. R. F. KIMBALL, Modification of the genetic effects of X rays by treatment after irradiation. *Proc. Intern. Genet. Symposia, 1956, Tokyo and Kyoto* (*Cytologia,* suppl. vol.), pp. 252–255, Science Council of Japan, Tokyo, 1957.
6. C. O. DOUDNEY and F. L. HAAS, Modification of ultraviolet-induced mutation frequency and survival in bacteria by postirradiation treatment. *Proc. Natl. Acad. Sci. U. S.* **44,** 390–401 (1958).
7. R. LATARJET, P. MORENNE, and R. BERGER, Un appareil simple pour le dosage des rayonnements ultraviolets émis par les lampes germicides. *Ann. inst. Pasteur* **85,** 174–184 (1953).
8. E. L. POWERS and C. F. EHRET, Radiation effects on cells, genetics or physiology? *Proc. 1st Intern. Conf. Peaceful Uses Atomic Energy, Geneva, 1955,* **11,** 266–271 (1956).
9. N. A. MITCHISON, Evidence against micronuclear mutation as the sole basis for death at fertilization in aged, and in the progeny of ultraviolet irradiated *Paramecium aurelia. Genetics* **40,** 61–75 (1955).
10. R. F. KIMBALL, Inheritance of mutational changes induced by radiation in *Paramecium aurelia. Genetics* **34,** 412–424 (1949).
11. A. HOLLAENDER and C. W. EMMONS, Wavelength dependence of mutation production in

the ultraviolet, with special emphasis on fungi. *Cold Spring Harbor Symposia Quant. Biol.* **9,** 179–186 (1941).

12. H. J. Muller, The manner of production of mutations by radiation. In *Radiation Biology* (A. Hollaender, ed.), Vol. I, pp. 475–626, McGraw-Hill Book Co., New York, 1954.
13. C. P. Swanson, The effects of ultraviolet and X-ray treatment on the pollen tube chromosomes of *Tradescantia*. *Genetics* **27,** 491–503 (1942).
14. B. P. Kaufmann and A. Hollaender, Modification of the frequency of chromosomal rearrangements induced by X-rays in *Drosophila*. II. Use of near-ultraviolet radiation. *Genetics* **31,** 368–375 (1946).
15. C. P. Swanson, The effect of supplementary factors on the radiation-induced frequency of mutation in *Aspergillus terreus*. *J. Cellular Comp. Physiol.* **39,** *Suppl.* **1,** 27–38 (1952).
16. S. Wolff and H. E. Luippold, Metabolism and chromosome-break rejoining. *Science* **122,** 231–232 (1955).
17. A. Hollaender, D. Billen, and C. O. Doudney, The modification of X-ray-induced mutations in *Escherichia coli* by pre- and posttreatment. *Radiation Research* **3,** 235 (1955).
18. N. H. Giles, Radiation-induced chromosome aberrations in *Tradescantia*. In *Radiation Biology* (A. Hollaender, ed.), Vol. I, pp. 713–761, McGraw-Hill Book Co., New York, 1954.

RADIATION RESEARCH 10, 498 (1959)

ANNOUNCEMENT

THE SOCIETY OF NUCLEAR MEDICINE

750 North Michigan Avenue, Chicago 11, Illinois, Delaware 7-3511

Sixth Annual Meeting

The sixth annual meeting of The Society of Nuclear Medicine will be held at the Palmer House, Chicago, Illinois, Thursday, Friday, and Saturday—June 18–20, 1959.

Additional information may be obtained by writing to Samuel N. Turiel, Administrator, The Society of Nuclear Medicine, 750 North Michigan Avenue, Chicago 11, Illinois.

EMERY L. JAFFE, M.D.
President

RADIATION RESEARCH **10**, 499–506 (1959)

Hydrogen Iodide Production in Radiolysis of Organic Liquids Containing Dissolved Iodine: Cyclohexane, *n*-Hexane, Benzene[1]

GISUKE MESHITSUKA[2] AND MILTON BURTON[3]

Department of Chemistry, University of Notre Dame, Notre Dame, Indiana

1. INTRODUCTION

Efforts to find significant HI production in γ-ray radiolysis of cyclohexane containing dissolved iodine have been repeatedly unsuccessful; G(HI) has been found by various investigators to be < 0.5 (*1*), < 0.3 (B. Besancon, private communication), and "negligible" (*2*). Consequently, a view has developed that H atoms are clearly *not* produced in radiolysis of any organic liquids. Speculations regarding the mechanism of radiolysis, of methanol (*3*) for example, have been complicated by the necessity of inclusion of this view. On the other hand, studies by Dewhurst (*4*) on the radiolysis of liquid *n*-hexane almost certainly require the assumption that H-atom production is involved in one of the elementary decomposition processes. The studies reported herein were performed in order to establish conditions of observable HI production; they show that illusorily low values of G(HI) may result from reactions both during and after irradiation.

2. EXPERIMENTAL PROCEDURE

2.1 Materials

Cyclohexane (Eastman Kodak spectro grade) was used without further purification. *n*-Hexane (Phillips pure grade) was subjected successively to passage through a silica gel column, azeotropic distillation with methanol, extraction of methanol with water and finally passage through silica gel. Benzene (Merck ACS reagent grade) was recrystallized three times prior to use.

[1] Contribution from the Radiation Project operated by the University of Notre Dame, and supported in part under U. S. Atomic Energy Commission Contract AT(11-1)-38. This paper was presented at the International Congress of Radiation Research, Burlington, Vermont, August 11–15, 1958.

[2] Permanent address: Department of Chemistry, Faculty of Science, Osaka University, Osaka, Japan.

[3] To whom requests for reprints of this article should be addressed.

The 20-ml samples of the various substances in Pyrex vessels (ca. 60-ml capacity) were completely degassed in successive distillations prior to exposure in an underground source (*5*).

2.2. Irradiation and Dosimetry

Irradiation by Co^{60} γ-rays followed the techniques conventional in this laboratory except as otherwise noted. The dose rate for cyclohexane irradiation was 6.70 $\times$ 10^{20} ev liter^{-1} min^{-1}; for *n*-hexane 5.74 $\times$ 10^{20} ev liter^{-1} min^{-1}; and for benzene 7.65 $\times$ 10^{20} ev liter^{-1} min^{-1}. Dosage was determined by Fricke dosimeter technique (*6*) using the value $G(Fe^{+++})$ = 15.6 (*6–8*) with appropriate corrections for the electron densities.

In all the cases studied in this work, iodine was added to the liquid at known concentration before the radiolysis.

2.3. Determination of Hydrogen Iodide

Determination of hydrogen iodide resultant from radiolysis involved extraction into water and employment of pH or ultraviolet absorption techniques. In a typical set of runs, samples were cooled to liquid nitrogen temperature immediately after irradiation, distilled water was added to the solid samples, and the samples were melted while being shaken. The HI was completely removed by successive extraction with water (total 100 ml) in a separatory funnel. Thereafter, any iodine introduced into the water in that process was extracted by three successive extractions with cyclohexane, thus destroying all I_3^- and leaving only I^- in the water. An unirradiated solution was treated in the same way to yield a reference solution. The I^- ion production was determined by ultraviolet absorption at 226 mμ (ϵ = 14,000 at 25°C) (*9, 10*).

In the case of benzene, direct ultraviolet determination of I^- was compared with a determination of I_3^-. In that case a small amount of I_2 was added to the final aqueous solution (after extraction with cyclohexane), and the amount of I^- was calculated from $[I_2]$ (ϵ = 746 for 460 mμ at 25°C) and $[I_3^-]$ (ϵ = 26,400 for 353 mμ at 25°C) by use of the known equilibrium constant (*10*). The agreement between I^- directly determined and I^- determined from $[I_2]$ and $[I_3^-]$ was good; the inference is that any C_6H_6 left in the aqueous extract after extraction with cyclohexane was without effect on the ultraviolet absorption by I^- at 226 mμ.

In a few cases in which the HI production was relatively high, a direct pH determination with a Beckman Model G pH meter gave results in good agreement with those obtained by ultraviolet absorption spectrometry (see Table I).

The principal point of departure from past procedures involves the technique of extraction with water. We have established that the observed yield of HI is sensitive to the time interval between irradiation and extraction. All efforts were made to reduce this interval to zero. It is apparent in Section 3 that the ideal situation

TABLE I

APPARENT $G(HI)$ AS A FUNCTION OF TIME AFTER 1-HOUR IRRADIATION ($[I_2] = 2 \times 10^{-2}\ M$)

Sample	Time		
	0	1 hr	3 days
Cyclohexane	0.99 1.05[a]	0.86	0.27
n-Hexane	1.36 1.34[a]	1.10	1.13

[a] Ultraviolet absorption.

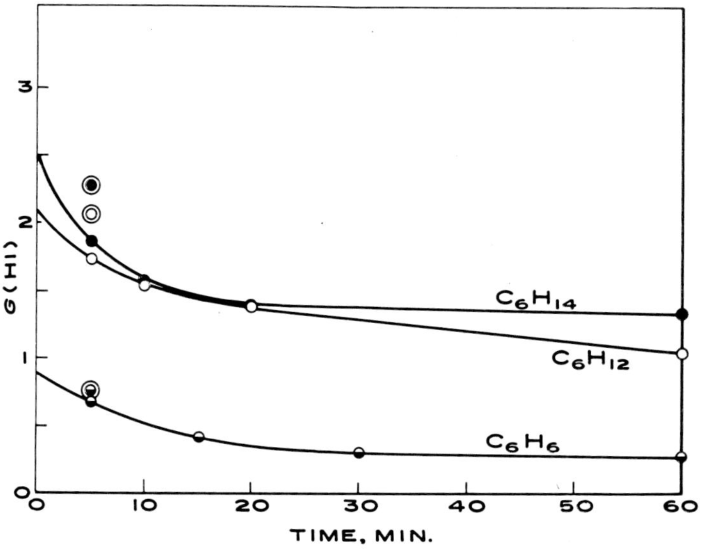

FIG. 1. Apparent $G(HI)$ as a function of irradiation time; solutions of $2 \times 10^{-2}\ M$ I_2 in *n*-hexane and cyclohexane, $4 \times 10^{-2}\ M$ I_2 in benzene. The double circles in each case represent irradiations with water present (~0.15 ml of H_2O per 20-ml sample).

involves an extrapolation to zero interval succeeding zero time of irradiation. Indications of the extraction technique are consequently given with the results.

3. RESULTS

Table I shows that the apparent $G(HI)$ decreases with increase of the time interval between irradiation of samples (cyclohexane, *n*-hexane) and aqueous extraction. During that time interval the samples were maintained under vacuum so that the effects were not attributable to secondary contamination. In these experiments,

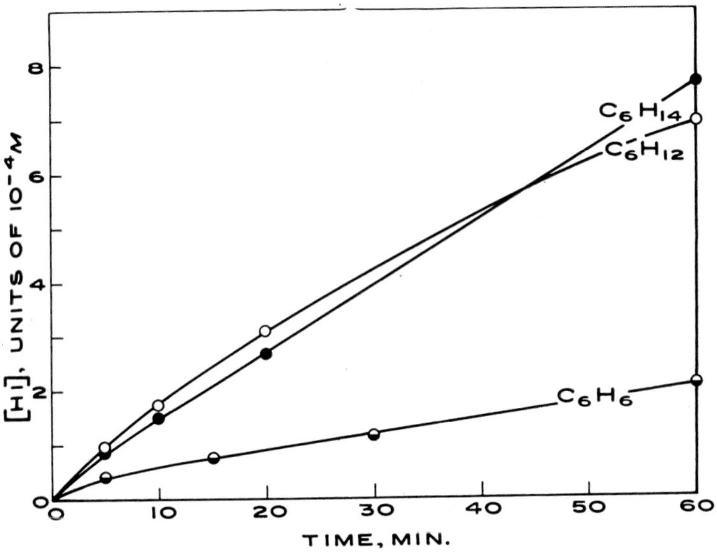

FIG. 2. HI production as a function of irradiation time; solutions as in Fig. 1

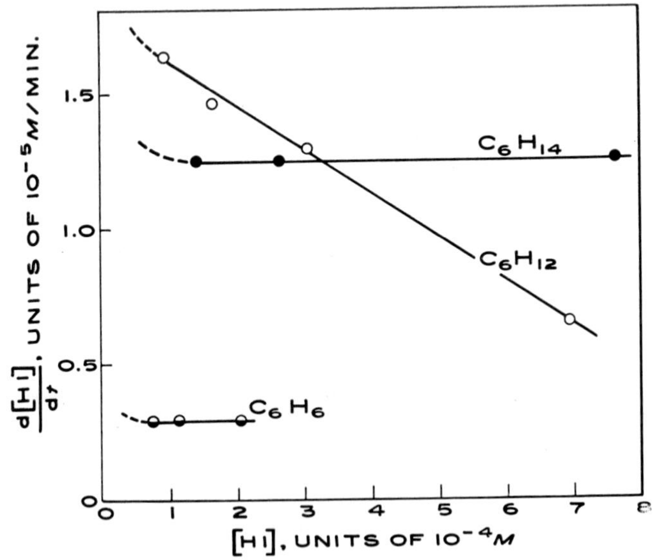

FIG. 3. Rate of HI production as a function of its concentration; solutions as in Fig. 1

hydrogen iodide was determined by pH measurement unless otherwise indicated. In the two cases noted in the table, the values determined from pH were checked by ultraviolet absorption.

Figure 1 shows the results of some studies of the effect of time of irradiation on apparent G(HI) from solutions in all three solvents. In each case extraction followed immediately on irradiation. The apparent G(HI) decreases with irradiation time in all cases; in n-hexane and benzene the decrease seems to be toward a limiting value at higher irradiation time. The rough extrapolated values of G(HI) at zero irradiation time for cyclohexane, n-hexane, and benzene are, respectively, about 2.1, 2.5, and 0.9. Also shown in Fig. 1 are three values of G(HI) obtained on 5-minute irradiation of solutions saturated with water (i.e., about 0.15 ml of water had been added and shaken into the hydrocarbon solution). Doubtless, presence of the water interferes with disappearance of HI by some secondary reaction.

Figure 2 shows increase of HI concentration in the samples as a function of time of irradiation. Figure 3 shows the tangents to the curves of Fig. 2 at various times, d[HI]$/dt$, plotted as a function of HI concentration. As is indicated also by Fig. 1, the apparent rates of HI production in n-hexane and benzene become constant after an initial period of irradiation; in cyclohexane the rate decreases linearly with HI concentration.

Figure 4 shows the effects of I_2 concentration on apparent G(HI) in the three systems. For this series of studies 20-ml samples were irradiated for 5 minutes in the presence of about 0.15 ml of water. Plotted in the same figure as a function of I_2 concentration are the values of $-\Delta G(H_2)$; i.e., the decreases in $G(H_2)$ resultant

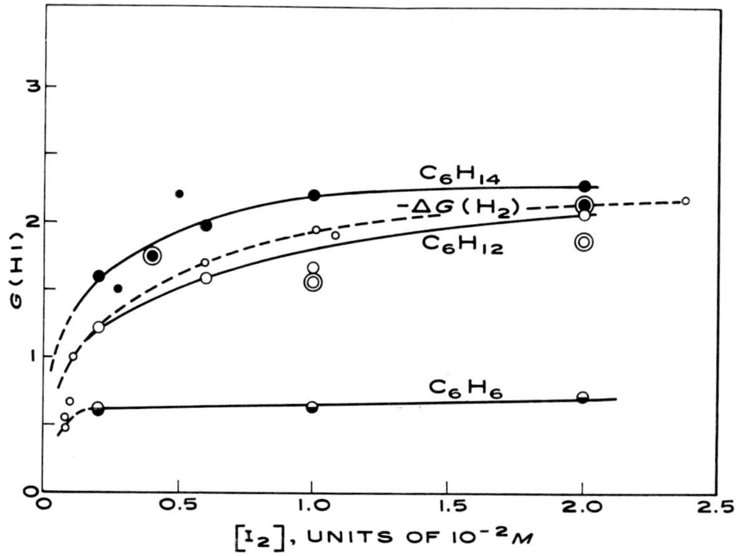

FIG. 4. Variation of G(HI) with iodine concentration in three liquids which contain about 0.15 ml of H_2O per 20-ml sample. The single circles of large size represent 5-minute irradiations; the double circles represent 20-minute irradiations. Included in the figure are small circles representing $-\Delta G(H_2)$ for n-hexane ● (*4*) and cyclohexane ○ (*1*). The dashed line represents $-\Delta G(H_2)$ in cyclohexane.

from addition of I_2 to cyclohexane (*1*) and *n*-hexane (*4*). The latter points fit the G(HI) curve fairly well.

4. DISCUSSION

In these experiments the amount of I_2 consumed was in all cases less than 4% of the amount initially present. Thus, a reasonable assumption is that in all cases the rate of the process represented by

$$\text{Sample} \rightsquigarrow \text{HI} \qquad (1)$$

is invariant during the course of the reaction. Figure 3 means, then, that in *n*-hexane and benzene rates of HI disappearance become constant after attainment of a certain concentration of HI and that in cyclohexane the rate of such disappearance becomes first order in HI concentration.

4.1. n-Hexane

We write in addition to reaction 1

$$\text{Sample} \rightsquigarrow \text{X} \qquad (2)$$
$$\text{HI} + \text{X} \rightsquigarrow \text{P} \qquad (3)$$

where X is some product which can react with HI to yield P, a stable product. If the reaction rates may be represented by $r_1 > r_2$ and if r_3, represented by

$$r_3 = k_3\,[\text{HI}]\,[\text{X}] \qquad (4)$$

is fairly rapid, HI accumulates with irradiation time until r_3 eventually equals r_2. But

$$d[\text{HI}]/dt = r_1 - r_3 \qquad (5)$$

so that, when $r_3 \rightarrow r_2$,

$$d[\text{HI}]/dt \rightarrow r_1 - r_2 \qquad (6)$$

and is constant if, as indicated for r_1, r_2 is also fairly constant during the course of the reaction.

In this picture X is an unsaturated entity and reaction 3 is merely the addition of HI to that entity. According to Dewhurst (*4*), for *n*-hexane G(unsaturates) averages 1.19 as determined in the presence of several scavengers other than I_2. Figures 1 and 4 clearly indicate $G(\text{HI}) > 2$. Thus $r_1 > r_2$, as required by the suggested mechanism, and HI addition is generally considered to be fairly rapid (*11*, *12*). In correspondence to equation 6

$$G_s(\text{HI}) = G_1 - G_2 \qquad (7)$$

where the G's are for HI production in the steady state and in reactions 1 and 2 respectively. From Fig. 3 G_s(HI) is calculated to be 1.29, and, since G_2 can be taken to be Dewhurst's value of 1.19, it follows that $G_1 = 2.48$, in good agreement with the zero irradiation value of $\sim$2.5 extrapolated from Fig. 1 or the value of $\sim$2.3 which may be estimated from Fig. 4.

4.2. Benzene

The similarity of the curves for *n*-hexane and benzene in Fig. 3 suggests a similar process so far as HI production is concerned. If we assume the same schemes, G_2 (i.e., the 100-ev yield of X which can react with HI) is calculated from equation 7, by introducing data obtained from Fig. 1 and Fig. 3, to be $0.9 - 0.23 \approx 0.7$.

4.3. Cyclohexane

In cyclohexane HI disappearance seems to become first order in HI concentration after attainment of a certain concentration of HI. Thus, in this region

$$d[\mathrm{HI}]/dt = r_1 - k[\mathrm{HI}] \qquad (8)$$

The slope of the straight line in Fig. 3 gives $k = 1.61 \times 10^{-2}$ min^{-1}. A clue to the interpretation of the first-order dependence shown in equation 8 may be afforded by the fact that the rate of HI disappearance was found to be much greater during irradiation than afterward. This fact means that during irradiation HI may be reacting with some intermediate species or that some intermediate species may be catalyzing the HI disappearance reaction.

The conclusion, $G(\mathrm{HI}) \sim 2.1$ in cyclohexane solution, is (as seen from Fig. 4) very close to the value $-\Delta G(H_2) \sim 2.2$ formerly given for the effect of iodine on hydrogen yield (*1*). A reasonable inference, based on this result alone, is that HI is formed by reaction of atomic H with iodine and that $-\Delta G(H_2)$ in this case represents a simple scavenging reaction. If this view should prove correct, the mechanism of cyclohexane radiolysis previously suggested (*1*) could be greatly simplified.

5. SUMMARY

Radiolysis of cyclohexane, *n*-hexane, and benzene solutions containing dissolved iodine gives hydrogen iodide with initial $G(\mathrm{HI})$ estimated to be, respectively, about 2.1, 2.5, and 0.9. Low yields of HI previously observed are attributed in part to rapid reactions of HI with intermediate products during irradiation. In the case of cyclohexane, an alternative possibility is HI disappearance catalyzed by some intermediate. In addition, in all cases, postirradiation disappearance of HI also occurs. The kinetics are examined, and a tentative interpretation is offered. In benzene, $G_2 \sim 0.7$ is, in the scheme suggested, the 100-ev yield of a species which can react rapidly with HI.

These results may lead to modification of previously expressed views (*1*) of the mechanism of cyclohexane radiolysis.

RECEIVED: October 27, 1958.

REFERENCES

1. M. BURTON, J. CHANG, S. LIPSKY, and M. P. REDDY, Radiation protection in cyclohexane. *Radiation Research* **8,** 203–213 (1958).
2. R. W. FESSENDEN and R. H. SCHULER, On the use of iodine as a radical detector in hydrocarbon radiolysis. *J. Am. Chem. Soc.* **79,** 273–276 (1957).
3. G. MESHITSUKA and M. BURTON, Radiolysis of liquid methanol by Co^{60} gamma-radiation. *Radiation Research* **8,** 285–297 (1958).
4. H. A. DEWHURST, Radiation chemistry of organic compounds. II. *n*-Hexane. *J. Phys. Chem.* **62,** 15–20 (1958).
5. M. BURTON, J. A. GHORMLEY, and C. J. HOCHANADEL, Design of an inexpensive high-intensity gamma source. *Nucleonics,* **13,** No. 10, 74–77 (1955).
6. R. M. LAZO, H. A. DEWHURST, and M. BURTON, The ferrous sulfate radiation dosimeter. *J. Chem. Phys.* **22,** 1370–1375 (1954).
7. C. J. HOCHANADEL and J. A. GHORMLEY, A calorimetric calibration of gamma ray actinometers. *J. Chem. Phys.* **21,** 880–885 (1953).
8. R. H. SCHULER and A. O. ALLEN, Yield of the ferrous sulfate radiation dosimeter. *J. Chem. Phys.* **24,** 56–59 (1956).
9. H. FROMHERZ and W. MENSCHICK, Ueber die Lichtabsorption der Alkalihalogenide in waesserigen Loesungen. *Z. phys. Chem.* (*Leipzig*) **B7,** 439–467 (1930).
10. A. D. AWTREY and R. E. CONNICK, The absorption spectra of I_2, I_3^-, I^-, IO_3^-, $S_4O_6^{--}$, and $S_2O_3^{--}$. Heat of the reaction $I_3^- = I_2 + I^-$. *J. Am. Chem. Soc.* **73,** 1842–1843 (1951).
11. P. KARRER, *Organic Chemistry* 54 (1950).
12. S. F. O'CONNOR, L. H. BALDINGER, R. R. VOGT, and G. F. HENNION, Solvent effects in addition reactions. I. Addition of hydrogen bromide and chloride to cyclohexane and 3-hexane. *J. Am. Chem. Soc.* **61,** 1454–1456 (1939).

RADIATION RESEARCH 10, 507–515 (1959)

Radiation Effects on Aqueous Solutions of S-(2-Aminoethyl)thiuronium Salts[1]

DONALD R. ANDERSON AND BETTY J. JOSEPH

Department of Radiobiology, School of Aviation Medicine, USAF, Randolph Air Force Base, Texas

INTRODUCTION

Compounds that may protect biologic systems against the adverse effects of ionizing radiation have become of increasing practical importance. Additional information on the behavior of such protective agents may lead to a better understanding of their mode of action, as well as enhance their value as investigative tools in radiobiological research.

In 1949, Patt *et al.* (*1*) reported that rats could be protected against radiation effects with the —SH compounds cysteine and glutathione. Bacq *et al.* (*2*) demonstrated the protective action of several amines and sulfhydryl compounds including 2-mercaptoethylamine (MEA). Doherty and Burnett (*3*), while investigating compounds related to MEA, discovered that mice given *S*- (2-aminoethyl) thiuronium (AET) survived lethal doses of radiation. Subsequently, Doherty and his associates reported on the protective activity of a large number of mercaptoguanido compounds and their derivatives (*4*).

AET is unstable in solution. Shapira *et al.* (*4*) postulated an equilibrium wherein the AET in a neutral solution is transformed through a cyclic intermediate to the active protective form, 2-mercaptoethylguanidine (MEG). In this form the —SH group is available for reaction and is readily oxidized to the disulfide guanidinoethyldisulfide. The authors state that AET was quantitatively converted to MEG on neutralization to pH 7.0, and that MEG was stable at all pH's. Shapiro (*5*) investigated the chemical properties of AET in buffered solutions and found that an equilibrium did in fact exist, but that it shifted with time, temperature, and pH.

A report from this laboratory (*6*) concerning radiation effects on the enzyme creatine phosphokinase described the protective activity of AET salts in a simple biologic system. These observations led to a further investigation of the radiation

[1] This work was conducted at the Radiobiological Laboratory of the University of Texas and the United States Air Force, Austin, Texas, and was supported (in part) with funds provided under Contract AF 41(657)-149 and the School of Aviation Medicine.

effects on aqueous solutions of AET. Results of this investigation are presented in this report.

MATERIALS AND METHODS

All chemicals, unless otherwise stated, were of analytical reagent grade and used without further purification. Solutions were made with glass-distilled water (four times distilled).

p-Chloromercuribenzoic acid (CMBA) was reprecipitated three times according to the method of Boyer (*7*).

The AET salts were synthesized by Brois (*8*).[2] Solutions were made up in equimolar tris (hydroxymethyl)aminomethane (Tris) buffer of pH 8.5 to 9.0. The resulting solutions were at pH 7.2 to 7.4. Aliquots were irradiated in siliconed vials topped with parafilm and a screw cap.

The pH measurements were made with a Beckman Model G pH meter with a glass electrode.

A Co^{60} facility was used for irradiation (*9*). The exposure dose rate routinely used was 2000 r/min.

Two methods have been used in this investigation to determine the concentration of free sulfhydryl groups.

1. *Amperometric titration*. The apparatus and procedure described by Benesch *et al.* (*10*) were used with the following modifications. The bridge from the reference electrode was a glass U-tube filled with 30% KCl in 1.5% agar. It was replaced daily. A G.E. Model 32C galvanometer was used. The titrations were more conveniently carried out with 1 μM of thiol in a total volume of 60 ml, titrating with 10^{-4} *M* $AgNO_3$ from a calibrated burette. The presence of 0.01% gelatin in this mixture gave more stable and reproducible current readings. Galvanometer readings were made with each 2-ml increment of $AgNO_3$. The end point was obtained by plotting current versus milliliters of $AgNO_3$ and extrapolating the linear portion of the line to zero current. Figure 1 illustrates titrations of cysteine and AET dinitrate.

2. *Spectrophotometric measurement of mercaptide formation with CMBA*. This reaction has been studied and described by Boyer (*7*). The determinations reported here were made in the following manner: A volume containing 0.5 μM of thiol was diluted to 8.5 ml. One milliliter of 0.5 *M* Tris buffer, pH 7.15, and 0.5 ml of 10^{-3} *M* CMBA were added. Approximately 10 minutes after mixing, the optical density was read in a Beckman DU spectrophotometer at 255 mμ. Measurements of the rate of reaction showed that it goes to completion almost immediately. Cysteine was also used as a check on the reproducibility and validity of this method.

Deoxygenation was accomplished by dispensing the solution in ampoules. The

[2] Analysis calculated for AET dinitrate, $C_3H_{11}O_6SN_5$: C, 14.69; H, 4.52; S, 13.08; N, 28.56. Found: C, 14.69; H, 4.46; S, 13.05; N, 28.22.

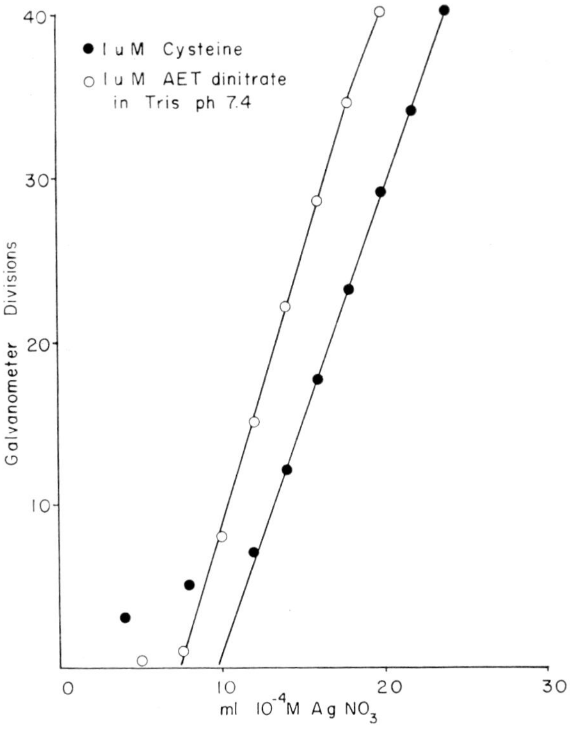

FIG. 1. Amperometric titration of sulfhydryl groups of MEG formed from AET dinitrate compared with cysteine.

ampoules were then alternately evacuated and filled with argon at atmospheric pressure. The argon was bubbled through alkaline pyrogallol[3] and dried prior to admission to the evacuated ampoule. This procedure was repeated ten times, and the ampoules were then heat-sealed with argon in the gas phase. Control samples were sealed in ampoules with air in the gas phase.

Samples were saturated with oxygen by bubbling 100% oxygen through the solution in ampoules for 10 minutes, after which the ampoules were sealed.

RESULTS AND DISCUSSION

Since aqueous solutions of the AET salts are acid, pH approximately 4.0, a buffer was required to maintain a pH at which the equilibrium favored the MEG form. Dale *(11)* has described "protection effects" in solutions containing two or more solutes. This protection varies not only in proportion to the relative amounts of the solutes but also according to their respective capabilities to act as acceptors

[3] Fifteen grams of pyrogallol in 25 ml of water added to 150 ml of 30% KOH.

TABLE I

G VALUES FOR AET DINITRATE BUFFERED WITH INCREASING CONCENTRATIONS OF TRIS AND PHOSPHATE BUFFERS TO pH 7.2 TO 7.4

AET concentration	*Buffer concentration*	*Tris*	*Phosphate*
10^{-4} *M*	1×10^{-4} *M*	7.9	—
10^{-4} *M*	2×10^{-4} *M*	8.0	7.9
10^{-4} *M*	3×10^{-4} *M*	7.9	8.1
10^{-4} *M*	4×10^{-4} *M*	8.0	7.6
10^{-3} *M*	1×10^{-3} *M*	15.3	15.5
10^{-3} *M*	2×10^{-3} *M*	15.7	15.4
10^{-3} *M*	3×10^{-3} *M*	15.3	15.9

TABLE II

DETERMINATION OF SULFHYDRYL GROUPS BY AMPEROMETRIC TITRATION SHOWING THE AMOUNT OF MEG FORMED BY CYCLIZATION OF THE AET SALT

pH	*Number of determinations*	*Per cent of theoretical —SH*
7.0	2	74, ± 0
7.1	3	73, ± 0
7.2	6	72, ± 2
7.3	4	74, ± 3
7.4	6	73, ± 1
7.5	4	74, ± 1

for radicals. In order to evaluate the influence of the Tris buffer on the radiation effect on AET, a series of samples containing buffer in one to four times the molar concentration of the AET salt were irradiated. Tris and phosphate buffers were used; however, an equimolar concentration of phosphate was not sufficient to bring a 10^{-4} *M* solution of AET dinitrate to pH 7.2. *G* values[4] were calculated and are shown in Table I.

Solutions of all the AET salts buffered with an equimolar concentration of Tris to pH 7.0 to 7.5 maintained for at least 3 hours an equilibrium in which 70 to 75% of the AET was in the MEG form with —SH groups available to react with the silver ions (Table II) or CMBA. In samples that had remained at room temperature for 6 hours a 10 to 15% decrease in titratable —SH groups was noted.

The destruction of the —SH groups of MEG is directly proportional to the radiation dose, as shown in Fig. 2. The same linear plot is obtained with data from amperometric titrations and spectrophotometric determinations. Barron and Flood (*12*) have also demonstrated a linear relationship to dose in the oxidation of a number of other thiols by ionizing radiation.

[4] That is, the number of molecules changed per 100 ev of energy absorbed.

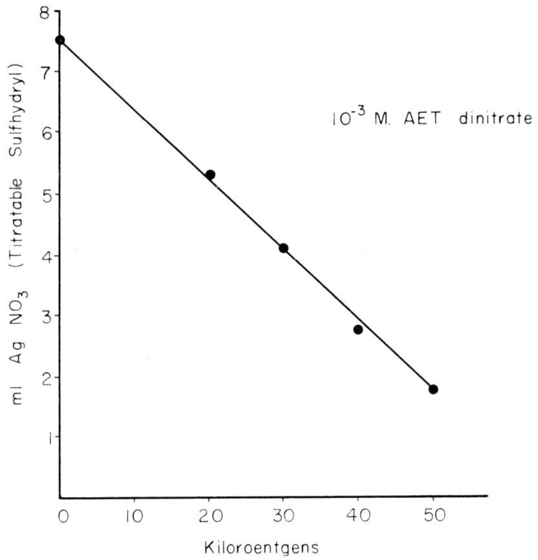

FIG. 2. Titratable sulfhydryl groups versus γ-radiation: 1 μM of AET dinitrate, pH 7.4.

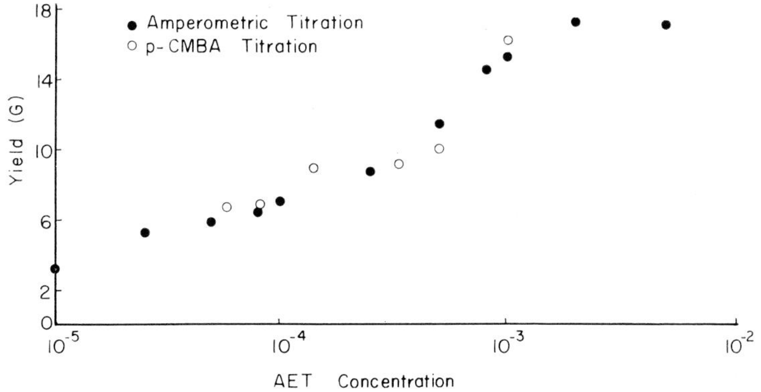

FIG. 3. Yield versus concentration. AET dinitrate buffered with equimolar Tris to pH 7.2 to 7.4.

G values were calculated by assuming 1.76×10^{12} ion pairs formed in aqueous solutions per roentgen of Co^{60} γ-radiation (*13*). Values obtained with data from both methods are in good agreement (Fig. 3). There is an apparent plateau at the higher concentrations. We were unable to extend the upper limit of these observations, however, because of the restrictions imposed by the available dose rate of the Co^{60} source. Yields for 10^{-3} *M* solutions of various salts of AET are listed in Table III.

TABLE III
COMPARISON OF RADIATION YIELDS OF VARIOUS AET SALTS

AET salt, $10^{-3}M$	*G value*	
	Amperometric titration	*Spectrophotometric determination*
AET dinitrate	15.3	16.2
AET dibromide	14.8	12.6
AET dichloride	11.6	11.8
AET sulfate	12.2	10.8
AET diacetate	0	0

Values for all salts except the acetate are greater than 3.0, suggesting a radiation-induced chain-type reaction.

The reason for the anomalous behavior of the acetate salt of AET is not clear. The addition of an equimolar concentration of acetate ion to solutions of the nitrate salt had no effect on the concentration of available —SH groups in the solution. Previous work at this laboratory showed that the acetate salt of AET offered little or no protection against radiation damage to the enzyme creatine phosphokinase. Two possible explanations might be (1) steric hindrance which prevents the cyclization of buffered AET diacetate to the MEG form, or (2) an inherent instability of the diacetate salt in crystalline form.

It is of interest to determine if the radiation effect is altered in the presence or absence of dissolved O_2. Figure 4 shows the results of an experiment in which a series of deoxygenated and control samples were irradiated. The G values were calculated and found to be 9.0 and 16.9. A second series of samples was saturated with O_2 and irradiated, with controls. In this case there was no significant difference in the two curves.

Since the presence of dissolved O_2 during irradiation enhances the production of HO_2 and H_2O_2, the results would indicate that these radicals, in addition to the OH radical, are significantly involved in the oxidation of MEG in aqueous solutions by ionizing radiation.

The high yields obtained in aqueous solutions of AET salts may suggest that the protective capacity of these compounds is a result of their ability to compete successfully with biologic molecules in radical capture; i.e., they act as a "radical scavenger." Several investigators have presented evidence, however, that AET is readily protein-bound, probably through a disulfide linkage, and that this complex is relatively insensitive to radiation-induced radicals. For example, Shapiro (*5*) added labeled AET to human serum and found 44% of the activity protein-bound and only 18% in the —SH form. This suggests the possibility that sensitive biologic molecules may be temporarily shielded from radiation damage by coupling with a protective compound which is later removed through normal metabolic processes.

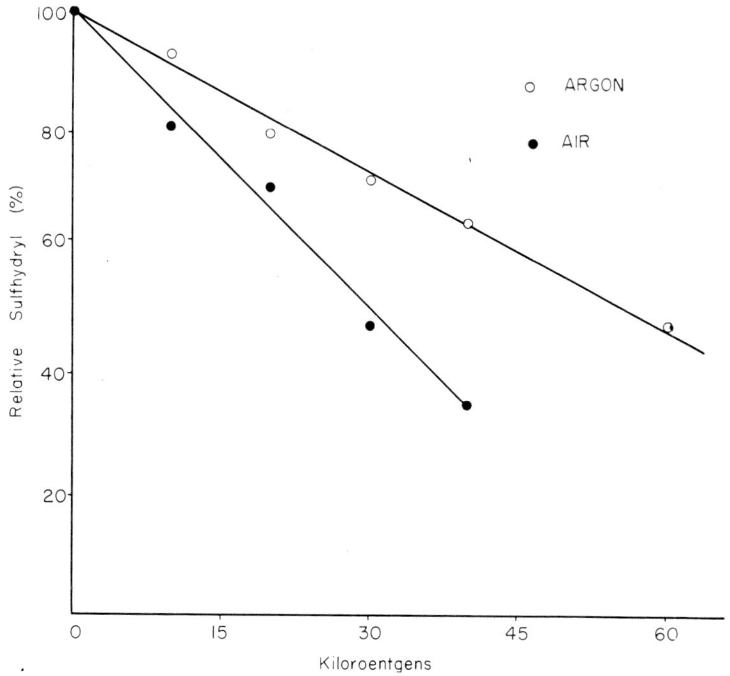

FIG. 4. Titratable sulfhydryl groups versus γ-radiation showing the effect of the presence of oxygen: 10^{-3} M AET dinitrate buffered with equimolar Tris to pH 7.4.

Both reactions may be a part of the mechanism through which AET affords protection against radiation damage.

SUMMARY

Aqueous solutions of the protective compound AET, buffered to favor the formation of the active MEG form, showed marked sensitivity to ionizing radiation as measured by a reduction in concentration of —SH groups. Two methods of determining the concentration of —SH groups were used, with comparable results.

The destruction of —SH groups of MEG is directly dependent on radiation dose. The G values vary from 3.2 at 10^{-5} M to 17.1 at 5×10^{-3} M AET. The high yield suggests that a chain-type reaction may account for the radiation sensitivity. In deoxygenated samples the radiation effect was significantly decreased.

It is suggested that the protective activity of AET involves not only the sensitivity to radiation of the free —SH group but also the capacity of the compound to couple with sensitive biologic molecules and shield them from radiation damage.

ACKNOWLEDGMENTS

The authors wish to thank Stanley J. Brois for supplying the AET salts used in this study, the Physics and Engineering Section of this laboratory for the use of the Co^{60} facility and the dosimetry, Henry Schlattner for the construction of the rotating platinum electrode, and A/2C Michael D. Cragin for technical assistance.

RECEIVED: May 13, 1958

REFERENCES

1. H. M. PATT, E. B. TYREE, R. L. STRAUBE, and D. E. SMITH, Cysteine protection against X-irradiation. *Science* **110**, 213 (1949).
2. Z. M. BACQ, A. HERVE, J. LECOMTE, P. FISCHER, J. BLAVIER, G. DECHAMPS, H. LEBIHAN, and P. RAYET, Protection contre le rayonnement X par la β-mercaptoethylamine. *Arch. intern. physiol.* **59**, 442–447 (1951).
3. D. G. DOHERTY and W. T. BURNETT, JR., Protective effect of *S*,2-aminoethylisothiuronium·Br·HBr and related compounds against X-radiation death in mice. *Proc. Soc. Exptl. Biol. Med.* **89**, 312–314 (1955).
4. R. SHAPIRA, D. G. DOHERTY, and W. T. BURNETT, JR., Chemical protection against ionizing radiation. III. Mercaptoalkylguanidines and related isothiuronium compounds with protective activity. *Radiation Research* **7**, 22–34 (1957).
5. B. SHAPIRO, The behavior of the radiation protective agent AET in aqueous solutions and human serum. School of Aviation Medicine, USAF, Report 21 (1958).
6. D. R. ANDERSON, Some effects of ionizing radiations on creatine phosphokinase. School of Aviation Medicine, USAF, Report 115 (1958).
7. P. D. BOYER, Spectrophotometric study of the reaction of protein sulfhydryl groups with organic mercurials. *J. Am. Chem. Soc.* **76**, 4331–4337 (1954).
8. S. J. BROIS, The reaction of ethylenimine with thiourea and its derivatives. School of Aviation Medicine, USAF, Report 15 (1958).
9. J. A. AUXIER, A high level Co^{60} irradiation facility. School of Aviation Medicine, USAF, Report 40 (1955).
10. R. E. BENESCH, H. A. LARDY, and R. BENESCH, The sulfhydryl groups of crystalline proteins. I. Some albumins, enzymes and hemoglobins. *J. Biol. Chem.* **216**, 663–676 (1955).
11. W. M. DALE, The effect of X-rays on the conjugated protein *d*-amino-acid oxidase. *Biochem. J.* **36**, 80–85 (1942).
12. E. S. G. BARRON and V. FLOOD, Studies on the mechanism of action of ionizing radiations. VI. The oxidation of thiols by ionizing radiations. *J. Gen. Physiol.* **33**, 229–241 (1950).
13. F. T. FARMER, G. STEIN, and J. WEISS, Chemical actions of ionizing radiations on aqueous solutions. Part I. Introductory remarks and description of irradiation arrangements. *J. Chem. Soc.* **1949**, 3241–3245.

RADIATION RESEARCH 10, 515–521 (1959)

Primary Processes in the Flash Photolysis of Ovalbumin and Constituents[1]

L. I. GROSSWEINER[2] AND W. A. MULAC

Argonne National Laboratory, Lemont, Illinois

INTRODUCTION

It is well known that the absorption of ultraviolet light by proteins induces significant permanent changes in almost all measurable properties (*1*). The purpose of these experiments is to investigate the primary photochemical acts by means of the flash photolysis of ovalbumin and certain constituent amino acids and related compounds. Flash photolysis work with simpler compounds has shown that aromatic free radicals can be detected, owing to resonance stabilization, thus suggesting that the lifetimes of free radical intermediates of amino acids and proteins might also be sufficiently long for detection (*2*). The experimental method, in brief, consists in irradiating with an intense light flash the air-free solutions in a fused silica cell and then, after a preset time interval, taking the optical absorption spectrum with a weaker "spectroflash" lamp as the source. In this way, one obtains the absorption spectrum of the transient photochemical products within 10 μsec of flash irradiation. For most of these experiments, the irradiation flash lamp duration was 25 μsec, with a maximum effective light output of 5×10^{19} quanta, from 200 to 500 mμ, into a 35-cc sample in a 25-cm-long cell. The absorption spectra were taken with a 10-μsec-duration spectroflash lamp on the Gaertner L 234 quartz prism spectrograph using Kodak 103-F spectroscopic plates. The concentrations of solute were chosen to give an optical density of unity for a 1-cm path at the peak of the aromatic absorption band (e.g., ~1 m*M* phenol in H_2O). The chemicals used were analytical grade and were not further purified. Other experimental details are reported elsewhere (*3*).

RESULTS

Earlier experiments have shown that air-free, aqueous solutions of ovalbumin (Nutritional Biochemical Corp.) display a short-lived absorption spectrum after flash irradiation into the aromatic band (*4*). The transient spectrum shows two

[1] Based on work performed under the auspices of the U. S. Atomic Energy Commission.
[2] Department of Physics, Illinois Institute of Technology.

prominent absorption regions—a very broad band in the visible, and a series in the ultraviolet headed by a distinct band at 412 mμ (27 mμ half-width). The details of the visible absorption show broad overlapping bands with shoulders at 585 and 528 mμ and partially resolved peaks at 478 and 426 mμ. Comparison experiments with the constituent chromophoric amino acids and related aromatics showed that the visible band is associated with the indole group, and the 412 mμ band and series with the phenol group. Phenylalanine, cystine, histidine, and the peptide linkages make a negligible contribution to the observed transient spectrum. It is convenient to discuss the flash photolysis of the phenol and indole substituents separately.

Phenol Derivatives

Flash irradiation of phenol in air-free aqueous solutions of pH 7 and pH 12 (0.01 *M* NaOH), and in ethanol, carbon tetrachloride, and cyclohexane gives, in each case, a characteristic transient absorption spectrum showing a distinct band near 402 mμ followed by diffuse overlapping bands at shorter wavelengths (Table I). In ethanol solutions, which were studied in greater detail, identical short-lived transients of comparable intensity were obtained with freshly prepared solutions exposed to a single weak flash and with solutions which had previously been exposed to considerable flash irradiation. This establishes that the transient species in question is an initial product and is not due to further decomposition of permanent irradiation products. The lifetime of the transient is less than 50 μsec, but a careful determination of the kinetics was not possible because of an overlapping absorption of much longer duration. The substituted phenols—anisole, tyrosine, and glycyltyrosine—give transient absorption spectra which closely resemble those from phenol (Table I).

In the assignment of the spectra to particular species, a satisfactory explanation of the following is considered necessary:

1. Similar transient spectra appear in the different organic solvents and in distilled water; particularly note that hydrogen atom abstraction is impossible from carbon tetrachloride.

2. The spectra obtained from phenol and the phenolate ion show prominent similarities.

3. Solutions of phenol or anisole in ethanol show very similar transient spectra.

The assignment of the transients to molecular triplet states is unlikely, because very similar spectra are obtained from different compounds, permanent decomposition occurs, and, most important, triplet spectra invariably show broader bands with an intensity distribution nearly symmetrical about the center. We therefore assign the transients to free radicals, of which only two are consistent with the above results, the phenoxy free radical and the phenol radical cation. The phenoxy free radical in the gas phase, however, has been identified by Porter

TABLE I

TRANSIENT ABSORPTION SPECTRA FROM PHENOL DERIVATIVES AND RELATED COMPOUNDS

Solute	*Solvent*	*Transient spectra*		
		Prominent bands[a]	*Shoulders*	*Diffuse series*[b]
Phenol (Me)	Water #	403 (14)	427	387, 375, 356, 338, ···
Phenol (Me)	Ethanol (USI)	401 (11)	428	382, ···
Phenol (Me)	Cyclohexane (EOC)	396 (11), 368		350, ···
Phenol (Me)	Carbon tetrachloride (Mal)	402 (11)	418	387, 372, ···
Phenol (Me)	0.01 M NaOH	402 (5)		391, 374, 358, 346, ···
Anisole (EK)	Ethanol	401 (4)		385, ···
L-Tyrosine (Me)	Water	412 (31)	433	393, ···
Glycyl-L-tyrosine (NBC)	Water	408 (27)	427	392, ···
Catechol (Mat)	Ethanol	385, 370		370, ···
Resorcinol (EK)	Ethanol	431, 412	470	398, ···
Hydroquinone (Mat)	Ethanol	412	450	399, ···
Benzoquinone (Mat)	Ethanol	429, 411	437	404, ···
4,4′-Dihydroxybiphenyl (EK)	Ethanol	624, 459, 440		411, ···
Benzyl alcohol (EK)	Ethanol	317	334	305, ···
Benzyl bromide (Mat)	Ethanol	317, 306	330	298, 296, ···
Benzylamine (Mat)	Ethanol	313, 306		306, ···

[a] Figures in parentheses are the half-widths.

[b] Resolved bands; when this figure corresponds to a prominent band, it indicates a totally unresolved band to shorter wavelengths of the prominent band.

Note: Me—Merck; EK—Eastman Kodak; NBC—Nutritional Biochemical; Mat—Matheson; USI—U.S. Industrial Chemicals; EOC—Eastman Organic; Mal—Mallinckrodt; #—triply distilled water.

and Wright (*2*) as a diffuse band at 292 mμ and in E. P. A. glass by Norman and Porter (*5*) as a continuous band below 287 mμ, which is consistent with the assignments of the related benzyl, thiophenyl, and diphenylmethyl free radicals (*2*, *5*, *6*). It is, therefore, unlikely that the spectrum we observed in liquids is the phenoxy free radical, as one would not expect such marked differences between the gas and solid phases. The alternative and preferred assignment is to the phenol radical cation, produced by photoejection of an electron from phenol. The energy requirements for such a process cannot be satisfied entirely by the maximum available photon energy of about 6 ev. Appearance potential data show that the energy required for ejection of an oxygen lone-pair electron is near 9 ev (*7*). The energy deficit must be supplied by the solvation energy of the cation and electron, so that the process is favorable only in condensed phases. (A possible alternative mechanism is the indirect action of the photoexcited solvent on the solute, but this appears unlikely, particularly in aqueous solutions where light absorption by oxygen-free water in fused silica cells in negligible.) An admittedly very rough estimate of the solvation energy of the radical cation in organic solution can be made from the Born formula (*8*). With effective values for the atomic radius of 2 A and for the dielectric constant of 2, the free energy of solvation is nearly 4 ev. The magnitude of this result indicates that solvation energy could indeed supply the deficit. The proposed primary step is

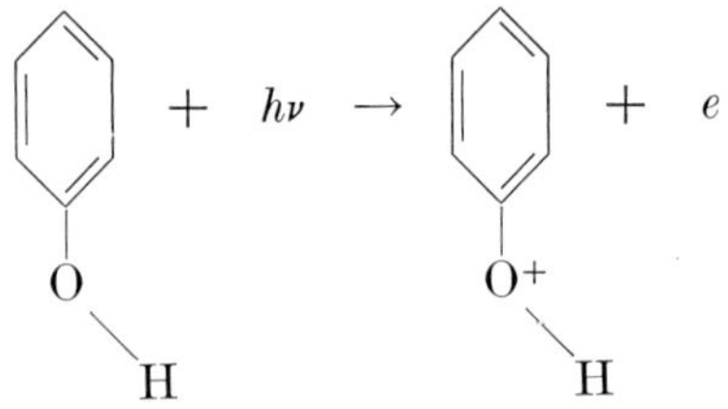

(1)

For anisole, the analogous process gives the anisole radical cation, whose spectrum would be quite similar. In the photolysis of the phenolate ion, however, where photo-oxidation is more favorable, the primary product is the phenoxy free radical, equation 2:

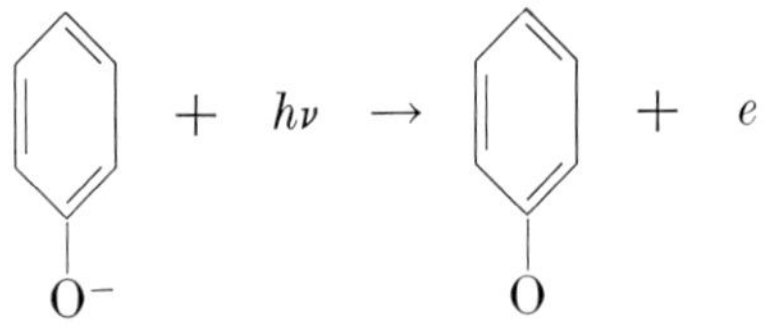

(2)

The detection of the assumed radical cation spectrum can be explained if a rapid proton capture occurs, equation 3:

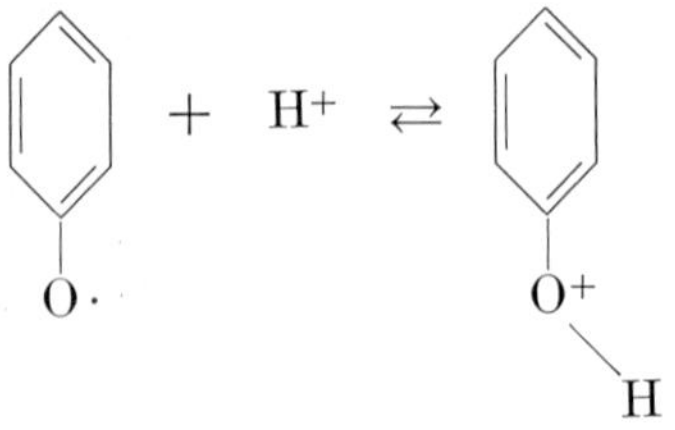

(3)

This requires the phenol radical cation to be a much weaker acid than aqueous molecular phenol, which is about 98% dissociated at pH 12. However, the contribution of hydration to the difference in the dissociation energies of phenol and phenol radical cation is approximately the sum of the hydration energies of the phenolate ion and the phenol radical cation, and it is not unreasonable to assume that measurable amounts of the cation are present in equilibrium after the flash irradiation. We would expect to find evidence for the phenoxy free radical spectrum at 290 mμ, and a comparison of the transient spectra from aqueous phenol at pH 7 and pH 12 shows a lower photographic density on the latter in this region, indicating that association is probably proceeding some 50 μsec after the irradiation flash. The assignment of this spectrum to the phenol radical cation is supported by the work of Norman and Porter (*5*) on the photolysis of aniline in E. P. A. glass. In addition to the expected anilino free radical spectrum at 309 mμ, they found a transient spectrum to which our work bears a very close resemblance, showing a single sharp band at 429 mμ and a weaker continuous absorption from 405 mμ to shorter wavelengths. They assign this spectrum to the aniline radical cation, so that our assignment of the phenol radical cation is analogous to this result.

The results of flash photolysis of some related compounds will be summarized briefly. Ethanol solutions of catechol and resorcinol gave transient spectra of the same general appearance, the former showing two bands of approximately equal intensity at 385 and 370 mμ and a continuous absorption into the ultraviolet; for the latter the bands are at 431 and 412 mμ. Hydroquinone (and benzoquinone) in ethanol solutions showed the characteristic semiquinone absorptions reported by Lewis and Bigeleisen (*9*) in E. P. A. glass and by Bridge and Porter (*10*) in water-ethanol solutions. Solutions of 4,4′-dihydroxybiphenyl in ethanol showed an interesting transient spectrum consisting of narrow short-lived bands at 459 and 440 mμ and broad long-lived bands (some milliseconds) at 624 and 411 mμ. Pyrogallol and benzoic acid in ethanol gave no detectable transients. Finally, benzyl alcohol, benzyl bromide, and benzylamine in ethanol showed bands near 317 and 305 mμ, which, as previously mentioned, have been assigned to the benzyl radical.

Indole Derivatives

The transient spectra obtained with air-free solutions of indole and substituted indole derivatives in aqueous and ethanol solutions show a very broad, continuous absorption through the visible region. A densitometric analysis of the spectrum plates showed that there are broad, overlapping bands, whose positions are given in Table II, with the more prominent peaks underlined. The agreement between the peak locations of the transient spectra from the different substances is considered as sufficiently close to indicate a single or very similar transient species, noting for these complex molecules with diffuse transient spectra that specific assignments are more speculative than for the phenol derivatives. The only likely common product is the 3-indolyl free radical, produced from indole by the splitting-off of a hydrogen atom from the position 3 carbon on the pyrrole ring, and from the

TABLE II

TRANSIENT ABSORPTION SPECTRA FROM INDOLE DERIVATIVES

Solute	*Solvent*	*Transient spectra*[a]
Indole (Mat)	Water #	579, 536, 495, 458, 437, ···
Indole (Mat)	Ethanol (USI)	598, 515, (overlapping) 439, ···
3-Indoleacetic acid (MCB)	Water	598, (overlapping) 439, 424, ···
3-Indoleacetic acid (MCB)	Ethanol	(unresolved, overlapping)
DL-Tryptophan (Me)	Water	515, 493, 457, 424, ···
L-Tryptophan (Pf)	Ethanol	519, (overlapping)
Glycyl-L-tryptophan (NBC)	Water	523, 476, 432, ···

[a] Peak wavelengths of resolved bands indicated; underlined bands are more prominent.

Note: Mat—Matheson; MCB, Matheson, Coleman, and Bell; Me—Merck; Pf—Pfanstiehl; NBC—Nutritional Biochemical; USI—U.S. Industrial Chemicals; #—triply distilled water.

substituted indoles by rupture of the side chain at the 1–2 carbon bonds. It is also possible, however, that rupture may occur at the 2–3 carbon bonds of the side chain, giving the 3-indolylmethyl (skatole) free radical, whose absorption spectrum would be similar to that of the 3-indolyl free radical. In either case, these results indicate that the opening of the pyrrole ring is a secondary reaction.

Extrapolating the above results to the photochemistry of aqueous ovalbumin, we propose that the primary processes are the photoejection of electrons from tyrosine, leaving tyrosine radical cations on the protein chain, and the rupture of tryptophan side chains, with the splitting-off of either 3-indolyl or skatole free radicals. Electron ejection is consistent with the conclusions of Debye and Edwards (*11*) about the long-lived phosphorescence of frozen alkaline solutions of phenol, tyrosine, and bovine serum albumin. When oxygen is present in solution, the photoejected electron probably reduces water, with the formation of HO_2 radical, which explains the rapid uptake of oxygen by ovalbumin during irradiation (*12*). Further, the splitting of the tryptophan group in the side chain leaves reactive sites on the protein between adjacent peptide linkages, so that further reactions might involve breaking of the chain at these points, as proposed by Mitchell and Rideal (*13*). We find no evidence for unique assumptions about electronic energy transfer for long distances along the protein chain.

SUMMARY

Aqueous solutions of air-free ovalbumin show a transient optical absorption spectrum after flash irradiation into the aromatic band. Comparison experiments with constituent dipeptides, amino acids, and aromatic chromophores show that the transient spectrum results from the photochemical effects on the tyrosine and tryptophan groups. The primary processes proposed are the photoejection of electrons from tyrosine radicals and the breaking of tryptophan radicals in the side chains.

ACKNOWLEDGMENT

The authors wish to thank Dr. N. K. Bridge of the British Rayon Research Association (Manchester, England) for valuable discussions and suggestions while he was a Research Associate at this laboratory.

RECEIVED:

REFERENCES

1. I. M. CLAESSON, The effect of ultraviolet light on *Helix pomatia* hemocyanin and bovine serum albumin as studied by the changes in the ultraviolet spectrum and sedimentation behavior. *Arkiv Kemi* **10**, 1–102 (1956); this paper includes a bibliography of review papers on the effects of ultraviolet light on proteins.
2. G. PORTER and F. J. WRIGHT, Primary photochemical processes in aromatic molecules. Part 3. Absorption spectra of benzyl, anilino, phenoxy and related free radicals. *Trans. Faraday Soc.* **51**, 1469–1474 (1955).
3. L. I. GROSSWEINER and M. S. MATHESON, The kinetics of the dihalide ions from the flash photolysis of aqueous alkali halide solutions. *J. Phys. Chem.* **61**, 1089–1095 (1957).
4. L. I. GROSSWEINER, Metastable states of photoexcited ovalbumin and constituents. *J. Chem. Phys.* **24**, 1255–1256 (1956).
5. I. NORMAN and G. PORTER, Trapped atoms and radicals in rigid solvents. *Proc. Roy. Soc.* **A230**, 399–414 (1955).
6. G. PORTER and M. W. WINDSOR, Observation of short-lived free radicals in solutions. *Nature* **180**, 187–188 (1957).
7. J. D. MORRISON and A. J. C. NICHOLSON, Studies of ionization efficiency. Part II. The ionization potentials of some organic molecules. *J. Chem. Phys.* **20**, 1021–1023 (1952).
8. M. BORN, Volumen und Hydratationswärme Der Ionen. *Z. Physik* **1**, 45–48 (1920).
9. G. N. LEWIS and J. BIGELEISEN, Photochemical reactions of leuco dyes in rigid solvents. Quantum efficiency of photooxidation. *J. Am. Chem. Soc.* **65**, 2419–2423 (1943).
10. N. K. BRIDGE and G. PORTER, Primary photoprocesses in quinones and dyes. I. Spectroscopic detection of intermediates. *Proc. Roy. Soc.* **A244**, 259–275 (1958).
11. P. DEBYE and J. O. EDWARDS, A note on the phosphorescence of proteins. *J. Chem. Phys.* **20**, 236–239 (1952).
12. D. T. HARRIS, Observations on the velocity of the photooxidation of proteins and amino acids. *Biochem. J.* **20**, 288–292 (1926).
13. J. S. MITCHELL and E. K. RIDEAL, Photochemical reactions in monolayers. II Photochemistry of proteins. *Proc. Roy. Soc.* **A167**, 342–367 (1938).

RADIATION RESEARCH **10**, 522–531 (1959)

Specification of Radiation Quality[1]

HARALD H. ROSSI

Radiological Research Laboratory, Columbia University, New York, New York

INTRODUCTION

The pioneering experiments by Zirkle (*1*) and a multitude of succeeding studies have established that the biological effectiveness of ionizing radiation depends not only on the amount of energy absorbed but also on the spatial distribution of energy deposition. Since the energy is imparted in or near the tracks of charged particles, it has been considered convenient to express the heterogeneity of energy deposition in terms of the linear density of energy *loss* in these tracks. The term *linear energy transfer* (LET) has been coined by Zirkle *et al.* (*2*) for this purpose. Using this concept one may express radiation quality as a distribution of dose in LET, specifying the fraction of the dose deposited in each LET interval. Theoretical computations of such distributions have been performed for neutrons (*3*) and for electromagnetic radiations (*4, 5*). An instrument has been developed (*6*) for the experimental determination of the LET distribution of dose delivered by charged particles heavier than electrons. As a result of studies performed with this instrument it has become apparent that the concept of LET distribution of dose has certain limitations. It is the purpose of this presentation to discuss these limitations and to propose an alternate parameter that may be used to express radiation quality.

LIMITATIONS OF LET CONCEPT

Statistical Fluctuations

The loss of kinetic energy of charged particles is discontinuous and consequently subject to statistical fluctuations. Hence, the LET attributed to a particle of a given type and energy is actually a *mean* which may be determined theoretically on the basis of quantum-mechanical probabilities and experimentally by averaging over a large number of individual particles. If, employing the "track segment method," one irradiates a thin biological sample of thickness ΔX with a homogenous beam of charged particles having a LET, L, the energy, ΔE, expended by indi-

[1] Based on work performed under U. S. Atomic Energy Commission contract AT-30-1-Gen-70.

vidual particles will deviate from the mean value $L\ \Delta X$ to an extent that depends on the magnitude of ΔX, as well as on the energy which the particles can dissipate in a single collision. Because of the first of these factors, the spread in observed values of $\Delta E/\Delta X$ is greater, the smaller the thickness. Thus, for example, it is greater in the nucleus of a cell than in the cell as a whole. Because the maximum energy that can be lost in a collision depends on the mass of the moving particle, the spread will be larger for electrons than for protons having the same LET.

If one is not dealing with short portions of trajectories of monoenergetic particles, the dose is distributed over a range of LET values. Modification of this distribution due to statistical fluctuations results in "experimental" LET spectra that depend on the size of the tissue sample in which they are evaluated and that differ from "theoretical" LET spectra (*7*). Thus, although representation of dose in LET may be a convenient summary abstraction, it is related to the actual pattern of energy deposition in a manner that is not simple.

Change in LET along Track (d^2E/dx^2)

Protons of energies of 1 Mev and 30 kev and electrons of 2 kev energy all have approximately the same LET of about 30 kev/μ. These particles have not only markedly different penetration, but, more important, they maintain a LET which is, say, within 10% of the above value, over distances which vary from several microns in the case of the more energetic proton down to magnitudes of the order of atomic diameters for the electron. Thus the *same* dose delivered in the *same* LET interval may be deposited along a few long track sections or along many short ones. If the length of these sections is of the order of the dimensions of sensitive biological structures, this difference may be of importance, since incomplete passage through the structure may not result in inactivation. Even in the case of radiochemistry where effects on isolated molecules are under study, the length of individual track sections over which the LET remains within a certain interval are of importance when they are comparable to the diffusion lengths of activated products.

Lateral Extension and Curvature of Track

The LET has been defined as the "linear rate of loss of energy (locally absorbed) by an ionizing particle traversing a material medium" (*8*). The expression in the parentheses indicates the existence of an ambiguity which cannot be clearly resolved. The column of primary ionizations which defines a particle track is invariably surrounded by spurs produced by electrons (δ-rays) ejected with sufficient energy to produce ionization. The range of such secondaries is usually short compared with the residual range of the primaries. In the case of electrons, however, it is possible that any fraction of the primary energy is transferred, and in case one-half is transferred the track will fork into two equal prongs. In a computation of

LET spectra produced by X-rays (*5*) it was found that these spectra depended on the cutoff point beyond which a secondary electron is no longer considered part of the track of the primary electron.

In the case of heavy particles the δ-ray range is always small, but nuclear interactions of various types may produce energetic secondaries of various kinds, particularly at high energies.

Even when the δ-ray range is short compared with the range of the primary particle, it may be long compared with the dimensions of a sensitive structure, and, in this case, energy which is lost by the primary particle inside the structure is absorbed outside. This basic distribution cannot be materially modified by diffusion of active radicals when the δ-ray range exceeds the diffusion length.

Near the end of the electron range the track curvature becomes very pronounced. When the radius of curvature becomes comparable to the dimensions of sensitive sites, the mean "local" energy deposition increases for the same LET. Finally, when the radius of curvature becomes comparable to ion spacing, the LET concept becomes meaningless.

DISTRIBUTION OF DOSE IN Y

Definition of Y

The difficulties enumerated above are eliminated if, instead of expressing the radiation quality in terms of the energy imparted along the particle track, one relates the critical parameter to the energy which is absorbed in a small mass of the irradiated material as a result of the essentially instantaneous passage of a charged particle through or near the volume, including any energy that might be deposited by secondary and higher order radiations. Each such passage will be termed an *event*. The energy imparted in an event is independent of dose rate. Because of its isotropic properties the sphere is the preferable shape for the test volume. Therefore in the following discussion, events occurring in spherical volumes will be considered.

Assume an isolated, small (e.g., 1-cm diameter) mass of tissue is irradiated by thermal neutrons. Since quanta resulting from capture in hydrogen have an exceedingly high probability of escaping without the production of secondary electrons, virtually all the dose is delivered by 600-kev protons from the (n, p) reaction with nitrogen.[2] Hence, all interactions contribute the same energy through the agency of identical particles.

Consider a volume in this tissue that is spherical in shape and has a diameter that is much larger than the particle range. In this case the number of events is proportional to the cube of the diameter, d, and each event contributes the same energy, E_0 (i.e., 600 kev).

[2] For purposes of simplicity, the contribution of the C^{14} recoils will be neglected in this discussion.

If the sphere diameter is much less than the range, virtually all events are due to particles originating outside the sphere, and the latter may be considered to be in a uniform flux of particles, all of which traverse it completely. In this case the number of events is proportional to the square of the diameter, and the energy deposited per event is proportional to the diameter.

Define now the parameter, Y, as *the energy imparted in an event divided by the sphere diameter*. Note that, although the preceding and the following illustrations may be concerned with particle "tracks," this definition does not involve the spatial distribution of energy deposition inside the sphere.

Idealized Y Distribution of Dose

Neglecting statistical fluctuations and lateral extension and curvature of tracks, one may derive relations between $D(L)$, the distribution of dose in LET, and $D^*(Y)$, the "idealized" distribution of dose in Y. Despite the omission of the above factors, such approximations are useful in establishing the basic aspects of the Y concept.

From considerations given in the preceding section it is evident that, in the case of a sphere that is much larger than the range, Y for any event is inversely proportional to the diameter ($Y = E_0/d$). For a small sphere Y is essentially independent of diameter. If a particle has a LET, L, and traverses along an intercept which has a length that is a fraction, K, of the diameter, Y is equal to KL.

Thus the idealized distribution of the dose in Y, $D^*(Y)$, in the case of a comparatively large d of 0.1 mm (100 μ) is approached by a delta function at E_0/d = 600/100 = 6 kev/μ. Some contributions must be made, however, by events due to particles crossing the surface of the sphere. These deposit energies of less than E_0, and their contribution results in a "tail" (Fig. 1).

When d is very small it may be shown (see the Appendix) that with $D^*(L)$ as the distribution of dose in L

$$D^*(Y) = 3Y^2 \int_Y^{L_{\max}} \frac{D(L)\,dL}{L^3} \tag{1}$$

Equation 1 is valid for any irradiation conditions. In the case under discussion, $D(L)$ is given by

$$D(L) = \frac{1}{E_0}\left(\frac{dE}{dL}\right)_{\text{proton}}$$

Thus

$$D^*(Y) = \frac{3Y^2}{E_0} \int_{E_y}^{E_0} \frac{dE}{L(E)^3} \tag{2}$$

where E_y is the energy corresponding to $L = Y$.

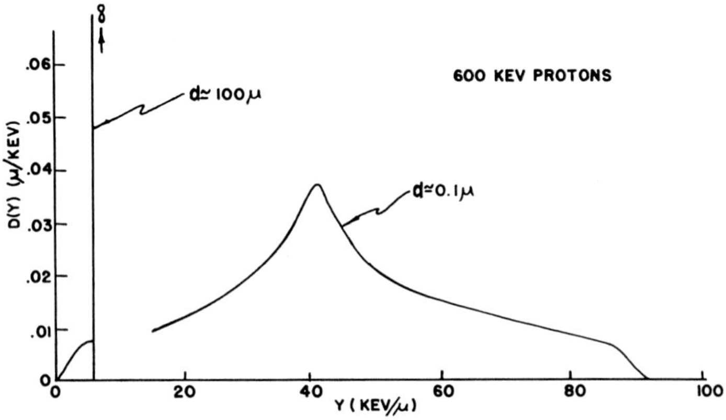

FIG. 1. Idealized Y distribution of dose for 600-kev protons in tissue for 100-μ sphere and 0.1-μ sphere.

This curve is indicated schematically in Fig. 1. With kev/μ as the unit for Y, the maximum Y is 91, corresponding to a traversal at maximum LET across a major diameter.

When the sphere diameter is comparable to the particle range, a theoretical evaluation of the Y spectrum is a complex problem, since variations in track length as well as in L must be considered. It will be seen, however, that Y_{max} increases as $1/d$ only if d is larger than the proton range. The latter is about 10 μ. For a sphere of this diameter Y_{max} is equal to the average value of the LET over the entire range of a 600-kev proton (60 kev/μ). For values of d that are less than 10 μ, Y_{max} increases only to the extent that the mean LET in a major traversal can increase. When the sphere has a diameter of the order of 0.1 μ, the change in LET during any traversal is negligible, and Y_{max} and the entire distribution $D(Y)$ remain the same as long as the assumptions made in this section are valid.

Actual Y Distribution of Dose

The degree to which the above simplifications are admissible must depend largely on the types and energies of the charged particles involved. At any rate, statistical fluctuations must distort the idealized shape, particularly when d becomes small.

Experiments with monoenergetic neutrons indicate (*9*) that idealized and actual distributions agree well for neutron energies above 1 Mev and values of d of the order of 1 μ. At lower neutron energies there is considerable discrepancy. Figure 2 shows experimental results for 500-kev *neutrons* for spheres of 1.5-μ, 3-μ, and 6-μ diameters. The idealized curve for $D(Y)$ was obtained from equation *1*, using $D(L)$ values given by Boag (*3*) and taking into account contributions made by protons beyond the peak of the Bragg curve. The reasons for the shape of the experimental curves, together with curves obtained at other neutron energies, will be given in

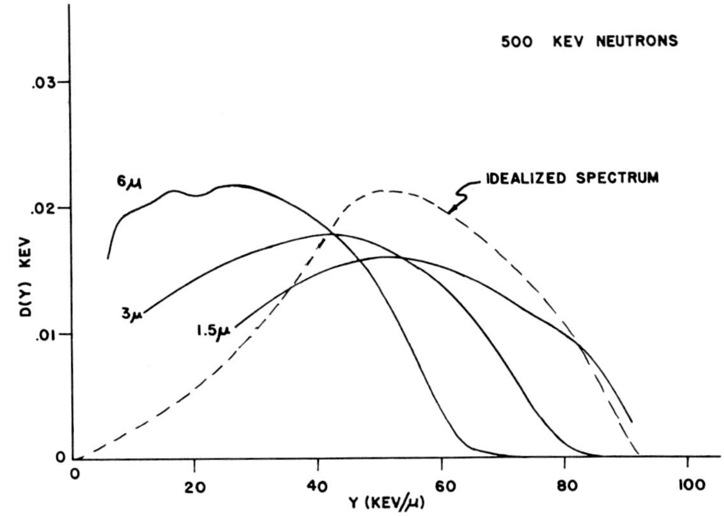

FIG. 2. Idealized Y distribution for 500-kev neutrons for small spheres and experimental Y distributions for 1.5-μ, 3-μ, and 6-μ spheres.

another publication (*9*). Figure 2 is presented here merely to indicate that, for a neutron energy that is not very low and spheres that are smaller than most cell nuclei, the Y distribution can be quite different from the one that might be inferred from the LET spectrum.

Local Dose and Frequency of Events

Each event imparts an increment of dose which may be called a "local" dose· Frequently the local dose is larger than the *mean* dose imparted to the irradiated object as a whole. The representation $D(Y)$ may be used not only to determine the fraction of the dose delivered at any Y but also to evaluate the local dose and to determine the probability of such an occurrence.

In a unit density sphere having a diameter of d microns, an event of magnitude Y delivers an energy of $Y \times d$ kev to a volume of $(\pi d^3/6) \times 10^{-12}$ cm^3. This corresponds to a dose of $(6Y/\pi d^2) \times 10^{12} \times 1.6 \times 10^{-11} = 30.6Y/d^2$ rads.

For each rad of mean dose, $D(Y)$ rads are delivered per kev/μ interval at Y. Hence, the number of events corresponding to Y is $D(Y)d^2/30.6Y$.

For example, when tissue is exposed to 500-kev neutrons, the fraction of the dose delivered at a Y between 79.5 kev/μ and 80.5 kev/μ is 0.01 for 1.5-μ-diameter sphere (Fig. 2). Each event contributes an energy of $80 \times 1.5 = 120$ kev, which results in a local dose of $30.6 \times 80/1.5^2 = 1090$ rads. For each rad of mean tissue dose the frequency of this event is $0.01 \times (1.5)^2/(30.6 \times 80) = 9.2 \times 10^{-6}$. Hence, such an event will occur in one out of 100,000D randomly selected spheres, if D is the dose in rads.

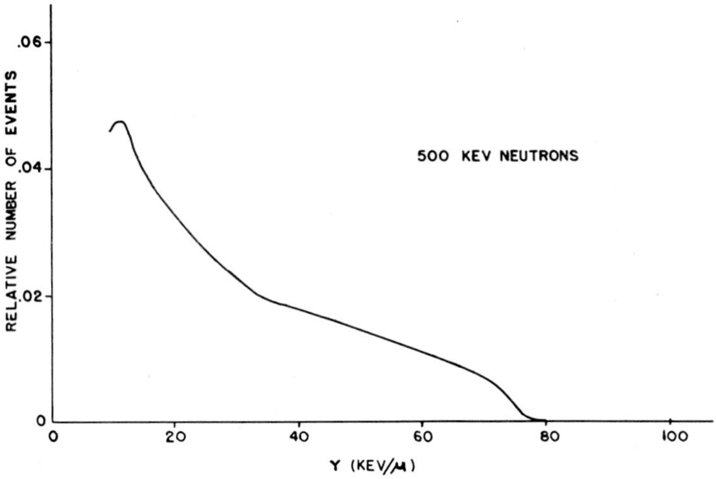

FIG. 3. Number of events versus Y for 500-kev neutrons; $d = 3\ \mu$

The frequency, F, of the occurrence of any event corresponding to a Y larger than some lower limit, $Y_{\min}$ is given by

$$F = \int_{Y_{\min}}^{Y_{\max}} \frac{D(Y)d^2}{30.6Y}\, dY \quad \text{per rad of mean dose}$$

Numerical evaluation of this integral for $d = 1.5\ \mu$ and $E_n = 500$ kev (Fig. 2) gives $F = 1.32 \times 10^{-3}$ for $Y_{\min} = 20$ kev/μ, (the lowest value determined). Hence it may be concluded that per rad of mean dose only one in about 750 spheres will contain events with Y in excess of 20 kev/μ.

Since the dose per event is proportional to Y, a curve relating the relative *number* of events to Y may be obtained by dividing $D(Y)$ by Y. Figure 3 shows such a curve for $d = 3\ \mu$ and $E_n = 500$ kev. Note that most of the events are small.

DISCUSSION

The detector of the LET spectrometer (*6*), which is a spherical shell of tissue-equivalent plastic filled with tissue-equivalent gas, has been designed to simulate small spheres of unit density tissue. The instrument may readily be used to obtain $D(Y)$ spectra except for limitations in resolution. Since the energy loss is measured on the basis of ionization, Y must be determined in units of W/d, where W is the average energy expended in the production of an ion pair. Furthermore, when the number of ion pairs is small, fluctuations in avalanche formation in the proportional counter cause broadening of the true distribution. In most cases thus far investigated the effect of these disturbances has been negligible.

Measurements at high neutron energies may be used to derive $D(L)$ spectra

(*7*, *9*) that are similar to those computed by Boag (*3*). Such $D(L)$ spectra cannot be evaluated at neutron energies below about 500 kev because of incomplete particle traversal, even in the smallest spheres that can at present be simulated. On the basis of data obtained at high energies it may be anticipated that the availability of smaller counters will make it possible to obtain $D(Y)$ spectra for smaller spheres, but measured $D(L)$ spectra will be consistently different from those that are computed theoretically because of marked statistical fluctuations that must occur in small samples.

Since the counter reproduces the actual processes taking place in tissue rather faithfully, it would appear that the information obtained with this device is of more explicit value than the more abstract representation $D(L)$. All existing theories of the biological action of radiation, such as the "target" theory, the "activated water" theory, and the intermediate "diffusion" theory, postulate mechanisms accounting for differences in RBE, which are based on differences in local deposition of energy within certain volumes of the irradiated material. The extent of these volumes may vary or be unknown, but $D(Y)$ spectra for a wide range of diameters should include the information required.

Since there is at present no reason to prefer the $D(Y)$ spectrum corresponding to a definite diameter and since in many cases (as in Fig. 2) the variation with d is considerable, a representation of radiation quality in terms of $D(Y)$ must be given by a series of spectra covering a rather wide range of d, which might cover values from 10 μ to $10^{-2}\mu$. Information of this type is complete but also complex, and for some purposes (e.g., personnel protection) the single distribution $D(L)$ may be more practical.

Correlation of chemical and biological effects with $D(L)$ is still quite sparse, and as yet apparently no correlation with $D(Y)$ has been even attempted. Because of this uncertainty, the concept of Y has been expressed as a symbol without having been given a name, and it is recommended that for the present Y be considered as an alternate rather than a preferable index of radiation quality.

SUMMARY

Radiation quality has been commonly expressed in terms of the LET of the ionizing particles that deliver the absorbed dose. The detailed mechanism of energy loss of charged particles is such that there is a very complex relation between LET and the energy deposited in some small region of the irradiated tissue.

The parameter Y is defined as the energy imparted to a small sphere divided by the sphere diameter. Representation of the dose in Y for a range of diameters yields information on the spatial distribution of energy, as well as on the local dose and the frequency with which such a dose is delivered.

It is believed that this representation may prove useful in fundamental radiobiological and radiochemical studies.

APPENDIX

Relation between D(L) and D(Y)

In a sphere which is randomly traversed by particles traveling in straight lines, the distribution, $P(x)$, of path intercepts of length x is (*6*)

$$P(x) = 2x/d^2 \qquad (x \leq d)$$

where d is the sphere diameter.

The energy deposited by particles having an intercept, x, and a LET, L, is xL. Hence, the relative dose distributed by these particles is $2x^2L/d^2$. The fraction of the total dose at L contributed between x and $x + dx$ is

$$\Delta(x)\, dx = K(2x^2L/d^2)\, dx$$

where K is a normalizing factor which may be obtained from

$$\int_0^d \Delta(x)\, dx = 1$$

Thus

$$K = 3/2Ld$$

and

$$\Delta(x)\, dx = 3x^2\, dx/d^3$$

Define Y as the energy deposited in a traversal divided by the sphere diameter. Thus

$$Y = xL/d$$

and

$$dY = dxL/d$$

Then the fraction of the dose delivered between Y and $Y + dY$ is

$$\Delta(Y)\, dY = 3Y^2\, dY/L^3 \qquad (Y \geq L)$$

If the dose is delivered in a range of LET with the dose between L and $L + dL$ being $D(L)\, dL$, then

$$d[D(Y)] = 3Y^2 D(L)\, dL/L^3$$

is the differential contribution to $D(Y)$ due to particles having a LET, L. Hence

$$D(Y) = 3Y^2 \int_Y^{L_{\max}} D(L) d\, dL/L^3$$

ACKNOWLEDGMENTS

The author is indebted to W. Rosenzweig for helpful discussions and to M. Lubert for the preparation of Figs. 1, 2, and 3.

RECEIVED: July 7, 1958

REFERENCES

1. R. E. ZIRKLE, Biological effectiveness of alpha particles as a function of ion concentration in their paths. *Am. J. Cancer* **23**, 558–567 (1935).
2. R. E. ZIRKLE, D. F. MARCHBANK, and K. D. KUCK, Exponential and sigmoid survival curves resulting from alpha and X-irradiation of *Aspergillus* spores. *J. Cellular Comp. Physiol.* **39**, *Suppl.* **1**, 75–85 (1952).
3. J. W. BOAG, The distribution of linear energy transfer or "ion density" for fast neutrons in water. *Radiation Research* **1**, 323–341 (1954).
4. D. V. CORMACK and H. E. JOHNS, Electron energies and ion densities in water irradiated with 200 Kev, 1 Mev and 25 Mev radiation. *Brit. J. Radiol.* **25**, 369–381 (1952).
5. M. DANZKER, N. D. KESSARIS and J. S. LAUGHLIN, Absorbed dose and linear energy transfer in radiation experiments. *Radiology* in press. By courtesy of the authors the manuscript was made available prior to publication.
6. H. H. ROSSI and W. ROSENZWEIG, A device for the measurement of dose as a function of specific ionization. *Radiology* **64**, 404–411 (1955).
7. H. H. ROSSI and W. ROSENZWEIG, Measurements of neutron dose as a function of linear energy transfer. *Radiation Research* **2**, 417–425 (1955).
8. Report of the International Commission on Radiological Units and Measurement (ICRU). *Natl. Bur. Standards (U. S.) Handbook* **No. 62** (1956).
9. W. ROSENZWEIG and H. H. ROSSI, Determination of the quality of the absorbed dose delivered by monoenergetic neutrons. *Radiation Research* **10**, 532–544 (1959).

RADIATION RESEARCH 10, 532–544 (1959)

Determination of the Quality of the Absorbed Dose Delivered by Monoenergetic Neutrons[1]

W. ROSENZWEIG AND H. H. ROSSI

Department of Radiology, Columbia University, New York, N. Y.

In order to allow a more precise characterization of the quality of ionizing radiation, a spherical proportional counter has been developed at this laboratory. It was shown (*1*) that because of its shape the pulse-height spectrum obtained with this counter could under certain conditions be subjected to a mathematical analysis in order to obtain the distribution of the dose in the LET (linear energy transfer) of the ionizing particles. Actual measurements on Pu-Be and Po-B neutron sources and on 3-Mev neutrons from a deuterium (*d*, *n*) reaction were performed and reported (*2*). At that time a comparison was made with calculations by Boag (*3*) based on the LET versus energy curve for protons in water. Some differences between the calculated and observed spectra were found and possible causes discussed. Subsequent measurements indicated that the differences could not be completely explained on the basis of experimental error and that the measured spectrum must differ from the calculated one because of physical factors that are more fundamental. The calculated spectrum uses the concept of the LET of a particle at a point. This is a useful abstraction which can never be quite approached in a physical measurement. The gas volume of the counter must take a finite sample from the track of the ionizing particle. If the sample is very small there will be large statistical fluctuations in the energy loss of the particle owing to the discontinuous nature of the collision process and the possible loss of energetic δ-rays to the counter wall. This effect will be minimized by making the sample larger, but in this case the ionizing particle loses so much energy that it can no longer be characterized by a single LET. It has already been pointed out (*4*) that the counter measurement presents a picture which resembles more closely events that take place in a sphere of tissue under irradiation.

The present work is a study of the pulse-height spectra and resultant dose distributions for monoenergetic neutrons as a function of neutron energy and also sample size. The neutrons were produced at a Van de Graaff generator at the follow-

[1] Based on work performed under Contract AT-30-1-GEN-70 for the U. S. Atomic Energy Commission.

ing energies: 0.2, 0.5, 1.0, 2.0, 3.0, and 4.0 Mev by the tritium (p, n) reaction; 6.0 and 8.0 Mev by the deuterium (d, n) reaction. For the thickness of target used, it was estimated that the spread of neutron energies was ±30% at 0.2 Mev, ±15% at 0.5 Mev, ±10% at 1.0 Mev, and ±5% or less at the higher energies. Two 4-inch spherical proportional counters were used with electrode structures as described elsewhere (*2*). One had a tissue-equivalent conducting plastic wall (from now on referred to as the TE counter), and the other was identical with the first except that it had a 1/32-inch aluminum liner on the inner surface (the Al counter). Both were operated with tissue-equivalent gas under a continuous gas flow condition. The TE counter can be considered to be equivalent to a spherical biological structure surrounded by tissue; the Al counter is equivalent to the same structure but completely isolated. Whereas the former will record recoil protons which originate both within and without the sphere, the latter will record only those which arise from within. The effective size of this equivalent sphere was varied by operating the counter at pressures of 5, 10, 20, and 40 mm of mercury. Taking into account the actual physical size of the counter one obtains a correspondence between counter gas pressure and the effective diameter of an equivalent sphere of unit density tissue:

Pressure	*Sphere diameter*
5 mm	.75 μ
10 mm	1.5 μ
20 mm	3 μ
40 mm	6 μ

The energy calibration under a given set of operating conditions was effected by means of a collimated Cm^{244} α-source, and the pulses from the counter were sorted on a Los Alamos 100-channel analyzer.

Pulse-height spectra were obtained at all energies and pressures with the TE counter. The Al counter was used at each pressure only for those energies which yielded an appreciable gas contribution. The results of the measurements will be presented in three different ways.

1. The pulse-height spectrum: This is a plot of the relative number of pulses falling into a given unit pulse-height interval versus pulse height. Since the pulse height is proportional to the energy deposited in the spherical volume during the traversal of a single ionizing particle, the ordinate of this plot gives the frequency of occurrence of traversals in which a given amount of energy is deposited.

2. The dose as distributed in energy-event size: This distribution is obtained by multiplying the ordinate of the pulse-height spectrum by the abscissa and plotting this product versus the pulse height. Since the abscissa is the same as before, the ordinate of this plot gives the relative dose which is imparted to the sphere by events lying in a given unit event size (pulse-height) interval.

3. The dose as distributed in LET: As mentioned previously, whenever conditions permit, the pulse-height spectrum may be analyzed to yield this distribution.

An analysis was made whenever all particles lose only a small fraction of their energy in traversing the sphere (this excludes all 6-μ-diameter measurements) and/or when the Al counter measures less than 10% of the TE counter dose. The ordinate of this plot gives the relative dose imparted to the sphere by events in a given LET interval.

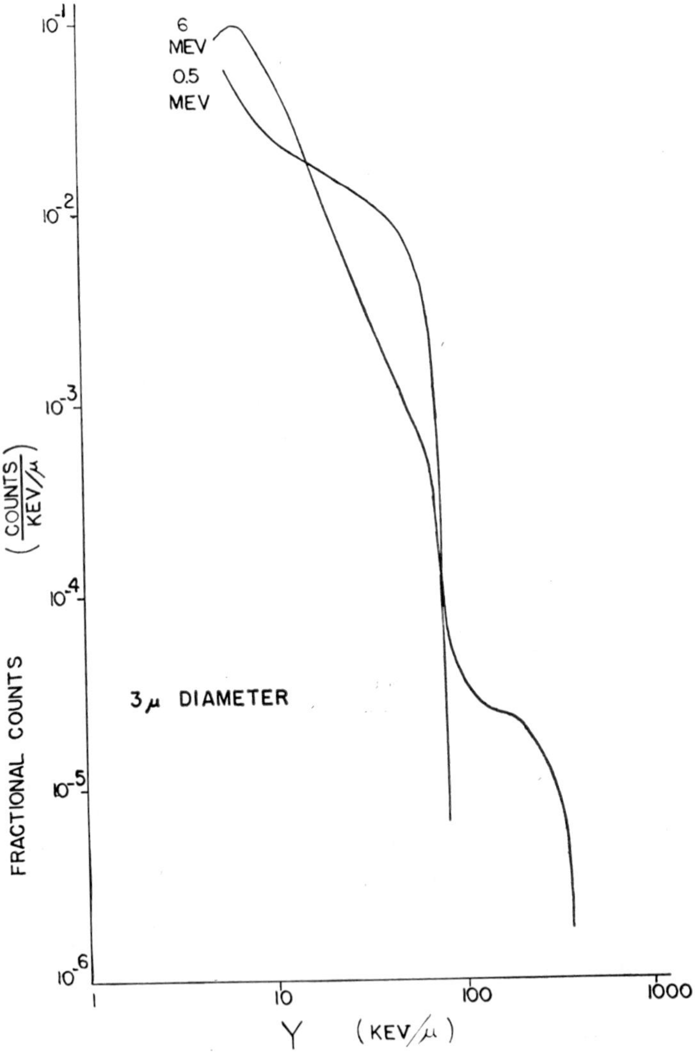

FIG. 1. Example of pulse-height spectra for 0.5-Mev and 6-Mev neutrons in a 3-μ-diameter tissue sphere surrounded by tissue.

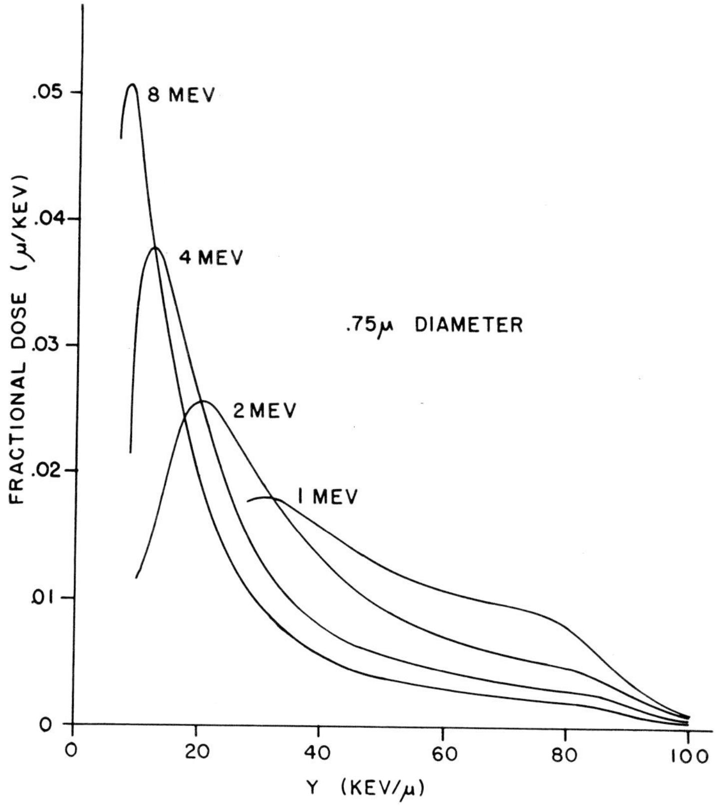

FIG. 2. Dose absorbed in a 0.75-μ-diameter tissue sphere surrounded by tissue as distributed in Y for neutrons in the range 1 Mev to 8 Mev.

As an example of pulse-height spectra, Fig. 1 shows a logarithmic plot for 0.5-Mev and 6-Mev neutrons in a 3-μ-diameter tissue sphere surrounded by tissue walls. The curves are normalized to give a total area of 1 (i.e., one event), and the abscissa is in units of energy-event size in kiloelectron volts divided by the sphere diameter in microns and is designated by the symbol Y (kev/μ) (*5*). All the measured curves have these general features in common: Most of the pulses are small. For small diameters there is an abrupt drop in the vicinity of 92 kev/μ which represents protons of highest average LET traversing a major diameter of the sphere. As the diameter goes up, this drop must occur at lower values of Y, as will be explained below. At high neutron energies events above this cutoff are also observed. These are due to carbon recoils and occur in greater abundance and extend to larger Y as the neutron energy is increased.

An exhaustive presentation of dose as distributed in Y is given in the next eight

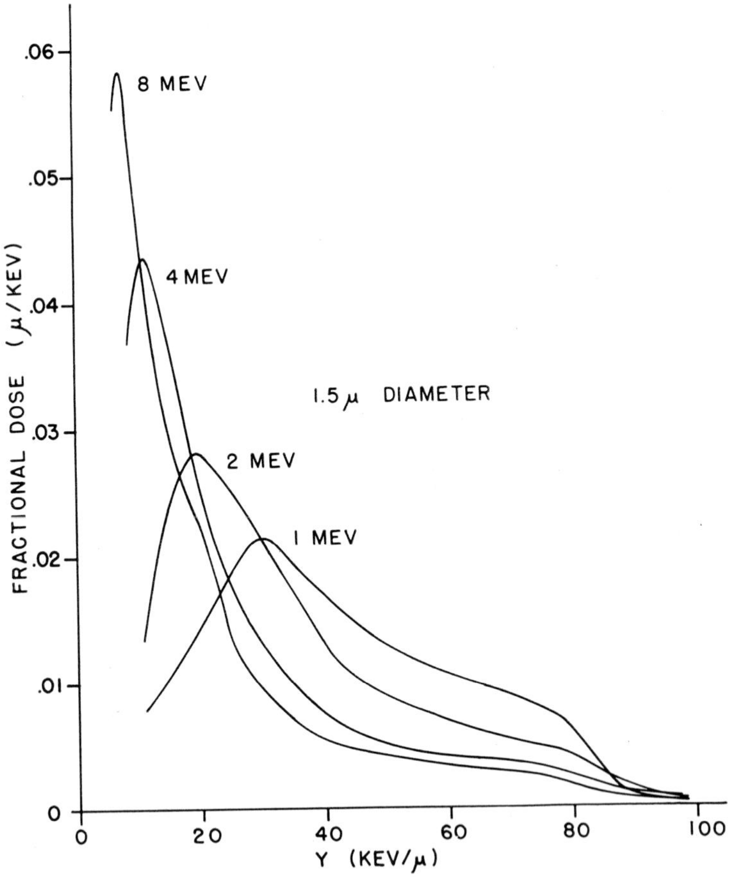

FIG. 3. Dose absorbed in a 1.5-μ-diameter tissue sphere surrounded by tissue as distributed in Y for neutrons in the range 1 Mev to 8 Mev.

figures. Figures 2 to 5 contain families of curves for the TE counter in the range of energies from 1 to 8 Mev for each of the four samples sizes used. Figures 6 to 9 contain curves for both the TE counter and the Al counter at 0.2 and 0.5 Mev for all four sample sizes except for two cases. Each of the TE counter curves is normalized to unit area (i.e., unit dose), and the parameter Y is used as the energy-event size variable. In order to obtain the absolute value of the event size in kiloelectron volts it is only necessary to multiply Y by the sphere diameter.

In order to describe completely the behavior of these curves with variation in neutron energy and sample size a detailed mathematical analysis would be required which will not be given here. A general discussion can be given, however, if the physical properties of LET versus energy (Bragg curve) and range versus energy for

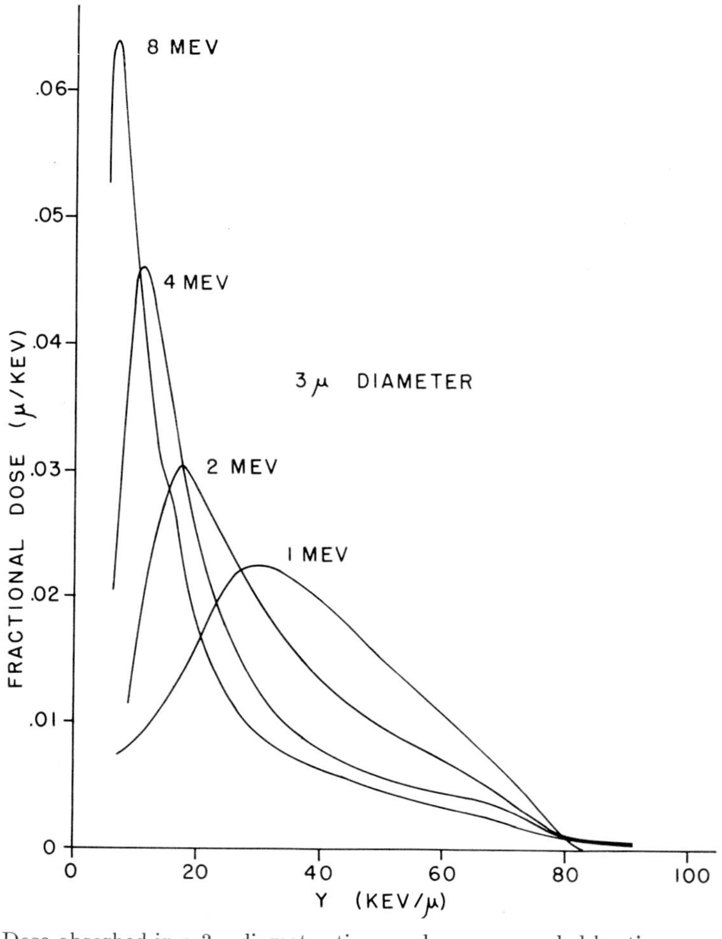

FIG. 4. Dose absorbed in a 3-μ-diameter tissue sphere surrounded by tissue as distributed in Y for neutrons in the range 1 Mev to 8 Mev.

protons are kept in mind. The location of the break at large Y must be consistent with the largest amount of energy which a proton can spend in traversing a major diameter of the counter. When the diameter is small, e.g., 0.75 μ, protons near the Bragg peak can cross a major diameter with an LET near 92 kev/μ without losing too much energy, thus giving rise to a Y of 92 kev/μ. As the diameter is increased the proton can maintain an LET of 92 kev/μ for only part of its traversal, the rest being spent at progressively lower LET. Hence, the maximum Y will decrease with increasing diameter. This trend can be observed on the curves for all energies except when the neutron energy becomes so low that the range of the most energetic

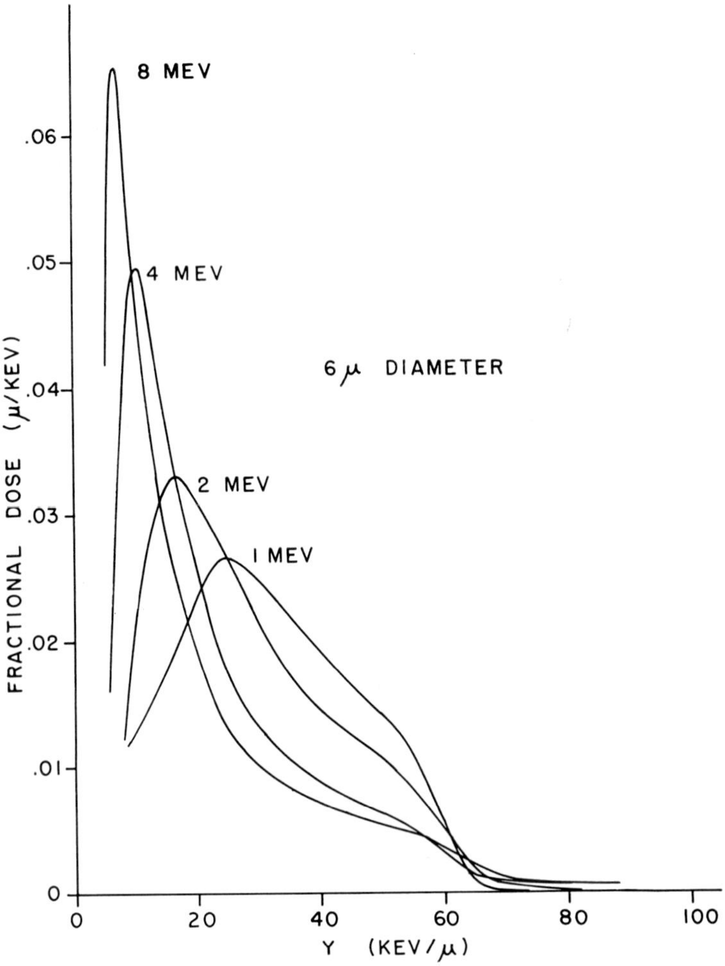

FIG. 5. Dose absorbed in a 6-μ-diameter tissue sphere surrounded by tissue as distributed in Y for neutrons in the range 1 Mev to 8 Mev.

recoil protons becomes less than the major diameter of the sphere. Under such circumstances the maximum observed Y will be the neutron energy divided by the sphere diameter. For the case of 0.2-Mev neutrons in the 6-μ sphere the maximum observed Y is about 40 kev/μ, which is reasonable when the smear in neutron energy is taken into account. It may also be observed from the shapes of the curves that the average Y increases as the neutron energy is decreased, reaching a maximum (for the 1.5-μ, 3-μ, and 6-μ spheres) at 0.5 Mev and decreasing again at 0.2 Mev.

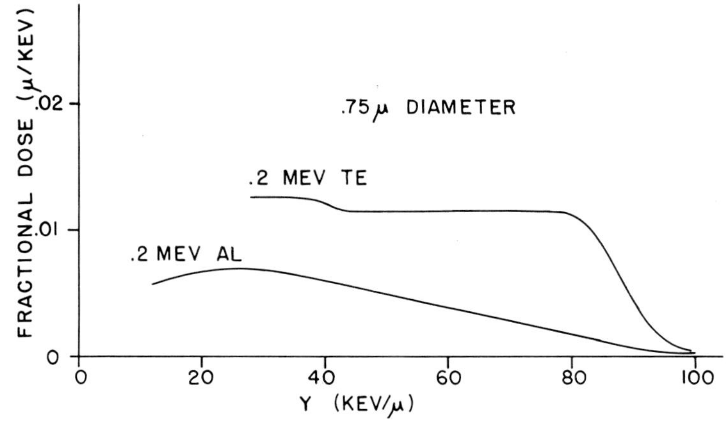

FIG. 6. Dose absorbed in a 0.75-μ-diameter tissue sphere surrounded by tissue (TE) or isolated (Al) as distributed in Y for 0.2-Mev and 0.5-Mev neutrons.

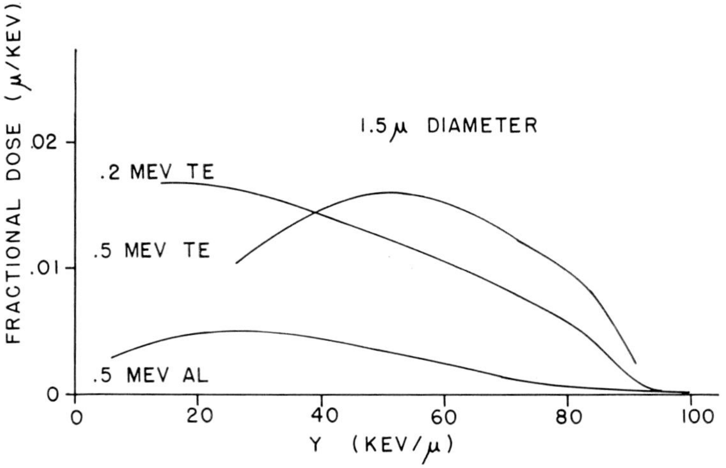

FIG. 7. Dose absorbed in a 1.5-μ-diameter tissue sphere surrounded by tissue (TE) or isolated (Al) as distributed in Y for 0.2-Mev and 0.5-Mev neutrons.

This behavior may be biologically significant, indicating a possible maximum in the biological effectiveness of neutrons in the vicinity of 0.5 Mev.

Most of the Al counter measurements made are included in Figs. 6 to 8. These curves are not normalized to unity but give the correct fractional dose compared with the total dose as determined with the TE counter. As is to be expected, the fractional dose due to recoil protons originating in the gas volume becomes smaller as the neutron energy is increased for a given sample size. Also, for a given energy,

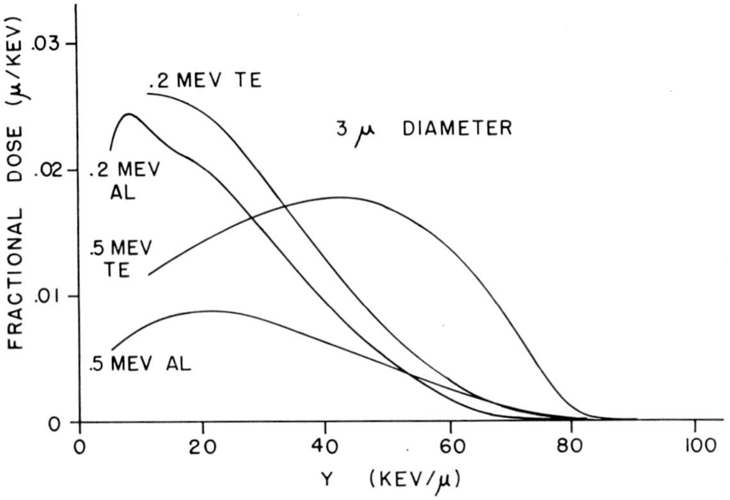

FIG. 8. Dose absorbed in a 3-μ-diameter tissue sphere surrounded by tissue (TE) or isolated (Al) as distributed in Y for 0.2-Mev and 0.5-Mev neutrons.

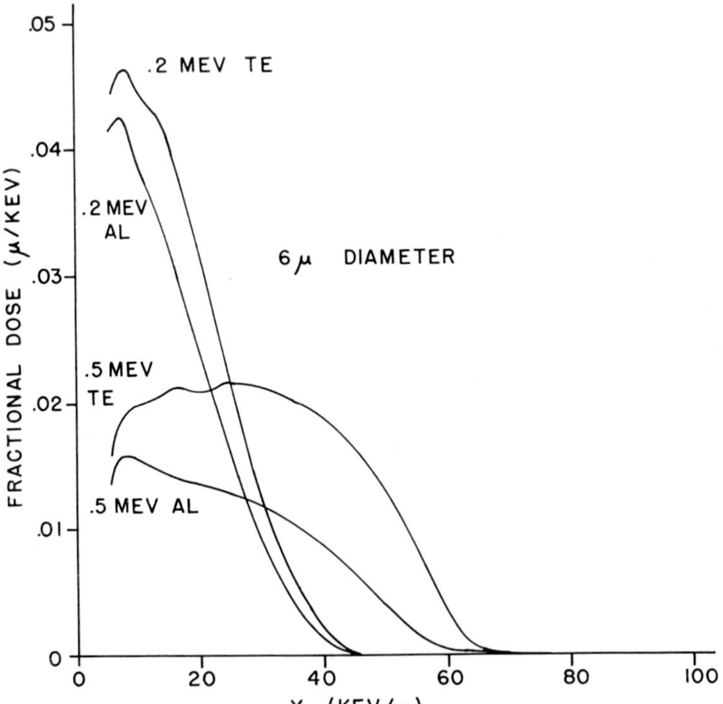

FIG. 9. Dose absorbed in a 6-μ-diameter tissue sphere surrounded by tissue (TE) or isolated (Al) as distributed in Y for 0.2-Mev and 0.5-Mev neutrons.

TABLE I

Ratio of the Absorbed Dose Measured in the Al Counter to that Measured in the TE Counter

Neutron energy (Mev)	*Sphere diameter (μ)*			
	0.75	*1.5*	*3*	*6*
0.2	0.42	—	0.78	0.82
0.5	—	0.26	0.38	0.57
1	0.10	0.14	0.21	0.31
2			0.10	0.15
3				0.11

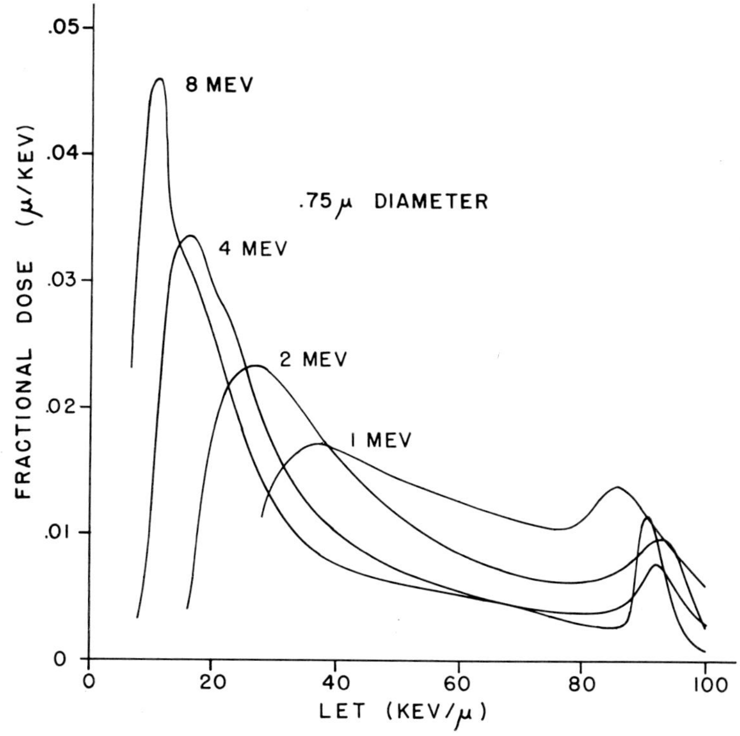

Fig. 10. Dose as distributed in LET for neutrons in the range of 1 Mev to 8 Mev. Effective counter diameter 0.75 μ.

the fraction decreases with decreasing sample size. The results of these measurements are presented in Table I, which gives the ratio of the dose measured in the Al counter to that measured in the TE counter. As may be observed from the table, in the case of 0.2-Mev neutrons in 3-μ and 6-μ spheres almost all the dose is due to particles

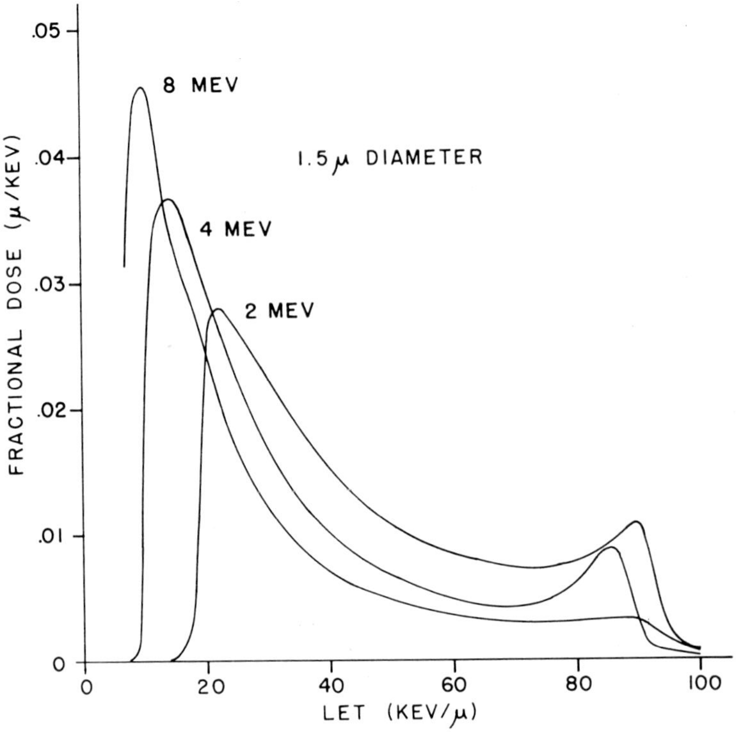

FIG. 11. Dose as distributed in LET for neutrons in the range of 2 Mev to 8 Mev. Effective counter diameter 1.5 μ.

originating within the sphere. For a biological system the implications are that the absorbed dose at a particular location is characterized by the hydrogen content of an increasingly smaller surrounding volume as the neutron energy decreases. Thus, at 0.2 Mev variations in hydrogen content within distances of about 1 μ must result in corresponding variations in absorbed dose.

In those instances where conditions permitted, analyses of the pulse-height spectra were made to yield dose versus LET curves. These curves, normalized to unit area (unit dose), are shown in Figs. 10 to 12. It is felt that the condition of small energy loss in the counter is already violated for some of the large energy events in the 3-μ sphere but that the curves in general still give a good representation. The behavior of the curves with energy is in approximate accordance with Boag's calculations (*3*). Both the calculations and the measurements indicate an increase in average LET with decreasing energy. It is of interest to note that if the calculated spectra were continued to lower energies a maximum average LET would be found in the range of about 0.5 Mev because of the characteristics of the

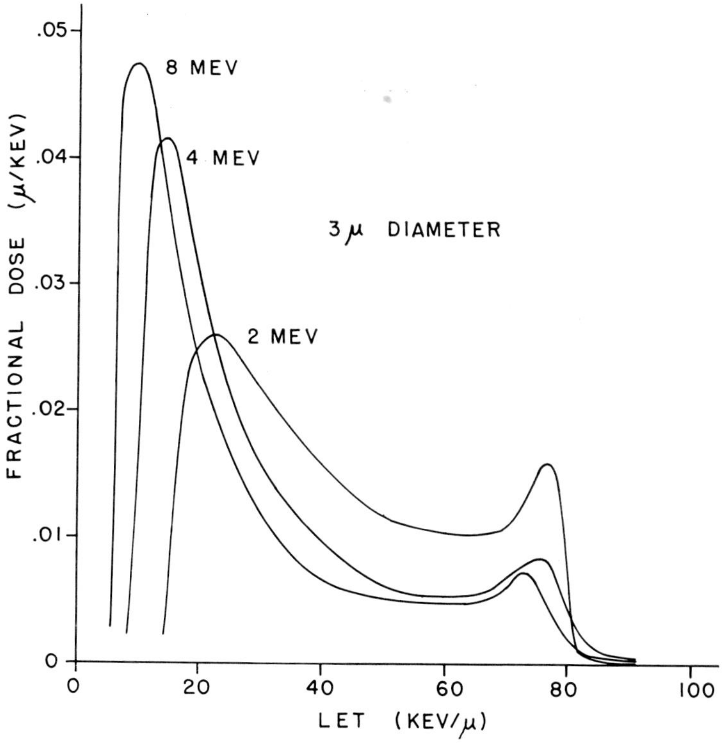

FIG. 12. Dose as distributed in LET for neutrons in the range of 2 Mev to 8 Mev. Effective counter diameter 3 μ.

Bragg curve. The significance of such a calculation, however, is limited by the considerations given above with respect to samples of finite size.

Finally, it must be mentioned that the results presented here are subject to some experimental error which would tend to distort the spectra slightly. Notable among these are slight drifts in gas multiplication and in the electronic system. These will manifest themselves mostly at low gas pressures (0.75-μ and 1.5-μ spheres) and protracted measurements (which were required at neutron energies of 0.2 and 0.5 Mev). Also, inherent in a proportional counter measurement is its finite resolution which tends to have a broadening effect on the observed spectra. Since this depends approximately inversely on the square root of the energy lost by the particles in the counter volume, the largest effect will again take place for small sample sizes (0.75 μ and 1.5 μ). On the basis of published data (*6*) involving a cylindrical proportional counter it is to be expected that this spread is at most $\pm 6\,\%$ for the smallest energy events measured.

It is felt that the radiobiologist performing neutron irradiations can benefit greatly from interpreting the results of his own experiments in light of the findings presented in this paper. It must be borne in mind that, if the variation in the parameters LET or Y are responsible for corresponding variations in the relative biological effectiveness (RBE) of radiation, then the RBE of neutrons is inextricably related to the neutron energy. Existing discrepancies in the RBE of "fast" neutrons may be attributable to the failure of taking this variation into account. It must further be noted that on a microscopic level, particularly at low neutron energies, the picture depends greatly on the size of the biological structure under consideration. The two factors which enter here are the local hydrogen content which affects the magnitude of the total absorbed dose and the actual physical size compared to the range of the recoil protons which affects the detailed energy deposition as illustrated by the dose versus Y curves.

ACKNOWLEDGMENTS

The authors are indebted to Mr. M. Lubert who assisted in the evaluation of the data. The large Los Alamos Van de Graaff generator was made available through the good offices of Dr. J. Sayeg. The generous assistance of Dr. J. J. McKibben and his staff is also gratefully acknowledged. The Cm^{244} α-source used in the calibration of the proportional counter was provided by Argonne National Laboratory.

RECEIVED: September 5, 1958

REFERENCES

1. H. H. ROSSI and W. ROSENZWEIG, A device for the measurement of dose as a function of specific ionization. *Radiology* **64,** 404–410 (1955).
2. H. H. ROSSI and W. ROSENZWEIG, Measurements of neutron dose as a function of linear energy transfer. *Radiation Research* **2,** 417–425 (1955).
3. J. W. BOAG, The distribution of linear energy transfer or "ion density" for fast neutrons in water. *Radiation Research* **1,** 323–341 (1954).
4. H. H. ROSSI and W. ROSENZWEIG, Limitations of the concept of linear energy transfer. *Radiology* **66,** 105 (1956).
5. H. H. ROSSI, Specification of radiation quality. *Radiation Research* **10,** 522–531 (1959).
6. A. BISI and L. ZAPPA, Statistical spread in pulse size of the proportional counter spectrometer. *Nuovo cimento* **2,** 988–994 (1955).

RADIATION RESEARCH 10, 545–551 (1959)

Deoxyribonuclease II Activity in Lymphoid Tissues of Rats[1]

E. R. GORDON, E. GASSNER, S. OKADA, AND L. H. HEMPELMANN[2]

Division of Experimental Radiology, University of Rochester School of Medicine, Rochester, New York

INTRODUCTION

It has been established that the total activity[3] of deoxyribonuclease II (DNase II) in the spleen (*1–3*) and thymus glands (*3*) of rats is unchanged during the first 24-hour period of tissue atrophy induced by total-body X-irradiation. This observation could be explained in several ways. Any satisfactory hypothesis, however, must take into account the fact that cell death and subsequent disappearance of cell fragments are not accompanied by a parallel loss of total DNase activity from lymphoid organs. The present paper presents indirect evidence that the radiosensitive lymphocytic centers contain little DNase II activity. Such evidence was gained from a study of the change in DNase II activity during the first week after exposure and from observations of the action of cortisone on the DNase II activity in lymphoid tissues. Experimental data are also presented to show that the alteration in DNase II activity results primarily from the direct action of ionizing radiation rather than from an indirect action mediated by some physiological mechanism.

METHODS

Male Sprague-Dawley rats weighing 180 to 200 gm were used. They were kept in individual cages and fed ground Purina fox chow. When only one day elapsed between treatment and sacrifice, the animals were starved but had free access to water. In the experiments lasting a week, the nonirradiated controls were pair-fed with the experimental animals to exclude possible effects of the partial starvation which follows radiation exposure.

In the first experiments, the entire bodies of rats were sham-irradiated or irradiated with 756 r of 250-kvp X-rays with the following radiation factors: 18

[1] Supported, in part, by a grant from the U. S. Atomic Energy Commission.

[2] With the technical assistance of B. Schlegel.

[3] *Total activity* refers to enzymatic activity contained in the whole organ. *Specific activity* is defined as enzymatic activity per milligram of wet tissue.

r/min, 15 ma, aluminum parabolic filter 0.42 mm, with 0.5 mm Cu and a target-to-animal distance of 25 cm. For partial-body irradiation, the rats were anesthetized with sodium pentothal and placed in a plastic cylinder which fitted snugly in a lead cylinder (1/4 inch thick). This shielded the upper part of their bodies to the xiphoid process. Seven or eight animals so shielded were irradiated simultaneously using the above factors. Sham-irradiated controls were treated the same way but not placed under the X-ray tube. The scattered radiation in the region of the shielded thymus gland was measured by means of a 100-r Victoreen chamber placed in the presumed location of the thymus in a phantom consisting of rice packed in the plastic and lead cylinders. At best, this dose is only an approximation of the actual dose received by the gland, since the radiation flux changes rapidly in this region. Thus, moving the chamber from the site of the gland 1 cm in either direction along the cylindrical axis changed the dose from 50 to 170% of the presumed thymic dose.[4]

In one experiment, cortisone acetate (Merck) was injected intramuscularly as a single large dose (10 mg per 100 gm of body weight); in a second experiment, smaller doses (1 mg per 100 gm of body weight) were injected daily for one week.

The tissues were homogenized in distilled water, diluted 1:100 with water, and assayed for DNase II activity by the method used by Kowlessar *et al.* (*4*).

RESULTS

The data in Fig. 1 were obtained from one of two similar experiments showing the DNase activity of the spleen and thymus glands of irradiated and pair-fed control rats during the first week after exposure. These charts indicate that, at this dose of total-body irradiation, atrophy of the spleen and thymus was almost complete by the third day. Thereafter, the organ weights of the irradiated rats remained constant without gross evidence of regeneration. A twofold elevation of the specific DNase activity over the level seen in nonirradiated controls occurred during the initial period of radiation-induced atrophy. After the third day after exposure, the specific activity fell rapidly and approached the control value by the seventh day. The total enzymatic activity of spleen and thymus decreased to about one-third that of the controls by the end of the first week after irradiation. The weights of the spleen and thymus obtained from control animals decreased slightly, but the total and specific DNase activity remained constant in these organs.

The data in Table I show the organ weights and enzymatic activities of lymphoid tissues of animals treated either with a single large dose of cortisone or with repeated smaller doses. Twenty-four hours after the former treatment, there was loss of weight of the spleen and thymus glands, which was more pronounced in the

[4] The authors wish to thank Dr. A. L. Carsten for the use of his shielding apparatus and for providing information about its scattering properties.

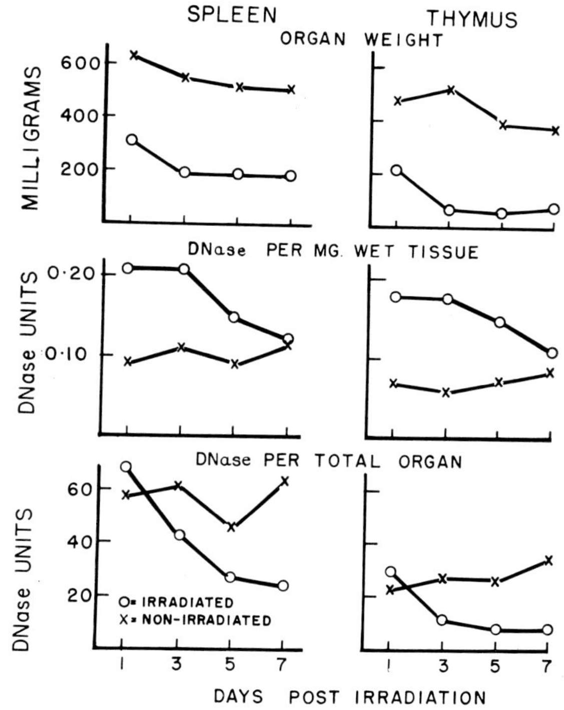

FIG. 1. Changes in organ weight and DNase II activity during first week after irradiation. Units of DNase II activity represent change in optical density measured at 600 mμ. This is one of two typical experiments using five rats per point.

thymus. There was a moderate increase in the specific activity but no significant change in the total activity of the organs. The change in specific activity was less than that observed 24 hours after exposure of rats to a lethal dose of X-rays but was comparable in magnitude to that produced by 150 r (S. Okada, unpublished data). The decrease in total DNase activity produced by repeated small doses of cortisone resembled that noted one week after exposure to 756 r, an $LD_{75(30)}$.

Table II shows the mean enzymatic activity of the spleen and thymus glands of rats exposed to partial-body or total-body X-irradiation. The reduction in weight and change in enzymatic activity in the irradiated spleen was of the same magnitude regardless of whether the entire body or only its lower half was exposed. When the thymus was shielded, however, there was an increase of 147% in the specific activity over that observed in the nonirradiated controls. The measured dose of scattered X-rays in the region of the thymus was 30 r when the partly shielded rice phantom was irradiated with 756 r of X-rays (S. Okada, unpublished data).

TABLE I

EFFECT OF CORTISONE ON DNASE II ACTIVITY OF LYMPHOID TISSUE

Tissue	*Groups of 10 animals*	*Organ weight*[a] *(mg)*	*DNase activity*[b] *per milligram wet tissue*[a]	*DNase activity per organ*[a]
Part A. Tissue Activity 24 Hours after Administration of 10 Mg of Cortisone Acetate per 100 Gm of Body Weight				
Spleen	Control	620 ± 73	0.262 ± 0.043	162 ± 25
	Cortisone	548 ± 72	0.361 ± 0.066	197 ± 46
Thymus	Control	429 ± 71	0.129 ± 0.015	53 ± 11
	Cortisone	327 ± 46	0.205 ± 0.045	67 ± 20
Part B. Tissue Activity 7 Days after Daily Injection of 1 Mg of Cortisone Acetate per 100 Gm of Body Weight				
Thymus	Control	519 ± 27	0.064 ± 0.015[c]	33 ± 10
	Cortisone	196 ± 12	0.110 ± 0.020[c]	21 ± 1

[a] ± standard deviation.

[b] Enzymatic activity is expressed in terms of change in optical density at 600 mμ per milligram of wet tissue.

[c] Assay values differ from those reported above owing to a change in the substrate. Whereas it was formerly prepared by the method of Kay *et al.* (*5*), that used for Part B was purchased from the California Foundation for Biochemical Research.

TABLE II

PARTIAL-BODY IRRADIATION AND WHOLE-BODY IRRADIATION ON TISSUE DNASE II 24 HOURS AFTER EXPOSURE

Tissue (15 rats/group)	*Type of X-ray exposure*	*Organ weight*[a] *(mg)*	*DNase activity*[b] *per milligram wet tissue*[a]	*DNase activity per organ*[a]
Spleen	Nonirradiated	569 ± 58	0.224 ± 0.055	127 ± 28
	Lower body exposed	297 ± 51	0.389 ± 0.058	116 ± 22
	Total body exposed	282 ± 37	0.450 ± 0.050	127 ± 17
Thymus	Nonirradiated	526 ± 58	0.086 ± 0.010	45 ± 7
	Lower body exposed	390 ± 66	0.126 ± 0.022	49 ± 9
	Total body exposed	295 ± 61	0.208 ± 0.027	60 ± 10

[a] ± standard deviation.

[b] Enzymatic activity is expressed in terms of change in optical density at 600 mμ per milligram of wet tissue.

DISCUSSION

As has been pointed out (*1–3*, *6*), the specific DNase II activity of the spleen and thymus increases during the first day after whole-body irradiation. The present experiments show that the enzymatic activity does not continue to increase beyond this time. During this early period of rapidly changing enzymatic activity, almost all adult lymphocytes are lysed and the resulting cell fragments disappear from the lymphoid organs (*7–9*). This suggests that the lymphocytes present before irradiation did not contribute appreciably to the total DNase activity as measured in the organs. Supporting this hypothesis is the report (*2*) that the dose of whole-body irradiation (400 r) required to cause a maximal increase in DNase II activity in rat spleen is the same as that needed to destroy almost all adult lymphocytes within 24 hours (*7–9*). The decline in DNase II activity described in the spleen and thymus after the third day postirradiation cannot be attributed to further rapid changes in cell types (*10*) but could be associated with altered function of radioresistant cells surviving at this time. Either of the two following changes in cellular function could apply: (1) metabolic alterations prior to regeneration of lymphocytes, or (2) diminution of the activity of nucleolytic enzymes once phagocytized nuclear fragments have been digested. The latter explanation implies that at least part of the early increase in DNase activity is associated with *in situ* degradation of DNA-containing nuclear fragments (*3*), presumably occurring in tissue macrophages. This would be analogous to the increase in activity of acid phosphatase (*11*) and peptidases (*12*) noted as reticular cells are transformed into macrophages in the appendices of irradiated rabbits.

A single large dose of cortisone acetate which produces lymphocytolysis similar to that resulting from X-ray exposure (*13*) caused an increase in specific activity comparable in degree to that seen after a sublethal dose of X-rays. A similar observation has been reported by Weymouth (*14*) in mice given hydrocortisone. This would seem to support the hypothesis that the alteration in specific enzymatic activity is correlated with the loss of adult lymphocytes and disappearance of nuclear fragments.[5] Daily administration of cortisone caused profound atrophy of the thymus, greater than that observed one week after exposure to a single lethal dose of X-rays. In contrast to the specific enzymatic activity of the irradiated gland which soon returned to an approximately normal level, the specific DNase II activity in the thymus of the cortisone-treated animals remained higher than normal one week after start of treatment. This could be explained by the fact that there is continued destruction of lymphocytes throughout the entire period of cortisone administration.

The experiments involving total-body and partial-body exposure were done in an attempt to determine whether the change in enzymatic activity of the thymus gland was due to the direct action of X-rays or whether it could be an indirect effect presumably mediated through the adrenal glands. Such an indirect effect of X-rays on the weight and histological appearance of the shielded thymus gland has been described (*15*). The results seem to indicate that the increase in observed enzymatic activity of the thymus is greater than that which would be expected from the approximately 30 r of scattered X-rays in the region of the shielded gland. This may

[5] Current studies in this laboratory using a histochemical technique for localizing DNase II in lymphoid tissue confirm the impression that lymphoid centers contain little DNase activity.

be deduced from two observations: First, the observed change corresponds in magnitude to that noted after 100 r of X-rays given to the entire body (S. Okada, unpublished data) and, second, the change in enzymatic activity of the thymus (S. Okada, unpublished data) and spleen (*2*; S. Okada, unpublished data) is linearly proportional to the dose of total-body X-irradiation between 50 and 200 r. It is safe to conclude, however, that any such indirect effect of radiation on lymphoid tissue is almost completely masked by the more pronounced direct effect when the entire body is exposed.

SUMMARY

1. When compared with that of control rats, the specific DNase II activity in spleens and thymus glands of irradiated rats was elevated during the first 3 days after exposure and fell almost to a normal level by the end of the first week. The total activity of the organs decreased to about one-third that of the control values on the seventh day after exposure.

2. The injection of cortisone acetate caused an increase in specific DNase II activity of the spleen and thymus gland comparable to that noted after a sublethal dose of total-body X-irradiation.

3. A moderate increase in specific activity of DNase II was noted when the thymus gland was shielded from the incident radiation.

4. The early increase in specific activity of DNase II noted in lymphoid tissue after irradiation was correlated with the loss of lymphocytic centers which probably contain little enzymatic activity.

5. It was shown that the observed effects on lymphoid tissue were largely due to the direct action of radiation on adult lymphocytes, although there may have been a slight indirect effect of radiation on lymphoid tissue.

RECEIVED: March 24, 1958

REFERENCES

1. N. M. FELLAS, I. MESCHAN, P. L. DAY, and C. D. DOUGLAS, Effect of total body X-irradiation on desoxyribonuclease activity of rat spleen. *Proc. Soc. Exptl. Biol. Med.* **87,** 231–233 (1954).

2. C. D. DOUGLAS and P. L. DAY, Effect of various doses of total body X-irradiation on total amount of desoxyribonuclease II in rat spleen. *Proc. Soc. Exptl. Biol. Med.* **89,** 616–617 (1955).

3. S. OKADA, E. R. GORDON, R. KING, and L. H. HEMPELMANN, Effect of X-ray exposure on desoxyribonuclease II activity in lymphoid tissue. *Arch. Biochem. Biophys.* **70,** 469–476 (1957).

4. O. D. KOWLESSAR, K. I. ALTMAN, and L. H. HEMPELMANN, The effect of ionizing radiation on desoxyribonuclease activities of body fluids. I. The effect of total body exposure on urinary excretion of desoxyribonuclease. *Arch. Biochem. Biophys.* **52,** 363–372 (1954).

5. E. R. H. KAY, N. S. SIMMONS, and A. L. DOUNCE, An improved preparation of sodium deoxyribonucleate. *J. Am. Chem. Soc.* **74,** 1724–1726 (1952).

6. N. B. KURNICK, B. W. MASSEY, and G. SANDEEN, Desoxyribonucleases and desoxyribonuclease inhibitor of hematopoietic tissue: The effect of radiation. *Ann. N. Y. Acad. Sci.* **75**, 61–70 (1958).
7. O. A. TROWELL, The sensitivity of lymphocytes to ionizing radiation. *J. Pathol. Bacteriol.* **64**, 687–704 (1952).
8. P. D. H. DEBRUYN, The effect of X-rays on the lymphatic nodule with reference to the dose and relative sensitivities of different species. *Anat. Record* **101**, 373–404 (1948).
9. N. L. PETRAKIS, Quantitative histologic analysis of the early effects of whole-body irradiation on the mouse thymus. *Radiation Research* **5**, 569–572 (1956).
10. R. G. MURRAY, *Histopathology of Irradiation from External and Internal Sources* (W. Bloom, ed.), Chapters 7 and 9, McGraw-Hill Book Co., New York, 1948.
11. W. L. DOYLE, Distribution of phosphatase in the rabbit appendix after X-irradiation. *Am. J. Anat.* **87**, 79–117 (1950).
12. W. L. DOYLE, Peptidase distribution in lymphatic tissue. *J. Biophys. Biochem. Cytol.* **1**, 221–236 (1955).
13. O. A. TROWELL, Action of cortisone on lymphocytes *in vitro*. *J. Physiol. (London)* **119**, 274–285 (1953).
14. P. P. WEYMOUTH, The effect of a single systemic X-irradiation of the C57BL mouse on the nucleodepolymerases of the thymus. *Radiation Research* **8**, 307–321 (1958).
15. C. P. LEBLOND and G. SEGAL, Differentiation between the direct and indirect effects of roentgen rays upon organs of normal and adrenalectomized rats. *Am. J. Roentgenol. Radium Therapy* **47**, 302–306 (1942).

RADIATION RESEARCH 10, 552–570 (1959)

Some Radiological Applications of Gamma-Ray Transport Theory

M. J. BERGER AND L. V. SPENCER

National Bureau of Standards, Washington, D. C.

1. INTRODUCTION

The theory of the penetration and diffusion of γ-rays, developed extensively in recent years (*1–4*), has so far been applied mainly to engineering problems such as the shielding of nuclear reactors. We should like to present here some applications of radiological interest, together with a brief indication of some of the available methods of calculation. Our topic is the spatial pattern of energy dissipation by γ-radiation in bounded water media. Two situations are considered: (1) an isotropic source (e.g., a radioactive isotope) distributed within the medium, and (2) a narrow pencil of radiation incident on a semi-infinite medium. Numerical results are presented for a source energy of 1.28 Mev[1] (between the two Co^{60}-source energies of 1.33 and 1.17 Mev).

Boundary conditions are schematized by the assumption that radiation cannot return to the bounded medium once it has left it.[2] To establish the spatial pattern of energy dissipation, we calculate the transfer of energy (by absorption or scattering) from γ-rays to electrons, but disregard the displacement of the electrons while they are slowed down and dissipate the energy along their paths. In the energy region below 1.28 Mev considered here, the electron displacement (some fraction of the electron range) is quite small compared to the comparable quantity (mean free path between interactions) for γ-radiation.[3] In a comparison of calculated and experimental results, an approximate adjustment will be made for electron displacement.[4]

The calculations to be presented are based on a combination of the following

[1] 1.28 Mev corresponds to a Compton wavelength $\lambda = 0.511/1.28 = 0.4$.

[2] This would be very nearly the case for a water phantom surrounded by air. Solid objects in the vicinity of the phantom, however, such as walls and furniture, would reflect some soft radiation (peaking at ~200 kev) back into the phantom.

[3] At an energy of 1.28 Mev, the ratio of the electron range to the γ-ray mean free path is 0.036, and at lower energies it is even smaller.

[4] An accurate treatment of electron displacement, for the case of a 40-Mev bremsstrahlung beam penetrating into water, has been given by Brysk (*5*).

techniques: (1) analytical evaluation of the unscattered and once-scattered radiation flux, (2) evaluation of the multiply-scattered flux by the moment method (*1*), and (3) random sampling (Monte Carlo) to take into account boundary effects (*4, 6*). The analytical calculations, although exact, are not sufficient because radiation scattered more than once contributes importantly to the energy dissipation. The extension of the analytical calculations to higher orders of scattering is rather impracticable. The moment method is in part analytical and in part numerical. It is the most powerful of the three techniques but subject to the limitation that it assumes an unbounded and homogeneous medium. The Monte Carlo method is almost entirely numerical and therefore laborious, but it has the advantage of being applicable to problems with boundary conditions of any complexity. The various techniques complement each other and are most efficient in combination.

2. INTERNAL SOURCE

We consider a bounded medium in which an isotropic source, i.e., a source emitting photons uniformly in all directions, is distributed in some specified manner. The objective of our considerations is the spatial distribution function, $F(r)$, of the energy dissipation; $F(r)\,dV$ is the *fraction* of the energy emitted by the source that is dissipated in a volume element, dV, in the neighborhood of a point r in the medium. The following situations will be considered in succession: a point-isotropic source in an infinite medium, in a medium with a spherical boundary, and in a medium with an arbitrary boundary; a distributed isotropic source in a medium with an arbitrary boundary.

2.1. Point-Isotropic Source in an Infinite Medium

The fractional energy dissipation in a shell of thickness dr and radius r around the source in an infinite medium will be denoted as $4\pi r^2 F_\infty(r)\,dr$. It is convenient to separate $F_\infty(r)$ into two components,

$$F_\infty(r) = F_\infty^{\,0}(r) + F_\infty^{\,S}(r) \qquad (1)$$

where $F_\infty^{\,0}(r)$ represents energy dissipation by previously unscattered photons, and $F_\infty^{\,S}(r)$ dissipation by scattered photons. The analytical expression for the unscattered component is

$$F_\infty^{\,0}(r) = \frac{e^{-\mu_0 r}}{4\pi r^2}\,\mu_0' \qquad (2)$$

where $\mu_0 = \mu(E_0)$ is the narrow-beam attenuation coefficient, and $\mu_0' = \mu'(E_0)$ is the energy absorption coefficient at the source energy E_0.[5]

[5] The distance $1/\mu_0$ is called a mean free path. For $E_0 = 1.28$ Mev and a water medium, $\mu_0 = 0.0625\ \text{cm}^{-1}$ and $\mu_0' = 0.0295\ \text{cm}^{-1}$. Reference *7* contains a tabulation of $\mu(E)$, and reference *8* a tabulation of $\mu'(E)$. The quantity $E_0 F_\infty^{\,0}(r)$ represents an "absorbed dose" in rads, if r is expressed in cm, μ_0 in cm^{-1}, μ_0' in cm^2/gm (i.e., if the linear energy absorption coefficient is multiplied by the density of the medium), and E_0 in units of 100 ergs.

To determine $F_\infty^S(r)$, we first consider its moments

$$M_n = \frac{1}{n!}\int_0^\infty (\mu_0 r)^n F_\infty^S(r) 4\pi r^2\, dr \tag{3}$$

for various values of n. The moment of lowest order, M_0, can be calculated from first principles. The entire energy emitted by the source must be dissipated somewhere in the infinite medium, so that

$$\int_0^\infty F_\infty(r) 4\pi r^2\, dr = 1 \tag{4}$$

By integration over equation 2 one finds that

$$\int_0^\infty F_\infty^0(r) 4\pi r^2\, dr = \frac{\mu_0'}{\mu_0} \tag{5}$$

It follows from equations 1, 4, and 5 that

$$M_0 = 1 - \frac{\mu_0'}{\mu_0} = 0.527 \tag{6}$$

The transport equation governing the diffusion of γ-radiation is reduced, according to the moment method, to a system of integral equations which can be solved numerically to yield moments-in-r of *even* order. For a 1.28-Mev source in water, one finds that[6]

$$M_2 = 3.5336\, M_0 ; \qquad M_4 = 6.6388\, M_0 ; \qquad M_6 = 10.2333\, M_0 \tag{7}$$

We now approximate $F_\infty^S(r)$ by a function $\tilde{F}_\infty^S(r)$, which has the appropriate qualitative features and has the same first four even moments as $F_\infty^S(r)$, i.e., a function which satisfies the conditions

$$\frac{1}{n!}\int_0^\infty (\mu_0 r)^n \tilde{F}_\infty^S(r) 4\pi r^2\, dr = M_n \qquad n = 0, 2, 4, 6 \tag{8}$$

For large r, $F_\infty^S(r)$ is approximately exponential. For small r it has a spatial dependence similar to that of the once-scattered flux which goes as $1/r$. The approximating function is therefore chosen to be[7]

$$\tilde{F}_\infty^S(r) = (A_1 e^{-C_1 r} + A_2 e^{-C_2 r}) \frac{1}{r} \tag{9}$$

[6] To keep the calculation internally consistent, it is necessary to compute the intermediate results, i.e., the moments, to a greater number of significant figures than the energy dissipation distribution.

[7] For a general discussion of this type of moment-fitting procedure, see references *9* and *10*. These references also contain practical prescriptions for calculating the parameters of the approximating function from the moments. Note that there is an error in equation C2 of reference *10*, where D_j^3 should be replaced by D_j^2.

It is convenient to rewrite equation 9 in such a form that the disposable parameters are dimensionless:

$$\tilde{F}_{\infty}^{S}(r) = \mu_0\, r(A_1' e^{C_1'\mu_0 r} + A_2' e^{C_2'\mu_0 r}) \frac{e^{-\mu_0 r}}{4\pi r^2}\, \mu_0' \tag{10}$$

When the parameters A_1', A_2', C_1', and C_2' are adjusted so that the four conditions of equation 8 are satisfied, they are found to have the values

$$\begin{aligned} A_1' &= 1.325 & C_1' &= 0.0314 \\ A_2' &= -0.461 & C_2' &= -0.244 \end{aligned} \tag{11}$$

The distribution $F_{\infty}^{S}(r)$ has been calculated extensively by the moment method for different source energies and materials (*3*).[8] The results are available in the form of "buildup factors" defined as

$$B(r) = \frac{F_{\infty}(r)}{F_{\infty}^{0}(r)} = 1 + \frac{F_{\infty}^{S}(r)}{F_{\infty}^{0}(r)} \tag{12}$$

Note that, according to equations 2 and 10,

$$B(r) = 1 + \mu_0\, r(A_1' e^{C_1'\mu_0 r} + A_2' e^{C_2'\mu_0 r}) \tag{13}$$

2.2. Point-Isotropic Source in a Bounded Spherical Medium

We consider a scattering medium in the form of a sphere of radius R, and a point source at the center of the sphere (see Fig. 1). The energy dissipation at a distance r from the source will be denoted as $F_R(r)$, and its components as $F_R(r)$ and $F_R^S(r)$. Unscattered radiation within the sphere is not affected by the presence of the boundary, so that

$$F_R^{0}(r) = F_{\infty}^{0}(r) \tag{14}$$

The amount of scattered radiation within the sphere is reduced, however, because it is no longer possible for radiation to be scattered into the sphere from the surrounding region. Therefore $F_R^{S}(r)$ is smaller than the corresponding infinite medium distribution, $F_{\infty}^{S}(r)$, by an amount that increases as the boundary is approached.

The calculation of $F_R^{S}(r)$ is a boundary problem which—in the present state of the art—can be done only with the aid of random sampling (Monte Carlo). The Monte Carlo method is a form of analog experimentation, carried out with paper and pencil or with an electronic computer, and based on the construction and evaluation of model γ-ray trajectories. A trajectory is characterized by the energies and directions of the γ-ray immediately before (or immediately after) each scattering, the path lengths between successive scatterings, and the number of scatterings that occur before absorption terminates the trajectory. Each of these char-

[8] An extension of the tabulations in reference *3* is now in progress at the National Bureau of Standards.

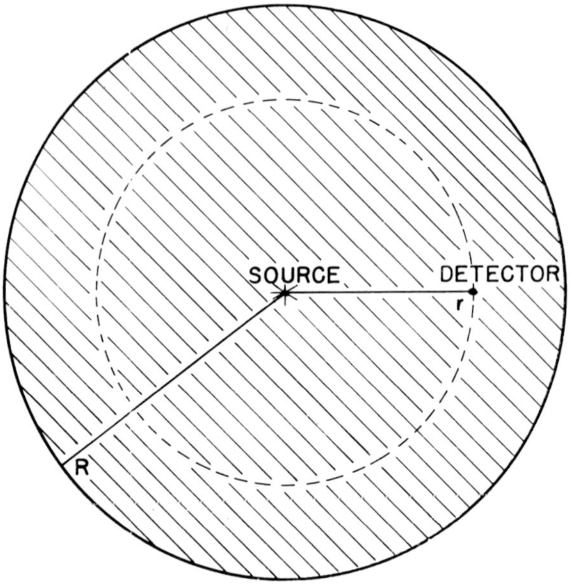

FIG. 1. Medium with spherical boundary and a point-isotropic source at its center.

acteristics is a random quantity with a statistical distribution determined by the scattering and absorption cross sections for γ-radiation. A model trajectory is obtained by selecting its characteristic parameters through random sampling. For example, in order to determine the deflection associated with a scattering, one may set up a number of angular regions such that a deflection into any of these regions is equally likely, choose one of these regions at random, and identify the desired deflection angle with the mid-point (or some other representative point) of the chosen region.[9] The Monte Carlo method separates the multiple-scattering process into a succession of elementary events to which the boundary conditions can readily be applied. When calculating the radiation present in a bounded medium, one constructs model trajectories by the same rules as if the medium were unbounded, except that trajectories are cut short as soon as they go outside the boundaries. A large set of model trajectories serves as the basis for an estimate of the radiation flux or other related quantities. By scoring the distance, r, from the source at which each interaction takes place, and the amount of energy dissipated in the interaction, one obtains an estimate of $F_R(r)$ [or of $F_R^S(r)$, if the energy dissipated in the first interaction in each trajectory is disregarded].

The infinite-medium distribution, $F_\infty^S(r)$, can be calculated to a given accuracy by the moment method with much less work than the bounded-medium distribu-

[9] In practice, more sophisticated selection techniques are used. See, e.g., reference *6*.

tion, $F_R^S(r)$, can be calculated by the Monte Carlo method. The difference between these two distributions will turn out to be at most 16% in the present calculations, and can generally be expected to be small. Under these circumstances it is advantageous to make a direct Monte Carlo estimate of the difference $F_\infty^S(r) - F_R^S(r)$. This can be accomplished by constructing model trajectories as if the medium were unbounded and interpreting them as follows. In each trajectory, energy dissipation is recorded and scored only for interactions that satisfy two conditions: (1) They must occur in a sphere of radius R around the source. (2) At least one preceding interaction in the same trajectory must have taken place at a distance from the source greater than R, i.e., outside the sphere boundary.

A measure of the reduction of energy dissipation due to the presence of the boundary is given by the ratio $F_R(r)/F_\infty(r)$. This ratio can be expressed in the form

$$\frac{F_R(r)}{F_\infty(r)} = 1 - \frac{F_\infty^S(r) - F_R^S(r)}{F_\infty(r)} \tag{15}$$

Figure 2 contains plots of $F_R(r)/F_\infty(r)$ versus r, for spherical media with radii $\mu_0 R = 0.5$, 1, 2, 3, and 4 mean free paths. These results are based on a calculation of $F_\infty(r)$ by the moment method and an estimate of $F_\infty^S(r) - F_R^S(r)$ by the Monte Carlo method. The reduction of energy dissipation is seen to be confined to a region no farther than approximately one mean free path from the boundary. The maximum reduction (at the boundary) ranges from 6% for $\mu_0 R = 0.5$ to 14.5% for $\mu_0 R = 4$. The explanation for this lies in the increasing proportion of scattered to unscattered radiation as the distance from the source is increased, and in the fact that only the amount of scattered radiation is reduced owing to the presence of the boundary. As will be shown below, the per cent reduction of energy dissipation by scattered radiation is practically independent of the radius of the bounded medium.

2.3. Point-Isotropic Source in a Medium with an Arbitrary Boundary

The Monte Carlo results used to evaluate equation 15 can be represented by the empirical formula

$$\frac{F_\infty^S(r) - F_R^S(r)}{F_\infty^S(r)} = ae^{-b\mu_0(R-r)} \tag{16}$$

where the parameters have the values $a = 0.16$ and $b = 3.1$. It is noteworthy that equation 15 is a function of $R - r$ only, but not of R or r separately. This means that the boundary effect for scattered radiation, as represented by the ratio $[F_\infty^S(r) - F_R^S(r)]/F_\infty^S(r)$, depends only on the distance from the boundary but is independent of the distance from the source and of the radius of curvature of the boundary. This suggests that formula 16, or a similar formula with different numerical parameters at other source energies, will provide a good representation of the

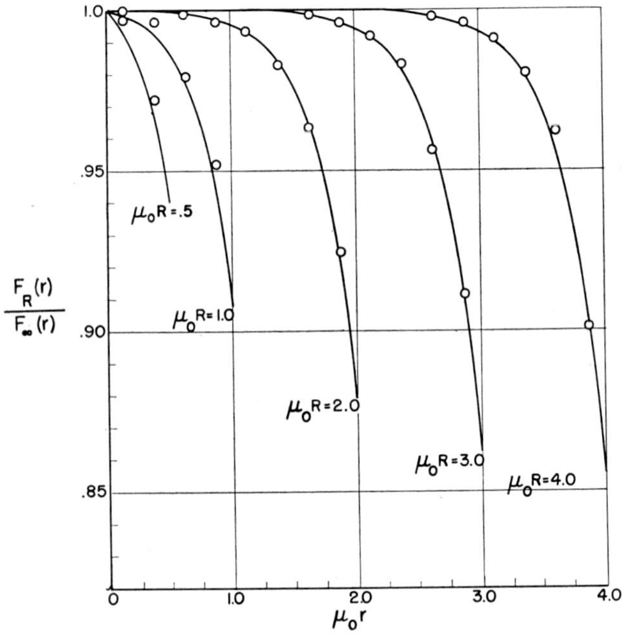

FIG. 2. Reduction of energy dissipation near a spherical boundary [source arrangement as shown in Fig. 1, source energy 1.28 Mev, μ_0 (water) = 0.0625 cm^{-1}]. $F_R(r)$ is the energy dissipation in a sphere of radius R, at a distance r from the center. $F_\infty(r)$ is the corresponding energy dissipation at a distance r from a source in an infinite medium.

boundary effect for other boundary geometries (if the radius of curvature of the boundary surface is larger than, say, 0.5 mean free path).

Support for this conjecture can be obtained from an independent Monte Carlo calculation (*11*) pertaining to the emergence of radiation from a semi-infinite medium that contains a plane-monodirectional source. This calculation can be interpreted as yielding the energy dissipation reduction factor at a plane boundary,

$$\frac{F_\infty{}^S(R) - F_R{}^S(R)}{F_\infty{}^S(R)} = a, \qquad \text{for very large } R. \tag{17}$$

One obtains a = 0.22, 0.17, and 0.067 for source energies E_0 = 0.66, 1.0, and 4.0 Mev, respectively. By interpolation one arrives at a value a = 0.15 for E_0 = 1.28 Mev, which is consistent with the value a = 0.16 found in the present calculation. The agreement is an indication that the boundary effect is insensitive in regard to the geometry of the boundary as well as in regard to the geometry of the source.

2.4. Distributed Isotropic Source in a Medium with an Arbitrary Boundary

We now consider a source characterized by a distribution function $S(r)$, where $S(r)\,dV$ is the *fraction* of the photons that are emitted in a volume element, dV, around the point r. The corresponding energy dissipation distribution, $F(r)$, or its components $F^0(r)$ and $F^S(r)$, are obtained by regarding the distributed source as consisting of a collection of point sources and integrating over energy dissipation distributions for point sources. For the unscattered component one has the exact integral relation

$$F^0(r) = \int_V dV' S(r') F_\infty{}^0(|r - r'|) \tag{18}$$

where the integration extends over the volume V occupied by the source. The corresponding approximate relation for the scattered component is

$$F^S(r) = [1 - ae^{-b\mu_0 L(r)}] \int_V dV' S(r') F_\infty{}^S(|r - r'|) \tag{19}$$

where the factor $1 - ae^{-b\mu_0 L(r)}$ is a boundary correction analogous to formula 16, with $L(r)$ the distance of the point r from the nearest boundary.[10] If the medium and source have spherical symmetry, the integral relations are relatively simple. Let $4\pi r'^2 S(r')\, dr'$ denote the fraction of the γ-rays emitted at distances between r' and $r' + dr'$ from the center of a medium of radius R. The corresponding energy dissipation distributions are[11]

$$F^0(r) = \frac{2\pi}{r} \int_0^R S(r') r'\, dr' \int_{|r-r'|}^{r+r'} F_\infty{}^0(r'') r''\, dr'' \tag{20}$$

$$F^S(r) = \frac{2\pi}{r} [1 - ae^{-b\mu_0(R-r)}] \int_0^R S(r') r'\, dr' \int_{|r-r'|}^{r+r'} F_\infty{}^S(r'') r''\, dr'' \tag{21}$$

3. EXTERNAL SOURCE

A narrow pencil of radiation is assumed to be incident perpendicularly on a semi-infinite medium that is bounded on the left by the plane $z = 0$ and occupies the entire space to the right of that plane. We want to determine the fraction $2\pi\rho F(\rho, z)\, dz\, d\rho$ of the energy injected by the source into the medium which is dissi-

[10] The applicability of this approximate boundary correction is subject to restrictions. It is assumed that the point r is not in the vicinity of more than one boundary, as would be the case, for example, in the interior of a very thin slab. Moreover, the validity of formula 16 has been established only for source-boundary separations greater than 0.5 mean free path. It seems plausible, however, that formula 16 will remain an adequate approximation even for shorter separation distances. In any case, if the distance $|r - r'|$ from the source point r' is small, the principal contribution to the energy dissipation at r is due to the unscattered γ-rays [i.e., $F_\infty{}^0(|r - r'|) \gg F_\infty{}^S(|r - r'|)$], so that the boundary correction is of little importance.

[11] The volume integral over the source distribution is reduced to two spatial integrations (with respect to r' and r'') and an angular integration over an azimuth which yields the factor 2π. For the details of the reduction in spherical as well as in other geometries, see reference *12*, p. 592.

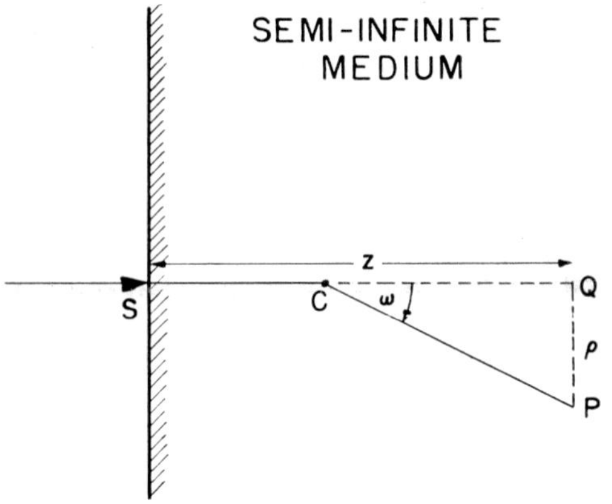

FIG. 3. Narrow beam of radiation incident on a semi-infinite medium. Geometry of single scattering.

pated in a volume element $2\pi\rho\, d\rho\, dz$ at depth z and at a radial distance ρ from the line of incidence (see Fig. 3).[12]

3.1. Method of Calculation

This problem could be treated efficiently by a procedure analogous to that used for the internal source; i.e., the determination of the corresponding infinite-medium distribution, $F_\infty(\rho, z)$, by the moment method is practicable though more difficult than that of $F_\infty(r)$ because a two-variable problem must be solved. Suitable computational techniques have been developed, and a pilot calculation has been completed,[13] which is not fully applicable to the problem at hand, however.

We therefore fall back on a combination of analytical and Monte Carlo calculations, setting

$$F(\rho, z) = F^0(\rho, z) + F^1(\rho, z) + F^{MS}(\rho, z) \tag{22}$$

where $F^0(\rho, z)$, $F^1(\rho, z)$, and $F^{MS}(\rho, z)$ represent the contributions to the energy dissipation by unscattered, once-scattered, and multiply-scattered radiation, respectively.

[12] A calculation of a similar nature, in which the emphasis was placed on the spectral distribution of the scattered radiation, has been briefly reported by Bruce and Johns (*13*).

[13] L. V. Spencer, to be published. In this pilot calculation, a symmetrical source was assumed that emits in two opposite directions, i.e., along the negative as well as the positive z-axis. For deep penetrations, the flux distribution resulting from the symmetrized source is not significantly different from that of an ordinary monodirectional source; at the source plane $z = 0$ it is greater by a factor of 2. For shallow penetrations of interest in radiological applications, the difference between the fluxes in the two cases are neither negligible nor well known.

Unscattered radiation is attenuated exponentially and concentrated along the direction of incidence, so that

$$F^0(\rho, z) = \frac{\delta(\rho)}{2\pi\rho} e^{-\mu_0 z} \mu_0' \qquad (23)$$

where $\delta(\rho)$ is the Dirac delta function.[14]

For moderate penetration depths, the contribution $F^1(\rho, z)$ is important and determines characteristic features of $F(\rho, z)$. An analytical evaluation of this component is therefore helpful. The necessary derivation is illustrated by Fig. 3, in which S represents the effective source, C the point at which the first scattering takes place, ω the deflection resulting from that scattering, and P the point at which the energy dissipation is to be calculated. The deflection angle is related to the energies E_0 and E of the γ-rays before and after the first scattering by the Compton relationship

$$\cos \omega = 1 - \frac{mc^2}{E} + \frac{mc^2}{E_0} \qquad (24)$$

where mc^2 is the electron rest energy (0.511 Mev).

A beam of photons of energy E_0 is attenuated by a factor $e^{-\mu_0 s}$ while traversing the distance $s = \overline{SC}$. A fraction $k(E_0, E)\, dE\, ds$ of the attenuated beam is scattered in the neighborhood of C, between s and $s + ds$, such that the photon energy is lowered to a value between E and $E + dE$. The Klein-Nishina scattering coefficient, $k(E_0, E)$ is given by

$$k(E_0, E) = \frac{2.494 \times 10^{-25} N mc^2}{E_0^2} \cdot \left[\frac{E_0}{E} + \frac{E}{E_0} - 2\left(\frac{mc^2}{E} - \frac{mc^2}{E_0}\right) + \left(\frac{mc^2}{E} - \frac{mc^2}{E_0}\right)^2\right] \qquad (25)$$

where N is the number of electrons per cubic centimeter of the medium. The scattered beam is further attenuated by a factor $e^{-\mu(E)t}$ while traversing the distance $t = \overline{CP}$. The energy dissipation by once-scattered radiation between t and $t + dt$ is proportional to dt, to the photon energy, E, and to the energy dissipation coefficient, $\mu'(E)$. In summary, the energy dissipated between t and $t + dt$ by photons with energies between E and $E + dE$ that have been scattered between s and $s + ds$ has the average value

$$K e^{-\mu_0 s} k(E_0, E)\, dE\, ds e^{-\mu(E) t} E \mu'(E)\, dt \qquad (26)$$

where K is the number of photons emitted by the source. We now change variables from s and t to ρ and z, which describe the position of the point in P cylindrical

[14] $\delta(\rho) = 0$ if $\rho \neq 0$; $\int_0^\infty \delta(\rho)\, d\rho = 1$. Note that $2\pi \int_0^\infty F^0(\rho, z)\rho\, d\rho = e^{-\mu_0 z}\mu_0'$.

coordinates (see Fig. 3). Thus

$$\left.\begin{aligned} \rho &= \overline{QP} = t \sin \omega \\ \text{and} \qquad z &= \overline{SQ} = s + t \cos \omega \end{aligned}\right\} \tag{27}$$

The differential element $ds\,dt$ in equation 26 must accordingly be replaced by

$$\begin{vmatrix} \dfrac{\partial s}{\partial z} & \dfrac{\partial s}{\partial \rho} \\ \dfrac{\partial t}{\partial z} & \dfrac{\partial t}{\partial \rho} \end{vmatrix} d\rho\, dz = \frac{1}{\sin \omega}\, d\rho\, dz = \frac{1}{2\pi\rho \sin \omega}\, 2\pi\rho\, d\rho\, dz \tag{28}$$

We now divide expression 26 by KE_0, express s and t as functions of ρ and z, make the substitution of equation 28, and integrate with respect to E, in order to obtain the fractional energy dissipation, $F^1(\rho, z)$, by once-scattered radiation in the volume element $2\pi\rho\, d\rho\, dz$ around the point (ρ, z). It is assumed that $s > 0$, so that the deflection angle, ω, cannot be smaller than

$$\omega' = \cos^{-1} \frac{z}{\sqrt{\rho^2 + z^2}} \tag{29}$$

Nor can ω exceed π. According to equation 24, the energy must therefore lie between the limits

$$E'' = \frac{mc^2}{(mc^2/E_0) + 2} \leq E \leq \frac{mc^2}{(mc^2/E_0) + 1 - (z/\sqrt{\rho^2 + z^2})} = E' \tag{30}$$

The final result is

$$\begin{aligned} F^1(\rho, z) = \frac{1}{2\pi\rho E_0} \int_{E''}^{E'} & \frac{k(E_0, E) E \mu'(E)}{\sin \omega} \\ & \cdot \exp\left[-\mu_0 \left(z - \rho \frac{\cos \omega}{\sin \omega} \right) - \mu(E) \frac{\rho}{\sin \omega} \right] dE \end{aligned} \tag{31}$$

A Monte Carlo estimate of the multiply-scattered component $F^{MS}(\rho, z)$ can be made by a procedure quite similar to that discussed in Section 2.2. Model trajectories are constructed by random sampling, and the amounts of energy dissipated at various (ρ, z) locations are scored. Trajectories are terminated when they leave the semi-infinite medium, i.e., when z becomes negative. In order to separate out the contribution to the energy dissipation by multiply-scattered radiation, scores are kept only for losses of energy that occur in the second or subsequent interactions in each trajectory.

An estimate of the boundary effect can also be made by a direct Monte Carlo computation of the difference

$$F_\infty^S(\rho, z) - F^S(\rho, z) = F_\infty^S(\rho, z) - F^1(\rho, z) - F^{MS}(\rho, z) \tag{32}$$

This requires the scoring of energy losses in interactions occurring at positions $z > 0$ that have been preceded in the same trajectory by at least one interaction occurring at position $z < 0$.

3.2. Illustrative Results

Boundary effect. Figure 4 shows the results of a Monte Carlo estimate of the ratio $[F_\infty^S(\rho, z) - F^S(\rho, z)]/F_\infty^S(\rho, z)$. The reduction of the energy dissipation due to the presence of the boundary is appreciable only within approximately one mean free path from the boundary. The reduction is a strongly increasing function of the radial displacement (reaching a value of 40% for $\mu_0 z = 0$ and $\mu_0 \rho = 3$).

Energy dissipation distributions. Figure 5*A* contains curves of

$$(2\pi\rho/\mu_0 \mu_0')e^{\mu_0 z}F^1(\rho, z)$$

versus $\mu_0 \rho$ for different penetration depth: $\mu_0 z$. Note that the radial distributions $F^1(\rho, z)$, multiplied by $e^{-\mu_0 z}$, tend to a common limit for $\mu_0 \rho = 0$, regardless of the depth of penetration. As $\mu_0 z \to 0$, the slopes of the distribution; for small $\mu_0 \rho$ become progressively steeper until a limiting discontinuing curve is reached when $\mu_0 z = 0$.

Figure 5*B* contains plots of $(2\pi\rho/\mu_0 \mu_0')e^{\mu_0 z}F^S(\rho, z)$ versus $\mu_0 \rho$ for different penetration depths $\mu_0 z$. They are based on a combination of the results of Fig. 5*A* with

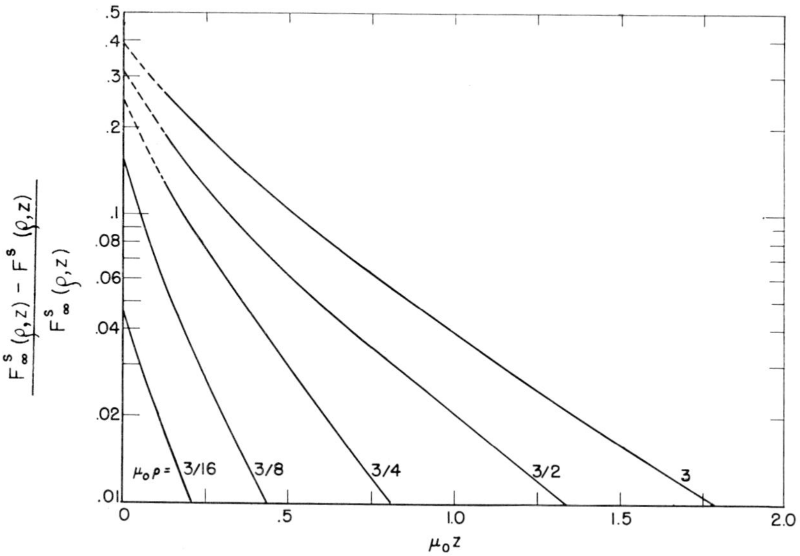

FIG. 4. Reduction of energy dissipation near the boundary of a semi-infinite medium [source arrangement as shown in Fig. 3, source energy 1.28 Mev, μ_0 (water) = 0.0625 cm^{-1}]. $F^S(\rho, z)$ is the energy dissipation by scattered radiation at depth z, and at a distance ρ from the axis of the incident beam. $F_\infty^S(\rho, z)$ is the corresponding energy dissipation at the same position in an infinite medium.

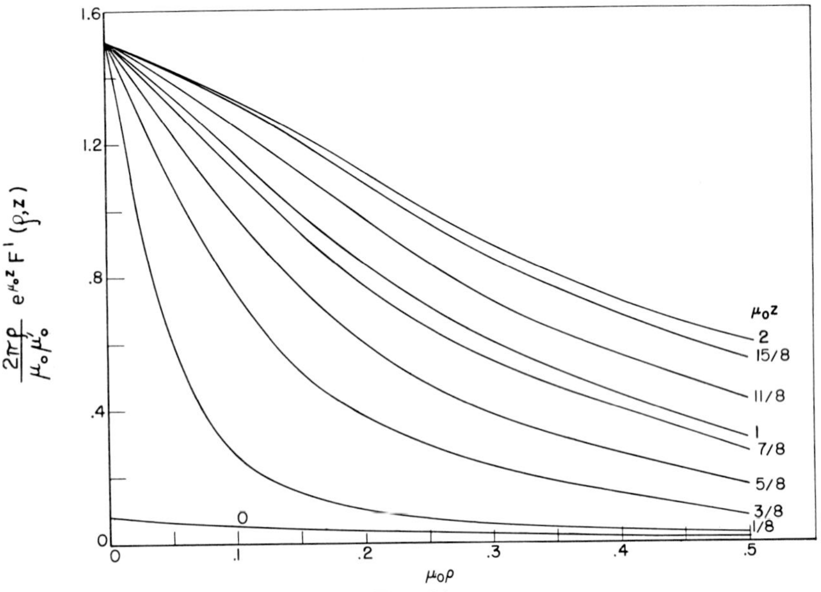

FIG. 5*A*

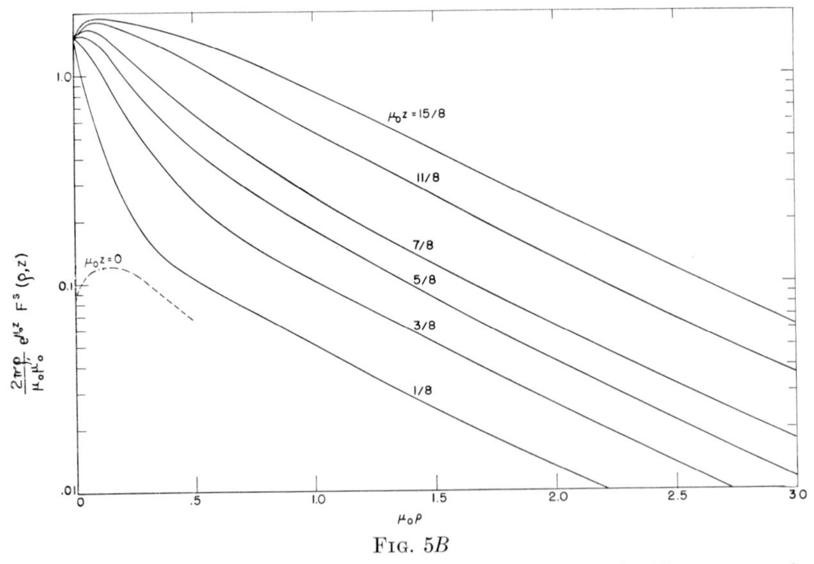

FIG. 5*B*

FIG. 5. Distribution of energy dissipation about the axis of an incident narrow beam, at various penetration depths z. [Source arrangement as in Fig. 3, source energy 1.28 Mev, μ_0 (water) = 0.0625 cm^{-1}, μ_0' (water) = 0.0295 cm^{-1}]. The factor $2\pi\rho/\mu_0\mu_0'$ makes the quantity plotted dimensionless. The additional factor $e^{\mu_0 z}$ is introduced for convenient graphical presentation. *A*, energy dissipation by singly-scattered radiation. *B*, energy dissipation by singly-scattered and multiply-scattered radiation.

a Monte Carlo estimate of $F^{MS}(\rho, z)$. The contribution $F^1(\rho, z)$ of once-scattered radiation is predominant for small values of $\mu_0 \rho$, and there is again a common intercept of the radial distributions at $\mu_0 \rho = 0$. But, compared to the curves in Fig. 5*A*, the maxima of the radial distributions are shifted from $\mu_0 \rho = 0$ to larger values of $\mu_0 \rho$, the shift being an increasing function of the depth of penetration.

Buildup factor. The fraction of the energy dissipated between z and $z + dz$ is

$$
\begin{aligned}
2\pi \int_0^\infty \rho F(\rho, z)\, d\rho\, dz &= e^{-\mu_0 z}\mu_0'\, dz + 2\pi \int_0^\infty F^S(\rho, z)\rho\, d\rho\, dz \\
&= e^{-\mu_0 z}\mu_0'\, dz B(z)
\end{aligned}
\tag{33}
$$

where $B(z)$ is a quantity commonly denoted as buildup factor. By integration over the radial distributions in Fig. 5*B* one finds that in the range of depths $0 \leq \mu_0 z \leq 2$ the buildup factor can be represented with an accuracy of 1 to 2% by the formula

$$B(z) = 1.11 + 0.99\mu_0 z \qquad \text{(source energy 1.28 Mev, water medium)} \tag{34}$$

Radial spread of energy dissipation. To get a clear picture of the radial spread of the beam as it penetrates into the semi-infinite medium, it is useful to introduce the fraction

$$p(\rho, z) = \frac{2\pi \int_0^\rho \rho' F(\rho', z)\, d\rho'}{2\pi \int_0^\infty \rho' F(\rho', z)\, d\rho'} \tag{35}$$

of the energy dissipated at depth z at radial distances less than or equal to ρ. Figure 6 contains a contour map that illustrates the radial spread of the energy dissipation with increasing depth of penetration. Contour lines in the ρ–z plane are given along which $p(\rho, z)$ has fixed values. When one of these contours is rotated about the z-axis, it encloses a volume within which is dissipated a fraction, p, of the energy injected by the source into the semi-infinite medium. The quantity $p(0, z) = 1/B(z)$ is the ratio, at depth z, of the energy dissipated on the axis of incidence to the total energy dissipated at the same depth. This ratio is 0.91 at the boundary of the medium, decreases to 0.58 at a depth of 10 cm, and is only 0.43 at a depth of 20 cm. Thus, even though the incident beam is sharply defined, the radial spread of the energy dissipation is marked.

3.3. Comparison with an Experiment

Johns and his collaborators (*14*) have made careful measurements of the depth-dose distribution in a water phantom (in effect, a semi-infinite medium) due to incident circular beams of Co^{60} radiation. These experimental results provide a means for checking our calculations. The quantity in terms of which a comparison will be made is the percentage depth dose, defined by Johns as the ratio of the dose

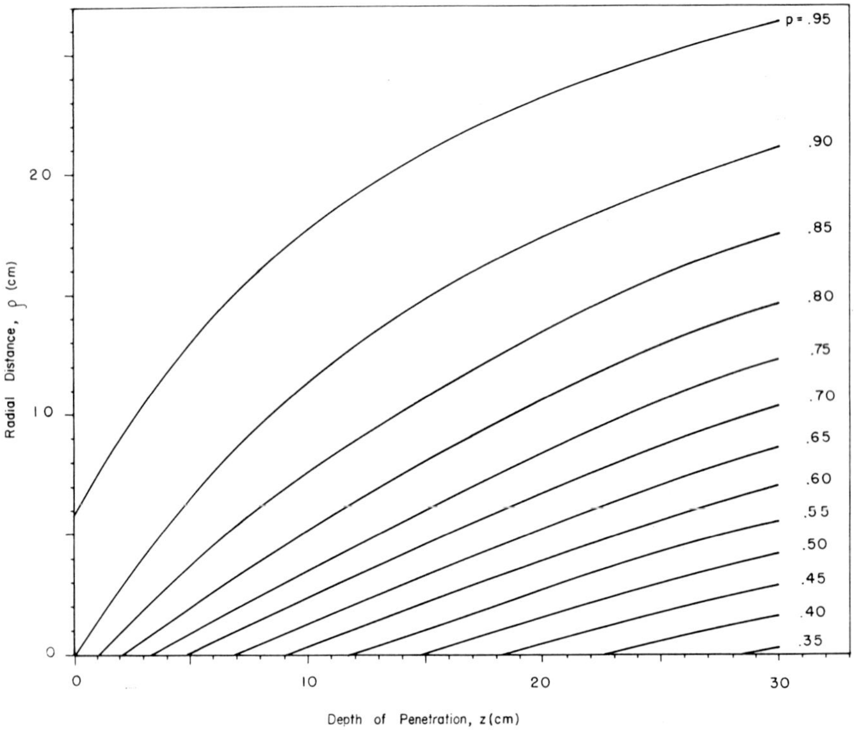

FIG. 6. Contour diagram indicating the radial spread of a narrow beam as it penetrates into a semi-infinite medium. The diagram is based on the results shown in Fig. 5. The contours pertain to the quantity $p(\rho, z)$ which represents the fraction of the energy dissipated at depth z that is dissipated at distances from the beam axis that are greater than ρ.

at a given depth on the axis of the incident beam to the maximum dose on the axis. The percentage depth dose, $P_\rho(z)$, at depth z, resulting from a circular beam of radius ρ, can be expressed as follows in terms of the distribution functions and integral quantities introduced in Sections 3.1 and 3.2:

$$P_\rho(z) = \frac{2\pi \int_0^\rho \rho' F(\rho', z)\, d\rho'}{2\pi \int_0^\rho \rho' F(\rho', \hat{z})\, d\rho'} \times 100 = \frac{p(\rho, z) B(z) e^{-\mu_0 z}}{p(\rho, \hat{z}) B(\hat{z}) e^{-\mu_0 \hat{z}}} \times 100 \qquad (36)$$

where $\hat{z}$ is the depth at which $2\pi \int_0^\rho \rho' F(\rho', z)\, d\rho$ is a maximum. The second part of equation 36 is a consequence of equations 33 and 35. The percentage depth dose can be calculated with the values of $p(\rho, z)$ from Fig. 6 and values of $B(z)$ from formula 34.

The conditions of the experiment differ somewhat from those assumed in the calculations so that a number of adjustments have to be made prior to a comparison.

Electron displacement. The experimental results pertain to the energy dissipation $F^*(\rho, z)$ by electrons set in motion by γ-rays, whereas the calculation is for the energy transfer, $F(\rho, z)$, from γ-rays to secondary electrons. The secondary electrons tend to move in the forward direction so that the peak of $F^*(\rho, z)$ occurs not at the surface of the medium but at a depth corresponding roughly to an electron range and found experimentally to be of the order of 0.5 cm. At depths greater than the range of the secondary electrons, the γ-ray flux and electron flux are approximately in equilibrium so that the distribution $F^*(\rho, z)$ closely follows the distribution $F(\rho, z)$, except for a slight displacement toward greater depths due to electron travel; i.e., $F^*(\rho, z) \sim F(\rho, z - \delta)$ where δ is a small and approximately constant distance of the order of an electron range.[15] If the comparison between experiment and calculation is made for the percentage depth dose as defined by equation 36, with $\hat{z} = 0.5$ cm, and if the comparison is confined to depths $z > \hat{z}$, the influence of electron travel is practically eliminated.

Source energy. The calculation was done for an assumed source energy of 1.28 Mev, whereas the experimental source consisted of the two Co^{60} lines (1.33 and 1.17 Mev) plus some softer radiation. The narrow-beam attenuation coefficient of the radiation from the experimental source was found by Johns to have the value 0.0660 cm^{-1}, as compared to the theoretical value 0.0625 cm^{-1} at 1.28 Mev. The calculation was adjusted to the experimental source energy on the basis of the assumption that the pattern of energy dissipation is insensitive to small changes of the source energy, provided all distances are expressed in units of mean free paths of the source radiation, i.e., if $F(\rho, z)$ is regarded as a function of $\mu_0 \rho$ and $\mu_0 z$. The percentage depth dose was converted from one source energy to another by a rescaling procedure in which all distances are multiplied by a factor

$$\alpha = \frac{\mu_0(1.28 \text{ Mev})}{\mu_0(\text{expt})} = \frac{0.0625}{0.0660} = 0.947 \qquad (37)$$

Thus

$$P_\rho(z) \,|_{\text{expt}} = P_{\alpha\rho}(\alpha z) \,|_{1.28 \text{ Mev}} \qquad (38)$$

Source geometry. In the calculation the incident beam of radiation was assumed to consist of parallel rays, whereas the experimental source consisted of a slightly divergent bundle of rays. In radiological language, the calculation was for an infinite source-to-skin distance (SSD), whereas the experimental SSD was no greater than ~100 cm. Johns introduces an inverse-square-law correction factor

$$f = \frac{P_\rho^{s_1}(z)}{P_\rho^{s_2}(z)} = \left(\frac{s_1 + \hat{z}}{s_2 + \hat{z}}\,\frac{s_2 + z}{s_1 + z}\right)^2 \qquad (39)$$

[15] For a theoretical analysis of this situation, for a higher source energy, see reference *5*.

which relates the percentage depth doses for two different source-to-skin distances, s_1 and s_2. The inverse-square-law correction factor (equation 39) is strictly applicable only to beams of zero cross-sectional area (field size), for which the depth dose on the beam axis is contributed wholly by unscattered radiation. For beams of finite cross section, the correction factor is expected to be somewhat too large, because scattered radiation, which is not governed by an inverse square law, also contributes to the depth dose on the axis. It has been found experimentally (for $s_1 = 100$ cm and $s_2 = 80$ cm) that for field sizes up to 100 cm^2 equation 39 is correct to within 1%, and that for larger field sizes up to 400 cm^2 the true value of f is only a few per cent smaller than that given by equation 39.

In Table I a comparison is made between experimental and calculated percentage depth doses for field sizes ranging from zero to 400 cm^2, and for a source-to-skin distance of 100 cm. The experimental values are taken directly from Table 1 of reference *14*. The calculated values were obtained by an evaluation of equation 36 (with $\hat{z} = 0.5\alpha = 0.473$ cm), followed by a source energy correction according to equation 38, and a source geometry correction according to equation 39, with a factor $f = [100.473/(100 + z)]^2$ that converts the percentage depth dose from an infinite SSD to an SSD of 100 cm. The calculated results are not expected to be accurate to more than two significant figures; the third significant figure is essentially the result of interpolation and is given to facilitate intercomparisons. The calculated and experimental results generally agree to within 1 to 2% except at the greatest depth (20 cm) where the discrepancies are of the order of 5%. For the beams with field sizes of 200 and 400 cm^2, the geometric correction is not quite

TABLE I

Percentage Depth Dose for Cobalt-60 Radiation (Source-to-Skin Distance 100 Cm)
(Comparison of calculated values with the experimental results of Johns *et al.*, *14*)

Beam area, $\pi\rho^2$ (cm^2)		*Depth, z (cm)*										
		0.5	*2*	*4*	*6*	*8*	*10*	*12*	*14*	*16*	*18*	*20*
0	Expt.	100.0	87.9	73.8	62.3	52.7	44.7	38.0	32.2	27.2	23.0	19.5
	Calc.	100.0	87.9	74.1	62.4	52.6	44.4	37.6	31.8	27.0	22.8	19.3
20	Expt.	100.0	91.7	81.0	70.6	61.0	52.3	44.8	38.5	33.1	28.5	24.4
	Calc.	100.0	93.6	82.2	70.7	60.4	51.9	44.5	37.9	32.2	27.2	23.1
50	Expt.	100.0	93.0	83.2	73.6	64.2	55.5	48.0	41.5	35.9	31.1	27.0
	Calc.	100.0	94.8	84.2	74.1	64.5	55.4	47.7	40.7	34.8	29.7	25.4
100	Expt.	100.0	94.0	84.8	75.6	66.5	57.9	50.4	44.0	38.4	33.6	29.2
	Calc.	100.0	95.0	86.1	76.1	66.9	58.3	50.6	43.4	38.5	32.3	27.8
200	Expt.	100.0	94.5	85.7	76.9	68.3	60.3	53.1	46.7	41.1	36.3	32.0
	Calc.	100.0	95.4	87.0	77.8	69.1	60.8	53.4	46.6	40.4	35.0	30.4
400	Expt.	100.0	94.6	86.4	78.2	70.1	62.5	55.4	49.2	43.7	38.8	34.5
	Calc.	100.0	95.5	87.8	79.6	71.5	63.7	56.5	49.9	43.8	38.4	33.7

accurate, and the calculated values in Table I should be raised by a few per cent. On the whole, considering the imperfect match between the conditions of the calculation and the experiment, the agreement is satisfactory. It thus appears entirely feasible to carry out depth-dose determinations by calculation, with an accuracy sufficient for radiological purposes.

4. SUMMARY

Gamma-ray transport theory is applied to the calculation of energy dissipation in bounded water media under conditions approximating those found in radiological problems. A combination of analytical, numerical, and Monte Carlo techniques is used. Two typical situations are considered: (1) a medium in which an isotropic source of radiation is distributed; (2) a medium irradiated by an external beam of radiation. The spatial pattern of energy dissipation is worked out in detail for a source emitting 1.28-Mev photons. The results of problem 2 are applied to the calculation of the depth dose produced by the irradiation of a medium with Co^{60} beams with cross-sectional areas up to 400 cm^2. The calculated depth-dose distributions are in good agreement with experimental distributions obtained by Johns and his collaborators.

ACKNOWLEDGMENT

The authors are indebted to Mrs. I. Reingold and Mr. J. A. Doggett for their help with the numerical work.

RECEIVED: June 16, 1958

REFERENCES

1. L. V. SPENCER and U. FANO, Penetration and diffusion of X-rays. Calculation of spatial distributions by polynomial expansion. *J. Research Bur. Standards* **46,** 446–456 (1951).
2. U. FANO, Gamma ray attenuation. *Nucleonics* **11,** No. 8, 8–12 (1953); **11,** No. 9, 55–61 (1953).
3. H. GOLDSTEIN and J. E. WILKINS, JR., Calculations of the penetration of gamma rays. U.S. Atomic Energy Commission Report NYO-3075 (June 30, 1954).
4. U. FANO, L. V. SPENCER, and M. J. BERGER, Penetration and diffusion of X-rays. To be published in the *Encyclopedia of Physics*, Vol. 38/2, Springer, Berlin.
5. H. BRYSK, Spatial distribution of energy dissipation by high-energy X-rays. *Phys. Rev.* **96,** 419–425 (1954).
6. H. A. MEYER, ed., *Monte Carlo Methods*, proceedings of a symposium held in 1954, John Wiley & Sons, New York, 1956.
7. G. WHITE GRODSTEIN, X-ray attenuation coefficients from 10 kev to 100 Mev. *Natl. Bur. Standards (U. S.) Circ.* **583** (1957).
8. Report of the International Commission of Radiological Units and Measurements (ICRU). *Natl. Bur. Standards (U. S.) Handbook* **No. 62** (1956).
9. L. V. SPENCER, Penetration and diffusion of X-rays: Calculation of spatial distributions by semi-asymptotic methods. *Phys. Rev.* **88,** 793–803 (1952).
10. M. J. BERGER, Penetration of gamma radiation from a plane monodirectional oblique source, *J. Research Natl. Bur. Standards* **56,** 111–128 (1956).

11. M. J. BERGER and J. DOGGETT, Reflection and transmission of gamma radiation by barriers: Semianalytic Monte Carlo calculation. *J. Research Natl. Bur. Standards* **56**, 89–98 (1956).
12. S. GLASSTONE, *Principles of Nuclear Reactor Engineering*, D. Van Nostrand, New York, 1955.
13. W. R. BRUCE and H. E. JOHNS, Monte Carlo calculations on the spectrum of scattered radiation produced in water by X-ray beams of interest in radiotherapy. *Radiology* **68**, 100–101 (1957).
14. H. E. JOHNS, E. R. EPP, D. V. CORMACK, and S. O. FEDORUK, Depth dose data diaphragm design for the Saskatchewan 1000 curie cobalt unit. *Brit. J. Radiol.* **25**, 302–308 (1952).

RADIATION RESEARCH 5, 571–583 (1959)

A Study of Comparative Protection against Lethality of Triethylenemelamine, Nitrogen Mustard, and X-Irradiation in Mice[1,2]

EDWIN I. GOLDENTHAL,[3] M. V. NADKARNI,[4] AND PAUL K. SMITH

Department of Pharmacology, The George Washington University, School of Medicine, Washington, D. C.

INTRODUCTION

A number of compounds, among them cysteine (*2*, *3*), cysteamine (β-mercaptoethylamine) (*4*), and sodium nitrite (*5*), afford significant protection in experimental animals against a lethal dose of x-rays, especially when administered prior to irradiation. The nitrogen mustards and related alkylating compounds such as triethylenemelamine (TEM) show carcinostatic and pharmacological actions similar to those produced by X-rays and have therefore been termed "radiomimetic." Philips (*6*) has summarized these similarities, and although the parallelism is by no means perfect the effects of the alkylating agents and X-irradiation have many features in common. Of a number of compounds studied to ascertain their protective effect on the toxicity of nitrogen mustard (HN2) (*7–9*), cysteine was found to be the most effective. Cysteine and cysteamine have been used clinically as an effective measure against nausea and vomiting accompanying X-irradiation and HN2 therapy (*4*, *10*).

The present report describes a comparison of the protective action of cysteine, cysteamine, and sodium nitrite on the toxicity of nitrogen mustard, triethylene-

[1] A preliminary abstract (*1*) was published in the *Proceedings of the American Association for Cancer Research*.

[2] This investigation was supported by research grants from the Damon Runyon Memorial Fund for Cancer Research (DRG-42G), the American Cancer Society (CH-30), the National Cancer Institute, National Institutes of Health (C-2326), and the U. S. Atomic Energy Commission (AT (30-1)-1107).

[3] A part of this material is from a dissertation presented by Edwin I. Goldenthal in partial fulfillment of the requirements for the Ph.D. degree. Present address: Division of Pharmacology, Food and Drug Administration, Department of Health, Education, and Welfare, Washington, D. C.

[4] Present address: Cancer Chemotherapy National Service Center, National Cancer Institute, National Institutes of Health, Bethesda, Maryland.

melamine, and X-irradiation. An attempt is made to explain the observed results of these protection experiments in terms of the chemical reaction between the alkylating drugs and the protective compounds.

MATERIALS AND METHODS

Mice

Adult C_3H, CFW, and $DBA/_2$ mice weighing between 20 and 25 gm were used in this investigation. The animals were housed in plastic cages and fed a diet of Purina laboratory chow and tap water. All animals were observed for 28 days after treatment.

Irradiation

A cylindrical wooden box, 16 cm in diameter and 9 cm in height, with a plastic top was used to house the mice during irradiation. The box contained ten radial compartments. Control and experimental animals were placed individually in alternate compartments. A deep-therapy standard X-ray machine was used[5] with the following physical factors: 200 kv, 20 ma, 0.5 mm copper filter, 1.0 mm aluminum filter, and an output of 79 r/min.

Protection Studies

Intraperitoneal doses of TEM (4.5 mg/kg body weight) or of nitrogen mustard, methylbis(2-chlorethyl)amine hydrochloride (4.0 mg/kg body weight), killed all C_3H mice between 3 and 7 days after injection. An exposure of 900 r of X-rays produced a similar response. At least two groups of eleven mice of different sex were used for each dose of HN2 or TEM, and ten mice in the irradiation experiments. Solutions of drugs were freshly prepared. L-Cysteine hydrochloride, neutralized to pH 7, at a dosage of 1000 mg/kg or sodium nitrite at a dosage of 125 mg/kg in a phosphate buffer at pH 7.4 was injected intraperitoneally 30 minutes prior to the toxic dose of HN2, TEM, or irradiation. Cysteamine benzoate was neutralized to pH 7 and injected intraperitoneally 5 minutes prior to irradiation or 30 minutes prior to HN2 or TEM at a dosage of 150 mg/kg. When TEM or HN2 was administered, the intraperitoneal injection was made contralateral to that of the protective agents.

In vitro Interaction

To determine the role which direct chemical reaction might play in the reduction of toxicity, each of the protective compounds was mixed and allowed to react with HN2 or TEM before being injected intraperitoneally into C_3H mice. Dosages identical to the preceding experiments were employed, and the same experimental conditions prevailed.

[5] Through the courtesy of the Department of Radiology, The George Washington University Hospital, Washington, D. C.

To examine the possibility of a chemical reaction of the sulfhydryl protective compounds with HN2 and TEM, TEM (4.5 mg) was added to an aqueous solution of cysteine (150 mg) or cysteamine (150 mg) at room temperature, and each of these solutions was injected intraperitoneally into groups of six CFW mice at various time intervals after mixing at a dosage equivalent to 4.5 mg/kg of TEM. HN2 (4.0 mg) was allowed to react with cysteine or cysteamine at room temperature, and the solution was injected intraperitoneally into groups of six CFW mice at a dosage equivalent to 4.0 mg/kg of HN2 at known time intervals after mixing. Cysteine and cysteamine were reacted with TEM and HN2 in varying proportions at 37°C, and at various intervals the progress of the reaction was determined by measuring the free sulfhydryl groups by the nitroprusside test. The reaction products were chromatographed in two solvent systems, and the compounds localized with ninhydrin.

Isolation of TEM:Cysteine Product

To ascertain the nature of the reaction between TEM and cysteine, 5 mM of TEM and 10 mM of cysteine were dissolved in water, mixed, and placed in a water bath at 55°C for 3 hours. No detectable free sulfhydryl groups were present. The solution was then lyophilized, the solid dissolved in a minimum amount of water, and ethanol added to a final concentration of 60%. The precipitate was centrifuged off, redissolved, and the above process repeated twice. The final precipitate was washed with acetone and dried. No toxicity to CFW mice was observed after injection of the purified compound up to 1000 mg/kg body weight. The purified product was tested for its carcinostatic properties, as compared against a TEM control, by measuring the survival time of $DBA/_2$ mice inoculated with leukemia 1210.[6] TEM and the reaction product each were injected into tumor-bearing mice on alternate days until all animals were dead, and the average survival time of each group was compared.

Oxidation of TEM:Cysteine Product

The reaction products of TEM and cysteine, cysteine, and cystine were oxidized by placing a small amount of the compound on filter paper and then adding two drops of hydrogen peroxide. Taurine and cysteic acid also were chromatographed simultaneously.

Sulfhydryl Measurements

The nitroprusside test was employed to measure the presence of free sulfhydryl groups. Micropipets were used to measure exact aliquots of the solution to be tested. The aliquot was placed on a spot plate, and one drop each of a 10% solution of sodium hydroxide and a freshly prepared 1% solution of sodium nitroprusside were

[6] Through the courtesy of Dr. L. W. Law, National Cancer Institute, National Institutes of Health, Bethesda, Maryland

added. The time required for the disappearance of the purple color was taken as a measure of the quantity of free sulfhydryl groups present. Sulfhydryl content was estimated on a numerical scale of 1 to 4 plus, a standard curve being constructed with known quantities of cysteine or cysteamine.

Chromatography

Whatman No. 1 filter paper was used for chromatography. The chromatograms were developed in three solvent systems: (1) methyl ethyl ketone:propionic acid: water (2:1:2 v/v); (2) acetone:water (3:2 v/v); and (3) phenol saturated with water.

Radioactivity Measurements

Radioactive samples of urine and administered solutions were plated directly at constant geometry on aluminum disks. Chromatograms were cut into strips 3 cm square and assayed for radioactivity. Strips showing activity were further divided into 1-cm strips and recounted in order to determine more accurately the exact location of radioactivity. The counting equipment consisted of a windowless gas-flow (natural gas) proportional counter.

Studies with Cysteine and HN2-C^{14}

To ascertain whether a chemical combination between HN2 and cysteine occurred *in vivo* during the course of a protection experiment, methyl-labeled HN2-C^{14} was injected intraperitoneally into groups of three male C_3H mice at a dosage of 4.0 mg/kg. Cysteine was administered subcutaneously to two groups of three male C_3H mice at a dosage of 1000 mg/kg followed by an intraperitoneal injection of HN2-C^{14} 30 minutes later. In a separate experiment, HN2-C^{14} (4.0 mg) was mixed with cysteine (1000 mg) for 1 hour and injected intraperitoneally into two groups of three male C_3H mice at a dosage equivalent to 4.0 mg/kg of HN2. The per cent urinary excretion of radioactivity was calculated. Each urine sample was co-chromatographed in two solvent systems along with the reaction product of HN2-C^{14} and cysteine.

RESULTS

Protection Studies

Protection in the various pretreated groups in terms of per cent survival of mice is tabulated in Table I. Since differences in the response of males and females were not evident, the results are not grouped according to sex. Striking differences have been revealed in the degree of protection obtained by prior administration of the compounds. None of the compounds protected against the toxicity of TEM. Each of the three compounds afforded protection against X-irradiation. Cysteine provided substantial protection against the toxicity of HN2; cysteamine gave only partial protection; and sodium nitrite gave little, if any, protection.

In Vitro Interaction

The per cent survival of the mice administered the compounds immediately after mixing is shown in Table II. Here again, differences between the behavior of HN2 and TEM are evident. HN2 lost its toxicity immediately on mixing with either cysteine or cysteamine, but mixing with sodium nitrite had no effect. TEM did not lose its toxicity immediately on mixing with any of these compounds.

The rate of reduction in toxicity of TEM when mixed with cysteine or cysteamine was approximated by injecting the mixture into mice at various intervals after mixing and observing the mortality. The results, shown in Table III, indicate a complete disappearance of toxicity of TEM 4 hours after being mixed with either cysteine or cysteamine. TEM alone under similar conditions retained its biological activity. This indicated that a chemical reaction probably occurred between TEM and cysteine or cysteamine. Further evidence for this was obtained by demonstrating that, whenever TEM was in excess stoichiometrically, the free sulfhydryl groups in the reacting mixture had completely disappeared after 5 hours of reaction (Table IV). When either cysteine or cysteamine was present in a 2:1 or 3:1 molecular ratio, some free sulfhydryl groups remained even after 24 hours. Evidence for the formation of new compounds was obtained by paper chromatography. The com-

TABLE I

PROTECTION OF MICE PRETREATED WITH CYSTEINE, CYSTEAMINE, OR SODIUM NITRITE AGAINST THE TOXICITY OF X-RAYS, HN2, OR TEM

	X-Rays (900 r)		*HN2 (4.0 mg/kg)*		*TEM (4.5 mg/kg)*	
Pretreatment	*Survivals*	*Per cent survival*	*Survivals*	*Per cent survival*	*Survival*	*Per cent survival*
None	5/140	4	1/55	2	0/48	0
Cysteine (1000 mg/kg)	23/30	73	22/22	100	0/22	0
Cysteamine (150 mg/kg)	58/80	69	22/80	28	0/33	0
Sodium nitrite (125 mg/kg)	21/30	66	5/66	8	0/22	0

TABLE II

PER CENT SURVIVAL OF MICE ADMINISTERED LETHAL DOSE OF HN2 OR TEM IMMEDIATELY AFTER MIXING WITH SELECTED COMPOUNDS

	HN2 (4.0 mg/kg)		*TEM (4.5 mg/kg)*	
Compounds mixed	*Survivals*	*Per cent survival*	*Survivals*	*Per cent survival*
None	1/55	2	0/48	0
Cysteine (1000 mg/kg)	39/40	98	0/22	0
Cysteamine (150 mg/kg)	22/22	100	0/22	0
Sodium nitrite (125 mg/kg)	0/22	0	0/22	0

TABLE III

EFFECT OF REACTION TIME ON PER CENT MORTALITY OF MICE ADMINISTERED A MXTURE OF TEM AND CYSTEINE OR CYSTEAMINE

		TEM + cysteine[a]		*TEM + cysteamine*[a]	
Time after mixing (hours)	*Number of mice*	*Deaths*	*Per cent mortality*	*Deaths*	*Per cent mortality*
0	6	6	100	6	100
1	6	6	100	6	100
2	6	4	67	6	100
4	6	0	0	0	0
6	6	0	0	0	0

[a] 150 mg/kg of cysteine or cysteamine and 4.5 mg/kg of TEM injected intraperitoneally.

TABLE IV

LOSS OF FREE SULFHYDRYL GROUPS OF TEM:CYSTEINE AND TEM:CYSTEAMINE MIXTURES

Hours	*TEM:cysteine*					*Cysteine*	*TEM:cysteamine*					*Cysteamine*
	1:1	*2:1*	*3:1*	*1:2*	*1:3*		*1:1*	*2:1*	*3:1*	*1:2*	*1:3*	
0	++++	++++	++++	++++	++++	++++	++++	++++	++++	++++	++++	++++
1	++++	++++	+++	++++	++++	++++	++++	+++	+++	++++	++++	++++
2	+++	+++	++	+++	+++	++++	+++	++	++	+++	+++	++++
3	++	++	++	+++	+++	++++	++	+	+	++	+++	++++
4	++	+	+	+++	+++	++++	+	+	−	++	+++	++++
5	+	−	−	++	++	++++	+	−		+	+++	++++
6	+			+	++	++++	−			+	+	++++
12	−			+	+	++++				−	+	++++
24				+	+	++++					+	++++

pounds were localized with ninhydrin. The R_f values for the reaction products of TEM and cysteamine, of HN2 and cysteamine, and of HN2 and cysteine are different from those of the original sulfhydryl compounds or its oxidized forms (Table V).

Chromatography of the lyophilized product of TEM and cysteine in two solvent systems showed that two compounds had been formed during the reaction, neither of which corresponded to cysteine, cystine, or TEM. One of these compounds produced a much greater intensity in color after ninhydrin treatment than the other compound. After three reprecipitations with ethanol, the dry product represented a recovery of 38% of theory. This compound gave a single spot with ninhydrin (Fig. 1) and corresponded to the spot of greater intensity. The elemental analysis of the compound[7] calculated on the basis of the proposed structure (Fig. 2) $C_{18}H_{33}N_9S_3O_6$ was: C, 38.09%; H, 5.86%; N, 22.21%; and S, 16.94%. Found: C,

[7] Analysis by Oakwold Laboratories, Alexandria, Virginia.

TABLE V

R_f VALUES OF REACTION PRODUCTS IN PHENOL:WATER AND METHYL ETHYL KETONE SOLVENT SYSTEMS

Reaction product	*Phenol:water*	*Methyl ethyl ketone*
Cysteamine	0.81	0.42
Cystamine	0.38	0.09
TEM + cysteamine	0.82	0.32
HN2 + cysteamine	0.70	0.35
Cysteine	0.56	0.28
Cystine	0.18	0.06
HN2 + cysteine	0.70	0.02

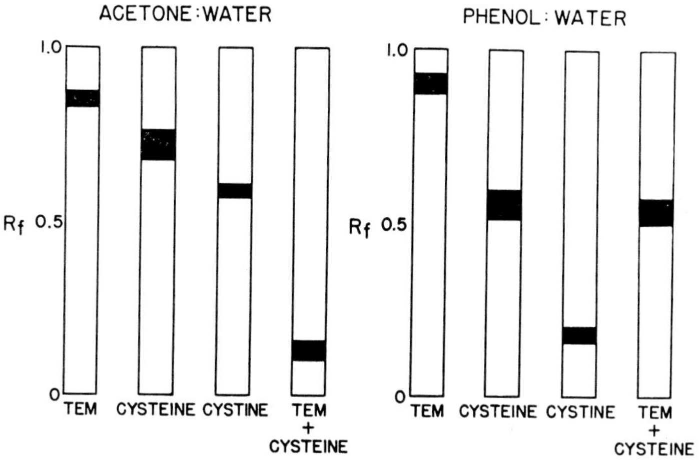

FIG. 1. Chromatograms of reaction product of TEM and cysteine

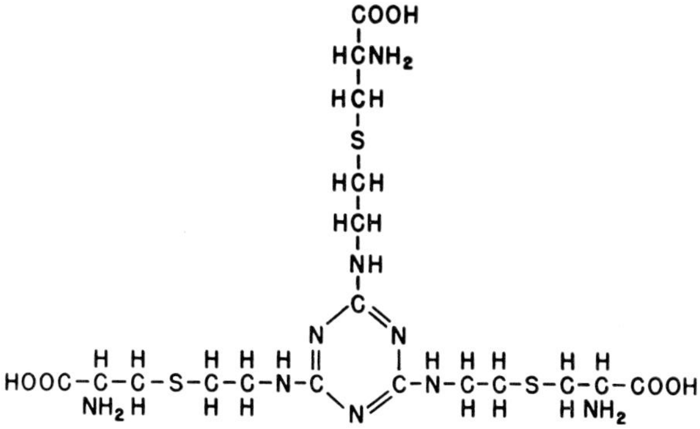

FIG. 2. Proposed structural formula for reaction product of TEM and cysteine

TABLE VI

R_f VALUES OF REACTION PRODUCT OF TEM AND CYSTEINE BEFORE AND AFTER TREATMENT WITH HYDROGEN PEROXIDE

Reaction product	*Phenol saturated with water*	*Acetone: water*
Cysteine	0.56	0.73
Cysteine + H_2O_2	0.13	0.61
Cystine	0.18	0.59
Cystine + H_2O_2	0.08	0.60
Purified TEM:cysteine product	0.53	0.13
Purified TEM:cysteine product + H_2O_2	0.12	0.61
Cysteic acid	0.11	0.62
Taurine	0.31	0.71

TABLE VII

EFFECT OF TEM:CYSTEINE PRODUCT ON SURVIVAL TIME OF L-1210 LEUKEMIC DBA/2 MICE

Compound	*Number of mice*	*Dosage (mg/kg)*	*Survival time (days)*
No treatment	12	—	6.12 ± 0.59
TEM	12	0.75	9.29 ± 0.55
TEM:cysteine product	12	100	6.20 ± 0.36
TEM:cysteine product	12	250	6.30 ± 0.49

TABLE VIII

LOSS OF FREE SULFHYDRYL GROUPS OF HN2:CYSTEINE AND HN2:CYSTEAMINE MIXTURES

Minutes	*HN2 : cysteine*			*Cysteine*	*HN2 : cysteamine*			*Cysteamine*
	1 : 1	*2 : 1*	*1 : 2*		*1 : 1*	*2 : 1*	*1 : 2*	
0	++++	++++	++++	++++	++++	++++	++++	++++
10	++	—	+	++++	+	+	++	++++
20	—		+	++++	—	—	+	++++
30			—	++++			—	++++
40				++++				++++
50				++++				++++
60				++++				++++

38.17%; H, 6.33%; N, 22.64%; and S, 16.92%. The neutralization equivalent: calculated, 189.23; found, 192.03. No distinct melting point could be obtained with the compound. The compound expanded at 190°C, followed by shrinking immediately thereafter, and turned brown at 200°C. It appears that three molecules of cysteine react with one molecule of TEM through the sulfhydryl group of cysteine

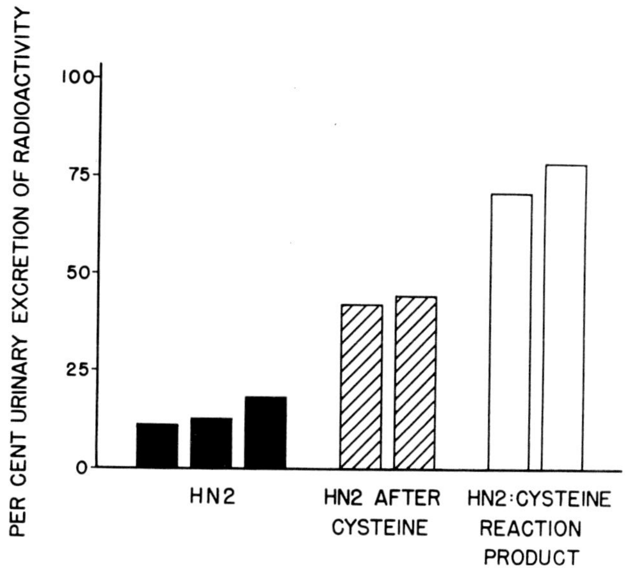

FIG. 3. Comparison of the effect of cysteine on the 24-hour urinary excretion of radioactivity after HN2-C^{14} administration.

with the ethylenimino group of TEM. The results of chromatography with the oxidation products of this compound, shown in Table VI indicate that one of the oxidized products is cysteic acid. To test the toxicity of the TEM:cysteine derivative, the reaction product was administered to mice at doses up to 1000 mg/kg, and no deaths were observed. When tested against leukemia 1210 the results shown in Table VII indicate that this compound possesses no carcinostatic activity even at massive dosages.

When HN2 was mixed with cysteine or cysteamine and injected into mice at an estimated LD_{100} dose of HN2 at various time intervals after mixing, a complete loss of toxicity of HN2 was observed even when injections were made immediately after mixing. The rate of disappearance of free sulfhydryl groups, as measured by the nitroprusside test, in mixtures of HN2 and cysteine or cysteamine is shown in Table VIII. Evidence for the instantaneous formation of a new compound was obtained by paper chromatography (Table V), the compounds being localized with ninhydrin color reaction.

Radioactive Studies

The comparison of the effect of cysteine on the urinary excretion of HN2-C^{14} is shown in Fig. 3. When cysteine was administered 30 minutes prior to HN2, the urinary excretion of radioactivity rose to an average value of 42.8%, as compared

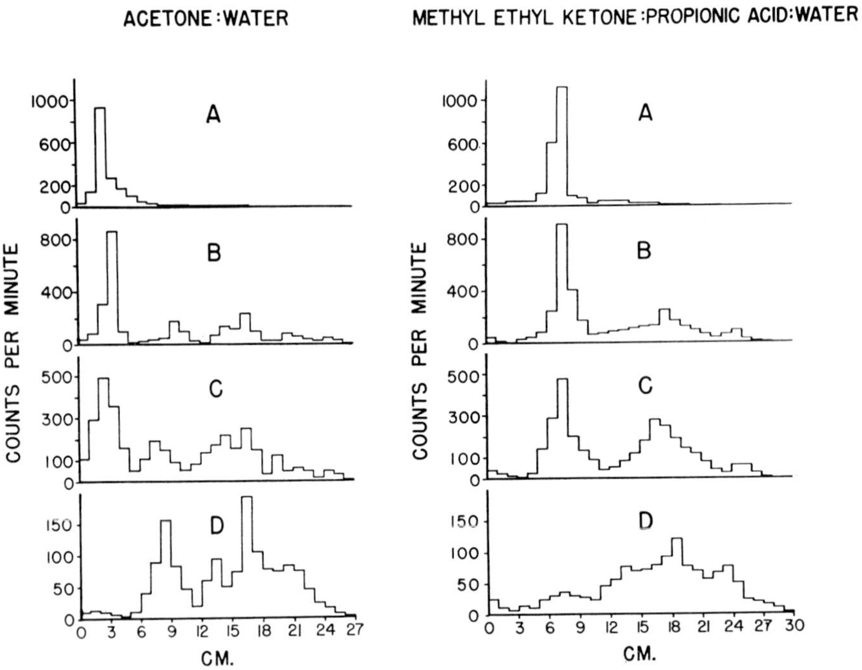

FIG. 4. Radioactivity distribution on chromatograms showing the effect of cysteine on the urinary excretion of HN2-C^{14}. *A*, reaction product of HN2-C^{14} and cysteine. *B*, urine of mice administered the reaction product of HN2-C^{14} and cysteine. *C*, urine of mice administered cysteine 30 minutes before HN2-C^{14}. *D*, urine of mice administered HN2-C^{14}.

to 14.7 % when HN2-C^{14} was administered alone. The results of chromatograms of these urines are shown in Fig. 4. The evidence indicated that a new compound which corresponded to that of the reaction product appeared in the urine of mice pretreated with cysteine. It is apparent that some of the administered HN2 combined with the cysteine in the animal body, and the reaction product was excreted in the urine.

DISCUSSION

Prior administration of cysteine, cysteamine, or sodium nitrite showed substantial protection against the lethal effects of a single dose of X-rays on mice, the results being in agreement with those of other investigators. When tested against other radiomimetic agents, the same compounds showed a variable response as protective agents. Excellent protection against the lethality of HN2 was obtained with cysteine, less protection with cysteamine, and very little, if any, with sodium nitrite. No protection was obtained against the toxicity of TEM with any of the agents used. It is possible that the low degree of protection obtained with cysteamine against nitrogen mustard toxicity was due to a limitation of dosage necessitated by considerably higher toxicity of cysteamine as compared to cysteine. This observation is in agreement with the results obtained by Salerno and Friedell (*11*), who found that the magnitude of protection of these compounds against the toxicity of HN2 was directly proportional to the molar dosage.

It has been demonstrated that HN2 is capable of reacting with either cysteine or cysteamine within a very short time. This difference in reaction rates between HN2 and TEM is probably due to the ethylenimino moieties of TEM requiring a longer time for intramolecular rearrangement to a reactive form. As demonstrated by *in vitro* experiments the reaction between the sulfhydryl compounds and TEM required several hours, and it is probable that TEM has exerted its toxic effects before any inactivation could occur. In contrast, HN2, a more reactive compound, is inactivated almost immediately.

In general, the evidence is consistent with the assumption that sulfhydryl-containing compounds serve as absorbing material for the oxidants formed in intracellular water after X-irradiation. This action may be an indirect one, and a compound such as cysteine may reduce the availability of oxygen and hence the yield of these free radicals (*12*). If this is the case, one would not expect sodium nitrite to reduce the toxicity of HN2 or TEM, since this compound acts in X-ray protection presumably by producing a methemoglobinemia. Brandt and Griffin (*7*) presented evidence to show that the reduction of toxicity of HN2 by cysteine was not merely an inactivation of HN2 by direct combination in the blood stream. They observed a moderate lowering of the white blood count, but not so great a leukopenia as with HN2 alone. Several of the mice pretreated with cysteine developed tumors, as one would expect with HN2 alone. This observation could be explained on the basis of a large percentage of the HN2 combining with cysteine so that the actual amount of free HN2 present in the animal would be well below the toxic level. Furthermore, others (*13*, *14*), using rabbits, reported a protective effect on the leukopenia induced by HN2 when L-cysteine was coadministered. This occurred only if cysteine was administered prior to HN2 and lends support to a chemical combination *in vivo* of cysteine and HN2.

The results obtained with labeled HN2 clearly demonstrate that this nitrogen mustard combines with cysteine *in vivo*. Approximately 14% of the injected radioactivity was excreted in the urine in 24 hours when HN2 was administered alone, as compared to 43% when the mice were pretreated with cysteine. Mice pretreated with cysteine before HN2 administration excrete a new compound in the urine. This has been shown to be the reaction product of the two compounds. There is partial breakdown of the reaction product of HN2 and cysteine when administered to mice. It appears from these experiments that the protection observed in animals pretreated with cysteine and then administered HN2 is, at least in part, due to a chemical inactivation *in vivo*. TEM, which reacts slowly *in vitro*, retained its toxicity, whereas the more reactive HN2 was rapidly inactivated.

SUMMARY

A comparison was made of the protective action of cysteine, cysteamine, and sodium nitrite against the lethality in mice by X-irradiation, nitrogen mustard, or triethylenemelamine. Striking differences were revealed in the degree of protection obtained by the preadministration of the compounds. All compounds afforded some protection against the lethal effects of X-irradiation. Substantial protection against the lethality of HN2 was obtained with cysteine, and some protection with cysteamine. None of the compounds gave measurable protection against TEM.

Chemical interaction of HN2 or TEM with cysteine or cysteamine *in vitro* was demonstrated. The reaction of HN2 with cysteine or cysteamine was instantaneous, whereas that between TEM and cysteine or cysteamine required several hours. It is suggested that the difference in reactivity may explain the differences in the degree of protection afforded by the sulfhydryl-containing compounds.

The *in vitro* reaction product of TEM with cysteine was isolated and purified. The probable structure of the reaction product is suggested. This compound was shown to be inert with respect to toxicity as well as carcinostatic effects on leukemia-1210.

A threefold increase in the urinary excretion occurred when cysteine was preadministered to mice as compared to HN2 alone. A compound corresponding to the R_f of the reaction product appeared in this urine. The suggestion is made that the mechanism of cysteine protection is through direct chemical inactivation of HN2.

RECEIVED: June 26, 1958

REFERENCES

1. M. V. NADKARNI, E. I. GOLDENTHAL, and P. K. SMITH, Observations on the comparative protective action of certain compounds against the lethal effects of triethylene melamine, nitrogen mustard, and X-radiation. *Proc. Am. Assoc. Cancer Research* **1,** 34–35 (1954).
2. H. M. PATT, D. E. SMITH, E. B. TYREE, and R. L. STRAUBE, Further studies on modification of sensitivity to X-rays by cysteine. *Proc. Soc. Exptl. Biol. Med.* **73,** 18–21 (1950).
3. H. M. PATT, E. B. TYREE, R. L. STRAUBE, and D. E. SMITH, Cysteine protection against X-irradiation. *Science* **110,** 213–214 (1949).
4. Z. M. BACQ, G. DECHAMPS, P. FISCHER, A. HERVE, H. LEBIHAN, J. LECOMTE, M. PIROTTE, and P. RAYET, Protection against X-rays and therapy of radiation sickness with β-mercaptoethylamine. *Science* **117,** 633–636 (1953).
5. L. J. COLE, V. P. BOND, and M. C. FISHLER, Preprotection of mice against X-irradiation mortality by sodium nitrite. *Science* **115,** 644–646 (1952).
6. F. S. PHILIPS, Recent contributions to pharmacology of bis(2-haloethyl) amines and sulfides. *Pharmacol. Revs.* **2,** 281–323 (1950).
7. E. L. BRANDT and A. C. GRIFFIN, Reduction of toxicity of nitrogen mustards by cysteine. *Cancer* **4,** 1030–1035 (1951).

8. G. W. Howe, H. N. Marvin, and C. L. Spurr, Evaluation of choline and related substances as antitoxic agents to nitrogen mustard *in vivo*. *Texas Repts. Biol. Med.* **10,** 39–44 (1952).
9. M. L. Mitchell and R. J. Girerd, Effect of growth hormone and antibiotics upon nitrogen mustard treated rats. *Proc. Soc. Exptl. Biol. Med.* **83,** 615–618 (1953).
10. A. S. Weisberger, R. W. Heinle, and B. Levine, Effect of l-cysteine on nitrogen mustard therapy, *Am. J. Med. Sci.* **224,** 201–211 (1958).
11. P. R. Salerno and H. L. Friedell, *U. S. Atomic Energy Comm. Nuclear Sci. Abstr.* **9,** (1955).
12. H. M. Patt, Protective mechanisms in ionizing radiation injury. *Physiol. Revs.* **33,** 35–76 (1953).
13. A. S. Weisberger and R. W. Heinle, The protective effect of cysteine on leucopenia induced by nitrogen mustard. *J. Lab. Clin. Med.* **36,** 872–876 (1950).
14. A. S. Weisberger, R. W. Heinle, and B. Levine, Some structural requirements for prevention of leukopenia induced by nitrogen mustard. *J. Clin. Invest.* **31,** 217–222 (1952).

RADIATION RESEARCH **5**, 584–596 (1959)

Effects of Nonirradiated Protoplasm on Recovery of Amoebae Exposed to Supralethal Doses of Fission Neutrons[1,2]

EDWARD W. DANIELS AND HOWARD H. VOGEL, JR.

Division of Biological and Medical Research, Argonne National Laboratory, Lemont, Illinois

INTRODUCTION

It has been shown that the giant amoeba *Pelomyxa illinoisensis* is relatively sensitive to X-rays (*1*, *2*). On the other hand, *Pelomyxa carolinensis* is about ten times as radioresistant (*3*, *4*), and the large uninucleated species, *Amoeba proteus*, is also highly resistant to X-rays (*5*). The relatively high sensitivity of *P. illinoisensis* to ionizing radiations suggested that it might be a useful unicellular system for analysis of the comparative biological effects of X-rays, γ-rays, and fission neutrons. As a preliminary step in this investigation and in order to compare the relative biological effectiveness of two radiations, dose-survival curves were constructed for *P. illinoisensis* after exposure to fission neutrons and to Co^{60} γ-rays. Cell division data were obtained from irradiated cells kept in isolation. With this information available, it was possible to find out whether or not transplanted, nonirradiated protoplasm had the capacity to prevent death in pelomyxae exposed to supralethal doses of fission neutrons. Previous work (*1*, *6*) had shown that supralethally X-irradiated *P. illinoisensis* would recover after fusion with nonirradiated cells or with certain portions of nonirradiated, centrifuged cells. The induction of recovery in this giant amoeba by similar procedures after irradiation with fission neutrons will be reported in this paper.

METHODS AND MATERIALS

Pelomyxa illinoisensis cells were washed free from other organisms and then put into a phosphate buffer (*7*) which was used as the culture medium. Before irradiation, they were placed in 1-ml cone-shaped plastic vials which were sealed with Scotch tape and fastened in the center of a plastic exposure cage (16 inches × 16 inches) designed for irradiation of mice (*8*). In all experiments, randomly se-

[1] This work was performed under the auspices of the U. S. Atomic Energy Commission.

[2] Preliminary reports of this work were presented before the American Society of Zoologists, August, 1957 (Abstracts 110 and 111; *Anat. Record.*, Vol. 128).

lected vials of amoebae were used as controls and were treated in the same manner as the exposed vials except for irradiation. Temperature (24°C) and relative humidity (50%) were controlled during irradiation by a climatizer unit. About a half hour after the amoebae were irradiated with either fission neutrons or γ-rays, they were washed, isolated, and fed with ciliates (*Paramecium caudatum*) and flagellates (*Chilomonas paramecium*).

The neutron exposures were carried out in a radiation chamber (*8*) at the thermal column of Argonne's CP-5 research reactor. Fast neutrons were obtained by Zirkle's method (*9*) in which the thermal column of a reactor is used in conjunction with a plate of uranium to convert slow neutrons to fission neutrons. The spectrum within the radiation chamber at CP-5 has been described for neutron energies between 0.5 and 6 Mev (*10, 11*).

Comparative dosimetric methods (Sigoloff chemical dosimeters—water-equivalent and anhydrous tetrachloroethylene; Victoreen r-chambers calibrated against Rossi tissue-equivalent chambers; photographic emulsion techniques used by Tochilin *et al.* at USNRDL) indicated that the total dose rate at the animal exposure position was approximately 31 rep/min with CP-5 operating at 2000 kw. This total was composed of 24 rep/min of fission neutrons and 6.5 rep/min of γ-ray contamination. In this paper the total dose of fission neutrons includes the 15 to 20% γ-ray component.

Four separate exposures to Co^{60} γ-radiation were carried out in the high-level gamma room (*12*) at an intensity of 25 r/min. All irradiated cells were kept a minimum of 10 days after irradiation, more than twice the mean time to death for the lethally irradiated animals. When kept for longer periods, the cells which survived 10 days after exposure usually gave rise to mass cultures.

The centrifugation was done in a cold room (1°C) with a Lourdes centrifuge. All materials other than the organisms were precooled during the preceding night. The cells were rounded by agitation and then put into ice-cold water in a centrifuge tube which contained a cushion of 10% neutralized gum arabic. The cells were centrifuged at a radius of 10 cm for 10 minutes, exclusive of acceleration and deceleration. The centrifugal forces used ranged from 700 to 6700 $\times$ *g*. The stratified amoebae were transferred immediately after centrifugation to a plastic dish containing ice water. Within 20 minutes after centrifugation, during which time they maintained the stratified condition, they were cut into thirds. The cutting device consisted of a 5-mm section of the cutting edge of a thin razor blade. The cell portions were kept separated from each other and placed in the laboratory which was kept at a temperature between 24° and 26°C. All protoplasmic systems were transferred by the method of microfusion, and the resultant cells were isolated and cultured individually (1). The heavy third portions were the most difficult to fuse, since they often disintegrated when stabbed with a microneedle. When this occurred, the cell membrane would burst and liberate its contents into the culture medium.

RESULTS

Radiation Effects

Dose-survival curves. Complete survival curves for the amoebae are presented here after single exposures both to Co^{60} γ-rays and to fission neutrons at approximately equal intensities. The 10-day survival data are illustrated graphically in Fig. 1 as dose-survival probit regression lines following each radiation. Each datum represents 25 cells. The lethal range after γ-irradiation was found to be approximately from 13,000 to 21,000 r; such exposures required from 9 to 14 hours at the dose rate utilized. On the other hand, only 5 to 7 hours of fission neutron irradiation (9000 to 13,000 rep) was necessary to produce death in amoebae during the 10-day period after exposure.

The apparent difference in the slopes of the two probit regression lines (Fig. 1) is probably not significant, as can be seen in Fig. 2, which represents a sigmoid dose-survival curve for γ-irradiated amoebae. The points representing neutron exposures were obtained by multiplying the values for neutron dose in kilorep by a factor of 1.5, an estimated figure for relative biological effectiveness (RBE). It appears from this graph that both sets of points fit the line quite well; a common

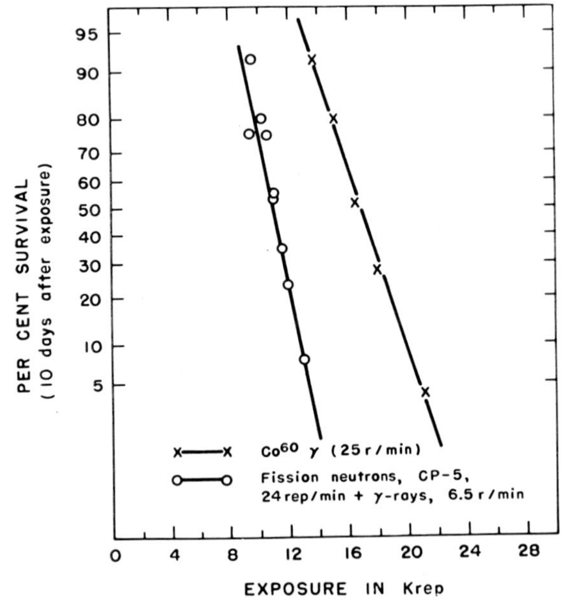

FIG. 1. Per cent survival of *Pelomyxa illinoisensis* after exposure to fission neutrons and to Co^{60} γ-rays (probit regression lines). Each point represents 25 cells which were irradiated and isolated at the beginning of the experiment. The survival data were calculated from the exposed cells or their offspring. X——X: Co^{60} γ(25 r/min); O——O: fission neutrons, CP-5, 24 rep/min. + γ-rays, 6.5 r/min.

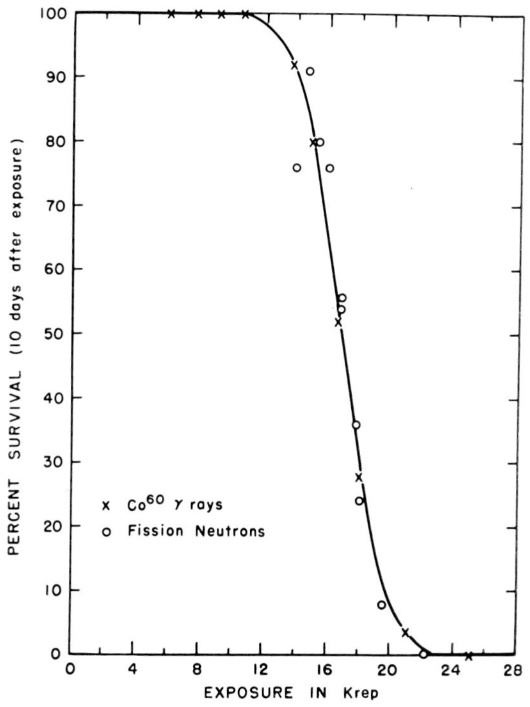

FIG. 2. Dose-survival curve for *Pelomyxa illinoisensis* after single exposures to fission neutrons and Co^{60} γ-rays. A factor of 1.5 was used for relative biological effectiveness (RBE) to superimpose the neutron points (from Fig. 1) upon the γ-ray curve. (Thus, the actual dose of neutrons received by the organisms was that shown in Fig. 2 divided by 1.5.)

regression line could be drawn. Thus, in Fig. 1, the neutron probit regression line can be superimposed on the γ-line by multiplying by the factor of 1.5. A value for the RBE of the two radiations then can be determined. For 50% survival, the RBE would be

$$\frac{17{,}000 \text{ rep } (\gamma)}{11{,}000 \text{ rep (n)}} = 1.5$$

These data indicate that for this biological effect and under the conditions of this experiment fission neutrons were approximately one and a half times as effective as Co^{60} γ-rays.

The time of death after comparable doses of the two radiations was remarkably similar: The mean time of death with its standard error after a lethal γ-ray exposure (25 kr) to 25 cells was 4.2 ± 0.4 days. The mean time of death in a similar group of 25 cells after a single lethal neutron dose of 14.8 krep (8 hours) was 4.4 ± 0.1 days.

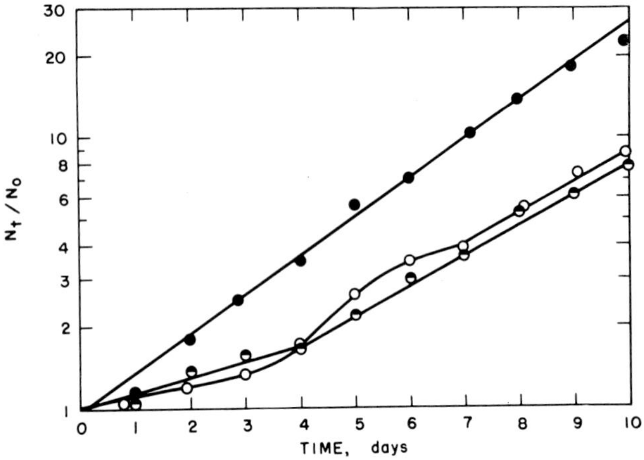

FIG. 3. Rate of cell division in fission neutron-irradiated amoebae, single cell clones: ●, nonirradiated controls (50 clones); ○, 9500-rep fission neutrons, exposure 5¼ hours (25 clones, 92% survival, Fig. 1); ◓, 11,000-rep fission neutrons, exposure 6 hours (50 clones, 55% survival, Fig. 1). N_t is the total number of cells at time t. N_t/N_0 = ratio of total number of surviving cells over the surviving clones at time t.

Effects of irradiation on the rate of cell division. The effects of single exposures of fission neutrons on the division rates of amoebae are illustrated in Fig. 3. The rate of division is inhibited in both groups of neutron-irradiated amoebae shown. Similar inhibition of the rate of cell division was observed after comparable γ-irradiation. In each case, the irradiated cells had essentially recovered to the control rate of division by the first week after exposure.

Effects of Microfusion

It had already been established that an 8-hour irradiation with fission neutrons (approximately 15,000 rep) was lethal to all amoebae within a 10-day period (Fig. 1). In the following work, involving the effects of microfusion after irradiation, a supralethal dose of 30,000 rep neutrons was used. This exposure of 15 to 16 hours' duration was at least twice that required to produce the $LD_{99(10)}$.

Nonirradiated, noncentrifuged protoplasm. Nonirradiated protoplasm from *P. illinoisensis* cells, when transferred into supralethally neutron-irradiated cells prevented death in 91% of the irradiated cells (Table I). Each of these organisms divided at least once within 10 days after exposure, and representative clones that were kept for further study each gave rise to mass cultures of some 30 cells within a month after irradiation. One cell, which did not divide at any time after irradiation and microfusion, died one month after exposure. All of 158 irradiated, nonfused cells which were isolated died, as well as all of some 1000 irradiated cells which were kept in mass cultures. Each of 45 isolated, nonirradiated control cells survived and divided at least once within the 10-day period of study.

TABLE I

PER CENT SURVIVAL AND MEAN CELL DIVISIONS OF SUPRALETHALLY NEUTRON-IRRADIATED AMOEBAE FUSED WITH DIFFERENT NONIRRADIATED CELL PORTIONS

Experimental procedures	*Original number of cells*	*Cells surviving 10 days (%)*	*Irradiation to first cell division (days ± S. E.)*	*First to second cell division (days ± S. E.)*	*Second to third cell division (days ± S. E.)*
Nonirradiated controls	45	100	2.2 ± 0.2	2.3 ± 0.1	2.4 ± 0.2
Nonirradiated portion fused with irradiated cell	33	91	4.0 ± 0.3	2.3 ± 0.4	2.2 ± 0.2
3000 × *g* portions fused with irradiated cell					
Light third	28	54	4.6 ± 0.5	2.0 ± 0.3	2.3 ± 0.4
Middle third	24	92	5.5 ± 0.6	2.4 ± 0.3	2.3 ± 0.3
Heavy third	26	96	5.6 ± 0.5	2.4 ± 0.2	2.1 ± 0.2
6700 × *g* portions fused with irradiated cell					
Light third	23	13	3.0 ± 0.6	1.8 ± 0.8	3.3 ± 0.8
Middle third	26	89	4.6 ± 0.4	2.2 ± 0.2	1.8 ± 0.1
Heavy third	22	96	5.1 ± 0.2	2.6 ± 0.3	1.3 ± 0.3

The mean time required for the first cell division in the irradiated, fused group which received nonirradiated protoplasm was approximately 2 days longer than that for the nonirradiated, nonfused controls (Table I). It appears that this delay was due entirely to the consequences of irradiation, since isologous fusion of nonirradiated *P. illinoisensis* organisms causes little, if any, delay. Similarly, the fusion of nonirradiated, *P. carolinensis* giant amoebae does not cause a delay in cell division (*13*). There was no delay in either the second or third divisions in the neutron-irradiated cells which received nonirradiated protoplasm (Table I). This is also true after supralethal X-irradiation followed by fusion with nonirradiated protoplasm (*1*). Cell lines that survived 10 days after supralethal irradiation and microfusion usually gave rise to mass cultures when kept for longer periods.

The volume of nonirradiated protoplasm introduced into the irradiated cells was estimated by visual comparison of rounded cells prior to fusion at a magnification of 90 times. In some cases, the diameters were measured and the relative volumes were calculated from these. Every irradiated cell survived that received an amount of nonirradiated protoplasm equal to or greater than its own volume, and it either gave rise to a mass culture or showed evidence of this capacity. Cells that contained an excess of irradiated protoplasm survived, provided this quantity did not exceed roughly 15 parts to 1 part nonirradiated protoplasm. Thus, it appears that recovery can occur, provided a certain minimum of nonirradiated protoplasm is introduced into the supralethally irradiated cell.

Nonirradiated centrifuged protoplasm. The intracellular components appear randomly distributed in the normal pelomyxa cell, and, since the protoplasm is almost constantly changing from sol to gel or vice versa in some part of the living cell, the protoplasm in the sol is consistently being mixed. The majority of these amoebae contain around 200 nuclei (*14*, *15*) distributed randomly; Fig. 4*A* shows a typical cell taken from a stock culture. Centrifugation brings about a stratification of components within the cell. Some of these strata can be seen with the light microscope (Fig. 4, *B*, *C*, and *D*). Nuclei and mitochondria migrate toward the centrifugal pole during 10 minutes of centrifugation at 715 × *g* (Fig. 4*B*); the mitochondria stain bright crimson and can be seen concentrated in the centrifugal half of the cell. Figure 4, *C* and *D*, shows a similar stratification of nuclei after centrifugation for 10 minutes at 3000 × *g* and 6700 × *g*, respectively. The nuclear stratum does not migrate further toward the heavy pole at the higher centrifugal force. Many food vacuoles migrate to the extreme centrifugal pole, however, as the 6700 × *g* force is applied (Fig. 4*D*); these vary in size, shape, and density, whereas the nuclei are much more uniform in these aspects. Most of the crystal-like components migrate toward the heavy pole of the cell at relatively low centrifugal forces, less than 1000 × *g*. The bulk of the fine particulates (0.1 to 0.3 μ), which are smaller than acid–fuchsin staining mitochondria (0.5 to 2.0 μ), migrate out of the light third portion at between 1000 and 6700 × *g*.

Survival of the nonirradiated, nonfused light and heavy thirds was limited to several hours, whereas the middle thirds lived much longer and frequently regenerated the missing parts of the cell.

Addition of the protoplasm from the middle third or heavy third portions of nonirradiated cells centrifuged at 3000 or 6700 × *g* prevented death in 89 to 96% of supralethally fission neutron-irradiated recipients (Table I). Although the volume of the injected protoplasm was not precisely measured, it was apparent that a relatively small quantity of donor protoplasm from the middle third and

---

FIG. 4. Whole mounts and sections of *Pelomyxa illinoisensis* cells showing the effects of centrifugation. *A*, noncentrifuged control cell showing the many randomly distributed nuclei (*n*). *B*, a 5-μ section of a cell after centrifugation for 10 minutes at 700 × *g*. Nuclei are stratified (*n*) as are mitochondria (*m*), although mitochondria also extend throughout the nuclear stratum; arrows indicate food vacuoles. *C*, whole mount of a cell after centrifugation for 10 minutes at 3000 × *g*; *n*, nuclear stratum; microscopic examination showed no nuclei above or below this stratum. Very few food vacuoles are seen in this section. *D*, whole mount of cell after centrifugation for 10 minutes at 6700 × *g*. The cytoplasm at the light centripetal position, *a*, contains no nuclei; these are confined to portion *b*, which was nearly pulled into two parts by the centrifugal force; almost all nuclei are in the lower part of *b* (upper or centripetal part of the heavy ball-shaped portion). Many food vacuoles can be seen in section *c*.

Magnification was 145× for each figure. *A*, *C*, and *D* were fixed in Schaudinn's fluid and stained with Delafield's hematoxylin. *B* was fixed in osmium tetroxide and stained by Altman's acid–fuchsin method. The centrifugal poles in *B*, *C*, and *D* are directed toward the bottom of the page.

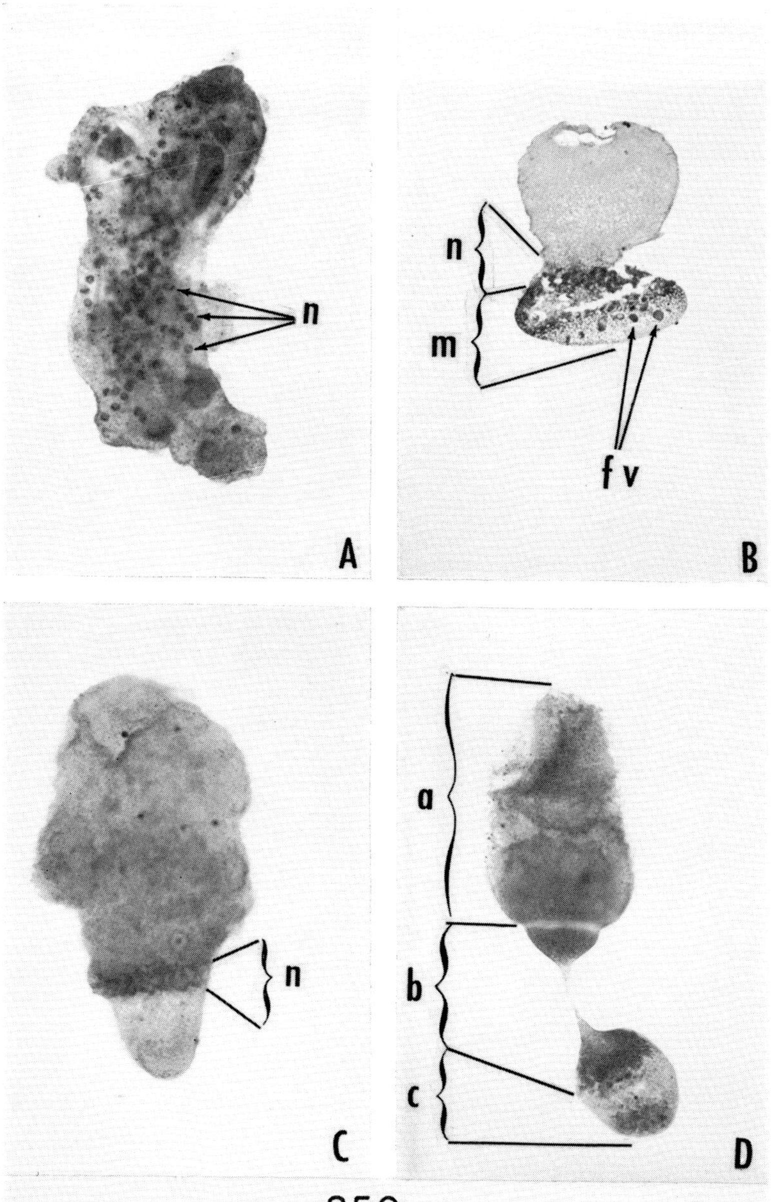

FIG. 4

particularly from the heavy third portions brought about recovery in the irradiated cell. The components required for recovery appeared to be most concentrated in the heavy third, next most concentrated in the middle third, and least concentrated in the light third portion. The survival data of successfully fused cells agree with those obtained previously for *P. illinoisensis* which were supralethally X-irradiated and then fused either with whole protoplasm (*1*) or with centrifuged halves of nonirradiated cells (*6*).

After the transfer of cytoplasm from the light third of nonirradiated, centrifuged cells into supralethally neutron-irradiated cells, the latter frequently died at the usual postirradiation time. Death sometimes occurred even after the transfer of the entire contents of a light third cell portion. Half (54%) of the supralethally neutron-irradiated cells lived after fusion with light third portions which had been cut from cells centrifuged at 3000 $\times$ g for 10 minutes. Light portions taken from cells centrifuged at 6700 $\times$ g for a similar period of time prevented death in only 13% of fused protoplasts.

About three out of four of the fused cells that lived throughout the 10-day experimental period after supralethal exposure divided at least once during this time. Eventual death after 10 days occurred much more frequently in cells which did not divide at least once within 10 days after fusion. If a cell division occurred in any of the irradiated, fused cells, permanent recovery was essentially assured, since these daughter cells usually produced mass cultures when they were kept for this purpose. Table I shows that the mean times to the first cell division after supralethal neutron exposure and microfusion are delayed about 2 days. This delay occurred whether the nonirradiated protoplasm was from a noncentrifuged cell or from the light, middle, or heavy third portion of a centrifuged cell. The mean times to second and third cell divisions were not delayed in any of the experimentally fused groups in which nonirradiated protoplasm was used.

Time of microfusion after irradiation. In previous work (*1*) it was found that, within broad limits, the time of fusion subsequent to supralethal X-ray exposure did not significantly affect either survival or the time of occurrence of the first postirradiation cell division; the time during which fusion was effective extended from the end of the period of X-irradiation to about 1.5 days postirradiation. The results obtained from the neutron-exposed animals are very similar. The time lapse between neutron exposure and fusion with noncentrifuged, nonirradiated protoplasm varied between 1 and 29 hours. No correlation was obvious in the time lapse between irradiation and fusion and per cent survival, or time to first cell division.

Supralethally X-irradiated protoplasm. Supralethally X-irradiated protoplasmic systems will not prevent death or promote cell division if introduced by fusion into other supralethally X-irradiated cells (*6*). The same effect was obtained when supralethally neutron-irradiated cells were fused with supralethally X-irradiated cells. In the absence of fusion, the mean time of death with its associated standard error in 158 supralethally neutron-irradiated (30 krep) cells was 4.2 ± 0.04 days; in 164 supralethally X-irradiated (24 kr) cells the mean time of death was 4.6 ± 0.1 days (*6*). After this information was obtained, two groups of cells were simultaneously exposed to twice the lethal dose of neutrons and of X-rays, respectively. Twenty-one fusions were made in such a way that each fused protoplast contained approximately 1 part X-irradiated to 8 parts neutron-irradiated protoplasm; all fusions were made within 0.6 ± 0.1 day after exposure. None of these fused organisms survived or underwent cell division, and their mean time of death was 5.0 ± 0.1 days after irradiation. As far as per cent survival and cell division are concerned, the X-irradiated and neutron-irradiated protoplasmic systems are not mutually helpful.

DISCUSSION

Relative Biological Effectiveness of Fission Neutrons and Co^{60} Gamma-Rays

The relative biological effectiveness of two types of radiation may be defined as the ratio between doses of the two that produce equivalent specific biological changes. The RBE of γ-rays and fission neutrons is of particular interest because of the differences in the spatial distribution of energy absorbed from the two radiations. Gamma-rays, like X-rays, dissipate energy in tissue chiefly by means of recoil electrons, whereas fission neutrons dissipate energy largely by recoil protons. The pattern for neutrons is one of short, heavily ionized columns of tracks, relatively widely separated. In contrast, tracks from equal doses of γ-rays are more sparsely ionized, much longer, and thus less widely separated. It has already been demonstrated (*16*) that these two radiations are not strictly additive in producing some biological effects in mammals, and there is evidence that different mechanisms of lethality may be involved. It therefore seemed important to compare the lethal effects of these radiations on single cells and also to determine whether nonirradiated protoplasm would exhibit a protective effect in neutron-irradiated amoebae as it does in X-irradiated amoebae.

The results of these experiments have suggested an RBE of 1.5 between fission neutrons and Co^{60} γ-rays for 10-day survival after a single exposure. It is of interest that this is one of the lowest values for any of the biological systems tested at the CP-3′ and CP-5 reactors. In many different tests involving vertebrates fission neutrons were found to be two to six times as effective as Co^{60} γ-rays, and this figure has been as high as twenty to thirty for some invertebrate (*17*) and plant material.

The results of the experiments described in this paper do not suggest different mechanisms of lethality in the amoebae for X-rays, γ-rays, and fission neutrons. The mortality modes are the same after each radiation. The results of the protection experiments are remarkably similar, both qualitatively and quantitatively, after supralethal doses of X-rays (*6*) and neutrons. Protoplasmic systems that have been submitted to supralethal doses of fission neutron radiation will not prevent death or promote cell division when fused into supralethally X-irradiated amoebae. Since X-irradiated and neutron-irradiated protoplasmic systems are not mutually beneficial as far as cell division and survival are concerned, it can be concluded that they both destroy or inactivate the substance(s) in nonirradiated protoplasm which has been shown to be reparative in fusion experiments.

Radiation Protection

A number of compounds are known that prevent death when given before an otherwise lethal dose of ionizing radiation. At the present time, however, no chemically defined compounds are known that can effectively modify the development of damage and promote recovery in cells which have first been exposed to a lethal dose of ionizing radiation. On the other hand, it is well known that recovery has been brought about in some lethally irradiated animals as a result of the transfer of complex nonirradiated protoplasmic systems, usually consisting of large numbers of cells (*18–20*). In the giant amoeba it was found that only a part of the nonirradiated cell is necessary to prevent death, even in cells that had received supralethal doses of either X-rays or fission neutrons and, more recently, ultraviolet radiation (*21*, *22*).

The protective substance (or substances) appears to be present in the middle and heavy third of the centrifuged nonirradiated cell. Whether the donor cells were centrifuged at 3000 × *g* or at 6700 × *g*, 89 to 96% of irradiated cells fused with middle or heavy portions survived the 10-day period. This protection is similar to that achieved by fusing noncentrifuged, nonirradiated protoplasm into neutron-irradiated amoebae (91% survival in thirty-three fusions).

The light thirds retained some therapeutic capacity, provided the gravitational forces were not too high. In previous work with X-irradiated cells (*6*), it was shown that the protective material was present in some 86% of *light halves* of amoebae centrifuged at 700 × *g* but that, as the centrifugal force was increased, the percentage of effective light halves decreased directly with the gravitational forces used. Light portions of cells centrifuged at 5000 × *g* prevented death in only 3% of X-irradiated cells, and there was no protection at all when forces of 10,000 × *g* or more were used. Similarly, in the present experiments, more than half (54%) of the neutron-irradiated cells survived after fusion with light thirds from nonirradiated amoebae centrifuged at 3000 × *g*. When the centrifugal force was increased to 6700 × *g*, however, only 3 cells out of 23 such fusions survived.

It is clear from microscopic study of fixed material that the heavy and middle thirds contained the nuclei and most of the acid–fuchsin staining mitochondria. Since the nuclei and most of the mitochondria are centrifuged out of the still effective light portions at relatively low centrifugal forces, it does not appear that either of these components is necessary for the recovery of supralethally irradiated amoebae, as long as other nonirradiated essential cytoplasmic components are injected. The present evidence is that the finer particulates (0.1 to 0.3 μ), smaller than mitochondria, and/or the cytoplasm that suspends them, contain the reparative agent.

SUMMARY

1. Dose-survival curves were constructed for the giant amoeba, *Pelomyxa illinoisensis*, after exposure to Co^{60} γ-rays (25 r/min) and to fission neutrons (31 rep/min). Neutrons were approximately 1.5 times as effective as γ-rays in killing these cells within 10 days after exposure.

2. Protoplasm from nonirradiated amoebae was transferred by microfusion into supralethally neutron-irradiated cells (30,000 rep). This procedure prevented death in 91% of the irradiated cells. Surviving cells usually gave rise to mass cultures.

3. Living, nonirradiated amoebae were centrifuged and cut into heavy, middle, and light thirds. Each of these cellular portions was then fused into a different amoeba which had been irradiated with a supralethal dose of neutrons.

4. Addition of the protoplasm from the middle or heavy thirds of nonirradiated cells (centrifuged for 10 minutes at 3000 $\times$ g or at 6700 $\times$ g) prevented death in 89 to 96% of the supralethally neutron-irradiated recipients.

5. After fusion with the light third portion cut from cells centrifuged at 3000 $\times$ g, 54% of the neutron-irradiated amoebae survived. When the centrifugal force was increased to 6700 $\times$ g, the light portions prevented death in only 13% of fused protoplasts.

6. Although the nuclei and most of the mitochondria were centrifuged out of these light portions, many of them still proved to be effective in protecting the irradiated amoebae. It does not appear, therefore, that these components are essential for the recovery of supralethally irradiated amoebae, provided certain of the other cytoplasmic components are present.

7. The present evidence is that the finer particulates (0.1 to 0.3 μ), smaller than the acid–fuchsin staining mitochondria, and/or the cytoplasm suspending them, contain the reparative agent(s).

8. Cells supralethally irradiated with fission neutrons were fused with supralethally X-irradiated cells. As far as survival and cell division were concerned, these two irradiated protoplasmic systems were not mutually beneficial.

9. The results were not affected by changes in the interval between irradiation and fusion, over the range tested, 1 to 29 hours.

RECEIVED: July 22, 1958

REFERENCES

1. E. W. DANIELS, X-Irradiation of the giant amoeba, *Pelomyxa illinoisensis*. I. Survival and cell division following exposure. Therapeutic effect of whole protoplasm. *J. Exptl. Zool.* **130,** 183–197 (1955).
2. E. W. DANIELS, Recovery from lethal X-radiation injury in amoebae after injection of

centrifuged portions of nonirradiated cells. (Abstract) *Radiation Research* **5,** 604 (1956).

3. E. W. DANIELS, Studies on the effect of X-irradiation upon *Pelomyxa carolinensis* with special reference to nuclear division and plasmotomy. *J. Exptl. Zool.* **117,** 189–210 (1951).
4. R. WICHTERMAN, X-Irradiation of the giant amoeba, *Chaos chaos*. *Biol. Bull.* **113,** 359 (1957).
5. M. J. ORD, and J. F. DANIELLI, The site of damage in amoebae exposed to X-rays. *Quart. J. Microscop. Sci.* **97,** 29–37 (1956).
6. E. W. DANIELS, X-Irradiation of the giant amoeba, *Pelomyxa illinoisensis*. II. Further studies on recovery following supralethal exposure. *J. Exptl. Zool.* **137,** 425–442.
7. D. M. PACE, and B. W. MCCASHLAND, Effects of low concentration of cyanide on growth and respiration in *Pelomyxa carolinensis*, Wilson. *Proc. Soc. Exptl. Biol. Med.* **76,** 165-168 (1951).
8. H. H. VOGEL, JR., R. A. BLOMGREN, and N. J. G. BOHLIN, Gamma-neutron radiation chamber for radiobiological studies. *Nucleonics* **11,** No. 3, 28–31 (1953).
9. R. E. ZIRKLE, J. R. RAPER, E. F. RILEY, JR., and G. E. STAPLETON, Additivity of fast neutrons and gamma rays in their acute lethal action on mice. U. S. Atomic Energy Commission Report AECD-2328 (1945).
10. H. H. VOGEL, JR., D. L. JORDAN, G. KOHLER, E. TOCHILIN, and B. W. SHUMWAY, Neutron spectrum within the biological radiation chamber at CP-5. Semiannual Report of the Biological and Medical Research Division, Argonne National Laboratory, ANL 5732, pp. 110–112 (1957).
11. N. A. FRIGERIO and H. H. VOGEL, JR., Moderated neutron flux in the CP-5 biological facility. Semiannual Report of the Biological and Medical Research Division, Argonne National Laboratory, ANL-5841, pp. 123–127 (1957).
12. G. A. SACHER, D. GRAHN, S. LESHER, and K. HAMILTON, The γ-ray toxicity program: calibration and equipment. Quarterly Report of the Biological and Medical Research Division, Argonne National Laboratory, ANL-5378, pp. 91–94 (1955).
13. E. W. DANIELS, Cell division in the giant amoeba, *Pelomyxa carolinensis*, following X-irradiation. II. Analysis of therapeutic effects after fusion with nonirradiated cell portions. *J. Exptl. Zool.* **127,** 427–462 (1954).
14. R. R. KUDO, Observations on *Pelomyxa illinoisensis*. *J. Morphol.* **88,** 145–184 (1951).
15. J. F. MCCLELLAN, Observations on nuclear division in *Pelomyxa illinoisensis*. Ph.D. Thesis, University of Illinois (1954).
16. J. W. CLARK, D. L. JORDAN, and H. H. VOGEL, JR., Biological effects of fast neutrons and gamma rays. *Am. J. Roentgenol. Radium Therapy Nuclear Med.* **77,** 524–530 (1957).
17. T. N. TAHMISIAN and H. H. VOGEL, JR., Relative biological effectiveness of fast neutrons, gamma rays, and X-rays on grasshopper nymph ovarioles (*Melanoplus differentialis*). *Proc. Soc. Exptl. Biol. Med.* **84,** 538–543 (1953).
18. E. LORENZ, D. UPHOFF, T. R. REID, and E. SHELTON, Modification of irradiation injury in mice and guinea pigs by bone marrow injections. *J. Natl. Cancer Inst.* **12,** 197–201 (1951).
19. H. M. PATT, Protective mechanisms in ionizing radiation injury. *Physiol. Revs.* **33,** 35–76 (1953).
20. LEON O. JACOBSON, Modification of radiation injury in experimental animals. *Am. J. Roentgenol. Radium Therapy Nuclear Med.* **72,** 543–555 (1954).
21. E. W. DANIELS, Micrurgical studies on irradiated *Pelomyxa*. *N. Y. Acad. Sci.* in press.
22. E. W. DANIELS and H. H. VOGEL, JR., Protective component in nonirradiated protoplasm of amoebae. Second United Nations International Conference on the Peaceful Uses of Atomic Energy. A/Conf. 15/P/907 U.S.A., June (1958).

RADIATION RESEARCH 5, 597–603 (1959)

Synthesis of Porphine-like Substances Induced by Gamma-Irradiation[1]

A. SZUTKA, J. F. HAZEL, AND WALLACE M. McNABB

Department of Chemistry, University of Pennsylvania, Philadelphia, Pennsylvania

INTRODUCTION

Scientists in recent years have been attempting to find a probable agent for the formation of the organic milieu, which is often associated with the origin of life. It has been generally assumed that the temperature at the time of formation of the earth's surface was 100°C or less and that the atmosphere around the earth consisted of methane or carbon monoxide and carbon dioxide, ammonia or nitrogen, water, and probably hydrogen (*1–3a*). Under those primitive earth conditions, probable sources of energy responsible for the formation of simple organic compounds have been considered to be ultraviolet light, electric discharge, and ionizing radiations.

Following the above theories, Miller (*4*) studied the action of an electric discharge on a mixture of methane, ammonia, water, and hydrogen and was able to identify ten amino acids (glycine, *dl*-alanine, β-alanine, sarcosine, α-aminobutyric, aspartic, and glutamic acids), three hydroxy acids (glycolic, lactic, and α-hydroxybutyric acids), four aliphatic acids (formic, acetic, propionic, and succinic acids), and urea.

Miller's experiments were repeated and confirmed by Abelson (*3b*) and by Pasynskii and Pavlovskaya (*5*). A few years earlier Garrison and co-workers (*6*) showed that bombardment of aqueous solutions of carbon dioxide with 40-Mev helium ions produced formic acid and formaldehyde, among other products.

The formation of an organic acid (oxalic acid) was shown also by Hasselstrom and Henry (*7*) on β- or γ-irradiation of aqueous solutions of ammonium, calcium, and sodium bicarbonates as well as ammonium carbonate. They also showed that aqueous ammonium acetate on exposure to β-radiation forms, in addition to di- and tricarboxylic acids, small amounts of glycine and aspartic acid (*8*).

Paschke and co-workers (*9*) have irradiated solid ammonium carbonate and

[1] This paper was presented at the International Congress of Radiation Research, Burlington, Vermont, August 10–16, 1958.

found ammonium formate, glycine, possibly alanine, and one more unidentified amino acid.

The significance of porphyrins from the point of view of origin of life was discussed thoroughly by Calvin (*10*), Granick (*11*), and Oparin (*1*).

One of the purposes of this paper is to present another observation that may have a bearing on the formation of the organic milieu, this time involving the synthesis of more complex organic substances from simple precursors under the influence of irradiation.

EXPERIMENTAL PROCEDURE

It has been known that pyrrole and benzaldehyde when heated to about 180°C condense to form $\alpha,\beta,\gamma,\delta$-tetraphenylporphine (*12*) (Fig. 1) and $\alpha,\beta,\gamma,\delta$-tetra-

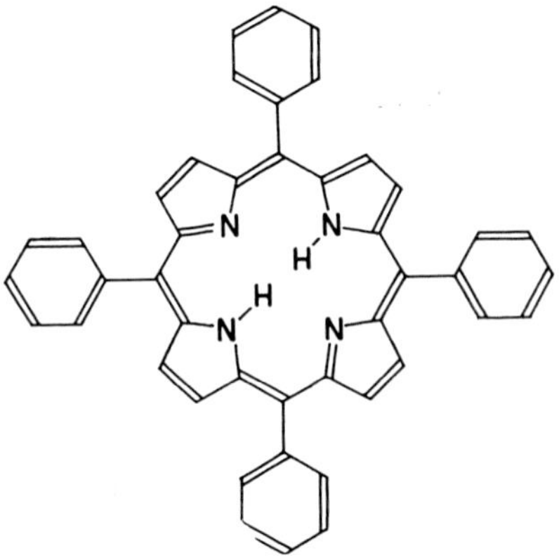

FIG. 1. $\alpha,\beta,\gamma,\delta$-Tetraphenylporphine molecule

phenylchlorine (*13*). The same system, with 5 ml of pyrrole, 10 ml of benzaldehyde, 10 ml of pyridine (all freshly redistilled), and 5 gm of zinc acetate, was used in our experiment. The pyridine serves as a solvent. Zinc acetate was found to increase the yield (*13, 14*). The mixture was placed in a screw-cap Pyrex tube with approximately 2 ml of air space above the liquid and irradiated with Co^{60} γ-rays for 10.0 hours at the rate of approximately 0.5 megaroentgen per hour. The solution removed from the irradiation vessel, reddish in color, was diluted with chloroform, treated with an equal volume of 6 *N* hydrochloric acid, and stirred vigorously for 3 hours. The acidic solution was then neutralized with ammonia. The chloroform solution, separated from the aqueous layer, was washed several times with distilled water and chromatographed on activated alumina, as suggested by Priesthoff and Banks (*14*), with fresh chloroform as eluent. Three chromatographic treatments removed most of the tarry products from the chloroform

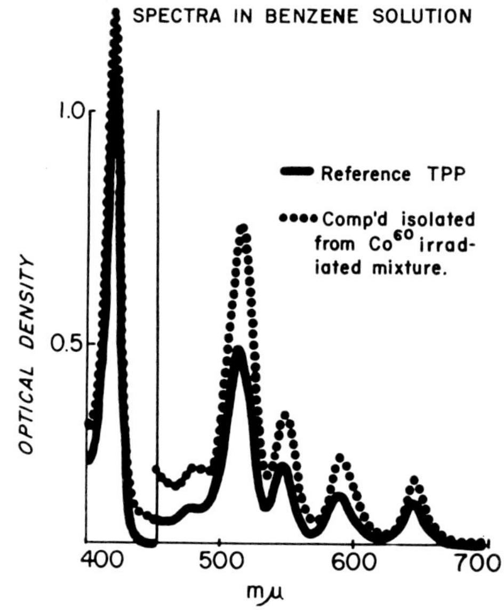

FIG. 2. Absorption spectra in benzene solution

solution, which was subsequently subjected to chromatography on a Magnesol column. The dark-green band was repacked into a second column, wetted with ether, and eluted with chloroform. The procedure was repeated until a single, clear band was obtained. The spectrum in a hand spectroscope showed the absorption bands characteristic for $\alpha,\beta,\gamma,\delta$-tetraphenylporphine. Figure 2 shows the spectra of $\alpha,\beta,\gamma,\delta$-tetraphenylporphine in benzene, prepared by the method of Ball *et al.* (*13*), and of the compound isolated from the irradiated mixture. Both spectra were found to be identical with those found in the literature (*15*, *16*).

It is well known that acid salts of $\alpha,\beta,\gamma,\delta$-tetraphenylporphine exhibit also the characteristic spectra (*16*, *17*). Therefore, part of the benzene solution of the reference compound and part of that isolated from the irradiated mixture were evaporated to dryness and treated with glacial acetic acid. To ensure complete solution both tubes were placed in a boiling water bath for 30 minutes. Both spectra were recorded on a Cary recording spectrophotometer and are shown in Fig. 3. They were found to be identical with those listed in the literature (*16*, *17*) except for a higher background of the spectrum of the compound isolated from the irradiated mixture. This indicates that some contamination was still present in the compound. An additional evidence of identity of the compound isolated from the irradiated mixture was obtained by formation of a zinc chelate. The reference $\alpha,\beta,\gamma,\delta$-tetraphenylporphine and the compound isolated from the irradiated mixture were dissolved in 10 ml of chloroform, treated with approximately 100 mg of crystalline

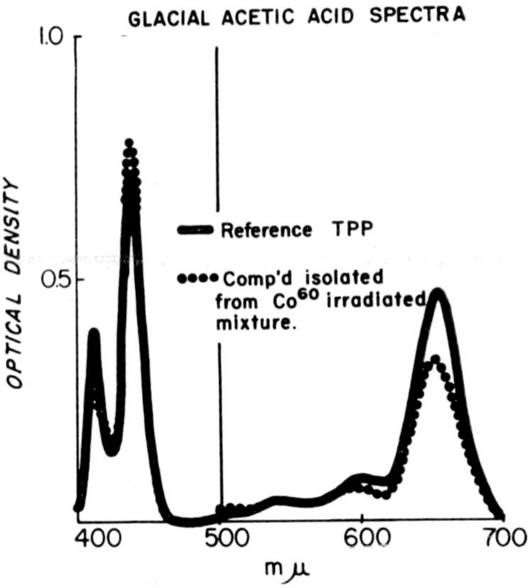

FIG. 3. Absorption spectra in glacial acetic acid

zinc acetate, and boiled for about 5 minutes. After cooling, anhydrous sodium sulfate was added, and the solution was filtered. The clear filtrate was evaporated to dryness, then dissolved in benzene. The spectra of the reference zinc chelate and the chelate of the compound isolated from the irradiated mixture agree with those obtained by Rothemund and Menotti (*18*) and by Dorough *et al.* (*16*).

On the other hand when an identical mixture of benzaldehyde, pyrrole, and zinc acetate in pyridine was kept in the dark for several days without irradiation, it became yellowish in color and no porphine-like products could be detected by the methods described previously.

The above results indicate that the synthesis of $\alpha,\beta,\gamma,\delta$-tetraphenylporphine from benzaldehyde and pyrrole was induced by γ-irradiation. Although the amount isolated in each of the five separate runs was in the microgram range, this quantity was sufficient to make positive identification.

DISCUSSION

Shemin (*19*) showed that the starting substances in the biosynthesis of porphyrins in living organisms were fairly simple compounds, glycine and succinic acid, i.e. substances which undoubtedly have arisen from the simpler hydrocarbons, ammonia and water (*3–5*), or ammonia, acetic acid, and water (*8*). The actual process of biosynthesis, however, takes place in many stages and requires for its accomplishment the presence of a highly organized living system containing numerous specific enzymes. In some instances the specific enzyme required in the biosynthesis can be replaced by purely chemical processes, as was shown by Scott (*20*) for the conversion of one of the precursors of δ-aminolevulinic acid to porphobilinogen. In addition to this, Treibs (*21*) found that the transformation of porphobilinogen to a mixture of porphyrins can also be achieved abiogenically at high temperatures and acidities. Corwin (*22*), Rothemund (*12*), and others synthesized porphine-like substances, but in all cases temperatures higher than those suggested for the primitive earth conditions were required.

On the other hand, the results of our experiment would imply that the synthesis of a porphine-like substance from simple precursors can be induced by γ-irradiation. The availability of these precursors in the primaeval earth conditions can scarcely be doubted. Garrison *et al.* (*6*) found aldehydes on irradiation of carbon dioxide in water with α-particles. Losanitsch and Jowitschitsch (*23*) submitted a mixture of carbon monoxide and methane to the action of silent discharges and obtained an oily condensation product containing aldehyde. Also the action of electric discharge on benzene and carbon monoxide results in benzaldehyde formation (*1*). Furthermore, Chichibabin (*24*) has shown that pyrrole is formed from acetylene and ammonia in the presence of catalysts (aluminum oxide, ferric oxide) at elevated temperature. It can be assumed, however, that electric discharges, solar radiation, or high-energy radiations can supply the energy necessary for activation, since pyrolidine and pyridine compounds were formed in a mixture of acetylene and ammonia irradiated with ultraviolet rays (*25*).

The energy necessary for the above reactions to occur was readily available in the primaeval earth conditions. It is generally considered that the possible sources of energy are solar radiation, electrical discharges, and the energy of the disintegration of the atoms of the naturally radioactive substances. On the basis of direct measurements obtained by sending rockets to great heights Sanderson and Hulbert (*26*) give the intensity of the ultraviolet radiation from 400 mμ downward as 4.8×10^{20} kcal/year. The second source of energy in the atmosphere of the earth are electrical discharges. The energy is estimated several orders lower, approximately 1.2×10^{15} kcal/year, taking into account the noisy discharges of thunderstorms. It may be that the energy of silent discharges in the atmosphere is quite considerable. There is also reason to suppose that thunderstorms were more frequent in primaeval times! The third source of energy is radioactive disintegration, which is estimated at the present time to be 4.1×10^{18} kcal/year. If we assume that the radioactivity of the earth was several times as great in the remote past as it is now on account of the breakdown of K^{40} and U^{235}, the total amount is estimated to be 2×10^{19} kcal/year (*1*). On this basis it may be supposed that enough radioactivity existed to accomplish the reactions proposed above.

Although our experiments utilized only high-energy radiation as a possible source of energy, we do not exclude other sources such as solar energy or electrical discharges.

SUMMARY

The present work indicates that porphyrin-like substances can be produced from simple precursors by irradiation. The availability of precursors and of energy has been discussed.

RECEIVED: September 15, 1958

REFERENCES

1. A. I. OPARIN, *The Origin of Life* (translated by A. Synge), 3rd ed., Academic Press, New York, 1947.
2. H. C. UREY, *The Planets*, Yale University Press, New Haven, Connecticut, 1952.
3. (*a*) P. H. ABELSON, The nature of the primitive environment. *Abstr. Am. Chem. Soc. 133rd Meeting, San Francisco* p. 53c (1958); (*b*) Amino acids formed in "primitive atmosphere." *Science* **124,** 935 (1956).
4. (*a*) S. L. MILLER, A production of amino acids under possible primitive earth conditions. *Science* **117,** 528–529 (1953); (*b*) Production of some organic compounds under possible primitive earth conditions. *J. Am. Chem. Soc.* **77,** 2351–2361 (1955); (*c*) The formation of organic compounds on the primitive earth. *Ann. N. Y. Acad. Sci.* **69,** 260–274 (1957); (*d*) Formation of organic compounds on the primitive earth. *Abstr. Am. Chem. Soc. 133rd Meeting, San Francisco* p. 52c (1958).
5. A. PASYNSKII and T. PAVLOVSKAYA, *Trudy I Sympoziuma po proiskhozhdeniu zhizni, Moscow, 1957*. Cited in ref. *1*, p. 180.
6. W. M. GARRISON, D. C. MORRISON, J. G. HAMILTON, A. A. BENSON, and M. CALVIN, Reduction of carbon dioxide in aqueous solutions by Ionizing Radiations. *Science* **114,** 416–418 (1951).
7. T. HASSELSTROM and M. C. HENRY, New synthesis of oxalic acid. *Science* **123,** 1038–1039 (1956).
8. T. HASSELSTROM, M. C. HENRY, and B. MURR, Synthesis of amino acids by beta radiation. *Science* **125,** 350–351 (1957).
9. R. PASCHKE, R. W. H. CHANG, and D. YOUNG, Probable role of gamma irradiation on origin of life. *Science* **125,** 881 (1957).
10. M. CALVIN, Chemical evolution and the origin of life. *Am. Scientist* **44,** 248–263 (1956).
11. S. GRANICK, Speculations on the origins and evolution of photosynthesis. *Ann. N. Y. Acad. Sci.* **69,** 292–308 (1957).
12. P. ROTHEMUND, New porphyrin synthesis. The synthesis of porphin. *J. Am. Chem. Soc.* **58,** 625–627 (1936).
13. R. H. BALL, G. D. DOROUGH, and M. CALVIN, A further study of the porphine-like products of the reaction of benzaldehyde and pyrrole. *J. Am. Chem. Soc.* **68,** 2278–2281 (1946).
14. J. H. PRIESTHOFF and C. V. BANKS, A new method of purifying $\alpha,\beta,\gamma,\delta$-Tetraphenylporphines. *J. Am. Chem. Soc.* **76,** 937–938 (1954).
15. D. W. THOMAS and A. E. MARTELL, Absorption spectra of para-substituted tetraphenylporphines. *J. Am. Chem. Soc.* **78,** 1338–1343 (1956).
16. G. D. DOROUGH, J. R. MILLER, and F. M. HUENNEKENS, Spectra of the metallo-derivatives of $\alpha,\beta,\gamma,\delta$-tetraphenylporphine. *J. Am. Chem. Soc.* **73,** 4315–4320 (1951).
17. C. V. BANKS and R. E. BISQUE, Spectrophotometric determination of zinc and other metals with $\alpha,\beta,\gamma,\delta$-tetraphenylporphine. *Anal. Chem.* **29,** 522–526 (1957).
18. P. ROTHEMUND and A. M. MENOTTI, Porphyrin studies. V. The metal complex salts of $\alpha,\beta,\gamma,\delta$-tetraphenylporphine. *J. Am. Chem. Soc.* **70,** 1808–1812 (1948).

19. D. Shemin, The biosynthesis of porphyrins. *Proc. 3rd Intern. Congr. Biochem., Brussels, 1955* pp. 197–204 (1956).
20. J. J. Scott, Synthesis of crystallizable porphobilinogen. *Biochem. J.* **62,** 6P (1956).
21. A. Treibs, "Chemische Grundlagen zur Biosynthese der Porphyrine. *Proc. 3rd Intern Congr. Biochem., Brussels, 1955* pp. 207–210 (1956).
22. (*a*) A. H. Corwin and E. C. Coolidge, A stepwise porphyrin synthesis. *J. Am. Chen Soc.* **74,** 5196–5197 (1952); (*b*) A. H. Corwin and V. L. Sydow, New method for po. phyrin synthesis. *J. Am. Chem. Soc.* **75,** 4484–4486 (1956).
23. S. M. Losanitsch and M. Z. Jowitschitsch, "Ueber chemische Synthesen mittels der dunklen electrischen Entladung. *Ber.* **30,** 135–139 (1897).
24. A. E. Chichibabin, *J. Russ. Phys.-Chem. Soc. (Chem.)*, **47,** (Otd. 1), 703 (1915) (cited in ref. 1).
25. C. Ellis and A. A. Wells, *The Chemical Action of Ultraviolet Rays* (rev. by F. F. Hayroth), p. 407, Reinhold Publishing Corp. New York, 1941.
26. J. A. Sanderson and E. O. Hulburt, in *Radiation Biology* (A. Hollaender, ed.), Vol. 2, p. 95, McGraw-Hill Book Company, New York, 1955.

Samuel Colville Lind

RADIATION RESEARCH **10,** 605–606 (1959)

Samuel Colville Lind: The First Eighty Years

If Samuel C. Lind had published only his doctoral dissertation, his name would still be known to every physical chemist. In this thesis he demonstrated that the formation of hydrogen bromide from its elements is not, as was expected, a bimolecular reaction but conforms to a complicated rate equation containing a fractional exponent, an additive term, and two empirical constants. This work was completed in Leipzig in 1905, and now, fifty-four years later, his equation, including the values of the constants, still stands as essentially correct. It is quoted in every monograph on kinetics and in practically all texts of physical chemistry as the classical example of a reaction whose kinetics are at once complex and understandable.

As we all know, Dr. Lind did not rest content with this one classical contribution but has gone ahead in many ways to add to our knowledge of physical chemistry. To date he has published over 160 scientific papers, nor is the list closed. To most chemists, his fame rests chiefly on his many fundamental and valuable studies of radiation chemistry. He was a pioneer in this field of science; indeed, it would not be much of an exaggeration to say that the appearance, in 1912, of his paper on the α-particle-induced formation of ozone marked the beginning of the quantitative study of radiation chemistry. As aids to his measurements of radiochemical reactions, he developed a number of original and useful experimental techniques, including a practicable method of radon purification, a simple but reliable and versatile electroscope, and a method of preparing small thin-walled bulbs, capable of containing radon but of transmitting α-particles. No account of Dr. Lind's contributions to radiation chemistry would be complete without mention of his ionization theory of the chemical effects of penetrating radiation. Although this theory in its original form (as the ion-cluster theory) may at present seem an oversimplification, at the time it was introduced in explanation of the radiation chemistry of simple gases it did a great deal to establish order in a chaotic field. In a more general form, the ionization theory is still a useful and essential part of radiation chemistry.

Dr. Lind's first studies of radiation chemistry were made at the laboratory of Madame Curie in Paris and at the Institute for Radiation Research at Vienna. His attempts to continue these investigations, after returning to this country, met obstacles which would have discouraged a less determined man. Unable to obtain the use of radium, he resigned his academic position at the University of Michigan and joined the U. S. Bureau of Mines at Golden, Colorado. There he devoted four years of arduous work (under conditions which would shock and horrify the health monitors of our present A.E.C. institutions) to the extraction and purification of radium from carnotite ores. After he and his associates had extracted 8.5 grams of pure radium, he was allowed the use of half a gram for his scientific studies. These were carried on at Golden, at Reno, and finally at the University of Minnesota. Many of his experimental measurements of the chemical effects of α-particles were made in this period, from 1918 to 1942.

Few men have contributed in as many different ways to the progress of chemistry as has Dr. Lind. He has served effectively as a teacher, author, editor, research worker, executive, and consultant. He studied in four countries and earned degrees from three universities. He has given unstintingly of his time for the advancement of scientific education and of the science of chemistry. Among other similar activities, he served on the International Radium Standards Commission, the Committee on Professional Training, and the National Advisory Health Council; for twenty years he was Editor of the *Journal of Physical Chemistry*; and he has acted as president of the American Electrochemical Society and of the American Chemical Society. It is not surprising that he has been awarded many honors. The universities of Colorado, Washington and Lee, and Michigan have granted him honorary degrees. He received the Nichols medal in 1926 and the Priestly medal in 1952. He was made a member of the National Academy of Sciences in 1930 and of the American Philosophical Society in 1940.

Those of us who are fortunate enough to know him personally—and it is a goodly number, for he has never been niggardly with his friendship—count as red-letter days those occasions when Dr. and Mrs. Lind (more affectionately, Lindy and Tottie) visit our communities. Although Dr. Lind has never tolerated nonsense in the fields of science and education, he has a broad understanding and tolerance of differences among individuals. He is as much at home with mountaineers and back-country farmers, whom he meets on his fly-fishing trips, as with his professional colleagues. He is outspoken and quick to accept a challenge; but, although he obviously enjoys a good fight, he never harbors a grudge. His autobiography would make fascinating reading, but I am sure it will never be written. He will never have time to write of his past, being much too preoccupied with the business and pleasure of "making more past."

Professor Robert Livingston
Department of Chemistry
University of Minnesota
Minneapolis, Minnesota

RADIATION RESEARCH 10, 607–609 (1959)

The Radiation Chemistry of Gases: Introduction to the Symposium[1]

LEON M. DORFMAN

Argonne National Laboratory, Lemont, Illinois

It is an enjoyable occasion under any circumstances to join in celebrating the eightieth birthday of a fellow scientist. But it is a unique privilege indeed to be permitted to do honor to a fellow scientist who, on his eightieth birthday, is an active contributor to a field of research which owed its inception and development largely to his pioneering work. Those of us who share, with Dr. S. C. Lind, a common interest in the study of radiation chemistry felt that a symposium held in his honor would be most appropriately constituted if it were to consist of current research reports rather than historical surveys. It is in this way that we have chosen to extend to Dr. Lind our best wishes for a continued happy life and many more fruitful years of research.

* * *

A most important basic question, of broad significance in the radiation chemistry of gases, concerns the relative importance of ionization and excitation in the primary process and the role played by ions and by neutral species, both free radicals and excited molecules, in the complexity of secondary reactions which may occur. Little doubt remains about the general importance of ions in the radiation chemistry of gases, a fact which was recognized by Lind many years ago. During the last few years a good deal of research and discussion has centered about the role of ions in the secondary reactions. But the data which may uniquely and quantitatively establish this role in detail have only begun to appear.

The primary process consists of (1) excitation and (2) ionization, and it is generally thought that in molecular systems roughly half the energy expended in the gas goes into electronic excitation. For the rare gases this fraction is significantly less than half. This assumption rests largely on two types of fairly carefully ob-

[1] Based on a paper presented before the annual meeting of the Radiation Research Society, Pittsburgh, May 18–20, 1959, as part of the Symposium on Radiation Chemistry of Gases in honor of Dr. S. C. Lind on the occasion of his eightieth birthday. The Symposium was organized by Dr. Leon M. Dorfman, and he and Dr. A. O. Allen served as chairmen of the sessions.

tained data: the ionization potentials of gaseous molecules, and the energy necessary to produce an ion pair in various gases. It is fairly clear, however, that a knowledge of the energies and the populations of the various excited states to which the ions may be raised is necessary in answering this question. At the present time it may be considered that the precise quantitative partition of energy between ions and excited molecules has not been established. Nor is this question answered in the present symposium.

Among the variety of secondary reactions which may occur are the following: (3) neutralization, (4) unimolecular dissociation of ions, (5) ion-molecule reactions, involving either parent ions or fragment ions, (6) free radical reactions, of which there are several different types, and (7) reactions of excited molecules. There is a good deal of evidence which indicates that free radicals are of course formed and contribute in a major way to most radiation chemical reactions. On the other hand, there are a number of cases in which the over-all chemistry does not seem susceptible of explanation on the basis of a free radical model alone. Many decomposition products are known to be formed in processes which do not involve a free radical precursor.

The demonstration, in mass spectrometer studies, that ion-molecule reactions occur with high efficiency has had a profound influence on our thinking about mechanisms in gas phase systems. It has been shown, from the new information on cross sections for these reactions and from earlier data on neutralization cross sections, that ion-molecule reactions should compete overwhelmingly with neutralization processes.

The present symposium presents evidence, both experimental and theoretical, on many of these points. The paper by Stevenson considers the average energies of molecular ions and, by a treatment involving the quasi-equilibrium rate theory and information about appearance potentials, draws an important conclusion about the relative probability of occurrence of ion-molecule reactions (in cases where those involve the parent ion) and unimolecular dissociation of ions. The theoretical study of Magee and Funabashi examines the likelihood of cluster formation in irradiated gases and draws attention to those conditions under which small clusters may actually be formed. Some mass spectral evidence for ion-molecule reactions in alkyl iodide systems is discussed in the paper by Pottie, Barker, and Hamill. The paper by Schaeffer and Thompson presents one of the few clear-cut phenomenological evidences for an ionic mechanism in a radiation chemical reaction. The paper by Jones on the very interesting system nitrogen-oxygen-water is a good example of the complex results that can be found in radiation chemical systems. The paper on acetylene, by Dorfman and Wahl, presents some interesting new evidence which is thought to indicate the role of excited molecules. Lampe's work on ethylene provides evidence for both free radical processes and ionic reactions. The thorough study of butane, by Kuppermann and Burton, is concerned with a slightly different area of gas-phase radiation chemistry, namely, reactions in an electric discharge. A comparison is made with radiolysis results for the same compound.

RECEIVED: February 16, 1959

RADIATION RESEARCH **10**, 610–621 (1959)

On the Average Energies of Molecular Ions[1]

D. P. STEVENSON

Shell Development Company, Emeryville, California

INTRODUCTION

The rational discussion of the mechanism of chemical reactions induced by ionizing radiation, with particular reference to the role played in these reactions by ions, requires certain information concerning relative kinetics of the primary processes. In particular there is required knowledge of the relative kinetics of the reactions

$$M \rightsquigarrow M^* \quad (1)$$

$$M \rightsquigarrow M^+ + e^- \quad (2a)$$

$$M^+ + e^- \rightarrow M^* + h\nu \quad (2b)$$

$$M^+ \rightarrow F_i^+ + G_i$$

$$M^+(F^+) + M(N) \rightarrow P^+ + Q \quad (2c)$$

Mass spectrometric measurements (*1*, *2*) have provided sufficient information on the rates of reactions (2c) to show that at atmospheric pressure and reasonable dose rates such reactions are very fast compared to recombination reactions (2a) (*3*). The quasi-equilibrium rate theory of the origin of mass spectra (*4*) provides a means of deducing the kinetics of the unimolecular dissociation reaction (2b) from mass spectrometric data. Furthermore, the characteristic parameter of the quasi-equilibrium rate theory of the origin of mass spectra indirectly provides a means of evaluating the relative frequency of reactions 1 and 2 from mass spectrometric measurements.

The characteristic parameter of the quasi-equilibrium rate theory is the average excitation energy, $\bar{\epsilon}$, with which molecule ions are formed by electron impact-induced

[1] Based on a paper presented before the annual meeting of the Radiation Research Society Pittsburgh, May 18–20, 1959, as part of the Symposium on Radiation Chemistry of Gases in honor of Dr. S. C. Lind on the occasion of his eightieth birthday. The Symposium was organized by Dr. Leon M. Dorfman, and he and Dr. A. O. Allen served as chairmen of the sessions.

ionization: that is, it is the usual parameter of an energy distribution function. The average energy expended in the formation of molecule ions is the sum of $\bar{\epsilon}$ and the ionization potential of the molecule. Under the assumption of the essential applicability of the quasi-equilibrium rate theory to mass spectra, $\bar{\epsilon}$ can be related to two observable mass spectral qualities. The first portion of this paper briefly describes these relations and the method of evaluation of $\bar{\epsilon}$.

Inasmuch as there are questions (*5*) concerning the general validity of the quasi-equilibrium theory, it was deemed desirable to obtain an independent check on the $\bar{\epsilon}$ calculated by means of the theory. It is possible, when sufficient data are available, to calculate an average energy required to form a molecule ion by methods independent of the theory. The second section of this paper describes this method and gives results. The remainder of the paper presents a brief discussion of the significance of the comparison of the results of the two preceding sections.

Average Ion Energies from the Quasi-Equilibrium Rate Theory of the Origin of Mass Spectra

For molecule ions to which the quasi-equilibrium rate theory of dissociation of Eyring and co-workers (*4*) is applicable, it can be shown that the fraction, f_p, of the molecule ions remaining undissociated at a time, t, after formation is given by

$$f_p = \int_0^{\epsilon_1} D(\epsilon)\, d\epsilon + \int_{\epsilon_1}^{\epsilon_{\max}} D(\epsilon) e^{-k(\epsilon)t}\, d\epsilon \tag{3}$$

where $D(\epsilon)$ is the characteristic distribution in excitation energy, ϵ, with which molecule ions are formed by impact with electrons of energy E_e. The distribution function is normalized in the range $0 \leq \epsilon \leq \epsilon_{\max}$, where $\epsilon_{\max} < E_e - I^z + E(T)$, and I^z and $E(T)$ are the ionization potential and thermal vibrational energy of the molecule, respectively. The lowest dissociation limit of the molecule ion is represented by ϵ_1. All energies, ϵ, are measured relative to the vibronic ground state of the molecule ion. The total specific rate of dissociation of the molecule ions of excitation energy, ϵ, is given by $k(\epsilon)$, and

$$k(\epsilon) = \sum_{i=1}^{n} k_i(\epsilon) \tag{4}$$

where the specific rates of the individual dissociation processes, i, are functions of ϵ_i/ϵ, where ϵ_i is the critical energy (dissociation limit) of the ith process. Equation 3 states that molecule ions as formed are of two types: stable (those with excitation energies less than the lowest dissociation limit, ϵ_1) and metastable (those with excitation energies greater than ϵ_1).

In order to apply equation 3 to the interpretation of the mass spectrum of a substance or, conversely, to deduce properties of molecule ions from the mass spectrum, it is necessary to have knowledge of the nature of the excitation energy distribution function, $D(\epsilon)$. There are theoretical reasons (*6*) for believing that $D(\epsilon)$ should approach zero as ϵ goes to zero and that $D(\epsilon)$ should be small for large ϵ. From the results of measurements of the dependence of f_p on the energy of the ionizing electrons, E_e, one can conclude that for $E_e >$ ca. $2I^z$, ϵ_{max}, the high energy cutoff of $D(\epsilon)$, becomes essentially independent of E_e. This confirms the theoretical expectation (*6*) that the probability of formation of highly excited states of the ions should be small.

The experimental evidence for the statement in the preceding paragraph is shown in Figs. 1 to 4, where f_p versus E_e curves are shown for various typical hydrocarbons. All the substances show the same general behavior, i.e., a rapid decrease of f_p for E_e immediately greater than the first appearance potential of a fragment ion in the mass spectrum ($I^z + \epsilon_1$) followed by a rapid approach to a constant asymptote such that f_p is independent of E_e for $E_e > 2I^z$.

A one-parameter distribution function that has the essential characteristics that are required is

$$D(\epsilon) = \frac{\pi}{2}\frac{\epsilon}{\bar{\epsilon}^2} e^{-(\pi/4)(\epsilon/\bar{\epsilon})^2} \tag{5}$$

which has 95% of its area in the range $0 \leq \epsilon \leq 2\bar{\epsilon}$, though it is normalized to the range $0 \leq \epsilon \leq \infty$. An analytically more convenient distribution function that has been used in the interpretation of the mass spectra of propane (*6*) and some simple alcohols (*7*) is

$$D(\epsilon) = \frac{1}{\epsilon_{max}} = \frac{1}{2\bar{\epsilon}} \tag{6}$$

In the following discussion we shall compare average excitation energies, $\bar{\epsilon}$, that may be computed from observed values of f_p and ϵ_1 for some simple hydrocarbons for the distribution functions (equations 5 and 6). In the following section of this paper we shall indicate an alternate method of calculation of the average excitation energy with which molecule ions are formed that is independent of assumptions of the form of the excitation energy distribution function, thus providing a test of the reliability of the calculations based on equations 3, 5, and 6.

Inasmuch as it is necessary to assume a rather simple form for the excitation energy distribution function, $D(\epsilon)$, it is reasonable to make a further simplification of equation 3 as follows: We rewrite equation 3 as

$$f_p \cong \int_0^{\epsilon_1'} D(\epsilon)\, d\epsilon \tag{7}$$

where ϵ_1' is an energy (greater than ϵ_1) such that $k_1(\epsilon_1')t = 1$. That is, we approximate the second term of equation 3 by taking $e^{-k(\epsilon)t} = 1$ for $k(\epsilon)t \leq 1$ and $e^{-k(\epsilon)t} = 0$ for $k(\epsilon)t \geq 1$. For a typical mass spectrometer the transit time, t, of ions from their point of origin to the ion detector is $\sim 10^{-5}$ sec; thus ϵ_1' is obtained as a solution of the equation $k_1(\epsilon_1') = 10^5$ sec^{-1}. We assume the unimolecular rate constants to be of the classical form (*4*):

$$k_i(\epsilon) = s_i \, \nu_i \left(1 - \frac{\epsilon_i}{\epsilon}\right)^{S-1} \tag{8}$$

where s_i is the steric factor in the range 1 to 10^{-3}, ν_i is a reaction frequency, and $S = 3N - 6$ is the number of degrees of vibrational freedom of an N-atomic molecule. We take $s_i\nu_i \sim 10^{14}$ sec^{-1} for a bond dissociation process and $\sim 10^{12}$ sec^{-1} for a four-center disproportionation process.

That $s_i\nu_i$ for disproportionation reactions must be the order of 10^{-2} times those for bond dissociation reactions follows from the relative frequencies of such processes as $C_4H_{10}^+ \rightarrow C_3H_7^+ + CH_3$, and $C_4H_{10}^+ \rightarrow C_3H_6^+ + CH_4$. The former, with the larger critical energy, is also the one with the larger frequency of occurrence.[2]

Substitution of equations 5 and 6 into equation 7 gives, respectively, for f_p

Exponential distribution $\qquad f_p = 1 - e^{-(\pi/4)(\epsilon_1'/\bar{\epsilon})^2} \qquad (9)$

Uniform distribution $\qquad f_p = \epsilon_1'/2\bar{\epsilon} \qquad (10)$

and inversion of equation 8 gives

$$\epsilon_1' = \frac{\epsilon_1}{1 - (10^5/s_i \, \nu_i)^{1(S-1)}} \tag{11}$$

The vanishing current appearance potentials of ions in the mass spectrum of a substance are believed to be measures of the minimum energy required of the ionizing electrons for the formation of the ion. Hence the difference between the appearance potential of a fragment ion and that of the parent ion should be a measure of ϵ_i for the fragment ion. If the quasi-equilibrium rate theory is rigorously applicable to the dissociation of molecule ions, the difference between the appearance potential of a fragment ion and that of the parent ion should measure, ϵ_i', as has been indicated by Friedman and co-workers (*5*). Evidence on this question is ambiguous. In the case of the two important primary dissociation reactions of the ethane ion,

$$C_2H_6^+ \rightarrow C_2H_5^+ + H \tag{12}$$

$$C_2H_6^+ \rightarrow C_2H_4^+ + H_2 \tag{13}$$

the differences between the appearance potentials of fragment and parent ions have been reported to be, 1.2_7 and 0.5_0 ev, respectively (*8*). From thermochemical data

[2] That the frequency factor, ν, for a bond dissociation process is of the order 10^{14} secs^{-1} has been experimentally shown from measurements of the variation in the fraction of benzene ions ($C_6H_6^+$) that dissociate to $C_6H_5^+ + H$ with the residence time of the $C_6H_6^+$ ions in a mass spectrometer ion source. Unpublished results of the present author.

and direct measurements of the ionization potentials of the molecules ethane and ethylene and the ethyl radical there may be calculated, for ϵ_{12} and ϵ_{13}, 1.17 ev and 0.2_7 ev, respectively. If it is assumed that all 18 degrees of freedom participate, it would be expected, from equation 11, that, for equation 13, $\epsilon'_{13} = 1.42\ \epsilon_{13}$; and, for equation 12, $\epsilon'_{12} = 1.64\ \epsilon_{12}$. Thus for the case of rigorous applicability of the quasi-equilibrium theory the expected differences between fragment and parent ion appearance potentials would be 1.92 ev and 0.38 ev, respectively, for equations 12 and 13. There is essential agreement between $A(C_2H_4^+) - A(C_2H_6^+)$ with ϵ'_{13} (0.5_0 versus 0.38); and $A(C_2H_5^+) - A(C_2H_6^+) = 1.2_7$ agrees with the calculated ϵ_{12}, not with the estimated ϵ'_{12}.

Inasmuch as we wish to apply the quasi-equilibrium theory to the calculation of the average energy with which molecule ions are formed by electron impact, we shall accept the consequences of the theory and associate ϵ_1' with the differences between the vanishing current appearance potential of the lowest energy fragment and parent ion, despite the conflicting evidence on the question.

The necessary data and the results of calculations of $\bar{\epsilon}$ from equations 9 and 10 are summarized in Table I. In those cases where there is disagreement between data in the published literature and results obtained in these laboratories, we have arbitrarily selected our data.

Friedman, *et al.* (*7*) have made similar calculations for some of the molecules considered in Table I, but, as is discussed below, these authors made a different assumption with respect to the relation between appearance potential differences and the critical energies for processes than is done here.

The foregoing discussion of ion energies, based on equation 3, obviously breaks down completely where $\epsilon_1 \leq 0$, as would appear to be the case for such substances as CCl_4, SiH_4, and $Pb(CH_3)_4$, that have undetectable intensity of parent ions in their mass spectra. In such cases one should presumably consider the secondary dissociation reactions of the ions formed in primary processes, treating each primary fragment ion as the parent of its set of secondary fragments. Our present understanding of mass spectra does not permit such calculations.

Ion Energies from Mass Spectrometric Appearance Potentials

Experimentally, appearance potentials of ions in mass spectra have been defined in two manners. These appearance potentials, termed the vanishing current (V.C.) and linear extrapolation (L.E.), correspond to the two methods of interpreting the initial portions of the ionization efficiency curves (ion current versus ionizing electron energy) of the ions of the mass spectrum of a substance. As has been discussed by Mariner and Bleakney (*9*), these two appearance potentials of ions are to be associated with the least energy (V.C.) and average energy (L.E.) required for the formation of the ion and the associated neutral fragments (if any). If the interpretation of the L.E. appearance potentials suggested by Mariner and Bleakney

TABLE I

EXCITATION ENERGIES FROM QUASI-EQUILIBRIUM RATE THEORY OF THE ORIGIN OF MASS SPECTRA

Molecule	*Process*	ϵ'	f_p	$\bar{\epsilon}$ *Eq. 9*	$\bar{\epsilon}$ *Eq. 10*	*References*
Methane	$CH_4^+ \rightarrow CH_3^+ + H$	1.2_7	0.49_8[a]	1.3_6	1.2_8	b, c
Acetylene	$C_2H_2^+ \rightarrow C_2H^+ + H$	6.0_0	0.67_4[a]	5.0_0	4.4_5	d, e
Ethylene	$C_2H_4^+ \rightarrow C_2H_2^+ + H_2$	2.9_8	0.43_5	3.5_0	3.4_3	e, f
Ethane	$C_2H_6^+ \rightarrow C_2H_4^+ + H_2$	0.5_0	0.12_6	1.2_1	1.9_8	g, h
Propylene	$C_3H_6^+ \rightarrow C_3H_5^+ + H$	2.2_8	0.18_7	4.4_4	6.1_0	e, i, j
Propane	$C_2H_8^+ \rightarrow C_3H_7^+ + H$	0.4_6	0.10_8	1.2_1	2.1_3	e, i, j
n-Butane	$C_4H_{10}^+ \rightarrow C_3H_6^+ + CH_4$	0.5_3	0.08_6	1.5_7	3.0_8	e, h
Benzene	$C_6H_6^+ \rightarrow C_6H_5^+ + H$	4.4_8	0.55_0	4.4_5	4.0_7	e, k
n-C_6H_{14}	$C_6H_{14}^+ \rightarrow C_4H_8^+ + C_2H_6$	0.5_0	0.07_9	1.5_5	3.1_6	e
Phosphine	$PH_3^+ \rightarrow PH^+ + H_2$	2.7_0	0.38_0	3.4_6	3.5_6	e

[a] Lack of agreement with data shown in Fig. 1 is due to systematic error resulting from neglect of instrumental discrimination against low m/q ions (H^+, H_2^+, C^+, CH^+) in computation of data for Fig. 1.

[b] L. G. Smith, *Phys. Rev.* **51,** 663 (1937).

[c] C. A. McDowell and J. W. Warren, *Discussions Faraday Soc.* **No. 10,** 53 (1951).

[d] Tate, Smith, and Vaughan, *Phys. Rev.* **48,** 525 (1935).

[e] Unpublished measurements, present author.

[f] Kusch, Hustrulid, and Tate, *Phys. Rev.* **52,** 843 (1937).

[g] J. A. Hipple, *Phys. Rev.* **53,** 530 (1938).

[h] D. P. Stevenson and J. A. Hipple, *J. Am. Chem. Soc.* **64,** 1588 (1942).

[i] J. Delfosse and W. Bleakney, *Phys. Rev.* **56,** 256 (1939).

[j] D. P. Stevenson and J. A. Hipple, *J. Am. Chem. Soc.* **64,** 2769 (1942).

[k] Hustrulid, Kusch, and Tate, *Phys. Rev.* **54,** 1037 (1938).

(*9*) is accepted, then the average energy acquired by a molecule in the ionization process will be

$$\bar{A}(M^+) = \sum_i f_i \bar{A}_i \tag{14}$$

where f_i and $\bar{A}_i$ are the fractional intensity and L.E. appearance potential, respectively, of the ith ion in the mass spectrum of M. The f_i can be taken from the mass spectrum of the substance corresponding to any ionizing electron energy in the range (greater than ca. $2I^z$ to $3I^z$) where the relative intensities of the ions in the mass spectrum are independent of the ionizing electron energy (see Figs. 1 to 4).

To the extent that the ionization efficiency curve of an ion has two or more linear branches, it is of course necessary to determine the L.E. appearance potential by extrapolation of the "highest electron energy" linear segment. Examples of such

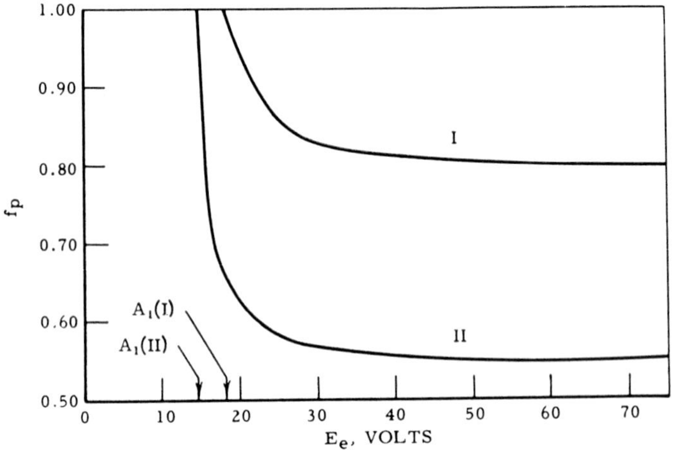

FIG. 1. Variation of parent ion fraction, f_p, with ionizing electron energy, E_e: I, acetylene II, methane. A_1(I), the appearance potential of C_2H^+ from C_2H_2; A_1(II), the appearance potential of CH_3^+ from CH_4.

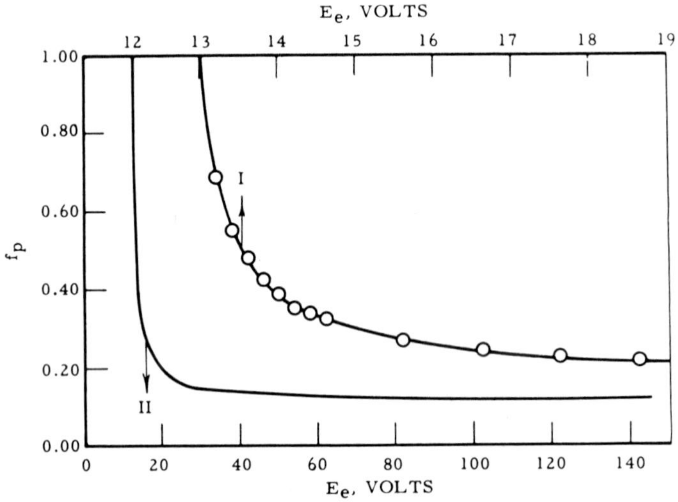

FIG. 2. Variation of parent fraction, f_p, with ionizing electron energy, E_e, for ethane. Upper curve (I) shows the initial portion of lower curve, (II).

behavior are to be found in the cases of the CH_2^+, CH^+, and C^+ ions of the methane mass spectrum (*10*).

Linear extrapolation appearance potentials and the associated fractional intensities of ions in the mass spectra of the various substances considered in the

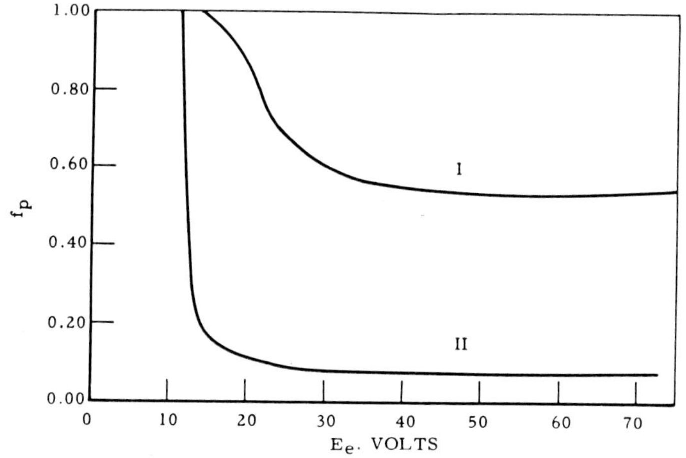

FIG. 3. Parent ion fraction, f_p, versus ionizing electron energy, E_e: I, benzene; II, n-butane.

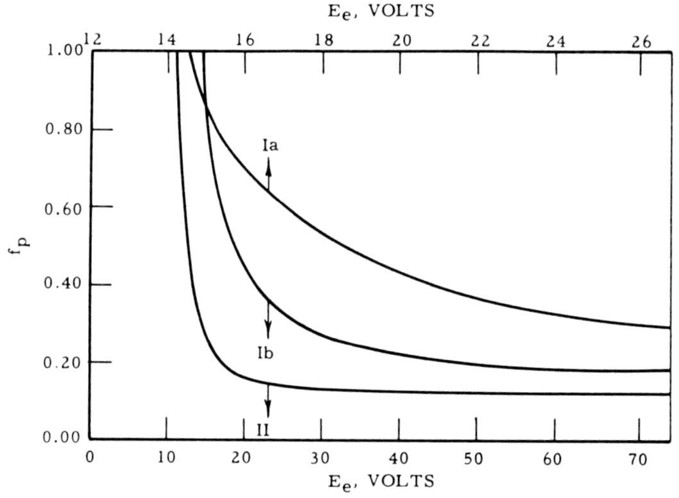

FIG. 4. Variation of f_p with E_e: Ia, Ib, propylene; II, propane.

previous section of this paper were obtained from the literature, supplemented as necessary by measurements made by the present author. The average ionization energies, $\bar{A}(M^+)$, computed by means of equation 14, are given in the second column of Table II. In Table III the data for propylene are given as a more or less typical example.

The average excess or excitation energy, $\bar{\epsilon}$, with which the ion (M^+) is formed is to be associated with the difference between the average appearance potential,

TABLE II

AVERAGE IONIZATION ENERGIES, $\bar{A}(M^+)$, OF MOLECULES

Molecule	$\bar{A}(M^+)$[a]	$I_0^z(M)$[b]	$\bar{\epsilon}$
Methane	15.0	12.99	2.0
Acetylene	15.2	11.41	3.8
Ethylene	13.9	10.52	3.4
Ethane	14.8	11.65	3.1
Propylene	16.6	9.73	6.9
Propane	14.2	11.08	3.1
n-Butane	13.6	10.81	2.8
Benzene	15.5	9.25	6.2
n-Hexane	13.8	10.5_8[c]	3.2
Phosphine	13.3	10.1_1[c]	3.2

[a] References essentially those given in Table I.
[b] From K. Watanabe, *J. Chem. Phys.* **26,** 542 (1957), with exceptions.
[c] Discussed in text.

TABLE III

APPEARANCE POTENTIALS (L.E.) AND FRACTIONAL INTENSITIES OF IONS OF THE PROPYLENE MASS SPECTRUM

Ion(i)	f_i[a]	$\bar{A}_i(ev)$[b]	*Ion*	f_i	$\bar{A}_i$
$C_3H_6^+$	0.189	11.6	$C_3H_5^{++}$	0.002	33.
$C_3H_5^+$	0.306	14.6	$C_3H_4^{++}$	0.007	36.
$C_3H_4^+$	0.078	14.5	$C_3H_5^{++}$	0.006	38.
$C_3H_3^+$	0.192	17.3	$C_3H_2^{++}$	0.009	38.
$C_3H_2^+$	0.071	24.9			
C_3H^+	0.032	28.4	CH_3^+	0.007	$21._2$
C_3^+	0.006	35.4	CH_2^+	0.004	$26._8$
			CH^+	0.002	~30.
$C_2H_4^+$	0.006	17.	C^+	0.001	~35.
$C_2H_3^+$	0.088	16.2			
$C_2H_2^+$	0.020	19.2			
C_2H^+	0.004	~30.			
C_2^+	0.001	~40.			

[a] Characteristic of 75-volt ionizing electrons and the gas at ~125°C.
[b] Electron energy scale calibrated by taking $\bar{A}(A^+) = 15.8$ ev.

$\bar{A}(M^+)$, and the lowest ionization potential, $I_0^z(M)$, of the molecule. Thus we have

$$\bar{\epsilon} = \bar{A}(M^+) - I_0^z(M) \quad (15)$$

The ionization potential, $I_0^z(M)$, may be obtained from the vanishing current appearance potential or preferably by the photoionization method (*11*). In column

3 of Table II are given the appropriate ionization potentials of the various substances used to calculate the $\bar{\epsilon}$ given in column 4. All except those for n-hexane and phosphine were taken from the work of Watanabe (*11*). In the case of n-hexane, we determined the difference between the vanishing current appearance potential of $C_4H_{10}^+$ (ex n-butane) and $C_6H_{14}^+$ (ex n-hexane) and combined this difference with Watanabe's (*11*) ionization potential of n-butane to obtain the ionization potential of n-hexane. The ionization potential of phosphine was obtained by comparison of the vanishing current appearance potential of PH_3^+ with that of argon (Ar^+), taking $I_0^z(Ar) = 15.76$ ev.

DISCUSSION

Comparison of the average excitation energies with which ions are formed as calculated from equation 14, shown in Table II, with those from equations 9 and 10, shown in Table I, indicate generally excellent agreement between results of the different methods of calculation. This agreement is very satisfying from several points of view. In the first place, it gives grounds for trusting the validity of the average excitation energies that we have obtained and conclusions based on these average energies—for example, the validity of the relative frequency of simple excitations and ionizations that may be calculated by intercombination of these results with measurements of W, the average energy dissipated by ionizing radiation in forming an ion pair (*12*). In the second place, the agreement between the two methods of evaluating the ion excitation energies provides substantiation for the general applicability of the quasi-equilibrium rate theory to mass spectra. This latter conclusion is of particular importance to radiation chemistry because this theory is the only approach currently available to understanding the kinetics of the primary reaction process (equation 2b).

Prior to discussing the kinetic implications of our results we should indicate several conclusions concerning the energetics of the ionization process. First, we note that the excitation energies calculated from the uniform excitation energy distribution function (equation 10 and Table I) are in better agreement with the results of Table II than are those from the modified exponential excitation energy distribution function (i.e., ex equation 9). This result is pleasing in view of the analytical simplification this permits in efforts to obtain integrals of equations such as equation 3.

The results given in Tables I and II indicate that there is a tendency for unsaturated hydrocarbon molecule ions to be formed with greater excitation energies than are saturated hydrocarbon molecule ions. Further, there appears to be no marked change in the magnitude of excitation energy with molecular complexity in the alkane series. This conclusion is at variance with that of Friedman *et al.* (*7*). The reason for this disagreement is in part our association of ϵ_1' with the difference between the vanishing current appearance potential of the fragment and parent ions, whereas Friedman *et al.* (*7*) associated this difference with ϵ_1. As the molecular complexity increases (i.e., as S increases), equation 11 indicates that the ratio, ϵ_1'/ϵ_1, increases quite rapidly. The agreement between the results given in Tables I and II would appear to provide substantiation of our identification of ϵ_1' with $A_1 - A_P$ rather than the identification made by Friedman *et al.* (7).

It was pointed out in the Introduction that for gases at atmospheric pressure reactions of the type of equation 2c are very fast compared to the neutralization reactions (2a). From the results that have been obtained above we may now make an estimate of the nature of the competition between reactions 2b and 2c in determining the fate of the molecule ions formed in excitation processes (equation 2). If we take the collision frequency at atmospheric pressure to be about 10^{10} sec^{-1}, the question that is to be answered is, what is the fraction of molecule ions that will have decomposed in 10^{-10} sec? From the mass spectrometric data we know the fraction of molecule ions that remain undecomposed after 10^{-5} sec. If from equation 11 we define a quantity, ϵ_1'',

$$\epsilon_1'' = \left[\frac{1 - (10^5/s_1\,\nu_1)^{1/S-1}}{1 - (10^{10}/s_1\,\nu_1)^{1/S-1}}\right]\epsilon_1' \qquad (16)$$

then by analogy to equation 10 we would have

$$f_p(10^{-10}\text{ sec}) = \epsilon_1''/2\bar{\epsilon} \qquad (17)$$

We use the expression for f_p corresponding to the uniform excitation energy distribution function because the $\bar{\epsilon}$ from equation 10 of Table I are in better agreement with the $\bar{\epsilon}$ computed from equation 15 (Table II).

In Table IV are given for the substances considered in Tables I and II the quantities $\bar{\epsilon}$, ϵ_1''/ϵ_1', and $f_p(10^{-10}$ sec). As indicated above, we have taken $s_1\nu_1 = 10^{14}$ sec^{-1} for processes involving simple bond dissociation and $s_1\nu_1 = 10^{12}$ sec^{-1} for disproportionation reactions.

TABLE IV

PARENT FRACTIONS, f_p, AT 10^{-10} SEC AFTER IONIZATION

Molecule	$\bar{\epsilon}$	ϵ''/ϵ'	$f_p(10^{-10}$ *sec*)
Methane	1.2_8	1.71	0.85
Acetylene	4.4_5	1.52	1.
Ethylene	3.4_3	2.83	1.
Ethane	1.9_8	3.04	0.38
Propylene	6.1_0	1.98	0.37
Propane	2.1_3	2.05	0.22
n-Butane	3.0_8	2.09	0.18
Benzene	4.0_7	2.06	1.
n-Hexane	3.1_6	3.36	0.27
Phosphine	3.5_6	2.28	0.87

Examination of the results given in Table IV reveals that for simple molecule ions such as those of methane and phosphine, or the unsaturated hydrocarbons such as acetylene, ethylene, and benzene, the rate of dissociation reactions (2b) are slow compared to those of ion molecule reactions (2c) that may take place. For the more complex alkanes, and presumably alkenes, the rates of dissociation of the molecule ions are comparable with the rates that have been found for bimolecular reactions of the ions with molecules, and reactions of fragment ions (in 2c) must be considered along with reactions of the molecule ions.

RECEIVED: December 10, 1958

REFERENCES

1. D. P. STEVENSON and D. O. SCHISSLER, Rate of the gaseous reactions $X^+ + YH = XH^+ + Y$. *J. Chem. Phys.* **23,** 1353 (1955).
2. H. M. ROSENSTOCK and C. E. MELTON, Metastable transitions and collision-induced dissociations in mass spectra. *J. Chem. Phys.* **26,** 314–322 (1957).
3. D. P. STEVENSON, Ion-molecule reactions. *J. Phys. Chem.* **61,** 1453-6 (1957).
4. K. KRAUS, A. L. WAHRHAFTIG, and H. EYRING, Mass spectra and the chemical species produced by the impact of low energy electrons. *Ann. Rev. Nuclear Sci.* **5,** 213–241 (1955).
5. L. FRIEDMAN, F. A. LONG, and M. WOLFSBERG, Ionization efficiency curves and the statistical theory of mass spectra, *J. Chem. Phys.* **26,** 714–715 (1957).
6. H. M. ROSENSTOCK, M. B. WALLENSTEIN, A. L. WAHRHAFTIG, and H. EYRING, Absolute rate theory for related systems and the mass spectra of polyatomic molecules. *Proc. Natl. Acad. Sci. U.S.* **38,** 667–678 (1952).
7. L. FRIEDMAN, F. A. LONG, and M. WOLFSBERG, Study of mass spectra of the lower aliphatic alcohols. *J. Chem. Phys.* **27,** 613–622 (1957).
8. D. P. STEVENSON and J. A. HIPPLE, Ionization and dissociation by electron impact: normal butane, isobutane, and ethane. *J. Am. Chem. Soc.* **64,** 1588–1594 (1942).
9. T. MARINER and W. BLEAKNEY, A note on the significance of appearance potentials of ions in a mass spectrometer. *Phys. Rev.* **72,** 807–814 (1947).
10. C. A. MCDOWELL and J. W. WARREN, The ionization and dissociation of molecules by electron impact. *Discussions Faraday Soc.* **No. 10,** 53–65 (1951).
11. K. WATANABE, Ionization potentials of some molecules. *J. Chem. Phys.* **26,** 542 (1957).
12. J. WEISS and W. BERNSTEIN, The current status of *W*, the energy to produce one ion pair in a gas. *Radiation Research* **6,** 603–610 (1957).

RADIATION RESEARCH 10, 622–635 (1959)

The Clustering of Ions in Irradiated Gases[1,2]

JOHN L. MAGEE AND KOICHI FUNABASHI[3]

Department of Chemistry, University of Notre Dame, Notre Dame, Indiana

INTRODUCTION

The Lind cluster theory (*1*) of the radiation chemistry of gases was based on the known ability of gaseous ions to form clusters (*2*, *3*). Later theoretical considerations of Eyring *et al.* (*4*) shifted the emphasis to free radical mechanisms with the inadvertent result that not only clusters, but to a large extent ions, were ignored in subsequent development of radiation chemistry theory. Recent investigations of ion-molecule reactions in mass spectroscopy (*5*, *6*) have led to a realization of the important role of ions in the radiation chemistry of gases, and a reconsideration of the effects of clustering is indicated.

The importance of clustering of ions has been recognized in physical processes. Bloom and Margenau (*7*) have investigated a cluster model to explain mobility measurements in rare gases (*8*), and Tohmfor and Volmer (*9*) have studied the kinetics of formation of nuclei by ions in condensing gases.

This paper presents a brief consideration of the general theory of the clustering of ions in gases. A systematic comparison of the theory with experiment is impossible because data are not available. However, some comparison is attempted, and a brief consideration of the possible effects of clustering on the radiation chemistry of gases is made.

ENERGETICS OF CLUSTER FORMATION

Let us consider the clustering of an ion[4] A^+ in a gas composed of neutral molecules B. The general clustering reaction can be written

[1] Based on a paper presented before the annual meeting of the Radiation Research Society, Pittsburgh, May 18–20, 1959, as part of the Symposium on Radiation Chemistry of Gases in honor of Dr. S. C. Lind on the occasion of his eightieth birthday. The Symposium was organized by Dr. Leon M. Dorfman, and he and Dr. A. O. Allen served as chairmen of the sessions.

[2] Contribution from the Radiation Project operated by the University of Notre Dame, and supported in part under U. S. Atomic Energy Commission Contract AT(11-1)-38.

[3] Permanent address: Nanzan University, Showa-ku, Nagoya, Japan.

[4] In the formulas of this paper, we shall indicate the ions as *positive*. It is recognized that negative ions also form clusters. Furthermore, all ions are singly charged. It is considered unlikely for a doubly charged ion to persist long enough to form a cluster.

$$A^+ + nB \rightarrow A^+B_n \qquad (n = 1, 2, 3 \cdots) \tag{1}$$

The energy change in this reaction can be divided into three terms:

$$E_n = E_{ne} + E_{nl} + E_{nc} \tag{2}$$

where E_{ne} is the energy change due to alteration of the electrostatic field of the ion by the cluster, E_{nl} is the energy of intermolecular attraction of the neutral molecules (such as leads to liquefaction of the gas at low temperature), and E_{nc} is the energy of any specific chemical interaction in the cluster.

We shall be interested in the possibility for the occurrence of large clusters, and so it is useful to consider the behavior of E_n for large n. Let us say that a cluster is spherical in shape with radius b. Elementary electrostatics gives us an estimate of the electrostatic energy as

$$E_{ne} = -\frac{e^2}{2a}\left(1 - \frac{1}{K}\right)\left(1 - \frac{a}{b}\right) \tag{3}$$

where a is the radius of the ion A^+, and K is the dielectric constant of the neutral molecules. Although as an estimate of the electrostatic energy equation 3 is admittedly rough, its principal features should be valid.

There is a finite and rather small limit to the total amount of electrostatic energy which a cluster can have (for $b \rightarrow \infty$). Thus the electrostatic binding energy per neutral molecule goes to zero as the cluster size increases. The derivation of equation 3 is in agreement with the origin of the energy as due to the polarizability of the neutral molecule in the coulomb field. Thus the electrostatic binding energy of a neutral molecule varies inversely as the fourth power of its distance from the charge.

Steric considerations lead to a shell model for the structure of small clusters. For a given A^+ and B there should be n_1 neutral molecules which are essentially equivalent in a first shell, n_2 in a second, etc. Since $r_2 \approx 2r_1$, the electrostatic binding of a first-shell molecule should be about sixteen times as great as that of a second-shell molecule.

An estimate of E_{nl} for a large cluster can be made as

$$E_{nl} = -n\epsilon_1 + 4\pi b^2 \tau \tag{4}$$

where ϵ_1 is the heat of vaporization of the liquid form of B, and τ is its surface tension. Since $b^2 \propto n^{2/3}$, for large clusters the last term becomes negligible, and E_{nl} decreases linearly with cluster size.

It is impossible to make a general estimate of the E_{nc}, since the formation of a chemical bond is a specific chemical effect. It is certain, however, that the energy of such an effect saturates for a very small cluster size, possible with the first neutral molecule. It is also expected that positive ions should have larger binding energy than negative ions due to this term. Positive ions should always have a certain amount of chemical unsaturation, whereas negative ions may not.

The complete energy of reaction 1 can be written as

$$E_n = -\epsilon_x - \frac{e^2}{2a}\left(1 - \frac{1}{K}\right) - n\epsilon_1 + \frac{e^2}{2b}\left(1 - \frac{1}{K}\right) + 4\pi b^2\tau \tag{5}$$

where ϵ_x is a constant term taken for specific chemical binding.

Introduction of

$$b = \left(\frac{3v_0}{4\pi}\right)^{1/3} n^{1/3} \tag{6}$$

where v_0 is the volume of a single molecule, allows an explicit expression for E_n as a function of n:

$$E_n = -\epsilon_x - \frac{e^2}{2a}\left(1 - \frac{1}{K}\right) - n\epsilon_1 + \frac{e^2}{2}\left(\frac{4\pi}{3v_0}\right)^{1/3}\left(1 - \frac{1}{K}\right) n^{-1/3} + 4\pi\left(\frac{3v_0}{4\pi}\right)^{2/3} \tau n^{2/3} \tag{7}$$

APPLICABILITY OF EQUILIBRIUM TREATMENT

In irradiated gases, ions have lifetimes which vary with the rate of irradiation. In most systems of interest in radiation chemistry, lifetimes of ions are long compared with the time required for clustering. For such systems, cluster formation can be treated as an equilibrium process. The considerations of this paper are specifically concerned with such cases. This section considers the limits of validity of such an equilibrium treatment.

Consider an irradiated gas in a steady state:

$$\frac{dn_+}{dt} = \frac{dn_-}{dt} = I - k'n_+^2 = 0 \tag{8}$$

where n_+ and n_- are the concentrations of the ions, I is the rate of ion pair production per unit volume, and k' is the recombination coefficient. The coefficient k' for a number of molecules has been measured by Mächler (*10*).

The steady-state concentration is

$$n_+ = \sqrt{\frac{I}{k'}}$$

The mean life of an ion is

$$t_+ = \frac{n_+}{I} = \frac{1}{\sqrt{Ik'}} \tag{9}$$

The rate of the clustering process is proportional to the square of the pressure at low pressures, where a three-body process is required, but is proportional to the pressure at high pressures, where a bimolecular mechanism becomes effective. The rate constant (sec^{-1}) can thus be written as

$$\kappa = \frac{\alpha p^2}{1 + \beta p} \tag{10}$$

where α and β are constants characteristic of the clustering gas, and p is its pressure. A consideration of these processes was first given by Thomson (*3*).

The criterion for applicability of an equilibrium clustering theory is that the quantity κt_+ is much greater than unity. In Fig. 1 there is a graph of the logarithm of the rate of irradiation against the logarithm of the pressure under conditions such that κt_+ equals unity for air. There is also a plot of the rate of irradiation such that the air doubles its energy content in 1 minute, owing to the absorbed radiation. Although each substance has slightly different parameters, it is clear from this figure that the equilibrium theory is always applicable for systems of chemical interest in steady state.

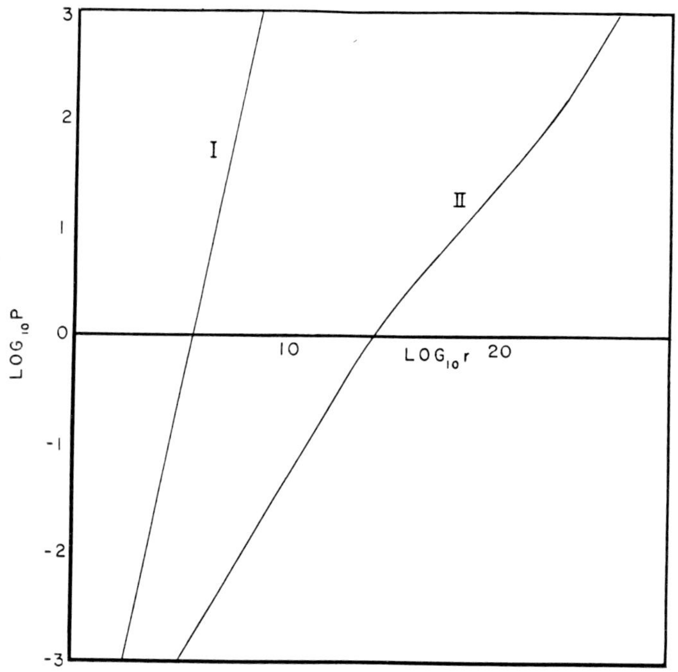

FIG. 1. Relation between rate of irradiation (r, roentgens per second) and pressure of clustering gas (in atmospheres). The equilibrium treatment is valid to the left of line II. Along line I, the rate of energy absorption is high enough to double the energy content of a gas, initially at 300°K, in 1 minute.

EQUILIBRIUM THEORY OF CLUSTER FORMATION

Consider a gas in which ions of the type A^+ and its various clustered forms A^+B_n are in a long-term steady condition. Equation 1 describes the system. Let us call the concentration of unclustered ions c_0, and let the concentration of A^+B_n be c_n. The total concentration of ions, c, is always so small that the concentration of neutral molecules, c_B, is unaffected by the clustering. Conservation of charge requires that

$$\sum c_n = c \qquad (n = 0, 1, 2 \cdots) \tag{11}$$

where the summation extends over all positive ions:

$$\sum K_n \frac{c_0}{c} c_B^{\,n} = 1 \qquad (n = 0, 1, 2 \cdots) \tag{12}$$

where the K_n's are equilibrium constants for the reaction 1. They can be obtained from statistical mechanics in a straightforward way. The individual terms in this summation give the distribution of clustered ions:

$$K_n = \frac{Q_n}{Q_0 Q_B^{\,n}} \exp\left(\frac{-E_n}{kT}\right) \tag{13}$$

where Q_n is the partition function of the nth cluster per unit volume, Q_B is the partition function of the neutral molecule per unit volume, and E_n is the cluster energy given in equation 7.

The evaluation of K_n requires certain approximations which make it convenient to consider two special cases: for "large" clusters and for "small" clusters. The terms "large" and "small" will be defined more precisely later.

EQUILIBRIUM THEORY FOR LARGE CLUSTERS

For "large" clusters we can write

$$Q_n = \frac{[2\pi(m_A + nm_B)kT]^{3/2}}{h^3} \frac{8\pi^2(8\pi^3 A_n B_n C_n)^{1/2}(kT)^{3/2}}{\sigma_n h^3} \cdot \left[1 - \exp\left(\frac{-h\bar{\nu}}{kT}\right)\right]^{-(3n-3)} \tag{14}$$

where A_n, B_n, and C_n are moments of inertia, σ_n is the symmetry number, and $\bar{\nu}$ is an appropriate average frequency. (The assumption is explicitly made at this point that A and B are monatomic, but this will not limit the subsequent treatment.)

The concentration of ions in the nth type of cluster can be given as

$$c_n = c_0 \alpha x^n \exp\left(-\beta n^{-1/3} - \gamma n^{2/3}\right) \tag{15}$$

where

$$\alpha = \frac{Q_n}{Q_0}\left[1 - \exp\left(-\frac{h\bar{\nu}}{kT}\right)\right]\exp\left[\frac{\epsilon_x}{kT} + \frac{e^2}{2akT}\left(1 - \frac{1}{K}\right)\right]$$

$$x = \left(1 - \exp\frac{-h\bar{\nu}}{kT}\right)^{-3}\frac{c_{\mathrm{B}}}{Q_{\mathrm{B}}}\exp\frac{\epsilon_1}{kT}$$

$$\beta = \frac{1}{2}\left(\frac{4\pi}{3v_0}\right)^{1/3}\frac{e^2}{kT}\left(1 - \frac{1}{K}\right)$$

$$\gamma = 4\pi\left(\frac{3v_0}{4\pi}\right)^{2/3}\frac{\tau}{kT}$$

According to hypothesis, the condition exists for large clusters, so let us consider n to be a continuous variable. The quantity α is a slowly varying function of n and can be taken as constant if the range of variation is not too great. Equation 15 gives the distribution function of clusters. It can be approximated as the gaussian function:

$$\frac{c_n}{c} = \frac{1}{\sqrt{\pi}\Delta}\exp\left[-\left(\frac{n - n^*}{\Delta}\right)^2\right] \tag{16}$$

where n^* is the most probable cluster size and must satisfy the relation

$$\ln x + \tfrac{1}{3}\beta n^{*-4/3} - \tfrac{2}{3}\gamma n^{*-1/3} = 0 \tag{17}$$

and Δ is given by

M

$$\Delta = \left(\frac{1}{9}\,\frac{2\beta - \gamma n^*}{n^{*7/3}}\right)^{-1/2} \tag{18}$$

The distribution function given in equation 16 is normalized so that

$$\int_{-\infty}^{\infty}\frac{c_n}{c}\,d(n - n^*) = 1$$

and the treatment above is approximately valid only if $n^* \gg \Delta$. For the special case that $x = 1$, we have

$$n_1^* = \frac{1}{6}\,\frac{e^2}{\tau v_0}\left(1 - \frac{1}{K}\right) \tag{19}$$

It can be seen from an elementary consideration of the equilibrium of the gas B with its liquid phase that x is the saturation ratio (for temperatures below the critical temperature):

$$x = \frac{c_{\mathrm{B}}}{c_{\mathrm{BS}}} = \frac{P_{\mathrm{B}}}{P_{\mathrm{BS}}} \tag{20}$$

where c_{BS} and P_{BS} are the concentration and pressure of the saturated gas.

There is a constant of dimension temperature for each gas, defined as

$$\theta = \frac{8\pi(3v_0/4\pi)^{2/3}\tau}{3kn_1^{*1/3}} \tag{21}$$

which allows a simplification of the formulas for $\ln x$ and Δ:

$$\ln x = \frac{\theta}{T}\frac{\nu - 1}{\nu^{4/3}} \tag{22}$$

where $\nu = n^*/n_1^*$. Also

$$\Delta = \left[6n_1^* \frac{T}{\theta}\left(\frac{\nu^{7/3}}{4 - \nu}\right)\right]^{1/2} \tag{23}$$

The maximum for $\ln x$ occurs when $\nu = 4$, and at this point

$$\ln x_{\max} = 0.47 \frac{\theta}{T} \tag{24}$$

Equations 22, 23, and 24 are in reduced variables and apply to all gases. Another characteristic temperature of a gas is given by

$$T^* = 0.47\theta \tag{25}$$

For temperatures below T^* the value of $x_{\max}$ is greater than e.

For values of $x > 1$ it is clear that no long-term steady state for clusters is possible. Since the gas is supersaturated, all clusters must grow without limit. The general relation between $\ln x$ and ν is given in Fig. 2. The portion of the curve indicated by the dotted line is for values of ν at which the distribution function goes through a minimum. This is the "critical cluster size" of the theory of condensation (*9, 11*), the cluster size at which the free energy decreases as the cluster grows. The equilibrium theory of cluster formation breaks down as supersaturation conditions approach the maximum in the $\ln x$ versus ν curve.

Figure 3 shows the behavior of Δ as a function of ν.

In Table I values of the parameters v_0, n_1^*, θ, and T^* are given for representative gases.

EQUILIBRIUM THEORY FOR SMALL CLUSTERS

Under conditions of great interest in radiation chemistry, gases are frequently far below their saturation pressures, and the calculated values of n^* for the most probable cluster size are in the vicinity of 1, or even less. Clearly the large cluster treatment is inapplicable under such conditions. For such small clusters the structure must be treated explicitly. The following consideration is intended to give an approximation which is useful in this region.

The first several molecules of a cluster are expected to fill a "shell" in which the neutral molecules have approximately the same binding energy. We can use an

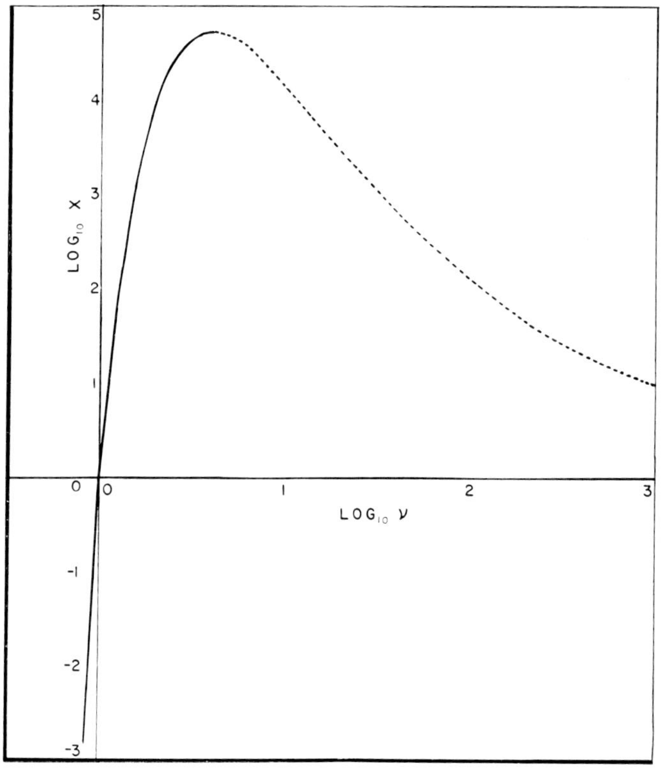

FIG. 2. Relation between the saturation ratio, x, and the most probable cluster size (in reduced units, $\nu = n^*/n_1^*$).

expression analogous to equation 15 for the ion distribution of first-shell cluster:

$$c_n = c_0 \alpha_n x_1^{\ n} \tag{26}$$

where

$$x_1 = \left[\left(1 - \exp\frac{-h\bar{\nu}}{kT}\right)\right]^{-3} \frac{c_\mathrm{B}}{Q_\mathrm{B}} \exp\left(\frac{\epsilon_1}{kT}\right) \tag{27}$$

and ϵ_1 is the appropriate binding energy to be taken for the first shell. Also

$$\alpha_n = \frac{Q_n}{Q_0}\left[\left(1 - \exp\frac{-h\bar{\nu}}{kT}\right)\right]^{3n} \tag{28}$$

where Q_n is the partition function which is possibly, but not necessarily, expressed in the form of equation 14.

By hypothesis the clusters are small, and thus a satisfactory description is ob-

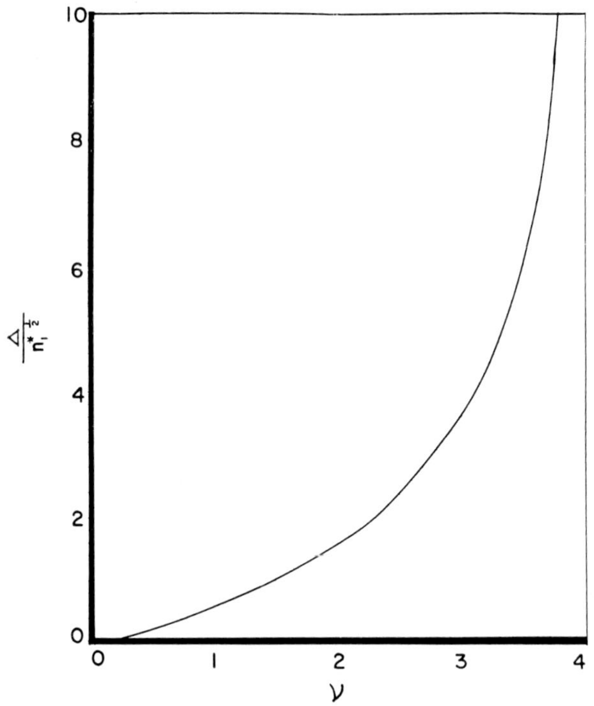

FIG. 3. Relation between root mean square deviation, Δ, and the most probable cluster size (in reduced units, $\nu = n^*/n_1^*$).

tained by neglecting larger clusters. The condition for conservation of charge leads to

$$1 + \sum_{n=1}^{n_1} \alpha_n x_1^n = \frac{c}{c_0} \tag{29}$$

when n_1 is the coordination number of the shell. The distribution of cluster sizes is

$$\begin{aligned} \frac{c_0}{c} &= \left[1 + \sum_{n=1}^{n_1} \alpha_n x_1^n\right]^{-1} \\ \frac{c_j}{c} &= \alpha_j x_1^j \left[1 + \sum_{n=1}^{n_1} \alpha_n x_1^n\right]^{-1} \qquad (j = 1, 2, \cdots, n_1) \end{aligned} \tag{30}$$

From the general nature of these functions it is clear that for some value of x_1, say x_1^*, we have $c_1 = c_{n_1}$, or

$$\alpha_1 x_1^* = \alpha_{n_1} x_1^{*n_1} \tag{31}$$

TABLE I
MOLECULAR CONSTANTS FOR LARGE CLUSTERS

Gas	τ *(ergs/cm₂)*	$v_0 \times 10^{23}cm^3$	n_1^*	θ	T^*
H_2	9.017	1.32	164.83	21.45	10.1
N_2	27.581	2.66	26.26	193.1	90.8
O_2	38.357	2.28	22.80	254.0	119.4
CO	29.420	2.79	25.32	215.3	101.2
CO_2	64.043	4.41	7.16	969.1	455.5
NO	52.859	1.66	30.84	256.3	120.5
N_2O	64.561	5.07	5.87	114.5	538.2
Cl_2	73.706	4.42	8.25	1065.0	500.6
H_2O	224.157	0.97	14.93	966.9	454.4
Ar	37.252	2.06	28.39	214.3	100.7
Kr	40.885	2.44	25.34	273.5	128.6
Xe	54.341	3.44	14.55	550.5	258.7
CH_4	39.086	2.91	20.56	315.4	148.2
C_2H_6	49.157	3.24	18.52	441.2	207.4
C_2H_2	58.352	3.88	10.65	710.2	333.8
C_2H_4	49.165	4.85	10.25	703.3	330.6
C_6H_6	61.153	7.62	6.58	1370.0	643.9

Let us define a new variable, y, which is equal to *unity* at this point:

$$\begin{aligned} y &= \kappa x_1 \\ 1 &= \kappa x_1^* \end{aligned} \tag{32}$$

From equation 31 this gives

$$\alpha_{n_1} = \kappa^{n_1 - 1}\alpha_1 \tag{33}$$

From equation 28 it is evident that $\alpha_1 < \alpha_2 < \alpha_3 \cdots < \alpha_{n_1}$. The α's are not simple quantities, since they depend on details of the structure of the clusters. However, they tend to increase by geometric progression. A simple model for first-shell clusters is obtained by the approximation

$$\alpha_n = \kappa^{n-1}\alpha_1 \tag{34}$$

which interpolates the intermediate values of α_n. The distribution is now

$$\begin{aligned} \frac{c_0}{c} &= \left[1 + \frac{\alpha_1}{\kappa}\sum_{n=1}^{n_1} y^n\right]^{-1} \\ \frac{c_j}{c} &= \frac{\alpha_1}{\kappa} y^j \left[1 + \frac{\alpha_1}{\kappa}\sum_{n=1}^{n_1} y^n\right]^{-1} \qquad (j = 1, 2, \cdots, n_1) \end{aligned} \tag{35}$$

A typical set of distributions is shown in Fig. 4. Since α_1/κ is expected to be 10 or more, first-shell clustering can be described simply:

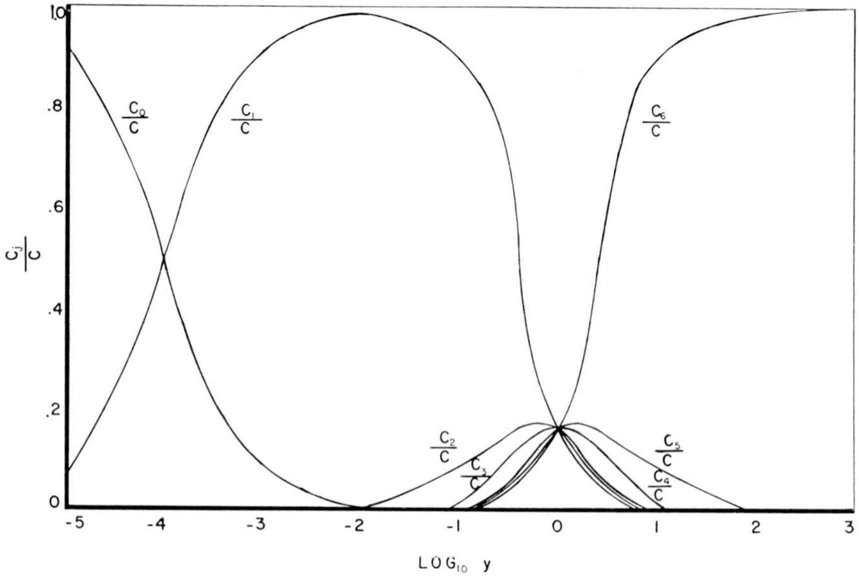

FIG. 4. Cluster distribution for $n_1 = 6$ and $\alpha = 10^4$: y is a linear function of the pressure.

$0 < y < \frac{\kappa}{\alpha_1}$	essentially no clustering
$\frac{\kappa}{\alpha_1} < y < 1$	the cluster c_1 dominates
$1 < y$	the cluster c_{n_1} dominates

In the vicinity $y \approx 1$, all the clusters $c_2 \cdots c_{n_1-1}$ have their maxima.

Values of α_1/κ for typical gases are shown in Table II.

APPLICATION OF CLUSTER THEORY

Data are not available for a systematic comparison of the theory presented here with experiment. As far as the authors know, there are no results at all in the large cluster region. In the first-shell cluster region, data of Munsen and Hoselitz (*8*) can be used. This region is best described by a plot on a pressure-temperature diagram of the lines separating the no-cluster, one-cluster, and n_1-cluster conditions. According to equation 27 for x_1, it is suggested that plots of log c_B versus T^{-1} should be essentially straight lines for the conditions

$$y = 1$$

$$y = \frac{\kappa}{\alpha_1}$$

TABLE II

CONSTANTS FOR SMALL CLUSTERS AT $T = 300°K$

Gas	α_1	κ	α_1/κ
Ar	3.5×10^4	16	2.2×10^3
Kr	1.4×10^5	22	6.4×10^3
Xe	3.2×10^5	28	1.2×10^4

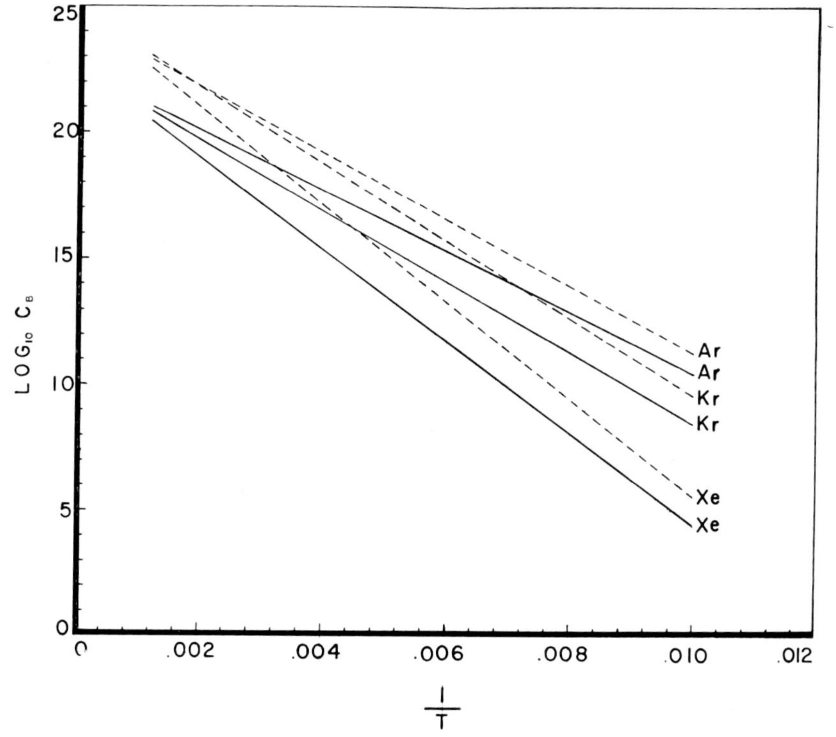

FIG. 5. Effect of temperature on cluster distributions of Ar, Kr, and Xe. For each system, below the solid line there is no clustering; above the dotted line there is full clustering in the first shell; and in the region between the two lines clusters of type c_1 dominate. C_B is the number of molecules per unit volume.

Such plots for $Li^+ - Ar$, $Li^+ - Kr$, and $Li^+ - Xe$ are shown in Fig. 5. The molecular constants required for these calculations are obtained from Margenau (*12*) and Hirschfelder *et al.* (*13*). Table III summarizes the comparison with experiment.

EFFECTS OF CLUSTERING ON THE RADIATION CHEMISTRY OF GASES

We shall now consider briefly the possible effects of clustering on chemical mechanisms in irradiated systems. All gaseous systems are expected to show significant

TABLE III

COMPARISON WITH EXPERIMENT

Ion	Gas	Temperature (K)	$\frac{c}{1-c}$[a] Experiment	$\frac{c}{1-c}$[a] Theory	r[b] Experiment	r[b] Theory
Li^+	Ar	195	>10	>10	2	4
	Ar	290	<1/3	0.3	1	1
	Kr	290	>10	2	2	1
	Kr	360	<2	1/4	1	1
	Xe	290	>20	>10	2	4
	Xe	300		3	1	1

[a] c, fraction of clustered ions.

[b] r, average number of molecules clustered.

changes in mechanism and yield as conditions are altered so that clustering increases. Heretofore it does not seem to have been realized that large cluster sizes occur only near saturation of a gas, and experimental data in this region are not available.

Consider an irradiated system in which there is no clustering. Immediately after formation, the parent ions dissociate, and/or rearrange, and react with neutral molecules. Ion-molecule reactions continue until the most stable ionic species remain. Radicals are formed in the sequence, and they react in typical ways. Charge neutralization may result in additional reaction or formation of radicals. If the pressure in such a system is increased so that the ions form clusters, all the steps in the sequence can be altered. All ion-molecule reactions involve "sticky" collision, and at higher pressures clustering may prevent completion of reactions which are normal at lower pressures. This effect is similar to the "cage effect" in liquids. Of course, the most exothermic ion-molecule reactions should be affected last, since they are expected to require the least time for completion. As a general rule it is perhaps the neutralization reaction which would be affected first, since the most stable ionic form is involved and would be clustered at the lowest pressure.

The remarks thus far have been addressed to single-component systems. Interesting possibilities exist for the induction of chemical reaction in small components of mixture through the mechanism of clustering. Although it has not been considered explicitly in this paper, it is clear that clustering in mixtures would involve its various components in characteristic manners and that a small component may cluster preferentially. It is possible that preferential reaction of a small component could result from preferential clustering. At present, selective effects are usually attributed to charge or excitation transfer (*14*, *15*).

In conditions which allow formation of large clusters, it is possible that specific ion-catalyzed reactions could be obtained between clustered molecules in the sense originally suggested by Lind (*1*).

ACKNOWLEDGMENTS

The authors would like to thank Miss Elizabeth L. Atkins and Mr. Joseph Chen for their assistance in the calculations. They would also like to acknowledge valuable discussion with Radiation Project Staff members, particularly Professor Milton Burton, Professor W. H. Hamill, Dr. W. H. Taylor, and Dr. G. von Bünau.

RECEIVED: December 22, 1958

REFERENCES

1. S. C. LIND, *The Chemical Effects of Alpha Particles and Electrons*, p. 663, Chemical Catalog Co., New York, 1928.
2. P. LANGEVIN, L'ionsation des gaz. *Ann. chim. et phys.* **28,** 289–384 (1903).
3. J. J. THOMSON, Recombination of gaseous ions, the chemical combination of gases and monomolecular reactions. *Phil. Mag.* **47,** 337–378 (1924).
4. H. EYRING, J. O. HIRSCHFELDER, and H. S. TAYLOR, Chemical reactions and ionization processes. *J. Chem. Phys.* **4,** 479–491 (1936).
5. D. P. STEVENSON and D. O. SCHISSLER, Reactions of gaseous molecule ions with gaseous molecules. IV. Experimental method and results. *J. Chem. Phys.* **29,** 282–294 (1958).
6. F. H. FIELD and F. W. LAMPE, Reactions of gaseous ions. VI. Hydride ion transfer reactions. *J. Am. Chem. Soc.* **80,** 5587–5592 (1958).
7. S. BLOOM and H. MARGENAU, Ion clustering. *Phys. Rev.* **85,** 670–673 (1952).
8. J. R. MUNSEN and K. HOSELITZ, The mobility of alkali ions in gases. *Proc. Roy. Soc.* **A172,** 43–50, (1950).
9. G. TOHMFOR and M. VOLMER, Die Keimbildung unter dem Einfluss electrischer Ladungen. *Ann. Physik* **33,** 109–131 (1938).
10. W. MÄCHLER, Über Druck- und Temperaturabhängigkeit des Wiedervereinigungskoeffizienten und der Ionisation durch Gammastrahlen in Luft und Kohlensäure. *Z. Physik* **104,** 1–33 (1936).
11. H. REISS, Theory of the liquid drop model. *Ind. Eng. Chem.* **44,** 1284–1288 (1952).
12. H. MARGENAU, On the forces between positive ions and neutral molecules. *Philosophy of Science* **8,** 603–613 (1941).
13. J. O. HIRSCHFELDER, C. F. CURTISS, and R. BIRD, *Molecular Theory of Gases and Liquids*, p. 1110, John Wiley & Sons, New York, 1954.
14. E. ZUBLER, W. H. HAMILL, and R. R. WILLIAMS, JR., Ion pair yield in the X-ray decomposition of hydrogen bromide in rare gas atmospheres. *J. Chem. Phys.* **23,** 1263–1267 (1955).
15. M. BURTON and J. L. MAGEE, Charge transfer in the radiation chemistry of gases. *J. Phys. Chem.* **56,** 842–845 (1952).

RADIATION RESEARCH **10**, 636–654 (1959)

Decomposition of *n*-Butane in an Electric Discharge[1,2]

ARON KUPPERMANN[3] AND MILTON BURTON

Department of Chemistry, University of Notre Dame, Notre Dame, Indiana

1. INTRODUCTION

Interest in the chemical effect of an electric discharge dates back to 1796 when several Dutch chemists (*1*) subjected gaseous hydrocarbons to sparking and observed the appearance of oil droplets and an increase of 40% in the volume of the gas. One of the first attempts to explain the mechanism of electric discharge reactions was that of Lind (*2*), who suggested an ion-cluster theory to explain the high yields of conversion of electrical to chemical energy. Lunt and Emeléus (*3*, *4*) de-emphasized the importance of ionic mechanisms and interpreted the phenomena on the basis of reactions of neutral free radicals, and Bradford and Finch (*5*) suggested that these radicals resulted from electronic excitation processes as opposed to thermal ones. Recent work has tended to support these views. Wiener and Burton (*6*) used kinetic and tracer methods in the study of an atmospheric pressure discharge through methane. Ethylene (*7*) and ethane (*8*) were similarly investigated. A successive excitation mechanism of transfer of energy from the electrons in the discharge to free radicals was proposed by Burton and Magee (*9*) and applied to the methane discharge (*10*). The results of this recent work are consistent with the view that ionic reactions are unimportant, that the kinetic temperature of the molecules is not high, and that electronic excitation of neutral free radicals plays a dominant role.

[1] Based on a paper presented before the annual meeting of the Radiation Research Society, Pittsburgh, May 18–20, 1959, as part of the Symposium on Radiation Chemistry of Gases in honor of Dr. S. C. Lind on the occasion of his eightieth birthday. The Symposium was organized by Dr. Leon M. Dorfman, and he and Dr. A. O. Allen served as chairmen of the sessions.

[2] Contribution from the Radiation Project of the University of Notre Dame, supported in part under U. S. Atomic Energy Commission Contract At(11-1)-38 and U. S. Navy equipment loan Contract Nonr-06900. This paper is an abstract from a thesis presented by Aron Kuppermann in partial fulfillment of the requirements for the degree of Doctor of Philosophy at the University of Notre Dame.

[3] American Oil Co. Fellow at the University of Notre Dame during part of the work reported. Present address: Noyes Chemical Laboratory, University of Illinois, Urbana, Illinois.

The work here reported was undertaken with the purpose of determination of the applicability of these views to a more complex molecule. Ionic reactions may play an important role in the radiation chemistry of gases (*11*, *12*) because of the relatively large values for the reaction cross sections of ions with molecules (*13*). The question of whether they may be important in electrical discharge chemistry is, therefore, re-examined. It has recently been shown that molecular detachment processes are important in the radiation chemistry of ethane (*14*). Consequently, the possible importance of similar reactions in the electric discharge decomposition of *n*-butane is also examined.

2. EXPERIMENTAL PROCEDURES

2.1. Chemicals

n-Butane, *i*-butane, and argon were supplied by the Matheson Co. The first two were 99.9% pure (extra-pure grade), and the last was 99.8% pure. Deuterium was supplied by the Stuart Oxygen Co. and had an isotopic purity of 99.5%. These purities were checked by mass spectrometric analysis (see Section 2.3 below), and the gases were used without further purification. The *n*-C_4D_{10} was prepared by successive equilibrations of *n*-butane with D_2 on a platinum catalyst at 150°C. Analysis showed it to be 99.5% pure in D atoms with respect to total H + D.

2.2. Equipment and Technique

The apparatus used was a modification of the one devised by Wiener and Burton (*6*) and is shown in Fig. 1. This modification permitted runs in the pressure range 10 cm Hg to 1 atm. It consisted essentially of two calibrated bulbs, B_1 and B_2, of about 35 cm^3 each, a discharge tube, *D*, and the stopcocks, manometers, etc., necessary for introducing and removing known amounts of gases into and from the main portion of the apparatus. Details of the discharge tube are shown in Fig. 2. The interelectrode distance was about 2 mm. The electrodes were made of nickel. The cathode, *C*, was water-cooled and inserted into the system through a brass plug, *P*, which fitted snugly a ground-glass standard-taper joint. Vacuum tightness between the plug and the cathode insertion tube was achieved with the help of Apiezon Q wax. The anode, *A*, sat on a ground-glass collar, *X*. Two thermocouples, P_1 and P_2, enclosed in glass sleeves were located close to the discharge region, one just before it and one just after it. The tips of these sleeves were very thin so as to allow good thermal contact between the thermocouples and the gas.

The discharge was operated by a variable 5000-volt 300-ma direct-current power supply. A resistor in series with the power supply could be varied between 0 and 300 kΩ and permitted control of the current.

The technique consisted in filling bulb B_2 (Fig. 1) and the tube connecting it to bulb B_1 with mercury, and introducing a known amount of gas into the remaining 90 cm^3 of the system. The mercury was then allowed to flow at a controlled rate

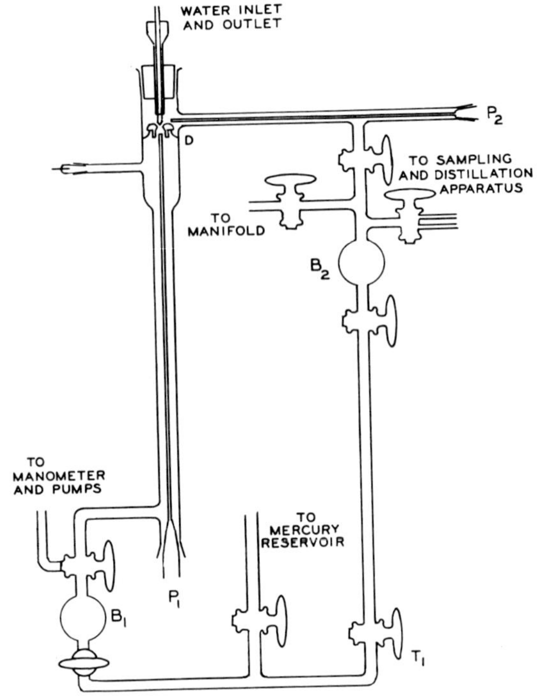

FIG. 1. Discharge apparatus.

from B_2 to B_1 through the flow stopcock T_1 while the discharge was on. This forced a known amount of gas (about 40% of the total) through the discharge. The voltage, current, and flow time were measured. The amount of gas in the system after the run was determined, and samples for analysis were collected.

2.3. Analyses

All analyses were carried out with a Consolidated Engineering analytical mass spectrometer, Model 21-103A. Standard fragmentation patterns for the deuterated ethylenes and acetylenes determined by Mohler *et al.* with a similar instrument (*15*, *16*) were used. For the several deuteromethanes, the API patterns (*17*), also established with a similar instrument, were used, except that the CD_3^+ ion current in CD_3H was taken as 43.3% (instead of 27.7%) of the parent ion current, according to a correction mentioned by McNesby and Gordon (*18*). The deuterium-containing samples were divided in a LeRoy still (*19*) into three fractions, the C_4 and C_3 fraction, the C_2 fraction, and the fraction containing the methanes and hydrogens. These fractions were then analyzed mass spectrometrically, by means of the fragmentation patterns mentioned above.

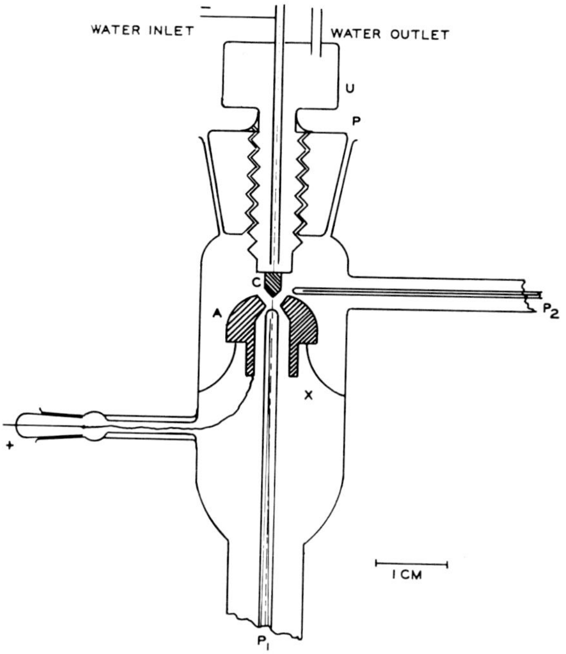

Fig. 2. Details of discharge tube.

3. RESULTS

3.1. n-Butane

Three pressures were used: 10, 30, and 50 cm Hg. Higher pressures than 50 cm Hg were not practicable because the rapid formation of carbon filaments between the electrodes shorted out the discharge. The appearance of the discharge was that of a cylinder about 1 mm in diameter and about 2 mm long extending between the electrodes. Its position would jump around several times during a run. The color of the discharge was sometimes blue and sometimes yellow. During each run the voltage would vary appreciably in an erratic manner, whereas the current would be more stable. This voltage variation was as large as $\pm 30\%$ in some of the runs at 50 cm Hg. In a typical experiment, of 0.514 mM of n-C_4H_{10} at 10.4 cm Hg pressure introduced into the discharge system, only 0.177 mM actually passed the discharge. The amount of decomposed n-C_4H_{10} was 0.094 mM. The nature and amount of gaseous products, in millimoles, were as follows:

Hydrogen	0.0591	Propylene	0.0122
Methane	0.0206	Diacetylene	0.0012
Acetylene	0.0216	Vinylacetylene	0.0016
Ethylene	0.0366	Butadiene	0.0020
Ethane	0.0106	Butene	0.0027
Propyne	0.0032	Benzene	0.0002

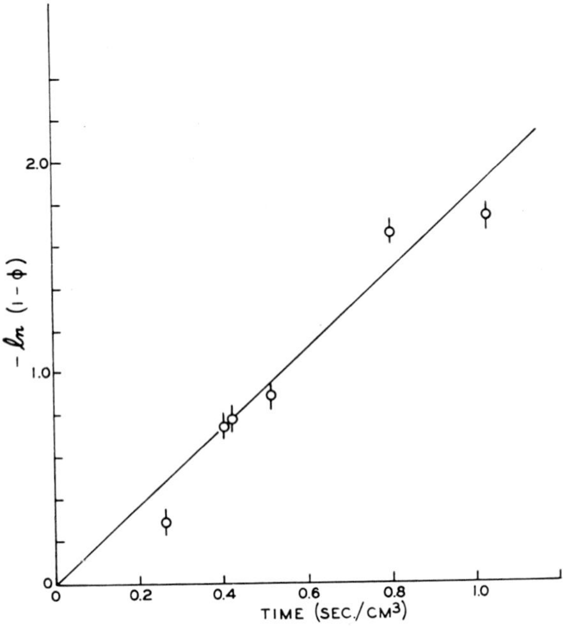

FIG. 3. Plot of $-\ln(1 - \phi)$ versus reciprocal flow rate, t. $p_0 = 10.1$ cm Hg; $V = 455$ volts; $I = 9.0$ ma; slope $= 1.78$ cm³/sec.

Nongaseous products seemed always to be produced; in this run, by material balance, their average empirical formula was calculated to be $CH_{2.3}$.

In general, the temperature of the thermocouple just preceding the discharge did not change during the run, whereas after it the temperature of the thermocouple increased between 30 and 40°C. This second thermocouple was located about 1 mm away from the discharge. When it was introduced directly into the discharge, its Pyrex enclosure melted.

At each pressure p_0, voltage V, and current I, runs were made at several flow rates.

For each set of runs at approximately the same p_0, V, and I, the quantity $-\ln(1 - \phi)$, where ϕ is the fractional decomposition of the n-butane that passed through the discharge, was plotted against the reciprocal flow rate, t, and in all cases straight lines were obtained, for values of ϕ up to 85%. Figure 3 is a typical example of these straight lines. The values of the slopes, k, of these straight lines, as well as the quantity $k' = kV^{-1}I^{-1/2}$, are given in Table I.

The compositions of the gaseous products formed depended mainly on the pressure of the discharge. The facts about the stoichiometry of the over-all decomposition reaction are summarized in the following two average equations:

$p_0 = 10.1$ cm Hg

$$n\text{-}C_4H_{10} \rightarrow 0.63H_2 + 0.22CH_4 + 0.18C_2H_2 + 0.51C_2H_4 + 0.14C_2H_6 + 0.027C_3H_4 + 0.19C_3H_6 + 0.04C_3H_8 + 0.023C_4H_2 + 0.019C_4H_4 + 0.022C_6H_4 + 0.035C_4H_8 + 0.0013C_6H_6 + \frac{1}{n}(CH_{2.5})_n$$

$p_0 = 50.0$ cm Hg

$$n\text{-}C_4H_{10} \rightarrow 1.17H_2 + 0.12CH_4 + 0.37C_2H_2 + 0.20C_2H_4 + 0.010C_2H_6 + 0.014C_3H_4 + 0.031C_3H_6 + 0.030C_4H_2 + 0.012C_4H_4 + 0.001C_4H_6 + 0.038C_4H_8 + 0.0045C_6H_6 + \frac{2.4}{n}(CH_{2.2})_n$$

The last term in each of these two equations represents the sum total of the non-gaseous products as determined by material balance. In some runs very small amounts of octane were found in the gaseous products.

The values of $G(—C_4H_{10})$—number of n-butane molecules decomposed per 100 ev absorbed—did not depend markedly on the voltage, current, or flow rate. The average value of $G(—C_4H_{10})$ in these runs was about 16.

3.2. n-Butane + n-Butane-d_{10}

Several runs were made with mixtures of n-C_4H_{10} and n-C_4D_{10}. Table II shows the isotopic composition of the hydrogens and methanes formed, and Table III that of the acetylenes and ethylenes. The reason that the results for the runs at the low pressure are missing from Table III is that at 10 cm Hg the ethanes are important products, but the fragmentation patterns of the several deuteroethanes were not available. The unraveling of the mass spectra of the mixtures of acetylenes

TABLE I

VARIATION OF RATE CONSTANTS WITH VOLTAGE AND CURRENT

p_0 (*cm Hg*)	V (*volts*)	I (*ma*)	k (*cm*^{3}/*sec*)	$k' \times 10^3$ ($cm^3 \cdot sec^{-1} V^{-1} ma^{-1/2}$)
10.1	550	4.5	0.62	0.53
10.1	455	9.0	1.78	1.3
10.0	385	15.5	2.08	1.4
30.0	815	5.2	0.52	0.28
29.9	560	11.5	1.50	0.79
30.1	420	17	1.40	0.81
49.9	430	12	0.72	0.48
49.9	260	30	0.65	0.45
49.9	275	86	1.16	0.45

TABLE II

ISOTOPIC COMPOSITION OF HYDROGENS AND METHANES IN n-BUTANE + n-BUTANE-d_{10} RUNS

Mole % n-C_4D_{10}	p_0 (cm Hg)	$[C_4H_{10}]/[C_4D_{10}]$	$[HD]/[H_2]$	$[D_2]/[H_2]$	$[HD]^2/[H_2][D_2]$	$[CH_4]/[DC_4]$	$[CH_3D]/[CD_4]$	$[CH_2D_2]/[CD_4]$	$[CHD_3]/[CD_4]$
30	10.0	2.3	0.73	0.16	3.3	10.5	7.0	4.0	3.6
60	10.0	0.67	2.28	1.61	3.3	0.68	0.87	0.84	1.39
40	50.0	1.5	1.21	0.45	3.3	3.7	4.1	3.0	2.8
60	50.0	0.67	2.86	2.20	3.6	0.32	0.71	1.04	1.49

TABLE III

ISOTOPIC COMPOSITION OF ACETYLENES AND ETHYLENES IN n-BUTANE + n-BUTANE-d_{10} RUNS

Mole % n-C_4D_{10}	p_0 (cm Hg)	$[C_2HD]/[C_2H_2]$	$[C_2D_2]/[C_2H_2]$	$[C_2HD]^2/[C_2H_2][C_2D_2]$	$[C_2H_3D]/[C_2H_4]$	$[C_2H_2D_2]/[C_2H_3D]$	$[C_2HD_3]/[C_2H_4]$	$[C_2D_4]/[C_2H_4]$
40	50.0	1.28	0.43	3.8	0.41	0.55	0.81	1.14
60	50.0	3.12	2.30	4.2	0.66	0.53	0.46	0.55

and ethylenes for the runs at 50 cm Hg was achieved by successively "peeling off" the contributions of C_2D_4, C_2D_3H, $C_2D_2H_2$, and C_2DH_3 and completing the analysis by solving the system of four equations obtained from peaks at m/e 28, 27, 26, and 13.5. Only $C_2H_3^{++}$ from C_2H_4 and C_2HD^{++} from C_2HD contribute to this last peak, and, as a result, the accuracy obtained by this method is much higher than if peaks at m/e 25 or 24 were used.

In all n-C_4H_{10} + n-C_4D_{10} runs the region of the mass spectra of the products between m/e 58 and m/e 68 was carefully observed. After subtracting out the contribution to these peaks due to undecomposed butane-d_{10}, no residues, within the accuracy of the mass spectrometer, were left. This indicates that no partially deuterated butanes were detectable in the products. However, some C_4HD was formed in all these runs.

3.3. n-Butane + Deuterium

A few runs were made with mixtures of n-butane and deuterium. The isotopic compositions of some of the products are summarized in Table IV. Some C_4HD was found among the products, but no deuterobutanes were detected.

3.4. n-Butane + Argon

Some kinetic runs were made at 50 cm pressure with mixtures in pressure ratios of 10 n-butane to 40 A. The slope of k of the straight line obtained by plotting $-\ln(1 - \phi)$ against t is 2.3 ml/sec, and the value of $k' = kV^{-1}I^{-1/2}$ is 1.4 × 10^{-3}

cm³ sec⁻¹ (ma)⁻¹ᐟ². The average composition of the main gaseous products, relative to acetylene, together with the corresponding values for the pure n-butane runs, is given in Table V.

3.5. *i-Butane*

For comparison purposes, a run was made with pure i-butane at 10 cm Hg. The stoichiometry of the over-all reaction was:

$$i\text{-}C_4H_{10} \rightarrow 0.70H_2 + 0.33CH_4 + 0.23C_2H_2 + 0.20C_2H_4 + 0.13C_2H_6 + 0.065C_3H_4 + 0.24C_3H_6 + 0.078C_3H_8 + 0.022C_4H_2 + 0.027C_4H_4 + 0.027C_4H_6 + 0.034C_4H_8 + \frac{1}{n}(CH_{2.3})_n$$

3.6. *Irradiation of n-Butane by 1.5-Mev Van de Graaff electrons*

Also for comparison purposes, two runs were made in which n-butane was bombarded by 1.5-Mev Van de Graaff electrons. Table VI contains the composition of

TABLE IV

Isotopic Composition of Products in n-Butane + Deuterium Runs

Mole % D_2	*30*	*30*
p_0 (cm Hg)	*50*	*10*
$[HD]/[H_2]$	0.44	0.19
$[D_2]/[H_2]$	1.66	2.36
$[HD]^2/[H_2][D_2]$	0.12	0.015
$[CH_3D]/[CH_4]$	0.32	0.151
$[CH_2D_2]/[CH_4]$	0.09	0.02
$[C_2HD]/[C_2H_2]$	0.34	0.06
$[C_2D_2]/[C_2H_2]$	0.028	—
$[C_2HD]^2/[C_2H_2][C_2D_2]$	4.2	—
$[C_2H_3D]/[C_2H_4]$	0.17	—
$[C_2H_2D_2]/[C_2H_4]$	0.022	—

TABLE V

Composition of Gaseous Products, for Pure n-Butane and for n-Butane + Argon Mixtures

Total pressure (cm Hg)	*n-C_4H_{10} pressure (cm Hg)*	*A pressure (cm Hg)*	$\frac{[H_2]}{[C_2H_2]}$	$\frac{[CH_4]}{[C_2H_2]}$	$\frac{[C_2H_4]}{[C_2H_2]}$	$\frac{[C_2H_6]}{[C_2H_2]}$	$\frac{[C_3H_6]}{[C_2H_2]}$
10	10	0	3.4	1.2	2.8	0.78	1.05
50	50	0	2.9	0.33	0.49	0.03	0.07
50	10	40	2.6	0.64	1.1	0.05	0.02

TABLE VI

COMPOSITION OF GASEOUS PRODUCTS FOR 1.5-MEV ELECTRON BOMBARDMENT AND ELECTRIC DISCHARGE RUNS IN PURE *n*-BUTANE

Pressure (cm Hg)	*Type of run*	ϕ (%)	$[H_2]/[CH_4]$	$[C_2H_2]/[CH_4]$	$[C_2H_4]/[CH_4]$	$[C_2H_6]/[CH_4]$	$[C_3H_8]/[CH_4]$
10	1.5-Mev electrons	12	2.5	—	2.7	2.4	2.7
10	Discharge	64	2.8	0.80	2.3	0.6	0.2
50	1.5-Mev electrons	45	3.2	—	1.0	2.0	1.7
50	Discharge	59	6.7	2.7	1.3	0.1	0.2

the gaseous products formed in these runs, relative to methane, together with the corresponding values for the electric discharge runs in pure *n*-butane.

4. DISCUSSION

4.1. Character of the Discharge

Cooled cathode glow discharges in air at pressures up to 1 atm have been observed and studied (*20–23*). The main conclusions are that they behave similarly to the low-pressure ones, with the exception that the average temperature of the gas in the cathode dark space is estimated to be 400°C at 10 cm Hg and 700°C at 1 atm (*20*). With that exception the similarity laws are obeyed (*22*). The implication is that the normal cathode fall, V_n, is about the same at low and high pressures. The product of the pressure, p, by the length, d_n, of the cathode dark space, the ratio of the normal electric field, X, in the positive column to the gas pressure, and the electron temperature, T_e, in the positive column are also about the same at low and high pressures (*24*). However, these equalities should be taken as order of magnitude, rather than exact relationships, since a very large pressure extrapolation is involved.

Previous papers from this laboratory (*6, 7*) considered the atmospheric pressure discharges through methane and ethylene as high-pressure glow discharges. In the electric discharge work here reported, the voltages and current densities observed are also characteristic of glow discharges. In low-pressure glow discharges the normal cathode fall, V_n, for several polyatomic gases (*25*) lies between 200 and 500 volts. The value of V_n for the high-pressure glow discharges prevalent in this research should also lie in this range. The energy distribution function of the electrons leaving the dark space, as experimentally determined by Chaudhri (*26*), shows a maximum at eV_n, where e is the electronic charge. The value of pd_n for many gases (*27*) lies between 0.3 and 0.9 cm × mm Hg. This indicates that at 50 cm Hg the length of the cathode dark space should lie in the range 6 to 20 μ, and at 10 cm Hg in the range 30 to 100 μ. These lengths are of the same order of magnitude as the mean free path of the electrons in the gas at these pressures. It is at the end of the cathode dark space that most ionization occurs. Most of the power dissipated in the cathode dark space is spent heating the cathode (and is removed by the cooling water), the rest going into the production of ions and heating of the gas (*22*). In the positive column the field strength is much lower than in the cathode dark space and the average electron energy is of the order of a few electron volts as described in Section 4.2. In order to interpret the high efficiency of conversion of electrical into chemical energy, it is necessary to assume that most of the energy dissipated in the positive column produces chemical reactions. At the end of the positive column, close to the anode, the field strength increases again and further ionization occurs.

The model here assumed for the electrons and ions in the discharge is then the following. Electrons generated at the cathode, by positive ion bombardment and other causes, are accelerated in the cathode dark space, whose length is of the order of a few tens of microns, and most of them acquire an energy of about 200 ev. Most of this energy is lost by ionization and excitation of the gas molecules as, together with the electrons generated in the ionizing collisions, they go through the negative glow. They then go through the Faraday dark space and enter the positive column, where their average energy is low, probably not more than a few electron volts. As they leave the positive column, whose length is roughly equal to the interelectrode distance ($\sim$2 mm), they are accelerated in the anode glow, producing in unit time the same number of ions to flow into the positive column as flow out at the other end into the Faraday dark space. Except in the cathode dark space, almost the entire current is carried by the electrons. Very close to the cathode, however, it is entirely carried by the positive ions.

The diameter of the discharge we used was of the order of magnitude of 1 mm. The cross-sectional area of the interelectrode space through which the entire gas flowed was of the order of 20 mm^2. The reciprocal flow rates used in the experiments varied from 0.16 to 1.82 sec/cm^3, corresponding to flow velocities of 31 to 2.7 cm/sec. If the discharge filled the entire interelectrode annular region and had a thickness of 1 mm, the average residence time, τ, of a molecule in the discharge would vary from about 32 msec to about 37 msec. The diffusion coefficient, D, of gases, at standard temperature and pressure, varies from 0.1 to 1 cm^2/sec (*28*). The average distance a molecule passing through the interelectrode space had to diffuse transversally in order to get into the discharge was about $\Delta x = 3$ mm. The mean diffusion time, θ, corresponding to this distance is given by the Einstein equation (*28*):

$$\theta = \frac{(\Delta x)^2}{2D} > 45 \text{ msec}$$

This indicates that, if nonturbulent flow conditions existed, not all molecules would flow through the discharge. However, the geometry of the flow path tended to induce turbulence. If this turbulence were sufficient to make all molecules flow through the discharge, the average residence time of the molecules would be about one-tenth of the values given above, and hence would vary from about 0.32 to 3.7 msec. These are order-of-magnitude calculations.

For a fixed gas pressure, the current density of a glow discharge is independent of current. This means that the cross-sectional area of the discharge is proportional to the current. If this cross section is a circle, its diameter is proportional to the square root of the current. If, however, it is approximately rectangular with one of its dimensions fixed, the other dimension varies linearly with current. Hence, the average residence time of a molecule in the discharge can be proportional to a power of the current which varies between ½ and 1, depending on the geometry of the discharge.

4.2. Electron Energy Distribution in the Positive Column

It is normally difficult to measure experimentally the energy distribution of the electrons in an electric field in a gas (*29*). It is especially difficult under the experimental conditions described here, in which the length of the discharge was only about 2 mm and the duration less than a minute. However, in recent years, considerable progress in the theory of these distributions has been made.[4] It seems desirable to use this knowledge in estimating the electron energy distribution expected in the experiments here reported.

The values of X/p in the positive columns of these experiments were of the order of magnitude of 20 volts cm^{-1} (mm Hg)$^{-1}$. The electron drift velocities for these values of X/p have been measured for several molecular gases (*30, 31*), and all of them are of the order of 10^7 cm/sec. The current densities in the *n*-butane runs were of the order of 10^{10} electrons sec^{-1} cm^{-2}. These values furnish a concentration of 10^{12} electrons/cm^3. On the other hand, the *n*-butane density was of the order of 10^{19} molecules/cm^3. Consequently, the electron concentration is much lower than the molecular concentration, and the theory of Holstein (*32*) is applicable to the situation encountered in these discharges. Barbiere (*33*) applied this theory to helium and argon. A very important conclusion was that the distribution functions obtained showed a sharp cutoff very close to the first excitation energy, even when the excitation cross section was low. This result would indicate that, if in the present discharges there existed a reasonable concentration of species such as butyl or other radicals having a first excitation potential lower than that of butane, this potential would determine the upper limit of the energy of the electrons in the positive column, and these species would be the main agent of energy absorption from the electrons. In other words, the maximum energy of the electrons is very nearly equal to the lowest excitation energy available among the important species in the discharge. That it is reasonable to assume that a relatively high concentration of radi-

[4] An excellent review of this field is given in L. B. Loeb, *Basic Processes of Gaseous Electronics*, Chapter IV, University of California Press, Berkeley, California, 1955.

cals, especially butyl radicals, exists in the discharge will be shown in Sections 4.5 and 4.6. In addition, the intense visible light produced by the discharge must be due to species other than *n*-butane, since the first optically allowed electronically excited state of nonaromatic hydrocarbons (*34*) lies usually in the vacuum ultraviolet region. On the other hand, the light observed could have come from electronically excited radicals.

An approximate value of the average energy, E_{av}, of the electrons in the positive column can be computed by assuming that all collisions between the electrons and molecules are elastic and then introducing an estimated correction factor. This assumption of elastic collisions furnishes (*35*) the expression

$$E_{av} = 0.605 \frac{Xe}{\sigma N \alpha^{1/2}}$$

where X is the field intensity, e the electronic charge, σ the elastic collision cross section of the electrons with the molecules, N the number density of the molecules, and α the fractional energy loss of the electrons per collision. For elastic collisions α would be $2\ m/M$, where m is the electronic mass and M the molecular mass. However, since in fact inelastic collisions occur, a larger value of α should be used. This quantity is not known for $n\text{-}C_4H_{10}$, but a value of 0.002 may be estimated on the basis of the experimental values for NH_3 and CO_2 (*36*). The value of X for the 50-cm-Hg runs was of the order of 1000 volts/cm. The elastic collision cross section of electrons of 1-ev energy with butane (*37*) is 14.4 A^2. At 400°K these values give $E_{av} = 0.8$ ev. If the theoretical elastic value $\alpha = 2m/M = 0.935 \times 10^{-5}$ had been used, the unrealistic value 8.5 ev would have resulted. Consequently, the approximate calculation of E_{av} depends entirely on the choice of α, which is relatively arbitrary. However, the work of Barbiere (*31*) permits one to state that this average energy should be lower (but not very much lower) than the lowest excitation energy of the important species present in the positive column, which is, as mentioned, the cutoff energy. This conclusion implies that no ions are formed in the positive column and that whatever ions do exist there have drifted in from the anode glow region. It also implies that it is not necessary to assume the successive excitation mechanism postulated by Burton and Magee (*9, 10*) on the basis of a cutoff energy smaller than the dissociation energy of the weakest bond in the system.

4.3. Thermal Reactions

The mean free path of *n*-butane molecules at room temperature is 1.4 μ at 10 cm Hg pressure and 0.28 μ at 50 cm Hg. These results are computed by using a molecular cross section of 16 A^2 calculated from the van der Waals b constant for *n*-butane. The number of collisions per second a butane molecule undergoes is about 2.4×10^8 at 50 cm Hg. For the maximum residence time of 3.7 msec mentioned in Section 4.1 this corresponds to a maximum total number of collisions in the discharge of 0.9×10^6 at 10 cm Hg to 4.5×10^6 at 50 cm Hg. At higher temperatures the collision rate is lower. Even if the temperature throughout the discharge were as high as the upper limit of 700°C obtained in the atmospheric-pressure glow discharge through air (see Section 4.1), the value of $e^{-E/RT}$ for $E = 40$ kcal would only be about 2×10^{-9}, and the fractional decomposition of the butane would be negligible if it were due solely to thermal reactions. In addition, even if the temperature in the very small cathode dark space were high, as mentioned in Section 4.1, the gas molecules would rapidly cool down as they left this region before thermal decomposition could take place. Also, the temperature indicated by the thermocouple located right after the discharge is only about 55° to 65°C, tending to point to an average discharge temperature of not more than 100°C. Finally, as will be shown in Section 4.5, the interpretation of the runs with *n*-butane + *n*-butane-d_{10} mixtures also supports the view of a low temperature of the gas in the discharge. Such low temperatures are normally observed in low-pressure glow discharges (*20*).

4.4. Ion-Molecule Reactions

From the fact that there exists no mechanism for formation of positive ions in the positive column and that the electric current in that region is carried almost exclusively by the electrons, it is reasonable to conclude that the contribution of ion-molecule reactions to the chemistry occurring in that region is relatively small and that most of the chemical energy comes from the energy dissipated by the electrons in inelastic collisions that do not produce ionization. In so far as the negative glow and cathode dark space are concerned, most of the energy of the ions is dissipated in heating the cathode, as pointed out in Section 4.1, so that even in this region the amount of chemistry due to ion-molecule reactions seems to be unimportant. In addition, the butane molecules can spend only a very small fraction of the residence time in this region, owing to its small size compared to that of the positive column. These arguments tend to indicate that ion-molecule reactions, in spite of their relatively large cross section, are probably unimportant under the conditions of our experiments.

4.5. Methane Formation

Recently, Dorfman (*14*) has shown that in the radiolysis of ethane an appreciable amount of CH_4 is formed by a molecular detachment process, i.e., by a process in which all four hydrogen atoms of the CH_4 formed come from the same C_2H_6 molecule. The question arises as to whether a similar process occurs in the electric discharge decomposition of *n*-C_4H_{10}. Information on this point is contained in the runs with *n*-C_4H_{10} + *n*-C_4D_{10} mixtures. The argument that follows is essentially that of Dorfman. In it we shall consider the methane-d_4 and -d_3 only, since the analysis for the others is inaccurate owing to lack of calibration of the mass spectrometer.

Let it be assumed that all methane is formed from reactions of free methyls *only*.

Then, the following statements can be made about the distribution of H and D atoms among the methanes. (1) If the methane is formed by recombination of methyl radicals and hydrogen atoms, then $[CD_4]/[CD_3H] = [C_4D_{10}]/[C_4H_{10}]$ will be true to a good first approximation. There may be a small error due to minor isotope effects in the primary process. (2) If the methane is formed in reactions in which thermal methyl radicals abstract hydrogen atoms from butane molecules, the isotopic distribution can be predicted on the basis of the isotope effects determined for the reactions of thermal methyl radicals with ethane (*38–40*). The assumption in such a case is that essentially the same isotope effect occurs in the thermal reactions of methyl radicals with n-C_4H_{10} molecules. These values lead to $[CD_4]/[CDH_3] = (0.2)[C_4D_{10}]/[C_4H_{10}]$ at 25°C or $(0.3)[C_4D_{10}]/[C_4H_{10}]$ at 400°C. (3) If the methane is formed in hydrogen abstraction reactions by "hot" methyl radicals, the isotope effect should be much smaller and the relation $[CD_4]/[CD_3H] \leqslant [C_4D_{10}]/[C_4H_{10}]$ should be obeyed. The final conclusion is that, if all methane is formed from reactions of free methyl radicals only, then $(0.2)[C_4D_{10}]/[C_4H_{10}] \leqslant [CD_4]/[CD_3H] \leqslant [C_4D_{10}]/[C_4H_{10}]$.

If, on the other extreme, it is assumed that all methane is formed by molecular detachment processes, there should be no CD_3H formed, since Wiener and Burton (*6*) found that practically no exchange occurred among the methanes in the atmospheric pressure discharges through $CH_4 + CD_4$ mixtures. Consequently, all CD_3H formed should be attributed to methyl radical reactions.

From the data of Table II it follows that for all four runs $[CD_4]/[CD_3H] \doteqdot (0.5) [C_4D_{10}]/[C_4H_{10}]$. Let superscripts r denote molecules formed by free radical reactions. Then, since $[CD_4^r]/[CD_3H]$ must necessarily be $\geqslant (0.2)[C_4D_{10}]/[C_4H_{10}]$, it follows that $[CD_4^r]/[CD_4] \geqslant 0.4$, the equality sign holding only if the radical reactions involve thermal methyls at 25°C.

The other product of these abstraction reactions should be C_4H_9. An indication that these radicals are indeed present is given by the small amount of octane vapor found in the gaseous products, by the fact that the empirical formula of the nongaseous residue is close to that of octane, and also because Lind and Glockler (*41*) found that octane is one of the main components of the liquid fraction collected when butane at atmospheric pressure is passed through a bank of ozonizers. On the other hand, no C_4D_9H is found in the n-C_4H_{10} + n-C_4D_{10} runs. The apparent inconsistency of having methyls abstract hydrogens from butane molecules without detecting even minimal abstraction by the butyl radicals disappears if it is assumed that the methyls are slightly "hot" to the extent of being able to overcome the activation energy of about 9 kcal (*42*) of the abstraction reaction, whereas the butyl radicals are at the temperature of the discharge. The probability factor of the abstraction reaction just mentioned is about 10^{-3} (*42*). Even if we assume that for abstraction by butyl instead of methyl radicals this factor is 10^{-4}, between 1% and 10% of the butyl radicals should abstract hydrogen atoms during their residence in the discharge even if the temperature were as low as 200°C. This suggests that the molecular temperature in the discharge is below 200°C. If indeed the CD_3 radicals are "hot," then the ratio $[CD_4^r]/[CD_4]$ should be much larger than the 0.4 value obtained on the assumption that they were thermal radicals at 25°C. This suggests that this ratio is probably close to unity and that molecular detachment processes in the formation of methane from *n*-butane in an electric discharge process are either absent or present in small amounts, being much less important than in the radiation chemistry of ethane. It may be noted that in the case of methane (*6*) evidence of the lack of molecular detachment of hydrogen was also found.

A mechanism by which "hot" methyls and "cold" butyls could be formed is the following. The methyls would be formed from electronically excited butyls, which receive their electronic excitation by inelastic collisions with electrons in the discharge. If the excited butyl formed had an energy about 0.5 ev above that necessary for decomposing into CH_3 and C_3H_6, the methyl would come off with a kinetic energy of 0.4 ev, owing to the conservation of momentum, which would be sufficient to make hydrogen abstraction occur at every collision. Additional evidence supporting this view is given by the fact that in a mixture containing 10 cm Hg of n-C_4H_{10} and 40 cm Hg of A (see Table V) less methane is formed than in 10 cm Hg of pure n-C_4H_{10}, indicating that the methyls are cooled down by the argon. Also, in the n-$C_4H_{10} + D_2$ runs (see Table IV) CH_3D is formed but no C_4H_9D is detected. The "cold" butyls could be formed principally by the abstraction of hydrogen atoms from butane by "hot" methyls, or, to a smaller extent, by the rupture of a C—H bond in electronically excited butane molecules, in which case practically all the excess energy would be given to the H atoms.

4.6. Kinetics and Mechanism

The kinetic results described in Section 3.2 are interpreted as meaning that the over-all reaction is first order in butane. The approximate ½ power dependence in current is interpreted, according to the observations at the end of Section 4.1, as being entirely due to the variation of the size and geometry of the discharge with current, as proposed by Reddy and Burton (*7*). The dependence on voltage is attributed to an effect on the average energy of the electrons, as discussed in Section 4.8.

In a system like the present one in which high fractional decompositions unavoidably occur, it is difficult to unravel primary from secondary products. Consequently, any detailed mechanism that is proposed will undoubtedly contain an appreciable amount of speculation and as such cannot be shown to be unique. The important features it should explain are: the main products of the reaction, the over-all first-order kinetics, and the existence of CH_3, C_4H_9, C_2H, CH_2, C_2H_3, and H as important intermediates, as shown by the isotopic studies (Tables II, III, and IV). Many such mechanisms can be suggested, but it serves no special purpose to do so in detail. A very simplified mechanism which has the correct kinetic behavior and which explains some of the important features observed is as follows:

$$C_4H_{10} \rightsquigarrow CH_3 + C_3H_7 \quad (1)$$

$$C_4H_{10} \rightsquigarrow 2C_2H_5 \quad (2)$$

$$CH_3 + C_4H_{10} \rightarrow CH_4 + C_4H_9 \quad (3)$$

$$C_2H_5 + C_4H_{10} \rightarrow C_2H_6 + C_4H_9 \quad (4)$$

$$C_3H_7 + C_4H_{10} \rightarrow C_3H_8 + C_4H_9 \quad (5)$$

$$C_4H_9 \rightsquigarrow CH_3 + C_3H_6 \quad (6)$$

$$C_4H_9 \rightsquigarrow C_2H_5 + C_2H_4 \quad (7)$$

$$C_4H_9 + C_2H_5 \rightarrow C_6H_{14} \quad (8)$$

Steady-state treatment of this "chain" mechanism (which differs from ordinary chains in that propagation steps 6 and 7 are endothermic and are nourished by the discharge) furnishes a first-order rate law for the butane decomposition. Actually, other reactions must compete with steps 4 and 5 in order to explain the formation of acetylene and some of the intermediates.

4.7. Yields

As mentioned at the end of Section 3.1, the average value of $G(-C_4H_{10})$ in these runs was about 16. The maximum that could be expected, as calculated from the observed stoichiometry and tables of heats of formation, is about 34 (*42*), corresponding to an average efficiency of conversion of electric to chemical energy of about 50%. Considering that about 30% of the energy input is dissipated in the cathode dark space as thermal and ionization energy, this result corresponds to a chemical efficiency of about 70% in the positive column. The explanation of this high efficiency lies in the fact that, owing to the low energies of the electrons in this column, the amount of excess energy introduced into the radicals to decompose them, which appears as degraded thermal energy of the products, is very small; i.e., almost all electronic excitation energy is used in producing chemical effects.

4.8. Dependence of Products on Pressure, Electron Energy, and Structure

As indicated in Section 4.2, the average energy of the electrons should depend on X/N or X/p_0, and, since in glow discharges X/p_0 is independent of p_0, the average energy of the electrons at pressures of 10 cm Hg pressure and 50 cm Hg should be the same. On the other hand, it was found that X/p_0 was higher at the lower pressure; such a result suggests that the behavior of the high-pressure unconstricted glow discharge is not exactly equivalent to that of the low-pressure constricted one. Consequently, it may be expected that the average energy of the electrons in the discharge at 10 cm Hg is higher than in the discharge at 50 cm Hg. If this view is correct, the CH_3 and C_2H_5 radicals formed in the discharge at 10 cm Hg should be "hotter" than those formed in the discharge at 50 cm Hg, with a better chance of formation of CH_4 and C_2H_6, respectively, by hydrogen abstraction processes. The stoichiometric equations given in Section 3.1 show indeed that less CH_4 and C_2H_6 is formed at the higher pressure. The main differences between the composition of the products in the discharge runs and in the 1.5-Mev electron bombardment runs is attributed to the fact that energy absorption is due mainly to the butane molecules and that the average energy of the electrons is high compared to that in the discharge, so that different kinds of processes may occur. A consequence is that one should expect relatively more C_2H_6 and C_3H_8, compared to CH_4, in the high-energy electron bombardments than in the discharge reactions, which is indeed found, as shown in Table VI. This difference should be more pronounced in the runs at 50 cm Hg than in those at 10 cm Hg, as is also the case.

As expected on structural grounds, the stoichiometric equation given in Section 3.5 shows that in *i*-butane relatively more CH_4 and less C_2H_4 is formed than in *n*-butane.

5. SUMMARY

The effects of an electric discharge on *n*-C_4H_{10}, as well as on mixtures of *n*-C_4H_{10} with *n*-C_4D_{10}, D_2, and A, respectively, in the pressure range 10 to 50 cm Hg, have been studied and examined in the light of the theory of the physical phenomena governing the discharge. The products formed in pure *n*-C_4H_{10} were compared with those formed in pure *i*-C_4H_{10} and with those formed by irradiation of *n*-C_4H_{10} by 1.5-Mev electrons. The behavior of the discharge indicates that it is probably of the glow type. In the discharge through pure *n*-C_4H_{10}, the rate of disappearance of this substance is first order in *n*-C_4H_{10} and order ½ to 1 in current. The amount of products in the gas phase ranges from 40 to 90% of the total. The main gaseous products are hydrogen, acetylene, ethylene, and methane. The average efficiency of conversion of electrical to chemical energy found in the work reported was about 50%. It was concluded that ionic reactions are probably unimportant, that the temperature of the discharge is relatively low (i.e., probably less than 100°C), that molecular detachment of methane from *n*-C_4H_{10} is not important, and that the results are consistent with a mechanism of energy input involving energy transfer from the electrons in the discharge to radicals (probably butyls) via excitations of low-lying electronic states of these radicals. It is not necessary to assume a successive excitation mechanism of these radicals. Finally, it was concluded that, when the excited butyls decompose, the lighter fragments formed (such as methyls) are "hot."

RECEIVED: December 29, 1959

REFERENCES

1. Reported by M. FOURCROY, Sur trois espèces différentes de gaz hydrogène carboné, retirées de l'éther et de l'alcool par différens procédés. *Ann. chim. Paris* [1] **21,** 48–71 (1797).

2. S. C. LIND, The theory of chemical action in electrical discharge. *Trans. Am. Elec. Soc.* **53,** 25–34 (1928).
3. R. W. LUNT and K. G. EMELÉUS, Chemical reaction in ionized gases. *Nature* **137,** 404 (1936).
4. R. W. LUNT, Chemical reaction in electrical discharges. *Trans. Faraday Soc.* **32,** 1691–1700 (1936).
5. B. W. BRADFORD and G. I. FINCH, The mechanism of ignition by electric discharges. *Chem. Revs.* **21,** 221–244 (1937).
6. H. WIENER and M. BURTON, Decomposition of methane in an electrical discharge. *J. Am. Chem. Soc.* **75,** 5815–5823 (1953).
7. M. P. REDDY and M. BURTON, Decomposition of ethylene in an electric discharge. *J. Am. Chem. Soc.* **79,** 813–820 (1957).
8. J. STURM, Decomposition of ethane in an electric discharge. Thesis, University of Notre Dame, 1956.
9. M. BURTON and J. L. MAGEE, Successive excitation by low-energy electrons: General principle. *J. Chem. Phys.* **23,** 2194–2195 (1955).
10. M. BURTON and J. L. MAGEE, Successive excitation by low-energy electrons: Application to electric discharge in methane. *J. Chem. Phys.* **23,** 2195–2196 (1955).
11. O. A. SCHAEFFER and S. O. THOMPSON, The role of ions in the radiation induced exchange of hydrogen and deuterium. *J. Am. Chem. Soc.* **80,** 553–558 (1958).
12. G. G. MEISELS, W. H. HAMILL, and R. R. WILLIAMS, JR., The radiation chemistry of methane. *J. Phys. Chem.* **61,** 1456–1461 (1957).
13. D. P. STEVENSON and D. O. SCHISSLER, Rate of the gaseous reactions, $X^+ + YH = XH^+ + Y$. *J. Chem. Phys.* **23,** 1353–1354 (1955).
14. L. M. DORFMAN, Radiolysis of ethane: Isotopic and scavenger studies. *J. Phys. Chem.* **62,** 29–33 (1958).
15. F. L. MOHLER, V. H. DIBELER, L. WILLIAMSON, and H. DEAN, Mass spectra of deuteroacetylenes, monodeuterobenzene, and deuteronaphthalenes. *J. Research Natl. Bur. Standards* **48,** 188–192 (1952).
16. V. H. DIBELER, F. L. MOHLER, and M. DE HEMPTINNE, Mass spectra of the deuteroethylenes. *J. Research Natl. Bur. Standards* **53,** 107–111 (1954).
17. Catalog of Mass Spectral Data, American Petroleum Institute Research Project 44, Carnegie Institute of Technology, Pittsburgh, Pennsylvania, August 31, 1950, Serial Nos. 444, 456, 457, 458.
18. J. R. MCNESBY and A. S. GORDON, Photolysis of acetone. *J. Am. Chem. Soc.* **76,** 1416–1418 (1954).
19. D. J. LEROY, An apparatus for the low temperature fractionation of small gas samples. *Can. J. Research* **B28,** 492–499 (1950).
20. A. VON ENGEL, R. SEELIGER, and M. STEENBECK, Über die Glimmentladung bei hohen Drucken. *Z. Physik* **85,** 144–160 (1933).
21. N. A. GAMBLING and H. EDELS, High pressure glow discharge in air. *Brit. J. Appl. Phys.* **5,** 36–39 (1954).
22. G. FRANCIS, *Handbuch der Physik* (S. Flügge, ed.), Vol. XXII, 2nd ed., pp. 193–194, Springer, Berlin, 1956.
23. A. VON ENGEL, *Ionized Gases*, p. 209, Oxford University Press, Oxford, 1955.
24. Reference *22*, pp. 70–82.
25. J. D. COBINE, *Gaseous Conductors*, p. 217, McGraw-Hill Book Company, New York, 1941.
26. R. M. CHAUDHRI, Distribution of energy among the cathode rays of a glow discharge. *Nature* **148,** 727–728 (1941).
27. Reference *22*, p. 93.
28. W. JOST, *Diffusion in Solids, Liquids, Gases*, p. 25, Academic Press, New York, 1952.

29. L. B. Loeb, *Basic Processes of Gaseous Electronics*, p. 269, University of California Press, Berkeley, California, 1955.
30. N. E. Bradbury and R. A. Nielsen, Absolute values of the electron mobility in helium, *Phys. Rev.* **49,** 388–393 (1936); R. A. Nielsen and N. E. Bradbury, Electron and negative ion mobilities in oxygen, air, nitrous oxide and ammonia. *Ibid.* **51,** 69–75 (1937); R. A. Nielsen, Absolute values of the electron drift velocity in nitrogen, helium, neon and argon. *Ibid.* **50,** 950–954 (1936).
31. E. J. Lauer, Mechanisms of positive and negative corona in hydrogen and argon between coaxial cylindrical electrodes over an extended pressure range. *J. Appl. Phys.* **23,** 300–307 (1952).
32. T. R. Holstein, Energy distribution of electrons in high frequency gas discharges. *Phys. Rev.* **70,** 367–384 (1946).
33. D. Barbiere, Energy distribution, drift velocity and temperature of slow electrons in helium and argon. *Phys. Rev.* **84,** 653–658 (1951).
34. R. W. Ditchburn, Absorption cross sections in the vacuum-ultraviolet. III. Methane. *Proc. Roy. Soc.* **A229,** 44–62 (1955).
35. P. M. Morse, W. P. Allis, and E. S. Lamar, Velocity distributions for elastically colliding electrons. *Phys. Rev.* **48,** 412–419 (1935).
36. H. S. W. Massey and E. H. S. Burhop, *Electronic and Ionic Impact Phenomena*, p. 279, Oxford University Press, New York, 1952.
37. V. E. Brüche, Wirkungsquerschnitt und Molekelbau in der Kohlen wasserstaffreike: CH_4-C_2H_6-C_3H_8-C_4H_{10}, *Ann. Physik* **396,** 387–408 (1930).
38. A. F. Trotman-Dickenson, The reactions of methyl radicals. *Quart. Rev.* **7,** 198–220 (1953).
39. F. O. Rice and R. E. Varnerin, Activation energies of reactions of methyl radicals with organic molecules. *J. Am. Chem. Soc.* **77,** 221–224 (1955).
40. F. O. Rice and T. A. Vanderslice, The relative activation energies of removal of primary, secondary and tertiary hydrogen atoms by methyl radicals. *J. Am. Chem. Soc.* **80,** 291–293 (1958).
41. S. C. Lind and G. Glockler. IV. The chemical effects of electrical discharge in butane. Fractionation of the liquid products. *J. Am. Chem. Soc.* **51,** 3655–3660 (1929).
42. A. Kuppermann, Decomposition of *n*-butane in an electric discharge. Thesis, University of Notre Dame, 1955.

RADIATION RESEARCH **10**, 655–663 (1959)

Radiation-Induced Reactions in the N_2-O_2-H_2O System[1,2]

A. RUSSELL JONES

Oak Ridge National Laboratory, Oak Ridge, Tennessee

INTRODUCTION

Nitric acid was found to be the major initial product when moist air was subjected to electron bombardment.[3] It was formed in amount stoichiometrically equivalent to the hydrogen of the water initially present and then disappeared on continued irradiation, re-forming water and producing a stoichiometric amount of nitrogen dioxide. Both formation and destruction were linear functions of the energy input. This behavior was noted as a by-product of investigation of solid-gas reactions (*1*). Since the phenomenon had not been previously reported, some further work was done.[3]

Soddy (*2*) reported that the collection of pure radon by condensation at low temperature was impossible if air was present, owing to the simultaneous condensation of nitrous oxide. Lind and Bardwell (*3*) found that ozone and acid-forming oxides of nitrogen were simultaneously formed along with a smaller amount of nitrous oxide when air in a flow system was exposed to α-rays. Cloetens (*4*) manometrically monitored mixtures of nitrogen, oxygen, and radon: the pressure decreased, then partially recovered, and finally decreased monotonically. Pshezhetsky and his collaborators (*5–8*) demonstrated that the yields of nitrogen oxides were very nearly equal for electrons and gamma rays absorbed in liquid air and in air at room temperature.

[1] Based on a paper presented before the annual meeting of the Radiation Research Society, Pittsburgh, May 10–20, 1959, as part of the Symposium on Radiation Chemistry of Gases in honor of Dr. S. C. Lind on the occasion of his eightieth birthday. The Symposium was organized by Dr. Leon M. Dorfman, and he and Dr. A. O. Allen served as chairmen of the sessions.

[2] Work performed for the U. S. Atomic Energy Commission at the Oak Ridge National Laboratory, Oak Ridge, Tennessee, operated by Union Carbide Corporation.

[3] Initial measurements were made in collaboration with Dr. R. H. Johnsen, summer employee in 1957 on leave from Florida State University, Tallahassee, Florida, and a preliminary report was given to the Nuclear Technology Symposium, American Chemical Society Meeting San Francisco, April 18, 1958: A. R. Jones and R. H. Johnsen, Chemical features of the fixation of nitrogen by irradiation of moist air.

The corrosion of metals in the presence of water vapor in Argonne's CP-3 heavy-water reactor led to a number of studies (*9–13*), the conclusions of which were that nitrogen and oxygen combined in the gas phase to produce a low equilibrium concentration of nitrogen oxides when exposed to reactor radiation. However, if water vapor and a metal which could react with nitric acid were present, fixation of nitrogen continued. Similar studies by the British (*14*) indicated that nitrate ion production in the nitrogen-oxygen-water system was independent of oxygen concentration. The fixation of nitrogen by the action of reactor radiations on air has been discussed by both Russian (*15*) and American (*16*) authors, with the latter stating that ordinary dry air provided the highest yields of nitrogenous compounds.

Thus the radiation chemistry of air is of practical interest because the corrosive effects of the products influence the design and operation of nuclear reactors, and because the oxidation of nitrogen under the action of ionizing radiation is one of the possible effective methods of utilizing atomic energy for bringing about chemical synthesis. In addition, the availability of the system and its initial simplicity have caused it to be the subject of many studies of the relations between primary activation processes (by heat, light, electrical discharge, and ionizing radiation) and subsequent chemical reactions.

EXPERIMENTAL PROCEDURE

The experiments were performed in a gold-plated brass cell (Fig. 1) which contained a 380-ml cavity of oval cross section, 10 cm in length. The gaseous contents were irradiated with a 100-μa beam of 1.0-Mev electrons which was admitted

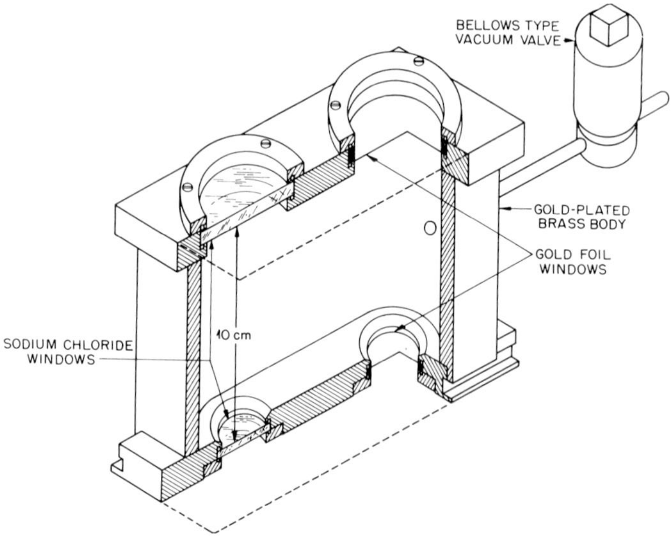

FIG. 1. Cell for electron irradiation and infrared analysis of gas mixtures.

through a 2-mil gold-foil window. The exposure was periodically interrupted, and the progress of chemical change within the system was analyzed by infrared spectrophotometry over the 4000 to 650-cm^{-1} region through a pair of sodium chloride windows sealed to the cell. For analytical comparison, absorbance-partial pressure curves were made for the substances of interest (with the cell brought to atmospheric pressure with Drierite-dried air). Attempts were made to determine the water vapor content of the system in some experiments by mass spectrometric analysis after irradiation.

A duplicate cell on which was mounted a strain-type pressure pickup was irradiated under the same conditions, and the pressure change caused by the radiation-induced formation of water from a stoichiometric mixture of hydrogen and oxygen in the presence of a drying agent (fused KOH) was used to determine the dose rate. This dosimeter requires acceptance of the ion-pair yield of 3.9 determined by Lind (*17*) for the same system admixed with radon in a glass vessel in the presence of mercury vapor. The dose rate was calculated to be 1.73×10^{20} ev/min for the air system.

RESULTS

In the presence of water vapor, the electron bombardment of moist air produced nitric acid at a rate linear with dose and independent of the concentration of water vapor up to 11 mm, the highest concentration which could be examined with sodium chloride windows in the cell. The data are summarized in Fig. 2 for a number of concentrations of water vapor, and in Fig. 3, where the relationships for all the products are indicated. At the concentration of nitric acid equal to the maximum permissible concentration as calculated stoichiometrically for the hydrogen present in the initial amount of water, the nitric acid began to disappear under continued irradiation and continued to disappear linearly with dose. During the disappearance of the nitric acid, a stoichiometric amount of nitrogen dioxide was produced with the same G yield. Subsequent to the decomposition of the nitric acid, nitrogen dioxide was produced at a lower rate, and one which decreased slightly with dose, apparently asymptotically approaching a limiting G value (Fig. 3). Although the presence subsequent to the decomposition of the nitric acid of a substantial fraction of the initial concentration of water was established by mass spectrometry, the results were quite erratic.

The other major product of the irradiation of moist air was nitrous oxide, which was produced at a rate independent of water vapor concentration over the experimental range. The 100-ev yield decreased with dose, apparently asymptotically approaching a limiting value (Figs. 3 and 4). In addition to selective infrared absorption caused by the major products, some absorption bands were observed which appeared to be caused by intermediates whose concentrations remained too low for quantitative determination (Fig. 3). Ozone was rapidly formed and apparently disappeared just before the nitric acid concentration reached maximum. In experi-

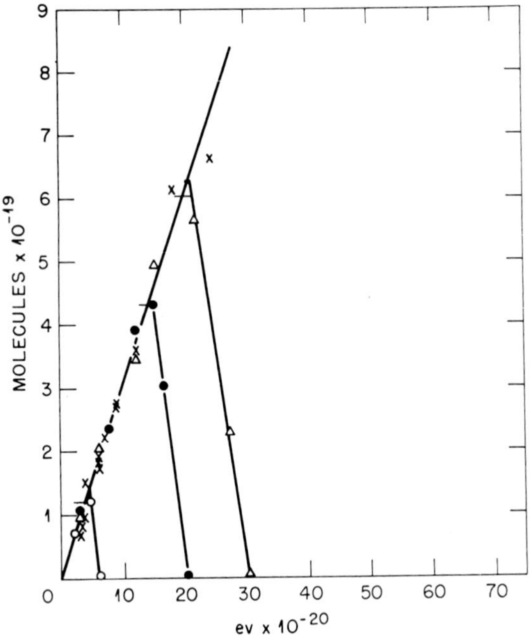

FIG. 2. Production and destruction of nitric acid from air as a function of dose. All data are included for experiments in which the partial pressure of water varied from 0.25 to 2.5 mm. Above that pressure aqueous-nitric acid precipitated within the cell at room temperature. Short horizontal lines represent the calculated maximum HNO_3 for three experiments for which disappearance is shown.

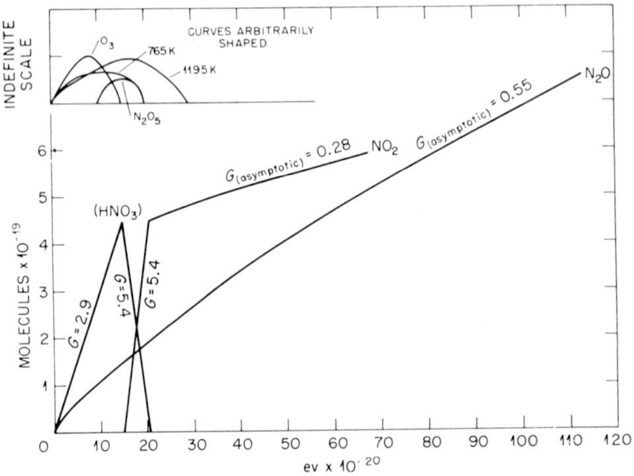

FIG. 3. Chemical production as a function of dose for a typical experiment.

ments with low concentrations of water, nitrogen pentoxide appeared momentarily just before all of the water was used up.

When nitrogen dioxide was added to moist air before irradiation, no nitric acid or nitrogen pentoxide appeared. Instead (Fig. 5), more nitrogen dioxide was formed at a nearly linear rate—the same as obtained after the nitric acid decomposed in the previous experiments. When fresh moist air was added to an irradiated system which had not yet reached its calculated maximum nitric acid concentration, the maximum reached was an amount of nitric acid stoichiometrically equal to that calculated from the sum of the amounts of water added. When fresh moist air was

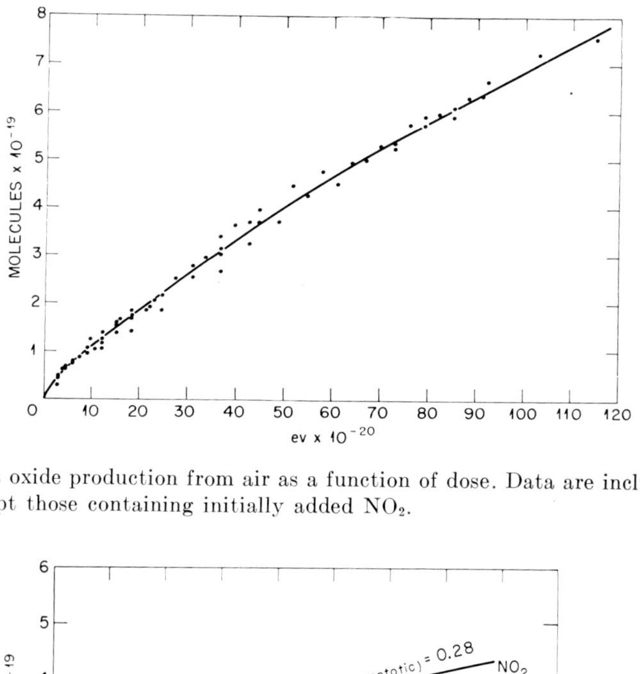

FIG. 4. Nitrous oxide production from air as a function of dose. Data are included for all experiments except those containing initially added NO_2.

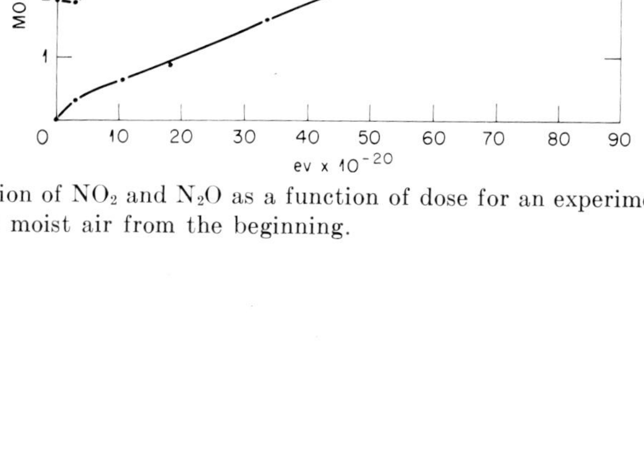

FIG. 5. Production of NO_2 and N_2O as a function of dose for an experiment with nitrogen dioxide present in moist air from the beginning.

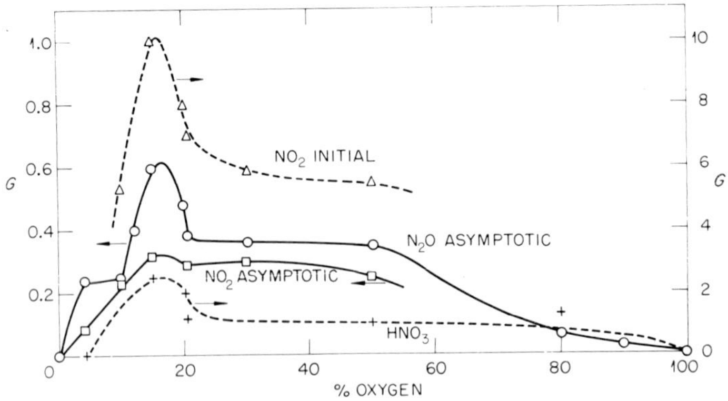

FIG. 6. G values as a function of oxygen concentration.

TABLE I

G VALUES AS A FUNCTION OF OXYGEN CONCENTRATION

Figures	O_2 (%)	G_{N_2O} (*asymptotic*)	G_{HNO_3} (*production*)	G_{HNO_3} (*destruction*)	G_{NO_2} (*initial*)	G_{NO_2} (*asymptotic*)
—	0	0	0	0	0	0
1	4.2	0.24	0	0	0	0.08
2	10.0	0.25	1.50	−5.3	5.3	0.22
3	12.4	0.40	—	—	—	—
4	15.4	0.60	2.25	−10.0	10.0	0.32
5	20.1	0.48	2.00	−8.0	8.0	—
6	Air	0.38	1.20	−7.0	7.0	0.29
7	30.3	0.36	1.10	−5.9	5.9	0.30
8	50.2	0.35	1.04	−5.5	5.5	0.25
9	80.0	0.065	1.37	—	—	—
10	90.2	0.03	0.58	—	—	—
—	100.0	0	0	0	0	0

added to an irradiated system in which the nitric acid had completely decomposed, its effect was unnoticeable spectrophotometrically when the irradiation was resumed: nitrous oxide and nitrogen dioxide continued to form at their asymptotic rates.

When powdered sodium chloride was added to the cell, its presence had no effect on the G values of the products after the surface was conditioned in the same manner as the sodium chloride window surface by exposure to air and radiation (*1*). However, the presence of excess gold surface (as gold foil) within the cell greatly decreased the yield of nitric acid. The rate of production of nitrous oxide did not appear to be affected. No nitrogen dioxide, nitrogen pentoxide, or ozone was perceptible. A partial coverage of the gold cell wall with a nonvolatile hydrocarbon grease (to simulate an increase in the minute amount of rubber gasket material exposed within the cell) effectively prevented the formation of ozone and nitrogen oxides other than nitrous oxide, the rate of production of which was not affected. Rapid formation of carbon dioxide occurred.

A series of moist nitrogen-oxygen mixtures, wherein the ratio of nitrogen to oxygen was varied although the total pressure was atmospheric, was irradiated, and the experimental results are presented in Table I and Fig. 6. Trace amounts of water, probably less than 0.3 mole %, were present in all runs. The only chemical change noted when moist oxygen was irradiated was the formation of a slight amount of ozone. With moist nitrogen, there was no indication of any change on irradiation. In none of these experiments were any of the following compounds observed: ammonia, nitrogen pentoxide, nitric oxide, nitrous acid, hydrogen peroxide.

DISCUSSION

The marked dependence on oxygen concentration of the G values for the production of nitrous oxide, the production of nitric acid, the subsequent destruction of nitric acid, the initial production of nitrogen dioxide, and the asymptotic production of nitrogen dioxide are clearly shown. Each of the G's reached a maximum value at about 15% oxygen content. All data on the effect of varying the nitrogen-oxygen ratio were collected without disturbance of the interior surface of the cell. During each such period, the G values obtained were quite reproducible. The fact that all the G values listed above peak at about 15% oxygen indicates that the percentage of oxygen present in the system is probably the dominant factor in the change of G values in this region.

At low oxygen concentrations it was found that inhibition of the production of nitric acid was more sensitive to the presence of minute traces of nitrogen dioxide than was the case at higher oxygen ratios. This, and the inhibiting effects of organic material and of additional gold surface (a catalyst for oxygen atom recombination),[4] indicates the importance of the radiation products of oxygen.

The lack of chemical change noted when moist nitrogen was irradiated seems to refute the claim (*14*) that nitrate production in the nitrogen-oxygen-water system is independent of oxygen concentration. It is probable that in the British experiments a sufficient amount of water was decomposed to furnish the necessary oxygen.

Since both the production and destruction of nitric acid are apparently noncompetitive processes, they would seem to involve different intermediates. The disappearance of ozone from the system at the moment nitric acid begins to break down, the inhibiting effects of nitrogen dioxide, excess gold surface, and organic material make reasonable the assumption that the radiation-produced reagent leading to the formation of nitric acid is ozone, and the destructive agent is some

[4] Private communication from P. Harteck.

nitrogen-containing product of the action of radiation on nitrogen dioxide. The assumption also follows from the lowered fixation yield after the nitric acid cycle—that is, the lower fixation yield in the presence of nitrogen dioxide, which, in conjunction with the fact that the same initial species are produced by the impingement of high-voltage electrons on the system throughout the experiment, indicates that the initial intermediate containing nitrogen reacts with nitrogen dioxide to produce nitrogen molecules, or that nitrogen dioxide disturbs the formation of the long-lived nitrogen-containing intermediate during the secondary stages of the primary process—as by absorption of subexcitation electrons, negative ion formation, or reaction with a precursor of the long-lived nitrogen-containing intermediate.

There seems no reason to doubt that the gas phase reactions for the nitrogen-oxygen system under the influence of radiation as tabulated by Harteck and Dondes (*16*) include the intermediates responsible for the formation and destruction of nitric acid, and the problem is to discover in what manner water molecules interfere temporarily with the interaction of the agents to produce NO_2.

Experiments with electron bombardment at controlled voltages (*6–8*) have confirmed earlier work of a similar nature (*18*); the formation of nitrogen oxides appears to begin when the electrons are sufficiently accelerated to be able to ionize the nitrogen molecules, and the rate of formation is increased when the accelerating potential reaches the value corresponding to the formation of atoms and atomic ions of nitrogen. Since there are no corresponding rate changes at the critical potentials of oxygen, it could be concluded that only atomic or molecular ions of nitrogen actively participate in the formation. However, the production of nitrogen oxides has been explained[4] (*16*) purely as a consequence of the interaction of neutral species.

To this author it appears that at this time there is no method for differentiating the actions of ions and of neutral species in this system and that the reactions probably proceed by many paths.

SUMMARY

The exposure of moist nitrogen-oxygen mixtures to electron bombardment was shown to lead directly to the formation of nitric acid and nitrous oxide. After complete exhaustion of the water, the nitric acid disappeared with the formation of water and a stoichiometric amount of nitrogen dioxide. Subsequent to the decomposition of the nitric acid, nitrogen dioxide was produced at a much lower rate, and the total nitrogen fixation yield was decreased. The production and destruction of nitric acid were linear functions of the energy input, as was the formation of nitrogen dioxide from the nitric acid. There was a marked dependence of the G values for all these chemical changes on the oxygen concentration, with maximum values reached in every case at about 15 mole % oxygen.

[5] Students of the Massachusetts Institute of Technology Engineering Practice School at the Oak Ridge National Laboratory.

ACKNOWLEDGMENTS

The author is indebted to Dr. C. J. Hochanadel, Dr. R. L. Platzman, Dr. S. C. Lind, Dr. P. S. Rudolph, and Dr. R. H. Johnsen for their suggestions and criticism; and to the latter and to G. R. Seiler[5] and E. C. Hansen[5] for their help in collecting the data.

RECEIVED: December 17, 1958.

REFERENCES

1. A. R. JONES, Radiation-induced reactions of potassium bromide with air. *Science* **127,** 234 (1958).
2. F. SODDY, Radioactivity. *Ann. Rept. Chem. Soc.* **8,** 269–301 (1911).
3. S. C. LIND and D. C. BARDWELL, Ozonization and interaction of oxygen with nitrogen under alpha radiation. *J. Am. Chem. Soc.* **51,** 2751–2758 (1929).
4. R. CLOETENS, Action des particules alpha sur les melanges d'azote et d'oxygene. *Bull. soc. chim. Belges* **45,** 97–112 (1935).
5. S. YA. PSHEZHETSKY, I. A. MYAZNIKOV, and N. A. BUNEEV, Formation of ozone in liquid oxygen under the action of fast electrons. *Collection Papers Radiation Chem., Publ. Acad. Sci.U.S.S.R.* 133–141 (1955).
6. S. YA. PSHEZHETSKY and M. T. DMITRIEV, Kinetics of nitrogen oxidation induced by electron bombardment. *Doklady Acad. Nauk U.S.S.R.* **103,** 647–650 (1955).
7. S. YA. PSHEZHETSKY, Some regularities of the mechanism and kinetics of simple radiation-chemical reactions. *Conf. Acad. Sci. U.S.S.R. Peaceful Uses Atomic Energy, Publ. Acad. Sci. U.S.S.R.* Division of Chemical Sciences, pp. 64–78 (1955).
8. M. T. DMITRIEV and S. YA. PSHEZHETSKY, Kinetics and mechanism of the oxidation of nitrogen under electron impact. *All-Union Conf. Appl. Radioactive Stable Isotopes and Radiation Nat'l. Econ. and Sci. Publ. Acad. Sci. U.S.S.R.* Division of Chemical Sciences (1957). (Abstract in translation in AEC-Tr-2925, pp. 4–5.)
9. A. O. ALLEN and S. GORDON, Formation of acid in heavy water pile moderator. University of Chicago Metallurgical Laboratory Report CC-3412 (1945).
10. A. O. ALLEN, T. W. DAVIS, and C. J. HOCHANADEL, Fixation of nitrogen by pile radiation and acid formation in the argonne pile. Oak Ridge National Laboratory Report ORNL-Mon-C-390 (1947).
11. W. H. MCCORKLE, Heavy water in nuclear reactors. *Nucleonics* **11,** No. 5, 21–25 (1953).
12. W. PRIMAK and L. H. FUCHS, Transportation of matter and radioactivity by ionized air corrosion. *Phys. Today* **7,** No. 9, 15–16 (1954).
13. W. PRIMAK and L. H. FUCHS, Nitrogen fixation in a nuclear reactor. *Nucleonics* **13,** No. 3, 38–41 (1955).
14. J. WRIGHT, J. K. LINACRE, W. R. MARSH, and T. H. BATES, Effect of radiation on heterogeneous systems of air or nitrogen and water. *Proc. 1st Intern. Conf. Peaceful Uses Atomic Energy, Geneva, 1955,* **7,** 560–563 (1956).
15. V. I. VESELOVSKY, Radiation-chemical processes in inorganic systems. *Proc. 1st Intern. Conf. Peaceful Uses Atomic Energy, Geneva, 1955,* **7,** 599–609 (1956).
16. P. HARTECK and S. DONDES, Producing chemicals with reactor radiations. *Nucleonics* **14,** No. 7, 22–25 (1956).
17. S. C. LIND, Chemical action produced by radium emanation, I. *J. Am. Chem. Soc.* **41,** 531–551 (1919).
18. O. H. WANSBROUGH-JONES, The interaction of oxygen with nitrogen after collision with electrons. *Proc. Roy. Soc.* **A127,** 511–529 (1930).

RADIATION RESEARCH **10**, 644–670 (1959)

Ion-Molecule Reactions of Methyl and Ethyl Iodides[1,2]

R. F. POTTIE, R. BARKER, AND W. H. HAMILL[3]

Department of Chemistry, University of Notre Dame, Notre Dame, Indiana

INTRODUCTION

The relevance of mass spectrometry to the study of chemical reactions between ions and molecules was recognized twenty years ago by Glockler and Lind (*1*). Recent studies have been concerned mostly with hydrocarbons. Reactions of halogen-containing compounds which have been reported so far involve only the hydrogen halides. Examples are

$$HX^+ + HX \rightarrow H_2X^+ + X \tag{1}$$

where X is Cl or Br (*2*), and the analogous reaction (*3*)

$$HCl^+ + CH_4 \rightarrow H_2Cl^+ + CH_3 \tag{2}$$

We find that methyl and ethyl iodides react similarly, forming ions of the types R_2I^+ and RHI^+, where R is CH_3 or C_2H_5. Other reactions of less clearly defined types have also been found.

EXPERIMENTAL PROCEDURE

The instrument used was a CEC Model 21-103A mass spectrometer, modified so that both ionizing and repeller voltages could be measured with a potentiometer. Further modification enabled ionizing voltages to be set to a minimum of 5.4 volts and magnetic scanning to be carried out over several mass units.

Appearance potentials were determined by vanishing current methods, both the extrapolated difference method of Warren (*4*) and the initial logarithmic method of Lossing (*5*) being employed. In some instances where secondary ion intensities at maximum pressure were very low, appearance potentials were estimated by linear

[1] Based on a paper presented before the annual meeting of the Radiation Research Society, Pittsburgh, May 18–20, 1959, as part of the Symposium on Radiation Chemistry of Gases in honor of Dr. S. C. Lind on the occasion of his eightieth birthday. The Symposium was organized by Dr. Leon M. Dorfman, and he and Dr. A. O. Allen served as chairmen of the sessions.

[2] Contribution from the Radiation Project operated by the University of Notre Dame and supported in part under U. S. Atomic Energy Commission Contract AT-(11-1)-38.

[3] Correspondence and requests for reprints should be sent to Professor Hamill.

extrapolation. The voltage scale was calibrated either from the appearance potential, A, of the primary ion or from that of an added standard.

Secondary ions were characterized by the linear dependence of ion current on the square of the inlet pressure and also by the decrease of ion current with increasing repeller field strength.[4] Appearance potential measurements of both primary and secondary ions assist in establishing their genetic relationship, since it is expected, and commonly observed, that $A(S^+) = A(P^+)$ for

$$P^+ + M = S^+ + N \tag{3}$$

That is to say, primary ions are assumed to react in their ground states.

The cross section, σ, for reaction 3 is given by the following equation (*6*):

$$\sigma = \frac{I_{S^+}}{I_{P^+}} \frac{1}{dC_M}$$

where I is ion current, C_M is concentration of molecules M in the ionization chamber, and d is the distance from the center of the electron beam to the exit slit (1.31 mm).

Values of C_M are directly proportional to the partial pressure of M in the inlet storage bulb. The proportionality constant was established by measuring the saturation ion current, I_+, to the negatively biased repeller plate of the ionization chamber (*6*). It is expected that

$$I_+ = QI_elC_M \tag{4}$$

where Q is the cross section for ionization, I_e is the electron current, l is the length of the electron path, and C_M is the concentration of molecules. As a test of our experimental arrangement, ion current versus reservoir pressure was measured for argon, krypton, hydrogen, methane, cyclopropane, and neopentane at 70-volt ionizing voltage and 10-μa ionizing current. With $Q = 3.52 \times 10^{-16}$ cm^2 for argon, our values of Q agree adequately with previously reported values (*7*, *8*). From the mean values of $K = C_M/$(reservoir pressure) at each of several pressures up to 400 μ, we find $K = 1.67 \times 10^{10}$ molecules cc^{-1} μ^{-1} with a very small upward trend at the higher pressures.

Sensitivities for primary ions have been found constant up to rather high pressures. Thus, at 70-volt ionizing voltage and 40-volt cm^{-1} repeller field strength, the ion intensities at $m/e = 14$, 14.5, and 15 for 4 to 418 μ of ethane are quite linear with reservoir pressure.

[4] It is, of course, established that secondary ion current varies as the inverse square root of the repeller field strength. In practice, under our experimental conditions, the applied repeller voltage does not adequately describe the effective field within the ionization chamber for small values. Diminishing ion current establishes the useful upper limit of repeller field strength. The useful domain between these limits (ca. 10 to 40 volt cm^{-1}) is often insufficient for a fully quantitative test.

TABLE I

APPEARANCE POTENTIALS OF IONS FROM METHYL IODIDE

Primary ions	A (ev) This work	A (ev) Reported	Secondary ions	A (ev)
CH_3I^+	(9.55)	9.6[b]	$C_2H_6I^+$	9.5 ± 0.2
HI^+	11.1 ± 0.4		$CH_3I_2^+$	11.2 ± 0.1
I^+	13.1 ± 0.2	12.9[b]	I_2^+	13.0 ± 0.2
CH_2I^+	13.2 ± 0.2		CHI_2^+	14.3 ± 0.2
CHI^+	14.1 ± 0.2		CI_2^+	18.4[a]
CI^+	17.5 ± 0.2; 17.9[a]			

[a] Except for these two measurements obtained by linear extrapolation, the vanishing current method was used.

[b] From reference *9*.

Under normal operating conditions peaks differing by a single mass unit cannot be adequately resolved at m/e in excess of 200. The metastable suppressor overcomes this difficulty although greatly reducing the ion current. Assignment of m/e in the region 150 to 280 is facilitated by the fact of a linear dependence of m/e versus distance from a reference peak on the chart. At high m/e the graphical dependence was nonlinear but smooth, requiring several mass standards. Substances chosen for this purpose and their molecular masses were: methylene iodide 268; trimethylene iodide 296; tetramethylene iodide 310; hexamethylene iodide 338; 1,1,2-tribromopropane 278, 280, 282, 284. The diiodides gave only one significant peak in the region of interest, that corresponding to the molecular mass. The four isotopic molecular masses of tribromopropane were particularly useful for identifying the ion from ethyl iodide at $m/e = 283$.

RESULTS

Methyl iodide. Secondary ions were observed in the mass spectrum of methyl iodide at m/e values of 157, 254, 266, 267, and 269, which correspond to $C_2H_6I^+$, I_2^+, CI_2^+, CHI_2^+, and $CH_3I_2^+$, respectively. Both repeller field strength and pressure dependence were characteristic of ion-molecule reactions. Appearance potentials for both primary and secondary ions appear in Table I. The following processes are indicated.

$$CH_3I^+ + CH_3I \rightarrow C_2H_6I^+ + I \quad (5)$$

$$I^+ + CH_3I \rightarrow I_2^+ + CH_3 \quad (6)$$

or

$$CH_2I^+ + CH_3I \rightarrow I_2^+ + C_2H_5 \quad (7)$$

$$CI^+ + CH_3I \rightarrow CI_2^+ + CH_3 \quad (8)$$

$$CHI^+ + CH_3I \rightarrow CHI_2^+ + CH_3 \quad (9)$$

$$HI^+ + CH_3I \rightarrow CH_3I_2^+ + H \quad (10)$$

Appearance potential data are incapable of distinguishing between reactions 6 and 7. Neither is it possible to decide on the basis of the energetics.[5] From the appearance potential for CH_2I^+ in Table I we obtain $\Delta H_f(CH_2I^+) = 257$ kcal mole^{-1}. The heats of reactions 6 and 7 are -7 kcal and -4 kcal, respectively, so that neither can be eliminated on the ground of endothermicity. As a final test, the ionization efficiency curves for primary and secondary ions must be superposable, with use of an appropriate scale factor (*6*). Both ions meet this requirement equally well over a wide range of ionizing voltages, and it is therefore impossible to decide between them.

Ethyl iodide. Secondary ions were found at values of m/e equal to 185, 254, 255, 266, 267, 269, 283, and 312. Appearance potentials of all significant primary ions containing iodine and of all secondary ions are listed in Table II with the exception of CI_2^+, which could not be measured owing to its low intensity and its proximity to the abundant CHI_2^+ ion.

From these results we conclude that the following reactions occur:

$$C_2H_5I^+ + C_2H_5I \rightarrow C_4H_{10}I^+ + I \quad (11)$$

$$C_2H_5I^+ + C_2H_5I \rightarrow C_4H_{10}I_2^+ \quad (12)$$

$$HI^+ + C_2H_5I \rightarrow C_2H_5I_2^+ + H \quad (13)$$

$$CH_2I^+ + C_2H_5I \rightarrow CH_3I_2^+ + C_2H_4 \quad (14)$$

$$CHI^+ + C_2H_5I \rightarrow CHI_2^+ + C_2H_5 \quad (15)$$

$$CI^+ + C_2H_5I \rightarrow CI_2^+ + C_2H_5 \quad (16)^5$$

$$I^+ + C_2H_5I \rightarrow HI_2^+ + C_2H_4 \quad (17)$$

$$HI^+ + C_2H_5I \rightarrow I_2^+ + C_2H_6 \quad (18)$$

In addition to the self-reactions it was found that $C_3H_8I^+$ occurs in a mixture of methyl and ethyl iodides. The proximity of the appearance potentials of methyl iodide (9.55 ev) and ethyl iodide (9.47 ev) precludes the possibility of distinguishing between the following reactions:

$$CH_3I^+ + C_2H_5I \rightarrow C_3H_8I^+ + I \quad (19)$$

$$C_2H_5I^+ + CH_3I \rightarrow C_3H_8I^+ + I \quad (20)$$

[5] Appearance potentials and heats of formation of ions used here are from F. H. Field and J. L. Franklin, *Electron Impact Phenomena and the Properties of Gaseous Ions*, Academic Press, New York, 1957. Other heats of formation employed, in kcal mole^{-1}, are: CH_4, 17.9; C_2H_4, 12.5; C_2H_6, 20.2; CH_3I, 4.5; C_2H_5I, 0.6; H, 52.1; I, 25.5; CH_3, 32.5; C_2H_5, 25.2; C_2H_3, 64.

TABLE II

APPEARANCE POTENTIALS OF IONS FROM ETHYL IODIDE

Primary ions	*A (ev)* *This work*	*A (ev)* *Reported*	*Secondary ions*	*A (ev)*
$C_2H_5I^+$	9.4 ± 0.1	9.6[b]	$C_4H_{10}I^+$	9.4 ± 0.2
HI^+	11.7_5 ± 0.2; 12.4[a]	11.7[b]	$C_4H_{10}I_2^+$	9.5 ± 0.1
CH_2I^+	14.1 ± 0.1	13.7[b]	$C_2H_5I_2^+$	11.5 ± 0.4
I^+	15.1 ± 0.2; 15.9[a]	14.8[b]	I_2^+	11.6 ± 0.4; 12.5[a]
CHI^+	15.7 ± 0.2		$CH_3I_2^+$	14.1 ± 0.2
H_2I^+	17.9 ± 0.5		CHI_2^+	15.2 ± 0.4
CI^+	20.2 ± 0.4		HI_2^+	15.7[a]
			CI_2^+	—

[a] These values were obtained by linear extrapolation.
[b] From reference *10*.

It was also found that adding methane to methyl iodide strongly increased the peak at $m/e = 143$. It is clear that the species CH_4I^+ is being produced, but we have not identified the primary ion. There is no enhancement of the peak at $m/e = 143$ (viz., $C^{13}H_3I$) in methyl iodide alone at high pressure.

Cross sections for the preceding ion-molecule reactions are listed in Table III. Maximum heats of formation, ΔH_f, have been determined for secondary ions on the assumed basis that reactions are thermoneutral. These values are given in the last column of Table III.

Heats of formation of some primary ions. From methyl iodide it was found that $A(I^+) = 13.1$ ev, and if we assign this to process 21 the corresponding $\Delta H_f(I^+) = 274$ kcal is in good agreement with the accepted value of 267 kcal. For ethyl iodide $A(I^+) = 15.1$ ev, but the analogous reaction 22 leads to the impossibly high value of $\Delta H_f(I^+) = 323$ kcal. The best description appears to be given by reaction 23 for which $\Delta H_f(I^+)$ is 264 kcal.

$$CH_3I \rightarrow I^+ + CH_3 + e \quad (21)$$

$$C_2H_5I \rightarrow I^+ + C_2H_5 + e \quad (22)$$

$$C_2H_5I \rightarrow I^+ + CH_4 + CH + e \quad (23)$$

From ethyl iodide $A(HI^+) = 11.7$ ev. If we postulate process 24:

$$C_2H_5I \rightarrow HI^+ + C_2H_4 + e \quad (24)$$

then $\Delta H_f(HI^+) = 257$ kcal mole^{-1}, which compares well with the accepted value of 246 kcal. For methyl iodide the observed $A(HI^+)$ was not satisfactorily reproducible. The measured value of $A(HI^+) = 11.1 \pm 0.4$ ev is much lower than

TABLE III

Cross Sections of Ion-Molecule Reactions of Methyl and Ethyl Iodides

Reaction	$\sigma \times 10^{16}$ cm^2 — *Gradient (volt cm⁻¹)* 4.0	10.0	40	ΔH_f[a] *(sec ion)*
$CH_3I^+ + CH_3I \rightarrow C_2H_6I^+ + I$	5.6	3.4	—	204
$I^+ + CH_3I \rightarrow I_2^+ + CH_3$	14.3	5.3	2.6	239
$CH_2I^+ + CH_3I \rightarrow I_2^+ + C_2H_5$	31.0	12.2	7.1	237
$CI^+ + CH_3I \rightarrow CI_2^+ + CH_3$	58	17.5	5.3	—
$CHI^+ + CH_3I \rightarrow CHI_2^+ + CH_3$	132	36	10.8	—
$HI^+ + CH_3I \rightarrow CH_3I_2^+ + H$	162	51	22.6	199
$HI^+ + C_2H_5I \rightarrow I_2^+ + C_2H_6$	13.5	5.1	4.4	266
$I^+ + C_2H_5I \rightarrow HI_2^+ + C_2H_4$	5.1	2.2	1.3	254
$CHI^+ + C_2H_5I \rightarrow CHI_2^+ + C_2H_5$	343	115	27	—
$CH_2I^+ + C_2H_5I \rightarrow CH_3I_2^+ + C_2H_4$	42.3	11.2	2.6	244
$HI^+ + C_2H_5I \rightarrow C_2H_5I_2^+ + H$	20.0	6.2	3.1	193
$C_2H_5I^+ + C_2H_5I \rightarrow C_4H_{10}I^+ + I$	3.5	1.8	0.6	189
$C_2H_5I^+ + C_2H_5I \rightarrow C_4H_{10}I_2^+$	1.44	0.24	0.04	214
$CI^+ + C_2H_5I \rightarrow CI_2^+ + C_2H_5$	25.5	8.7	2.0	—
$CH_3I^+ + C_2H_5I \rightarrow C_3H_8I^+ + I$				199
or	3	—	—	
$C_2H_5I^+ + CH_3I \rightarrow C_3H_8I^+ + I$				194

[a] Values of ΔH_f represent upper limits and are based on thermoneutrality.

the only previously reported value of 13.2 ± 0.6 ev (*8*). The latter value would be expected from the accepted $\Delta H_f(HI^+)$ if the process is

$$CH_3I \rightarrow CH_2 + HI^+ + e \tag{25}$$

The only process leading to CH_2I^+ from methyl iodide is 26, and the measured $A(CH_2I^+)$ = 13.2 ev. The corresponding value of $\Delta H_f(CH_2I^+)$ is 256 kcal mole⁻¹. Unfortunately none of the possible mechanisms for CH_2I^+ formation from ethyl iodide yields a confirmatory value.

$$CH_3I \rightarrow CH_2I^+ + H + e \tag{26}$$

Of the several possible assignments which can be considered for the formation of CHI^+ from methyl and ethyl iodides, the two following are the most nearly consistent:

$$CH_3I \rightarrow CHI^+ + 2H + e \tag{27}$$

$$C_2H_5I \rightarrow CHI^+ + CH + H + H_2 + e \tag{28}$$

The corresponding values of $\Delta H_f(CHI^+)$, based on the observed appearance potentials, are 227 and 207 kcal mole^{-1}, respectively.

There are also several possible processes leading to CI^+ as well as a considerable uncertainty in the appearance potentials. For methyl iodide the mode of decomposition is very probably 29, leading to $\Delta H_f(CI^+) = 348$ kcal mole^{-1}. For ethyl iodide either of the processes 30 or 31 would be acceptable, since the corresponding values of $\Delta H_f(CI^+)$ are 330 and 354 kcal mole^{-1}, respectively.

$$CH_3I \rightarrow CI^+ + H_2 + H \tag{29}$$

$$C_2H_5I \rightarrow CI^+ + CH_3 + 2H \tag{30}$$

$$C_2H_5I \rightarrow CI^+ + CH_2 + H + H_2 \tag{31}$$

The reaction leading to the formation of $C_4H_{10}I_2^+$, the ionic dimer of ethyl iodide, will be discussed elsewhere (*11*) and is listed in Table III for the sake of completeness.

SUMMARY

Ion-molecule reactions from methyl iodide, ethyl iodide, and their mixture have been observed in the mass spectrometer. Appearance potentials of the important primary ions and of all secondary ions and the reaction cross sections have been measured.

RECEIVED: December 18, 1958

REFERENCES

1. G. GLOCKLER and S. C. LIND, *The Electrochemistry of Gases and Other Dielectrics*, p. 364, John Wiley & Sons, New York, 1939.

2. D. O. SCHISSLER and D. P. STEVENSON, Reactions of gaseous molecule ions with gaseous molecules. II. *J. Chem. Phys.* **24,** 926 (1956).

3. F. H. FIELD and F. W. LAMPE, Reactions of gaseous ions. V. Methane-hydrogen chloride and methane-hydrogen sulfide. *J. Am. Chem. Soc.* **80,** 5583–5587 (1958).

4. J. W. WARREN, Measurement of appearance potentials of ions produced by electron impact using a mass spectrometer. *Nature* **165,** 811 (1950).

5. F. P. LOSSING, A. W. TICKNER, and A. J. BRYCE, The ionization potentials of the deuterated methanes. *J. Chem. Phys.* **19,** 1254 (1951).

6. D. P. STEVENSON and D. O. SCHISSLER, Reactions of gaseous ions with gaseous molecules. IV. Experimental method and results. *J. Chem. Phys.* **29,** 282–294 (1958).

7. F. W. LAMPE, J. L. FRANKLIN, and F. H. FIELD, Cross sections for ionization by electrons. *J. Am. Chem. Soc.* **79,** 6129 (1957).

8. J. W. OTVOS and D. P. STEVENSON, Cross-sections of molecules for ionization by electrons. *J. Am. Chem. Soc.* **78,** 546–552 (1956).

9. H. BRANSON and C. SMITH, Electron impact studies in CH_4, CH_3Cl, CH_3Br, and CH_3I. *J. Am. Chem. Soc.* **75,** 4133–4138 (1953).

10. A. P. IRSA, Electron impact studies on C_2H_5Cl, C_2H_5Br, and C_2H_5I. *J. Chem. Phys.* **26,** 18–22 (1957).

11. R. F. POTTIE and W. H. HAMILL, Persistent ion-molecule collision complexes of organic halides. To be published.

RADIATION RESEARCH 10, 671–679 (1959)

The Exchange of Hydrogen and Deuterium in the Presence of Electrons and Ultraviolet Radiation[1,2]

O. A. SCHAEFFER AND S. O. THOMPSON

Chemistry Department, Brookhaven National Laboratory, Upton, New York

INTRODUCTION

In a previous publication (*1*) it was reported that the radiation-induced exchange of hydrogen and deuterium is an ion chain process. It was found that the ion yield was large 18,000 exchanges per ion pair at 100 mm pressure. The nonradical nature of the reaction was demonstrated by the fact that Kr and Xe have no affect on the thermal and photochemical reaction, but these rare gases even in small amounts practically stop the radiation-induced process.

This work has been extended to a study of the atom and ion reactions occurring simultaneously in the same vessel. It was found possible to obtain information concerning the chain termination of the ion reaction. In addition the present work contains an analysis of the ion chain mechanism from the standpoint of the energetics and measured cross sections of the various interactions between hydrogen and the rare gases and their associated ions. In this way it has been found possible to understand the previously reported moderate inhibition of the ion reaction with additions of any of the rare gases.

EXPERIMENTAL PROCEDURE AND RESULTS

The experimental procedure for the irradiation of H_2-D_2 mixtures where helium was added as a rare gas impurity has been previously described (*1*). The results when large amounts of helium are present are shown in Fig. 1.

To study the effect on H_2-D_2 mixtures when they were simultaneously exposed to electrons and ultraviolet radiations, a cell was constructed as shown in Fig. 2.

[1] Based on a paper presented before the annual meeting of the Radiation Research Society, Pittsburgh, May 10–20, 1959, as part of the Symposium on Radiation Chemistry of Gases in honor of Dr. S. C. Lind on the occasion of his eightieth birthday. The Symposium was organized by Dr. Leon M. Dorfman, and he and Dr. A. O. Allen served as chairmen of the sessions.

[2] Research performed under the auspices of the U. S. Atomic Energy Commission.

The main features of the cell included two sets of windows, ⅛-inch quartz plates and 5 mg/cm^2 mica windows, a small side arm for holding distilled mercury, and a mercury reservoir system. The cell had a gas volume of 90 cc. This arrangement permitted the cell to be thoroughly pumped to a residual pressure of 5×10^{-7} mm

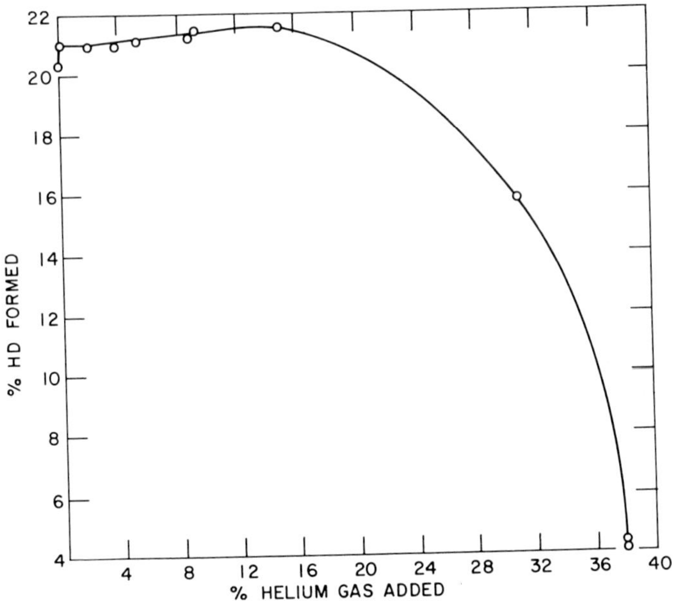

FIG. 1. Radiation-induced exchange in the presence of helium.

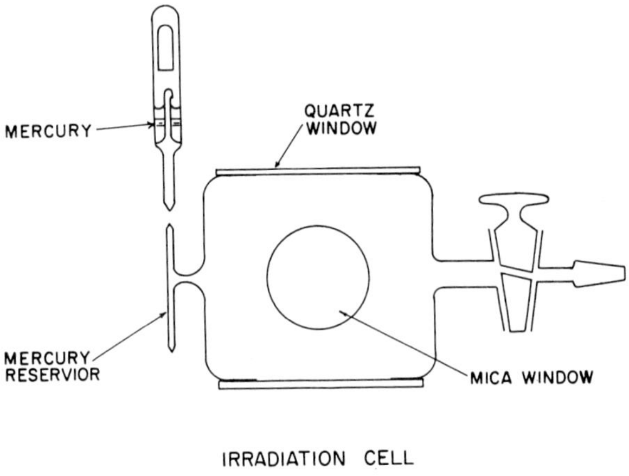

FIG. 2. Cell used for the simultaneous irradiation with ultraviolet and 2-Mev electrons.

TABLE I

EXCHANGE OF H_2 AND D_2 IN THE PRESENCE OF 2-MEV ELECTRONS AND ULTRAVIOLET LIGHT

Experimental conditions	*Conversion to HD (% of mixture)*
Electrons alone	21.6 ± 1.2
Electrons + mercury	14.1 ± 1.8
Electrons + mercury + ultraviolet	10.4 ± 1.7
Mercury + ultraviolet	6.4 ± 0.1
Electrons + mercury + ultraviolet + Xe	6.1 ± 0.1

and allowed the cell to be stabilized by electron irradiation before any mercury was added.

The radiations were 2-Mev electrons produced by a Van de Graaff accelerator and ultraviolet radiation of 2537-A wavelength produced by a low-pressure mercury discharge tube. The sources were arranged so that their beams would enter the cell at right angles and would suffer as little scattering as possible.

The gases used were of the highest purity commercially available. The hydrogen and deuterium were purified by passing through a palladium thimble heated to 700°C. The mixtures of the gases were made manometrically to an accuracy of about 1%.

The procedure for making an irradiation was as follows. The cell was pumped to a residual pressure of 5×10^{-7} mm for 5 to 6 hours and was filled with 100 mm of an equimolar mixture of H_2 and D_2. The cell was placed in a jig for irradiation and was irradiated with electrons until the gas mixture produced reproducible quantities of HD for a given electron dose. It was found necessary to precondition the cell surfaces in this way in order to have reproducible results. For the simultaneous irradiations with electrons and ultraviolet light, mercury was added to the evacuated cell by breaking the breakseal and distilling some droplets into the side arm. The breakseal portion was sealed off and mercury was introduced into the cell itself, then the hydrogen was added.

The irradiation dose time of the cell was standardized to 620 to 630 seconds for both electrons and ultraviolet radiation. The quantity of electrons was 500 μcoulombs; the quantity of photons was constant but was not accurately known.

The irradiated gases were analyzed for H_2, HD, and D_2 with a mass spectrometer. The method and accuracy have been described elsewhere (*1*).

The experimental results are presented in Table I.

DISCUSSION

When hydrogen is irradiated with ionizing radiations, H_2^+ ions are formed predominantly as the initial product of the ionization. However, because of the large cross section for the reaction

$$H_2^+ + H_2 \rightarrow H_3^+ + H$$

the H_2^+ has only a fleeting existence so that most of the positive ionization in hydrogen is rapidly converted to H_3^+. There is some H^+ formed, both initially and as a result of collisions involving repulsive final electronic states. The H_3^+ can then act as a chain carrier to cause an exchange in a mixture of H_2 and D_2 by

$$H_3^+ + D_2 \rightarrow H_2 + HD_2^+$$

By adding the rare gases it is possible to study this relatively simple system and show the importance of ions in gas phase radiation chemistry.

Energetics of the Ion Reactions

When rare gases are added to the irradiated mixture, a number of reactions resulting in hydride ion formation are possible. Table II summarizes most of these reactions and gives a value for the energy in terms of the bond energy of the rare gas hydride ion, $E(RH^+)$, and the energy, X, for the reaction of the rare gas ion and hydrogen. The energy values used for this computation are given in Table III. The second reaction in Table II has been studied in a mass spectrometer (*2*) for Kr, Ar, and Ne. It was shown that this reaction for all the rare gases has a large rate constant with zero heat of activation, and hence all the values of $-X$ must be negative, i.e., exothermic. From this one can say that the bond energy of ArH^+ is greater than 52 kcal, that of KrH^+ is greater than 93 kcal, and that of XeH^+ is greater than 102 kcal.

Reaction 3 has not been observed by Stevenson and Schissler for Ar or Kr, although from an energy standpoint one would clearly expect a reaction. One can conclude from the results that reaction 3 has a lower cross section than reaction 2. In Table III a value for the bond energy of HeH^+ is listed as 54 kcal (*4*). The value was calculated (*5*) by a Wang ionic-polar type of wave function and could easily be in error by the 6 kcal required to make reaction 3 exothermic for helium. If this were the case, then, as the bond energy for NeH^+ would be still larger, reaction 3 would also be possible for neon. Hence, it is likely that reaction 3 can take place for all the rare gases.

We have preliminary confirmation of this in a mass spectrometer study. A Consolidated Nier mass spectrometer was operated with a large H_2 pressure behind the leak. Also it was possible to introduce rare gases into the tube itself. When this was done the H_2^+ peak was relatively independent of the presence of rare gas. However, the H_3^+ peak was severely reduced in intensity by the addition of He, Ar, or Kr. These results[3] suggest that the rare gases are reacting with the H_2^+ and competing with the formation of H_3^+.

[3] We are indebted to Mr. A. P. Irsa for these results.

TABLE II

ION REACTIONS OF THE RARE GASES AND HYDROGEN

Reaction[a]	Helium	Neon	Argon	Krypton	Xenon[b]
1. $RH^+ = R + H^+$ Energy $= E(RH^+)$	$E(HeH^+)$	$E(NeH^+)$	$E(ArH^+) > 52$	$E(KrH^+) > 93$	$E(XeH^+) > 102$
2. $R^+ + H_2 = RH^+ + H$ Energy $= -X_R$	$-X_{He}$ $= -E(HeH^+) - 147$	$-X_{Ne}$ $= -E(NeH^+) - 81$	$-X_{Ar}$ $= -E(ArH^+) + 52$	$-X_{Kr}$ $= -E(KrH^+) + 93$	$-X_{Xe}$ $= -E(XeH^+) + 102$
3. $R + H_2^+ = RH^+ + H$ Energy $= Y_R$	Y_{He} $= 60 - E(HeH^+)$ $= -X_{He} + 207$	Y_{Ne} $= 60 - E(NeH^+)$ $= -X_{Ne} + 141$	Y_{Ar} $= 60 - E(ArH^+)$ $= -X_{Ar} + 8$	Y_{Kr} $= 60 - E(KrH^+)$ $= -X_{Kr} - 33$	Y_{Xe} $= 27 - E(XeH^+)$ $= -X_{Xe} - 42$
4. $R + H_3^+ = RH^+ + H_2$ Energy $= Z_R$	Z_{He} $= 74 - E(HeH^+)$ $= -X_{He} + 221$	Z_{Ne} $= 74 - E(NeH^+)$ $= -X_{Ne} + 155$	Z_{Ar} $= 74 - E(ArH^+)$ $= -X_{Ar} + 22$	Z_{Kr} $= 74 - E(KrH^+)$ $= -X_{Kr} - 19$	Z_{Xe} $= 41 - E(XeH^+)$ $= -X_{Xe} - 61$

[a] R is a rare gas atom.
[b] This value is for $XeH^+ = Xe^+ + H$, as this is for the lowest ionic state of XeH^+.

TABLE III

ENERGY OF ION REACTIONS OF RARE GASES AND HYDROGEN

Reaction	*Energy (kcal/mole)*	*Reference*
$He = He^+ + e$	563	*3*
$Ne = Ne^+ + e$	497	*3*
$Ar = Ar^+ + e$	364	*3*
$Kr = Kr^+ + e$	323	*3*
$Xe = Xe^+ + e$	280	*3*
$H_2 = H_2^+ + e$	356	*3*
$H = H^+ + e$	313	*3*
$H_3^+ = H_2 + H^+$	74	*4*
$HeH^+ = He + H^+$	54	*4*
$H_2 = H + H$	103	*4*

Reaction 4 is exothermic for Kr and Xe, but whether the reaction is endothermic or exothermic for Ar, Ne, and He is not definite. If reaction 3 goes, as seems the case, then the bond energies of ArH^+, NeH^+, and HeH^+ are all larger than 60 kcal. If these bond energies are also smaller than 74 kcal, reaction 4 will not go for Ar, Ne, and He.

Mechanism of the Reaction

Based on the energy considerations and the previous radiation-induced exchange results (*1*), the following reaction mechanism is proposed.

Chain initiation $$H_2^+ + H_2 \rightarrow H_3^+ + H \quad (1)$$

Ion chain $$H_3^+ + D_2 \rightarrow H_2 + HD_2^+ \quad (2)$$

Initiation inhibition (R is any rare gas) $$H_2^+ + R \rightarrow RH^+ + H \quad (3)$$

Chain inhibition (R is Kr or Xe only) $$H_3^+ + R \rightarrow RH^+ + H_2 \quad (4)$$

Enhancement $$R^+ + H_2 \rightarrow RH^+ + H \quad (5)$$

(R is He, Ne or Ar only) $$RH^+ + H_2 \rightarrow R + H_3^+ \quad (6)$$

Chain termination $$H_3^+ + M^- \rightarrow H_2 + H + M \quad (7a)$$

or

$$H_3^+ \cdot M + e^- \rightarrow H_2 + H + M \quad (7b)$$

The ion chains are initiated by reaction 1 and propagated by reaction 2. The addition of a rare gas inhibits the reaction by 3 and 4, 3 being possible for any rare gas whereas 4 is possible only for Kr or Xe. This explains the inhibition of moderate amounts of any rare gas and the severe inhibition of Kr and Xe. If all the ion reactions have comparable rate constants, then reaction 4 is much more effective in inhibiting the reaction mechanism than reaction 3 as 4 removes the ion chain carriers; and 3 competes with the formation of the chain carrier. As the chains are very long, 10,000 or so, it is reasonable to expect that the addition of even a small concentration of a gas which can undergo reaction 4 will markedly inhibit the reaction, as is indeed observed with Kr and Xe. On the other hand, reaction 3 inhibits the reaction by competing with the formation of the chain carrier reaction. One would then expect that inhibition by this reaction would become important only when the concentration of R is comparable to that of H_2. This is in accord with the observations with addition of He, Ne, and Ar. Previously (*1*) we had ascribed the inhibition of Kr and Xe to a charge exchange reaction which is energetically unfavorable.[4] The present mechanism avoids this difficulty and at the same time affords an explanation of the inhibiting nature of Ar, Ne, and He.

Reaction 5 takes place for all the rare gases; however, reaction 6 takes place only for He, Ne, and Ar. Reactions 5 and 6 explain the increased yield of the reaction observed at low rare gas concentration[5] for He, Ne, and Ar (*6*).

The particular type of curve one would get for exchange rate versus rare gas concentration would depend on the relative rates of the various ionic reactions. The relative rate of reaction 1 versus reaction 3 determines the extent of inhibition; production of H_3^+ by reactions 5 and 6 relative to that from reaction 1 determines the relative enhancement of the reaction.

The Reaction in the Presence of Ultraviolet and 2-Mev Electrons

To investigate the possibility that the radical reaction is inhibited by the ion reaction, or vice versa, the exchange of H_2 and D_2 was studied in the presence of ultraviolet radiation and 2-Mev electrons. If there is no interaction, then the amount of exchange should be additive; if there is some interaction, as

$$\text{Ion} + \text{radical} \rightarrow \text{No ion or no radical}$$

then the extent of exchange will be less than the sum of both reactions independently. As is seen in Table I, with both ultraviolet and 2-Mev electrons simultaneously the yield is lower than with either radiation alone. Evidently there is an interaction.

From Table I it is seen that with added Xe the radical reaction yield is unchanged. One can then conclude that the electrons have no effect on the radical reaction. The only difference with and without Xe is that the H_3^+ ions are converted to XeH^+ in the presence of Xe. The H_3^+ cannot reduce the radical yield substantially without

[4] Pointed out to us in a private communication by R. L. Platzman.

[5] We should like to acknowledge helpful correspondence with S. C. Lind on this point.

introducing considerable exchange. This is seen from a consideration of the relative concentrations of H_3^+ and H during the reactions. The concentrations can be calculated from the rate constants and the measured rate of HD production. For the radical chain

$$H + D_2 \rightarrow HD + D$$

the specific rate constant is 1.4×10^{-16} cm³/molecule-sec (*1*), and for the ion chain the specific rate constant is 1.4×10^{-9} cm³/molecule-sec (*2*). The ion and radical concentrations are easily calculated and are listed in Table IV. The concentration of H without ultraviolet is calculated from the previous results (*1*) on experiments with xenon and no ultraviolet. It was found that the exchange yield was reduced by about a factor of 1000 by adding xenon. The calculated radical concentration is over 10^5 times the calculated ion concentration, and thus the small ion concentrations are not likely to be effective in the removal of H atoms.

The radicals, however, do reduce the ion yield and so do inhibit the ion chain. This can come about by an increase in ion recombination caused either by H atoms forming H^- ions which then rapidly react with H_3^+ or by cluster formation as $H_3^+ \cdot H$ which may be more easily neutralized by electrons than H_3^+. In fact, in order to have the long chain, H_3^+ must not be easily neutralized by an electron, and it is probably only such clusters or negative ions that easily neutralize a free H_3^+ ion.

The reaction is terminated by a reaction which neutralizes H_3^+, as indicated in reaction 7a or 7b. Whether the neutralization takes place homogeneously in the gas phase or on the walls is not clear. From our previous results we concluded that in our system the neutralization took place in the gas phase. However, as pointed out, this may have been due to impurities in the hydrogen. The recombination in the electron reaction alone cannot be due to H atoms or H atom clusters. The present result would then be such that a 10^5-fold increase in H atom concentration caused by the ultraviolet would essentially stop the exchange reaction. Hence if neutralization in the absence of ultraviolet is due to clusters they must be clusters of the type $H_2 \cdot H_3^+$.

TABLE IV

RADICAL AND ION CONCENTRATIONS IN THE ULTRAVIOLET- AND 2-MEV ELECTRON-INDUCED HYDROGEN-DEUTERIUM EXCHANGE

Ion or Radical	*Concentration (molecules/cc)*
H_3^+	1.6×10^5
H without ultraviolet	2×10^8
H with ultraviolet	7×10^{11}
H_2 (100 mm pressure)	4×10^{18}

SUMMARY

The mechanism for the radiation-induced exchange of hydrogen and deuterium in the presence of the rare gases is studied from considerations of the individual ion molecule reaction rate constants and energy changes. A mechanism is proposed which accounts adequately for the experimental facts. The mechanism involves H_3^+ as the ion chain carrier, with rare gas inhibition by the formation of RH^+, where R is a rare gas. Moderate inhibition is caused by reaction with H_2^+, and marked inhibition is caused by reaction with H_3^+. The rare gases then fall into two sets: He, Ne, and Ar, showing moderate inhibition at moderate concentrations, and Kr and Xe, showing marked inhibition even at trace concentrations. For the rare gases He, Ne, and Ar, the reaction $R^+ + H_2 \rightarrow RH^+ + H$ followed by the reaction $RH^+ + H_2 \rightarrow R + H_3^+$ is energetically possible and causes an enhancement of the reaction. The reaction is studied in the simultaneous presence of ultraviolet and electron radiations. It is shown that there is an interaction between the ion and radical reactions and that the increased presence of hydrogen atoms inhibits the ion reaction. It is suggested that the reaction may terminate by the neutralization of ion molecule clusters with free electrons.

RECEIVED: December 23, 1958

REFERENCES

1. S. O. THOMPSON and O. A. SCHAEFFER, The role of ions in the radiation induced exchange of hydrogen and deuterium. *J. Am. Chem. Soc.* **80**, 553–558 (1958).
2. D. P. STEVENSON and D. O. SCHISSLER, Reactions of gaseous molecule ions with gaseous molecules. IV. Experimental method and results. *J. Chem. Phys.* **29**, 282–294 (1958).
3. F. H. FIELD and J. L. FRANKLIN, *Electron Impact Phenomena*, pp. 243–246, Academic Press, New York, 1957.
4. J. O. HIRSCHFELDER, C. F. CURTISS, and R. B. BIRD, *Molecular Theory of Gases and Liquids*, pp. 1061–1103, John Wiley & Sons, New York, 1954.
5. C. A. COULSON and W. E. DUNCONSON, Comparison of wave-functions for HeH^{++} and HeH^+. *Proc. Roy. Soc.* **A165**, 90–115 (1938).
6. S. C. LIND, Note on radiation-induced exchange of hydrogen. *J. Phys. Chem.* **62**, 1601 (1958).
7. H. EYRING, J. O. HIRSCHFELDER, and H. S. TAYLOR, The theoretical treatment of chemical reactions produced by ionization processes. Part I. The ortho-para hydrogen conversion by alpha-particles. *J. Chem. Phys.* **4**, 479–491 (1936).

RADIATION RESEARCH 10, 680–690 (1956)

The Radiation Chemistry of Acetylene

I. Rare Gas Sensitization. II. Wall Effect in Benzene Formation[1,2]

LEON M. DORFMAN AND A. C. WAHL[3]

Argonne National Laboratory, Lemont, Illinois

INTRODUCTION

In the radiolysis of acetylene, polymerization to form cuprene (*1*) and cyclization to form benzene (*2*, *3*) account for virtually all the reacted acetylene. At low conversion, 21% of the acetylene forms benzene, and it has been shown (*3*) that the ratio of cyclization to polymerization is independent of pressure over a substantial range above 100 mm, and of absorbed radiation intensity. The indication from this kinetic study was that the reaction involves a complete duality of primary process in which the transient precursors of the benzene and the polymer are distinct and do not interact with each other in any way. This is in contrast with an earlier suggestion (*2*) that the polymer and the benzene originate from a common trimer intermediate.

The proposal was made that the separate primary processes might involve ionization on the one hand and electronic excitation by electron impact on the other, the primary precursor of benzene being an excited acetylene molecule, possibly in a triplet state. This speculation seemed the more inviting on the basis of published (*4*) data on the excited states of acetylene, the lowest of which was found to have molecular constants almost identical with those of benzene.

To obtain evidence bearing on the possible role of electronic excitation in the cyclization, an investigation of the rare gas-sensitized radiolysis of acetylene, with a special emphasis on benzene formation in the helium-sensitized reaction, has been carried out. The radiation sensitization of the acetylene polymerization by rare gases in mixtures with acetylene has long been known from the classic studies

[1] Based on a paper presented before the annual meeting of the Radiation Research Society, Pittsburgh, May 18–20, 1959, as part of the Symposium on Radiation Chemistry of Gases in honor of Dr. S. C. Lind on the occasion of his eightieth birthday. The Symposium was organized by Dr. Leon M. Dorfman, and he and Dr. A. O. Allen served as chairmen of the sessions.

[2] Based on work performed under the auspices of the U. S. Atomic Energy Commission.

[3] Present address: Department of Chemistry, The University of Chicago, Chicago, Illinois.

of Lind and his collaborators (*5*). The present study was undertaken on the basis of the following consideration. In the helium-sensitized radiolysis there is an important difference in the primary process as compared with the direct radiolysis in which both ionization and excitation can, of course, take place. Since the sensitization involves energy transfer to acetylene from either a helium ion or an excited helium atom, it can be readily seen that the result in either case will be ionization of the acetylene. If the collisional transfer is from a helium atom in the 2^1P or 2^3P state, or the metastable 2^1S or 2^3S state, and the helium returns to the ground 1^1S state, then ionization of the acetylene will occur, since all excited states have energies in excess of 19.7 ev (*6*), and the ionization potential of acetylene is 11.4 volts (*7*). There is, in fact, direct experimental evidence (*8*) of the ionization of acetylene by excited helium atoms. Collision with ^1P or ^3P atoms with transitions to the lower-lying S states cannot produce electronic excitation of the acetylene, since transitions from the higher S and P terms to the $2S$ and $2P$ states all involve less than 4.7 ev, which is probably insufficient to raise the acetylene molecule to its lowest excited state. Therefore only ionized states of acetylene will be formed in the sensitization by excited helium atoms. If collision with helium ions occurs, then charge transfer will ionize the acetylene, the ionization potential of helium being 24.6 volts (*9*).

Thus, in the helium-sensitized radiolysis of acetylene, electronically excited neutral acetylene is eliminated as a primary transient, an ionized state of acetylene always resulting from the collisional transfer. If an excited neutral acetylene molecule is indeed the primary precursor of benzene, then the cyclization reaction should be eliminated in the helium-sensitized radiolysis.

In addition to the helium-sensitized radiolysis, sensitization by argon, krypton, and xenon has also been examined. The work with helium led, of necessity, to an investigation of the direct radiolysis in the low-pressure region for the following reason. To preserve the condition helium $\gg$ acetylene in order that the electron fraction of helium should be very much greater than that of acetylene in the sensitized runs, it was necessary to use low pressures (ca. 7 mm) of acetylene, and for comparison purposes the formation of benzene in the direct radiolysis in this pressure region had also to be determined.

EXPERIMENTAL PROCEDURE

The preparation and purity of the gases used was as follows. Matheson Co. acetylene was degassed at $-150°C$ and then subjected to distillation three times at $-125°C$. Mass spectrometric analysis disclosed no impurities, which therefore amounted to certainly less than 0.1%. Helium from three separate sources was used. In some runs, ordinary tank helium was used without further purification. In two runs, research-grade helium, obtained from Air Reduction Co., was used. Analysis of this helium showed the following: nitrogen 0.05%, oxygen 0.01%. In six other runs, tank helium was purified by bubbling it through a column of sodium-potassium alloy specifically to remove oxygen which might conceivably have an inhibitory effect. Analysis of this purified helium showed: oxygen $<0.004\%$; nitrogen $<0.017\%$. The argon, krypton, and xenon were all research-grade gases, obtained from Air Reduction Co., and were used without further purification. Analysis of these gases showed the following impurity content: the argon contained 0.06% nitrogen, 0.01% oxygen; the krypton contained $<0.15\%$ nitrogen, $<0.01\%$ oxygen; the xenon contained 0.13% nitrogen, $<0.01\%$ oxygen.

The source of radiation was a Van de Graaff accelerator delivering a 1-Mev electron beam. The electron beam entered the reaction cell through a 2-mil-thick stainless steel window so that the peak energy of the electrons incident on the gas was approximately 0.8 Mev. Beam currents of 30 to 60 μa were used, the majority of runs being carried out at about 55 μa. At these currents, with the cell window 1½ inches below the accelerator window, the required irradiation times ranged from ½ minute in some of the sensitized runs to 45 minutes in the low-pressure direct radiolysis.

Glass reaction cells of two different sizes were used. Two cylindrical cells with a window at one end, with inside diameter 35 mm, over-all length approximately 18 cm, and total volume 165 cc, were used in most of the runs. A large spherical cell, total volume 1031 cc, consisting of a 1-liter bulb connected to a 30-mm fernico seal to which the stainless steel window was fastened, was used in a series of runs. The precise volume ratio of these cells was 6.25. The condition of the reaction cell wall was not identical in all the runs. The change in surface condition resulted from the deposition, during each run, of a very thin layer of cuprene polymer, for which there is no known solvent. For six runs (the initial pair and two subsequent sets before which the cell was opened) the surface was completely clean at the start of the irradiation. For another six runs the polymer layer was rather incompletely removed by the mechanical action of water, and the cell was subsequently degassed. In the remainder the surface had accumulated a polymer layer of varying thickness. The reproducibility of the results regardless of the previous history of the surface indicated quite clearly that the reaction rates were unaffected by the condition of the surface.

The benzene analysis was performed spectrophotometrically with a Cary recording spectrophotometer, Model 14R, by measuring the 2530-A benzene absorption in the gas after each run. The absorption spectrum from 2300 to 2700 A was recorded after each run with a 10-cm absorption cell, and in addition the 2530-A peak was separately recorded by using the slowest scan rate and highest sensitivity of the instrument. The limit of sensitivity of the analysis was somewhat better than 0.1 μM of benzene. The amount of benzene formed in the direct radiolysis in the small cells usually exceeded 0.8 μM, and in the spherical cell it was usually greater than 4 μM. Although it was necessary to establish only the linearity with pressure of the benzene absorption curve, and thus to determine the relative amounts of benzene for purposes of this investigation, an absolute calibration was nevertheless carried out in the following way. At the high end of the pressure range a known pressure of benzene was introduced directly into the absorption cell, and the 2530-A peak measured. In the lower range where this method was not feasible, known quantities of benzene were formed in direct radiolysis runs at higher acetylene pressure, where the fraction of acetylene going to benzene is known (*3*) with moderately good accuracy, and introduced into the absorption cell. From these measurements, calibration points on the same absorption curve were obtained.

The amount of acetylene reacting was determined simply by measuring the initial and final pressures on a manometer which was read with a cathetometer. The minute amounts of hydrogen formed were, of course, removed before the final pressure reading was taken. In runs at the lower acetylene pressures these readings were taken in a small analytical volume (ca. 9 cc) into which the acetylene had been condensed. In order to minimize any possible loss of benzene, the stopcocks in this part of the vacuum system were lubricated with silicone grease. In the sensitized runs the rare gas was very slowly pumped off after the run through two traps, at −195°C, in which the condensables, acetylene and benzene, were trapped. After reading the final pressure the entire condensable fraction was condensed into the ultraviolet absorption cell for measurement. In the xenon-sensitized runs the rare gas was not pumped off before reading, but the final and initial pressures were measured for the total of xenon and acetylene.

RESULTS AND DISCUSSION

Benzene Calibration

The calibration curve for benzene analysis by measurement of the ultraviolet absorption at 2530 A, over the range 1 to 12 μM of benzene, is shown in Fig. 1. The ordinate represents the optical density, and the abscissa the amount of benzene present in the ultraviolet absorption cell, which has a volume of 30.0 cc. The solid circles represent points obtained by introducing a known pressure of benzene directly into the ultraviolet absorption cell. The remainder of the points were obtained from runs at moderately high pressure, for which the amount of benzene was calculated on the basis of the previously determined (*2*, *3*) 21% conversion of acetylene to benzene.

The optical density is linear, or at least very nearly so, in the benzene pressure so that the 2530-A peak height is an adequate representation, for the purpose of the present investigation, of the amount of benzene formed. It should be understood that the interpretation of the results of this investigation is not dependent on the absolute calibration for benzene, a relative determination of benzene forma-

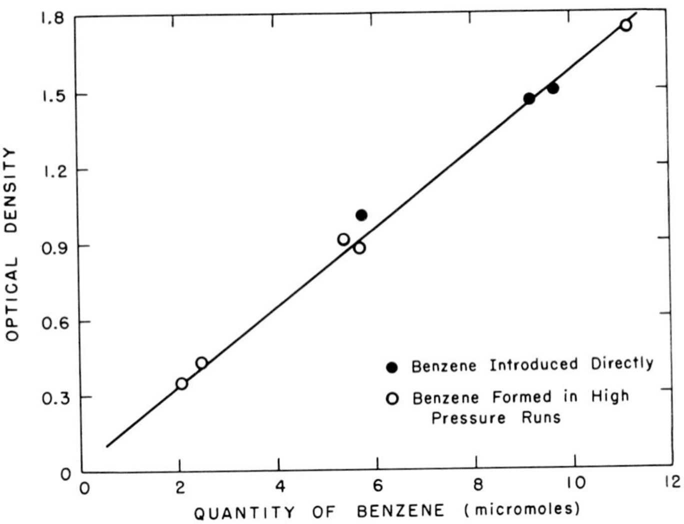

FIG. 1. Calibration for benzene analysis by ultraviolet absorption at 2530 A.

tion being sufficient. Nevertheless the absolute calibration is useful for purposes of reference. The calibration constant, obtained from Fig. 1, for the optical density per micromole of benzene is 0.165 ± 0.011. That is, a peak height of 16.5 chart divisions is obtained for 1 μM of benzene, and the sensitivity of the measurement is approximately 0.07 μM.

Rare Gas Sensitization

The details of ten runs on the helium-sensitized radiolysis using the cylindrical cells are shown in Table I. The data in the table show the initial pressure of acetylene and the pressure of helium, the electron fraction of helium, the diminution in acetylene pressure, and the number of moles of acetylene reacting. In analyzing for benzene several runs were combined in the ultraviolet absorption cell to increase the quantity of benzene, if any were formed. These combined runs are indicated in the table by brackets and consisted of runs 8 and 9, 19 and 21, and 26 through 29. The results of the benzene analysis may be summarized by stating that no benzene was detected in any of these runs, with the possible exception of the combination of the last four, in which a total of 71 μM of acetylene reacted, and for which an absorption was barely discernible. It is clear, therefore, that in the helium-sensitized radiolysis of acetylene, in contrast with the direct radiolysis, cyclization to benzene is essentially eliminated, as anticipated on the basis of the reasoning set forth in the Introduction.

In addition to the helium-sensitized radiolysis, sensitization by argon, krypton,

TABLE I

Helium-Sensitized Radiolysis of Acetylene

Run No.	Pressure (mm)		Electron fraction of helium	$-\Delta P_{C_2H_2}$ (mm)	C_2H_2 reacting (moles × 10^6)
	Acetylene	Helium			
8	7.20	675	0.93	1.93	17.2
9	7.20	675	0.93	1.84	16.4
11[a]	6.83	590.3	0.93	2.28	20.4
12[a]	6.83	590.3	0.93	2.07	18.5
19[a, b]	7.99	661.9	0.92	2.12	15.5
21[a]	5.87	523.2	0.93	1.65	14.7
26[a, b]	7.54	603	0.92	2.29	16.7
27[a, b]	7.54	603	0.92	2.66	19.4
28	7.43	534	0.91	2.01	17.9
29	7.43	492	0.90	1.94	17.3

[a] Helium purified through NaK column.
[b] Cylindrical cell of slightly smaller volume, 135 cc, used in these runs.

TABLE II

Rare Gas-Sensitized Radiolysis of Acetylene

Run No.	Pressure (mm)		Electron fraction of rare gas	$-\Delta P_{C_2H_2}$ (mm)	C_2H_2 reacting (moles × 10^6)	Benzene formed (moles × 10^6)
	Acetylene	Rare gas				
36[a]	34.24	170 A	0.86	5.88	42.9	0.1
37[a]	34.24	170 A	0.86	5.83	42.6	0.1
54	23.21	127.9 A	0.88	7.81	69.6	0.1
15	23.10	245.8 Kr	0.96	2.8	25	0.1
13	29.48	117.7 Xe	0.94	2.2	20	0.1
53	22.13	108.2 Xe	0.95	4.53	40.4	0.2

[a] Cylindrical cell of slightly smaller volume, 135 cc, used in these runs.

and xenon has also been examined for benzene formation. The results of six runs with these rare gases are shown in Table II. The figures in the last column show that barely measurable quantities of benzene were formed, rather than amounts of the order of 1 to 3 μM which would be formed in the direct radiolysis for the quantities of acetylene reacting in these particular runs. The very small amount of benzene which was formed is to be attributed to that small fraction of the incident energy which is absorbed directly by the acetylene and results in cyclization as well as polymerization. Otherwise it is clear that in the radiolysis sensitized by argon, krypton, and xenon, as well as by helium, the cyclization reaction is eliminated.

Pressure Dependence and Wall Effect in the Direct Radiolysis

It seemed advisable, for comparison purposes, to have data on benzene formation in the direct radiolysis at the low acetylene pressures used in the helium-sensitized radiolysis. This was particularly so in view of the fact that no benzene at all was detected in most of the helium-sensitized runs, whereas on the basis of a 21% conversion to benzene for that fraction of the acetylene which reacts as a result of direct absorption of energy, rather than by sensitization, a detectable quantity would have been expected.

The results of a series of twenty-five runs demonstrate that the rate of benzene formation in the direct radiolysis does indeed decrease with decreasing pressure in the low-pressure region. There is no need to tabulate the details of all these runs, since the over-all result is quite adequately represented in Fig. 2. Nevertheless the details of a few of these runs are shown in Table III. The amount of acetylene reacted was such that the quantity of benzene formed in these runs ranged from 0.6 to 5.5 μM with the cylindrical cells, and was as high as 10 μM with the large spherical cell. At the lowest pressure used with the cylindrical cells, the products of four separate identical runs were combined for ultraviolet analysis to bring the amount of benzene formed to 1.2 μM.

The data are shown in Fig. 2, in which the fraction of the reacted acetylene which forms benzene is plotted as a function of the initial acetylene pressure. The open circles are for runs in the cylindrical cells. The fraction of acetylene forming benzene,

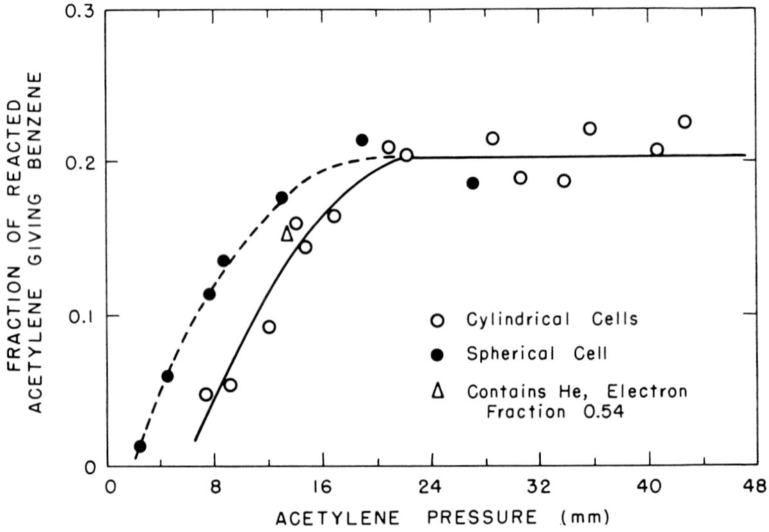

FIG. 2. Pressure dependence and wall effect in benzene formation in the direct radiolysis of acetylene.

TABLE III

BENZENE FORMATION IN THE DIRECT RADIOLYSIS—TYPICAL RESULTS

Run No.	*Acetylene pressure (mm)*	*Pressure decrease (mm)*	*Acetylene reacting (moles × 10^6)*	*Benzene formed (moles × 10^6)*	*Fraction of reacted acetylene forming benzene*
14	40.72	7.99	76.9	5.5	0.21
66	12.06	1.91	17.8	0.58	0.098
60[a]	4.59	0.83	47.3	1.02	0.065
74[a]	13.06	1.86	110.5	6.7	0.18

[a] Large spherical cell used in these runs.

which has been shown (*3*) to be invariant with pressure at higher pressures, maintains its value of 0.2 down to the region around 20 mm. With further decrease in pressure it is clear that the fraction forming benzene begins to fall off quite sharply, reaching a value of approximately 0.04 at a pressure of 8 mm. There is one point on this curve (indicated by a triangle) which represents a run containing a small amount of helium, the electron fraction of helium being only 0.54 for this run. The fraction of reacted acetylene going to benzene has been calculated for only that part of the energy which has been directly absorbed by the acetylene. As may be seen, the point lies very close to the curve. The estimate of directly absorbed energy based on electron fraction would, if anything, be slightly low, so that the point would lie even closer to the curve than is indicated.

The decrease in benzene formation at the lower pressures (in contrast with its invariance over an extensive range of increasing pressure) can be logically attributed to a wall effect. If one of the transient precursors of the benzene, either monomer or dimer, has a sufficiently long lifetime, it will diffuse to the wall where it may be deactivated before the trimer can be formed. It seems unlikely that the trimer transient would have a sufficiently long lifetime to diffuse to the wall, since only a molecular rearrangement would be required to form benzene. This diffusion-dependent deactivation will then compete with benzene formation at low pressures as determined by the transient lifetime and the mean path length to the walls. The evidence which establishes that such an explanation is substantially correct was obtained from the runs with the spherical cell for which the mean path length to the walls is considerably greater than for the cylindrical cells. The average distance to the walls for this cell—0.75 times the radius (*10*)—is approximately 4.5 cm, whereas for the small cylindrical cells it is considerably less, probably between 2 and 3 cm. The solid circles in Fig. 2 represent runs with the spherical cell. The decrease in benzene formation is again observed, but the curve is now significantly shifted to lower pressures as expected, because of the longer time of diffusion to the walls.

From these observations it is possible to draw some interesting and important conclusions about the characteristics of the benzene precursors. The root-mean-square molecular velocity at 25°C is approximately 5×10^4 cm sec^{-1} for a molecule having the mass of the monomer, and 3.3×10^4 cm sec^{-1} for the dimer mass. Since the average distance to the wall is 4.5 cm, we can conclude that the lifetime of one or both of these transients is at least 10^{-4} sec and may be considerably greater, since the mean path length to the walls is certainly greater than the average distance. If these transients are electronically excited states of acetylene or of the dimer, this would rule out the singlet state as a possibility, since the radiative lifetime for the singlet is more than three orders of magnitude too short. The following is also noteworthy. At a pressure of 10 mm the collison frequency at 25°C would be approximately 8×10^7 sec^{-1}. Thus, on the average, the transients must survive at least 8000 collisions with acetylene molecules in the ground state in order to reach the walls. This means that the elementary reactions involved in the cyclization do not have the characteristics normally attributed to ion-molecule reactions which apparently occur with high cross section and unity collision efficiency. The reasonable possibilities are an excited molecule in a triplet state or perhaps a free radical.

It is of interest to compare this pressure effect on benzene formation in the radiolysis of acetylene with the analogous data from the photochemical reaction. The photochemical studies show that in both the photolysis (*11*) at 1849 A and the mercury—photosensitized reaction (*12*) the quantum yield for benzene formation does indeed fall off at low pressures. In the photolysis it begins to decrease at 25 to 30 mm, and it has decreased more than tenfold at 2 mm; in the photosensitized reaction it declines sharply below 20 mm. There is, however, a striking difference in these photochemical studies as contrasted with the radiolysis, in that the quantum yield for polymerization shows an identical decline at low pressures, the fraction of acetylene going to benzene remaining constant down to a few millimeters, the lowest pressures investigated. From the present investigation it is clear that in the radiolysis the polymerization yield does not show a decrease corresponding to that of the cyclization at low pressures. It may be that the polymerization yield does not decrease at all at lower pressures, but this cannot be shown definitively from the present investigation because of an uncertainty, owing to the contribution of the slow electron component of the scattered secondaries, in calculating the relative absorbed intensity at lower pressures.

From these new observations (1) that benzene formation is eliminated in the rare gas-sensitized radiolysis of acetylene, whereas the polymerization yield is apparently unchanged (*5*), and (2) that the benzene yield is sharply reduced at lower pressures owing to a wall effect, taken together with the earlier kinetic studies (*3*), it seems a reliable conclusion that the acetylene radiolysis involves at least a duality of primary process. A consideration of the conditions under which the wall effect is manifested indicates the likelihood that the transient precursors of the benzene are excited molecules in a triplet state. On the basis of these observations and the foregoing discussion, the suggested mechanism for the direct radiolysis involves ionization:

$$C_2H_2 + e = C_2H_2^+ + 2e \tag{1}$$

which may result in polymerization through a series of ion-molecule reactions:

$$C_2H_2^+ + C_2H_2 = C_4H_3^+ + H \tag{2}$$

which have been observed (*13,14*) in the mass spectrometer; or, as well, by means of a free radical chain which may be initiated by either ionization or excitation:

$$H + C_2H_2 = C_2H_3 \xrightarrow{C_2H_2} \text{Polymer} \tag{3}$$

Cyclization occurs quite independently as a result of electronic excitation by electron impact:

$$C_2H_2 + e = C_2H_2^* + e \tag{4}$$

$$C_2H_2^* + C_2H_2 = (C_2H_2)_2^* \xrightarrow{C_2H_2} C_6H_6 \tag{5}$$

In the sensitized radiolysis ionization by charge transfer occurs, leading to polymerization. Dissociative ionization apparently occurs to only a small extent in both the direct ionization (*15*) and the charge transfer ionization (*14*).

SUMMARY

In the rare gas-sensitized radiolysis of acetylene, with helium, argon, krypton, and xenon, cyclization to benzene, an important process in the direct radiolysis, is completely eliminated. In the direct radiolysis the fraction of reacted acetylene going to benzene, which is constant at 0.2 at high pressures, is found to decrease sharply at very low pressures. This is shown to be due to a wall effect. From a consideration of the experimental conditions it is shown that benzene precursors reaching the wall have a lifetime of at least 10^{-4} sec.

These new observations, together with the earlier kinetic studies, are consistent with a mechanism involving a complete duality of primary process in which the precursors of the polymer and of benzene are distinct. It is suggested that ionization of the acetylene leads to polymerization, whereas cyclization requires electronic excitation of the acetylene, probably to a triplet state.

ACKNOWLEDGMENTS

It is a pleasure to acknowledge the many stimulating discussions, based on a common desire to arrive at a unified understanding of the radiation chemistry and photochemistry of acetylene, with our colleagues, Drs. R. L. Platzman and Max S. Matheson. We are indebted to Mr. C. Plucinski for performing the mass spectrometric analysis, and to Mr. R. H. Lowers for carrying out the Van de Graaf irradiations.

RECEIVED: January 16, 1959

REFERENCES

1. S. C. Lind, D. C. Bardwell, and J. H. Perry, The chemical action of gaseous ions produced by alpha particles. VII. Unsaturated carbon compounds. *J. Am. Chem. Soc.* **48,** 1556–1575 (1926). (There are several early studies of acetylene, the works of Lind and his collaborators being the most extensive.)
2. C. Rosenblum, Benzene formation in the radiochemical polymerization of acetylene. *J. Phys. Chem.* **52,** 474–478 (1948).
3. L. M. Dorfman and F. J. Shipko, The β-particle radiolysis of acetylene. *J. Am. Chem. Soc.* **77,** 4723–4726 (1955).
4. C. K. Ingold and G. W. King, Excited states of acetylene. *J. Chem. Soc.* **1953,** 2702–2755.
5. S. C. Lind and D. C. Bardwell, The chemical action of gaseous ions produced by alpha particles. VIII. The catalytic influence of ions of inert gases. *J. Am. Chem. Soc.* **48,** 1575–1584 (1926).
6. G. Herzberg, *Atomic Spectra and Atomic Structure*, p. 65, Dover Publications, New York, 1944.
7. K. Watanabe, Ionization potentials of some molecules. *J. Chem. Phys.* **26,** 542–547 (1957).
8. W. P. Jesse and J. Sadauskis, Ionization by alpha particles in mixtures of gases. *Phys. Rev.* **100,** 1755–1762 (1955).
9. C. E. Moore, *Atomic Energy Levels*, Vol. I, p. 5, National Bureau of Standards, Circular No. 467, 1949.
10. S. C. Lind, *The Chemical Effects of Alpha Particles and Electrons*, p. 94, Chemical Catalog Co., New York, 1928.
11. M. Zelikoff and L. M. Aschenbrand, Vacuum ultraviolet photochemistry. Part III. Acetylene at 1849 Å. *J. Chem. Phys.* **24,** 1034–1037 (1956).
12. S. Shida, Z. Kuri, and T. Furuoya, Mercury photosensitized polymerization of acetylene. *J. Chem. Phys.* **28,** 131–135 (1958).
13. F. H. Field, J. L. Franklin, and F. W. Lampe, Reactions of gaseous ions. II. Acetylene. *J. Am. Chem. Soc.* **79,** 2665–2669 (1957).
14. R. Barker, W. H. Hamill, and R. R. Williams, Jr., Ion-molecule reactions of acetylene. *Abstr. Am. Chem. Soc., 132nd Meeting A.C.S., New York* p. 46S (1957).
15. D. P. Stevenson, On the average energies of molecular ions, *Radiation Research* **10,** 610–621 (1959).

RADIATION RESEARCH 10, 691–701 (1959)

The Direct Radiolysis and the Radiation-Sensitized Hydrogenation of Ethylene[1]

F. W. LAMPE

Humble Oil and Refining Company, Research and Development Division, Baytown, Texas

INTRODUCTION

The lack of information in the literature pertaining to the radiation chemistry of ethylene is quite surprising. There have been, to the author's knowledge, only four papers dealing with this subject published since 1925.

Mund and Koch (*1*), in probably the first investigation into the radiolysis of ethylene, observed the formation of liquid hydrocarbons, as well as an evolution of permanent gases ($CH_4 + H_2$) whose rate of formation appeared to be about 10% of the rate of ethylene disappearance. Somewhat later Lind *et al.* (*2*) studied α-particle radiolysis in more detail and found ethylene to react with an ion-pair yield of 5.1, with hydrogen and methane formation occurring with a combined ion-pair yield of about 0.8. Using the values of Jesse and Sadauskis (*3*) for the average energy required to produce an ion pair, these ion-pair yields correspond to G values of -18.2 and 2.9, respectively. No other products were reported by these authors.

Lewis *et al.* (*4*) reported the γ-ray-induced polymerization of ethylene at room temperature and pressures ranging from 17 to 109 atmospheres. They observed the formation of white solid polyethylene with G values for ethylene consumption being very dependent on total dose and ranging from 0 to as high as 2000.

Recently an electron radiolysis of ethylene has been reported (*5*) in which gaseous reaction products consisting of butane, acetylene, hydrogen, methane, ethane, and butene were observed; the liquid products consisted of C-6 and C-8 aliphatic hydrocarbons, aromatics, and olefins. Quantitative energy yield values, if measured in this work, were not available to the author.

The literature situation regarding the radiation-induced hydrogenation of ethylene is similar to that of the direct radiolysis. Lind *et al.* (*2*) report a few in-

[1] Based on a paper presented before the annual meeting of the Radiation Research Society, Pittsburgh, May 18–20, 1959, as part of the Symposium on Radiation Chemistry of Gases in honor of Dr. S. C. Lind on the occasion of his eightieth birthday. The Symposium was organized by Dr. Leon M. Dorfman, and he and Dr. A. O. Allen served as chairmen of the sessions.

conclusive experiments under conditions which most probably would not give results much different from those obtained in the direct radiolysis. Mikhailov *et al.* (*5*) mention that dilution of the ethylene with hydrogen did affect both the conversion of ethylene and the yield of gaseous products.

With such a scarcity of information on an important compound, ethylene radiation chemistry seemed to us to be a field in need of much investigation.

EXPERIMENTAL PROCEDURE

The radiation employed in this work was the electron beam from a 2-Mev Van de Graaff electrostatic accelerator. In all experiments the accelerating voltage was maintained at 2.0 Mv and the electron beam current at approximately 5 μa.

The irradiation vessels and procedures have been described previously (*6*). The radiation-induced polymerization of acetylene was used as a dosimeter; the details of the method were described in a previous publication (*7*).

Phillips research-grade ethylene, having a stated purity of 99.9+ mole %, was frozen out in liquid nitrogen and then allowed to distill slowly into an evacuated (10^{-6} mm) storage bulb on the vacuum system. The middle third of the frozen-out sample was collected. Hydrogen was obtained from the Matheson Company, and argon from the Air Reduction Sales Company. Both were used without further purification.

Quantitative analysis of C-1 through C-6 hydrocarbons was accomplished by gas liquid partition chromatography. The use of two columns, consisting of hexadecane and benzyl cellosolve substrates on 40- to 60-mesh crushed firebrick support, enabled complete separation and determination of all hydrocarbon con-

TABLE I

100-Ev Yields in Ethylene Radiolysis at 25°C

Compound	*G (75 mm)*	*G (150 mm)*
C_2H_4	−14.2 ± 2.3	−15.5 ± 1.8
H_2	1.14 ± 0.28	1.28 ± 0.19
CH_4	0.13 ± 0.02	0.12 ± 0.02
C_2H_2	1.52 ± 0.04	1.46 ± 0.10
C_2H_6	0.40 ± 0.01	0.27 ± 0.10
C_3H_6	0.26 ± 0.02	0.23 ± 0.04
C_3H_8	0.33 ± 0.02	0.11 ± 0.03
n-C_4H_{10}	0.50 ± 0.03	0.48 ± 0.05
cis-C_4H_8-2	0.21 ± 0.12	0.12 ± 0.04
trans-C_4H_8-2	0.12 ± 0.02	0.14 ± 0.05
1-C_4H_8 (or iso)	0.17 ± 0.04	0.14 ± 0.04
n-C_5H_{12}	0.13 ± 0.05	0.06 ± 0.02
n-C_6H_{14}	0.16 ± 0.06	0.13 ± 0.04

stituents in the aforementioned range. Hydrogen was determined mass spectrometrically.

RESULTS AND DISCUSSION

Ethylene radiolysis. The gaseous products of the direct electron radiolysis of ethylene and their 100-ev yields for initial ethylene pressures of 75 and 150 mm are shown in Table I. All such G values were obtained by the measurement of initial slopes of plots in which the amount of substance formed (or consumed, as in the case of ethylene) was plotted versus the energy absorbed. A typical such plot showing acetylene and ethane formation at 150 mm is shown in Fig. 1.

The course of the reaction, as reflected by the G values, appears to be independent of initial ethylene pressure. Although there is a variation in the G values for ethane and propane with pressure that is outside the estimated experimental error, it is more likely, in the author's opinion, that the observed variation is from an experimental source rather than being characteristic of the reaction. In addition, the complexity of the reaction, as indicated by the presence of twelve gaseous products, is made even more evident when it is realized that only about one-third

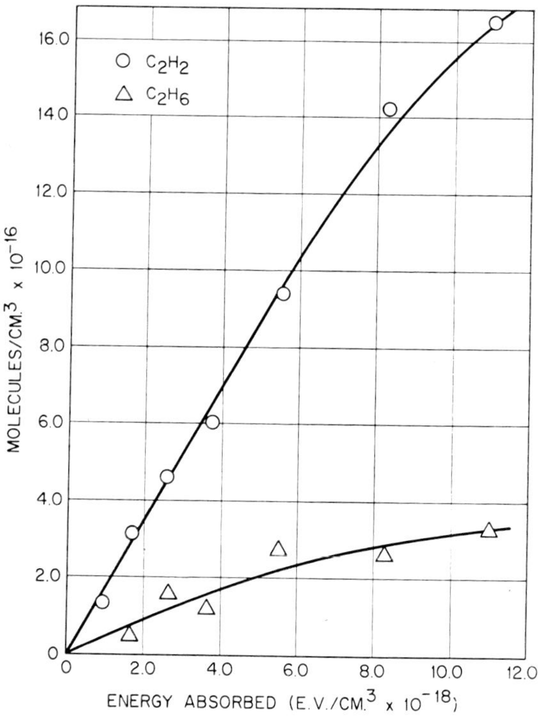

FIG. 1. Acetylene and ethane formation at 150 mm in the direct radiolysis of ethylene.

of the ethylene that has reacted is accounted for by the gaseous products. Thus polymerization of ethylene to a material of low vapor pressure must be the predominating process.

The near equality of the hydrogen and acetylene G values immediately suggests that their formation is similar to that involved in the mercury-photosensitized decomposition of ethylene (*8*); in this case, acetylene and hydrogen are formed as the result of the decomposition of an excited ethylene molecule. However, a serious objection to this suggested mode of formation is the apparent independence of $G(C_2H_2)$ with respect to pressure. Collisional deactivation of excited ethylene, which results in a decrease in the quantum yield of the mercury-photosensitized decomposition (*8*) and which would be expected to result in a decrease in $G(C_2H_2)$, will, of course, be more probable at higher pressures. Although the data in Table I refer to only a twofold variation in pressure, the results of experiments in which the pressure is increased severalfold by the addition of argon (and which are presented in a later section) confirm the conclusion that acetylene most probably is not formed from a unimolecular decomposition of excited ethylene.

One of the many ion-molecule reactions observed in ethylene (*9*, *10*), namely,

$$C_2H_3^+ + C_2H_4 \rightarrow C_2H_5^+ + C_2H_2 \quad (1)$$

produces acetylene, and it is tempting to consider reaction 1 as the source of the acetylene. However, one is still faced with the difficulty of explaining the nearly equal hydrogen formation rate, the origin of the many other gaseous products, the polymerization, and the ultimate results of the many other known ion-molecule reactions, some of which are more probable than reaction 1. Thus, although we feel that the key to the understanding of the radiation chemistry of ethylene lies in the ion-molecule reactions, we have so far been unsuccessful in relating all the ion-molecule reactions and their consequences to the observed results of the ethylene radiolysis.

Radiolysis of ethylene-argon mixtures. To investigate further the effect of total pressure on the radiolysis of ethylene, we carried out experiments in which varying amounts of argon were added to 75 mm of ethylene. The observed G values, de-

TABLE II

EFFECT OF ARGON ON THE RADIOLYSIS OF ETHYLENE

Component	*"G" for argon partial pressure of:*			
	0 mm	*75 mm*	*150 mm*	*225 mm*
C_2H_4	−14.2	−25 (−30)	−40 (−46)	−42 (−61)
C_2H_2	1.52	3.0 (3.2)	3.6 (4.9)	4.3 (6.6)
C_2H_6	0.396	0.58 (0.84)	0.78 (1.3)	0.77 (1.7)
n-C_4H_{10}	0.505	0.89 (1.1)	1.0 (1.6)	1.1 (2.2)

fined in this instance by the number of molecules formed or consumed per 100 ev of energy *absorbed by ethylene*, and determined in the same manner as those shown in Table I, are shown in Table II. The values shown parenthetically were calculated by dividing the values obtained in the absence of argon by the fraction of the energy absorbed by ethylene. Thus, these would be the observed values if all the energy absorbed by the argon was as effective in producing reaction as is energy absorbed by the ethylene. Figure 2 shows typical results for the product formation in a mixture of 75 mm of ethylene and 75 mm of argon.

The increase in the G values with argon concentration is evidence of interaction between argon and ethylene—that is, energy is somehow transferred from the argon to the ethylene, be it a transfer of charge or of excitation. Such transfer manifests itself as an increase in the rate of ethylene conversion, an effect that has been noted previously in acetylene (*11*, *12*), butadiene (*12*), and several inorganic

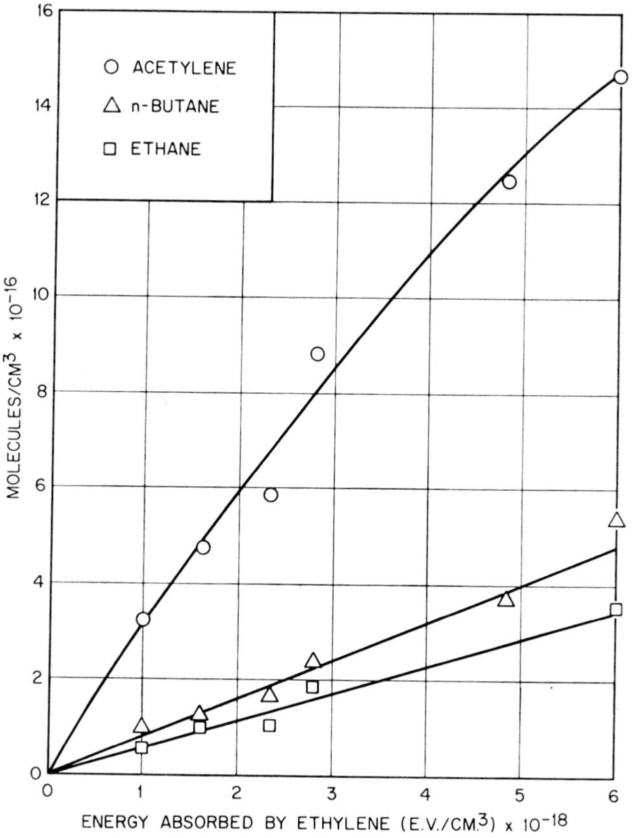

FIG. 2. Product formation in radiolysis of ethylene (75 mm)-argon (75 mm) mixture.

TABLE III

EFFECT OF ARGON ON THE COURSE OF THE RADIOLYSIS

Component	*Relative G at argon partial pressure of:*			
	0 mm	*75 mm*	*150 mm*	*225 mm*
C_2H_4	9.4	8.3	11	9.8
C_2H_2	1.0	1.0	1.0	1.0
C_2H_6	0.26	0.19	0.22	0.18
n-C_4H_{10}	0.33	0.30	0.28	0.26

gas radiolyses (*11*). The G values shown in Table III are those of Table II but calculated relative to $G(C_2H_2) = 1$. The fact that $G(C_2H_2)/G(—C_2H_4)$ is independent of pressure over a wider range than is shown in Table I is confirmatory evidence that acetylene is not formed in a unimolecular dissociation of excited ethylene. If acetylene were formed in this way, all reaction paths of ethylene conversion would have to be unimolecular also, and that is very unlikely. Although there may be a trend in the $G(C_4H_{10})/G(C_2H_2)$ ratio with argon pressure, the observed variation is within experimental error and, in our opinion, should be considered as constant. The constancy, or rather the very small variation in relative G values with varying argon pressure, indicates that the distribution of entities derived from ethylene and responsible for the observed reaction is the same whether the ethylene receives the initial energy from 1.7-Mv electrons or from argon ions and/or excited argon atoms. It thus appears that the immediate precursors to the major products are identical whether argon or ethylene absorbs the electron beam energy. Moreover, the very high specific reaction rates of the ion-molecule reactions initiated by electron impact on ethylene (*9*, *10*) force one to conclude that such reactions are occurring in irradiated ethylene. Therefore, although the evidence is certainly not compelling, it is at least suggestive that the following processes represent the argon-ethylene interaction:

$$A^+ + C_2H_4 \rightarrow C_2H_4^+ + A$$

$$A^* + C_2H_4 \rightarrow C_2H_4^+ + A$$

where A^* represents an argon atom in an excited state that is at least 10.5 volts above the ground state.

Comparison of the G values of Table II with the values in parentheses indicates that the energy transfer from argon to ethylene is surprisingly efficient, especially at low argon partial pressures. As the argon partial pressure is increased, however, the efficiency seems to decrease, as would be expected because of the increased probability of argon ion-electron recombination and of collision of argon-excited atoms with argon with degradation of the energy.

Sensitized hydrogenation of ethylene. Photosensitized hydrogenation reactions are based on the initial formation of hydrogen atoms by the interaction of an excited metal atom with molecular hydrogen (*8*). The hydrogen atoms so formed attack a substrate to initiate the observed chemical conversion. For example, in the mercury-photosensitized hydrogenation of ethylene (*8*), the following mechanism explains the experimental facts at room temperature:

$$Hg(^3P_1) + H_2 \rightarrow 2H + Hg(^1S_0) \quad (1)$$

$$H + C_2H_4 \rightarrow C_2H_5 \quad (2)$$

$$C_2H_5 + C_2H_5 \rightarrow C_2H_6 + C_2H_4 \quad (3)$$

$$C_2H_5 + C_2H_5 \rightarrow C_4H_{10} \quad (4)$$

The quenching cross section of ethylene for $Hg(^3P_1)$ atoms is about eight times as large as that of hydrogen (*8*); consequently, even at high ratios of hydrogen to ethylene a considerable amount of energy is absorbed by the ethylene. However, under hydrogenation conditions the total pressure of the system is high, and the consequences of energy absorption by the ethylene (unimolecular dissociation of excited ethylene to acetylene and hydrogen) is kept to a minimum by deactivating collisions. In other words, under hydrogenation conditions reaction 6 is favored over reaction 5, and reactions 1 to 4 completely account for the observations:

$$C_2H_4^* \rightarrow C_2H_2 + H_2 \quad (5)$$

$$C_2H_4^* + M \rightarrow C_2H_4' + M \quad (6)$$

In reaction 6 the prime denotes a lower state of excitation than the asterisk.

Now consider the case of subjecting a mixture of hydrogen and ethylene to ionizing radiation. The absorption of energy by hydrogen will produce ionization, i.e.,

$$H_2 \rightsquigarrow H_2^+ + e \quad (7)$$

and reaction 7 will be followed very quickly by reaction 8 (*13, 14*):

$$H_2^+ + H_2 \rightarrow H_3^+ + H \quad (8)$$

Neglecting the admitted possibility of proton transfer from H_3^+ to ethylene, we can expect H_3^+ to undergo only neutralization, i.e.,

$$H_3^+ + e \rightarrow H_2 + H \text{ (or 3H)} \quad (9)$$

The result, of course, of reactions 7 to 9 is that an ionization event in hydrogen has resulted in the formation of two or four hydrogen atoms. These hydrogen atoms will initiate the chemical conversion of ethylene through reactions 2 to 4.

However, there is a complicating factor here that is not present in the photosensitized situation. As in the photosensitized case, the ethylene (containing 16 electrons as compared to 2 for hydrogen) will absorb appreciable amounts of energy even at high ratios of hydrogen to ethylene. Here the similarity ends, for the consequences of energy absorption by ethylene are independent of pressure, as shown in the first two sections of this paper, and reactions 7 to 9 followed by reactions 2 to 4 will not account completely for the results. The rather unselective consequences of energy absorption by ethylene will be superimposed on the mechanism of reactions 7 to 9 followed by reactions 2 to 4.

The solution to the problem of improving the specificity of hydrogen atom initiation by ionizing radiation lies in the fact that rare gas ions will abstract hydrogen atoms from hydrogen (*13*). For example, if we were to irradiate argon-hydrogen mixtures, the following would occur, in addition to reactions 7 to 9:

$$A \rightsquigarrow A^+ + e \tag{10}$$

$$A^+ + H_2 \rightarrow AH^+ + H \tag{11}$$

$$AH^+ + e \rightarrow A + H \tag{12}$$

Thus energy absorption by argon has identical results to that by hydrogen. In addition, since argon will absorb energy at a much greater rate than hydrogen and somewhat faster than ethylene, the addition of argon to a hydrogen-ethylene system should result in increased specificity with respect to hydrogen atom attack.

The irradiation of mixtures of 30 mm of ethylene, 300 mm of hydrogen, and partial pressures of argon ranging from zero to 400 mm provided the following experimental facts:

1. The only significant products are *n*-butane, ethane, acetylene, and propane, which account for about 70 to 80% of the ethylene reacted. This is in contrast with the results for pure ethylene.
2. The initial rate of acetylene formation is independent of argon concentration.
3. The initial rates of formation of butane and ethane increase with argon concentration.
4. The ratio of ethane to butane increases markedly at very high conversions.
5. Propane is a minor constituent except in experiments at the highest argon pressures that were carried to high ethylene conversion. Restricting ourselves to rates extrapolated to zero time, we may neglect propane for the moment.

These facts are consistent with the occurrence of reactions 2 to 4 and 7 to 12 and with the acetylene formation occurring only as the result of energy absorption by ethylene. Assuming these reactions we can easily see that under conditions of constant hydrogen and ethylene concentrations

$$\left[\frac{R(C_4H_{10})}{R(C_2H_2)}\right]_0 = \alpha + \beta(A) \tag{13}$$

and

$$\left[\frac{R(C_2H_6)}{R(C_2H_2)}\right]_0 = \alpha' + \beta'(A) \tag{14}$$

with

$$\frac{\beta'}{\beta} = \frac{k_3}{k_4} \tag{15}$$

Since ethylene is depleted very rapidly, the acetylene formation rate decreases very rapidly with conversion. Hence, it is essential to extrapolate rate ratios to zero time. In Fig. 3 is shown the butane-to-acetylene ratios as a function of "the time of irradiation" at various partial pressures of argon (denoted in millimeters by the number on each line of Fig. 3). The intercepts of Fig. 3 are the ratios of the initial formation rates defined in equation 13. A similar plot was constructed for the determination of the initial values of $R(C_2H_6)/R(C_2H_2)$.

In accordance with equations 13 and 14, Fig. 4 shows the initial rate ratios plotted against argon pressure. The functions are linear, as the mechanism requires. The ratio of the slopes, k_3/k_4, is found to be 0.39, which is in fair agreement with the value of the ratio of disproportionation to combination of ethyl radicals obtained from mercury diethyl photolysis but considerably higher than that found from azoethane and diethyl ketone photolyses (*8*).

If ethane is formed not only by reaction 3 but by some additional process, a high value would be expected. The fact that propane is formed and becomes significant at high conversions suggests the presence of methyl radicals. We propose that in this system the following reaction is producing methyl radicals:

$$H + C_2H_5 \rightarrow 2CH_3 \tag{16}$$

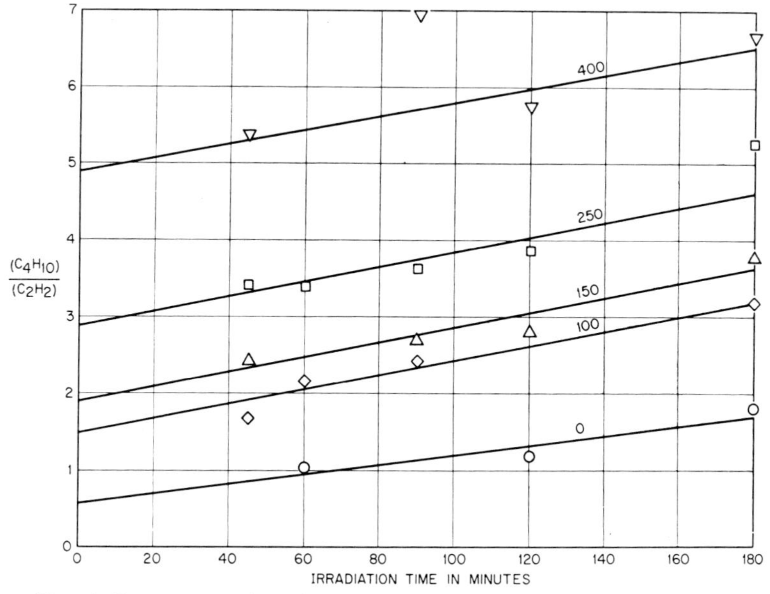

FIG. 3. Butane-acetylene formation rate ratio as a function of time.

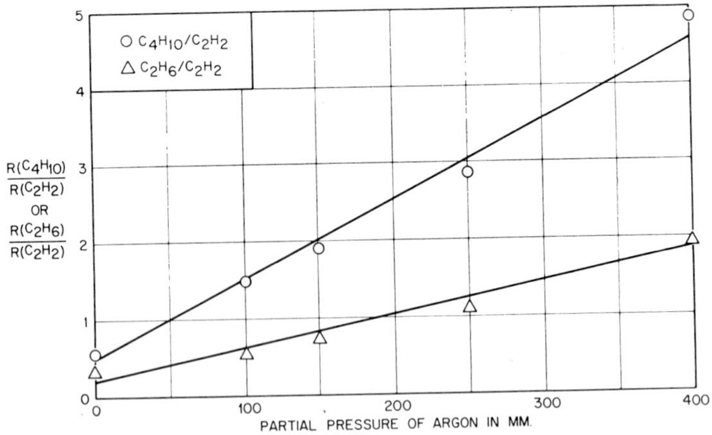

FIG. 4. Effect of argon pressure on initial formation rate ratios.

and that propane is formed by

$$CH_3 + C_2H_5 \rightarrow C_3H_8 \tag{17}$$

The additional ethane is formed either by combination of methyl radicals or, equivalently, by the stabilization of the excited ethane molecule formed in equation 16. The presence of propane appears to rule out the explanation advanced for the high value of k_3/k_4 found in mercury diethyl photolysis, namely, energy carryover from the primary step.

The experimental facts thus seem to be in agreement with the mechanism given by equations 2 to 4, 7 to 12, and 16 and 17 being superimposed on the normal radiolysis of ethylene. The degree to which the sensitized hydrogenation predominates depends on the concentration of the noble gas. In this particular case, reaction 16 probably could be suppressed by reducing sufficiently the intensity of radiation. Regardless of whether this reaction does or does not occur, however, the noble gas radiation-sensitized reactions appear to provide a useful method for the generation of hydrogen atoms.

SUMMARY

In the electron radiolysis of pure ethylene, some dozen gaseous products, increasing in mass up to *n*-hexane, are formed. The major products are acetylene, hydrogen, *n*-butane, and ethane. The *G* values for formation of the gaseous products and for disappearance of the ethylene are independent of pressure. Polymerization of ethylene to nonvolatile material appears to be the predominant reaction, however, since the gaseous products account for only about one-third of the ethylene reacted.

When argon is added to ethylene, an energy transfer occurs which accelerates the reaction but does not cause any large change in the course of the reaction. This is interpreted as suggestive of ethylene ion formation as a result of energy transfer.

The irradiation of argon-hydrogen-ethylene mixtures shows that specific radiation-sensitized hydrogen atom initiation is feasible. This is due to the rapid reaction of argon ions with hydrogen molecules that was first observed in mass spectrometers.

RECEIVED: January 26, 1959

REFERENCES

1. W. MUND and W. KOCH, Changes in gaseous hydrocarbons under the action of radium emanation. *Bull. soc. chim. Belgique* **34,** 119–126 (1925).
2. S. C. LIND, D. C. BARDWELL and J. H. PERRY, The chemical action of gaseous ions produced by alpha particles. VII. Unsaturated compounds. *J. Am. Chem. Soc.* **48,** 1556–1575 (1926).
3. W. P. JESSE and J. SADAUSKIS, Ionization of pure gases and the average energy to make an ion pair for alpha and beta particles. *Phys. Rev.* **97,** 1668–1670 (1955).
4. J. G. LEWIS, J. J. MARTIN, and L. C. ANDERSON, Gamma-activation of syntheses—polymerization of ethylene. *Chem. Engr. Prog.* **50,** 249–255 (1954).
5. B. M. MIKHAILOV, V. G. KISELEV, and V. S. BOGDANOV, Radioactive chemical conversions of organic compounds. Part 3. Conversions of ethylene under the action of fast electrons. *Izvest. Akad. Nauk S.S.S.R. Otdel. Khim. Nauk* No. 5, 545–549 (1958).
6. F. W. LAMPE, High energy electron irradiation of methane. Remarks on the reaction mechanism. *J. Am. Chem. Soc.* **79,** 1055–1058 (1957).
7. F. W. LAMPE, High energy electron irradiation of neopentane. *J. Phys. Chem.* **61,** 1015–1016 (1957).
8. E. W. R. STEACIE, *Atomic and Free Radical Reactions*, 2nd ed., Reinhold Publishing Corporation, New York, 1954.
9. D. O. SCHISSLER and D. P. STEVENSON, Reactions of gaseous molecule ions with gaseous molecules. II. *J. Chem. Phys.* **24,** 926 (1956).
10. F. H. FIELD, J. L. FRANKLIN, and F. W. LAMPE, Reactions of gaseous ions. I. Methane and ethylene. *J. Am. Chem. Soc.* **79,** 2419–2429 (1957).
11. S. C. LIND AND D. C. BARDWELL, The chemical action of gaseous ions produced by alpha particles. VIII. The catalytic influence of ions of inert gases, *J. Am. Chem. Soc.* **48,** 1575–1584 (1926).
12. R. C. PALMER and D. C. BARDWELL, Polymerization by soft X-rays of unsaturated organic gases with and without acceleration by admixture of noble gases. Presented at the 134th National Meeting of the American Chemical Society, Chicago, Illinois, September 7–12, 1958.
13. D. P. STEVENSON and D. O. SCHISSLER, Rate of the gaseous reactions $X^+ + YH = XH^+ + Y$. *J. Chem. Phys.* **23,** 1353–1354 (1955).
14. H. EYRING, J. O. HIRSCHFELDER, and H. S. TAYLOR, The theoretical treatment of chemical reactions produced by ionization processes. *J. Chem. Phys.* **4,** 479–491 (1936).

RADIATION RESEARCH **10,** 703–704 (1959)

AUTHOR INDEX

A

Alt, H. L., 148
Anderson, Donald R., 507
Atherton, D. R., 130
Augenstine, Leroy, 89

B

Baldwin, W. F., 387, 397
Barber, Albert A., 167
Barker, R., 664
Beam, Carl A., 449
Bennett, Winifred, 273
Binkley, W. W., 37
Berger, M. J., 552
Birge, Ann C., 433, 449
Bond, V. P., 20
Brauer, Ralph W., 80
Burton, Milton, 499, 636

C

Clark, J. W., 148
Cohen, J., 197
Cole, A., 418
Cole, Sibyl, 273
Cooper, J. A. D., 148
Crist, Robert, 357

D

Dacquisto, Michael P., 118
Daniels, Edward W., 584
Dorfman, Leon M., 607, 680

E

Easterday, O. D., 20
Elkind, M. M., 283, 296
Entenman, Cecil, 67

F

Funabashi, Koichi, 622

G

Gaither, Nenita, 490
Garrison, Warren M., 273
Gassner, E., 545
Goldenthal, Edwin I., 571
Goodwin, Paul N., 6
Gordon, E. R., 545
Grossweiner, L. I., 515
Gunter, S. E., 418

H

Hamill, W. H., 664
Hartnett, Anne Rimkus, 357
Haymond, Herman R., 273
Hazel, J. F., 597
Hempelmann, L. H., 545
Hutchinson, F., 477

J

Jackson, Kenneth L., 67
Jones, A. Russell, 655
Jordan, D. L., 148
Joseph, Betty J., 507
Jowsey, J., 213, 234, 243, 258, 323

K

Kalbach, Harvey, 80
Keller, N., 130
Kent, Sidney P., 380
Kimball, R. F., 490
Krebs, John S., 80
Krise, George M., 410
Kuppermann, Aron, 636

L

Lampe, F. W., 691
Leone, Charles A., 357
Livingston, Robert, 605

M

McBeth, Carolee, 357
McCabe, L. J., 37
McNabb, Wallace M., 597
Madsen, K. A., 48
Magee, John L., 622
Marshall, J. H., 197, 213, 234, 243, 258, 323
Meshitsuka, Gisuke, 499
Metcalf, D., 313
Michelakis, A. M., 37
Moh, C. C., 13
Mulac, W. A., 515
Murray, Raymond G., 347

N

Nadkarni, M. V., 571
Noyes, Howard E., 400
Nygaard, Oddvar F., 462

O

Okada, S., 545

P

Parkinson, John E., 63
Potter, Richard L., 462
Pottie, R. F., 664

Q

Quastler, Henry, 402

R

Rambach, W. A., 148
Rosenzweig, W., 532
Ross, D. A., 477
Rossi, Harald H., 522, 532
Rowland, R. E., 213, 234, 243, 258, 323

S

Salthouse, T. N., 387, 397
Salunkhe, D. K., 48
Sayeg, Joseph A., 176, 433, 449
Schaeffer, O. A., 671
Schwarz, Drew, 1
Shen Han, T. M., 37
Sicard, M. A., 1
Simon, M., 48
Sinclair, W. K., 418
Smith, Douglas E., 335
Smith, Paul K., 571
Spalding, J. F., 176
Spencer, L. V., 552
Stevenson, D. P., 610
Storer, John B., 180
Stover, Betsy J., 130
Strang, V. G., 176
Sutton, Harriet, 283, 296
Szutka, A., 597

T

Thompson, S. O., 671
Tobias, Cornelius A., 449

V

Van Bekkum, D. W., 339
Vogel, Howard H., Jr., 148, 584
Vos, O., 339

W

Wahl, A. C., 680
Wensinck, F., 339
White, V. K., 197
Wilbur, Karl M., 167
Wilcox, William S., 112
Williams, Clyde M., 410
Wilson, Stella M., 490
Withrow, R. B., 13
Woese, Carl, 370
Wolfrom, M. L., 37

Y

Yanders, Armon F., 30

Z

Zucker, Marion, 402

RADIATION RESEARCH 10, 705–710 (1959)

SUBJECT INDEX

A

Acetic acid-oxygen solutions, radiation-induced oxidation, GARRISON *et al.*, 273
Acetylene, radiolysis, rare gas sensitization, wall effect in benzene formation, DORFMAN AND WAHL, 680
Alpha and other recoil heavy particles, effect on acute mortality and survival time in mice, BOND AND EASTERDAY, 20
S-(2-Aminoethyl)thiuronium salts, effects of X-irradiation on SH-groups, ANDERSON AND JOSEPH, 507
Amoebae, effects of nonirradiated protoplasm on recovery of organisms exposed to supralethal doses of fission neutrons, DANIELS AND VOGEL, JR., 584
Animals, small, chronic irradiation source for, NOYES, 400
Antioxidant activity of mammalian tissues, effects of X-irradiation, BARBER AND WILBUR, 167
Aqueous solutions, kinetics of indirect effects of ionizing radiation, HUTCHINSON AND ROSS, 477

B

Bacillus megaterium spores, radiation destruction of plaque forming ability of, WOESE, 370
Bean (*Vicia faba*) root tips, X-ray induced chromatid aberrations, reversal of far-Red potentiating effect by red radiant energy, MOH AND WITHROW, 13
Bone, canine calcium metabolism, Ca^{45} and bone growth, MARSHALL *et al.*, 243
  diffuse activity and long term exchange, MARSHALL *et al.*, 258
  microradiographic measurements of mineral density, ROWLAND *et al.*, 234
  microscopic studies of deposition in three dimensions, MARSHALL *et al.*, 197
  quantitative autoradiography, MARSHALL *et al.*, 213
 human, microradiography of radium in, ROWLAND *et al.*, 323
Bone marrow, effects of single and divided doses of X-irradiation in partially shielded rats. MURRAY, 347
n-Butane, decomposition in an electric discharge, KUPPERMANN AND BURTON, 636
Butyl bromides, gamma radiolysis, WILCOX, 112

C

Ca^{45} metabolism in canine bone, bone growth and, MARSHALL *et al.*, 243
  diffuse activity and long term exchange, MARSHALL *et al.*, 258
  microscopic studies of deposition in three dimensions, MARSHALL *et al.*, 197
  quantitative autoradiography, MARSHALL *et al.*, 213
Carbon nuclei and other radiations, LET experiments, survival of haploid yeast, SAYEG *et al*, 449
Calorimetric measurements on a Caesium-137 teletherapy unit, GOODWIN, 6
$Caesium^{134}$, as chronic radiation source for small animals, NOYES, 400
Caesium-137 teletherapy unit, calorimetric measurements, GOODWIN, 6
Carbohydrates, effects of ionizing radiations on, WOLFROM *et al.*, 37
Carbon nuclei, "accelerated" and other radiations, effects on survival of haploid yeast, dosimetry of cyclotron beams, BIRGE AND SAYEG, 433
Cell division in epidermis of insect, relation to radiation injury, BALDWIN AND SALTHOUSE, 387
Cell division, X-ray sensitivity, ultraviolet sensitivity, and photoreactivation in yeast, ELKIND AND SUTTON, 273

Chromatid aberrations, in X-irradiated *Vicia*, reversal of far-red effect by red, MOH AND WITHROW, 13
Clustering of ions in irradiated gases, MAGEE AND FUNABASHI, 622
Cobalt^{60} gamma irradiation, rat, effect of pitressin on polydipsia and polyuria following, WILLIAMS AND KRISE, 410
Cysteine, cysteamine and sodium nitrite, effects against toxicity of nitrogen mustard, triethylenemelamine and X-irradiation, GOLDENTHAL *et al.*, 571
protection of the irradiated ground squirrel, SMITH, 335

D

Death in mice irradiated with specific organs protected, QUASTLER AND ZUCKER, 402
Decomposition of *n*-butane in an electric discharge, KUPPERMAN AND BURTON, 636
Deoxyribonuclease II activity in lymphoid tissues of X-irradiated rats, GORDON *et al.*, 545
Deoxyribonucleic acid metabolism in various tissues of rat following X-irradiation, NYGAARD AND POTTER, 462
Dogs, beagle, metabolism of Pu^{239} in, STOVER *et al.*, 130
effect of internal emitters on red cell survival, PARKINSON, 63
Dose delivered by monoenergetic neutrons, determination of quality of absorbed, ROSENZWEIG AND ROSSI, 532
Dosimetry of cyclotron beams used in irradiation of yeast with carbon nuclei and other radiations, BIRGE AND SAYEG, 433
Drosophila, sperm, effect of dose rate on genetic damage from fast electrons, YANDERS, 30

E

Electric discharge, decomposition of *n*-butane, KUPPERMANN AND BURTON, 636
Electrons, fast, effect of dose rate on genetic damage in *Drosophila* sperm, YANDERS, 30
high speed, effect on carbohydrates, WOLFROM *et al.*, 37
and ultraviolet radiation, exchange of hydrogen and deuterium, SCHAEFFER AND THOMPSON, 671
Energies, average, of molecular ions, STEVENSON, 610
Erythrocytes, survival in beagle dogs, effects of internal emitters, PARKINSON, 63
Ethylene, direct radiolysis and radiation sensitized hydrogenation of, LAMPE, 691
Exchange of hydrogen and deuterium in the presence of electrons and ultraviolet radiation, SCHAEFFER AND THOMPSON, 671

F

Fe^{59} incorporation in gamma and neutron irradiated rats, RAMBACH *et al.*, 148

G

Gamma irradiation, (Co^{60}), effect of high doses on seedling growth, SICARD AND SCHWARTZ, 1
of cyclohexane, *n*-hexane, benzene (containing dissolved iodine), with production of hydrogen iodide, MESHITSUKA AND BURTON, 499
and neutron radiation, effects on Fe^{59} incorporation in the rat, RAMBACH *et al.*, 148
of plants, carrots and potatoes, morphological and biochemical changes, MADSEN *et al.*, 48
of pyrrole and benzaldehyde with production of porphine-like substances, SZUTKA *et al.*, 597
Gamma radiolysis of butyl bromides, WILCOX, 112
Gamma rays, helium ions, protons and neutrons, effects of oxidation of aqueous acetic acid, GARRISON *et al.*, 273
transport, theory, radiological applications, BERGER AND SPENCER, 552
Gases, irradiated, chemistry of, DORFMAN, 607
clustering of ions in, MAGEE AND FUNABASHI, 622
Gastrointestinal radiation syndrome, role of bile secretion, JACKSON AND ENTENMAN, 67

Genetic damage from fast electrons in *Drosophila* sperm, effect of dose rate, YANDERS, 30
Growth of seedlings following exposure to high doses of radiation, SICARD AND SCHWARTZ, 1

H

Hydrogen and deuterium, exchange in the presence of electrons and ultraviolet radiation, SCHAEFFER AND THOMPSON, 671
Hydrogen iodide production in radiolysis of organic liquids containing dissolved iodine, MESHITSUKA AND BURTON, 499

I

Indirect effect of ionizing radiation on aqueous solution, kinetics of, HUTCHINSON AND ROSS, 477
Indirect inactivation of macromolecules in solution by ionizing radiation, method of analysis, AUGENSTINE, 89
Insect, epidermis, radiation damage, reversible effects, BALDWIN AND SALTHOUSE, 397
  Rhodnius prolixus, radiation damage in epidermis related to cell division, BALDWIN AND SALTHOUSE, 387
Internal emitters, effects on red cell survival in beagle dogs, PARKINSON, 63
Iodides, methyl and ethyl, ion-molecule reactions, POTTIE *et al.*, 664
Ion-molecule reactions of methyl and ethyl iodides, POTTIE *et al.*, 664
Ionizing radiation on aqueous solutions, kinetics of indirect effects. HUTCHINSON AND ROSS, 477
Ions, clustering, in irradiated gases, MAGEE AND FUNABASHI, 622
  molecular, average energies, STEVENSON, 610
Irradiation, alpha, roentgen, and ultraviolet, production of mutation in *Paramecium aurelia*, postirradiation treatment with streptomycin, KIMBALL *et al.*, 490
  chronic, source for small animals, NOYES, 400

L

Lethal irradiation sites of action in division of yeast cells, ELKIND AND SUTTON, 296
Lind, S. C. The First 80 years, LIVINGSTON, 605
Linear energy transfer (LET), specification of radiation quality, ROSSI, 522
Lymphocyte homeostasis in the mouse, long term effects of whole body irradiation, METCALF, 313

M

Metabolism of Ca^{45} in canine bone, microradiographic measurements of mineral density, ROWLAND *et al.*, 234
  of Pu^{239} in adult beagle dogs, STOVER *et al.*, 130
Mice, acute mortality and survival time, heavy particle irradiation, BOND AND EASTERDAY, 20
  female, ability to respond to gonadotropin (FSH) hormone after irradiation, SPALDING *et al.*, 176
  long term effect of whole-body irradiation on lymphocyte homeostasis, METCALF, 313
  modes of radiation death following exposure with different organs protected, QUASTLER AND ZUCKER, 402
  non-recuperable injury caused by ionizing radiation, KREBS *et al*, 80
  rate of recovery from radiation damage and its possible relationship to life shortening, STORER, 180
  X-irradiation, acquired radioresistance, DACQUISTO, 118
    infected lesions of the tongue in relation to bacteremia following, VOS *et al.*, 339
Microradiography of radium in human bone, ROWLAND *et al.*, 323
Monkeys, *Rhesus*, X-irradiated paper electrophoretic analyses of serum, LEONE *et al.*, 357
Morphological and biochemical changes in carrots and potatoes following gamma-irradiation, MADSEN *et al.*, 48
Mortality, mouse, following exposure to heavy

particle irradiation, BOND AND EASTERDAY, 20

N

Neutrons, fission, supralethal doses to amoebae, effects of nonirradiated protoplasm on recovery of organism, DANIELS AND VOGEL, JR., 584
monoenergetic, determination of quality of absorbed dose, ROSENZWEIG AND ROSSI, 532
protons, and other radiation, specification of radiation quality, ROSSI, 522
Nitric acid-oxygen-water reactions induced by radiation, JONES, 655
Non-ionizing radiation as an agent in altering X-radiation effects, MOH AND WITHROW, 13
Nuclear Medicine, Society of, Annual Meeting, 1959, 498
Southwestern Society, 1959 Meeting, following p. 270

O

Ovalbumin and constituents, flash photolysis of, GROSSWEINER AND MULAC, 515
Ovulation induced by injected hormones in heavily irradiated female mice, SPALDING *et al.*, 176
Oxidation of aqueous acetic acid-oxygen solutions upon irradiation, GARRISON *et al.*, 273

P

Paramecium aurelia, radiation-induced mutation, effect of streptomycin treatment, KIMBALL *et al.*, 490
Photolysis, flash, of ovalbumin and constituents, GROSSWEINER AND MULAC, 515
Pitressin, depressing effects on post-irradiation polydipsia and polyuria in the rat, WILLIAMS AND KRISE, 410
Plants, carrots and potatoes, morphological and biochemical changes produced by gamma-irradiation, MADSEN *et al.*, 48
Plutonium^{239}, metabolism in adult beagle dogs, STOVER *et al.*, 130
Porphine production by γ-irradiation of pyrrole and benzaldehyde, SZUTKA *et al.*, 597
Protection studies, comparative, of compounds against radiation and radiomimetic agents, GOLDENTHAL *et al.*, 571

Q

Quality determination, absorbed dose delivered by monoenergetic neutrons, ROSENZWEIG AND ROSSI, 532

R

Rabbit, retina, X-irradiation effect on glycogen content and histology, KENT, 380
Radiation chemistry, of acetylene, rare gas sensitization, wall effect in benzene formation, DORFMAN AND WAHL, 680
of carbohydrates, WOLFROM *et al.*, 37
effects on aqueous solutions of AET ANDERSON AND JOSEPH, 507
flash photolysis of ovalbumin, GROSSWEINER AND MULAC, 515
gamma radiolysis of butyl bromides, WILCOX, 112
of gases, DORFMAN, 607
hydrogen iodide production in radiolysis of organic liquids containing dissolved iodine, MESHITSUKA AND BURTON, 499
method of analysis of indirect inactivation of macromolecules in solution, AUGENSTINE, 89
Radiation dosimetry, calorimetric measurements on a Caesium-137 teletherapy unit, GOODWIN, 6
specification of radiation quality, ROSSI, 522
Radiation-induced reactions in the N_2–O_2–H_2O system, JONES, 655
Radioactive calcium in canine bone, bone growth and, MARSHALL *et al.*, 243
diffuse activity and long term exchange, MARSHALL *et al.*, 258
microradiographic measurements of mineral density, ROWLAND *et al.*, 234
microscopic studies of deposition in three dimensions, MARSHALL *et al.*, 197
quantitative autoradiography, MARSHALL *et al.*, 213

Radiological application of gamma-ray transport theory, BERGER AND SPENCER, 552
Radiolysis, direct, and radiation sensitized hydrogenation of ethylene, LAMPE, 691
Radioresistance, acquired, X-irradiation of mice, DACQUISTO, 118
Radium in human bone, microradiography of, ROWLAND *et al.*, 323
Rat, effects of gamma and neutron irradiation on Fe^{59} incorporation, RAMBACH *et al.*, 148
effect of X-irradiation on DNA metabolism in various tissues, NYGAARD AND POTTER, 462
partially shielded, effects of single and divided dose of X-radiation on bone marrow, MURRAY, 347
post irradiation polydipsia and polyuria, effect of pitressin in, WILLIAMS AND KRISE, 410
and rabbits, effect of X-irradiation on antioxidant activity of tissues, BARBER AND WILBUR, 167
role of bile secretion in the gastrointestinal radiation syndrome, JACKSON AND ENTENMAN, 67
X-irradiation, DNase activity in lymphoid tissues following, GORDON *et al.*, 545
Recovery of amoebae, exposed to supralethal doses of fission neutrons, effect of non-irradiated protoplasm, DANIELS AND VOGEL, JR., 584
from radiation damage and its possible relationship to life shortening in mice, STORER, 180
from radiation induction of mutation in *Paramecium aurelia* by streptomycin treatment, KIMBALL *et al.*, 490
studies in X-irradiated mice, KREBS *et al.*, 80
Relative biological effects at extreme ranges of LET, survival of haploid yeast, SAYEG *et al.*, 449
of gamma and X-irradiation on yeast, SINCLAIR *et al.*, 418
Retina, rabbit, changes after X-irradiation, KENT, 380
Reversible effects of X-irradiation of insect epidermis, BALDWIN AND SALTHOUSE, 397

S

Seedling growth, effect of high doses of radiation on, SICARD AND SCHWARTZ, 1
Sera from irradiated monkeys, paper electrophoretic analyses, LEONE *et al.*, 357
Spores of lysogenic *Bacillus megaterium*, destruction of plaque forming ability of, WOESE, 370
Squirrel, hibernating and nonhibernating, protection by cysteine after irradiation, SMITH, 335
Symposium on radiation chemistry, introduction, DORFMAN, 607
Synthesis of porphine-like substances induced by γ-irradiation, SZUTKA *et al.*, 597

T

Theory of gamma-ray transport, radiological applications, BERGER AND SPENCER, 552
Tongue lesions and bacteremia in X-irradiated mice, VOS *et al.*, 339

X

X-irradiation of bone marrow of partially shielded rats, MURRAY, 347
(200kvp and 22Mevp) and $Cobalt^{60}$ radiation, RBE on yeast survival curves, SINCLAIR *et al.*, 418
destruction of plaque forming ability of lysogenic *Bacillus megaterium* by, WOESE, 370
effect on antioxidant activity of mammalian tissues, BARBER AND WILBUR, 167
on aqueous solutions of S-(2-Aminoethyl) thiuronium salts, ANDERSON AND JOSEPH, 507
ground squirrel, protection by cysteine, SMITH, 335
of insect epidermis, injury related to cell division, BALDWIN AND SALTHOUSE, 387
reversible effects, BALDWIN AND SALTHOUSE, 397
macromolecules in solution analysis of results, method for, AUGENSTINE, 89

mice, acquired radioresistance, DACQUISTO, 118
with different organs protected, manner of subsequent death, QUASTLER AND ZUCKER, 402
effect on ovulation, SPALDING *et al.*, 176
lesions of the tongue and development of bacteremia in, VOS *et al.*, 339
long term effects on lymphocyte homeostasis, METCALF, 313
and neutron irradiation, rate of recovery and its possible relationship to life shortening, STORER, 180
non-recuperable injury, KREBS *et al.*, 80
monkeys, paper electrophoretic analyses of serum, LEONE *et al.*, 357
of rabbit retina, effects on glycogen content and histology, KENT, 380
and radiomimetic chemicals, action of protective substances, GOLDENTHAL *et al.*, 571
rats, effect on DNA metabolism in various tissues, NYGAARD AND POTTER, 462
DNase activity in lymphoid tissues, GORDON *et al.*, 545
role of bile secretion in gastrointestinal syndrome, JACKSON AND ENTENMAN, 67
sites of action of lethal effects in division of yeast cells, ELKIND AND SUTTON, 296
X-ray sensitivity in yeast, relation between division, UV sensitivity, and photoreactivation, ELKIND AND SUTTON, 273

Y

Yeast, haploid, survival, effects of accelerated carbon nuclei and other radiations, dosimetry of cyclotron beams, BIRGE AND SAYEG, 433
survival, effects of carbon nuclei and other radiations, biological experiments, SAYEG *et al.*, 449
relation between division and X-ray sensitivity, UV sensitivity and photoreactivation, ELKIND AND SUTTON, 273
RBE of X- and gamma-irradiation, SINCLAIR *et al.*, 418
sites of action of lethal irradiation, ELKIND AND SUTTON, 296